The Visual History of Type

The Visual History of Type

The Visual History of Type
Paul McNeil

Is the aleph, that place in Borges from which the entire world is visible simultaneously, anything other than an alphabet?
Georges Perec

For Lynne

Published in 2017
by Laurence King Publishing Ltd
Laurence King Student & Professional
An imprint of Quercus Editions Ltd
Carmelite House
50 Victoria Embankment
London EC4Y 0DZ
Tel: +4420 7841 6900
Fax: +44 20 7841 6910
Email: enquiries@laurenceking.com
www.laurenceking.com

Reprinted 2018, 2019, 2021

A catalogue record for this book is available from the British Library.
ISBN: 978-1-78067-976-1

Designed by Paul McNeil
Typeset in Linotype Univers
www.muirmcneil.com

Printed in China

LAURENCE KING

MIX
Paper from
responsible sources
FSC® C008047

Papers used by Quercus are from well-managed forests and other responsible sources.

contents

For more than 500 years type and typography have been the primary instruments of printing and publishing, activities which are no less significant in the development of civilization than the invention of the wheel. In the twenty-first century we are witnessing an unprecedented shift in the ways in which we relate to typographic technologies. In addition to their predominant role in mass communications, they have become central to many of our social interactions. Type is everywhere today, from the printed pages to the mobile devices in our hands and from our everyday personal exchanges to the global cityscape. Yet many people are oblivious to its presence.

Matthew Carter, probably the most eminent type designer of his generation and certainly the most prolific, said in an interview for the 2007 documentary film *Helvetica*, 'you find yourself sitting next to some nice person on a plane or a train and they ask you sooner or later what you do and if you say "type designer", they generally look completely blank'. Why is this the case? If Carter were a fashion designer, an architect or an illustrator, people outside of the creative industries would have a far greater appreciation for what he does for a living and for its consequences. But for a designer of type, the reaction is not only inevitable but also entirely appropriate.

Type is easily disregarded because, as Gerard Unger, another renowned type designer, has said, 'It is almost impossible to look and read at the same time: they are different actions.' A reader can never be conscious of the act of reading while doing so because, should he or she become momentarily aware of the visible presence of a body of text, at that precise instant it will cease to perform its primary function of conveying language. This is, of course, a matter of degree in specific contexts: novels function differently from newspaper headlines, for example, and tickets operate differently from billboard ads. Nevertheless, the principle holds true to a lesser or greater extent in all situations. The early printing trade was always very secretive and it is no coincidence that it was traditionally known as 'the black art'. The dichotomy between reading and seeing words is equivalent to a blind spot where the message they convey is very likely to be read, recognized and retained while its vehicle – its formation as a visual object – usually goes unnoticed. This capacity to hide in plain sight is the secret that gives type its performative power, enabling it to influence communications subliminally in order to create a mood, provide a tone of voice, evoke emotional responses and disclose information progressively through emphasis and diminution.

This book sets out to promote an awareness of the enormous potential contained within these signs that are so taken for granted and to communicate, clearly and concisely, the stages of the development of type in relation to cultural and technological narratives. It is a unique survey intended for graphic design practitioners, students of typography and general readers interested in the history of communications and visual culture. *The Visual History of Type* addresses its subject from a broad perspective. It provides a definitive overview of the major typefaces produced since the advent of printing in the 1450s until the present day, with an emphasis on the direct, faithful representation of key historical type designs presented in their original specimens or, where more suitable, in alternative contemporary settings.

Throughout the history of printing, type specimens and catalogues have been published by foundries and printers to promote their services. Until the arrival of the computer these were used extensively as a tool to select fonts, to plan typographic designs and to make comparative studies between typefaces. Designed explicitly to draw attention to the appearance of typefaces, specimens are often very well-considered utilitarian artefacts that reflect the visual tropes of their times. However, they are often overlooked in graphic design histories and have never before been collected into a single, comprehensive volume. More than 320 typefaces are represented in the specimens featured in this edition, many of them widely regarded as the finest representatives of the typographic canon. Designs such as Garamond and Baskerville are upheld as 'classics' because they have proven time after time to be readable, versatile and unobtrusive, particularly in extended bodies of text. Their effectiveness as book typefaces is the product of a delicate balance between the unity of the character set and the diversity of individual letterforms.

Because generations of readers have found these familiar forms effortlessly legible, generations of printers and publishers have depended on them, time and again. As a result, they have endured many changes in technologies and fashions and have become accepted as benchmarks of excellence, efficiency and beauty. But the objective of this volume is to present an accurate picture of every stage of the development of type and it therefore includes a number of typefaces that may have only survived in use for short periods as a result of changes in trends, markets or technologies. Many of these typefaces were designed for display use at large sizes rather than as body text – to attract attention first and to convey words second. Although they might seem ostentatious, localized, antiquated or even ugly, these designs are as significant to this narrative as those that could be deemed more worthy. *The Visual History of Type* also includes a number of groundbreaking experimental designs that may never have been published commercially but that opened up new directions in the development of the field.

Advancement in type design has always been very slow. When type designer Dave Farey said 'Nothing I have done is original. It's all based on the 26 letters of the alphabet...', he was referring to a persistent feature that has made type design a particularly conservative field. Although it would be possible to construct an infinite variety of letterforms, the demands of the reading process necessarily confine designers to the conventional limits of the alphabetic skeleton. If a character fails to represent a linguistic unit, it just isn't a character. Type is therefore always obliged to look to the past by referencing pre-existing forms which are universally accepted and understood. As a result, much of its lineage has involved a series of successive adaptations of longstanding designs to new technologies – for instance, in the transition of a typeface from machine composition to a digital format.

The heritage of type and lettering is deeply rooted in this tradition of revivalism, with the most enduring faces being subjected to repeated reinterpretations, conditioned by the constraints of new technologies, the intentions and skills of designers, and the vagaries of fashion.

Because of these limitations, similarities between designs are inevitable even when they are not deliberate, calling into question the nature of originality in type design and encouraging copying, plagiarism and piracy, issues which have afflicted it throughout its history.

The Visual History of Type is sequenced on a timeline that follows the publication dates of the typefaces shown or their first known implementations. It is arranged in seven sections separated into the following major historical and technological phases:

1450– The period which witnessed the invention of printing with movable type and the instigation of practically every feature that has defined typographic design ever since.

1650– The era of European expansion which saw the loosening of the roman letter from its humanistic roots during the Baroque and Enlightenment periods that created the foundations of the modern era.

1800– The century when typography was used to meet the voracious needs of commerce during the Industrial Revolution, resulting in an explosion of new technologies, typeforms and ideas.

1900– The half century afflicted by global wars that precipitated the rise of the avant-garde creative movements to challenge social conventions in order to create a wide variety of innovative forms.

1950– The postwar period of consolidation when graphic design became a specialist profession in its own right, directed towards service and objectivity in visual communications.

1980– The final decades of the twentieth century, marked by a shift from mechanical to digital technologies, triggering a reconfiguration of design practices along with an expansion of their scope.

2000– The early decades of the twenty-first century when digital type design matured in line with rapid advancements in digital communication technologies and corresponding social functions.

In the organizational structure of this book the use of a conventional type classification scheme has deliberately been avoided because such schemes have proven faulty in a number ways. The arcane terminology they use is itself the product of historical evolution and as a result lacks both consistency and consensus, causing confusion by identifying typefaces on the arbitrary basis of various historical, geographical or other associations, or of a fragmentary assortment of visual attributes. Type classification schemes also give the illusion of mapping everything possible within the scope of the design of letters and in doing so have reactionary effects that inhibit potential for development. While some typefaces may fall comfortably under a single classification, others may amalgamate different characteristics to cross existing boundaries or to transcend them altogether, as has been the case increasingly since the advent of digital type design. In this light, it is clear that classification schemes should only be used as pragmatic guides to a terrain where many other useful connections can also be made.

The Visual History of Type works with a more stable terminology intended to be descriptive rather than definitive, using four relatively durable visual categories: serif, sans serif, script and blackletter. These are helpfully supplemented by an extendable system of keywords that refer either to the historical associations of the typeface shown or to its major visual attributes. All typefaces or type families are displayed on individual spreads that are arranged in a consistent manner throughout. In all instances, images of original type specimens or, where more suitable, their contemporary applications, are supported with succinct summaries of the development, appearance and usage of each design, locating it within its historical context. In addition, tabular sections provide useful key data as indicated in the guide opposite.

It should be noted that this edition focuses on those language groups that use type set in the Latin alphabet, in particular Europe and the United States. Equivalent work on non-western typographic histories is needed by experts in these areas, as they are likely to provide new revelations that may call into question many of our preconceptions.

In 1992 Ellen Lupton and J. Abbot Miller proposed that 'a canon of ideally proportioned letterforms has yielded to a flexible genetic code capable of breeding an infinity of new species' in a short review of the status of type in contemporary graphic design. Lupton and Miller's stated objective in their *Natural History of Typography* was to map what they saw as a major cultural shift occurring in the last decades of the twentieth century 'away from an understanding of letters as stable reflections of handwriting or an ideal classical past toward a view of typography as the endless manipulation of abstract relationships'. Referencing the theory of evolution throughout, the authors traced the cultural development of type design through a series of ideological phases culminating in this late-twentieth-century paradigm shift, where unprecedented forms were emerging from computers that allowed designers for the first time to take direct control of their production processes. At the same time, new critical theories were overturning prevalent assumptions about neutrality in contemporary communications and design practices. The synergy of these influences provided a generation of designers with both the attitudes and the means to face what was seen as a new frontier.

But the work shown throughout this volume suggests that the 'flexible genetic code' which Miller and Lupton had observed was not new at all. A dominant theme of *The Visual History of Type*, demonstrated in all of the examples shown, is the extraordinary flexibility, contextuality and redundancy of language represented in type, driven for over 500 years by a persistent tension between the humanistic, gestural origins of letters and the systematic, analytical nature of their mechanized forms. Their DNA is easily identifiable as the alphabet, the resilient core onto which all Latin typographic structures are attached. For thousands of years, this spectacular code has been subjected to myriad changes in appearance in its daily use in reading matter and in the environment as it constantly adapts to transformations in media, technologies, languages, aesthetics and ideologies, while always remaining perfectly the same.

Paul McNeil
February 2017

A guide to the typeface tables

Ty The original name of the typeface
Ca Typeface categorization as either a Serif, Sans Serif, Script or Blackletter
Ke Keywords referring either to historical associations or governing visual features of the typeface
Te The technology for which the typeface was originally created
Da The first publication date of the typeface, or its first known implementation
De The originator of the typeface: its founder, punch cutter, calligrapher, designer or design director
Fo The type foundry or printer that originally published the typeface
Co The country of the original publishing type foundry

Characteristics
The key features of the typeface shown in the specimen and the table, based solely on visual attributes. General identifying characteristics are the relationship of the lower case x-height to the ascender height, the relative proportions of thick and thin strokes within glyphs, the relationship of the angles of strokes to their terminals, the jointing formation of serifs to strokes, and the shapes of serifs, where applicable. Unique features of selected letterforms are also itemized

Connections
A list of preceding or succeeding typefaces that may have influenced the design of the type shown or been influenced by it

Availability
An indication of the source from which the type was available in a digital format at the time of printing

Specimen
The title of the printed type specimen or example shown with publication details and page dimensions to the nearest 5mm. Image sources are listed on page 672

140-150

In fifteenth-century Europe, rapid social changes fuelled a pressing need for the efficient and economical reproduction of written documents. Until that time, books were hand-copied by monks and lay scribes. This was a slow, labour-intensive process for a limited group of literate people. A revolution was brought about with the invention of printing using movable type, initially for the commercial publication of short documents, and soon afterwards for the first mass-produced book, Johannes Gutenberg's 42-line Bible of 1455.

The art of printing combined a number of features from existing technologies, such as paper-making methods that had evolved from the textile industry and the adaptation of presses first used for wine making. Its most significant innovation, however, was the cutting and casting of movable metal type, a process that remained in use, almost unchanged, until the late nineteenth century. To manufacture type, a pattern for each character was carved into the end of a steel bar – a punch – that was then struck into a soft copper blank. This impression was inserted into a mould into which a molten metal alloy was poured, cooling quickly to become hard. The resulting reversed images of letters could be handled in minutes, assembled and locked in a frame, coated in ink and then impressed onto paper to make a page of text.

Printing spread at a remarkable speed. Within 50 years of its invention, more than 1,000 printers had set up workshops in over 200 cities across Europe. Early printed editions were intended to resemble the handmade books that preceded them, so the typefaces cut by the first German printers were close interpretations of the angular blackletter scripts of the day. As printing progressed from city to city, new designs for letterforms were adapted to match regional manuscript styles to address the requirements of indigenous readers.

When printing reached Italy, the fulcrum of humanist thinking during the Renaissance, letterforms started to evolve into the styles with which we are familiar today. This step in the development of typography was an expression of contemporary Italian tastes and attitudes, motivated by a rediscovery of classical Greco-Roman culture, rather than the result of any particular technical innovations.

Early humanist typefaces derived their capital letters from Roman inscriptions while the lower case was adapted from the formal handwriting of Italian scribes. Gradually, punch cutters began to improve the appearance and efficiency of characters by making the best use of their own production methods, rather than simply seeking to copy handwritten letters. Nicolas Jenson and Francesco Griffo skilfully advanced these possibilities in the design of type, creating a blueprint for its future direction that continues to bear an influence after 500 years.

The printing press started a revolution that changed society irrevocably. The first mass medium, it released medieval culture from the limitations of orality and writing by precipitating the spread of knowledge and ideas in an unprecedented manner. Through the new practice of publishing, a single communication could be reproduced indefinitely and disseminated to a geographically dispersed audience in an almost limitless time frame. For an expanding group of literate people, printing facilitated the ability of the individual to make intellectual and ideological choices by providing verifiable information. Affordable, portable books also lent themselves to acts of solitary reading – internalized, self-reflexive experiences that stimulated new ideas about the autonomy of the individual in relation to others and to society. This had a galvanizing effect on the development of personal rights and liberties. Over the next three centuries these new ways of thinking brought about profound challenges to institutional control, leading to dramatic religious reforms, radical sociopolitical changes, and new scientific modes of inquiry that initiated the modern era.

Gutenberg's Bastarda

Ty	**Gutenberg's Bastarda**
Ca	**Blackletter**
Ke	**Bastarda**
Te	**Letterpress**
Da	**1454**
De	**Johannes Gutenberg**
Fo	**Johannes Gutenberg**
Co	**Germany**

Characteristics

a	Single-storeyed
d	Curved uncial stem
f long s	Long, pointed descender
h	Curved uncial form
r s	Alternate forms
y	Medieval form
ff fi fl ll pp	Ligatures
&	Medieval form

aCOORS

abcdefghi

moprstuxz

Connections

Gutenberg's Textura	1455
Zainer's Gotico-Antiqua	1468
Caxton's Bastarda	1476
The Wittenberg Bastarda	1508

Availability

Not available

Specimen

Indulgentia. Johannes Gutenberg, Mainz, 1454 (201x279mm)

Tradition has it that Johannes Gutenberg (c1398–1468) invented the art of printing in around 1450. However, historical evidence presents a much more complex picture of a number of activities occurring at multiple locations in southern Germany during the mid-fifteenth century, with several individuals involved in developing printing techniques. Johannes Gutenberg did not invent the printing press but was the first to demonstrate the practical use of movable type, not in the form of the magnificent 42-line Bible for which he is famous (pp14–15) but for much less ambitious commercial reasons.

Since the eleventh century, indulgences and pardons had been awarded by the Church for the remission of sins, earned either by prayer or through donations. An indulgence took the form of a preset document with a space left for the name of a penitent as proof of his or her right to divine forgiveness. For the Church, this involved costly, labour-intensive procedures where thousands of identical documents would be written by hand.

Gutenberg's inestimable contribution to printing was devised to solve this problem. The invention of movable type allowed the production of uniform indulgences in large quantities, rapidly and at a reasonable price. An experienced goldsmith, Gutenberg formulated a durable alloy of lead, tin and antimony. He also invented a method for creating moulds for letters into which the metal would be poured. The resulting characters were cast on uniform bodies so that they would align accurately within a frame. Once the type was composed, locked into the frame and inked, it was impressed on either paper or vellum to create a printed text. Since individual letters could be moved, rearranged and reused, an almost infinite variety of texts could be produced.

The indulgence shown here uses two sizes of type and large initials engraved in wood, with spaces left for the name of the penitent and the date to be inserted by hand. The larger type is the same Textura blackletter that would be used for the text of the 42-line Bible the following year, and the smaller gothic type is known as Bastarda, a contemporary fifteenth-century script. To imitate scribal practices in handwritten documents, many alternate characters were used, including ligatures, abbreviations and contractions.

Gutenberg may have printed indulgences from 1452, but the earliest that survive were made in 1454. Thirty copies of the example shown remain, although how many were printed is not known. However, they must have been highly lucrative. A similar surviving document was published in as many as 140,000 copies.

s inspecturis **Paulinus** Chappe Cōsiliari9 Ambasiator z pcurator generalis Serenissimi
Rū Sāctissim9 ixpo pr z dūs nr dūs Nicolaus diuia puidētia pp quit9 Afflictiōī Regni Cypri
se crucis xpi hostes Theucros z Saracenos gratis cōcessit omiby xpifideliby vbilibet ōstitutis
pie exhortādo qui infra trieniū a prima die Oaÿ Anni dūi Occcclÿ icipiēdū p defēsiōe catho
nis magis uel min9 put ipoz videbitur ōsciētÿs pcūtoriby uel nūc9 substitutis pie erogaue
egulares p ipos eligēdi ōfessioniby eoz auditis- p cōmissis etiā sedi aplice reseruatis excessiby
iby p vna vice tātū debitā absolutiōe impēdere z penitētiā salutarem iniūgere Recnō sī d
ōicationum suspensionū z interdicti alÿsqz sentencÿs cēsuris z penis ecclesiasticis a iure uel ab
existūt absoluere-Iniūcta p modo culpe penitētia salutari uel alÿs q de iure fuerit iniūgēda
esan propter amissionē loqle ōfiteri nō poterit signa ōtriciōis ostēdēdo plenissimā oīm pccoz
uerint Indulgentiā ac plenariā remissiōe semel in vita z semel in mortis articulo ipis aūcte
p eos facta si supuixerint aut p eoz heredes sī tūc trāsierit Sic tamē qp post indultū ōcessum
uadā alia die ieiunēt-legittimo ipedimēto ecclesie pcepto regulari obseruātia pnia iniūcta
ditis in dicto āno uel eius parte-anno sequēti uel alias quam primū poterint ieiunabūt Et sī
iuniū cōmode adimplere nequiuerit Confessor ad id electus in alia ōmutare poterit caritatis
ōdo tū ex ōfidentia remissionis hmōi qp absit peccare nō psumāt Alioqui dicta cōcessio quo ad
e et remissio quo ad pcta ex ōfidentia ut pmittitur ōmissa nullius sint roboris uel momenti
ōsbergh et fredonia ... Rma Colonii ... iuxta dictum indultū
ierito huiusmodi indulgentÿs gaudere debet-In veritatis testimoniū sigillū ad hoc ordinatū
i Datū Colonie Anno dūi Occccliiÿdie vero ... mensis ...

ssime absolutionis et remissionis in vita

ihesus xps p suā sanctissimā et pÿssimā miaz te absoluat Et aūcte ipis beatoz qz petri z pauli
a z tibi ōcessa Ego te absoluo ab omiby pccis tuis ōtritis ōfessis z oblitis Etiā ab omiby casiby
icūqz grauiby sedi aplice reseruatis Recnō a quibuscūqz excōicationū suspensionū z interdicti
asticis a iure uel ab hoie pmulgatis si quas incurristi dando tibi plenissimā oīm pccoz tuoz
ues sancte matris ecclie in hac parte se extendūt-In noīe patris z filÿ z spiritus sancti Amen

arie remissionis in mortis articulo

ut supra Ego te absoluo ab omiby pccis tuis ōtritis ōfessis et oblitis restituendo te vnitati
ndo tibi penas purgatorÿ quas propter culpas z offensas incurristi dando tibi plenariā oīm
ues sancte matris ecclie in hac parte se extendūt-In noīe patris z filÿ z spiritus sancti Amen

Gutenberg's Textura

Ty	**Gutenberg's Textura**
Ca	**Blackletter**
Ke	**Textura**
Te	**Letterpress**
Da	**1455**
De	**Johannes Gutenberg**
Fo	**Johannes Gutenberg**
Co	**Germany**

Characteristics

Heavy, upright letters
Angled junctions
Vertical emphasis
a Double-storeyed with closed upper loop
d Angled uncial stem
h i m n Strokes terminate in points at foot
ff ft ve Ligatures

Connections

Hopyl's Textura	1506
Weiss-Gotisch	1936
Bastard	1990
FF Johannes G	1991

Availability

FF Johannes G is a digital revival available
from FontFont and resellers

Specimen

42-line Bible. Johannes Gutenberg, Mainz,
1455 (391x274mm)

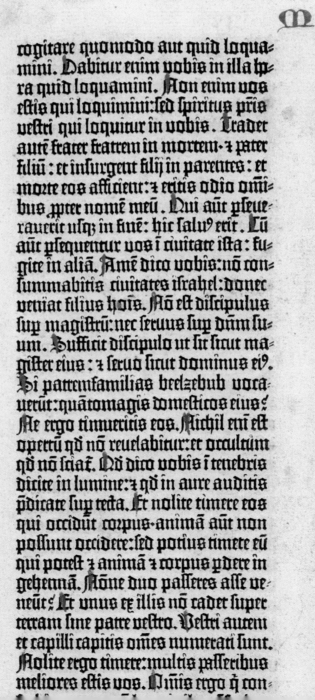

The innovations in printing technology attributed to Johannes Gutenberg (c1398–1468), working in Mainz, Germany, in the early 1440s, were so significant that he is regarded as one of the leading figures of his time.

His invention of printing types that were movable, interchangeable and reusable marked the first step in a progression away from the medieval towards the modern era. The advent of printing in Europe instigated the dissemination of literacy and knowledge on a mass scale and, in doing so, it transformed the future of Western society and culture.

Gutenberg's 42-line Latin Bible, published in 1455, is thought to be the first substantial book ever printed with movable type in Europe.

This type was cut, probably with the assistance of Peter Schöffer, to replicate the book hand widely used in Germany during the fifteenth century for missals and liturgical manuscripts. Known as Textura or Textualis, it is a formal alphabet with heavy, upright letters. Its letterforms are tall and narrow, emphasizing parallel verticals, with stroke junctions that are sharply angular. Only a few strokes show any curvature, mainly in the capitals.

Ascenders and descenders are stout, and strokes terminate in diamond-shaped swellings. In order to achieve a faithful representation of handwriting, the typeface used in the 42-line Bible contains almost 300 different individual glyphs, including a large number of alternate character contours as well as abbreviations and ligatures, where common sequences of two or more letters are joined together on a single type body.

Although the 42-line Bible was the first major book ever printed, it is nothing short of a masterpiece. The work of Gutenberg and his craftsmen demonstrates

remarkable expertise in terms of composition, presswork and book production. Carefully formulated inks gave a crisp, clear impression on high-quality paper or on the fine vellum that was used for a small part of the print run. A solemn majesty is imparted by the pages of the 42-line Bible, although to modern eyes the dense vertical strokes of its Textura type might look spiky and rigid and therefore be perceived as illegible. However, Gutenberg's editions should not be judged out of context. They equalled the manuscripts they sought to imitate, presenting texts with a harmony and vigour that remain unsurpassed.

The Subiaco Type

Ty	**The Subiaco Type**
Ca	**Blackletter**
Ke	**Gotico-Antiqua**
Te	**Letterpress**
Da	**1465**
De	**Konrad Sweynheym and Arnold Pannartz**
Fo	**Sweynheym & Pannartz**
Co	**Italy**

Characteristics
Long ascenders and descenders
Blunt baseline serifs
a Double-storeyed
d Upright stem
g Double-storeyed, narrow
h Curved uncial form
t Arrow-headed
y Straight tail

AGMRS
abcdefghi
moprstuyʒ

Connections

Zainer's Gotico-Antiqua	1468
Jenson	1470
The Golden Type	1890
Subiaco	1902

Availability
Not available

Specimen
Lucius Coelius Lactantius, *De divinis institutionibus*. Sweynheym and Pannartz, Subiaco, 1465 (328x230mm)

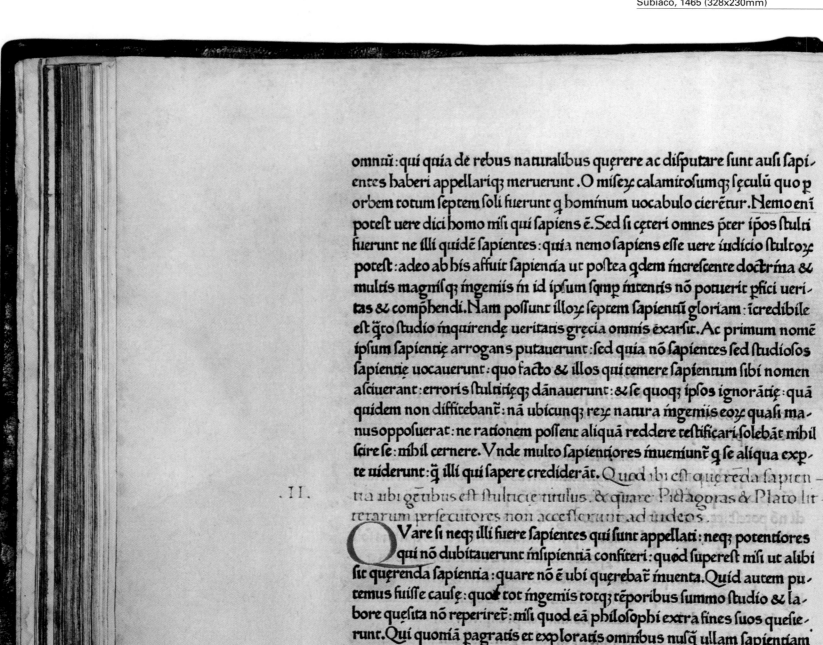

The Subiaco typeface represents a milestone in the history of printing and typography. In the opinion of the eminent British typographer Stanley Morison, it is 'entitled to rank as the first humanistic or roman type'.

The art of printing was brought to Italy from Germany by two monks, Konrad Sweynheym (?–1476) and Arnold Pannartz (?–1477), who founded the first press at the Benedictine monastery in Subiaco in 1464. Sweynheym is thought to have mastered his printing skills working with Johannes Gutenberg in Mainz, and Pannartz

probably came from Cologne. In 1467, Sweynheym and Pannartz relocated their press to Rome, but during their three-year tenure at Subiaco they printed four handsome editions using typeface designs never seen before.

In order to cater for the demands of an Italian readership, books were required that used familiar Italian characters in an indigenous style. Sweynheym and Pannartz therefore substituted the blackletter type used in early German books for a new letterform of their own design that was based largely on

contemporary Italian book hands. Their new alphabet is not an exclusively roman form but a hybrid of the features of letters of the Middle Ages and of the Renaissance, known as a Gotico-Antiqua (Gothic-Roman) or Fere-Humanistica (Semi-Humanist) type. It retains many residual traces of the German Textura with its exaggerated vertical stress, comparatively heavy, square contours and slight overall compression. The key characteristics of the Subiaco type are its long ascenders and descenders, with blunt baseline serifs that give a strong vertical emphasis overall.

The impression made by the Lactantius edition shown here is one of an evenly toned body of text framed within generous page margins. The project was brilliantly executed, with the design of the type and the diligence of the presswork clearly intended to result in a book closely resembling a work of fine calligraphy. This is remarkable, considering that Sweynheym and Pannartz were novices.

The fact that their typeface was recut in 1902 for the editions of the Ashendene Press (pp172–73) is further evidence of its enduring excellence.

Ty	**Zainer's Gotico-Antiqua**
Ca	**Blackletter**
Ke	**Gotico-Antiqua**
Te	**Letterpress**
Da	**1468**
De	**Günther Zainer**
Fo	**Günther Zainer**
Co	**Germany**

Characteristics

Open, rounded letterforms
Long ascenders and descenders
Round form ligatures
a Double-storeyed with closed upper loop
d Curved uncial stem
g Open lower bowl, rounded shape
h Curved uncial form

ADERS

abcdefghi

mopqrstuxy

Connections

The Subiaco Type	1465
Von Speyer's Roman	1470
The Troy Type	1892
Chaucer Type	1896

Availability

Morris Troy is a digital version of William
Morris's Troy type revival, available from
the P22 Type Foundry and resellers

Specimen

Evengelium Nicodemi incipit feliciter.
Günther Zainer, Augsburg, c1473
(276x200mm) Source: BNF

alius dixit·leprosus eram·& mundauit me.Rñ verũt
iuxei·legem habemus·mulierem in testimoniũ nõ ve
nire. Et alij quidã· ex multitudine iuxeoų & msrum
clamauerunt dicentes. Iste homo ppBa est·demonia
ei subiecta sunt.Dicit pplatus· quare & toctoribų vtis
non sunt subiecta. Rñxerunt pplato·nescimus.Alij
aũt dixerunt· Lazarum quaxriduanũ·mortuum· su
scitauit.Nõ audiens preses·tremefactus ad omnem
multitudinem.Quid vultis effundere sanguinem in
nocentem·Et quocans nichoxemũ & xij·viros qui di
xerunt·non ẽ natus ex fornicatõne·dixit·Quid faciã
Qm sedicõ sit in pplõ.Vicunt illi·nescims·ipsi vixeãt
Item quocans omnẽ multitudinẽ iuxeoų· dixit.Sci
tis·cp psuetuxo est i pascha·vt dimittã vobÿ vnũ vin
ctum·habeo aũt insignẽ in carcere·homicidã· qui di
ctur barrabas. In iBu vero·nullam culpam inuenio
mortis.Quem ergo vultis vobis dimittã·Clamaue
runt iuxei barrabam. Dicit pplatus·quid faciemus
xe iBu. Rñxerunt iuxei oms·crucifigat.Non es ami
cus cesaris·si hũc dimittis·cp dicit se filium xei·& re
gem·ne forte velis hũc regem esse·non cesarem·Tunc
furore repletus·dixit pplatus.Semp sediciosi fuistis
& qui p vobis fuerunt·ptrarium eis fuistis.Rñxerũt
iuxei.Qui sunt p nobis·xeus vester·qui eripuit vos
xe dura egiptioų seruitute·& eduxit vos p mare ó egi
pto·sicut p aridam·& in heremo cibauit nos manna·
& eduxit vobis aquam xe petra·& potauit vos·& leges
xedit vobis·& in alijs oibų irritatus est·& voluit vos
occixere.Sed ópxecatus ẽ moyses p vobis· quẽ post
modum lapidare voluistis.Nunc dicitis. Quia re
gem non habemus. Et exurgens cepit exire.Clama
u erũt iuxei.Regem habemus·cesare·nõ iBm.Rñdit
pplatus.Nam & magi obtulerũt ei munera sic regi.

Et audiens herodes a magis qp rex natꝰ esset ·voluit eū occidere. Quo ꝯgnito pater eius ioseph tulit eum ⁊ matrem eius· ⁊ fugerūt in egiptum. Audiensꝗ herodes ꝑdidit infantes iudeoꝝ qui nati sunt in bethleem. Et audiens pplatus· facto silentō in ipło dixit· Ergo hic est quem querebat herodes. Dicūt ei· hic est· accipiens eū· misit ad herodem dicens. Innocens ego sum a sanguine iusti huiꝰ· vos videritis· ⁊ ꝑfectus est pplatus his verbis· dicens sentenciam aduersus iħm. Genus tuum ꝓbauit te regem· ꝓpterea ꝓcipio te primum flagellari ħm statuta prioꝝ principū. Deinde alleuari in cruce· in loco quo tentus es· ⁊ duos malignos tecum quoꝝ nomina sunt hec Dysmas ⁊ Gesmas. Et exiētibus de ꝓtorio· ⁊ duo latrones cum eo· venerūt cū eo ad locum. Et expoliauerunt eum vestimentis suis· ⁊ ꝑcinxerunt cum lintheo ⁊ coronam de spinis imposuerunt sup caput eius. Similiter ⁊ duos latrones cum eo suspenderunt Dysmas a dextris· ⁊ Gesmas a sinistris. Iħs vero dixit. Pater Parce· ⁊ dimitte illis qp nesciunt quid faciunt· ⁊ diuiserunt sibi vestimēta eiꝰ Steteruntꝗ ppli ⁊ irriserunt eum principes sacerdotū ⁊ iudices eoꝛū intra semetipos loquentes. Alios saluos fecit· nunc seipm saluum faciat si filius dei est· descendat de cruce· deludebant quoꝗ eum milites· ⁊ accipientes acetum ⁊ fel· offerebant ei bibere dicentes. Si tu es rex iudeoꝝ· libera temetipm. Accipiens autē longinus miles lanceam· aperuit latus eius ⁊ exiuit sanguis ⁊ aqua. Iussit aūt pplatus pro sentencia scribi titulum lụis hebiacis· grecis· ⁊ latinis· ħm qd dixerunt iudei· hic est rex iudeoꝝ. Vnus aūt ex his latronibus qui suspensi sunt noie Gesmas dixit ei· Si tu es xps libera temetipm ⁊ nos. Rndit Dysmas· ⁊ ꝯturbauit eū dicens. Non times deum· qui in hoc iudicō es· nos enī digne ea que gessimꝰ recipimꝰ· hic nil mali fecit

In the late fifteenth century, some of the finest books were printed in types that were hybrids of gothic and roman forms, based partly on Textura and partly on the formal hand of the Italian scholars of the fourteenth century – in particular, that of Petrarch. Known as Gotico-Antiqua (Gothic-Roman) or Fere-Humanistica (Semi-Humanist), these types were first seen in the publications of German printers working in Italy (pp16–17).

The Gospel of Nicodemus was printed in 1468 by Günther Zainer (?–1478), the first printer in Augsburg, where he was active from that date. During his career he produced about 80 books of a consistently high quality, including the first-ever printed calendar and two editions of the Bible in the German language.

Zainer's Gotico-Antiqua is a rounded letterform with wide, open proportions, and ascenders and descenders that resemble those of roman type, but with neither its serifs nor the terminals of Textura. The ascenders and descenders are also proportionately longer than those of Textura, giving a comparatively light appearance to printed pages and drawing the eye across the lines of text with ease.

Letter shapes are well differentiated and very readable but somewhat lacking in variation, with blunt strokes ending at the baseline. The capital letters are the least resolved aspect of the typeface, showing considerable irregularity in their appearance, resulting from an inconsistent mixture of roman and gothic influences.

The Gotico-Antiqua style remained in regular use in Germany for less than three decades. After 1485, other blackletter typefaces became more popular. Its most notable revival was in the nineteenth century, when William Morris used it as the model for the Troy and Chaucer types of the Kelmscott Press.

Jenson

Ty	**Jenson**
Ca	**Serif**
Ke	**Old Style, Venetian**
Te	**Letterpress**
Da	**1470**
De	**Nicolas Jenson**
Fo	**Nicolas Jenson**
Co	**Italy**

Characteristics

Capitals to ascender height
D H N S Wide
M Serifs on the inside of stems
M Top serifs
Q Long tail
a f Top terminals
b d p q Tilted bowls
e Small eye and extending oblique bar
f Extended arch
h Non-uncial form
i j Small dot offset to right
y Straight tail

ADMQR
abcdefghij
lmoprstuy

Connections

The Golden Type	1890
The Doves Type	1900
Cloister Old Style	1913
Adobe Jenson	1996

Availability

Digital types based on Jenson's Roman are widely available

Specimen

Eusebius Pamphilus, *De evangelica praeparatione*. Nicolas Jenson, Venice, 1470 (335x232mm)

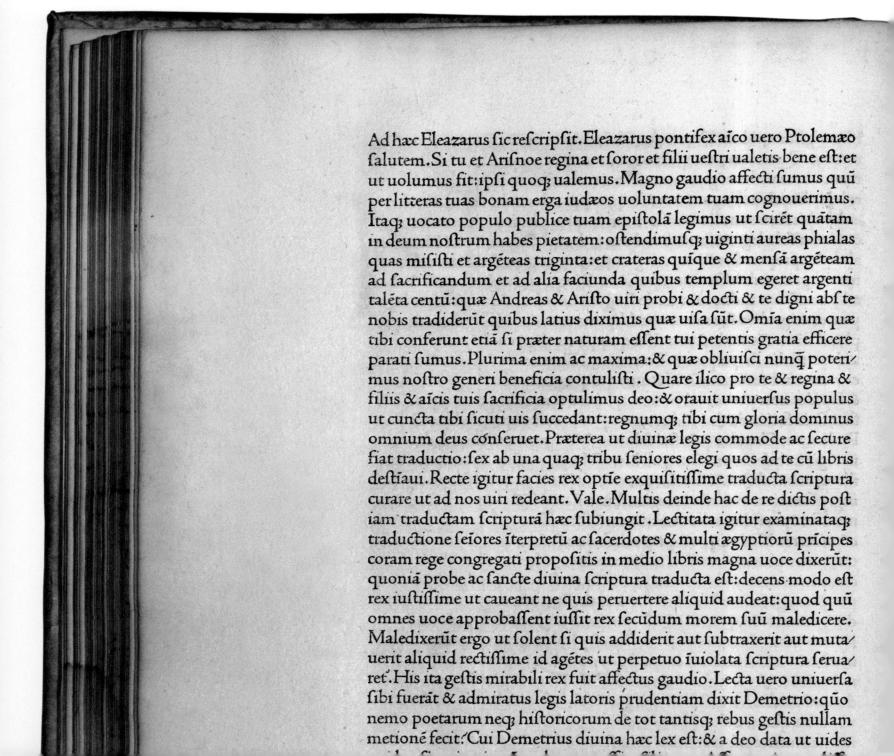

Nicolas Jenson (c1420–80) trained originally as a goldsmith and was employed as Master of the French Royal Mint at Tours. In 1458, King Charles VII despatched him to Germany to master the new craft of printing and type production in Mainz, the city where Gutenberg was then working. Jenson later returned briefly to France with his newly acquired skills, but soon afterwards he travelled to Italy.

In 1468 he established himself as the first non-German printer and publisher in Venice. Rapidly becoming one of the most prolific printers of his time, he published around 150 editions and distributed them throughout Europe. He excelled as a punch cutter. Beginning with classical works set in roman type, he progressed to devotional books, papal publications and Bibles set in Rotunda, a blackletter used extensively in southern European printing at the time. Although neither his type nor the punches used to make them have survived, Jenson's books have served as a source of inspiration ever since.

His roman type, designed following typographic models drawn from contemporary Italian manuscripts, marks a turning point in the history of printing. A blueprint for all that followed, it continues to influence type design today. An advertisement of 1482 claimed that Jenson's editions 'do not hinder one's eyes, but rather help them and do them good. Moreover, the characters are so intelligently and carefully elaborated that the letters are neither smaller, larger nor thicker than reason or pleasure demand'.

Elegant but not austere, the pages of Jenson's *De evangelica praeparatione* use a single size of type throughout with plain capitals employed as initials. Letters are full-bodied but finely cut, with a moderate contrast between thick and thin strokes. The capitals follow the proportions of classical Roman inscriptions although they are large – standing as tall as the ascenders – and some are relatively wide.

The lower case shows direct influences of contemporary Italian calligraphy with the strokes of a broad pen evident in many letterforms. Serifs are strong and steeply sloped: those in the lower case transition smoothly into stems, while those on the capitals are square and unbracketed.

Nicolas Jenson's work elevated the nascent craft of printing to a fine art. The balanced proportions of his letters, the evenness of their spacing and the restrained overall tone of his pages demonstrate why he was acclaimed above other printers working in fifteenth-century Italy and why his work has remained a cornerstone in the history of typography.

Von Speyer's Roman

Ty	**Von Speyer's Roman**
Ca	**Serif**
Ke	**Old Style, Venetian**
Te	**Letterpress**
Da	**1470**
De	**Johann and Vindelin von Speyer**
Fo	**Johann and Vindelin von Speyer**
Co	**Italy**

Characteristics

Capitals to ascender height
A High crossbar
A Foot serifs on the inside of stems
D E H N S Wide
M Serifs on the inside of stems
Q Long tail
a Small, steeply angled bowl
b d p q Tilted bowls
e Small eye
h Curved uncial form
i Small dot
y Angled with short, straight tail

AEPQS
abcdefghi
moprstuy

Connections

The Subiaco Type	1465
Jenson	1470
Ratdolt's Roman	1477
Bremer Antiqua	1922

Availability

Not available

Specimen

Saint Augustine, *De civitate Dei*. Johann and Vindelin von Speyer, Venice, 1470 (420x278mm)

The brothers Johann and Vindelin von Speyer were among the first emigrants from Germany to instigate the printing movement in Italy and have been credited by some as the originators of movable type in the Italian or Roman style. Among other contenders are Konrad Sweynheym and Arnold Pannartz (pp16–17), Nicolas Jenson (pp20–21) and Adolf Rusch.

The Von Speyer brothers began work in Venice in 1468 when Johann was granted an exclusive licence for all print production in the city. This monopoly ended on his death in 1470, when Vindelin took over the press. Vindelin maintained the same care and attention to quality and detail that had characterized Johann's work in the publications produced after his brother's death. Between 1470 and 1477 he issued over 70 major editions. He also produced five types that demonstrate exquisite craftsmanship, three of which were blackletter styles probably employed for their economical use of space.

For the printing of Saint Augustine's *De civitate Dei* in 1470, the Von Speyer brothers cut an exceptionally graceful and delicate font that is considered by many to qualify as the first roman typeface. It was modelled on a contemporary Italian manuscript style known as Scrittura Umanistica. Almost as handsome as the type of Nicolas Jenson, the design is executed with great technical skill and presented in generously proportioned pages that are the product of immaculately even presswork.

'Many roman types of varying degrees of purity and attractiveness were used by Italian printers of this period,' wrote D. B. Updike in 1937. 'It was reserved for John and Wendelin de Spire to show a roman type which today appears roman to us. In the fount used … this very modern quality can be clearly recognized.'

legitur: confiderent nihil effe diuturnum in quo eft aliquid extremum: & oĩa feculorum fpacia definita: fi æternitati interminate comparentur : non exigua exiftimanda effe fed nulla. Ac per hoc. fi non quinque uel fex : uerum etiam fexaginta milia fiue fexcenta aut fexagefies aut fexceties milia dicerent ãnoɤ: aut itidem per totidem totiens multiplicaretur hęc fumma: ubi iam nullum numeri nomē haberemus ex quo deus hominem fecit: fimiliter quęri poffȝ cur ante nõ fecerit. Dei quippe ab hominis creatione ceffatio retrorfus aeterna fine initio tanta eft: ut fi ei conferatᷓ qͫmlibȝ magna & ieffabilis numerofitas temporum: quę tamen fine conclufa certis fpaciis terminatur: nec faltem tãta uideri debeat : quanta fi humoris breuiffimam guttam uniuerfo mari etiam quantum oceanus circumfluit comparemus: quoniam iftorum duorũ unum quidem perexiguum eft : alterum incomparabiliter magnum: fed utrunque finitum . Illud uero temporis fpacium quod ab initio aliquo progreditur .& aliquo termino coercetur: magnitudine quantacũque tendatur: comparatum illi quod initium non habȝ: nefcio utrum pro minimo an potius pro nullo deputandum eft . Huic enim fi a fine uel breuiffima fingillatim momenta detrahantur: decrefcente numero licȝ tam igenti ut uocabulum non iueniat retrorfum redeundo: tanquam fi hominis dies ab illo in quo nunc uiuit ufqȝ ad illum in quo natus eft detrahas : ᷓqͩndoque ad initiũ illa detractio pducetᷓ . Si autem detrabantur retrorfus in fpacio quod a nullo cępit exordio : nõ dico fingillatim minuta momenta uel horarum: aut dieɤ aut menfium aut ãnorũ etiam quantitates : fed tam magna fpacia quanta illa fumma compraehendit annorum: quę iam dici a quibuſlibȝ computatoribus: non poteft: quae tamē momentoɤ minutatim detractione confumitᷓ: & detrahantᷓ hęc tanta fpacia non femel atque iterum fępiufqȝ fed femper: quid fit: quid agitur: quãdo nũq ad initium quod omnino nullum eft puenitur? Quapropter quod nos modo quęrimus poft quinque milia & quod amplius excurrit annorum: poffent & pofteri etiam poft annorum fexcenties milies eadem curiofitate requirere fi intantum haec mortalitas hominum exoriendo & occumbendo & imperita perfeuerarȝ infirmitas . Potuerunt & qui fuerunt ante nos ipfis recentibus hominis creati temporibus iftam mouere quęftionem. Ipfe denique primus homo uel poftridie uel eodē die pofteaᷓq factus eft: potuit inquirere cur non ante fit factus . Et quandocunque antea factus effȝ : non uires tunc alias & alias nunc uel etiam poftea ifta de initio reɤ tęporaliũ cõtrouerfiam reperirȝ.

Cᷓ xiii: De reuolutione feculorum quibus certo fine concluſis uniuerfa femper feundem ordinem eandemqȝ fpem redita

HAnc autem fe philofophi mundi huius nõ aliter putauerunt poffe uel debere diffoluerȝ: nifi ut circuitus temporum induceret: qbus eadem femper fuiffent: renouata atque repetita in rerum natura: atque ita deinceps fore fine ceffatione affeuerarent uolumi uenientium preterentiumque feculorum

Ty	**Caxton's Bastarda**
Ca	**Blackletter**
Ke	**Bastarda**
Te	**Letterpress**
Da	**1476**
De	**Johan Veldener**
Fo	**William Caxton**
Co	**UK**

Characteristics

Ornate capitals

Looped ascenders

d Angled uncial stem

f long s Long, pointed descender

r s Alternate forms

w Tall

be da de ha he oo pr re th Ligatures

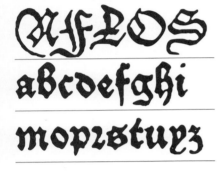

Connections

Gutenberg's Bastarda	1454
Zainer's Gotico-Antiqua	1468
Upper Rhine Bastarda	1485
The Wittenberg Bastarda	1508

Availability

Not available

Specimen

Geoffrey Chaucer, *The Canterbury Tales*.
William Caxton, London, 1476
(262x175mm)

And many a iacke of duyr haſt thou ſold
That hath be this hoot and this cold
Of many a pilgrym haſt thou criſtis curs
For of thy perſely yet fare they the wers
Now tel on gentil roger be thy name
But I pray the be not wroth for game
A man may ſay ful ſoth in game and pley
Thow ſaiſt ſoth ſayde Roger be my fey
But ſoth pley quade pley as the flemyng ſaith
And therfore harry baily be thy feyth
Be thow not wroth ar we departen here
Though that my tale be of an hoſtillere
But natheles I wil not telle it yet
But or we departe Iwis thou ſhalt be qwyt
And therwith al he lowgh and made chere
And ſayde his tale as ye ſhul aftir here

      Here endith the cokis prolog ✠
      And begynneth his tale ✠

A Prentis whilom duelt in our cyte
      Of craft of vitaillers was he
As gaylard he was as goldſmyth in þ ſhalbe
Brown as a bery a proper felalbe
With lokkis I kembid ful fetouſly
Daunce he coude wel and iolily
Than he was clepid Perkyn Reuelour
He was as ful of loue and paramour
As is the hyue ful of hony ſwete
Wel was the wenche þ with hym mighte ſlepe
And at euery bridale wolde he ſynge & hoppe

William Caxton (c1420–c1491) introduced the art of printing to England. He was not, however, a printer in the sense of being directly involved in presswork and he certainly did not cut his own type. Rather, he was a pragmatic, visionary businessman who understood the value of printing in furthering his interests in the new trade of publishing and bookselling.

He had first recognized the potential of the new technology while working in various locations in the Low Countries and in Germany, the birthplace of printing in Europe. After venturing into bookselling, he set up his own press in Bruges, publishing seven editions, including the first book printed in the English language. In 1476, Caxton re-established himself in London, bringing with him a team of skilled craftsmen from Europe, together with all of the equipment and materials they needed to set up the first printing press in England.

One of his earliest publications was Chaucer's *Canterbury Tales*, a judicious choice for the first major book for the English market. Its first edition was published in 1476 and the second, illustrated with woodblock prints, in 1483. For the first edition, shown here, Caxton chose a type designed to appeal to an educated readership. Cut for him by Johan Veldener, an experienced Flemish punch cutter, it was based on the gothic handwriting then extensively used in European universities. Known as Bastarda, its ornate, angular forms and numerous ligatures had evolved from Textura (pp14–15) specifically for the production of non-religious documents.

During his lifetime, William Caxton published over 100 editions, most of them in the English language. At a time when most European books were printed in Latin, Caxton's carefully considered programme of well-crafted vernacular editions addressed the requirements of a new secular, literate class in England, while transforming and elevating the status of their native language at the same time.

Ty	**Ratdolt's Rotunda**
Ca	**Blackletter**
Ke	**Rotunda**
Te	**Letterpress**
Da	**1482**
De	**Erhard Ratdolt**
Fo	**Erhard Ratdolt**
Co	**Germany**

Characteristics

Ornate capitals

Short ascenders and descenders

Flat stroke terminals at baseline

Arabic numerals

a Double-storeyed with closed upper loop

d Curved uncial stem

g Closed tail

h Curved uncial form

r s Alternate forms

Connections

Availability

Not available

Specimen

Euclid, *Elementa geometriae*. Erhard
Ratdolt, Venice, 1482 (270x197mm)

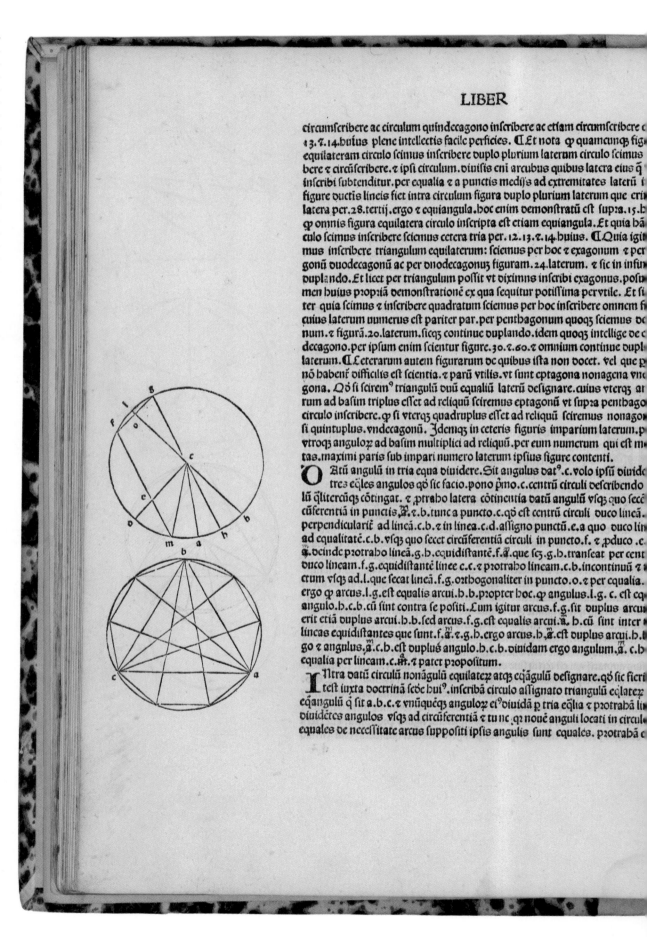

Erhard Ratdolt (1447–1528) of Augsburg was one of a large number of pioneering German printers who emigrated to Italy. Ratdolt set up a press in Venice in 1476, but a decade later he returned to Augsburg to establish a print workshop there.

One of the most productive printers of his time, Ratdolt is renowned for the quality of his editions. He also introduced a number of ingenious innovations. He was the first printer to make use of a title page in one of his books, and in 1486 he published the first formalized type specimen ever printed. It was an extensive document, with one Greek typeface, three romans and ten sizes of Rotunda, the blackletter style shown here in his edition of Euclid's *Elementa geometriae*.

The first large-scale printed scientific text, the *Elementa geometriae* became essential reading for Renaissance scholars and went through many editions in the sixteenth century. A generously proportioned publication, it is considered an early masterpiece of typographic craft, showing great care and attention to detail in its design, presswork and finishing. In addition to a spectacular title page with a unique ornamental border, the book features hundreds of decorated woodcut initials and around 420 intricate geometric scientific diagrams. Originally thought to have also been woodcuts, recent research suggests that the diagrams may actually have been printed from fine metal rules or castings.

The text in Ratdolt's edition is in the Rotunda blackletter, a style that Nicolas Jenson had first cut in 1474. It was modelled on a scribal hand common in fifteenth-century southern Europe that was based primarily on gothic traditions, but that also has the beginnings of some roman tendencies. A hierarchy of two sizes of type is used throughout Ratdolt's *Elementa geometriae* with a mix of ornate roman initials and smaller two-line text capitals that are characteristic of the Rotunda form.

Creussner's Schwabacher

Ty	Creussner's Schwabacher
Ca	Blackletter
Ke	Schwabacher
Te	Letterpress
Da	1485
De	Friedrich Creussner
Fo	Friedrich Creussner
Co	Germany

Characteristics

A H M S	Distinctive forms
a	Single-storeyed
d	Curved uncial stem
f long s	Long descender
g	Open tail, flat top-stroke
h	Curved uncial form

AHGMS
abcdefghi
moprstuvx

Connections

Alte Schwabacher	1835
Offenbacher Schwabacher	1900
Schneidler Schwabacher	1913
Ehmcke Schwabacher	1914

Availability

A digital version of a revival from 1913, Schneidler Schwabacher, is available at typOasis

Specimen

Konrad Celtis, *Proseuticum ad Fridericum III*. Friedrich Creussner, Nuremberg, c1487 (203x135mm)

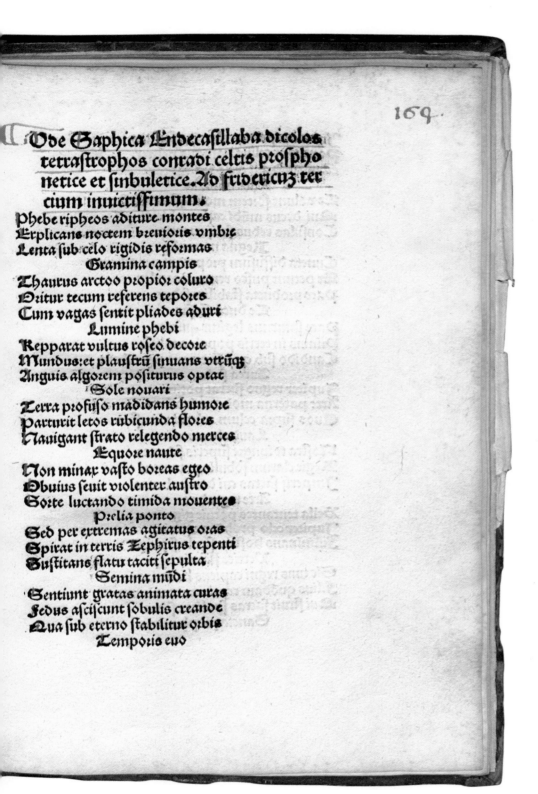

Friedrich Creussner was a German printer and publisher who was active in Nuremberg from 1472 to 1496. Very little is known about his life, but around 180 of his publications have survived. Most of these are broadside single sheets and educational textbooks of relatively short extent. Despite the modesty of his output, his presswork was executed to a very high standard and is distinguished by his implementation of seven different styles of blackletter type.

Proseuticum ad Fridericum III, shown here, is a comparatively small volume, printed around 1487 in a style of blackletter that Creussner had first used two years previously. This style of letter, called Schwabacher, had developed from Textura (pp14–15), with the additional influence of contemporary humanist type designs from Italy.

Because it bore a closer resemblance to ordinary German handwriting than Textura, during the first half of the sixteenth century Schwabacher became the most popular and widespread typeface for publications concerning secular and educational subjects in Germany. It was particularly ubiquitous in printing from Nuremberg during that period. However, after about 1550 its popularity declined and it became used selectively as a secondary type in much the same way that italic is used nowadays with roman.

Creussner's Schwabacher has several distinctive characteristics, most notably the softening of the angularities of Textura by means of curved strokes, and the relatively even visual balance between upper and lower case letters. In earlier blackletter typefaces, the capital letters had shown a great deal of variation and often bore no formal relationship to the lower case forms, but with Schwabacher the design of both is consistent and harmonious.

Ty	**Griffo's Roman / Bembo**
Ca	**Serif**
Ke	**Old Style**
Te	**Letterpress**
Da	**1495**
De	**Francesco Griffo**
Fo	**Aldus Manutius**
Co	**Italy**

Characteristics

A	Flat apex
G	No spur
J	Descends below baseline
K	Bowed arms
M	Splayed
R	Wide leg
T	Opposing serifs
W	Crossed centre-strokes
a	Double-storeyed, small bowl
f	Extended arch
g	Double-storeyed, ear thickens at right

ABENRS
abcdefghi
moprstuy

Connections

Garamond's Roman	c1538
Centaur	1914
Poliphilus	1920
Bembo	1929

Availability

Monotype Bembo is available from
Monotype and resellers

Specimen

Pietro Bembo, *De Aetna*. Aldus Manutius,
Venice, 1495 (176x129mm)

rominium memorabile:nam de hoc poe
tae uersu (si recte memini) nobis pueris
nondum inter grammaticos conuenie-
bat : qua quidem in readhuc illi arbi-
trum si quaerunt; plane uideo eam cōtro
uersiam posse dirimi a Niso tuo ;a quo ne
scio q̃ blande caeteri hospites suscipian-
tur ;te certe (ut illi dicerent) etiam elegan
tiorem remisit: Sed sequere.   B.   F.
Taurominii cum ueterum monumento
rum reliquiae plures uisuntur, templa ,
sepulchra, aquaeductus:quin saepe teme
re graeca numismata passim effodiuntur
áffabre facta illa quidem , neq; in aes modo insculpta ; sed in argentum , sed in au-
rum; quod etiam Syracusis plurimum ,
et ferè per totam insulam euenit :tum eti
am coctile theatrum adhuc manet paulo,
q̃ id , quod Romae uidimus ,minus ;nisi
ꝗ illud amphitheatrum est: quae quidem omnia eò inspexi diligentius ; ꝗ
te recordabar plurimum semper uete-

rum hominum imaginibus, monumen
tísque, tanq̃ uirtutum illorum, et gesta-
rum rerum testibus, oblectari.   Vrbs
ipsa loco praecelso, atq; edito sita, et mõ
tium angulo promissa in pelagus pro-
spectum maris Ionii late hinc inde do-
minatur: theatrum ultimam anguli ru
pem insedit, qua collis cõspicuus ante
omnem urbem in circum planitiem du
cens audentior procurrit in mare ; atq;
hinc fluctibus, inde urbe medius ipse ter
minatur. E Taurominitano demissi iu
go, et littore paulatim relicto, uallémq;
ingressi; quam a leua Aetnae radices, a
dextra Taurominitani montes effici-
unt; per eam Randatium usq; peruenì-
mus nouum oppidum, et in Aetnae radicibus, qua parte mediterranea despe-
ctat, situm. iter totum a Taurominio no
bis quatuor, et uiginti mil. pass. comfe-
ctum est. uallis sonoro, et ppetuo flumine
scinditur, et irrigatur. Platani numerosa

In 1495, 15 years after Nicolas Jenson's death, a new roman typeface appeared in Venice, one of the major centres of printing in the late fifteenth century. This design became the progenitor of all old-style typefaces, setting a new standard for typographic excellence. The type was cut for the Venetian printer and publisher Aldus Manutius (1449–1515) by Francesco Griffo (1450–1518) for use in *De Aetna*, a short travelogue written by the young Italian humanist poet Pietro Bembo.

Aldus Manutius is one of the most revered names in typographic history, although he was certainly neither a punch cutter nor a pressman. A scholar, businessman and publisher, he eschewed books on religious subjects, instead producing editions of classical texts in Latin, Greek and Italian that reflected the humanist cultural sensibilities of the day. His ambition was to print definitive works that were meticulously edited and of the highest production standards.

Manutius's books were the perfect vehicles for Francesco Griffo's types. Griffo was the first punch cutter whose designs were as much a product of their technology as they were a reflection of the humanist manuscript hands on which they were modelled. Using consummate craft skills, Griffo exploited type production techniques and materials to cut and cast types that were more precise and more refined than had been achieved previously.

As Nicolas Jenson had done in 1470, Griffo based his capitals on Roman monumental inscriptions, with the lower case developed from contemporary humanistic scripts that were themselves rooted in the ninth-century Carolingian minuscule. The delicacy of his roman type contrasts with Jenson's earlier, heavier letterforms. The stress of the letters is angled and the serifs in the lower case characters are oblique and sharply cut. These curve gracefully into the stems of letters that are themselves full and rounded. One of the main characteristics that distinguished Griffo's types from earlier Venetian forms is the way in which the capitals stand at a lower height than the ascenders of the lower case letters so that in bodies of text they do not obtrude.

Manutius became enormously successful and his work was highly influential on the burgeoning class of literate professionals in Renaissance Italy. His publications were groundbreaking, both formally and ideologically, as were the roman types in which they were set.

Ty	**Griffo's Italic / Aldine Italic**
Ca	**Serif**
Ke	**Old Style Italic**
Te	**Letterpress**
Da	**1501**
De	**Francesco Griffo**
Fo	**Aldus Manutius**
Co	**Italy**

Characteristics

A	Angled apex
G	Spur serif
M	Splayed
P	Open bowl
Q	Long tail
W	Centre-strokes meet at apex
a	Single-storeyed
b h k l	Serifed ascender only
g	Inclined to left
k	Closed bowl
p q	Serifed descender only
et fa fi fp fr if	Ligatures

ACMPQR
abcdefghi
moprstux

Connections

Availability

Bembo Italic is available from Monotype and resellers

Specimen

C. Plinii secundi novocomensis epistolarum libri decem. Aldus Manutius, Venice, 1508 (150x90mm)

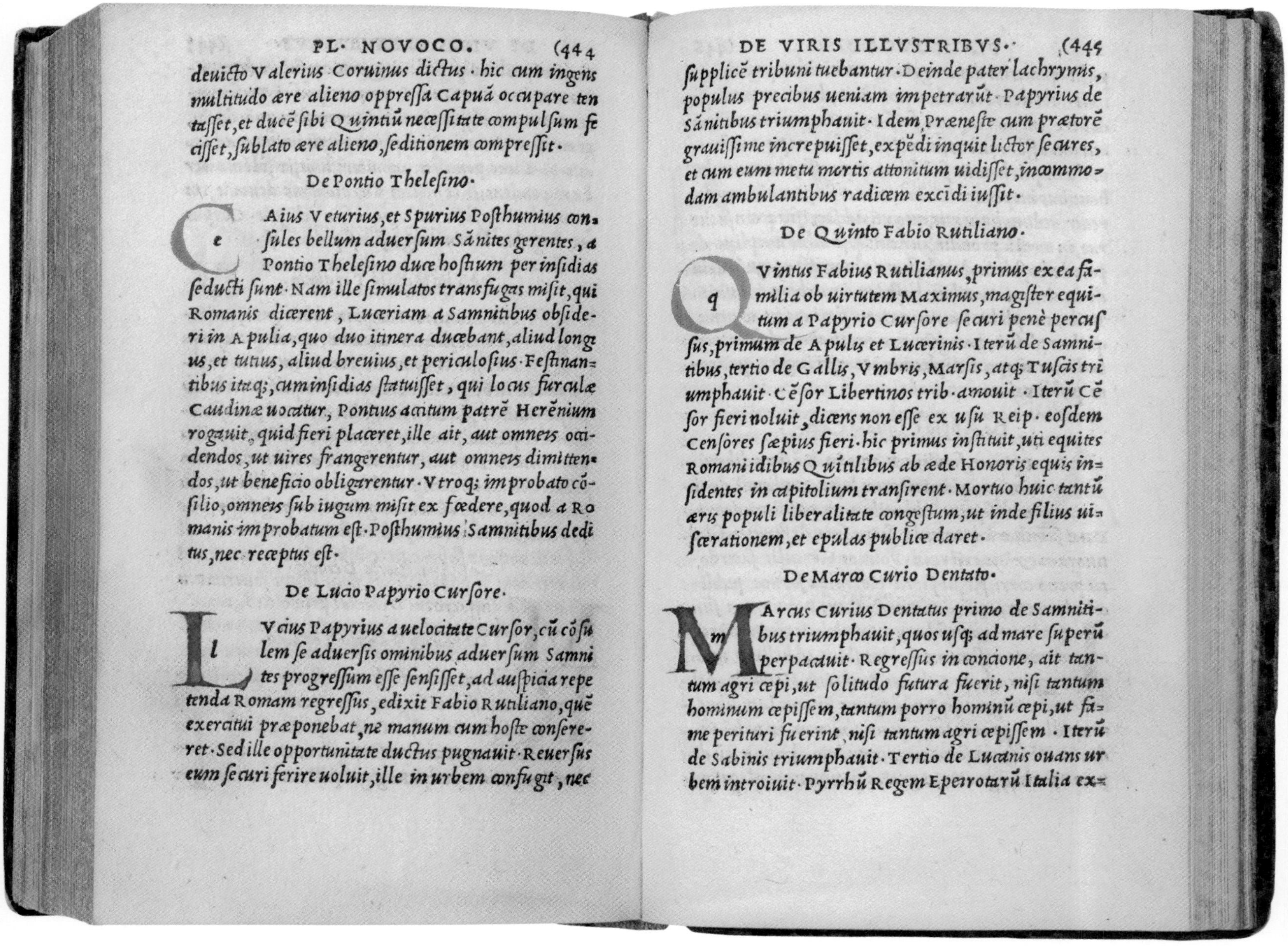

1501

The roman types of Francesco Griffo (1450–1518) were not his only enduring contribution to typographic history. Towards the end of the fifteenth century, when most books were large and heavy, the need arose for a smaller, cheaper, portable publication format suited to the requirements of a new, mobile class of literate professionals across Europe. To meet this demand, Aldus Manutius (1449–1515) commissioned Griffo to cut a new, space-saving form: the italic.

Manutius was an astute businessman as well as a scholar and a publisher, as attentive to profit as to quality. Intending to publish mass editions of the classics and appreciating the economy of the papal chancery hand, he had the first italic type cut in 1500, issuing his first pocket-sized, cheap volumes the following year. Manutius's new series of books had a number of unique distinguishing features. The text was meticulously edited in a plain setting without commentaries or other additions. It was printed on a fine, lightweight paper in an exceptionally small, narrow format (approximately 150x90mm) and it was set in Griffo's tiny italic typeface. First appearing in a 1501 edition of Virgil, Griffo's Italic was a remarkable invention. Nowadays, and for centuries, italic has been thought of as a subsidiary to roman, to be used selectively within bodies of text to provide emphasis or contrast: a compressed, slanted letterform that is different from the upright letters while remaining harmonious and even in tone. However, the italic form was originally conceived as a completely autonomous typeface, designed specifically to be used on its own throughout small-format publications.

Griffo's cut of the first italic on a rectangular body was an exceptional technical achievement. Despite its diminutive size and extremely compact fit, he managed to retain many of the features of cursive handwriting, with regularly inclined letterforms and flowing extenders. Renaissance scribes used roman capitals in cursive chancery hands, and Griffo followed this practice in the design of his italic type. As with his earlier roman (pp30–31), these are shorter than the ascenders of the lower case so that they do not obtrude visually. Inclined capitals matching the italic lower case were not introduced until the 1550s (pp58–59).

Griffo's blueprint for the italic form was not without flaws. Because it was modelled on scribal hands, it included as many as 60 ligatures, complicating the compositor's work and giving the impression of a script that was described by the type historian A. F. Johnson as 'hasty'. Nevertheless, the convenience of the small Aldine Press books ensured their popularity, resulting in the widespread distribution of Griffo's new italic across Europe.

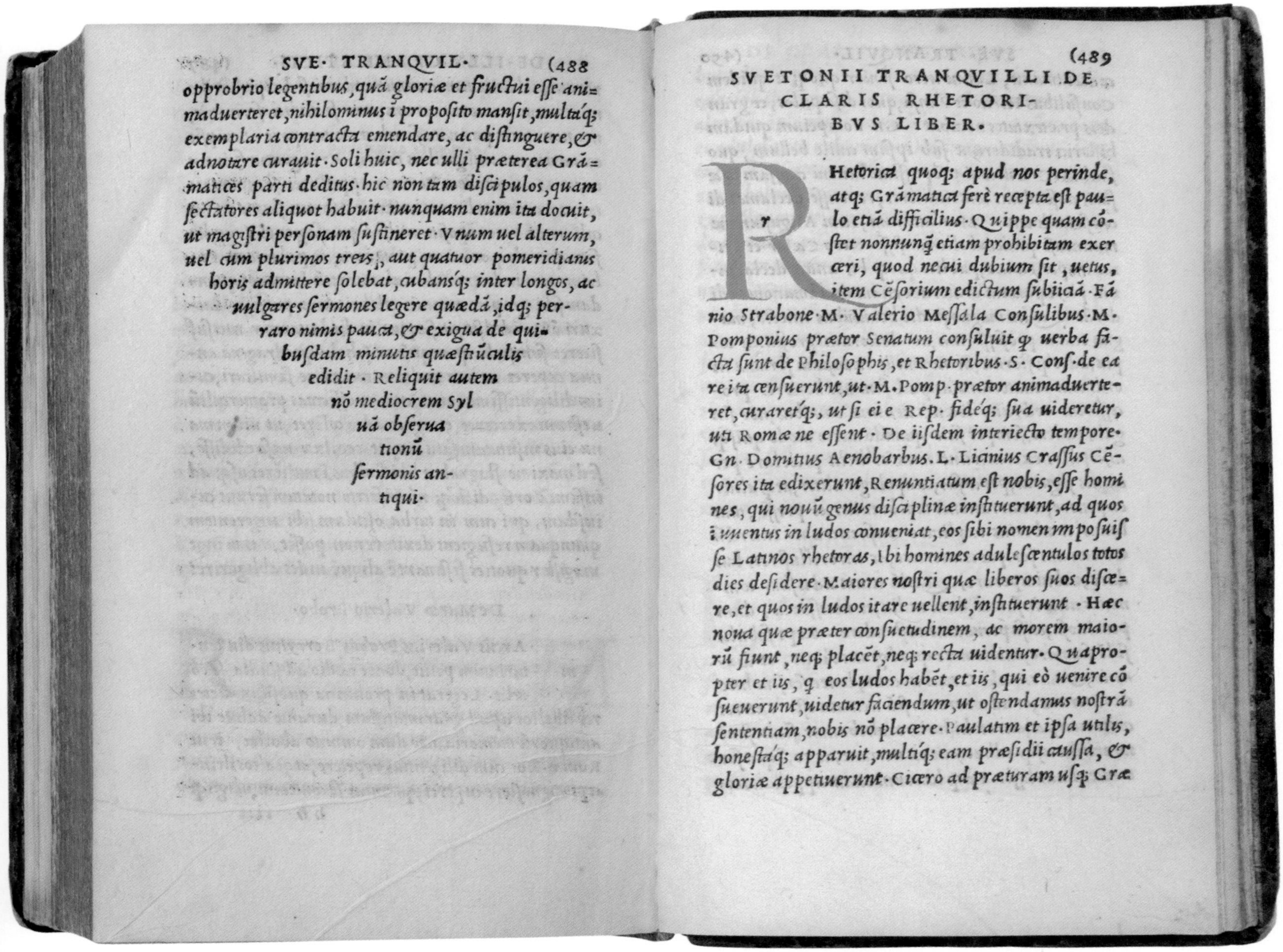
SVE· TRANQVIL· (488
opprobrio legentibus, quā gloriæ et fructui esse ani=
maduerteret, nihilominus ĩ proposito mansit, multaq;
exemplaria contracta emendare, ac distinguere, &
adnotare curauit· Soli huic, nec ulli præterea Grã=
matices parti deditus· hic non tam discipulos, quam
sectatores aliquot habuit· nunquam enim ita docuit,
ut magistri personam sustineret· Vnum uel alterum,
uel cum plurimos treis, aut quatuor pomeridianis
horis admittere solebat, cubansq; inter longos, ac
uulgares sermones legere quædã, idq; per-
raro nimis pauca, & exigua de qui-
busdam minutis quæstiũculis
edidit· Reliquit autem
nõ mediocrem Syl
uã obserua
tionũ
sermonis an-
tiqui·

(489
SVETONII TRANQVILLI DE
CLARIS RHETORI-
BVS LIBER.
R
Hetorica quoq; apud nos perinde,
atq; Grãmatica ferè recepta est pau=
lo etiã difficilius· Quippe quam cõ-
stet nonnunq̃ etiam prohibitam exer
ceri, quod necui dubium sit, uetus,
item Cẽsorium edictum subiiciã· Fã
nio Strabone· M· Valerio Messala Consulibus· M·
Pomponius prætor Senatum consuluit q; uerba facta sunt de Philosophis, et Rhetoribus· S· Cons· de ea
re ita censuerunt, ut· M· Pomp· prætor animaduerte-
ret, curaretq;, ut si ei e Rep· fideq; sua uideretur,
uti Romæ ne essent· De iisdem interiecto tempore·
Gn· Domitius Aenobarbus· L· Licinius Crassus Cẽ-
sores ita edixerunt, Renuntiatum est nobis, esse homi
nes, qui nouũ genus disciplinæ instituerunt, ad quos
iuuentus in ludos conueniat, eos sibi nomen imposuis
se Latinos rhetoras, ibi homines adulescentulos totos
dies desidere· Maiores nostri quæ liberos suos discæ=
re, et quos in ludos itare uellent, instituerunt· Hæc
noua quæ præter consuetudinem, ac morem maio-
rũ fiunt, neq; placẽt, neq; recta uidentur· Quapropter et iis, q̃ eos ludos habẽt, et iis, qui eò uenire cõ
sueuerunt, uidetur faciendum, ut ostendamus nostrã
sententiam, nobis nõ placere· Paulatim et ipsa utilis,
honestaq; apparuit, multiq; eam præsidii caussa, &
gloriæ appetiuerunt· Cicero ad præturam usq; Græ

Ty	**Hopyl's Textura**
Ca	**Blackletter**
Ke	**Textura**
Te	**Letterpress**
Da	**1506**
De	**Wolfgang Hopyl**
Fo	**Wolfgang Hopyl**
Co	**France**

Characteristics

Heavy, upright letters

Angled junctions

Vertical emphasis

a Double-storeyed with closed upper loop

d Angled uncial stem

h i m n Strokes terminate in points at foot

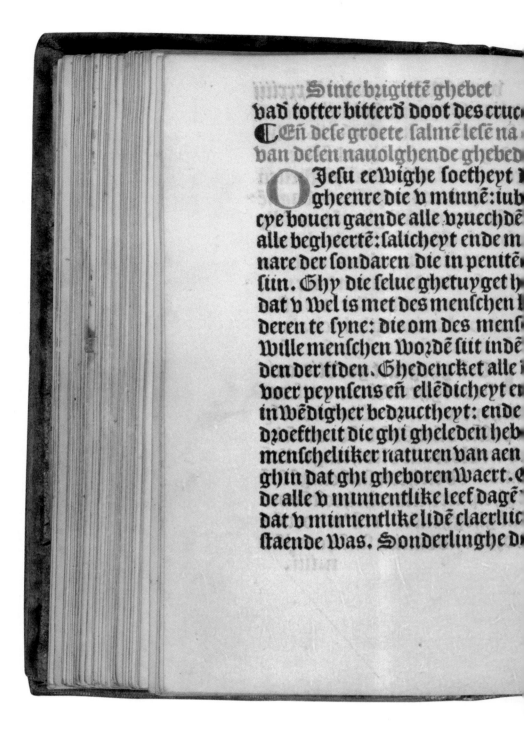

Connections

Caslon Black	1763
Manuskript-Gotisch	1899
Cloister Black	1904
Monotype Old English Text	1935

Availability

English Textura is a digital revival available from Hoefler & Co. and resellers

Specimen

Book of Hours, *Ghetyden van onser liever vrouwen*. Wofgang Hopyl, Paris, c1506 (160x120mm)

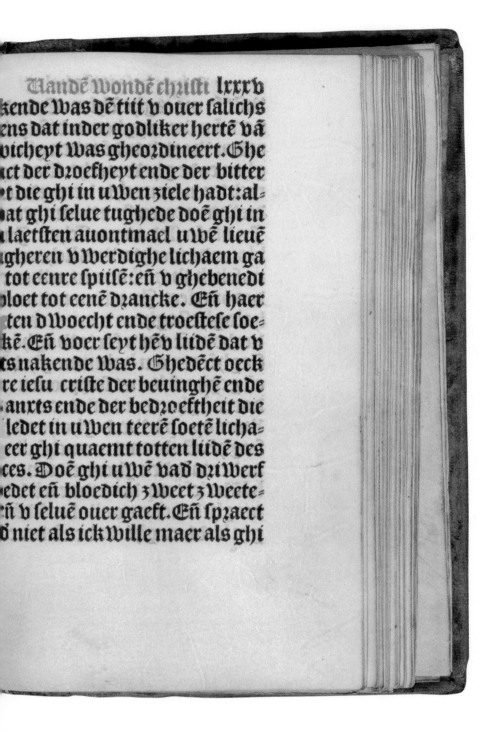

Very little is known about the origins and early career of Wolfgang Hopyl (?–1522) but he is thought to have been born in either Utrecht or The Hague. He is known to have worked with various associates from 1489 as a printer and type founder in Paris, a major publishing centre at the turn of the sixteenth century. His business activities were diverse, with commissions from clients in several European cities, and he was particularly successful in the publication of books for the rapidly expanding English market prior to the advent of printing in England.

Hopyl designed a new form of blackletter Textura typeface that broke with the traditions of German and Low Country types such as those used by Gutenberg (pp14–15). His design is simpler and sharper, resembling the proportions and contours of Textualis Formata, the scribal hand then widely used in England.

As a result, Hopyl's Textura became popular with early English printers such as Wynkyn de Worde and Richard Pynson at a time when English culture, along with its visual and typographic preferences, was influenced more by Germanic than by Roman traditions. Hopyl's typeface has subsequently inspired many revivals and is commonly considered the progenitor of an English blackletter heritage, often being identified as 'Old English Text'.

As its name suggests, one of the key features of Textura type was its capacity to provide a very even overall visual texture to the printed page. To achieve consistent spacing in text blocks that were justified to make rectangular areas early printers relied heavily on the use of a combination of extended, contracted and hyphenated words. The ampersand, derived from the Latin word *et*, is one of the few such abbreviations that remains in use today.

Ty	**The Wittenberg Bastarda**
Ca	**Blackletter**
Ke	**Bastarda**
Te	**Letterpress**
Da	**1508**
De	**Melchior Lotter**
Fo	**Melchior Lotter**
Co	**Germany**

Characteristics

Short ascenders and descenders
Large x-height
M Distinctive asymmetrical form
a Single-storeyed
d Curved uncial stem
f long s Long, pointed descender
g Closed tail
h Curved uncial form

AfMRS
abcdefghi
moprstuvz

Connections

Gutenberg's Bastarda	1454
Zainer's Gotico-Antiqua	1468
Caxton's Bastarda	1476
Upper Rhine Bastarda	1485

Availability

Not available

Specimen

Heinrich von Schleinitz, *Als Ich vormals.*
Melchior Lotter, Leipzig, 1510
(278x195mm)

reychs ordnunge/dir Freytags nach sanct Johannis baptiste schirsten rechter tageczeyt/alhie czu Freybergk/auff vnserm Slosse/vor denenn/so wir nach bemelter ordnung aldo czuhaben/vnd niderczusetzen gedenckenn/czuerscheynen/ ernent vnd vorbescheiden/das du/als wir deins vnbestendigen schreibens/dein czuuorsicht in rechtsflucht gestellet vormerckē/vnnutzlichē anfichtest. So thun wir doch dakegen berurten vnsernn/dir vormals czugeschickten vorbeschiedt/ crafft obgemelter ordnung Repetirn. Vnd nachdem das geleite ins reichs ordnunge begriffen/vnd wir vermogens derselben vnsern vorbeschiedt gestellet ꝛc. Sal doch an vns czum vberflus/wan du vnsern vorbeschiedt/krafts der ordnunge czuersuchen annympst/dich vnnd die ihenigen. So du vngeferlich mit bringst/vnd massen/wie es die ordnung des orts gibt/mit vnserm schrifftlichen geleitte/auff ernante czeyt czuuorsehē/auch nichts mangeln/mit vorsicherung/ du kompst ader nicht/wollen wir vnsernthalben/bemelter des heiligenn reichs ordnung gentzlichen genuge thun/vnd hirmitte getan/auch wes vns im falh deynner vorflucht vnd aussenbleybens/als dan forder geyn dir czuhandeln geburt/nichts begeben haben. Datū ịFreibergk vndter vnserm Secret. Mitwoch nach dem sontag Jubilate. Anno.xv.c.decimo.   In dem selbenn brieff thut mir hertzog Heinrich rechtsflucht vnnd vnbestendig schreyben czumessen/mit was grunde solichs geschehen magk/ist aus vorgemelten schrifften/vnd meynem vorgewandten vleis/recht czubekomen/leichtlich czuuermercken. Vnd ab wol solich brieff anczweyffel/bey allen menschen vorordenlichen vorbeschiedt/ nicht czuachten ist. Dieweil aber doch etzwas Keyserlicher Maiestat vnd des heiligen reichs ordnung/mit wenig wortten/darinne angeczeiget/mich mit geleit czuuorsehen/vñ ich kom ader nicht/Keyserlicher ordnung gentzlich gnugk czuthun/bewilliget ist/wie dem volge geschehen/wirdt sich hirnach befinden. Vff das hertzog Heinrich/weygerung des rechten/darauff alle sein vorberurte handelung gestelt ist/nicht stat gegeben/vnd mein recht vorgangk erreichenn mocht. Hab ich darnach/in meinem offenn brieffe/den ich hertzog Heinrich abermals mit czweyenn erbarn mannen/in beywesenn eins offenbaren schreybers czugesannt/angesatztenn rechts tag czubesuchen angenomen/nach seiner gethanenn vorwillung/vnnd wie sich aus crafft Keyserlicher ordnung geburt/ sicherung czu vnd von solichem tage/gesonnen/wie dan aus nachuolgendem/ desselben meyns briues inhalt clerlicher czubefinden ist.   Dem hochgebornen fursten herrn Heynrichen hertzogen czu Sachssen ꝛc. Hebe ich Heynrich von Sleynitz ꝛc Obermarschalh/in dieser meiner schrifft czuerkennen. Als ich kurtz nach Letare nechstuergangen/aus meiner nodturft ewer furstliche wird angesucht/mir nach laut Romischer keyserlicher Maiestat vnnd des heiligenn reichs ordnung recht czupflegen. Daruff mir Dinstages nach Quasimodogeniti/ein offen brieff/in scheyn eins vorbeschiedes czukomen/den ich vorbemelter ordnung/vnd dem rechtenn vngemeß befunden/deshalben/darein czuwilligē/ nicht vnbillich beswert gewest/vñ dy czeit in meiner antwort/auch nachuolgēde in meinem verslossen brieffe/ewer furstliche wird/vmb ordenliche vorbeschiedt/ czu vberflus/ferner erinnert/des ich bis am mōtag nach Lætate iungst verschinnen/gemägelt. So mir aber desselbē tages/ewer furstlichē wird offenner brieff/ yberreicht ist/darinne ewer furstlich wird/angeczeigte vormeinte vorbeschiedt clerē/das der nach ordnūg/des heillgē reichs sal geacht sein/auch mich vñ mein

nenn beyſtandt czu vnnd von beſtymptem tag/ nach auſzweyſſung vilberurter
ordnung/ſicher czugeleitten erbietten. Wiewol die czeit/darinne mir diſz alles
hat widerfaren ſollen verlauffen/aus dem vnd anderm/der letzten Ewer furſt⸗
lichen wird ſchrifft inhalts/ich mein recht in ander wege czuſuchenn fug vnnd
vrſach het. Offt das aber mein begirlicher wille/dieſer ſachen rechtlichenn auſz
trag czuhaben/vermarckt werde/wil ich abgotwil vff Freitag nach ſant Johã⸗
nes baptiſta tag ſchirſt volgende vor ewer furſtlichen wirdenn Reten vff dem
Slos ſreyberg/gegen vnnd wider ewer furſtlichen wird/mein rechtliche clag
anſtellen/nach inhalt Romiſcher keyſerlicher Ma. vnd des heiligen reichs ord⸗
nung/vnd anders nicht/rechtens gewartten. So ferne mir bey gegenwerttigen
diſz briues czeygern/nach auſweyſung berurter ordnung/vnd ewerm erbietten/
des ich ewer furſtliche wird hirmit thu erinnern/genugkſam geleyt/geſchickt
wirdt. Vñ in mangel deſſelben/auch ſuſt/wil ich in ichtes/vilberurter ordnung
entkegen/nicht gewilliget/ader was mir daraus geburen magk/nicht begeben
haben. Dauon ich in dieſem meynem briue offentlich proteſtire. Datũ vnder
meinem petzſchir ſreitags nach dem Sontag Exaudi. Anno dñi. xv. c. decimo.

   Wiewol ich mich vorſehen/hertzog Heinrich/wurd aus betrachtung der
billickeit/mir nach vorigem ſeinem erbietten/ſicherung vnd gleyt geſchickt ha⸗
ben/vff das ich mich mit beyſtandt/vnd ander meiner nodturfft/czu ſolichem
rechts tag/hette ſchicken mogen/es iſt aber nicht geſchehen/Sunder hertzog
Heinrich hat vff die czeit mein geſchickten/ein offenenn brieff gegeben/des in⸗
halt hirnach begriffen iſt.   Als wir lauts zweyer vnſer ſchrifft/der datum
montags nach dem ſontag Quaſimodogeniti/vnd dinſtags nach dem Son
tag Jubilate/alles iungſten verſchynne. Dir Heinrich von Sleynitz/auff dein
anſuchen/nach vermogen des heiligen reichs ordnung/vff Freytage nach ſant
Johans baptiſte ſchirſten alher gein ſreybergk/vor vnſere rete/tage ernennet
vnd angeſetzt/vnd das an vns/wu du den ſelben vorbeſchiedt crafft der ord⸗
nunge/czuerſuchẽ annympſt/dich vñ die ihenigen/So du vngeferlich mitbrin⸗
gen wirdeſt/inn maſſen wie die ordnunge/des orts gibet/mit vnſerm ſchrifftli⸗
chen gleitte gnugſam czuuerſehen/nichts mangeln ſolde ꝛc. des du/ab du ey⸗
niche begrunte ſache/gein vns rechtlichen czuuorfuren gehabt hetteſt/bis auff
ſolche rechtliche aus vbung/billich wereſt/erſettigt geweſenn. Nachdem vnns
aber/von der ſelben czeit/bis auff hewtte dato/von dir/ab du gedachte vnſere
tageſatzung/an/ader nicht anczunemen/gedechteſt/keyn vormeldung geſcheen
Sundern bynnen des/vnd vber bemelten vnnſern vorbeſchiedt. haſt du eyne
vnwarhafftige ſchrifft/wie vnns die/von vnſern herrn frunden/vnnd andern
czugeſchickt/ausgehenn laſſen/vns weytter damit anczururen/des wir. So dir
eher ader rechts beliebte/billicher verſchonet. In welicher deyner ſchrifft/du
dich czubeſchmuckung/deyner vnrumlichen handle/vorkerter dewttung/vnnd
offentlicher lugen/czugebrauchenn nit geſchempt. Vnd wiewol wir gein Chur
furſten. furſtenn vnnd ſtenden weliche die auſſage der geſchickten von Heſſenn
czu Molhawſen haben angehort. Ader der warhafftigen bericht entpfangen.
auch ane vnſere weyttere antwort. deyns ertichten czumeſſens/enſchuldigt. So
erfordert doch vnſer gelegenheyt/weyl vns ſolichs/vber vnſern bemelte gegebẽ
vorbeſchiedt. võ dir begegẽt/vns des/vñ ander deiner czunottigũg/gein vnſern
hern frundẽ vñ verwãdtẽ/do bey wir vns liebe ere vñ rechts vorſehẽ czuuorant⸗

                                     a iij

Bastarda, a form of blackletter based on gothic handwriting, was widespread in Germany and France during the fifteenth century. It was commonly used for non-scholarly and non-devotional documents considered to be of limited value or importance. Early printers designed local Bastarda typefaces specifically in order to print editions in regional languages. The example shown here was very local indeed, confined to the town of Wittenberg, from where its name is derived.

This typeface was first cut in 1508 in Leipzig for the press of Melchior Lotter (1470–1549). Born in Aue in the Ore Mountain region, he was the head of a family of printers who were leading agitators in the German Reformation, the Protestant movement that rejected the doctrines and practices of the late-medieval Catholic Church.

Lotter and his son, also named Melchior, both worked closely with Martin Luther, one of the leaders of the Protestant reform movement, in the production of several publications disseminating Protestant views, including their enormously influential *Das Newe Testament*. The accessibility of Luther's translation of the New Testament into vernacular German had a resounding impact on the Church as well as on German culture and on global politics.

The overall distinguishing characteristic of the Wittenberg Bastarda is the brevity of the lower case ascenders and descenders, resulting in a large-sized letterform in comparison with other gothic typefaces of the time. For the same reason, pages set in the Wittenberg Bastarda have an unusually dense, tightly packed appearance.

Ty	Wagner's Fraktur
Ca	Blackletter
Ke	Fraktur
Te	Letterpress
Da	1513
De	Leonhard Wagner and Johann Schönsperger
Fo	Johann Schönsperger
Co	Germany

Characteristics

Fragmented letterforms
Narrow character width
Ascenders terminate at sharp points
Upper case 'Schnorkel' terminals
a Single-storeyed
d Curved uncial stem
f long s Long, pointed descender
g Open tail, flat top-stroke
h Curved uncial form

Connections

Breitkopf Fraktur	1750
Unger-Fraktur	1793
Fette Fraktur	c1835
Weiss Fraktur	1913

Availability

Not available

Specimen

Das Gebetbuch Kaiser Maximilians I.
Johann Schönsperger, Augsburg, 1513
(280x195mm)

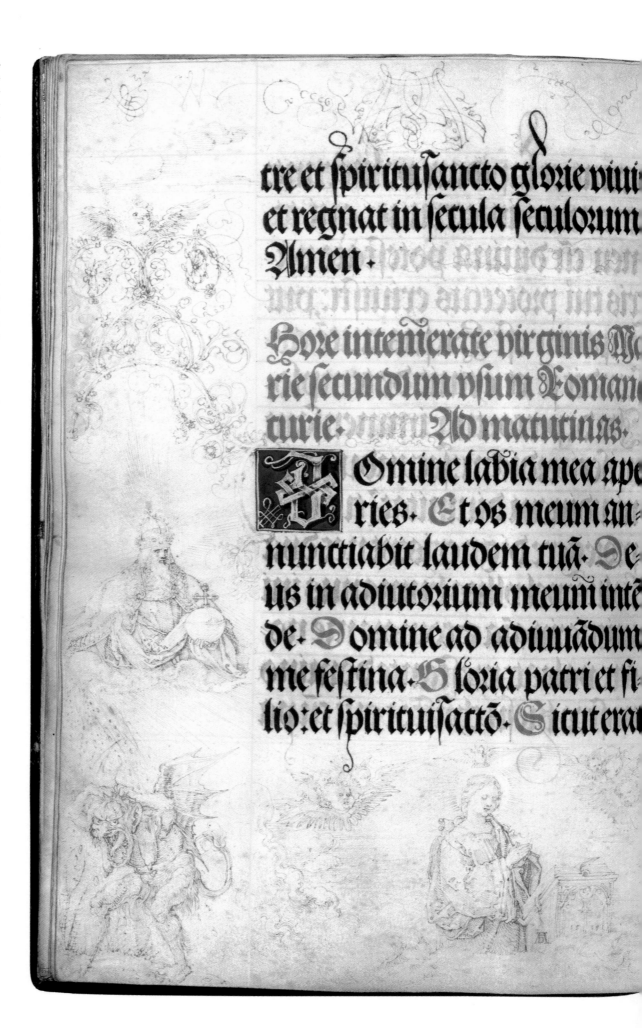

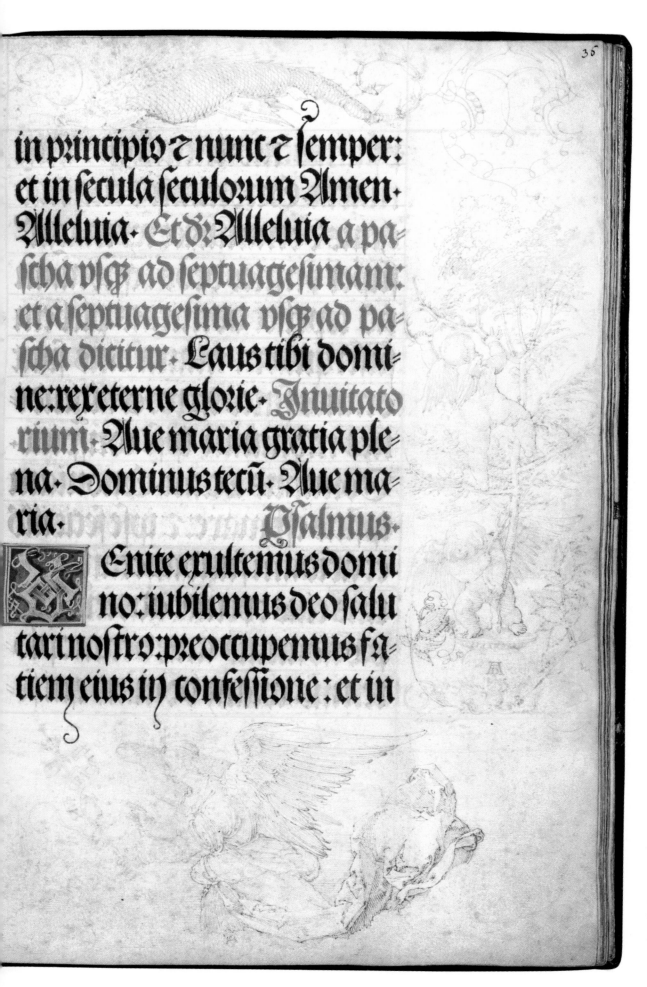

At the end of the fifteenth century, many German books were printed in the dense, angular gothic type known as Textura (pp14–15), but less scholarly and more secular editions were set in the rounder Schwabacher (pp28–29) or Bastarda fonts (pp36–37).

When the Holy Roman Emperor Maximilian the First (1459–1519) inaugurated a new library in 1513, he started by commissioning a prayer book, specifying that a new typeface should be created especially for its production, rejecting existing types as too antiquated, commonplace or ugly for such a project. The calligrapher, Leonhard Wagner, was ordered to design a typeface based on the Bastarda handwriting used by German chancery scribes while Johann Schönsperger was commisioned to cut punches and cast and set type. *Das Gebetbuch Kaiser Maximilians I* was subsequently printed on vellum and distributed for embellishment by the leading artists of the day. The result ranks alongside Gutenberg's 42-line Bible as a masterpiece of early German book production.

The new typeface rapidly supplanted other German gothic forms and became known as Fraktur. This name, derived from the same root as the English 'fracture', denotes its fragmentary linear character. Fraktur is characterized by its restless appearance in bodies of text, with letterforms that are angular in contrast to the smoothly modulated curves of roman scripts. Fraktur's letters are narrow and pointed by comparison with Schwabacher, making it a more economical type in its use of space. The terminations of the ascenders, rising to sharp points, are also notably different. Departing from early gothic traditions, the upper case is essentially calligraphic, with terminals that German scribes have described as 'Schnorkel', or elephants' trunks.

When the Protestant Reformation swept across Germany on a wave of printed propaganda, much of this material was set in the new Fraktur type. Its appearance made it easy for readers not only to recognize textual content as new and radical but also to differentiate Protestant views from Catholic ones: Protestants published in vernacular German, using Fraktur, whereas Catholics printed in Latin, using roman types. This distinction made Fraktur very popular in Germany and led to its becoming identified increasingly as a symbol of national identity. It subsequently became widespread in areas under German influence across Central Europe. Over the succeeding centuries, roman gradually displaced it, although Fraktur persisted in those territories where German remained the spoken language.

Ty	**Arrighi's Second Italic**
Ca	**Serif**
Ke	**Old Style Italic**
Te	**Letterpress**
Da	**1527**
De	**Ludovico Vicentino degli Arrighi**
Fo	**Ludovico Vicentino degli Arrighi**
Co	**Italy**

Characteristics

Long ascenders and descenders
Serifed terminals
e Small eye
g No ear
p Flat foot serif
x Wide
ct st Ligatures
. Large lozenge shape

ACMQR
abcdefghi
moprstux

Connections

Tagliente's Italic	1524
Blado Italic	1923
Le Griffe	1973
Poetica	1992

Availability

Not available

Specimen

Marco Girolamo Vida, *De arte poetica*.
Ludovico Vicentino degli Arrighi, Rome,
1527 (210x140mm)

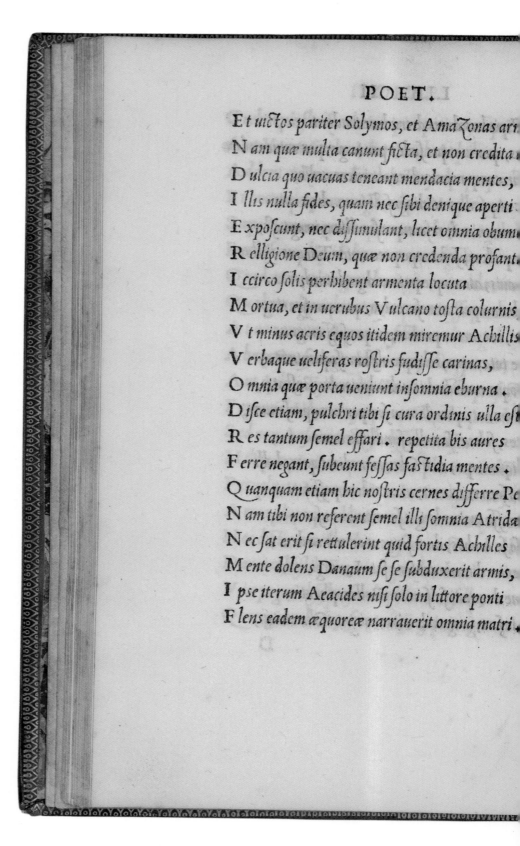

POET.

E t uictos pariter Solymos, et AmaZonas ar

N am quæ multa canunt ficta, et non credita

D ulcia quo uacuas teneant mendacia mentes,

I llis nulla fides, quam nec sibi denique aperti

E xposcunt, nec dissimulant, licet omnia obum

R elligione Deum, quæ non credenda profant

I ccirco solis perhibent armenta locuta

M ortua, et in uerubus Vulcano tosta colurnis

V t minus acris equos itidem miremur Achillis

V erbaque ueliferas rostris sudisse carinas,

O mnia quæ porta ueniunt insomnia eburna .

D isce etiam, pulchri tibi si cura ordinis ulla es

R es tantum semel effari . repetita bis aures

F erre negant, subeunt sessas fastidia mentes .

Q uanquam etiam hic nostris cernes differre Po

N am tibi non referent semel illi somnia Atrida

N ec sat erit si rettulerint quid fortis Achilles

M ente dolens Danaum se se subduxerit armis,

I pse iterum Aeacides nisi solo in littore ponti

F lens eadem æquoreæ narrauerit omnia matri

LIB. II

Q uin etiam reges cum dant mandata ferenda,

C uncta canunt prius ipsi, eadem mox carmine eodem

M isfi oratores repetunt nihil ordine uerso,

N on sic Ausonius Venulus, legatus ab Arpis

C um redit Aetoli referens responsa tyranni .

A ltum aliis assurgat opus . tu nocte, dieque

E xiguum meditator, ubi sint omnia culta,

E t uisenda nouis iterumque, iterumque figuris .

Q uod si longarum cordi magis ampla uiarum

S unt spatia, angustis cum res tibi finibus arcta,

I n longum trahito arte . uiæ tibi mille trahendi,

M ille modi . nam ficta potes multa addere ueris,

E t petere hinc illinc uariarum semina rerum .

N onne uides, ut nostra Deos in prælia ducant,

H os Teucris, alios Danais socia arma ferentes,

C ertantesque inter se odiis, donec pater ipse,

C oncilium uocet, atque ingentes molliat iras :

C um secura tamen penitus natura Deorum

D egat, et aspectu nostro summota quiescat .

A ddunt infernasque domos regna inuia uiuis,

D

Ludovico Vicentino degli Arrighi (1475–1527) was a professional scribe who was appointed to the Apostolic Chancery in Rome in about 1515. His most celebrated and influential work was *La operina*, a handwriting manual published in 1522. This short pamphlet, 32 pages printed from woodblocks rather than movable type, was the first of several publications by Arrighi that offered instruction in the execution of the elegant contemporary Italian script known as Cancelleresca Corsiva, or Chancery Cursive.

Arrighi entered the field of printing and publishing in 1524 in partnership with Lautizio Perugino, a goldsmith who is thought to have worked as his punch cutter. The *De arte poetica* shown here is printed in Arrighi's second italic type, a skilful adaptation of his own Cancelleresca Corsiva hand. Discernment and close attention to detail are evident in all aspects of this edition, not only in the elegant page design, with its generous margins and wide interlinear spaces, but also in the assurance with which the Cancelleresca Corsiva has been translated into typographic form.

The second italic is a large typeface with a very consistent stroke angle and long ascenders and descenders. Serifs have replaced the rounded terminals that were employed in Arrighi's first italic type. Very few ligatures are used and there are no decorative swash letters. Arrighi's italics were vastly superior to those produced by his contemporaries and were widely copied by other foundries.

Arrighi's italic types were revived in the twentieth century by designers such as Stanley Morison and Frederic Warde, whose interpretation of them was used as the italic for Centaur (pp196–97). In recent times, Robert Slimbach has reinterpreted Arrighi's letters in highly effective digital designs, including his Poetica family (pp506–507) and Adobe Jenson Italic (pp556–57).

Ty	**Colines's Roman**
Ca	**Serif**
Ke	**Old Style, French**
Te	**Letterpress**
Da	**1528**
De	**Simon de Colines**
Fo	**Simon de Colines**
Co	**France**

Characteristics

b	Flat top serif
b d o p q	Round bowls
e	Small eye and oblique bar
g	Large lower bowl
i j	Small dot offset to right
v	Vertex below baseline
.	Decorative lozenge shape

ABGNRS
abcdefghi
moprstuv

Connections

Jenson	1470
Griffo's Roman	1495
Estienne's Roman	1537
Garamond's Roman	c1538

Availability

Not available

Specimen

Johannes Chrysostomus, *Liber contra gentiles*. Simon de Colines, Paris, 1528 (197x143mm)

adiuuetur,quãtumᶜᴨ gratia,atᴄᴨ authoritate apud eũdem va=
leas,bonorum cõmodis experiri.quã ego in fententiã fcriberē
plura,nifi te tua fpôte fatis incitatũ effe viderem,& hoc quic=
quid attigi,nõ feci inflammãdi tui caufa,fed teftificãdi potius
amoris fummi erga te mei:qui cupiã ad eius te gloriæ faftigiũ
omni ftudio eniti,omnibus neruis contẽdere,ad quod fane ex
hominib⁹ noftris ad reip.gubernacula antehac accitis pauci=
fimi afpirarũt,dum illorũ animis parua admodum,feu nulla
potius elegãtium ftudiorũ, ingeniorúmve cura obreperet. In
quã ego curã,ac cogitationẽ fic te incũbere velim,vt tibi pla=
ne perfuafum fit,nõ poffe te ex quoquã alio operæprecio me=
lius, q̃ ex eo quod tu iuuandis bonarũ literarũ ftudijs feceris,
nomen iftud ab iniuria obliuionis affertũ immortalitati com
mendare.Cuius quidẽ immortalitatis,qua dixi potiffimũ ra=
tione,parandæ,tametfi,quod modo fum teftatus, haudquaᵍ̃
negligentẽ te effe fcio,tamen nihilominus id ego hic apud te
rurfus & facio,& fæpius pofthac facere inftitui:quod gymni=
corũ certaminũ fpectatores facere confueuere. Illi enim cur=
fores eos clamore,hortatu,fauore, etiam atᴄᴨ etiã profequun
tur,non qui poftremi in ftadio currũt,magno ab æmulis in=
teruallo relicti,fed qui metæ iam proximi de reportãdo victo
riæ præmio,pro fe quifᴄᴨ,puluerulenti nauiter concertant.Po
ftremũ illud erit,vt tibi feparatim cõmendem nõ tantum ftu
dia,fed & fortunas quoᴄᴨ Dionyfij tui,cuius fuprà mentionẽ
feci,hominis linguarũ trium cognitione ornati,eiufdemᴄᴨ fi
de erga te,ftudio,amore(nihil poffum præftãtius dicere)tuo=
rũ nemini cõcedentis:quæ partes te ipfum ad illũ,quod facis,
& diligẽdum,& ornãdum moximopere animare debẽt. Illu=
ftrabit, mihi crede, iftius dignitatis amplitudinẽ beneficiorũ
abs te in illũ collatorũ magnitudo. quem nos & quia tuus,&
quia te dignus,hoc eft & probus,& doctus,& quia nos diligit,
femperᴄᴨ dilexit,in primis amamus, carumᴄᴨ habemus.Be=
ne vale & Brixium tuũ vt amas,amare nunq̃ define. Lutetiæ
ex ædibus noftris XIIII Calend. Apriles. M. D. XXVIII.

DIVI IOANNIS CHRY
SOSTOMI LIBER CONTRA GENTILES
Babylæ epiſcopi ac martyris vitam continens,
Germano Brixio Altiſſiodoreñ. interprete.

Ominus noster IESVS ad crucis ſup
plicium iamiam acceſſurus, ac mor=
tem illam viuificam moriturus, illa
ipſa nocte poſtrema, dum diſcipu=
los ad ſe ſuos ſemotis arbitris vocaſ=
ſet, apud eos quum permulta verba
alia fecit, eoſdem plurimarum rerum cõmonefaciẽs,
tum inter alia, & tale quiddã ad eos locutus eſt. Amen
amen dico vobis, qui credit in me, opera quæ ego fa=
cio, & ille faciet, & his maiora faciet. Atqui multi o=
lim alij magiſtri extitere, qui & diſcipulos habuerũt,
& miracula item oſtentarunt, quemadmodum iacti=
tantes gloriantur gentiles, verũtamen illorum nemo
vnquam eiuſmodi orationem vſurpare, ac ne animo
quidem verſare auſus eſt. neq̃ ſane poſſint è gentili=
bus aliqui, etiam ſi nullius illos mendacij pudeat, com
mõſtrare huiuſmodi elogium, ſermonémve apud ſe
extare. ſpectra quidem certe demortuorum, neq̃ nõ
cadauerum quorundam ſimulachra qui repræſenta=
rent, multi multos apud ſe nouarum, mirandarúmq̃

b.j.

Influenced by roman types from Italy, the work of Parisian printers such as Robert Estienne, Simon de Colines and Antoine Augereau signalled the beginnings of a golden era of French typography in the sixteenth century.

Six years after Henri Estienne's death in 1520, his son Robert (pp46–47) took over his printing and publishing business from the elder Estienne's former assistant, Simon de Colines (1480–1546), who had married Henri's widow in 1522. As a consequence, Colines established his own workshop in the same street. He was widely admired for the outstanding craftsmanship of his presswork and came to be regarded as the most accomplished Parisian typographer working in the 1520s and 1530s. He was a prolific printer, publishing more than 700 titles, most of which were small-format editions of Greek and Latin classics.

The typographer and historian Robert Bringhurst said that Colines 'cut lucid and beautiful type at a crucial moment: when the Latin and Greek alphabets were still engaged in their historic metamorphosis from manuscript to metal'. Although the design of the type seen in his publications is attributed to him, the craftsmen who cut the punches for the romans used by both Colines and Estienne remain unknown, like many others before and since. However, since exclusive types were used by the Estienne family's presses, it is almost certain that they were produced under the direct supervision of Colines.

The Colines roman of 1528, shown here, is set in sizes equivalent to 14 and 16.5 point. They clearly resemble the type first used by Nicolas Jenson in *De evangelica praeparatione* in 1470 (pp20–21), but do not copy it slavishly. Although the fit of the letters is much tighter and the cut is sharper, capitals are of similar height to Jenson's, and the overall weight is even but dense, with comparatively short ascenders and descenders allowing for close line spacing. The clarity of the Colines typeface is enhanced by accomplished presswork, showing a balance of different type sizes in a well-proportioned page layout that is framed by generous margins.

The Basel Italic

Ty	**The Basel Italic**
Ca	**Serif**
Ke	**Old Style Italic**
Te	**Letterpress**
Da	**1537**
De	**Unknown**
Fo	**Sebastian Gryphius**
Co	**Switzerland**

Characteristics

Capitals: inclined, inconsistent angles
Lower case: large x-height, strong incline
A P Swashes
M N R V Variable incline
O Q upright
g Large upper bowl

CEPQS
abcdefghi
moprstuxy

Connections

Granjon's Italic	1560
Jannon's Italic	1621
Van Dijck's Italic	1689
Caslon's Italic	c1725

Availability

Not available

Specimen

Claude Rosselet, *Epigrammata*. Sebastian Gryphius, Lyon, 1537 (198x149mm)

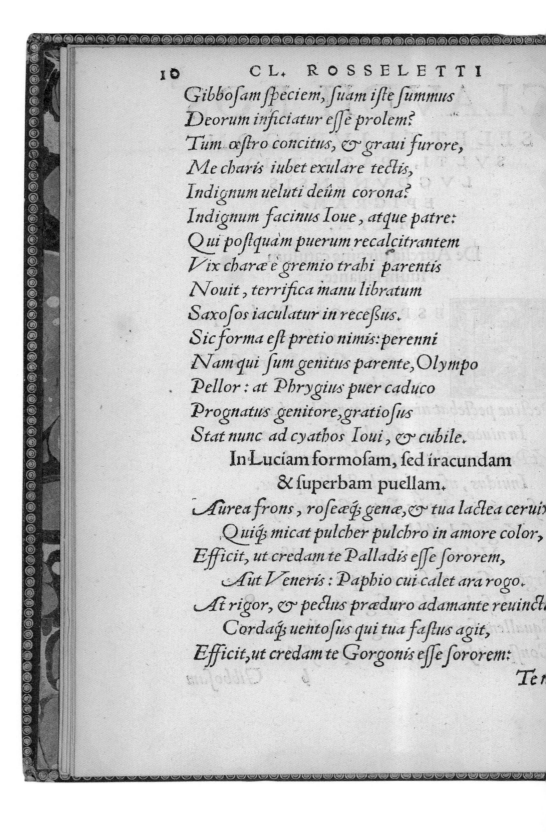

10   CL. ROSSELETTI

Gibbosam speciem, suam iste summus
Deorum inficiatur esse prolem?
Tum æstro concitus, & graui furore,
Me charis iubet exulare tectis,
Indignum ueluti deûm corona?
Indignum facinus Ioue, atque patre:
Qui postquam puerum recalcitrantem
Vix charæ e gremio trahi parentis
Nouit, terrifica manu libratum
Saxosos iaculatur in recessus.
Sic forma est pretio nimis: perenni
Nam qui sum genitus parente, Olympo
Pellor: at Phrygius puer caduco
Prognatus genitore, gratiosus
Stat nunc ad cyathos Ioui, & cubile.
      In Luciam formosam, sed iracundam
            & superbam puellam.
Aurea frons, roseæq; genæ, & tua lactea ceruix
      Quiq; micat pulcher pulchro in amore color,
Efficit, ut credam te Palladis esse sororem,
      Aut Veneris: Paphio cui calet ara rogo.
At rigor, & pectus præduro adamante reuincta
      Cordaq; uentosus qui tua fastus agit,
Efficit, ut credam te Gorgonis esse sororem:
                              Te

EPIGRAMMATA.　II

Te natura ferox noluit esse deam.
Si faciem eximiam facilis mens æquiparasset,
　Nulla foret supera pulchrior arce Venus.
　　Hominis uita, & mors.
Omnia quàm celeri pereunt mortalia lapsu?
　Nostraq; quàm subito frigore uita cadit?
Tam cito non perdit uarium rosa pulchra colorem:
　Tam cito nec liquidis bulla recedit aquis.
Heu breue nigrãtem fugimus post tẽpus ad Orcũ:
　Cunctaq; mors sæua pallida falce metit.
Nec quo abeas scitur: scimus quam soluimus orã:
　Et grauior nullo fit redeunte dolor.
In uario cursu morimur pueriq; senesq;:
　Omnibus hoc certum est: certa nec hora uenit.
　　Candido lectori.
Si iuuat hac nostra spatiari lector arena,
　Atque oculis uersus uoluere forte meos,
Expendas trutina leni, quæcunque licenter
　Scripta mihi riuo liberiore fluunt.
Sic uolui potius, quàm inter luxum otium abuti:
　Et iuuenile æuum deperijsse mihi.
Si bene quid, certe ueniam hac in parte probandus:
　Si male quid, toruum pone supercilium.
Inter odoratos sunt noxia gramina flores:
　　　b　2　　　　Est

The sixteenth century has been called 'the age of italics'. It is thought that in Italy, their birthplace, more books were typeset in them than in roman during the period. Originally, italics were lower case alphabets only, accompanied by upright roman capitals (see pp32–33), but after 1524, various attempts were made to design capitals with a corresponding incline, and by the middle of the century, sloping capitals had become the norm. Initially, though, working without reference to any calligraphic models, printers apparently experienced great difficulties in producing a satisfactory and harmonious italic upper case.

Epigrammata of Claudius Rosselettus, shown here, was printed by Sebastian Gryphius in 1537. Gryphius (1492–1556) was the son of a German printer, from whom he learned his trade. In around 1520 he established a press in Lyon, a major centre of the printing industry at that time. His editions were prized for their clean design and accurate presswork, and, as a result, he gained a reputation as the 'Prince of the Lyon book trade'.

Except for the roman headings, *Epigrammata* is set entirely in a new style of italic, acquired by Gryphius from an anonymous type founder working in Basel, from where the type gets its name. It is regarded as the progenitor of the italics used with old-style types. Letterforms are generous in width and more circular than earlier chancery models. The lower case has a large x-height and inclines considerably more than earlier models, while the upper case is an odd assortment of disparate letters of greatly variable inclination. The M, N, V and R have the least consistent angles, while the O and Q are upright. Despite its peculiar features, the Basel italic became an extremely popular typeface and was used for more than 30 years by most of the printing houses of Europe.

For a considerable time, the italic style was regarded as an autonomous alphabet, to be used independently. Gradually, however, it came to be thought of as a subsidiary typeface to roman, to be applied only for emphasis, citation and in preliminary matter.

Ty	**Estienne's Roman**
Ca	**Serif**
Ke	**Old Style, French**
Te	**Letterpress**
Da	**1537**
De	**Robert Estienne**
Fo	**Robert Estienne**
Co	**France**

Characteristics

	Long ascenders and descenders
A	Pointed apex
G	Inward serif on the upright
M	Single top serif
P	Open bowl
R	Curved, sweeping leg
i	Dot offset to right
v	Vertex below baseline

ACFMR
abcdefghi
moprstuxy

Connections

Griffo's Roman	1495
Colines's Roman	1528
Garamond's Roman	c1538
Granjon's Roman	1560

Availability

Not available

Specimen

Guillaume Du Bellay, *Exemplaria literarum.*
Robert Estienne, Paris, 1537 (213x151mm)

194

maxima beneficia)hæc inquam amicitia quam isti
adeò subuertere cōnituntur, longe firmioribus in-
nititur radicibus, quàm vt machinis huiusmodi
conuellere eam possint, aut vos in amicum & so-
cium Regem cōcitare, cuius nulla in vos nisi ficta
commemorari possit iniuria: imò verò qui maio-
rum suorum exemplo ornamento semper esse vo
bis studuerit,atque vsui: quémque nemo sit morta
lium,infirmū experturus vel hostem vel amicum.

Reuerendissimi, illustrissimi , inclyti , generosi,
splendidi,amplissimi,spectabiles,& prudētes amici,
fœderati ac socii, Deum Optimū Maximum de-
precor, opes ac dignitates vestras vt tueatur, atque
etiam augeat.Datum Lutetiæ Parisiorum, Calend.
Feb.Anno Do. M, D. X X X I I I I.

195

Ad Imperii ordines

DE INDICENDI COMMVNIS
Chriſtianorum omnium concilii ratione, Chri-
ſtianiſſimi Regis epiſtola.

FRANCISCVS Dei gratia Frācorū Rex, &c.
Reuerēdiſſimis, illuſtriſſimis, inclytis, generoſis,
ſplendidis, ampliſſimis, ſpectabilibus,& prudēti-
bus ſacri Romani Imperii electoribus, Principi-
bus,equitibus, ciuitatibus, earúmque magiſtrati-
bus, ac cæteris vniuerſis & ſingulis ordinibus, a-
micis,fœderatis, & ſociis chariſſimis,   s.

VPERIORIBVS
ad vos literis, quum ad
quaſdam reſponderem
paſſim apud veſtrates in
me diſſeminatas calū-
nias, obiter vobis, am-
pliſſimi ordines,meum
ſuper indicendo com-
muni Chriſtianorū cō-
cilio, ſenſum, animum, & expectationem ſigni-
ficaui: id quod fortaſſe tum feciſſem accuratius ac
diligentius, ſi vel leuem coniecturam habuiſſem
fore vnquam vt (quod poſtea & literis multorū &
ſermone omnium ad me perlatum eſt) iſta quo-
rūdam obtrectatione ſugillarer:me ſcilicet ad eam
rem vltro ſeſe accingenti Pontifici moram vnum

n.ii.

Robert Estienne (1503–59) was the son of Henri Estienne, an eminent Parisian printer and bookseller. A Protestant scholar, he rose to become the leading French printer of the sixteenth century at a time when publishing took on a pivotal role in the development of new political, social and religious ideas. Estienne was as committed to education as he was to biblical and classical learning, producing a series of grammars, thesauri and lexicons intended to facilitate public access to theological knowledge. Also issued in editions for younger readers, some of these remained in use throughout the sixteenth and seventeenth centuries.

Estienne's work was distinguished not only by its scholarship but also by the fine quality of his printing. He introduced many rational innovations in his publications, in which roman and italic types of exceptionally high quality were used to differentiate meanings in text. His French Bible of 1533 was the very first to assign numbers to verses, a practical innovation of enduring value.

In the early 1530s, Estienne produced the first set of Latin typefaces to be designed as a completely coordinated series, with a collection of matched sizes ranging from approximately 6 to 42 point, the largest movable type that had ever been cut and cast until that time. Overall, Estienne's Roman is light in weight with a gentle stroke contrast. It is evident that he must have based his designs on Francesco Griffo's type for *De Aetna*, published by Aldus Manutius in 1495 (pp30–31). The details of many letter contours correspond closely to those of Griffo, such as the cupped apex of the A and the serifs that face inwards on the uprights of G and M. Capitals are not as tall as lower case ascenders so that, like the *De Aetna* type, they balance well in bodies of text.

In 1539, Estienne was appointed Imprimeur du Roi (Printer to the King), although this official status failed to protect him from the hostility of the French religious establishment. He was eventually forced to emigrate to Switzerland in 1551 in order to escape persecution, establishing a press in Geneva where he continued to publish Protestant editions, including many of John Calvin's writings.

Estienne's rationalized system of type sizes, his many other technical innovations and his accomplished typography had a huge impact on sixteenth-century French printing and on the future of typography.

Ty	**Garamond's Roman**
Ca	**Serif**
Ke	**Old Style, French**
Te	**Letterpress**
Da	**c1538**
De	**Claude Garamond**
Fo	**Claude Garamond**
Co	**France**

Characteristics

Top serifs have downward slope
Q Long tail
R Leg below baseline
T Inclined left-hand top serif
a Small bowl
e Small eye

ACEMRS
abcdefghi
moprstuyz

Connections

Stempel Garamond	1924
Garaldus	1957
Sabon	1967
Adobe Garamond	1989

Availability

Digital types based on Garamond's Roman
are widely available

Specimen

Dominique Jacquinot, *L'usaige de
l'astrolabe, avec un traicté de la sphère.*
Jean Barbé, Paris, 1545 (177x130mm)

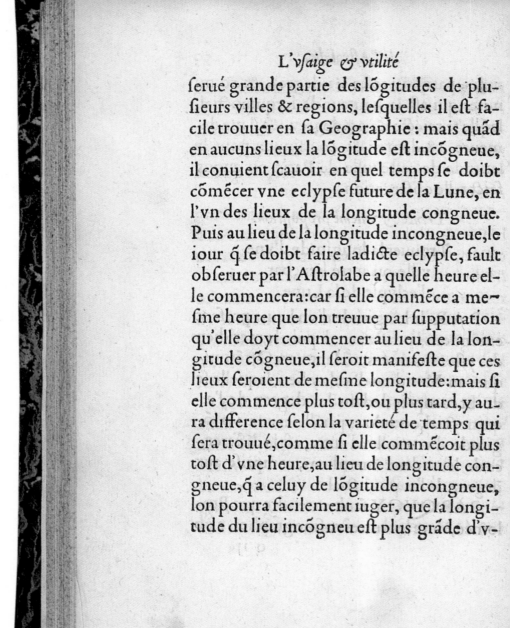

L'vsaige & vtilité

serué grande partie des lógitudes de pluſieurs villes & regions, leſquelles il eſt facile trouuer en ſa Geographie : mais quãd en aucuns lieux la lógitude eſt incógneue, il conuient ſcauoir en quel temps ſe doibt cómécer vne eclypſe future de la Lune, en l'vn des lieux de la longitude congneue. Puis au lieu de la longitude incongneue, le iour q̃ ſe doibt faire ladicte eclypſe, fault obſeruer par l'Aſtrolabe a quelle heure elle commencera: car ſi elle cómméce a meſme heure que lon treuue par ſupputation qu'elle doyt commencer au lieu de la longitude cógneue,il ſeroit manifeſte que ces lieux ſeroient de meſme longitude:mais ſi elle commence plus toſt,ou plus tard,y aura difference ſelon la varieté de temps qui ſera trouué,comme ſi elle commécoit plus toſt d'vne heure,au lieu de longitude congneue,q̃ a celuy de lógitude incongneue, lon pourra facilement iuger, que la longitude du lieu incógneu eſt plus grãde d'v-

de l'Astrolabe. 51

ne heure, qui vault 15. degrez, que celle du lieu a nous cõgneu. Et semblablemẽt fault entendre des autres differences de temps, selon la valeur des degrez, en prenãt tousiours 15. degrez pour vne heure, & quatre minutes pour chacun degré.

POVR exẽple, ie treuue dedans Ptolomée, que la longitude de la ville de Paris est de 23. degrez, & qv'ne eclypse de la Lune doibt cõmencer audict lieu a trois heures apres minuict : sur ce poinct ie veulx scauoir combien Tubinge ville renommée a de lõgitude, pour ce faire i'obserue audict lieu le temps que se faict ladicte eclypse, et treuue son commencement a trois heures, 24. minutes apres minuict, qui sont 24. minutes, valant 6. degrez plus tard, q̃ dans Paris, lesquelz ie adiouste a la lõgitude de Paris, pour autant que le commencement de l'eclypse sy faisoit plus tost : & par ce moyen ie congnois que Tubinge a vingt & neuf degrez de longitude.

o iij

By the second quarter of the sixteenth century France had displaced Italy as the epicentre of the printing and publishing trade. In Paris books were being produced to the highest standards, with an unprecedented sophistication in design and accuracy in presswork.

The elegant roman types of Claude Garamond (c1510–61) were among the most significant contributions to the French printing industry. Having learned the craft of punch cutting with Antoine Augereau in Paris, Garamond established himself as an independent type founder in around 1538. In his short career he cut at least 34 different types, including 17 romans and 7 italics. The most enduring of these is a group of roman types he produced in the mid-1530s that drew inspiration from Francesco Griffo's letters of 1495 (pp30–31).

While Garamond's work was not particularly innovative, he used his prodigious technical skills to refine Griffo's Aldine design, cutting letters with restraint and assurance. Garamond's Roman provides a light, even overall tone to bodies of extended text, with a sense of fluency and balance that is largely due to its spacing. The characters have a consistent appearance, with a meticulous alignment and fit between them. Like Griffo's design, capitals are slightly shorter than the ascenders so as not to obtrude, contributing to the harmony of the page. The designs of capitals, lower case and italics (pp50–51) are coordinated, providing printers with the first comprehensively organized collection of typefaces. They formed a blueprint that continued to influence printing and type founding in France for over a century.

Since its inception, Garamond has been one of the most popular typefaces in the history of typography, and has probably been the subject of more imitations, reinterpretations and revivals than any other. Almost every major foundry in the world has published a typeface in Garamond's name. However, due to gaps in early historical records, many of these have been misattributed, with romans actually based on Jean Jannon's Caractères de l'Université from a century later (pp62–63), and italics referencing those of Garamond's contemporary, Robert Granjon (pp58–59). It was not until 1926 that these errors were identified by Beatrice Warde, but by then many type foundries, including Monotype and ATF, had already released type families erroneously believed to be revivals of Garamond's work. These misattributions persist to the present day.

Ty	**Garamond's Italic**
Ca	**Serif**
Ke	**Old Style Italic, French**
Te	**Letterpress**
Da	**c1545**
De	**Claude Garamond**
Fo	**Claude Garamond**
Co	**France**

Characteristics

Italic lower case with roman capitals
y Long, curved tail
as ff fi fl fr is st us Ligatures
& Distinctive

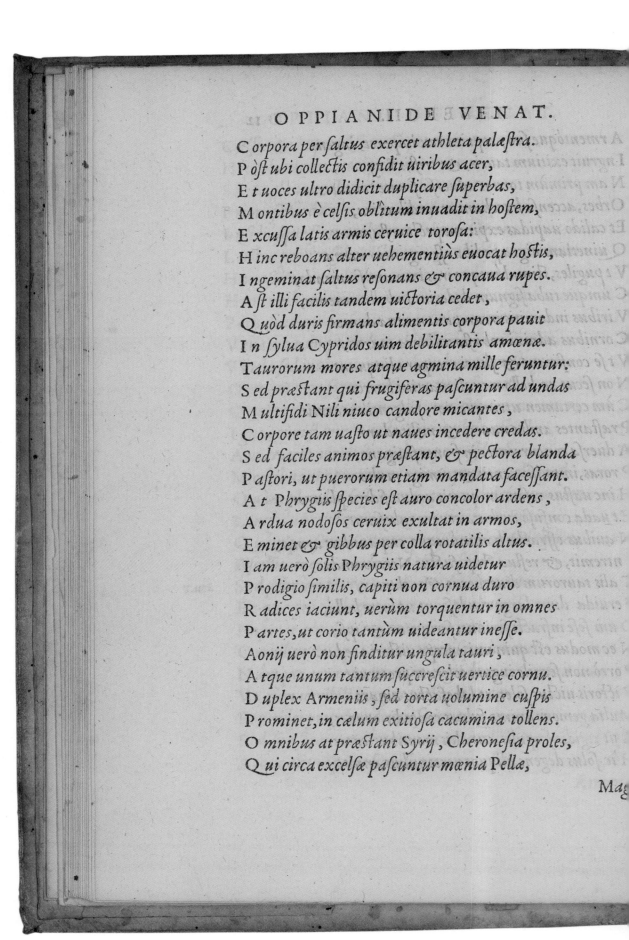

Connections

Griffo's Italic	1501
Granjon's Italic	1560
Stempel Garamond Italic	1924
Adobe Garamond Italic	1989

Availability

Digital types based on Garamond's Italic
are widely available

Specimen

Oppian, *De venatione libri IV*. Michel de
Vascosan, Paris, 1555 (233x170mm)

LIBER II.

Magnanimi, fortes, generosi, marte feroces,
Cornupetæ, torui, riuales, atque superbi,
Alto mugitu atque horrenda uoce tonantes:
Nec tamen aut pingues immensa mole grauantur
Corporis, aut macri spoliantur robore iusto,
Temperiem mediam sortiti munere diuûm,
Et cursu rapidi & uiolento robore fortes.
Illos (ut perhibent) Erithæa magnus abegit
Alcides, tolerans infracto corde laborem,
Cùm procul Oceano triplicem certamine uicit
Geryonem in speculis altis, uictórque redibat,
Populea circum uelatus tempora fronde:
Cùm uarios iterum uersaret adire labores,
Non quos præciperet Iuno, aut Eurystheus acer:
Principis Archippi Pellæ mandata parabat,
Immensus quando exundabat campus ad imas
Emblonij montis radices, quippe fluenta
Vorticibus rapidis in agros torquebat Orontes
Aequoris oblitus, nymphǽque retentus amore
Cautibus è celsis labens obduxerat agros
Aptos seminibus, Melibæam linquere nolens.
Stipabant etenim montes, cingente corona,
Vdo tollentes utrinque cacumina campo.
Arduus aduerso stabat Dioclæus ab ortu,
Læuáque & occasus Emblonius ora tenebat,
Turbidus in medio campo stagnabat Orontes,
Vt muros unda reflua tumefactus obiret.
Sic igitur Pellam cingebat tanta uorago,
Vt meritò appellaretur peninsula quondam.

E

Claude Garamond (c1510–61) was the most renowned punch cutter in Europe during the sixteenth century and his work had an impact on the course of typographic history that continues to the present day. However, very little is known about his origins or the circumstances of his life. Until recently, he was thought to have been born in the 1480s and to have learned his craft working for Geoffroy Tory, but recent research has revealed that he was apprenticed to the printer Antoine Augereau from around 1525 until 1534, when Augereau was executed for his religious faith.

The first original typefaces cut by Garamond date from the 1530s. After many years spent as an apprentice and journeyman, he became a master of his trade and established himself as an independent type founder from around 1538, remaining productive until his untimely death in 1561. It is now considered probable that he was born in 1510, the date which until recently had been mistakenly understood as the first year of his apprenticeship.

In 1543 Claude Garamond relocated his workshop near to the press of his brother-in-law, the printer Pierre Gaultier. There, between 1543 and 1550, he cut punches for new italic characters following the Venetian models first made by Francesco Griffo for Aldus Manutius.

The example shown here, set in a size equivalent to around 16.5 point, is as well considered and expertly cut as his roman (pp48–49). The lower case letters show a slightly varied angle of inclination, enhanced by the conventional use of broad, upright capitals as initials and within the body text. A flowing calligraphic appearance is emphasized by the use of many ligatures that draw on European scribal traditions.

Like his romans, Garamond's sprightly italics impart a very light and even overall tone to bodies of extended text. However, despite their evident qualities, Garamond's italics were not quite as widely accepted by printers and publishers as those of his contemporary Robert Granjon (pp58–59).

Amphiareo's Capitals

Ty	**Amphiareo's Capitals**
Ca	**Decorative**
Ke	**Capitals**
Te	**Xylography**
Da	**1556**
De	**Vespasiano Amphiareo**
Fo	**Curtio Troiano di Navo**
Co	**Italy**

Characteristics

Woodcut initial capitals
Elaborate multi-line decorative forms

Connections

Pouchée's Decorated Alphabets	c1820
The Alphabet	2001
Amphiareo	2002
Gothic Majuscules	2003

Availability

Not available

Specimen

Opera di Frate Vespasiano Amphiareo da Ferrara. Curtio Troiano di Navo, Venice, 1556 (150x200mm)

Vespasiano Amphiareo (1501–63), a Franciscan monk, was one of the most famous and successful calligraphers working in Italy during the sixteenth century. Born in Ferrara, he worked as a writing master, teaching penmanship in Florence and subsequently in Venice, where he remained for over 30 years.

He made claims to be the originator of the Cancelleresca Bastarda script, a less formal and rounder sixteenth-century italic hand than that of Ludovico Vicentino degli Arrighi (pp40–41). In 1556, Amphiareo published a writing manual, *Opera di Frate*

Vespasiano Amphiareo da Ferrara ... nella quale si insegna a scrivere varie sorti di lettere. The publication was a huge success, running to over 20 editions and remaining in print for decades.

In his treatise, Amphiareo provides very little practical guidance on calligraphic techniques. The *Opera di Frate Vespasiano Amphiareo* serves more as a copy book, showing wood engravings of model alphabet specimens, most of which are derived from the earlier chancery hand of Giovanni Antonio Tagliente. Among a large number of specimens of these

italic scripts is a collection of particularly exuberant decorated capital letters.

These are notable as the regulated, printed renditions of illuminated capitals designed for use as initials in manuscripts and books of the time. Amphiareo's Capitals can be considered the precursors of both ornamental letters of the eighteenth and nineteenth centuries (pp116–17), and of the more recent lineage of alphabets designed solely for display use rather than in text – where, like Amphiareo's Capitals, letters often function firstly as eye-catching forms and secondly as vehicles for text.

Civilité

Ty	**Civilité**
Ca	**Script**
Ke	**Formal, Unconnected**
Te	**Letterpress**
Da	**1557**
De	**Robert Granjon**
Fo	**Robert Granjon**
Co	**France**

Characteristics

Round, upright character construction
Many alternate characters
d v Elongated, angled flourishes

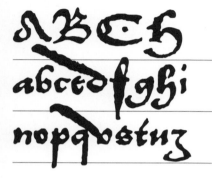

Connections

Amphiareo's Cancelleresca Bastarda	1554
Cottrell's Engrossing	c1765
Ronde	1809
St Augustine Civilité	1992

Availability

St Augustine Civilité, a digital revival, is
available from Hoefler & Co. and resellers

Specimen

Gautier de Châtillon, *Alexandreidos libri
decem*. Robert Granjon, Lyon, 1558
(200x142mm)

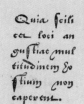

Robert Granjon's Civilité typeface has its origins in a cursive script that was seen extensively in northern European countries during the sixteenth century. Scribes originally used it to draw up commercial contracts, terminating many of its characters with long, trailing flourishes. Despite their ornamental appearance, these were employed not for decoration but to prevent fraudulent amendments.

Robert Granjon (1513–90), a French type founder, proposed that his country should adopt what he called a *lettre françoise*, believing that France, like Italy and Germany, should have a typeface based on its national hand, particularly for publications set in the vernacular and for educational purposes. Taking the standard contractual script as his model, he cut an extensive body of types, including over 50 alternate characters and ligatures, together with 12 terminal flourishes intended to both decorate the text and allow for its expansion to fit page widths where necessary. Granjon printed about 20 editions in Civilité (meaning 'good manners') between 1557 and 1562.

Despite the exceptional refinement of his design, Granjon's attempt to rival the italic form did not take hold in France, only being used sporadically. Its main disadvantage was that it was complicated for printers and compositors to implement. The many ligatures and variant characters were not easy or economical to set. While the original handwritten manuscript could be extended or contracted at will to fit any suitable line length in the process of writing, the task of setting the Civilité type was constrained by the fixed size of whatever terminal sorts were available.

Civilité enjoyed greater success in the Netherlands. Granjon supplied Plantin, among others, with his script types and they were widely copied, despite the fact that Granjon had been granted the protection of a royal monopoly for ten years in 1557.

Like many other script types, Civilité left little impression on the development of typography in Europe. Surviving as something of a historical curiosity, it is, nevertheless, one of the most sophisticated typeforms ever devised.

Ty	**Granjon's Roman**
Ca	**Serif**
Ke	**Old Style, French**
Te	**Letterpress**
Da	**1560**
De	**Robert Granjon**
Fo	**Robert Granjon**
Co	**France**

Characteristics

A	Cupped apex
E F X Y	Narrow
K R	Serifless tails
M	Splayed
v	Vertex below baseline

ABEMRS
abcdefghi
moprstuy

Connections

Garamond's Roman	c1538
Plantin	1913
Joanna	1931
Galliard	1978

Availability

A digital version of a 1928 revival is available from Linotype and resellers

Specimen

Livy, *Romanae historiae*. George Corvinus, Frankfurt am Main, 1568 (380x230mm)

440   T. LIVII HIST. AB VRBE COND.

Syphax rex Numidarum.

socios,& nouos adijcerent, in Africam quoq; fpem extenderunt. Syphax erat rex Numidarum, fubitò Carthaginienfibus hoftis factus. ad eum centuriones tres legatos miferunt,qui cum eo amicitiam focietatemq; facerent:& polliceretur,fi perfeueraret vrgere bello Carthaginienfes, gratam eam rem fore fenatui populoq; Romano,& adnixuros, vt in tempore, & benè cumulatam gratiam referant. Grata ea legatio barbaro fuit. collocutusq; cum legatis de ratione belli gerendi,vt veterum militũ verba audiuit, quàm multaru rerum ipfe ignarus effet, ex comparatione tam ordinatæ difciplinæ animaduertit. Tum primùm,vt pro bonis ac fidelibus focijs facerent,orauit,vt duo legationem referrent ad imperatores fuos:vnus apud fefe magifter rei militaris remaneret.

Numidarum gens ad pedeftria bella rudis.

neret.rudem ad pedeftria bella Numidarum gentem effe,equis tantum habilem. Ita iam inde à principijs gentis maiores fuos bella geffiffe, ita fe à pueris infuetos:fed habere hoftem pedeftri fidentem marte, cui fe æquari robore virium velit. & fibi pedites comparandos effe:& ad id multitudine hominũ regnum abundare:fed armandi ordinãdiq; & inftruendi eos,artẽ ignorare.omnis, velut fortè congregata turba fua infcia, ac temeraria effet. Facturos fe in præfentia quod vellet,legati refponderũt:fide accepta, vt remitteret extemplò cum,fi imperatores fui non comprobaffent factum. Q. Statorio nomen fuit, qui apud regẽ remanfit. Cum duobus Romanis relata Numidafq; legatos in Hifpaniam mifit ad capiendã fidem ab imperatoribus Romanis,ijfdem mandauit,vt protinus Numidas,qui intra portas, feu præfidia Carthaginienfium auxiliares effent,ad tranfitionem perlicerent.Et Statorius ex multa iuuentute regi pedites confcripfit:ordinatosq; proximè morem Romanum inftruendo, & decurrendo figna fequi,& feruare ordines docuit:& operi, alijsq; inftitutis militaribus ita affuefecit,vt breui rex nõ equiti magis fideret,quàm pediti:collatisq; æquo campo fignis,iufto prælio Carthaginienfem hoftẽ fuperaret.Romanis quoq; in Hifpania legatorũ regis aduentus magno emolumento fuit. nanq; ad famã eorum tranfitiones crebrę abNumidis cœptę fieri.Ita cum Syphace Rom.iuncta amicitia eft.Quod vbi Carthaginienfes acceperũt,extemplò ad Galã in parte altera Numidię(Maffyla ea gens vocatur)regnantem legatos mittunt. Filiũ Gala Mafaniffam habebat,feptem & decem annos natum,

Mafaniffa regis Gale filius.

cæterùm iuuenem ea indole,vt iam tum appareret, eius regnum opulentius quàm quod accepiffet,facturũ. Legati quoniam Syphax fe Romanis iunxiffet, vt potentior focietate eorũ aduerfus reges populosq; Africæ effet, docent melius fore Galæ quoq; Carthaginienfibus iungi quamprimum,

By the middle of the sixteenth century France occupied the leading role in European printing and publishing and Paris had become the centre of a flourishing book trade, with many craftsmen contributing to it. Claude Garamond's refined roman typefaces had a huge influence on their activities, with many punch cutters applying their skills to imitating his designs rather than attempting anything original.

One notable exception was Robert Granjon (1513–90), who, although better known for his vibrant italics and his non-Latin designs, also excelled in cutting roman typefaces that were discerning reinterpretations of Garamond's forms.

The son of a Parisian bookseller, Granjon was also by far the most prolific punch cutter of his day. It has been estimated that he completed approximately 90 different types during his career, including around 15 roman designs and 30 italics (pp58–59) in addition his innovative Civilité script (pp54–55). He also developed several fonts for musical notation, including one that became the most widely disseminated in Europe until the mid-eighteenth century.

Granjon's typefaces were much sought after by printers and publishers across Europe. He travelled extensively to work as a punch cutter and an engraver in cities such as Lyon, Geneva, Antwerp and Frankfurt, as well as Paris, contributing to the operations of many leading printers such as Christophe Plantin.

In 1578 Granjon emigrated to Rome, where he worked until 1589 on the development of types in Middle Eastern scripts required by Catholic missionaries, contributing to the very earliest editions printed in oriental languages.

Granjon's later roman types were highly sophisticated designs. The 1560 example shown here, in a publication from 1568, displays his finely cut gros-romain type, a size approximately equivalent to 16 point. Compared to those of his contemporaries, these letters are full of vitality and personality; Stanley Morison considered them 'equal to Garamond's'.

The original punches and matrices for 40 of Robert Granjon's types survive today in the Plantin-Moretus Museum in Antwerp. The best of these were used by Monotype as the basis for its Plantin typeface in 1913.

Ty	**Granjon's Italic**
Ca	**Serif**
Ke	**Old Style Italic, French**
Te	**Letterpress**
Da	**1560**
De	**Robert Granjon**
Fo	**Robert Granjon**
Co	**France**

Characteristics

Italic lower case with swash italic capitals
F Heavy mid-stroke
K R Serifless leg
y Long, curved tail
& Distinctive

ADERZ
abcdefghi
moprstuxz

Connections

Griffo's Italic	1501
Garamond's Italic	c1545
Jannon's Italic	1621
Van Dijck's Italic	1689

Availability

Digital types based on Granjon's italics are widely available

Specimen

Jean Cousin, *Livre de perspective*. Jean le Royer, Paris, 1560 (419x277mm)

Robert Granjon (1513–90) was the most prolific type founder in sixteenth-century Paris, an international centre for printing and publishing at the time. Although he produced many very fine roman designs (pp56–57) and a large number of non-Latins, his most enduring achievements are his Civilité script types (pp54–55) and a series of vibrant italic designs, a letterform in which he excelled.

Granjon cut approximately 30 italic types in a wide variety of styles, ranging in size from the equivalent of 6.5 point to approximately 42 point, which at the time was the largest font of its kind ever cut in France. Granjon's italics had a more pronounced slant, a finer weight and a more rigorous cut than those of his contemporaries. Their contours evolved over 40 years of development that progressed through four distinct stages, from tentative early attempts in the 1540s to typefaces with full-blooded personalities, based on emphatically slanted characters, in the mid-1560s.

After this phase, the letterforms started to become somewhat more compact and upright, and in the final stage of their evolution Granjon's italic characters demonstrated an exuberantly spiky appearance with a marked contrast of thick and thin strokes, decorated with many swashes and flourishes.

This example shows a flamboyant intermediate Granjon italic from 1560 in a size equivalent to 16.5 point. It is notable for the integration of sloping capitals with the lower case replacing the upright capitals that had been conventionally used in chancery italic types. Unlike many previous failed attempts by other punch cutters to create a compatible italic upper case, Granjon's new capitals were far more regular and more complementary to the lower case.

Granjon's designs, with their many alternate characters and extravagant swash capitals, became the prototype for italic types until the earlier Arrighi model was revived in the 1920s.

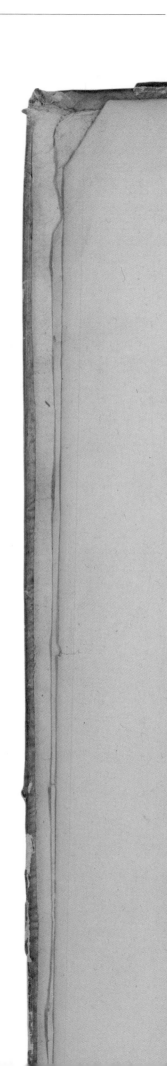

L'IMPRIMEVR AV LECTEVR.

SI pour mon commencement, *Amy Lecteur*, i'entreprens imprimer liures difficiles & de grands frais, cela ne me doit estre imputé à temerité ou folie, comme on faict communement à touts ceux qui ne suiuent l'opinion deprauee des bons menasgiers du temps present, qui disent.

Qu'vn chascun doit auec peu de despence
Acquerir biens qui soient de grand' substance:

car par l'institution qu'on m'a donnee depuis mon ieune aage, i'ay tousiours estimé que l'humaine felicité consistoit à s'employer pour le public: considerant plustost le proffit que la Republique pouuoit rapporter de nostre labeur, que l'aquisition des grans biens & tresors du monde. Ainsi aussi ont vescu touts ceux qui ont voulu suiure la vertu, comme toutes histoires nous tesmoignent: & moy les desirant imiter, selon la vacation en laquelle il a pleu à Dieu m'appeller: m'estant presenté par maistre Iehan Cousin (en l'art de Portraicture & Peincture non infime à Zeusis, ou Appelles) vn liure de la pratique de Perspectiue, par luy composé, & les figures pour l'intelligence d'iceluy necessaires, portraittes de sa main sus planches de bois : i'ay accepté laditte offre, & ay taillé la plus grand' part desdittes figures, & quelques vnes qui au parauant estoient encommencees par maistre Aubin Oliuier, mon beau frere, les ay paracheuees, & mises en perfection, selon l'intention dudit Autheur: sçachant que le present liure d'onera instruction à vn million d'hommes de bien portraire toutes choses apres le naturel, sans trauail de corps & d'esprit, ains plustost auec grand contentement qui procedera de la raison, que trouueras dans cest œuure descritte. Ce qui n'est chose de peu de pris, veu que si nous voulons considerer tout ce qui est soubz la concauité des cieux, nous confesserons la Portraiture estre mere & tutrice de touts arts, & de ce qui est digne de memoire. Cela nous tesmoigne assez Iosephus en son liure de la guerre des Iuifs, quand il parle de deux Colomnes, l'vne de terre, & l'autre de cuiure, qui furent construittes par les filz d'Adam auant le deluge, sur lesquelles les sept Arts Liberaux estoient descrites &

Ty	**Van den Keere's Roman**
Ca	**Serif**
Ke	**Old Style, Dutch**
Te	**Letterpress**
Da	**c1570**
De	**Hendrik van den Keere**
Fo	**Officina Plantiniana**
Co	**The Low Countries / Belgium**

Characteristics

Open, rounded characters
Large x-height
Sharply incised forms
Short ascenders and descenders
A Cupped apex
E Heavy mid-stroke
R Leg below baseline
T Inclined left-hand top serif
a Small bowl
e Small eye

ADEGV
abcdeghil
moprstuv

Connections

Garamond's Roman	c1538
Renard	1992
DTL Van Den Keere	1994
Poynter Oldstyle	1997

Availability

DTL Van Den Keere is available from the Dutch Type Library and resellers

Specimen

Specimen characterum. Christophe Plantin, Antwerp, c1585 (208x280mm)

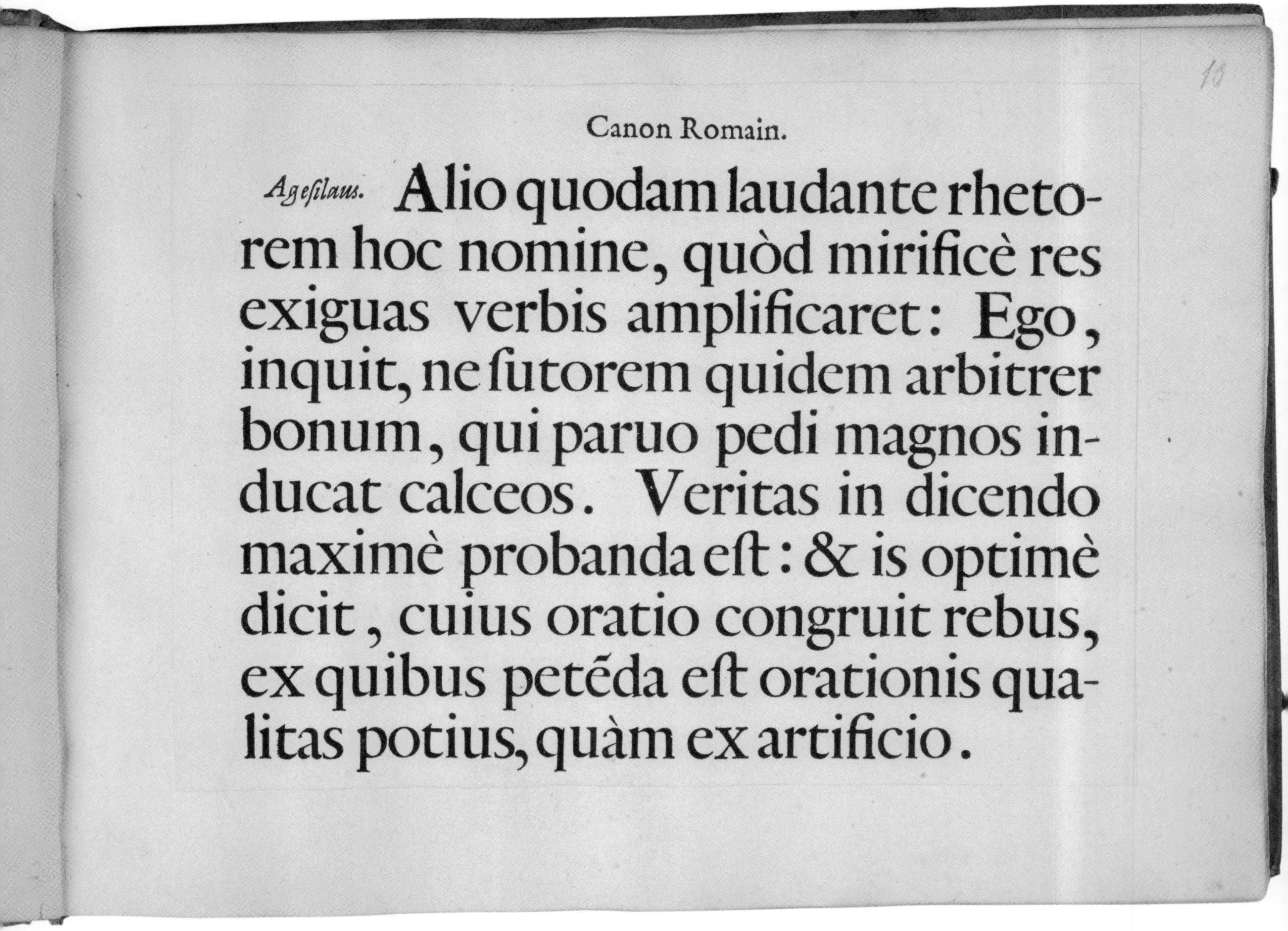

Canon Romain.

Agesilaus. Alio quodam laudante rhetorem hoc nomine, quòd mirificè res exiguas verbis amplificaret: Ego, inquit, ne sutorem quidem arbitrer bonum, qui paruo pedi magnos inducat calceos. Veritas in dicendo maximè probanda est: & is optimè dicit, cuius oratio congruit rebus, ex quibus petẽda est orationis qualitas potius, quàm ex artificio.

By the mid-sixteenth century, Antwerp had become one of the most important cities in northern Europe, a cultural hub with a thriving publishing industry. At its heart was the printing business of Christophe Plantin (1520–89), a French émigré whose workshop ran more than 20 presses at the peak of its operations in 1575. Plantin's fine editions were set in French types, such as those cut by Robert Granjon and Claude Garamond, far surpassing those of his local competitors.

In 1570, Hendrik van den Keere (c1540–80) of Ghent became Plantin's main supplier of punches. He was largely unknown until recently, as for centuries his types were held in closed storage at Plantin's workshop in Antwerp, now the Plantin-Moretus Museum. Van den Keere's work was only rediscovered in the 1950s, in a unique collection of some 40 sets of original punches and matrices, along with a large quantity of business documents that provide an extraordinarily detailed picture of the activities of a sixteenth-century type foundry.

Van den Keere died prematurely from an injury in 1580, having worked with Plantin for only 12 years. In that time, he made a huge number of types that were widely seen across Europe through his client's business activities. He cut as many as 12 blackletter faces, some of which were enormously successful in the late sixteenth century, when the form was still in common use in northern Europe. However, his enduring legacy is a series of roman typefaces. Influenced by Garamond's designs (pp48–49), they are slightly more compact and heavier, while remaining open and unostentatious. Their most notable feature, the tall x-height, was motivated more by economic demands than aesthetic considerations. To save space in printing while also using less metal, Plantin had instructed Van den Keere's predecessor, Robert Granjon, to shorten the descenders and ascenders of the Garamond types owned by the company so that they could be cast on bodies smaller than the ones for which they had been designed. When Van den Keere took over the operation, he continued to make these adaptations, integrating them into his original types.

Hendrik van den Keere is acknowledged today as one of the most skilled punch cutters of the Low Countries, whose work links the great French Renaissance types of the sixteenth century and the robust Dutch designs of the seventeenth.

La plus grande Romaine.

Heraclitus Ephesius. Interrogatus aliquando, cur file-ret, vt vos, inquit, loquamini.

Gloria tibi Dñe.

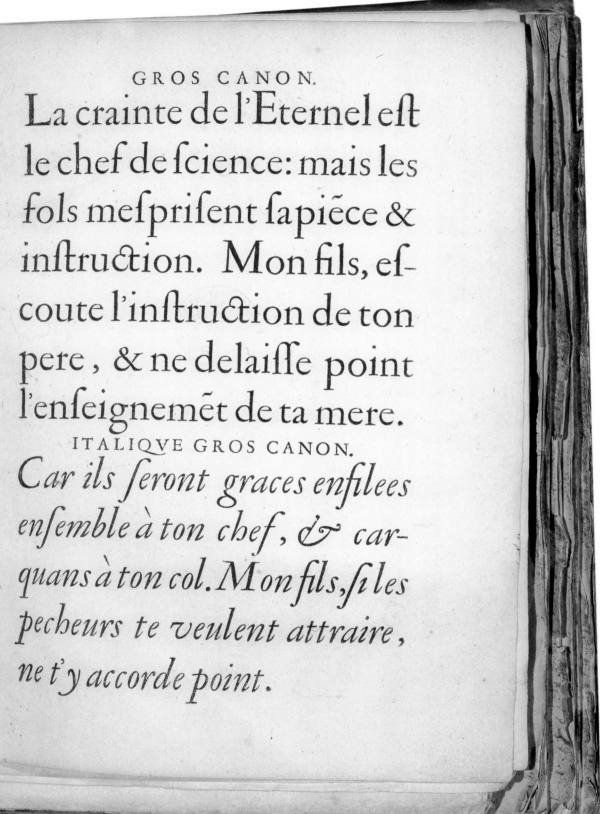

GROS CANON.

La crainte de l'Eternel est
le chef de science: mais les
fols mesprisent sapiéce &
instruction. Mon fils, es-
coute l'instruction de ton
pere , & ne delaisse point
l'enseignemēt de ta mere.

ITALIQVE GROS CANON.

Car ils seront graces enfilees
ensemble à ton chef, & car-
quans à ton col. Mon fils, si les
pecheurs te veulent attraire,
ne t'y accorde point.

Ty	**Jannon's Roman and Italic**
Ca	**Serif**
Ke	**Old Style, French**
Te	**Letterpress**
Da	**1621**
De	**Jean Jannon**
Fo	**Jean Jannon**
Co	**France**

Characteristics

E N	Wide
a	Long upper arch; small, steeply inclined bowl
b d p q	Tilted axis
e	Small eye, heavy bottom
i m n r	Steep, cupped upper serifs
s v	Narrow

EMNSV
abcdefghi
oprstuy*aefg*

Connections

Monotype Garamond	1922
Simoncini Garamond	1961
ITC Garamond	1975
Jannon Pro	2010

Availability

Jannon Pro is a digital revival available from the Storm Type Foundry and resellers

Specimen

Espreuves des caractères nouvellement taillez. Jean Jannon, Sedan, 1621 (229x164mm)

PETIT CANON.

S'ils diſent, Vien auec nous , ten-
dons des embuſches pour tuer :
aguettons ſecretement l'innocent
encores qu'il ne nous ait point fait
le pourquoy. Engloutiſſons-les
comme vn ſepulcre, tous vifs, &
tous entiers cõme ceux q̃ deſcen-
dent en la foſſe. Nous trouuerons
toute precieuſe cheuance , nous
remplirons nos maiſons de butin.

ITALIQVE PETIT CANON.

Tu y auras ton lot parmi nous , il n'y
aura qu'vne bourſe pour nous tous.
Mon fils , ne te mets point en chemin
auec eux : retire ton pied de leur ſen-
tier. Car leurs pieds courent au mal,
& ſe haſtent pour reſpandre le ſang.

Jean Jannon (1580–1658) ranks among the leading representatives of French typography of the first half of the seventeenth century. A Swiss-born Protestant, he worked in the printing workshops of the Estienne family in Paris for some years. However, to escape persecution for his religious beliefs, in 1610 he moved to Sedan, where he was employed at the printing office of the Calvinist Academy as 'Imprimeur de son Excellence et de l'Academie Sédanoise'.

In 1615, with the type, punches and matrices at the Calvinist Academy printing office becoming worn out from repeated use, Jannon began cutting his own letters so that he would not need to purchase new type from Paris, at a time when ongoing religious and political conflicts would have made it difficult to do so. Six years later he issued his typefaces in the first type specimen book ever published in France. His early letterforms clearly owe a great deal to Claude Garamond's designs from almost a century earlier (pp48–51), but they demonstrate a vitality and confidence of their own. Jannon's types are very similar to Garamond's, but with grander baroque forms that are more asymmetrical and irregular in their axis and inclination.

Sharply cut, even and light in colour, they are most immediately recognizable by the shape of the lower case a, which has a long upper arch extending above a bowl that is smaller and more steeply inclined than Garamond's. Other notable differences include the cupped triangular serifs on the stems of such characters as i, m, n and r, which are also steep.

Several of Jannon's matrices and types were purchased by the French Royal Printing Office in 1641, although they were apparently little used in the seventeenth century. When these were officially published 200 years later, in an 1845 specimen of the Imprimerie Nationale in Paris, they were misattributed to Claude Garamond and subsequently served as the source for many designs believed to be Garamond revivals by companies such as American Type Founders, Monotype and Linotype. Doubts about their provenance, first raised by Jean Paillard in 1914, were investigated by Beatrice Warde in the 1920s and continue to be researched today by the type historian James Mosley.

Jean Jannon's typefaces are now recognized as some of the most graceful and brilliantly cut of the seventeenth century, although all that survives of his work are three sizes of matrices in the collections of the Imprimerie Nationale.

1950-1961

Although the foundations of the modern age are firmly embedded in the Renaissance with the advent of printing and publishing, its form was determined by the economic, scientific and social revolutions of the seventeenth and eighteenth centuries.

The seventeenth century was an era of global expansion, when independent European nations grew economically and physically, many seeking to build empires through exploration, conquest and colonization. It was also a period of extended religious and political conflict that often resulted in brutal violence. The philosophical and cultural movement that followed during the Enlightenment emphasized free thinking, reason and critique in a reaction to the dogmatic fundamentalism of the preceding years. The Enlightenment world view held that the universe was logical and understandable and that the historical trajectory of mankind was one of improvement. Science was perceived as the instrument of its progression. Philosophers such as Rousseau, Voltaire and Diderot asserted that, rather than passively accepting the orders of established institutions, individuals had the right – as well as the capacity – to think for themselves and to act accordingly.

During the seventeenth century very few technical improvements in printing and publishing were made, but in 1692 a significant conceptual advance was instigated in France when the Académie Française commissioned a rationally constructed alphabet, the Romain du Roi. This was a typographic landmark of the Age of Reason that signalled the beginnings of a totally new way of understanding visual communications. Whereas previous typefaces had evolved naturally over time from formal scripts, the Romain du Roi was the systematic output of a purely logical process, with letterforms constructed on grids before being cut into metal.

The Romain du Roi was not a particularly effective typeface. However, in a less severe form, its approach became a key principle of the next stage of type design, marking a move away from calligraphic letters towards those that began to be understood as products of technologies and as elements in visual systems, much in the way that component parts operate in machines.

The typefaces that followed its influence are often classified as 'transitional' designs because of their intermediate position between the old styles of the Renaissance and the designs that came afterwards, at the end of the eighteenth century. Transitional typefaces are identified by features that follow rational principles, with a higher contrast than old-style faces, a vertical stroke axis and sharp, bracketed serifs. These characteristics are evident in Pierre-Simon Fournier's types from the 1760s, but were achieved with even greater success by John Baskerville in a type design that is a model of Enlightenment thinking. Although he is known today primarily for his type, Baskerville's numerous improvements to paper, ink and printing processes had an equally decisive impact on the course of typographic history.

A number of type founders drew on Baskerville's techniques and letterforms to create typefaces in the late 1700s and early 1800s that are now described as 'modern'. Among the first, and among the most influential, were Firmin Didot from Paris and Giambattista Bodoni of Parma. Their typefaces are identified by their abrupt vertical stress and extreme stroke contrast, with flat serifs and horizontals that are hairline-thin. Embodying scientific and classical ideals, the modern types are a dazzling expression of the Age of Reason. Although they are harsh on the eye and not easy to read in text, they reconceived the ways in which type could be used, permanently changing the direction of visual communications.

The Fell Types

Ty	**The Fell Types**
Ca	**Serif**
Ke	**Old Style, Dutch**
Te	**Letterpress**
Da	1672
De	**Peter de Walpergen**
Fo	**Oxford University Press**
Co	**UK**

Characteristics

	Short ascenders and descenders
A	Cupped apex
Q	Long, heavy tail
f h i k l m n r	Thin, flat bottom serif
g	Narrow, hooked ear
p q	Flat bottom serif
s	Narrow
&	Distinctive form

ACEMQS
abcdefghi
orstuya*efg*

Connections

Availability

A digital revival of the Fell Types is available from Hoefler & Co. and resellers

Specimen

John Fell, *A Specimen of the Several Sorts of Letter Given to the University.* Oxford University Press, Oxford, 1695 (208x132mm)

By the end of the seventeenth century the printing industry was well established in England, although very little type of English origin was available. For a century and a half the Crown had regulated the trade so restrictively that a type-founding industry had no chance to develop. As a result, during the seventeenth century English printers were forced to import their types, largely from the Netherlands.

One of the first to recognize the detrimental effects of this dependency was John Fell, Bishop of Oxford. To promote 'the cause of learning' in England he began to assemble a comprehensive collection of types for the Oxford University Press in 1667, writing: 'The foundation of all success must be layd in doing things well, and I am sure that will not be don with English letters.' In addition to acquiring several typefaces from France, Germany and the Netherlands, Fell contracted a German type founder, Peter de Walpergen (1646–1703), to cut a number of fonts that are known today as 'the Fell Types' and that remain in the possession of the Oxford University Press.

The Fell Types are comparable to the designs of Jean Jannon (pp62–63). In the Fell roman, a narrowing of the round letters and a high degree of contrast are evident. Ascenders and descenders are notably short, giving larger sizes a squat appearance. In the lower case, thin, flat serifs are found at the base of vertical stems, a feature that later distinguished classical and modern types. The slant of the Fell italic has the same lack of uniformity as Jannon's, but the capitals show slight differences. In the lower case italic the ovals are wide, and ascenders and descenders are short.

With their many imperfections, the Fell Types have been considered by some as visually crude and technically inept. Type historian Harry Carter's view, for example, was that 'The pieces of type differ in height to an extent that horrifies a type-founder and tries the patience of a machine manager', but he went on to argue that these faults contribute favourably to their singular personality.

Despite their obvious technical and aesthetic deficiencies, the Fell Types were among the very first fonts cast in England, forming a bridge between the seventeenth-century Dutch old styles of Miklós Kis (pp68–69) and Christoffel van Dijck (pp70–71) and the seminal eighteenth-century designs of William Caslon (pp76–77).

Two Line English Roman.

ABCDEFGHIKLM NOPQRSTV &c.

Pater noster qui es in cœlis, sanctificetur nomen tuum. Veniat regnum tuum: fiat voluntas tua, sicut in cœlo, ita etiam in terra. Panem noftrum ---

Two Line English Italick.

ABCDEFGHIKLMNOP QRSTVUWXYZ J Æ

Pater noster qui es in cœlis, sanctificetur nomen tuum. Veniat regnum tuum: fiat voluntas tua, ficut in cœlo, ita etiam in terra. Panem noftrum ---

Double Pica Roman.

ABCDEFGHIKLMNOPQR STVUWXYZ ABCDEFGHIK-

PAter noster qui es in cœlis, sanctificetur nomen tuum. Veniat regnum tuum: fiat voluntas tua, ficut in cœlo, ita etiam in terra. Panem noftrum quotidianum da nobis hodie. Et remitte nobis debita noftra, ficut & remittimus debitoribus noftris. Et ne nos inducas in tentationem, fed libera nos ab illo malo. AMEN.

Double Pica Italick.

AABCDEFGHIJKLMM NOPQRSTVUWXYZ ÆÆ

PAter noster qui es in cœlis, fanctificetur nomen tuum. Veniat regnum tuum: fiat voluntas tua, ficut in cœlo, ita etiam in terra. Panem noftrum quotidianum da nobis hodie. Et remitte nobis debita noftra, ficut & remittimus debitoribus noftris. Et ne nos inducas in tentationem, fed libera nos ab illo malo. Amen.

Ty	**Kis's Roman**
Ca	**Serif**
Ke	**Old Style, Dutch**
Te	**Letterpress**
Da	**1687**
De	**Miklós Kis**
Fo	**Miklós Kis**
Co	**Netherlands**

Characteristics

A	Pointed apex
G	Has spur
M	Splayed
Q	Long tail
T	Outward-sloping serifs on top-stroke
W	Stepped centre-strokes
a	Narrow
b d p q	Oblique stress
c e	Bottom-heavy
g	Narrow, ball ear
o	Vertical stress
u	Flat top serifs

ACEMST
abcdefghi
moprstuvz

Connections

Availability

FB Kis is a digital revival available from the Font Bureau and resellers

Specimen

Lorenzo Magalotti, *Saggi di naturali esperienze*. Giovanni Filippo Cecchi, Florence, 1691 (364x248mm)

LXXXVIII.

ESPERIENZE
INTORNO AL-
LA PRESSIONE
DELL'ARIA.

*Altra inven-
zione di vaso
per uso della
medesim' es-
perienza.*

FIGURA
XXX.

da quest'esperienza, pensammo ad un altro vaso, come A B C, persuadendoci di poter con esso più facilmente ovviare così al trapelar dell'aria, come alla difficultà di muovere innanzi, e 'ndietro il legnetto. S'empiè dunque d'argentovivo il suddetto vaso per la bocca A, avendo prima serrata l'altra C, ed appoggiatala sul piumaccetto, come nell'esperienza antecedente s'insegnò di fare. Indi legata intorno al legnetto la vescica A B C, si tuffò quello sotto l'argento della bocca A (vedi figura xxIx.) sicchè l'ambra venisse a posare in B, sur un pezzetto di panno, come l'altro attaccato al vetro. Messi poi sull'argento parecchi minuzzoli di paglia minutissimamente trita, si mandò giù la vescica, legandola immediatamente sotto la rivolta della bocca A. Fatto il voto s'incominciò a scaldar l'ambra in sul panno con muover per di fuora in qua, e 'n la il manico del legnetto, ed a presentarla, quando si credea già calda,

*Ambra dentr'
al voto nõ tira*

or a questo, or a quel minuzzolo, che nella caduta dell'argento rimanevano sparsi per la palla, ma non si vedde mai, che alcuno ne venisse tirato.

*Ragguaglio di
particolarità,
per le quali si
revoca in dub-*

Avvertasi però, che non è da starsene in conto alcuno a quest'esperienza, ne da attribuire assoluta-

Miklós Kis (1650–1702) was a Calvinist priest and teacher from Hungary who travelled to Holland in 1680 on the orders of his bishop to commission the printing of a Hungarian Bible. When this venture proved unsuccessful, he decided to take on the task himself and became an apprentice at the workshop of Dirk Voskens, an eminent Dutch punch cutter. Kis showed a prolific talent in cutting type, becoming expert in only three years.

Over the next decade he printed a number of religious texts while gaining an international reputation as a punch cutter, so much so that Cosimo de' Medici, the Grand Duke of Tuscany, offered him a position at his court. Kis declined. Devoted to publishing religious books and Bibles, he returned to Hungary in 1690 to establish a new press, leaving type and many matrices in Leipzig, apparently hoping to sell them. However, he made many enemies in Hungary due to his radical views on education and publishing during a time of religious and political upheaval.

After Kis died in 1702 his work was largely forgotten. However, the stock he had left in Leipzig came into the possession of the Ehrhardt foundry which issued a specimen showing a large range of his types in the 1720s. Over many years and through many business acquisitions, his matrices eventually ended up in 1919 at the Stempel foundry where they were misattributed to a Dutch punch cutter named Anton Janson who also worked in Leipzig. This design was later revived by Linotype in 1937 as Janson, then again as Janson Text in 1954, and finally in 1985 when it was digitized. Monotype's 1937 Ehrhardt is another revival, named after the foundry in which the matrices had survived. It was not until 1954 that research proved their source to be the exceptional work of Miklós Kis.

Compared to earlier old-style models, the Kis type of 1687, set here in a size equivalent to 20 point, is more finely cut and provides better spatial economy due to the tight fit of the letters. In some respects it is similar to Fleischman's Roman (pp78–79), although it is far more regular. Kis's letters are characterized by a strong contrast between thick and thin strokes with a vertical stress overall. It has a medium x-height, with sharply cut, oblique serifs, except for the u and the flat hairlines on descenders.

It took over 250 years for the achievement of Miklós Kis to be recognized, but the nature of typography is such that his typeface, although revived, is still erroneously named Janson. Legible and economical, it remains one of the most reliable typefaces for bookwork.

LXXXIX.

tare, che dall'argentovivo steſſo ſi laſciaſſe alcuna ſpezie di feccia in ſul panno, ſicchè poi ſtrofinatavi l'ambra ne riceveſſe un leggero appannamento, il qual turaſſe l' inviſibili bocche di quelle vie, ond' eſce la virtù ſua , il qual ſoſpetto tanto più crebbe, quanto che già ſapevamo trovarſi alcuni liquori, de'quali bagnata l'ambra , e tutte l' altre gioie di ſimigliante virtù dotate ricuſan d'attrarre ; ma eſſendoſi poi veduto, che la medeſim' ambra arrotata ſur un altro panno lavato, e rilavato in argentovivo tirava tuttavia con gran forza, ſi credè , che il panno del vaſo poteſſe per avventura nuocerle coll' umidità della gomma inzuppata nell' attaccarlo. Fu perciò meſſa in cambio di panno una ſtriſcetta di camoſcio appiccata con cera lacca a fine di sfuggire l'inzuppamento dell'umido ; ma queſta diligenza ancora fu vana, poichè , o voto, o pieno d'aria che ſi foſſe il vaſo , o l'ambra non tirò mai : che è quanto poſſiamo con verità dire d'un' eſperienza tentata per tante vie inutilmente.

ESPERIENZE INTORNO ALLA PRESSIONE DELL'ARIA.

L'ambra, e l' altre ſuſtanze elettriche, bagnate d'alcuni liquori, non tirano.

ESPERIENZA

Per riconoſcere qual ſarebbe il moto dell' inviſibili eſalazioni del fuoco nel voto

Ty	**Van Dijck's Roman and Italic**
Ca	**Serif**
Ke	**Old Style, Dutch**
Te	**Letterpress**
Da	**1689**
De	**Christoffel van Dijck**
Fo	**Christoffel van Dijck**
Co	**Netherlands**

Characteristics

Vertical stress
Large capitals
A Cupped apex
A E H N D High contrast
Q Long, heavy tail
R Straight leg, serifed
a Narrow
c e Sharp exit strokes
g Narrow, unevenly weighted lower bowl
u Hairline serifs

AEGQRS
abcdefghi
orstuya*efg*

Connections

Kis's Roman	1687
Caslon	c1725
Monotype Van Dijck	1935
DTL Elzevir	1992

Availability

DTL Elzevir is a digital revival available from Dutch Type Library and resellers

Specimen

Terence, *Comediae*. Cantabrigiae Typis Academicis, Cambridge, 1701 (295x240mm)

2

ANDRIÆ ARGUMENTUM,

C. SULPICIO APOLLINARI AUCTORE

Sororem falso creditam meretriculæ,
Genere Andriæ, Glycerium vitiat Pamphilus:
Gravidaque facta, dat fidem, uxorem fibi
Fore hanc: nam aliam pater ei defponderat
Gnatam Chremetis: atque ut amorem comperit,
Simulat futuras nuptias; cupiens, fuus
Quid haberet animi filius, cognofcere.
Davi fuafu non repugnat Pamphilus.
Sed ex Glycerio natum ut vidit puerulum
Chremes, recufat nuptias, generum abdicat:
Mox filiam Glycerium infperato agnitam
Dat Pamphilo hanc, aliam Charino conjugem.

P. TE-

3

P. TERENTII ANDRIA.
PROLOGUS.

POETA cum primum animum ad fcribendum ap-
Id fibi negotî credidit folum dari,   [pulit,
Populo ut placerent, quas feciffet fabulas.
Verum aliter evenire multo intellegit.
Nam in prologis fcribundis operam abutitur,   5
Non qui argumentum narret, fed qui malevoli
Veteris poetæ maledictis refpondeat.
Nunc, quam rem vitio dent, quæfo, animum advortite.
      Menander fecit Andriam & Perinthiam.
Qui utramvis recte norit, ambas noverit.   10
Non ita diffimili funt argumento: fed tamen
Diffimili oratione funt factæ ac ftylo.

A 2   Quæ

Christoffel van Dijck (1606–69) was a Dutch printer, type founder and engraver who produced fonts for the compact editions of the Elsevier publishing house, a company renowned for the quality of its work in the Netherlands and the surrounding countries. Van Dijck was born in what is now Germany and arrived in Amsterdam shortly before 1640, where he worked first as a journeyman goldsmith and soon after as a type founder. He was considerably more successful in his craft than in business. During his early years, he often found himself in debt and was occasionally forced to turn over his equipment and assets to creditors.

After 1650 his business appears to have become stable and prosperous, but four years after his death the entire inventory of his workshop was sold at auction. Several of his types, punches and matrices were acquired by the printer and bookseller Daniel Elsevier. Subsequently, due to a succession of business mergers and other transactions over many years, almost all of it was lost or melted down for scrap. Only four of his original types survive, an italic and three blackletters now kept in the Enschedé collection.

The types of Van Dijck and his Dutch contemporaries continued to be influenced by predecessors like Garamond (pp48–51) but marked the beginnings of a transition that would follow several decades later in the development of typefaces that were radically different to the traditional forms of the Renaissance. The Van Dijck types shown here demonstrate slight traces of a departure from calligraphic sources. They are differentiated from those of Garamond by their sharper cut and a more geometric approach to their construction.

The general impression of the page is one of clarity and economy. The contrast between horizontal strokes and stems is more pronounced than the old style, and the serifs are delicately cupped, with a few exceptions, such as the u. Overall, the stress is vertical, although the c and e are inclined. The lower case has a relatively large x-height with short ascenders. Capital letters are large and wide, with many exhibiting a powerful stroke contrast. The italic is of an equally sharp cut, with a distinctly cursive character and a consistent incline.

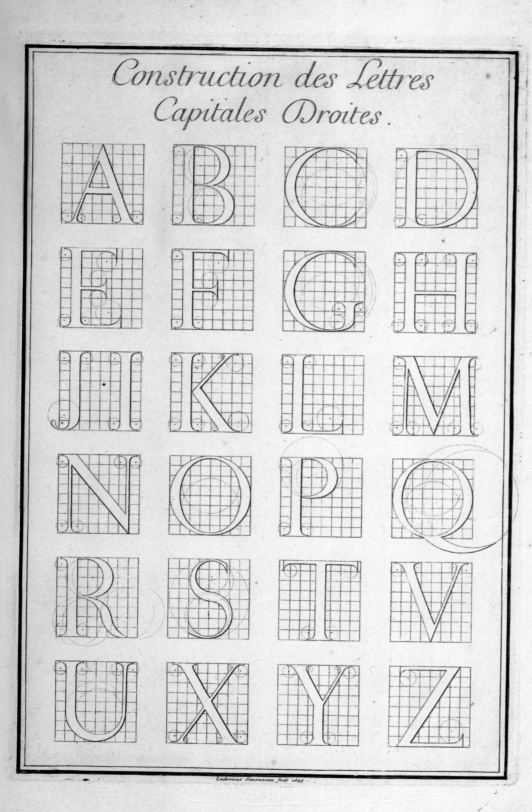

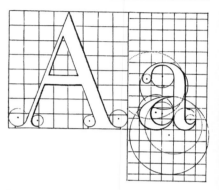

Ty	The Romain du Roi
Ca	Serif
Ke	Transitional
Te	Copper Engraving
Da	1695
De	Louis Simonneau and Philippe Grandjean
Fo	Imprimerie Royale
Co	France

Characteristics

Based on square grids 8 units wide
Vertical stress
Thin strokes with high contrast
Sharp, unbracketed serifs

Connections

LaPolice BP	2006
Romain BP	2007
Royal Romain	2008
SangBleu	2008

Availability

Not available

Specimen

Description et perfection des arts et métiers, des arts de construire les caractères. Académie Royale des Sciences, Paris, 1704 (475×310mm) Source: BNF

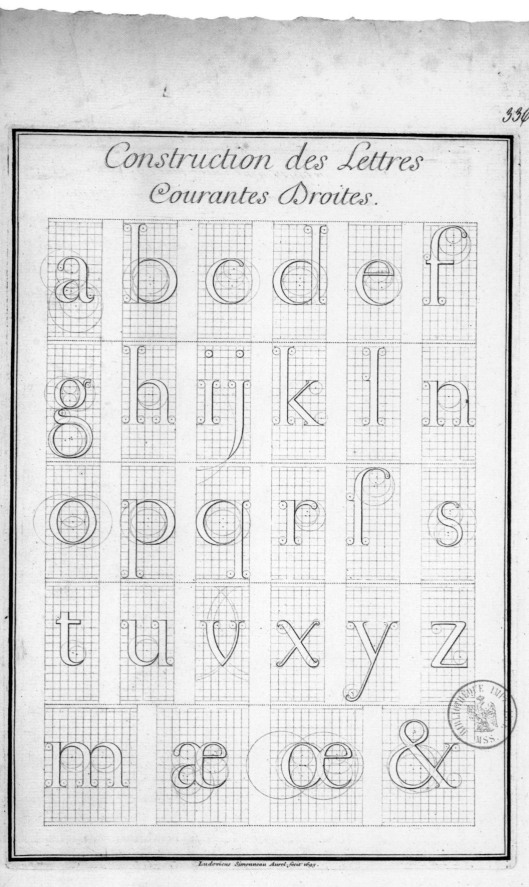

The late seventeenth-century saw the beginnings of a period defined by its rejection of traditional norms as European society began to be transformed by new scientific and philosophical theories. In 1692, a significant cultural development was instigated in the field of printing and type design when the French Academy of Sciences commissioned a rationally constructed alphabet named the Romain du Roi. This initiative was the origin of a radical new direction in letterform design that would have a huge impact on the future of typography.

The design of the typeface was supervised by the Bignon Commission, a government-appointed group comprising two academics and two clergymen, one of whom was also an engineer. With a mission to document 'the techniques used in the practice of the arts' so that contemporary manufacturing methods would be recorded in detail, they chose to begin with 'the Art which preserves all others': printing.

Disregarding the influence of handwriting that had underpinned the design of type since its inception, the letters of the Romain du Roi were constructed systematically, with the individual parts of letterforms treated as elements in an overall design scheme. Based on two different grids divided into squares – 8x8 units for capitals and 15x8 units for the lower case – letter constructions were documented in large copperplate engravings by Louis Simonneau while the cutting of the types was assigned to Philippe Grandjean (pp74–75).

Typographically, the commission's prototype is far from satisfactory. It is awkward both in proportion and contour, and lacking in evidence of humanity. However, its analytical approach had a liberating effect on the direction of typography throughout Europe at a time when improvements in printing methods, papers and inks afforded new possibilities. The Romain du Roi introduced many new ideas that, in a less rigid form, would become the characteristics of modern type design: a shift of stress to the vertical, much greater contrast between thick and thin strokes, and sharp, bracketed serifs. Above all, its analytical approach signalled a move away from letters derived from handwriting towards those that began to be perceived as products of technological processes and as component parts in systems of visual differentiation.

The impact of the Romain du Roi would continue directly for the next century, influencing the type designs of Fournier (pp82–85), Fleischman (pp78–79) and Baskerville (pp80–81), and eventually leading to the modern types of Didot (pp90–91) and Bodoni (pp96–97).

The Romain du Roi

Ty	**The Romain du Roi**
Ca	**Serif**
Ke	**Transitional**
Te	**Letterpress**
Da	**1702**
De	**Louis Simonneau and Philippe Grandjean**
Fo	**Imprimerie Royale**
Co	**France**

Characteristics

Vertical stress
Thin strokes with high contrast
Capitals to ascender height
Most capitals have uniform width
Sharp, bracketed hairline serifs
A Pointed apex
M Splayed
R Curved leg
b d h l Flat top serifs
g Narrow, bulbous ear
l Central spur to left side
t Short, flat top

AEGMRS
abcdefghij
lmoprstuy

Connections

Fleischman's Roman	1739
Fournier's Roman	1764
Didot	1784
Bodoni	1788

Availability

Various digital revivals are available

Specimen

Medailles sur les principaux evenements du regne de Louis le Grand. Imprimerie Royale, Paris, 1702 (433x288mm)
Source: BNF

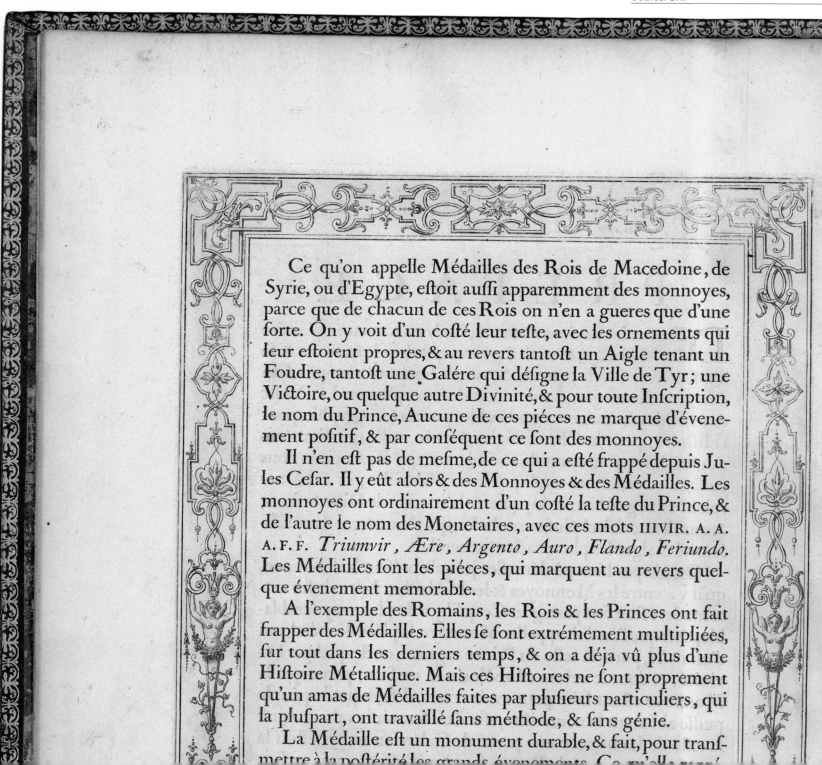

The Bignon Commission's deliberations on behalf of the French Academy of Sciences (pp72–73) resulted in the commissioning of a series of types cut by Philippe Grandjean (1666–1714) for the exclusive use of the Imprimerie Royale.

The Romain du Roi typeface was literally 'the King's Roman', the official type of the French state under Louis XIV. Cut and cast by the Imprimerie, the type was rigorously protected by law against any unauthorized duplication. It is highly likely that Grandjean based his type on original drawings produced by members of the commission rather than Simonneau's

engraved letters, since Grandjean is known to have started cutting the first size of the type in 1696, when Simonneau's work could not have been complete.

While Grandjean's type is distinctly geometric by comparison to any previous designs, it is much softer and more humanistic than the stiff, mechanical letters of the commission on which it was based. Grandjean clearly ignored Simonneau's more extreme forms, like the g, v and x, and his italic is much more serviceable than the awkwardly inclined roman style shown in the engravings. Grandjean's letters have a stress in the

vertical axis, and a considerable contrast between thick and thin strokes. There are bracketless, almost hairline serifs on many capitals, as well as the p, u and r, while the l, j and all of the ascenders have double serifs; the lower case l has a curious spur on the side and there is a short, flat top on the t, both of which are also found in Simonneau's engravings. Because the type was cut to fit a mathematical structure, capitals are the same height as ascenders. They therefore look somewhat large and disproportionate to the lower case. Many previous types had been subtler, with a reduced capital height to avoid this imbalance.

The first book to use the Romain du Roi type was not published until 1702, a decade after the project's inception. *Medailles sur les principaux evenements du regne de Louis le Grand* is a luxurious and immaculately produced publication, reflecting the extravagance of the reign of Louis XIV.

Tobias Smollett's critique of Louis XIV's regime might also apply to the book's design. He described it as 'an ostentation of fastidious pomp, a prodigality of expense, an affectation of munificence, an insolence of ambition and a haughty reserve of deportment.'

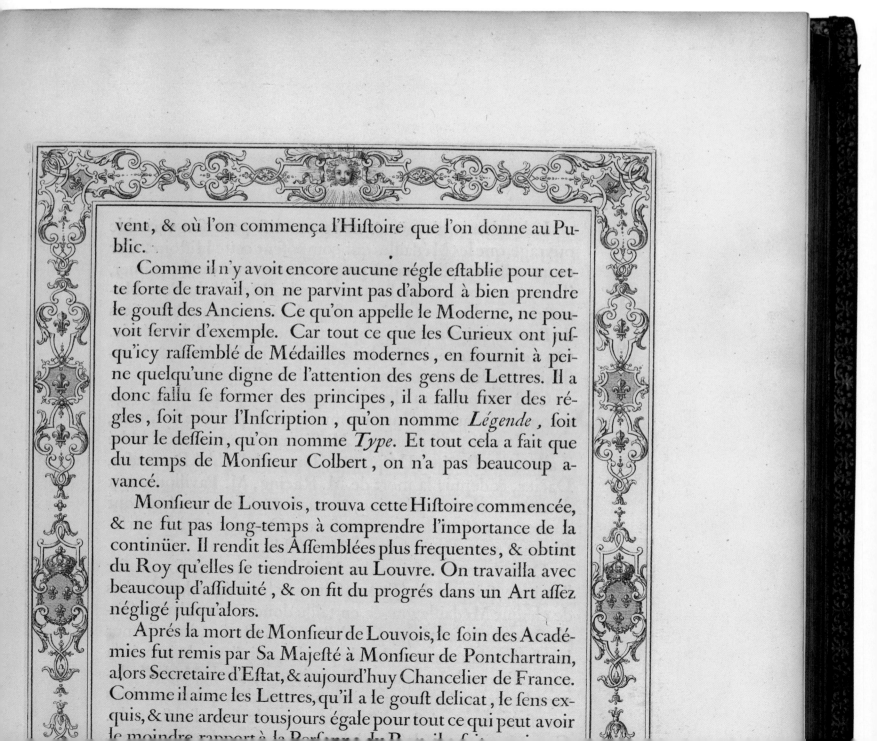

Ty	**Caslon**
Ca	**Serif**
Ke	**Old Style, Dutch**
Te	**Letterpress**
Da	**c1725**
De	**William Caslon**
Fo	**William Caslon**
Co	**UK**

Characteristics

A	Cupped apex
C	Double serifs
G	No spur
Q	Long, heavy tail
R	Straight leg
T	Outward-sloping serifs on top-stroke
Q &	Ornate

ACJMQT
abcdefghij
orstuy*aefg*

Connections

The Fell Types	1672
Baskerville	1757
Caslon 540	1902
Adobe Caslon	1990

Availability

Digital revivals are widely available

Specimen

A Specimen by William Caslon. William Caslon, London, 1734 (527x420mm)

A S P E

By WILLIAM CASLON, Letter

ABCD
ABCDE
ABCDEFG
ABCDEFGHI
ABCDEFGHIJK
ABCDEFGHIJKL
ABCDEFGHIKLMN

French Cannon.

Quousque tandem abutere, Catilina, pati-

Quousque tandem

abutere, Catilina,

patientia nostra?

Two Lines Great Primer.

Quousque tandem

DOUBLE PICA ROMA
Quousque tandem abutere, lina, patientia nostra? qua nos etiam furor iste tuus elu quem ad finem sese effrenata ABCDEFGHIJKLMN

GREAT PRIMER ROMAN
Quousque tandem abutere, Catilin tientia nostra? quamdiu nos etia ror iste tuus eludet? quem ad fin se effrenata jactabit audacia? nih nocturnum præsidium palatii, ni bis vigiliæ, nihil timor populi, nih ABCDEFGHIJKLMNOP

ENGLISH ROMAN.
Quousque tandem abutêre, Catilina, nostra? quamdiu nos etiam furor iste tuus quem ad finem sese effrenata jactabit a nihilne te nocturnum præsidium palati urbis vigiliæ, nihil timor populi, nihil fus bonorum omnium, nihil hic muni ABCDEFGHIJKLMNOPQRST

PICA ROMAN.
Melium, novis rebus studentem, manu sua Fuit, fuit ista quondam in hac repub. virtus fortes acrioribus suppliciis civem perniciosum acerbissimum hostem coërcerent. Habemus natusconsultum in te, Catilina, vehemens, & non deest reip. consilium, neque autoritas h dinis: nos, nos, dico aperte, consules desum ABCDEFGHIJKLMNOPQRSTV

SMALL PICA ROMAN. No 1.
At nos vigesimum jam diem patimur hebescere acie autoritatis. habemus enim hujusmodi senatusconsul rumtamen inclusum in tabulis, tanquam gladium reconditum: quo ex senatusconsulto confestim inter esse, Catilina, convenit. Vivis: & vivis non ad dam, sed ad confirmandam audaciam. Cupio, P esse clementem: cupio in tantis reipub. periculis ABCDEFGHIJKLMNOPQRSTVUV

SMALL PICA ROMAN. No 2.
At nos vigesimum jam diem patimur hebescere acie autoritatis. habemus enim hujusmodi senatusconsul rumtamen inclusum in tabulis, tanquam gladium reconditum: quo ex senatusconsulto confestim inter esse, Catilina, convenit. Vivis: & vivis non ad dep

I M E N

...ler, in Chifwell-Street, LONDON.

Double Pica Italick.
...fque tandem abutere, Catili-
patientia noftra? quamdiu
...tiam furor ifte tuus eludet?
...e ad finem fefe effrenata jac-
CDEFGHIJKLMNO

Great Primer Italick.
...fque tandem abutére, Catilina, pa-
...a noftra.? quamdiu nos etiam fu-
...te tuus eludet? quem ad finem fefe
...ata jaɛtabit audacia? nihilne te
...rnum præfidium palatii, nihil ur-
...giliæ, nihil timor populi, nihil con-
CDEFGHIJKLMNOPQR

English Italick.
...ue tandem abutere, Catilina, patientia nof-
...quamdiu nos etiam furor ifte tuus eludet?
...ad finem fefe effrenata jaɛtabit audacia?
...te noɛturnum præfidium palatii, nihil ur-
...iliæ, nihil timor populi, nihil confenfus bo-
...omnium, nihil hic munitiffimus habendi fe-
CDEFGHIJKLMNOPQRSTVU

Pica Italick.
...a, novis rebus ftudentem, manu fua occidit.
...uit ifta quondam in hac repub. virtus, ut viri
...crioribus fuppliciis civem perniciofum, quam a-
...num hoftem coërcerent. Habemus enim fenatuf-
...m in te, Catilina, vehemens, & grave: non deeft
...nfilium, neque autoritas hujus ordinis: nos, nos,
...rte, confules defumus. Decrevit quondam fenatus
DEFGHIJKLMNOPQRSTVUWXYZ

Small Pica Italick. No 1.
...vigefimum jam diem patimur hebefcere aciem horum
...is. habemus enim hujufmodi fenatufconfutum, verum-
...clufum in tabulis, tanquam gladium in vagina recon-
...quo ex fenatufconfulto confeftim interfeɛtum te effe, Ca-
...onvenit. Vivis: & vivis non ad deponendam, fed ad
...ndam audaciam. Cupio, P. C., me effe clementem:
...tantis reipub. periculis non diffolutum videri: fed jam
DEFGHIJKLMNOPQRSTVUWUXYZ

Small Pica Italick. No 2.
...vigefimum jam diem patimur hebefcere aciem horum au-
...habemus enim hujufmodi fenatufconfultum, verumtamen
...in tabulis, tanquam gladium in vagina reconditum —
...natufconfulto confeftim interfeɛtum te effe, Catilina, con-
...Vivis: & vivis non ad deponendam, fed ad confirman-
...daciam. Cupio, P. C., me effe clementem: cupio in tantis

Pica Black.
And be it further enacted by the Authority
aforefaid, That all and every of the faid Exchequer Bills to be made forth by virtue of
this Aɛt, or fo many of them as fhall from
ABCDEFGHIJKLMNOPQRST

Brevier Black.
And be it further enacted by the Authority aforefaid, That all and every
of the faid Exchequer Bills to be made forth by virtue of this Aɛt, or fo
many of them as fhall from time to time remain undifcharged and uncan-
celled, until the difcharging and cancelling the fame purfuant to this Aɛt,

Pica Gothick.
ATTA ƲNSAR ΦN ÍN ҺIMINAM VEIҺNAI
NAMꝜ ΦEIN UIMAI ΦINDINASSNS ΦEINS
VAIRΦAI VIAGA ΦEINS SVE ÍN ҺIMINA

Pica Coptick.
Ϧεn ογαρχη ⲁ⳰ϯ ⲑⲁⲙⲓⲟ ⲛⲧⲫⲉ ⲛⲉⲙ ⲡⲕ-
ⲁϩⲓ· ⲡⲓⲕⲁϩⲓ ⲇⲉ ⲛⲉ ⲟγⲁⲑⲛⲁⲧ ⲉⲣⲟϥ ⲡⲉ ⲟγⲟϩ
ⲛⲁⲧⲥⲟⲃⲧ ⲟγⲭⲁⲕⲓ ⲛⲁϭⲭⲏ ⲉⲭⲉⲛ ⲫⲛⲟγⲛ ⲟγⲟϩ
ⲟγⲡⲛⲁ ⲛⲧⲉϥϯ ⲛⲁϭⲛⲏⲟγ ϩⲓⲭⲉⲛ ⲛⲓⲙⲱⲟγ· ⲟ·

Pica Armenian.
 Արձակ Թագաւոր՝ երկիր և ծովու, որոյ ական
և պատուէր՝ որպէս և է իւր մէծ Աստուծոյ
իւր բանն և պատմաՀնւմ 'ի վեր քան զամ
Թագաւորաց. և ձայնց լայնութի, որպէս երկին

Englifh Syriack.
ܘܐܡܪ ܝܗܘܐ ܐܝܣ ܐܠܗܐ ܟܗܝܐ ܐܝܚܕܐ
ܘܚܙܐ ܣܒܪ ܢܐܠܐ ܪܢܐ ܚܝ ܘܚܠܝܣܕܝ
ܟܕ ܠ ܣܐܚ ܐܠ ܣܬܚ ܟܕ ܣܪ ܝܚܚܚܪ

Pica Samaritan.
ⵣⵀⵏⵉⵣ ⵉ ⵣ ⵣⵀ ⵀⵀ ⵏⵉⵣ ⵏⵉⵣⵏ
ⵏⵉⵣ ⵏⵉⵣⵏ ⵉⵏ ⵉⵏⵉⵣ ⵏⵉⵏⵉⵏ ⵏⵉⵏⵉⵏ
ⵏⵉⵣ ⵏⵉⵣⵏ ⵏⵉⵏⵉⵏ

Englifh Arabick.
لا يلي لك الله آخر غيري ۞ لا تاخذ لك صورة ۞ ولا تمثيل كل ما
في السماء من فوق ۞ وما في الارض من اسفل ۞ ولا ما في
الماء من تحت الارض ۞ لا تسجد لهن ۞ ولا تعبدهن ۞
فاني انا الرب الهك الاه غيور ۞ اجتزي ذنوب الابا من

Hebrew with Points.
בְּרֵאשִׁית בָּרָא אֱלֹהִים אֵת הַשָּׁמַיִם וְאֵת הָאָרֶץ : וְהָאָרֶץ
הָיְתָה תֹהוּ וָבֹהוּ וְחֹשֶׁךְ עַל־פְּנֵי תְהוֹם וְרוּחַ אֱלֹהִים
מְרַחֶפֶת עַל־פְּנֵי הַמָּיִם : וַיֹּאמֶר אֱלֹהִים יְהִי אוֹר וַיְהִי־אוֹר :
וַיַּרְא אֱלֹהִים אֶת־הָאוֹר כִּי־טוֹב וַיַּבְדֵּל אֱלֹהִים בֵּין הָאוֹר

William Caslon (1693–1766) was the first printer in England to achieve prestige and prosperity thanks, in part, to government policies that had impeded English type founding and printing for centuries. Until he started to manufacture fonts in the 1720s, most printers were forced to import their typefaces from the Netherlands, as the type industry was almost non-existent in England.

Before turning to type production, Caslon had trained as an engraver, setting up independently in 1716 and opening his own type foundry a few years later. The design of his first types, produced in around 1725, was directly influenced by Dutch designs of the time, such as those of Christoffel van Dijck (pp70–71) and Dirk Voskens, but he introduced the sensibilities of the English baroque style with a liveliness of modelling and variation of form that was lacking in contemporary Dutch types.

Caslon's early letterforms are somewhat sturdier than many earlier old-style typefaces, with a relatively even contrast between thick and thin strokes. The axis of curves is almost completely vertical, and the serifs are notably stout. On close inspection, some individual character contours show minor inconsistencies, giving a blotchy overall impression, especially in the small sizes. However, the idiosyncrasies of Caslon's few eccentric letters give his types an animated rhythm that contributes greatly to their congenial appearance. A body of text set in Caslon has a visual effect that is inviting, pleasing to the eye and very comfortable for reading at length.

Caslon's typefaces were an instant success in Britain and the United States, where they were used extensively, most notably for the first printed version of the United States Declaration of Independence in 1776. As a result of the enduring success of William Caslon's work, the art of printing in England began to improve, soon becoming the equal of anywhere in the world. At the same time, the craft of type founding was resurrected as a thriving trade. Despite the many innovations that consequently followed, Caslon's remained the types of choice for most printers in the country until well into the nineteenth century. No longer forced to rely on foreign imports, English printers could now work with domestic types that proved so dependable that the expression 'when in doubt, use Caslon' became a popular maxim in the trade.

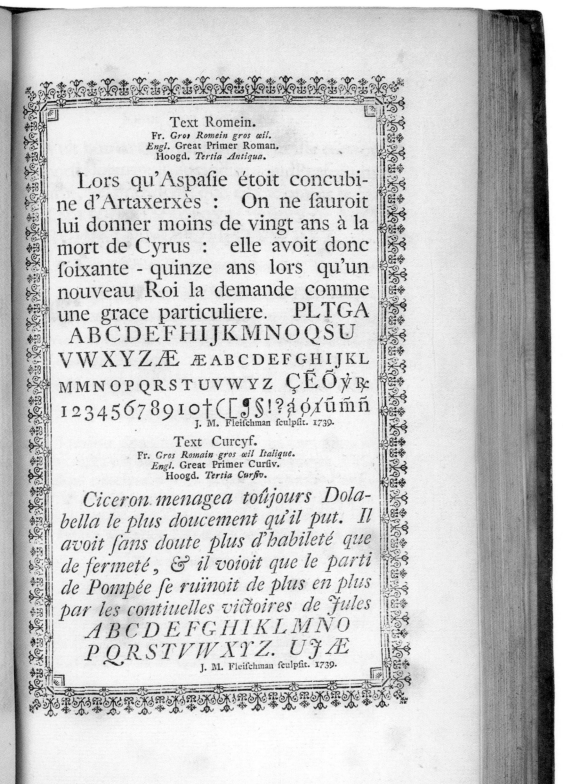

Ty	**Fleischman's Roman**
Ca	**Serif**
Ke	**Transitional**
Te	**Letterpress**
Da	**1739**
De	**Joan Michaël Fleischman**
Fo	**Joh. Enschedé en Zonen**
Co	**Netherlands**

Characteristics

Mixed vertical and angled stress

Cupped serifs on lower case ascenders

E Long arms

E F L T Z Forked serifs

J Descends below baseline

M Square proportion

T Outward-sloping serifs on top-stroke

g Narrow, bulbous ear

ACEJMQ
abcdefghij
orstuy*aefg*

Connections

Bulmer	1792
DTL Fleischmann	1992
Fenway	1998
Farnham Text	2004

Availability

DTL Fleischmann is available from Dutch Type Library and resellers

Specimen

Proef van letteren. Enschedé, Haarlem, 1768 (210x125mm)

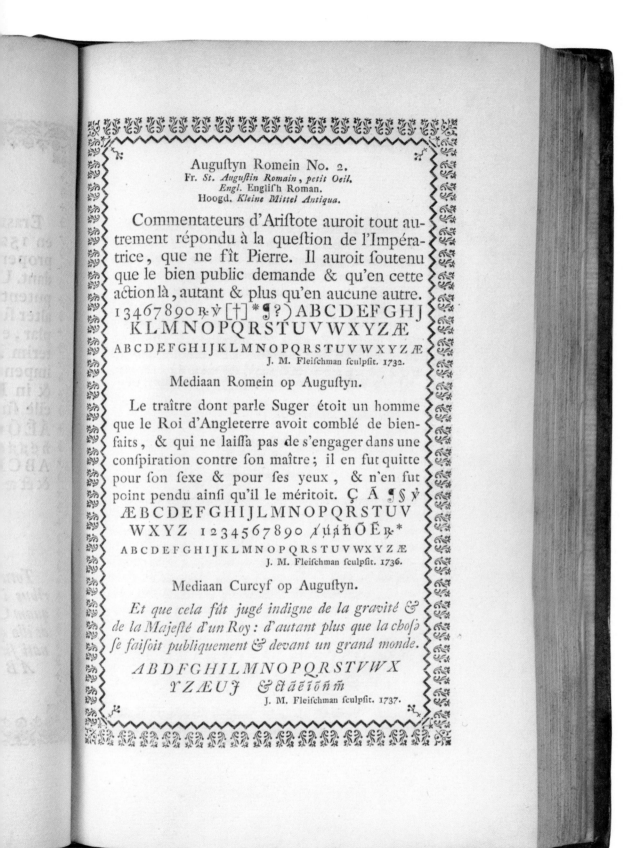

In the mid-eighteenth century there was a dynamic shift in the design of type. The groundbreaking work of John Baskerville, Pierre-Simon Fournier and Joan Michaël Fleischman signalled a departure from the old styles first cut in the Renaissance, laying the foundations for the rationalist neoclassical faces of Didot and Bodoni.

Joan Fleischman (1701–68) was born in Germany. He worked in Holland from 1728, where he was employed as a journeyman punch cutter at various type foundries until setting up on his own. From 1743 onwards he worked predominantly for the highly respected Enschedé foundry in Haarlem, cutting almost 100 types in a wide variety of styles, including romans, italics, blackletters, and non-Latins such as Greek, Armenian and Arabic.

The typefaces shown are from the Enschedé specimen of 1768, issued a few months after Fleischman's death. Made between 1732 and 1739, they demonstrate his exceptional skills as a punch cutter. To achieve lighter strokes and sharper curves, Fleischman used better tools and finer materials than his contemporaries. His type sparkles on the page, mixing vertical and oblique stresses within letterforms that have a large x-height and a strong contrast between thick and thin strokes. The formation of serifs rejects traditional norms in favour of a playfully irreverent approach. Serifs are notably variable, forked on several capitals, while on some of the lower case ascenders they are cupped. These features clearly anticipate the designs of Didot and Bodoni.

Fleischman's Roman is traditionally classified as a transitional typeface, an awkwardly relative term locating it – and types like it – somewhere between the Renaissance and the Enlightenment. The typographer Robert Bringhurst has described the style somewhat more succinctly as 'rococo'.

Ty	**Baskerville**
Ca	**Serif**
Ke	**Transitional**
Te	**Letterpress**
Da	**1757**
De	**John Baskerville**
Fo	**John Baskerville**
Co	**UK**

Characteristics

Vertical stress

Capitals lower than ascender height

A High crossbar and pointed apex

C Top and bottom serifs

E Long bottom stroke

J Descends below baseline

Q Swash-like tail

R Straight, flared leg

g Open tail

ACEJMQ
abcdefghij
orstuyaefg

Connections

Caslon	c1725
Fry's Baskerville	1766
Monotype Baskerville	1923
Mrs Eaves	1996

Availability

Digital revivals are widely available

Specimen

Type Specimen and Proposal for Printing of the Works of Virgil. John Baskerville, Birmingham, 1754 (280x220mm)

PUBLII VIRGILII
MARONIS
BUCOLICA
GEORGICA
ET
AENEIS

Ad optimorum Exemplarium fidem recensita.

TO THE PUBLIC.

JOHN BASKERVILLE propofes, by the advice and affiftance of feveral learned men, to print, from the Cambridge edition corrected with all poffible care, an elegant edition of Virgil. The work will be printed in quarto, on this writing royal paper, and with the letter annex'd. The price of the volume in fheets will be one guinea, no part of which will be required till the book is delivered. It will be put to prefs as foon as the number of Subfcribers fhall amount to five hundred whofe names will be prefixt to the work. All perfons who are inclined to encourage the undertaking, are defired to fend their names to JOHN BASKERVILLE in Birmingham; who will give fpecimens of the work to all who are defirous of feeing them.

Subfcriptions are alfo taken in, and fpecimens delivered by Meffieurs R. and J. DODSLEY, Bookfellers in Pall Mall, London. MDCCLIV.

P. VIRGILII MARONIS

BUCOLICA

ECLOGA I. cui nomen *TITYRUS*.

MELIBOEUS, TITYRUS.

Tityre, tu patulæ recubans fub tegmine fagi,
  Silveftrem tenui Mufam meditaris avena:
Nos patriæ fines, et dulcia linquimus arva,
Nos patriam fugimus: tu Tityre lentus in umbra
Formofam refonare doces Amaryllida filvas.
T. O Melibœe, Deus nobis hæc otia fecit:
Namque erit ille mihi femper Deus; illius aram
Sæpe tener noftris ab ovilibus imbuet agnus:
Ille meas errare boves, ut cernis, et ipfum
Ludere quæ vellem, calamo permifit agrefti.
M. Non equidem invideo; miror magis: undique totis
Ufque adeo turbatur agris. en ipfe capellas
Protenus æger ago: hanc etiam vix Tityre duco.
Hic inter denfas corylos modo namque gemellos,
Spem gregis, ah! filice in nuda connixa reliquit.
Sæpe malum hoc nobis, fi mens non læva fuiffet,
De cœlo tactas memini prædicere quercus.
Sæpe finiftra cava prædixit ab ilice cornix.
Sed tamen, ifte Deus qui fit, da, Tityre, nobis.
T. Urbem, quam dicunt Romam, Melibœe, putavi
Stultus ego huic noftræ fimilem, quo fæpe folemus
Paftores ovium teneros depellere fœtus.
Sic canibus catulos fimiles, fic matribus hædos
Noram; fic parvis componere magna folebam.

At the start of the eighteenth century, old-style typefaces were the norm; by the end, the radical modern styles of Bodoni and Didot had become dominant. Central to this significant change in the direction of typographic design were the innovations of John Baskerville (1706–75), an English maker of japanned wares who was also an expert writing master and letter carver.

Late in life Baskerville set up as a printer, applying his professional skills to produce a series of books that have few rivals in the history of printing. Although self-taught, he was relentless in his pursuit of perfection, involving himself in every detail of the print production process. He made numerous improvements to the paper, ink and the printing press itself to achieve results that were more sharply cut and lighter than any previous design. He developed smooth, glazed paper and, using his knowledge of japanning, formulated his own dense black ink. To maintain the highest standards he would print a run of 2,000 to obtain 1,500 copies.

Baskerville's typefaces are the result of his ambition to improve on those of William Caslon (pp76–77). Unlike the theoreticians who had designed the Romain du Roi at the turn of the century (pp72–73), his work was informed by an expert understanding of pen-drawn letters. In the mid-eighteenth century, writing masters began to hold their pens at right angles to the baseline to create sharply defined forms with an upright stress. This practice influenced the consistency of the stroke construction of Baskerville's type, which had an increased contrast between thick and thin strokes, making the serifs sharper and more tapered, with a shift to vertical in the axis of rounded letters. Character proportions are wide and regular, with open counterforms and curved strokes that are circular. Baskerville's skills as a writing master are evident in the flowing curves of the italic and occasional distinctive swashes.

In 1757, after years in development, Baskerville published his first edition, a handsome collection of Virgil with ample margins, widely spaced headings and deep, open leading. This was followed by some 50 further classics. His work did not meet with universal approval from his British competitors, some of whom accused him of 'blinding all the readers in the nation; for the strokes of your letters, being too thin and narrow, hurt the eye'. In Europe, however, he became highly respected, notably by Fournier and Bodoni who later cut letterforms of even greater contrast. The refined dignity of Baskerville's typefaces has never been exceeded. His work informed everything that followed.

Ty	**Fournier's Roman**
Ca	**Serif**
Ke	**Transitional**
Te	**Letterpress**
Da	**1764**
De	**Pierre-Simon Fournier**
Fo	**Pierre-Simon Fournier**
Co	**France**

Characteristics

Vertical stress
Light overall weight
Contrast between thick and thin strokes
Minimal bracketing on serifs
Capitals to ascender height
Wedge-shaped serifs on ascenders
c e Tilted axis

ACJMQR
abcdefghij
koprstuvy

Connections

The Romain du Roi	1702
Baskerville	1757
Monotype Fournier	1925
Source Serif Pro	2014

Availability

Monotype Fournier is available from
Monotype and resellers

Specimen

Manuel typographique. Pierre-Simon
Fournier, Paris, 1764–66 (180x125mm)

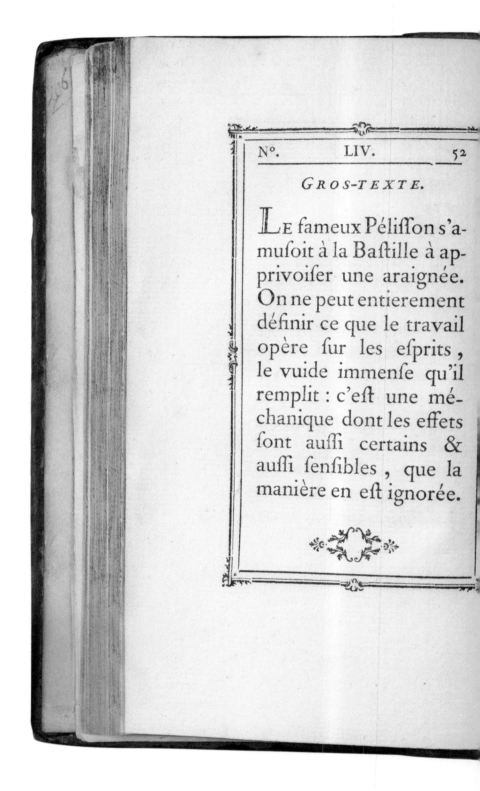

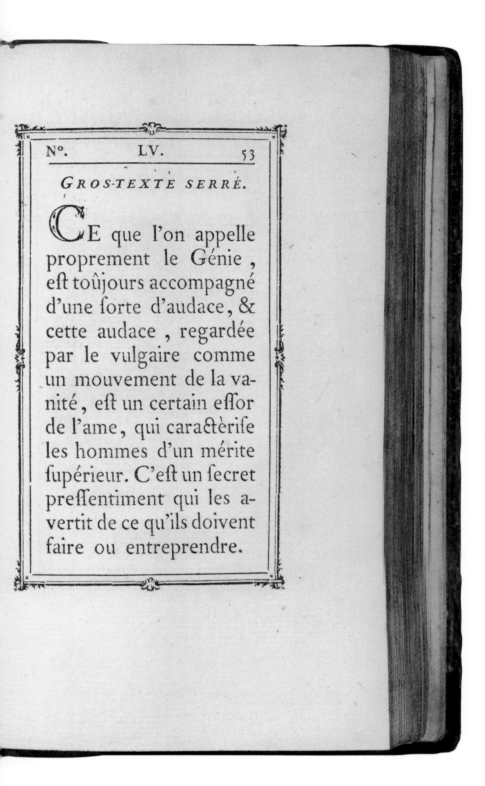

N°. LV. 53

GROS-TEXTE SERRÉ.

CE que l'on appelle proprement le Génie, eſt toûjours accompagné d'une ſorte d'audace, & cette audace, regardée par le vulgaire comme un mouvement de la va-nité, eſt un certain eſſor de l'ame, qui caractèriſe les hommes d'un mérite ſupérieur. C'eſt un ſecret preſſentiment qui les a-vertit de ce qu'ils doivent faire ou entreprendre.

Pierre-Simon Fournier (1712–68) was the foremost type founder working in France during the eighteenth century. Fournier le Jeune, as he was known, was one of four generations involved in the French printing and type-founding industry. His father, Jean-Claude Fournier, was manager of the Le Bé foundry in Paris from 1698 until 1729, and for a short time Fournier le Jeune worked there. By 1736 he had set up his own business producing large type punches and engravings of printers' ornaments.

Fournier made a number of significant contributions to the history of printing and publishing. In the course of his career he made numerous improvements to techniques of cutting and casting type. He also wrote extensively about printing practice and its historical development. In addition, he established a number of important typographic conventions, including the standardization of type measurement in the original point system. This is regarded as one of his most enduring contributions to typography.

It is estimated that Fournier le Jeune may have cut as many as 60,000 punches in the production of around 150 typefaces, some spanning huge ranges of size, from 5 to 108 point. Many of his types were also offered in sets of coordinated styles, along with related fonts of typographic ornaments, a progenitor of the way in which type families are configured today.

The typefaces that Fournier and his successors created were a continuation of the Romain du Roi style (pp74–75), adapted for their own time. While his designs retained features of earlier models, many new ideas were incorporated, marking the beginnings of a transition towards the more austere style that Didot and Bodoni would make popular later in the century. Fournier's types had a greater vertical stress than the old-style types, a larger contrast between thick and thin strokes, and little or no bracketing on the serifs. They were also much lighter and more delicate in overall weight. The matching height for ascenders and capitals anticipated the later modern types, while the influence of the old style persisted in the angled serifs on the ascenders, together with the tilted axes on the c and e.

Ty	**Fournier's Italic**
Ca	**Serif**
Ke	**Transitional Italic**
Te	**Letterpress**
Da	**1764**
De	**Pierre-Simon Fournier**
Fo	**Pierre-Simon Fournier**
Co	**France**

Characteristics

Light overall weight
Contrast between thick and thin strokes
Character construction derived from roman forms
Moderate ascenders and descenders
Consistent angle of incline
Wide, rounded arches

ACQMR
abcdefghij
koprstuvy

Connections

The Romain du Roi	1702
Wilson	1768
Monotype Fournier	1925
Corundum Text	2006

Availability

Monotype Fournier is available from Monotype and resellers

Specimen

Manuel typographique. Pierre-Simon Fournier, Paris, 1764–66 (180x125mm)

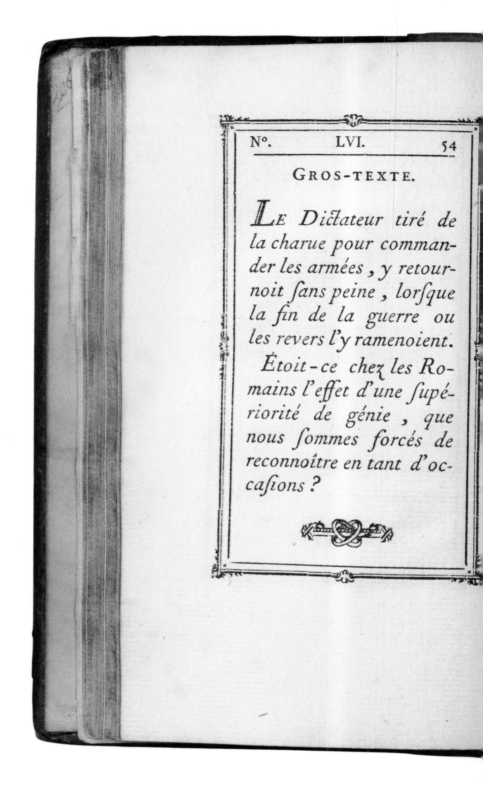

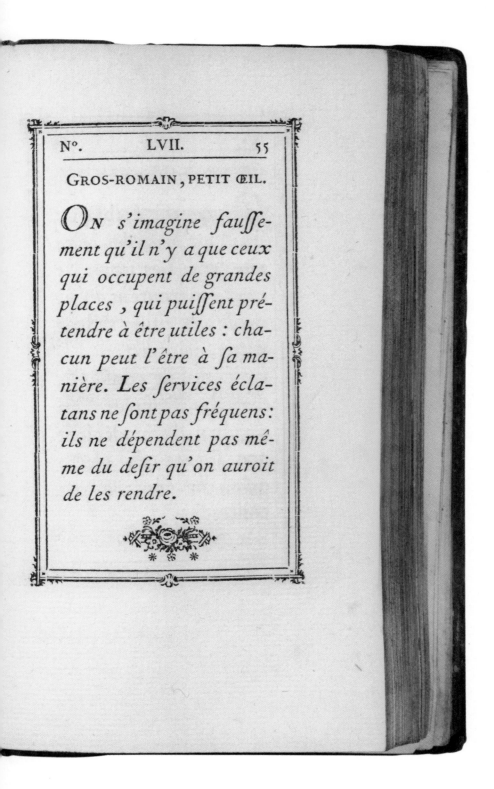

The italic types cut by Pierre-Simon Fournier (1712–68) in the mid-eighteenth century are often admired for their originality and readability. The type historian Harry Carter described them, for example, as 'the most legible of all italics'. Like Fournier's corresponding romans (pp82–83), the lively qualities of his italic letters reveal the ingenuity of Fournier's working methods in developing a completely new style informed by a profound understanding of the old.

Departing from earlier conventions, Fournier's Italic is characterized by a pronounced stroke contrast and the use of serifs on lower case characters in a manner that suggests the heritage of engraved lettering rather than a calligraphic tradition. Unlike the chancery italics of the Renaissance period, they have the qualities of a type derived logically from the roman form in order to harmonize with it. An even rhythm is provided in bodies of text by wide, rounded arches, a tall x-height and relatively short ascenders and descenders with a very consistent angle of incline.

By rationalizing and simplifying many features of familiar old-style letterforms, Fournier's types were much more balanced than the harshly mathematical alphabets that had been introduced by the Imprimerie Royale at the beginning of the eighteenth century (pp72–75). They were also considerably more convivial and were largely responsible for accustoming educated readers to a logical, progressive approach to the appearance of text, laying the foundation for the modern styles made popular by Didot and Bodoni soon after.

GREAT PRIMER. No I.

Quousque tandem abutere, Catilina,
patientia noftra? quamdiu nos etiam
furor ifte tuus eludet? quem ad finem
fefe effrenata jactabit audacia? nihilne
te nocturnum præsidium palatii, nihil
urbis vigiliæ, nihil timor populi, nihil
confensus bonorum omnium, nihil hic

A B C D E F G H I J K L M N

No 2.

Quousque tandem abutere, Catilina, patientia noftra? quamdiu nos etiam furor ifte tuus eludet? quem ad finem fefe effrenata jactabit audacia? nihilne te
nocturnum præsidium palatii, nihil urbis vigiliæ, nihil timor populi, nihil

A B C D E F G H I J K L M N O

Italick.

*Quousque tandem abutere, Catilina, pa-
tientia noftra? quamdiu nos etiam furor
ifte tuus eludet? quem ad finem fefe effrenata jactabit audacia? nihilne te nocturnum præsidium palatii, nihil urbis
vigiliæ, nihil timor populi, nihil confen-
A B C D E F G H I J K L M N O*

Ty	**Wilson**
Ca	**Serif**
Ke	**Transitional**
Te	**Letterpress**
Da	**1768**
De	**Alexander Wilson**
Fo	**Alexander Wilson & Sons**
Co	**UK**

Characteristics

Vertical stress

Capitals lower than ascender height

A High crossbar and pointed apex

C Top serif only on larger sizes

J Descends below baseline

Q Long, heavy tail

R Curved leg

Q & Ornate

ACJMQR
abcdefghij
orstuy*aefg*

Connections

Baskerville	1757
Fontana	1936
Georgia	1996
Miller	1997

Availability

Foundry Wilson is a digital revival
available from the Foundry and resellers

Specimen

A Specimen of Printing Types. Alexander
Wilson & Sons, Glasgow, 1783
(230x155mm)

ENGLISH ROMAN. NO 3.

Quoufque tandem abutere, Catilina, patientia
noftra? quamdiu nos etiam furor ifte tuus eludet? quem ad finem fefe effrenata jactabit audacia? nihilne te nocturnum præfidium palatii,
nihil urbis vigiliæ, nihil timor populi, nihil
confenfus bonorum omnium, nihil hic munitiffimus habendi fenatus locus, nihil horum o-
ra vultufque moverunt? patere tua confilia non
fentis? conftrictam jam omnium horum confcientia teneri conjurationem tuam non vides?
quid proxima, quid fuperiore nocte egeris? ubi
fueris, quos convocaveris, quid confilii ceperis,
quem noftrum ignorare arbitraris? O tempora,
o mores! Senatus hoc intelligit, conful vidit:
hic tamen vivit. vivit? immo vero etiam in fe-
ABCDEFGHIJKLMNOPQRS

Englifh Italick.

Quoufque tandem abutere, Catilina, patientia nof-
tra? quamdiu nos etiam furor ifte tuus eludet?
quem ad finem fefe effrenata jactabit audacia? ni-
hilne te nocturnum præfidium palatii, nihil urbis
vigiliæ, nihil timor populi, nihil confenfus bonorum
omnium, nihil hic munitiffimus habendi fenatus lo-
cus, nihil horum ora vultufque moverunt? patere
tua confilia non fentis? conftrictam jam omnium
horum confcientia teneri conjurationem tuam non
vides? quid proxima, quid fuperiore nocte egeris,
ubi fueris, quos convocaveris, quid confilii ceperis,
quem noftrum ignorare arbitraris? O tempora,
o mores! Senatus hoc intelligit, conful vidit: hic
ABCDEFGHIJKLMNOPQRST

Alexander Wilson (1714–84) established the Wilson type foundry in partnership with John Baine in 1742 and set up shop in Glasgow in 1762. Wilson was an exceptionally cultured man, a surgeon and professor of astronomy as well as a type founder. His foundry employed some of the most highly skilled craftsmen of the time, including William Miller, Richard Austin and Johann Christian Bauer, and its work was highly respected by the Scottish printing trade. Foremost among Wilson's customers were the printers to the University of Glasgow, who used many of his typefaces exclusively in their editions of the classics.

Wilson's earliest types, like Caslon's, were modelled on the Dutch old style, but his later designs began to show the influence of John Baskerville's work (pp80–81). The type historian Harry Carter wrote that 'Baskerville imported into typography the flowing curves, long hairlines and general love of symmetry of the contemporary writing masters. Wilson took the letter-forms of Baskerville but kept to an older style of shading.'

Wilson's type had the large lower case x-height, wide proportions and incised qualities that made Baskerville's letters so graceful, but its high contrast between thick and thin strokes anticipates the Scotch Roman (pp112–13) that followed it some years later. Lively and robust at the same time, and characterized by heavy, squared serifs, the Wilson types are notable for their excellent fit and even colour at both large and small point sizes.

Wilson's design was revived in 1936 by Giovanni Mardersteig at the Monotype Corporation for machine composition and was published under the name of Fontana. It was revived again digitally in 1993 from original specimens by David Quay and Freda Sack for the Foundry. Their reinterpretation faithfully reconstructed the original roman and italic and added new styles to complete a family of three weights, complemented by a set of printers' flowers from the same source.

Ty	**Cottrell's Scripts**
Ca	**Script**
Ke	**Formal, Connected**
Te	**Letterpress**
Da	**1774**
De	**Thomas Cottrell**
Fo	**Thomas Cottrell**
Co	**UK**

Characteristics

Thin, even stroke width
Long ascenders and descenders
Swash capitals
Small x-height
Entry strokes and exit strokes allow characters to link

Agrippa beginning Jerusalem

Connections

The Grover Cursorials	c1700
The Bâtarde Coulée Script	c1742
Didot's Anglaise	1809
Snell Roundhand	1966

Availability

Not available

Specimen

A Specimen of Printing Types by Tho. Cottrell. Thomas Cottrell, London, 1774 (275x171mm)

Engrossing.

And be it further hereby enacted, That the Mayors, Bailiffs, or other head Officers of every Town and placeproortr te, and City within this Realm being Justice or Justices of Peace, shall have the same authority by virtue of this Act, within the limits and precincts of their Jurisdictions, as well out of Sessions, as at their Sessions, if they hold

A B C D E F G H I K L M N O P Q R S T U V

Double Pica Script.

Then Agrippa said unto Paul, Thou art permitted
to speak for thyself. Then Paul stretched forth the hand,
and answered for himself: I think myself happy King
Agrippa, because I shall answer for myself this day
before Thee, touching all the things whereof I am ac=
cused of the Jews: especially, because I know thee to
be expert in all customs and questions which are among
the Jews: wherefore I beseech thee to hear me patiently.
My manner of life from my youth, which was at
the first among mine own nation at Jerusalem, know
all the Jews; which knew me from the beginning (if
they would testify) that after the most straitest sect of
our religion, I lived a Pharisee. And now I stand
and am judged for the hope of the promise made of God
unto our fathers: unto which promise our twelve tribes,
instantly serving God day and night, hope to come: for
which hope's sake, King Agrippa, I am accused of
the Jews. Why should it be thought a thing incredible
with you that God should raise the dead? I verily
thought with myself that I ought to do many things
contrary to the name of Jesus of Nazereth: which things
I also did in Jerusalem: and many of the saints did
I shut up in prison having received authority from the
chief priests; and when they were put to death I gave
my voice against them. And I punished them oft in
every synagogue and compelled them to blaspheme; and
being exceedingly mad against them, I persecuted them
A B C D E F G H I J K L M N O P 2
R S T U V W X Y Z A B C D E F G H I

Thomas Cottrell (?–1785) was a resourceful English punch cutter and letter founder. He served his apprenticeship in the foundry of William Caslon, but in 1757 Cottrell and a co-worker, Joseph Jackson, lost a dispute with their employer concerning wages. When they unexpectedly found themselves dismissed, Cottrell and Jackson established their own foundry.

Among other innovations, Cottrell was the first British type founder to cut script types. In England, a country with a negligible early history in the practice of type founding, there is very little evidence of the design of any earlier types based on scribal hands like those found in Italy, France or Germany. The notable founders of the eighteenth century, such as Caslon and Baskerville, had attempted nothing at all in these styles.

Cottrell's Engrossing, shown far left, commissioned in around 1765 by William Richardson, is a mechanization of the standard scribal hand used for English legal documents at the time. It is a relatively faithful but somewhat fragmentary reproduction of its source.

In 1774 Cottrell introduced a technical innovation that began a new international typographic trend. In his Double Pica script, shown here, he attempted to imitate a formal hand based on an Italian manuscript model. To achieve this, he fitted letters together side by side with as little spacing as possible and with entry and exit strokes that aligned to mimic the uninterrupted flow of script.

Many other English founders soon started to devise their own script typefaces in response to Cottrell's idea. Within a few years, many of these new designs began to demonstrate the characteristics of formal 'modern' types, with a greater differentiation of thick and thin strokes, as they replicated the Roundhand practised by English writing masters of the time with increasing accuracy.

These types were very quickly copied by many Continental founders, who called the form Anglaise as a reference to its country of origin. This more refined Anglaise style was admired and copied by the Didots (pp90–91) and developed into the standard typographic script of the nineteenth century. Although the original Cottrell script types were among the best of their time, they soon fell into disuse as fashions moved on.

LE VINGT ET UN.

Couplets chantés par une des élèves
DE MADAME HÉMART,

DONT LE PENSIONNAT EST ÉTABLI RUE DE LA PÉPINIÈRE.

Un beau modèle est sous nos yeux;
C'est Minerve, c'est la prudence:
Qu'il seroit pour nous glorieux
D'en bien prendre la ressemblance!
Saisissons cet ensemble heureux,
Et ces détails remplis de grace:
Le succès, quoique un peu douteux,
Peut favoriser notre audace.

Oui, Madame, à la Vérité
Rendons cet hommage sincère,
Nous trouvons en vous la bonté
Et les tendres soins d'une mère.

Ty	**Didot**
Ca	**Serif**
Ke	**Modern**
Te	**Letterpress**
Da	**1784**
De	**Firmin Didot**
Fo	**Didot**
Co	**France**

Characteristics

Vertical stress
Thin strokes with high contrast
Sharp, unbracketed serifs
Most capitals have uniform width
E Heavy, bracketed serifs
J Narrow tail sits on baseline
M Narrow
Q Curved tail below letter
R Curved leg
W Stepped centre-strokes

ACEMQR
abcdefghij
orstuy*aefg*

Connections

Bodoni	1788
HTF Didot	1991
Linotype Didot	1991
Didot Elder	2004

Availability

Various digital revivals are available

Specimen

Spécimen des nouveaux caractères de la fonderie et de l'imprimerie de P. Didot, l'aîné. Pierre Didot, Paris, 1819 (250x180mm)

LE QUINZE.

Cette épître se trouve en tête de mon édition in-folio des œuvres de Boileau, en deux volumes, tirée seulement à 125 exemplaires, dont Sa Majesté a daigné agréer la dédicace.

AU ROI.

SIRE,

D'un monarque guerrier, l'un de tes fiers aïeux,
Despréaux a chanté le courage indomptable,
La marche menaçante et le choc redoutable,
Les assauts, les combats, et les faits merveilleux.
LOUIS, applaudis-toi d'un plus heureux partage.
Plus beau, plus fortuné, toujours cher à la paix,
Ton règne ami des lois doit briller d'âge en âge;
Tous nos droits affermis signalent tes bienfaits.
Le ciel t'a confié les destins de la France:
Qu'il exauce nos vœux, qu'il veille sur tes jours!
De ta carrière auguste exempte de souffrance
Que sa bonté pour nous prolonge l'heureux cours!

The Didots were an illustrious family of printers, type founders and papermakers who served the French Crown for nearly two centuries. Among their many accomplishments are the development of stereotyping and the invention of a national standard for type measurement, but their most enduring legacy is a series of typefaces.

When Pierre Didot (1761–1853) inherited the family business in 1789 he set about redirecting it towards the production of collectible books designed to be appreciated as objects. They were luxuriously bound, large-format publications with sumptuous illustrations and set in an elegant series of types that his brother Firmin (1764–1836) had begun to design some years earlier.

Pierre used the smooth, calendered paper that had been pioneered by John Baskerville (pp80–81) to give a sharper impression than had previously been possible, permitting the reproduction of more delicate letterforms. Firmin took advantage of the improved stock by refining typefaces he had first introduced for their father, François-Ambroise (1730–1804). His new types were influenced by the recent work of Baskerville and were a continuation of the rationalizations made in the typefaces of Pierre-Simon Fournier (pp82–85) and the earlier Romain du Roi, cut by Philippe Grandjean (pp74–75) nearly a century earlier. Didot's new designs were first seen in 1784 and are considered by many to be the first truly modern type, predating the designs of Didot's Italian competitor, Giambattista Bodoni. The originator of the form remains unproven, although it is evident that Bodoni and the Didots influenced each other.

The specimen shown here is a late example of the Didot style, cut by Vibert for Pierre Didot in 1819. Didot's original typefaces have a vertical axis, very high contrast between heavy black stems, and extremely thin connecting strokes of the same weight as the serifs, which are hairline and unbracketed. They are far more spartan and geometric than Bodoni's letters. For example, where Bodoni's serifs are joined to stems with a gently curved bracket and the lower case serifs are slightly concave, Didot's are completely straight and join at a severe right angle.

Rational, progressive and nuanced, Didot's typefaces incorporate scientific and classical ideals in a late expression of Enlightenment thinking. They reformulated the ways in which type could be conceived and how it has been conceived ever since, decisively changing the course of typographic history.

Ty	**Gil's Roman and Italic**
Ca	**Serif**
Ke	**Old Style, Dutch**
Te	**Letterpress**
Da	**1787**
De	**Jerónimo Gil**
Fo	**Jerónimo Gil**
Co	**Spain**

Characteristics

	Even contrast
A	Angled apex
E	Wide bottom stroke
M	Splayed
e	Small eye
f	hooked arch
g	Large lower bowl
i	Large dot
v	Vertex below baseline

ACEMS
abcdefghi
orstuy*aefg*

Connections

Kis's Roman	1687
Van Dijck's Roman	1689
Caslon	c1725
Geronimo	1997

Availability

Geronimo is a digital revival available from the Enschedé Font Foundry

Specimen

Caracteres de la Imprenta Real en 1793.
Imprenta Real, Madrid, c1793
(215x155mm)

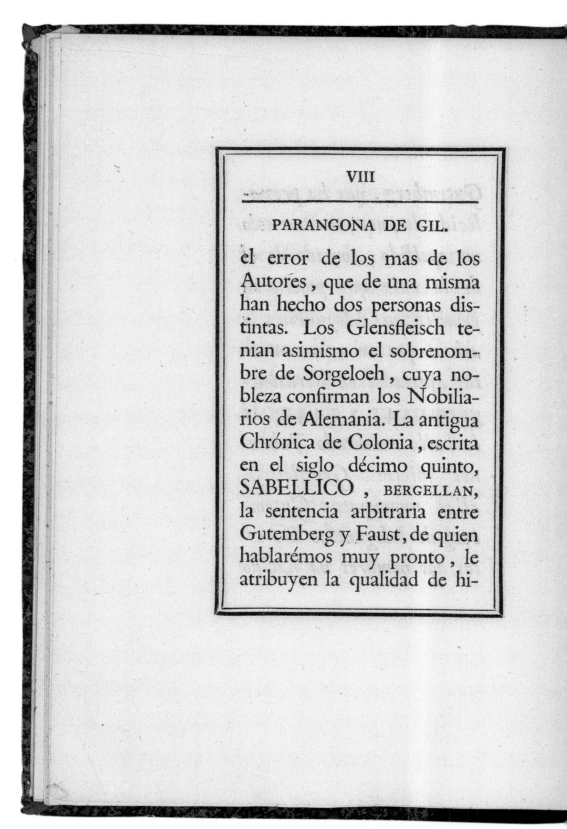

VIII

PARANGONA DE GIL.

el error de los mas de los Autores, que de una misma han hecho dos personas distintas. Los Glensfleisch tenian asimismo el sobrenombre de Sorgeloeh, cuya nobleza confirman los Nobiliarios de Alemania. La antigua Chrónica de Colonia, escrita en el siglo décimo quinto, SABELLICO, BERGELLAN, la sentencia arbitraria entre Gutemberg y Faust, de quien hablarémos muy pronto, le atribuyen la qualidad de hi-

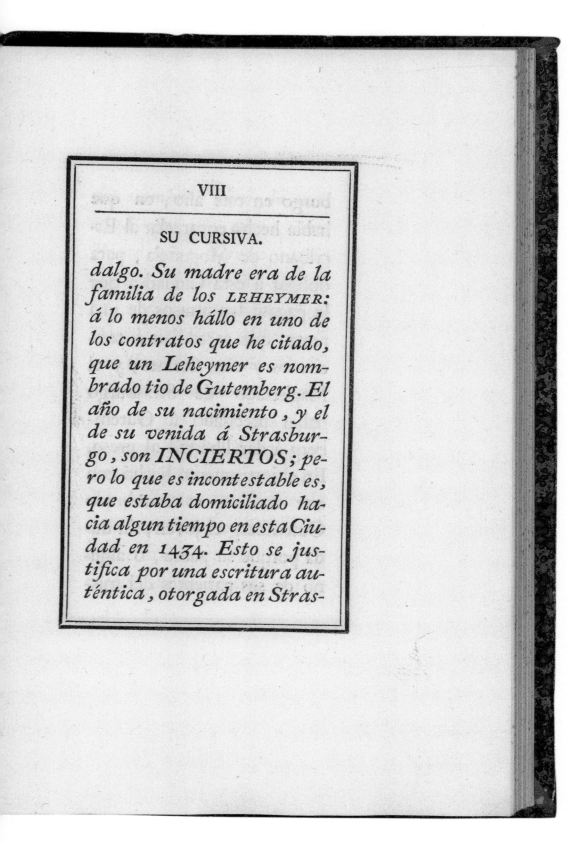

VIII

SU CURSIVA.

dalgo. *Su madre era de la familia de los* LEHEYMER: *á lo menos hállo en uno de los contratos que he citado, que un Leheymer es nombrado tio de Gutemberg. El año de su nacimiento, y el de su venida á Strasburgo, son* INCIERTOS; *pero lo que es incontestable es, que estaba domiciliado hacia algun tiempo en esta Ciudad en 1434. Esto se justifica por una escritura auténtica, otorgada en Stras-*

In the late eighteenth century the Spanish printing industry began to flourish. After more than two centuries of underdevelopment, the output of Spain's foremost printing houses began at last to achieve standards comparable to the most prestigious printers in Europe. A new national acknowledgement of the value of publishing in the dissemination of knowledge led to a rapid growth in the book market.

Faced with this growing demand and a shortage of types, Spanish printers trained some of the country's most skilled craftsmen in the art of punch cutting, thus liberating the Spanish printing industry from its dependence on imported type and establishing an indigenous type-design industry.

Jerónimo Antonio Gil (1731–98) was one of the earliest Spanish punch cutters. Originally trained as an engraver of medals and coins, he was commissioned to establish a foundry for the Royal Library in Madrid. Here he produced an enormous collection of very lively and idiosyncratic types, used most famously for the exquisite edition of *Don Quixote* printed by Joaquín Ibarra in 1780. The specimen from 1787 displays Gil's titling and text faces in both roman and italic styles. Uniquely Spanish in their appearance, the cut of his typefaces are also much more sophisticated than those of any of his contemporary countrymen.

Before the golden age of punch cutting in Spain most of the important books were printed in typefaces imported from the Netherlands, and Gil's letters, unsurprisingly, show a strong Dutch influence. This was his main point of reference, together with indigenous Spanish calligraphic forms that informed the design of his italics. Gil's roman characters have the appearance of Dutch old-style type, with a reduced contrast and a generous x-height in the lower case. In the larger sizes, ascenders and descenders are even shorter than in text sizes, creating a lively rhythm in bodies of extended setting.

Although Jerónimo Gil's typefaces do not follow the international trend of the time for the neoclassical style of European contemporaries like Bodoni or Didot (pp96–97, 90–91), they demonstrate the energetic expressiveness of an enlightened era in Spanish printing.

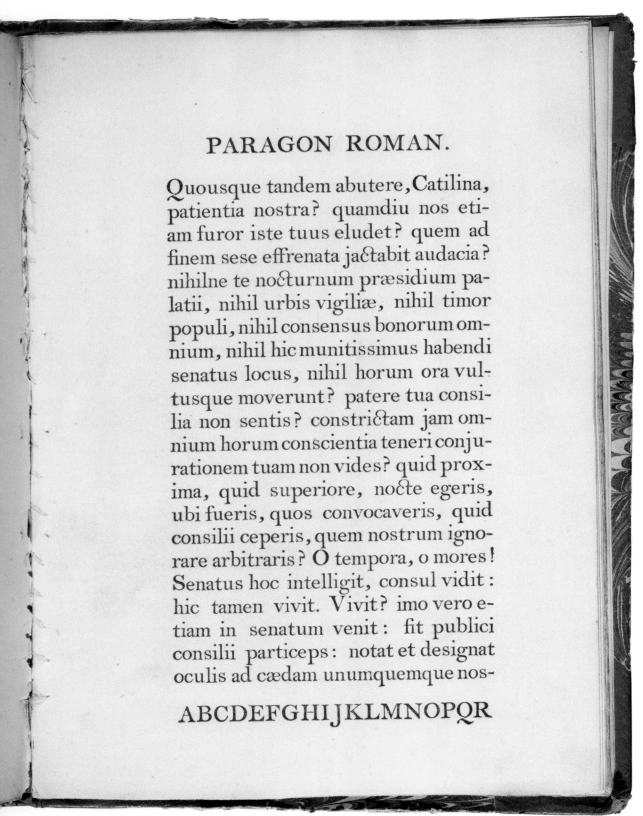

PARAGON ROMAN.

Quousque tandem abutere, Catilina, patientia nostra? quamdiu nos etiam furor iste tuus eludet? quem ad finem sese effrenata jactabit audacia? nihilne te nocturnum præsidium palatii, nihil urbis vigiliæ, nihil timor populi, nihil consensus bonorum omnium, nihil hic munitissimus habendi senatus locus, nihil horum ora vultusque moverunt? patere tua consilia non sentis? constrictam jam omnium horum conscientia teneri conjurationem tuam non vides? quid proxima, quid superiore, nocte egeris, ubi fueris, quos convocaveris, quid consilii ceperis, quem nostrum ignorare arbitraris? O tempora, o mores! Senatus hoc intelligit, consul vidit: hic tamen vivit. Vivit? imo vero etiam in senatum venit: fit publici consilii particeps: notat et designat oculis ad cædam unumquemque nos-

ABCDEFGHIJKLMNOPQR

Ty	**Bell**
Ca	**Serif**
Ke	**Transitional**
Te	**Letterpress**
Da	**1788**
De	**Richard Austin**
Fo	**John Bell**
Co	**UK**

Characteristics

Capitals to ascender height, heavier than lower case

K k R Curved tail ends in flat serif

Q Curved tail below letter

g Double-storeyed, large ear

ACJMQR
abcdefgijk
orstuy*aefg*

Connections

Bulmer	1792
Thorne's Modern	1800
Scotch Roman	1812
Monotype Bell	1931

Availability

Bell is available from Monotype and resellers

Specimen

A Specimen of Printing Types Cast at Bell & Stephenson's Original British Letter Foundry. British Letter Foundry, London, 1789 (220x150mm)

PARAGON ITALIC.

*Quousque tandem abutere, Catilina,
patientia nostra? quamdiu nos etiam
furor iste tuus eludet? quem ad finem
sese effrenata jactabit audacia? nihilne te nocturnum præsidium palatii,
nihil urbis vigiliæ, nihil timor populi,
nihil consensus bonorum omnium, nihil hic munitissimus habendi senatus
locus, nihil horum ora vultusque moverunt? patere tua consilia non sentis?
constrictam jam omnium horum conscientia teneri conjurationem tuam non
vides? quid proxima, quid superiore,
nocte egeris, ubi fueris, quos convocaveris, quid consilii ceperis, quem nostrum ignorare arbitraris? O tempora,
o mores! Senatus hoc intelligit, consul vidit: hic tamen vivit. Vivit? imo
vero etiam in senatum venit: fit publici consilii particeps: notat & designat
oculis ad cædem unumquemque nostrum. Nos autem viri fortes satisfa-*

ABCDEFGHIJKLMNOPQ

John Bell (1745–1831), an English publisher of periodicals and newspapers, advertised one of his publications in 1787 with the declaration that 'J. Bell flatters himself that he will be able to render this the most perfect and in every respect the most beautiful book, that ever was printed in any country'.

Impressed by contemporary French typefaces cut by Firmin Didot, with their razor-sharp contrast, Bell hired Richard Austin (c1765–1832), a young but highly skilled punch cutter and wood engraver, to produce a new typeface for this undertaking at his British Letter Foundry.

Bell and Austin's design is less austere than the French models it followed. It is a sharply serifed face with a vertical stress, similar to Didot in its contrast but more like Baskerville in its smooth stroke transitions and the use of bracketed, rather than flat, serifs. It anticipated the success of Austin's Scotch Roman (pp112–13) by two decades.

The Bell typeface introduced a well-considered innovation. Traditionally, text numerals were designed to fit alongside words set in lower case letters by following the same structural principles, some sitting on the baseline and others hanging below it. Bell was the first typeface to break with that tradition. The numerals are larger than lower case letters, sitting on the baseline, but are carefully proportioned to a slightly smaller height than the capitals. This trend was subsequently taken up in several other type designs.

John Bell's British Letter Foundry closed within two years and his typeface fell into disuse. It was rapidly forgotten in England, as typographic tastes shifted dramatically with the introduction of lithography at the beginning of the nineteenth century. In the United States, though, Bell was copied as early as 1792, and it remained in popular use there throughout the nineteenth century.

In 1926 Stanley Morison unexpectedly discovered a survival of Bell in an American type specimen and, impressed by its clarity, arranged for its revival for machine composition by the Monotype Corporation, released in 1931.

Ty	**Bodoni**
Ca	**Serif**
Ke	**Modern**
Te	**Letterpress**
Da	**1788**
De	**Giambattista Bodoni**
Fo	**Giambattista Bodoni**
Co	**Italy**

Characteristics

| Vertical stress, thin strokes with high contrast |
| Most capitals have uniform width |
| Sharp, unbracketed serifs |
| **J** Slight hook below baseline |
| **M** Narrow |
| **Q** Tail centred below letter |
| **R** Straight and curved leg alternates |

ACJMQR
abcdefghij
orstuy*aefg*

Connections

Bauer Bodoni	1926
ITC Bodoni	1995
Filosofia	1996
Parmigiano	2013

Availability

Various digital revivals are available

Specimen

Manuale tipografico. Giambattista Bodoni, Parma, 1818 (320x220mm)

XLIV

al contrario si può far l'occhio in proporzione più piccolo, affinchè le righe da più larghi bianchi disgiunte, più svelte campeggino; benchè a tale intento non sia questo mezzo nè l'unico, nè il migliore.

Che però più necessaria si è la variata proporzione della larghezza, la quale potendo crescere finchè l'*o* si appressi alla figura circolare, a misura che più si va rotondando più distinta riesce la scrittura, e più capace d'uno spiccante contrasto di sottili tratti e di grossi, come di chiaro e oscuro. Ma per altra parte con meno lettere vien così la riga a compirsi, e però a crescere la mole del libro; cosa, che sebbene anco altronde non sia sempre senza sconcio, pur

XLV

potrebbesi per avventura comporta-
re se mai non s'avessero a stampar
versi, che vogliono ciascuno per sè
far la sua comparsa interi in una sola
riga. Onde per non dovervi adoperar
carattere molto minore di quello,
che altrimenti alla grandezza delle
pagine si converrebbe, non v'è talora
miglior compenso che di ristringer
le lettere senza accorciarle; poichè
meno rotonde elle possono pure aver
garbo. La proporzione della larghezza alla spalla non ricevendo legge
che dal piacer degli sguardi, con-
vien solo badare di non offenderli
con troppo bislunghi caratteri, quali
ne veggiamo in alcun libro d'oltre-
monti, anche delle più eleganti stam-
perie, per esempio negl'Inni di San-

Although John Baskerville's achievements were largely unappreciated in England, his elegant, plain book designs were greatly admired abroad, influencing eighteenth-century French, German and Italian printers and type founders.

Giambattista Bodoni (1740–1813), an accomplished typographer, was notably responsive, taking Baskerville's techniques and ideas to an extreme conclusion. A third-generation Italian printer, he intended to visit Baskerville in England as a young man but he fell ill and had to cancel his journey. He was subsequently appointed to establish and manage the press of the Duke of Parma in 1768. After initially printing from type imported from France he soon began his own ambitious programme of type design.

Bodoni's typefaces evolved progressively during his long and successful career, starting in the 1770s with transitional letterforms that resemble those of Pierre-Simon Fournier and developing in the 1790s to typefaces of a narrower underlying armature, with an overall geometric construction, an extreme contrast between thick and thin strokes, and hairline serifs with minimal brackets. These later types, for which he became renowned, were cut and cast with great skill and accuracy, providing remarkably subtle variations of weight and width, and retaining the finest hairline strokes even at the smallest sizes.

In the *Manuale tipografico*, published posthumously in 1818, Bodoni identified four principles of typography from which 'all beauty would seem to proceed': regularity, clarity, good taste and charm. He printed his editions with meticulous skill and care, using rich black inks on smooth, calendered paper. His page designs framed classical texts with a dignity and simplicity that is spectacular. The wide margins, capacious interlinear spaces, ample letter spacing and frugal use of ornament all serve to enhance his sharply printed typefaces.

Bodoni rapidly became one of the most widely admired type designers of his time. In 1825 the printer and historian Thomas Hansard wrote that his types had a 'beautiful and perfect appearance, which we find it difficult and highly expensive to equal'. Bodoni's letters, like those of his French contemporary Firmin Didot, are undeniably handsome, but the rather austere and dazzling forms of modern types are neither inviting nor comfortable to read when set in long texts. They look much more effective at larger sizes, foreshadowing the era of display types that followed them at the turn of the nineteenth century.

Bulmer

Ty	**Bulmer**		
Ca	**Serif**		
Ke	**Transitional**		
Te	**Letterpress**		
Da	**1792**		
De	**William Martin**		
Fo	**Shakspeare Printing Office**		
Co	**UK**		

Characteristics
C Vertical serifs
E Long bottom stroke
G Open
J Descends below baseline
Q Sweeping, curved tail
R Curved tail
a c f Large ears
g Appears to lean backwards, small upper bowl and curved ear

AGJMQR
abcdefghij
orstuy*aefg*

Connections

Baskerville	1757
Bell	1788
Thorne's Modern	1800
Caledonia	1938

Availability
Bulmer is widely available

Specimen
The Dramatic Works of Shakespeare.
Printed by W. Bulmer & Co. for J. & J. Boydell, London, 1802 (380x305mm)

48   MUCH ADO ABOUT NOTHING

SCENE III

THE STREET.

Enter Dogberry and Verges, with the Watch.

Dogb. Are you good men and true?

Verg. Yea, or else it were pity but they should suffer salvation, body and soul.

Dogb. Nay, that were a punishment too good for them, if they should have any allegiance in them, being chosen for the prince's watch.

Verg. Well, give them their charge, neighbour Dogberry.

Dogb. First, who think you the most desartlefs man to be constable?

1 Watch. Hugh Oatcake, sir, or George Seacoal; for they can write and read.

Dogb. Come hither, neighbour Seacoal: God hath blefsed you with a good name: to be a well-favoured man is the gift of fortune; but to write and read comes by nature.

2 Watch. Both which, master constable,——

Dogb. You have; I knew it would b——

In 1786, George Nicol, bookseller to King George III, commissioned the printing of a new edition of the works of William Shakespeare. Nicol appointed William Martin (1757–1830) to cut types for it 'in imitation of the sharp and fine letters used by the French and Italian printers'. William was the brother of Robert Martin, John Baskerville's apprentice and successor, and is thought to have acquired his knowledge of the art of punch cutting at the Birmingham foundry.

Looking for a printer capable of producing the highest quality presswork, Nicol also secured the services of William Bulmer, and the Shakspeare Printing Office was established under the firm of W. Bulmer and Co. The collaboration between Bulmer and Martin proved highly successful: Bulmer's printing was meticulous and Martin's types were of an exceptional integrity, combining grace with functionality. The historian Daniel Berkeley Updike described Martin's types as 'delicate and spirited, thoroughly English'. They were influenced by the modern typefaces of Didot and Bodoni but owed much more to Baskerville's transitional style. The Bulmer typeface shares its vertical stress and balanced stroke contrast, but is taller and narrower than its predecessor, with more finely cut serifs.

The publication of the first part of Boydell's Shakespeare in 1791 was an immediate success and the completion of the work, in nine volumes, in 1810 is regarded as marking an epoch in British typography. A revival of Martin's types was undertaken in 1928 by Morris Fuller Benton for ATF, using Bulmer's original editions as reference. In the early 1930s Monotype cut another version for the Nonesuch Press that was released commercially in 1939.

MUCH ADO ABOUT NOTHING 49

This is your charge; You shall comprehend all vagrom men; you are to bid any man stand, in the prince's name.

2 Watch. How, if he will not stand?

Dogb. Why then, take no note of him, but let him go; and presently call the rest of the watch together, and thank God you are rid of a knave.

Verg. If he will not stand when he is bidden, he is none of the prince's subjects.

Dogb. True, and they are to meddle with none but the prince's subjects:——You shall also make no noise in the streets; for, for the watch to babble and to talk, is most tolerable, and not to be endured.

2 Watch. We will rather sleep than talk; we know what belongs to a watch.

Dogb. Why, you speak like an ancient and most quiet watchman; for I cannot see how sleeping should offend: only, have a care that your bills be not stolen:——Well, you are to call at all the alehouses, and bid those that are drunk get them to bed.

2 Watch. How, if they will not?

Dogb. Why then, let them alone till they are sober; if they make you not then the better answer, you may say, they are not the men you took them for.

2 Watch. Well, sir.

Dogb. If you meet a thief, you may suspect him, by vir-

Ty	**Unger-Fraktur**
Ca	**Blackletter**
Ke	**Fraktur**
Te	**Letterpress**
Da	**1793**
De	**Johann Friedrich Unger**
Fo	**Johann Friedrich Unger**
Co	**Germany**

Characteristics

Thin strokes with high contrast
Capitals simplified, single stroke forms
Roman numerals
A B V Simplified contours
a Single-storeyed
a i r t u Flat foot serif
d Curved uncial stem
f long s Long, pointed descender
g Open tail
h Curved uncial form

ADFRS
abcdefghi
moprstuz

Connections

Wagner's Fraktur	1513
Breitkopf Fraktur	1750
Didot	1784
Walbaum's Fraktur	c1803

Availability

Unger Fraktur is available from RMU
Typedesign and resellers

Specimen

Johann Friedrich Unger, *Probe einer neuen Art Deutscher Lettern.* Berlin, 1793
(172x101mm)

4

Deutschen Lettern zu unbekannt war, und sich nicht in die, Deutschen Augen gewöhnlichen Schriftzüge versetzen konnte: — genug der Versuch mißlang abermals. Nun wollte ich, wiewohl ungern, die für mich so reitzende Aussicht, etwas zur Verbesserung der Deutschen Lettern beizutragen, vorläufig aufgeben, als Herr Didot mir meldete: er habe in der Königlichen Bibliothek zu Paris ein sehr schönes Manuscript gesehen, und sey geneigt, nach diesem, und mit Zuziehung meiner ihm gesandten Zeichnungen noch eine Deutsche Schrift zu versuchen. Er that es, und darauf erfolgten denn die Lettern, die auf der letzten Seite dieser Blätter abgedruckt sind.

Ich enthielt mich alles Urtheils darüber, ließ einige Abdrücke davon machen, und legte sie Männern von entschiedenem Kunstgeschmacke vor. Ihr Urtheil fiel einstimmig ungünstig aus, und es mußte mir

5

natürlich leid thun, meinem edlen Freunde Didot, der durchaus wissen wollte, wie sein Versuch aufgenommen wäre, so wenig Aufmunterndes sagen zu können. Es war mir um so empfindlicher, je gewisser ich wußte, daß er sich bloß auf Antrieb der uneigennützigsten Freundschaft in seinen überhäuften Geschäften unterbrochen, und diese undankbare Arbeit übernommen hatte.

Beinahe zu derselben Zeit gab Herr Rath Lampe eine Probe neuer Deutscher Lettern heraus, welche er nach seiner Idee von dem sonst sehr geschickten Schriftschneider und Gießer Herrn Gollner in Halle hatte verfertigen lassen. Diese ist im Ganzen, wenigstens entfernt, einigermaßen der von Didot geschnittenen ähnlich; doch hat letztere vollkommnere Zeichnung und Grundstrich, und verräth überhaupt einen größern Meister. Auch diese von Lampe und Gollner versuchte

The Age of Reason and the revolution that followed soon afterwards in France provoked much debate across Europe during the last years of eighteenth century. In Germany a discussion was prompted concerning the need for a plain, rational blackletter typeface to represent the country internationally. Unger-Fraktur, a radical response to this requirement, was a visible manifestation of Enlightenment thinking in Germany.

The typeface was designed by Johann Friedrich Unger (1753–1804), a printer and publisher from Berlin. For several years prior to establishing his own type foundry in 1780 Unger had been the licensed distributor of Firmin Didot's modern roman type (pp90–91) in Germany but had found little success selling it to printers for whom Fraktur (pp38–39) had been the accepted national style for almost three centuries.

Didot himself had made three attempts to cut a reformed Fraktur to suit the requirements of the German-speaking market, but none of them had proved satisfactory. Eventually, with Didot's support, Unger undertook the slow, laborious task of learning to cut types, and by 1793 had produced a set of designs intended to harmonize with the severe elegance of Didot's modern face.

In his rationalization of the Fraktur design, Johann Unger sought to capture what he called the 'Helle und Zarte' – brightness and delicacy – of the roman script. He rounded off the corners of the Fraktur lower case and rationalized the capitals, removing their ornate 'Schnorkel' terminals (p39). Throughout, he made the letter contours much simpler and less ambiguous than earlier designs. The type was accompanied by numerals that followed the Latin model rather than the gothic. The resulting form is open, delicate and somewhat similar to a Schwabacher (pp28–29).

Like Didot and Bodoni, Unger-Fraktur imparts an extremely light colour to the printed page, but it has not been universally regarded as aesthetically satisfactory or legible. Stanley Morison, for example, described it as 'a pallid abomination'. Regardless, Unger's modern Fraktur proved highly influential to the development of subsequent nineteenth-century German typographic styles.

6

Schrift fand keinen Beifall. Man zog immer noch die alte gewöhnliche vor, und diese beiden Männer erhielten für ihre gute Absicht nicht einmal den öffentlichen Dank, den sie doch gewiß verdienten, wenn auch gleich ihre Erfindung nicht so ausfiel, daß sie gebraucht werden konnte.

Dergleichen unglücklich ausgefallene Versuche hätten mich nun allerdings abschrecken, und zur gänzlichen Aufgebung meiner Idee bewegen müssen, wenn sie nicht zu fest bei mir gehaftet, und mich unablässig angespornt hätte. Hierbei nicht stehen zu bleiben, und sie, aller Schwierigkeiten ungeachtet, auszuführen, war mein lebhaftes Bestreben. Ich wandte mich zu diesem Endzweck an verschiedene Deutsche Stahlschneider, stieß aber jedesmal auf Schwierigkeiten und Einwendungen. Auch machten sie entweder zu hohe Forderungen, oder ihre Zeit war zu eingeschränkt, als

7

daß sie sich auf so manche, wahrscheinlich vergebliche Versuche einlassen konnten. Nun entschloß ich mich, selbst einigen Unterricht im Stahlschneiden zu nehmen, wobei mir mein Holzschneiden so gut zu Statten kam, daß ich jene Kunst im Allgemeinen sehr bald faßte.

Durch anhaltende Übung und wahrlich mit Anstrengung meines ganzen Vorrathes von Geduld, gelang es mir endlich, diese Schrift, welche ich dem sachverständigen Publikum itzt vorlege, zu Stande zu bringen. Mit was für ganz unerwarteten Schwierigkeiten, sowohl in der Behandlung des Stahls, als auch bei der Ausführung der Schriftzeichen selbst, ich kämpfen mußte, kann nur derjenige sich vorstellen, der sich mit ähnlichen Arbeiten befaßt, und, ohne eine dazu erhaltene Vorschrift oder ein nachzuahmendes Modell, lediglich seine Phantasie zur Richtschnur hat. Bei aller Abweichung von den alten

1-800

At the end of the eighteenth century industry was expanding at an unprecedented rate in Great Britain. Manufacturing processes for the mass production of goods, revolutionized by technological advances, began to depend on increasingly efficient production methods and cheap labour. Rapid population growth followed in industrialized cities as people moved from rural areas to find work.

The Industrial Revolution placed demands on visual communications that were not solely a product of technological advances. From the turn of the nineteenth century, increasing commercial competition required type to work harder on posters and hoardings in the dense, fast-moving environment of the city, where for the first time it had to shout in short bursts in order to compete for attention. This resulted in a proliferation of big, bold display faces, with many founders and wood-type producers experimenting liberally with variations of existing designs or creating new ones without any particular historical points of reference to constrain them. At this time of unprecedented invention, letterforms would be modified, decorated, thickened, expanded or condensed at will in the production of a huge number of novel alphabets. Many were short-lived, but others had a lasting influence on the development of typographic design.

The earliest of the display types to be cut in both wood and metal were fat faces, Egyptian slab serifs and grotesque sans serifs, all originating in the first quarter of the nineteenth century. Fat face types were thickened versions of modern styles with elephantine vertical strokes and hairline horizontals. Early slab serifs were equally brash, with rectangular serif blocks protruding from the stems, often at the same thickness as the body strokes, their forms anticipating the more nuanced letters of the Clarendon types devised in the 1850s. The prototypical sans serifs were heavy display faces in capitals only, but a wide range of styles and weights rapidly evolved during the latter half of the century in a number of German type foundries.

The Industrial Revolution in Britain introduced several significant innovations in printing technologies. Steam-driven presses replaced hand-operated ones in 1814 and rotary presses, capable of producing printed output six times faster than previously, were introduced in the 1840s. Electrotyping was invented in the late 1830s to make mechanical reproductions of engravings that could be incorporated with movable type for printing. This technology made the copying of letterforms a rapid and easy process, contributing to a huge increase in the number of display typefaces created during the period.

The composition of text type was transformed by the introduction of line-casting machines, first Ottmar Mergenthaler's Linotype in 1886 and then the Monotype a year later. Line casting allowed type to be selected via a keyboard, typeset and redistributed into the machine automatically after use. This accelerated production time to approximately 15 per cent of that of manual composition, providing huge labour savings while also using materials far more cost-effectively than ever before.

As typesetting and printing speeds increased exponentially, so too did punch cutting. In 1884 Linn Boyd Benton invented the Benton Pantograph, a device that automated the painstaking process of creating punches. With the Pantograph a character drawing could be scaled to any size and could be compressed, expanded or varied in its line weights to compensate for different conditions. The almost limitless range of typographic variants that was possible as a result signalled a shift away from the understanding of letters as physical archetypes with origins in handwriting. In the huge variety of late nineteenth-century typefaces, the alphabet began to be manipulated as a system of flexible design elements for visual communication rather than a set of symbols anchored in tradition.

Two Lines Great Primer, No.1. New.

Quousque tandem abutere, Catilina, patientia nostra? quamdiu nos
etiam furor iste tuus eludet? quem-
ad finem sese effrenata jactabit a-
udacia? nihilne te nocturnum præ
ABCDEFGHIJKLMNOPQRST
UVWXYZŒ ABCDEFGHIJKLM
NOPQRSTUVWXYZŒ £1234567890

Ty	**Thorne's Modern**
Ca	**Serif**
Ke	**Modern**
Te	**Letterpress**
Da	**1800**
De	**Robert Thorne**
Fo	**Robert Thorne**
Co	**UK**

Characteristics

Vertical stress
Thin strokes with high contrast
Capitals to ascender height
Most capitals have uniform width
Sharp, bracketed serifs
M Narrow
Q Looped tail below letter
R a t Tail turns upwards
a c f j r y Ball terminals
b No serif at foot
g Double-storeyed with teardrop ear
t Curved bracket connects stem and bar

ACJMQR
abcdefghij
mopqrstuv

Connections	
Bell	1788
Thorne's Fat Face	c1806
Scotch Roman	1812
Brunel	2008

Availability

Not available

Specimen

*Robert Thorne's Specimen of Printing
Types.* Robert Thorne, London, 1803
(233x150mm)

Two-Lines English. No. 1. New.

Quousque tandem abutere, Catilina, patientia nostra? quamdiu nos etiam furor iste tuus eludet? quem ad finem sese effrenata jactabit audacia? nihilne te nocturnum præsidium palatii, nihil urbis vigiliæ, nihil timor populi, nihil consensus bonorum omnium, nihil hic munitissim

ABCDEFGHIJKLMNOPQRSTUVWXY ZÆŒ ABCDEFGHIJKLMNOPQRSTUVWXYZÆŒ £1234567890 1802

Robert Thorne (1754–1820) was among the most resourceful of the London type founders working at the beginning of the nineteenth century, a time when the city was at the forefront of typographic innovation. He took over the foundry of Thomas Cottrell (pp88–89), to whom he had been apprenticed, in 1794, nine years after the latter's death, releasing his first specimen in the same year. This was essentially an updated edition of his predecessor's specimen, showing Cottrell's work, following a long-standing tradition in the trade. It contained a variety of book types and collections of large display letters cast in sand for which Cottrell had become well known.

By 1798, Thorne had started to cut his own typefaces, and by the turn of the century he had begun to respond to the huge demand for types in the modern style that had become the height of fashion in the wake of the designs of Didot and Bodoni. Other British founders were resistant to the change in public tastes, begrudging being forced to abandon more familiar, more robust designs, but Thorne did not share this view.

He first presented his new letterforms in his specimen of 1803, where he described them as 'Improved Printing Types'. His were the first English typefaces in the modern style, with a sharp overall appearance based on strong vertical stress, a high contrast between thick and thin strokes, and fine, bracketed serifs. They instantly met with considerable commercial success, causing other type founders to follow Thorne's example. Edmund Fry issued a specimen including several modern faces in the same year, and similar designs from Caslon and Figgins came soon after.

Robert Thorne subsequently developed many popular typefaces, including the fat face (pp108–109), his pumped-up display version of the modern, which in turn was exported to France, the birthplace of the style. He also relocated his company, renaming it the Fann Street Foundry. On his death in 1820 this was purchased by William Thorowgood, who had no previous experience in the type-founding business. As a consequence, many of the typefaces identified as Thorowgood's in later Fann Street Foundry specimens are actually Robert Thorne's work.

Ty	**Walbaum**
Ca	**Serif**
Ke	**Modern**
Te	**Letterpress**
Da	**c1803**
De	**Justus Erich Walbaum**
Fo	**Justus Erich Walbaum**
Co	**Germany**

Characteristics

Vertical stress
High stroke contrast
Large x-height
Unbracketed serifs
C G S s Wedge serifs without spurs
K k Bar joins arm and leg to stem
R Curved right leg
b No foot serif
g Small upper bowl, large lower bowl
t Unbracketed cross-stroke, flat top

ACKMRS
abcdefghij
orstuy*aefg*

Connections

Didot	1784
Monotype Walbaum	1933
Berthold Walbaum	1975
Basilia	1978

Availability

Walbaum is widely available

Specimen

Walbaum Schriften: Antiqua, Kursiv, Fraktur. F. A. Brockhaus, Leipzig, c1910 (280x220mm)

WALBAUM-ANTIQUA

WALBAUM-KURSIV

Corps 6 — Nonpareille 1140 — Min. ca. 4 kg à M. 9.50

Die Herstellung von Druckkomplexen erfordert Genauigkeit und Sicherheit. Der Künstler kann auf dem Plattenmaterial oder auf dem zum Umdruck bestimmten Papier nicht erst herumprobieren. Hinwegzubringende Korrekturen sind stets eine mißliche, meistens zeitraubende Sache, daher ist es jederzeit ratsam, daß vorerst eine möglichst ausgearbeitete Skizze hergestellt werde, nach welcher der Druckkomplex geschaffen werden kann. Beim Mehrfarbendruck mit Farbenteilplatten, welch letztere nacheinander und übereinander

Um rationell arbeiten zu können, ist man bestrebt, die technischen Hindernisse möglichst zu verringern. Andererseits muß aber auch berücksichtigt werden, daß in der geschickten Benützung jener vom Arbeitsmaterial gebotenen, oft hinderlichen Eigenschaften der Stil der Technik liegt, durch welchen die Ausdrucksweise von Anfang an bestimmt angegeben erscheint. Es muß der sachlich künstlerische

Petit 1141 — Min. ca. 5 kg à M. 8.60

...eitende Farbengraphiker wird in ...den gegebenen technischen Mitteln ...cheinung der Naturobjekte muß ...gabe eine Übersetzung erfahren. ...tographie die möglichst spiegel- ...rebt, so liegt der Hauptreiz der

Die Entwicklungsgeschichte des Farbendruckes geht aus von der primitiven Handkolorierung des einfarbigen Holzschnittes. Es blieb lange Zeit das Prinzip vorherrschend, eine mehr oder weniger tonrichtig ausgearbeitete Zeichenplatte als Grundlage zu benützen und diese durch Farbenzugabe zu ergänzen und

Borgis 1142 — Min. ca. 6 kg à M. 7.90

...her, als man den Einfluß ...uf Glas noch nicht kannte, ...deutung als heute; es wurde ...m Mattieren und Verzieren ...Heute aber bedient man sich ...Sandstrahlgebläses, das die

Nichtsdestoweniger spielt aber die Ätzkunst in der Glastechnik doch noch eine hervorragende Rolle, da sie die Ausführung tiefer und sehr korrekter Linien gestattet und insofern besonders modulationsfähig ist, daß im Gegensatze zur Arbeit mit dem jetzt

Korpus 1143 — Min. ca. 6 kg à M. 7.40

...Mainz in dem berühmten ...Psalters das erste datierte ...Lettern fertiggestellt war, ...l VII., der damalige König ...von der epochemachenden ...nd Nutzen zu ziehen. Er

Erst im Jahre 1470 wurde von drei deutschen Buchdruckergesellen, die man eigens hierzu über den Rhein hatte kommen lassen, in den Räumen der alten Sorbonne die erste Druckerei eingerichtet und das erste Buch in Frankreich gedruckt. Die

Cicero 1144 — Min. ca. 7 kg à M. 7.20

...s ja wohl möglich ist, ...laneten unseres Sonnen- ...uf dem Mars oder der ...-menschenartige Wesen, ...ner Kultur und als der

Das älteste Denkmal in dem ausgebreiteten vedischen Literaturkreise und somit wohl das älteste literarische Denkmal überhaupt sind die Hymnen des Rigveda, sofern sie,

Mittel 1145 — Min. ca. 7 kg à M. 7.10

...e Geist ist immer wirksam, er kann die einförmigen, ...nicht dulden, er will ihnen Leben und Gestalt geben

Tertia 1146 — Min. ca. 8 kg à M. 6.80

...Entwicklung der deutschen Schiffahrt
...AMBURG-AMERIKA-LINIE 67890

Text 1147 — Min. ca. 10 kg à M. 6.50

Nationalökonomie und bürgerliches Recht

Corps 28 — Doppelmittel 1148 — Min. ca. 12 kg à M. 6.10

Originalradierungen von Menzel

Bestellbox (left)

...r die Bestellung von
...baumschriften
...lten folgende Schrift-
nummern:

Walbaum-Antiqua
793. 5 Punkt. Min. ca. 2 kg.
794. 6 Punkt. Min. ca. 4 kg.
795. 8 Punkt. Min. ca. 5 kg.
796. 9 Punkt. Min. ca. 5 kg.
797. 10 Punkt. Min. ca. 6 kg.
798. 12 Punkt. Min. ca. 6 kg.
4 Punkt (kleines Bild). Min. ca. 7 kg.
4 Punkt (großes Bild). Min. ca. 7 kg.
800. 16 Punkt. Min. ca. 8 kg.
801. 20 Punkt. Min. ca. 10 kg.
802. 28 Punkt. Min. ca. 12 kg.
803. 36 Punkt. Min. ca. 14 kg.
804. 48 Punkt. Min. ca. 16 kg.

Walbaum-Kursiv
805. 6 Punkt. Min. ca. 4 kg.
806. 8 Punkt. Min. ca. 5 kg.
807. 9 Punkt. Min. ca. 5 kg.
808. 10 Punkt. Min. ca. 6 kg.
809. 12 Punkt. Min. ca. 7 kg.
810. 14 Punkt. Min. ca. 7 kg.
811. 16 Punkt. Min. ca. 8 kg.
812. 20 Punkt. Min. ca. 10 kg.
813. 28 Punkt. Min. ca. 12 kg.

Walbaum-Fraktur
814. 5 Punkt. Min. ca. 2 kg.
815. 6 Punkt. Min. ca. 4 kg.
816. 8 Punkt. Min. ca. 5 kg.
817. 9 Punkt. Min. ca. 5 kg.
Punkt (kleines Bild). Min. ca. 6 kg.
Punkt (großes Bild). Min. ca. 6 kg.
Punkt (kleines Bild). Min. ca. 7 kg.
Punkt (großes Bild). Min. ca. 7 kg.
Punkt (großes Bild). Min. ca. 7 kg.
Punkt (kleines Bild). Min. ca. 7 kg.
Punkt (großes Bild). Min. ca. 7 kg.
824. 16 Punkt. Min. ca. 8 kg.
825. 20 Punkt. Min. ca. 10 kg.
826. 28 Punkt. Min. ca. 12 kg.
827. 36 Punkt. Min. ca. 14 kg.
828. 48 Punkt. Min. ca. 16 kg.

Justus Erich Walbaum's roman typefaces represent one of the most significant departures from the blackletter tradition in the history of German typography.

Walbaum (1768–1839) was born in Steinbach, Brunswick. A skilled engraver and metal caster, he turned to lettercutting at the age of 30, starting his own type foundry at Goslar. Five years later he moved to Weimar, and in 1836 he sold his business to the F. A. Brockhaus type foundry in Leipzig. Brockhaus was eventually taken over by H. Berthold AG in 1918. As a result, many of Walbaum's matrices and original types survive today.

The design of Walbaum's roman was heavily influenced by the types of Firmin Didot (pp90–91) and Giambattista Bodoni (pp96–97), and it ranks alongside them as a defining work of the Enlightenment movement. But whereas Didot can be regarded as an authentic expression of the Age of Reason, Walbaum's letterform is a distinctly German interpretation of neoclassical ideals. It is no coincidence that Walbaum also produced a Fraktur typeface at the same time, designed to sit harmoniously alongside his roman.

Some consider Walbaum superior to the types that inspired it. Its rational, robust qualities and slight irregularities provide a warmth and readability that are lacking in the French and Italian forms. Walbaum is not as extreme as either Didot or Bodoni, with a less severe stroke contrast and gently bracketed serifs. The x-height of the lower case is tall, providing an open appearance, with a firm, square skeleton to the design of the individual letters.

During Walbaum's lifetime his typefaces were highly admired but his work was forgotten almost immediately after his death, partly because of the prevalence of Fraktur in Germany, and partly because changes in nineteenth-century tastes had moved away from the neoclassical. Since he was not a printer and therefore left no publications bearing his imprint, his work was completely overlooked.

It was only in the twentieth century, with the return to popularity of the typefaces classified as 'modern', that the beauty and functionality of his types achieved the recognition they deserve. Walbaum was revived and recut by many foundries, most notably Monotype during the 1930s. It has gone on to influence a number of contemporary designs.

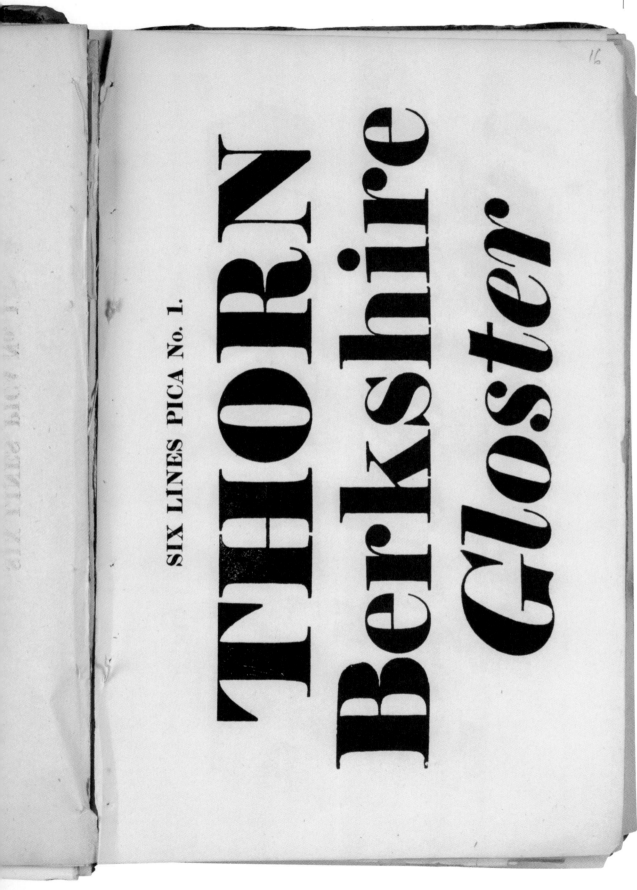

SIX LINES PICA No. 1.

THORN
Berkshire
Gloster

Ty	**Thorne's Fat Face**
Ca	**Serif**
Ke	**Modern**
Te	**Letterpress**
Da	**c1806**
De	**Robert Thorne**
Fo	**Fann Street Foundry**
Co	**UK**

Characteristics

Vertical stress

Extreme contrast of fat and thin strokes

Capitals to ascender height

Most capitals have uniform width

Sharp, unbracketed serifs

Q Looped tail below letter

R a t Tail turns upwards

a c f j r y Ball terminals

g Double-storeyed with teardrop ear

ACMQR
abcefgh
morstuv

Connections

Poster Bodoni	1920
Thorowgood	1950
Pistilli	1964
F37 Bella	2011

Availability

Many digital revivals are available

Specimen

A Specimen of the Printing Types in the Fann Street Foundry. W. Thorowgood & Co., London, 1821 (230x145mm)

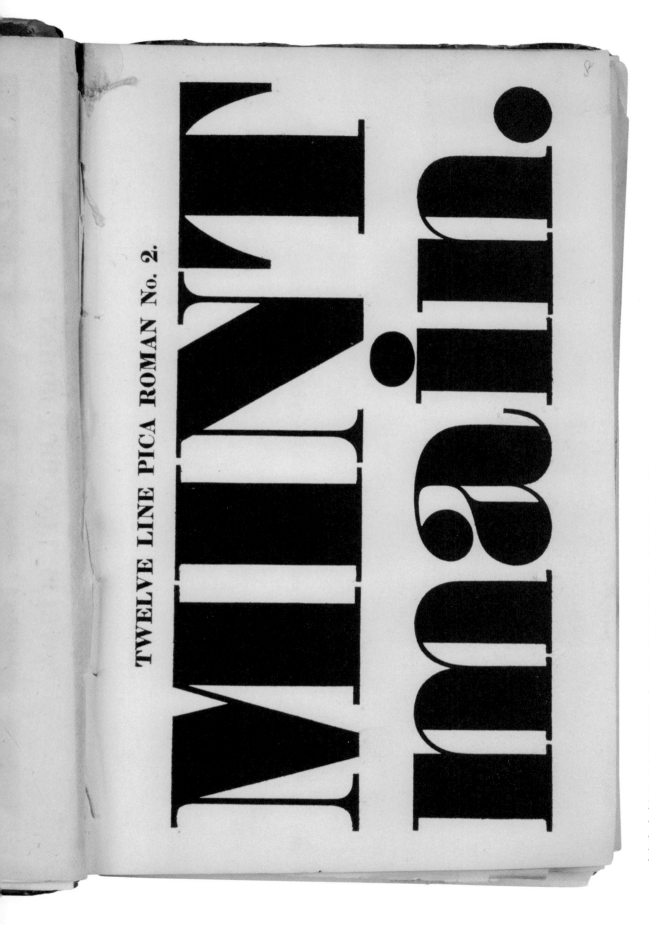

TWELVE LINE PICA ROMAN No. 2.

The early part of the nineteenth century was a period of enormous expansion of industry and commerce, particularly in England. As markets grew, so too did the demand for advertising, and many English founders designed types intended solely to address the demands of poster advertising. The earliest of these were the fat faces and Egyptians, both attributed to Robert Thorne (1754–1820), who had pioneered the development of the modern typeface in England at the turn of the century. Thorne probably had experience in creating display types as an apprentice to Thomas Cottrell, who was renowned for his large sand-cast letters.

Thorne adapted his modern style to make a bigger, bolder, blacker design than any before, specifically for use on posters and hoardings in dense city environments. In his Fat Face the thick strokes of Thorne's modern letterform are swollen to an extreme thickness and joined abruptly to connecting strokes and serifs that remain hairline-thin. The overall appearance is one of massive contrast in an alphabet that is ingeniously designed to be both obese and sprightly at the same time. Much playful variation is contributed by alternations of stroke endings, which range from bracketed and flat hairline serifs to triangular wedges and colossal ball terminals.

The fat faces, first seen in use around 1806, appalled many people. One critic, Thomas Hansard, described them as having 'preposterous disproportions'. However, they were remarkably successful. They attracted attention both to themselves and to the messages they carried and in the process brought about a transformation in the ways in which people interacted with text. Posters showing huge, bold words presented short, fragmented propositions, overturning the conventions of discursive reading and permanently changing the paradigm of social communications.

The fat letters were only the beginning of display types, as Thorne's Fann Street Foundry competed fiercely with other London foundries, such as Caslon and Figgins, to create increasingly extreme designs. Thorne's achievement as an innovator in type design was documented posthumously when William Thorowgood, a newcomer to the trade, who acquired Thorne's foundry after his death, published Thorne's specimen in 1821. During the next century, almost every major foundry would issue its own version of Thorne's Fat Face.

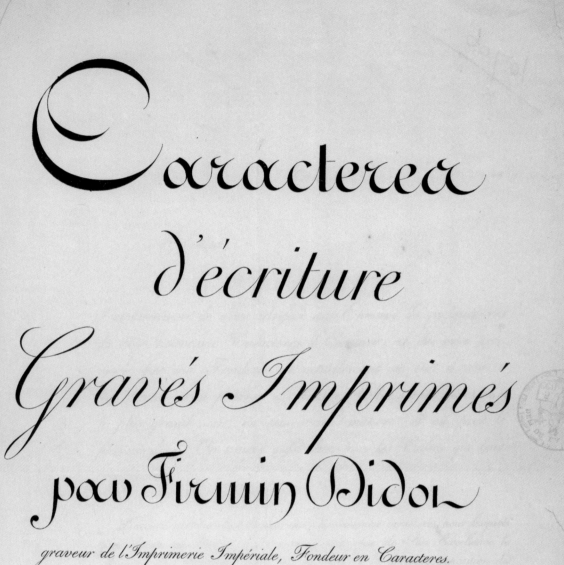

Caractères
d'écriture
Gravés Imprimés
par Firmin Didot

graveur de l'Imprimerie Impériale, Fondeur en Caracteres.

Paris, rue du Regard, Faubourg S.-Germain.

Division.

Bureau.

Préfecture
du Département de la Seine.

Par Brevet
d'Invention.

Ty	Didot's Anglaise and Ronde Scripts
Ca	Script
Ke	Formal, Connected
Te	Letterpress
Da	1809
De	Firmin Didot
Fo	Firmin Didot
Co	France

Characteristics

High contrast

Finely cut strokes

Scripts match neoclassical modern styles

Montpell
Ferrare
Bagnières

Connections

Cottrell's Double Pica Script	1774
Didot	1784
Parisian Ronde	1878
French Script	1905

Availability

Not available

Specimen

Caracteres d'écriture gravés, imprimés par Firmin Didot. Firmin Didot, Paris, 1809 (382x305mm)

Anglaise, the inclined script shown on this page in Firmin Didot's finely cut example of 1809, was so called because the style was based on English Roundhand, a calligraphic script of the 1600s that was produced using a sharply pointed nib instead of a traditional flat one. By the mid-eighteenth century the change from the use of the broad, square-cut pen to a pointed writing implement had had a transformative effect and English Roundhand had become the dominant script across Europe and the United States.

In the Roundhand script all letterforms are written at a constant slant, and the thickness of strokes is determined solely by the judicious control of pressure when writing, giving an extreme contrast of heavy downstrokes and fine hairlines. At the same time, baroque and rococo fashions ushered in a taste for curves and flourishes, while the revival of classical ideas introduced an analytical approach to letter construction. The combination of these influences began to be seen in the Romain du Roi (pp72–75) and reached its zenith in the severe romans of Didot (pp90–91) and Bodoni (pp96–97). Didot's Roundhand typeface also reflects that heritage.

Ronde, the round, upright typeface shown at far left, designed by Firmin Didot in 1809, is based on an elegant formal script widely used by seventeenth-century French state officials. This was a development of a hand of the 1600s that was closely related to Civilité type (pp54–55). Ronde is considered to be emblematic of a French Renaissance style in the way that Fraktur type is known as a German design.

The notable characteristics of a page set in Ronde are deep interlinear spaces, long ascenders and descenders, and large, flourished capitals. Its heavy strokes are very nearly upright, giving the characters a rounded overall appearance that is generally easy to read. Didot's Ronde is a very readable script typeface, with an extreme stroke contrast that allows it to match with both his groundbreaking roman (pp90–91) and the graceful Anglaise shown here.

Paris, ce   *1809.*

Monsieur,

J'ai l'honneur de vous adresser une Epreuve de quelques-uns de mes nouveaux Caracteres d'Ecriture, et de vous prévenir que ma Fonderie est actuellement en état d'exécuter les Fontes qu'on pourrait en desirer. Elles seront faites avec le plus grand soin, en très-bonne matiere, et au prix le plus modéré. On trouve aussi chez moi les Casses qui leur conviennent.

L'accueil extrêmement flatteur que ces nouveaux caracteres, pour lesquels j'ai obtenu un Brevet d'Invention, ont reçu de Son Excellence le Ministre de l'Intérieur, ainsi que du Juri, à la derniere exposition des objets d'art, me donne lieu de croire que cet avis vous sera agréable. J'aurais desiré mettre sous vos yeux plusieurs lignes de mes Caracteres d'écriture Ronde, Coulée, Bâtarde, et Anglaise; mais la disposition et la largeur de la page qui tient à cette Circulaire ne m'ont pas permis d'y placer un texte ou ils pussent tous être employés.

Firmin Didot Graveur de l'Imprimerie Impériale,
rue du Regard, n° 1, Faub. S. G.

Double Pica Roman.

Quousque tandem abutere, Catilina, patientia nostra? quamdiu nos etiam furor iste tuus eludet? quem ad finem sese effrenata jactabit audacia? nihilne te nocturnum præsidium palatii, nihil urbis vigiliæ, nihil timor populi, nihil consensus bonorum omnium, nihil hic munitissimus habendi senatus locus, nihil horum ora vultusque moverunt? patere tua consilia non sentis? constrictam jam omnium horum conscientia teneri conjurationem tuam non vides? quid proxima, quid superiore nocte egeris, ubi fue-

ABCDEFGHIJKLMNOPQ
RSTUVWXYZÆŒ
ABCDEFGHIJKLMNOP
QRSTUVWXYZÆ
ABCDEFGHIJKLMNOPQRSTUVX
£1234567890

Ty	**Scotch Roman**
Ca	**Serif**
Ke	**Modern**
Te	**Letterpress**
Da	**1812**
De	**Richard Austin**
Fo	**William Miller**
Co	**UK**

Characteristics

Vertical stress
Thin strokes with high contrast
Capitals to ascender height
Sharp, bracketed serifs
Capitals heavier than lower case
Most capitals have uniform width
M Narrow
Q Looped tail below letter
R a t Tail turns upwards
a c f j r y Ball terminals
g Double-storeyed with teardrop ear

ACJMQR
abcdefghij
orstuy*aefg*

Connections

Thorne's Modern	1800
De Vinne	1890
Caledonia	1938
Scotch Modern	2008

Availability

Various digital versions of Scotch Roman are available

Specimen

Specimen of Printing Types. William Miller, Edinburgh, 1813 (290x210mm)

Double Pica Italic.

Quousque tandem abutere, Catilina, patientia nostra? quamdiu
nos etiam furor iste tuus eludet?
quem ad finem sese effrenata jactabit audacia? nihilne te nocturnum præsidium palatii, nihil urbis vigiliæ, nihil timor populi,
nihil consensus bonorum omnium,
nihil hic munitissimus habendi senatus locus, nihil horum ora vultusque moverunt? patere tua consilia non sentis? constrictam jam
omnium horum conscientia teneri
conjurationem tuam non vides?
quid proxima, quid superiore nocte egeris, ubi fueris, quos convocaveris, quid concilii ceperis, quem
nostrum ignorare arbitraris?
ABCDEFGHIJKLMNOP
QRSTUVWXYZÆ
ABCDEFGHIJKLMNOPQRSTUVW

Following the designs of Didot and Bodoni, the severe modern letter became the prevalent style used in early nineteenth-century printing and publishing. In 1812, Richard Austin (c1765–1832), an English engraver and punch cutter who had previously produced the Bell types for the British Letter Foundry (pp94–95), cut a new type that referenced this contemporary trend, but which was considerably more practical and less mechanical.

Austin's new designs were first published in the specimens of two Scottish foundries, Wilson & Sons in 1812 and William Miller a year later. They also appear in the 1819 specimen of Austin's own Imperial Letter Foundry. These Scottish types were later imported into the United States by the Samuel Dickinson Foundry of Boston in the 1840s. They were extensively copied and modified by other American foundries and by the late nineteenth century had become known as 'Scotch Face' or 'Scotch Roman'.

Like Bodoni and Didot, Scotch Roman has a sharply vertical axis and high stroke contrast, with horizontal serifs and large ball terminals where appropriate. Capitals are also large, reaching the same height as the ascenders. However, in Scotch Roman a number of new features are introduced to make it more effective in body text as well as at larger sizes. The lower case x-height is very tall, with proportionally short ascenders and descenders. Stroke widths are modulated and serifs, while wide and sharp, are bracketed to the stems.

Scotch Roman achieved enormous popularity in nineteenth-century Britain, and even more so in the United States, becoming the dominant style there at the time. Its letter construction was the model for the development of other types such as Clarendon (pp132–33). Updated versions of Scotch Roman were released by a number of type foundries for machine composition in the early twentieth century, including Linotype and Monotype.

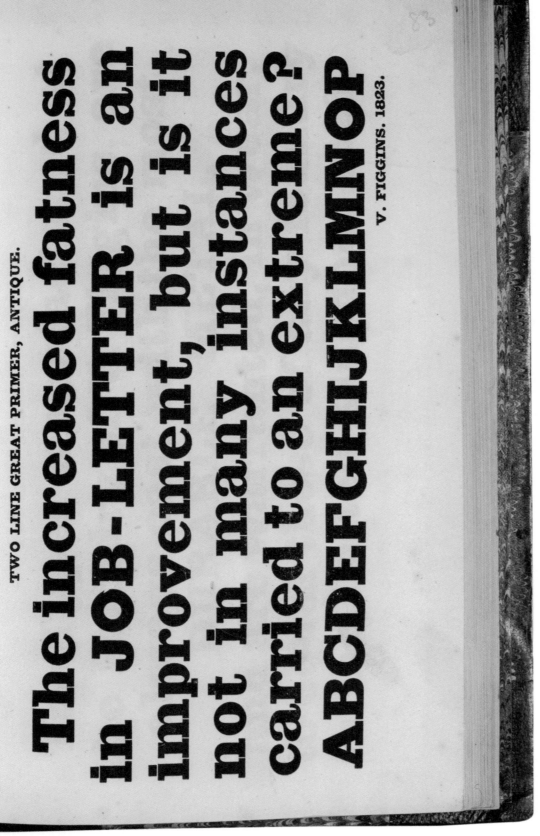

TWO LINE GREAT PRIMER, ANTIQUE.

The increased fatness in JOB-LETTER is an improvement, but is it not in many instances carried to an extreme? ABCDEFGHIJKLMNOP

V. FIGGINS. 1823.

Ty	**Figgins's Antique**
Ca	**Slab Serif**
Ke	**Egyptian**
Te	**Letterpress**
Da	**1815**
De	**Vincent Figgins**
Fo	**Vincent Figgins**
Co	**UK**

Characteristics

Thick strokes with slight contrast
Wide body
Large x-height
Heavy, rectangular slab serifs
R a t Tail turns upwards
a c f r Rounded swelling at upper terminals
g Double-storeyed, flat lower bowl
y Rounded swelling at tail

AGMRS
abcefghi
morstuy

Connections

Thorowgood's Egyptian	1821
Rockwell	1934
Giza	1994
Sentinel	2009

Availability

Not available

Specimen

Specimen of Printing Types. Vincent Figgins, London, 1823 (242x158mm)

FOUR-LINE PICA, ANTIQUE.

HOUSEHOLD
Birmingham
£1234567890
V. FIGGINS.

Vincent Figgins (1766–1844) began his career in type founding at the age of 16 as an apprentice to Joseph Jackson in London. Lacking the resources to acquire Jackson's workshop after the latter's death, he set up on his own in 1792 and went on to become one of the most successful type founders of his generation.

Figgins first displayed typefaces with slab serifs under the name Antique in his 1815 specimen book, although they became better known as Egyptians. Some have suggested that Robert Thorne (1754–1820) originated the design. Thorne had cut several sizes of type with slab serifs and had set trial specimens of them before his death in 1820. After William Thorowgood purchased his business Thorne's settings appeared in the Fann Street Foundry specimen of 1821, where the types were first given the name 'Egyptian'. The origin of this usage has been the subject of much conjecture (pp120–21), but the most reasonable explanation is that it is an oblique allusion to antiquity and to the exotic, following the fashion in the early nineteenth century for anything associated with Egypt, inspired by Napoleon's expedition there in 1798.

The early Egyptians were bold, novel types for use primarily on posters and hoardings. Their distinctive features are their slab serifs, unbracketed rectangles that are the same thickness as the horizontal parts of the letters. The structure of the letterforms, particularly the lower case, is evidently modelled on Thorne's modern face, with strokes thickened to give an overall boldness and a slight contrast of thick and thin, and with curved strokes reducing in weight at junctions to vertical strokes, as in the lower case a, d and g. Descenders and ascenders are very short at larger sizes, and capitals have a uniform width.

Like many other new styles, when the Egyptians appeared they were considered by many to be typographic monstrosities. However, they were very successful commercially, reflecting the industrialized ethos of the period and influencing the development of the more modulated forms of the Ionic and Clarendon styles developed in the 1840s (pp130–31, 132–33), along with such extravagances as the Italian and French Antique designs (pp118–19, 138–39).

Pouchée's Decorated Alphabets

Ty	**Pouchée's Decorated Alphabets**
Ca	**Decorative**
Ke	**Capitals**
Te	**Letterpress**
Da	**c1820**
De	**Louis Pouchée**
Fo	**Louis Pouchée**
Co	**UK**

Characteristics

Fat face character construction
Letters contain images of fruit, flowers, animals, musical instruments, agricultural tools, Masonic symbols, abstract designs

Connections

Fournier's Decorated Types	1764
Fry's Ornamented	1796
Didot's Decorated Capitals	c1800
Gillé's Lettres Ombrées Ornées	c1820

Availability

Not available

Specimen

Specimens of Stereotype Casting from the Foundry of L. I. Pouchée. London, c1820 (250x200mm)

In the early nineteenth century Louis John Pouchée (1782–1845) was a major manufacturer of printers' ornaments, pictorial stock-blocks and a series of decorative wood alphabets that are unsurpassed for their quality, originality and vivacity.

An entrepreneur with extensive business experience, Pouchée established a foundry in Lincoln's Inn Fields, London, in 1818, importing new mechanical type-founding equipment from France, probably to produce stereotype castings. His highly efficient production processes allowed him to undercut and outsell all of the London foundries, effectively breaking a trading cartel. This made him extremely unpopular in the industry and his business was forced to close in 1830, probably as a result of financial failure. Soon afterwards, Pouchée's equipment, stock and materials were sold at auction to his competitors, who dumped the advanced machinery he had been using, although the Caslon foundry took possession of some of his assets.

When Caslon ceased trading in 1937, the Monotype Corporation purchased part of their inventory, including 23 Pouchée wood-engraved alphabets which were eventually donated to the St Bride Printing Library in London. The patterns were misattributed for many years as Victorian curiosities made by a different foundry that operated later in the century, and it was not until 1966 that their true source was identified. Historical research was later corroborated by the chance discovery of a single surviving copy of the catalogue of about 1820 shown here, *Specimens of Stereotype Casting from the Foundry of L. I. Pouchée*.

In the creation of some of the most exuberant letterforms ever to have been made for letterpress printing, Pouchée and his craftsmen designed a total of 34 fat face ornamented alphabets up to 26 lines high (over 100mm), engraved from single blocks of end-grain boxwood as master patterns for the production of metal printing plates. Intended as eye-catching elements for posters and handbills, they featured finely cut images of fruit, flowers, animals, instruments, agricultural tools, Masonic symbols and abstract designs.

The original wood letters for 25 of the ornamented alphabets presented in Pouchée's specimen have survived. They were diligently proofed in their entirety by Ian Mortimer, using iron hand-presses, over a period of almost three years, and were published as *Ornamented Types: Twenty-Three Alphabets from the Foundry of Louis John Pouchée* in 1993.

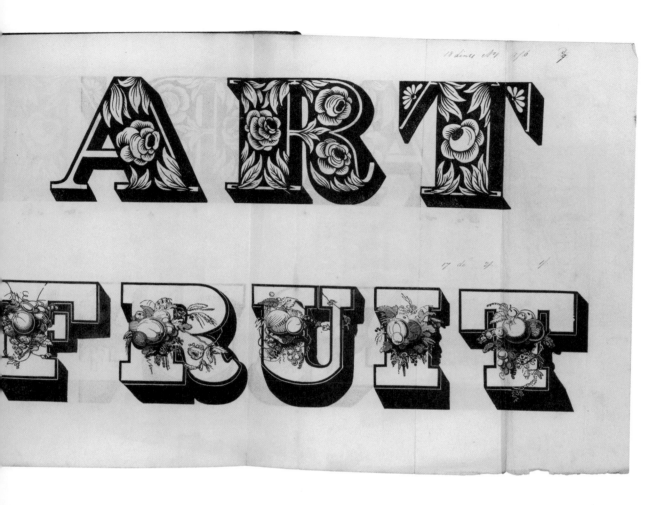

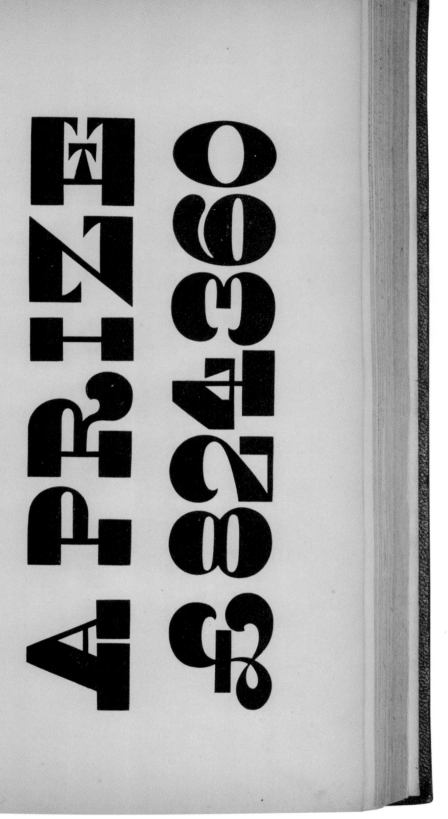

SEVEN-LINE PICA ITALIAN.

A PRIZE
8824360

Ty	**Italian**
Ca	**Serif**
Ke	**Modern, Reversed Contrast**
Te	**Letterpress**
Da	**1821**
De	**Unknown**
Fo	**Caslon & Catherwood**
Co	**UK**

Characteristics
Reversed contrast
Thick horizontal strokes and slab serifs
Hairline verticals
Reversed serifs

ABCDE
JKLMQ
RSTUZ

Connections
French Clarendon	c1860
Slab Sheriff	2009
Karloff	2011
Maelstrom	2012

Availability
A number of digital revivals of Italian
are available

Specimen
*Specimen of Printing Types by Henry
Caslon.* Henry Caslon, London, 1843
(250x155mm)

ITALIAN.

FIVE-LINE PICA.

BRISTOL

TWO-LINE GREAT PRIMER.

CHESTERFIELD,
£1234567890.

CASLON.

Italian, first shown by the Caslon & Catherwood foundry in 1821, is one of the earliest display types and one of the most eccentric. Designed to attract attention by defying readers' expectations, Italian was the work of an ingenious individual who reversed the logic of letterform construction in order to make it stand out in the increasingly saturated visual environment of the nineteenth century. Italian's design took all of the extreme individual characteristics of the fat face (pp108–109) and inverted them. The usual thick vertical strokes in the roman character were reduced to hairlines, the thin horizontal strokes were fattened, and all tapered shapes were reversed so that serifs joined to stems by their points.

Italian was not unsuccessful in the first half of the nineteenth century. In 1830, Caslon & Catherwood expanded its range by introducing a Shaded variant, and in 1846 Vincent Figgins released a slightly more condensed version complemented by a lower case. This was the final stage of the development of Italian by English type founders, although it continued to be produced both as metal and wood type up to the 1860s by foundries and manufacturers across Europe and until the mid-1880s in the United States. Though the popularity of Italian remained limited, it created a vogue for horizontally stressed types that influenced designs of the late nineteenth century, including the more elegant French Antique and French Clarendon styles (pp138–39).

It is difficult to evaluate a typeface that defies norms as flagrantly as the Italian, although few other type styles throughout the history of printing have provoked such hostile reactions from so many people. In 1938 the historian Nicolete Gray wrote that it had been 'much, and quite rightly, abused', going on to condemn it emphatically as 'a crude expression of the idea of perversity'. In more recent times, Peter Bil'ak, writing about his digital revival, Karloff, described the Italian with more equanimity as an example of 'skilled and deliberate ugliness'.

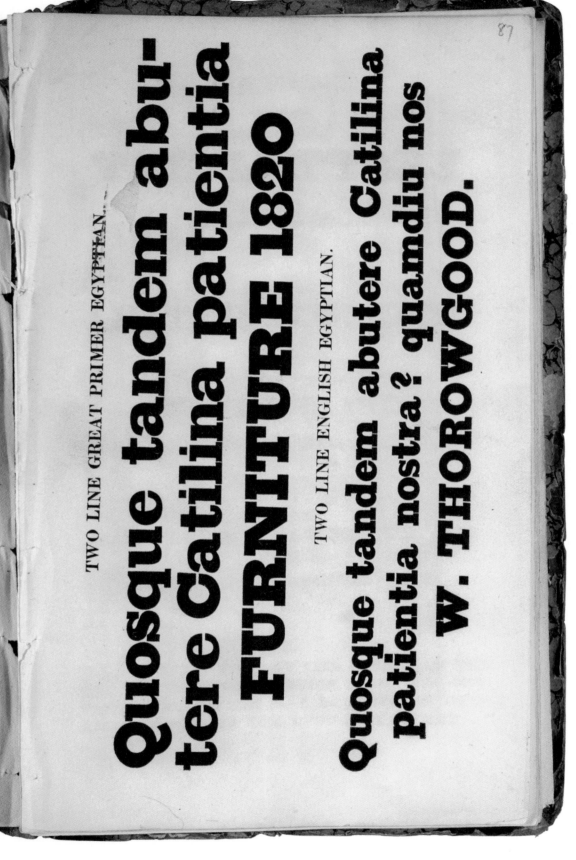

TWO LINE GREAT PRIMER EGYPTIAN.

Quosque tandem abu-
tere Catilina patientia
FURNITURE 1820

TWO LINE ENGLISH EGYPTIAN.

Quosque tandem abutere Catilina
patientia nostra? quamdiu nos
W. THOROWGOOD.

Ty	**Thorowgood's Egyptian**
Ca	**Slab Serif**
Ke	**Egyptian**
Te	**Letterpress**
Da	**1821**
De	**Robert Thorne**
Fo	**Fann Street Foundry**
Co	**UK**

Characteristics

Thick strokes with slight contrast

Wide body

Large x-height

Heavy, rectangular slab serifs

Q Curved tail below letter

R Flat foot serifs

a c f r y Square terminal

g Double-storeyed

i Small square dot

ACEQRS
abdehim
nopqrstu

Connections

Figgins's Antique	1815
Rockwell	1934
Giza	1994
Sentinel	2009

Availability

Not available

Specimen

A Specimen of the Printing Types in the Fann Street Foundry. W. Thorowgood & Co., London, 1821 (230x145mm)

FOUR LINE PICA EGYPTIAN.

THE LOTTERY DRAWS JUNE 12, & £3567 89. R. THORNE 4

From the evidence currently available, it is not possible to ascertain the originator of the slab serif type style. It is attributed to either Vincent Figgins (1766–1844) (pp114–15) or Robert Thorne (1754–1820) (pp108–109), although the name 'Egyptian' is first recorded in use to name types from Thorne's foundry. A satirical piece that described novel display lettering as 'Fashionable Egyptian Sign-Boards' had appeared in a book in 1806, but no Egyptian slab serif is documented until 1810 when it appeared on a lottery handbill printed from a woodblock.

When Robert Thorne died in 1820, the Fann Street Foundry was sold at auction to William Thorowgood (?–1877), who is said to have made the purchase with the proceeds from a state lottery draw. In the auction catalogue, six sets of matrices are listed under the heading 'Egyptian'. These all appeared in the first specimen book issued by Thorowgood directly after the purchase.

The examples shown here – Two Line Great Primer Egyptian, Two Line English Egyptian and Four Line Pica Egyptian – are from Thorowgood's second specimen, published in 1821. This catalogue was printed from 132 pages that had been composed by Thorne before his death but not printed previously. It represents an accurate inventory of his stock, although some new additions are featured. Despite the fact that it shows Thorne's name at the foot, the Four Line Pica Egyptian is one of these additions, cut after Thorne's death under Thorowgood's supervision.

Thorowgood went on to issue new specimens regularly, adding more typefaces, including Frakturs, Greeks and Russian types purchased from German foundries. In 1828 he took over the type foundry of Edmund Fry, which had a large collection of non-Latin types. Robert Besley (pp132–33) became a partner in the firm in 1828, taking over the foundry on Thorowgood's retirement in 1849, when it was renamed Robert Besley & Co.

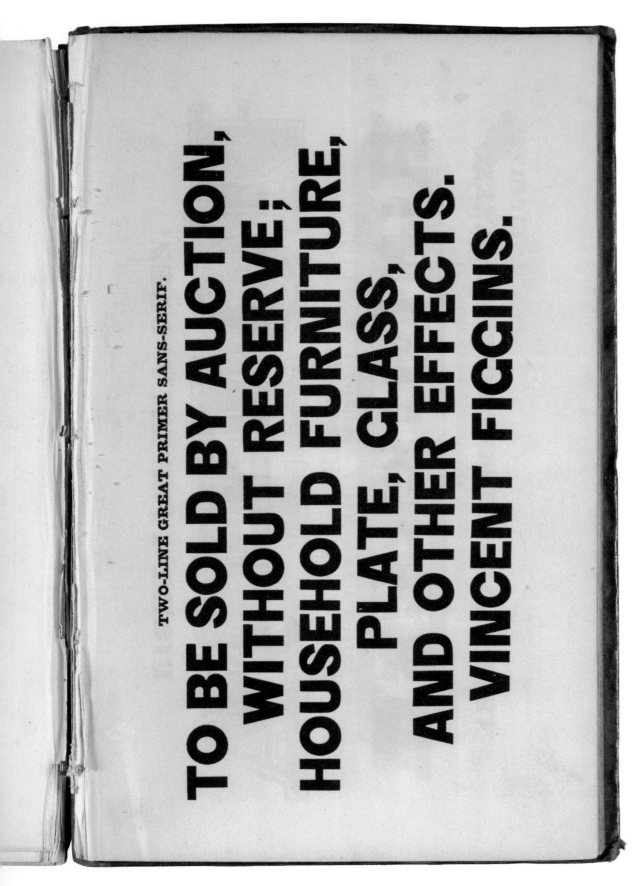

TWO-LINE GREAT PRIMER SANS-SERIF.

TO BE SOLD BY AUCTION, WITHOUT RESERVE; HOUSEHOLD FURNITURE, PLATE, GLASS, AND OTHER EFFECTS. VINCENT FICCINS.

Ty	**Figgins's Sans Serif**
Ca	**Sans Serif**
Ke	**Grotesque**
Te	**Letterpress**
Da	**1832**
De	**Vincent Figgins**
Fo	**Vincent Figgins**
Co	**UK**

Characteristics

Monoline

Capitals only

Even character widths

C G O Geometric, circular

C G S Flat terminal

G Small spur

S Uneven balance

ABCDEG HMNOP RSTUVY

Connections

Thorowgood's Grotesque	1832
Royal Gothic	c1870
Akzidenz-Grotesk	c1898
Figgins Sans	2008

Availability

Figgins Sans is a digital revival available from Shinntype and resellers

Specimen

Specimen of Printing Types. Vincent Figgins, London, 1832 (242x155mm)

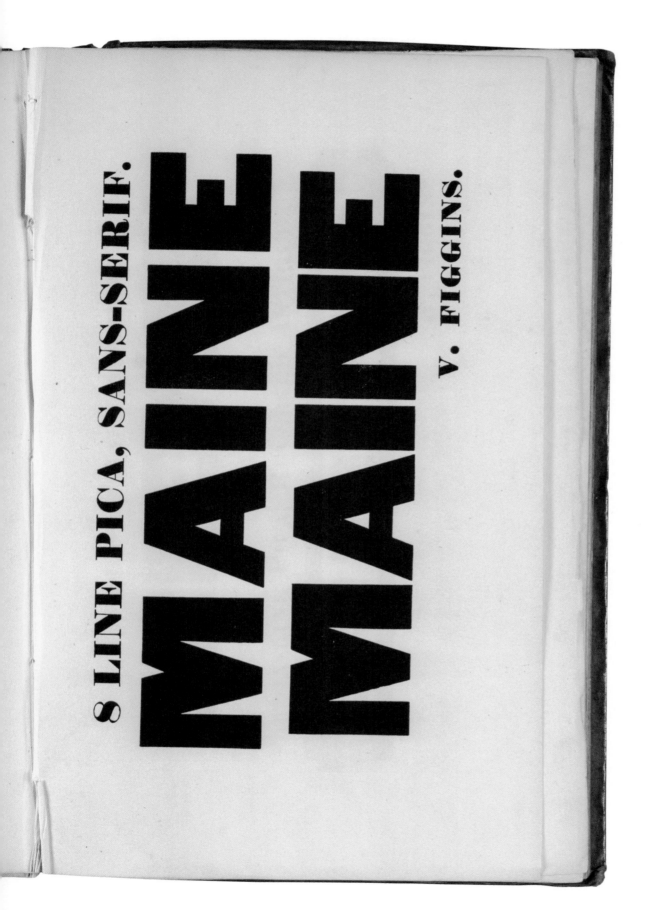

8 LINE PICA, SANS-SERIF.

MAINE
MAINE

V. FIGGINS.

The first sans serif type appeared as a single line setting in capitals under the name 'Egyptian' in William Caslon IV's specimen book of 1816. His business was sold to Blake, Garnett & Co., who included it in their specimen book of 1819. It seems to have been a tentative experiment, as the form was only seen sporadically over the next few years. But in 1832 dense black, somewhat awkward versions appeared under the name 'Sans-Serif' in the specimen book of Vincent Figgins (1766–1844), shown here. In the same year, William Thorowgood (?–1877) displayed a specimen under the name of 'Grotesque' (pp124–25).

Figgins's Sans Serif was in capitals only, intended for use in titling and advertising, with heavy, black letters that are remarkably uniform in width, a feature deriving from recent modern face designs. In the 1832 specimen only three sizes of sans serif capitals are shown, but within a year he had expanded his range of sans serifs to ten sizes, including a huge 20-line pica, and soon afterwards he added open and condensed versions. Figgins clearly recognized that a sans serif could be as black and dominant as any fat face or slab serif letterform.

The most important and obvious characteristic of the sans serif form is its absence of serifs. This has been said to have been achieved by severing the serifs from an Egyptian slab serif typeface, although there are several structural differences, such as the leg of the R and the rudimentary G. A more geometric construction method suggests itself, with its origins in contemporary architectural lettering. The letters are monoline, with strokes that appear to be of equal thickness, although the horizontals are slightly thinner than the verticals, and some strokes are reduced in weight at junctions with others.

The use of these new typefaces was limited almost exclusively to large headlines, with body text remaining in roman type. Lighter weights and lower case designs were only fully explored later in the nineteenth century. It wasn't until the late 1950s that sans serif types began to be fully accepted as effective and versatile tools of typographic communication.

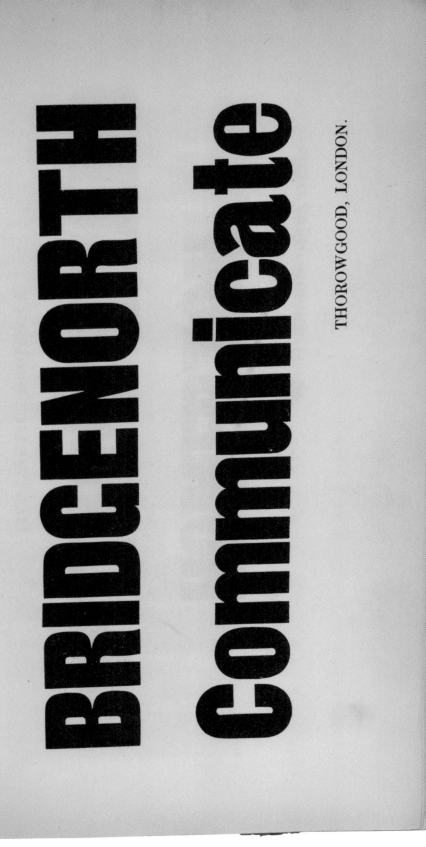

SEVEN LINE GROTESQUE.

BRIDGENORTH

Communicate

THOROWGOOD, LONDON.

Ty	**Thorowgood's Grotesque**
Ca	**Sans Serif**
Ke	**Grotesque**
Te	**Letterpress**
Da	**1832**
De	**William Thorowgood**
Fo	**Fann Street Foundry**
Co	**UK**

Characteristics

Capitals monoline, even, rectangular

Condensed heavy characters

S s Uneven balance

a e g Irregular stroke widths

BCDEGR aceimn ostu

Connections

Grotesque No. 9	1906
Aurora-Grotesk IX Halbbreit	1928
Schmalfette Grotesk	1954
Compacta	1963

Availability

Not available

Specimen

Fann Street Letter Foundry: Specimen of Printing Types. W. Thorowgood & Co., London, 1835 (275x165mm)

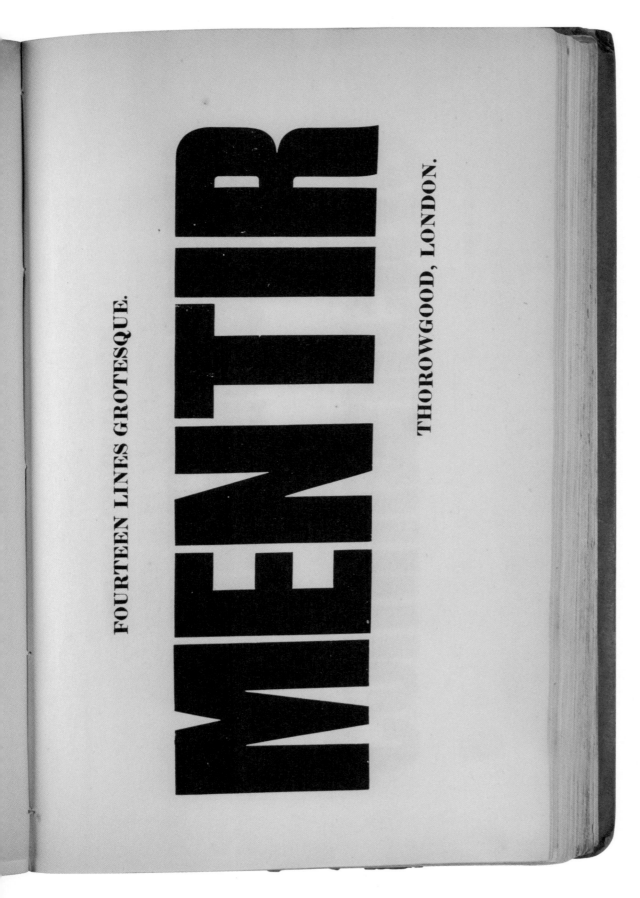

FOURTEEN LINES GROTESQUE.

MENTIR

THOROWGOOD, LONDON.

In 1832, Vincent Figgins (1766–1844) published the first commercially successful sans serif letters for use in titling (pp122–23). In the same year, William Thorowgood (?–1877) displayed sans serif specimens under the name of 'Grotesque'. The origins of this word are obscure, although it was probably used as a mildly perjorative reference, implying both oddity and ugliness. Indeed, until comparatively recently, sans serif typefaces have routinely been considered inferior to those with serifs and were frequently condemned as inadequate for many tasks. Other curious names were given to these early sans serif forms, including Doric and gothic, the latter term presumably due to the fact that the early types in this style were heavy, black letters, vaguely recalling medieval gothic types. There was as yet no generally agreed name for letters without serifs, though grotesque survives today as a synonym for the sans serif, largely as a result of its use in Germany, where the form was developed in the late nineteenth century.

Thorowgood's Grotesque was a condensed black type. In the upper case it was virtually monoline, with a rectangular vertical emphasis and very even character widths. Thorowgood was the only early type founder brave enough to experiment with the design of a lower case, drawn only at the Seven Line size shown at far left. The complexity of strokes in the lower case necessitated much variation in stroke width. In the 1835 specimen shown here the lower case was set as 'communicate', a word that did little to champion the merits of a sans serif lower case as it emphasized faults in the design. It is immediately evident that the compact sequence of -mmuni- has little in common visually with the final syllable, -cate, which is far looser and more varied in its stroke formation.

With such tentative and rudimentary beginnings, it is hardly surprising that other English foundries avoided developing their own lower case sans serifs. However, within a short time the trade had accepted that the grotesque was more effective than other styles in advertising applications. The design was recognized as being more capable of creating visual impact than fat faces and Egyptians, since the elimination of serifs permitted greater simplicity, density and scale on posters, hoardings and handbills. Many English printers exploited the assertiveness of sans serifs at display sizes, set in capitals only, until later in the century when more effective lower case letters were developed.

Fette Fraktur

Ty	**Fette Fraktur**
Ca	**Blackletter**
Ke	**Fraktur**
Te	**Letterpress**
Da	**c1835**
De	**Johann Christian Bauer**
Fo	**Joh. Peter Nees & Company**
Co	**Germany**

Characteristics

Vertical stress
Extreme contrast of thick and thin strokes
Simplified Fraktur capitals
Lower case has spiky gothic character
Ornamental flourishes
a Single-storeyed
d Curved uncial stem
f p long s Long, pointed descender
g Open tail
h Curved uncial form

ABCM
abcdefghi
koprstuz

Connections

Thorne's Fat Face	c1806
Fette Kanzlei	c1830
Fette Haenel-Fraktur	c1840
Hoyer-Fraktur	1935

Availability

Fette Fraktur is available from Linotype and resellers

Specimen

Bauer type specimen. Bauersche Giesserei, Frankfurt, c1880 (280x229mm)

Fette Fraktur is one of the most commonly seen surviving blackletter typefaces today, although this may have as much to do with its ready availability as any instrinsic merits in the design. It was cut by the prolific German punch cutter Johann Christian Bauer (1802–1867) around 1835 and first released by Joh. Peter Nees & Company. By the 1950s Fette Fraktur had become the property of the Stempel foundry, which reissued it as a face for photocomposition. It was later converted into a digital type and distributed by Linotype in a very popular typeface bundle during the 1980s and 1990s.

Fette Fraktur is among the most authoritative of the Frakturs, cut only in an ultrabold weight. Like many typefaces created in the early nineteenth century, it is a stylistic cross-breed, probably best described as a fat face variant of Fraktur: a reinterpretation for the German market of the extremely heavy versions of nineteenth-century modern faces such as Thorne and Thorowgood's fat faces (pp108–109).

Like them, Fette Fraktur was intended to be used big and bold in display advertising rather than in text. The typeface is characterized by the spiky gothic character of the lower case letters, with only their ornamental flourishes making them broken letters, while the curvaceous capitals are more typical of conventional Fraktur typefaces.

Due to their negative associations with the Nazi regime in mid-twentieth-century Germany, the use of blackletter types became unacceptable in post-war years, and for a time Fraktur was only seen in communications where a folksy, traditional Germanic flavour was required. Recently it has been somewhat rehabilitated, being popularized internationally by heavy metal, goth, punk and hip-hop graphic styles that address a youth culture motivated by a vague sense of rebellious individualism. But where once blackletter was the everyday writing system of a nation, today it remains an ostentatious curiosity with intensely historical undercurrents.

Neueste fette Fraktur.

-Erzeugniß unserer Gießerei. — Eingetragen zum Schutze gegen Nachbildung.

No. 189. Corps 36. Minimum 15 Kilo.

achrichten, Freischütz & Reform

No. 190. Corps 48. Minimum 18 Kilo.

ibisches Tageblatt 45

No. 191. Corps 60. Minimum 20 Kilo.

Reichs=Anzeiger

No. 192. Corps 72. Minimum 24 Kilo.

elder 2 Zeitung

No. 193. Corps 84. Minimum 28 Kilo.

er 7 Journal

Bauer'sche Gießerei in Frankfurt am Main.

Schnellpressendruck der Buchdruckerei der Neuen Frankfurter Presse.

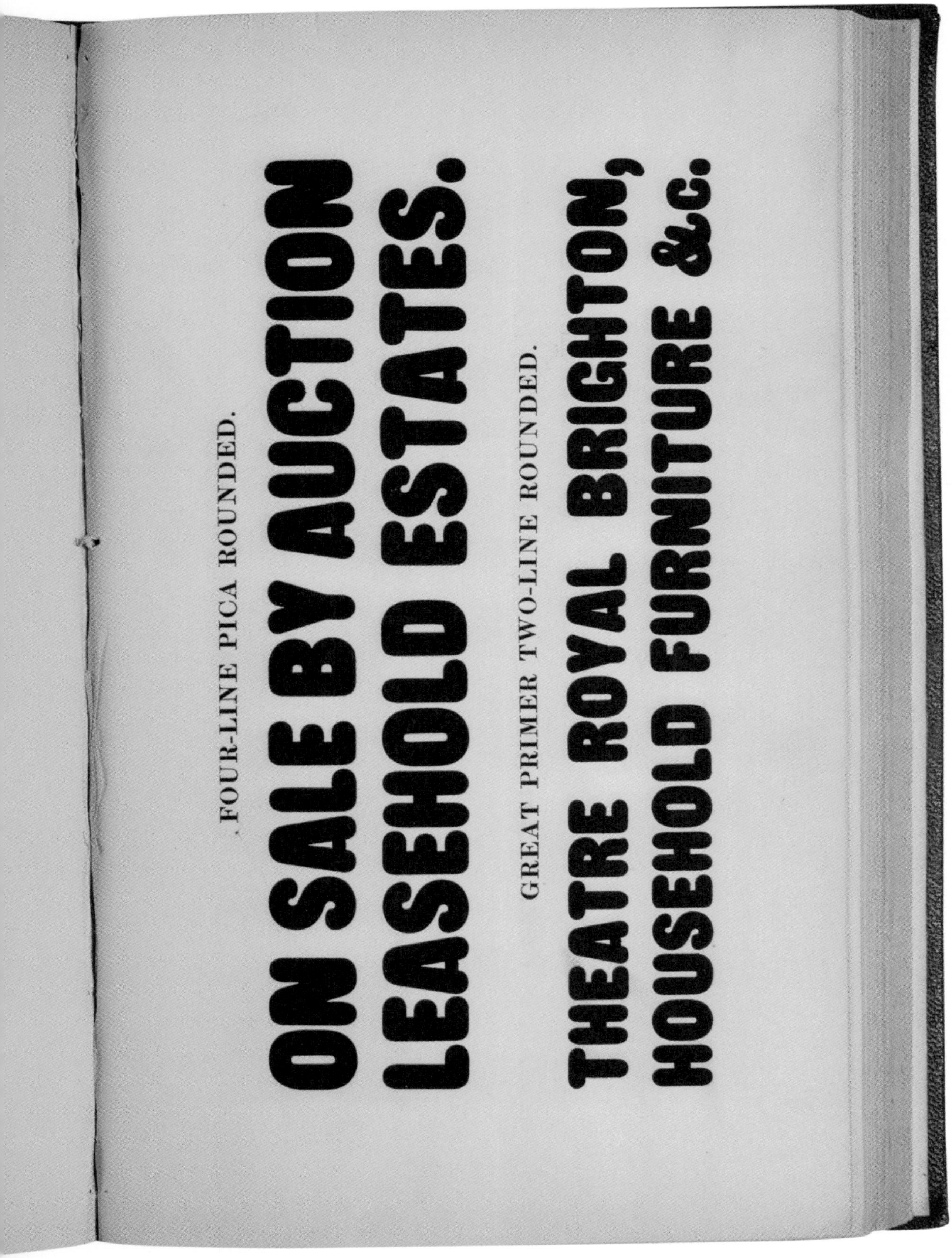

FOUR-LINE PICA ROUNDED.

ON SALE BY AUCTION LEASEHOLD ESTATES.

GREAT PRIMER TWO-LINE ROUNDED.

THEATRE ROYAL BRIGHTON, HOUSEHOLD FURNITURE &c.

Ty	**Caslon Rounded**
Ca	**Sans Serif**
Ke	**Capitals**
Te	**Letterpress**
Da	**1841**
De	**Unknown**
Fo	**Caslon**
Co	**UK**

Characteristics

Capitals only

Construction based on a condensed sans serif form with corners rounded off

ABCDEG HLNORS TUY&c.

Connections

Brauer Neue	1974
VAG Rounded	1979
Frankfurter	1981
FF Din Round	2010

Availability

Not available

Specimen

Specimen of Printing Types by Henry Caslon. Henry Caslon, London, 1843 (250x155mm)

FOUR-LINE ROUNDED, OPEN.

ON SALE BY AUCTION
LEASEHOLD ESTATES.

GREAT PRIMER TWO-LINE ROUNDED, OPEN.

THEATRE ROYAL BRIGHTON,
HOUSEHOLD FURNITURE &c.

In the first half of the nineteenth century, many founders and wood-type producers expanded their repertoires by experimenting freely with variations of existing designs to make novel typefaces. For example, a serif face could be thickened into a slab serif, or slabs could be removed to produce a sans serif. The basic forms could be expanded or condensed and a limitless range of other interventions could be made, such as inlines, outlines, ornaments and shadows.

One of the easiest possible modifications was to simply mill the corners of the letters in order to produce a rounded typeface. Gothic Round Condensed was the first wood type of this style, a round-cornered sans serif appearing in the 1838 catalogue of George Nesbitt, a prominent New York wood-type manufacturer. Subsequently, many wood letters were cut in rounded styles in the United States, where they became popular in the second half of the nineteenth century.

The first round foundry type produced in Europe is shown in Caslon's *Specimen of Printing Types*, published in 1843 in both a plain and an ornamented version, which the historian Nicolete Gray described as 'rather more sleek than most of the letters of this period'. It was probably not particularly successful, as it was not widely copied by Caslon's competitors; Gray noted that 'It is Caslon's invention, considerably developed by them, but never touched by the other founders'. However, the typeform was adapted by various German foundries and has served as the blueprint for a number of pneumatic designs produced throughout the twentieth century.

DOUBLE PICA IONIC.

Quousque tandem abutere, Catilina, patientia nostra? quamdiu nos etiam furor iste tuus eludet? quem ad finem sese effrenata jactabit audacia? nihilne te nocturnum præsidium palatii, nihil urbis vigiliæ, nihil

ABCDEFGHIJKLMN
ABCDEFGHIJKLMNOPQR
£ 1234567890

In the State Lotteries, now wisely abolished by the Legislature, the risk was so greatly against the adventurer, that, according to the Schemes, the buyer of the whole Lottery would lose half his money. Few, therefore, but the imprudent, the inconsiderate, & the

CASLON.

Ty	**Caslon's Ionic**
Ca	**Serif**
Ke	**Clarendon**
Te	**Letterpress**
Da	**c1844**
De	**Unknown**
Fo	**Caslon**
Co	**UK**

Characteristics

Vertical stress
Thick strokes with moderate contrast
Wide body
Moderate x-height
Heavy, bracketed slab serifs
M Narrow
Q Sweeping, looped tail
R a t Tail turns upwards
a c f j r y Ball terminals
g Double-storeyed with teardrop ear

AMQRS
abcefghij
noprstuv

Connections

Clarendon	1845
Century Schoolbook	1918
Egizio	1955
Farao	1998

Availability

Not available

Specimen

Specimen of Printing Types. H. W. Caslon & Co., London, c1844 (250x155mm)

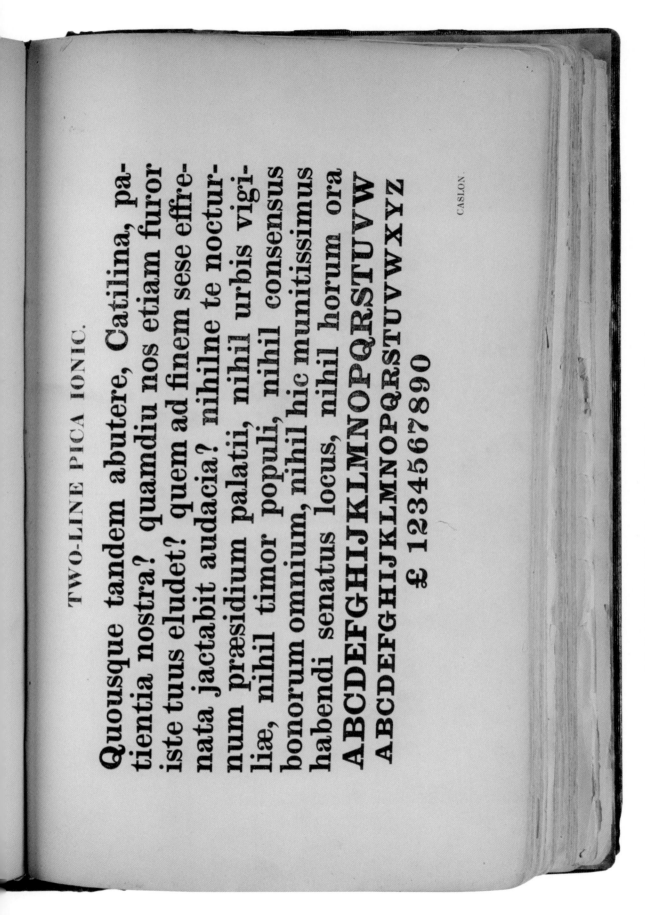

TWO-LINE PICA IONIC.

Quousque tandem abutere, Catilina, patientia nostra? quamdiu nos etiam furor iste tuus eludet? quem ad finem sese effrenata jactabit audacia? nihilne te nocturnum præsidium palatii, nihil urbis vigiliæ, nihil timor populi, nihil consensus bonorum omnium, nihil hic munitissimus habendi senatus locus, nihil horum ora ABCDEFGHIJKLMNOPQRSTUVW ABCDEFGHIJKLMNOPQRSTUVWXYZ £ 1234567890

CASLON.

The name Ionic appeared for the first time in a type specimen of the Blake & Stephenson (later Stephenson, Blake & Co.) foundry of around 1833, where it was used to title an outline letter. It was also employed by some early Victorian type founders as an alternative name for the Egyptian slab serif style (pp120–21).

Originally seen at large sizes in architectural and industrial lettering, the early Ionic typeface was described by the historian Nicolete Gray as 'an Egyptian with the slab serif bracketed and a definite differentiation between the thick and thin strokes'. However, comparison with late modern faces such as Thorne's Modern (pp104–105) or Scotch Roman (pp112–13) suggests that Ionic is more likely to be a development of these styles, with the stroke weight made heavier overall. The Ionic design was cut as type at the Caslon foundry in the early 1840s and first presented in the *Specimen of Printing Types* by Henry Caslon IV, probably printed in 1844.

In comparison with the Egyptians cut by Vincent Figgins (pp114–15) and Robert Thorne, characters are lighter overall with softer contours. There is also a greater differentiation between thick and thin strokes. Where the serifs in the Egyptians are stout, rectangular blocks, in the Caslon design they are thinner, less dominant, and, like the late modern style, bracketed, with curved transitions at the stroke joints.

Caslon's design directly influenced the development of Clarendon by the Fann Street Foundry in 1845, a form with which it is synonymous. Adaptations of the Ionic style were later used in newspapers because of their legibility and resilience in newsprint. These versions of the Ionic, designed specifically for newspaper reproduction, were usually monoline letters of large x-height with very short ascenders and descenders, open counters and thick, bracketed serifs.

TWO LINES GREAT PRIMER EXTENDED CLARENDON.

The municipal institutions of England gave the people a taste for self government and laid the foundation of British Freedom, and the

£1234567890

FREEHOLD HOUSES.

TWO LINES ENGLISH EXTENDED CLARENDON.

The municipal institutions of England gave the people a taste for self government, and laid a foundation for British Freedom and promoted the extension of British Commerce.

FARM IMPLEMENTS

Producing £234,890 Annually.

HUNTINGDON.

ROBERT BESLEY AND CO., LONDON.

Ty	**Clarendon**
Ca	**Serif**
Ke	**Clarendon**
Te	**Letterpress**
Da	**1845**
De	**Robert Besley**
Fo	**Fann Street Foundry**
Co	**UK**

Characteristics

Vertical stress

Thick strokes with moderate contrast

Wide body

Moderate x-height

Heavy, bracketed slab serifs

M Narrow

Q Sweeping looped tail

R a t Tail turns upwards

a c f j r y Ball terminals

g Double-storeyed with teardrop ear

AMQRS
abcefghij
korstuy

Connections

Ionic	c1844
Rockwell	1934
Craw Clarendon	1955
Archer	2003

Availability

Clarendon is widely available

Specimen

Fann Street Letter Foundry: A General Specimen of Printing Types. Robert Besley & Co., London, c1857 (280x220mm)

FIVE LINES CLARENDON EXTENDED.

FREEHOLD LAND Important Sale £16,348

CANON EXTENDED CLARENDON.

The municipal and commercial greatness of England. £12,345,678 COMMUNICATE

ROBERT BESLEY AND CO. LONDON.

Fat faces, grotesques and heavy slab serif types called 'Egyptians' were seen increasingly in the first decades of the nineteenth century, being widely used to attract attention at large sizes in posters and display advertising. By the mid-1830s smaller sizes of slab serif types began to occasionally find their way into books, usually for listings, charts or tables.

The Clarendon typeface was originated in 1845 by Robert Besley, working with his punch cutter, Benjamin Fox, at the Fann Street Foundry, London. It was influenced by Caslon's Double Pica Ionic (pp130–31), issued the year before, and on its release it achieved huge success in the burgeoning advertising and printing industries. This was due partly to its effectiveness in display applications and also to its functionality in providing emphasis in text settings. Clarendon matched well with contemporary text faces in the modern style, offering an alternative to italics that was especially useful for references such as dictionary entries. These were the very first bold types specifically designed for setting alongside text type. Clarendon's popularity led Besley to protect the design under the English Ornamental Design Act of 1842. When the registration expired three years later many competing foundries raced to cut and cast their own copies. As a result, the name Clarendon came to represent not a single typeface, but an entire category of slab serifs.

Clarendon's letters are relatively heavy overall, with a slight contrast between thick and thin strokes rather than the uniform weight of many Egyptians. They have a large x-height and short ascenders and descenders. The square serifs are thinner than those on Egyptians and have a subtle bracketing. Letterform construction owes much to contemporary text faces based on the roman model rather than the Egyptian style. This is evident in the shapes of the a, e, g and t, and the tail of the R, which terminates in an upward curve rather than a squared serif; the a, c, g and r end in ball terminals like those of the modern style. Early Clarendons were also often slightly compressed, making them suitable for setting in text.

With the advent of new bold text types during the late nineteenth century Clarendon was used less for emphasis in text and is nowadays considered a display type. Repeatedly revived and adapted for each new technological generation, its boldly assertive forms found frequent applications in newspapers, advertising, packaging and signage throughout the twentieth century.

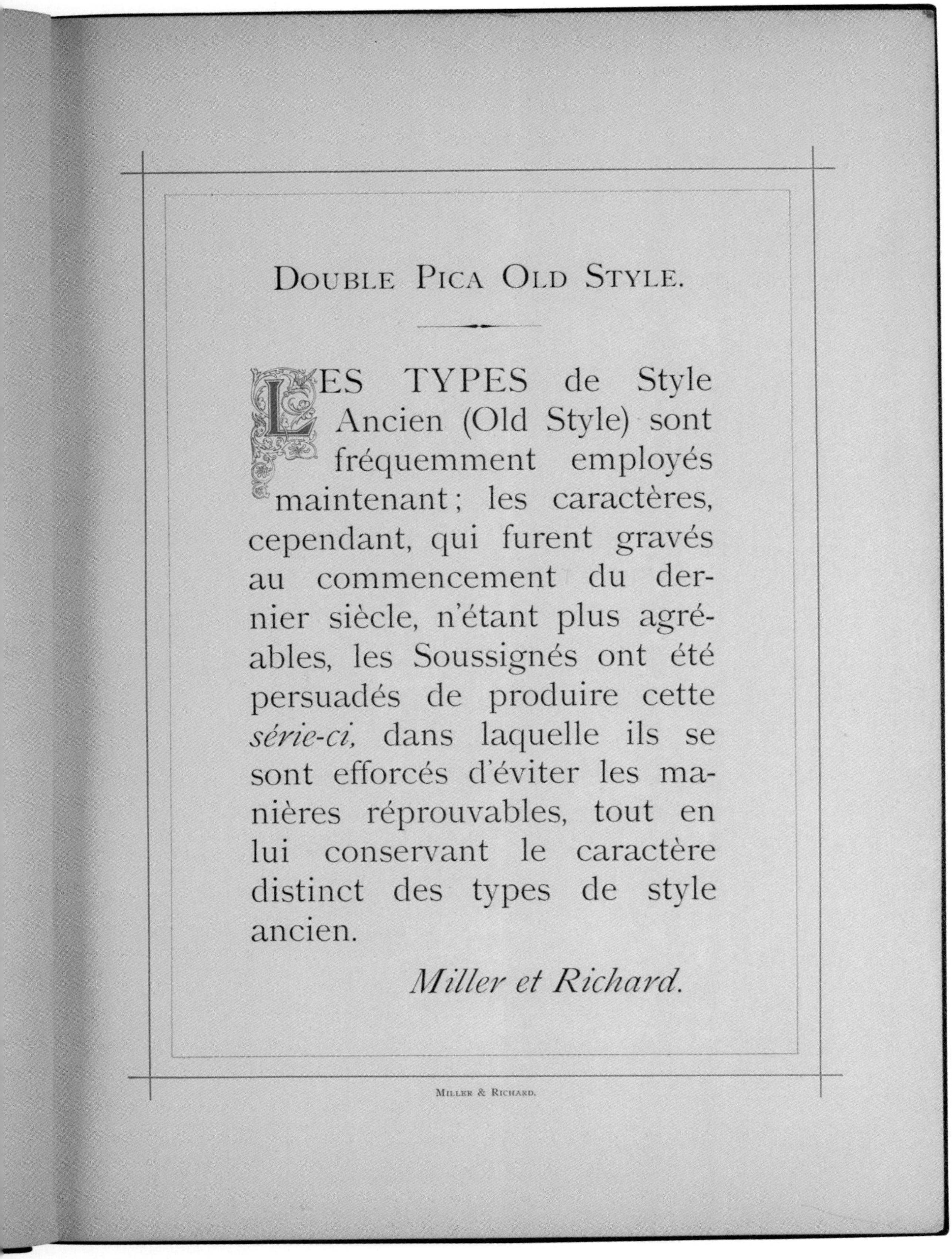

DOUBLE PICA OLD STYLE.

LES TYPES de Style Ancien (Old Style) sont fréquemment employés maintenant ; les caractères, cependant, qui furent gravés au commencement du dernier siècle, n'étant plus agréables, les Soussignés ont été persuadés de produire cette *série-ci,* dans laquelle ils se sont efforcés d'éviter les manières réprouvables, tout en lui conservant le caractère distinct des types de style ancien.

Miller et Richard.

MILLER & RICHARD.

Ty	**Phemister's Old Style**
Ca	**Serif**
Ke	**Old Style**
Te	**Letterpress**
Da	**c1858**
De	**Alexander Phemister**
Fo	**Miller & Richard**
Co	**UK**

Characteristics

Vertical stress
Thick, short, bracketed serifs
Most capitals have uniform width
E S Wide
M W Narrow
T Splayed top serifs
e Open eye
g Double-storeyed, angled lower bowl

AEMST
abcdefghi
orstuy*aefg*

Connections

Caslon	c1725
Bookman Oldstyle	1901
Monotype Old Style	1901
Century Oldstyle	1909

Availability

Various digital revivals are available

Specimen

Specimens of Old-Style Types. Miller & Richard, c1868 (275x200mm)

GREAT PRIMER OLD STYLE.

———————

TYPE of the OLD STYLE of face is now frequently ufed—more efpecially for the finer clafs of book work; as however the faces which were cut in the early part of the laft century are now unpleafing both to the eye of the critic and to the general reader, on account of their inequality of *fize* and confequent irregularity of *ranging*, the Subfcribers have been induced to produce this feries, in which they have endeavoured to avoid the objectionable peculiarities, whilft retaining the diftinctive characteriftics of the mediæval letters. The feries is complete from Double Pica to Pearl, with all the intermediate bodies, and has Roman and Italic Accents to each fount.

Miller & Richard.

MILLER & RICHARD.

During the 1850s a series of books with historical themes was published by the Chiswick Press, set in a revival of Caslon's old-style types. These editions met with considerable success, precipitating a general move away from the gaunt modern types that were widespread in bookwork at the time and a return to the friendlier styles of earlier days, remodelled to fit comfortably with the tastes of contemporary readers.

The first nineteenth-century old-style revival was cut by Alexander Phemister (1829–94) for the Scottish foundry Miller & Richard in about 1858, shortly before he emigrated to the United States. Phemister's typeface was a curious hybrid of modern and old-style forms, attempting to improve the Renaissance model by imposing rational values and regulated features on it. In their 1868 specimen, Miller & Richard indicated that their old styles were intended to overcome what they described as the 'objectional peculiarities ... of the mediaeval letters'.

In Phemister's design, the usually high contrast of the modern face is much reduced, resulting in a very pale overall colour that has something of the even appearance of the old style, although the overall stress is vertical. Serifs are thick, short and deeply bracketed to the stems. The letterforms are very round and have a number of eccentric features, such as the bowl of the lower case g and various ligatures that evoke an antique impression. Elsewhere modern forms are retained, such as in the a, with its sprung bowl, the e with its open counter, and the t with its ascending upper terminal. Unlike classical capitals with their undulating width variations, Miller & Richard's upper case letters have proportions that are approximately equal throughout, another feature borrowed from the modern face.

The new style, much admired and much copied by other British type foundries, spread quickly to Germany and the United States. It was extensively used as a text type well into the twentieth century, particularly in magazines and journals. As a result of Phemister's work, Miller & Richard gained an international reputation, while Phemister's typefaces had a significant effect on type design trends, influencing the resurgence of old-style revivals for machine composition during the 1920s and 1930s.

Ty	**Figgins's Antique No. 3**
Ca	**Serif**
Ke	**Clarendon**
Te	**Letterpress**
Da	**1860**
De	**Vincent Figgins**
Fo	**Vincent Figgins**
Co	**UK**

Characteristics

Vertical stress

Thick strokes with moderate contrast

Condensed body

Heavy, bracketed slab serifs

Q Sweeping, curved tail

R a t Tail turns upwards

a c f g r y Ball terminals

g Double-storeyed

AEGMRS abcdefghi koprstuvy

Connections

Clarendon	1845
Egyptienne Bold Condensed	c1850
French Clarendon	c1860
Rosewood	1994

Availability

Adobe's Rosewood is a digital revival of a similar type in capitals only

Specimen

Specimen Book of Type and Borders, Cast on Point Bodies: Catalogue of Printing Materials. R. H. Stevens & Co., London, 1929 (280x220mm)

ANTIQUE SERIES No. 3.

5 A 10 a   60 Point Col. 6

BOLDER FOUNT
The Modern Hom

5 A 8 a   48 Point Col. 6

IMPROVED PRODUC
Durable Antique Type

20 A 80 a   18 Point Col. 6   15 lbs.

SHIPMENT OF EXPORT ORDERS
Having had a varied and extensive experience, exceeding a century, of the Foreign and Colonial Trade we

40 A 160 a   11 Point Col. 6

IMPORTANT HINTS ON SHIPP
Goods intended for shipment must be more securely packed to ensure their transit than goods going from one p to another by railway. Dry goods she be packed in waterproof cases, and u

24 A 100 a   14 Point Col. 6   14 lbs.

UTILISING SPACE IN THE STOCKROOM
Lax methods of storing away material mean waste of space, and material unhandily piled requires too much time for its removal. The space may be wasted by lack of equipment or

40 A 180 a   9 Point Col. 6

EXPORTERS SHOULD INSURE THE GO
To arrive at the value for insurance the se should add to the original costs all subsequ charges payable in respect of them, the fre dock dues, and so on, so that the amount sta shall represent the actual value of the good the consignee's warehouse. Ignorance of w

12 A 45 a   30 Point Col. 6

RELIABLE REPRODUCTIONS FROM
Excellent progress has been made in th
art of Advertisement writing, and cleve

R. H. STEVENS & Co. Ltd.   **126**   SOUTHWARK ST., LONDON

ANTIQUE SERIES No. 3.

10 A   35 a   36 Point Col. 6   25 lbs.

ORDER PRINTING MATERIALS
From the Southwark Foundry and Every Description can be supplied

40 A 160 a   10 Point Col. 6   10 lbs.

MODERN METHODS IN COMMERCE
Probably one of the most striking things about the world of commerce is its rapid progress from cumbersome methods to its present efficient state. Business has been transformed from inaccurate guessing to almost an exact science. The revolution

33 A 125 a   12 Point Col. 6   13 lbs.

BUSINESS GROWTH AND TRANSPORT
Not so many years ago business of every kind was circumscribed by the lack of facilities of transportation. It was limited to the small territory lying immediately about the seat of manufacture, because there was no practical

36 A 150 a   7 Point Col. 6   6 lbs.

SELLING DIRECT FROM PRODUCER TO CONSUMER
A step beyond the organisation of the retail business and containing yet another factor of economy is the method of organisation in which the manufacturer sells directly to the consumer. The plans are not as new as the retailing combination, but their success has been great. Ordinarily the manufacturer sells to the jobber, the jobber in turn to wholesaler, the wholesaler to the retailer, and from him the product passes to the consumer. In each one of these deals there must also be the expense of the transfer from

45 A 190 a   8 Point Col. 6   8 lbs.

THE FORM OF ORGANISATION ADOPTED BY BIG COMPANIES
It was early recognised by business men that some form of organisation was necessary to the carrying on of a large enterprise. The reasons for this are evident. Private concerns depend upon the fortunes of one man corporations are self-perpetuating and stable. In the one-man business or partnership, personality plays a big part. Many of our big concerns have been built around the personality of one man. But it must not be understood that corporations eliminate personality. One man does not and cannot personally supervise all the work, yet through organisation

48 A 200 a   6 Point Col. 6   5 lbs.

THE EXERCISING OF CONTROL IN A LARGE ORGANISATION
From an analysis of the functions of a large business, the next step is an examination of its sources of authority, and here again we discover more than one definition or, in other words, a variety of methods under which control may be exercised. Every business has to have a fountain head or an ownership element which constitutes its primal authority and control. The form of this ownership is of no material importance whether it is vested in an individual in a partnership or in a body of stockholders. The essential fact is that this ownership constitutes the head of all business organisation, and subordinate to this authority are ranged the three departments of production, selling and accounting, by

60 A 250 a   5 Point Col. 6   4 lbs.

THE INDUCEMENTS TO INDIVIDUAL EFFORT IN LARGE BUSINESS CORPORATIONS
As the big institutions have increased in size, in this country, a perfect system has been demanded and, as usual, has been met. So perfect is the organisation of some of the large companies that the working ability not only of each plant, but of each individual employee, is known. A well-known leading manufacturer when asked what was the great factor in his institute that took the place of the incentive of ownership, said: "The deadly parallel." By this he meant that an exact report of each man is kept. There is an average below which no man's work can go, and as any man shows ability to advance, the position is always waiting for him. Each man knows that his work is more carefully watched than if an employer were with him all the time. He knows that his efforts are measured, that there is a dead line below which he cannot drop and possibilities of advance ahead if he shows ability above the average. Inducements for individual effort are even greater in a large

14 A 60 a   24 Point Col. 6   18 lbs.

THE SOUTHWARK TYPE FOUNDRY, LONDON
Merchants and Representatives who receive indents from abroad for Types and Printing Materials are invited to make known the wants of Correspondents and may depend upon complete satisfaction being a

R. H. STEVENS & Co. Ltd.   127   SOUTHWARK ST., LONDON

Vincent Figgins (1766–1844) was a British punch cutter and type founder who worked as an apprentice to Joseph Jackson from 1782 and set up his own foundry ten years later. His was one of the most important London type foundries of the nineteenth century. Figgins is credited with cutting the first slab serif or Egyptian typeface, which he released under the name 'Antique' in 1815 (pp114–15), and with the early commercial development of the sans serif (pp122–23).

When he retired in 1836, his sons Vincent II and James took over the management of the foundry, continuing to expand its catalogue with new designs and extensions to existing ranges. After the death of Vincent II in 1860, the business was continued by James and by his son, James II. For the last years of the firm's history, it was run by R. H. Stevens, another of Figgins's grandsons, whose 1929 catalogue is shown here. In 1933 the company merged with P. M. Shanks & Sons.

In the latter half of the nineteenth century, the Figgins foundry produced several refined versions of fashionable Clarendon types, retaining the robustness of Figgins's slab serif style, but with stronger contrast between thick and thin strokes. One such design is shown here. Figgins's Antique No. 3, originally cut in 1860, is an attractively condensed version in text and display sizes, with very thick serifs bracketed to stems with notably deep arcs.

Ty	**French Antique**
Ca	**Slab Serif**
Ke	**Egyptian, Reversed Contrast**
Te	**Letterpress**
Da	**1862**
De	**Unknown**
Fo	**Various**
Co	**UK**

Characteristics

Reversed contrast
Condensed proportions
Large, thick slab serifs

ABCDEQRSTZ
abcdefghijklm
opqrstuwxyz

Connections

Italian	1821
Figaro	1940
Manicotti	2010
Maelstrom	2012

Availability

Various digital versions of French Antique
and French Clarendon styles are available

Specimen

*Specimens of Wood Type by W. H.
Bonnewell & Co.* London, c1870
(310x250mm)

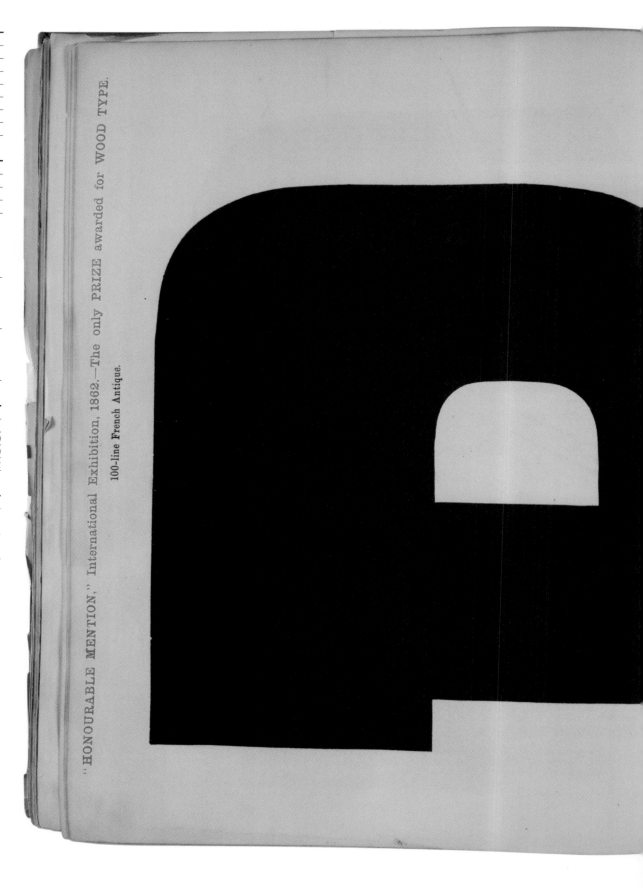

"HONOURABLE MENTION," International Exhibition, 1862.—The only PRIZE awarded for WOOD TYPE.

100-line French Antique.

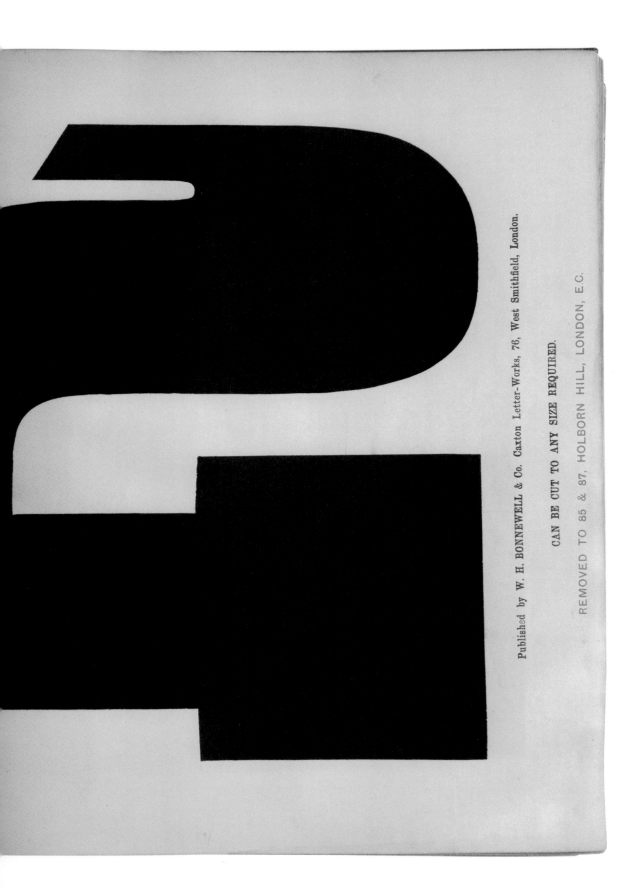

Published by W. H. Bonnewell & Co. Caxton Letter-Works, 76, West Smithfield, London.

CAN BE CUT TO ANY SIZE REQUIRED.

REMOVED TO 85 & 87, HOLBORN HILL, LONDON, E.C.

To satisfy the voracious appetite for exotic typefaces for use on posters and advertisements in Great Britain and the United States during the nineteenth century, many existing designs were subjected to radical modifications by foundries and wood-type manufacturers. Among the most effective and attractive of these were the French Antique and French Clarendon type styles that originated during the 1860s.

These designs were cross-breeds between the letters first seen in Caslon & Catherwood's specimen of Italian in 1821 (pp118–19) and two closely related slab serif styles, Egyptian (pp120–21) and Clarendon (pp132–33). As in the Italian, the axis of contrast was inverted in these new types so that the traditionally thick vertical strokes of the roman character became thin and the thinner horizontal strokes became thick. As a consequence, serifs became a dominant design feature, often assuming massive proportions as blocks either bracketed or bolted to the tops and bottoms of stems. These sometimes occupied more than half the overall height of characters, which were often also greatly condensed in order to emphasize the effect.

The Connecticut wood-type manufacturer William Page first showed a French Clarendon in 1865 and the style was rapidly copied and distributed by other wood-type producers throughout the United States. French Antiques and French Clarendons became dominant display types after the mid-1860s with an extensive range of variant styles, although they would finally fade from fashion at the end of the century as tastes turned towards less eccentric forms.

Readily familiar as the alphabets seen on circus posters and on 'wanted' notices in western movies, these typefaces have become widely regarded today as visual signifiers of the Wild West frontier in the nineteenth century.

Ty	**Latin**
Ca	**Serif**
Ke	**Wedge, Glyphic**
Te	**Letterpress**
Da	**c1870**
De	**Unknown**
Fo	**Stephenson, Blake & Co.**
Co	**UK**

Characteristics

Sharp, wedge-shaped serifs
Consistent bold weight across all widths
A Top serif
A H V-shaped crossbar in narrow variants
C c e t Bulging, hooked tail
V v W w Foot serifs
f r Hooked arch
f t Narrow
j y Hooked tail

ACMRW abcdefghij koprstuvy

Connections

Chisel	1939
Saracen	1992
Latino	2000
Infini	2015

Availability

Latin is widely available

Specimen

Specimen of Printing Types, etc.
Stephenson, Blake & Co., Sheffield, 1902
(242x155mm)

CANON BOLD LATIN.

MARINE Romans

TWO LINES GREAT PRIMER BOLD LATIN.

NORTHERN Monument

TWO LINES ENGLISH BOLD LATIN.

HEMINGSTONE Remunerator

DOUBLE PICA BOLD LATIN.

MERIONETHSHIRE £1234567890 Eastern Merchant

STEPHENSON, BLAKE & Co.

GREAT PRIMER BOLD LATIN.

Bournemouth Residence
EDINBURGH MANSIONS
Roman Ornaments

PICA BOLD LATIN.

ELEGANT HOUSEHOLD FURNITURE
Prominent American Senators
Temperance Demonstration in 1898.

LONG PRIMER BOLD LATIN.

BRIGHTON FURNITURE COMPANIES
Numerous Specimens from Amsterdam Museum
NORTHAMPTON SANATORIUMS

BREVIER BOLD LATIN.

Rotherham Amateur Dramatic Society
MAGNIFICENT METROPOLITAN ENTERTAINMENT
Donations and Subscriptions amount to £860.

NONPAREIL BOLD LATIN.

PENINSULAR AND ORIENTAL STEAMSHIP COMPANY
Forthcoming Conference of 2380 French and American Merchants
MILITARY TOURNAMENT AT PORTSMOUTH

PEARL BOLD LATIN.

Mercantile Transactions with Foreign Countries in the Eighteenth Century
PROSPECTUSES OF MANCHESTER AND DISTRICT THEATRE COMPANIES
Metropolitan Museum of Continental Specimens opened 1897.

STEPHENSON, BLAKE & Co.

During the nineteenth century, meteoric growth in the mass production of consumer goods led to a proportionate increase in the demand for publicity material. To fuel the flood of posters, handbills and advertisements that followed, type founders raced to supply new, attention-grabbing typefaces. Released from the traditional confines of both the book and the pen, designers of type were free to experiment with a wide range of ideas, from the most short-lived, ornate novelties to such enduring inventions as the first sans serif, slab serif and ultrabold serif typefaces. Their

explorations signalled the beginnings of the relationship between design and industry that endures today.

The Latin typefaces of the Stephenson, Blake & Co. foundry, originally published in the early 1870s, represent two different contemporary innovations. First, the Latin family is differentiated not by changes in weight – it is consistently bold – but by changes in width, from a tall Condensed to an expansive Wide, giving it the flexibility to fit a range of possible spaces while maintaining the same characteristics. Second, Latin is distinguished by its sharp,

wedge-shaped serifs, which emulate letters carved in stone, wood or metal as opposed to handwriting. Latin characters show the charming inconsistencies of a form that had no prescribed standard. To bear the weight of the large triangular serifs, strokes are necessarily thick, with a minimum contrast and a vertical axis to curved strokes.

The style was later identified with its own classification: Latin or Glyphic. Although it was never as widely used nor as influential as some other nineteenth-century forms, it remains a sharp, eye-catching design.

FIVE LINES BOLD LATIN CONDENSED.

MITRES
Roman

FOUR LINES BOLD LATIN CONDENSED.

HEROINE
Bondmen

CANON BOLD LATIN CONDENSED.

MERIONETH
£423890
Nomination

STEPHENSON, BLAKE & Co.

TWO LINES GREAT PRIMER BOLD LATIN CONDENSED.

HARMONIUMS
Merchantmen

TWO LINES ENGLISH BOLD LATIN CONDENSED.

MEDICAL REGISTER
American Company

DOUBLE PICA BOLD LATIN CONDENSED.

EDINBURGH MERCHANT
Monuments in Hindustan

GREAT PRIMER BOLD LATIN CONDENSED.

EMINENT DRAMATIC AUTHORS
Erection of Museums in 1898

PICA BOLD LATIN CONDENSED.

POPULAR LECTURE ON ENGLISH HISTORY
Manufactures from Germany and France

LONG PRIMER BOLD LATIN CONDENSED.

ESTABLISHMENTS IN DORCHESTER AND BRIGHTON
Detailed Estimate of Household Furniture, £3620.

BREVIER BOLD LATIN CONDENSED.

PRONOUNCING DICTIONARIES OF THE EUROPEAN LANGUAGES
Elementary Treatise on Landscape Gardening by Robinson

NONPAREIL BOLD LATIN CONDENSED.

LITHOGRAPHS OF COUNTRY AND SUBURBAN RESIDENCES NEAR BRADFORD
Recommendations from Competent European Authorities during 1900.

STEPHENSON, BLAKE & Co.

Ty	**Royal Gothic**
Ca	**Sans Serif**
Ke	**Grotesque**
Te	**Letterpress**
Da	**c1870**
De	**Unknown**
Fo	**Patent Type-Founding Company**
Co	**UK**

Characteristics

Irregular widths

Mixture of round and square forms

C O S Rounded

G Has spur

L S T Wide

g Square, open tail

t Square, tall ascender

AEGMRS
abcdeghi
koprstu

Connections

Thorowgood's Grotesque	1832
Folio	1957
Compacta	1963
Impact	1965

Availability

Not available

Specimen

Specimens of Types by P. M. Shanks & Sons. London, c1910 (242x155mm)

ROYAL GOTHIC.

170 a, 90 A   6 POINT.   6 lbs.

MANCHESTER AMATEUR HORTICULTURAL SOCIETY
The Exhibition Committee herewith announce Fourteen Competitions open
123   to Amateur and Professional Gardeners next Monday   480

120 a, 70 A   8 POINT.   8 lbs.

LARGE AMERICAN STEAMBOAT COMPANIES
Special Turbine Steamers for International Exhibition
4150   Handsome Accommodation Provided   5368

110 a, 56 A   10 POINT.   10 lbs.

METROPOLITAN BANKING ASSOCIATION
Having many Branches established throughout
42   England and several correspondents   80

85 a, 45 A   12 POINT.   12 lbs.

CONTINENTAL INTELLIGENCE
Latest Descriptive Telegrams Received
8970   Ministerial Movement   4635

75 a, 30 A   18 POINT.   18 lbs.

COMBINED INDUSTRIES
Great International Exhibition
12 Continental Markets 19

54 a, 21 A   24 POINT, No. 1.   20 lbs.

MENTON OINTMENT
Remarkable Experiments
73 Graphic Details 89

P. M. SHANKS & SONS, LTD., LONDON.
90

ROYAL GOTHIC.

60 a, 24 A   24 POINT, No. 2.   24 lbs.

SPECIAL NOTICE
Manchester Meeting

50 a, 18 A   30 POINT.   30 lbs.

CIRCULATION
Morning Standard

40 a, 15 A   36 POINT.   36 lbs.

HAMPSHIRE
Merton Council

30 a, 15 A   48 POINT.   48 lbs.

DESIGNER
Grand Home

30 a, 12 A   60 POINT.   60 lbs.

FINE Hand

P. M. SHANKS, & SONS LTD. LONDON.
91

The Patent Type-Founding Company was established in London by John Huffam King in 1855. It was sold two years later and traded as P. M. Shanks from 1881 until its merger with the Figgins foundry in 1933 to form Stevens, Shanks & Sons.

The Patent foundry's Royal Gothic typeface was cut and cast in around 1870. It is an extrabold sans serif with a relatively strong stroke contrast, providing considerable variation in colour. Showing its heritage in the English grotesques from the early part of the nineteenth century, Royal Gothic is notable for the irregular widths of many characters, such as the very wide S, T and L, and for its equally erratic mixture of curved and square forms. The rounded C, O and S, in particular, look out of place in an otherwise very rectilinear alphabet. Nevertheless, its predominant squareness gives Royal Gothic a distinctively tight fit and a dense, blocky impression that can be seen as a forerunner to later imposing display types such as Folio Bold (pp344–45) and Compacta (pp366–67).

A few years after the Patent foundry release, Royal Gothic made its first appearance in the United States, published in a Marder, Luse & Co. catalogue in 1887, followed shortly afterwards in various other founders' specimens, where it often appeared under the name of London Gothic and in a bold italic variant entitled Charter Oak.

143

Ronaldson Old Style

Ty	**Ronaldson Old Style**
Ca	**Serif**
Ke	**Old Style**
Te	**Letterpress**
Da	**1884**
De	**Alexander Kay**
Fo	**MacKellar, Smiths & Jordan**
Co	**USA**

Characteristics

Vertical stress

Thin strokes throughout

Most capitals have uniform width

C E F G L S Z Bracketed, angled serifs

E S Wide

M W Narrow

T Protruding top serifs

a Rounded bowl

e Open eye

g Double-storeyed, angled lower bowl

ACEMT
abcdefghij
orstuya*efg*

Connections

Phemister's Old Style	c1858
Binny Old Style	1863
Bookman Oldstyle	1901
ITC Tiffany	1974

Availability

Ronaldson Regular is a digital revival
available from Canada Type and resellers

Specimen

*New and Original Series of Old Style
Types*. MacKellar, Smiths & Jordan Co.,
Philadelphia, c1885 (240x155mm)

SMALL PICA OLD STYLE, No. 4.   PATENTED.

JAMES RONALDSON, the son of William Ronaldson, was born in 1768, at Gorgie, near Edinburgh, and died in Philadelphia in 1842. In 1794 he came to Philadelphia, aboard the sailing-vessel Providence. Shortly after his arrival he renewed his intimacy with Archibald Binny, with whom he was on friendly terms when in Scotland. For a year or two after his arrival in this country, Ronaldson carried on a biscuit bakery. His establishment was destroyed by fire in 1796, so that he found himself out of an occupation. It is related that about this time he encountered Binny in an ale-house; their acquaintance ripened into a friendly intimacy, and they shortly learned each other's views and prospects. The natural result was a copartnership between them, beginning Nov. 1, 1796, establishing the first permanent type-foundry in the United States. Ronaldson, who furnished the greater portion of the capital, assumed control of the financial department of the business. Binny, who was a practical type-founder, and had carried on the business in Edinburgh, contributed his tools, stock of metal, and types, and superintended the manufacturing department. The *connection proved mutually advantageous, and a prosperous business was the result. American printers, who had hitherto relied upon British founders for their supply*

ABCDEFGHIJKLMNOPQRSTUVWXYZ

1234567890

I WALK'D alone upon the Battery,
And look'd upon the waters as they roll'd—
A crystal sheet, with many a crumpled fold—
Up through the Narrows from the distant sea.
Vessels in multitude lay safe in port;
And some were outward bound with flowing sails,
And others, stain'd and batter'd by the gales,
Yet full of treasure, came to pay their court
To the proud island city by the sea:
While shell-like skiffs were skurrying everywhere,
Skimming like sea-birds most capriciously,
As if now on water,—then as if in air.

The MacKellar, Smiths & Jordan Co.   *Sansom Street, Philadelphia.*

PICA OLD STYLE, No. 4.   PATENTED.

JAMES RONALDSON, the son of William Ronaldson, was born in 1768, at Gorgie, near Edinburgh, and died in Philadelphia in 1842. In 1794 he arrived at Philadelphia in the sailing-vessel Providence. Shortly after his arrival he renewed his acquaintance with Archibald Binny, whom he had formerly known when living in Scotland. For a year or two after his arrival in this country Ronaldson carried on a biscuit bakery. His establishment was destroyed by fire in 1796; by this disaster he found himself out of an occupation. It is related that about this time he encountered Binny in an ale-house; their acquaintance ripened into a friendly intimacy, and they soon learned each other's views and prospects. The natural result was a copartnership was formed by them, beginning Nov. 1, 1796, establishing the first permanent type-foundry in the United States. Ronaldson furnished the greater part of the capital, and assumed control of the financial branch of the *business. Binny, who was a practical type-founder, and had carried on the business in Edinburgh, contributed his tools, stock of metal, and types, and took*

ABCDEFGHIJKLMNOPQRSTUVWXYZ

1234567890

TWICE I received a wholesome castigation
For stealing to the Battery to play
Without parental leave and approbation;
I'll not forget it to my latest day.
I told a rather hesitating story,
Not quite in keeping with my course in youth;
It may have been a crooked allegory,
And did not run in straight lines with the truth.
I bless the rod, and bless the hand that wielded,
Although it made my youthful shoulders tickle.

The MacKellar, Smiths & Jordan Co.   *Sansom Street, Philadelphia.*

In the mid-nineteenth century, a renewed interest in the convivial typefaces of the Renaissance era, initially used in setting historical publications, led to the revival of the old-style model updated to suit contemporary tastes. Following Miller & Richard's old style of around 1858 (pp134–35), several new interpretations appeared. One of these – Ronaldson Old Style, cut for MacKellar, Smiths & Jordan by Alexander Kay (1827–1905) in 1884 – became the bestselling American text typeface for almost 40 years. Kay was a Scottish-born punch cutter, known for his expert work on behalf of several English foundries, who had emigrated to the United States in 1854.

Ronaldson Old Style has a pallid overall appearance, with consistently thin strokes conforming to nineteenth-century typographic fashions. Like a modern face its stress is vertical, although its colour has the evenness of the old style. Its most evident characteristic is the use of heavy, angled serifs bracketed to most letters. These are particularly prominent on the eccentric T, where they protrude from the top bar like wings.

Ronaldson Old Style had become very popular by the turn of the twentieth century, particularly in the American book trade, and it was promptly copied by various other foundries. The upright roman was offered with an inclined version for use as an italic that was not well received by printers. As a result the roman was often paired awkwardly with non-matching italics from other typefaces. It was not until the 1920s that old-style designs were matched effectively with italics modelled on Renaissance chancery scripts (pp32–33).

Although the nineteenth-century old styles had a significant influence on the typographic innovations of the 1920s and 1930s, Ronaldson survived only in copies made for machine composition under various names by Monotype, Linotype and several other foundries. It was digitally recut for the first time in 2008 by Canada Type in the OpenType format, their revival offering extensive typographic features such as alternates, ligatures, small capitals and a range of variant numeral sets.

Ty	**Blackfriars Roman**
Ca	**Serif**
Ke	**Old Style, Reversed Contrast**
Te	**Letterpress**
Da	**c1890**
De	**Unknown**
Fo	**Blackfriars Type Foundry**
Co	**UK**

Characteristics

A	Serif at apex
G J	Spur
R	Concave, curved tail
U	Spurs
V v W w	Foot serifs
e	Angled cross-stroke
y	Hooked tail

AGRUW
abcdefghij
koprstuvy

Connections

Italian	1821
French Clarendon	c1860
French Antique	1865
Adobe Wood Type 1	1990

Availability

Drury Lane NF is a digital revival available from Nick's Fonts and resellers

Specimen

Catalogue Showing Type Faces, Borders & Brass Rules. Blackfriars Type Foundry, London, 1925 (290x225mm)

BLACKFRIARS ROMAN SERIES.

9 A 18 a — 48 POINT — About 24 lbs.

GUNS AND GAME
Britain's Wild Geese

10 A 26 a — 36 POINT — About 20 lbs.

SPECIMEN PRODUCED
Finest During Recent Years

18 A 44 a — 24 POINT — About 16¾ lbs.

GOOSE SHOOTING COMMENCES
Gatherings Encountered Daily 123456

24 A 60 a — 18 POINT — About 12⅝ lbs.

ON THE EAST COAST of England gatherings of geese being encountered

56 A 140 a — 9½ POINT — About 8 lbs.

ON SEVERAL OCCASIONS A SOLITARY goose, or a little party of geese, having much darker plumage than greylags, and seemingly somewhat darker than pinkfeet, have been seen following different kinds of food on portions of

44 A 114 a — 12 POINT — About 10½ lbs.

SIX DIFFERENT VARIETIES OF wild geese are more or less familiar to wildfowlers in this country and it is remarkable to what extent the pursuit

60 A 150 a — 8 POINT — About 6 lbs.

REFERRING TO THE FEEDING HABITS OF British wild geese is a reminder that the various species reveal much diversity of taste in the selection of food, and the careful study of this fact has often enough led to much success in goose shooting. For example, the experienced wildfowler is tolerably well assured that he

52 A 132 a — 10 POINT — About 8 lbs.

DURING A NUMBER OF SEASONS THE only geese to be shot were of the pink-footed variety. Next, on some marshes close inland, along the East Coast, casual bean geese were secured by way of a change. After that brent

78 A 196 a — 6 POINT — About 4½ lbs.

THE WILDFOWLER IN GREAT BRITAIN MUST LAY ASIDE guns and outfit on March 1st, as the shooting season ends on that day, but for keen sportsmen the close season is by no means a dull period. Fortified with further experiences in the shooting of geese, ducks, and plover, a number of people will be anxious to extend their armament in one or other direction so as to make fuller use of the opportunities coming their way. Thus, within a brief while they will interview their chosen gunmaker, knowing that to ensure fulfilment of their needs the

For Durability, the Ⓑ︎Ⓣ︎Ⓕ︎ Products are Unrivalled

125

BLACKFRIARS ITALIC SERIES.

10 A 20 a   48 POINT   About 24 lbs.

IMPERSONATION
Specialism in Acting

12 A 26 a   36 POINT   About 20½ lbs.

HISTORIC CHARACTERS
Versatility Simply Amazing

18 A 48 a   24 POINT   About 16 lbs.

SHAKESPEAREAN MASTERPIECES
Distinguished Actor Delighted Audience

24 A 60 a   18 POINT   About 12 lbs.

THE STAGE HISTORY of popular modern actors proves that temperament

56 A 140 a   9½ POINT   About 8 lbs.

SPECIALISM HAS BECOME MORE RIGID and stabilised in its scope. Looking back at stage history, under the different conditions from our time, we find that the leading actors had a wider range of characters. Burbage apparently created

46 A 118 a   12 POINT   About 10½ lbs.

UNDER MODERN CONDITIONS OF acting every player is now more or less restricted in his range of parts, if the artist is to be suitable to the character

66 A 160 a   8 POINT   About 6½ lbs.

THE ACTOR, BEFORE HE SPECIALISES, WOULD do well to serve an apprenticeship in a variety of parts. By playing a number of different parts at the beginning of his career the actor is enabled to find his forte. But it has to be said that nowadays, with the passing of the stock system, there are few opportunities for actors and actresses to be

54 A 136 a   10 POINT   About 8 lbs.

WITH REFERENCE TO THE OLDEN DAYS it may be averred by the modern that the old stock company acting was made up of specialism Each actor had his particular line of business, juvenile, heavy man, walking gentleman 12345

78 A 190 a   6 POINT   About 4½ lbs.

ANOTHER ADVERSE FACT OF SPECIALISM IS THAT IT OFTEN prevents a player from exploiting the full power of his talent. If Mr. Henry Ainley, for example, had not broken away from his juvenile line his histrionic position would have been considerably lowered. Moreover, if a player gets a name for a particular kind of part he has to wait for an engagement till that special part comes along. But under the present system of the stage we are confronted with the fact that specialism is a

For Borders & Brass Rules, see end of Catalogue

As the printing industry rapidly expanded to meet commercial demands in the nineteenth century, manual typecasting processes proved too slow. To improve matters, a number of inventors worked on the development of automated production processes. One successful solution was the Rotary Typecasting Machine, a device that could cast 1,000 types a minute, invented by Frederick Wicks (1840–1910), a former newspaper proprietor. In 1899 Wicks entered into a contract with the *Times* newspaper to supply any required daily quantity of brand-new type, eliminating the labour-intensive system of redistributing used type for resetting by hand.

The Wicks Rotary Typecasting Company produced a range of typefaces for their machines, most of them copies of commonly used foundry types, but Blackfriars Roman was an original design. It was named after the London street where the business was located.

Blackfriars Roman is an eccentric typeface, characterized by apparent imbalances resulting from the use of horizontal strokes that are thicker than vertical strokes, in a similar manner to the French Antique style (pp138–39). This impression is emphasized by the excessive weight of the serifs and the addition of horizontals in locations such as the apex of the A, the foot of the W and the small spurs on characters such as G and U. As in Caslon's extraordinary Italian (pp118–19), stroke contrast is reversed in Blackfriars Roman, although the effect is far less jarring than it is in the earlier type. Despite all of its oddities, Blackfriars is remarkably coherent as a design. This is largely accountable to serif formations that follow deeply angled curves, providing relatively smooth transitions between different strokes.

By 1909 Wicks casters had been superseded by faster machines that were capable of simultaneous typecasting and composition, and the business was taken over. Still casting type, the new company was called the Blackfriars Type Foundry. Their first catalogue, produced in 1908, presented all of the Wicks typefaces and several new designs. The business closed in 1931 and its matrices were eventually bought by the Stephenson, Blake foundry.

Ty	**Breite Grotesk**
Ca	**Sans Serif**
Ke	**Grotesque**
Te	**Letterpress**
Da	**1890**
De	**Unknown**
Fo	**J. G. Schelter & Giesecke**
Co	**Germany**

Characteristics

	Capitals to ascender height
	Most capitals have uniform width
A	Low crossbar
B E F P R S	Wide
C c e	Angled terminals
G	Has spur
M	Narrow
R	Curved leg
S s	Flat terminals
a	Double-storeyed, curve at foot
f	Narrow, terminals flush at right
g	Double-storeyed
i j	Square dots
t	Narrow, angled top terminal

AGMRS
abcdeghi
kmoprstu

Connections

Akzidenz-Grotesk	c1898
Monotype Grotesque	c1926
FF Bau	2002
Dada Grotesk	2007

Availability

FF Bau is a digital revival available from FontFont and resellers

Specimen

Typographische Mitteilungen von J. G. Schelter & Giesecke. Schriftgiesserei J. G. Schelter & Giesecke, Leipzig, 1897 (210x145mm)

J. G. SCHELTER & GIESECKE IN LEIPZIG.

BREITE MAGERE GROTESK.   Geschützt.

No. 1303. Tertia (16 P.).† 20 a 8 A. 2,7 kg.

Eschbachers neuere Erzählungen
ROMANZEITUNG

No. 1304. Text (20 P.).† 15 a 6 A. 3 kg.

Blüten Alpenveilchen Nelke
SCHNEEGLOCKEN

No. 1305. 2 Cicero (24 P.).† 12 a 5 A. 3,4 kg.

ROSE Märchen REBE

No. 1306. Doppelmittel (28 P.).† 10 a 4 A. 3,9 kg.

Deutsche Miscellen

No. 1307. 3 Cicero (36 P.).† 8 a 4 A. 4,5 kg.

Aus neuer Zeit

No. 1308. 4 Cicero (48 P.).† 6 a 3 A. 6 kg.

Heilsarmee

No. 1309. 5 Cicero (60 P.).† 4 a 2 A. 8 kg.

Germane

67 b

J. G. SCHELTER & GIESECKE IN LEIPZIG.

GROTESK MIT GEMEINEN.

No. 1135. Petit (8 P.). 53 a 21 A. 1,5 kg.

Reglement für die AUSBILDUNG und PRÜFUNG für den Staatsdienst

No. 1136. Korpus (10 P.). 41 a 17 A. 2 kg.

METHODE zu einer dauerhaften Konservirung der FARBEN

No. 1137. Cicero (12 P.). 34 a 14 A. 2,3 kg.

Deutsche Klassiker ZEITSCHRIFT Fremdwörterbücher

No. 1138. Mittel (14 P.). 30 a 12 A. 2,5 kg.

SAMMLUNG volkswirtschaftlicher SCHRIFTEN

No. 1139. Tertia (16 P.). 20 a 8 A. 2,8 kg.

Grundsätze STUDIE Denkspruch

No. 1140. Text (20 P.). 15 a 6 A. 3 kg.

BIBEL Kirchenlieder KREUZ

No. 1141. 2 Cicero (24 P.). 12 a 5 A. 3,7 kg.

Handel POST Verkehr

No. 1142. Doppelmittel (28 P.). 10 a 4 A. 4,7 kg.

SÜD Central OST

No. 1143. Kanon (36 P.). 8 a 4 A. 6,7 kg.

Handzeichnen

No. 1144. Missal (66 P.). 4 a 2 A. 9,4 kg.

Relation

67

Immediately after the invention of electrotyping, a rapid chemical reproduction process used in printing from the mid-1800s, the copying of typefaces became widespread. This proliferation, compounded by a paucity of contemporary documentation and a lack of historical research, has meant that the history of the origins and early development of the sans serif remains a matter of speculation.

However, there is strong evidence that the Leipzig type foundry J. G. Schelter & Giesecke was a significant contributor to the advancement of the form. In 1890, their Breite Grotesk was presented for the first time in a type specimen along with several other sans serifs. In the maelstrom of similar unidentified typefaces available at the time, its distinctive appearance is the result of a number of new features that do not appear to have been copied from other typefaces. Although Schelter & Giesecke gave no description of Breite Grotesk in their 1890 specimen, contemporary advertisements published by the foundry demonstrate that they intended the style to be used for creating emphasis in contrast with other types in advertising and jobbing work.

The basic proportions of Breite Grotesk are similar to those of a slightly earlier Schelter & Giesecke sans serif named Breite Etienne. It also demonstrates a number of inventive features that are found in Akzidenz-Grotesk (pp152–53), which it predates by several years. Breite Grotesk's capitals are of uniform width, departing completely from the varied proportions of the old-style Renaissance roman. Capitals that were traditionally narrow, such as B, E, R and S, were widened, and conventionally wide characters, such as M, O and W, were condensed so that widths were balanced throughout. The oval counterform resulting from the compression of the O is also seen in many lower case characters, such as b, d, p and q, giving the bowls of these letters smooth transitions of curves to stems. Lower case ascenders and capitals have the same height, making the latter appear somewhat dominant.

Breite Grotesk's rationalized features were significant innovations that had far-reaching consequences for the direction of the sans serif in the twentieth century – a form that, in the digital era, has become the predominant typographic norm in almost all visual communications.

Ty	**The Golden Type**
Ca	**Serif**
Ke	**Old Style, Venetian**
Te	**Letterpress**
Da	**1890**
De	**William Morris**
Fo	**Kelmscott Press**
Co	**UK**

Characteristics

Capitals to ascender height
Almost monolinear
Thick strokes and slab serifs
E Wide central arm
G No spur
J Descends below baseline
M N Flat serifs at top of stems
Q Long tail below letter
R Concave, curved tail
b d h k l Angled serif at top of ascender
i j Angled serif at top of stem
y Straight tail

EGNQR abcdefghij koprstuy

Connections

Jenson	1470
Cloister Old Style	1913
Italia	1974
ITC Golden Type	1989

Availability

ITC Golden Type is available from Linotype and resellers. P22 Morris Golden is available from P22 and resellers.

Specimen

Sulkhan-Saba Orbeliani, *The Book of Wisdom and Lies*. Kelmscott Press, London, 1894 (210x145mm)

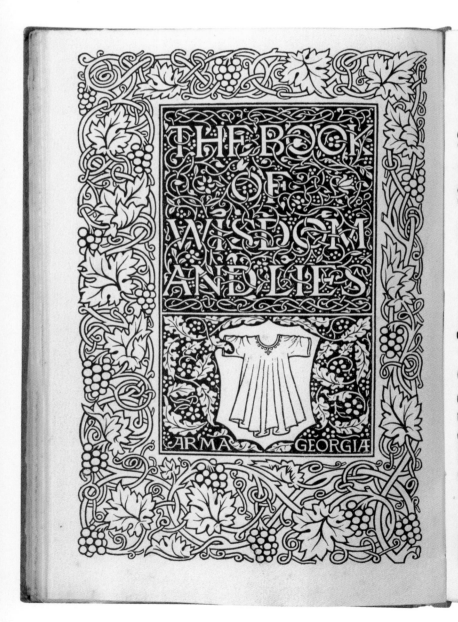

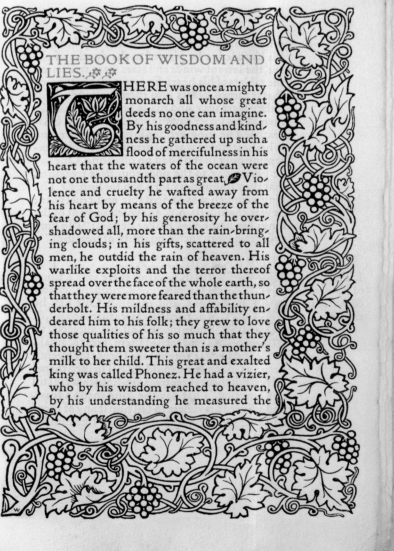

The most celebrated private press in the history of printing was founded in 1891 by William Morris (1834–96). He established the Kelmscott Press with the aim of using sixteenth-century printing techniques to publish books 'which would have a definite claim to beauty, while they should be easy to read and should not dazzle the eye'.

Morris was internationally renowned for his furniture, stained glass, wallpaper and textile designs, for his literary works and for his revolutionary socialist ideals. His work was underpinned by a romantic view of past culture as an amorphous field stretching back to the Middle Ages, when art and manufacture were thought

to be inseparable. In seeking a model for the design of the first type to be used at the Kelmscott Press, Morris chose to imagine the typefaces of Nicolas Jenson (pp20–21), a type founder working in 1470s Italy, as the finest examples of medieval letterforms. Jenson was clearly a Renaissance man whose types derived from humanistic scripts. However, this historical inaccuracy was no obstacle to Morris in his search for the archetypal gothic form.

Morris initially traced over photographic enlargements of Jenson's letters supplied by Emery Walker and proceeded to draw his own characters, aiming to capture the

spirit of the originals rather than duplicate them. Punches were cut from these drawings by Edward Prince, who later worked for the Doves (pp156–57) and Ashendene presses (pp172–73). The typeface was cut in one size only, equivalent to 14 point, and named after *The Golden Legend,* the first book planned for publication by the Kelmscott Press.

The type is significantly heavier than Jenson's original roman, fulfilling the need for full-blooded letterforms that could stand up to the densely packed, opulent illustrations and borders in Kelmscott Press editions like *The Book of Wisdom and Lies* shown here. The Golden Type's

character contours are somewhat laboured, almost monolinear, with heavy cross-strokes and serifs. The influence of robust nineteenth-century industrial typefaces such as Clarendon (pp132–33) is also evident.

The extravagant style and technical accomplishment of the Kelmscott Press books caused a sensation when they were published, and had a major influence on the growth of the private-press movement in England. Although Morris declined to release the Golden Type for sale, type founders around the world were quick to copy it, many seeking to improve it to address contemporary requirements.

XXIV.
The caliph
of Bagdad
and the
poor Arab

LEON TOLD THE KING A TALE.

THE caliph of Bagdad went to hunt, &, while galloping along, lost sight of his lords; only one vizier followed him. Overcome by hunger, he saw in a desolate spot a black tent. They rode up to it, & saw an Arab with three kids, his whole wealth. They dismounted and asked for food. The Arab killed a kid, cooked it, brought it and set it before them. The caliph ate nothing but the marrow. The Arab asked the vizier: "Why has the caliph eaten nothing?" The vizier replied: "He never eats anything but the marrow." The Arab arose, went and slew the two remaining kids, made ready their marrow, and brought it to the caliph. The vizier said: "Does thy mighty majesty see what this humble, poor Arab is doing? I swear by thy head that the rich and the generous could not do the like! The rich man always keeps a thousandfold more than he gives away, but this man has sacrificed everything he had to feed thee." The caliph gave his staff to the Arab and said: "Come to me, no one will shut my door against thee; I shall reward thee." The caliph rode away that day, and next day the Arab took the staff and went to him, opened the door, and entered. The caliph stood praying, with his back to the door, and did not see the Arab. The latter asked: "What is the

48

caliph doing, alternately prostrating himself & standing up?" The servants said: "He is praying." It happened that the Arab not only was ignorant of the nature of prayer, but had not even heard God's name, so he asked: "What is he praying for?" They answered: "He is asking God for wealth." The Arab said: "Instead of begging from him, I shall ask for what I want from Him of whom he asks; He will give it to me." When he had said this he went away. The caliph saw neither his coming in nor going out. The Arab came to his tent, and began to do what he had seen the caliph doing, and said: "O Thou of whom the caliph begs for wealth, give to me also, for I am very poor!" He prayed with a fervent heart. After some days, he took his tent away and pitched it in another place. While he was digging out a hole for the hearth, he found a chamber full of gold and silver. The Arab shut it up again, took the staff, set forth, came to the caliph, and bowed before him. The caliph said to him: "Why didst thou not visit me before?" The Arab told him all that had happened: "I asked of Him of whom thou didst ask, and He gave me a vault full of gold and silver; now give me a clerk to make an inventory thereof, & command that the treasure be brought to thee." The caliph sent the clerk to write down everything. The vizier looked at him, and said: "A poor Arab had three kids; he killed them for thee.

e   49

H·BERTHOLD A·G

Halbfette Akzidenz-Grotesk

82631. 4/6 Punkt. Min. ca. 2 kg.

Unter den vielen neuen Ausgrabungen und Entdeckungen ist die der alten Stadt Ostia eine der bedeutendsten zu nennen. Die Besteigung sowie Erforschung des höchsten Berges der Erde, Mont Everest genannt, zählt heute zu den allerneuesten Unternehmungen unserer Forscher, konnte aber bisher nicht
PLASTISCHE KÜNSTE IM ALTEN UND NEUEN GRIECHENLAND

82632. 5/6 Punkt. Min. ca. 3 kg.

Im griechischen Altertum glaubte man allgemein, daß den Göttern Opferduft und Weihrauch wohlgefällig sei. Olympische Spiele, welche aus Griechenland stammen, zeigen die verschiedensten Wettkämpfe, insbesondere den Ringkampf, wobei jeder Gelegenheit hat, vollendete
KANT ALS BEOBACHTER DES MENSCHLICHEN LEBENS

82633. 6 Punkt. Min. ca. 4 kg.

Das Münchener Haus auf der Zugspitze wird jeden Sommer von mehreren tausend Personen besucht. Trotzdem das Bergkraxeln alle Jahre seine Opfer fordert, finden sich immer wieder Touristen, welche durch allzugroßen Wagemut Leben und Gesundheit
WANDERUNGEN DURCH DAS SCHWEIZER GEBIRGE

82634. 8 Punkt. Min. ca. 5 kg.

Edel sei der Mensch, hilfreich und gut! De Im Automobil von Mainz bis Königsberg ist bei weitem teurer als eine Eisenbahnfahrt zweiter Klasse für dieselbe Strecke, denn
12345 MODERNE WAGEN-TYPEN 67890

82635. 10 Punkt kl. Bild. Min. ca. 6 kg.

Bedarfsartikel für die verschiedensten Gewerbe bekommt man bestimmt am vorteilhaftesten in Spezial-Geschäften
ELEKTRISCHE STROM-LIEFERUNGEN

82636. 10 Punkt gr. Bild. Min. ca. 6 kg.

Fremdsprachliche Lehrbücher sind nur Hilfsmittel, denn unmittelbarer Verkehr lehrt besser und schneller
LANGENSCHEIDT'SCHE METHODE

82637. 12 Punkt. Min. ca. 6 kg.

Oft ist das Leben nur ein Traum Manchmal ist im menschlichen Leben der Zufall entscheidend
GRAPHISCHE KUNSTANSTALT

82638. 14 Punkt. Min. ca. 7 kg.

Die Sonderausstellung im Märkischen Museum
FRIEDRICH DER GROSSE

82639. 16 Punkt. Min. ca. 8 kg.

Arbeit ist des Bürgers Z Industriestadt Spandau
MASCHINEN-VERKAUF

82640. 20 Punkt. Min. ca. 10 kg.

Beachtenswert bei Dampfschiffahrten
RHEIN 12 EMS

82641. 24 Punkt. Min. ca. 10 kg.

Moderne Stiefel
FILZSCHUH

82642. 28 Punkt. Min. ca. 12 kg.

Radiumbäder
KUR-PARK

82643. 36 Punkt. Min. ca. 14 kg.

Elektrizität
FUNKEN

82644. 48 Punkt. Min. ca. 16 kg.

Neuheit
WERK

82645. 60 Punkt. Min. ca. 20 kg.

Saiten
HORN

N 180 a

Ty	**Akzidenz-Grotesk**
Ca	**Sans Serif**
Ke	**Grotesque**
Te	**Letterpress**
Da	**c1898**
De	**Unknown**
Fo	**Berthold**
Co	**Germany**

Characteristics

Capitals to ascender height
A Low crossbar
C c G S s e Angled terminals
G Has spur
M Narrow, square
Q Short, curved tail
R Straight, angled leg
a Double-storeyed, curve at foot
f j r t Vertical terminals
g Single-storeyed
i j Square dots
t Flat top-stroke, curve at foot
y Curved tail

AGMQR
abcefghij
koprstuy

Connections

Venus	1907
Edel-Grotesk	c1914
Helvetica	1957
Theinhardt	2009

Availability

Akzidenz-Grotesk is available from Berthold and resellers

Specimen

Type foundry specimens. H. Berthold AG, Leipzig, 1920s (297x210mm)

H·B·E·R·T·H·O·L·D A·G

Fette Akzidenz-Grotesk

82477a. 5/6 Punkt. Min. ca. 3 kg.

Unter unseren modernen Dramatikern war es keinem
so wie Ibsen gelungen, die Anerkennung seiner Werke
zu erleben und den Erfolg in Ruhe genießen zu können
KLEINES THEATER IN DER KÖNIGGRÄTZER STRASSE

82478. 6 Punkt. Min. ca. 4 kg.

Seit dem Zeitalter der Entdeckungen, da Amerika
durch Christoph Columbus gesichtet wurde, sind
schon mehr als vierhundert Jahre dahingegangen
FAHRTEN AUF DEM MITTELLÄNDISCHEN MEERE

82480. 8 Punkt. Min. ca. 5 kg.

Edel sei der Mensch, hilfreich und gut!
Interessantes aus dem Thüringer Wald
HEIMLICHE GESCHICHTEN VON MACK

82481. 10 Punkt kl. Bild. Min. ca. 6 kg.

Reizende Neuheiten in Blusen für
junge Mädchen zu billigen Preisen
KAUFHAUS ZUM GRÜNEN STERN

82482. 10 Punkt gr. Bild. Min. ca. 6 kg.

Obst ist eine gesunde und leicht
bekömmliche Speise für Kranke
345 FRUCHTKONSERVEN 789

82483. 12 Punkt. Min. ca. 6 kg.

Pianos liefern in allen Arten
und Preislagen schnellstens
GEBRÜDER WEIDENSTOCK

82484. 14 Punkt. Min. ca. 7 kg.

Chinesische Kreppseide
Japon und Taffet-Chiffon
HOCHFEINE ROBEN

82485. 16 Punkt. Min. ca. 8 kg.

Arbeit ist des Bürgers
Lederwaren-Industrie
KINDERSCHUHE

82486. 20 Punkt. Min. ca. 10 kg.

Soldauer Zeitung
Verlagsdruckerei
MARKUSHOF

82487. 24 Punkt. Min. ca. 10 kg.

Rund um Sofia
FERIENFAHRT

82488. 28 Punkt. Min. ca. 12 kg.

Mundschenk
WEIN-HAUS

82489. 36 Punkt. Min. ca. 14 kg.

Kinderball
GEORGIA

82490. 48 Punkt. Min. ca. 18 kg.

Rausch
NATUR

82491. 60 Punkt. Min. ca. 24 kg.

Stand
HERD

82492. 72 Punkt. Min. ca. 30 kg.

Buch
ZION

N 180 b

Akzidenz-Grotesk is a sans serif typeface originally released by the Berthold Type Foundry at the end of the nineteenth century. Free from the quirks of the fashionable display types of the era and structurally functional, it was the first sans serif to achieve widespread popularity and is considered the progenitor of today's grotesque typeface designs. However, it owes its existence more to marketing activities than to a type design initiative. Berthold promoted Akzidenz-Grotesk to the trade as a range of coordinated weights and styles, although in fact it initially consisted of a collection of individual typefaces that resembled one another more by coincidence than intention.

Between about 1893 and 1926 Berthold purchased 18 other foundries, most of which held similar stock. During this process they rationalized the various sans serif typefaces they acquired, renaming them as members of the Akzidenz-Grotesk family. Over time, as its range of weights and styles expanded, the integration of several well-proportioned sans serifs into the collection became the major factor that contributed to its subsequent success, although the provenance of most of these designs has not been documented.

Akzidenz-Grotesk has little variation in stroke weight. Its x-height is larger than most typefaces from the turn of the century, and ascenders and descenders are short, allowing economical use of space. Its extensive range and utilitarian qualities also allowed it to be set in bodies of text, a practice that was uncommon at that time, since the grotesque was generally regarded as a subordinate form for use only in commerce and display. This new implementation transformed the potential of the sans serif.

The success of Akzidenz-Grotesk created a new market for sans serif display typefaces and many competitive products were soon released, most notably the Bauer foundry's Venus (pp182–83) and ATF's News Gothic and Franklin Gothic (pp174–75). During the 1930s, Akzidenz fell from favour as designers embraced geometric sans serifs such as Futura, but it became widely used again during the 1950s, when the Swiss Style of typographic design called for plain, robust letters, and it inspired important new sans serif designs like Univers and Helvetica.

Contemporary digital versions of Akzidenz-Grotesk are the result of a 1950s Berthold project directed by Günter Gerhard Lange, in which the type family was enlarged and rationalized without compromising the equanimity of the original typeface.

1900-1

During the early years of the twentieth century, as industrialized cities in Europe and the United States continued to grow, increasing numbers of people began to feel disillusioned by existing forms of social organization, cultural production and traditional belief systems. After the horrors of World War I, this resistance to accepted norms consolidated into several avant-garde artistic, literary and philosophical movements that arose to challenge social institutions and the attitudes they represented.

These initiatives are now grouped conveniently under the banner of 'modernism', although they could not have been more diverse geographically, politically or conceptually, encompassing a variety of movements ranging from art nouveau to Dada and from art deco to Futurism. Although they may have been motivated by different forces, a shared objective of the members of these groups was the intention to divorce themselves from the history of Western art, design and literature in order to originate completely unprecedented forms. The work that was generated as a result completely rewrote the agenda for creative production in the twentieth century and had a major impact on the fields of commercial art, typography and printing.

The work of many progressive designers active in Europe after World War I had strong ideological foundations, particularly in Germany, Russia and Eastern Europe. Modernist communication design of the post-war period rejected long-standing traditions associated with ornamentation in favour of bold verbal and visual statements that were often underpinned by radical social and political agendas. Cutting-edge materials, technologies and production methods were exploited to celebrate the functional aesthetic of the built environment and of the machine.

Many typographic designers of the time began to explore the possibilities of geometric construction and the manipulation of positive and negative space. They used existing sans serif typefaces or created grid-based, modular, often single-case alphabets for use in their designs. Among many others Herbert Bayer's Universal, Jan Tschichold's Transito and Josef Albers's Kombinations-Schrift are examples of pioneering work that heavily influenced the commercial design arena, with Paul Renner's groundbreaking Futura creating an insatiable global trend for the use of geometric types on its release in 1927.

The typographic developments of the first half of the twentieth century took place against the backdrop of the rapid expansion of technologies for machine composition along with a corresponding decline in traditional type-founding activities. While the Linotype line-caster was the international industry standard in newspaper and magazine printing at the turn of the century, by 1907 the Monotype casting machine had become its serious rival, capable of setting type in a wide range of sizes, using an improved keyboard that copied the efficient layout of a typewriter.

The contribution made to typographic history by the casting-machine manufacturers was not solely in the impact of their technological advances, but also in their commissioning of many of the most widely used and enduring typefaces of the twentieth century. In the 1920s the Monotype Corporation established a comprehensive programme to research and reconstruct some of the greatest typefaces from most historical periods, while also publishing many new designs from leading contemporary typographers. This typographic renaissance had a major effect on the improvement of printing and publishing standards during the period.

Ty	**The Doves Type**
Ca	**Serif**
Ke	**Old Style, Venetian**
Te	**Letterpress**
Da	**1900**
De	**Emery Walker, Percy Tiffin and Edward Prince**
Fo	**The Doves Press**
Co	**UK**

Characteristics

Large capitals to ascender height	
Square, unbracketed serifs	
Wedge serifs on ascenders	
D H N S Wide	
J Descends below baseline	
M N Top serifs	
R Concave, curved right leg	
W Crossed centre-strokes	
a Double-storeyed, small bowl	
d p q Oblique bowls	
e Small eye, oblique bar	
f Wide arch	
i j Small offset dot	
j Short descender	
y Straight, serifless tail	
z Angled serifs	

ACJMRW
abcdefghij
koprstuy

Connections

Jenson	1470
The Golden Type	1890
Cloister Old Style	1913
Centaur	1914

Availability

A digital revival is available from Typespec and resellers

Specimen

Robert Browning, *Men and Women*. Doves Press, London, 1908 (235x165mm)

EVELYN
Hope

BEAUTIFUL EVELYN HOPE IS DEAD
  Sit and watch by her side an hour.
That is her bookshelf, this her bed;
  She plucked that piece of geranium-flower,
Beginning to die too, in the glass.
  Little has yet been changed, I think—
The shutters are shut, no light may pass
  Save two long rays thro' the hinge's chink.

Sixteen years old when she died!
  Perhaps she had scarcely heard my name—
It was not her time to love: beside,
  Her life had many a hope and aim,
Duties enough and little cares,
  And now was quiet, now astir—
Till God's hand beckoned unawares,
  And the sweet white brow is all of her.

Is it too late then, Evelyn Hope?
  What, your soul was pure and true,
The good stars met in your horoscope,
  Made you of spirit, fire and dew—
And just because I was thrice as old,
  And our paths in the world diverged so wide,
Each was nought to each, must I be told?
  We were fellow mortals, nought beside?

22

No, indeed! for God above
  Is great to grant, as mighty to make,
And creates the love to reward the love,—
  I claim you still, for my own love's sake!
Delayed it may be for more lives yet,
  Through worlds I shall traverse, not a few—
Much is to learn and much to forget
  Ere the time be come for taking you.

But the time will come,—at last it will,
  When, Evelyn Hope, what meant, I shall say,
In the lower earth, in the years long still,
  That body and soul so pure and gay?
Why your hair was amber, I shall divine,
  And your mouth of your own geranium's red—
And what you would do with me, in fine,
  In the new life come in the old one's stead.

I have lived, I shall say, so much since then,
  Given up myself so many times,
Gained me the gains of various men,
  Ransacked the ages, spoiled the climes;
Yet one thing, one, in my soul's full scope,
  Either I missed or itself missed me—
And I want and find you, Evelyn Hope!
  What is the issue? let us see!

Evelyn
Hope

23

Like the fifteenth-century original by Nicolas Jenson that inspired it (pp20–21), the Doves Type has been admired by many as one of the most beautiful in typographic history. Its story is also one of the most enduring. In 1893 Thomas James Cobden-Sanderson (1840–1922) established the Doves Bindery in Hammersmith, and in 1900 he founded the Doves Press in partnership with Emery Walker (1851–1933), an expert in printing and engraving who had previously worked with William Morris in the production of fine editions (pp150–51) at the nearby Kelmscott Press.

When Walker and Cobden-Sanderson set out to create an original typeface for their new venture, Walker hoped, he said, to achieve 'the closest copy I could make or get made of Nicolas Jenson's type'. He appointed the type designer Percy Tiffin from his own photo-engraving company to draw the letters, based on enlarged tracings of a 1492 edition of Leonardo Aretino's *Historiae Florentini populi*, with capitals from Nicolas Jenson's *Pliny* of 1476. The type was cut by Edward Prince in one size only, equivalent to 16 point, and cast by Miller & Richard. This was the only typeface the Doves Press used in the 40 publications they produced between 1900 and 1917, including their iconic edition of the King James Bible. The Doves Press books had a huge influence on the revival of private-press printing in the twentieth century. They were completely unadorned by decoration or illustration, the precisely printed type acting alone in the design of clear and legible pages with spacious margins. The only embellishments were elegant initials and flourishes added by master calligraphers like Edward Johnston and Graily Hewitt.

Cobden-Sanderson and Walker had fundamentally different aspirations for the Doves Press and over time their working relationship became strained. By 1908 the press was in dire financial difficulties and when the partnership was dissolved the following year a bitter dispute ensued. To prevent Walker from gaining access to the Doves Type, the only assets remaining in the business, Cobden-Sanderson secretly dumped all of the punches, matrices and type into the Thames at Hammersmith Bridge between 1913 and 1917 on hundreds of evening walks.

The story of the Doves Type remained a typographic legend for over a century until 2014, when British type designer Robert Green had the Thames at Hammersmith Bridge searched by a team of divers. The small quantity of sorts they recovered informed the design of Green's digital revival of the Doves Type, making it a highly accurate and very serviceable digital interpretation of the original.

Ty	**Eckmann-Schrift**
Ca	**Blackletter**
Ke	**N/A**
Te	**Letterpress**
Da	**1900**
De	**Otto Eckmann**
Fo	**Klingspor**
Co	**Germany**

Characteristics

Brushstroke construction
Mix of straight blackletter forms with flowing curves
Concave strokes
Unornamented undulating strokes
Japanese calligraphic impression

ABCRST
abcdefghij
koprstuvy

Connections

Auriol	1901
Behrens-Schrift	1902
Arnold Böcklin	1904
Fanfare	1927

Availability

Eckmann-Schrift is available from Linotype and resellers

Specimen

Schriften und Ornamente nach Entwürfen von O. Eckmann. Rudhard'sche Giesserei, Offenbach, c1903 (270x210mm)

 Eckmann — Gesetzlich geschützt!

1421 Nonpareille · 6 Punkte — Undurchschossen
Der Sinn für Wahrheit, Schönheit und Recht, obgleich er am Ende in jedem einigermaßen Gebildeten und in geordneten Gesellschaftszuständen lebenden bis zu einem gewissen Grade mit Notwendigkeit durch den Einfluß der Umgebung selbst erweckt wird, kann und muß doch geübt werden, um Kraft und Geltung zu erlangen. Wie anders überlegt und schließt der ans Denken gewöhnte, durch Wissenschaft erleuchtete Gelehrte, als der, der sich nur mit körperlichen Arbeiten beschäftigt. Wie ganz anders erglüht der vom lieben gewiegte und am Busen der Geschichte großgezogene Mann für Recht und Gerechtigkeit, als der einem noch unklaren innern Drang folgende Jüngling.

Durchschossen — Satz etwa 4 Kilo, das Kilo M. 9.50
An jede Generation stellt das Leben neue Anforderungen. Der Typus des modernen Deutschen hat seine schwachen Seiten auf dem Gebiet ästhetischer Bildung. Es fehlt ihm an äußerer Kultur und Festigkeit der Form, wie an einem innern Verhältnis zur bildenden Kunst. Nach künstlerischen Genüssen, die eine Erziehung des Auges und des Herzens voraussehen, hat er kein Bedürfnis. Er fühlt sich mit dem äußeren Auge und mit der Seele überhaupt nicht. Diesen Unzulänglichkeiten muß aus Gründen der Erhaltung unserer Nation und aus Rücksicht auf unsere Volkswirtschaft entgegengearbeitet werden.

1422 Petit · 8 Punkte — Undurchschossen
Wann hätten die Deutschen nicht mit wahrer Lust das Geschäft betrieben, ihre großen Männer durch Vergleichungen mit anderen zu verkleinern und sich somit der Freude zu berauben, daß so viel Edelbäume in Germaniens Wäldern gewachsen sind? Im Auslande ist man stolz genug, die nationalen Genies als den Stolz der Nation zu betrachten, in Deutschland sieht man vor allem, was ihnen an der vermeintlichen Vollkommenheit fehlt.

Durchschossen — Satz etwa 5 Kilo, das Kilo M. 8.20
Die Arbeit ist nicht mehr die schwere Bürde, unter der das Menschengeschlecht seufzt, sie ist der eigentliche und wesentliche Inhalt unseres Daseins. Diese Auffassung mußte sich dem Menschen aufdrängen, sobald ihm die Früchte seines Fleißes vor Augen standen, sobald die Arbeit ihm Quellen des Wohlbehagens erschloß, die ihm bis dahin unzugänglich waren.

1422a Borgis · 9 Punkte — Undurchschossen
Es kommt nicht so sehr darauf an, daß einem Kinde viel gelehrt, sondern daß der Wunsch zu lernen in ihm geweckt werde. Nur zu oft wird das Wissen in einer so langweiligen Form geboten, daß jeder Wunsch nach Belehrung davor erstarrt oder gänzlich vergeht. Gelingt es, die Liebe zum Lernen zu erwecken, so folgt das Lernen von selbst nach.

Durchschossen — Satz etwa 5 Kilo, das Kilo M. 7.90
Das Glück liegt nicht in den Dingen, sondern in der Art und Weise, wie sie zu unseren Augen, zu unseren Herzen stimmen; ein Ding ist dem einen viel wert, was ein anderer mit keinem Finger anrühren möchte, und mancher wird unglücklich, wo ein anderer sein Glück gefunden hätte.

1423 Korpus · 10 Punkte — Undurchschossen
Das beste bürgerliche Erbe ist die Kraft und die äußere Möglichkeit, Reichtum zu erwerben, nicht der feste Besitz. Jener höchste Stolz starker Geister, alles durch sich selbst geworden zu sein, ist ein echt bürgerlicher, im Gegensatz zu dem aristokratischen Stolz auf historischen Ruhm und ererbtes Gut. Riehl

Durchschossen — Satz etwa 6 Kilo, das Kilo M. 7.70
Jede menschliche Natur will ihre bestimmte Konsumtion von Kummer und Sorge haben, je nach der Konstitution, und bleiben die reellen aus, so muß die Phantasie welche schaffen, kann sie das aber nicht, dann grämt man sich aus Weltschmerz.

1424 Cicero · 12 Punkte — Satz etwa 6 Kilo, das Kilo M. 7.30
Die wahre Bildung besteht nicht in totem Wissen und leerem Gedächtniskram, sondern in lebendiger Entwickelung des Gemüts und der Urteilskraft des Verstandes.

1425 Mittel · 14 Punkte — Satz etwa 7 Kilo, das Kilo M. 7.—
Die Sucht, sich in großen Worten zu berauschen, stiftet keinen Nutzen, sie verhindert bloß an nützlichen Taten.

1426 Tertia · 16 Punkte — Satz etwa 8 Kilo, das Kilo M. 6.80
In Träumen steckt nicht nur Allmacht, sondern auch Ohnmacht.

1427 Text · 20 Punkte — Satz etwa 9 Kilo, das Kilo M. 6.60
Liebe ist Gleichklang der Seelen, oder sie ist nichts.

1427a 2 Cicero · 24 Punkte — Satz etwa 10 Kilo, das Kilo M. 6.50
James Watt, der Erfinder der Dampfmaschine

1428 Doppelmittel · 28 Punkte — Satz etwa 11 Kilo, das Kilo M. 6.30
Einzug JULIUS CAESARS in Rom

4

Eckmann

Gesetzlich geschützt !

1429 3 Cicero · 36 Punkte   Satz etwa 14 Kilo, das Kilo M. 6.—

Richard WAGNERS Parsifal

1430 4 Cicero · 48 Punkte   Satz etwa 20 Kilo, das Kilo M. 5.50

Bismarcks Memoiren

1431 5 Cicero · 60 Punkte   Ganzer Satz](12 a 3 A) etwa 23 Kilo, halber Satz (6 a 2 A) etwa 13 Kilo, das Kilo, M. 5.30

Genf PARIS Ems

1432 6 Cicero · 72 Punkte · Auf Hohlfuß   Ganzer Satz (12 a 3 A) etwa 25 Kilo, halber Satz (6 a 2 A) etwa 15 Kilo, das Kilo M. 5.30

Sang an Aegir

1507 7 Cicero · 84 Punkte · Auf Hohlfuß   Ganzer Satz (8 a 3 A) etwa 30 Kilo, halber Satz (4 a 2 A) etwa 17 Kilo, das Kilo M. 5.40

Dante Heine

1508 8 Cicero · 96 Punkte · Auf Hohlfuß   Ganzer Satz (8 a 3 A) etwa 35 Kilo, halber Satz (4 a 2 A) etwa 20 Kilo, das Kilo M. 5.30

Niederland

Rudhard'sche Gießerei in Offenbach · M

5

Jugendstil was an art and design movement that flourished in Germany in the mid-1890s and continued to the first decade of the twentieth century. A German expression of art nouveau, it was a reaction against established traditions in the arts. Jugendstil sought to harmonize constructed forms with the natural environment, inspired by flowers, vegetation, abstract linear curves and Oriental crafts.

One of the most influential and active figures in the Jugendstil movement was Otto Eckmann (1865–1902). After rejecting painting, Eckmann dedicated himself to the applied arts and worked as a commercial artist, book designer and teacher. In 1898 he produced some striking lettering for the cover of a play called *Johannes*, by Hermann Sudermann.

Carl Klingspor, head of the Rudhard'sche Foundry, was so impressed by Eckmann's cover and his title-page designs that he commissioned him to design a new display typeface. The result was Eckmann-Schrift. At a time when German designers were questioning the political, aesthetic and functional values of the indigenous Fraktur letterform (pp38–39) in relation to roman typefaces, Eckmann's Jugendstil design neatly merged the two competing styles while simultaneously proclaiming its independence from the constrictions of the past.

Suggesting the motion of a brush, the strokes of Eckmann-Schrift's letterforms alternate in an ebb and flow between taut medieval blackletter constructions and gently flowing natural curves that are concave in many strokes. Avoiding superfluous flourishes, the letters retain the simplicity of Textura (pp14–15), but are characterized by soft undulations that give the impression of the animated motion of both roman letterforms and Japanese calligraphy.

Eckmann-Schrift was rapidly adopted for a wide range of applications. The attitude it embodied had a strong influence on the modern sans serif typeface designs that superseded it in the early decades of the twentieth century. Unlike many other blackletter types, its warmly expressive letters have survived several generations of printing technology and it is still available today in digital form.

Ty	**Auriol**
Ca	**Serif**
Ke	**Old Style, Stencil**
Te	**Letterpress**
Da	**1901**
De	**George Auriol**
Fo	**Deberny & Peignot**
Co	**France**

Characteristics

Curving, brushlike strokes
Unconnected stencil structure
Oblique stress

AMQRS abcdefghij koprstuv

Connections

Grasset	1898
Arnold Böcklin	1904
Robur Noir	1909
Hobo	1910

Availability

Auriol is widely available

Specimen

Manuel français de typographie moderne.
François Thibaudeau, Paris, 1924
(225x155mm)

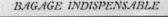

8   *BAGAGE INDISPENSABLE*

par le temps qui court, c'est au contraire l'imprimeur qui doit c[...]
après eux, aller les solliciter à domicile et par conséquent subi[...]
effets de la concurrence. ❦ Ici nous touchons à un problème par[...]
lier à notre temps, qui s'applique au fonctionnement de la gra[...]
industrie et que ne connurent point nos ancêtres : l'organisation[...]
travail, de la main-d'œuvre, et l'unification des prix en imprim[...]
La question de l'établissement des devis de travaux a provoqué d'[...]
reuses initiatives qui semblent devoir conduire à une solution effic[...]
❦ A ce tableau nous ajouterons la part prise par la publicité[...]
grandes firmes de fonderie pour initier le monde lettré aux essai[...]
modernisation des éléments du Livre, d'où il résulte que certains n[...]
d'artistes français, par exemple, sont devenus aussi caractéristi[...]
de forme typographique définie que le sont restées pour le passé[...]
créations des Jenson, des Garamond et des Didot, et que, po[...]
mise en œuvre de son matériel, l'imprimeur se trouve de plus en [...]
en présence de demandes formulées techniquement et de précis[...]
d'exécution, quand lui seul autrefois se reconnaissait le privilèg[...]
les fixer. Cela du reste pour nous amener logiquement à établir —[...]
ce qui nous concerne — que l'enseignement de la Typographie est s[...]
du domaine exclusif de la technique et de la main-d'œuvre d'ate[...]
pour conquérir de nouveaux milieux d'adaptation ; qu'il y a co[...]
quemment nécessité de créer un lien, une unification de prati[...]
entre ces éléments d'exécution à différents degrés, en tenant com[...]
des intérêts communs aux parties, qui peuvent se formuler de la fa[...]
suivante, savoir : *qu'il y a avantage pour l'imprimeur à recevoir des pr[...]*
rendus exécutables par une parfaite mise au point préalable ; autant que [...]
le client, des projets parlants, c'est-à-dire clairement exprimés, lui assure[...]
d'abord une exécution exacte de ce qu'il désire, puis lui feront réaliser l'éc[...]
mie de toute la série des recherches et des recommencements qui marq[...]
forcément cette période de tâtonnements quand on la pratique comme autr[...]
par épreuves successives. 🙢🙢🙢🙢🙢🙢🙢🙢🙢🙢🙢🙢🙢🙢

II
Notions de Typographie
& Vocabulaire technique.

L'ATELIER DE COMPOSITION.
½ Quand le stagiaire ou l'apprenti typographe pénètre dans l'atelier qui groupe le *matériel* dont il vient apprendre la manipulation, quel que soit l'emplacement affecté à cette division de l'*imprimerie*, la disposition logique du mobilier veut que son œil soit frappé tout d'abord par l'originale silhouette des *rangs*, accolés en dos-d'âne, sur lesquels se *montent* les *casses*. Appuyés aux murs sont les *rayons*, supportant casses et *casseaux*; puis son regard va de là au *lingotier*, au *casier aux interlignes*, à la *filetière*; enfin le *marbre* sur son *pied*, garni de tiroirs à *bardeaux*, d'un *porte-formes* en x, d'un tiroir à *coins*, à

George Auriol (1863–1938), born Jean-Georges Huyot, was a French commercial artist. He was known primarily as an illustrator, but was highly skilled in a wide range of media. He has been called the 'quintessential art nouveau designer', a master of the style characterized by its sensual curved lines and natural forms, which became fashionable in Europe in the late nineteenth century.

Auriol was an influential figure in Parisian avant-garde circles and was closely associated with many of the leading artists of the period, including Van Gogh, Toulouse-Lautrec, Erik Satie and Eugène Grasset, who designed his curvaceous Grasset typeface for Peignot & Sons in 1898. Two years later, Auriol was also invited by Georges Peignot to contribute to the foundry's growing catalogue of types in inventive new styles.

The result, Auriol, rapidly became one of the signature typefaces of the French art nouveau movement. Showing the influence of Japanese calligraphy, it is distinguished by its warm, organic contours, composed from brush-drawn, unconnected stencil strokes that are flowing and rationally structured at the same time.

Auriol achieved international popularity in the early twentieth century and was widely used as display type in books, posters and advertising. Just as Edward Johnston's famous alphabet (pp202–203) has become known as 'London's handwriting', Auriol is closely identified with Paris. The typeface has frequently been copied in the century since its inception. In 1979, during a revival of interest in the art nouveau period, it was re-released by Deberny & Peignot with new bold and black weights designed by Matthew Carter, who also took the opportunity to revive Auriol's harmonious sets of flower and vignette ornaments.

Ty	**Bookman Oldstyle**
Ca	**Serif**
Ke	**Old Style**
Te	**Letterpress**
Da	**1901**
De	**N/A**
Fo	**American Type Founders**
Co	**USA**

Characteristics

Large x-height
Short ascenders and descenders
C G S Barbed serifs
E F Angled top serifs
G Has spur
T Oblique, splayed serifs
g Double-storeyed, oblique lower bowl, small round ear

ACEGST
abcefghij
koprstuy

Connections

Ronaldson Old Style	1884
Cheltenham	1902
Bureau Roman	1997
Bookmania	2011

Availability

Bookman Oldstyle is widely available

Specimen

American Specimen Book of Type Styles.
American Type Founders, Jersey City,
1912 (280x230mm)

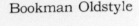

Bookman Oldstyle

72 Point   3 A $7 25   4a $4 55

REMINDER
Hauling Car

60 Point   3 A $6 55   4a $4 20

MARINERS
Flying Slowly

48 Point   4 A $4 25   6a $3 25

NAMED JUDGES
Reward Endeavors

36 Point   4 A $2 75   6a $2 25

AMERICAN HOUSE
Beautifying Expensively
Mighty Forces Growing

420

Bookman Oldstyle

5 A $2 25   9 a $2 00 $4 25

HUMOROUS DEPOSITOR
The University of Rushmorely
Southern Merchants Complain

5 A $1 70   10 a $1 80 $3 50

ADVISE HONEST SOLDIER
Interesting Indictments Expected
Home Discipline Gained Strength

6 A $1 55   14 a $1 70 $3 25

DINERS REJOICED
Enjoy March Banquet
Ninety Invited Guests

10 Point   18 A $1 25   36 a $1 25 $2 50

ELEVEN HOUSES RANSACKED
Daring Burglar Entered Fine Homes
Along the North Shore Drive During
Month of March and Secured a Large
Amount of Clothing and Rare Jewels

9 A $1 60   18 a $1 65 $3 25

DRIVERS HIT HORSES
Insulting Rich Bystanders
Discourage Mean Actions

9 Point   19 A $1 25   38 a $1 25 $2 50

STRONG MANSION CONSTRUCTED
Artistic Decorations Recently Completed
Delightful Garden and Beautiful Lawns
Remarkable Exterior Commented Upon
Magnificent Summer Resorts Described

13 A $1 45   26 a $1 55 $3 00

FIREMAN RISKED FORTUNE
Sharpers Captured Near Cleveland
Remember Seven Eventful Nights

8 Point   20 A $1 10   40 a $1 15 $2 25

NUMEROUS ENTERPRISING FRIENDS
Generous Support Secured The Nominations
Bright Orations and Wonderful Pyrotechnics
Dignified Candidates Rejected and Dismissed
Lavish Display of Silk Hats and Frock Coats

15 A $1 35   32 a $1 40 $2 75

KEMPBURG COUNCIL RESIGNED
Resignations Handed Mayor Separately
Taxpayers Making Mysterious Inquiries
Report Short $1234567890 Makes Denial

6 Point   23 A $0 95   47 a $1 05 $2 00

BOSTON STAPLE BINDERS AND POPULARITY
The Machine Has Been a Boon to Printers in General
Handsome Type Faces Are Cast on American Line
New History of Printing and Its Great Development
Celebrated Resorts in Germany and Other Countries
Government Exercises Influence in New Possession
Beautiful Sentiment $1234567890 Celebrate Prosperity

A M R r y of The ❧

These Special Characters are furnished with each font, except the Ornament,
that being furnished with sizes from 6 to 12 Point inclusive

421

Bookman Oldstyle was a standard in the repertoire of almost every printing office for much of the twentieth century as a type that could be trusted for clear, legible text settings as well as for display applications.

It is not an original typeface design but a remote descendant of the old style cut by Alexander Phemister in the late 1850s for the Scottish type foundry Miller & Richard by adapting an even earlier old style (pp134–35). The ubiquity of Phemister's Antique Old Style led several American type foundries to make copies of the design under a variety of different names. In 1901, the Bruce Type Foundry made refinements to their version, renaming it Bartlett Oldstyle. When Bruce was taken over by American Type Founders in the same year, they kept it in their catalogue but changed the name to Bookman Oldstyle. It continued to be cast at the Bruce foundry under both names until the plants were amalgamated in 1906. Over the ensuing decades, almost all type foundries created versions of Bookman, including Linotype, Monotype, Ludlow, Intertype, Bitstream and ITC.

Bookman Oldstyle was intended as a book face and was often chosen as a more contemporary alternative to Caslon (pp76–77), with a cleaner cut and more regular serifs. It has very sturdy contours but is legible even at small sizes due to its subtle modulation between thick and thin strokes and its open counters. The x-height is generous; ascenders and descenders are consequently very short. With the expansion of advertising, Bookman also proved effective for headlines. In the 1960s it gained popularity in display applications, partly due to its large range of swash characters, which fitted well with the flamboyant design trends of the period.

Bookman's most recent and most comprehensive revival is by Mark Simonson. His version, Bookmania, takes advantage of digital technologies in the production of a family with an impressively wide range. The Bookmania collection consists of five weights, italics, multiple sets of numbers, stylistic alternates, ligatures, small capitals and several swash sets for all variants. Containing over 3,000 glyphs in each weight, it is emphatically the most all-encompassing Bookman ever produced.

Ty	**Copperplate Gothic**
Ca	**Serif**
Ke	**Capitals**
Te	**Letterpress**
Da	**1901**
De	**Frederic W. Goudy**
Fo	**American Type Founders**
Co	**USA**

Characteristics

Large capitals and small capitals only
Monoline character construction
Short hairline serifs
A Flat serifed apex
E F Short middle arm
R Straight, angled leg

AKMW HEIBR CGQSJ

Connections

Blair	1900
Monotype Engravers	1902
Bank Gothic	1930
Luxury	2002

Availability

Copperplate Gothic is widely available

Specimen

American Specimen Book of Type Styles.
American Type Founders, Jersey City,
1912 (280x230mm)

LIGHT COPPERPLATE GOTHIC

24 Point No. 10   6 A $

HUMOROUS QUESTION

24 Point No. 9   7 A $

CONSTRUCTION MACHINES

18 Point No. 10   9 A $

DISHONEST BROKERS RETURN

18 Point No. 9   11 A $

MODERN ENTERPRISES DEMOLISHED

THE ECONOMIC CLUB OF BOSTON

REQUESTS THE HONOR OF YOUR COMPANY AT AN INFORMAL DINNER ON THE EVENING
OF WEDNESDAY, THE FIRST OF JUNE, ONE THOUSAND NINE HUNDRED
TWELVE, AT HALF AFTER SIX O'CLOCK, AT

THE GREAT NORTHERN HOTEL

SUBJECT FOR DISCUSSION

IS THE OVER-CAPITALIZATION OF OUR RAILROADS AN EVIL

SPEAKERS

JAMES S. MONTGOMERY, JR.   PROF. CHARLES LEON MORTON   DOCTOR MARCUS RADBURN
REV. PERCY ANDERSON   FRED WARREN ATHERINGTON   MAYOR HENRY MARKSON
DOCTOR ROBERT BOYCE KOTH   ANDREW H. CONARSIE   DAVID M. ROTHERFORD
PROFESSOR GEORGE N. NOSTRON WILL PRESIDE

RECEPTION WILL BE HELD AT HALF AFTER SIX   DINNER AT SEVEN

SPEAKING FROM HALF AFTER EIGHT UNTIL HALF AFTER TEN

STRONG $1234567890 FIGURES

12 Point No. 8   13 A $1 50

MERITORIOUS DESIGNS
CABINET RENUMBERED

6 Point No. 4   21 A $

REHEARSING WONDERFUL DRAMA
DIGNIFIED CHARACTER PRESENTE
CHOICE MIDNIGHT PERFORMANC

12 Point No. 7   16 A $1 50

INGENIOUS KINGS CONFER
HEROIC MAIDEN HONORED

6 Point No. 3   26 A $

ROMANTIC SUMMER GARDENS PURCHAS
MODERNIZED FINANCIERS DESIRED MON
ANCIENT COLONIAL MANSIONS SEARCH

12 Point No. 6   19 A $1 50

REMARKABLE SOUVENIR PRIZES
CURIOUS GERANIUM EXHIBITION

6 Point No. 2   32 A $

MUSCULAR GENTLEMEN EXHIBIT GREAT ENDURAN
STRENUOUS EXERCISE RECOMMENDED BY PHYSICI
MANY EXTRAORDINARY ACROBATIC ACHIEVEMEN

12 Point No. 5   24 A $1 50

ENTHUSIASTIC JUVENILE SERENADER
MAGNIFICENT SPRINGTIME COSTUMES

6 Point No. 1   37 A $

BEAUTIFUL STRAINS OF INSPIRING MUSIC DELIGHT LOVE
ALPINE MOUNTAIN CLIMBER ENJOYING SPECIAL PRIVILE
PERFUMED BREEZES PERMEATE THE GENTLE ATMOSPHE

674

HEAVY COPPERPLATE GOTHIC

24 Point No. 30   6 A $2 50

HUMOROUS QUESTION

24 Point No. 29   7 A $2 50

CONSTRUCTION MACHINES

18 Point No. 30   9 A $2 00

DISHONEST BROKERS RETURN

18 Point No. 29   11 A $2 00

MODERN ENTERPRISES DEMOLISHED

ANNOUNCEMENT

THE FIRM OF

MARKTON, BUCKRAND & COMPANY

MINING ENGINEERS

WISH TO INFORM THEIR MANY CUSTOMERS THAT THEY HAVE
ASSOCIATED WITH THEM IN THE CAPACITY OF
MASTER DRAUGHTSMAN

MR. EDGAR MURTENS

WHO WILL DIRECT THE DRAUGHTING DEPARTMENT AT
THE OFFICES OF THIS COMPANY

No. 2345 MONTGOMERY STREET

HUDSON, N. J.

CHARLES MARKTON, MANAGER

SOAPS
AND
PERFUMES

VALUABLE HINTS
ON THEIR MAKE
AND GRADE

COPYRIGHTED
1908

MASON & SON
NEW YORK

Auriol Ornament

STRONG $1234567890 FIGURES

12 Point No. 28   13 A $1 50

MERITORIOUS DESIGNS
CABINET RENUMBERED

12 Point No. 27   16 A $1 50

INGENIOUS KINGS CONFER
HEROIC MAIDEN HONORED

12 Point No. 26   19 A $1 50

REMARKABLE SOUVENIR PRIZES
CURIOUS GERANIUM EXHIBITION

12 Point No. 25   24 A $1 50

ENTHUSIASTIC JUVENILE SERENADER
MAGNIFICENT SPRINGTIME COSTUMES

6 Point No. 24   21 A $1 00

REHEARSING WONDERFUL DRAMAS
DIGNIFIED CHARACTER PRESENTED
CHOICE MIDNIGHT PERFORMANCES

6 Point No. 23   26 A $1 00

ROMANTIC SUMMER GARDENS PURCHASED
MODERNIZED FINANCIERS DESIRED MONEY
ANCIENT COLONIAL MANSIONS SEARCHED

6 Point No. 22   32 A $1 00

MUSCULAR GENTLEMEN EXHIBIT GREAT ENDURANCE
STRENUOUS EXERCISE RECOMMENDED BY PHYSICIAN
MANY EXTRAORDINARY ACROBATIC ACHIEVEMENTS

6 Point No. 21   37 A $1 00

BEAUTIFUL STRAINS OF INSPIRING MUSIC DELIGHT LOVERS
ALPINE MOUNTAIN CLIMBER ENJOYING SPECIAL PRIVILEGE
PERFUMED BREEZES PERMEATE THE GENTLE ATMOSPHERE

675

Copperplate Gothic was designed by Frederic W. Goudy (1865–1947) in 1900, and its successive weights and widths were subsequently drawn by Clarence Marder. It was first released by American Type Founders in 1901. The name of the typeface reflects its origins in the style of lettering often used during the nineteenth century, when copperplate engraving was a widely used printing technique. This kind of lettering was popular in professional communications such as business stationery and visiting cards.

Copperplate Gothic is a capitals-only typeface, with small capitals in the lower case register. The name Gothic – an American term for sans serif – is misleading, although Copperplate Gothic's monolinear strokes are an attribute that it shares with the sans serif style. However, its strokes have tiny, unbracketed serifs throughout, a characteristic that has been inherited from the origins of the type in engraved lettering. This feature is not only stylistic. It also usefully serves to emphasize the corners of the type in the printing process, ensuring that the characters appear crisply defined on paper.

There are nine weights and styles in the Copperplate Gothic series, each of which is designated by an alphanumeric code. The first part of the naming system relates to width and weight and the second to the height.

Despite the lack of a lower case, Copperplate Gothic is readable at small sizes because of its even contour, open shapes and wide spaces. Sturdy and sharp at the same time, Copperplate Gothic is suited to settings with open letter spacing, even at small sizes. Since its release it has maintained its usefulness in corporate design, particularly in its expanded versions, which impart an understated, well-established and authoritative tone.

Ty	**Behrens-Schrift**
Ca	**Blackletter**
Ke	**N/A**
Te	**Letterpress**
Da	**1902**
De	**Peter Behrens**
Fo	**Klingspor**
Co	**Germany**

Characteristics

Calligraphic and geometric strokes
Straight horizontals and verticals joined
by curved strokes
E V W Angled serif terminals
a Double-storeyed, large bowl
d Curved uncial stem
f long s Long descender
g Single-storeyed
h Square uncial form

ABCJRSW
abcdefghij
koprstuvy

Connections

Eckmann-Schrift	1900
Schelter-Antiqua	1906
Jessen-Schrift	1930
ITC Honda	1970

Availability

Behrens-Schrift is widely available

Specimen

Behrens: Schriften, Initialen und Schmuck.
Rudhard'sche Giesserei, Offenbach, c1902
(270x210mm)

Behrens=Schrift

Origi
Erzeu

1515a 2 Cicero · 24 Punkte   Satz etwa 10 Kilo, das Kilo III

Grundzüge einer Formenlehre für Buchdruc
1897   Kunstgewerbe=Museum Berlin   189

1516 Doppelmittel · 28 Punkte   Satz etwa 11 Kilo, das Kilo II

Deutsche und italienische Inkunabel
1892   Reichsdruckerei · Berlin   190

1517 3 Cicero · 36 Punkte   Satz etwa 14 Kilo, das Kilo I

Die Ästhetik der Druckschri
307   Heinrich Wallau   65

1518 4 Cicero · 48 Punkte   Satz etwa 20 Kilo, das Kilo II

Häusliche Kunstpfleg
24 Paul Schultze 9

14

Original
Erzeugnis

Behrens=Schrift

1510   5 Cicero · 60 Punkte   Ganzer Satz (14 a · 3 A) etwa 23 Kilo.   Halber Satz (7 a · 2 A) etwa 13 Kilo.   Das Kilo M. 5.30

Schatz der Armen
58 Maeterlinck 31

1520   6 Cicero · 72 Punkte · Auf Hohlfuß   Ganzer Satz (12 a · 3 A) etwa 23 Kilo.   Halber Satz (6 a · 2 A) etwa 13 Kilo.   Das Kilo M. 5.50

Meine Beichte!
2 Leo Tolstoi 4

1521   7 Cicero · 84 Punkte · Auf Hohlfuß   Ganzer Satz (8 a · 3 A) etwa 28 Kilo.   Halber Satz (4 a · 2 A) etwa 16 Kilo.   Das Kilo M. 5.40

Antike Kunst

15

Typographic reform was one of the major concerns of the German architect and designer Peter Behrens (1868–1940). He believed that, like architecture, typography provided 'the most characteristic picture of a period, and the strongest testimonial of spiritual progress'. Behrens wanted to instigate a new typographic paradigm for the twentieth century by creating a typeface that grew naturally out of German traditions but that would also embody 'the new spiritual and material matter of the epoch'. His intention was to create a uniquely German type, using logical construction methods to combine the power of blackletter, the grace of the humanist roman hand and the philosophy of Jugendstil, a German expression of the art nouveau movement.

Behrens-Schrift, the first typeface he designed, is a composite of these ideas. In contrast to the ornate gothic styles that dominated German type design at the beginning of the century, Behrens-Schrift features calligraphic strokes that have been rationalized in order to provide a readable, even and open typeface. Throughout, straight horizontals and verticals are counterbalanced by curved strokes with a flowing, natural feel, terminating in angled serifs that appear to be painted with a brush. These Jugendstil traits are particularly visible in letters such as the E, W, V, d, e and g.

In the handsome type specimen produced for Behrens-Schrift, the designer compared the act of reading to 'watching a bird's flight or the gallop of a horse. Both seem graceful and pleasing, but the viewer does not observe details of their form or movement. Only the rhythm of the lines is seen by the viewer, and the same is true of a typeface.'

After initial difficulties in finding a type founder who would accept Behrens's ideas, in 1901 the Klingspor foundry eventually agreed to manufacture and release Behrens-Schrift the following year. Six years later, Klingspor also published Behrens-Kursiv, an italic variant. Behrens-Schrift was a resounding success in Germany, balancing national heritage with a broader international outlook. It was widely used in both bookwork and advertising, and was adopted by the German government for use at the 1904 World's Fair held in the United States.

Ty	**Cheltenham**
Ca	**Serif**
Ke	**Clarendon**
Te	**Letterpress**
Da	**1902**
De	**Bertram Goodhue**
Fo	**Linotype / ATF**
Co	**USA**

Characteristics

	Large capitals to ascender height
	Tall ascenders, short descenders
A	Apex extends to left
C	No lower serif
E	Short mid-stroke
E F L	Wide
G	Spur serif
W	Crossed centre-strokes
f t	Narrow
g	Open lower bowl

ACEGW
abcdefghij
korstuyaefg

Connections

Clarendon	1845
The Golden Type	1890
Bookman Oldstyle	1901
ITC Cheltenham	1975

Availability

Cheltenham is widely available

Specimen

American Specimen Book of Type Styles.
American Type Founders, Jersey City,
1912 (280x230mm)

Cheltenham Bold

5 A $2 70   8 a $2 30 $5 00

36 Point

REVIEWS MYSTIC RITES
Displayed Handsome Shirts
Daring Explorer Astonished

30 Point

6 A $1 95   10 a $2 30 $4 25

FURNISHED SUPERB ACTORS
Heartily Endorse Banking Method
Determined Members Considering

24 Point

6 A $1 70   13 a $1 80 $3 50

PRINTER BUYS WITH CONFIDENCE
Design Improved Machinery Throughout
Handsome Souvenir Recently Presented

18 Point   10 A $1 60   20 a $1 65 $3 25

INTERESTING SUBJECT
Cause and Effect Relations
Debated by Omega Society

10 Point   18 A $1 20   37 a $1 30 $2 50

EDITOR STARTS ON JOURNEY
Mysterious Machines Being Rebuilt
Public Mints Are Continuing to Run
They Experienced Severe Reverses
Prolong Financial Embarrassments

14 Point   14 A $1 50   26 a $1 50 $3 00

MONSTER SHIPS OPERATED
Floating Palace Developed Speed
Makes Glad Orient and Occident

8 Point   22 A $1 10   45 a $1 15 $2 25

SCIENCE CANDLE BRIGHTLY BURNING
Emanating Rays Light Pathway of Progress
Humanity Recipient of Noted Improvement
Sanguine Expectations Crown Experimenter
Obscure Indefatigable Individuals Contribute

12 Point   17 A $1 30   33 a $1 45 $2 75

NOTED GRANGER EXHIBIT CLOSES
Mammoth Farm Production This Season
Best Cash Prize for Enterprising Farmer
Awards $1234567890 Handsome Medal

6 Point   24 A $0 90   48 a $1 10 $2 00

THE ORIGINAL UNIVERSITY OF TYPE DESIGN
Strong Type Families: the American Type Founders
Company Issues Have Given the Printing Industry a
Greater Business-Compelling Value for its Products
Than Any Other Known Ally or Industry Catering to
Successful Typographers. Recognized Appreciation
Evidenced Through $1234567890 the Rapid Increase

178

Cheltenham Bold in Practical Display

KING
OF ALL TYPE

The
Cheltenham
Family

¶ The sovereignty of the Cheltenhams in the big world of advertising has been thoroughly established. The growing popularity of the new members which have recently been added is an indication that this most pleasing type family will remain in favor for many years to come. When we consider the versatility and dignity of this monarch of display, we readily appreciate the reason for its phenomenal success. The progressive printers and publishers buying liberal weight fonts are certain to give the Cheltenhams first place in their composing rooms. Never in the history of type casting has the printing trade been presented with such variety and harmony in a single series of type faces. Its intrinsic worth and great adaptability is acknowledged by all. Sold in weight fonts at our regular body type prices

Chap-Book Border   Twentieth Century Ornaments   Cheltenham Paragraph Mark

Cheltenham, or 'Chelt' as it was referred to by generations of American printers, is one of the most ubiquitous typefaces of the twentieth century. It was designed in 1896 by an architect, Bertram Goodhue (1869–1924), in collaboration with Ingalls Kimball (1874–1933), the director of the Cheltenham Press, after which it is named.

Cheltenham was not modelled on a single historical source. It was originally conceived as a book typeface based on legibility studies that had indicated readers could identify specific characters by recognizing their upper parts. As a consequence, the design featured long ascenders and short descenders. However, Cheltenham's sturdy structure lent it readily to display typography, showing the influences of the solid Clarendon (pp132–33) typefaces widely used during the nineteenth century, and of the highly fashionable types of the Arts and Crafts movement, such as the Golden Type (pp150–51).

Initially naming the typeface Boston Old Style, Goodhue drew the original letters at 14 inches tall, with minimum contrast between thick and thin strokes, a narrow set width, and thick, bracketed serifs like those of Clarendon. The capital letters were comparatively wide and the lower case letters had a small x-height.

American Type Founders' prolific type designer Morris Fuller Benton (1872–1948) is thought to have then developed the final typeface for production. Although trial cuttings were made in 1899, the face was not completed until 1902. It was subsequently released by both Mergenthaler Linotype and ATF, the latter going on to add some 23 further variants, all of them adapted from the original design by Benton.

Cheltenham was also copied by almost every other major type foundry. As the most extensively used American advertising type of the era, it became known as the 'king of the display faces'. Its overwhelming popularity in headline settings persisted until fashions changed in the 1930s, when geometric sans serif and slab serif typefaces upstaged every other style.

Ty	**Della Robbia**
Ca	**Serif**
Ke	**Old Style**
Te	**Letterpress**
Da	**1902**
De	**Thomas M. Cleland**
Fo	**American Type Founders**
Co	**USA**

Characteristics

B P R	Open bowl
H N	Wide
J	Spur serif on right
M	Splayed, high vertex
R	Wide, curved leg
a	Sloped stem
b	Spur serif
e	Oblique bar
i j	Diamond-shaped dot
. ,	Diamond-shaped dot

BEJMRS
abcdefghij
koprstuvy

Connections

Windsor	1905
Weiss	1926
ITC Korinna	1974
Cantoria	1986

Availability
Della Robbia is widely available

Specimen
American Specimen Book of Type Styles.
American Type Founders, Jersey City,
1912 (280x230mm)

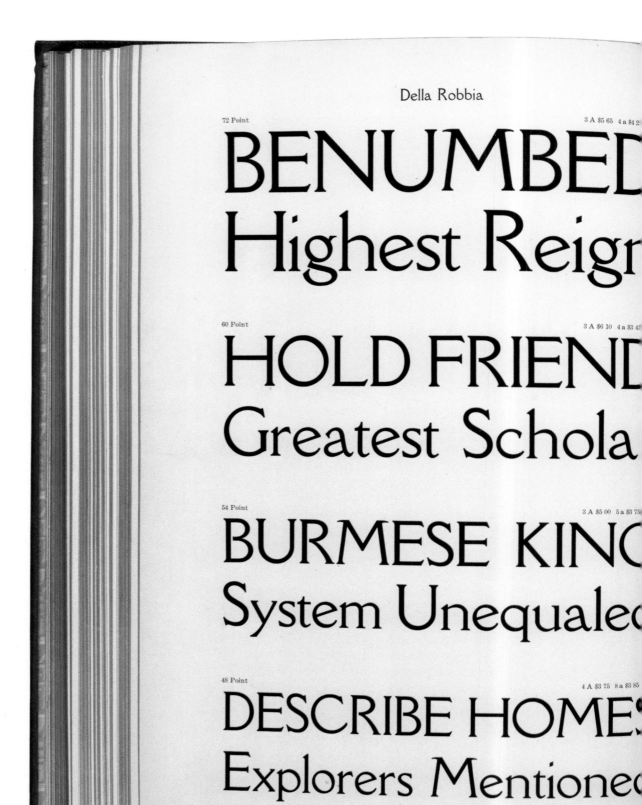

Della Robbia

72 Point   3 A $5 65   4 a $4 2

BENUMBED
Highest Reign

60 Point   3 A $6 10   4 a $3 4

HOLD FRIEND
Greatest Schola

54 Point   3 A $5 00   5 a $3 75

BURMESE KINC
System Unequaled

48 Point   4 A $3 75   8 a $3 85

DESCRIBE HOME
Explorers Mentioned

406

Della Robbia

42 Point   5 A $3 25   9 a $3 05 $6 30

HAULING ENGINES
Describe Either Method

36 Point   4 A $2 40   9 a $2 70 $5 10

FRAME HOUSE BURNED
Experiment Bringing Motive

30 Point   5 A $2 05   11 a $2 20 $4 25

SECURE NOVEL MAGAZINE
Greatest Medical Board Instructor

24 Point   7 A $1 85   12 a $1 65 $3 50

HOME KNIGHTS REVISE DECISION
Undisturbed Historical Emblems Retained

18 Point   9 A $1 60   18 a $1 65 $3 25

EXECUTIVE HONORED
BERMINGHAM HEROES
Historical Medals Discovered

10 Point   18 A $1 25   36 a $1 25 $2 50

PUBLISHES HANDSOME DESIGNS
FURNISHED PRINTED PROGRAM
By Committee for the Great Celebration
Mayor and Other Prominent Men There
Oration by State Senator John Monroe

14 Point   13 A $1 45   26 a $1 55 $3 00

GENUINE DEMANDS SIGNED
FIGURES DISGUISE MEANING
Remarkable History of Government

8 Point   23 A $1 15   46 a $1 10 $2 25

PROGRESSIVE PRINTERS USING AMERICAN
LINE TYPE PRODUCE HANDSOME DESIGNS
Della Robbia will Aid in Every Way to Give Your
Printing that Dignified and Fashionable Style Which
Meets the Approval of the Most Fastidious Customer

12 Point   16 A $1 35   33 a $1 40 $2 75

FINANCIAL STRINGENCY RELIEVED
MERCHANTS PREDICT PROSPERITY
Crisis of the Financial World Safely Passed
Secured Amount $1234567890 Philanthropist

6 Point   26 A $1 00   52 a $1 00 $2 00

BECAUSE OF ITS ATTRACTIVE VARIETY OF SIZES
LEADING EXPONENTS OF TYPOGRAPHY ADMIRE
THE FASHIONABLE DESIGNS SET IN DELLA ROBBIA
It Possesses an Individuality of its own that Produces the Artistic
Effects so Much Desired by Up-to-date Houses Throughout the
Country and Which has Led Master Printers to Adopt this Face
For Use on All Work that $1234567890 is of an Artistic Nature

407

Thomas Maitland Cleland (1880–1964) was an eminent American designer, painter and illustrator. Throughout his career, he was a vociferous advocate for traditional values who fiercely opposed modern trends in typography and type design in the early part of the twentieth century. 'You can no more dispense with the essential features of the written or printed Roman alphabet', he said, 'than you can dispense with the accents and intonations of human speech. This is simplification for simpletons, and these are block letters for blockheads.'

He produced Della Robbia, his only typeface, when he was 20 years old. Named after Luca della Robbia (1400–82), a renowned Florentine sculptor of the early Renaissance, Cleland's design combined a full-bodied old-style lower case with a set of capitals that were a considered and scholarly recreation of majuscule letters from inscriptions on fifteenth-century monuments and buildings in Florence.

Originally commissioned by the Bruce Type Foundry in New York, Della Robbia was issued by American Type Founders in 1902. Although in direct competition with the world-beating Cheltenham series, Della Robbia appealed to printers worlwide. It became an instant bestseller and was supplemented in 1918 with a light variant drawn by Morris Fuller Benton.

Never less than forthright in his views, Thomas Maitland Cleland later disowned Della Robbia, despite its enormous success all over the world, having been cut for machine composition by Monotype and issued in the foundry type catalogues of both Stephenson, Blake & Co. and Deberny & Peignot.

Ty	**Subiaco**
Ca	**Blackletter**
Ke	**Gotico-Antiqua**
Te	**Letterpress**
Da	**1902**
De	**Emery Walker and Sydney Cockerell**
Fo	**The Ashendene Press**
Co	**UK**

Characteristics

Long ascenders and descenders
Blunt baseline serifs
A High crossbar, small aperture
E F Narrow
M Splayed, no serifs at apex or vertex
R Wide, straight leg
T Serpentine top bar
a Double-storeyed
d Upright stem
g Double-storeyed
h Curved uncial form
t Arrow-headed
ct Flourished
fi fu ti tu Ligatures

ABEMR
abcdefghi
koprstuvy

Connections

The Subiaco Type	1465
Zainer's Gotico-Antiqua	1468
The Golden Type	1890
The Troy Type	1892

Availability

Not available

Specimen

The XI Bookes of the Golden Asse:
Containing the Metamorphosie of Lucius
Apuleius. Ashendene Press, London, 1924
(300x210mm)

THE FIFTEENTH CHAPTER. ❡HOW FOTIS TOLD
TO APULEIUS, WHAT WITCHCRAFT HER MIS-
TRESSE DID USE.

WHEN I was a bed I began to call to minde all the sorrowes and griefes that I was in the day before, untill such time as my love Fotis, having brought her mistresse to sleepe, came into the chamber, not as shee was wont to do, for she seemed nothing pleasant neither in countenance nor talke, but with sowre face and frowning looke, gan speake in this sort, Verily I confesse that I have been the occasion of all thy trouble this day, and therewith shee pulled out a whippe from under her apron, & delivered it unto mee saying, Revenge thy selfe of me mischievous harlot, or rather slay me.

❡And thinke you not that I did willingly procure this anguish and sorrow unto you, I call the gods to witnesse. For I had rather myne owne body to perish, than that you should receive or sustaine any harme by my meanes, but that which I did was by the commandement of another, and wrought as I thought for some other, but behold the unlucky chance fortuned on you by my evill occasion.

❡Then I, very curious & desirous to know the matter, answered, In faith (quoth I) this most pestilent & evill favoured whip which thou hast brought to scourge thee withal, shal first be broken in a thousand pieces, than it should touch or hurt thy delicate and dainty skin. But I pray you tell me, how have you been the cause and mean of my trouble & sorrow? For I dare sweare by the love that I beare unto you, and I will not be perswaded, though you your selfe should endeavour the same, that ever you went to trouble or harm me: perhaps sometimes you imagined an evil thought in your mind, which afterwards you revoked, but that is not to bee deemed as a crime.

❡When I had spoken these words, I perceived by Fotis eys being

58

wet with tears, and well nigh closed up, that shee had a desire unto pleasure, & specially because shee embraced and kissed me sweetly. And when she was somewhat restored unto joy, she desired mee that shee might first shut the chamber doore, least by the untemperance of her tongue, in uttering any unfitting words, there might grow further inconvenience. Wherewithall she barred and propped the doore, and came to me againe, & embracing me lovingly about the necke with both her armes, spake with a soft voice and said, I doe greatly feare to discover the privities of this house, and to utter the secret mysteries of my dame. But I have such a confidence in you and in your wisedome, by reason that you are come of so noble a line, and endowed with so profound sapience, and further instructed in so many holy & divine things, that you will faithfully keepe silence, and that whatsoever I shall reveale or declare unto you, you would close them within the bottome of your heart, and never discover the same: for I ensure you, the love that I beare unto you, enforceth mee to utter it. Now shal you know all the estate of our house, now shal you know the hidden secrets of my mistres, unto whome the powers of hel do obey, & by whom the celestiall planets are troubled, the gods made weake, and the elements subdued, neither is the violence of her art in more strength & force, than when she espieth some comly yong man that pleaseth her fancie, as oftentimes it hapneth, for now she loveth one Boetian a fair and beautiful person, on whom she employes al her sorcery and enchantment, and I heard her say with mine own ears yesternight, that if the Sun had not then presently gon downe, & the night come to minister convenient time to worke her magicall enticements, shee would have brought perpetuall darkenes over all the world her selfe. And you shall know, That when she saw yester night, this Beotian sitting at the Barbers a polling, when she came from the Baines shee secretly commanded me to gather some of the haire of his head which lay dispersed upon the ground, and to bring it home.

59

CHAPTER XV
How Fotis told to Apuleius, what witchcraft her mistresse did use

Inspired by the work of William Morris in his pursuit of perfection in printing at the Kelmscott Press (pp150–51), a number of small presses were established in England towards the end of the nineteenth century. One of the leading members of the private-press movement was C. H. St John Hornby, who established the Ashendene Press in 1895 in the summerhouse of his parents' home. For his earliest publications he bought founders' typefaces, but after moving to commercial premises in London in 1899 he decided to commission his own type.

His friend Emery Walker of the Doves Press (pp156–57) designed two typefaces for the Ashendene Press, named Subiaco and Ptolemy, working in collaboration with Sydney Cockerell. Usually considered the superior of the two, Subiaco was closely modelled on the pioneering work of Konrad Sweynheym and Arnold Pannartz at the Subiaco monastery in Italy in 1465 (pp16–17), a hybrid typeface combining the features of letters of the Middle Ages and of the Renaissance, known as a Gotico-Antiqua.

The eminent punch cutter Edward Prince, who worked for both the Kelmscott and Doves presses, cut Hornby's type in a single size, equivalent to 18 point. The result was a very well-considered revival of the original Sweynheym and Pannartz type, interpreting its combination of calligraphic, gothic and Latin features with assurance. Apart from the absence of the archaic long s and a lack of abbreviations the two are practically identical.

Subiaco became the main typeface used in Ashendene Press publications from 1902 until its closure in 1935. The 1924 publication shown here uses it to great effect in an austere body of plain text. Stanley Morison considered the design of the Ashendene books 'a spectacular achievement', a model of typographic restraint with spacious margins, precisely set type, little superfluous decoration and immaculate presswork.

Ty	**Franklin Gothic**
Ca	**Sans Serif**
Ke	**Grotesque**
Te	**Letterpress**
Da	**1904**
De	**Morris Fuller Benton**
Fo	**American Type Founders**
Co	**USA**

Characteristics

C c S s e	Angled terminals
G	Angular spur
Q	Short, curved tail
R	Straight, angled leg
a	Double-storeyed, slight curve at foot
f r t	Vertical terminals
g	Double-storeyed, small ear
i j	Square dots
t	Flat top-stroke
y	Curved tail

AGMQR
abcefghij
koprstuy

Connections

News Gothic	1908
Monotype Grotesque	c1926
Trade Gothic	1948
ITC Franklin Gothic	1980

Availability

Franklin Gothic is widely available. ITC Franklin Gothic is available from Monotype and resellers

Specimen

American Specimen Book of Type Styles. American Type Founders, Jersey City, 1912 (280x230mm)

Franklin Gothic

96 Point — 3 A $9 60 4a $6 15

THE Dog

84 Point — 3 A $7 70 4a $5 10

Cat RUNS

72 Point — 3 A $7 65 4a $4 90

KINGS Dine

60 Point — 3 A $6 05 4a $3 90

Made BRICKS

48 Point — 3 A $4 00 6a $3 85

PUMAS LEAPING
Demands Regular

42 Point — 4 A $3 55 6a $3 00

ANCIENT MANSION
Special Employment

738

Franklin Gothic

36 Point
4 A $2 65 7 a $2 55 $5 20

ASTRONOMER WROTE
Prominent Incorporator
Linguist Bought Stones

30 Point
5 A $2 20 8 a $2 05 $4 25

SPEAKER REFORMS GUIDE
Great Entertainer Preparing
Englishman Leaving Gotham

24 Point
5 A $1 65 11 a $1 85 $3 50

HUSKY SAILOR DROPS ANCHOR
Considered Beautiful Decorations
Nervous Printer Became Alarmed

18 Point
8 A $1 50 17 a $1 75 $3 25

FOUND NEW NECKTIE
Near Manchuria Rocks
Mariners Hunt Caribou

10 Point
16 A $1 20 32 a $1 30 $2 50

YOUNG UNITYPE OPERATOR
Philadelphia Detective Sighed
Expert Chemist Puzzled Child
Inquisitive Woman Explaining

8 Point
19 A $1 10 38 a $1 15 $2 25

FAMOUS PEDESTRIANS EXHAUSTED
Octogenarian Breaks Walking Record
Jumping From Bunker Hill Monument
New Type Bought by Country Printer

14 Point
12 A $1 40 24 a $1 60 $3 00

HELD BRAVE COMPOSITOR
Delightful Winter Excursions
Police Capture Daring Youth
Constable Examined Burglar

6 Point
21 A $0 90 44 a $1 10 $2 00

MARINER STRANDED ON BARREN ISLAND
Large Steamer Abandoned by Mutinous Crew
Dangerous Insects Infested Tropical Country
Horse Thief Departing From Oklahoma Town
Faithful German $1234567890 Won Reward

12 Point
14 A $1 25 29 a $1 50 $2 75

OLDEST MEMBERS PROTESTING
Regulations Strenuously Enforced
Denverite Closely Guarding Secret
Beautiful $1234567890 Damsels

5 Point
22 A $0 90 46 a $1 10 $2 00

COMPOSITOR TRYING TO ESTABLISH NEW RECORD
Pied Eight Pages of Four Point While Sprinting Around
Seven Stonemen Kept Busy Justifying Magazine Pages
Alleged Printer Served Apprenticeship With Carpenter
Proofreader Wore Out Fourteen Beautiful Blue Pencils

739

In the early 1900s, Morris Fuller Benton (1872–1948) worked on a series of similar sans serif typefaces for American Type Founders that would have a lasting influence on American graphic design. These included Globe Gothic, Lightline Gothic, Alternate Gothic and News Gothic. The most enduring, Franklin Gothic, was designed in 1904 and released a year later.

'Gothic' was a somewhat confusing term commonly given to sans serif typefaces originating in the United States at the beginning of the twentieth century. Equivalent to the European 'grotesque', it is probable that printers and founders derived the name from the blackletter gothics of the medieval period, not for any actual physical resemblance but for the word's connotations of both blackness and unfamiliarity.

Franklin Gothic was intended to be a face for newspapers and advertising. It was initially released in two upright weights, but further variants were added as sales increased, starting with Condensed and Extra Condensed, and companion italics five years later. Benton's design was greatly influenced by American woodcut gothic faces and contemporary sans serif designs from Germany such as Akzidenz-Grotesk (pp152–53). Franklin Gothic is a bold alphabet with a large x-height and a very moderate stroke contrast, except for a thinning at the junctions of curved strokes with stems. Its anatomical characteristics are drawn directly from humanist roman forms, as demonstrated in the double-storeyed lower case g, which is typical of early roman letters and is a key differentiator between American and European sans serif traditions.

By the mid-1920s the ATF catalogue offered more than 50 sans serif typefaces, and designs like Franklin Gothic were rapidly eclipsed by newer styles, looking inceasingly antiquated by comparison with highly fashionable geometric sans serifs such as Futura and Kabel. During the resurgence of interest in humanist sans serifs in the 1950s, the requirements of designers looking for a sleek, rational style were met by new designs like Univers and Helvetica, and traditional faces like Franklin Gothic were pushed further to the background. It was not until 1980 that Franklin Gothic found a new lease of life in a considered revival by the International Typeface Corporation. ITC Franklin Gothic became an American bestseller, perfectly suited to ITC's flamboyant style without losing the power of Benton's original design.

Ty	**Windsor**
Ca	**Serif**
Ke	**Old Style**
Te	**Letterpress**
Da	**1905**
De	**Unknown**
Fo	**Stephenson, Blake & Co.**
Co	**UK**

Characteristics

E F G T	Angled serifs
G	Spur serif
M	Splayed, with upper serifs
P R	Large bowl
W	Low apex with serif
a h m n	Sloped right-hand stem
e	Oblique crossbar
f	Narrow, non-kerning, hooked arch
o	Backward incline

BEGMR
abcefghi
koprstuy

Connections

Belwe	1907
Clearface	1907
Cooper Old Style	1919
Heroine	2009

Availability

Windsor is available from Linotype and resellers

Specimen

Printing Types: Borders, Initials, Electros, Brass Rules, Spacing Material, Ornaments. Stephenson, Blake & Co., Sheffield, 1924 (290x220mm)

Windsor

72 Point   5 A, 6; about 32 lb.

BRUGES
Church Bell

60 Point   5 A, 6 a; about 29 lb.

WINDSOR
River Steamer

48 Point   5 A, 10 a; about 24 lb.

MELBOURNE
British Naval Base

36 Point   6 A, 15 a; about 22 lb.

HAND STITCHER
Essential machine when
hand labour is expensive

STEPHENSON, BLAKE & Co. Ltd.   228   SHEFFIELD and LONDON

Windsor Elongated

72 Point   5 A, 6 a; about 19 lb.

FINE SPECIMENS
The Windsor Elongated

60 Point   5 A, 8 a; about 15 lb.

SEAPORT
Heliogravure

48 Point   7 A, 12 a; about 15 lb.

EMIGRANTS
Quebec Province

36 Point   9 A, 18 a; about 12 lb.

HANDKERCHIEF
Belfast Manufacturer

30 Point   12 A, 22 a; about 11 lb.

YOUNG BRIGADIER
Leads victorious advance

24 Point   18 A, 36 a; about 10 lb.

DRAMATIC PERFORMER
Historic Shakespearean Revival
Edinburgh Repertory Theatre

18 Point   24 A, 50 a; about 8 lb.

EASTERN STEAMER DEPARTS
Laden with valuable cargo for Australia
Estimated gross worth £1234567890

14 Point   32 A, 64 a; about 7 lb.

INVALUABLE TYPE FOR JOURNALS
Copy writers appreciate this elongated typeface
which is extremely narrow in set

12 Point   44 A, 90 a; about 6½ lb.

MOST POPULAR BRITISH TYPE FAMILY
The Windsor Family comprises eight series of varied widths
and strengths suitable for every display purpose

10 Point   44 A, 90 a; about 5 lb.

WINDSOR ELONGATED FOR COMMERCIAL PRINTER
Designed to meet the requirements of the General Printing Office
this popular family is in constant use in technical magazines

STEPHENSON, BLAKE & Co. Ltd.   237   SHEFFIELD and LONDON

Advertising expanded dramatically at the turn of the twentieth century as the supply of manufactured goods increased. This resulted in an urgent need for eye-catching typefaces, and many bold new display designs, such as Pabst, Belwe, Cheltenham (pp168–69), Clearface (pp180–81) and Cooper Old Style, were developed to meet the demand.

Windsor is a British contribution to this trend. It is an old-style serif typeface cut between 1905 and 1910 at the Sheffield type foundry Stevenson, Blake & Co. Windsor's design has often been attributed to Eleisha Pechey (1831–1902), although it is more likely that the type was drawn by anonymous staff members in the foundry's drawing office.

Windsor has a distinctly English, Edwardian feel. Its letters are modelled on contemporary and nineteenth-century revivals of old-style designs such as Bookman and Ronaldson (pp144–45), but their proportions, shallow stroke angles and rounded serifs show tendencies of the flowing natural curves seen in art nouveau designs, which were becoming increasingly popular during the time of Windsor's conception. It was cut in a range of styles, including Light, Bold, Ultra Heavy and Bold Outline. Two variant forms, Windsor Extra Bold Condensed and Windsor Elongated, shown on this page, are worthy of note as excellent examples of compressed display typefaces. With long oval forms that made for attractive settings with high impact, they were as well received and widely used as the standard-width type.

After a short initial period of popularity, Windsor fell into disuse for several decades, until the swinging sixties, when Victorian and Edwardian design became the height of fashion in the UK. Today a number of proprietary digital versions are available, some with minor differences to the original cuts. Of these, Linotype's offering is among the most faithful and most comprehensive.

Ty	Schelter-Antiqua
Ca	Serif
Ke	Gotico-Antiqua
Te	Letterpress
Da	1906
De	Unknown
Fo	J. G. Schelter & Giesecke
Co	Germany

Characteristics

A K N R	Curved oblique strokes
B P R	Open bowl
E	Gothic form, high middle arm
M N	Alternate forms
U V W	Curved stems, narrow top aperture
d	Gothic form
f	Narrow, non-kerning
g	Double-storeyed, open lower bowl
t	Narrow, flat foot serif

AEJMPW
abchdefghij
koprstuwz

Connections

Eckmann-Schrift	1900
Behrens-Schrift	1902
Della Robbia	1902
Souvenir	1914

Availability

Not available

Specimen

Schriften und Zierat. Schriftgiesserei J. G.
Schelter und Giesecke, Leipzig, c1912
(286x225mm)

DAS MASCHINENWESEN

Mühevolle, rastlose Tätigkeit auf gewerblich technischem Gebiete einerseits, Vertiefung und Ordnung in allen Zweigen der Naturwissenschaft andererseits haben im Laufe des vorigen Jahrhunderts der Erkenntnis Bahn gebrochen, daß Objekte der Außenwelt nicht der Laune des Zufalls, nicht der blinden Willkür ihr Dasein verdanken, daß vielmehr die Hervorbringung des allereinfachsten natürlichen oder künstlichen Gegenstandes eine Aufeinanderfolge von Zuständen und Wirkungen erfordert, welche man wegen der Gleichartigkeit ihres Vorkommens bei den verschiedensten Dingen als ein gemeinsames Prinzip, nämlich das der Entwicklungslehre, erkannt hat. In der Technik ist das Prinzip selbstverständlich; es folgt schon aus dem Begriff der Arbeit und der Tatsache, daß nur durch Arbeit die Körper ihren Ort oder die Formen ändern können. Im *Maschinenbau* gilt schon lange das Prinzip, daß für jede neue Form, die hergestellt werden soll, auch neue Formen der Werkzeuge und der dieselben tragenden und bewegenden Maschinen notwendig sind. Durch die bahnbrechenden Entdeckungen der großen Forscher des vorigen Jahrhunderts und die Entwicklung einer Wissenschaft der Technik ist die Zusammensetzung zwischen den natürlichen und künstlichen Produkten hergestellt, indem erwiesen wurde, daß für beide Arten das Entwicklungs-, das Anpassungsprinzip, maßgebend ist. Die unbewußte Wirkung der Naturkräfte und die bewußte Tätigkeit jedes Menschen arbeiten nach dem gleichen einheitlichen großen Prinzip der allmähligen Entwicklung und Anpassung an die bestehenden Zwecke oder Bedingungen. Wenn es möglich wäre, auf dieser

Geschützt

Schelter & Giesecke, Schriftgießerei, Leipzig

J 31

17292. Mittel Schelter-Antiqua No. 24 . Initial aus Serie 597

J. G. Schelter & Giesecke was a German type foundry and manufacturer of printing presses, established in 1819 in Leipzig by Johann Schelter and Christian Giesecke. Among the many typographic innovations the company pioneered were some of the earliest grotesque typefaces cast in the mid- to late 1800s (pp148–49).

By the end of the nineteenth century public tastes were moving away from the gaunt and ornate book types of the period towards new designs that were intended to be easier to read. Schelter & Giesecke entered this market in 1906 with Schelter-Antiqua, presented to the trade in a detailed specimen that included an essay describing its unique qualities and a warning against copyright infringement.

Influenced by the highly fashionable Jugendstil aesthetic, Schelter-Antiqua is a hybrid of Fraktur and roman forms in the tradition of the Gotico-Antiqua (pp16–17) but with a tendency towards the Latin form. The foundry invested a great deal of care in its design, ensuring that it was legible and spacious, with a robust contour that used no fragile hairline strokes. Schelter-Antiqua has a notably soft appearance with many distinctive features.

Having invested so much into a comprehensive series featuring many variants – from condenseds to semibolds – the foundry was inevitably keen to protect it legally. However, many imitations soon appeared. One of these, Souvenir, became highly successful, outlasting its predecessor by several decades. Souvenir was drawn, originally in a single weight, by Morris Fuller Benton and released by ATF in 1914. After a long period of popularity it fell into obscurity along with Schelter-Antiqua until 1971, when Ed Benguiat revived it for the International Typeface Corporation during a resurgence of interest in the art nouveau and art deco styles. ITC Souvenir became an international bestseller, and many associate it today with the American design aesthetic of the 1970s rather than with its older European roots.

Ty	**Clearface**
Ca	**Serif**
Ke	**Old Style**
Te	**Letterpress**
Da	**1907**
De	**Morris Fuller Benton**
Fo	**American Type Founders**
Co	**USA**

Characteristics

A	Flat apex extends to left
M	Narrow, high vertex
V W	Overlapping oblique strokes
a	Deep curve at top arch
a k r v w y	Ball terminals
e	Oblique crossbar
f	Narrow, non-kerning
g	Double-storeyed, ear above upper bowl

AJMQW
abcdefghij
orstuya*aefg*

Connections

Bookman Oldstyle	1901
Century Oldstyle	1909
Clearface Gothic	1910
ITC Clearface	1979

Availability

Clearface is widely available

Specimen

American Specimen Book of Type Styles.
American Type Founders, Jersey City,
1912 (280x230mm)

Clearface Bold

72 Point   3 A \$6 80 4 a \$4 45

FRIGHTENS
Staunch Limb
Display Fines

60 Point   3 A \$5 25 5 a \$4 05

KIND BROKER
Returned Names
Distrusts Burglar

48 Point   4 A \$3 85 7 a \$3 70

NOBLE DESIGNER
Marvelous Historians
Romans Entertaining

292

Clearface Bold

42 Point 5 A $3 45 8 a $3 10 $6 55

BEING DETERMINED
Remarkable Elimination
Hebrew National Society

36 Point 5 A $2 70 8 a $2 35 $5 65

INTERESTING PRINTERS
Handsome Mansions Rebuilt
Construct Greatest Buildings

30 Point 6 A $2 20 10 a $2 05 $4 25

SECURED HONEST MEMBERS
Unprecedented Multitudes Remain
Metropolitan Avenues Being Clean
Government Employing Detectives

24 Point 7 A $1 80 12 a $1 70 $3 50

EXERTS THEIR OBSCURED MUSCLE
Gymnastic Event Unexpectedly Continued
Secure Inspired Exhilarating Performance
Big Contractor Erected Beautiful Libraries

293

At the turn of the twentieth century, the market for advertising typefaces was increasingly competitive and the major type foundries were keen to meet the requirements of customers who wished to differentiate their work by using the most up-to-date lettering styles. American Type Founders was notably responsive to such demands.

In 1905 the prolific Morris Fuller Benton (1872–1948) drew the first version of Clearface in a single bold weight with the collaboration of his father, Linn Boyd Benton. Its design process developed in parallel with his work on Century Oldstyle (pp186–87) with which it has much in common.

The regular weight of Clearface was the first to be released in 1907, appearing in the 1909 ATF catalogue. By 1912 the catalogue also listed light and heavy variants, along with italics for each, and featured Clearface Gothic, a sans serif variant that shared few attributes with its serif counterpart other than its basic proportions.

Clearface achieved considerable popularity and was either licensed or copied by manufacturers of foundry type, along with all of the makers of composing machines, including Linotype, Intertype, Monotype and Ludlow, some of whom added their own styles to the range. The Clearface family appeared in ATF's monumental 1923 specimen book, but soon afterwards, as typographic fashions shifted towards sans serif designs, its use declined in advertising and display applications. It was then seen very little until the resurgence of interest in early twentieth-century typographic style during the 1960s and 1970s.

Ty	**Venus**
Ca	**Sans Serif**
Ke	**Grotesque**
Te	**Letterpress**
Da	**1907**
De	**Unknown**
Fo	**Wagner & Schmidt**
Co	**Germany**

Characteristics

Most capitals have uniform width
B R Small upper bowl
C c S s e g Angled terminals
E H High crossbar
G No spur, high arm
R Straight, angled leg
a Double-storeyed
f Narrow
g Single-storeyed, hooked tail
t Narrow, tall, angled top-stroke
y Hooked tail

ABEGMR
abcdefghij
koprstuvy

Connections

Akzidenz-Grotesk	c1898
Edel-Grotesk	c1914
Monotype Grotesque	c1926
Folio	1957

Availability

Venus is available from Linotype and resellers

Specimen

Venus type specimen. Bauersche Giesserei, Frankfurt, c1907 (279x205mm)

Sans serif typefaces were increasingly seen in Germany during the early years of the twentieth century, particularly in the work of practitioners of the Neue Typographie. Venus is one of the most instantly recognizable of these, since it was one of the most commonly used typefaces in the publications and posters produced by the Bauhaus printing workshop. Although not geometrically constructed, it conformed to the school's principles, and because it was readily available it was one of the first sans serifs to have been implemented in extended bodies of text.

The Wagner & Schmidt type foundry was established by Ludwig Wagner and Robert Arthur Schmidt in Leipzig in the 1880s. Specializing in punch cutting and engraving, the company marketed and sold matrices of its original typefaces to other European type foundries, where they would subsequently be cast and sold under their own proprietary names.

Venus is an original Wagner & Schmidt design, issued by the Bauer type foundry between 1907 and 1910. A development of the nineteenth-century grotesque style, it has a charming and eccentric personality underlying its plain forms. Offered in a wide range of weights and widths, Venus is easily distinguished from other grotesques by a number of idiosyncratic features, such as the unusually high crossbar of the B, E and F, the small bowl of the R and the alternate double-storey g in the bold weight.

Although hugely popular in the early part of the twentieth century, Venus did not survive the technological transitions to machine composition, photosetting or the digital era. However, with a very extensive range of variant styles, including unusual left-slanted weights, it is still familiar today as the typeface that is extensively used in German cartographic production.

BAHNHOF-STR

Dame

Unterröcke in Barche
Unterröcke in Tuch .
Morgenröcke in vers

Abend-Cape
M. 12.50 13.75 14.7

Jackets farbig und sc

Blusen {a
a
a

Kinder

Kinderkleider, bedruc
Kinderkleider, Wollst
Kinderkleider, Velout
Kinderkleider, Halbtu
Kinderkleider, reinwo
Kinderkleider, prima
Kinderkleider, elegan

Für die

Waschwannen, Zink
Waschzober, beste Q
Füllfässer, Zink . . . . .
Wringmaschinen, I.
Plättbretter, bezogen
Wirtschaftswagen
Gaskocher, 2 Kochlöch
Reibemaschinen . . .

KAFFEE
Porz
we
Gemüseschüsseln,
Saucieren, verschiede
Kartoffelschüsseln
Kaffeetassen

EINHARD

KASSEL — AM LUTHER-PLATZ

Corps 10 Weiss-Umrahmung Nr. 2270/71

swerte Angebote

ektion

.. M. 1.75	2.50	3.25
.. M. 5.25	6.40	7.85
.. M. 6.30	8.70	11.40

tel Neu eingetroffen! Erbitte höfl. Ihren Besuch!
.50 20.50 21.75 usw.

. M. 6.30	7.75	9.80
.... M. 1.80	2.50	3.70 usw.
.... M. 4.75	6.30	10.75 usw.
.... M. 7.50	9.25	12.50 usw.

Tücher und Decken

Damen-Plaids	M. 2.40	3.25	bis 29.50
Auto-Schals	M. 1.40	2.80	bis 23.75
Spitzen- und Tüll-Schals	M. 4.30	8.75	bis 69.50

Damen-Westen, Seelenwärmer } in sehr großer Auswahl und Extra-Preisen
Schulterkragen, Blusenschoner }

Reisedecken Wolle, Kamelhaar usw.	M. 6.50	8.80	bis 115.00
Schlafdecken	M. 3.20	6.80	bis 60.80
Wagen- und Schlittendecken	M. 8.50	9.80	bis 110.50

Herren-Artikel

0,75	Farb. Oberhemden, Zephir..	M.	4.25 4.75
1.35	Manschetten, pr. Lein., ½ Dtzd.	M.	2.50 3.75
2.60	Herren-Kragen, 5 f., ½ Dtzd.	M.	2.75 4.80
3.40	Krawatten, nur neueste Formen	M.	1.90 2.25
4.75	Hosenträger, aparte Muster...	M.	2.30 4.60
6.25	Auto-Schals, gestrickte	M.	0.95 1.85
14.50	Kragenschoner, weiß u. farbig	M.	1.25 3.50

Meine **DEVISE** lautet:
Überraschende Auswahl
Erstklassige Qualitäten
Größtmöglichste
Preiswürdigkeit

tschafts-Artikel

Emaille

0	Schmortöpfe ohne Ring	Pfg. 34 67 94
5	Schmortöpfe mit Ring .	Pfg. 44 76 98
0	Waschschüsseln	Pfg. 48 63 86
0	Küchenschüsseln....	Pfg. 14 26 36
5	Seifenhalter	Pfg. 24
0	Milchkannen mit Bügel	Pfg. 42 48 63
5	Behälter für Seife Garnitur	Pfg. 76 84 98
5	Marktkörbe mit emailliert. Einsatz	M. 1.25

Für die Küche

Holztabletts mit Einlage .	M.	0.95 1.35
Tischbestecke ... Paar	M.	0.66 0.87
Tee-Eier, vernickelt	M.	0.48 0.86
Kopfbürsten	M.	0.66 0.94
Kleiderbürsten	M.	0.66 0.94
Holz- oder Kohlenkasten ..	M.	2.30
Küchenstuhl, gestrichen	M.	2.45
Küchentisch, gestrichen	M.	4.90

VICE 9 Teile, ff. dekoriert **2.75, 3.50, 9.25, 12.50, 24.75**

Glas

Press-Glas-Garnitur „Diamant"
Beste Steinschliff-Imitation

0.35	Dessertteller	M. 0.25
0.46	Eisschalen mit Henkel	M. 0.35
0.97	Kuchenteller	M. 0.95 1.30
2.42	Kompottschalen, rund	M. 0.34 0.75
	Zuckerschalen mit Fuß	M. 0.45 0.64

Porzellan
dekoriert

Speiseteller, flach oder tief	M.	0.46
Dessertteller	M.	2.46 2.84
Beilageschalen	M.	1.94 2.38
Kartoffelschüsseln	M.	2.63

Reklameschrift Block

H·BERTHOLD A·G

82310. 8 Punkt. Min. ca. 5 kg.

Edel sei der Mensch, hilfreich und gut!
Unsere Block steht wie ein Fels in dem
Kommen und Gehen der Modeschriften
DER BESTE ERFOLG IST STETS REKLAME

82312. 10 Punkt. Min. ca. 6 kg.

Porträts in allen Größen werden
hier sauber und gut angefertigt
KUNSTHANDLUNG FRITZ WEBER

82313. 12 Punkt kl. Bild. Min. ca. 6 kg.

Herbst- und Frühjahrsmode
erregen lebhaftes Interesse
NEUHEITEN IN SEIDENROBEN

82314. 12 Punkt gr. Bild. Min. ca. 6 kg.
Zusatz 82314a. Min. ca. 1 kg.

Elegante Damen-Wäsche
in tadelloser Ausführung
12345 CHEMNITZ 67890

82315. 14 Punkt. Min. ca. 7 kg. Zusatz 82315a. Min. ca. 1,2 kg.

Rheinisches Winzerfest
LIEDER ZUR HARFE

82316. 16 Punkt. Min. ca. 8 kg. Zusatz 82316a. Min. ca. 1,4 kg.

Arbeit ist des Bürge
SEIDENMÄNTEL

82317. 20 Punkt. Min. ca. 10 kg. Zusatz 82317a. Min. ca. 1,7 kg.

Weihnachtsfeier
PROGRAMM

82318. 24 Punkt. Min. ca. 10 kg. Zusatz 8231Ba. Min. ca. 1,7 kg.

Körperpflege
VOLKSBAD

82319. 28 Punkt. Min. ca. 12 kg. Zusatz 82319a. Min. ca. 2 kg.

Lieder-Buch
MUSIKHAUS

82320. 36 Punkt. Min. ca. 14 kg. Zusatz 82320a. Min. ca. 2,5 kg.

Druckerei
REISBACH

82321. 48 Punkt. Min. ca. 16 kg. Zusatz 82321a. Min. ca. 2,8 kg.

Kuratel

82322. 60 Punkt. Min. ca. 20 kg. Zusatz 82322a. Min. ca. 3,6 kg.

Nabe

82323. 72 Punkt. Min. ca. 25 kg. Zusatz 82323a. Min. ca. 4,6 kg.

HEIM

82324. 84 Punkt. Min. ca. 30 kg. Zusatz 82324a. Min. ca. 5,5 kg.

Start

82325. 96/84 Punkt. Min. ca. 36 kg. Zusatz 82325a. Min. ca. 6,5 kg.

Reis

Als 6 Punkt kann unsere FETTE AKZIDENZ-GROTESK Nr. 82478 benutzt werden

In den Graden von 12 Punkt großes Bild an werden die nachstehend abgedruckten
Figuren in Form eines Zusatz-Sortiments abgegeben

a b d n o p s H C D E F K L N O R S // ST T

O 30c

Ty	**Block**
Ca	**Sans Serif**
Ke	**Geometric**
Te	**Letterpress**
Da	**1908**
De	**Hermann Hoffmann**
Fo	**Berthold**
Co	**Germany**

Characteristics
Dense black weight
Roughened contours
Large x-height with minimal descenders
C c S s Vertical terminals
K k Upward curving arm
R Upward curving tail
S Alternate versions
SS ST Ligatures

AGMQRS
abcefghij
koprstuy

Connections

Hermes	1911
Bernhard Bold Condensed	1912
Lo-Type	1914
Berlin Sans	1994

Availability
Berthold Block is available from Berthold
and resellers

Specimen
Type foundry specimens. H. Berthold AG,
Leipzig, 1928? (290x215mm)

H·BERTHOLD A·G

Schwere Block

83510. 60 Punkt. Min. ca. 25 kg. Zusatz 83510 a. Min. ca. 4 kg.

Stahlwerk
MÜNSTER

83511. 72 Punkt. Min. ca. 30 kg. Zusatz 83511 a. Min. ca. 5 kg.

Bauland
SEDNITZ

83512. 84 Punkt. Min. ca. 40 kg. Zusatz 83512 a. Min. ca. 6 kg.

Europa

83513. 96 Punkt. Min. ca. 45 kg. Zusatz 83513 a. Min. ca. 7 kg.

Memel

In allen Graden werden die nachstehend abgedruckten Figuren in Form eines Zusatz–Sortiments abgegeben

$ A B C D E E F H L M N R $ / // // T

Die Grade 10, 12, 14, 16, 20, 24 Cicero werden als Plakatschriften in Holz geliefert

○ 30 e

The Berthold Type Foundry released Block in 1908. It was designed by Hermann Hoffmann (1856–1926), a German type designer who had worked as a newspaper editor in Berlin, then been appointed as director of Berthold in 1895.

Geometrically constructed sans serif forms are generally considered to have originated several years after the publication of Block, with designs like Edward Johnston's Railway Type of 1916 (pp202–203) and Jakob Erbar's groundbreaking 1922 typeface (pp224–25). There is, however, no denying the brutally robust geometric structure that underlies the uneven edges of Block's seriless letterforms from 1908.

Like other Berthold types of the time, such as Louis Oppenheim's Lo-Type, the origins of Hoffmann's design can be discovered in the lettering of contemporary advertising posters from Berlin, in particular the work of Lucian Bernhard (pp298–99). The hand-painted headlines of Bernhard's exceptional designs for clients such as Bosch and Manoli are precisely replicated in Block's irregular forms, which, like the lettering they referenced, were intended to achieve maximum impact in advertising and posters.

With its distinctively thickset characters, wavering contours, colossal x-height and extremely stunted descenders, Block made a unique contribution to twentieth-century German design. It became a staple for job printing there for many decades and was hugely influential on subsequent designs.

In the late 1970s Berthold updated Block for photocomposition, adding weights and compatible italics to offer a more extensive range of typographic options.

Ty	**Century Oldstyle**
Ca	**Serif**
Ke	**Old Style**
Te	**Letterpress**
Da	**1909**
De	**Morris Fuller Benton**
Fo	**American Type Founders**
Co	**USA**

Characteristics

Vertical stress
Moderate stroke contrast
Most capitals have uniform width
Large x-height
A Angled apex
J Descends below baseline, hooked
M Narrow
Q Curved tail
W Centre-strokes meet at serifed apex
a Double-storeyed, large bowl
g Double-storeyed

AJMQW
abcdefghij
orstuya*aefg*

Connections

Phemister's Old Style	c1858
Century Expanded	1900
Bookman Oldstyle	1901
Clearface	1907

Availability

Century Oldstyle is widely available

Specimen

American Specimen Book of Type Styles.
American Type Founders, Jersey City,
1912 (280x230mm)

Century Oldstyle

72 Point   3 A $6 25   4 a $4 55 $10 80

RICH KINGS
Strange Mind

60 Point   3 A $5 35   5 a $4 35 $9 70

BRIDES HOME
Royal Grenadier

48 Point   4 A $3 95   7 a $3 90 $7 85

HONEST BINDERS
Design Knife Handle

42 Point   4 A $3 00   8 a $3 25 $6 25

GRAND COMEDIANS
Stage Manager Excited
Delighted Social Parties

234

Century Oldstyle

The Century was a popular American magazine in circulation during the latter part of the nineteenth century. It was set in contemporary typefaces that were descendants of modern styles like Scotch Roman (pp112–13). At the small point sizes used in the magazine, the type's exaggerated stroke contrast and thin contours were extremely pale in text, rendering it hard to read. Concerned by these deficiencies, *The Century*'s publisher, Theodore De Vinne, commissioned a new typeface from Linn Boyd Benton (1844–1932) of the newly formed American Type Founders.

36 Point   5 A $2 65   8 a $2 45 $5 10

REMARKABLE METHOD
Serious Conditions Detected

30 Point   5 A $2 00   10 a $2 25 $4 25

ENTERPRISING COUNCILMEN
Graduating Exercise Unexplained

24 Point   6 A $1 65   13 a $1 85 $3 50

MODERNIZED RAILROAD SCHEMES
Distinguished Scholar Receiving Mention
Banking Question Becoming Complicated

Benton's new design, named Century Roman, first appeared in the magazine in the November 1895 edition. A typeface that was much more readable at smaller sizes, it featured an increased x-height and a more even stroke contrast than its predecessor. Century Roman was also slightly compressed to permit more characters per line and even line breaks in the magazine's two-column format.

18 Point   10 A $1 50   20 a $1 75 $3 25

BEAUTIFUL RESIDENCE
Charming Landscape Scene
Fragrant Rosebush Garden

10 Point   17 A $1 15   32 a $1 35 $2 50

PROMPT RETURN MENTIONED
Greater Energy Recently Displayed
Real Estate and Government Bonds
Tremendous Deal Lately Negotiated

The success of the Century Roman design led Benton and his son, Morris Fuller Benton, to develop further variants. The new typefaces, Century No. 2 and Century Expanded, were wider and more evenly proportioned, and the latter immediately became so popular that the original Century Roman was soon replaced by several other new variants. By 1912 the ATF catalogue no longer offered the original typeface, but featured 64 pages on the other members of the Century series – which, as a result, has come to be regarded as the world's first coordinated type family.

14 Point   14 A $1 40   26 a $1 60 $3 00

STRENUOUS PERFORMANCES
Audience Extends Congratulations
Enthusiastic Manager Applauding

9 Point   20 A $1 15   38 a $1 35 $2 50

EUROPEAN PRINTERS WELCOMED
Artistic Designer Promoting Harmony
Wonderful Combination Demonstrated
Magnificently Colored Pictures Bought

One of its members, Century Oldstyle, was drawn by Morris Fuller Benton between 1908 and 1909. It was released at a time when heavier types with bracketed serifs were returning to popularity. Sharing few visual attributes with the other typefaces of the Century family, it was probably given the name for marketing purposes, anticipating that the success of the earlier face would carry over. Its design is a revival of Alexander Phemister's old style (pp134–35), cut for Miller & Richard around 50 years earlier, with a fairly large x-height, short ascenders and descenders, large capitals and strong old-style serifs. Since its release, Century Oldstyle has been highly regarded for its easy readability and has been widely used in magazines and editorial work.

12 Point   17 A $1 30   32 a $1 45 $2 75

SCIENTIFIC DOCUMENT REQUIRED
Original Mechanical Contrivance Sought
Reconsidering $1234567890 Propositions

8 Point   21 A $1 05   42 a $1 20 $2 25

EXTRAORDINARY REPORT SUBMITTED
Interesting Resolution Immediately Endorsed
Some Propositions Receive Unanimous Vote
Prospective Members Becoming Very Active

11 Point   17 A $1 25   35 a $1 50 $2 75

EXCITED COMPETITORS RECOGNIZED
Chromatic Selections Rendered Every Night
Many Celebrated Philanthropists Organizing
Resorts Unusually Crowded During August

6 Point   23 A $0 90   46 a $1 10 $2 00

BEAUTIFUL HOMESTEAD FINELY DECORATED
Colonial Architecture Greatly Admired by Contractor
Grand Paintings Procured From European Countries
Charming Lawns and Picturesque Sloping Meadows
Hunting Party Lost in the Wilds of Southern Montana
Splendid Receptions $1234567890 Lavish Entertainment

235

HERMES-GROTESK

No. 2012. corps 36. Min. 18 Ko.

Glaube und Heimat
KUNST-VEREIN

No. 2013. corps 48. Min. 23 Ko.

Kursbericht 35

No. 2014. corps 60. Min. 26 Ko.

Musikabend

No. 2015. corps 72. Min. 34 Ko.

Reichsamt

No. 2016. corps 96/84. Min. 42 Ko.

Enoshof

7815

Ty	**Hermes-Grotesk**
Ca	**Sans Serif**
Ke	**Geometric**
Te	**Letterpress**
Da	**1911**
De	**Wilhelm Wöllmer**
Fo	**Wöllmer Type Foundry**
Co	**Germany**

Characteristics

Character construction emphasizes straight vertical strokes
Small rounded corners at terminals
C c G g S s Angled terminals
E Angled terminal on centre arm
G No spur
M High vertex
e r t Vertical terminals
i j Square dots

AEGMQR
abcefghij
koprstuy

Connections

Royal Gothic	c1870
Block	1908
Lo-Type	1914
Klavika	2004

Availability

FB Hermes is a digital revival available from the Font Bureau and resellers

Specimen

Hermes-Grotesk specimen. Wöllmer Type Foundry, 1911? (282x200mm)

SCHMALE HALBFETTE HERMES-GROTESK

No. 2059. corps 36. Min. 14 Ko.

Deutsche Uhren-Industrie
3 SCHWARZWALD 5

No. 2060. corps 48. Min. 18 Ko.

Konzert-Haus CLOU

No. 2061. corps 60. Min. 19 Ko.

Bansin 18 Goslar

No. 2062. corps 72. Min. 22 Ko.

Herbst-Moden

No. 2063. corps 96|84. Min. 32 Ko.

Korbmöbel

7817

The Wöllmer Type Foundry was established by Wilhelm Wöllmer, who had founded a commercial printing business in Berlin in 1854. Ten years later he added the foundry, which operated until 1938.

The Hermes-Grotesk typeface was issued by Wöllmer in 1911. At the turn of the century, many German foundries published sans serif display types under a variety of names, often licensing the products of other foundries. As a result, their true origins can be difficult to trace. Hermes has frequently been confused with Hermann Hoffmann's 1908 typeface, Block (pp184–85), and its design is often attributed to him. However, it is more likely to have been drawn by Wöllmer himself, an experienced type designer who also specialized in blackletter and script faces.

Although it shares qualities of robustness and bulk with Block, the similarity ends there. Hermes-Grotesk is a much more nuanced form, based on a more complex geometry. Its clean contours feature small rounded corners at terminals that soften the line, suggesting the wear and tear of presswork. Hermes is distinguished by the straightness of its vertical strokes, which allow very compact settings that are dense and powerful. This visual trait was first seen in the earliest grotesques (pp124–25) and developed further during the twentieth century in condensed types such as Aurora-Grotesk, Compacta (pp366–67) and Impact (pp372–73).

Hermes-Grotesk was a stalwart of the printing industry in its time, but it soon fell into disuse as fashions and technologies changed over ensuing decades. In 1995, Matthew Butterick drew a digital revival for the Font Bureau, and in 2010 he expanded the Hermes family with additional weights, italics and alternate glyphs.

Ty	**Imprint**
Ca	**Serif**
Ke	**Old Style**
Te	**Letterpress**
Da	**1912**
De	**Frank Hinman Pierpont**
Fo	**Monotype**
Co	**UK**

Characteristics

Top serifs wedge-shaped	
A	Angled top
E F L S T	Wide
a	Large bowl
g	Small lower bowl
t	Very narrow

AEJQRS
abcdefghij
orstuya*efg*

Connections

Caslon	c1725
Plantin	1913
Miller	1997
Arnhem	1999

Availability

Imprint is available from Monotype
and resellers

Specimen

Monotype specimen book. Lanston
Monotype Corporation, London, 1931
(290x230mm)

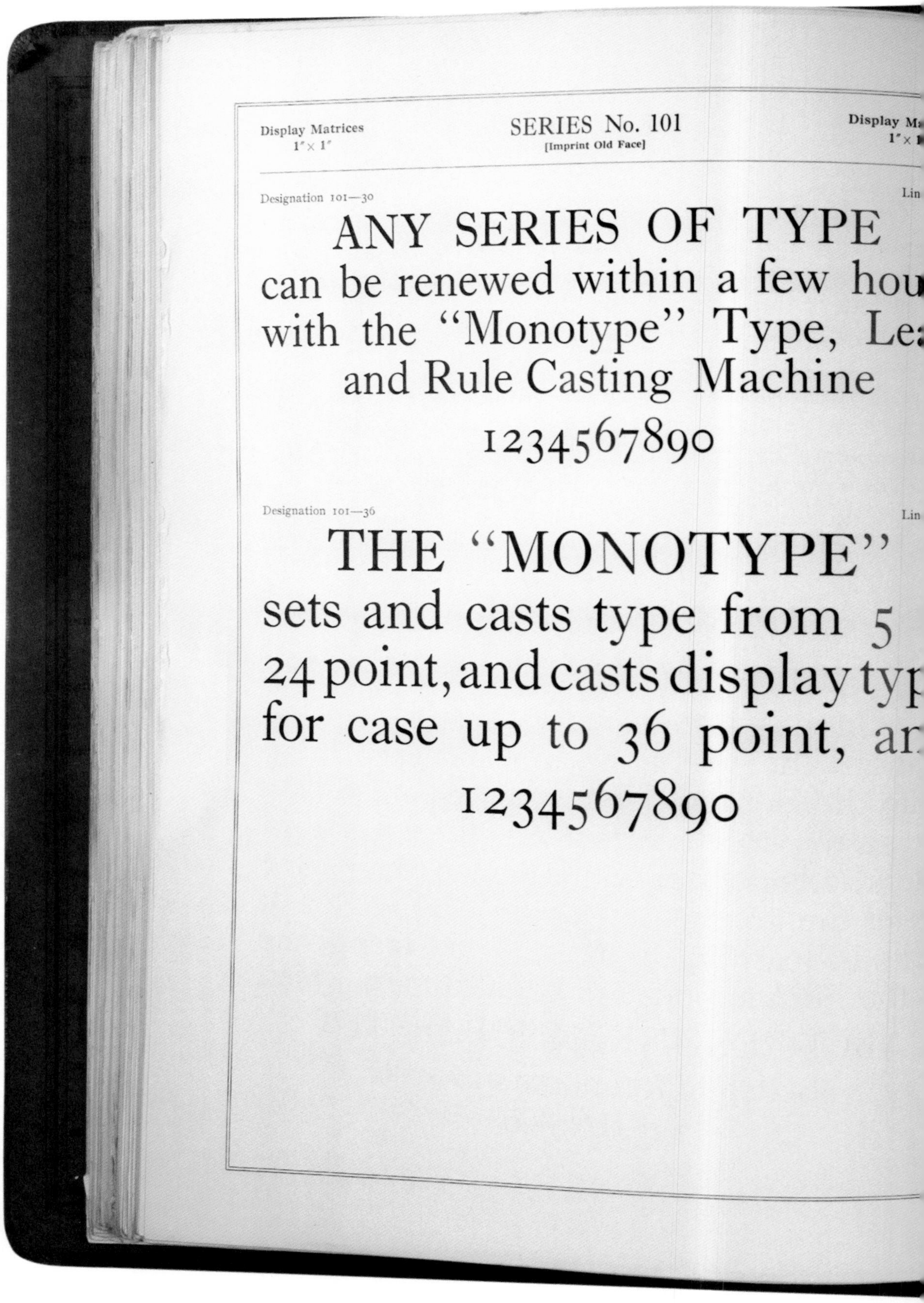

Display Matrices
1″ × 1″

SERIES No. 101
[Imprint Old Face]

Display Ma
1″ ×

Designation 101—30

Lin

ANY SERIES OF TYPE
can be renewed within a few hou
with the "Monotype" Type, Le
and Rule Casting Machine
1234567890

Designation 101—36

Lin

THE "MONOTYPE"
sets and casts type from 5
24 point, and casts display typ
for case up to 36 point, an
1234567890

SERIES No. 101
[Imprint Old Face]

Display Matrices
1″ × 1″

Display Matrices
1″ × 1″

Designation 101—18

Line ·181

On the greatest and most useful of all inventions, the invention of alphabetical writing, Plato did not look with much complacency. He seems to have thought that the use of letters had operated on the human mind as the use of the go-cart in learning to walk, or of corks in learning to swim is said to operate on the human body. It was a support which soon became indispensable to those who used it which made vigorous exertion first unnecessary and then impossible. The powers of the intellect would, he conceived, have been more fully developed without this delusive aid. Men would have been compelled to exercise the understanding and the memory, and, by deep and assiduous meditation,

ABCDEFGHIJKLMNOPQRSTUVWXYZ

12345 abcdefghijklmnopqrstuvwxyz 67890

Designation 101—24

Line ·2364

On the greatest and most useful of all inventions, the invention of alphabetical writing, Plato did not look with much complacency. He seems to have thought that the use of letters had operated on the human mind as the use of the go-cart in learning to walk, or of corks in learning to swim is said to operate on the human body. It was a support which

ABCDEFGHIJKLMNOPQRSTUV

abcdefghijklmnopqrstuvwxyz

1234567890

At the beginning of the twentieth century, an increasing number of printers installed the new Monotype and Linotype composing machines for setting type, although most of the typefaces available to them at the time were inferior imitations of foundry types.

This situation improved in 1912, when the first significant typeface cut specifically for mechanical composition appeared. It was commissioned from the Monotype Corporation by J. H. Mason (1875–1951) and Gerard Meynell for use in *The Imprint*, a periodical for the printing trade. Mason was the journal's editor and head of the book production department at the Central School of Arts and Crafts in London.

The new typeface, originally called Imprint Old Face, was cut by technicians in the Monotype Drawing Office under the direction of Frank Hinman Pierpont. Mason had anticipated that it would be an adaptation of eighteenth-century Caslon types, configured to suit the new casting machines, but the Monotype designers gave Imprint an individual personality with an orderly structure and sharply drawn contours.

Imprint has a larger x-height than most old-style faces, with comparatively short ascenders and descenders. Like Monotype Plantin (pp194–95), the letter contours are sturdy and very legible without being heavy. The original design included an extremely wide range of special characters for foreign languages, together with alternative lining and non-lining figures.

The Imprint journal achieved an excellent reputation in the printing trade but was not financially successful and it ceased publication within only a year. The typeface, however, proved emphatically that the Monotype casting machine could produce results that surpassed the finest hand-set composition, and it was extensively used in editorial and book design throughout the twentieth century. A digital revival was released by Monotype in 2001.

Ty	**Nicolas-Cochin**
Ca	**Serif**
Ke	**Transitional**
Te	**Letterpress**
Da	**1912**
De	**Georges Peignot**
Fo	**Peignot & Sons**
Co	**France**

Characteristics

	Large, tall capitals
	Tall ascenders with small x-height
A	Angled apex extends to left
C	Protruding lower stroke
M	Splayed
N	Oblique stroke extends to left at head
R	Wide, curved leg
S	Inclined

ACMRS
abcdefghij
korstuyaefg

Connections

Bernhard Modern	1937
Cochin	1977
Mantinia	1993
FF Oneleigh	1999

Availability

Nicolas-Cochin is available from Linotype and resellers

Specimen

Spécimen général des fonderies. Deberny & Peignot, Paris, 1926 (260x190mm)

LE NICOLAS-COCHIN   4ᵉ Catégorie

50 a 15 A   Rom. 2173 - Ital. 2231 - c. 14   3 k. 40

Depuis dix ans, nous avons vu se développer, plus qu'on ne l'avait jamais vu en France, le goût des styles disparus. Tandis que des commerçants et des antiquaires intéressés cherchent à maintenir, dans toute son ardeur, l'engouement du public pour les meubles, les bibelots ou les œuvres d'art des époques classiques, des artistes, fermes partisans des.....

1234567890 — 1234567890

LES BIBLIOPHILES   ÉDITION DE LUXE

50 a 15 A   Rom. 2174 - Ital. 2232 - c. 16   4 k. 20

Depuis dix ans, nous avons vu se développer, plus qu'on ne l'avait jamais vu en France, le goût des styles disparus. Tandis que des commerçants et des antiquaires intéressés cherchent à maintenir, dans toute son ardeur, l'engouement du public pour les meubles, les bibelots ou les œuvres d'art des époques classiques

1234567890 — 1234567890

BEAU MOBILIER   APPARTEMENT

30 a 10 A   Rom. 2158 - Ital. 2233 - c. 18   3 k. 90

Depuis dix ans, nous avons vu se développer, plus qu'on ne l'avait jamais vu en France, le goût des styles disparus. Tandis que des commerçants et des antiquaires intéressés cherchent à maintenir, dans toute son ardeur,

1234567890 — 1234567890

EXPOSITION   DÉCORATION

FONDERIES DEBERNY & PEIGNOT, 14, RUE CABANIS, PARIS

LE NICOLAS-COCHIN

30 a 10 A   Rom. 2160 - Ital. 2234 - c. 24 petit œil   6 k. 40

Quand on veut plaire dans le monde, il faut se résoudre à se laisser apprendre beaucoup de choses qu'on sait par des personnes qui les ignorent. L'inutile se donne une raison d'être.

Maximes et Pensées de Chamfort.

1234567890 — *1234567890*

ALENÇON   *TERGNIER*

30 a 10 A   Rom. 2162 - Ital. 2235 - c. 24 gros œil (sans talus)   8 k. 40

La vie contemplative est souvent misérable. L'on doit agir plus, penser moins et ne pas se regarder vivre. C'est...

Un Recueil de Proverbes.

123568o — *123568o*

MARNE   *RHONE*

Les longues du bas sont fondues sur corps 32

FONDERIES DEBERNY & PEIGNOT, 14, RUE CABANIS, PARIS

I - 10
RÉSUMÉ DES
LABEURS

Charles-Nicolas Cochin (1715–90), a Parisian engraver and illustrator, was a leading light in French artistic circles during the reign of King Louis XV in the eighteenth century. In addition to creating a large number of exquisite original drawings, Cochin illustrated more than 200 books and produced many designs for paintings and sculptures. Although he was not involved in the process of cutting and casting type, his engravings were frequently captioned or titled by hand in slender, late baroque letters that are distinguished by their incised contours, sharp serifs and elongated ascenders, in a style that greatly influenced the type designs of Baskerville, Didot and Bodoni.

One of the finest revivals of Cochin's engraved letters is the typeface named after him that was designed by Georges Peignot (1872–1915) for the Peignot & Sons type foundry in 1912 and cut by Charles Malin. The irregular qualities of incised copper are echoed in Peignot's design, which drew inspiration from the master engraver's letters without following the forms specifically. Peignot's Nicolas-Cochin type features very tall ascenders, long, sharply cut serifs and strokes that imitate the curved lines of letterforms cut with a burin.

In 1977 Matthew Carter expanded Peignot's typeface for photocomposition as a family in three styles. Named Cochin, this revival is available in digitized form. An alternative digital version that is rounder, more evenly proportioned and less archaic than Nicolas-Cochin was also released by Linotype in 2004.

Ty	**Plantin**
Ca	**Serif**
Ke	**Old Style**
Te	**Letterpress**
Da	**1913**
De	**Frank Hinman Pierpont**
Fo	**Monotype**
Co	**UK**

Characteristics

A	Flat apex
M	Splayed
P	Open bowl
Q	Blunt tail, terminates vertically
a	Double-storeyed, large bowl
b d h	Wedge-shaped top serifs
g	Double-storeyed, blunt ear
j	Stem has very slight curve
k	Blunt leg, terminates vertically
t	Very narrow

AEMPQ
abcdefghij
orstuya*efg*

Connections

Granjon's Roman	1560
Imprint	1912
Times New Roman	1932
DTL Van Den Keere	1994

Availability

Plantin is available from Monotype and resellers

Specimen

Monotype specimen book. Lanston Monotype Corporation, London, 1931 (290x230mm)

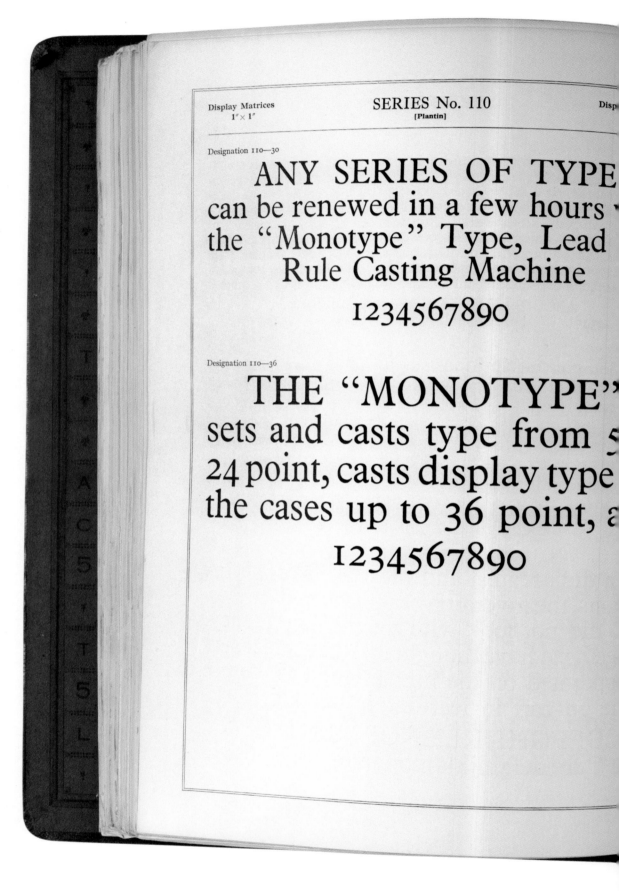

Display Matrices
1″ × 1″

SERIES No. 110
[Plantin]

Designation 110—30

ANY SERIES OF TYPE
can be renewed in a few hours
the "Monotype" Type, Lead
Rule Casting Machine
1234567890

Designation 110—36

THE "MONOTYPE"
sets and casts type from 5
24 point, casts display type
the cases up to 36 point, a
1234567890

SERIES No. 110
[Plantin]

Display Matrices
1″ × 1″

Display Matrices
1″ × 1″

gnation 110—42

Line ·4576

"MONOTYPE"
s the very best that can be
btained in type, leads,
ules, borders and spac-
ng material, and in the
uality equal in every way

gnation 110—48

Line ·5268

"MONOTYPE"
neans the best that is
o be obtained in type,
eads, rules and spac-
ng material, and in a

In 1913 the British Lanston Monotype Corporation issued Plantin on the initiative of the its works manager, Frank Hinman Pierpont, to fulfil the need for a text typeface suitable for printing on smooth art paper.

As a model Pierpont chose a sixteenth-century type cut by Robert Granjon that he had discovered at the Plantin-Moretus Museum, housed in the Antwerp type foundry of Christophe Plantin (1520–89), after whom the new face was named, somewhat erroneously since Plantin was not involved in cutting type. However, the significance of the Monotype revival lies less in its historical context and more in the fact that it was made to exploit modern production techniques. Punch cutters had always compensated for the effect of ink spread in the design of type by making strokes thinner than they would look when printed, but by 1913, improvements in paper manufacturing had resulted in the availability of smooth, coated stock that no longer required such adjustments.

Plantin was cut by Fritz Stelzer under Pierpont's supervision. He adapted the sixteenth-century prototype to make a readable, robust typeface suited to printing on the new papers. To increase legibility in text, it was given short ascenders and descenders, a large x-height and a slightly condensed width. Plantin's thin strokes were thickened in proportion to heavier stems in order to improve reproduction. The top serifs on lower case letters such as b and r are distinguished by their wedge-shaped appearance, which is particularly pronounced in bold variations. The result is an all-purpose typeface that shares the robust qualities of Monotype Imprint (pp190–91): sturdy enough for use on art paper but compact in relation to its size, and thus economical and pleasant to read.

Plantin has been used in publishing and advertising extensively since its release, both as a text typeface and in display applications. It has influenced the development of many other designs, and served as a key source for Times New Roman (pp280–81) in the 1930s.

Ty	**Centaur**
Ca	**Serif**
Ke	**Old Style, Venetian**
Te	**Letterpress**
Da	**1914**
De	**Bruce Rogers**
Fo	**Monotype**
Co	**USA**

Characteristics

E	Serifs on centre bar
J	Descends below baseline
M	Splayed, top serifs face outwards
R	Wide, curved leg below baseline
a r	Pen-formed terminal
e	Oblique crossbar extending to right
j	Pen-formed terminal curves downwards
o	Left-inclined axis

AEJMRS
abcdefghij
orstuya*efg*

Connections

Cloister Old Style	1913
Bembo	1929
Dante	1957
Adobe Jenson	1996

Availability

Centaur is available from Monotype and resellers

Specimen

New Series of the Centaur Types of Bruce Rogers and the Arrighi Italics of Frederic Warde. Monotype, London, 1929 (290x210mm)

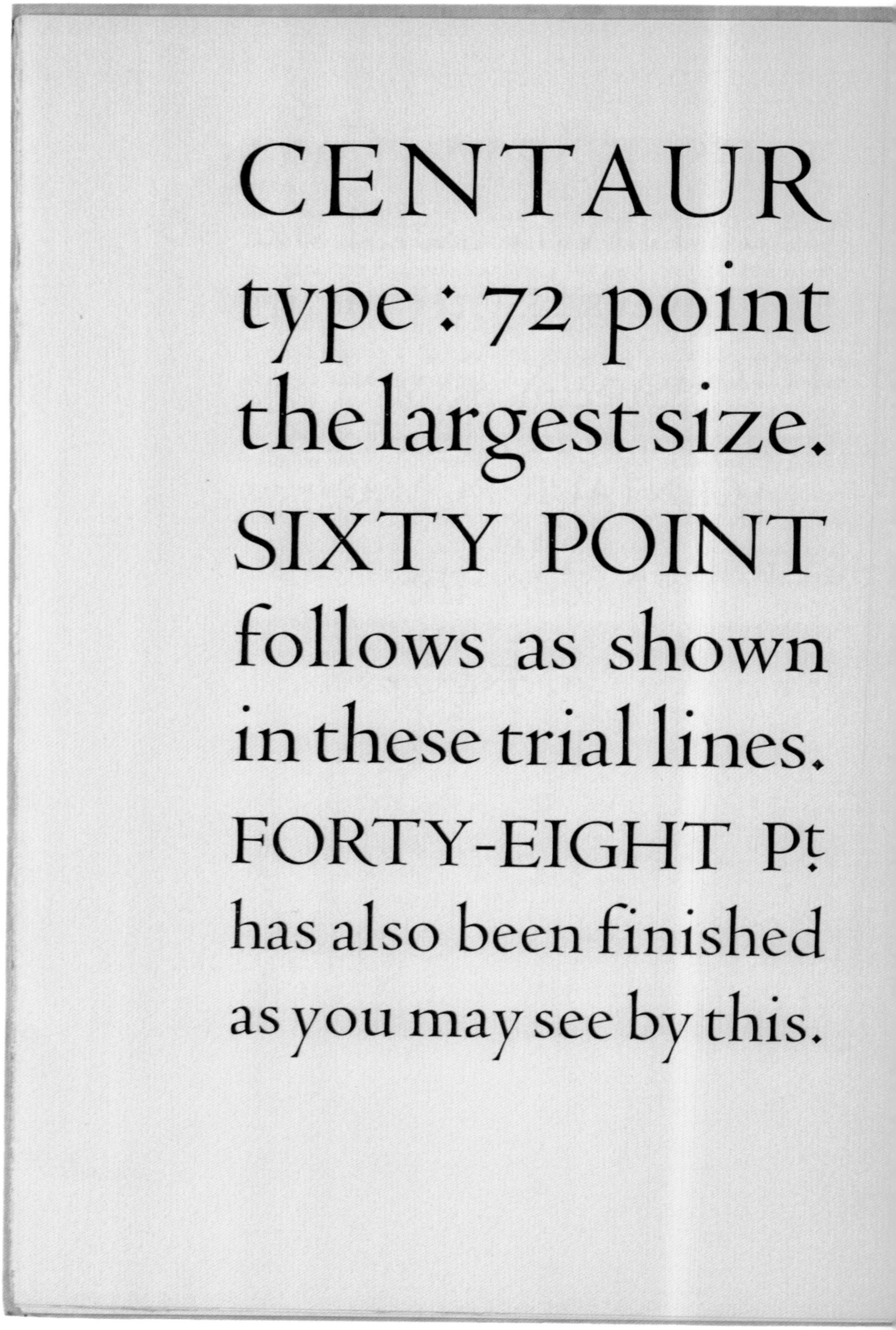

CENTAUR type : 72 point the largest size.

SIXTY POINT follows as shown in these trial lines.

FORTY-EIGHT Pt has also been finished as you may see by this.

THIS FORTY-TWO point is a very useful size not always easy to obtain. THIRTY-SIX POINT IS furnished, as are all the founts, with the figures 1234567890. CENTAUR ON THIRTY PT. can be seen in these three trial lines which show also: ÆŒQu£$& .,:;-!?

COMPOSITION MATRICES

COMPOSITION SIZES NOW BEGIN with 24 pt, (of which this is a specimen) and include 22 pt, 18 pt, 16 pt, 14 pt, 12 pt, & 10 pt. TWENTY-TWO POINT CAN BE CAST ON 24 point bodies and supplies a convenient type for folio volumes—catalogues of art collections, etc.

Centaur is among the most sophisticated of the numerous twentieth-century reinterpretations of the Venetian type cut by Nicolas Jenson in 1470 (pp20–21). Bruce Rogers (1870–1957), a prodigiously talented American typographer, was commissioned to design it for the Metropolitan Museum of Art in 1914.

Rogers intended to make a typeface that would emphasize the calligraphic qualities of its source. He worked from photo enlargements of Jenson's type, first drawing over the letters with a flat pen, then correcting them with white paint and judiciously reinterpreting the forms where appropriate. The type was cut from his drawings by Robert Wiebking and cast for the exclusive use of Rogers and his client by Barnhart Brothers & Spindler. Initially used in upper case by the museum in 1914, the typeface was named Centaur after the title of the first book set in it: *The Centaur*, designed by Rogers and published the following year.

Centaur was well received and, due to popular demand, Rogers agreed to make the type available in a Monotype version for machine composition that was issued in 1929. It was originally cut as a roman only, but at Rogers' request Monotype added an italic based on drawings by Frederic Warde (1894–1939), named Arrighi. Because Jenson's Roman did not have a companion italic, Warde used the types cut by Ludovico degli Arrighi in 1524–27 as his models. He shortened the ascenders so that the italic would balance visually with Centaur's height and created a new set of matching inclined capitals.

Centaur was an eminently readable but exceptionally delicate typeface. Rogers himself was aware of its limitations, writing prophetically: 'It is a little too elegant and thin for our modern papers and methods of printing, and seen at its best when printed on dampened hand-made or other antique papers, with more impressions than you can ordinarily get a pressman to put on it.'

In more recent photocomposition and digital incarnations Rogers' misgivings are borne out. Although these revivals are accurate reproductions of the original type they fail to compensate for digital or offset litho printing methods, resulting in settings that can look emaciated and hard to read at smaller sizes.

Ty	**Edel-Grotesk**
Ca	**Sans Serif**
Ke	**Grotesque**
Te	**Letterpress**
Da	**c1914**
De	**Unknown**
Fo	**Wagner & Schmidt**
Co	**Germany**

Characteristics

Most capitals have uniform width
B R Small upper bowl
C c S s e g Angled terminals
E H High crossbar
G Has spur, high arm
R Straight, angled leg
a Double-storeyed
f r t Narrow
g Single-storeyed
t Angled top-stroke

BCGKS
abcdefhi
komprst

Connections

Breite Grotesk	1890
Akzidenz-Grotesk	c1898
Venus	1907
FF Bau	2002

Availability

Not available

Specimen

Edel-Grotesk type specimen. Wagner &
Schmidt, Leipzig, date unknown
(270x210mm)

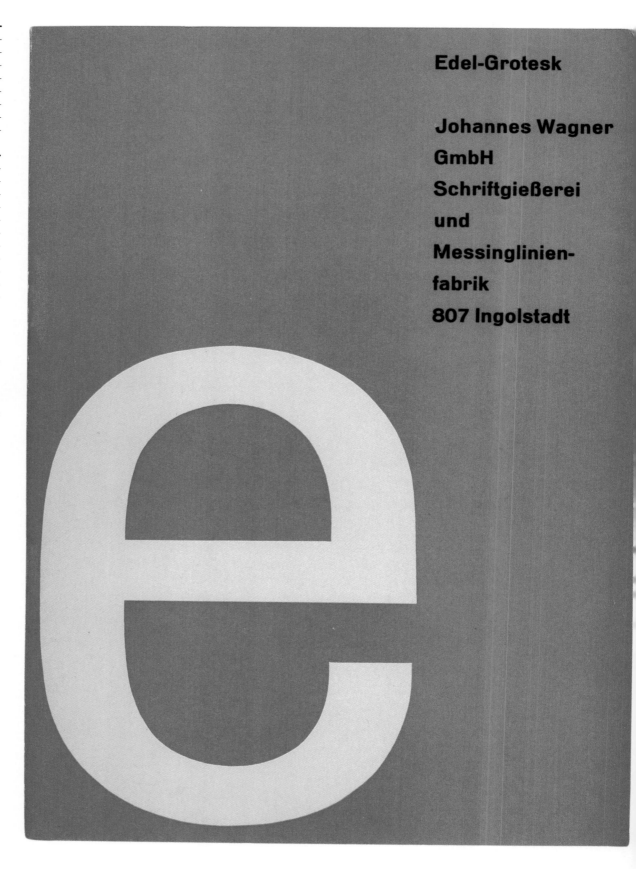

Edel-Grotesk

Johannes Wagner
GmbH
Schriftgießerei
und
Messinglinien-
fabrik
807 Ingolstadt

The history of the origins and early development of the sans serif in Germany at the beginning of the twentieth century is shrouded in obscurity. This is largely the result of a general absence of documentation for the rapid proliferation of types being produced and a lack of established conventions for naming them.

The situation is further complicated by the confusion caused by widespread copying at the time. Albrecht Seemann's *Handbuch der Schriftarten* (Handbook of Typefaces), published in 1926, went to considerable lengths to clarify matters by listing the product ranges of German foundries under category headings. In the Grotesk section of the handbook there are a number of typefaces published by competing type foundries that appear to be identical but are listed under different names.

It is probable that these fonts originated at Wagner & Schmidt, a Leipzig punch-cutting and engraving company, since, in addition to casting their own types, a large part of their business was the sale of matrices of their original designs to other foundries throughout Europe. Buyers would include them in their product ranges and market them as their own. Venus (pp182–83), released in 1907 by the Bauer Foundry, was one such design.

The identical designs shown in Seemann's handbook are thought to originate in a type of the early 1900s originally named Wotan, attributed to Johannes Wagner (1888–1965) and cut by Wagner & Schmidt before 1914. The design is based on nineteenth-century German wood-type grotesques ('Wotan' translates to English as 'wooden'). Its matrices are probably the originals from which at least ten identical versions from various foundries were produced under different names. The Aurora-Grotesk family, first released by the C. E. Weber foundry at around the same time, was probably cast from Wagner & Schmidt matrices. This version was extended with a wide range of variant styles cut and cast by Weber over many years. Jobbing print work using variants of these sans serif styles in a range of weights and widths was seen extensively in the early years of the twentieth century.

Edel-Grotesk dreiviertelfett

A B C D E F G H I J K L M
N O P Q R S T U V W X Y Z
1 2 3 4 5 6 7 8 9 0

Nr. 7706   Nonpareille (6 Punkt)   Min. etwa 4 kg   a 220 A 56

So mancher sagt, daß die Schneider die schlechtesten Anzüge und die Schuhmacher die schlechtesten Schuhe tragen; demnach müßten, logisch weitergedacht, auch

Nr. 7708   Petit (8 Punkt)   Min. etwa 5 kg   a 170 A 36

Gar oft hört man von Handwerkern, daß sie mit Drucksachen keine Kunden gewinnen

Nr. 7710   Korpus (10 Punkt)   Min. etwa 6 kg   a 120 A 30

Hier ist es eine große Aufgabe der Drucker, durch beweisende oder

Nr. 7712   Cicero (12 Punkt)   Min. etwa 7 kg   a 96 A 24

Man hat so etwas wie einen Werbefeldzug noch nicht an

Nr. 7714   Mittel (14 Punkt)   Min. etwa 7 kg   a 76 A 20

Werbung und Wirkung

Nr. 7716   Tertia (16 Punkt)   Min. etwa 8 kg   a 64 A 18

Gestalten und Setzen

Nr. 7720   Text (20 Punkt)   Min. etwa 11 kg   a 44 A 12

Monteur-Anzüge

Nr. 7724   2 Cicero (24 Punkt)   Min. etwa 12 kg   a 38 A 12

Der Grundsatz

Nr. 7728   Doppelmittel (28 Punkt)   Min. etwa 14 kg   a 32 A 10

Das neue Schulungsmaterial

Nr. 7735   3 Cicero (36 Punkt)   Min. etwa 16 kg   a 20 A 10

Unsere Eigenwerbung

Nr. 7748   4 Cicero (48 Punkt)   Min. etwa 20 kg   a 16 A 8

Ein Muster-Druck

Nr. 7760   5 Cicero (60 Punkt)   Min. etwa 20 kg   a 8 A 6

Gummitücher

Nr. 7772   6 Cicero (72 Punkt)   Min. etwa 25 kg   a 8 A 6

Musterbuch

Ty	**Goudy Oldstyle**
Ca	**Serif**
Ke	**Old Style**
Te	**Letterpress**
Da	**1915**
De	**Frederic W. Goudy**
Fo	**American Type Founders**
Co	**USA**

Characteristics

E L Bottom arm turns upwards
J Descends below baseline, hooked
P Open bowl
Q Sweeping tail below letter
R Wide leg
a Double-storeyed, large bowl
g Double-storeyed, upturned, pointed ear
i j Diamond-shaped dot
t Upturned serif on the arm

AEJPQR
abcdefghij
orstuya*efg*

Connections

Kennerley Old Style	1911
Deepdene	1927
University of California Old Style	1938
FF Oneleigh	1999

Availability

Goudy Oldstyle is widely available

Specimen

Book of American Types, Standard Faces.
American Type Founders, Jersey City,
1934 (279x210mm)

Goudy Oldstyle

72 Point   4A 6a
RICH
Spirits

60 Point   5A 7a
MODE
Highest

48 Point   5A 9a
NOTICE
Bright lad
leads class

42 Point   5A 10a
DANCED
Celebrated
big holiday

36 Point   6A 10a
HOME
Quaint

30 Point   7A 14a
FOUND
Musician
delighted

24 Point   8A 16a
NOTICES
Unfinished
framework

18 Point   12A 23a
MECHANIC
GIVES experts
usual warning

14 Point   17A 34a
EXPERIMENTS
BRIGHT magician
spent much time
unraveling tricks

12 Point   21A 40a
GRAND PICTURE
RECENT photographs
inspire many leading
theatrical promoters

10 Point   24A 48a
PERFECT SPECIMEN
SIMPLE design exhibited
considered very artistic
for modern typography

8 Point   27A 54a
CUT-COST EQUIPMENT
MODERN cabinets containing
leads and quads reduce labor
costs considerably. Efficiency
material creates large profits

6 Point   29A 58a
STIMULATING PRODUCTION
PROGRESSIVE printers recognize the
fact that economy lies in equipping
their plants with modern materials
and machinery. Now is the time, as
every minute lost swells the pay roll

Characters in Complete Font

ABCDEFGHIJKLM
NOPQRSTUVWX
YZ & $ 1234567890
abcdefghijklmnopq
rstuvwxyz ff fi fl ffi ffl ct
¶ ❦ . , - ' : ; ! ?

SMALL CAPS from 6 to 18 Point, and Oldstyle Figures
1234567890 in all sizes, are put up in separate fonts and furnished
only when specially ordered

:[32]:

1
2
3
4
5
6
7
8
9
0

60 Point Fi
set soli

Goudy Italic

★72 Point   3A 5a
Enlist

★60 Point   4A 7a
Restful

★48 Point   5A 9a
Singular

★42 Point   6A 10a
CREAM
Graphites

Characters in Complete Font

A B C D E F
G G H I J J K
L M N O P Q
R S T T U V
W X Y Y Z
& $ 1 2 3 4 5 6
7 8 9 0 a b c d e
f g h i j k l m n o
p q r s t u v w x
y z ff fi fl ffi ffl
Qu ct . , - ' ' : ; ! ?

★New Sizes

:[33]:

36 Point   6A 11a
PRINTERS
Harpsichord

30 Point   7A 14a
MECHANIC
English Subject

24 Point   9A 18a
INTRODUCED
Quaint Inhabitant

18 Point   14A 28a
MODERN SYSTEM
Large Mercantile Firm

14 Point   19A 36a
EXCURSION STEAMER
Delights Numerous Children

12 Point   24A 46a
BEAUTIFUL COMPOSITION
Hartford Sculptor Awarded Medal

10 Point   26A 52a
PRINTING LEADING MANKIND
Michigan College Students Enlightened
Bright Scholars Learning Graphic Arts

8 Point   29A 58a
ENFORCES FIRE PREVENTION RULES
Drastic Regulations Ordered by Advisory Board
Brilliant Artist Receives Highest School Award
Sculptor Beginning Statue Destined For Library

6 Point   33A 65a
AMERICAN TYPE STYLES INCREASE BUSINESS
National Advertisers Demand Latest Typographic Designs
Magnificent Craftsmanship Delighted Cultured Audience
Interesting Specimens Inspired Printers Attending Exhibits

Following the commercial success of his first typeface, Kennerley, Frederic W. Goudy (1865–1947) was commissioned by American Type Founders to create another. Issued in 1915 as Goudy Oldstyle, it became an instant bestseller. One of America's prodigiously gifted type designers, Goudy was a true perfectionist, striving always to find the ideal roman typeface. As for all of his types, he produced the original drawings for Goudy Oldstyle freehand.

Goudy Oldstyle is a well-balanced typeface with a strong personality and a few individual quirks that are typical of Goudy's work. Although its design was not based on a specific historical model, a fifteenth-century Venetian influence is evident in many of its attributes, most notably the proportions of the lower case and the use of rounded, slightly concave serifs. The full-bodied letters are characterized by a low contrast between thick and thin strokes and an oblique stress. A particular trait is the short descent of the lower case, which makes for tight settings that use vertical space very economically. Another exceptional feature of Goudy Oldstyle is the beautifully drawn classic capitals that are often used for title pages and headings.

On completing the type Goudy sold it outright to ATF on the understanding that the foundry would not interfere with his original designs. It went on to become one of the most successful typefaces ever produced by the foundry, the company publishing a 124-page specimen to promote it in 1927. However, because Goudy had sold the rights to his design, when the opportunity arose to extend it, development work was undertaken by the foundry's in-house designer, Morris Fuller Benton. Several additional variants were cut, all of which sold in great quantities, although Goudy received no compensation whatsoever, causing his relationship with ATF to deteriorate.

Satisfactory in both text and display environments, Goudy Oldstyle is one of the most popular typefaces of all time, frequently seen in packaging and advertising or wherever a gracious, readable and economical roman is needed.

Ty	**Johnston's Railway Type**
Ca	**Sans Serif**
Ke	**Geometric**
Te	**Lettering**
Da	**1916**
De	**Edward Johnston**
Fo	**N/A**
Co	**UK**

Characteristics

C c G S s e	Vertical terminals
G	No spur, no arm
M	High apex
O Q	Perfect circle
R	Wide, straight angled leg
S	Small upper arc
a g	Double-storeyed
i j	Diamond-shaped dot
l	Curved foot
o	Perfect circle
1	No serif

AGMQRS
abcefghij
kloprsty

Connections

Gill Sans	1928
Granby	1930
Brandon Grotesque	2010
Johnston 100	2016

Availability

ITC Johnston is available from Monotype and resellers. P22 Underground is available from P22 Type Foundry and resellers

Specimen

Photolithograph of the preliminary drawings for one-inch Railway type designs. Edward Johnston, 1916 (268x215mm)

Just before World War I, England's foremost calligrapher, Edward Johnston (1872–1944), was commissioned by the London Underground Electric Railway Company to design a new typeface as part of a plan to renew the company's image. To ensure that its communications would be unique and recognizable, the London Underground required lettering for its signage and publicity that would have 'the bold simplicity of the authentic lettering of the finest periods' and which would also belong 'unmistakably to the twentieth century'.

Johnston's sans serif type first appeared on an Underground poster in July 1916. The work of a master craftsman, it demonstrates the beauty and power of typography as a communication tool. Although it embodies an understanding of the history of the letterform in every detail, its reconciliation of humanistic and geometric forms is without precedent in the history of typography.

Johnston's upper case contours are based on the square and circular shapes of roman inscriptional capitals, and the lower case on the Italian script of the fifteenth century, the humanist minuscule. The Railway Type was exceptionally economical in its use of space. Drawn in a single weight, it was monoline, distinctive and remarkably legible, with every detail judiciously refined. Johnston established a precise balance of form and counterform not only in the letters, but also in the spacing between them, a consideration unknown in the grotesques of the day.

Protected by law, Johnston's Railway Type was used exclusively for nearly a century in London Underground's signage, publicity and posters, usually in capitals. However, it was not cut for presswork and in later years London Underground would use Stephenson, Blake's Granby (pp258–59) for text settings. In the 1980s, the type was recut digitally. This version, New Johnston, fell short of the original, with a large x-height and with many of Johnston's idiosyncratic traits eradicated. A decade later P22 Type Foundry issued a more accurate digital revival, and in 2016 Transport for London commissioned Monotype to remaster the typeface for its exclusive use, with a brief to restore its original features.

Johnston's radical innovations in the design of sans serif letters had a galvanizing effect on the direction of type design, influencing everything that came after it. His humanist, geometric sans serif was the original expression of the idea that a typeface could be a representation of its own time and place.

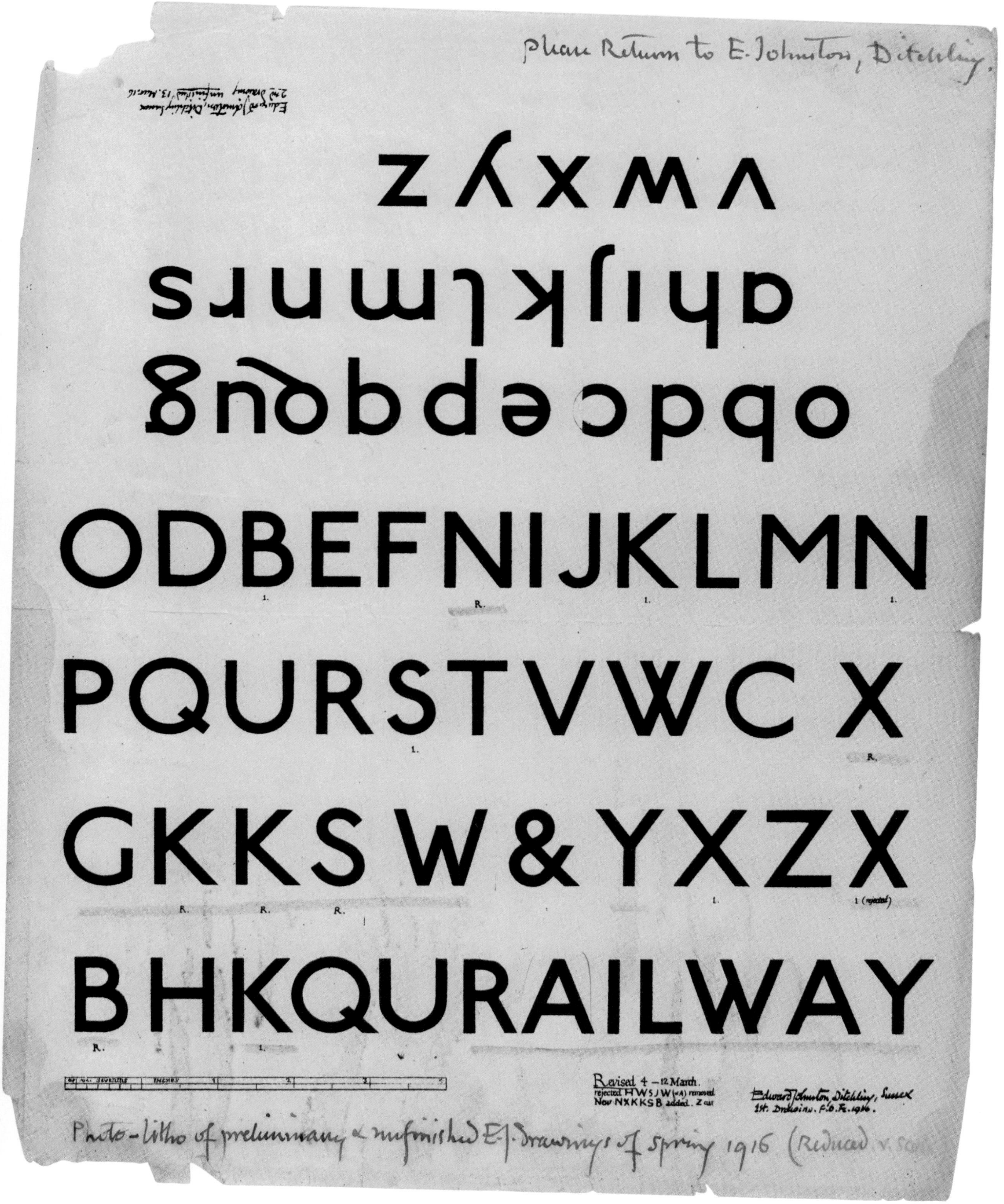

Please Return to E. Johnston, Ditchling.

Edward Johnston, Ditchling, Sussex
2nd Drawing, unfinished. 13. March. 16

z y x w v
w x y z

a h i j k l m n r s

o b d c e p q d u g

ODBEFNIJKLMN

PQURSTVWC X

GKKS W & YXZX

BHKQURAILWAY

Revised 4 – 12 March.
rejected H W S J W (&A) removed.
Now N X K K S B added. Z cut

Edward Johnston, Ditchling, Sussex
1st Drawing. F.O. Fe. 1916.

Photo-litho of preliminary & unfinished E.J. drawings of spring 1916 (Reduced. v. sca

Ty	**Parsons**
Ca	**Slab Serif**
Ke	**N/A**
Te	**Letterpress**
Da	**1917**
De	**Will Ransom**
Fo	**Barnhart Brothers & Spindler / ATF**
Co	**USA**

Characteristics

Alternate character set with elongated
ascenders and descenders

A Foot serifs face inwards

E F Mid-arm serif faces downwards

P R Open bowl

V W Curved right stem

a b d e g p Open bowl

e Small eye

f h i k t Serifs at head and foot face
opposite directions

f t Square form

g y Square tail

ABCERV
abcefghij
koprstvy

Connections

Cheltenham	1902
Pabst	1902
Hobo	1910
Artcraft	1912

Availability

Parsnip, a digital revival of Parsons, is
available from Nick's Fonts and resellers

Specimen

Specimen Book and Catalogue. American
Type Founders, Jersey City, 1923
(255x170mm)

Parsons Bold

Artistic Type Effects

An Origina
Type Desig

The
Family
Parsons Series
Parsons Italic
Parsons Bold

MANY artistic as
as exclusive e
in type arrange
without special
may be obtained
Parsons types. They are
different from any other
style and offer such a va
of possibilities that the de
will rarely ever grow tire
to the advertiser or the pr

The quaint auxiliaries accompa
the Parsons Family consist of the
Initials and Initial Decorators for
two colors. Whenever a color is u
these auxiliaries will add the att
touch sought by a discerning cli

The Parsons design is adapted for use in advertisemen
announcements, and all kinds of commercial printin

The Parsons Bol

88

Parsons Family

Pottery & China—

There is a beauty and originality in the designs and workmanship in our products of pottery and china. Vases and jardinieres of Oriental design, Chilean handmade earthen jugs, and a selection of exquisite masterpieces in china

Articles selected for out-of-town patrons

Foreign Agents in France, Italy, Persia, Greece, Siberia, Austria, China & Japan

Robert Whitelock Company

Jacksonville, Michigan

SPARTAN BORDER

BATIK

An artistic material to be had in many pleasing combinations

A fadeless washable cloth suitable for Studio Smocks Kimonos and Decorations

Samples furnished upon request

Elizabeth Hildrell
The Arts & Crafts Shop
Arlington

Who Reads Your Advertising?

Numerous pieces of printed matter daily find their way to the waste basket unread. Many are elegant specimens of advertising copy, but, not planned with more care, they are utterly worthless. Hardy Service offers advertisers a combination of typographical layout and copy writing that will eliminate much of this waste

Telephone John 375

Wilbur Hardy
Newton

89

Will Ransom (1878–1955) was so disillusioned by the misuse of his only typeface, Parsons, that he never attempted type design again in his long and illustrious career as a commercial artist.

In 1917, working as a freelance designer, Ransom drew up a distinctive style of lettering for advertisements promoting the Chicago department store Carson Pirie Scott and Co. Naming it Parsons after the store's advertising manager, the Barnhart Brothers & Spindler type foundry undertook the task of cutting it as type.

Ransom was reluctant to include the extremely long ascenders and descenders that characterized his advertising lettering in the typeface. He insisted the foundry advise printers that these should be used sparingly, with not more than one appearing in a line of setting. Accordingly, Parsons came with a disclaimer warning against the overuse of the extended b, d, g, h, k, l, p and y and double characters. However, the typeface became enormously fashionable in the 1920s and was very widely used in American motion picture titles and advertisements – frequently, to Ransom's horror, with a total lack of discrimination.

The foundry took every possible opportunity to maximize profits from the unprecedented success of Parsons. Over the next seven years they supplemented the original single weight with bold and italic versions, additional alternate characters, a set of decorative swash initials, numerous exotic borders and ornaments in one and two colours. Ransom was so disturbed by this exploitation of his original idea and by its continued mistreatment that he chose never to design any more typefaces. However, as the type historian Alexander Lawson said, 'while it lasted it was a wowzer, and the commercial printers had a wild time with it'.

Ty	**Century Schoolbook**
Ca	**Serif**
Ke	**Modern, Clarendon**
Te	**Letterpress**
Da	**1918**
De	**Morris Fuller Benton**
Fo	**American Type Founders**
Co	**USA**

Characteristics

Vertical stress with slight stroke contrast
Wide body
Moderate x-height
Heavy, bracketed serifs
M Narrow
Q Looped tail below letter
R a t Tail turns upwards
a c f j r y Ball terminals
b No serif at foot
g Double-storeyed with teardrop ear
t Curved bracket connects stem and bar

GMQRS
abcdefghi
orstyaefg

Connections

Scotch Roman	1812
Century Expanded	1900
Century Oldstyle	1909
Eames Century Modern	2010

Availability

Century Schoolbook is widely available

Specimen

Book of American Types, Standard Faces.
American Type Founders, Jersey City,
1934 (279x210mm)

Century Schoolbook and *Century Schoolbook Italic*

48 Point   5 A 8 a

BIG Liners 4

36 Point   5 A 10 a

Splendid MUSIC

30 Point   6 A 12 a

NICER Calculation 9

24 Point   8 A 14 a

HEROIC COMMANDER
Courageous Sailors Cited

18 Point   11 A 22 a

MANY GALLANT OFFICERS
SCOTCH Brigade Fought Bravely

16 Point   13 A 24 a

MODERN SOUTHERN MANSION
IDEAL Springtime Among Blossoms

14 Point   16 A 32 a

DESCRIBE INDUSTRIOUS NATIVES
UNIQUE Description of a Strange People

12 Point   20 A 40 a

PROMISING TESTIMONY READILY GIVEN
QUICK Decision Sought in Recent Market Case

10 Point   22 A 44 a

DELIGHTFUL SUMMERTIME EVENTS PROMISED
STEAMBOAT Outing Greatly Enjoyed by Society Children

8 Point   26 A 50 a

BRONZE TABLETS AND QUAINT ORIENTAL IDOLS SECURED
HISTORICAL Treasures are Given to Scientific Museum by Explorers

6 Point   28 A 55 a

MODERN DISTRIBUTION SYSTEM ADMIRED BY BRILLIANT EXECUTIVES
DISTINGUISHED Visitors Pouring Into Town for the Annual Manufacturing Exhibit

Characters in Complete Font

A B C D E F G H I J K L
M N O P Q R S T U V W X
Y Z & $ 1 2 3 4 5 6 7 8 9 0
a b c d e f g h i j k l m n
o p q r s t u v w x y z ff
fl ffi ffl . , - ' : ; ! ?

SMALL CAPS from 6 to 18 Point are put up separately
and furnished only when specially ordered

9 Point Century Schoolbook *and italic* carried in stock only at Fou

Century Schoolbook Italic

48 Point   5 A 8 a

Sight

36 Point   6 A 10 a

Dutiful

30 Point   6 A 12 a

Expedite

24 Point   8 A 14 a

Highlands

18 Point   11 A 22 a

Next Meeting

16 Point   13 A 26 a

SPORTSMEN
Displayed Grit

14 Point   16 A 32 a

REPRODUCED
Banking Capital

12 Point   20 A

KIND MOTH
Quarterly Book

10 Point   21 A

NEW SELECTI
Interesting Exam

8 Point   25 A

PENURIOUS OWN
Secured Competent

6 Point   30 A

RIDICULOUS INTERV
Diligent Steamship Repo

Characters in Complete
Font

A B C D E
G H I J K
M N O P Q
S T U V W
Y Z & $ 1 2 3
4 5 6 7 8 9 0
a b c d e f g
i j k l m n o p
q r s t u v
x y z ff fi fl ff
ffl . , - ' : ; !

:[86]:

Century Schoolbook Bold and Schoolbook Oldstyle

48 Point   4 A 7 a
LINK
River

36 Point   5 A 9 a
PURSE
Marked

30 Point   6 A 10 a
REPORT
Procured

24 Point   9 A 15 a
NUMBERS
Production

18 Point   11 A 21 a
ENDURANCE
Muscular boys
gain first prize

16 Point   12 A 22 a
NEIGHBORING
Educated youth
kindly advising

14 Point   14 A 27 a
IMPORT CIGARS
Charming oriental
aroma fills the air

12 Point   17 A 34 a
INCREASE PROFITS
Revival of business is
encouraging everyone

10 Point   20 A 40 a
THE GOLDEN SILENCE
Consider silently what a
man says, as words often
betray the speaker's mind

8 Point   23 A 44 a
THE ROAD TO GREATNESS
Many people say greatness is
but an eminence the ascent to
which is very steep and lofty

6 Point   26 A 52 a
A GOOD NATURED COUNTENANCE
Good nature is really more agreeable
than wit. It gives to the countenance
an air much more benign than beauty

Characters in Complete Font

A B C D E F G H I
J K L M N O P Q R
S T U V W X Y Z &
$ 1 2 3 4 5 6 7 8 9 0
a b c d e f g h i j k
l m n o p q r s t u
v w x y z ff fi fl ffi ffl
. , - ' : ; ! ?

Schoolbook Oldstyle

48 Point   5 A 8 a
Mined

36 Point   5 A 10 a
Intrudes

30 Point   6 A 12 a
Nice Bank

24 Point   9 A 15 a
MONITORS
Best Student

18 Point   12 A 23 a
QUICK WORK
RECENT Change

14 Point   17 A 32 a
FINE INTERVIEW
CURIOUS Merchants

12 Point   19 A 38 a
BEST AUTHORS
ENGLISH professor
writes love stories

10 Point   23 A 44 a
MIGHTY HUNTER
NOTED explorer wins
high honors in Africa

8 Point   25 A 50 a
MILITARY TACTICS
IMPRESSIVE ceremony
marked the arrival of
our victorious soldiers

6 Point   30 A 55 a
PHYSICAL AND MENTAL
HEALTHFUL recreation with
a proper diet is the best way
to prolong life and health

Characters in Complete Font

A B C D E F G H I J
K L M N O P Q R S
T U V W X Y Z & $
1 2 3 4 5 6 7 8 9 0
a b c d e f g h i j k
l m n o p q r s t u v
w x y z ff fi fl ffi ffl
. , - ' ' : ; ! ?

SMALL CAPS from 6 to 18 Point are put up in separate
fonts and furnished only when specially ordered

:[87]:

In 1915 Ginn & Co., an educational publishing house, commissioned Morris Fuller Benton of American Type Founders to cut a legible typeface for use in school textbooks. The result, Century Schoolbook, was a variant of ATF's highly successful Century series (pp186–87).

Research into reading and cognition guided Century Schoolbook's development. Benton drew on studies undertaken at Clark University which demonstrated that children quickly identified letterforms with contrasting weights if the lighter strokes maintained a visual density. The tests also revealed the importance of clear and open counterforms – the negative spaces within letters – in recognizing text at smaller reading sizes. Basing the new design on ATF's Century Expanded, Benton used the research data to determine stroke weights, character heights, apertures, letter spacing and word spacing in order to achieve a highly legible typeface for young readers.

Century Schoolbook is significantly heavier overall than Century Expanded, and demonstrates the heritage of both the late modern style (pp104–105) and that of the Clarendons (pp132–33). Key visual differentiators within the letterforms are somewhat exaggerated throughout. Century Schoolbook features prominent, blocky serifs that are gently bracketed with thick and thin strokes that are generally heavier than most serif typefaces, offset by generous white spaces within and between the letters. Over a period of five years, Benton expanded his design into a large series of typefaces.

Century Schoolbook is familiar to many people in English-speaking countries as the typeface they first learned to read with. It has been used as a reliable workhorse, not only for educational books but also for advertising, editorial design and brand communications.

Ty	**Bremer Antiqua**
Ca	**Serif**
Ke	**Old Style, Venetian**
Te	**Letterpress**
Da	**1922**
De	**Willy Wiegand and Louis Hoell**
Fo	**Bremer Presse**
Co	**Germany**

Characteristics

Capitals to ascender height	
A Serif at apex to left only	
D H N S Wide	
G No spur	
M Serifs on inside of stems, high vertex	
Q Short tail	
e Small eye and oblique bar	
h Non-uncial form	
i j Dot offset to right	
v w Cup-shaped	
y Cup-shaped, short tail	

AGMQS
abcdefghij
koprstuvy

Connections

Von Speyer's Roman	1470
The Doves Type	1900
Subiaco	1902
Johnston's Hamlet	1929

Availability

Not available

Specimen

Rudolf Borchardt, *Gartenphantasie.*
Bremer Presse, Munich, 1925
(250x175mm)

etwa vor, das Gebiet der Sommerblumen oder Annuellen (Einjahrsblumen wie man mit einem weder richtigen noch geschickten Worte sagt) im Sinne einer doppelten Modernität, der neuen deutschen Gartenvorstellungen und der neuen Weltblumenfülle, zu behandeln, und zu behandeln natürlich für den neuen Adepten, den halb empfänglichen, halb zaghaften, der neuen Thatsachen, das Publikum der Liebhaber die man wieder zu bilden, der Kenner, die man vorauszusetzen wünscht, und denen man alles, buchstäblich alles erst zu sagen und zu zeigen hat, vom Namen und Aussehen einer Salpiglossis superbissima angefangen bis zu der Thatsache, dass die stinkende kamillenblütige Mutterwurz Afrikas in ihren bisherigen Vorgärten ein fades Unkraut ist, und die den gleichen Namen tragende Matricaria eine edle Kulturpflanze, im Sinne der göttlichen Natur über die gemeine Natur hinausgeführt wie nur der zwischen Gemeinem und Göttlichem stehende, an beidem teilende Mensch es vermochte. Hier also steht die neue Gartenliteratur – und nicht nur an so wahllos herausgegriffenen Einzelpunkten – dem Liebhaber als das Mundstück Unterrichteter, ja als dasjenige von «Fachleuten», – um das widerwärtige Wort schon zu gebrauchen, – gegenüber, und vermittelt ihm mit einem unabsehbaren neuen Material zugleich Kriterien die es beherrschen sollen. Aber dies Material, das man nicht unabsehbar wie es ist, vorlegen kann, muss man selber vorher Kriterien der Wahl und Sichtung unterworfen haben. Die Arbeit an der Blume ist nicht eitel Meisterschaft, viel geistlose Unfeinheit des Handwerks, viel leerläufige Betriebsamkeit eines

22

geistig nicht geregelten, durch keinen gebieterischen Form-
sinn im Besteller beherrschten, in sich ganz wertlosen
Variierens um der Variation und Halbvariation willen
drängt sich aus der Kleinzüchterei her dem Handel auf,
verzwergt, was nicht zum Zwerge taugt, füllt, was nur
in ungefüllter Schlichtheit eine zarte Unschuld behält,
nennt das erste sich einstellende leberlila einer roten Art
schon blau, eine erste schmutzige Vergilbung weisser
Schönheiten schon Chromkönigin und überschreit sich,
stier an einander vorbeizüchtend, in neuen Unnamen, bis
die Zwerg-Päonien-Perfektions-Edel-Aster die würdige
Schwester des Prima-Edel-Oder-Tafel-Krebses gleicher
Krämerprägung geworden ist. Hier hätte die Front der
neuen Literatur gegen den « Fachmann » zu stehen, und
diese Front, um es mit warmherziger Offenheit zu sagen,
wird bislang weder fest, noch offensiv, noch einheitlich
genug gehalten. Hier hat man, um Kriterien der Wahl zu
finden, Liebhaber und nur Liebhaber zu sein. Was ein
Liebhaber ist, wie er sich bildet und wie er verfährt, hat
man, weil das in Deutschland verschollen ist, zugleich ein
wenig zu lernen und nicht nur zu lehren. Unter dem doppelten Zehrer des angeblichen Fachmanns-Rechtes und
eines falschen Dilettantismus erstickt wie eine verqueckte
und verseidete Wiese, liegt die echte und vornehme Lieb-
haberei bei uns in diesem wie in allen Stücken, und man
kann sie nicht befreien, ohne sich selber von den letzten Re-
sten schematischer Gewöhnungen ebenso befreit zu haben
wie von veralteten Sorten und kulturunwürdigen Arten.
Der Gegenstand kann nicht ausschliesslich empirisch

23

The Bremer Presse, directed by Willy Wiegand (1884–1961), was pre-eminent among the German private presses. It was a very short-lived operation, active only from 1911 to 1939, during an era of domestic political upheaval and rapid industrialization. Catering to a small bibliophile market, it was greatly influenced by the British private-press movement, most notably the work of the Doves Press (pp156–57). Like its English antecedent, Bremer rejected ornament and illustration in favour of typographic restraint. Wiegand regarded the creation of unique, distinctive typefaces as well as a renovation of craft printing skills as the most important aspects of the press's activities. In his view, 'The best jobbing type is that which one notices, the best book type is that which one forgets when reading. One cannot distinguish between them sharply enough.'

Wiegand designed the Bremer Antiqua types himself, basing their forms on the early Venetian designs of Adolf Rusch and Johann von Speyer (pp22–23), which he had researched during a visit to Italy in 1911. Fabricating the Bremer Presse typefaces was a lengthy collaborative process. Their sophistication is due largely to the contribution of Louis Hoell, one of the most expert and prolific German punch cutters working at the beginning of the twentieth century. He cut the first size of Bremer Antiqua in 16 point, at the Bauer Foundry, in 1913. A 12-point version of the Bremer Antiqua was completed in 1922, and an 11-point in 1925. A Greek type, a blackletter and a new roman style followed, but the three sizes of Bremer Antiqua remained the standard typeface of the Bremer Presse editions.

Today, the editions of the Bremer Presse are highly prized for austere, well-proportioned pages that are the product of unadorned typography, unique typefaces and painstaking presswork. In his appraisal of the Bremer Presse typeface, type historian Christopher Burke noted that it 'has its quirks, but, compared to most other private press typefaces, it is a model of restraint. Especially in the smaller, more sharply cut sizes, it seems to fulfil Wiegand's intentions.'

Ty	**Cooper Black**
Ca	**Serif**
Ke	**Old Style**
Te	**Letterpress**
Da	**1922**
De	**Oswald 'Oz' Cooper**
Fo	**Barnhart Brothers & Spindler**
Co	**USA**

Characteristics

Bold, rounded convex serifs
A Extended, rounded apex
M Splayed
O o Q Backward incline
f Narrow, non-kerning, hooked arch
i j Flat, elliptical dot

ACQRS
abefghi
rtyaefg

Connections

Windsor	1905
Robur Noir	1909
Cooper Old Style	1919
Goudy Heavyface	1925

Availability

Cooper Black is widely available

Specimen

Book of American Types, Standard Faces.
American Type Founders, Jersey City,
1934 (279x210mm)

Cooper Black

120 Point 3A 3a

OIL sold

96 Point 3A 3a

half 8

72 Point 3A 3a

BE paid

60 Point 3A 4a

3 days IN

48 Point 3A 4a

BOLD style

42 Point 3A 4a

4 stage HITS

36 Point 3A 4a

REAL position

30 Point 4A 7a

inspected HOMES

24 Point 5A 9a

PINK drape

18 Point 6A 13a

delighted FRIEN

14 Point 10A 20a

MAYOR greatly pleas

12 Point 13A 26a

BEAUTIFUL SPRING COA
finely tailored sport costu

10 Point 14A 28a

ENTRANCING MUSICAL DRA
collegiate glee club has rehea

8 Point 16A 32a

METROPOLITAN BUSINESS INCREA
builder receives many encouraging rep

6 Point 18A 36a

NOTED JURIST GIVES IMPORTANT DECI
this long disputed question satisfactorily se

Characters in Complete Font

A B C D E F G H I
K L M N O P Q R
T U V W X Y Z &
1 2 3 4 5 6 7 8 9
a b c d e f g h
j k l m n o p q
s t u v w x y
. , - ' : ; ! ? q .

:[116]:

Cooper Black Italic

120 Point 3A 3a

SIX tails

24 Point 5A 10a

HOME delights

18 Point 6A 15a

ndisputable STORY

14 Point 10A 23a

CHARMING lace displays

12 Point 13A 26a

nvestigated annual REPORTS

10 Point 14A 28a

ROWDS welcome arctic explorer

8 Point 16A 32a

ISCOVERS UNTOLD MINERAL WEALTH
oung traveler described unexploited region

6 Point 19A 38a

OMANTIC ADVENTURE LIES BEYOND HORIZON
anderlust victims always enjoy the wide open spaces

Characters in Complete Font

A B C D E F G H I J
K L M N O P Q R S
T U V W X Y Z & $
1 2 3 4 5 6 7 8 9 0
a b c d e f g h i
k l m n o p q r
t u v w x y z . ,
' : ; ! ? [ ] · — ( )

The following characters are fonted separately and furnished
only when separately ordered

B D E F G M N
P R T Y

96 Point 3A 3a

shift 4

72 Point 3A 4a

NO mail

60 Point 3A 4a

5 built UP

48 Point 3A 4a

MEN signed

42 Point 3A 4a

sold 28 LOTS

36 Point 3A 5a

REAL publicity

30 Point 4A 8a

duplicates ORDER

:[117]:

Some typefaces, like Cooper Black, are meant to be seen first and read second. It was designed by Oswald 'Oz' Cooper (1879–1940), a leading American typographer, illustrator and commercial artist active from around 1910 to 1940.

Cooper Black was released by the Barnhart Brothers & Spindler foundry in 1922 as a display version of the Cooper Old Style family, which had been issued three years earlier. The new heavyweight rapidly achieved far greater success than the design on which it was based, becoming the foundry's bestselling typeface during the mid-1920s. It continued to enjoy about 20 years of enormous popularity in both metal and wood versions and has been in widespread use ever since.

Cooper Black has an old-style construction and its contours show influences of other contemporary advertising types such as Windsor (pp176–77) and art nouveau and art deco styles. Its burly letterforms are simultaneously strong and soft, and the absence of sharp corners makes it very well suited to printing at large sizes in wood type. For a typeface with such an imposing body, Cooper Black exhibits an unexpected warmth and liveliness, particularly when set tightly. This is due partly to its bulbous serifs, short descenders, large lower case letters and tiny, gleaming white counterforms. A subtle flattening at the tops and bases of letters also gives the typeface stability; without this it would appear unsteady.

Despite its massive popularity, Cooper Black had its detractors in the trade, who discounted it as the 'Black Menace'. Cooper himself, one of the most brilliant lettering artists of his generation, did not hold it in high regard, saying, 'It's for far-sighted printers with near-sighted customers'. Despite his disaffection, however, it is for Cooper Black that he is best remembered today.

Ty	**Kombinations-Schrift**
Ca	**Sans Serif**
Ke	**Geometric, Modular, Stencil**
Te	**Lettering**
Da	**1923**
De	**Josef Albers**
Fo	**N/A**
Co	**Germany**

Characteristics

Character construction from squares, circles and quarter circles

Vertical openings separate downstrokes

Internal spaces equal to letter spaces, one-third of stroke width

Character height can be increased by adding modules

ABCEMRS
abcefghij
koprstuy

Connections

Futura Black	1929
Patrona Grotesk	c1931
Transito	1931
Bauhouse	2010

Availability

Architype Albers is available from the Foundry and resellers. P22 Albers is available from P22 Type Foundry and resellers

Specimen

This page: *Kombinationsschrift der Metallglas-Aktiengesellschaft*. Josef Albers, Offenburg, c1931 (296x210mm)
Opposite: Josef Albers, Illustrations of font combinations, c1926. In *Bauhaus* magazine No. 1, Dessau, 1931 (297x199mm)

Kombinationsschrift der Metallglas-Aktiengesellschaft Offenburg Baden

Entworfen von J. Albers, Bauhaus, Dessau,   Gebrauchsmusterschutz Nr. 118 623 2,
Alleinhersteller für Glasbeschriftung: Metallglas-Aktiengesellschaft Offenburg-Baden.

Die Kombinatiosschrift besteht aus nur 10 Grundformen.   Daraus sind alle Schriftzeichen zusammensetzbar:
Buchstaben, Ziffern, Umlaute, Akzente, Interpunktionen.

Die 10 Grundformen sind: $\underline{1}$ Kreis, $\underline{2}$ Gerade, $\underline{3}$ zweiseitig gerundete, $\underline{4}$ einseitig gerundete:

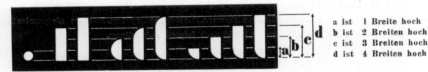

a ist 1 Breite hoch
b ist 2 Breiten hoch
c ist 3 Breiten hoch
d ist 4 Breiten hoch

I   IIc IId   IIIb IIIc IIId   IVa IVb IVc IVd

Die Grundformen sind in allen Größen lieferbar.
Doch empfiehlt sich, die leichter vermeßbaren Normalhöhen 8 12 16 20 24 28 32 40 44 48 cm zu wählen.
Diese Maße betreffen Mittel- + Oberlänge (wie bei b und A), welche die Größenwirkung der Schrift bestimmen.

Die Grundformen werden im allgemeinen in Milchglas gefertigt,
sie sind jedoch in allen Farben: Goldglas, rot, blau usw. lieferbar.

Das folgende Normalalphabet zeigt die gebräuchlichste Form und Proportion.
Daneben sind viele Form- und Maßvarianten möglich,
namentlich für Schriftfelder von außergewöhnlicher Höhe oder Breite.

abcdefghijklmnop
qrfstuvwxyzzk123
ABCDEFGHIJKLMNO
PQRSTUVWXYZäöçéš

own primarily as an abstract painter, [Jo]sef Albers (1888–1976) was also an [ac]complished designer, typographer [an]d photographer. A recurring theme [in] all of his work is the use of geometric [ar]rangements and systematic processes [in] the exploration of colour and form.

[De]signed between 1923 and 1931 during [hi]s time as a teacher at the Bauhaus, his [Ko]mbinations-Schrift alphabets exemplify [hi]s approach. One of the pioneers of [th]e Neue Typographie, or the New [Ty]pography, Albers was concerned with [th]e 'clarity of the message in its most [em]phatic form' and with typography [as] its medium. Kombinations-Schrift is [ab]solutely modern, reductivist and radical. [Th]e guiding principle behind its design [w]as to achieve a new economy for the [ar]rangement and implementation of type. [Th]e same objective is evident in Herbert [B]ayer's Universal Type (pp222–23) and [in] the work of many other typographic [d]esigners of the time.

[Al]bers intended Kombinations-Schrift to [b]e used as display lettering that would [b]e readable at a distance on advertising [bi]llboards and signage. It was not [d]esigned to be cut as type for use in print [b]ut rather to be engineered from glass, [pl]astic, metal or wood. One of the earliest [m]odular typefaces, it is constructed [sy]stematically from only three basic [g]eometric shapes: a square, a circle of [th]e same diameter as the square's length, [an]d a quarter circle of the same radius. [C]haracters assembled from these basic [c]omponent shapes are placed in [in]terconnected sequences, with character [st]rokes that are proportionate to their [in]ternal and external spaces, both [h]orizontally and vertically, in a fixed [r]elationship of three to one. The entire [d]esign space can thus be considered as [a] grid occupied by objects positionally [c]ontrolled to articulate meaning at all [le]vels, from micro to macro.

[T]he objective of this regulated approach [t]owards the construction of text, Albers [b]elieved, was beyond merely aesthetic [c]onsiderations. Its simplification and [c]larification of typographic messages was [in]tended to serve the social requirements [o]f 'everyday life, better than conventional [p]rinting … with its comparatively [c]omplicated composition'.

schwer lesbaren ansteigenden reihen auf tafel 4 unten sind für die lesbarkeit der schrift nicht maßgebend, weil die enge folge des formwechsels nur hier im system, nicht aber im schriftwort erscheint).

ein neuer vorteil ergibt sich aus der gleichen kegelbreite aller typen: jeder schriftsatz ist in seiner länge errechenbar. (bisher nur auf der schreibmaschine möglich). der ausgleich der buchstabenabstände ist bewußt vermieden worden. durch entsprechende verteilung der lücken innerhalb der vertikalen ist ein anderer ausgleich erreicht.

die kombinations-schriftzeichen sind in allen varianten ohne umzeichnen in schablonen verwendbar, da verbundene innenformen und stege fehlen.

die kombinationsschrift ermöglicht erstmalig, alle schriftzeichen einschließlich varianten, also jeden schriftsatz seitenvertauscht zu setzen sowohl in horizontaler wie vertikaler richtung.

alle wortbilder können somit außer vorwärts (links nach rechts) auch rückwärts (rechts nach links) und in beiden richtungen auch kopfstehend gedruckt werden, also in jeder spiegelschrift. das eröffnet ganz neue wirkungen für die reklame.

für montage-beschriftungen im besonderen, z. b. in holz, metall, karton, papier, für leuchtschriften, ergeben sich außer der schon genannten ersparnis an typen folgende vorteile: kein auszählen der benötigten einzelnen buchstaben nötig, also fortfall der buchstaben-liste, fortfall der empfindlichkeit (bruchgefahr) bei ausladenden oder dreigliedrigen buchstaben (K, L, M, T) bei überhängen und unterhängen.

derselbe gewinn wird sich bei stempelschriften zeigen und ganz besonders bei buchstaben aus sprödem material wie glas und porzellan.

die wirtschaftlich berechtigte forderung nach nurkleinschrift wird durch die kombinationsschrift nicht beeinflußt (die großbuchstaben gelten für die übergangszeit) und den vereinfachungsvorschlägen des alfabets (z. b. bezüglich f, v, ph, s, sch) von bayer, schmidt, schwitters, tschichold paßt sich die kombinationsschrift leicht an.

siehe auch: erste veröffentlichung der 1923 begonnenen normung von elementartypen in „offset" 1926 heft 7. weiter: hoffmanns schriftenatlas 1930.

---

von den alten jahrgängen der zeitschrift bauhaus sind noch vorhanden:

jahrgang	nr.		rmk.	
1927	nr. 3		1,—
1928	nr. 1		1,20
1929	nr. 1		2,—
1929	nr. 2		2,—
1929	nr. 3		2,—
1929	nr. 4		2,—

veranstaltungen winter 1931.

15. 1. 1931 dichter theodor däubler über „was ist tradition in der kunst?"

10. 2. 1931 klavierabend d. pianisten eduard erdmann-köln·

11. 3. 1931 konzertabend mit dem geiger professor adolf busch und rudolf serkin.

1. 4. 1931 universitäts-professor dr. dessauer-frankfurt a. m. über „kunst und technik".

2. 5. 1931 professor finlay freundlich vom einstein-institut über „die endlichkeit des weltraums als naturwissenschaftliches problem".

außerdem wird an einem z. zt. noch nicht feststehenden tage (voraussichtlich im februar) die tänzerin gret palucca mit ihrer tanzschule einen tanzabend veranstalten.

bauhaus-beleuchtungskörper
körting & mathiesen, leipzig w 35.

bauhaus-tapeten
hannoversche tapetenfabrik, gebr. rasch & co. gmbh., bramsche bei osnabrück.

bauhaus-mattglas
gewerkschaft kunzendorfer werke, kunzendorf n-l., kreis sorau.

bauhaus-stoffe
polytex - gesellschaft m. b. h. berlin sw 48, wilhelmstraße 107.

Neuland

Characteristics

Capitals only
Sans serif / blackletter construction
Convex strokes
Slight flares at junctions

ABCDEFG JKMNOP RSTUVZ

Connections

Lithos	1989
Manito	1990
Poster Black	1993
Othello	2002

Availability

Neuland is widely available

Specimen

Klingspor Schriften. Schriftgiesserei Gebr. Klingspor, Offenbach, 1954 (205x130mm)

Gebr. Klingspor, Offenbach am Main

NEULAND

basow	21046	Petit, 8 Punkte	Satz, 72 A, etwa 3,5 Kilo

DAS NEUE BÖRSENBLATT
WOCHENSCHRIFT FÜR DEN GESAMTEN
ÖSTERREICHISCHEN BUCHHANDEL

besaz	21047	Korpus, 10 Punkte	Satz, 60 A, etwa 4 Kilo

DRESSMAKING SALON
FRED DALTON & CO BALTIMORE
COLLECTION OF DRESSES

beseb	21048	Cicero, 12 Punkte	Satz, 46 A, etwa 4,5 Kilo

CHAMP DE MARS
UNE REVUE DES TROUPES
1234567890

besic	21049	Mittel, 14 Punkte	Satz, 36 A, etwa 5 Kilo

BREMER HERBSTMESSE
DER HANDEL

besod	21050	Tertia, 16 Punkte	Satz, 32 A, etwa 5,5 Kilo

FIGAROS HOCHZEIT
TONHALLE WEIMAR

besuf	21051	Text, 20 Punkte	Satz, 26 A, etwa 6,5 Kilo

BRUCKNER
DIE NEUE MUSIK

182

Gebr. Klingspor, Offenbach am Main

NEULAND

| 21052 | Doppelmittel, 28 Punkte | | Satz, 14 A, etwa 7 Kilo | biseh |

DAILY PRESS

| 21053 | 3 Cicero, 36 Punkte | | Satz, 10 A, etwa 10 Kilo | bisol |

PARSIVAL

| 21054 | 4 Cicero, 48 Punkte | | Satz, 8 A, etwa 15 Kilo | bosan |

BÜHNE

| 21424 | 5 Cicero, 60 Punkte | | Satz, 8 A, etwa 20 Kilo | bosiq |

SUIZA

| 21425 | 6 Cicero, 72 Punkte ⟨Hohlfuß⟩ | | Satz, 8 A, etwa 20 Kilo | bosor |

BERG

183

In the 1920s the German master calligrapher Rudolf Koch (1876–1934) set out to translate the dynamic energy of his woodcut illustrations into a compatible typeface. The result was Neuland, issued by Klingspor in 1923. Koch intended it to be a modernized display version of the blackletter type that was used in Germany at the time. In Neuland's design he attempted to preserve the flared, linear contours of the traditional style while integrating features of the geometric sans serif roman that designers like Jakob Erbar and Paul Renner were then developing.

Neuland was Koch's first ever attempt at mastering the art of punch cutting, a task he approached in the spirit of the medieval craftsmen he admired. Much of Neuland's character results from Koch's resourcefulness in overcoming the tight restrictions imposed by the tools and processes he used. He designed letters as he cut them, giving each an individual vitality while retaining its conformity to the character set. Neuland's capitals-only glyphs are drawn with a rugged energy that is clearly the outcome of this direct production method. Koch hand-cut the type in several point sizes, resulting in individual differences across the range, with exterior contours made by filing off the corners of metal quadrats, terminating letters in the gently flared points that are defining characteristics of the design.

The director of the Klingspor type foundry, Karl Klingspor, was less than enthusiastic about Neuland, calling it 'abominable, horrible, unbearably ugly', but then adding 'I am sure it will be a great success'. On its release, Neuland achieved excellent sales internationally. Eye-catching when set in tight blocks with little line spacing, its warm but imposing forms made it ideally suited to use in publicity, although most applications in which it first appeared made poor use of it.

Largely because of the absence of a blackletter tradition in the United States, Neuland became severed from its Germanic roots on its introduction there and immediately came to be identified with the handcrafted, folksy and ethnic. Through frequent use, it became a signifier of African and African-American culture, regardless of the lazy racial stereotyping that that implied, and regardless of the purposes for which its creator originally intended it.

Ty	**Lutetia**
Ca	**Serif**
Ke	**Old Style**
Te	**Letterpress**
Da	**1925**
De	**Jan van Krimpen**
Fo	**Joh. Enschedé en Zonen**
Co	**Netherlands**

Characteristics

E F S	Wide
J	Descends below baseline
Q	Long, curved tail below letter
a	No ear
b d p q	Wide bowl
e	Oblique crossbar
g	Double-storeyed, deep lower bowl
i j	Small dot to right of stem

AEJMQR
abcdefghij
orstuvyaefg

Connections

Centaur	1914
Perpetua	1930
Romulus	1936
Spectrum	1952

Availability

Lutetia Nova is a digital revival available from RMU Typedesign and resellers

Specimen

Lutetia type specimen. Joh. Enschedé en Zonen, Haarlem, c1925 (279x216mm)

---

cxxij · · · Actus Apostolorum

Cap. 28

Contradicentibus autem Judæis, coactus sum appellare Cæsarem, non quasi gentem meam habens aliquid accusare. Propter hanc igitur causam rogavi vos videre, et alloqui. Propter spem enim Israel catena hac circumdatus sum. At illi dixerunt ad eum: Nos neque litteras accepimus de te a Judæa, neque adveniens aliquis fratrum nuntiavit, aut locutus est quid de te malum. Rogamus autem a te audire, quæ sentis, nam de secta hac notum est nobis, quia ubique ei contradicitur.

CUM constituissent autem illi diem, venerunt ad eum in hospitium plurimi, quibus exponebat testificans regnum Dei, suadensque eis de Jesu ex lege Moysi et Prophetis a mane usque ad vesperam. Et quidam credebant his, quæ dicebantur: quidam vero non credebant. Cumque invicem non essent consentientes, discedebant dicente Paulo unum verbum: quia bene Spiritus sanctus locutus est per Isaiam prophetam ad patres nostros, dicens: Vade ad populum istum, et dic ad eos: Aure audietis, et non intelligetis: et videntes videbitis, et non perspicietis. Incrassatum est enim cor populi hujus, et auribus graviter audierunt, et oculos suos compresserunt, ne forte videant oculis, et auribus audiant, et corde intelligant, et convertantur, et sanem eos. Notum ergo sit vobis, quoniam gentibus missum est hoc salutare Dei, et ipsi audient.

Isai. 6, 9.
Mat. 13, 14.

ET cum hæc dixisset, exierunt ab eo Judæi multam habentes inter se quæstionem. Mansit autem biennio toto in suo conducto, et suscipiebat omnes, qui ingrediebantur ad eum. Prædicans regnum Dei, et docens, quæ sunt de Domino Jesu Christo, cum omni fiducia, sine prohibitione.

6

EPISTOLA

Beati Pauli Apostoli

ad Romanos

Caput I

PAULUS *servus Jesu Christi, vocatus Apostolus, segregatus in Evangelium Dei, quod ante promiserat per Prophetas suos in Scripturis sanctis de filio suo, qui factus est ei ex semine David secundum carnem, qui prædestinatus est Filius Dei in virtute secundum spiritum sanctificationis ex resurrectione mortuorum Jesu Christi Domini nostri, per quem accepimus gratiam, et Apostolatum ad obediendum fidei in omnibus gentibus pro nomine ejus, in quibus estis et vos vocati Jesu Christi: omnibus, qui sunt Romæ, dilectis Dei, vocatis sanctis: Gratia vobis, et pax a Deo Patre nostro, et Domino Jesu Christo.*

PRIMUM quidem gratias ago Deo meo per Jesum Christum pro omnibus vobis, quia fides vestra annuntiatur in universo mundo. Testis enim mihi est Deus, cui servio in Spiritu meo in Evangelio Filii ejus, quod sine intermissione memoriam vestri facio semper in orationibus meis: obsecrans, si quomodo tandem aliquando prosperum iter habeam in voluntate Dei veniendi ad vos. Desidero enim videre vos, ut aliquid impertiar vobis gratiæ spiritualis ad confirmandos vos: id est, simul consolari in vobis per eam, quæ invicem est, fidem

Act. 13, 2.

Jo. 22, 20.

Act. 6, 3.

7

Throughout his career Jan van Krimpen (1892–1958) was a forceful advocate for the highest standards in book typography conforming to classical values. His views could not be more clearly represented than in the understated beauty of his first typeface, Lutetia.

In 1923 Van Krimpen was commissioned by the Dutch Post Office to draw the lettering for a commemorative postage stamp to be printed by the prominent firm of Enschedé. Its satisfactory execution led Enschedé to invite him to design a new typeface. Lutetia was drawn the following year, cut and cast in 16 point only and first used in 1925 in a book that was a part of the Dutch contribution to the Exposition Internationale des Arts Décoratifs et Industriels Modernes in Paris. Appropriately, it was named Lutetia after the ancient Roman town that stood on the site of the French capital.

A twentieth-century hybrid serif combining old-style and baroque characteristics, Lutetia was quickly acknowledged as an innovative design that was markedly different from other romans being cut at the time, such as the recently revived version of Garamond. Although it is based on a Renaissance framework, Lutetia's contour has a crispness and streamlined elegance that is distinctly modern. Van Krimpen's roman capitals are exceptionally well proportioned, although he chose to use a wide E and F instead of the traditional narrow forms. Delicate, slightly cupped serifs provide a sense of forward movement and ascenders are tall, following the old-style model. References to Jenson are seen in the earless lower case a and the i, with its light dot to the right of the stem.

Lutetia's italic was inspired by sixteenth-century chancery scripts, but it was not a revival of a particular model. Van Krimpen based it on his own handwriting, which he had reformed after studying the work of Italian writing masters. It is somewhat wider and more legible than most chancery italics being explored at the time, but it is arguably somewhat too extravagant to work effectively as a companion to the roman.

Ty	**Monotype Fournier**	
Ca	**Serif**	
Ke	**Transitional**	
Te	**Letterpress**	
Da	**1925**	
De	**Stanley Morison**	
Fo	**Monotype**	
Co	**UK**	

Characteristics

Vertical stress
Light overall weight
Square serifs with slight bracketing
Capitals to ascender height
J Descends below baseline
M Narrow
R Curved right leg
W Crossed centre-strokes
b d h Angled upper serif
c e Tilted axis

ACJMRW
abcdefghij
orstuya*efg*

Connections

Fleischman's Roman	1739
Fournier	1764
Erdhart	1937
Source Serif Pro	2014

Availability

Monotype Fournier is available from Monotype and resellers

Specimen

Stanley Morison, *Fournier: A Specimen of a Classic Old Face*. Lanston Monotype Corporation, London, 1927 (210x145mm)

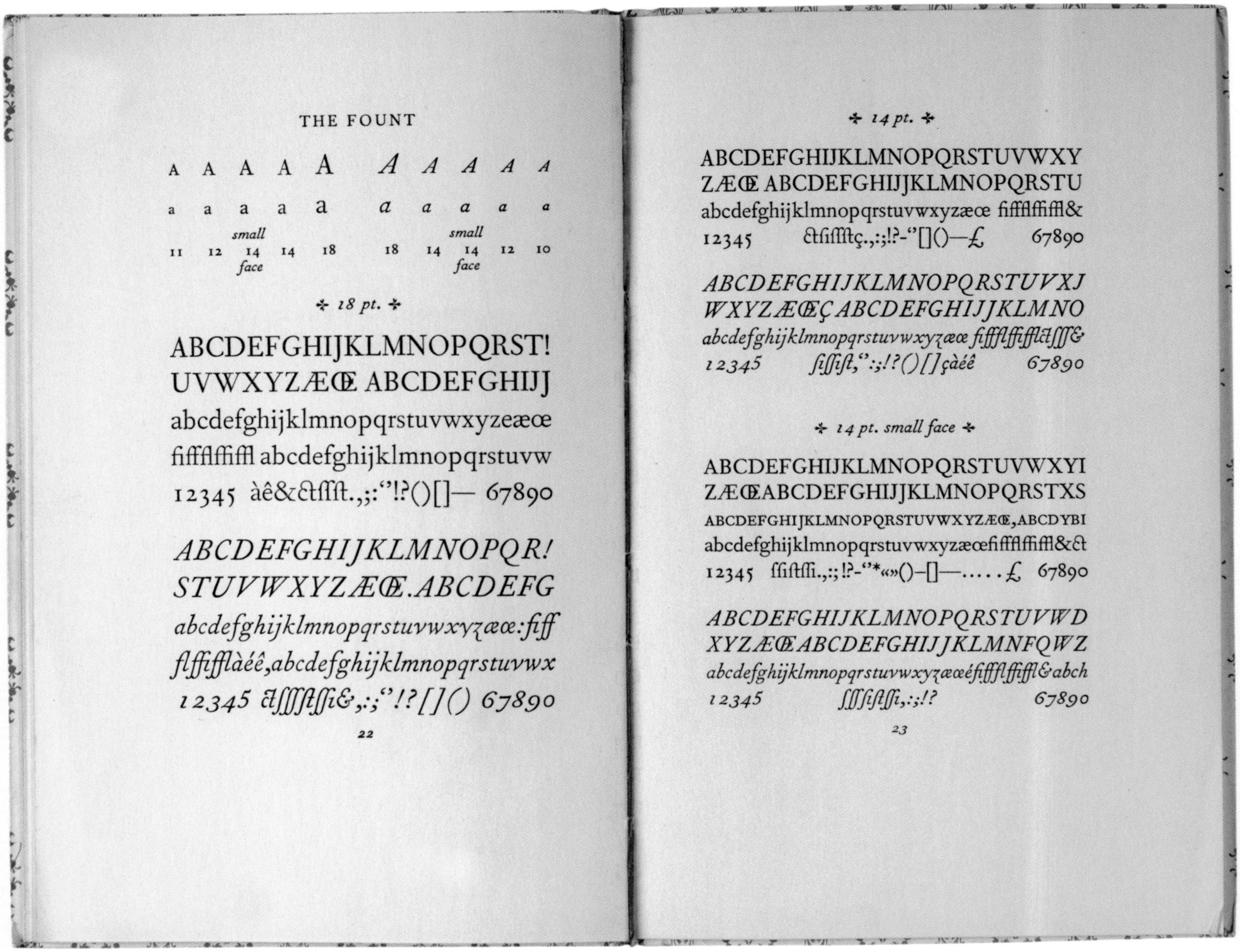

The Monotype Corporation's typographic adviser Stanley Morison (1889–1967) was one of the most influential typographers of the twentieth century. In the 1920s and 1930s he was responsible for a comprehensive programme of typeface releases for Monotype, many of which were historical revivals. Under his expert direction the company's collection of types for machine composition expanded greatly, informing the development of typography to the present day.

Morison was a great admirer of the late eighteenth-century types of the French type founder Pierre-Simon Fournier, and in 1924 he commissioned a Monotype revival based on specimens first shown in Fournier's 1764 *Manuel typographique* (pp82–83).

Fournier cut some of the most innovative typefaces of the eighteenth century. His lively designs were among the earliest of a baroque style that marked a transition from the influence of handwriting towards the rational modern forms created by Didot and Bodoni later in the century. Fournier's type designs are the product of both skill and scholarship, informed by the work of his contemporaries as well as his predecessors. The almost vertical stress of some of his letters references the Romain du Roi (pp72–75), while the proportions of some of his thin, narrow characters show the distinct influence of Fleischman (pp78–79).

Monotype's Series 185, released in 1925, is a revival of a face cut by Fournier in the 1740s. The Monotype design is delicate and open with letters that are relatively narrow. Capitals are particularly tall and therefore somewhat prominent in proportion to the lower case. Fournier has more vertical emphasis than old-style types, a low contrast between thick and thin strokes, and little or no bracketing on the serifs. It gives a clean impression with an even colour and provides excellent economy in text settings. The italic is a decorative style with unusual figures that demonstrate the influence of handwriting.

While Monotype Fournier is a worthy revival of a spirited original, it failed to achieve the success of contemporary Monotype typefaces such as Plantin, Baskerville, Garamond and Times New Roman and is rarely seen today.

ON ELIZABETHAN DRAMA

by Virginia Woolf

At the outset in reading an Elizabethan play we are overcome by the extraordinary discrepancy between the Elizabethan view of reality and our own. The reality to which we have grown accustomed is, speaking roughly, based upon the life and death of some knight called Smith, who succeeded his father in the family business of pitwood importers, timber merchants and coal exporters, was well known in political, temperance, and church circles, did much for the poor of Liverpool, and died last Wednesday of pneumonia while on a visit to his son at Muswell Hill. That is the world we know. That is the reality which our poets and novelists have to expound and illuminate. Then we open the first Elizabethan play that comes to hand and read how

I once did see
In my young travels through Armenia
An angry unicorn in his full career
Charge with too swift a foot a jeweller
That watch'd him for the treasure of his brow,
And ere he could get shelter of a tree
Nail him with his rich antlers to the earth.

Where is Smith, we ask, where is Liverpool?

And the groves of Elizabethan drama echo "Where?" Exquisite is the delight, sublime the relief of being set free to wander in the land of the unicorn and the jeweller among dukes and grandees, Gonzaloes and Bellimperias, who spend their lives in murder and intrigue, dress up as men if they are women, as women if they are men, see ghosts, run mad, and die in the greatest profusion on the slightest provocation, uttering as they fall imprecations of superb vigour or elegies of the wildest despair. But soon the low, the relentless voice, which if we wish to identify it we must suppose typical of a reader fed on modern English literature, and French and Russian, asks why, then, with all this to stimulate and enchant, these old plays are for long stretches of time so intolerably dull? Is it not that literature, if it is to keep us on the alert through five acts or thirty-two chapters, must somehow be based on Smith, have one toe touching Liverpool, take off into whatever heights it pleases from reality?

12

13

Preissig Antiqua

Ty	**Preissig Antiqua**
Ca	**Serif**
Ke	**Old Style, Geometric**
Te	**Letterpress**
Da	**1925**
De	**Vojtěch Preissig**
Fo	**Státní Tiskárna**
Co	**Czech Republic**

Characteristics

	Structure based on old-style armature
	Systematic linear construction method
	Short, straight wedge strokes throughout
	Thin, flat bracketless serifs
	Tall ascenders, short descenders
A	Pointed apex
G	No spur
J	Descends below baseline
M	Splayed
W	Stepped centre-strokes
a	Double-storeyed, small bowl
f	Narrow, non-kerning

AEJMQR
abcdefghij
orstuyaefg

Connections

Preissig Scrape	1914
Butterick	1928
Manuskript Antikva	1944
Tyfa	1960

Availability

Preissig Antikva Pro is a digital revival available from Storm Type Foundry and resellers

Specimen

Benjamin Franklin, *The Way to Wealth: The Preface to Poor Richard's Almanack for the Year 1758*. Random House, New York, 1930 (393x305mm)

more easily discharge them; but we have many others, and much more grievous to some of us. We are taxed twice as much by our idleness, three times as much by our pride, and four times as much by our folly; and from these taxes the commissioners cannot ease or deliver us by allowing an abatement. However, let us hearken to good advice, and something may be done for us; God helps them that help themselves, as Poor Richard says, in his almanack of 1733. > It would be thought a hard government that should tax its people one tenth part of their time, to be employed in its service. But idleness taxes many of us much more, if we reckon all that is spent in absolute sloth or doing of nothing, with that which is spent in idle employments or amusements that amount to nothing. Sloth, by bringing on diseases, absolutely shortens life.

Sloth, like rust, consumes faster than labour wears; while The used key is always bright. But dost thou love life, then do not squander time, for that's the stuff life is made of, as Poor Richard tells us. How much more than is necessary do we spend in sleep! forgetting that The sleeping fox catches no poultry. And that There will be sleeping enough in the grave, as Poor Richard tells us. If time be of all things

Vojtěch Preissig's aim in designing Preissig Antiqua was 'to protest against the mechanical roundness and polish of ordinary fonts by making an attempt at impeccable proportions'.

Preissig (1873–1944) was a Czech graphic artist, equally accomplished in typography, printmaking, design, illustration and painting. In 1910 he moved from Prague to the United States, where he worked as a teacher and freelance designer for 20 years. During this sojourn, the State Printing House in Prague invited him to

design an original typeface specifically for the Czech language, to be presented at the Exposition Internationale des Arts Décoratifs et Industriels Modernes in Paris in 1925. Preissig began the project in 1923 and worked painstakingly for two years on the typeface he named Preissig Antiqua.

His design made a feature of the diacritic marks that characterize the Czech writing system, directly affecting the shapes of the letters with which they appear. Because of this language-specific attribute, Preissig Antiqua can rightly be regarded

as the first truly Czech typeface. The skeleton of Preissig Antiqua is essentially that of a traditional old-style type, but the handmade, fractured energy of its contours strongly evokes a combination of both gothic and Cubist design styles. This is the result of Preissig's systematic linear construction method, making use of a series of straight wedges following a polygonal framework in incremental proportions in place of conventional rounded strokes. The abrupt termination of the strokes with flat bracketless serifs is another characteristic feature that

subsequently influenced many other Czech type designers, including Oldřich Menhart and Josef Týfa (pp358–59).

The 1925 Paris exhibition was the first international manifesto for Czech design culture, and Preissig Antiqua was recognized as a symbol of Czech independence, as a new nation with a distinct identity. Preissig modestly summarized his own achievement when he described the typeface as 'neither dull nor erratic, nor even a mere reflection or reproduction of the classics'.

take his business at night; while Laziness travels so slowly that poverty soon overtakes him. Drive thy business! let not that drive thee. And Early to bed, And early to rise, makes a man healthy, wealthy and wise, as we read in Poor Richard. So what signifies wishing and hoping for better times. We may make these times better if we bestir ourselves. As Poor Richard says, Industry need not wish, and He that lives upon hope will die fasting. There are no gains without pains; then Help hands, for I have no lands, or if I have they are smartly taxed. And, as Poor Richard likewise observes, He that hath a trade hath an estate, and He that hath a calling hath an office of profit and honour; but then the trade must be worked at and the calling well followed, or neither the estate nor the office will enable us to pay our taxes. If we are industrious we shall never starve; for, as Poor Richard says, At the working man's house hunger looks in, but dares not enter. Nor will the bailiff or the constable enter, for, as Poor Dick says,

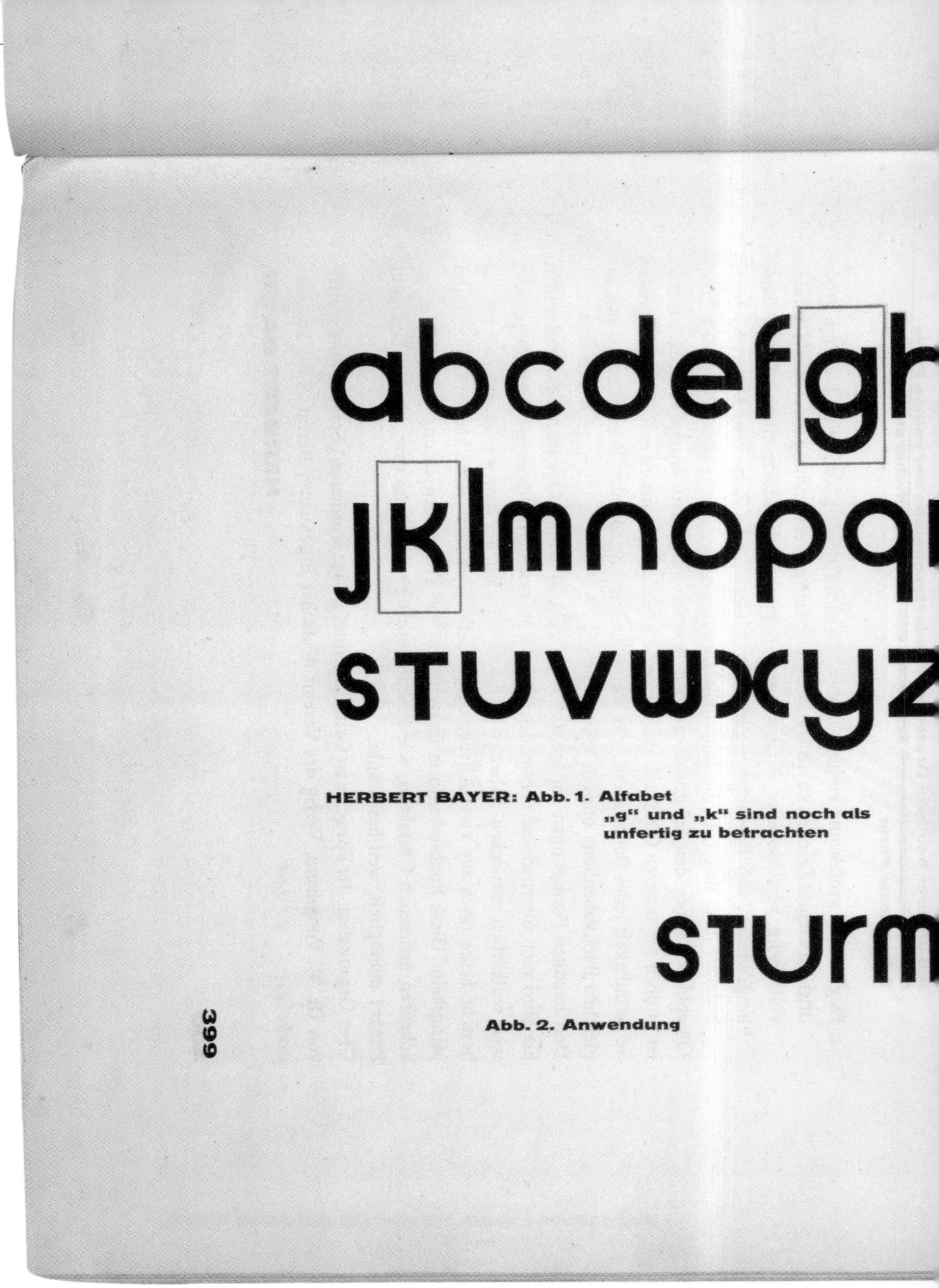

abcdefgh
jklmnopq
stuvwxyz

HERBERT BAYER: Abb. 1. Alfabet
„g" und „k" sind noch als
unfertig zu betrachten

sturm

Abb. 2. Anwendung

399

eispiel eines Zeichens
größerem Maßstab
äzise optische Wirkung

Ty	**Universal Type**
Ca	**Sans Serif**
Ke	**Geometric, Lower Case**
Te	**Lettering**
Da	**1925**
De	**Herbert Bayer**
Fo	**N/A**
Co	**Germany**

Characteristics

Geometric construction

Lower case only

Repeated modular forms

abcefgh ijklmopqr stuvxyz

Connections

Bayer Type	1933
ITC Bauhaus	1975
Chalet	1996
Architype Bayer	1997

Availability

Architype Bayer is available from the Foundry and resellers

Specimen

Offset, Buch und Werbekunst No. 7. Offset Verlag, Leipzig, 1926 (278x200mm)

Directly after graduating as a student at the Bauhaus, Herbert Bayer (1900–85) was appointed as head of its new printing and advertising workshop in Dessau. Under his direction, the workshop operated as a professional studio, moving away from traditional crafts towards the design of functional objects for mass production. What became known subsequently as Bauhaus typography was an integral aspect of the comprehensive reforms taking place at the school, reflecting the social, cultural and political climate of the time.

Herbert Bayer was one of several German designers of the period, including Josef Albers (pp212–13), Kurt Schwitters and Jan Tschichold (pp378–79), who were engaged in a radical reappraisal of text, not merely in terms of its appearance but as a vehicle for conveying language. They were less concerned with issues of typographic convention and more with the total reform of their writing system. While others sought to improve visual communications by inventing entirely new alphabets, Bayer's concerns were slightly more pragmatic. He believed that the use of upper case characters was archaic and redundant. 'The voice does not make capital sounds,' he said. 'Why then should the eye require them?' His proposal to eliminate them was particularly radical for German, in which many capitals are used.

In 1925, the school's director, Walter Gropius, commissioned Bayer to design a typeface to be used for all Bauhaus communications. Bayer took this opportunity to test his ideas by developing an idealized, rational alphabet. This became his Proposal for a Universal Typeface, a sans serif design whose letterforms were distilled to a bare minimum. Paying no reference to the stroke of the pen or cut of the chisel, the design is rigorously geometric and modular. Like the output of an industrial production line, a fixed set of components, constructed with pen and compass from circular arcs and straight lines, is repeated, rotated, reflected and assembled into a complete alphabet without capitals.

Envisaging Universal as an all-encompassing system that would eventually include different versions for handwriting, typewriting and printing, Bayer continued to refine his designs for the next five years. Although it was not cut as type at the time, Universal had a substantial effect on the exploration of typography in the late twentieth century and inspired a large number of typefaces, including ITC Ronda, ITC Bauhaus, Horatio (pp404–405), Blippo and many others. Architype Bayer, cut digitally by the Foundry in 1997, is a faithful interpretation of Bayer's original design.

Ty	**Erbar-Grotesk**
Ca	**Sans Serif**
Ke	**Geometric**
Te	**Letterpress**
Da	**1926**
De	**Jakob Erbar**
Fo	**Ludwig & Mayer**
Co	**Germany**

Characteristics

A	Low crossbar
C c S s e	Angled terminals
G	No spur
M	Splayed with pointed apex
Q	Straight, flat tail
R	Straight, angled leg
a	Double-storeyed
f t	Very narrow
g	Single-storeyed
i j	Square dots
t	Angled top, straight stem, no foot
y	Straight tail

AGMQR
abcefghij
koprstuy

Connections

Johnston's Railway Type	1916
Futura	1927
Kabel	1927
Neuzeit-Grotesk	1928

Availability

Erbar is available from URW and resellers

Specimen

Erbar-Grotesk specimen. Ludwig & Mayer, Frankfurt, c1927 (270x210mm)

HALBFETTE ERBAR-GROTESK

Nr. 6894   6 Punkte   Satz 3 Kilo   120a 48A

Der Stil eines Werkes ist nichts anderes als die Art, in der ein Künstler seinen Stoff gestaltet, in der ein Dichter vor allem sein Kunstmittel: die Sprache, zur Wiedergabe der Vorgänge und zur Charakteristik der Menschen gebraucht. Der Stoff des Dichters wird in der Regel ein Stück Leben, ein Stück von der

Nr. 6895   8 Punkte   Satz 4 Kilo   100 a 40A

Es ist noch kein Meister vom Himmel gefallen, es ist auch noch kein Meister geboren worden, aber die Meisterschaft kommt allemal nach und nach, leise und langsam, nicht von selbst, sondern durch Übung. Wer noch soviele Gaben und Anlagen

Nr. 6896   10 Punkte   Satz 5 Kilo   80a 28A

Jack London gehört zu den Toten, aber er ist in Wahrheit doch der jüngste unter den Lebenden. Er ist so unbelastet, wie nur ein Mensch sein kann, der früh und allein auf

Nr. 6897   12 Punkte   Satz 6 Kilo   70a 24A

Die Schriften Robert Schumanns über Musik und Musiker sind das schönste literarische Denkmal, das sich je ein Musiker gesetzt hat. Man kann dies

Nr. 6898   14 Punkte   Satz 7 Kilo   60a 24A

Für jeden Naturbeobachter ist es etwas ganz Selbstverständliches, unsere Wild- und Nutzbäume auf

Nr. 7023   16 Punkte   Satz 8 Kilo   50a 20A

Wie diese Kunst als Ausdruck der Empfindung und nicht der Erkenntnis aufgefaßt werden

Nr. 7024   20 Punkte   Satz 10 Kilo   40a 16A

Seit der Mitte des letzten Jahrhunderts machte in steigendem Maße sich

Nr. 7025   24 Punkte   Satz 12 Kilo   36a 14A

Wie die Menschheit die Erde erobert hat

Nr. 7026   28 Punkte   Satz 14 Kilo   30a 12A

Moderne Kunst und Dekoration

Nr. 7027   36 Punkte   Satz 16 Kilo   20a 8A

Volksbildung

Nr. 7028   48 Punkte   Satz 20 Kilo   16a 6A

Demokrat

Nr. 7029   60 Punkte   Satz 28 Kilo   16a 6A

Konzert

Nr. 7030   72 Punkte   Satz 30 Kilo   12a 4A

Station

Nr. 7031   84 Punkte   Satz 32 Kilo   10a 4A

Eichel

SCHRIFTGIESSEREI LUDWIG & MAYER FRANKFURT A·M

Die Buchstaben AMNVWÄ · AMNVWÄ sind spitz und stumpf vorhanden. Wir liefern auf Wunsch die eine oder andere Form

KRÄFTIGE ERBAR-GROTESK

ERSTE GARNITUR | ZWEITE GARNITUR

Nr. 6419   28 Punkte   Satz 14 Kilo   30a 12A | Nr. 6615   28 Punkte   Satz 13 Kilo   30a 12A

Gutenbergbilder
Modenakademie

Gutenbergdenkmal
Moden-Akademie

Nr. 6420   36 Punkte   Satz 15 Kilo   20a 8A | Nr. 6616   36 Punkte   Satz 15 Kilo   20a 8A

Cohen-Verlag
Frankfurt a+M

Teubner-Verlag
Frankfurt+Main

Nr. 6421   48 Punkte   Satz 20 Kilo   16a 6A | Nr. 6617   48 Punkte   Satz 17 Kilo   16a 6A

Opelräder

Opel-Werk

Nr. 6604   60 Punkte   Satz 24 Kilo   16a 6A | Nr. 6618   60 Punkte   Satz 24 Kilo   16a 6A

Baukunſt

Dichtkunst

Nr. 6605   72 Punkte   Satz 32 Kilo   16a 6A | Nr. 6619   72 Punkte   Satz 30 Kilo   16a 6A

Moden

Modern

Nr. 6606   84 Punkte   Satz 40 Kilo   16a 6A | Nr. 6620   84 Punkte   Satz 36 Kilo   16a 6A

Kohle

Kohlen

SCHRIFTGIESSEREI LUDWIG & MAYER FRANKFURT A·M

Die Buchstaben AMNVWÄ · AMNVWÄ sind in beiden Garnituren spitz
und stumpf vorhanden. Wir liefern auf Wunsch die eine oder andere Form

During the nineteenth century, the first sans serif typefaces were subordinate to the traditional roman form. They were bold slab serif or Clarendon display types from which the serifs had been removed, described as grotesque or grotesk in Europe and as gothic in the United States.

In 1916 Edward Johnston departed from this tradition in the unprecedented design of his lettering for the London Underground (pp202–203), a paradigm shift in the development of the sans serif form in the twentieth century. A few years later, in Germany, Jakob Erbar (1878–1935) began to experiment with 'a precise, mechanically-produced reading type in the form of a modern sans serif' for the Ludwig & Mayer foundry. Erbar, having studied lettering with Fritz Ehmcke and Anna Simons, who in turn had been students of Edward Johnston, aimed to design a typeface that would be based on the pure geometry of the circle and square but that would be highly legible, with letterforms free of any redundancies.

Intended as a display face for use in advertising, Erbar-Grotesk, the first truly geometric sans serif, was strikingly elegant for a design with such mathematical origins. Although it was drawn in the early 1920s, Ludwig & Mayer did not complete cutting it for machine composition until 1926, when it was issued in regular and bold weights and an upper case display variant named Lucina, followed by a light weight and an italic in 1927. Erbar-Grotesk's low x-height and long ascenders were among its key distinguishing features, and Ludwig & Mayer offered it in two alternative versions: one with a standard x-height, and one with a lower x-height and extremely long ascenders. Alternate forms with pointed apexes and vertices for capitals A M N V and W were also provided.

Paul Renner's Futura (pp230–31) is so similar to Erbar-Grotesk that some have suggested that he may have based his forms on it, although there is no evidence to support this view. Renner's design proved to be the most widespread and enduring of the geometric sans serifs, thanks largely to the international sales activities of its foundry, Bauer. The immediate success of both Erbar and Futura triggered an explosion of new geometric sans serifs from competing foundries, including Nobel, Vogue, Kabel, Metro, Neuzeit, Tempo, Spartan, Twentieth Century and many others.

Although Erbar was rapidly eclipsed by its many competitors, it remains a revolutionary sans serif design, an enduring icon of the Weimar era in Germany and of the zeitgeist of the 1920s.

Ty	**Monotype Grotesque**
Ca	**Sans Serif**
Ke	**Grotesque**
Te	**Letterpress**
Da	**c1926**
De	**Frank Hinman Pierpont**
Fo	**Monotype**
Co	**UK**

Characteristics

C c g J S s	Inconsistent terminals
G	Has spur
Q	Small, curved tail below letter
R	Curved leg
a	Double-storeyed, curve at foot
f r t	Vertical terminals
g	Double-storeyed
i j	Square dots
t	Narrow, flat top-stroke
y	Curved tail

AEGJRS
abcefghij
oqrstuwx

Connections

Akzidenz-Grotesk	c1898
Venus	1907
Edel-Grotesk	c1914
Arial	1982

Availability

Monotype Grotesque is available from
Monotype and resellers

Specimen

Monotype specimen book. Lanston
Monotype Corporation, London, 1931
(290x230mm)

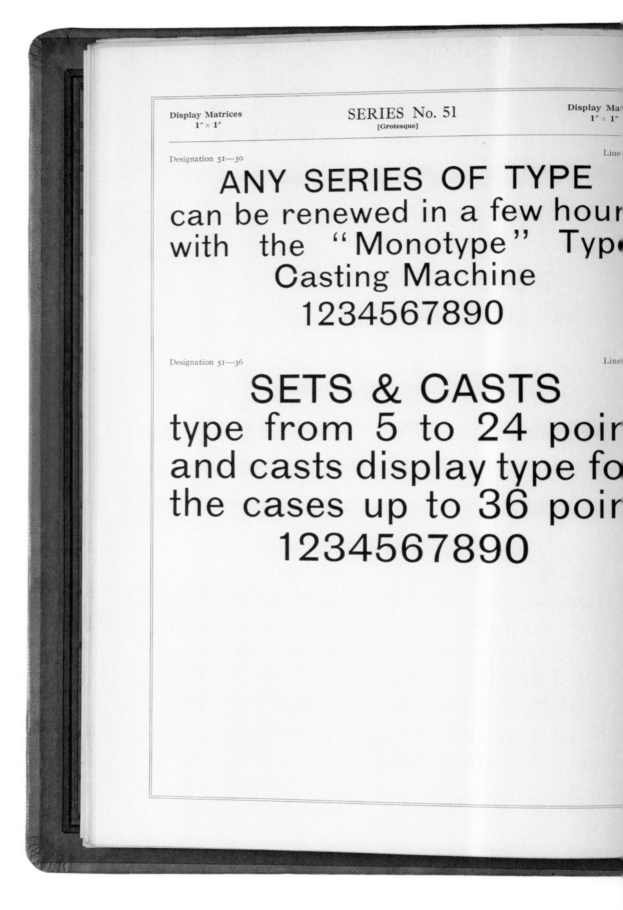

SERIES No. 51
[Grotesque]

Designation 51—72

Line ·793

PRINTERS can cast type from 5 to 72 point on the "Monotype" Super Cast-ing Machine and can also

Matrices for casting 60-point and 72-point sizes can only be used on the Super Caster

The contemporary typeface named Monotype Grotesque is the descendant of a group of loosely related sans serifs that originated in a design cut by Monotype in around 1926 under the direction of Frank Hinman Pierpont (1860–1937). It was introduced to address the company's need for a contemporary sans serif in its catalogue since the style was becoming very fashionable at the time.

The original Monotype Grotesque was based on various nineteenth-century sans serifs from Germany such as Ideal and Akzidenz-Grotesk (pp152–53). Like these earlier sans serif typeface families, Monotype Grotesque grew over several years to become a large group of associated independent typefaces rather than a logical series conforming to any overarching structure. Today we expect to find absolute consistency across the weights and styles of a typeface, but the Monotype Grotesque collection was never intended to coordinate in this way. Based on more natural family resemblances, each of its various styles had a mixture of shared traits and attributes that were unique to its width, weight or style.

In standard width variants such as Series No. 51, shown here, lower case letters a, e, g and t follow the model of twentieth-century English romans. Upper case characters are of nearly equal width, with the M, for example, almost square. One of the most notable features of Monotype Grotesque is the visible thinning of arcs that are tangential to stems.

Although they never achieved the huge international success of other sans serifs, the Monotype Grotesque typefaces were extensively used in the UK in the 1950s and 1960s as alternatives to Helvetica (pp346–47) and Univers (pp350–51), largely due to their ready availability for machine composition. The most popular of these, Monotype Grotesque Series No. 215, is the version that remains in use today as a digital font. This style also reputedly served as the model for the design of Arial (pp446–47), the typeface found today on personal computers everywhere.

Ty	**Weiss**
Ca	**Serif**
Ke	**Old Style**
Te	**Letterpress**
Da	**1926**
De	**Emil Rudolf Weiss**
Fo	**Bauer**
Co	**Germany**

Characteristics

Tapered, top-heavy stems
A Pointed apex, low crossbar
B S s Visually top heavy
M N No serifs at apex
U Foot at right stem
W Crossed centre-strokes
f Narrow, non-kerning
g Double-storeyed, straight ear
q Stem extends above bowl

BEMRSU
abcdefghij
koqrstuvy

Connections

The Doves Type	1900
Weiss Fraktur	1913
Centaur	1914
Schneidler Old Style	1936

Availability

Weiss is widely available

Specimen

Weiss type specimen. Bauersche
Giesserei, Frankfurt, c1926 (297x210mm)

WEISS ROMAN · THE BAUER TYPE FOUNDRY INC.

12 POINT 24A 47a

Gutenberg began with forty lines to a page, and after the printing of a few pages changed to forty-two lines, so as to save paper; he also enlarged the edition, reprinting the first few pages with forty-two lines to the page; this one has only forty. How long it took him to print the book, and when he finished it, we do not
CHARMING MONOGRAPHS ON FAMOUS AMERICAN AUTHORS

14 POINT 22A 42a

The public value of a public institution is dependent more on the use it makes of its collections than on the extent or worth of the collections themselves. There are some libraries we know of housing priceless material, yet that material is so inaccessible that the public service
HISTORICAL INDEX TO ROYAL FAMILIES OF NORWAY

16 POINT 18A 38a

An interesting account of the various styles and periods of Church Architecture, with special references to the points of agreement and difference between that of Scotland and
EXHIBITION OF ARTISTICAL WRITS AND DESIGNS

18 POINT 12A 26a

Jest-Book. Being a collection of the most brilliant jests
A Simplified way of Teaching the Learned Languages
FIRST EDITION OF THE NEW TESTAMENT

24 POINT 9A 19a

History of The International Labour Office
MUTUAL INSURANCE ASSOCIATION

WEISS ROMAN · THE BAUER TYPE FOUNDRY INC.

30 POINT 6A 10a

Humorous and Satirical Works
THE REIGNING FASHION

36 POINT 5A 7a

Romances and Proverbs
GRANITE NORWAY

48 POINT 4A 6a

Modern Sculptors
SPANISH TALES

60 POINT 3A 5a

Camden Road
FURNITURE

Emil Rudolf Weiss (1875–1942), a German poet, artist and designer, began work on his eponymous typeface during World War I but left it incomplete for a number of years. When the Weiss family was eventually published by the Bauer Foundry in Frankfurt in 1926, it became one of the most popular roman types to be issued for hand composition rather than by machine.

Although it does not directly reference any historical model, the key characteristics of Weiss follow the style of Italian types from the Renaissance. Its roots can be seen in the work of a number of type founders of that era, such as Aldus Manutius and Nicolas Jenson. Like its ancestors, Weiss has comparatively even strokes giving a low contrast overall. Renaissance influences are also in evidence in the design's sloping serifs and slightly top-heavy characters. With letter stems that are thicker at the top than the bottom and an almost geometric regularity overall, Weiss gives text settings a strikingly attractive, crisp rhythm. The combination of rational and calligraphic features distinguishes Weiss from many other contemporary interpretations of sixteenth-century types such as Schneidler Old Style (pp296–97).

Weiss was one of the earliest twentieth-century romans to be complemented by an authentic chancery italic based on the manuscript styles of Renaissance master calligraphers like Ludovico Vicentino degli Arrighi (pp40–41) and Giovanni Antonio Tagliente. Weiss was used most frequently for display purposes as a hand-set type until it became more widely available – and very popular – with the advent of photocomposition.

Ty	**Futura**
Ca	**Sans Serif**
Ke	**Geometric**
Te	**Letterpress**
Da	**1927**
De	**Paul Renner**
Fo	**Bauer**
Co	**Germany**

Characteristics

Capitals have classical proportions

Tall ascenders

A M V W Pointed apex

C c Vertical terminals

E F L S Narrow

M Splayed

S s Angled terminals

a g Single-storeyed

i j Round dots

j t Straight stem, no foot

v w Pointed apex

ACEMRS abcdefghij koprstuvy

Connections

Erbar-Grotesk	1922
ITC Avant Garde Gothic	1970
Avenir	1988
Brandon Grotesque	2010

Availability

Futura is widely available. Architype Renner is a digital revival of Renner's original characters, available from the Foundry and resellers

Specimen

Futura specimen No. 1. Bauersche Giesserei, Frankfurt, c1927 (297x210mm)

REN NER

FUTURA BAUERSCHE GIESSEREI, FRANKFURT A. M.

mager

Nr. 8320 20 Punkte
Min. 9,50 kg
14 A 50 a

DER OZEANFLUG CHAMBERLINS
Empfang auf dem Tempelhofer Feld
Besuch des Fliegers in Frankfurt a. M.

Nr. 8324 24 Punkte
Min. 11 kg
12 A 42 a

PUNKT UND LINIE ZU FLÄCHE
Technische Lehranstalten Dessau

Nr. 8328 28 Punkte
Min. 12 kg
10 A 36 a

MODERNE TYPOGRAPHIE
Die alte und neue Buchkunst

Nr. 8336 36 Punkte
Min. 14 kg
8 A 22 a

LIGNOSE FILM-PACK
Der werbende Trickfilm

Nr. 8348 48 Punkte
Min. 17 kg
6 A 18 a

REKLAME-BÜRO
Ein Bauhausbuch

FUTURA · DIE SCHRIFT UNSERER ZEIT

EN
NER

FUTURA BAUERSCHE GIESSEREI, FRANKFURT A. M.

halbfett

Nr. 8220 20 Punkte
Min. 9,50 kg
14 A 50 a

ERFOLGREICHE BUCH-AUTOREN
Wilhelm Speyer Lion Feuchtwanger
Radierungen zeitgemäßer Künstler

Nr. 8224 24 Punkte
Min. 11 kg
12 A 42 a

PRESSA KÖLN AM RHEIN 1928
Die heutige Zeitungsilluſtration

Nr. 8228 28 Punkte
Min. 12 kg
10 A 36 a

DIE RATIONELLE KÜCHE
Internationale Ausſtellung

Nr. 8236 36 Punkte
Min. 15 kg
8 A 22 a

KULTUR UND PRESSE
Arbeitsgemeinschaft

Nr. 8248 48 Punkte
Min. 19 kg
6 A 14 a

KÜNSTLERHEIM
Niederlahnstein

UTURA · DIE SCHRIFT UNSERER ZEIT

The plaque left on the Moon in July 1969 to commemorate the Apollo 11 space mission was set in Futura, an archetype of the modern era designed by Paul Renner (1878–1956). With its architectural construction, rigorous geometry and absence of decoration, Futura has become emblematic of the modernist movement that originated in Germany in the early years of the twentieth century. Although Renner was not affiliated with the Bauhaus, he espoused similar ideals and believed that modern typefaces should express modern conditions rather than archaic ones.

Commissioned by the Bauer Foundry, Renner worked for several years on Futura's development, possibly in response to the design of Jakob Erbar's groundbreaking geometric typeface (pp224–25). Renner's initial drawings were made with a pen, compass and ruler, using the circle, square and triangle as building blocks to construct characters that were extremely distilled abstractions of conventional roman letters. When a trial cut of the first version was made, Bauer thought some characters too experimental and Renner was asked to amend the unconventional lower case to resemble traditional forms more closely.

The final version of Futura, released in 1927, has a minimal, measured and industrial appearance, with every feature serving a defined purpose. The typeface is built logically from a limited range of simple geometric parts, which are duplicated, reflected and rotated to build a character set that achieves harmonious classical proportions, particularly in the upper case, which mirrors the structure of Roman inscriptional capitals. Like a traditional text typeface, the lower case has tall ascenders that stand above the capitals. Futura appears to be monolinear – the result of absolutely perfect symmetries – but this is, in fact, a subtle optical illusion intended to create visual balance. Strokes seem to be without any contrast but actually have a slight modulation. This is identifiable in the apparent circularity of the o, which is, in fact, slightly elliptical, and in the careful thinning of curves that are tangential to other strokes – where the right leg of the h meets its stem, for example.

Futura was expanded by Bauer in the years after its release into one of the earliest coordinated type systems, including a comprehensive range of weights with matching obliques and corresponding condensed families. Its immediate global success precipitated a flood of new geometric sans serif typefaces from competing foundries, and it remains one of the definitive sans serif types in the twenty-first century.

Kabel

Ty	**Kabel**	
Ca	**Sans Serif**	
Ke	**Geometric**	
Te	**Letterpress**	
Da	**1927**	
De	**Rudolf Koch**	
Fo	**Klingspor**	
Co	**Germany**	

Characteristics

A High crossbar, rests on points
C E F Arms have angled terminals
E F L Narrow
G No spur
W Crossed centre-strokes
a Double-storeyed
b Stem merges with bowl
e Oblique bar
f Cross-stroke does not extend to left
g Double-storeyed, open lower bowl
t Top is angled, curve at foot
v w y Angled terminals

AEGMW
abcdefghij
koprstuvy

Connections

Erbar-Grotesk	192
Koch Antiqua	192
Futura	192
Prisma	193

Availability
Kabel is widely available

Specimen
Kabel type specimen. Klingspor, Offenbach, c1927 (185x229mm)

---

62 a, 26 A, etwa 8 Kilo

and of iron
HE JUDGE

44 a, 16 A, etwa 9 Kilo

Stuttgart
ILLER

6 14 A, etwa 10 Kilo

in Köln
FRAU

2 a, 12 A, etwa 11 Kilo

urorte
STEIN

4 a, 10 A, etwa 14 Kilo

inder
SEN

21419   4 Cicero, 48 Punkte   Satz, 20 a, 10 A, etwa 20 Kilo

Saint Maurice

21420   5 Cicero, 60 Punkte   Satz, 14 a, 6 A, etwa 23 Kilo

Rembrandt
VAN RIJN

21421   6 Cicero, 72 Punkte   Satz, 10 a, 4 A, etwa 26 Kilo

Don Juan
BÜHNE

21422   7 Cicero, 84 Punkte   Satz, 10 a, 4 A, etwa 30 Kilo   Grobe Kabel

Merkur

21423   8 Cicero, 96 Punkte   Satz, 8 a, 4 A, etwa 35 Kilo

Kreuth

21532   8 Cicero, 96 Punkte (nur Großbuchstaben)   Satz 6 A, etwa 22 Kilo

REBE

Bruchzahlen ¼ ½ ¾ und % liefern wir bei nachfolgenden Kabel-Schriften in den Graden von 6 bis 16 Punkt mit: Leichte Kabel, Norm-Kabel, schmale Kabel, grobe Kabel, fette Kabel und schmale halbfette Kabel.

5

'People are always saying that I try to express my own personality in type design, but that is not at all true; on the contrary, I do my best to avoid such expressionism.' These are the words of Rudolf Koch (1876–1934), a leading German calligrapher, typographer and teacher.

It is surprising that a craftsman so renowned for his skills in the use of traditional methods should have been so keen to design a geometric typeface, but in the 1920s, when modernist ideas began to influence typographic tastes, he enthusiastically accepted the Klingspor foundry's invitation to do so.

Koch's contribution to the competitive sans serif market was Kabel, a monolinear design that had a similar geometric structure in the upper case to types such as Futura and Erbar, although the lower case is distinguished by a number of calligraphic characteristics.

Kabel reveals an interesting negotiation between modernist principles and traditional craftsmanship, exhibiting many personal and historical features that are hallmarks of Koch's design work. Indeed, Kabel could almost be considered a development of his 1922 Koch Antiqua, as it shares many of its character shapes and proportions, most notably its unusual g.

Koch's profound knowledge of the history of lettering is evident in Kabel's design, with lower case letterforms such as the a, e and g having their roots in the ninth-century Carolingian minuscule and upper case characters showing influences of even earlier monumental capitals from Roman inscriptions.

Kabel's stroke weights are more varied than most geometric sans serifs, and the terminals of some vertical and diagonal strokes are cut at a shallow angle. As a result, letterforms do not sit squarely on the baseline, making for a more animated and natural appearance than types such as Futura.

When Kabel was launched in 1927 it made a significant contribution to the German Neue Typographie movement. Together with Futura and Erbar, it had an explosive effect on contemporary typographic practice, transforming the visual landscape of the twentieth century. Over the ensuing years, Futura eclipsed the success of its competitors but Kabel remains a popular and versatile typeface.

In the 1970s, a revival of Kabel was issued by ITC. Like other ITC typefaces of the time, this version features an excessively large x-height created to cater for design tastes of the day, and should not be confused with the original.

Leichte Kabel

21401 2 Cicero, 24 Punkte   Satz, 40 a, 16 A, etwa 10 Kilo

Impressum van den catalogus
NIEUWES ADRESBOEK

21402 Doppelmittel, 28 Punkte   Satz, 34 a, 14 A, etwa 11 Kilo

Technische Hochschule
DARMSTADT

21403 3 Cicero, 36 Punkte   Satz, 26 a, 10 A, etwa 14 Kilo

Not too much Zeal
FOUR-MASTED

21404 4 Cicero, 48 Punkte   Satz, 22 a, 8 A, etwa 20 Kilo

Neues Rathaus
MÜNCHEN

21405 5 Cicero, 60 Punkte   Satz, 14 a, 6 A, etwa 23 Kilo

Musikschule
DRESDEN

21406 6 Cicero, 72 Punkte ⟨Hohlfuß⟩   Satz, 12 a, 6 A, etwa 23 Kilo

Erzgebirge
GRANIT

21407 7 Cicero, 84 Punkte ⟨Hohlfuß⟩   Satz, 10 a, 6 A, etwa 26 Kilo

Stickstoff

72206 Nonpareill
Bei der Ausstattung
stattung zu untersch
DIE ZEITSCHRIFTE

72208 Petit, 8 Pur
Kiezen is een ge
tieve voorkeur
DE HERLEVIN

72209 Borgis, 9 P
Es hat sich die
Stellung erobe
VORTRÄGE

72210 Korpus, 10
All business
press-copyin
THE TRADE

72212 Cicero, 12
Della stessa
IL RISORG

72214 Mittel, 14 P
Jahresberi
DIE NEU

72216 Tertia, 16 P
El termin
EL CON

2

Ty	**Broadway**
Ca	**Sans Serif**
Ke	**Geometric, Capitals**
Te	**Letterpress**
Da	**1928**
De	**Morris Fuller Benton**
Fo	**American Type Founders**
Co	**USA**

Characteristics

Extreme contrast of thick and thin strokes
Sharp joint between thick and thin strokes
A Low crossbar
B Curled open counter
E F High middle arm, shortest arm at top
M Splayed, pointed apex
S Alternate forms
g j p q y No descender

AMWX EHTBR CGDOS

Connections

Boul Mich	1927
Broadway Engraved	1928
Parisian	1928
ITC Manhattan	1970

Availability

Broadway is available from Monotype and resellers

Specimen

The Broadway Series. American Type Founders, New Jersey, c1928 (300x230mm)

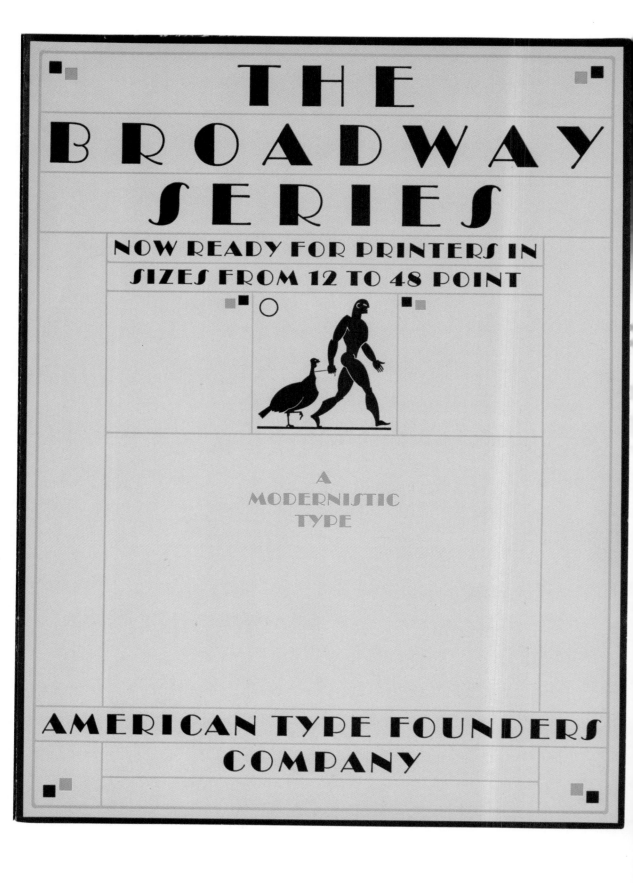

Few typefaces are as evocative of a specific time and place as Broadway, and few could be more appropriately named. As a typographic representation of the United States in the 1920s, Broadway instantly evokes the glitz and glamour of art deco and the jazz age.

The original display typeface was designed in 1928 in capitals only and was followed by a condensed variant in 1929, to which a lower case was added. Both were drawn by the prolific Morris Fuller Benton (1872–1948), chief typeface designer at American Type Founders. A Monotype copy was completed in 1929 with the addition of a lower case for the standard width, designed by Sol Hess, who also produced Broadway Engraved, a decorative variant.

Sharp geometry, enormous bulk and extreme stroke contrast are Broadway's major characteristics. The design seems to reappropriate the basic features of a nineteenth-century fat face (pp108–109) but, dramatically, it severs the serifs. In most of the characters, hairline strokes are used to describe contours, supporting heavyweight main strokes that meet with them at abrupt angles rather than in smoothly modulated curves.

Broadway is the most enduring of the many American art deco display typefaces of the time, such as Gallia, Boul Mich and Parisian (pp242–43). It had a long initial run of popularity before being discontinued by ATF in 1954, but it was rediscovered in the photocomposition years and has since been used frequently as a ready solution whenever a type is required to suggest an impression of the roaring twenties.

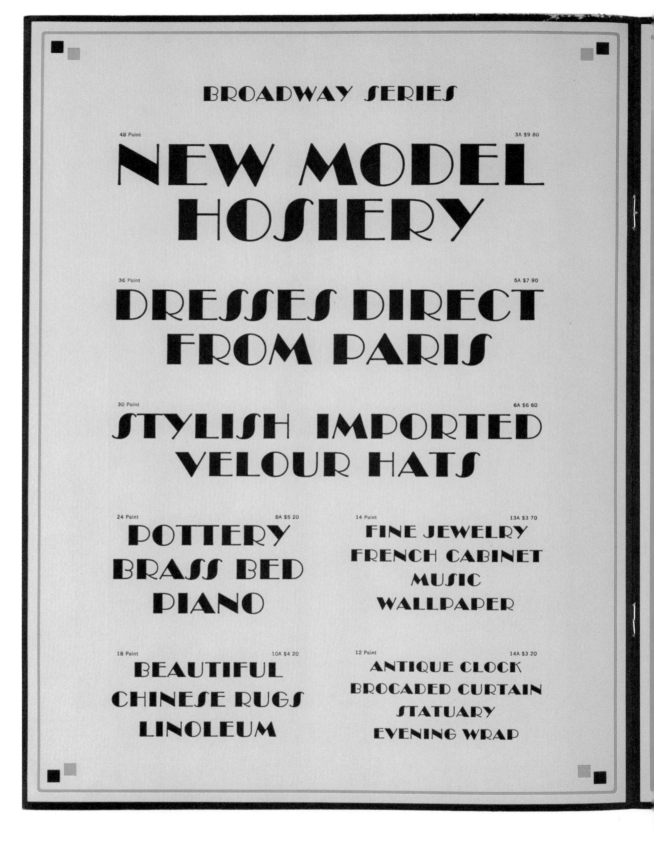

235

Ty	**Curwen Sans**
Ca	**Sans Serif**
Ke	**Geometric**
Te	**Letterpress**
Da	**1928**
De	**Harold Curwen**
Fo	**Curwen Press**
Co	**UK**

Characteristics

Tall ascenders and descenders
Small x-height
Large capitals
A M N Pointed vertices
G No spur
M Splayed
R Straight, angled leg
W Crossed centre-strokes
e Narrow, open bowl
g Double-storeyed with open lower bowl
t Tall stem

AGMRW abcdefghij koprstuvy

Connections

Johnston's Railway Type	1916
Kabel	1927
Gill Sans	1928
Regular	2012

Availability

Not available

Specimen

A Working Handbook of Types in Use at the Curwen Press. London, 1931 (180x135mm)

The Curwen Press was founded by John Curwen in 1863 to publish sheet music. In 1914, his grandson, Harold Curwen (1885–1949) took over its management. Under his direction, the press became a leader in the resurgence of fine British printing in the early twentieth century, with a diverse output that included books, posters and ephemera.

Harold Curwen had a lifelong interest in the arts having studied calligraphy with Edward Johnston at the Central School. Drawing on this experience, he began work on a geometric alphabet in 1911, but it was not until 1928 that this design was finally cut as a typeface for the exclusive use of the Curwen Press. During the two decades it took for Curwen Sans to reach completion, Edward Johnston had produced his seminal lettering for the London Underground (pp202–203) and Eric Gill's eponymous sans serif typeface (pp238–39) had been released by Monotype. Both were enormously influential on the development of the sans serif in the twentieth century, the latter becoming one of Monotype's bestsellers.

Despite its proximity to the designs of Johnston and Gill, Curwen Sans was little known until recent times as it was made solely for use in work produced by the Curwen Press – a print business, not a type foundry – and when the company ceased trading in the 1980s the typeface disappeared with it.

As a design, Curwen Sans deserves reappraisal. Like Johnston's or Gill's typefaces, the letters follow the classical proportions of Roman inscriptional capitals, but they are more geometric, sharing many properties with Rudolf Koch's Kabel (pp232–33), issued in 1927. The N and Z both feature sharp vertices, similar to those in Paul Renner's geometric Futura (pp230–31), and the crossed W is a distinctively classical feature. The Curwen Sans lower case is full of personality, if a little odd. It has a considerably smaller x-height than other geometric sans serifs, with longer ascenders and descenders. Its disparate character set contains a number of eccentric individuals, such as the g, which has similarities to Kabel's, and the unusual e with its opened eye.

It would be easy to mistake Curwen Sans for a whimsical derivative of the mainstream geometric sans serifs of the 1920s, as clients of the Curwen Press might have done at the time. Although no grand claims can be made about its historical significance, Curwen Sans is a truly groundbreaking achievement, unconfined by precedent or convention.

36 A QUICK BROW

30 N FOX JUMPED OV

24 R THIS LAZY DOG. A Q

18 ICK BROWN FOX JUMPED OV

12 THIS LAZY DOG. A QUICK BROWN FOX JUMP

18 1 2 3 4 5 6 7 8 9 0

CURWEN BLOCK CAPITALS AVAILABLE IN
12, 18, 24, 30 and 36 point

36

Since 1900, the essential features [24] of development have been brought about by the activities of two groups, i.e. the type-foundries and the book-artists, who, in some cases, collaborate. The book-artist is an artist who concentrates his efforts on the book, not merely as an illustrator, but as a supervisor of the whole process of its production.

CURWEN SANS-SERIF AVAILABLE IN
24 point

37

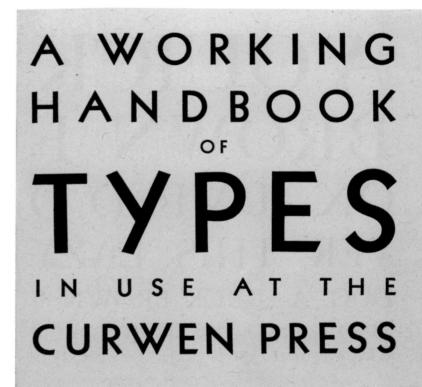

A WORKING
HANDBOOK
OF
TYPES
IN USE AT THE
CURWEN PRESS

JANUARY   1931

Ty	**Gill Sans**
Ca	**Sans Serif**
Ke	**Geometric**
Te	**Letterpress**
Da	**1928**
De	**Eric Gill**
Fo	**Monotype**
Co	**UK**

Characteristics

C c S s e r	Vertical terminals
G	No spur
M	High vertex
Q	Short, curved tail
R	Wide, curved leg
V W	Pointed vertex
a	Double-storeyed, curve at foot
b d p	Flat junction of bowl to stem
f	Narrow
g	Double-storeyed
i j	Round dots
t	Angled bracket connects stem and bar
y	Straight tail
f	Straight descending tail
p	Stem and bowl strokes overlap

GMQRSV
abcdefghij
prstyaefp

Connections

Johnston's Railway Type	1916
Kabel	1927
Granby	1930
Bliss	1996

Availability

Gill Sans is available from Monotype and resellers

Specimen

Gill Sans specimen sheet. Monotype Corporation, Salfords, c1940 (270x210mm)

THE STORY OF "MONOTYPE" GILL SANS, CONTINUED FROM THE OPPOSITE PAGE

REASONS *FOR CUTTING* GILL SANS: The Monotype Corporation had no ambition to start a new Fashion in display. That was the ambition of the "old style" typefounders, who had lost their great market for "body" founts, and therefore had to exploit the *face-cutting side* of their business. [That side is unknown to the "new style" typefounder who simply buys or hires ready-made matrices and casts founts on his "Monotype" caster.] The remarkable thing was not that *German* letter-founders were the first to follow the lead of a great English designer, but that *English* letter-cutting foundries were not. [12 pt. solid

WHEN, however, it became evident that **a "new" sans-serif** would **henceforth be in** *permanent demand*, **inasmuch as it fulfilled a permanent need** in certain 20th century forms of commercial printing, The Monotype Corporation stepped in with a *new design*. The stepping-in was done in order that its customers might be able to produce their own founts of decent sans-serif at something under half the cost of buying them. The *choice of a new design*, by an internationally famous letterer, was partly a matter of pride, but was also dictated by the need for a letter so perfectly **rational** that it would cut through all the quibbling about minor variations of form. This intention was specially manifested when the *"100 per cent. normal l.c."* was cut.

THE FIRST ORDERS for "Monotype" *Gill Sans* came from adventurous printers who had discovered that their customers would take seriously any work of art by Mr. Eric Gill, whether it were a statue, a wood-engraving, a stone-cut inscription or a type design. But the æsthetic intelligentzia do not form a *mass market*. **What started Gill Sans on its extraordinary career of popularity—what made it first challenge and then vanquish its only competitor, "Chelt."** in the jobbing field, was not the international fame of its designer amongst cultured people. **It was the discovery, by large print-buying firms (indeed, by one man in one such firm) that in "Monotype" Gill Sans there would be found the one perfect face for large-scale type** *standardization of printed matter* **other** *than continuous reading matter.* When it is realized that the vast majority of distinctively 20th century printing consists of something which is *not* continuous reading matter, it will be seen how important this discovery was.

The value of **STANDARDIZATION** itself had only begun to be realized, for most customers were still trying to *show each printer* how they wanted *each job*; only a few had been forced to save time by adopting certain rational **principles** of type-choice, layout, etc., and asking printers to conform to them. Mr. C. G. Dandridge of the L.N.E.R. had seen the economic value of standardizing the vast output of time-tables, posters, handbills, labels, and other ephemeral pieces. **"Monotype" GILL Sans** appeared as a face which was simple enough to be fool-proof as long as it was alone; a neutral face that asked for no special paper surface or decoration or layout style; **a face that would have a grave and candid beauty if it were simply let alone to do its work of conveying ideas.** [*continued overleaf*

COMPOSITION SIZES shown on this page: 18 rom., 14 rom. & ital., 12 to 7 pt. rom. & ital. combined in matrix-case with 275

262
Normal
Caps & lower case
Roman & Italic

LEFT: COMPOSITION Sizes, 262 roman & italic showing combination with Heavy 275

'Monotype'
Gill Sans 262
Roman from 72
to 14 displ. *Ital. 36-14*
Bold r. & *it.* **72 to 14**
DISPLAY sizes: *specimens*
available to any Master Printer

iii

Gill Sans was designed between 1927 and 1928 by the British artist, sculptor and letter carver Eric Gill (1882–1940). It was based on the lettering he had painted in 1926 for the fascia of Douglas Cleverdon's bookshop in Bristol. When Stanley Morison saw the hand-lettered sans serif capitals, he invited Gill to develop them into a type family to compete with geometric sans serifs from Germany, like Erbar, Futura and Kabel, which enjoyed huge commercial success across Europe during the late 1920s. Morison's acumen resulted in the release of Gill Sans by the Monotype Corporation in 1928.

Gill's design is hugely influenced by Edward Johnston's 1916 lettering for the London Underground (pp202–203), which Gill had worked on while apprenticed to Johnston. With the opinion that some of Johnston's letters were 'not entirely satisfactory', he set out to achieve an archetypal alphabet that, he said, would be 'foolproof'. Integrating Johnston's calligraphic principles with geometric construction methods and classical proportions, Gill Sans is at once a modern and traditional design. While its basic shapes are built from plain lines and arcs, its letterforms are modelled on the contours and proportions of Roman inscriptional lettering for the upper case, and on early Renaissance Venetian types for the lower case. This gives Gill Sans a warmth and humanity rarely seen in sans serif typefaces and contributes much to its readability in bodies of text.

In addition, each member of the family imparts its own individual personality. Unlike the interpolated weights of most contemporary types, Gill's were not generated algorithmically from a single master design but drawn with careful attention to specific features. With considerable input from the technicians at Monotype's Drawing Office, Gill Sans was published in four weights, italics, a condensed face and several display versions, including Gill Cameo and Gill Shadow. It quickly became the bestselling sans serif typeface in Great Britain.

Eric Gill's most enduring contribution to the history of design, Gill Sans, like the man himself, has not been without detractors. It has been notably criticized by some for having a regular weight that can look too dark and a light weight that can look spindly. However, it remains dignified and authoritative when set in capitals, and is exceptionally convivial in most text environments. Gill Sans has been used around the world for every application imaginable, communicating with an unassuming, clear and uniquely English tone of voice.

Ty	**Neuzeit-Grotesk**
Ca	**Sans Serif**
Ke	**Geometric**
Te	**Letterpress**
Da	**1928**
De	**Wilhelm Pischner**
Fo	**Stempel**
Co	**Germany**

Characteristics

Capitals have old-style proportions
Large x-height
C c G g e Angled terminals
G No spur
J Top bar to left
M Wide, low vertex
Q Short, straight tail
R Straight leg
S s Flat terminals
a Double-storeyed, straight stem
f r t Narrow, vertical terminals
g Single-storeyed
i j Round dots
l Curved foot
t Flat top-stroke
y Straight tail

ACEJMR
abcefghij
kloprstuy

Connections

Erbar-Grotesk	1922
Futura	1927
Nobel	1929
LL Brown	2011

Availability

Neuzeit-Grotesk is available from URW
and resellers

Specimen

Neuzeit-Grotesk type specimen.
D. Stempel AG, Frankfurt, c1932
(297x210mm)

3747 5 Punkt 2,5 kg 50 A 192 a

Die Kunst, ein Buch als Ganzes schön zu gestalten, hat niemals höher gestanden als in
Deutschland zur Zeit der Erfindung des Buchdrucks. Was Gutenberg und seine Genossen im engen Anschluß an die sichere Tradition der gotischen Handschriften geschnitten,
gegossen, gesetzt und gedruckt haben, hat keiner ihrer Nachfolger daheim oder im Aus-

DIE KUNST, EIN BUCH ALS GANZES SCHÖN ZU GESTALTEN, HAT NIEMALS HÖHER GESTANDEN ALS IN
DEUTSCHLAND ZUR ZEIT DER ERFIN-
DUNG DES BUCHDRUCKS. WAS GUTENBERG UND SEINE GENOSSEN IM
ENGEN ANSCHLUSS AN DIE SICHERE TRADITION DER GOTISCHEN HAND-

6984 6 Punkt 3 kg 46 A 176 a

Die Kunst, ein Buch als Ganzes schön zu gestalten, hat niemals höher gestanden als in Deutschland zur Zeit der Erfindung des Buchdrucks. Was
Gutenberg und seine Genossen im engen Anschluß an die sichere Tradition der gotischen Handschriften geschnitten, gegossen, gesetzt und

DIE KUNST, EIN BUCH ALS GANZES SCHÖN ZU GESTALTEN, HAT
NIEMALS HÖHER GESTANDEN ALS IN DEUTSCHLAND ZUR ZEIT
DER ERFINDUNG DES BUCHDRUCKS. WAS GUTENBERG UND
SEINE GENOSSEN IM ENGEN ANSCHLUSS AN DIE SICHERE

6986 8 Punkt 4 kg 40 A 142 a

Die Kunst, ein Buch als Ganzes schön zu gestalten, hat niemals höher gestanden als in Deutschland zur Zeit der Erfindung des Buchdrucks. Was Gutenberg und seine Genossen im engen Anschluß an die sichere Tradition der

DIE KUNST, EIN BUCH ALS GANZES SCHÖN ZU GE-
STALTEN, HAT NIEMALS HÖHER GESTANDEN ALS IN
DEUTSCHLAND ZUR ZEIT DER ERFINDUNG DES
BUCHDRUCKS. WAS GUTENBERG UND SEINE GENOS-

6987 9 Punkt 5 kg 38 A 130

Die Kunst, ein Buch als Ganzes schön zu gestalten,
hat niemals höher gestanden als in Deutschland zur
Zeit der Erfindung des Buchdrucks. Was Gutenberg

DIE KUNST, EIN BUCH ALS GANZES SCHÖN ZU
GESTALTEN, HAT NIEMALS HÖHER GESTANDEN
ALS IN DEUTSCHLAND ZUR ZEIT DER ERFIN-

6988 10 Punkt 5 kg 32 A 112

Die Kunst, ein Buch als Ganzes schön zu gestalten, hat niemals höher gestanden als in Deutschland zur Zeit der Erfindung des Buchdrucks. Wa

DIE KUNST, EIN BUCH ALS GANZES SCHÖN
ZU GESTALTEN, HAT NIEMALS HÖHER GE
STANDEN ALS IN DEUTSCHLAND ZUR ZEN

6989 12 Punkt 6 kg 28 A 92

Die Kunst, ein Buch als Ganzes schön z
gestalten, hat niemals höher gestande
als in Deutschland zur Zeit der Erfindun

DIE KUNST, EIN BUCH ALS GANZE
SCHÖN ZU GESTALTEN, HAT NIEMAL
HÖHER GESTANDEN ALS IN DEUTSCH

LEICHTE NEUZEIT-GROTESK

3748 14 Punkt 7 kg 26 A 84 a

Nachrichten aus Presse und Rundfunk · REPORTAGEN AUS DEM STADION

3749 16 Punkt 8 kg 22 A 72 a

Moderne Bauweisen von heute · SIEDLUNG AUF DEM LAND

3750 20 Punkt 10 kg 18 A 56 a

Physikalische Lehrformeln · JOURNAL DE PHYSIQU

3751 24 Punkt 11 kg 16 A 50 a

Magazine for printers · GRAPHISCHE HEFT

3752 28 Punkt 12 kg 10 A 34 a

Midsommarsdag · BUCHGEWERBE

3753 36 Punkt 15 kg 8 A 26 a

Gardinenstoff · KONFEKTION

3754 48 Punkt 18 kg 6 A 18 a

Ruderboot · FISCHERE

Like Paul Renner's Futura, Neuzeit is a typeface whose name boldly declares its own ambitions. The word translates into English as 'modern era', making a confident claim as an epoch-defining typeface, although this is something of an overstatement. Neuzeit-Grotesk is a serviceable and well-structured geometric sans serif family designed by Wilhelm Pischner (1904–89) between 1928 and 1930 for the Stempel foundry in four weights: light, regular, medium and bold. It was cut for machine composition and for hand-setting. The Neuzeit-Grotesk family was subsequently extended, with two condensed variants being released in the late 1930s, but due to World War II it was not until 15 years later that accompanying italics were added.

Compared with geometric sans serifs of its time, Neuzeit-Grotesk has one major point of difference. Its x-height is larger than most others, with shorter ascenders and descenders, giving a distinctive colour to bodies of text. Overall, the letterforms are wide, providing an open and even appearance on the page, although they are slightly compressed in the light and medium weights. Two characters were originally provided in alternate versions: a single- or double-storeyed a and a u with or without a stem.

In 1966, a new version of the typeface was developed by Stempel and Linotype. Designed for exclusive use as part of the corporate identity for the German engineering company Siemens, it was called Neuzeit S. Intended for reading extended bodies of text, the new design had some of the proportions but none of the geometric character of the original Neuzeit-Grotesk. The two typefaces have very little in common, although they are often confused with each other.

Despite its evident qualities, in a crowded marketplace the original Neuzeit-Grotesk was not extensively used until it was included in the DIN typeface series by the Deutsches Institut für Normung in 1970 as part of its standard for the design and application of lettering to be used in signage and technical documentation. In the DIN 30640 standard, two Neuzeit-Grotesk weights were redrawn, with all characters becoming slightly wider, descenders being elongated, and the alternate a and u from the original typeface integrated into the standard character set. Despite these modifications, the DIN implementation of Neuzeit-Grotesk maintained much of its original character.

FETTE NEUZEIT-GROTESK

andbuch der modernen Technik · TECHNISCHE LEHRANSTALTEN

ormschöne Möbel im Heim · EDELHOLZ-VERARBEITUNG

tahl- und Eisenwaren · ROSTFREIES BESTECK

Eiskunstlaufmeister · WINTERSPORTLER

Svensk Ordbok · SPRACHLEHRE

Calorimétrie · HEIZSONNE

Pentecost · LONDON

Parisian

Ty	**Parisian**
Ca	**Sans Serif**
Ke	**Geometric**
Te	**Letterpress**
Da	**1928**
De	**Morris Fuller Benton**
Fo	**American Type Founders**
Co	**USA**

Characteristics

Extreme contrast of thick and thin strokes
Large capitals
Elongated ascenders, short descenders
A Crossbar extends to left
B R Looped, open bowls
E F High middle arm
S s Sloped alternate
W Crossed centre-strokes
a Single-storeyed
r Looped arch
t Straight stem

ABERSW
abcdefghijk
lnopqrstuvy

Connections

Broadway	1928
Plaza	1975
New Yorker Type	1985
ITC Vintage	1996

Availability

Parisian is available from Monotype and resellers

Specimen

Parisian – An Advance Showing. American Type Founders, New Jersey, 1928 (300x230mm)

A Twentieth Century
Type Design

The

72 Point

FLOWERS
Beautiful Rose

42 Point

INDIAN RUG
Cleverly Designed

36 Point

IMPORTED GOWNS
Enthusiastic Buyer Rewarded

24 Point

FASHIONABLE SILK LINGERIE
Modern Designs Make Exhibits Interesting

12 Point

EDUCATIONAL VALU
COMMUNITY PRINTS
GENERALLY RECOGN

Printing has long exerted an e
and enlightening influence whic
asset to any community, whethe
or small. The industry is one i
the arts and crafts make a happ

Che

A B C
H I J
P Q I
W X Y
3 4 5
a b c d
m n o
w x y z

Prices and Schemes of Job Fonts

72 Point Caps 3A $13 00 Lowercase 4a $5 40 Complete $18 40
60 Point Caps 4A   9 60 Lowercase 6a 5 90 Complete 15 50
48 Point Caps 6A   9 10 Lowercase 9a 5 60 Complete 14 70
42 Point Caps 7A   7 70 Lowercase 10a 5 05 Complete 12 75
36 Point Caps 7A   6 00 Lowercase 11a 4 15 Complete 10 15
30 Point Caps 8A   4 75 Lowercase 14a 3 65 Complete   8 40

AMERICAN TYPE

Series

10 Point

CESSFUL PRINTERS ARE
AYS USERS OF MODERN
OR-SAVING EQUIPMENT

labor-saving devices tend generally
the standard of morale among the
in the composing room. An ample
of spacing material kept constantly
the compositors by alert apprentices
the spacing problem of most of its
and makes correct spacing possible

Font

E F G
M N O
T U V
$ 1 2
8 9 0
i j k l
s t u v
: ; ! ?

DERS COMPANY

For Commercial Printing
and Magazine Display

60 Point

BROADSIDE
Noted Engravings

48 Point

SILK HOSE
Modern Colors

30 Point

FURNITURE EXHIBITION
Manufacturers Anniversary Display

18 Point

RADIO MARVEL
Magnificent new models
give wonderful reception

14 Point

GRACE UNIVERSITY
Manhattan college celebrates
fiftieth anniversary with many
gatherings and athletic events

Prices and Schemes of Job Fonts

24 Point	Caps 10A $4 25	Lowercase 17a $3 05	Complete $7 30
18 Point	Caps 14A 3 60	Lowercase 30a 3 20	Complete 6 80
14 Point	Caps 19A 3 45	Lowercase 38a 2 85	Complete 6 30
12 Point	Caps 23A 3 15	Lowercase 46a 2 65	Complete 5 80
10 Point	Caps 26A 2 80	Lowercase 53a 2 40	Complete 5 20

From its origins in Paris during the first decades of the twentieth century, the art deco style quickly spread across the globe, influencing all creative disciplines from interiors to fashion and from architecture to advertising. It remained hugely popular until the late 1930s.

Typical attributes of the art deco style – clean geometric symmetries, sleek curves, strong vertical lines and aerodynamic forms – are all perfectly embodied in Parisian, a typeface designed by Morris Fuller Benton (1872–1948) for American Type Founders in 1928. Parisian bears a strong family resemblance to Broadway, Benton's design from the same year (pp234–35). However, where the latter seeks to evoke the flamboyant glitz of New York, Parisian is intended, through both its name and its appearance, to reflect the more seductive glamour of the French capital in the jazz age.

Like Broadway, Parisian has a razor-sharp contrast between thick and thin strokes but there the similarity ends. Parisian is markedly more slender and poised than its relative, and its bolder strokes are slightly flared. Lower case letters have a tiny x-height, offset by elongated ascenders whose height corresponds to that of the extravagant capitals. A notable feature is the distribution of weight onto single downstrokes only in most characters. These strokes make a strong contrast with the hairline curves that extend from them.

Parisian's slender, graceful style made it very popular for display, advertising and packaging applications, particularly for the fashion industry. Today, it still maintains the cool air of sophistication we readily associate with its era.

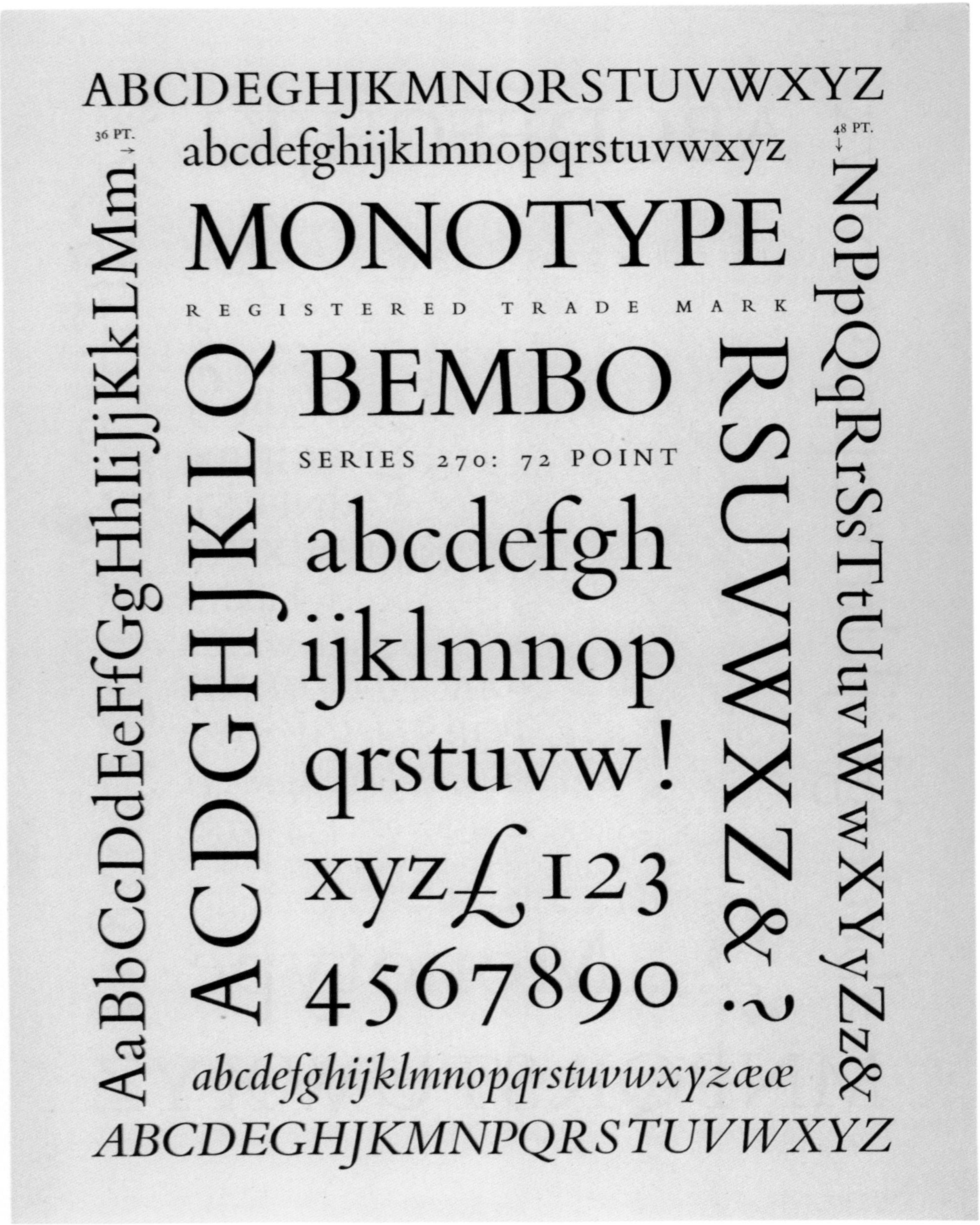

Bembo specimen sheet. Monotype Corporation, Salfords, c1940 (270x210mm)

Ty	**Bembo**
Ca	**Serif**
Ke	**Old Style**
Te	**Letterpress**
Da	**1929**
De	**Stanley Morison**
Fo	**Monotype**
Co	**UK**

Characteristics

A	Flat apex, high crossbar
G	No spur
J	Descends below baseline, slight hook
K	Curved arm
M	Splayed
Q	Tail below letter
R	Very wide, curved right leg
W	Crossed centre-strokes
a	Double-storeyed
f	Extended right arch
g	Double-storeyed
r	Upturned arch

AGJKRW
abcdefghij
orstuya*efg*

Connections

Griffo's Roman	1495
Poliphilus	1920
Lutetia	1925
DTL Haarlemmer	1995

Availability

Bembo is available from Monotype and resellers

Specimen

Bembo specimen sheet. Monotype Corporation, Salfords, c1940 (270x210mm)

ABCDEFGHJKL

abcdefghijklmnopqrstuvwx

yzfiflfffffiffl.,;:."'?!-1234567890

THE MONOTYPE
CORPORATION
LIMITED
Registered Office: 55-56
Lincolns Inn Fields
London, W.C.2.
Works: Salfords
nr. Redhill
Surrey

'MONOTYPE' BEMBO SERIES No. 270

30 point
ABCD
EGHIJK
MNPRST
UVWXYZ!
abcdefghijklm
nopqrstuvwxyz?
ABCDEGHJKMN
PQRSTUVWXYZ,
abcdefghijklmnopqrstuvw
xyz 1234567890 1234567890

A RENOWNED FACE — 'MONOTYPE' BEMBO —
shown in alphabets for your convenience when making layouts.
Composition sizes begin at 6 pt. Display sizes: 14, 16, 18, 22, 24, 30, 36, 48

60 & 72
point

REGISTERED
TRADE MARK

Monotype

60 POINT

MNPQRSTUWXYZ

During the 1920s the Monotype Corporation, under the direction of Stanley Morison, embarked on an ambitious programme to recut a large number of historic typefaces for machine composition. The last design in the series to be executed, Monotype Bembo, was one of the handsomest of the revivals and an enduring favourite of Morison's. Published in 1929, it has proved to be one of the most popular book types of the twentieth century.

Monotype Bembo was modelled on a type cut in 1495 by Francesco Griffo for *De Aetna*, a short travelogue by Pietro Bembo published by the Venetian printer and publisher Aldus Manutius (pp30–31). Griffo was one of the first punch cutters to break away from the constraining influence of the humanist manuscript hand. With consummate skill, he exploited type production technologies to cut and cast types that were more precisely formed than had ever been seen before.

Monotype Bembo is carefully constructed to replicate the sophistication of Griffo's designs within the production limitations of a type for machine composition. It maintains a calligraphic impression that is particularly evident in the smooth curves of its lower case letters and its sharp serif formation. A particular feature of Bembo, following one of Griffo's innovations, is the way in which the height of the capitals falls shorter than that of the lower case ascenders. In practical use these balanced proportions result in bodies of text that are light but even in colour overall, making Bembo very comfortable and easy to read at length.

The original roman model referenced by the new typeface was without an accompanying italic so Morison was compelled to find one elsewhere. He commissioned a design from the contemporary British calligrapher Alfred Fairbank, who based his version on a sixteenth-century chancery hand by Ludovico Vicentino degli Arrighi (pp40–41). However, this design was not accepted by Monotype as it failed to match well with the roman. A more sympathetic alphabet, modelled on a script by Arrighi's contemporary, Giovanni Antonio Tagliente, is the one that was finally implemented as Bembo Italic.

Bifur

Ty	**Bifur**
Ca	**Sans Serif**
Ke	**Geometric, Modular**
Te	**Letterpress**
Da	**1929**
De	**A. M. Cassandre**
Fo	**Deberny & Peignot**
Co	**France**

Characteristics

Capitals only
No counterforms
Modular geometric components
Two-tone linear version
Two-colour, two-part modular version

Connections

Prisma	193
Fregio Mecano	c193
Peignot	193
Baby Teeth	196

Availability

P22 Bifur is a digital revival including lower case, available from P22 Type Foundry and resellers

Specimen

Bifur type specimen. Deberny & Peignot, Paris, c1929 (265x175mm)

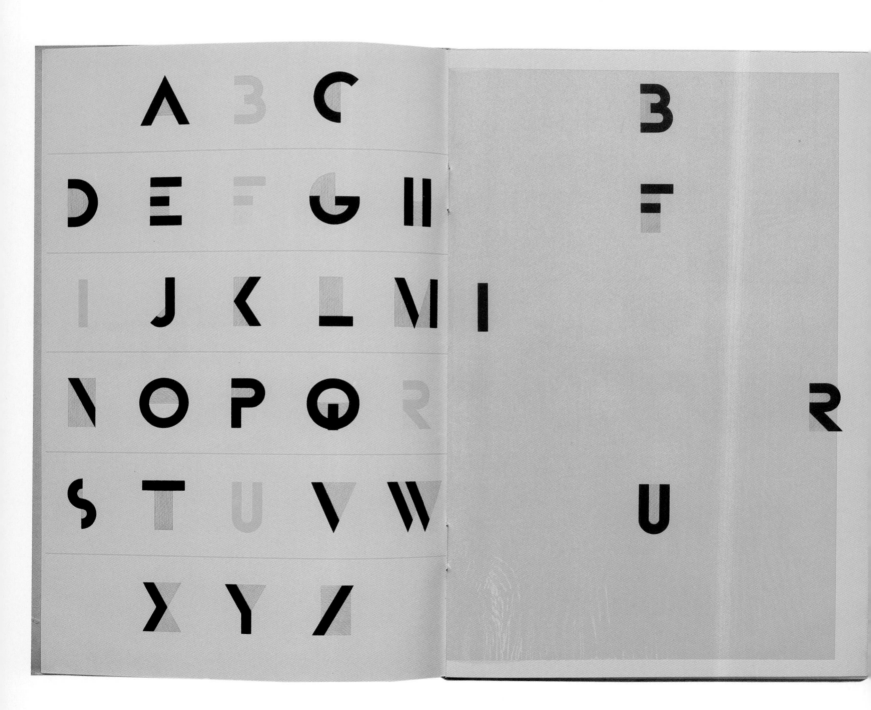

A. M. Cassandre (1901–68) was one of the most influential graphic artists of the twentieth century. His advertisement and poster designs are renowned for their seamless integration of type and image.

In 1925 he won first prize at the Exposition Internationale des Arts Décoratifs et Industriels Modernes in Paris for an art deco publicity poster named 'Au Bucheron'. The poster's lettering impressed Charles Peignot, director of the Deberny & Peignot foundry, so much that he appointed Cassandre to design for his company, beginning a relationship that would last for several years.

The year 1929 was an important one for the Deberny & Peignot foundry for two reasons. Firstly, Charles Peignot bought the rights to Paul Renner's groundbreaking Futura type (pp230–31) from the German foundry, Bauer. Secondly, Peignot issued Bifur, Cassandre's first typeface. Bifur escapes traditional classification but perfectly embodies the spirit of its age. One edition of its type specimen describes its objectives: 'Neither Cassandre, the artist who designed Bifur, nor ourselves, have wished to produce something "pretty". We wished to construct a publicity type; to suppress in each letter that which is unnecessary.'

Like other modular types of the time, Bifur broke down letterforms into simple geometric parts. It was released in two formats: a single two-tone face and a two-part, two-colour modular system in which the individual pieces of the letters could be arranged to create eye-catching layouts, like those of the type specimen shown below. Probably designed by Cassandre himself, this exceptional brochure has exceptionally high production values.

Bifur expresses modernist ideas that are similar to those being explored in geometric types made at the time by designers such as Josef Albers (pp212–13) and Herbert Bayer (pp222–23), but in a much more playful, flamboyant way. Where many other designs referenced machines and systems, Bifur was inspired by the modern city and by the glamour of art deco. Its conjunctions of bold circular, square and triangular shapes produced radically abstracted alphabetic forms that Adrian Frutiger later suggested were 'like a picture'. Reflecting on Bifur's impact, Charles Peignot said: 'There were no new or innovative typefaces which existed at the time. Bifur created a real scandal … Bifur was not a financial success, but in those happy days one could afford to take a few risks.'

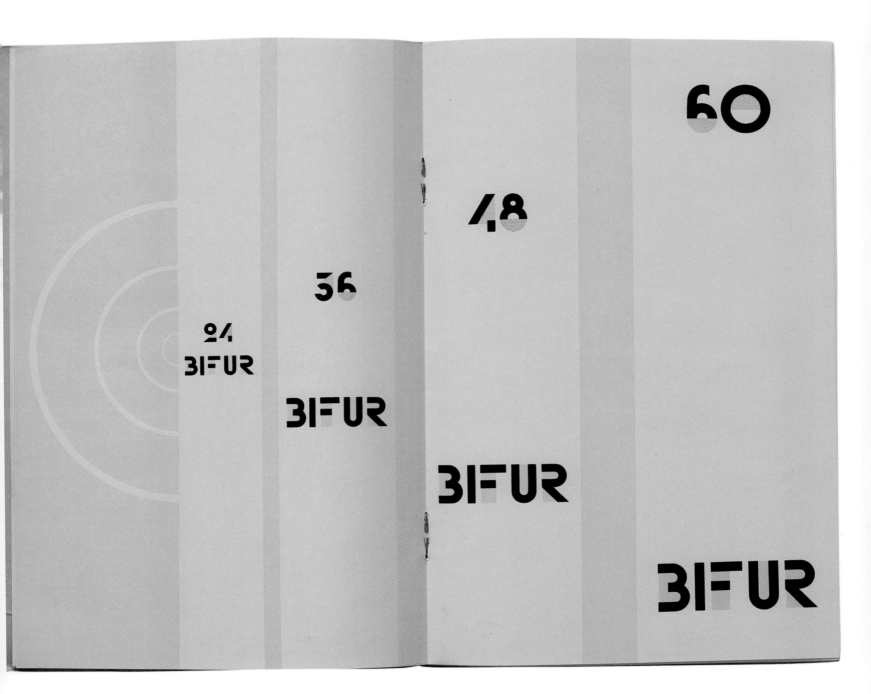

Ty	**Futura Black**
Ca	**Sans Serif**
Ke	**Geometric, Modular, Stencil**
Te	**Letterpress**
Da	**1929**
De	**Paul Renner**
Fo	**Bauer**
Co	**Germany**

Characteristics

Geometric character construction

Vertical openings between stems

Mixture of modular parts with unique custom features

ABEMOS
abceghij
koprstuy

Connections

Kombinations-Schrift	1923
Bragadoccio	1930
Transito	1931
Traffic	1973

Availability

Futura Black is widely available

Specimen

Futura Black type specimen. Bauersche Giesserei, Frankfurt, c1929 (250x180mm)

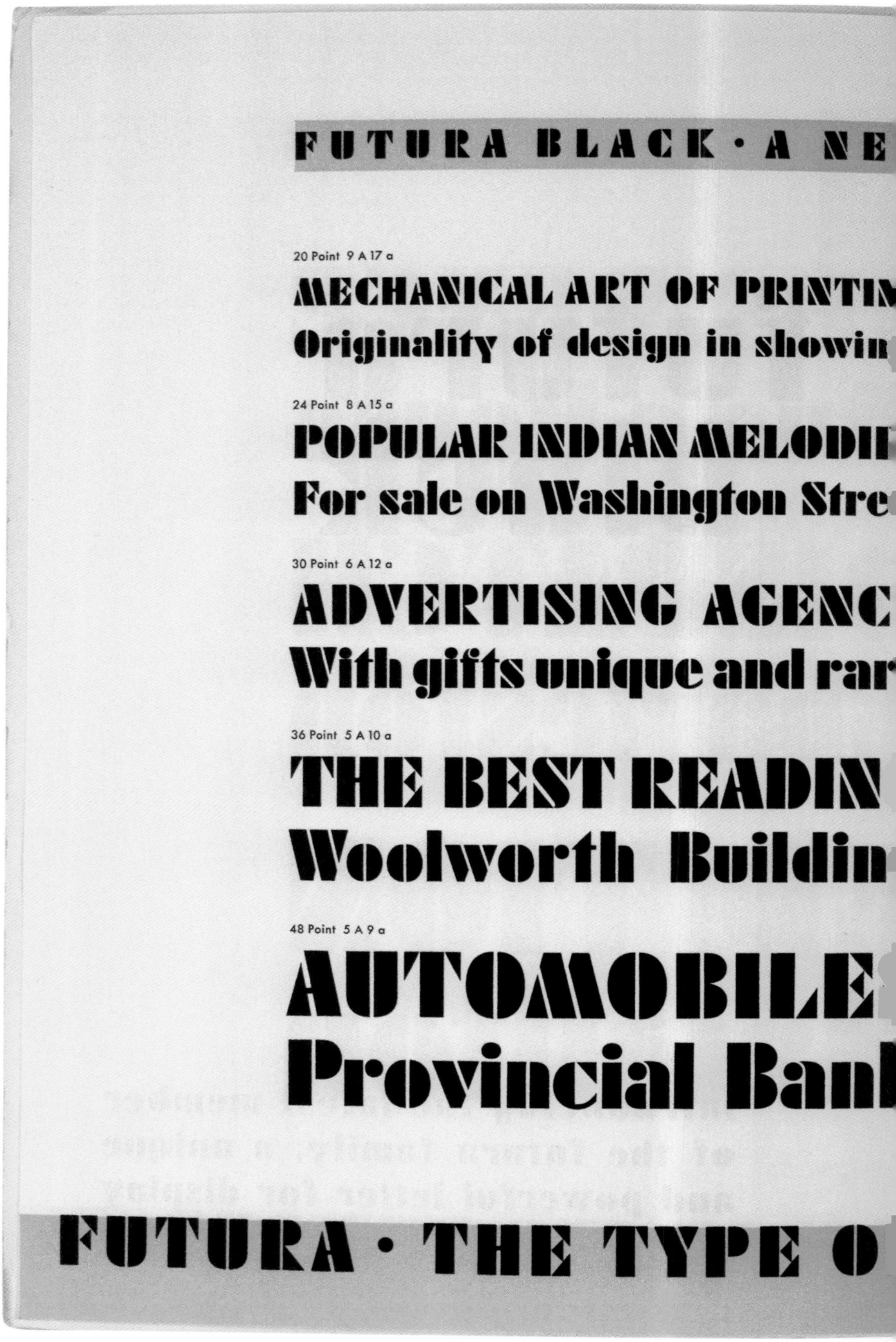

FUTURA BLACK · A NE

20 Point 9 A 17 a

MECHANICAL ART OF PRINTIN

Originality of design in showin

24 Point 8 A 15 a

POPULAR INDIAN MELODI

For sale on Washington Stre

30 Point 6 A 12 a

ADVERTISING AGENC

With gifts unique and rar

36 Point 5 A 10 a

THE BEST READIN

Woolworth Buildin

48 Point 5 A 9 a

AUTOMOBILE

Provincial Bank

FUTURA · THE TYPE O

ESIGN BY PAUL RENNER

int 5 A 8 a

RESIDENCE

Music House

Point 4 A 6 a

DISPATCH

Charleston

Point 3 A 4 a

EDITION

Hamilton

ODAY AND TOMORROW

In 1929 Paul Renner produced a typeface for the Bauer Foundry that appropriated the ideas of the geometric stencil alphabets Josef Albers had been developing since 1923 (pp212–13) and made them commercially successful. Confusingly, but not surprisingly, Bauer included Renner's new design in the Futura series, naming it Futura Black. It was common practice for foundries of the time to seek to increase sales by extending trusted product names to new types that were similar in attitude if not in form. Doing so suggested to customers that the new typeface would work well with existing types; this is certainly the case with the relationship of Futura Black to its namesake.

Futura Black is so similar to the Kombinations-Schrift stencil designs by Josef Albers that many have mistakenly attributed the typeface to him, although there is no evidence that he and Renner collaborated. Albers is known to have intended Kombinations-Schrift to be not a foundry type but rather machined from glass, plastic or metal for environmental signage. Renner's cutting a similar form as type, therefore, may be seen as commercially opportunistic rather than as an act of plagiarism.

On close inspection crucial differences between the two designs can be seen. Whereas Albers' type is constructed systematically from only three basic geometric shapes, Futura Black combines its apparently modular components with many custom character parts in order to make letters look conventional and thus easier to read, such as the angled strokes of the A and M, or the lower jaw of the e and c. By the same token, where Albers' designs were constructed from entirely separate pieces that could be assembled to make letters, Renner's characters were built as complete single units, only resembling modular forms. As a result they were far easier and quicker to use.

The illustrious German typographer Jan Tschichold was not an admirer of Renner's display face. In correspondence with Josef Albers about the development of another modular stencil typeface that he was working on, he said that he could not understand the success of 'the idiotic Futura Black'. Whatever its merits or faults, Futura Black was a type with a uniquely powerful and modern appearance at the time of its release, and its association with the Futura family ensured that it became one of the bestselling European display faces of its era.

Memphis

Ty	**Memphis**
Ca	**Slab Serif**
Ke	**Geometric**
Te	**Letterpress**
Da	**1929**
De	**Rudolf Wolf**
Fo	**Stempel**
Co	**Germany**

Characteristics

Monoline, geometric construction
Large x-height
A Flat top serif
C O Q a o Circular
G Straight, vertical spur
Q Tail terminates in flat serif
a Single-storeyed
e Circle divided by crossbar
f t Narrow
g Single-storeyed, short flat tail
i j Square dots
r Has a circle in place of arch
t Flat top
y Straight tail with flat serif

AGMQR
abcefghij
koprstuy

Connections

City	1930
Stymie	1931
Rockwell	1934
Lubalin Graph	1974

Availability

Memphis is available from Linotype and resellers

Specimen

Specimen Book of Linotype Faces.
Mergenthaler Linotype Company, New York, 1939 (260x185mm)

A-P-L MEMPHIS

72 Point (72△1038) Lower case alphabet, 911 points. Code word. ZAVON

72 Always insi

On quality 2

60 Point (60△1038) Lower case alphabet, 803 points. Code word. ZAVOH

60 Sugar plums

All times for th

54 Point (54△1038) Lower case alphabet, 736 points. Code word. ZAVOB

54 Exquisite taste

That gives you 3

48 Point (48△1038) Lower case alphabet, 651 points. Code word. ZAVNI

48 Satisfaction! Man

Fruits of different

42 Point (42△1038) Lower case alphabet, 571 points. Code word. ZAVME

42 Climes are brought

A registered dealer

A-P-L range also includes 6, 8, 10, 12, 14, 18, 24, 30 and 36 point sizes, inclusive

602

INOTYPE
MEMPHIS

FOUR USEFUL WEIGHTS:

IT · MEDIUM · BOLD · **EXTRA BOLD**

Though based on a century-old Egyptian design, Lino-type Memphis is far removed from its crude ancestors. A true contemporary face and the reflection of our scientific times, it combines the simplicity of functional form with the style-smartness useful for a variety of advertising composition and commercial printing. Memphis is available in a complete size range up to 144 point, in four useful related weights: Light, Medium, Bold and Extra Bold, each with an accompanying italic.

LINOTYPE

ENTHALER LINOTYPE COMPANY, BROOKLYN, N. Y.
rk City, Chicago, San Francisco, New Orleans. Canadian Linotype,
., Toronto, Canada. *Representatives in Principal Cities of the World*

Dr Rudolf Wolf (1895–1942) is remembered for two particular achievements: he is credited with the invention of the letter sequence commonly used in evaluating the appearance of typefaces – 'hamburgefontsiv' – and the creation of the first ever geometric slab serif, Memphis.

Wolf designed Memphis in 1929 at the Stempel foundry in Germany, where he worked as publicity manager. Memphis integrates the features of the vigorous Egyptian types that had been popular in the early part of the nineteenth century (pp114–15) with the systematic, rounded geometries of new, cutting-edge sans serifs such as Futura (pp230–31), Kabel (pp232–33) and Neuzeit-Grotesk (pp240–41). As a result, its letterforms are monolinear, giving a rational, bright impression. In order to achieve a streamlined appearance, the weight of curves tapers very slightly as they connect with stems and serifs. These are also thinner than the stems themselves, although they appear to be identical.

Memphis has a number of unique features. Both the lower case o and the capital O are perfect circles. The tail of th g is short and flat as is the foot of the t, allowing it to sit tightly next to letters that follow it, and the r has a circular ear that refers back to nineteenth-century Egyptian forms. Memphis quickly became one of the most popular typefaces of its era, appearing in print and advertising around the globe. After its introduction in 1929, various additions were made to the family. In 1933 Linotype introduced light and bold weights, and in 1934 companion italics were released, followed by a medium weight a year later. New versions of the family continued to be added for a decade, culminating with Memphis Extra Bold in 1939.

The overwhelming success of Memphis led to an explosion of geometric slab serifs as foundries around the world raced to provide competitive products. Several fashionable alternatives were released, but none were better suited to the principles of the New Typography than Memphis, a sharp reflection of the aesthetic of the machine age.

Ty	**Nobel**
Ca	**Sans Serif**
Ke	**Geometric**
Te	**Letterpress**
Da	**1929**
De	**Sjoerd Henrik de Roos and Dick Dooijes**
Fo	**Amsterdam Type Foundry**
Co	**Netherlands**

Characteristics

C c S s e r Angled terminals
G No spur
M High vertex
Q Short, curved tail
R Straight leg
a Double-storeyed
f Narrow
g Single-storeyed
i j Square dots
t Narrow, flat top-stroke
y Curved tail

AGMQR
abcefghij
koprstuy

Connections

Kabel	1927
Gill Sans	1928
Metro	1930
FB Nobel	1993

Availability

FB Nobel is available from Font Bureau and resellers. DTL Nobel is available from the Dutch Type Library and resellers

Specimen

Nobel type specimen. Amsterdam Type Foundry, Amsterdam, c1929 (270x210mm)

1

NOBEL LIGHT

8 point - no. 12497 - 60 x A, 120 x a, 42 x 1, - 5 lbs

De Magere Nobel neemt in de moderne typografie een aparte plaats in. De strenge zakelijkheid van haar vormgeving wordt verzacht door haar fijne tekening. Hierdoor is het mogelijke

DE MAGERE NOBEL KAPITALEN STAAN IN LIJN MET DE NORMALE EN ZIJN ALS AANVULLING OP DEZE

10 point - no. 12498 - 54 x A, 108 x a, 40 x 1, - 6¾ lbs

Le Noble Maigre possède un cachet très particulier. La sobriété quelque peu sévère de sa structure est adoucie par la finesse de son dessin

ON NE SAURAIT IMAGINER COMBIEN IL FAUT PARFOIS DE COMBINAISON ET DE

12 point - no. 12499 - 42 x A, 82 x a, 26 x 1, - 8 lbs

Few people read a book at one sitting, many read a mystery as if it were wine

NOBEL LIGHT CAPS, CAST IN LINE WITH THE NOBEL LIGHT, ARE VERY

14 point - no. 12500 - 38 x A, 76 x a, 26 x 1, - 9½ lbs

När man ser deras påkostade och välredigerade uppvisningar skulle

MED EN MODERN LASTKNEKT LASTAR EN ENSAM MAN MED

18 point - no. 12501 - 24 x A, 52 x a, 20 x 1, - 10¾ lbs

Es un rocío renaciente para

UNA INTERPRETACIÓN

24 point s - no. 12502 - 18 x A, 34 x a, 16 x 1, - 13 lbs

Een goed letterbeeld

WOLKENBANKEN

24 point l - no. 12503 - 16 x A, 30 x a, 16 x 1, - 12¾ lbs

Une bonne action

CHEMIN DE FER

30 point - no. 12504 - 14 x A, 26 x a, 14 x 1, - 16 lbs

Moderne tijden

HERFSTWIND

36 point - no. 12505 - 12 x A, 20 x a, 10 x 1, - 20 lbs

Merveilleuse

INDUSTRIE

48 point - no. 12506 - 10 x A, 18 x a, 8 x 1, - 28¾ lbs

De paden

KANSEN

60 point - no. 12507 - 6 x A, 12 x a, 6 x 1, - 30½ lbs

Second

ROND

72 point - no. 12508 - appr. 35 lbs

Heren

BERG

3

N

Hoewel van een ander genre, heeft de No bij de drukkers een even belangrijke plaat overen als onze Hollandse Mediæval- en

Le Noble a acquis rapidement un portante auprès des Imprimeurs ment parce que c'est un caract

A charming, whimsical co flower stories written by on

Många gånger under h lopp har mänskligheten

Sombreros de la es

Kunstavond in

Roméo et Jul

Planten in

Explorate

Het sch

Dame

Mon

NUM

8 point - no. 12509 - appr. 5 lbs

EL KAPITALEN-SERIE VORMT BIJ TAL
TWERKJES EN HANDELSDRUKWERKEN

10 point - no. 12510 - appr. 7 lbs

UVEAU PAR CRAINTE DE NE
AÎTRE, EST DEVENU SOUVENT

12 point - no. 12511 - appr. 8 lbs

NATIONAL ADVERTISING
ROMOTION ENSURE THE

14 point - no. 12512 - appr. 9½ lbs

JÄLP AV DESSA OCH
OTT OMDÖME SKALL

18 point - no. 12513 - appr. 10½ lbs

RICES Y ACTORES

24 point s - no. 12514 - appr. 13 lbs

CHTE WINTER

24 point l - no. 12515 - appr. 13 lbs

GLEMENTER

30 point - no. 12516 - appr. 16½ lbs

DERLAND

36 point - no. 12517 - appr. 19½ lbs

ENTELER

48 point - no. 12518 - appr. 27 lbs

INKEN

60 point - no. 12519 - appr. 30 lbs

ETITE

72 point - no. 12520 - appr. 35 lbs

TEM

5

NOBEL BOLD

8 point - no. 12521 - appr. 5 lbs

De moderne typografische ontwerper vindt in onze
Vette Nobel een machtig middel om op zakelijke
en toch sprekende wijze aan teksten en slagregels

DE VETTE NOBEL KAPITALEN HOUDEN WIJ OOK
ZONDER DE ONDERKAST STEEDS VOORRADIG

10 point - no. 12522 - appr. 7 lbs

Le Noble Gras est un caractère tout in-
diqué pour faire ressortir un texte ou un
titre. Le dessin est très soigné et on s'est

TRÈS DEMANDÉES, LES CAPITALES DE
CE BEAU CARACTÈRE SONT AUSSI

12 point - no. 12523 - appr. 8 lbs

Our businesslike modern Nobel
Bold is a type for advertising and

INTERNATIONAL COPYRIGHT
PROTECTION SORELY NEEDED

14 point - no. 12524 - appr. 9½ lbs

Vi får lov att känna den var-
ma och strålande glädjen att

OCH SÅ KOMMER DE TILL
MOTIONSINSTITUTET OCH

18 point - no. 12525 - appr. 10½ lbs

Es el resultado de más

ARTISTAS ITALIANOS

24 point s - no. 12526 - appr. 13 lbs

Opvallende letter

ZEER DUIDELIJK

24 point l - no. 12527 - appr. 13 lbs

Récit au Cercle

COLLECTIONS

30 point - no. 12528 - appr. 16½ lbs

Hoge bomen

ORNAMENT

36 point - no. 12529 - appr. 19½ lbs

Nouvelles

AUTEURS

48 point - no. 12530 - appr. 27 lbs

Somber

MOLEN

60 point - no. 12531 - appr. 30 lbs

Fleurs

JOUR

72 point - no. 12532 - appr. 35 lbs

Doek

TRED

Nobel has been pointedly described by Tobias Frere-Jones as 'Futura cooked in dirty pots and pans'. It is a geometric sans serif typeface designed by Sjoerd Henrik de Roos (1877–1962) and Dick Dooijes (1909–98) between 1929 and 1935 for the Amsterdam Type Foundry.

In 1927 Bauer had achieved instant international success with the release of Paul Renner's groundbreaking Futura. Like almost every other type manufacturer of the day, the Amsterdam Type Foundry wanted to feature a similar design in its catalogue and De Roos was briefed to update an existing sans serif, Berthold Grotesk, by giving it a more geometric appearance. De Roos was trained in the Arts and Crafts tradition and is considered to be Holland's first professional type designer. His design, executed by Dick Dooijes, is much more sophisticated than many of its competitors.

Like Metro (pp260–61) by W. A. Dwiggins and Kabel (pp232–33) by Rudolf Koch, Nobel was an attempt to reconcile the demand for modernist, machine-like geometric typefaces with older, more legible and more calligraphic approaches to the design of letters. Nobel overcomes the cold sterility of many other early geometric sans serifs with its highly readable lower case, using curves that are warm and delicately modulated. In its lightest version, Nobel shares many features with Futura, but in the roman and bold weights differences emerge that reveal a far less rigid structure.

Neither De Roos nor Dooijes considered Nobel a great personal accomplishment, although it became one of the bestselling sans serif types of the Amsterdam Type Foundry, remaining popular into the 1950s. It was, however, dismissed in the post-war period by designers who preferred the less mannered neutrality of nineteenth-century sans serifs like Akzidenz-Grotesk and it was little used in the photocomposition era.

In 1993, Nobel was revived by two digital foundries independently – the Dutch Type Library in Holland and Font Bureau in the United States – and it is widely seen today.

Bank Gothic

Ty	**Bank Gothic**
Ca	**Sans Serif**
Ke	**Geometric, Capitals**
Te	**Letterpress**
Da	**1930**
De	**Morris Fuller Benton**
Fo	**American Type Founders**
Co	**USA**

Characteristics

Capitals only
Monoline character construction
Square characters with rounded corners
C G J S Strokes terminate at angles
D Rounded
E F Short middle arm
R Straight, angled leg

AIKMW
HJDBR
CGQSU

Connections

Copperplate Gothic	1901
Agency FB	1990
Stratum	2004
Purista	2007

Availability

Bank Gothic is widely available

Specimen

Book of American Types, Standard Faces.
American Type Founders, Jersey City,
1934 (279x210mm)

BANK GOTHICS

BANK GOTHIC LIGHT

18 Point No. 10 10A
MECHANICS

18 Point No. 9 12A
REPRODUCED

12 Point No. 8 15A
SECURED HOME

12 Point No. 7 17A
CLEVER SALESMAN

12 Point No. 6 21A
SUPERIOR INSURANCE

12 Point No. 5 24A
ENTERPRISING EXHIBITOR

6 Point No. 4 21A
**BEAUTIFUL SUMMER GARDENS
TENNIS CHAMPION SURPRISED**

6 Point No. 3 25A
**AMERICAN PRESIDENT ENTERTAINED
REMARKABLE MECHANICAL EXHIBITS**

6 Point No. 2 29A
**ARTIST ILLUSTRATING WESTERN SCENERY
FIRM ESTABLISHING NORTHERN BRANCH**

6 Point No. 1 35A
**ARCHITECTURAL INSTITUTE GIVING EXHIBITION
BRILLIANT PAGEANT CLOSING ENTERTAINMENT**

BANK GOTHIC MEDIUM

18 Point No. 20 10A
EXTENDING

18 Point No. 19 12A
BENEVOLENT

12 Point No. 18 15A
GRAND SCENES

12 Point No. 17 17A
HISTORIC VOLUME

12 Point No. 16 21A
STEADY EMPLOYMENT

12 Point No. 15 24A
ENCOURAGING SYMPTOM

6 Point No. 14 21A
**INTERESTING COVER DESIGNS
PROMOTES REAL INVESTMENT**

6 Point No. 13 25A
**MODERNISTIC OFFICE STATIONERY
PRINTING INSTRUCTORS ENGAGED**

6 Point No. 12 29A
**DISTINCTIVE PRINTING RECEIVED AWARD
CUSTOMER DESIRES ARISTOCRATIC TYPE**

6 Point No. 11 35A
**ADMIRES DIGNIFIED COMMERCIAL STATIONERY
REPRODUCE FINE ENGRAVED ANNOUNCEMENT**

BANK GOTHIC BOLD

18 Point No. 30 9A
PRODUCE

18 Point No. 29 11A
DISTINGUIS

12 Point No. 28 13A
MODERN RADI

12 Point No. 27 16A
BANK TREASURE

12 Point No. 26 20A
ECONOMIC METHOD

12 Point No. 25 24A
DESIRABLE PRODUCTI

6 Point No. 24 21A
**SUBMIT INTERESTING REPO
NATIONAL BANK STATEMEN**

6 Point No. 23 25A
**UNUSUAL OPPORTUNITY OFFE
HANDSOMELY BOUND DICTION**

6 Point No. 22 29A
**COMPETENT MECHANIC MADE FORE
MANUFACTURING CONCERN PROSPE**

6 Point No. 21 34A
**INTERNATIONALLY PROMINENT TYPOGRA
EXHIBITED WONDERFUL PRINTING SPECIE**

CHARACTERS IN COMPLETE FONT

A B C D E F G H I J K L M N O P Q R S T U V W X Y Z &
$ 1 2 3 4 5 6 7 8 9 0 . , - ' ' : ; ! ?

CHARACTERS ARE THE SAME IN LIGHT, MEDIUM AND BOLD

FRANK PANKEY, JR.
TREASURER

GEORGE M. CHAPMAN
PRESIDENT

CHARLES E. MEISTER
CHEMIST

GIBSON-KINNEY COMPANY

MANUFACTURING CHEMISTS

MANUFACTURERS
FOR
BOTTLERS
EXCLUSIVELY
•
MEMBER OF
WESTERN MANUFACTURERS
OF SODA WATER
FLAVORS

ESTABLISHED 1896
TELEPHONE MAIN 1301

FLAVORS
CERTIFIED COLORS
ACIDS
COMPOUNDS
GINGER ALE
EXTRACTS
ETC.

1027 RIVER STREET

DANTOWN, IOWA

VOCATIONAL CAMEO 3616

:[140]:

BANK GOTHICS CONDENSED

BANK GOTHIC CONDENSED LIGHT

18 Point No. 40 13A
MODERN HOUSE

18 Point No. 39 15A
NCREASED ORDER

12 Point No. 38 17A
URCHASED BUILDING

12 Point No. 37 20A
MPROVING PRODUCTIONS

12 Point No. 36 25A
EPORT SPLENDID CONDITION

12 Point No. 35 29A
ANUFACTURERS CALLED MEETING

6 Point No. 34 25A
STINGUISHED LAWYER RECEIVED AWARD
ROPEAN THESPIANS HELD CONVENTION

6 Point No. 33 30A
HIBITING DIGNIFIED COMMERCIAL STATIONERY
PRODUCED FINE ENGRAVED ANNOUNCEMENTS

6 Point No. 32 35A
DERNISTIC EMBELLISHMENT PLEASED TYPOGRAPHER
FTSMAN CREATED MANY ORIGINAL COVER DESIGNS

6 Point No. 31 40A
Y CUSTOMERS ARE DEMANDING ARISTOCRATIC TYPE FACES
SPEROUS MANUFACTURING CONCERN PROMOTED FOREMAN

BANK GOTHIC CONDENSED MEDIUM

18 Point No. 50 12A
REGAL EMPIRES

18 Point No. 49 15A
STYLISH LINGERIE

12 Point No. 48 17A
MODERNIZED SKETCH

12 Point No. 47 19A
EXCLUSIVE ATMOSPHERE

12 Point No. 46 23A
BEAUTIFUL SUMMER GARDEN

12 Point No. 45 27A
INTERESTING COVER DESIGN SOLD

6 Point No. 44 25A
ARTIST ILLUSTRATING WESTERN SCENERY
FIRM ESTABLISHING NORTHERN BRANCH

6 Point No. 43 28A
ARCHITECTURAL INSTITUTE GIVING EXHIBITION
BRILLIANT PAGEANT CLOSES ENTERTAINMENT

6 Point No. 42 33A
CONCERN ORDERED MODERNISTIC OFFICE STATIONERY
MANY PROMINENT PRINTING INSTRUCTORS ENGAGED

6 Point No. 41 38A
AMERICAN PRESIDENT ENTERTAINED DISTINGUISHED ENVOYS
SHOWN NUMEROUS REMARKABLE MECHANICAL INNOVATIONS

BANK GOTHIC CONDENSED BOLD

18 Point No. 60 11A
RIGHT DESIGN

18 Point No. 59 13A
DESCRIBES SHIP

12 Point No. 58 15A
RURAL MERCHANTS

12 Point No. 57 17A
SPLENDID ATTRACTION

12 Point No. 56 21A
ORDERS COLORFUL GOWNS

12 Point No. 55 25A
FRENCH AIRPLANE TRIUMPHANT

6 Point No. 54 22A
BROKER SUBMITS EXCELLENT REPORT
MARKET NATIONAL BANK STATEMENTS

6 Point No. 53 26A
UNUSUAL OPPORTUNITY OFFERED DIRECTOR
HANDSOMELY EMBELLISHED DICTIONARIES

6 Point No. 52 31A
COMPETENT YOUNG CRAFTSMAN GETS PROMOTION
MACHINE MANUFACTURING CONCERN PROSPERED

6 Point No. 51 35A
INTERNATIONALLY PROMINENT TYPOGRAPHERS CONVENED
EXHIBITS SEVERAL WONDERFUL TYPOGRAPHIC SPECIMENS

CHARACTERS IN COMPLETE FONT

A B C D E F G H I J K L M N O P Q R S T U V W X Y Z &
$ 1 2 3 4 5 6 7 8 9 0 . , - ' ' ' : ; ! ?

CHARACTERS ARE THE SAME IN LIGHT, MEDIUM AND BOLD

FOR LARGER SIZES OF BANK GOTHIC CONDENSED MEDIUM SEE POSTER GOTHIC, PAGE 185

PEERLESS AUTOMATIC UNIT

•

THE PEERLESS AUTOMATIC UNIT WILL HANDLE THE FULL
RANGE OF STOCK, STARTING WITH 13-POUND FOLIO, UP TO
10 OR 12-PLY CARDBOARD. IT WILL ALSO FEED BLOTTERS,
ENVELOPES, TAGS, CARDS, AND EVEN CERTAIN FOLDED JOBS
THAT ARE TO BE IMPRINTED. THERE IS AN ENDLESS VARIETY
OF WORK WHICH THE PEERLESS WILL DO QUICKER AND
BETTER THAN CAN BE DONE ON A PRESS FED BY HAND

AMERICAN TYPE FOUNDERS SALES CORPORATION

AMERICAN
INSTRUMENTS OF UNUSUAL
EXCELLENCE

**KINGSMAN
PIANOS**

ON DISPLAY
AT THE MUSIC SHOW
HARMONY HALL

KINGSMAN PIANO COMPANY
PHILADELPHIA

:[141]:

Bank Gothic is a square geometric sans serif typeface designed by Morris Fuller Benton (1872–1948) for American Type Founders in 1930. Influenced by the commercial lettering of nineteenth-century engravings, it is an upper case alphabet using only rectilinear geometric shapes that have some similarities to those of City, a square slab serif by Georg Trump (pp256–57) published in the same year.

Benton's original Bank Gothic family consisted of five typefaces: Light, Medium, Bold, Light Condensed and Medium Condensed. These were cast for hand composition and were extensively used in business communications for several decades.

In the 1980s Linotype created a digital revival that included small capitals to map onto the lower case keys of the keyboard, but at the time Linotype only digitized the medium weight of the family. This typeface was never completed in PostScript and as a result it fell out of distribution during the early 1990s. In 2006, Linotype released a revised and expanded Bank Gothic for OpenType implementation, naming it Morris Sans. The new family's designer, Dan Reynolds, undertook a radical overhaul, rationalizing widths and weights and extending character sets which were augmented with newly designed lower case letters.

Ty	**City**
Ca	**Slab Serif**
Ke	**Geometric**
Te	**Letterpress**
Da	**1930**
De	**Georg Trump**
Fo	**Berthold**
Co	**Germany**

Characteristics

Monoline, geometric
Rectilinear with small, radiused corners
A No top serif
G No spur
K R Square leg
M High vertex
Q Vertical tail below letter
a Double-storeyed
f t Narrow
g Single-storeyed

AGKMQR
abcdefghij
koprstuvy

Connections

Eurostile	1962
Quadrato	1963
FF Magda Clean	1998
Cholla	1999

Availability

City is available from Berthold and resellers

Specimen

City type specimen. H. Berthold AG, Berlin, c1930 (297x210mm)

„if it's a

paramount

picture it's the best show

in town"

For as long as you have known motion pictures you have known one name to stand head and shoulders above the rest. Today Paramount's claim to leadership is greater than ever before in all its brilliant history. The proof is in this list of Paramount Pictures released in the past four months. This is a complete list – not a selected few – a record of successes without precedent! But Paramount is not content to rest on past performance. The pictures coming promise even more! If the theatre that now serves you does not show Paramount, present this list to the manager and demand what you are rightfully entitled to – the absolute best in motion picture entertainment.

Paramount Pictures
Paramount Famous Lasky Corp. Adolph Zukor, Pres., Paramount Bldg., N.Y.

Die
Vossische Zeitung
ist seit
zwei Jahrhunderten
das Blatt
der besten Familien

n Sie die „Vossische Zeitung" regelmäßig bekommen wollen, senden Sie uns diese Postkarte

rn Sie mir

VOSSISCHE ZEITUNG

Januar

Drucksache

Vossische Zeitung

Berlin SW 68

Kochstrasse 22

KT

leuten denk-

ode lücken-

starke Orga-

In the 1930s geometric slab serifs started to become almost as fashionable as the sans serifs on which they were based. Many printing offices and type foundries raced to include modern typefaces that resembled Memphis (pp250–51) and Stymie (pp278–79) in their catalogues.

City is a unique contribution to the slab serif category, designed by the distinguished German type designer Georg Trump (1896–1985) in 1930. Its rigidly geometric structure, composed of straight lines, rounded right-angled joints, square terminals and thick slab serifs, is modernist in every detail. It is a representation of its time: a typographic expression of urban architecture and the systematic construction methods of the machine age.

City's structures are based on the repetition, scaling and transposition of modular blocks that constitute the parts of the characters. Letter shapes are characterized by the consistent use of external circular arcs at stroke junctions to soften the hard rectilinear spaces of internal forms. The overall result is a highly coherent and straight-talking typeface. City was cut in three weights: light, medium and bold, each in roman and italic, and was released in 1930 by the Berthold Type Foundry in Berlin.

In 1935, City's appropriateness as a symbol of modernity was reinforced when Jan Tschichold used it for the titling of his seminal publication *Typographische Gestaltung* (Typographic Design), and it became one of the most successful display faces of its time.

Ty	**Granby**
Ca	**Sans Serif**
Ke	**Geometric**
Te	**Letterpress**
Da	**1930**
De	**Unknown**
Fo	**Stephenson, Blake & Co.**
Co	**UK**

Characteristics

	Moderate ascenders and descenders
A	Low crossbar
G	No spur, long stem, short arm
M	High vertex
Q	Straight, angled tail
R	Straight, angled leg
S	Small upper arc
a	Double-storeyed, straight stem
g	Single-storeyed
i j	Diamond-shaped dot
s	Narrow
t	Flat top
y	Short, curved tail
. ,	Diamond-shaped

AGMQRS
abcefghij
koprstuy

Connections

Johnston's Railway Type	1916
Gill Sans	1928
Bliss	1996
LL Brown	2011

Availability

Granby is available from Elsner+Flake and resellers

Specimen

Granby type specimen. Stephenson, Blake & Co., Sheffield, 1930s (270x210mm)

Granby

72 Point · 5 A, 6 a ; about 32 lb.

BOURNE
Public Draft

60 Point · 5 A, 8 a ; about 29 lb.

CRUSADER
Embarking for
the Holy Land

48 Point · 7 A, 12 a ; about 24½ lb.

MODERNISTIC
Granby is the type
face of the century

STEPHENSON, BLAKE & Co. Ltd.

SHEFFIELD and LONDON

Granby

42 Point   9 A, 16 a ; about 24 lb.

FOLK DANCING
Delightfully executed
by exuberant scholars

36 Point   10 A, 20 a ; about 22½ lb.

SPECIMEN NOTES
Handsome booklet gives
pleasure to typographers

30 Point   12 A, 22 a ; about 21 lb.

WHITE STAR CRUISES
Send for illustrated brochure
containing details of voyages

24 Point large face   18 A, 40 a ; about 17½ lb.

THE DESIGN OF OUR TIME
Displayed advertisements showing
this fine series promote stimulating
business relations with many clients

STEPHENSON, BLAKE & Co. Ltd.   SHEFFIELD and LONDON

The Granby type family was cut in 1930 and expanded during the following decade by Stephenson, Blake & Co. as they participated in the rush of type foundries to capitalize on the huge popularity of Monotype's Gill Sans (pp238–39) and the geometric sans serifs being introduced across Europe, such as Futura (pp230–31), Erbar (pp224–25) and Kabel (pp232–33). Stephenson, Blake's need to enter this competitive market was urgent, as these new bestsellers had swept aside the earlier grotesques that had made up a very large part of the company's stock.

Granby is so similar to Edward Johnston's Railway Type (pp202–203), designed for the exclusive use of the London Underground in 1916, that it is surprising action was not taken against the foundry for copyright infringement. Perhaps awkward questions were not asked because the businesses had a close association. Stephenson, Blake had cut the wood letters for the original Railway Type and was responsible for holding their patterns. Ironically, the London Underground soon became a major user of Granby in its print work, since Johnston's type had been cut for signage and display, not for machine composition. Until the 1970s, text in printed matter, including the iconic London Underground map, was set in Granby.

Eric Gill was a student of Johnston's, who had been involved in the design of the London Underground type. Some have considered his Gill Sans to be an improved and more balanced interpretation of Johnston's face, but in recent times Granby has also been reappraised and it can be argued that, far from a shallow imitation, the careful adjustments that were made to some of Johnston's more unorthodox characters, such as the R, e and s, suggest that Granby might be the superior type. It has been published digitally by Elsner+Flake although, regrettably, Granby has become somewhat lost nowadays among the teeming ranks of geometric sans serifs.

Ty	**Metro**
Ca	**Sans Serif**
Ke	**Geometric**
Te	**Letterpress**
Da	**1930**
De	**William Addison Dwiggins**
Fo	**Linotype**
Co	**USA**

Characteristics

C c S s e r	Vertical terminals
G	No spur
Q	Tail below letter
M	Splayed
R	Straight leg
a	Single-storeyed, curve at foot
f	Narrow, straight-angled cut at top
g	Single-storeyed
i j	Round dots
t	Small curve to right at foot
y	Straight tail

AGMQR
abcefghij
koprstuy

Connections

Gill Sans	1928
Neuzeit-Grotesk	1928
Nobel	1929
Gotham	2000

Availability

Metro is available from Linotype and resellers

Specimen

Specimen Book of Linotype Faces. Mergenthaler Linotype Company, New York, 1939 (260x185mm)

A·P·L

METRO BLACK No. 2

42 Point (42△1004) Lower case alphabet, 554 points. Code word, ZANBI.

PERSIAN LAMB FU
Coat of fine tight cu
and gloss black, $29

48 Point (48△1004) Lower case alphabet, 638 points. Code word, ZANCO.

SPORT COATS O
Pure virgin wool

60 Point (60△1004) Lower case alphabet, 803 points. Code word, ZANDU.

FALL SALE O
Blue and grey

72 Point (72△1004) Lower case alphabet, 965 points. Code word, ZANEF.

FOUR RUG
Selling at 8

All-Purpose Linotype matrices are also available in 6, 8, 10, 12, 14, 18, 24, 30 and 36 point sizes.

637 a

METROLITE No. 2 with METROBLACK No. 2

18 POINT, *Two-Letter*

OW IS ONE TO ASSESS AND EVALUATE A TYP

ow can one assess or evaluate a type face in terms

its esthetic design? Why do the pace-makers in

e art of printing rave over a specific face of type?

at do they see in it? Why is it so superlatively

easant to their eyes? **Good design is always prac-**

al design. And what they see in a good type design

partly, its excellent practical fitness to perform

work. It has a "heft" and balance in all of its parts

st right for its size, as any good tool has. Your good

(four point leaded)

OW **IS ONE TO ASSESS AND EVALUATE A TYP**

ow **can one assess or evaluate a type face in terms**

its **esthetic design? Why do the pace-makers in**

e **art of printing rave over a specific face of type?**

at **do they see in it? Why is it so superlatively**

easant **to their eyes?** Good design is always prac-

al design. **And what they see in a good type design**

partly, **its excellent practical fitness to perform**

work. **It has a "heft" and balance in all of its parts**

st **right for its size, as any good tool has. Your good**

(four point leaded)

ABCDEFGHIJKLMNOPQRSTUVWXYZ&
ABCDEFGHIJKLMNOPQRSTUVWXYZ&

bcdefghijklmnopqrstuvwxyz 1234567890 ($,.:;'-'?!)
bcdefghijklmnopqrstuvwxyz 1234567890 ($,.:;'-'?!)

Information: 18△74. Lower case alphabet, 236 points. Figures, .1107. Runs in 90 channel magazine. Code word. ZILFU. **Also avail-**
s **Metroblack No. 2 with Metrolite No. 2** (18△8).

647

When geometric sans serif typefaces first became the height of fashion in the 1920s type founders everywhere raced to bring their own proprietary versions to market. In 1928, American graphic designer William Addison Dwiggins (1880–1956) publicly criticized various typefaces of the time in his book, *Layout in Advertising.* Dwiggins's view was that sans serifs such as Erbar, Futura and Kabel were 'fine in the capitals and bum in the lower case'. The Mergenthaler Linotype Company responded by challenging him to create a typeface that addressed this criticism, starting a professional relationship that would endure for several decades.

When Dwiggins set out, at the age of 49, to improve on the geometric sans serifs of the day, it was the first time he had ever attempted to design type. However, he was a hugely accomplished graphic artist. Following his contention, his design for the Metro series differed radically from its competitors, particularly in the distinctive structure of its lower case. Dwiggins took care to retain the necessarily legible forms found in humanist romans, avoiding the sterility of pen-and-compass sans serifs.

Metro has a much warmer and subtler character than most early modern geometric types and is notable for the delicacy of its curves and angled terminals. The slanted apex of Metro's capital A, and the old-style contours of letters such as a, e and g, give a calligraphic feel to Dwiggins's letters, and American art deco tendencies are apparent throughout. Metroblack No. 2 was the first typeface in the Metro family to be released by Mergenthaler Linotype in 1930. Three further weights, Metromedium, Metrolite and Metrothin, were subsequently drawn up by Linotype's design office under Dwiggins's supervision, although Metrothin was never released.

Dwiggins ranks among the most influential graphic artists and type designers of the twentieth century. He went on to produce several other excellent text typefaces, including Electra (pp292–93) and New Caledonia. In 2013 Linotype took the opportunity to update his seminal Metro design for digital reproduction. The new typeface, Metro Nova, uses OpenType technology to build extensively on the solid foundations of the original Metro.

*MONOTYPE

PERPETUA

Series No. 239

ABCDEFGHJKLMNOPQRSTUVWXYZÆŒ&
ABCDEFGHIJKLMNOPQRSTUVWXYZ&1234567890

ABCDEGHJKMNQRSTUVXYZ
ABCDEFGHJKLMNPQRSTUWXYZ
abcdefghijklmnopqrstuvwxyzæœ
abcdefghijklmnoqrsuvwxyz 24pt. 5678

↑ 24 PT. ROMAN AND ITALIC   ↓ 42 PT. ROMAN AND ITALIC

ABCDEFGHKLN
MQRSTUWXYZ
abcdefghijklmnpqr
stuvwxyz *abcdefghj*
klmnopqrstuvwxyz&
ABCDEGHJKMNP
QRSTUVWXYZ42

THE MONOTYPE CORPORATION LTD
Registered Office: 55-56 Lincolns Inn Fields, London, w.c.2
*Head Office & Works: Salfords, Redhill, Sy.   *Registered Trade Mark*

abcdefghijklmnopqrstuvwxyz
abcdefghijklmnopqrstuvwxyz23

18 PT. ROMAN AND ITALIC CAPS. AND L.C.
60 PT. ROMAN AND ITALIC

ABCDGHJKQRUVWXZ&
BCDGHJKMNQSVWXYZ&.?
abcdefghjklmnpqtuvwxyz abc
defghjkmnpqrstuvwxyz

Ty	**Perpetua**
Ca	**Serif**
Ke	**Transitional**
Te	**Letterpress**
Da	**1930**
De	**Eric Gill**
Fo	**Monotype**
Co	**UK**

Characteristics

	Vertical stress
E	Wide middle bar
J	Descends below baseline
M	Splayed
Q	Short, curved tail below letter
R	Curved tail with flat foot
U	Has foot
a	Double-storeyed, upturned curve at foot
a c e	Sharp, serifless terminal
b d q	Flat junction of bowl to stem
g	Double-storeyed, straight ear
j	Sharp, curved tail

AEJMQR
abcdefghij
qrstuv*aefg*

Connections

Lutetia	1925
Joanna	1931
Spectrum	1952
Capitolium	1998

Availability

Perpetua is available from Monotype and resellers

Specimen

Perpetua specimen sheet. Monotype Corporation, Salfords, c1940 (270x220mm)

UVXYZ ABCD
abcdefghjkmpqrstuvxyz
ABCDEGHJKMNQRS
TUWXYZ *ABCDEFGHI*
JKLMNQRSTUVWXYZ
abcdefghjkmnpqrstuvwxyz
Perpetua 2 39

←30 AND 72 PT.   ↑ TOP PANEL, 36 PT.   ↓ BELOW, 48 PT.   30 AND 72 PT.→

ABCDGHJKMN
QRSTUVWXYZ
abcdefghjkmnpqr
stuvwxyz ; *abcdefg*
hijklmnpqrstuvwxyz
ABCDEGHJKMN
PQRSTUVXYZ&

Stanley Morison, typographic adviser to the Monotype Corporation, was the instigator of the design of Perpetua. His plan for the expansion of the Monotype Corporation's type library had begun with typefaces that re-engineered historical designs like Bembo, Garamond and Baskerville for machine composition. The next stage in Morison's strategy was the development of new, modern designs, starting with a book face. Suggesting a need for an 'ideal type', he commissioned Eric Gill (1882–1940) to produce what he called a 'type-design of the twentieth century worthy of a permanent place in the history of typography'.

Gill was a gifted English sculptor, designer and lettering artist who had no previous experience in the creation of type when he began initial sketches for the design in 1925, three years before the release of Gill Sans (pp238–39). A single roman weight of Perpetua was launched in 1930, along with a matching italic named Felicity. The italic had been designed as a sloped roman rather than a traditional cursive because Morison believed that this made for a more harmonious relationship with the roman, but it was rejected by Monotype and Gill was asked to return to the drawing board. His amended italic was more flowing in its construction, although it retained roman serifs. The completed family was finally released for machine composition in 1932, seven years after Morison had first approached Gill.

Although it does not conform to traditional type classification, Perpetua is usually described as a transitional form because of its late baroque attributes, such as its strong, vertical stroke contrast and bracketed serifs. It also bears distinctive traits that are characteristic of Eric Gill's approach to the construction of letters. With the proportions and contours of his stone-cut inscriptional lettering, Perpetua has an almost vertical stress, a pronounced contrast between thick and thin strokes, and sharp horizontal serifs. The x-height is extremely short in relation to proportionately long ascenders and descenders.

Perpetua had first been used by Gill in 1928 in a private printing of *The Passion of Perpetua and Felicity*. In an insert to the publication Gill expressed his views on the typeface, writing: 'In my opinion Perpetua is commendable in that, in spite of many distinctive characters, it retains that common-placeness and normality which is essential to a good book-type.'

Ty	**Beton**
Ca	**Slab Serif**
Ke	**Geometric**
Te	**Letterpress**
Da	**1931**
De	**Heinrich Jost**
Fo	**Bauer**
Co	**Germany**

Characteristics

Monoline, geometric construction
Small x-height
Long ascenders and descenders
C G O Q o Circular
G Vertical spur serif
K Curved tail
a Double-storeyed
f r t Narrow
i j Round dots
t Slab serif at foot
y Straight tail, serif extends to right

AGKMQ
abcefghij
koprstuy

Connections

Memphis	1929
Stymie	1931
Rockwell	1934
Lubalin Graph	1974

Availability

Beton is available from Linotype and resellers

Specimen

Beton type specimen. Bauersche Giesserei, Frankfurt, c1931 (297x210mm)

Etwas ganz

Chevrolet-Erfolg auch Ihr Erfo

Der neu

DER SCHNELL
ZUVERLÄSSIG
LASTWAGE

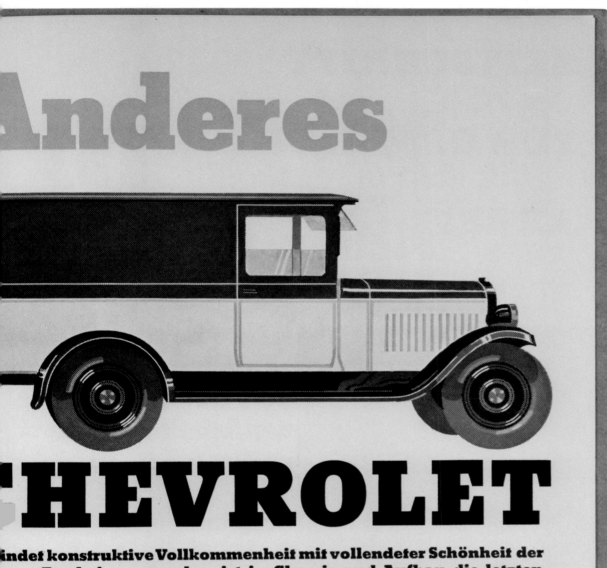

Beton is a geometric slab serif designed by Heinrich Jost (1889–1948) for Bauer between 1929 and 1931. Jost, who worked at the Frankfurt foundry for most of his career, was Bauer's art director from 1922 until his death in 1948. He was responsible for the creation of several typefaces, including Bauer Bodoni, a design that is widely regarded as one of the finest interpretations of Bodoni ever made.

Beton is a geometric slab serif typeface whose structure is based on classical letter proportions. Its name is German for concrete, suggesting its blocky, industrial impression. Compared to Rockwell (pp288–89), it has a smaller x-height and more subtle variations of stroke thickness and serif construction. Unusually for a geometric typeface, the lower case a is double-storeyed, and the foot serif of the y extends only to the right.

Beton does not function as a family of related weights in the logical way that is expected nowadays. Although produced originally in six styles, only four follow a loosely consistent progression: Beton Light, Beton Demi Bold, Beton Bold and Beton Extra Bold. The other two members of the family, Beton Bold Condensed and Beton Bold Compressed, have completely different characteristics, functioning more effectively as autonomous typefaces.

In the United States Beton was copied and adapted for machine composition by Intertype in 1934. Three years later Intertype added Beton Wide to fit two-letter matrices with the Extra Bold. Like the other members of the family, Beton Wide has a number of design features provided to address American tastes in slab serif designs more closely, including several alternate characters, a set of redesigned numerals and bracketed serifs.

Ty	**DIN 1451**
Ca	**Sans Serif**
Ke	**Geometric**
Te	**Various**
Da	**1931**
De	**Unknown**
Fo	**N/A**
Co	**Germany**

Characteristics

Monoline geometric character construction	
Contours built on centre lines	
Terminals may be rounded or flat	
G	No spur
Q	Short, straight tail
R	Straight leg
a	Double-storeyed
f t	Vertical terminals
g	Single-storeyed
i j	Square dots
t	Narrow, flat top-stroke
y	Curved tail

AGMQRS
abcefghij
kloprstuy

Connections

Helvetica	1957
Isonorm	1974
FF DIN	1995
T-Star Pro	2002

Availability

DIN is widely available

Specimen

DIN 1451 specifications. Deutsches Institut für Normung, Berlin, 1932 (297x210mm)

Seite 6

Normschriften
Engschrift Mittelschrift Breitschrift
mit Hilfsnetz gemalt   Hilfsnetz für Malschablonen
Beispiele

Fette Engschrift

Innerhalb eines Wortes   Alleinstehend

abcdefghijklmnopqrstuvwxl

yzßäöü&.,-:;!?") 1234567890

ABCDEFGHIJKLMNOPQRSTUVW

XYZÄÖÜ

Fette Mittelschrift

abcdefghijklmnopqrs

tuvwxyzßäöü&.,-:;!?")

1234567890ABCDEF

GHIJKLMNOPQRSTU

Seite 7

VWXYZÄÖÜ

Fette Breitschrift

abcdefghijklmn

opqrstuvwxyz

ßäöü&.,-:;!?")

1234567890

ABCDEFGHIJK

LMNOPQRSTU

VWXYZÄÖÜ

Mit Hilfsnetz oder Schablone gemalte Schriften zeigen von den auf der 1. Seite dargestellten Schriften kleine, zulässige Abweichungen, die durch die Forderung leichter Erkennbarkeit auf große Entfernungen und Konstruierbarkeit mit Lineal und Zirkel bedingt sind.

Große Buchstaben	= 7/7 h	Buchstabenabstand: eng	= 1/7 h
Kleine "	= 5/7 h	mittel	= 1,5/7 h
Strichdicke	= 1/7 h	breit	= 2/7 h

DIN has been used across the entire German road network since the 1930s. As familiar a part of the nation's visual landscape as Fraktur once was, it has become an unofficial emblem of German identity. As Erik Spiekermann has said, DIN is 'the magic word for everything that can be measured in Germany'.

In 1931 the Deutsches Institut für Normung, an organization established in 1917 to regulate quality standards, issued *DIN 1451 – Normschriften*, a set of instructions for the construction and application of lettering to be applied in public signage, vehicle demarcation and technical documentation. The document provided specifications for the design of DIN Schriften, a coordinated group of typefaces that had been developed from lettering that was then used by the Deutsche Reichsbahn – the pre-war German national railway.

The project began around 1923 under the supervision of an engineer, Ludwig Goller (1884–1964), although it is not known whether he was personally responsible for drawing the typefaces. Two core principles underpinned the design of DIN. Firstly, to enable efficient reproduction standards letterforms were rendered with compass and ruler on a grid. This was identical to the construction method of contemporary geometric typefaces made by Herbert Bayer (pp222–23), Joost Schmidt, Josef Albers (pp212–13) and others, although the intention was not the same. DIN was concerned only with pragmatic standards of performance rather than conceptual, aesthetic or ideological issues. Secondly, DIN was intended to be rendered with all kinds of instruments, from technical pens to engraving tools, for a wide range of media. Consequently, every character was designed around an invisible centre line to which monolinear stroke weight could be added, with terminals that could either be rounded or flat depending on the instrument used.

These engineered methods of construction deviated from the traditional type design techniques that followed the subtle movement of the hand. The result is a mathematical and monotone family of typefaces that are characterized by the recurrence of simple circular, vertical and horizontal strokes of the same width.

Joanna

Ty	**Joanna**
Ca	**Serif**
Ke	**Old Style**
Te	**Letterpress**
Da	**1931**
De	**Eric Gill**
Fo	**Monotype**
Co	**UK**

Characteristics

Almost vertical stress
Very low stroke contrast
Capitals lower than ascender height
Slab serifs
A Flat apex
J Descends below baseline
Q Curved tail below letter
R Wide downward-curved leg
W Serif at apex
a Double-storeyed, shallow curve at foot
b d q Flat junction of bowl to stem
f Wide, extended arch
g Double-storeyed, small lower bowl
w Serif at apex
y Straight tail

AJPQRW
abcdefghij
oqrstuyaefg

Connections

Granjon's Roman	1560
Perpetua	1930
Electra	1935
FF Scala	1991

Availability

Joanna is available from Monotype and resellers

Specimen

Eric Gill, *An Essay on Typography*. Hague & Gill, Pigotts, 1931 (200x125mm)

26 honour a successful contraption for boiling soap. ¶ It is a matter of satisfaction, therefore, that, in spite of our preoccupation with merely physical convenience, we have inherited an alphabet of such pre-eminent rationality and dignity as the Roman. A good example is the inscription on Trajan's Column at Rome, of which a plaster cast is in the Victoria & Albert Museum, London. ¶ Lettering is for us the Roman alphabet and the Roman alphabet is lettering. Whatever the Greeks or the Germans or the Russians or the Czecho-Slovaks or other people may do, the English language is done in Roman letters, and these letters may be said to have reached a permanent type about the first century A.D. ¶ Though in the course of the centuries innumerable variations in detail have been made, Roman letters have not changed essentially. Fourteen hundred years after the cutting of the Trajan inscription the tablet in Henry VII's chapel was inscribed, and no Roman would have found any difficulty in reading the letters. Eighteen hundred years after the time of Trajan & four hundred years after Henry VII, Roman letters are still made, & in almost the same way (e.g. the Artillery Monument, Hyde Park Corner).

¶ But, although the Roman alphabet has remain'd 27
essentially unchanged through the centuries, customs & habits of work have changed a great deal.
In the time of the Romans, say A.D. 100, when a
man said the word 'letters' it is probable that he
immediately thought of the kind of letters he was
accustomed to seeing on public inscriptions. Altho'
all sorts of other kinds of lettering existed (on wax
tablets, on papyrus, &c.) the most common kind
of formal lettering was the inscription in stone.
The consequence was that when he made letters
'as well as he could' it was the stone inscription
letter that he took as his model. He did not say:
Such and such a tool or material naturally makes
or lends itself to the making of such & such forms.
On the contrary, he said: Letters are such & such
forms; therefore, whatever tools & materials we
have to use, we must make these forms as well as
the tools and material will allow. This order of
procedure has always been the one followed. The
mind is the arbiter in letter forms; not the tool or
the material. This is not to deny that tools and
materials have had a very great influence on letter
forms. But that influence has been secondary, and
for the most part it has been exerted without the

Joanna, an unorthodox serif typeface designed by Eric Gill (1882–1940) between 1930 and 1931 was described by Robert Harling in 1976 as a 'typographical masterpiece which remains virtually unknown'. Gill himself considered it 'a book face free from all fancy business'.

Joanna was named after one of Gill's daughters, and it was originally created for hand composition at Hague & Gill, the press that Gill ran with Rene Hague, Joanna's husband. The typeface was first cut and cast for them in a small quantity by the Caslon foundry in only two sizes. For Joanna's design Gill took inspiration from the French Renaissance typefaces of Robert Granjon (pp54–59) and drew on the construction methods and forms of his own earlier typefaces, Cockerel, Gill Sans (pp238–39) and Perpetua (pp262–63).

A light but even old-style face notable for the unobtrusive size of its capitals, Joanna shows the clear influence of Granjon's type in the structure of its roman, although its regulated geometries, moderate stroke contrasts and crisp, rectangular serifs present a clean impression that also exhibits the rational modernity of the slab serif form.

The italic was intended as a book face in its own right, to be used for setting extended text rather than just for emphasis. It is a highly original and idiosyncratic design, with roman-shaped letterforms that have a tiny incline of only three degrees. The italic is also extremely narrow, distinguishing itself easily from the roman. In the original design there were no italic capitals, so that the lower case would be used with roman capitals, following the traditional practice originated by Francesco Griffo and Aldus Manutius in the early 1500s (pp32–33).

Gill's seminal tract, *An Essay on Typography*, shown here, was printed by Hague & Gill in 1931, using Joanna alone throughout. The book communicates his views on typographic design through both its form and its content. Gill's text is framed appropriately in an unadorned page layout with well-proportioned margins, and diligent presswork shows Joanna's capability as a text face. The Monotype Corporation recut Joanna for machine composition in 1937 for the exclusive use of J. M. Dent & Sons and, as a result, it only became generally available in 1958. In 1986, Monotype added several weights to the family, together with small capitals, ligatures and old-style figures, and re-released Joanna as a member of the first generation of digital typefaces.

Ty	**Johnston's Cancelleresca Corsiva**
Ca	**Serif**
Ke	**Old Style Italic**
Te	**Letterpress**
Da	**1931**
De	**Edward Johnston**
Fo	**Cranach Presse**
Co	**Germany**

Characteristics

Roman capitals
Italic lower case
Long ascenders curve to right
Long descenders curve to left

AEGMR
abcdefghij
koprstuvy

Connections

Tagliente's Italic	1524
Arrighi's Second Italic	1527
Blado Italic	1923
Poetica	1992

Availability

Not available

Specimen

Rainer Maria Rilke, *Duineser Elegien: Elegies from the Castle of Duino.* Cranach Presse, Weimar, 1931 (245x150mm)

THE EIGHTH ELEGY

umb creatures gaze with their whole vision out

Into infinity. our eyes alone

Would seem to be inverted, and like snares

Set all around them, compassing their free

Passage. what lies beyond, for us is only

Intelligible through the mask of beasts,

For in his early years we take the child,

Turn him about, and, so compelling him

Make him look backwards at all conformation,

Not over space, that in the glance of beasts

Dwells so profound. exempt from thought of death!

That's seen by us alone; the freeborn beast

Keeps his perdition evermore behind him,

And God before him; when he goes, he goes

Into eternity, like springs of water.

But never for a single day have we

Clear space before us, space wherein the flowers

Spring endlessly. the world, and still the world,

Never a nowhere, blank, without negation;

Pure space, surveillance-free, in which to breathe,

88

DIE ACHTE ELEGIE

Rudolf Kassner zugeeignet

Mit allen augen sieht die kreatur

Das offene. nur unsre augen sind

Wie umgekehrt und ganz um sie gestellt

als fallen, rings um ihren freien ausgang.

Was draussen ist, wir wissens aus des tiers

antlitz allein; denn schon das frühe kind

wenden wir um und zwingens, dass es rückwärts

gestaltung sehe, nicht das offne, das

im tiergesicht so tief ist. frei von tod.

ihn sehen wir allein; das freie tier

hat seinen untergang stets hinter sich

und vor sich Gott, und wenn es geht, so gehts

in ewigkeit, so wie die brunnen gehen.

Wir haben nie, nicht einen einzigen tag,

den reinen raum vor uns, in den die blumen

unendlich aufgehn. immer ist es welt

und niemals nirgends ohne nicht:

das reine, unüberwachte, das man atmet und

unendlich weiss und nicht begehrt. als kind

89

The Cranach Presse was founded in 1913 at Weimar, Germany, by the cosmopolitan diplomat Count Harry Kessler (1868–1937) to publish editions that sought, like the Doves Press (pp156–57), to achieve typographic clarity with the highest production values rather than mimic archaic models.

For its earliest publications, the Cranach Presse commissioned a roman type based on Nicolas Jenson's (pp20–21), drawn by Percy Tiffin under the supervison of Emery Walker, and cut by Edward Prince, the skilled punch cutter of the Kelmscott and Doves types. Asked to provide a companion italic lower case, the team ran into difficulties – with no contemporary model to follow, they had chosen to adapt a letterform drawn by the Venetian scribe Giovanni Antonio Tagliente in the 1520s, some 50 years after Jenson, and Kessler was not satisfied with their results.

He turned to the eminent British calligrapher Edward Johnston (1872–1944) to act as an adviser. At first, Johnston agreed only to provide sketches and notes to guide the punch cutter, but eventually Kessler persuaded him to produce finished drawings, which he started working on in about 1914. The Cranach Presse ceased operations during World War I and the project was postponed until 1925, when production resumed.

Kessler asked Johnston to create a set of companion capital letters for the lower case he had drawn before the war, but the task was beset with difficulties, compounded by the decade-long interval. When the new capitals were cut, they printed too heavily, looking squashed in test proofs, and had to be abandoned. As a result, the cursive was cast for text composition with roman capitals in 1931 for the book shown here, a bilingual edition of Rainer Maria Rilke's *Duineser Elegien*, translated into English by Vita Sackville-West.

Johnston's Cancelleresca Corsiva was not completely successful in itself. The requirement to follow Tagliente's letters clearly inhibited Johnston and, as a result, the typeface demonstrates a conflict between his talents as a calligrapher and the demands of a worthy historical revival. The 1931 Rilke edition was the only implementation of Johnston's italic. Two years later, the Cranach Presse closed down. Although something of a failed experiment, the significance of Johnston's Cancelleresca Corsiva lies in its influence on the development of the many old-style italic typefaces that followed.

Oz Cooper's Lettering

Ty	**Oz Cooper's Lettering**
Ca	**Sans Serif**
Ke	**N/A**
Te	**Lettering**
Da	**1931**
De	**Oswald 'Oz' Cooper**
Fo	**N/A**
Co	**USA**

Characteristics

Monoline with slightly uneven stroke weights and directions

Slightly rounded terminals follow stroke directions

A Flat apex, high crossbar

E F S Narrow

J Descends below baseline

M Splayed

Q Curved tail below letter

R Wide leg

W Stepped centre-strokes

a Double-storeyed

g Double-storeyed, oblique lower bowl

i j Round dots

AEJMRW
abcdefghij
orstuyaefg

Connections

Cooper Old Style	1919
Oz Handcraft BT	1990
ITC Highlander	1993
Oz	1999

Availability

ITC Highlander is a digital revival available from Monotype and resellers

Specimen

The Book of Oz Cooper. The Society of Typographic Arts, Chicago, 1949 (280x210mm)

158

159

Oswald 'Oz' Cooper (1879–1940) was a prominent American graphic artist who had a profound understanding of lettering and calligraphy, skills he used to articulate a wider range of personal expression than would be possible in type.

His lettering for a 1931 promotional calendar, one of a series made for his studio, Bertsch & Cooper, is among his finest work. The spirited styles used for headings and numerals are different for every month, but they demonstrate a consistent simplicity throughout that characterizes his approach. He later developed the forms in some display lettering exercises with serifless characters similar to those on the Bertsch & Cooper calendar, although the result was never cut into type as he had no interest in the sans serif as a letter for printing.

Cooper's alphabet has a modest x-height with long ascenders, giving classic old-style proportions to an otherwise relaxed, informal alphabet. The slightly uneven weight of brush-drawn strokes contributes further to the design's charm. Such imperfections give warmth and humanity to the letters in contrast to the tendency towards monotony that is common in more regular sans serif forms. The italics are true cursive designs, carefully drawn to complement the roman while maintaining their own design integrity.

In the 1990s British type designer Dave Farey (1943–) chose to translate Cooper's letters into type in order to create a new family that, he hoped, would stand out from other contemporary designs. 'At the same time,' he said, 'I did not want to create a design that was so distinctive, or so unusual, that it limited itself to just a few display applications.' Farey's revival, ITC Highlander, was released in 1993. Although it is undeniably a sans serif, Farey preferred to describe it as a 'soft terminal monoline', taking the view that the slightly rounded terminals help make the design easier to read than most sans serif styles.

Ty	**Patrona Grotesk**
Ca	**Sans Serif**
Ke	**Geometric, Modular, Stencil**
Te	**Letterpress**
Da	**c1931**
De	**V. Kánský**
Fo	**Slevarna Pisem**
Co	**Czech Republic**

Characteristics

38 individual geometric components
Modular construction
Stencil-like openings
Construction allows letterforms in many European writing systems
Construction allows letterforms in Cyrillic
Construction allows ornaments and patterns

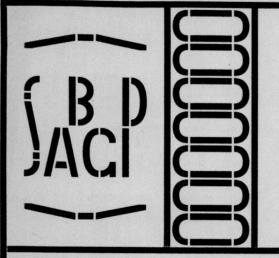

Connections

Kombinations-Schrift	1923
Fregio Mecano	c1933
Alpha-Blox	1944
PDU	2011

Availability

Not available

Specimen

Patrona type specimen. Slevarna Pisem, Prague, 1930s (270x210mm)

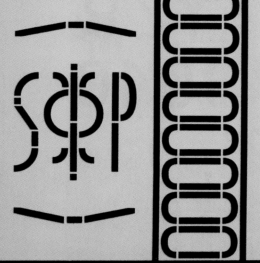

Patrona Grotesk is an ingenious Czech contribution to the early modernist project where the alphabet was reformulated as a system of variable parts that could be arranged as components in page layouts regulated by geometry.

Very little is known about Patrona Grotesk's history other than that it was designed by V. Kánský and issued by the Prague type foundry Slevarna Pisem in around 1931. 'Patrona' translates into English as 'cartridge', an appropriate name to represent the notion of a system of configurable units similar to machine parts. In the specimen shown here Patrona is described as 'a totally new concept for constructing upper case typefaces in both Roman and Cyrillic' from segments it describes as 'polotypes'.

Patrona was based on the breakdown of letterforms into 38 different component parts. These could be arranged as a series of disjointed monolinear shapes to construct an extensive variety of stencil-like capital letterforms in the Serbian, Bulgarian and Russian alphabets, as well as those of Western languages. In addition, a wide range of simple decorative borders and step-and-repeat patterns could be easily achieved with the same broken stencil effect.

The Patrona specimen claims that the advantage of its components to the user is that 'they are systematic: the exact size of each word can be established in advance to create a wide range of consistent forms, or to implement narrow or wide letters on demand, without any difficulties'. It goes on to suggest that Patrona is very economical due to its modularity, and highly suitable for advertising since its 'remarkable impact will be effective in newspapers and magazines'. There is scant evidence that this ever occurred, however, and other than its appearance in the spectacular specimen shown here, Patrona, like many other early modular typefaces, seems to have disappeared without a trace.

Prisma

Ty	**Prisma**
Ca	**Sans Serif**
Ke	**Geometric, Capitals**
Te	**Letterpress**
Da	**1931**
De	**Rudolf Koch**
Fo	**Klingspor**
Co	**Germany**

Characteristics

Geometric construction
Capitals only
Classical letter proportions
Smaller 4-line version
Larger 5-line version

Connections

Piccadilly	1973
Pump Triline	1975
Boymans	2003
Prismaset	2010

Availability

Prisma is widely available. Prisma Pro
is available from RMU Typedesign and
resellers

Specimen

Prisma specimen. Klingspor, Offenbach,
1930s (185x229mm)

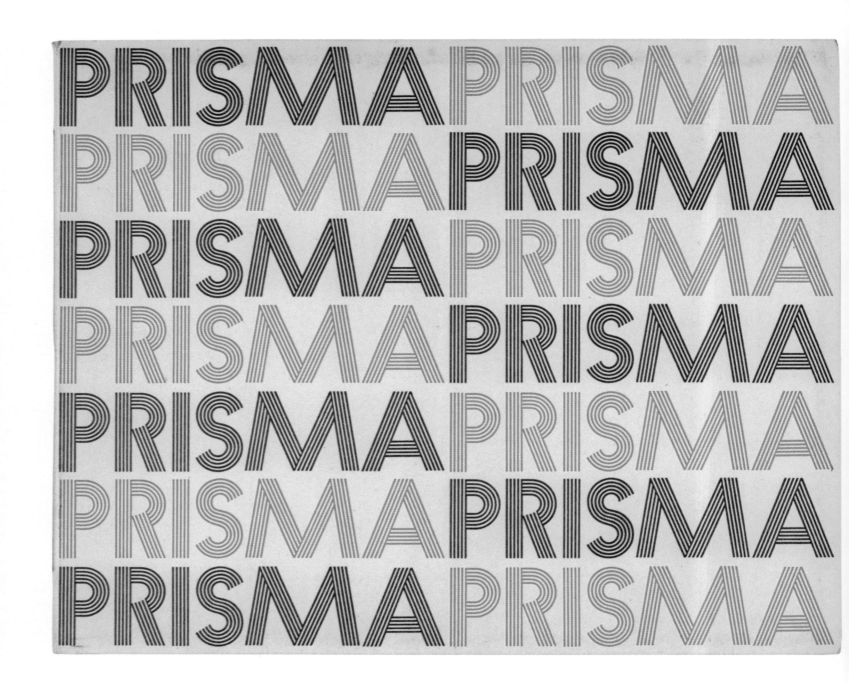

Rudolf Koch, the leading German calligrapher of his generation, is reported to have said: 'The task of creating a type with a pair of compasses and a straight-edge has always attracted me.' Although he was referring to the design of his Kabel typeface (pp232–33), it is with the drawing of Prisma that he came closest to reconciling his lettering with the purity of geometric form.

Prisma was released by the Klingspor foundry in 1931. Like Koch's Zeppelin typeface of 1929, Prisma was designed as a version of the bestselling Kabel family intended for display and headline setting.

Zeppelin is an upper and lower case inline version of Kabel, showing strong art deco influences, but Prisma is a much more complex form. It is a multilinear design in capitals only, where each character stroke is assembled from groups of thin black lines running in parallel. These emphasize the stroke structure by exposing the individual geometric elements from which each letter is built. A particular subtlety of Prisma's construction is that it was cut at two different optical scales. Its four smaller point sizes were each composed of four thin black strokes, whereas five lines were used in larger cuts of 48 point and

60 point. This attention to detail and scale gave a consistency to Koch's original design that is lacking in later revivals produced for different technologies.

A uniquely distinctive display typeface, Prisma became an instant commercial success regardless of its association with Kabel. It was subjected to numerous adaptations and additions during the photocomposition era, when the production of display faces became cost-effective. Many different manufacturers attempted their own versions, including Bauhaus Prisma, Futura Prism, Prisma Graphic, Prisma Neo and Prismania.

These interpretations offered a variety styles with many alternative combinations of lines, solids and white spaces, while also providing alternate letter shapes, many based on other Bauhaus-inspired typefaces of the time.

None could improve on the sophisticated linear geometries of Prisma until, in 2010, James Goggin released Prismaset (pp640–41), an analytical reinvention of Koch's design, reverse-engineered for digital technologies into an extensive collection of component typefaces that can be assembled into a wide variety of variant weights and styles.

Prisma

72720 Text, 20 Punkte   Satz, 24 A, etwa 4,5 Kilo

TEATRO DE BURGOS DON QUIJOTE DE LA MANCHA

72724 2 Cicero, 24 Punkte   Satz, 18 A, etwa 5 Kilo

DIE AUSSTELLUNG IM RATHAUS

72728 Doppelmittel, 28 Punkte   Satz, 14 A, etwa 5,5 Kilo

NOTIZIE VARIE MILANO

72736 3 Cicero, 36 Punkte   Satz, 12 A, etwa 7 Kilo

BUCHDRUCK MASCHINE

72743 4 Cicero, 48 Punkte   Satz, 10 A, etwa 10 Kilo

INVOICE

72760 5 Cicero, 60 Punkte   Satz, 8 A, etwa 12,5 Kilo

BERLIN

Figurenverzeichnis

**A B C D E F G H I
J K L M N O P Q
R S T U V W X Y
Z Ä Ö Ü $ - ? . ! &
1 2 3 4 5 6 7 8 9 0**

74510 Zu Korpus
Musik im Leben

84512 Zu Cicero
Beethoven-

74514 Zu Mittel
Come nasce

74516 Zu Tertia
Entwicklu

74520 Zu Text
Museo

74524 Zu 2 Cicero
Gesells

74528 Zu Doppelmi
Reise

74536 Zu 3 Cicero
Ma

Ty	**Stymie**
Ca	**Slab Serif**
Ke	**Geometric**
Te	**Letterpress**
Da	**1931**
De	**Morris Fuller Benton**
Fo	**American Type Founders**
Co	**USA**

Characteristics

Monoline, geometric construction
Moderate x-height
A Horizontal top serif
C O Q o Circular
G Has spur and wide arm
Q Short, curved tail below letter
a Double-storeyed, large round bowl
f Narrow, non-kerning
g Single-storeyed, short tail
t Narrow, flat foot
y Straight tail with flat serif

AGMQR
abcefghij
koprstuy

Connections

Memphis	1929
Rockwell	1934
Lubalin Graph	1974
Museo Slab	2009

Availability

Stymie is widely available

Specimen

Book of American Types, Standard Faces.
American Type Founders, Jersey City,
1934 (279x210mm)

After geometric sans serif typefaces had become an unstoppable global trend in the late 1920s, many type foundries began to explore the possibilities for creating geometric serif types, in effect adding thick rectangular serifs at the terminals of letters similar to those of Kabel or Futura. Memphis (pp250–51), designed by Rudolf Wolf for Stempel in 1929, was the first design of this sort to be released, precipitating a surge of competitors, including R. H. Middleton's Karnak, issued by Ludlow in 1931; Rockwell (pp288–89), issued by Monotype in 1934; and Heinrich Jost's Beton (pp264–65), issued by Bauer in 1936.

In 1931 American Type Founders entered this lucrative market, challenging Stempel's Memphis with Stymie, the name a pointed reference to blocking an opponent's line of attack. ATF's assiduous Morris Fuller Benton based Stymie on Litho Antique, a design from 1910, whose owner, the Inland Type Foundry, had been taken over by ATF a year later. In his adaptation of the earlier design, Benton redrew its rounded characters in an uncompromisingly geometric form and created a wide range of alternate letters. He also added an eccentric set of variant characters with extremely elongated ascenders and descenders for use in display settings, shown on the right.

Geometric slab serifs do not share the same heritage as Egyptians (pp114–15) or Clarendons (pp132–33), which have more natural contours based on visually adjusted thick and thin strokes. Stymie, like its competitors, is characterized by monoline strokes, purely geometric contours and a systematic progression of weights from a hairline light, shown on the left, to a very dense bold.

The geometric slab serif style quickly became almost as popular as its sans serif equivalents, combining the rigorous logic of Futura with the steady rhythms of the serif form, and typefaces like Stymie were seen frequently in advertisements and publicity material.

:[58]:

279

Ty	**Times New Roman**
Ca	**Serif**
Ke	**Transitional**
Te	**Letterpress**
Da	**1932**
De	**Victor Lardent and Stanley Morison**
Fo	**Monotype**
Co	**UK**

Characteristics

Vertical and oblique stress
Moderate stroke contrast
Most capitals have uniform width
Large x-height
Short ascenders and descenders
Sharp, bracketed serifs
C G Wide
Q Short, curved tail below letter
R Straight, angled leg
W Stepped centre-strokes, serif at apex
a Double-storeyed, large bowl
a c f r y Ball terminals
f r t Narrow
g Double-storeyed, large lower bowl
t Curved bracket connects stem and bar
w Stepped centre-strokes, serif at apex

AGQRW
abcdefghij
orstuya*efg*

Connections

Plantin	1913
Perpetua	1930
Georgia	1996
Capitolium	1998

Availability

Times New Roman is widely available

Specimen

Times New Roman type specimen.
Monotype Corporation, Salfords, c1940
(270x210mm)

'MONOTYPE'
327 TIMES NEW
ROMAN
SERIES 3

AN "OMNIBUS"
(ALL SIZE
IS SHOWN ON
ADVERTISING A

THIS page shows "Monotype" Times New Roman, Series No. 327, roman *and italic*, and Series 421, Times Semi-bold, set to different double and single column measures. It also shows a book page set in the 11 pt. of Series 327. The famous Penguin and Pelican sixpennies are standardized to "Monotype" Times New Roman. *The Listener* is one of the many periodicals set in this famous "Monotype" face. [11 pt.]

MANY TITLING FOUNTS
DISPLAY AND COMP.

are shown on the broadsheet of this folder. The size you are now reading is 6 pt., Series 327. An index of faces shown will be found on the back page.

AND THIS SEMI-BOLI
a deeper and more emphat
iant. *Note the well-formed*
The Cambridge University Pres
this series for its legible Pitt" 8vo

LONG DESCENDER SORTS

"Monotype" Times New Roman was for a year reserved by *The Times* for its own exclusive use, together with the many other related titling and bold series that had been cut by The Monotype Corporation at the paper's behest.

During that year, the public in general and the book publishers in particular were able to test the virtues of the new face under the searching conditions of high-speed rotary printing from curved stereoplates, on newsprint, with news-quality ink, in "news sizes" (e.g. 5 pt. to 9 pt. being the equivalents of the book printer's 8 pt. to 14 pt. normal range).

For the first time in typographic history since newspapers were invented in the seventeenth century, a type face specially designed for NEWS legibility was found to possess, not only the clarity and quick discrimination-value of literal legibility, but also the subtler quality of *readability*. Through all the handicaps of news production, its inherent dignity and its crisp, sure treatment of curve and serif shone out with recognizable charm.

Mr. Francis Meynell was amongst the first of the BOOK publishers to seize upon the new face when it became available. Soon its popularity in book circles was such as to call for the production of the special LONG DESCENDER SORTS shown on this "page".

The normal book measure is 21 picas; hence no face used in book work needs *very* short descenders. Some white "channel" is needed to carry the eyes back to the beginning of the next line. As "Monotype" Times New Roman in book lines needs in any case to be leaded or cast on a larger body, it can just as easily be cast with descenders g j p q y substituted for g j p q y.

When *The Times* entrusted to The Monotype Cor tion the task of cutting "the perfect newspaper f the preliminary optical research had shown the parative inefficiency of all-over thickening as a n of increasing legibility. Abandoning the model of (a 19th century jobbing face), *The Times* arrived far more compact, and infinitely more attractive, d in the "Old Face" category, which permits the *max normal differentiation of letters by thickening—no* whole face but—*the characteristic strokes.*

The paragraph above shows 12 point "Monot *Times* New Roman cast on a 14 point body with special long descenders; contrast with this parag set in 12 point with short descenders and leaded 2 pc Below, the 12 on 12 point is set solid.

Catalogue work and **JOBBING,** "Standardizati of typography and other cases where a wide rang sizes and **differentiation by weight** are required, proved the remarkable practicality of this face. Se illustrated and other PERIODICALS have already "redressed" in "Monotype" *Times* New Roman, one advantage which should not be overlooked is the range of sizes in roman *and italic* is unusually la Note the brilliantly cut 5½ and 6 point sizes.

For a miniature size, 5½ pt. "Monotype" Times New Roman is extremely legible. ABCDEFGHIJKLMNOPQRSTUVWXY ZÆŒ& ABCDEFGHIJKLMNOPQRSTUVWXYZÆ Œ abcdefghijklmnopqrstuvwxyzæœ& fiflffl ffiffl— £1234567890 ..;;"-!?O **†‡‖.—§.. *ABCDEFGHIJKLMNOPQRSTUVWXY ZÆŒ& abcdefghijklmnopqrstuvwxyzfiflffiffl ffiœ £1234567890 ::!?&*

WE HAVE AVAILABLE comparison of the same copy (precisely word-for set (a) in Ionic, (b) in Times New Rom both 9-pt., both to 13 ems. The copy ta depth in Ionic with 29 lines. Series 32 three-quarters of an inch and sets the words legibly in only 23 lines.

MONOTYPE" TIMES
ED SERIES)
OF THIS FOLDER
MENS ARE ON P. 4

FIRST ALL-SIZE SPECIMEN SHOWING OF "MONOTYPE"

Times WIDE 427:

ewest, and probably the most *36 point*

nportant of the "classic" book faces *30 point*

roduced for contemporary needs.

he extraordinary charm and legibility of the ITALICS of *18 point*
ese founts will be evident to every typographer. *Full normal*
rns (a "single type" advantage) are essential to any good
lic. It is also important to note that the letter-widths

any character in roman and italic respectively
decided independently, when the face is a
Monotype" face (single type).

[427
UICK BROWN FOX JUMPS OVER THE LAZY DOG
ick brown fox jumps over the lazy dog *abcdefghijklmnopq*
UICK BROWN FOX JUMPS OVER THE LAZY DOG [327
ick brown fox jumps over the lazy dog *abcdefghijklmnopq* [327

REMARKABLE LEGIBILITY

n point", says the modern publisher, "is too small
ze of type to be used in any book whose sales will
end, to some extent, on the verdict of over-worked
k-reviewers". For "ten point" read "small print" and
dictum is certainly just: midnight oil casts very un-
•urable shadows on literary work that happens to be
than EASY to read.

ut what does "ten point" mean to-day? These lines
printed in type of that size, but the print is the *optical*
valent of a legible eleven point—even of a (long
ender) twelve point. Being cast on a size larger body
eu of one point leading, these types are eleven point
s, though the face-size is ten point: i.e. the matrices
d have been (but were not) cast on "their own" ten
t body.

hese paragraphs show how "Monotype" Times Wide,
es 427, looks in 10 pt. to a measure of 21 picas. Our
imen Printing Department will gladly prepare, for
owner of "Monotype" machines who is contem-
ing the purchase of these matrices, TRIAL PAGE
OOFS in any specified size, measure, etc.

"MONOTYPE" TIMES WIDE

Some types look larger, size for size, than others, because they have unusually short descenders and ascenders. This allows more room for the "x" or middle part of the lower-case. A good newspaper type is one in which seven point manages to achieve almost as much legibility as a normal ten point book face. Hence every modern news text-face has a "large x" and short ascenders and descenders.

But only one modern news text-face has ever recognized the fact that a "large x" is bound to waste space *horizontally* (a very serious waste where *narrow* news columns are concerned)—unless curves such as those in e, p, q, etc., can be somewhat condensed, by way of compensation.

The imperceptible condensation of "Monotype" Times New Roman puts it in a class by itself as a news face. In the wider book measure, however, condensation is no asset. It was the charm of the *design and cut* of "Monotype" Times New Roman, not its relative condensation, which made book publishers hail the face with enthusiasm.

All the remarkable legibility-for-size of Series 327, "Monotype" Times New Roman, and all the charm of its crisp distinctive cut, are reflected in *this wider version, Series 427, for which it is safe to prophesy a most distinguished reception amongst book producers.*

427, 11 on 12
First two paragraphs leaded 1½ pts.

In 1931, the British Monotype Corporation was commissioned to develop a new typeface by the *Times* newspaper in response to a critical article written by Stanley Morison, Monotype's typographic adviser. In it, he had condemned the newspaper's poor print quality and the defective modern typeface that had survived in its pages for many years.

Morison proposed the design of a new type which, he wrote in a subsequent report to *The Times*, 'will tend towards the "modern", though the body of the letter will be more or less old-face in appearance'. His intention was to create a highly legible text typeface that was both economical in its use of space and appropriate to modern newspaper production methods. Working under Morison's supervision, Victor Lardent, an artist from the advertising department of *The Times*, drew up two alternative designs: a version of Eric Gill's Perpetua (pp262–63) with shortened extenders, and a radical new design modelled on Monotype Plantin 113 (pp194–95). The committee of *The Times* chose the second option and Times New Roman made its first appearance in the newspaper on 3 October 1932.

Incorporating features of old-style and transitional letterforms, Times New Roman is a hybrid that is free from both 'conscious archaism and conscious art', as Morison explained. It has balanced proportions that are similar to those of Plantin, but with a much higher contrast in the strokes of the letters, and with sharper serifs that are also steeply bracketed. Times New Roman is readily identified by its large x-height, short ascenders and descenders, and a slightly oblique stress that is more evident in the lower case than the upper.

After one year's exclusive use, Times New Roman was released for commercial sale when Monotype licensed it for Linotype and Intertype line-casting machines. It continued to be used, unchanged, by *The Times* for 40 years, but since 1972 the newspaper has updated it several times to suit new production technologies and different formats, while remaining faithful to Morison and Lardent's design. There has probably never been a more popular text face than Times New Roman or one with a wider influence. It has been used in every aspect of printed communications, from editorial work to advertising, and because of its distribution in computer operating systems, it has become one of the most familiar typefaces of all time. It continues to occupy a unique position in the typographic repertoire, not because of any relationship to a particular historical period but because it functions as faultlessly as it was intended to.

Ty	**Bayer Type**
Ca	**Serif**
Ke	**Geometric**
Te	**Letterpress**
Da	**1933**
De	**Herbert Bayer**
Fo	**Berthold**
Co	**Germany**

Characteristics
Originally lower case only
Modular geometric construction
Extreme contrast of thick and thin strokes
Short hairline serifs

abcefgh
ikmoprs
tuwxyz

Connections

Didot	1784
Thorne's Fat Face	c1806
Universal Type	1925
Al-Bro	1950

Availability
Architype Bayer is a digital revival
available from the Foundry and resellers

Specimen
Study for Bayer Type. Herbert Bayer,
c1930–32 (300x537mm)

Herbert Bayer said that the 1920s typographic revolution 'was not an isolated event but went hand in hand with a new social, political consciousness and consequently, with the building of new cultural foundations'. His Universal Type (pp222–23) had been conceived not as a stylization of alphabetic form but as a political statement: a revolutionary new system for social communication that was unencumbered by superfluous ornamentation or any reference to historical precedent.

The relative commercial success of the design work produced at the Bauhaus in the late 1920s and early 1930s was marked by a proportionate reduction in its idealistic social position, partly because of the German political climate of the time, and partly because most customers were unwilling to engage with it. Bayer's eponymous typeface, designed between 1930 and 1933, demonstrates this shift in attitude.

Bayer Type was commissioned by the Berthold Type Foundry for commercial use. In terms of construction, Bayer Type is similar to Universal in that it is drawn geometrically, with pen and compass, from repeated components, but it is far more mannered than its predecessor. Bayer Type is fashionable and stylized, with strong contrasts in the thicks and thins of the letterforms, unbracketed hairline serifs and classical ball terminals ending several strokes.

Bayer's original drawing, reproduced here, is in lower case only, but the final typeface released by Berthold was complemented by a very conventional and ungainly set of capitals, a form that Bayer had previously sought to eradicate from his design work and from the German language.

Berthold's final version, cut in light, medium and bold weights, is a visual compromise that is far more referential to historical Didot types (pp90–91) and fat faces than the letters shown here, particularly in the upper case. In its 1933 promotional brochure, Bayer Type is described as 'designed upon the sure basis of classical forms, but shows an obvious tendency to the present time', a markedly different time from the decade that had preceded it.

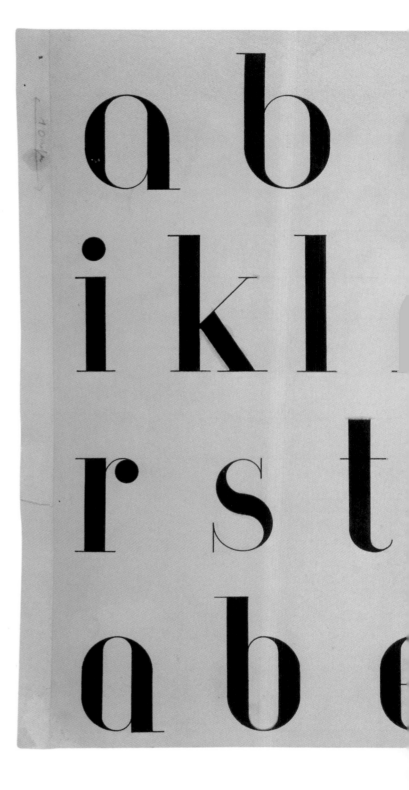

d e f g h
n o p q
v w x y z
h

Ty	**Fregio Mecano**
Ca	**Sans Serif**
Ke	**Geometric, Modular, Stencil**
Te	**Letterpress**
Da	**c1933**
De	**Giulio da Milano (?)**
Fo	**Nebiolo**
Co	**Italy**

Characteristics

Modular construction
20 individual geometric components
Graphic surface grid conceals joints
Variations of height, width, weight
Variations of serif configuration
Variations of ornament and pattern

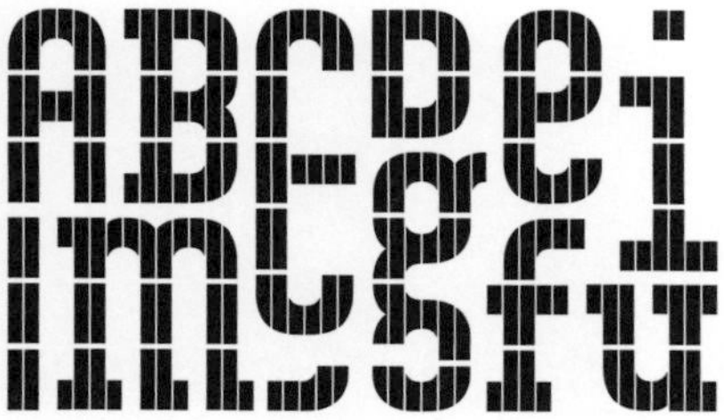

Connections

Kombinations-Schrift	1923
Patrona Grotesk	c1931
Fregio Razionale	1935
Tribasei	2006

Availability

Section Bold Condensed is a digital revival
available from Monotype and resellers.
Tribasei is a more extensive digital revival
available from Molotro

Specimen

Campionario caratteri e fregi tipografici.
Nebiolo, Turin, c1938 (260x175mm)

FREGIO MECANO

(Carattere scomponibile)

Minimo Kg. 2,50   Si vendono anche figure separate : minimo Kg. 1 per fig

SERIE 900

FREGIO MECANO

Si eseguisce anche
in legno con asta da
3-6-8-12-16 righe

NEBIOLO · TORINO

268

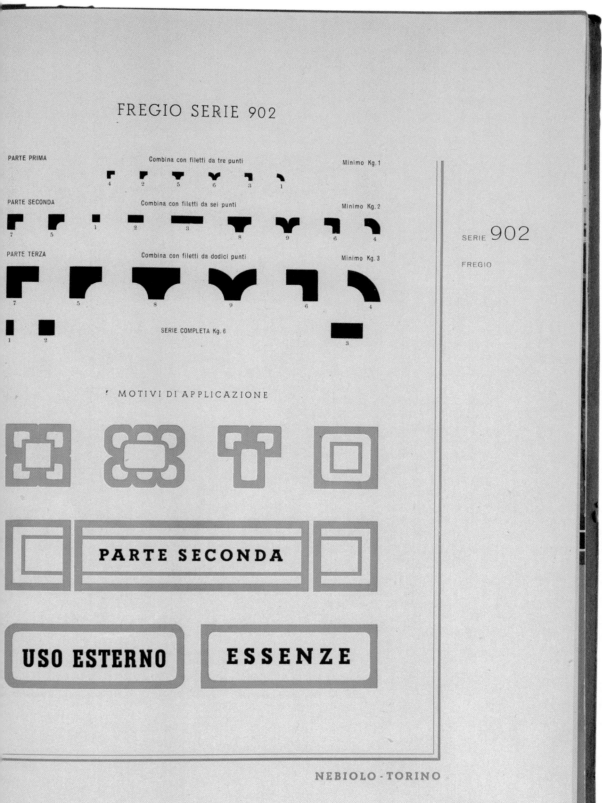

During the first half of the twentieth century, many designers explored the construction of modular typefaces, where letterforms were split into geometric parts that could be assembled in arrangements regulated by underlying grid structures. Fregio Mecano is one of the earliest, most inventive and most effective of these. Loosely translated into English as 'mechanical ornament', Fregio Mecano is described in a printed specimen as a collection of 'decomposable characters'. Issued by the Italian type foundry Nebiolo in the early 1930s, it was a modular typographic system designed for use in letterpress display applications.

The identity of the designer of Fregio Mecano is not known for certain, but it is attributed to the artist Giulio da Milano (1895–1990), who was the first director of the Nebiolo foundry in Turin from 1930 to 1936. He is known to have designed several other modular and geometric types that bear a close resemblance to Fregio Mecano, including Nebiolo's Neon and Fregio Razionale, both released in 1935.

Fregio Mecano's design was based on the decomposition of letterforms into 20 simple pieces that could be combined and recombined to construct an almost infinite variety of new typographic forms, including borders, patterns, alphabets and numerals. Incised vertical and horizontal lines within the segments themselves created a graphic grid that unified the appearance of the assembled forms and served to conceal the joints between them. By rearranging the pieces, constructed letters could achieve extensive variations of height, width or weight while maintaining a consistent appearance. It was also possible to create a slab serif alphabet simply by adding segments.

The Fregio Mecano typeface, like most letterpress designs based on modular elements, was not successful in terms of sales, largely because of the design complexities it presented to printers as a result of the time and expense its composition demanded. It fell into almost complete disuse, but due to a resurgence of interest in systems type in the twenty-first century, Fregio Mecano is now widely admired as one of the progenitors of the programmatic methods afforded by digital design technologies.

Ty	**Element**
Ca	**Blackletter**
Ke	**Textura, Geometric**
Te	**Letterpress**
Da	**1934**
De	**Max Bittrof**
Fo	**Bauer**
Co	**Germany**

Characteristics

Square, geometric construction

Compressed vertical emphasis

Consistent angles throughout

Counterforms and character spacing
evenly balanced

a Single-storeyed

d Angled uncial stem

f long s Long descender

h Roman form

ABCEFTU
abedfghij
koqrstuy

Connections

Tannenberg	1933
Deutschland Mager	1934
ITC Honda	1970
Klute	1997

Availability

Not available

Specimen

Element type specimen. Bauersche
Giesserei, Frankfurt, c1934 (210x100mm)

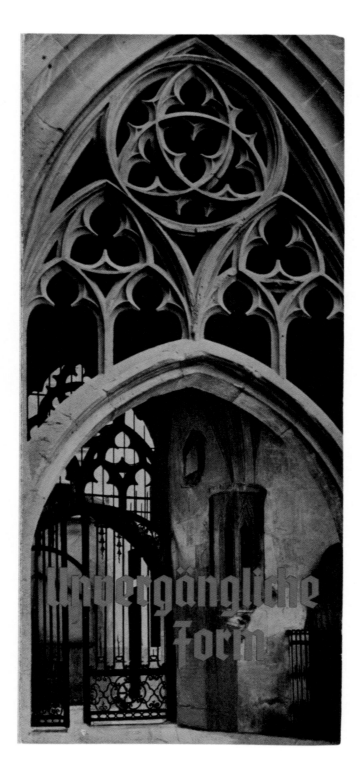

Die
aufstrebende
Schlankheit
der gotischen
Form

BAUERSCHE GIESSE

sentliches Merkmal der deutschen Schrift,

dem nun vollendeten Schnitt der schmalen

Element

besonders kräftigen und reinen Ausdruck.

ben die Fertigstellung dieses Schnittes nicht

zt, weil wir aus langer Erfahrung wissen,

der Erfolg einer Schrift beruht. Die Hand

mpelschneiders muß dem Geiste des Künst-

zur letzten Einzelheit gefolgt sein.

KFURT A · M · NEW YORK

Schmalfette Element

ift in den Graden von 12 bis 84 Punkt geschnitten

20 Punkt

Gemälde von Rembrandt

24 Punkt

Universität Tübingen

28 Punkt

Kölner Rundfunk

36 Punkt

Das gute Buch

48 Punkt

Hotel Wien

In Holz von 8 bis 20 Cicero geschnitten

Max Bittrof (1890–1972), a commercial artist and typographer from Frankfurt, designed Element in 1934 for the Bauer Foundry. It was the result of Bittrof's efforts to solve a uniquely German design problem. The persistent competition between two orthographic traditions – blackletter and roman – paralleled a long-standing conflict between nationalist and internationalist perspectives that eventually came to a head in the struggle between fascism and socialism in 1930s Germany. The search for a balance within its typeforms that would encapsulate the uniqueness of its culture, while at the same time presenting the state as a progressive global power, was not new. Many others, including Unger (pp100–101), Breitkopf and Walbaum (pp106–107), had sought to address the same issue in previous generations. By the 1930s, however, it had become a complex and pressing political problem.

When Element was released as a family in four weights by Bauer in 1934 it was part of a contemporary trend among German foundries for pared-down geometric blackletter typefaces that included Tannenberg, National and Gotenberg. All of these typefaces, including Element, attempted to amalgamate features of the blackletter with those of roman sans serif styles, removing superfluous elements in the search for a German character expressing rational modern values. They bear little relation to the folksy, decorative Frakturs that were officially endorsed by the state at the time.

Partly for functional reasons, these typefaces were widely used in exterior signage, but, largely due to the Nazis' outright rejection of modern design as *Kulturbolschewismus* (cultural Bolshevism), they were not widely adopted in Germany. Subsequently, negative associations with fascism and nationalist politics caused them to be reviled internationally as examples of 'jackboot gothics'.

Element and other short-lived, unpopular geometric blackletters survive as a record of the development of German design in turbulent pre-war conditions, with the pioneering contributions of designers like Max Bittrof only now beginning to be recognized.

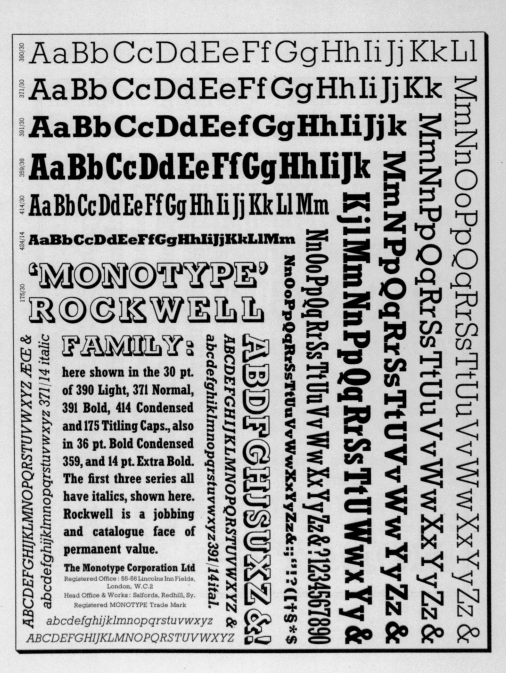

Ty	**Rockwell**
Ca	**Slab Serif**
Ke	**Geometric**
Te	**Letterpress**
Da	**1934**
De	**Frank Hinman Pierpont**
Fo	**Monotype**
Co	**UK**

Characteristics

Monoline, geometric construction

Large x-height

A Serif at apex

C G O Q o Almost circular

G No spur

Q Short tail below letter

a Double-storeyed

f Narrow, non-kerning

i j Round dots

t Narrow, angled top

y Flat tail, serif extends to left

AGMQR abcefghij koprstuy

Connections

Memphis	1929
Stymie	1931
Serifa	1967
PMN Caecilia	1991

Availability

Rockwell is available from Monotype and resellers

Specimen

Rockwell specimen sheet. Monotype Corporation, Salfords, c1940 (270x210mm)

By the 1930s, slab serif typefaces like Memphis (pp250–51) and Stymie (pp278–79) had become an essential part of the repertoire of almost every type foundry and printing office. In 1934 Frank Hinman Pierpont of the Monotype Corporation commissioned its drawing office to update No. 173, a typeface from 1913, in a style then known as Egyptian, featuring serifs that were rectangular, unbracketed and close in weight to the horizontal strokes of the letters.

The 1934 rationalization of No. 173 was released as Rockwell, the name borrowed from the company's American joint venture, Lanston Monotype. For many years American Type Founders' Stymie Bold and Monotype's Rockwell Bold were often mistaken for one another, not just because of their obvious similarities, but also as a result of commercial competition. Rockwell was occasionally listed as Stymie by Monotype and, to compound the confusion, the bold weight of the ATF type was named Rockwell at one point. These issues were probably not mere errors but rather attempts by the competing businesses to obstruct each other's marketing efforts.

Rockwell is fundamentally geometric but it is a far more nuanced face than Stymie. It has several atypical characteristics, including letter proportions based on classical forms, an even progression across its range of weights, and subtle differences in stroke and serif thickness. Its upper case O and lower case o are almost perfectly circular, but other characters are more modulated, particularly in the bold weight. Unusually for a geometric typeface, the lower case a is double-storeyed, and the ascender of the t is cut at a sharp angle, both features reflecting its origins in nineteenth-century Egyptians.

Slab serifs are versatile and sturdy, their evenness making them ideal for display and other applications requiring the reliability of a monoline typeface. Monotype Rockwell was produced in several variants that included italics and condensed versions, and it rapidly became the best performer of its kind in the twentieth century.

Albertus specimen sheet. Monotype Corporation, Salfords, c1940 (270x210mm)

Specimen text

MONOTYPE Registered Trade Mark

ALBERTUS 481

This distinctive type face is cut in 18, 24, 36, 48, 60 and (see over) 72 point. Display Matrices may be hired at *low cost* from our Lending Library at 54 Fetter Lane (1st floor), London, E.C.4

Other members of this Family are the Light 534, Titling 324, and the Bold Titling, Series 538

THE MONOTYPE CORPORATION LIMITED
Registered Office: 55-56 Lincolns Inn Fields, London, w.c.2
Head Office and Works: Salfords, Redhill, Surrey

abcDefG dgHhJjK kmnpQr qstuVvw WXxyZz 2345678

Ty	**Albertus**
Ca	**Serif**
Ke	**Wedge, Glyphic**
Te	**Letterpress**
Da	**1935**
De	**Berthold Wolpe**
Fo	**Monotype**
Co	**UK**

Characteristics

	Triangular serifs at terminals
A	Pointed apex, high crossbar
E	Arms terminate at angles
M	Vertical stems, high vertex
U	Has a foot on right stem
a	Double-storeyed, irregular bowl
b h m n	Top of arch reduces at stem
f	Angled terminal to cross-stroke
g	Double-storeyed, small lower bowl
i j	Large, round dot
3	Flat top

AEMRU
abcdefghij
koprstuvy

Connections

Optima	1958
Matrix	1986
Penumbra	1994
Infini	2015

Availability

Albertus is available from Monotype and resellers

Specimen

Albertus specimen sheet. Monotype Corporation, Salfords, c1940 (270x210mm)

MONOTYPE
ALBERTUS

SERIES NO. 481

72 PT. SHOWN HERE

abcdefghijklm
nopqrstuvwxyz
£1234567890 –
CDFGHIJKQV
WXYZ &⌐.,:;-"!?

Alternative sorts

&MTW

OTHER ALBERTUS SERIES: LIGHT; TITLING; BOLD TITLING

This page shows the largest size of a vigorous and sturdy display face that has already proved valuable when used for book jackets, showcards, and in packaging display. Alphabets of other (display) sizes, 18, 24, 36, 48 and 60 point are shown overleaf.

The Monotype Corporation Ltd., 55-56 Lincolns Inn Fields, London, w.c.2.   *Head Office and Works*: Salfords, Surrey

Albertus is based on bronze inscriptional lettering cut by Berthold Wolpe (1905–89), a German engraver, calligrapher, type designer, book designer and illustrator. Stanley Morison, typographic adviser to the British Monotype Corporation, greatly admired Wolpe's work and suggested that he should convert his lettering into a typeface. Dissatisfied with his initial attempts to reconstruct the letterforms, Wolpe reverted to taking direct rubbings of the original inscriptional capitals, resulting in an extremely successful typeface that was issued by Monotype in 1935.

Wolpe began his career in the 1920s at the renowned Offenbacher Werkstatt of Rudolf Koch (pp214–15, 232–33), a pre-eminent craftsman and type designer of the time. Koch's influence is evident in the design of Albertus as a type deeply rooted in the humanist tradition of classical letterforms but also showing a strong connection to the sans serif.

Wolpe's bronze lettering technique involved excising the material outside the letter contours to shape them from the perimeter, rather than from the interior, the usual way that letters in stone would be incised. This unorthodox process resulted in a design that stands midway between classical inscriptional letters and the modern sans serif, with bold, monoline strokes terminated by serifs that are reduced to sharply chiselled wedges.

Albertus was initially made available only as a titling face in capitals; a lower case roman was added in 1940, and later an italic that is notable for the narrowness of its character set. Wolpe took an ingenious approach to his design for Albertus, making a statement of great originality and purity. Its usefulness continued throughout the twentieth century, and it is still very popular today.

Ty	**Electra**
Ca	**Serif**
Ke	**Old Style**
Te	**Letterpress**
Da	**1935**
De	**William Addison Dwiggins**
Fo	**Linotype**
Co	**USA**

Characteristics

Narrow character widths
Tall capitals
Lower case has thick upper serifs and thin baseline serifs
J Descends below baseline
Q Sweeping tail below letter
b d p q Flat-topped bowl
f h m n Flat-topped arch
g Double-storeyed, small ear
t Flat top

AJKMQR
abcdefghij
orstuyaefg

Connections

Romulus	1936
Caledonia	1938
Fairfield	1940
Tyfa	1960

Availability

Electra is available from Linotype and resellers

Specimen

W. A. Dwiggins, *Emblems and Electra.* Mergenthaler Linotype Company, New York, 1935 (200x140mm)

William Addison Dwiggins (1880–1956) was a prominent American commercial artist who was as experienced in book design, advertising, illustration and calligraphy as he was in type design. He created Electra for the Linotype casting machine in 1935 as an attempt to capture the spirit of the machine age – 'to produce a fast-moving face a little out of the line of "old face" or "modern"'. The name Electra, he said, 'suggested itself as a possible expression of electric energy'.

Although Electra's construction loosely follows an old-style model, its strokes have the animation of brush-drawn forms. Thick upper serifs and thin baseline serifs are notable features of the design, giving a slight imbalance that adds a bounce to the visual rhythm of the text. Another unusual detail is the shallow upper arch of characters such as b, d, h, m, n, p and q. Dwiggins's rationale for their flat transition was that the sharp angles at junctions with stems added what he called 'snap' to the design. Electra's calligraphic characters are narrow and particularly large, and the capitals are comparatively tall. Alternative sets of short and long descenders were available in the original cut of the type.

In his 1926 essay 'Towards an Ideal Italic', Stanley Morison had proposed that most italic designs were unsatisfactory auxiliaries to roman because of their lack of similarity in appearance. Following his suggestion that a harmonious italic might be simply differentiated from roman by its angle of inclination alone, Dwiggins designed a pure 'sloped roman' for Electra with no traditional italic characteristics whatsoever. Like Van Krimpen's Romulus italic (pp294–95), Dwiggins's sloped roman was not well accepted and he designed a more conventional italic for Electra in 1944.

The Electra series was first released in the United States in 1935 where it was extensively used in editorial design and bookwork throughout the second half of the twentieth century, although it was not widely seen elsewhere.

A digital revival, published by Linotype in 1994, was accurate to Electra's contours but appeared somewhat pale and brittle on the printed page. LFA Aluminia, a more nuanced interpretation of Electra's unique qualities, was produced by Jim Parkinson for The Letterform Archive in 2017 for publication in Bruce Kennett's definitive *W. A. Dwiggins: A Life in Design*.

drawn to avoid the extreme contrast between "thick" and "thin" elements that marks most "modern" faces. The design is not based upon any traditional model, and is not an attempt to revive or to reconstruct any historic type. What the letter-draughtsman aimed to do is indirectly developed in the following:

COMMENT BY

W. A. D.

ON A NEW LINOTYPE FACE

. . . . Got in touch with Kobodaishi and had a long talk with him. You will remember him as the Patron Saint of the lettering art—great Buddhist missionary in old Japan.

I told him what I was doing with you people, and said that it would help us a lot if he could give us a kind of an idea what the type style was going to be in the next ten years—what was to be the fashionable thing, etc., etc.

He wouldn't say directly. He said: "The trouble with all you people is that you are always trying to reproduce Jenson's letters, or John de Spira or some of those Venetian people. You are always going back three or four hundred years and trying to do over again what they did then. What's the idea?"

"Well" I said, "we think those types were pretty good—about the best that anybody ever made, and we'd like to make some like them."

"But why *like* them?" he said. "You don't live in Venice in 1500. This is 1935. Why don't you do what *they* did: take letter shapes and see if you can't work them into something that stands for 1935? Why doll yourself up in Venetian fancy-dress costume and go dodging around in airplanes and automobiles dressed up *that* way?"

"I know" I said. "But you can't play tricks with the shapes of letters. If you do, people can't read 'em. People are used to type that looks like that, and you have got to keep mighty close to the old designs."

"Used to the 1500 types? Don't you believe it. People are used to newspaper types, and typewriter types. Your Venice types are just about as queer-looking to your friends in Hingham as Greek letters.

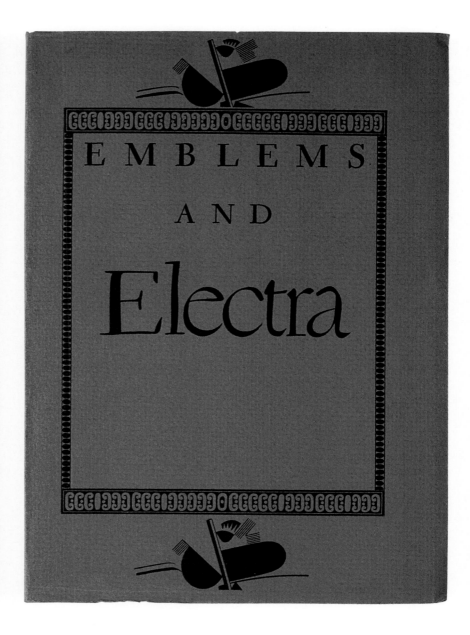

Ty	**Romulus**
Ca	**Serif**
Ke	**Old Style**
Te	**Letterpress**
Da	**1936**
De	**Jan van Krimpen**
Fo	**Joh. Enschedé en Zonen and Monotype**
Co	**Netherlands**

Characteristics

Old-style character construction
Wide, light characters
Long ascenders
Tall, light capitals
J Descends below baseline
M Splayed
Q Tail below letter
R Wide, downward-curved leg
W Stepped centre-strokes
a Double-storeyed, curve at foot
f Extended arch
g Double-storeyed, large upper bowl

AJMQW
abcdefghij
orstuyaefg

Connections

Electra	1935
Fairfield	1940
FF Scala	1991
Thesis	1994

Availability

Not available

Specimen

Romulus type specimen. Joh. Enschedé en Zonen, Haarlem, c1948 (210x130mm)

Since the beginnings of digital typography in the 1990s many designers have developed large extended families containing typefaces that fit into multiple classifications. Usually working from a common line at the very core of the character strokes, specific features like weight, width, serif shape and stroke modulation can be built up systematically, often with the aid of automated processes, to produce coordinated typeface groups. While belonging to different classes – sans and serif, for example – these have a coherent appearance that makes them well disposed to harmonious combinations in typographic applications. Rather than being obliged to seek different typefaces for contrast or continuity, graphic designers can rely on a single family. Martin Majoor's Scala (pp496–97) and Lucas de Groot's Thesis (pp538–39) are among the most effective and extensive examples of this 'superfamily' class available today.

The idea was not, however, an innovation of the digital era. It was first conceived in 1931 by Jan van Krimpen (1892–1958) with his Romulus typeface. The original family was the most comprehensive ever designed until that time. It included three serif types (Roman, Roman Semibold, Roman Bold Condensed) and four related sans serifs (Light, Normal, Semibold and Bold). All weights and sizes were designed to correspond to common centre lines. In addition, there were two kinds of serif italic which matched with the other styles, one a sloped roman and the other a traditional Cancelleresca Bastarda.

The serifed version of Romulus has the appearance of an old-style face but is more regular in its details than its antecedents. Its characters are wide, comparatively light and have a moderate stroke contrast. The capitals are very large in relation to the lower case but are also light in weight. The sloped roman version of the italic is an unusual innovation, also seen in Dwiggins's Electra (pp292–93), that is appealing but not easily distinguishable from the upright form, being similar not only in shape but in stroke thickness.

The first Romulus types to be released were cut by Enschedé and Monotype between 1931 and 1936, but the outbreak of World War II disrupted the project. After the war, Van Krimpen had lost interest in resuming work on Romulus and, although a digital revival by Dutch Type Library is in progress, it remains the relic of an incomplete but highly ambitious experiment.

ROMEIN Corps 24 No. 6619 9,5 kg 15 A 42 a

TYPOGRAPHIE IS HET vak van op eene juiste wijze plaatsen van druk-materiaal met het oog op een bepaald doel; van zoodanig de letters schikken, de ruimte verdeelen, het schrift beheerschen

ROMEIN Corps 20 No. 6617 8 kg 20 A 55 a

AANGEZIEN DRUKKEN IN wezen een middel is van vermenigvuldiging moet het drukwerk niet slechts goed zijn op zichzelf beschouwd maar ook goed voor een gemeen doel. Van zooveel te grooter wijdheid dit doel is des te strenger zijn de beperkingen den drukker opgelegd. Hij wage een proefneming

LETTERGIETERIJ JOH. ENSCHEDÉ EN ZONEN / HAARLEM

MEIN
orps 16
. 6615
7 kg
A 75 a

TYPOGRAPHIE KAN MEN OM schrijven als het vak van op een juiste wijze plaatsen van druk-materiaal met het oog op een bepaald doel; van zoodanig letters schikken, de ruimte verdeelen, en het schrift beheerschen, als noodig is om zooveel mogelijk het goed verstaan van den tekst door den lezer te bevorderen. Typographie is 't doeltreffende middel voor het bereiken van een in zijn wezen nuttig, en alleen bij toeval schoon, einde; want genieten van een 'voorbeeld' zal slechts zelden de juiste wensch van een lezer zijn. *Dus elke rangschikking van druk-materiaal die, met welk inzicht ook, tusschen den schrijver en den lezer wil treden is verkeerd. Hieruit volgt dat er bij het drukken van boeken die bedoeld zijn om gelezen te worden weinig plaats is voor typographisch schitteren. Zelfs eentonigheid en saaiheid in de zetwijze zijn ten opzichte van den lezer minder verkeerd dan typographische zonderlingheden en grappen. Van dat*

CURSIEF
Corps 16
No. 6616
7 kg
15 A 90 a

LETTERGIETERIJ JOH. ENSCHEDÉ EN ZONEN / HAARLEM

ROMEIN
Corps 36
No. 6623
11 kg
7 A 18 a

TYPOGRAPHIE kan men omschrijven als het vak van *oog op een bepaald doel; van zoodanig*

CURSIEF
Corps 36
No. 6624
10 kg
5 A 22 a

ROMEIN
Corps 28
No. 6621
10 kg
12 A 32 a

RANGSCHIKKING van drukmateriaal welke, met eenigerlei inzicht, tusschen den schrijver en *zijn om gelezen te worden weinig plaats is voor*

CURSIEF
Corps 28
No. 6622
8,5 kg
8 A 32 a

LETTERGIETERIJ JOH. ENSCHEDÉ EN ZONEN / HAARLEM

Ty	**Schneidler Old Style**
Ca	**Serif**
Ke	**Old Style, Venetian**
Te	**Letterpress**
Da	**1936**
De	**Ernst Schneidler**
Fo	**Bauer**
Co	**Germany**

Characteristics

	Almost monoline character construction
	Capitals to ascender height
	Angled and concave serifs
A	Pointed apex
K k	Arm and tail do not touch stem
M	Splayed, serifs at foot only
O o	Monolinear, circular
P	Open bowl
Q	Short, non-descending tail
R	Wide, straight leg
e	Small eye and oblique bar

AJKMPQ
abcdefghij
orstuyaefg

Connections

The Doves Type	1900
Kennerley Old Style	1911
Centaur	1914
PMN Caecilia	1991

Availability

Schneidler Old Style is available from Linotype and resellers

Specimen

Bauer Text type specimen. Bauersche Giesserei, Frankfurt, c1936 (297x210mm)

Spring type tonic

Refreshing as a May breeze playing across a flower-flecked meadow, a new text letter blooms! Bauer Text invigorates the written word with tonic charm. Clear, cleanly-cut, and open, this face meets the oft-voiced need for just such a modern body type. For Bauer Text, though faintly reminiscent of the well-loved Bookman, is a distinct and pleasing modern departure.

BAUER TEXT

It's effective in a wide range of uses. It's "neutral" in its influence upon accompanying display or caption faces. It "reads well" even when set solid in its smallest size. Bauer Text is herewith introduced in the first weight of a series, and in sizes from 8 to 48 point. Note in the following pages how adaptable it is, how legible in every adaptation. Bauer Text is available now. Full stocks insure prompt deliveries. Wire, 'phone, or write the Bauer representative nearest you, or

SOLDANS LIMITED · 5·11 THEOBALDS ROAD · LONDON, W.C.1

8 Point 28A 56a — The various processes of graphic art seem to enjoy successive spells of public favour, to sink for a while into comparative obscurity until changed economic conditions or the genius of one practitioner bring them once more into prominence. Etching rose to supreme heights with Rembrandt in mid-seventeenth century, but by the end of that century had already given place in universal estimation to line-engraving. Line-engraving was threatened by mezzotint and stipple, enjoyed a brief REVIVAL IN THE EARLY NINETEENTH CENTURY, TO MAKE WAY FOR WOOD-ENGRAVING.

10 Point 26A 53a — The 'sixties saw the triumph of reproductive work on wood, a triumph cut short by the perfecting of the various photo-mechanical processes. Etching, on the other hand, was re-born as an independent art with Jaque, Meryon, Haden, and Whistler, and has continued to enjoy immense popularity to the present day. It was, never A VERY SATISFACTORY METHOD OF BOOK ILLUSTRATION. ITS VERY

11 Point 26A 50a — looseness of technique made it unsuitable for a work of collaboration, and the modern illustrator of books employs it very rarely. Even in its own field it has felt the influence of the modern pleasure in straight lines and formal DESIGN. THE SKETCHINESS OF SOME OF THE OLDER MASTERS HAS

12 Point 24A 47a — been abandoned and a technique adopted which assimilates the products of the etcher's needle to those of the engraver's burin. It was to be expected, therefore, that this age should see a revival of pure line-engraving FOR ITS OWN SAKE, NOT AS A REPRODUCTIVE PROCESS, BUT

BAUER MAKERS OF FINE TYPES FOR MORE THAN A CENTURY

M 2

14 Point 22 A 42 a

as a personal means of expression. There is once more a market for engraved plates, prized either for themselves or as the decoration OF A FINE BOOK. THE REVIVAL OF LINE-ENGRAVING HAS

16 Point 18 A 38 a

already begun to win its triumphs, and one of its most successful exponents in England is Mr. Stephen Gooden. GOODEN WAS BORN IN LONDON IN 1892. AT

18 Point 12 A 26 a

Rugby, where he was educated, he already knew his genius did not lie in the direction of scholastic SUCCESSES, AND HE JOINED THE SLADE

24 Point 9 A 19 a

Delicate Roses and Animal Figures
EXQUISITE IVORY CARVINGS

30 Point 6 A 10 a

Brass Candle Sticks embossed
GEOMETRICAL DESIGNS

36 Point 5 A 7 a

Stained Glass Windows
THE MODERN ART

48 Point 4 A 6 a

Information Office
MASTERPIECES

BAUER MAKERS OF FINE TYPES FOR MORE THAN A CENTURY

Ernst Schneidler (1882–1956) was a German type designer, educator and publisher, and one of the finest calligraphers of his generation. He originally designed Schneidler Medieval in 1936 for the Bauer type foundry in Berlin. It was later called Schneidler Old Style, although it was also marketed as Bauer Text. The design takes its inspiration from the typefaces cut for Venetian printers in the Renaissance period. Although Schneidler Old Style does not follow any specific model, it reproduces the dignified tone of the types of Nicolas Jenson (pp20–21) and Aldus Manutius (pp30–31).

Schneidler Old Style is a considered attempt to replicate the appearance of early printing by exploiting a number of subtle optical strategies. Its contours follow the proportions of its Venetian models, with an x-height that balances well with ascenders and capitals that are quite large, like those of Jenson. However, Schneidler Old Style is almost monotone. Stroke contrast is very low, with horizontals that are only slightly narrower than stems. In addition, junctions are slightly rounded to match the serif terminals, which also have small concave indentations throughout. In use, these features impart a pale, even rhythm, with soft swellings that give the distinctly inky impression of a text that appears to have been printed from antique metal type.

Schneidler Old Style survives today as a delicate typeface that performs well in display applications and that is reasonably effective in text.

M 3

Ty	**Bernhard Modern**
Ca	**Serif**
Ke	**Old Style**
Te	**Letterpress**
Da	**1937**
De	**Lucian Bernhard**
Fo	**American Type Founders**
Co	**USA**

Characteristics

	Oblique stress
	High stroke contrast
	Small x-height
	Elongated ascenders and short descenders
A	Extended stroke at apex
J	Descends below baseline
M	Splayed
Q	Sweeping tail below letter
W	Crossed centre-strokes
a	Double-storeyed, round bowl
f	Narrow, non-kerning
g	Double-storeyed, small lower bowl
k	Upper bowl

AJMQW
abcefghijk
orstuya*efg*

Connections

Nicolas-Cochin	1912
Koch Antiqua	1922
Bernhard Fashion	1929
Belucian	1990

Availability

Bernhard Modern is widely available

Specimen

Bernhard Modern type specimen.
American Type Founders, New Jersey,
c1937 (275x190mm)

BERNHARD MODERN ROMAN

MARKwell the

MARKwell the b

MARKwell the bea

MARK well the bea

MARK well the beau

MARKwell the beautyo

MARK well the beauty of

MARK well the beauty of pages

MARK well the beauty of pages print

MARK WELL THE BEAUTY OF PAG
Mark well the beauty of pages printed with

MARK WELL THE BEAUTY OF PAGES
Mark well the beauty of pages printed with th

MARK WELL THE BEAUTY OF PAGES PRI
Mark well the beauty of pages printed with the care

A B C D E F G H I
J K L M N O P Q R
S T U V W X Y Z &
. , - ' ' " " : ; ! ? §
$ 1 2 3 4 5 6 7 8 9 0 ¢
a b c d e f g h i
j k l m n o p q r
s t u v w x y z

Characters " " are not made in 8 and 10 point

72
3A

60 p
3A

48 p
5A

42 p
5A

36 p
6A

30 p
7A

24 p
8A

18 po
14A 2

14 po
19A 3

12 po
22A 4

10 po
26A 5

8 po
28A 5

32

298

BERNHARD MODERN ITALIC

Bernhard Modern is a serif typeface designed by Lucian Bernhard (1883–1972) in 1937 for American Type Founders. A German émigré to the United States, Bernhard was an artist, teacher and prolifically talented designer. In 1928 he signed a contract with ATF and proceeded to produce around 36 typefaces during the following decades, including bestsellers like Bernhard Gothic, Bernhard Fashion and Tango.

Bernhard Modern was Lucian Bernhard's response to the popularity of the sharply defined faces of the early twentieth century which had been loosely based on letters from baroque copper engravings, such as Peignot & Sons' Nicolas-Cochin (pp192–93).

Bernhard Modern is a somewhat decorative typeface that is distinctive in display applications but remains reasonably effective in text. It has a crisp, calligraphic impression which echoes the cultivated poise of the art deco style, with a sharp contrast between thin and thick strokes and wide, splayed flat serifs. Like many of Bernhard's designs, it is an extremely tall typeface with a small x-height and elongated ascenders that extend above capitals that are already large. The ascender length is offset by relatively short descenders, providing an appearance of towering height without requiring excessive leading.

point 4a
MARK well the

point 6a
MARK well the b

point 10a
MARK well the bea

point 11a
MARK well the beau

point 11a
MARK well the beaut

point 13a
MARK well the beauty o

point 17a
MARK well the beauty of t

point 28a
MARK well the beauty of pages

point 38a
MARK well the beauty of pages printe

point 44a
MARK WELL THE BEAUTY OF PAG
Mark well the beauty of pages printed with t

point 52a
MARK WELL THE BEAUTY OF PAGE
Mark well the beauty of pages printed with th

point 58a
MARK WELL THE BEAUTY OF PAGES PR
Mark well the beauty of pages printed with the care

A B C D E F G H I
J K L M N O P Q R
S T U V W X Y Z &
. , - ' ' " " : ; ! ?
$ 1 2 3 4 5 6 7 8 9 0
a b c d e f g h i
j k l m n o p q r
s t u v w x y z Th

Characters " " are not made in 8 and 10 point

33

Ty	**Peignot**
Ca	**Sans Serif**
Ke	**Geometric**
Te	**Letterpress**
Da	**1937**
De	**A. M. Cassandre**
Fo	**Deberny & Peignot**
Co	**France**

Characteristics

Vertical stress

Moderate stroke contrast

Elongated ascenders

Conventional capitals

a e g h m n q r t Lower case characters have upper case contours

h Upper case form with ascender

AEGQRS
abcdefghij
knoprstuy

Connections

Universal Type	1925
Bifur	1929
Chambord	1945
Gerstner Original BQ	1987

Availability

Peignot is available from Linotype and resellers

Specimen

Le Peignot: Caractère dessiné par A. M. Cassandre. Deberny & Peignot, Paris, 1937 (320x245mm)

prouvent abondamment que la forme a bas de casse n'est autre, à son origine, que la forme A déformée à travers les siècles par les scribes jusqu'à l'invention de l'Imprimerie... Celle-ci, soucieuse, à ses débuts, d'imiter les manuscrits, adopta a minuscule, qui servit ensuite de thème à toutes les déformations décoratives. Ce qui est vrai pour a minuscule l'est aussi pour un grand nombre de lettres. D'ailleurs, si c, i, o, s, u, v, x, y, ont la même forme originelle, dans leur aspect "capitales" et dans leur aspect "bas de casse", c'est uniquement parce que ces formes simples s'écrivaient facilement et que la main des scribes n'a pas éprouvé le besoin de les simplifier.

Mais rien, dans la technique d'imprimerie, ne nous empêche de revenir aux formes classiques et nobles de la lettre et d'abandonner des formes bas de casse qui, avant peu, paraîtront aussi archaïques que les formes des caractères gothiques.

Une seule condition s'impose : le respect de la lisibilité; or, de toute évidence, un texte en capitales est moins lisible qu'un texte en bas de casse. Pourquoi ? Mais uniquement parce que le mot prend une forme rectangulaire monotone qui n'offre à l'œil aucun point de repère. Or, l'œil saisit la silhouette d'un mot, voire d'un groupe de mots; il n'épelle pas chaque lettre, il ne décompose pas le mot en lettres, ce qui, au contraire, est le fait du correcteur.

Cette habitude que l'œil a prise des longues du haut et du bas est de celles qui doivent être respectées, ce qui explique que, dans le PEIGNOT, nous ayons conservé ces auxiliaires indispensables à une lecture facile. Aucune de ces longues du bas et du haut n'est cependant anachronique : l, b, f, sont des capitales atrophiées ; h, k, sont des capitales que leur haste adapte à la lecture; p, q, y, sont des capitales dont la ligne est descendue. Seul de toutes les minuscules, d, de forme cursive, subsiste, mais, dans l'état actuel des habitudes de la lecture, il est impossible de le concevoir autrement.

Il se peut que ce principe nouveau heurte; mais, s'il est des habitudes respectables auxquelles il faut se plier, il en est d'autres qui se perdront facilement parce qu'elles n'ont aucune racine physiologique profonde dans l'individu. D'autres habitudes naîtront, et c'est parce qu'il en est ainsi que le Garamont ou le Didot eussent gêné l'œil des scribes du Moyen Age.

Le rythme de l'évolution de la forme des lettres à travers les siècles est lent, mais cela n'implique pas que cette évolution ne se poursuive. Les scribes ont mis dix siècles à déformer la capitale des Romains; l'Imprimerie aura mis cinq siècles à influencer la forme fondamentale des lettres.

ALPHABET

DEMI-GRAS C. 60

A A B b C c D d E E F f G G

H H I i J j K k L L M M N N

O O P P Q Q R R S S T T U U

V V W W X X Y Y Z Z

1 2 3 4 5 6 7 8 9 0

1 2 3 4 5 6 7 8 9 0

Peignot was designed by A. M. Cassandre (1901–68) for the French foundry Deberny & Peignot in 1937. Largely because of Cassandre's reputation as the leading poster designer in France during the art deco period, Peignot is often identified as a novel display typeface that exemplifies its flamboyant style. However, closer examination reveals a design of considerably more depth and integrity, based on a considered exploration of typographic form. Equally as radical and ambitious as the alphabets designed by Josef Albers (pp212–13), Herbert Bayer (pp222–23) and others a few years previously, Cassandre's typeface is notable for its amalgamation of upper and lower case characters in place of a conventional lower case.

In designing Peignot's letterforms, Cassandre researched the origins of roman type in the scribal writing of the early medieval era with the intention of achieving a perfected form stripped of any extraneous elements. He believed that many typographic attributes that the alphabet had accumulated over the centuries were ornamental redundancies and should be eradicated. Anticipating that doing so would lead to the next step in the evolution of the printed word, he proposed that 'There is no technical reason in printing why we cannot return to the noble classical shapes of the alphabet and discard the lower case forms'.

To achieve this revolutionary objective, Cassandre substituted 11 minuscule characters whose form was unique with hybrid versions of corresponding capital letters. Because his intention was for Peignot to be used as a book face, he added elongated ascenders and descenders to them where appropriate in order to maintain character differentiation in bodies of extended text.

Available in three upright weights, Peignot is a geometrically constructed typeface with a pronounced vertical stress and high contrast between thick and thin strokes. Graceful and well proportioned, it is characterized by its elongated extenders and the absence of serifs.

Unsurprisingly, Peignot did not bring about the next stage in literacy that Cassandre had hoped to achieve. In contradiction to its designer's intentions, however, it became a very popular typeface in posters, advertising and brand communications throughout the twentieth century.

Ty	**Stencil**
Ca	**Serif**
Ke	**Clarendon, Capitals, Stencil**
Te	**Letterpress**
Da	**1937**
De	**Gerry Powell**
Fo	**American Type Founders**
Co	**USA**

Characteristics

Character construction based on
Clarendon model
Bold capitals only
Small, rounded slab serifs
Narrow stencil bridges

ABCDEG
IJMOPQ
RSTUXZ

Connections

Tea-Chest	1939
Glaser Stencil	1970
FF Flightcase	1992
Le Corbusier	1999

Availability

Stencil is widely available

Specimen

Stencil type specimen. American Type
Founders, Jersey City, c1937 (279x216mm)

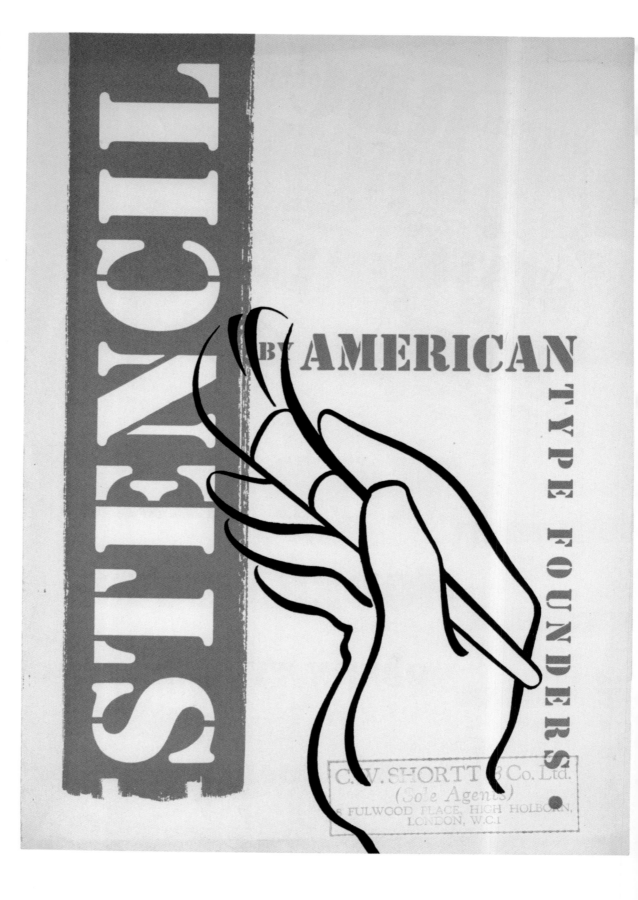

Stencilled lettering originated in texts produced at large sizes for German and French liturgical books of the seventeenth century. With the expansion of global trade in the late 1800s, the technique also became widely used in commerce. Product consignments could be rapidly and efficiently identified by branding them with stencilled letters, typically on wooden chests, for maritime transportation around the world. Stencils were necessarily simple to apply and had to be sufficiently resilient to survive repeated use without collapsing. Their lettering was utilitarian, economical with space and bold in weight in order to be easily recognized at a distance.

By the middle of the nineteenth century a number of proprietary devices were available for the production of trade stencils. These often consisted of thin metal plates carrying individual glyphs that could be interlocked to make word forms. They were sold in various lettering styles, some of which resembled thickened versions of Clarendon (pp132–33) or Didot (pp90–91), although the stencil forms have features that are the product of their own manufacture and usage. Stencil letters are inevitably robust in their construction. They are also distinguishable by their breaks, a result of the bridges that hold the stencil templates together to retain the negative spaces of the letters.

This basic industrial letterform was translated into display type in two competing designs released within a month of each other in 1937. The first was created by Robert Hunter Middleton (1898–1985) for the Ludlow typecaster, while Gerry Powell's (1899–?) version for American Type Founders was released very shortly afterwards. Both typefaces are faithful mechanical reproductions of original stencil forms. Virtually indistinguishable, they consist of capital letters with fat strokes, small bracketed serifs and softly rounded corners.

At the time of their release, bold, blocky typefaces were hugely popular and Stencil became a useful addition to the catalogues of many printing workshops. After World War II, when US military vehicles were identified with genuine stencils, Powell's typeface became widely used by designers as a signifier for any association with the US Army. Stencil's military connotations persist today in the host of digital versions that are available.

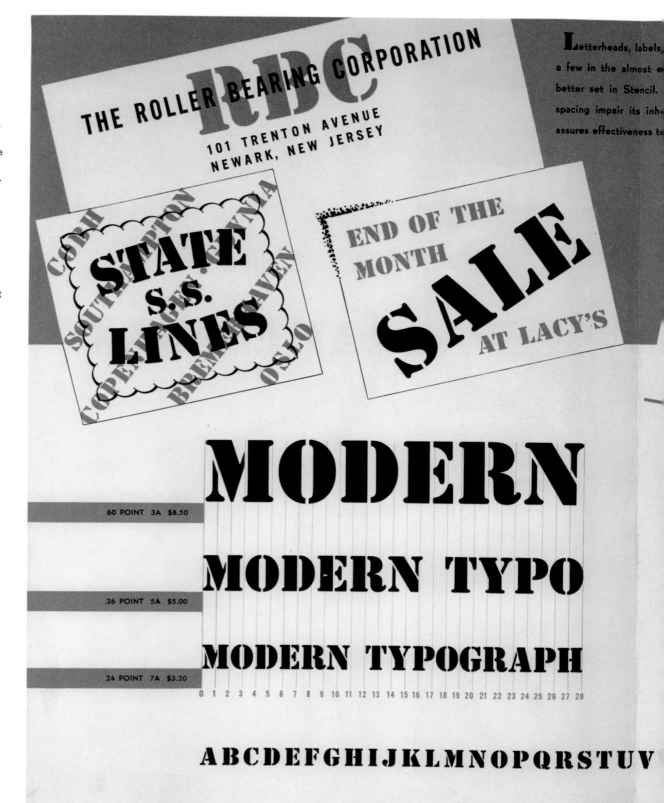

Ty	**Caledonia**
Ca	**Serif**
Ke	**Transitional**
Te	**Letterpress**
Da	**1938**
De	**William Addison Dwiggins**
Fo	**Linotype**
Co	**USA**

Characteristics

G	Open, no spur
J	Descends below baseline
Q	Short curved tail below letter
R	Curved tail
f	Large ear
g	Ear turns up
t	Unbracketed

AGJMQR
abcdefghij
orstuy*aefg*

Connections

Baskerville	1757
Bell	1788
Bulmer	1792
Scotch Roman	1812

Availability

Caledonia is available from Linotype and resellers

Specimen

A New Printing Type: Caledonia.
Mergenthaler Linotype Company,
New York, 1939 (200x140mm)

In 1938 the Mergenthaler Linotype Company invited W. A. Dwiggins (1880–1956) to renovate their version of Scotch Roman (pp112–13), a book type style that was seen everywhere at the time.

Considering Scotch Roman to be structurally deficient, Dwiggins attempted to amalgamate the best features of Baskerville, Bodoni and Didot into a new design. However, after struggling to achieve a harmonious and distinctive combination of modern and old styles, he abandoned this approach and turned to a type drawn by William Martin for William Bulmer in 1792 (pp98–99) as the cornerstone for his new typeface.

Caledonia, which takes its name from the Roman name for Scotland, has a very well-judged anatomy, with proportions that make for easy readability. Upper case and lower case are visually balanced, with capitals shorter than the ascenders of the lower case letters in order not to obtrude. The type has a vertical stress, with an x-height that is generous but not large, and a stroke contrast that is pronounced, although thin strokes hold well even at smaller sizes. Caledonia's calligraphic details reveal a playfulness that is typical of Dwiggins's work. Notably, ascenders are slightly thinner at the foot than at the top, giving a lively impression. Many characters also have their own internal logic. The a, for instance, has a heavy bottom terminal to the right, while the e is almost perfectly round. This varied approach to construction gives the type an animated appearance without becoming too eccentric or attention-seeking.

Dwiggins paid close attention to the appearance of the type at small sizes, particularly in the transitions of the curves into the vertical stems of, for example, the h, m, n and the left of the small u. The tops and bottoms of these arcs are very round, thin and open in a modern face style, but where they swell into the stem, the transitions become sharp points.

By combining the rational qualities of Bulmer with the more varied appearance of Scotch Roman, Dwiggins achieved a balanced typeface that quickly became one of the most successful ever produced in the United States. Maintaining its integrity across a range of printing conditions and materials, Caledonia has since been widely used in publishing and editorial work.

x

FIGURE 3   *On the trail*

hamıle nt
amulet pi
mhnjup

The next effort was a look at Baskerville and Bodoni and Didot, and all the designers who were working in that general direction. The results did not get very far: merely a rehash of the old forms without any improvement. (*fig.* 2) One was not trying for a *revival*, one wanted something modern and individual.

CALEDONIA   *xj*

FIGURE 4   *The Final Effort*

mhnjuf

dbosrt ag

Then, in pursuit of lively curves combined with a general "modern face" atmosphere, we turned to one of the types that Bulmer used, cut for him by William Martin around 1790—and here seemed a good place to start again. The Martin letters were more slender than the face one had in mind, so an attempt was made to add weight to the characters and still keep some of the Martin swing (*fig.* 3). The result of this last effort (*fig.* 4) was most promising; so we went on and finished the alphabets in the form shown in this text; and christened the face CALEDONIA because the project was inspired in

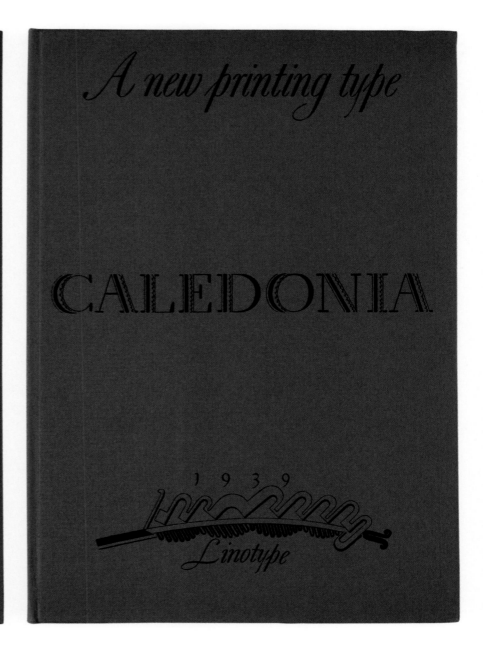

Ty	**Lydian**
Ca	**Sans Serif**
Ke	**Calligraphic**
Te	**Letterpress**
Da	**1938**
De	**Warren Chappell**
Fo	**American Type Founders**
Co	**USA**

Characteristics

A N	Angled apex extends to left
E F T	Angled terminals
U	Right stem extends to baseline
W	Crossed centre-strokes
e	Bevelled crossbar junction

AENORW
abcdefgijk
orstyaefg

Connections

Klang	1955
Optima	1958
ITC Tiepolo	1987
Harbour	1998

Availability

Lydian is widely available

Specimen

Lydian and Lydian Italic type specimen.
American Type Founders, New Jersey,
c1938 (297x210mm)

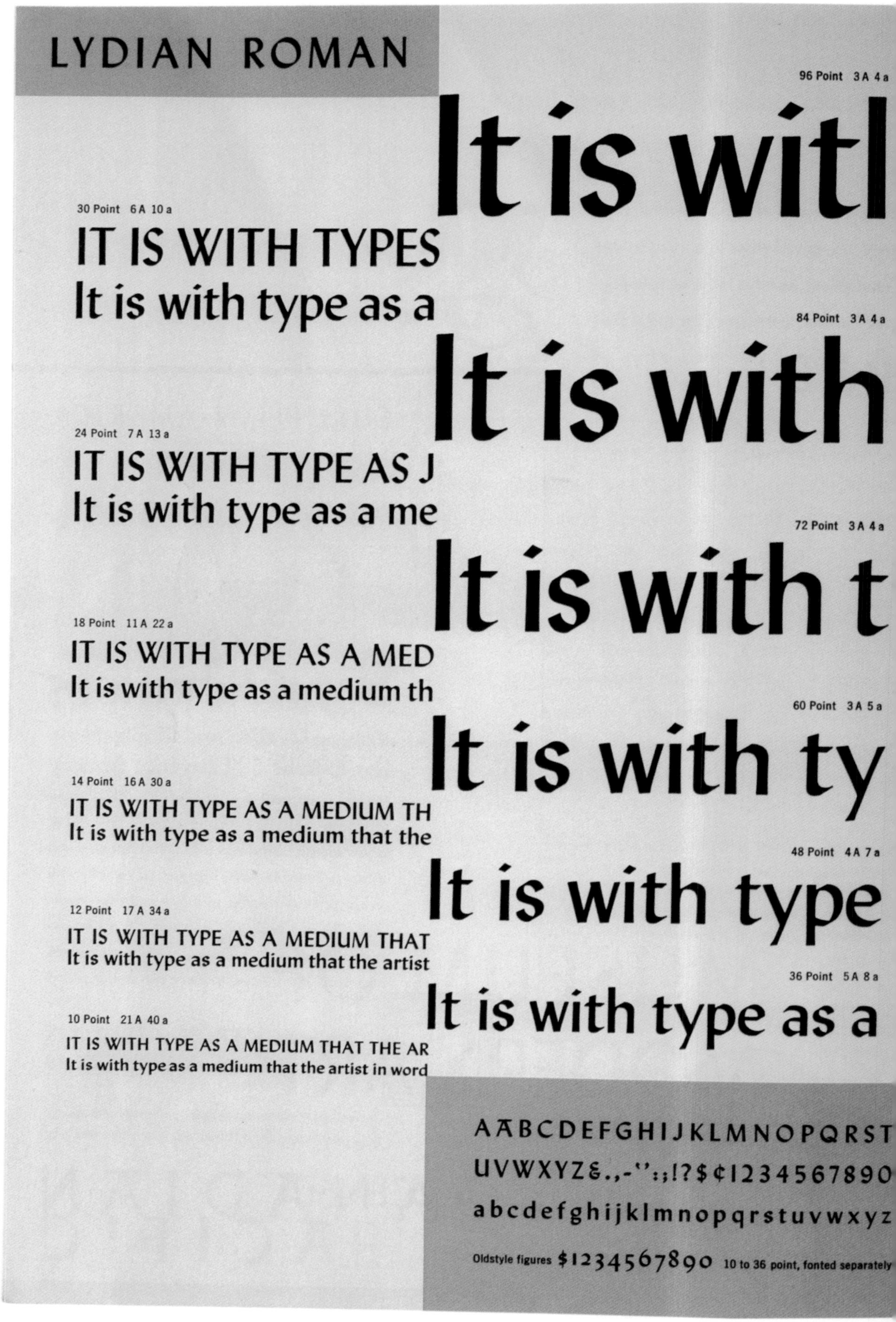

LYDIAN ROMAN

96 Point 3A 4a

It is witl

30 Point 6A 10a

IT IS WITH TYPES
It is with type as a

84 Point 3A 4a

It is with

24 Point 7A 13a

IT IS WITH TYPE AS J
It is with type as a me

72 Point 3A 4a

It is with t

18 Point 11A 22a

IT IS WITH TYPE AS A MED
It is with type as a medium th

60 Point 3A 5a

It is with ty

14 Point 16A 30a

IT IS WITH TYPE AS A MEDIUM TH
It is with type as a medium that the

48 Point 4A 7a

It is with type

12 Point 17A 34a

IT IS WITH TYPE AS A MEDIUM THAT
It is with type as a medium that the artist

36 Point 5A 8a

It is with type as a

10 Point 21A 40a

IT IS WITH TYPE AS A MEDIUM THAT THE AR
It is with type as a medium that the artist in word

AĀBCDEFGHIJKLMNOPQRST
UVWXYZ&.,-'':;!?$¢1234567890
abcdefghijklmnopqrstuvwxyz
Oldstyle figures $1234567890 10 to 36 point, fonted separately

LYDIAN ITALIC

96 Point 3A 4a

It is with

84 Point 3A 4a

It is withi

72 Point 3A 4a

It is with tr

60 Point 3A 5a

It is with typ

48 Point 4A 8a

It is with type a

36 Point 5A 9a

It is with type as a n

30 Point 6A 11a

IT IS WITH TYPES
It is with type as a t

24 Point 7A 14a

IT IS WITH TYPE AS I
It is with type as a med

18 Point 12A 24a

IT IS WITH TYPE AS A MEDI
It is with type as a medium tha

14 Point 16A 32a

IT IS WITH TYPE AS A MEDIUM TH
It is with type as a medium that the a

12 Point 19A 38a

IT IS WITH TYPE AS A MEDIUM THAT T
It is with type as a medium that the artist

10 Point 22A 44a

IT IS WITH TYPE AS A MEDIUM THAT THE ARTI
It is with type as a medium that the artist in word

ABCDEFGHIJKLMNOPQRST
VWXYZ&.,-'':;!?$¢1234567890
bcdefghijklmnopqrstuvwxyz

dstyle figures $1234567890 10 to 36 point, fonted separately

Around ten years after geometric types conquered the typographic scene during the 1920s their popularity began to wane a little and a variety of new alternatives started to come onto the market. In 1938 American Type Founders released one such design, a sans serif submitted to the company by Warren Chappell (1904–91), an American who had studied type design and punch cutting with Rudolf Koch (pp214–15, 232–33) in the early 1930s.

Lydian, named after the designer's wife, Lydia, is an unusual sans serif face with strongly calligraphic letter shapes that clearly show the influence of Koch's teaching. They give the impression of lettering made with a broad pen held at a 45-degree angle, particularly in the rounded capitals C, G, O and Q, but with stroke terminations that are square and almost flat throughout, providing a stable and clean appearance.

The original foundry type was cast by ATF and included an alternate capital A with an extended bar at the apex and a choice of lining or non-lining figures. Among the other members of the family introduced over the next decade the most successful is a very legible italic with an even more markedly pen-drawn structure.

Although the italic, shown on this page, gives the appearance of having been executed with the same instrument as the roman, it is somewhat freer and more natural, in a style unmatched by any other script at the time. Lydian Bold Condensed, added by Chappell in 1946, has the general character of the earlier faces, but with much greater emphasis on the vertical strokes, giving the effect of a simplified, romanized German blackletter.

Lydian was an immediate hit and it continued to be well used as a display and advertising type for several decades after its introduction.

Ty	**Reporter**
Ca	**Script**
Ke	**Informal, Connected**
Te	**Letterpress**
Da	**1938**
De	**Carl Winckow**
Fo	**Johannes Wagner**
Co	**Germany**

Characteristics

Informal, connected script

Imitates flow and texture of a dry brush

Long ascenders and descenders at varied angles

ABCMOS
abcdefghij
klnoprstuy

Connections

Kaufmann	1936
Brush Script	1942
Mistral	1953
Loupot	1998

Availability

Reporter #2 is widely available

Specimen

Reporter type specimen. Johannes Wagner, Berlin, c1936 (270x210mm)

Überall, wohin man in der Ausstellung blickt, wirken das vervielfältigte Bild und das gedrückte Wort auf uns

Nr. 9910   Korpus (10 Punkt)   Min. etwa 9 kg   130 a 60 A

Von Hamburg über Antwerpen, Southampton, Lissabon, Tanger, Algier nach Genua-Italien

Nr. 9912   Cicero (12 Punkt)   Min. etwa 10 kg   110 a 48 A

Auf der großen 9. Internationalen Handwerks-Ausstellung in Bremen

Nr. 9916   Tertia (16 Punkt)   Min. etwa 12 kg   78 a 32 A

Entdeckungen, Menschenschicksale in unserem Zeitalter

Nr. 9920   Text (20 Punkt)   Min. etwa 14 kg   60 a 24 A

Die Feier zur Grundsteinlegung in Ludwigshafen

Nr. 9924   2 Cicero (24 Punkt)   Min. etwa 16 kg   50 a 20 A

Ulmer Grasbahn-Rennen für Motorräder

Nr. 9928   Doppelmittel (28 Punkt)   Min. etwa 18 kg   40 a 16 A

Nr. 9936   3 Cicero (36 Punkt)   Min. etwa 20 kg   26 a 12 A

Nr. 9948   4 Cicero (48 Punkt)   Min. etwa 22 kg   16 a 6 A

Nr. 9960   5 Cicero (60 Punkt)   Min. etwa 26 kg   12 a 4 A

Nr. 9972   6 Cicero (72 Punkt)   Min. etwa 30 kg   12 a 4 A

Größere Grade
als Plakatschrift in Holz
bis 24 Cicero lieferbar

Reporter, released by the Johannes Wagner foundry in 1938, was the product of two years of painstaking work by Carl Winckow (1882–1952), an experienced German punch cutter. Johannes Wagner, the proprietor of one of Berlin's leading type foundries, had for some years intended to produce a more vigorous script than those available at the time. His plan was to cut a type based on an original brush-drawn alphabet but he was unable to find anyone who could produce a satisfactory script. Finally, in 1936, Winckow submitted a drawing presenting a few words that Wagner accepted as a starting point for further development.

Rather than proceeding to draw a set of single letters, Winckow began by hand-lettering complete words, their individual characters and sequences forming the basis for the final alphabet. By working in this way, he maintained a consistent bond between natural handwriting and typographic forms, ensuring that Reporter would be lively and authentic in its appearance. To give variety to the shapes of characters and their joining strokes, and to avoid excessive repetitions, Winckow also produced a large number of alternate characters and ligatures. For nearly two years he diligently cut more than 1,600 characters, treating each as a unique form.

The result of his efforts is a strikingly dynamic script that has a handwritten appearance in spite of the limitations of foundry setting. Reporter's strokes have the texture of dry brush-written letters with numerous small white marks inside their stems, emphasizing a sense of movement. Although the letters are not connected in the conventional sense, they flow together seamlessly and are aligned on a slightly irregular baseline, resulting in spontaneous, energetic settings. Winckow also created a simplified version, Reporter #2, omitting the internal white strokes.

The Wagner foundry went to great lengths to demonstrate Reporter's versatility in its publicity material and it attracted much interest among printers and designers when released in 1938. Combining boldness with informality, it has since found wide use in signage, posters and other display applications.

Ty	**Schadow-Antiqua**
Ca	**Slab Serif**
Ke	**Egyptian**
Te	**Letterpress**
Da	**1938**
De	**Georg Trump**
Fo	**C. E. Weber**
Co	**Germany**

Characteristics

Slightly condensed overall
Large x-height
Short ascenders and descenders
Light, square serifs
Q Short, straight tail below letter
a Double-storeyed, round bowl
f Narrow, rounded top-stroke
g Double-storeyed, shallow lower bowl
j Straight, angled tail
y Hooked tail

AEGMQR
abcdefghij
koprstuvy

Connections

Joanna	1931
Candida	1936
Melior	1952
FF Scala	1991

Availability

Schadow is available from MyFonts and resellers

Specimen

Schadow-Antiqua type specimen. C. E. Weber, Stuttgart, c1938 (297x210mm)

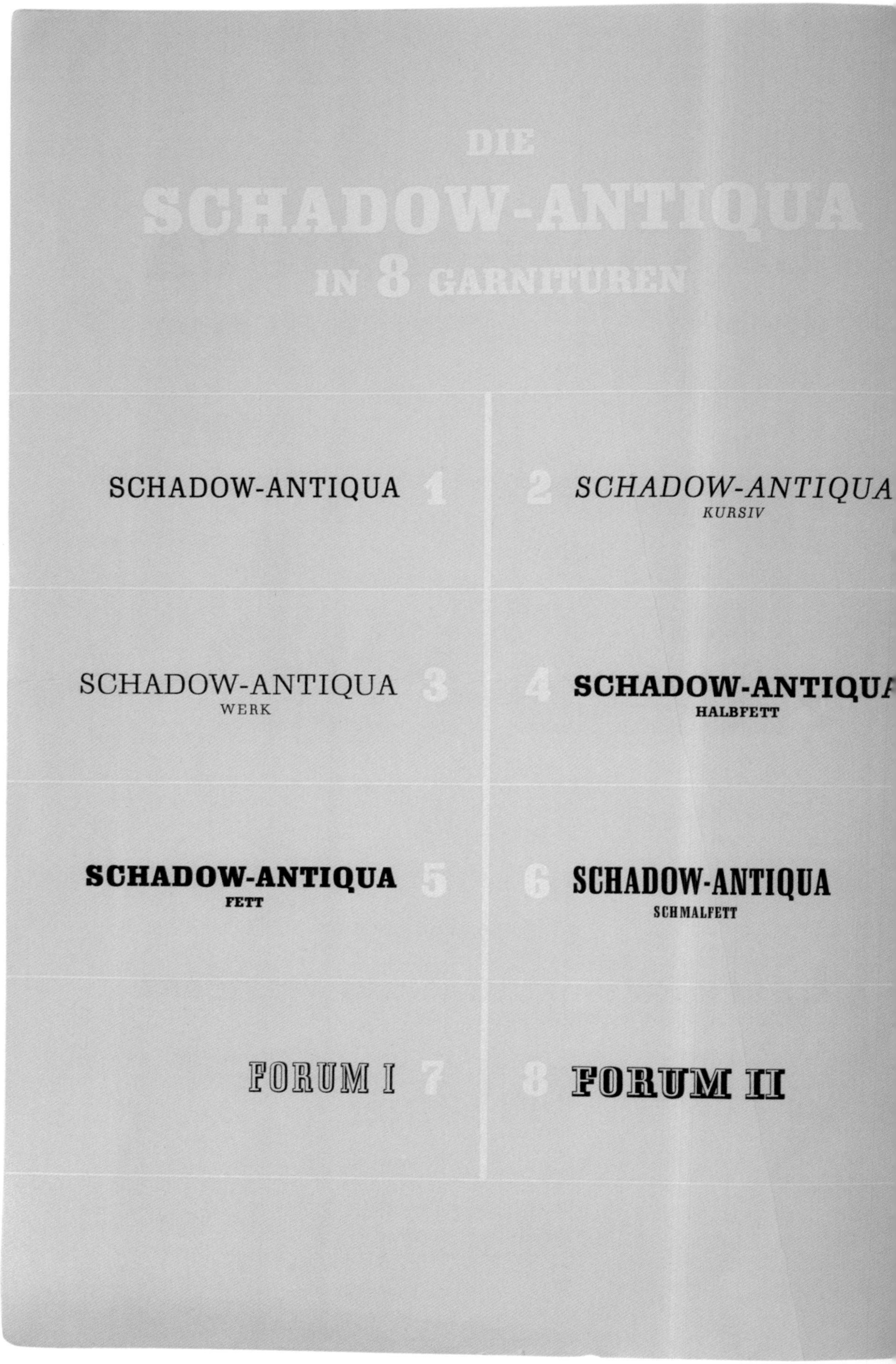

DIE
SCHADOW-ANTIQUA
IN 8 GARNITUREN

SCHADOW-ANTIQUA 1

2 SCHADOW-ANTIQUA
KURSIV

SCHADOW-ANTIQUA 3
WERK

4 SCHADOW-ANTIQUA
HALBFETT

SCHADOW-ANTIQUA 5
FETT

6 SCHADOW-ANTIQUA
SCHMALFETT

FORUM I 7

8 FORUM II

AN SIEHT ZWAR NICHT, WAS EIN MENSCH denkt, aber daß er denkt, sieht man. Die Seele läßt sich nicht malen, wohl aber die Beseeltheit. In den Blicken, Mienen, Gebärden, Haltungen besitzen wir sichtbare Anweisungen auf ein nicht Sichtbares. Wäre es anders, so könnte kein Maler und kein Bildhauer einem Menschenantlitz den Stempel des Geistes aufprägen. Wer die von Figuren wimmelnde Welt der Bilder durchwandert, begegnet hier und da den stillen Gestalten der Denker. Es gibt kaum einen Moment des geistigen Lebens, welcher nicht einem Künstler als Inspiration oder als Motiv gedient hat.

1479 5/6 P. etwa 3 kg 168 a 54 A   2 P. Durchschuß

ZWEI GRUNDFORMEN DES LEBENS SIND uns aus der Philosophie des Mittelalters überliefert: das tätige Leben, die vita activa und das beschauliche Leben, die vita contemplativa, das Wort beschaulich ist bestimmt keine glückliche Übersetzung von kontemplativ, da es einen Beigeschmack von gemütlicher Untätigkeit hat, richtiger wäre zu reden von einem besinnlichen Leben. Man unterschied die psychologischen Typen der Täter und der Denker. Nach außen hin sich abschließend und nach innen sich willig öffnend.

1480 6 P. etwa 3,5 kg 168 a 54 A   3 P. Durchschuß

IN DER SPANISCHEN KAPELLE SANTA Maria Novella in Florenz hat Andrea da Firenze die Helden der Kirche dargestellt. Eine in tiefes Nachdenken versunkene männliche Sitzfigur bedeutet die kontemplative Theologie, veranschaulicht aber den Denkenden im Zustande der Kontemplation. Das Buch im Arm, das gedankenschwere Haupt in die Hand gestützt, harrt die Gestalt des Weisen schon auf den Augenblick der Inspiration.

1481 7/8 P.   4,5 kg 140 a 44 A   2 P. Durchschuß

EMBRANDT HAT WIEDERHOLT Denkergestalten in ihren Klausen, lesend, schreibend, disputierend, einsam sinnend, gemalt. Über diese, Stilleben und Genrebild verbindende Gruppe der sogenannten Philosophen ragt hinauf in das Sinnbildliche, so Rembrandts Spätwerk, Aristoteles mit der Büste Homers. Es beruht in der tiefen Kontemplation.

1482 8 P. etwa 5 kg 140 a 44 A   3 P. Durchschuß

IM DEM MUTTERSCHOSS DER besinnlichen Gestimmtheit versteckt ruhen noch die Gedanken. Der Moment der Inspiration ist die Freude ihrer Geburt. Das Rätsel der Inspiration löst niemand. Wer unternahm, diesen Seelenvorgang zu beschreiben, ist fremden Gewalten gewichen.

1483 9/10 P. etwa 5 kg 108 a 34 A 2 P. Durchschuß

DIE MALEREI HAT, UM EINE Eintönigkeit zu vermeiden sowie Gegensätze sprechen zu lassen, öfter die Denkergestalten gleich paarweise auftreten lassen. Solche «Philosophenehepaare» hat auch Joos van Gent schon gemalt.

1484 10 P. etwa 5,5 kg 108 a 34 A 4 P. Durchschuß

SCHADOW-ANTIQUA

Europäische Buchgemeinschaft Düsseldorf

1485 12 P. Satz etwa 6 kg 80 a 26 A

Württembergische Möbelwerkstätte

1486 14 P. Satz etwa 7 kg 68 a 22 A

HUNTER ELECTRO COPYIST

1487 16 P. Satz etwa 8 kg 60 a 20 A

Aktuelle Rundfunkschau

1488 20 P. Satz etwa 9,5 kg 44 a 16 A

Bremer Handelsbank

1489 24 P. Satz etwa 10 kg 36 a 12 A

Fahrschule Endel

1490 28 P. Satz etwa 12 kg 30 a 10 A

Stahlindustrie

1491 36 P. Satz etwa 13,5 kg 18 a 8 A

Adreßbuch

1492 48 P. etwa 12 kg etwa 9,5 kg

Mercura

1493 60 P. etwa 17 kg etwa 12 kg

abcdefghijklmnopqrstuvwxyz1234567890ABCDEFGHIJKLMNOPQRSTUVWXYZ

Schadow-Antiqua represents a marked departure from the slab serif tradition to which it belongs. It was designed by Georg Trump (1896–1985) for the Stuttgart type foundry C. E. Weber in 1938. Trump created Schadow-Antiqua at a time when geometric slab serifs were the height of fashion in display applications. Rockwell (pp288–89), Stymie (pp278–79) and Trump's own City (pp256–57) were hugely popular at the time.

With its delicately modulated stroke contrast, slight compression and light, square serifs, Schadow-Antiqua was much more refined and better suited to general use in text. Like Eric Gill's Joanna (pp268–69), Schadow-Antiqua shows a combination of Egyptian and book-face characteristics although Trump's face is much more sturdy and unconventional.

The common features of Schadow-Antiqua's styles are its thin, flat serifs, a very subtle stroke contrast and a large lower case closely resembling that seen in typewriter faces. All weights share these family traits while avoiding the uniformity of many of today's type families. Drawn by hand, long before weights and widths could be interpolated automatically, the details of Schadow-Antiqua differ subtly from weight to weight. For example, in the regular, the Q has a short diagonal tail and the g has a closed lower bowl, while the book weight has a Q with a bent tail and a g with an open lower bowl.

In the 1950s Schadow-Antiqua was internationally successful but this did not last long. It soon became obsolete and, despite a digital revival by Bitstream in 2001, is seldom seen today.

University of California
Old Style

Ty	**University of California Old Style**
Ca	**Serif**
Ke	**Old Style**
Te	**Letterpress**
Da	**1938**
De	**Frederic W. Goudy**
Fo	**Monotype**
Co	**USA**

Characteristics

A	Apex extends to right
J	Descends below baseline
X	Curved, thinner stem
a	Blunt stem terminal
e	Oblique bar
f	Narrow, non-kerning
g	Ear curves upwards
u	Blunt stem terminal

AEJMQX
abcdefghij
orstuy*aefg*

Connections

Kennerley Old Style	1911
Goudy Oldstyle	1915
ITC Berkeley Oldstyle	1983
FF Scala	1991

Availability

ITC Berkeley Oldstyle is available from
Monotype and resellers

Specimen

Frederic W. Goudy, *Typologia*. University
of California Press, Berkeley, 1940
(270x175mm)

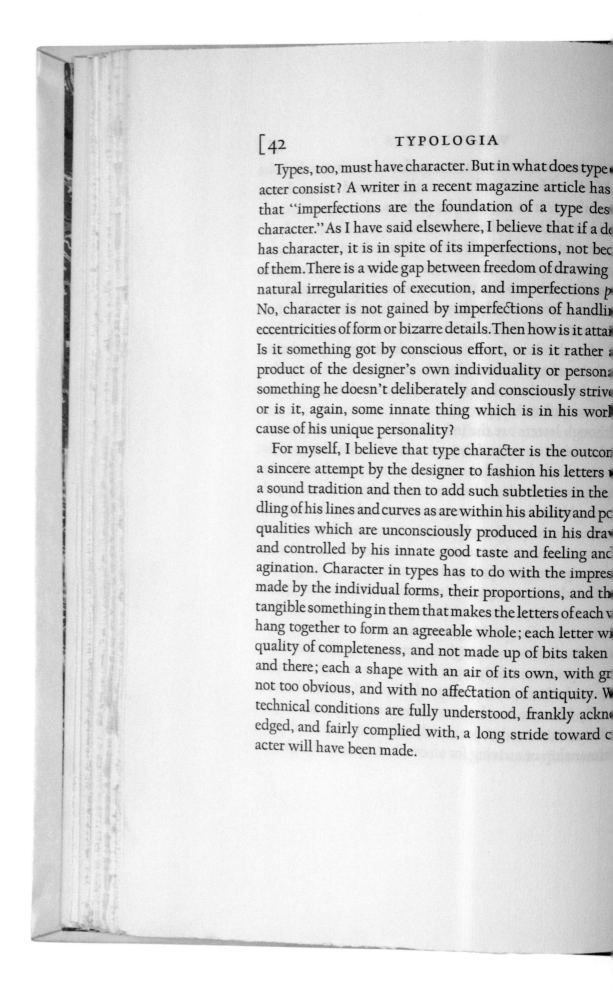

[42   TYPOLOGIA

Types, too, must have character. But in what does type
acter consist? A writer in a recent magazine article has
that "imperfections are the foundation of a type des
character." As I have said elsewhere, I believe that if a de
has character, it is in spite of its imperfections, not bec
of them. There is a wide gap between freedom of drawing
natural irregularities of execution, and imperfections p
No, character is not gained by imperfections of handli
eccentricities of form or bizarre details. Then how is it atta
Is it something got by conscious effort, or is it rather a
product of the designer's own individuality or persona
something he doesn't deliberately and consciously striv
or is it, again, some innate thing which is in his wor
cause of his unique personality?

For myself, I believe that type character is the outco
a sincere attempt by the designer to fashion his letters
a sound tradition and then to add such subtleties in the
dling of his lines and curves as are within his ability and po
qualities which are unconsciously produced in his dra
and controlled by his innate good taste and feeling and
agination. Character in types has to do with the impres
made by the individual forms, their proportions, and th
tangible something in them that makes the letters of each
hang together to form an agreeable whole; each letter wi
quality of completeness, and not made up of bits taken
and there; each a shape with an air of its own, with gr
not too obvious, and with no affectation of antiquity. W
technical conditions are fully understood, frankly ackn
edged, and fairly complied with, a long stride toward c
acter will have been made.

WHAT TYPE IS   43]

When a type design is good it is not because each individual letter of the alphabet is perfect in form, but because there is a feeling of harmony and unbroken rhythm that runs through the whole design, each letter kin to every other and to all.

One writer, in speaking of modern type design, says, "It is doubtful whether the type designer benefits from a close study of hand lettering," meaning a study of the manuscript hands of the past. In the main I am inclined to agree with him. I do find manuscript letters intensely interesting, but only occasionally do they suggest new type expressions to me. As a general thing I prefer to get my suggestions from a study of the earlier types that appeal to me, realizing of course that the types which I most admire were quite probably inspired by the very manuscript hands which I do not find of much use in my own work. With complete independence of calligraphy I attempt to secure, rather, the negative quality of unpretentiousness, and strive for the pure contour and monumental character of the classic Roman letters in the spirit of the best traditions, and avoid, as far as I am able, any fantastic quality or any exhibition of self-conscious preciosity.

My friend, Stanley Morison, has said, "The good type-designer knows that, for a new fount to be successful, it has to be so good that only very few recognize its novelty. If readers do not notice the consummate reticence and rare discipline of a new type it is probably a good letter. But if my friends think that the tail of my lower-case *r* or the lip of my lower-case *e* is rather jolly, you may know that the fount would have been better had neither been made." I am not sure that I accept his dictum completely, but inversely I have often said that when one friend or critic has found fault with the tail of an

In 1938 the type designer Frederic W. Goudy (1865–1947) was invited to draw a new typeface for the exclusive use of the University of California Press. Goudy accepted the task enthusiastically and a year later had built its foundations. He was pleased with his work; in fact, Goudy considered the design to be among his best. Originally called University of California Old Style, its first use was in Goudy's *Typologia*, shown here, published in 1940 by the press.

For many years, the typeface remained the property of the university and was not seen elsewhere, but in about 1958 it was renamed 'Californian' and a licence for the sale of the Monotype matrices was arranged. However, since the commercial release occurred during the last years of the Lanston Monotype Company in the United States, sales were poor, even though the typeface was well regarded.

Described in sales literature as adding 'an unmistakeable note of graciousness and quiet dignity to the most humdrum of printed pieces', University of California Old Style is a spacious, legible roman with a notably genial italic. The design is characterized by its calligraphic stress, smooth stroke-weight transitions, moderate x-height and square, solid serifs. These features combine in a highly readable face with a text colour that is light, even and easy on the eye.

University of California Old Style has been redrawn on a number of occasions and is better known today in the form of a photocomposition revival from 1983, when the International Typeface Corporation asked Tony Stan (1917–88) to revisit the Goudy design. His adaptation, ITC Berkeley Oldstyle, retains the sensibilities and dynamics of Goudy's original without being a slavish copy. A useful contribution in Stan's revival is the addition of three new weights – Medium, Bold and Black – which facilitate usage in a wide range of applications.

University of California Old Style balances easy readability with an honest dignity that is characteristic of Goudy's work. It is considered by many to be the finest typeface to have been produced by an American master craftsman whose typographic legacy remains unequalled.

Ty	**Chisel**
Ca	**Serif**
Ke	**Wedge, Glyphic, Decorative**
Te	**Letterpress**
Da	**1939**
De	**Robert Harling**
Fo	**Stephenson, Blake & Co.**
Co	**UK**

Characteristics

Character construction based on Latin
Wedge serifs
White inline contour
Small dropshadow to right
A Top serif at apex
C c e t Bulging, hooked tail
f r Hooked arch
f t Narrow
j y Hooked tail

ABCEMR
abcefghij
koprstuy

Connections

Latin	c1870
Tea-Chest	1939
Profil	1946
Saracen	1992

Availability

Chisel is available from URW and resellers

Specimen

Rich Fruity Latins. Stephenson, Blake & Co., Sheffield, c1960 (205x130mm)

Robert Harling (1910–2008) was a significant figure in twentieth-century British graphic design. As both an editor and a typographer, he bridged the gap between the gentlemanly commercial artists of the pre-war period and the professional graphic design practitioners who followed it.

Harling's lifelong fascination with graphic ephemera was influential in transforming contemporary popular taste in the UK, foreshadowing Pop Art and other 1960s design trends. In his twenties he co-founded and edited the groundbreaking journal *Typography*. As its editor he was responsible for the publication of articles on a broad range of subjects, many of which would be considered beneath the remit of typographic design at the time. As well as featuring contentious avant-garde design work from Europe, the journal explored such commonplace items as tea labels and tram tickets.

Harling's love of the vernacular and the everyday extended to his type designs. In addition to creating publicity material for the Stephenson, Blake foundry, he produced three popular display typefaces for the company. In 1938 he designed Playbill, followed by Chisel and Tea-Chest (pp316–17) in the next year. As their names suggest, all three are interpretations of letters associated with nineteenth-century commercial ephemera.

Chisel is based on Latin (pp140–41), a Victorian family of wedge-serifed display types in several widths that had been published by Stephenson, Blake & Co. in around 1870. In a playful tribute to the industrial age, Harling's design inscribes a sharp inline contour of variable width within the bodies of the Latin characters while adding a small dropshadow to the right. The effect, quite literally, is to cast a bright and friendly light on an otherwise austere form.

CHISEL

72 Point

ABCabc

60 Point

DEFdefgh

48 Point

GHIJKijkmn

36 Point

LMNOPQRSTU
opqrstuvwxyz-.

30 Point

VWXYZÆŒ&ABCDE
abcdefghijklmnopqr
tuvwxyzæœ
1234567890£$,.:;-!?

Chisel
expanded

48 Point
ABab

42 Point
CDEF!
cdefgh

36 Point
GHIJKL
ijklmno

30 Point
MNOPQR
pqrstuvx

18 Point
STUVWXYZ
abcdefghijkl
mnopqrstuv
wxyzæœ,.;:-!?'
&£$1234567

chisel
CHISEL

probably the most widely used
decorated letterform
hand tooled from Bold Latin Condensed

EXPANDED
expanded

hand tooled from Wide Latin

Ty	**Tea-Chest**
Ca	**Serif**
Ke	**Clarendon, Stencil, Capitals**
Te	**Letterpress**
Da	**1939**
De	**Robert Harling**
Fo	**Stephenson, Blake & Co.**
Co	**UK**

Characteristics

Bold, condensed capitals
Equal character widths
Short, bracketed serifs
Narrow stencil bridges

ABCEFGHJ KLMNOPQ RSTUWXYZ

Connections

Stencil	1937
Glaser Stencil	1970
Granite	1995
Le Corbusier	1999

Availability

Tea-Chest is widely available

Specimen

Tea-Chest: A Stencil Type. Stephenson, Blake & Co., Sheffield, c1950 (230x180mm)

3 SIZES OF TEA-CHEST

ABCDEFGHIJKL MNOPQRSTUVW

72 point   5 A; about 20 lb.

ABCDEFGHIJKLMN OPQRSTUVWXYZ12

60 point   5 A; about 13 lb.

ABCDEFGHIJKLMNOPQ RSTUVWXYZ&£!?234567

48 point   7 A; about 10 lb.

STEPHENSON BLAKE & CO LTD · THE CASLON LETTER FOUNDRY · SHEFFIELD

TEA-CHEST

A STENCIL TYPE

How strange that stencilled letter-forms have had no place in the spate of type designs which in recent years, has descended with such fury upon the unsuspecting printer and typographer. Stencils are certainly available and can be purchased from any shop dealing in artists' materials, but the so-called ease of handling of stencils is an overrated legend (as you will hear from any lettering artist) and the results are scarcely ever satisfactory. This is a pity, for the stencil character, if well-designed has many points in its favour.

Tea-chest is such a character. It is unusual, yet by no means bizarre or illegible. It is condensed, and will bring out those important words in a display with just the exact degree of emphasis. it is as suitable for use in the editorial pages of magazines as it is in the advertisement columns. Tea-chest is as useful for a letterhead as it is for a dust wrapper. Tea-chest is, in short, a display type which will find a ready place in the specification of the typographer and in the repertory of the printer and type-setter.

STEPHENSON BLAKE

STEPHENSON BLAKE & CO LTD · THE CASLON LETTER FOUNDRY · SHEFFIELD

The English typographer Robert Harling (1910–2008) created Tea-Chest for the Stephenson, Blake foundry in 1939. Unusually for a designer of his time, he found inspiration in a wide variety of artefacts from popular culture rather than from the typographic canon.

Tea-Chest exemplifies Harling's interest in the vernacular. It is a bold stencil face named after the trade lettering on which it was based. Originating in the late eighteenth century, these letters were stencilled crudely onto wooden crates for shipping on the high seas around the globe. Based on a condensed Clarendon form (pp136–137), they were necessarily simple to reproduce, bold and easy to read at a distance, and they were economical in their use of space.

Harling's typographic interpretation of these historic industrial letters is a display typeface in a single weight only: a bold condensed alphabet in capitals featuring short, thick, bracketed serifs that only extend to the outside of stems, and narrow stencil bridges giving the characters their uniquely utilitarian appearance.

Harling and Stephenson, Blake's intentions for Tea-Chest are revealed in the foundry's promotional brochure of the time: 'the stencil character, if well-designed has many points in its favour. Tea-chest is such a character. It is unusual, yet by no means bizarre or illegible. It is condensed, and will bring out those important words in a display with just the exact degree of emphasis. It is as suitable for use in the editorial pages of magazines as it is in the advertisement columns.'

Ty	**Fairfield**
Ca	**Serif**
Ke	**Old Style**
Te	**Letterpress**
Da	**1940**
De	**Rudolph Ruzicka**
Fo	**Linotype**
Co	**USA**

Characteristics

	High stroke contrast
A	Cupped, angled apex
J	Descends below baseline
K k	Bar links arm and tail to downstroke
M	Slightly splayed, angled vertex
Q	Sweeping tail below letter
R	Curved leg with flat serif
g	Double-storeyed, large upper bowl

AJKMQR
abcdefghij
orstuya*efg*

Connections

Joanna	1931
Electra	1935
Romulus	1936
Tyfa	1960

Availability

Fairfield is available from Linotype and resellers

Specimen

Specimen Book of Linotype Faces, 1940 Supplement. Mergenthaler Linotype Company, New York, 1940 (260x185mm)

II POINT

Linotype Fairfield

〜〜〜〜〜〜

HOW IS ONE TO ASSESS AND EVALUATE A TYPE FACE IN TERMS OF ITS ESTHETIC DESIGN? WHY DO THE PACE-MAKERS IN THE How is one to assess and evaluate a type face in terms of its esthetic design? Why do the pace-makers in the art of printing rave over a specific face of type? What do they see in it? Why is it so superlatively pleasant to their eyes? *Good design is always practical design.* And what they see in a good type design is, partly, its excellent practical fitness to perform its work. It has a "heft" and balance in all of its parts just right for its size, as any good tool has. Your good chair has all of its parts made nicely to the right size to do exactly the work that the chair has to do, neither clumsy and thick, nor "skinny" and weak, no waste of material and no lack of strength. And, beyond that, the chair may have been made by a man who worked out in it his sense of fine shapes and curves and proportions: it may be, actually, a work of art. The same thing holds for shapes of letters. And your chair, or your letter (if a true artist made it) will have, besides its good looks, a suitability to the *n*th degree to be sat in, or stamped on paper and read. That explains, in a way, why the experts rave over *How is one to assess and evaluate a type face in terms of its esthetic design? Why do the pace-makers in the art of printing rave over a specific face of type? What do they see in it? Why is it so superlatively pleasant to their eyes? Good design is al-*

(on thirteen point body)

How is one to assess and evaluate a type face in terms of its esthetic design? Why do the pace-makers in the art of printing rave over a specific face of type? What do they see in it? Why is it so superlatively pleasant to their eyes? *Good design is always practical design.* And what they see in a good type design is, partly, its excellent practical fitness to perform its work. It has a "heft" and balance in all of its parts just right for its size, as any good tool has. Your good chair has all of its parts made nicely to the right size to do exactly the work that the chair has to do, neither clumsy and thick, nor "skinny" and weak, no waste of material and no lack of strength. And, beyond that, the chair may have been made by a man who worked out in it his sense

(on twelve point body)

How is one to assess and evaluate a type face in terms of its esthetic design? Why do the pace-makers in the art of printing rave over a specific face of type? What do they see in it? Why is it so superlatively pleasant to their eyes? Good design is always practical design. And what they see in a good type design is, partly, its excellent practical fitness to perform its work. It has a "heft" and balance in all of its parts just right for its size, as any good tool has. Your good chair has all of its parts made nicely to the right size to do exactly the work that the chair has to do, neither clumsy and thick, nor "skinny" and weak, no waste of material and no lack of strength. And, beyond that, the chair may have been made by a man who worked out Jgjpqy

(on eleven point body with short descenders)

ABCDEFGHIJKLMNOPQRSTUVWXYZ&
ABCDEFGHIJKLMNOPQRSTUVWXYZ&
ABCDEFGHIJKLMNOPQRSTUVWXYZ&

abcdefghijklmnopqrstuvwxyzfiflffffiffl 123456789 [($£,.:;'-'?!*†‡§¶)] 123456789
abcdefghijklmnopqrstuvwxyzfiflffffiffl 123456789 [($£,.:;'-'?!†‡§¶)] 123456789*

Matrix Information: 11△146. Lower case alphabet, 131 points. Figures, .0761; comma, period and thin space, .038. Smallest slug on which this face will cast is 12 point; with short descenders on 11 point. Code word, ZIRIZ.

s-56

Rudolph Ruzicka (1883–1978) was a Czech designer and wood engraver who was employed for 50 years as a consultant to the Mergenthaler Linotype Company. In his work he took a distinctly modernist approach. Type, he observed, 'is made to be read, and that implies a reader ... He wants no interruptions of the process of following the printed thought ... type is after all, only a medium between writing and reading.'

12 POINT
Linotype Fairfield

HOW IS ONE TO ASSESS AND EVALUATE A TYPE FACE IN TER
OF ITS ESTHETIC DESIGN? WHY DO THE PACE-MAKERS IN T

How IS ONE to assess and evaluate a type face in terms of its esthetic design? Why do the pace-makers in the art of printing rave over a specific face of type? What do they see in it? Why is it so superlatively pleasant to their eyes? *Good design is always practical design.* And what they see in a good type design is, partly, its excellent practical fitness to perform its work. It has a "heft" and balance in all of its parts just right for its size, as any good tool has. Your good chair has all of its parts made nicely to the right size to do exactly the work that the chair has to do, neither clumsy and thick, nor "skinny" and weak, no waste of material and no lack of strength. And, beyond that, the chair may have been made by a man who worked out in it his sense of fine shapes and curves and proportions: it may be, actually, a work of art. The same thing holds for shapes of letters. And your chair, or your letter (if a true artist made it) will have, besides

How is one to assess and evaluate a type face in terms of its esthetic design? Why do the pace-makers in the art of printing rave over a specific face of type? What do they see in it? Why is it so superlatively pleasant to their eyes? Good

(on fourteen point body)

How IS ONE to assess and evaluate a type face in terms of its esthetic design? Why do the pace-makers in the art of printing rave over a specific face of type? What do they see in it? Why is it so superlatively pleasant to their eyes? *Good design is always practical design.* And what they see in a good type design is, partly, its excellent practical fitness to perform its work. It has a "heft" and balance in all of its parts just right for its size, as any good tool has. Your good chair has all of its parts made nicely to the right size to do exactly the work that the chair has to do, neither clumsy and thick, nor "skinny" and weak, no waste of

(on thirteen point body)

How is one to assess and evaluate a type face in terms of its esthetic design? Why do the pace-makers in the art of printing rave over a specific face of type? What do they see in it? Why is it so superlatively pleasant to their eyes? Good design is always practical design. And what they see in a good type design is, partly, its excellent practical fitness to perform its work. It has a "heft" and balance in all of its parts just right for its size, as any good tool has. Your good chair has all of its parts made nicely to the right size to do exactly the work that the chair has to do, neither clumsy and thick, nor "skinny" and weak,   Jgjpqy

(on twelve point body with short descenders)

ABCDEFGHIJKLMNOPQRSTUVWXYZ&
ABCDEFGHIJKLMNOPQRSTUVWXYZ&

ABCDEFGHIJKLMNOPQRSTUVWXYZ&

abcdefghijklmnopqrstuvwxyzfiflffflffifl 1234567 [($£,.:;'-'?!*†‡§¶)] 1234567
abcdefghijklmnopqrstuvwxyzfiflffflffifl 1234567 [($£,.:;'-'?!†‡§¶)] 1234567*

Matrix Information: 12△508. Lower case alphabet, 139 points. Figures, .083; comma, period and thin space, .0415. Smallest slug on which this face will cast is 13 point; with short descenders on 12 point. Code word, ZIRJO.

Linotype released Fairfield in 1940. In its design process, Ruzicka pointed out: 'the limitations accepted were those tending to the greatest economy of means, rather than those supposedly inherent in the machine.' Its overall form is an intriguing hybrid of the Venetian types of the sixteenth century and the later designs of Bodoni and Didot, but it also embodies the spirit of its own era. Although its contours are quite traditional, Fairfield's absence of ornamental details results in a typeface that is flowing, elegant and modern. Fairfield is notable for its fine, delicate stems, counters and curves. An abrupt contrast between thin and thick strokes with sharp, unbracketed serifs reflects the streamlined attributes of the art deco style. The balanced proportions of upper and lower case letters, x-heights, ascenders and descenders contribute to an even overall colour in bodies of text that is light but very easy to read.

For Fairfield's 1991 faithful revival as a digital typeface by Adobe Systems designer Alex Kaczun added bold and heavy weights, together with small capitals and old-style figures.

s-57

Ty	**SuperTipo Veloz**
Ca	**Serif / Sans Serif**
Ke	**Geometric, Modular, Capitals**
Te	**Letterpress**
Da	**1942**
De	**Joan Trochut Blanchard**
Fo	**Iranzo**
Co	**Spain**

Characteristics

Capitals only
Modular alternate characters
Modular character components
Alternate swash, flourish and ornamental
components

Connections

Kombinations-Schrift	1923
Patrona Grotesk	c1931
Fregio Mecano	c1933
Walker	1995

Availability

Superveloz is a digital revival available
from Typerepublic and resellers

Specimen

SuperTipo Veloz type specimen
broadsheet. SADAG, Barcelona, c1948
(320x220mm)

'SuperTipo Veloz' translates into English
as 'super speedy type'. It was a modular
typographic system designed for use in
letterpress display settings, released by
Fundición Tipográfica José Iranzo in
Barcelona in 1942.

Created by Catalan designer Joan Trochut
Blanchard (1920–80), it consisted of a
collection of letterform stems and parts in
a coordinated range of styles and weights.
These could be used as modular building
blocks to construct any number of
variations of abstract or alphabetic forms.
The components could be linked together
in lateral sequences or superimposed in
layers to create exciting and unpredictable
typographic effects. A secondary set of
additional forms, such as swashes, tails
and flourishes, could also be applied to
complement and extend the possibilities
of the basic system.

The son of a commercial printer, Trochut
Blanchard was concerned about the need
for quality design within tight commercial
constraints in the 1940s. At a time when
the printing industry in Spain was at a low
ebb, SuperTipo Veloz sought to address
the requirements of small print workshops
by providing a flexible system that could
be used both for composing display text
and as an exploratory design tool.

The system was intended to allow printers
to develop display settings without the
usual restrictions of lead type in order to
improve the quality of everyday jobbing
work, such as stationery, catalogues
and advertisements. Like many other
letterpress designs built from modular
elements, the opportunities offered by
SuperTipo Veloz were inevitably offset
by the considerable time, expense and
diligence its composition demanded.

In 2004 the designer's grandson, Alex
Trochut, collaborated with the Spanish
type designer Andreu Balius in the creation
of Superveloz, a faithful reinterpretation of
Trochut Blanchard's original system that
takes advantage of digital technologies to
provide a wide range of visual options.

1950

As international trade and industry started to recover after World War II, so did the demand for designed and printed business communications, while at the same time global publishing markets were beginning to make a resurgence. Propelled by advances in print production technologies, the ensuing opportunities for the communications industries precipitated a re-evaluation of ideas about the social functions and consequences of design.

In the 1950s an aspiration to achieve objectivity in communications was becoming a preoccupation of many members of the design profession, informed by the ideals of pre-war modernism. The sense of order and neutrality that many people desired in the wake of World War II resulted in an initiative that emerged from Switzerland to become one of the most influential design movements of the twentieth century. The International Typographic Style, also known as the Swiss Style, emphasized clear organization, navigation and readability in visual communication. The use of content-driven layouts, proportional grids, logical text alignments and plain-looking sans serif typefaces like Akzidenz-Grotesk brought a new sense of composure to contemporary graphic design. The prevalence of the Swiss Style led to a renewed interest in the simplicity of nineteenth-century grotesque forms, instigating the creation of several new sans serif typefaces deliberately stripped of idiosyncratic features, most notably Univers, Folio and Neue Haas Grotesk, later renamed Helvetica, all released in 1957.

The post-war increase in the supply and demand for design took place in the context of rapid advances in the technologies used to generate type, which marked a transition away from letterpress print production. Photocomposition was a short-lived phase in the history of typography but one that had a lasting effect on the industry. The first photosetting devices had been experimented with in the 1930s but started to be commercially viable only in the early 1950s when a variety of machines entered the market.

Photocomposition automated typesetting processes using photographic images of letters in ways that were far more economical, more flexible and quicker than had been possible within the restraints of metal type. Letters for photocomposition were located on negative film masters that were projected onto photo-sensitive paper, where they were positioned and scaled to desired configurations. Technically, the new machines proved effective for display work but less so for text setting. The quality of photographic outlines projected at different scales was variable, and the expense of the new technology was prohibitive for most jobbing printers.

In the 1960s, dry-transfer lettering arrived, placing type into the hands of designers for the first time. Letraset manufactured more than 1,200 dry-transfer typefaces, many of which were subsequently licensed to photocomposition manufacturers. Intended for use in headlines, this intermediate technology was accessible and cheap, mirroring the popular culture of the time with many playful, eye-catching typefaces.

Together, these new technologies transformed the design industry. An explosion of novel display types was seen in the 1960s and 1970s, instigating new approaches to the ways in which communications could be designed. Closer letter spacing than had previously been possible became highly fashionable with types designed not only for print but also for film and television. Combined with quick, cheap and efficient offset litho printing methods, the new technologies brought about a revolution in the operations involved in visual communications, shifting core activities away from traditional printing houses to designers, typographers and advertising agencies.

These changes stimulated the growth of the graphic design profession, placing control of the origination of printed communications into users' hands for the first time and leading directly to the digital revolution of the 1980s and 1990s.

Ty	**Al-Bro**
Ca	**Sans Serif**
Ke	**Geometric, Modern**
Te	**Photocomposition**
Da	**1950**
De	**Alexey Brodovitch**
Fo	**Photo-Lettering Inc.**
Co	**USA**

Characteristics

Geometric sans serif construction
Extreme contrast of thick and thin strokes
Ball terminals
E F Hairline mid-serif
a f k s Swash alternates
e Thick mid-stroke

ABEJKSU
aabceffg
kossrwx

Connections

Bodoni	1788
Bayer Type	1933
HTF Didot	1991
Albroni	1992

Availability

Albroni is a digital revival of Al-Bro by Nico
Schweizer. It is not currently available.

Specimen

Portfolio, No. 1. Zebra Press, Cincinnati,
1950 (327x257mm)

NEW LETTER: The signs and symbols of musical notation inspired the design of this new letter-face, which has just been announced. It was designed by Alexey Brodovitch, art director of *Harper's Bazaar* and *Portfolio*, who calls it the Albro Alphabet (after the first syllables of his name). It is being released through Photo-Lettering, Inc., New York.

j B G A M

g h i j m n

u v w x y z

1 2 3 4 5 6 7 8 9 ¢ $

Alexey Brodovitch (1898–1971) was a Russian-American graphic artist and photographer who single-handedly revolutionized American magazine design during the 1940s and 1950s. In his role as art director at *Harper's Bazaar*, he invested each monthly issue with a sequential design that had the qualities of a musical composition. To create energy and movement on static printed pages he used groundbreaking visual effects that exploited extreme contrasts of size, content, texture and colour to give the reader an experience that was both informative and visually stimulating.

In 1949 Brodovitch collaborated in the design and production of *Portfolio*, a publication that many consider the finest American design journal of the twentieth century. Form and content in *Portfolio* were inseparable. Its focus was on art and design topics, but it was intended at the same time to be an outstanding example of design itself. Advertising was excluded, and without its obstruction Brodovitch was liberated from any practical editorial or aesthetic restraints, making wildly imaginative layouts possible for a huge variety of content.

Portfolio No. 1 demonstrates the extensive range of subjects that inspired Brodovitch's design ideas. It included features on mathematics, musical notation, the Bodoni typeface (pp96–97) and the simply crafted artefacts of the early American Shaker communities. The design of the geometric typeface he produced for the winter 1950 edition's final spread is a distillation of all of these influences. Named Al-Bro – an abbreviation of Alexey Brodovitch – the new design clearly resembles Didot (pp90–91), one of Brodovitch's favourite typefaces. Although Al-Bro's letters show a more rounded and mathematical appearance, they share Didot's vertical stress and are similarly characterized by their extremely fine hairlines contrasted with very bold stems. In the ball terminals of several characters, such as the s and a, playful references to musical notation are clearly visible.

Portfolio was short-lived. Without any advertising revenue the magazine's extravagant production caused it to fail after only three issues. However, it is widely recognized today as one of the most significant publications in design history. Released by Photo-Lettering Inc. (pp356–57) for photocomposition, the Al-Bro typeface was soon lost among the thousands of typefaces in the foundry's catalogue, suffering a similar fate to the magazine itself, in spite of its many charms.

Ty	**Palatino**
Ca	**Serif**
Ke	**Old Style**
Te	**Letterpress**
Da	**1950**
De	**Hermann Zapf**
Fo	**Stempel**
Co	**Germany**

Characteristics

Large x-height
Short ascenders
E F L Narrow
J Descends below baseline, hooked
P R Open bowl
Q Sweeping tail below letter
R S X Y Calligraphic strokes
g Double-storeyed, large lower bowl
h m n Right foot serif to exterior only
t Crossbar below midline

AEJMPR
abcdefghij
norstyaefg

Connections

Weiss Antiqua	1928
Michelangelo	1950
Sistina	1951
Zapf Renaissance	1987

Availability

Palatino is available from Linotype and resellers

Specimen

Palatino type specimen. D. Stempel AG, Frankfurt, c1950 (297x210mm)

Palatino

6 point no. 5327 30 A 65 a 27 Fig. 1
Can the continued existence and survival of the independent type founder, of whatever nationality, be expected at this period of development in the graphic arts? In strict terms of economics of print

CAN THE CONTINUED EXISTENCE AND SURVIVAL OF THE INDEPENDENT TYPE

8 point s. f. no. 5328 25 A 53 a 24 Fig. 1   6
Can the continued existence and survival of the independent type founder, of whatever nationality, be expected at this period of development in the graphic arts? In

CAN THE CONTINUED EXISTENCE AND SURVIVAL OF THE INDEPEND

8 point l. f. no. 5330 21 A 44 a 21 Fig. 1   8
Can the continued existence and survival of the independent type founder, of whatever nationality, be expected at this period of developme

CAN THE CONTINUED EXISTENCE AND SURVIVAL OF T

10 point no. 5331 23 A 44 a 18 Fig. 1   9
Can the continued existence and survival of the independent type founder, of whatever nationality, be expected at this period of

CAN THE CONTINUED EXISTENCE AND SURVIVA

12 point s. f. no. 5332 21 A 40 a 18 Fig. 1   10
Can the continued existence and survival of the independent type founder, of whatever nationality, be expected at this

CAN THE CONTINUED EXISTENCE AND SURV

12 point l. f. no. 5333 18 A 35 a 13 Fig. 1   12
Can the continued existence and survival of the independent type founder, of whatever nationality,

CAN THE CONTINU ED EXISTENCE AND

When ordering Linotype matrices please use this column of point sizes.

Studies in the literature of Northern Europe
14 point no. 5334 16 A 30. a 12 Fig. 1

ART COLLECTION

New Advertising Art in a modern style
18 point no. 5335 11 A 23 a 10 Fig. 1

NEW ZEALAND

Quartet in C minor by Brahms
20 point no. 5336 9 A 15 a 8 Fig. 1

MUSIC SHOP

House of Representatives
24 point no. 5337 7 A 12 a 7 Fig. 1

KINGDOM

Saint Paul's Cathedral
30 point no. 5338 5 A 9 a 6 Fig. 1

PICTURE

New York Show
42 point no. 5339 4 A 7 a 4 Fig. 1

TOWN

Manufacture
54 point no. 5340 5 A 7 a 6 Fig. 1

SEND

Palatino Semi Bold

8 point s.f. no.5438 30A 50a 28 Fig.1 6🎵

Can the continued existence and survival of the independent type founder, of whatever nationality, be expected at this period of development in the graphic arts? In

CAN THE CONTINUED EXISTENCE
AND SURVIVAL OF THE INDEPEND

8 point l.f. no.5440 21A 42a 20 Fig.1 8🎵

Can the continued existence and survival of the independent type founder, of whatever nationality, be expected at this period of developme

CAN THE CONTINUED EXIS
TENCE AND SURVIVAL OF T

10 point no.5441 24A 44a 18 Fig.1 9🎵

Can the continued existence and survival of the independent type founder, of whatever nationality, be expected at this period of

CAN THE CONTINUED E
XISTENCE AND SURVIVA

12 point s.f. no.5442 22A 40a 17 Fig.1 10🎵

Can the continued existence and survival of the independent type founder, of whatever nationality, be expected at this

CAN THE CONTINUED
EXISTENCE AND SURV

12 point l.f. no.5443 18A 34a 14 Fig.1 12🎵

Can the continued existence and survival of the independent type founder, of whatever nationality,

CAN THE CONTINU
ED EXISTENCE AND

🎵 When ordering Linotype matrices please use this column of point sizes.

Life and Customs of the Indians in America   PRIMITIVE RACE
14 point no.5444 16A 29a 11 Fig.1

Great Events at the Saratoga Raceway   STRONGHOLD
18 point no.5445 10A 22a 10 Fig.1

European Imports in Demand   DUTCHMAN
20 point no.5446 9A 14a 8 Fig.1

Puerto Rico and Trinidad   JOURNEY
24 point no.5447 7A 11a 7 Fig.1

House of Commons   NATION
30 point no.5448 5A 9a 6 Fig.1

Modern Painter   IMAGE
42 point no.5449 4A 7a 4 Fig.1

Westminster   KING
54 point no.5450 5A 7a 5 Fig.1

Named after a sixteenth-century Italian writing master, Palatino was released by Stempel for Linotype machine composition in 1950. Its design was started two years earlier by Hermann Zapf (1918–2015), a German calligrapher who was then the foundry's art director. Palatino is one of several typefaces by Zapf that were inspired by monumental inscriptions carved during the time of the Roman Empire and by humanist typefaces of the Italian Renaissance, such as Jenson (pp20–21), whose letters have the calligraphic grace of those written with a broad-nib pen. But where Renaissance types tend to use small characters with a low x-height and proportionately long ascenders and descenders, Palatino is a much larger, wider, brighter and more open form.

The typeface's geniality and charm is due to Zapf's expertise as a calligrapher, and to his profound understanding of the technicalities of type design. He carefully considered manufacturing processes, print production methods and the effects of materials when developing his typefaces. Palatino was specifically designed with offset litho and gravure printing methods in mind. To compensate for the mediocrity of paper available in post-war Germany, Zapf gave its characters open counters and a stroke weight slightly more even and heavier than the norm for roman types. These enhancements made Palatino a reliable choice for editorial work in newspapers and magazines.

After its release in 1950 some designers criticized Palatino for its strong personality, expressing the view that, in comparison with more self-effacing types, its calligraphic details made it obtrusive in extended reading matter. Nevertheless, Palatino rapidly became very successful around the world. It has been adapted to virtually all technologies and remains one of the most well-used serif typefaces available today.

Ty	**Banco**
Ca	**Sans Serif**
Ke	**Geometric, Capitals**
Te	**Letterpress**
Da	**1951**
De	**Roger Excoffon**
Fo	**Fonderie Olive**
Co	**France**

Characteristics

All capitals character construction
Slight incline overall
Strokes are tapered top to bottom
C O P Q R S Strokes are disjointed

AHIMEFT CDGOQS BPRUJYZ

Connections

Jacno	1950
Choc	1955
ITC Banco	1997
Serge Black	2012

Availability

Banco is available from Monotype and resellers

Specimen

Banco type specimen. Fonderie Olive, Marseilles, c1951 (280x200mm)

In 1950 the Deberny & Peignot foundry was preparing to publish a new typeface by Marcel Jacno (1904–89), the leading designer and typographer working in post-war France. It was to be called simply Jacno. At that time, competition was fierce for fashionable display types in a volatile market. For foundries that hit on a successful design, sales could be lucrative, but disastrous otherwise.

The rivalry between Fonderie Olive and Deberny & Peignot was so intense that when one of Olive's in-house designers, Roger Excoffon (1910–83), saw a picture of Jacno's unpublished typeface in a magazine, he decided to create a new design that would completely outclass it. 'I hastily sketched a few letters in a style not identical but belonging to the same visual family', he later admitted. When presented with Excoffon's proposal, a playful and dynamic alphabet of capital letters, Marcel Olive is reported to have declared 'Banco!', a French expression meaning 'Let's do it!', which also conveniently mimicked 'Jacno'.

Designed and manufactured by Olive at breakneck speed, Banco was on the market within two months. Its appearance was striking: an imposing capital alphabet that is slightly inclined, it is top-heavy with broad strokes that are very subtly tapered from top to bottom. Its letters seem to be the brushwork of an energetic hand, a trait typical of Excoffon's painterly approach to display letters. The various parts of the characters are naturally constructed but often completely separate from each other, capturing the dynamism and humanity of calligraphic forms.

Banco became a meteoric bestseller that was equally popular with printers and designers, completely eclipsing Marcel Jacno's typeface. Its immense success revitalized Olive as a manufacturer of fashionable display typefaces and established Roger Excoffon as one of the most innovative type designers of his generation. When ITC commisioned Phill Grimshaw to design a digital revival in 1997, he usefully extended Banco with a very well-matched lower case and an accompanying light weight.

Ty	**Berling Antikva**
Ca	**Serif**
Ke	**Old Style**
Te	**Letterpress**
Da	**1951**
De	**Karl-Erik Forsberg**
Fo	**Berlingska**
Co	**Sweden**

Characteristics

Oblique stress
Moderate stroke contrast
Capital height lower than ascenders
Curving, bracketed serifs
M Slightly splayed
Q Tail below letter
R Curved leg
W Centre-strokes meet at apex
a g Double-storeyed

AGMRW
abcdefghij
orstuy*aefg*

Connections

Centaur	1914
Bembo	1929
Sabon	1967
Minion	1990

Availability

Berling is widely available

Specimen

Berling type specimen. Berlingska
Stilgjuteriet, Lund, c1951 (275x190mm)

BERLING ANTIKVA

Han äger en enastående mottaglighet för alla sinnesintryck och en lika enastående uttrycksförmåga att återge dessa i ord. Han är sålunda vår första betydande realist. Ett viktigt drag i den bellmanska dikten är den innerliga föreningen mellan ord och toner. Bellman skrev sångerna för att sjungas, och

12 p Berling antikva nr 4012
Min ca 6 kg 18 A 170 a

I regel målar Bellman tavlor, som är fyllda av glädjens fest och yra. Men ofta skymtar dödstanken och bildar en mörk bakgrund. Detta ger de uppsluppna visorna ett djupare perspektiv. Över de

12 p Berling antikva 2 p mellanslag

ABCDEFGHIJKLMNOPQRSTUVWXYZÅÄ
abcdefghijklmnopqrstuvwxyzåäö

Oförskräckt bekämpar han i dessa satirer fördomar och vidskepelse hos hög och låg, och han känner sig som en stridsman för

14 p Berling antikva nr 4014
Min ca 7 kg 30 A 114 a

ABCDEFGHIJKLMNOPQRSTUVWXY
abcdefghijklmnopqrstuvwxyzåäö

I sin hänförelse för det nya lyckorike, som man hoppades, att upplysningen

16 p Berling antikva nr 4016
Min ca 9 kg 30 A 90 a

ABCDEFGHIJKLMNOPQRSTUV
abcdefghijklmnopqrstuvwxyzåäö

Lenngren som har en tydligt
REDAN SOM UNG SKREV

20 p Berling antikva nr 4020
Min ca 11 kg 22 A 72 a

BERLINGSKA STILGJUTERIET · LUND

BERLING ANTIKVA

24 p Berling antikva nr 4024
Min ca 12 kg 18 A 56 a

Sin största betydelse har denna
GENOM SIN TRO KUNDE

28 p Berling antikva nr 4028
Min ca 14 kg 16 A 36 a

Under tiden kom han in
REGLER FÖR POESINS

36 p Berling antikva nr 4036
Min ca 17 kg 12 A 30 a

Nyromantikerna de
POETEN HAN ÄR

48 p Berling antikva nr 4048
Min ca 22 kg 10 A 18 a

Ord och tankar
MED ORDETS

60 p Berling antikva nr 4060
Min ca 33 kg 10 A 18 a

Musikaliska
STORDAG

BERLINGSKA STILGJUTERIET · LUND

Karl-Erik Forsberg (1914–95) was an illustrious Swedish artist, calligrapher and graphic designer. His most celebrated achievement was his 1954 *Bibeln med bilder av Rembrandt* (Bible with Pictures by Rembrandt). This was an exquisitely produced edition, set in Berling, a typeface of Forsberg's own design.

It was originally drawn for the Berlingska foundry in Lund. A single weight, Berling Antikva, was released in 1951 with a matching italic, and within the next eight years the family was expanded to a range of five weights. It is said to be the first Swedish serif typeface and it has been considered an icon of Scandinavian design ever since.

Like Jan Tschichold's Sabon (pp378–79), Berling features the classic attributes of old-style romans, with a well-proportioned x-height and ascenders that extend above the height of the capital letters in order to balance the latter proportionately with the lower case. With fine terminals and sharp, beak-like serifs Berling has higher contrast than most old-style typefaces. In photocomposition and early digital versions of the typeface this became problematic, since the horizontal strokes in the lighter weights were marginally too fragile in text settings at small sizes.

In 2004 the Swedish publisher Verbum commissioned a comprehensive digital redesign of Berling, working in collaboration with Linotype. Named Berling Nova, it was released in two optical sizes in order to provide a coordinated solution to both text and display applications.

Vendôme

Ty	**Vendôme**
Ca	**Serif**
Ke	**Old Style, French**
Te	**Letterpress**
Da	**1951**
De	**François Ganeau**
Fo	**Fonderie Olive**
Co	**France**

Characteristics

Stems slightly inclined
Long, sharp serifs
G No spur
M Splayed
R Curved, tapered leg
V v W w Pointed vertex, narrow
W Crossed centre-strokes
c e Bottom-heavy
g Double-storeyed, short ear

AGMRW
abcdefghij
koprstuy

Connections

Jannon's Roman and Italic	1621
Trump Mediaeval	1954
Meridien	1957
Galliard	1978

Availability

Vendôme is available from Linotype and resellers

Specimen

Vendôme type specimen. Fonderie Olive, Marseilles, c1951 (279x216mm)

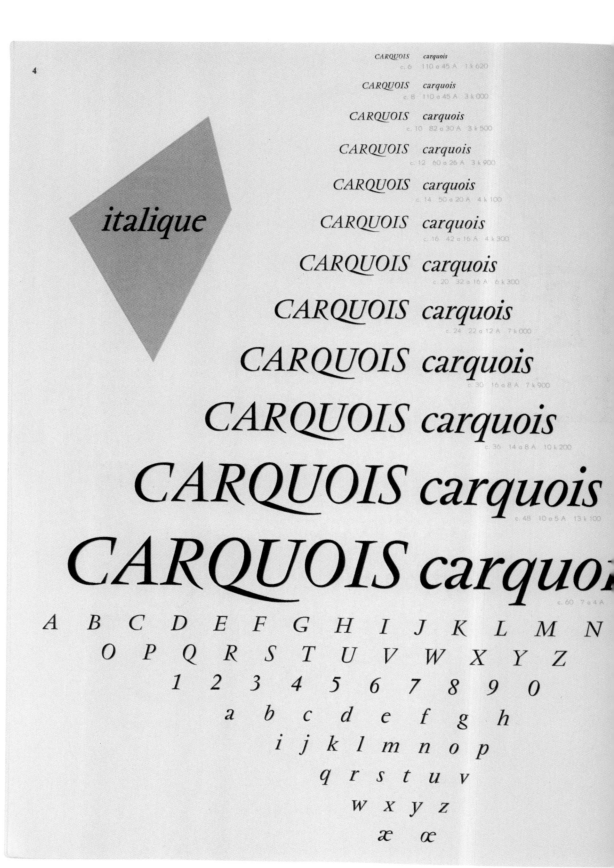

332

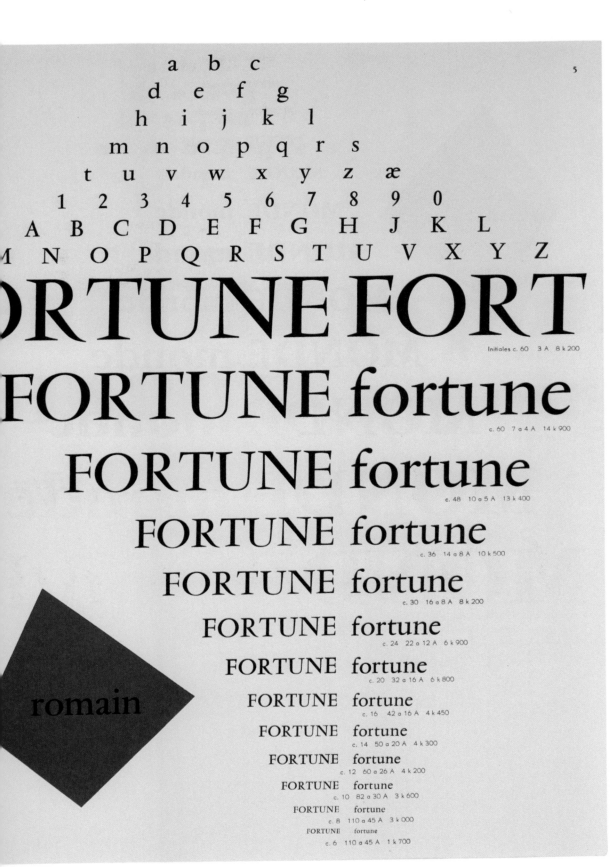

abc
defg
hijkl
mnopqrs
tuvwxyz æ
1234567890
ABCDEFGHIJKL
MNOPQRSTUVXYZ

ORTUNE FORT

Initiales c. 60 3 A 8 k 200

FORTUNE fortune

c. 60 7 a 4 A 14 k 900

FORTUNE fortune

c. 48 10 a 5 A 13 k 400

FORTUNE fortune

c. 36 14 a 8 A 10 k 500

FORTUNE fortune

c. 30 16 a 8 A 8 k 200

FORTUNE fortune

c. 24 22 a 12 A 6 k 900

FORTUNE fortune

c. 20 32 a 16 A 6 k 800

FORTUNE fortune

c. 16 42 a 16 A 4 k 450

FORTUNE fortune

c. 14 50 a 20 A 4 k 300

FORTUNE fortune

c. 12 60 a 26 A 4 k 200

FORTUNE fortune

c. 10 82 a 30 A 3 k 600

FORTUNE fortune

c. 8 110 a 45 A 3 k 000

FORTUNE fortune

c. 6 110 a 45 A 1 k 700

romain

Vendôme, an unorthodox interpretation of French Renaissance types, was the work of the artist, sculptor and stage designer François Ganeau (1912–83). Probably named after Place Vendôme, a square in Paris, the typeface was inspired by the work of Claude Garamond in the sixteenth century (pp48–49) and later types cut by Jean Jannon (pp62–63). It was the only post-war typeface manufactured by the Olive foundry not to have been designed by Roger Excoffon, although he was closely involved in its development. Throughout each stage of the design process, Ganeau, who had no previous experience in drawing type, would meet with him on a weekly basis for guidance.

Vendôme is characterized by its old-style contours and the vigour of its asymmetrical triangular serifs. Overall letter proportions and the contrast between thick and thin strokes closely follow the Garamond model that inspired them, giving the face a dignified, powerful appearance. The dynamic energy of the roman is provided by its knife-like serifs and equally sharp punctuation marks and accents, combined with the forward motion implied by a slight inclination of the stems. The italic is a sloped roman rather than a traditional form based on a chancery hand, giving a contemporary appearance and further reinforcing a lively overall impression.

Published in 1951, Vendôme was well received by the printing trade both in France and abroad. Although it had been intended for text, it was used mostly for advertising and publicity work for many years. It became very successful for Fonderie Olive and several variants were developed over the next five years under Excoffon's direction. François Ganeau's major contribution to typography, Vendôme took an approach to type design that recognized its own history while locating it within a contemporary frame.

Ty	**Melior**
Ca	**Serif**
Ke	**Transitional**
Te	**Photocomposition**
Da	**1952**
De	**Hermann Zapf**
Fo	**Stempel**
Co	**Germany**

Characteristics

Super-elliptical character construction
Square, bracketed serifs
Moderate stroke contrast
A Flat apex, no serif
G No spur
a g Double-storeyed

AGMRW
abcdefghij
koprstuy

Connections

Century Schoolbook	1918
Renault	1978
Utopia	1989
Velo Serif	2014

Availability

Melior is available from Linotype and resellers

Specimen

Melior type specimen. D. Stempel AG, Frankfurt, 1950s (210x100mm)

Melior's clean, clinical appearance is based on its elliptical curves and square, bracketed serifs. It was designed by Hermann Zapf (1918–2015) and released by the Stempel foundry in 1952.

It is thought that Zapf's typeface was a response to the ideas of Piet Hein, a Danish scientist, mathematician and poet who proposed that the super-ellipsoid form – a squared circle – provided an aesthetic unity superior to that of Euclidean geometry, writing that it was 'less obvious and less banal'. Architects, artists and designers from several disciplines experimented with super-ellipsoid shapes in the 1950s, and Melior represents Zapf's integration of its mathematical principles into the design of type.

Melior, its name meaning 'better' in Latin, was also the first typeface to be developed for photocomposition with Ikarus, a pioneering computer-aided type-design and digitizing system. It was made with the intention of becoming a multipurpose typeface for use in editorial publications as well as brand communications. To meet these requirements, legibility was rigorously tested across a wide range of materials and printing processes.

Melior is traditionally classified as a transitional serif, showing influences of rational eighteenth-century types like Baskerville (pp80–81) and Wilson (pp86–87). The Melior family's squared letterforms, vertical stress and balanced contrast of thick and thin strokes give the typeface a very upright, stable appearance while remaining easy to read. The design is relatively condensed in order to use space efficiently and to fit short lines of text in newspaper and magazine settings. Melior's inviting and efficient appearance made it a reliable typeface in editorial work for over 50 years.

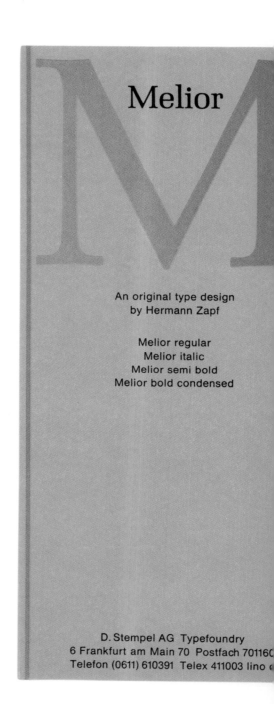

Melior

An original type design
by Hermann Zapf

Melior regular
Melior italic
Melior semi bold
Melior bold condensed

D. Stempel AG Typefoundry
6 Frankfurt am Main 70 Postfach 701160
Telefon (0611) 610391 Telex 411003 lino d

Melior regular

6
ff-Fasern herzustellen, sind hochwertige Einrichtungen erforderlich
8 sf
enz der Internationalen Forschungsgesellschaft für Medizin
8 lf
e la poésie française de la renaissance au romantisme
10
omwissenschaft ergeben sich ständig neue Aspekte
12 sf
onales Automobilrennen auf dem Nürburgring
12 lf
ll uvertyr på Konserthuset i Stockholm
14
he Kurzfilmtage in Recklinghausen
18
opments in Swedish Economy
24 sf
rimento di valute italiane
24 lf
deutscher Rundfunk
30
ndelsabkommen
36
ute des Indes
48
rmingham
60
estspiele

Melior italic

6
Den zweiten Höhepunkt erreichte die deutsche Buchkunst zur Zeit der Renaissance
8 sf
Ein Bericht über die Entwicklung des Hoch- und Tiefbaus im letzten Jahr
8 lf
Bunter Melodienreigen aus der Operette »Das Land des Lächelns«
10
Konferenz der Internationalen Forschung für innere Medizin
12 sf
Gute Erzeugnisse aus der fränkischen Keramik-Industrie
12 lf
Landschaftsbilder aus dem schönen Nordirland
14
El nuevo Mercado de Flores en Barcelona
18
Nouvelle édition revue et complétée
24 sf
Stenografisk maskinskrivning
24 lf
Gold- und Silberschmied
30
Agencia de patentes
36
Holidays in Italy
48
Schriftgießer
60
Handsatz

Melior semi bold

6
Die Geschichte der rheinischen Städtekultur von den Anfängen bis zur Gegenwart
8 sf
Notices sommaires des manuscrits grecs de la Bibliothèque de Reims
8 lf
Kolorierte Reproduktionen alter Kupferstiche und Lithographien
10
La lettre ornée dans les manuscrits du VIIIe au XIIe siècle
12 sf
Technische Formen und ihr Einfluß auf die Architektur
12 lf
Rheinisch-Westfälische Landesbank in Bochum
14
Centro oficial de contratación de moneda
18
Bauarbeiten im Londoner Freihafen
24 sf
Innehavare av nyttjanderätt
24 lf
Frankfurter Allgemeine
30
House of Commons
36
Decentramento
48
Información
60
Standbild

Ty	**Steile Futura**
Ca	**Sans Serif**
Ke	**Geometric**
Te	**Letterpress**
Da	**1952**
De	**Paul Renner**
Fo	**Bauer**
Co	**Germany**

Characteristics

C c S s e	Vertical terminals
C c G O o	Straight downstrokes
G	No spur
K	Arms touch stem at joint
Q	Short, angled tail
R	Upright leg
a	Double-storeyed, straight stem
c	Narrow
f r t	Narrow with vertical terminals
i j	Round dots
j	Straight tail
t	Flat top-stroke

AGEMQR
abcdefghij
koprstuvy

Connections

Futura Display	1932
Tasse	1994
Solex	2000
The Morgan Project	2001

Availability

Steile Futura is widely available

Specimen

Steile Futura type specimen. Bauersche Giesserei, Frankfurt, c1952 (297x210mm)

BAUERSCHE GIESSEREI · FRANKFURT AM MAIN W 13

15406 6 Punkt ca. 3 kg 48 A 170 a

Die Buchstaben, in denen die flüchtigen Laute der Sprache sichtbare Gestalt empfangen, nehmen unter den Werken der bildenden Kunst, zu denen diese zu rechnen sind, eine eigenartige Stellung ein. In einem, nicht in jedem Sinn willkürliche Bildungen, künstlich ersonnen und losgelöst von den Formen der Natur, wenn auch im einzelnen an sie erinnernd, fügen sich ihre Linien immer wieder zu der ihnen einmal bestimmten Figur zusammen. Ungleich den Schöpfungen der Plastik und Malerei, deren Motive, aus der Zerstreutheit des Zufalls zusammengefaßt, ihre Wirkung der Ausstrahlung eines durch den künstlerischen Willen neu geschaffenen Daseins verdanken, sind die SCHRIFTZEICHEN MEHR DEN WERKEN DER ARCHITEKTUR UND

15408 8 Punkt ca. 4 kg 40 A 140 a

Die Buchstaben, in denen die flüchtigen Laute der Sprache sichtbare Gestalt empfangen, nehmen unter den Werken der bildenden Kunst, darunter sie zu rechnen sind, eine eigenartige Stellung ein. In einem, nicht in jedem Sinn willkürliche Bildungen, künstlich erdacht und losgelöst von den Formen der Natur, wenn auch im einzelnen an sie erinnernd, fügen sich ihre Linien immer wieder zu der ihnen einmal bestimmten Figur zusammen. Ungleich den Schöpfungen der Plastik UND MALEREI, DEREN MOTIVE, AUS DER ZERSTREUTHEIT

15409 9 Punkt ca. 4,5 kg 36 A 126 a

Die Buchstaben, in denen die flüchtigen Laute der Sprache ihre sichtbare Gestalt empfangen, nehmen unter den Werken der bildenden Kunst, darunter sie zu rechnen sind, eine eigenartige Stellung ein. In einem, nicht in jedem Sinn willkürliche Bildungen, künstlich ersonnen und losgelöst von den Formen der Natur, wenn auch im einzelnen an sie erinnernd, FÜGEN SICH IHRE LINIEN IMMER WIEDER ZU DER

15410 10 Punkt ca. 5 kg 32 A 110 a

Die Buchstaben, in denen die flüchtigen Laute der Sprache sichtbare Gestalt empfangen, nehmen unter den Werken der bildenden Kunst, darunter sie zu rechnen sind, eine eigenartige Stellung ein. In einem, nicht in jedem Sinn willkürliche Bildungen, künstlich ersonnen und losgelöst von den Formen der Natur, wenn auch im einzelnen AN SIE ERINNERND, FÜGEN SICH IHRE LINIEN

15412 12 Punkt ca. 6 kg 28 A 100 a

Kein Meister fällt vom Himmel. Dieses alte Sprichwort hat seine Geltung behalten beim Handwerk wie bei der Kunst. Ausnahmslos gilt es bei der angewandten Kunst und beim KUNSTGEWERBE. HIER KOMMT ES FÜR

15414 14 Punkt ca. 7 kg 24 A 84 a

Das erfordert Begabung und eisernen Fleiß. Darum wird nicht jeder Künstler mit Erfolg an die kunstgewerblichen Aufgaben herantreten. Der Künstler ARBEITET NICHT MEHR FÜR EINEN

15416 16 Punkt ca. 7 kg 20 A 70 a

Erst diejenigen, die Gelegenheit hatten, einen Blick in seine buch- gewerbliche Werkstatt zu tun und ihn bei der Arbeit zu beobachten WERDEN ERKENNEN WIE VIEL

15420 20 Punkt ca. 8,5 kg 16 A 56 a

Der Meister kann sich nicht genug tun und wenn er die Aufgabe vor sich sieht, und sei es die kleinste, sucht er MIT VERSCHIEDENSTEN

Steile Futura is a condensed, rectilinear sans serif designed by Paul Renner (1878–1956). It is a more subtly modulated typeface than Futura (pp230–31), with which it has virtually nothing in common other than its name. Renner worked on it sporadically for many years, starting in 1932 with Futura Display, a square, blocky type drawn for Bauer. Subsequently, a lighter design with more rounded and modulated strokes, Renner Grotesk, was cast as a trial by the Stempel foundry in 1936. Renner Kursiv, an italic companion to the Grotesk, was then made after Bauer had taken over Stempel in 1938. This was a true cursive, marking a pronounced difference between Renner Grotesk and Futura. Renner's poor health during the 1940s slowed down the project's further development, but he returned to it in 1951, giving it the name Steile Futura ('Steile' meaning 'upright').

Although both are essentially geometric, Renner's approach to Steile Futura's construction was the precise opposite to that of Futura. Steile Futura's contours show clear influences of handwriting in contrast to the pure modularity of the earlier design. Conversely, where Futura follows classical traditions in its varied letter proportions and widths, Steile Futura uses the regular geometric rhythm of characters with relatively even widths – an innovative way of achieving an equally rational, modern appearance by completely different means. Steile Futura is unusual for a sans serif in being accompanied by a true italic rather than an inclined roman. The lower case italic a is single-storeyed, and suggestions of calligraphy are seen in the shapes of the italic e, h, k, m, n and u. Single-foot serifs at the base of many italic characters emphasize the impression.

In 1952 Bauer released the Steile Futura family in light, medium and bold, with italics corresponding to the two heavier weights. It was marketed under a variety of names in different territories and consequently also became well known to many as Bauer Topic.

BAUERSCHE GIESSEREI · FRANKFURT AM MAIN W 13

15424   24 Punkt   ca. 10 kg   14 A 50 a

Geschichte der Malerei und Plastik in Wort und Bild
Radierungen aus dem neunzehnten Jahrhundert
EIN LICHTBILDERVORTRAG IM GEMEINDEHAUS

15428   28 Punkt   ca. 10,5 kg   10 A 36 a

Internationale Boxkämpfe in Düsseldorf
Handels- und Gewerbeschule Offenbach
WINTERSPORT IM BAYERISCHEN WALD

15436   36 Punkt   ca. 14,5 kg   10 A 30 a

Fachzeitung für den Lederhandel
BERCHTESGADENER REISEBÜRO

15448   48 Punkt   ca. 15,5 kg   6 A 18 a

Die Erfindung Gutenbergs
HANDEL UND VERKEHR

Weitere Grade in Vorbereitung

«-,:?(")!';.»

A B C D E F G H I J K L M N O
P Q R S T U V W X Y Z Æ Œ
1 2 3 4 5 6 7 8 9 0

TOURISME		*distinguée*
c. 12 32 A		76 a 3 k 500
TOURISME		*distinguée*
c. 14 30 A	*abcdefghiklm*	92 a 4 k 600
TOURISME		*distinguée*
c. 16 24 A		60 a 5 k 100
TOURISME	*nopqrstuv.*	*distinguée*
c. 20 22 A		50 a 6 k 900
TOURISME		*distinguée*
c. 24 16 A	*w.xyzæœ*	32 a 7 k 500
TOURISME		*distinguée*
c. 30 12 A	*ff ll gu st*	24 a 8 k 500
TOURISME		*distinguée*
c. 36 10 A		20 a 10 k 300
TOURISME	*on ll*	*distinguée*
c. 48 6 A		14 a 12 k 500
TOURISME	*e distinguée*	
c. 60 5 A		10 a 14 k 200
TOURISME	*distinguée*	
c. 72 4 A		9 a 14 k 800

Ty	**Mistral**
Ca	**Script**
Ke	**Informal, Connected**
Te	**Letterpress**
Da	**1953**
De	**Roger Excoffon**
Fo	**Fonderie Olive**
Co	**France**

Characteristics

Informal, sloped, connecting script
Replicates flow and texture of pen
Lower case letters designed to link
accurately above or below baseline
Long ascenders and descenders at
variable angles

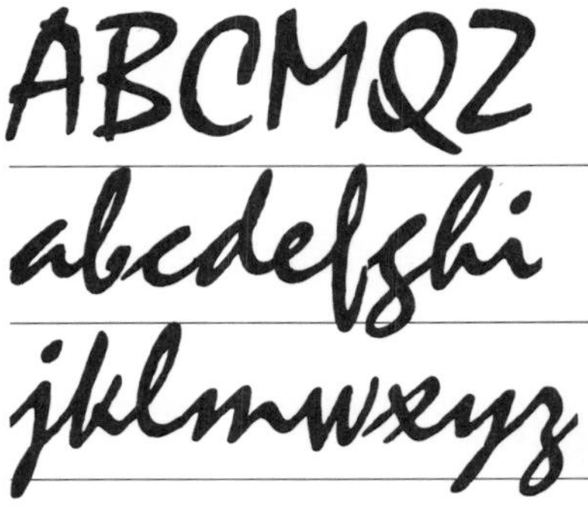

ABCMQZ
abcdefghi
jklmwxyz

Connections

Reporter	1938
Choc	1955
Forte	1962
Blog Script	2015

Availability

Mistral is available from Linotype and
resellers

Specimen

Mistral type specimen. Fonderie Olive,
Marseilles, c1951 (279x216mm)

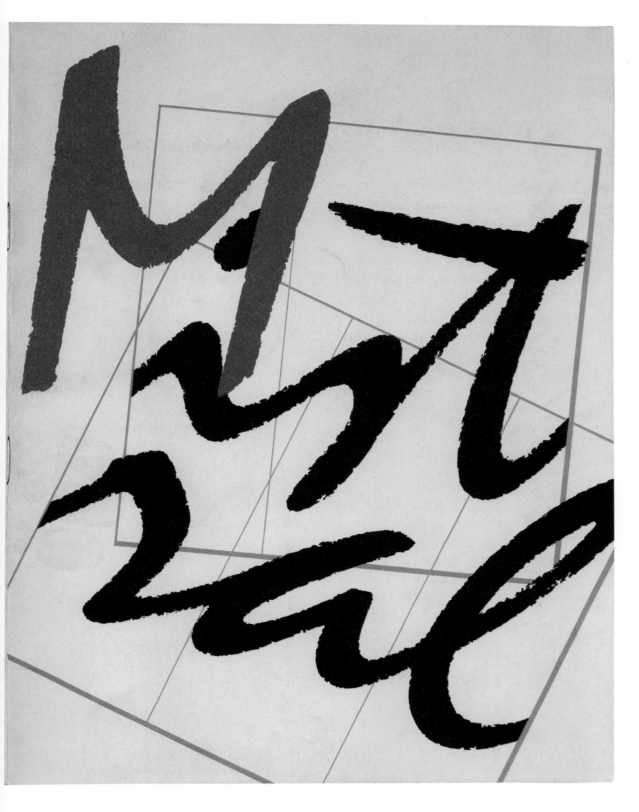

Mistral is a script typeface designed by Roger Excoffon (1910–83) for Fonderie Olive and released in 1953. It was an innovative solution to a long-standing typographic problem: how to create type that appeared to flow as naturally as handwriting within the fixed confines of its metal body. The project started as an attempt to represent genius in typographic form. In the hope of finding well-formed scripts on which to model Mistral, Excoffon researched and documented the handwriting of a number of eminent thinkers. However, on discovering no consistent relationship between manuscript and intellect, he decided to model the typeface on his own writing.

Mistral is an informal connected script of exceptional virtuosity and vitality. Whereas Excoffon's Banco (pp328–29) appeared to be constructed with brushstrokes, Mistral suggests the urgent flow and texture of a felt-tip or ballpoint pen. The lower case letters are carefully designed to connect sequentially in a natural manner. In order to instil the typeface with the vital energy of handwriting, Excoffon wanted letters to appear to move up and down spontaneously rather than be tethered to the baseline in a flat alignment. He knew that this effect would be technically impossible to achieve by copying directly from handwriting because it would result in rows of characters at random locations with their entry and exit strokes failing to link consistently. To solve the problem, Excoffon varied the positions of the letters within the bounds of their bodies, moving them above or below the baseline, but left the locations and angles of connecting strokes intact. Long ascenders and descenders at slightly different angles contributed to the effect, while providing a sense of forward motion. He also included several ligatures to vary the visual rhythm of lines of text, although these have not survived in digital versions of the typeface.

Mistral was released with great success in 1953, securing Excoffon's reputation as a type designer and inspiring him to design Choc (pp340–41). All of Excoffon's alphabets had a strikingly contemporary feel that contributed much to the look of French graphic design in the 1950s. By the middle of the decade, his typefaces were seen across Europe in every possible application from advertising to window displays and corporate logos.

Ty	**Choc**
Ca	**Script**
Ke	**Informal, Non-connected**
Te	**Letterpress**
Da	**1955**
De	**Roger Excoffon**
Fo	**Fonderie Olive**
Co	**France**

Characteristics

Informal, sloped, non-connected script
Replicates flow and texture of a fat brush
Ascenders and descenders at variable angles
Variation of thick and thin strokes
Small, tight counterforms

ABCMZ
abcdefghi
klmowxyz

Connections

Banco	1951
Mistral	1953
Calypso	1958
Sutturah	2011

Availability

Choc is available from Linotype and resellers

Specimen

Choc type specimen. Fonderie Olive, Marseilles, c1958 (279x216mm)

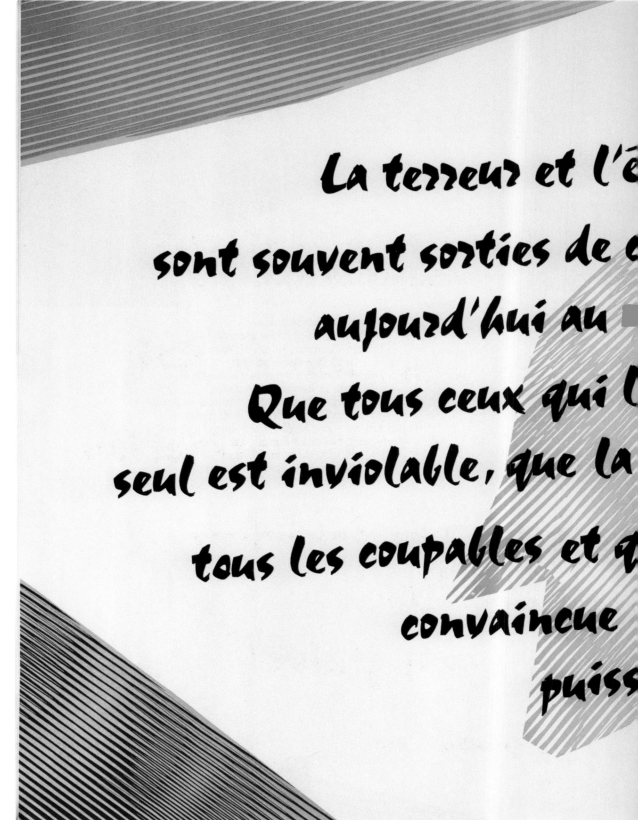

ante

ais; qu'elles y rentrent

e la loi!

tent sachent que le Roi

atteindra sans distinction

'y a pas une tête qui,

e criminelle,

apper à son glaive!

Vergniaud (1792)

Soon after the launch of Mistral in 1953 (pp338–39) Roger Excoffon (1910–83) began to experiment with a typeface along similar lines: a bold, non-connected script based on lettering made with brushstrokes. Not unlike the abstract paintings that were in fashion at the time, Choc looked natural and spontaneous, although in reality it was the product of a rigorous development process.

Choc was first intended as an emboldened version of Mistral, for which it was to be a supplementary series. Over time, Excoffon developed it further in a series of pencil drawings into a single independent script. He refined the drawings in meticulous detail to provide the direction of the type for execution by technicians at Fonderie Olive. Although Choc shares many of Mistral's characteristics – the capitals, in particular, follow similar contours – the concept underpinning each typeface is completely different. The design of Mistral focused on the composition of flowing word sequences, but Choc distilled individual letters and words into forcefully dense forms. Mistral was about continuity, whereas Choc was about fragmentation.

Choc's design exploits counterpoised contrasts throughout. Replicating the motion of a brush, like a raw version of Banco (pp328–29), its strokes are extremely heavy at the tops of letters and lighten somewhat towards the foot, with many of these thinner terminals showing an angry, torn quality. Unlike Mistral, Choc's letter shapes are highly irregular, with stems inclining at various angles. They appear to be fighting to maintain their balance on an unstable baseline, with some seeming to fall forwards (d, l, n, u, z), while others stand almost upright (e, h, m, s, v). Individual characters are defined by an asymmetrical stroke structure where acute angles interchange with flowing arcs in an aggressive rhythm. Their visceral energy is further emphasized by counterforms that are either extremely tight or non-existent.

The typeface was cast in nine sizes and released by Fonderie Olive in 1955, becoming an instant bestseller in editorial, advertising and jobbing work. Many more scripts were designed during the 1950s, and many have been designed since, but no others have achieved the knockout punch of Choc.

Ty	**Courier**
Ca	**Slab Serif**
Ke	**Typewriter, Monospaced**
Te	**Typewriter**
Da	**1955**
De	**Howard Kettler**
Fo	**IBM**
Co	**USA**

Characteristics
- Monospaced
- Monoline character construction with all strokes and serifs the same thickness
- Tall x-height
- Short ascenders and capitals
- Large, open counterforms
- **I i J j f** Wide
- **M m W w** Narrow
- **i j** Large round dot

ABGIMW

abcefg

imprty

Connections

Prestige Elite	1953
Letter Gothic	1956
FF Trixie	1991
Pitch	2012

Availability

Courier is widely available

Specimen

IBM Selectric Composer typeface portfolio. IBM United Kingdom, London, c1974 (297x210mm)

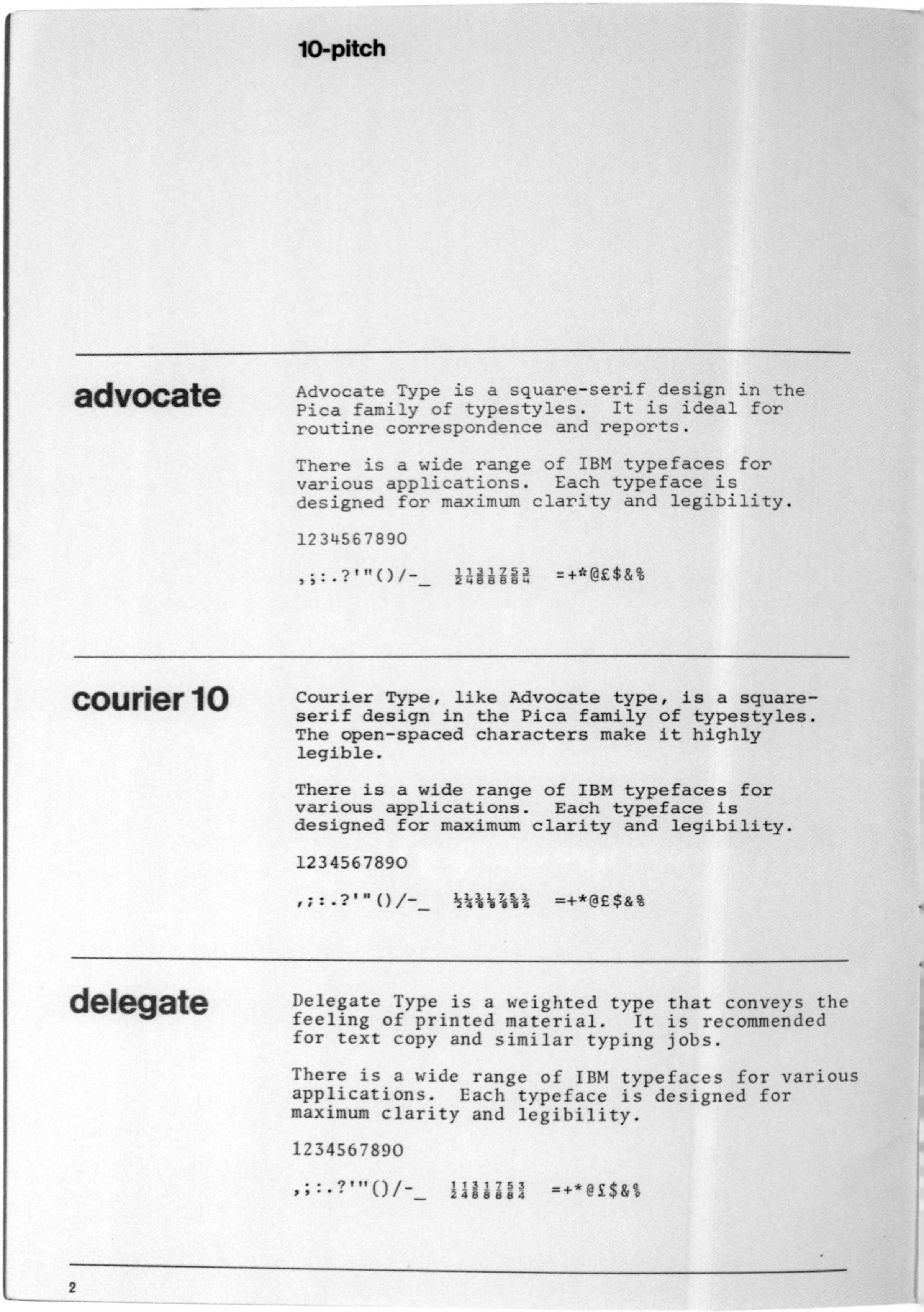

10-pitch

advocate

Advocate Type is a square-serif design in the Pica family of typestyles. It is ideal for routine correspondence and reports.

There is a wide range of IBM typefaces for various applications. Each typeface is designed for maximum clarity and legibility.

1234567890

,;:.?'"()/-_ ½ ¼ ⅜ ⅛ ⅞ ⅝ ¾ =+*@£$&%

courier 10

Courier Type, like Advocate type, is a square-serif design in the Pica family of typestyles. The open-spaced characters make it highly legible.

There is a wide range of IBM typefaces for various applications. Each typeface is designed for maximum clarity and legibility.

1234567890

,;:.?'"()/-_ ½ ¼ ⅜ ⅛ ⅞ ⅝ ¾ =+*@£$&%

delegate

Delegate Type is a weighted type that conveys the feeling of printed material. It is recommended for text copy and similar typing jobs.

There is a wide range of IBM typefaces for various applications. Each typeface is designed for maximum clarity and legibility.

1234567890

,;:.?'"()/-_ ½ ¼ ⅜ ⅛ ⅞ ⅝ ¾ =+*@£$&%

2

Courier was designed by Howard 'Bud' Kettler (1919–99) in 1955 as part of a typeface collection for IBM's manual typewriters that also included Prestige Elite and Letter Gothic. Courier is a monospaced slab serif typeface whose features are largely dictated by the construction of the bar typewriter mechanism for which it was created. The letters of manual typewriter faces must all fit onto striker arms that are the same size. When a key is depressed, a letter strikes the paper through a gate and the carriage advances a fixed distance. Consequently, every character must occupy exactly the same width, regardless of whether it is narrow or wide. This demands a number of adjustments in the design of the letters and in their spacing.

Courier is a '10-pitch' typeface, meaning that at its original size exactly ten letters side-to-side will fit one inch. It is a design with very well-structured proportions and contours, similar to Clarendon (pp132–33), with many compensations to provide an even overall balance. The capital height is small, fitting harmoniously with a rounded lower case that has a tall x-height, allowing for wide, open counterforms. Courier is completely monoline, with all strokes and serifs conforming to the same thickness in order to compensate for the erratic quality of manually typed output. Despite the extreme restrictions of the technology for which it was designed, Courier is exceptionally legible and economical at the same time.

IBM chose not to secure exclusive rights to the typeface and it soon became a typewriter industry standard. It was later revised and redrawn by Adrian Frutiger for the IBM Selectric Composer series of electric typewriters. The arrival of personal computing in the 1980s might have seen the end of Courier, but because it occupied so little digital memory it was included with computers and laser printers as the substitute that would automatically be printed in place of any font that was missing. Its monospaced features also made it useful in programming applications where columns of characters and figures had to be vertically aligned.

Courier is one of the most recognizable typefaces today, used extensively not only for its functionality but because it suggests a businesslike authenticity that seems free of contrivance. This is a surprising achievement for an alphabet so defined by the constraints of its own reproduction. Its name was originally to have been 'Messenger', but Kettler changed it for publication because, as a press advertisement explained: 'A letter can be just an ordinary messenger, or it can be the courier, which radiates dignity, prestige, and stability.'

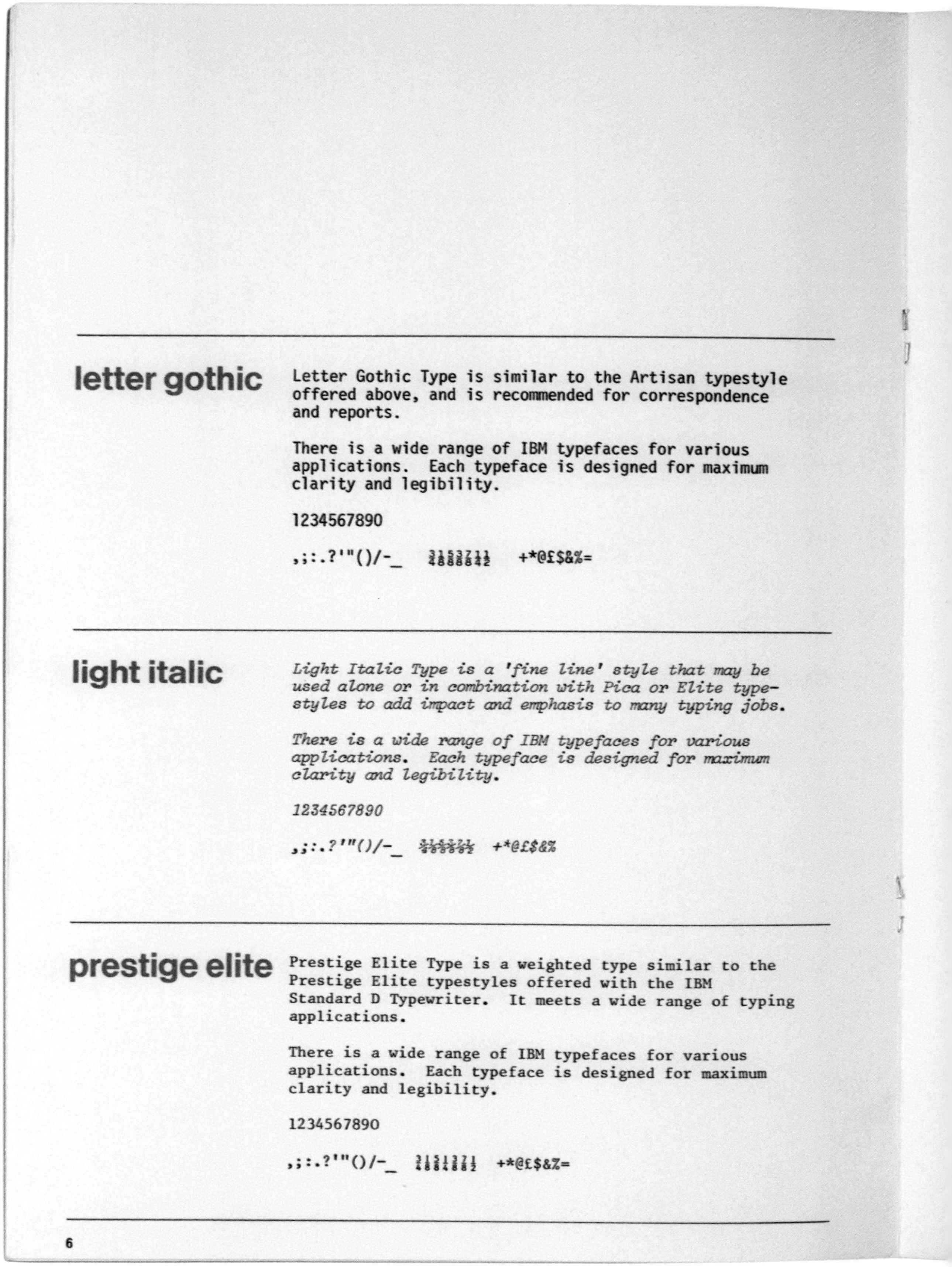

letter gothic

Letter Gothic Type is similar to the Artisan typestyle offered above, and is recommended for correspondence and reports.

There is a wide range of IBM typefaces for various applications. Each typeface is designed for maximum clarity and legibility.

1234567890

,;:.?'"()/-_ ¾⅛⅝⅜⅞¼½ +*@£$&%=

light italic

Light Italic Type is a 'fine line' style that may be used alone or in combination with Pica or Elite typestyles to add impact and emphasis to many typing jobs.

There is a wide range of IBM typefaces for various applications. Each typeface is designed for maximum clarity and legibility.

1234567890

,;:.?'"()/-_ ¾⅛⅝⅜⅞½ +@£$&%*

prestige elite

Prestige Elite Type is a weighted type similar to the Prestige Elite typestyles offered with the IBM Standard D Typewriter. It meets a wide range of typing applications.

There is a wide range of IBM typefaces for various applications. Each typeface is designed for maximum clarity and legibility.

1234567890

,;:.?'"()/-_ ¾⅛⅝¼⅜⅞½ +*@£$&%=

6

Ty	**Folio**
Ca	**Sans Serif**
Ke	**Grotesque**
Te	**Letterpress**
Da	**1957**
De	**Konrad Bauer and Walter Baum**
Fo	**Bauer**
Co	**Germany**

Characteristics

C c S s e g	Flat terminals
G	Has spur
Q	Hooked tail below letter
R	Curved, upright leg
a	Double-storeyed, curve at foot
f r t	Vertical terminals
i j	Square dots
t	Flat top-stroke
y	Curved tail

AGMQR
abcefghij
koprstuy

Connections

Royal Gothic	c1870
Akzidenz-Grotesk	c1898
Helvetica	1957
Forma	1968

Availability

Folio is available from Neufville Digital and resellers

Specimen

Folio type specimen. Bauersche Giesserei, Frankfurt, c1957 (279x216mm)

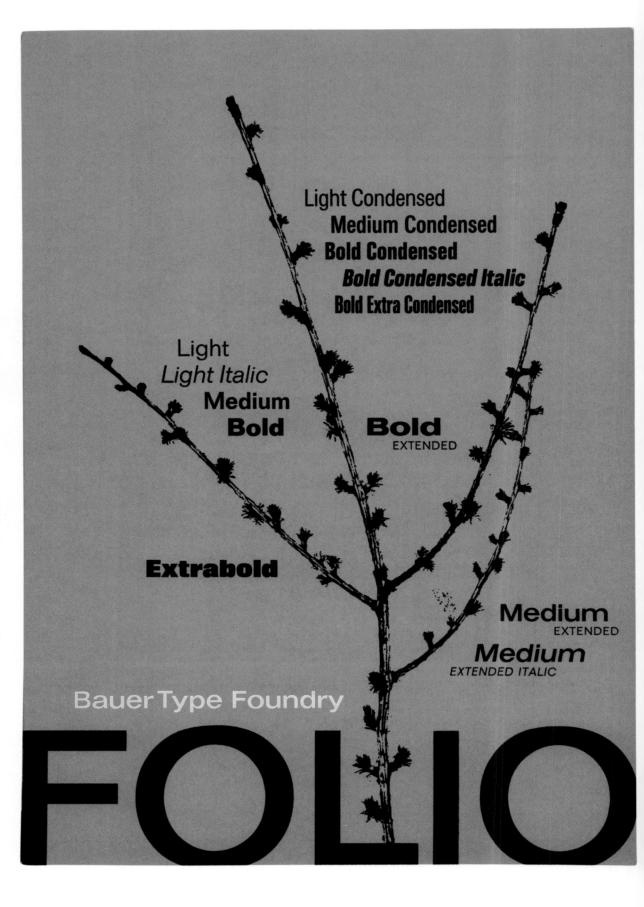

Folio was released in 1957, the same year as Helvetica (pp346–47) and Univers (pp350–51), at the high point of a decade in which a large number of new sans serif typefaces were issued, reflecting a shift in the design trends of the era.

During the 1950s typographers and designers began to turn against the geometric sans serifs that had been in fashion since the 1920s, favouring more subtle typefaces based on nineteenth-century grotesque models such as Akzidenz-Grotesk (pp152–53) and Venus (pp182–83). This precipitated an interest in the design community in improving the formulation of the grotesque style and led to a spate of new sans serif designs as foundries competed for a share of the lucrative global market.

A prime example of the new International Typographic Style, Folio was designed by Konrad Bauer (1903–70) and Walter Baum (1921–2007), highly experienced type designers who had been jointly responsible for several bestselling designs for the Bauer type foundry. Their intention for Folio, like Max Miedinger's for his design of Helvetica, was to develop a rational typeface that improved on the nineteenth-century grotesque form by smoothing out its more idiosyncratic features. Folio is modelled more closely on Akzidenz-Grotesk than Helvetica or Univers, with a smaller x-height than either. Folio also features a subtler stroke contrast that is increasingly evident in heavier weights. There are some notable differences between Folio's characters and its competitors', such as the lower case a and the capital G and Q. Unlike Helvetica, Folio was also conceived as a comprehensive programme of typefaces, consisting of 12 different versions by 1965.

Folio achieved some success in the United States partly due to the effectiveness of Bauer's international marketing and distribution activities and partly because it was licensed to Intertype for machine composition. Although it is a distinctive contribution to the category of sans serif typefaces, Folio has always been overshadowed by Helvetica and Univers, two bestsellers that have continued to dominate the sans serif market since their arrival. Folio remains an underrated design that deserves wider recognition and wider use.

FOLIO LIGHT

abcdefghijklmnopqrstuvwxyz ABCDEFGHIJKL MNOPQRRSTUVWXYZ $¢£1234567890&.,:;'-)!?""

Ligatures ff, fi, fl available in sizes from 6 to 14 point

FOLIO LIGHT ITALIC

abcdefghijklmnopqrstuvwxyz ABCDEFGHIJKL MNOPQRRSTUVWXYZ $¢£1234567890&.,:;'-)!?""

Ligatures ff, fi, fl, ft available in sizes from 6 to 14 point

FOLIO MEDIUM

abcdefghijklmnopqrstuvwxyz ABCDEFGHIJKL MNOPQRRSTUVWXYZ $¢£1234567890&.,:;'-)!?""

Ligatures ff, fi, fl available in sizes from 6 to 14 point

FOLIO BOLD

abcdefghijklmnopqrstuvwxyz ABCDEFGHIJ KLMNOPQRRSTUVWXYZ $¢£1234567890&.,:;'-)!?""

FOLIO EXTRABOLD

abcdefghijklmnopqrstuvwxyz ABCDEFGHIJKL MNOPQRRSTUVWXYZ $¢£1234567890&.,:;'-)!?""

FOLIO LIGHT CONDENSED

abcdefghijklmnopqrstuvwxyz ABCDEFGHIJKL MNOPQRRSTUVWXYZ $¢£1234567890&.,:;'-)!?""

FOLIO MEDIUM CONDENSED

abcdefghijklmnopqrstuvwxyz ABCDEFGHIJKL MNOPQRRSTUVWXYZ $¢£1234567890&.,:;'-)!?""

Ty	**Helvetica**
Ca	**Sans Serif**
Ke	**Grotesque**
Te	**Letterpress**
Da	**1957**
De	**Max Miedinger**
Fo	**Haas**
Co	**Switzerland**

Characteristics

C c S s e g	Flat terminals
C O Q 0	Oval counterforms
G	Has spur
Q	Straight, angled tail
R	Curved, upright leg
a	Double-storeyed, curve at foot
f r t	Vertical terminals
i j	Square dots
t	Flat top-stroke
y	Flat, hooked tail

AGMQR
abcefghij
koprstuy

Connections

Akzidenz-Grotesk	c1898
Folio	1957
Univers	1957
Unica	1980

Availability

Helvetica is available from Linotype and resellers

Specimen

Helvetica type specimen. D. Stempel AG, Frankfurt, 1960s (210x210mm)

ABCDEFGHIJKLMNOPQR
STUVWXYZ &.,-:;'!?()/ $ 1234567890 £
abcdefghijklmnopqrstuvwxyz

8 pt sf	L1237	26 A	51 a	21 Fig.1
8 pt lf	L1238	24 A	48 a	21 Fig.1
10 pt sf	L1239	28 A	47 a	18 Fig.1
10 pt lf	L1240	25 A	43 a	18 Fig.1
12 pt	L1241	22 A	39 a	16 Fig.1
14 pt	L1242	18 A	28 a	13 Fig.1

8 sf — The basic character in a type design is determined by the uniform design characteristics of all letters in the alphabet. However, this alone does not determine the standard of the type face and the quality of composition set with it. The appearance is something complex which forms itself out of many details, like form, proportion, ductus, rhythm etc. If everything harmonizes, the total result will be more than the sum of its components. The only reliable basis for THE DESIGN OF A TYPE IS A POSITIVE FEELING

10 sf — The basic character in a type design is determined uniform design characteristics of all letters in the alp However, this alone does not determine the standard type face and the quality of composition set with appearance is something complex which forms its of many details, like form, proportion, ductus, rhyth If everything harmonizes, the total result will be mo THE SUM OF ITS COMPONENTS. THE ONLY REL

8 lf — The basic character in a type design is determined by the uniform design characteristics of all letters in the alphabet. However, this alone does not determine the standard of the type face and the quality of composition set with it. The appearance is something complex which forms itself out of many details, like form, proportion, ductus, rhythm etc. If everything harmonizes, the total RESULT WILL BE MORE THAN THE SUM OF IT

10 lf — The basic character in a type design is determined by the uniform design characteristics of all letters the alphabet. However, this alone does not determine the standard of the type face and the quality composition set with it. The appearance is some complex which forms itself out of many details FORM, PROPORTION, DUCTUS, RHYTHM E

12 — The basic character in a type design is determined by the uniform design characteristics of all letters in the alphabet. However, this alone does not determine the standard of the type face and the quality of composition set with it. The appearance is something complex which forms itself out of many details, like form, proportion, ductus, rhythm If everything harmonizes, the total result will be more than the sum of its components. The only reliable basis for the design of a type is a positive feeling for form and style. ORDER TO BE ABLE TO REALIZE THE CONCEPT OF A TYPE FACE THE FUR

14 — The basic character in a type design is determined by the uniform design characteristics of all letters in the alphabet. However, this alone does not determine the standard of the type face and the quality of composition set with it. The appearance is something complex which forms itself out of many details, like form, proportion, ductus, rhythm etc. If everything harmonizes, the total result will be more than the sum of its components THE ONLY RELIABLE BASIS FOR THE DESIGN OF A TYPE IS A P

Helvetica Medium

5772	14 A	20 a	10 Fig.1
5773	10 A	20 a	9 Fig.1
5774	8 A	12 a	7 Fig.1
5775	7 A	10 a	6 Fig.1
5776	5 A	9 a	6 Fig.1
5777	4 A	6 a	4 Fig.1
5778	3 A	5 a	3 Fig.1
93424	4 A	5 a	3 Fig.1
93425	4 A	4 a	3 Fig.1

16 Technical journal of engineering drawing for the students

18 Hand-catalogue of postage-stamps for collectors

24 sf Production per hour of a rotary machine

24 lf Electronic engineering principles

30 Consignment for inspection

42 Bank of Jefferson City

48 Nautical science

60 Force landing

72 Bookbinder

30 SOUTH AFRICA COMPANY

In the late 1950s Eduard Hoffmann (1892–1980), director of the Haas Type Foundry in Switzerland, decided that the foundry needed a new sans serif in its portfolio to compete with Akzidenz-Grotesk (pp152–53), a favourite among Swiss graphic designers at the time. A freelancer, Max Miedinger (1910–80), was commissioned to design it. Originally released for hand composition as Neue Haas Grotesk in 1957, Miedinger's new typeface was not unlike Akzidenz, but cleaner and more refined. Helvetica acquired its name in 1960, when Stempel adapted it for Linotype composition.

It is a rounded sans serif typeface with a large x-height and strokes terminating consistently either horizontally or vertically, giving a particularly robust and self-possessed appearance to individual characters in comparison with earlier sans serifs that follow a more natural line, like Akzidenz-Grotesk. Designer Mike Parker, who was involved in Helvetica's production at Stempel, reflected on its formal qualities in 2007: 'It is so firm. It is not a letter that is bent to shape. It's a letter that lives in a powerful matrix of surrounding space. It's brilliant when it's done well.' Helvetica is a type built for efficiency, deliberately stripped of remarkable features. There are very few eccentricities in its letterforms and no features that might connect to any obvious historical reference points. As a result, Helvetica rapidly became the typeface of choice for many modern designers. It resonated with the post-war ideals of clarity, accuracy and objectivity that later became known as the Swiss Style or International Typographic Style.

Over the next three decades the Helvetica family was expanded with new weights, widths and variants. In 1983, to control its unbridled growth, Helvetica was updated by Linotype and renamed Neue Helvetica (pp452–53), a system with a huge number of variations within a cohesive organizational framework.

Helvetica became a household name in the 1980s, bundled with computer systems since the advent of desktop publishing. Today it is everywhere. It is probably the most widely used typeface of all time and it has been copied endlessly. Helvetica has become so familiar – not only to designers but to almost everyone – that it goes barely noticed. To serve as a vehicle for communication in this way might be seen as the highest possible achievement for a typeface. But for a few within the design profession, Helvetica's global ubiquity implies a dull homogeneity and lack of discernment. As Erik Spiekermann, one of its most vociferous critics, has commented: 'You have to breathe, so you have to use Helvetica.'

Ty	**Meridien**
Ca	**Serif**
Ke	**Old Style**
Te	**Photocomposition**
Da	**1957**
De	**Adrian Frutiger**
Fo	**Deberny & Peignot**
Co	**France**

Characteristics

Capitals lower than ascender height
Sharp, cupped serifs
G No spur
M Splayed stems
V v W w Pointed vertex
c e Bottom-heavy
f Narrow, non-kerning
g Double-storeyed, short flat ear
y Flat serif on straight tail

AGMRW
abcdefghij
orstuy*aefg*

Connections

Jenson	1470
Latin	c1870
Vendôme	1951
Galliard	1978

Availability

Meridien is widely available

Specimen

Meridien type specimen. Deberny & Peignot, Paris, 1957 (297x230mm)

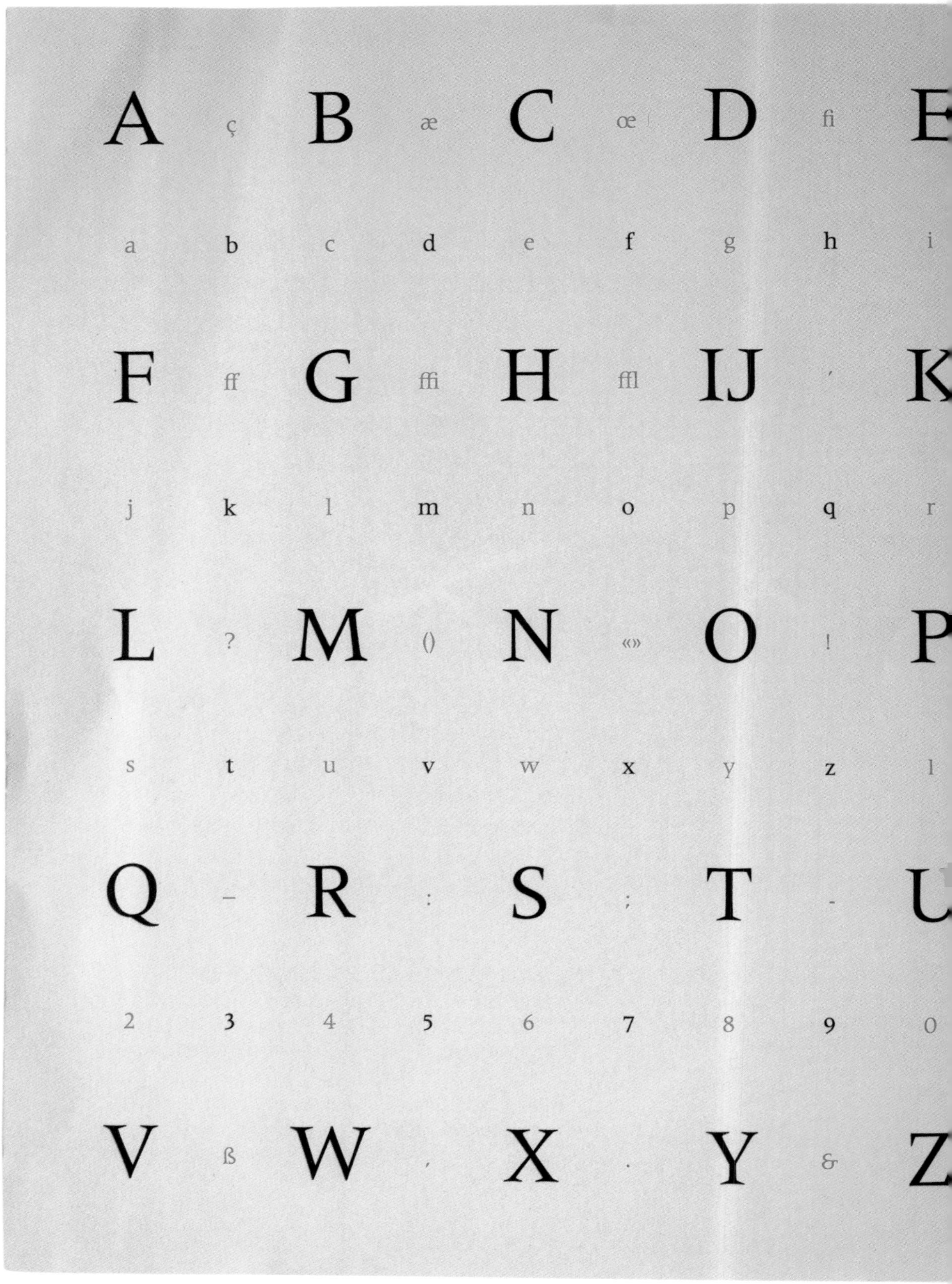

6 - 5600   195 a 45 A - 43 l. - 2,15 k

La terre de France est remarquable par la netteté de sa figure, par les différences de ses régions, par l'équilibre général de cette diversité de parties qui se conviennent, se groupent et se complètent assez bien. Une sorte de proportion heureuse existe en ce pays entre l'étendue des plaines et celle des montagnes, entre la surface totale et le développement des côtes; et sur les côtes mêmes, entre les falaises, les roches, les plages qui bordent de calcaire, de granit ou de sable le rivage de la France sur trois mers. la France est le seul pays d'Europe qui possède trois fronts de mer distincts. Quant aux ressources de surface ou de fond, on peut dire que peu de choses essentielles à la vie manquent à la France. Il s'y trouve
LA TERRE DE FRANCE EST REMARQUA

c. 24 - 5607   30 a 10 A - 35 l. - 6,82 k

La terre de France est remarquable par la netteté de sa figure, par les différences de ses régions et l'équilibre général de cette diversité de parties qui se conviennent, se groupent et se
LA TERRE DE FRANCE EST REM

8 - 5601   145 a 32 A - 43 l. - 2,72 k

The ages-old struggle between royal and baronial powers dominates the story of England in the 13th Century. As this struggle was fought to an effective decision between the time of John's ascent to the throne in 1199 and the death of Edward I in 1307, England was shaping itself for the modern age. There was no talk of 'the rights of man' or the sovereign power of 'the people.' Yet the nation was unwittingly playing with such revolutionary concepts, and the leading actor in the unfolding drama was King John, who was to become so unenviably famous. As in all
THE AGES-OLD STRUGGLE BETWEEN ROY

c. 20 - 5606   59 a 12 A - 35 l. - 5,60 k

La terre de France est remarquable par la netteté de sa figure, par les différences de ses régions, par l'équilibre général de la diversité de parties qui se conviennent, se groupent et se complètent assez bien
LA TERRE DE FRANCE EST REMARQ

c. 10 - 5602   81 a 33 A - 39 l. - 3,18 A

Jede Nation hat Eigentümlichkeiten, wodurch sie von den andern unterschieden wird, und diese sind es auch, wodurch die Nationen sich untereinander getrennt, sich angezogen oder abgestoßen fühlen. Die Äußerlichkeiten dieser innern Eigentümlichkeit kommen der andern meist auffallend widerwärtig und im leidlichsten Sinne lächerlich vor. Diese sind es auch warum wir eine Nation immer weniger achten als sie es verdient. Die Innerlichkeiten hinge-
JEDE NATION HAT EIGENTÜMLICHKEITE

c. 16 - 5605   69 a 20 A - 37 l. - 4,81 k

The ages-old struggle between royal and baronial powers dominates the story of England in the 13th Century. As this struggle was fought to an effective decision between in the time of John's ascent to the throne in 1199 and the death of Edward I in 1307, England was shaping itself
THE AGES-OLD STRUGGLE BETWEEN RO

c. 12 - 5603   65 a 27 A - 37 l. - 3,51 k

La terre de France est remarquable par la netteté de sa figure, par les différences de ses régions, par l'équilibre général de cette diversité de parties qui se conviennent, se groupent et se complètent assez bien. Une sorte de proportion heureuse existe en ce pays entre l'étendue des plaines et celle des montagnes, entre la surface totale et le développement des côtes;
LA TERRE DE FRANCE EST REMARQUAB

c. 14 - 5604   59 a 24 A - 37 l. - 3,88 A

Jede Nation hat Eigentümlichkeiten, wodurch sie von den andern unterschieden wird, und diese sind es auch, wodurch die Nationen sich untereinander getrennt, sich angezogen oder abgestoßen fühlen. Die Äußerlichkeiten dieser inneren Eigentümlichkeit kommen der andern meistens auffallend widerwärtig und im leidlichsten Sinne
JEDE NATION HAT EIGENTÜMLICHKEITNE

Adrian Frutiger (1928–2015), designer of over 100 typefaces, considered Meridien, released by the French foundry Deberny & Peignot in 1957, to be among his best work. A glyphic, old-style serif type, it was the first realization of Frutiger's ideas about creating visual harmony in the construction of letterforms.

He started the Meridien project in 1954, drawing on three quite disparate historical influences to inform the design process. The most evident of these is François Ganeau's Vendôme typeface (pp332–33), published only six years earlier by Deberny & Peignot's main competitor, Fonderie Olive. Nicolas Jenson's Venetian type (pp20–21) from 1470 was also an important point of reference for the skeletons of Meridien's letterforms, which Frutiger based on enlargements of Jenson's characters. Much of their individual personality is inspired by the nineteenth-century Latin style, with its relatively even contours and sharp, triangular serifs (pp140–41).

Meridien was intended to be a typeface for setting in extended bodies of text. To avoid the brittleness of the Latin form the construction of Meridien's characters avoids the use of straight stems, which are all slightly concave so that strokes are heavier and more stable at the ends. These barely noticeable swellings give a lively expression to the type, with the intention of promoting legibility. To further support the flow of reading, Meridien also has a relatively large x-height and strong, angular serifs throughout, with no exceptions – Frutiger was keen to exclude any rounded terminals, which he felt would damage the integrity of the design.

Meridien's capitals are relatively small and unobtrusive in order to contribute to the type's overall rhythm, the feature that was most important to Frutiger. This, he thought, was the aspect of the design that would be most useful in stimulating reading. As he said later: 'I wanted readers to have the feeling they were strolling through a forest, rather than through a suburb with dour, straight houses.'

Ty	**Univers**
Ca	**Sans Serif**
Ke	**Grotesque**
Te	**Letterpress**
Da	**1957**
De	**Adrian Frutiger**
Fo	**Deberny & Peignot**
Co	**France**

Characteristics

C c S s e g Flat terminals
G No spur
K k Arms touch stem at joint
Q Flat tail on baseline
R Curved, upright leg
a Double-storeyed, straight stem
f r t Vertical terminals
i j Square dots
t Angled top-stroke
y Straight tail

AGMQR
abcefghij
koprstuy

Connections

Helvetica	1957
Forma	1968
Unica	1980
Imago	1982

Availability

Univers is available from Linotype and resellers

Specimen

Univers specimen. Deberny & Peignot, Paris, 1957 (290x225mm)

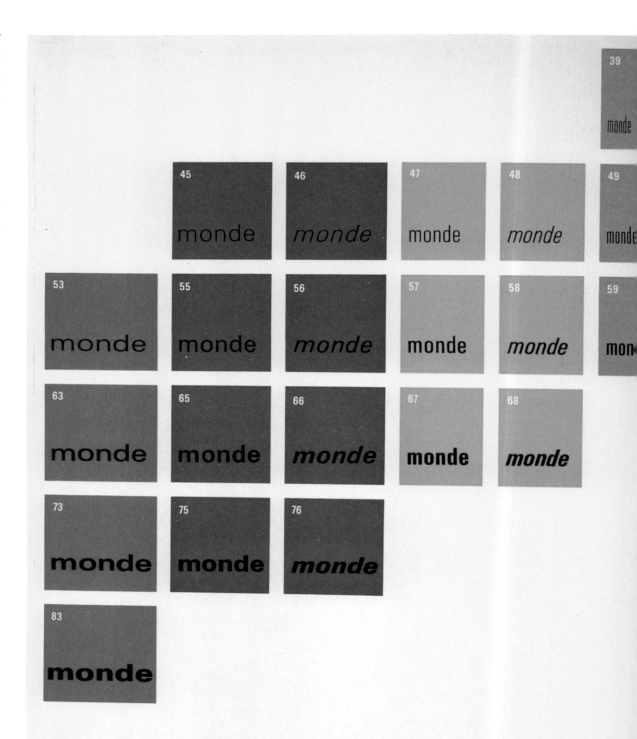

21 variations sur un thème uniq

univers

20 variantes

4 graisses

7 chasses

7 italiques

Deberny Peignot 18 rue Ferrus Paris Por 79-79

Les perfectionnements de la technique des Fondeurs et les immenses possibilités des procédés de composition photographique, manuelle ou mécanique, ont accru le rythme de création des caractères. Ceux-ci, le plus souvent inspirés par le besoin de nouveauté, sont essentiellement soumis aux caprices de la mode et passent avec elle. Ces soucis décoratifs répondent à la nécessité d'agrémenter la «vision» d'un texte. L'imprimerie utilise des caractères de base; ceux-ci, assez curieusement, ne correspondent plus actuellement au style de notre époque mais nous ont été légués par le passé; ainsi le Garamont par la Renaissance, le Baskerville par les Encyclopédistes, le Didot et le Bodoni par l'Empire et, récemment, l'Europe de l'entredeux guerres. Ainsi donc le vingtième siècle n'utilise-t-il presque universellement pour la transmission imprimée de la pensée que des signes dont la forme a été soit définitivement fixée il y a deux siècles, soit imprimée par eux. Il s'agit là d'un décalage anachronique qui démontre que notre époque peut encore chercher son expression propre dans ce domaine.

L'alliance traditionnelle de la Typographie et de l'Architecture s'est toujours manifestée au cours des grandes périodes de civilisation. Leurs correspondances secrètes se traduisent alors par la permanence d'une façon de vivre et l'unité d'un style dans toutes les formes d'expression artistiques.

Notre siècle, traversé par des bouleversements profonds, sociaux, économiques ou politiques et jusqu'ici aveuglé par le progrès industriel s'est lentement détaché des racines humanistes; étant mouvement par essence, on pourrait croire qu'il n'a pas encore manifesté la continuité d'un style essentiel qui, seul, eût déjà permis la cristallisation d'une typographie fondamentale. En fait, à l'aube de la seconde moitié du siècle, nous avons le recul nécessaire pour jeter un regard en arrière. Il est facile de découvrir à travers les tâtonnements et les erreurs, le fil directeur dont l'architecture actuelle et la typographie Univers expriment les concordances profondes et l'aboutissement.

La typographie Univers manifeste la consécration du style Antique. Apparemment, issue de la pierre lithographique vers les années 1890, l'antique exprime une volonté de rigueur à une époque où l'Art et l'Architecture exhaltent encore les souvenirs d'une pseudo-Renaissance. Toutefois, l'essor industriel, les transformations radicales de la vie économique et sociale libèrent peu à peu l'architecture de ces conventions périmées. Vers 1920, l'apparition en Allemagne du Futura, de l'Erbar et du Kabel expriment le triomphe de l'esprit de géométrie. Leurs auteurs croyaient éliminer toute nuance personnelle issue de la sensibilité d'un artiste pour atteindre la rigueur abstraite d'un code absolu. La lettre s'intégrait à l'édifice rationaliste dont les manifestations dans le domaine de l'architecture, du mobilier ou de l'automobile, se traduisaient par un style dépouillé, strictement soumis à l'exigence des nouveaux matériaux, le béton, le tube, etc... Aujourd'hui, ces mêmes matériaux assouplis par la perfection de la Technique obéissent à leur tour aux exigences d'un humanisme renaissant. Ainsi s'impose un retour à des formes plus inspirées par l'esprit de finesse.

Avec l'UNIVERS, Adrian Frutiger n'a eu d'autres soucis que de nous apporter une typographie du plus juste équilibre entre cet esprit de finesse et l'esprit de géométrie.

The Univers family was designed by the prodigious Swiss type designer Adrian Frutiger (1928–2015) between 1954 and 1957. Although often thought of as a Swiss typeface, Univers was made while he was working in France for the Deberny & Peignot foundry. It was commissioned in response to the technological advances in printing and production brought about by the advent of photocomposition.

Like Helvetica, released in the same year, Univers is based on the archetypal sans serif forms of Akzidenz-Grotesk (pp152–53). However, Univers is somewhat more severe than Helvetica, with every superfluous feature excised. Frutiger removed the eccentricities of the traditional grotesque to produce a design that is sharply cut, unobtrusive and supremely versatile. With Univers, Frutiger initiated a trend towards a large x-height in the sans serif form. The stiff geometry seen in many twentieth-century sans serifs was replaced with subtle arcs that are slightly squared to produce a very balanced and legible typeface in both text and display applications. Vertical and horizontal stroke widths contrast only slightly and, like Helvetica, they are consistently terminated, either horizontally or vertically, to give a determined quality to each letterform.

Univers was the first typeface whose construction was developed as a cohesive system from the outset. To create a series of related styles that were diverse but harmonious, Frutiger unified every element of the family within a strict modular framework. He devised a two-digit numerical matrix for each member of the family in order to distinguish one version from another and to avoid the vagueness of traditional descriptors such as light, bold, compressed, expanded and so on. The first digit for each typeface referred to stroke weight, and the second to character width, with odd numbers being assigned to upright styles and even numbers to italics. Frutiger continued to improve the Univers system cyclically, working in collaboration with technicians to add new weights and to expand the family with many non-Latin writing systems, such as Greek, Cyrillic and Arabic. Originally drawn in 21 weights and styles, the Univers family has now grown to a collection of 44 typefaces.

Frutiger himself did not regard Univers as his greatest achievement, saying in a 1979 interview that it 'does not now have much actual interest. It is in fact the shape and character of a particular epoch – the 60s.' Nevertheless, Univers is a landmark in the history of typography. Integrating rational design with timeless elegance, it remains one of the most popular typefaces available.

Ty	**Optima**
Ca	**Sans Serif**
Ke	**Humanist, Flared**
Te	**Letterpress**
Da	**1958**
De	**Hermann Zapf**
Fo	**Stempel**
Co	**Germany**

Characteristics

C G	Open
D O Q	Wide
E F L S	Narrow
M	Splayed
N	Lightweight verticals
S	Slightly top-heavy, tilted to right
a g	Double-storeyed
e	Bowl open and wide
f t	Narrow

ACEGMS
abcdefghij
koprstuy

Connections

Stellar	1929
Lydian	1938
Syntax	1969
SangBleu	2008

Availability

Optima is available from Linotype and resellers

Specimen

Optima type specimen. D. Stempel AG, Frankfurt, c1958 (297x210mm)

Optima

8 point s.f. no.1200 29 A 55 a 27 Fig.1   6
A letter is a designed area. It is a pattern made within a space. Its outlines have the effect of motion. It begins and ends. The things are true about the shapes of letters that

A LETTER IS A DESIGNED AREA. IT IS A PATTERN MADE WITHIN A SPACE

8 point l.f. no.1202 23 A 45 a 21 Fig.1   8
A letter is a designed area. It is a pattern made within a space. Its outlines have the effect of motion. It begins and ends. The things are true about

A LETTER IS A DESIGNED AREA IT IS A PATTERN MADE WITHIN

10 point no.1203 27 A 45 a 20 Fig.1   9
A letter is a designed area. It is a pattern made within a space. Its outlines have the effect of motion. It begins and ends. The

A LETTER IS A DESIGNED A REA. IT IS A PATTERN MADE

12 point s.f. no.1204 24 A 40 a 18 Fig.1   10
A letter is a designed area. It is a pattern made within a space. Its outlines have the effect of motion. It begins

A LETTER IS A DESIGNED AREA. IT IS A PATTERN M

12 point l.f. no.1205 20 A 33 a 13 Fig.1
A letter is a designed area. It is a pattern made within a space. Its outlines have the effect of

A LETTER IS A DESIG NED AREA. IT IS A PA

When ordering Linotype matrices please use this column of point sizes

Studies in the literature of Eastern Europe   ART COLLECTIONS
14 point no. 5694 18 A 29 a 11 Fig.1

News from the other side of the earth   PULVERIZATION
18 point no. 5695 12 A 22 a 10 Fig.1

Lost in the Australian Deserts   IN ENGLAND
24 point s.f. no. 5696 9 A 14 a 8 Fig.1

Publics in Industrial World   FURNITURE
24 point l.f. no. 5697 8 A 12 a 7 Fig.1

Report from Mexico   MODERN
30 point no. 5698 6 A 9 a 6 Fig.1

The Power Show BOILERS
36 point no. 5699 5 A 8 a 5 Fig.1

Examinations HAND
48 point no. 5700 4 A 5 a 4 Fig.1

In 1950 the renowned German calligrapher Hermann Zapf (1918–2015) was researching historical letterforms at the Basilica di Santa Croce in Florence when he discovered a fifteenth-century marble tomb whose inlaid capitals were highly unusual. They had classical Roman proportions but lacked traditional serifs. In his excitement to make a visual record of his extraordinary find Zapf realized that he had run out of paper. As a result, he hastily drew his first sketches for Optima on an Italian banknote.

Zapf worked on the design for two years, refining character shapes and proportions, before submitting his final drawings to the Stempel foundry for cutting and casting for hand-setting. Optima was released by Stempel in 1958, and by Linotype for machine composition in 1960. Zapf's intention for his new typeface was, he said, 'to produce a good, readable face, which would not be as monotonous and tiring as a normal sans serif, simple and self-explanatory in its forms.' With Optima, he bridged the gulf separating serif and sans serif typefaces: traditional serifs have been replaced by gently curved flares at the terminals of strokes, highly reminiscent of stone-cut letters.

Following Roman inscriptional models, Zapf designed Optima with harmonious proportions based on classical geometry. True to this heritage, it has wide, full-bodied lower case characters, following the delicate relationships of traditional types of the Renaissance, and capitals that closely resemble the Roman inscriptions that first inspired the design. Characters have a decisive contrast of thick and thin strokes with a vertical stress. Following the modern convention of sans serif designs like Helvetica or Univers, Optima's italic is a slanted version of the roman.

With his Optima design Zapf fused two fundamentally opposed typographic traditions into one of the most spirited humanist sans serifs in the history of visual communication. Settings in Optima project a gently incised, handmade appearance, combining the evenness and clarity of sans serif type with the vivacity of Renaissance letterforms and the majesty of classical Roman inscriptions.

Royal Brierley Crystal

Modern homes demand modern glass

The up-to-date household is incomplete without Royal Brierley Crystal – the glass which gives distinctive dignity and added charm to both table and sideboard. Write for copy of illustrated booklet showing »Royal Brierley Crystal«, together with prices.

STEVENS & WILLIAMS LTD. / STOURBRIDGE

Ty	Transport
Ca	Sans Serif
Ke	Grotesque
Te	Signage / Lettering
Da	1959
De	Jock Kinneir and Margaret Calvert
Fo	N/A
Co	UK

Characteristics

A	Low crossbar
C c S s e g	Angled terminals
G	Has spur
M	High vertex
Q	Straight, angled tail
R	Straight, angled leg
a	Double-storeyed, small curve at foot
f t	Angled terminals
i j	Round dots
l	Hooked tail
t	Tall, angled top-stroke
y	Flat, hooked tail

AGMQR
abcefghij
koprstuy

Connections

Akzidenz-Grotesk	c189
Helvetica	195
Akkurat	200
Lettera-Txt	200

Availability

New Transport is a digital revival available from A2-Type and resellers

Specimen

Traffic Signs for Motorways: Final Report of the Advisory Committee. Ministry of Transport, HMSO, London, 1962 (250x155mm)

Figure 1. Form and proportion of capital letters, where employed, for all uses except in route-numbers (see figure 4) and telephone numbers (see figure 5). (Paragraph 15)

36

37

In planning the construction of Britain's first motorway in the 1950s an urgent need for a more efficient road signage system was recognized. Until then a chaotic assortment of signs was in use on Britain's roads. An all-capitals alphabet designed by Hubert Llewellyn-Smith had been officially instated in 1933, but older signs featured a random variety of alphabets supplied by their manufacturers. In the early days of motoring, legibility had not been an issue, but with the rapid expansion of road transport after the war it was becoming a pressing concern.

The Ministry of Transport's Advisory Committee on Traffic Signs for Motorways appointed the accomplished British designer Jock Kinneir (1917–94) and his assistant Margaret Calvert (1936–) to develop a new motorway signage system in 1957. Kinneir said that they started working on the design by asking: 'What do I want to know, trying to read a sign at speed?' Their solution was based on the proposition that every sign should operate as a schematized map, intended for drivers to be able to read as quickly and as efficiently as possible.

Although Kinneir and Calvert had not been briefed to design a custom typeface, they were convinced that improving on the capital letters then in use would be beneficial to road safety and that a combination of upper and lower case would be more legible. The basis for their lettering was Akzidenz-Grotesk (pp152–53), the classic sans serif that had also been the model for Helvetica and Univers.

In developing their letterforms Kinneir and Calvert introduced features that owed much to Edward Johnston's Railway Type (pp202–203), such as the high vertex of the upper case M and the curved foot of the lower case l that mirrors the distinctive tails of the a and t. Designed to eliminate ambiguities between letters and thus optimize recognition, these features also contributed a far more relaxed and inviting sensibility to British road signage than the geometric lettering then in use on many European road signs (pp266–67).

After comprehensive testing in 1958 Kinneir and Calvert's signage was first introduced on the M1 motorway the next year. They were later commissioned to extend the system for implementation throughout the entire British road network. Later named Transport, the typefaces, in bold and medium weights, remain the only ones permitted on UK road signs.

Amiable yet rigorous, the system has become a blueprint for modern road signage all over the world. However, like much of the best typographic design, the typefaces used on Kinneir and Calvert's signs have performed so efficiently for so long that most people are completely unaware of them.

Figure 2. Form and proportion of lower-case letters. (Paragraph 15)

Ty	**Various**
Ca	**Various**
Ke	**Various**
Te	**Photocomposition**
Da	**1960**
De	**Various**
Fo	**Photo-Lettering Inc.**
Co	**USA**

Availability
House Industries offer an online service to provide digital versions of selected Photo-Lettering Inc. settings.

Specimen
Alphabet Thesaurus Nine Thousand.
Photo-Lettering Inc., New York, 1960
(305x230mm)

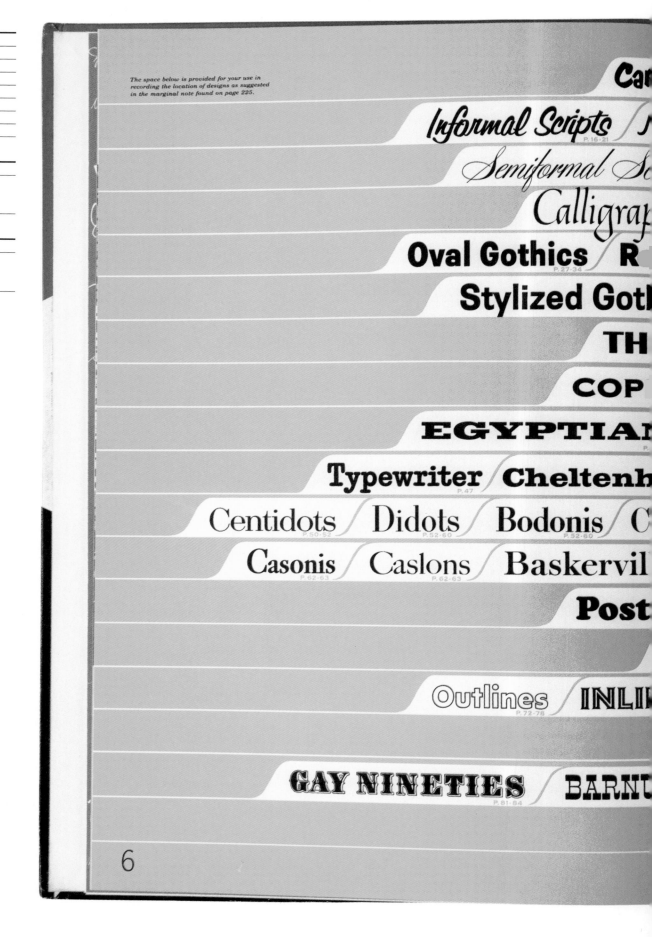

Chalks / Blurbs / Balloons 1
P.10-16 P.15 P.10-16 P.15

Brush Scripts / Stylized Scripts 2
P.17-21 P.16-21 P.21

mal Scripts / Upright Formals 3
P.22-23 P.21

at Pens / UNCIALS 4
P.25-26 P.25,71

hics / Grotesks / Parallel GOTHICS 5
P.27-34 P.32-33 P.35-38

imated GOTHICS / INTERLOCKS 6
P.38-40 P.38-40

THIN sans serifs 7
P.40-42

TES / MONTgomerys / Monroes 8
P.42-43 P.42-43 P.42-43

ock Serifs 9
P.44-47, 49-50

mer / Clarendon / Century 10
P.49 P.49-50 P.50-52

ENGRAVERS / Latins/Animated 11
P.55-57,61 P.60-61 P.60-61

lmers / Garamonds / ROMANS 12
P.64 P.63 P.64-67

omes / STENCILS 13
P.68 P.69

icans / Medievals / Old English 14
P.70 P.71 P.70-71

adeds / CONTOURS 15
P.72-78 P.72-78

NOVELTIES GALORE 16
P.79-80

amentals 17
P.81-84 P.726-727

PHOTO-LETTERING TECHNIQUES 18
P.724-740

7

In the 1960s Photo-Lettering Inc. in New York was one of the largest and most successful companies using photocomposition for the production of typography and layouts. It was founded by Ed Rondthaler (1905–2009) in the late 1930s to exploit the commercial potential of the first phototypesetting device, the Rutherford Photo-Lettering Machine, and was a mainstay of the New York advertising industry until the inception of desktop publishing in the 1990s.

Photocomposition automated processes to set type with photographic images of letters that were far more economical, more flexible and quicker than was possible within the restraints of metal type. It transformed the way printed matter was produced, and, in tandem with the development of offset litho printing, brought about a revolution in the operations involved in print production, shifting key activities away from both traditional printing houses and lettering artists to designers, typographers and advertising agencies. The transition precipitated the growth of the design profession, placing control of the origination of printed communications into users' hands for the first time and leading to the digital revolution of the 1980s and 1990s.

With its almost infinite variety of photographic manipulations of letters and words, Photo-Lettering Inc. offered unprecedented possibilities in the design of type, triggering an explosion of new typefaces. Alphabets for phototypesetting were drawn in ink on glass panels by experienced lettering artists and took around 200 hours to complete. This was far quicker and cheaper than traditional type production for letterpress printing, which required lengthy processes using extensive skills and materials.

Alphabet Thesaurus Nine Thousand, the 1960 Photo-Lettering catalogue shown here, is named after the number of types it contains, of which some are redrawings of classic types, some are new designs and some are photo-distorted variants of existing ones. Many fine headline types were produced for Photo-Lettering Inc. by a large number of lettering artists, including Herb Lubalin, Milton Glaser and Ed Benguiat. However, the massive proliferation of faces and the short-term, ephemeral nature of their applications had the effect of debasing the value of individual typefaces, many of which became buried in the sheer bulk of the offering. The spread shown here illustrates the huge extent of Photo-Lettering Inc.'s range rather than any individual design.

Ty	**Tyfa**
Ca	**Serif**
Ke	**Modern**
Te	**Letterpress**
Da	**1960**
De	**Josef Týfa**
Fo	**Grafotechna**
Co	**Czech Republic**

Characteristics

Vertical axis

High stroke contrast

Thin, unbracketed serifs

Thick / thin stroke changes at junctions

AGMRW
abcdefghij
orstuya*efg*

Connections

Didot	1784
Joanna	1931
Schadow-Antiqua	1938
Basilia	1978

Availability

Tyfa Antikva is available from Storm Type Foundry and resellers

Specimen

Oldřich Hlavsa, *Typographia 2: Fotosazba.* SNTL (Nakladatelstoi technicke literatury), Prague, 1981 (250x150mm)

JOSEF TÝFA, TÝFOVA ANTIKVA, 1959—60, GRAFOTECHNA

ABCDEFGHI
JKLMNOPRST
UVWXYZ
&1234567890
abcdefghijkl
mnopqrstuvw
xyz.,:!?

Die Schriftgestaltung des 20. Jah
Streben charakterisiert, eine Sch
den zeichnerischen Details von
freimacht und den Anforderung
Drucktechniken entspricht. Mit a
unter Wahrung optimaler Leserl

540

JOSEF TÝFA, TÝFOVA KURZÍVA, 1959—60, GRAFOTECHNA

ABCDEFGHI JKLMNOPRST QUVWXYZ &1234567890

abcdefghijkl mnopqrstuvw xyz.,:!?

rts ist durch das
ntwerfen, die sich in
chen Vorlagen
gegenwärtigen
Worten, der Schrift
den Ausdruck

541

In 1960 a national competition was held in Czechoslovakia to choose the best new typeface for book work. The winning entry was designed by Josef Týfa (1913–2007), an experienced and respected Czech graphic designer who had decided to specialize in type.

Týfa's winning typeface was originally cut by Grafotechna in both foundry metal and for machine composition and was issued shortly afterwards for phototypesetting. Although the design became popular and successful in Czechoslovakia, it remained largely unknown internationally due to Cold War politics. Efforts were made in the 1970s to license the design to the International Typeface Corporation in America, but communication through the Iron Curtain proved impossible and the plan was abandoned.

It was not until 1998 that Tyfa was finally issued globally by ITC as a result of the work of the Czech type designer František Štorm. In 1995 he undertook an extensive digital adaptation of the typeface, making a number of subtle improvements with Josef Týfa's active collaboration.

Although the structure of Tyfa shows old-style tendencies, its contours are neoclassical. Like Didot (pp90–91) or Bodoni (pp96–97), it is essentially a modern type design, with regulated geometries, a vertical axis, a pronounced contrast between thick and thin strokes, and thin serifs with no bracketing at their joints to the stems. However, Tyfa is notable for its interchanges between thick or thin letter parts at unexpected locations, which lend it the very affable and informal qualities of pen-drawn lettering.

The heritage of Czech type design is evident in Tyfa, which shares some of the attributes of earlier work by Vojtěch Preissig (pp220–21), Rudolph Ruzicka (pp318–19) and Oldřich Menhart, but Tyfa, like its predecessors, has a strongly non-conformist personality of its own, drawn from unfamiliar sources of inspiration. 'In the past, type design was primarily based on the aesthetic values of the faces', Josef Týfa remarked. 'Mine were inspired by the forms of modern architecture.'

Ty	**Ad Lib**
Ca	**Sans Serif**
Ke	**Grotesque, Casual**
Te	**Letterpress**
Da	**1961**
De	**Freeman Craw**
Fo	**American Type Founders**
Co	**USA**

Characteristics

Uneven character construction

Rough, square-cut counterforms

Uneven baseline

Alternates and ligatures

Invertible characters

ABGIMR
abcefghi
koprstuy

Connections

Bingo	1996
FF Folk	2003
Ed Interlock	2004
Burbank	2007

Availability

Ad Lib is widely available

Specimen

Ad Lib type specimen. American Type Founders, Jersey City, 1961 (210x93mm)

FGHIJKL
MNOPQR
STUVWX
YZABCD
ZABCDE
FGHIJKL
MNOPQR
STUVWX
KLMNOP
FGHIJKL
MNOPQR
ZABCDE
FGHIJKL

Designers, printers, typographers and advertisers who have expressed a desire for a n "casual" type will enjoy working with Ad Lib, ATF's crisp new letter of manifold use. It was de by versatile graphic artist Freeman Craw, well known for his Clarendons and Moderns. Althou spirit and technique of Ad Lib are free and spo this latest design follows consistently sound, ba and normal letter forms. Since it is related to ot ATF Gothics, Ad Lib combines well with them, as well as with its more distant cousins, e.g. the Bodonis, Centurys, Baskerville, etc. Close fitting of Ad Lib requires minimum word spacing.

Several imaginative innovations in type desi have made possible maximum freedom and vari in typographic arrangement. For instance . . .

Features:

1. Variant characters are supplied to give variety characters which repeat in the same word or headline. These are logical, subtle variations as would occur in a custom-lettered headline.

E *or* E, N *or* N, O *or* O, R *or* R,
S *or* S, T *or* T, a *or* a, c *or* c, e *or* e
f *or* f, g *or* g, l *or* l, m *or* m, o *or* o,
r *or* r, s *or* s, t *or* t, 0 *or* 0

Note: These variants, however, may be used eith at random with the regular characters or with careful design-layout intent. Regular and varia versions are clearly marked on the type body and should be stored in the same type case compartm

Ad Lib

THE spontaneous

ATF INNOVATION: cocoanuts

send Albuquerque cocoanuts

AND-LETTERED LOOK. This new approach to type design

pecial alignment allows certain characters to
nverted to make even more variants (for instance,
re are four versions of 'o'). These "turnabouts"
marked ◊ on the body.

or **q**, **d** *or* **p**, **n** *or* **u**, **p** *or* **d**, **q** *or* **b**,
or **o**, **u** *or* **n**

ll further variety is available in ligatures:

H Th ff

ere are special characters which are not regularly
pplied in font schemes:

% – () ¢

ABCDEEFGHIJKLMNNOO
PQRRSSTTUVWXYZ&TH
Th$12345678900¢aabccd
eeffgghijkllmmnnoopqrrss
ttuvwxyz.,:;-'?!?""""()*%-ff

AD LIB IS AVAILABLE
NOW FROM
YOUR NEAREST
ATF TYPE DEALER

Ad Lib is a display typeface designed in 1961 by Freeman Craw (1917–) for American Type Founders. Craw, an eminent American designer and art director, had a long-standing working relationship with ATF, having previously designed a number of the foundry's typefaces, most notably Craw Clarendon and Craw Modern.

At first glance Ad Lib resembles the sans serifs of the period, in particular Folio (pp344–45) and Helvetica Bold (pp346–47), but the visual conflict between its uneven external contours and its rough, square-cut interior forms makes it a mocking caricature of the earnest functionality of the grotesques on which it was based. Ad Lib's handmade effect, giving the impression of a woodcut print, was achieved by cutting the letters out of black sheet material with scissors. Its style has much in common with Ben Shahn's blocky hand lettering from the 1940s and 1950s.

The complete typeface, shown in ATF's 1961 specimen, featured alternate designs for a number of characters, intended to provide a spontaneous, hand-lettered look. In addition, it was vertically aligned on a jauntily uneven baseline so that several characters could be flipped over to form additional alternates, such as d for p, n for u, and vice versa. Little used in practice, these ingenious alternate characters were soon discontinued.

Although it was originally cast in metal for hand-setting, Ad Lib's design can be seen as a response to the newfound freedoms of 1960s photocomposition techniques. It became extremely popular from the early to mid-1960s, finding enormous success in TV and film title sequences, particularly for cartoons. Ad Lib's novel and ephemeral nature continues to reflect the spirit of its time.

Ty	**Antique Olive**
Ca	**Sans Serif**
Ke	**Humanist, Reversed Contrast**
Te	**Letterpress**
Da	**1962**
De	**Roger Excoffon**
Fo	**Fonderie Olive**
Co	**France**

Characteristics

Very tall x-height
Short ascenders and capitals
Most capitals have uniform width
Elliptical arcs
C c S s e g Vertical terminals
G No spur, tall vertical
K k Arms touch stem at joint
Q Short, angled tail
R Straight, angled leg
a Double-storeyed
a f r t Vertical terminals
i j Flat, elliptical dots
t Curved junction with cross-stroke
y Straight tail

AGEMQR abcefghij koprstuy

Connections

Frutiger	1976
FF Balance	1993
FF Legato	2004
Signo	2014

Availability

Antique Olive is available from Linotype and resellers

Specimen

Antique Olive type specimens. Fonderie Olive, Marseilles, c1960 (340x210mm)

Antique Olive is a sans serif typeface designed between 1955 and 1962 by Roger Excoffon, typographer and art director at Fonderie Olive. The project, originally called Catsilou, was the realization of Excoffon's vision for a new typography that was the product of scientific principles rather than the recycling of historical tropes. Excoffon intended to achieve what he described as 'the exact representation of the unconscious alphabet in each of us … the ideal alphabet.' The design was based on extensive research by Excoffon, José Mendoza y Almeida and Gérard Blanchard, who investigated graphology, the history of typography and the studies into legibility and the physiology of reading that were undertaken in the early twentieth century by the opthamologist Dr Émile Javal (pp612–13).

The result of these explorations was a sans serif with an unusual inversed stress. All of Antique Olive's letters are heavier at the top than at the base, and horizontal strokes are thicker than vertical ones throughout. These features influence the formation of positive and negative shapes within letters and words to guide the reader's eye comfortably along lines of text. In addition, wherever possible, strokes terminate vertically (c, e, s, for example), further enhancing the reading process by allowing consecutive letters to flow together in sequences rather than as autonomous objects. Antique Olive has an exceptionally large x-height – it only just falls short of the capitals – with proportionally short ascenders and descenders. In spite of some unfamiliar forms, Antique Olive is remarkably readable and highly effective in both headline settings and bodies of text.

The typeface was originally released in a wide ultrabold weight, Antique Olive Nord, in 1958, followed four years later by the complete family produced in four weights, light roman, italic, bold and black, along with a wide extrabold and ultrabold (Antique Olive Compact and Nord) as well as condensed variants. It was intended to compete with the new grotesques that were taking over the world of graphic design in the late 1950s, such as Helvetica (pp346–47) and Univers (pp350–51).

A latecomer to a highly competitive market, Antique Olive was well received but did not achieve the unparalleled success of its competitors outside France. This was partly because its unusual character did not conform to current trends. The work of a master typographer, it has, however, maintained an excellent reputation due to the integrity and vibrancy of its letterforms, which stand out in sharp contrast to the cold neutrality of the more ubiquitous sans serifs.

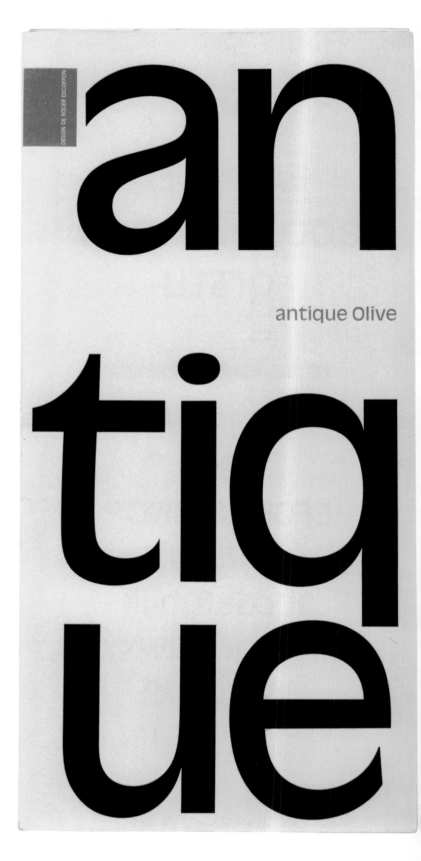

antique Olive

c. 48

ABCDEFGHIJKLMNOPQRSTUV
WXYZŒ&1234567890AIÉEÉÈ

abcdefghijklmnopqrstuvwx
yzàáâbçdéeêéëéfghiklmnñôöpú

c. 36

ABCDEFGHIJKLMNOPQRSTUVWWXYZ 12
34567890Æ&ŒABCDEÉÈÉEÉFGHIKLMNÒ

abcdefghijklmnopqrstuvwwxyzœæíû

c. 30

ABCDEFGHIJKLMNOPQRSTUVWXYZ123456789

abcdefghijklmnopqrstuvwwxyzàbçdéémnoü

c. 24

ABCDEFGHIJKLMNOPQRSTUVWXYZ ÆŒ1234567890ÉÈÉ

abcdefghijklmnopqrstuvwwxyzàâbçdéémnôöpqrstüyz

c. 20

ABCDEFGHIJKLMNOPQRSTUVWXYZ &1234567890?ABCDEFGHMNUZ

abcdefghijklmnopqrstuvwwxyzæœàáâbçdéèéëghîmnôöpqrstüü

c. 16

ABCDEFGHIJKLMNOPQRSTUVWXYZ Æ&Œ1234567890ABCDEEEFGHIKLMNOPQRSTVXYZ

Ty	**Eurostile**
Ca	**Sans Serif**
Ke	**Geometric**
Te	**Letterpress**
Da	**1962**
De	**Aldo Novarese**
Fo	**Nebiolo**
Co	**Italy**

Characteristics

Super-elliptical letterform structure
A M N V W Flat apexes
C c S s e g Flat terminals
G No spur
K Bar links arm and leg to downstroke
Q Angled tail longer on interior of letter
R Short leg
a Double-storeyed
f Narrow
g Single-storeyed
i j Square dots
r Wide, curved arch
t Crossbar wide on right, upturned tail
y Stepped strokes, curved tail

AGKMR abcefghij koprstuy

Connections

Bank Gothic	1930
Microgramma	1952
Vitesse	2006
Forza	2010

Availability

Eurostile is widely available

Specimen

Eurostile type specimen. Nebiolo, Turin, c1962 (297x210mm)

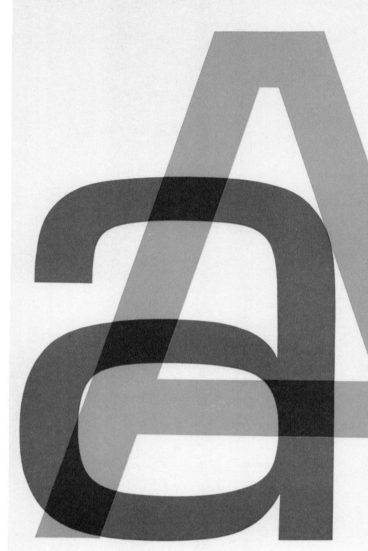

Oggi l'artista grafico sceglie ed impiega i carat... funzione non soltanto della loro leggibilità, ma ... del loro contenuto estetico e più particolarr... della loro adattabilità alla funzione di massa di c... Il blocchetto del testo assume in tali casi un ... prossimo a quello di un fondo omogeneo, di to... più o meno grigia a seconda dello spessore d... della serie adottata e da ciò nasce l'importa... avere un'assortimento di serie assai ricco i... stessa famiglia. Con la famiglia **Eurostile** la N... si è proposta di offrire ai grafici uno strumento ... colarmente idoneo a conseguire tali risultat... tratto saliente della personalità di questo cara... libero da retorica e conformismo, consiste nella ... dratura delle lettere tradizionalmente circolar... unita ad un'accentuata linearità determina ... monia architettonica ed un'intensità di ritm... consentono di ottenere effetti nuovi ed interes... nello stampato. Un accorgimento importante è ... quello di avere diminuito il rapporto di altezz... maiuscolo e minuscolo in confronto alle tradiz... proporzioni, il che ha consentito di disegnare a ... denti e discendenti poco accentuate, con il po... risultato di una maggior compattezza di colore fr... e riga aumentando la leggibilità nei corpi piccoli e...

Sintesi
evolutiva
del
nostro
tempo

monde graphique, qui a déjà accordé sa faveur
Microgramma, réserve maintenant le même ac-
il favorable à l'**Eurostile**, qui en est essentiel-
ent la dérivation. Stimulés par ce succès, nous
mes en train d'enrichir le nombre de ses variantes. L'**Eurostile** est une
ression de notre époque, dans laquelle les caractères linéales sont
s doute parmi les plus répandus. Par ces créations au style si ca-
téristique et inimitable, Nebiolo offre au monde graphique le moyen
l pour réaliser un imprimé moderne. Aujourd'hui plus que jamais
iste se soucie de l'harmonie esthétique de la page: les blancs,
ignes, les fonds, la couleur sont étroitement mêlés dans le jeu
uel qui est à l'origine d'une composition parfaitement équili-
e. Parmi ces éléments, le caractère joue toujours un rôle
s important; dans la plupart des cas il est, pour ainsi dire,
rotagoniste. Sous l'aspect technique et artistique, l'**Eu-
tile** a toutes les qualités nécessaires à réaliser typo-
phiquement l'idée de l'artiste. Parmi les variantes qui
rent ici il y en a deux toutes récentes qui ont peut-
e le plus d'intérêt au point de vue de la publicité et
a composition typographique: ce sont les séries
sse étroite normale et compacte. La pro-
ine variante de l'**Eurostile** sera la série **demi-
sse étroite**, à présent en cours d'exécution.

CIETÀ NEBIOLO 🔷 TORINO

Eurostile
une synthèse
de l'évolution
de
notre temps

In 1952 the Nebiolo foundry in Italy released Microgramma, a geometric sans serif available only in capitals. It was designed by Alessandro Butti (1893–1959) in collaboration with Aldo Novarese (1920–95). A decade later Novarese decided to revise and extend it, creating a lower case and reducing the size of the upper case proportionately. He also added condensed and compact versions to the original five styles.

The 1962 design, Eurostile, became one of the most popular and recognizable typefaces of the time. Its distinctive super-elliptical letter contour – neither round nor rectangular – was already a familiar part of the visual landscape, seen in everything from fashion design to television screens, reflecting the technological optimism of the space age. It was, as Novarese himself remarked, an 'unmistakable outline, well matching the feverish activity all around us'.

The most obvious attributes of Eurostile, apart from its super-elliptical letterforms, are its large x-height and even stroke contrast. The rectangular shapes of the letters allow for an extremely tight fit, resulting in a visibly geometric and rhythmic quality in headlines and bodies of text. The square geometry also gives a number of distinctive features to individual character constructions.

Once a first choice among graphic designers for use in headlines, Eurostile has fallen into relative obscurity today. Novarese suggested in the 1960s that it should be 'considered a symbol of our present times, as other faces were the expression of other periods of the past'. Perhaps a victim of its own success, Eurostile's appearance now seems more appropriate to the latter.

Compacta

		Characteristics	Connections	
Ty	**Compacta**	Heavy, rectilinear strokes	Schmalfette Grotesk	1954
Ca	**Sans Serif**	Small, vertical internal spaces	Impact	1965
Ke	**Geometric**	Tight letter spacing	Helvetica Inserat	1966
Te	**Instant Lettering**	Extremely compressed	Brauer Neue	1974
Da	**1963**	Extremely large x-height		
De	**Letraset / Frederick Lambert**	Short ascenders and descenders		
Fo	**Letraset**			
Co	**England**			

ABCDEMRS
abcdefghij
kmoprstuy

Availability
Compacta is widely available

Specimen
Letraset catalogue. London, 1970
(230x265mm)

42

COMPACTA

ABCDEFGHIJKLMNOPQRSTUVWXYZ
abcdefghijklmnopqrstuvwxyz
1234567890
&?!ß€$(;)

Pica

635 144pt 42.2mm
636 144pt 42.2mm
637 120pt 35.0mm
638 120pt 35.0mm
639 96pt 27.9mm
640 96pt 27.9mm
641 84pt 24.5mm
642 84pt 24.5mm
643 72pt 21.1mm
644 72pt 21.1mm
645 60pt 17.5mm
646 60pt 17.5mm
647 48pt 14.0mm
648 48pt 14.0mm
649 42pt
650 36pt
651 30pt
1872 24

Compacta was the very first typeface published by Letraset in 1963 using its dry-transfer lettering system, a method for creating headline settings to be used in camera-ready artwork, the standard production process for offset litho printing in the 1960s.

Compacta was created by lettering artists at Letraset's in-house type studio working in collaboration with the English graphic designer and educator Frederick Lambert. The design of the letterforms was heavily influenced by Schmalfette Grotesk, a

capitals-only typeface made by German typographer Walter Haettenschweiler in 1954. This earlier type had become hugely popular internationally after being used for headlines by Willy Fleckhaus in his exceptionally well-structured page layouts for the groundbreaking German magazine *Twen*. Because Schmalfette Grotesk was unobtainable in the UK, Compacta found a ready market and immediately became enormously successful.

Compacta is an extremely bold and condensed display typeface designed

around its tight internal vertical spaces. As its name suggests, it is intended to be spaced very tightly so that external and internal spaces correspond with each other. The rectilinear structure of letter contours, with their minute curves and counterforms, makes for dense word settings with high impact, inevitably offset by a loss of legibility and visual balance at smaller point sizes.

Compacta was originally available in two weights, with an oblique and an outline version; light and black were added later.

With the advent of instant dry-transfer lettering, graphic designers rather than trained compositors were able to manipulate headline settings for the first time, directly and cheaply, leading to an explosion of novel display typefaces and instigating new approaches to the ways in which printed matter could be designed in the 1960s and 1970s. Closer letter spacing than had previously been possible became highly fashionable, also influencing the look of phototypesetting, which, unlike letterpress, could be specified with negative spacing values.

43

COMPACTA BOLD

ABCDEFGHIJKLMNOPQRSTUVWXYZ

abcdefghijklmnopqrstuvwxyz

1234567890

&?!ßE$(;)\\《[8

1112 144pt 42.2mm

1113 144pt 42.2mm

1114 120pt 35.0mm

1115 120pt 35.0mm

1116 96pt 28.0mm

1117 96pt 28.0mm

1118 84pt 24.5mm

1119 84pt 24.5mm

1120 72pt 21.0mm

1121 72pt 21.0mm

1122 60pt 17.6mm

1123 60pt 17.6mm

1124 48pt 14.0mm

1125 48pt 14.0mm

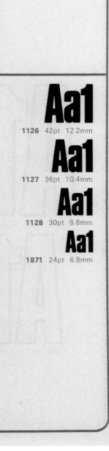

1126 42pt 12.2mm

1127 36pt 10.4mm

1128 30pt 8.8mm

1871 24pt 6.8mm

Ty	**Quadrato**
Ca	**Sans Serif**
Ke	**Geometric, Typewriter, Monospaced**
Te	**Typewriter**
Da	**1963**
De	**Arturo Rolfo**
Fo	**Olivetti**
Co	**Italy**

Characteristics

Monospaced

Monoline character construction with all strokes and serifs the same thickness

Tall x-height

Short ascenders and capitals

Large, open counterforms

Small, radiused corners

I i J j f Wide, serifed

M m W w Narrow

i j Large dot

AEGIQRS
abcefgi
lmprstz

Connections

Prestige Elite	1953
Courier	1955
Letter Gothic	1956
Nitti	2008

Availability

LL Valentine is a digital revival available from Lineto and resellers

Specimen

This page: Olivetti Quadrato specimen letter. Olivetti, Ivrea, c1964 (297x210mm)
Opposite: Quadrato 'A' technical drawing. Olivetti, Ivrea, 2005 (297x210mm)

olivetti

Egregio Signore,

      La pregheremmo di dedicare qualche attimo di attenzione a questa lettera: è stata compilata con una Olivetti PRAXIS 48 ossia con un modello di macchina per scrivere elettrica la cui novità essenziale consiste, oltre che nel meccanismo di scrittura, soprattutto nella dimensione.

      La PRAXIS 48 è infatti una macchina per scrivere elettrica che, mentre sul piano qualitativo offre tutte le garanzie degli altri maggiori modelli per ufficio, presenta, rispetto a questi, due ulteriori vantaggi: non crea problemi di spazio e può essere installata dovunque, anche sullo scrittoio di uno studio privato, e in secondo luogo, data l'estrema semplicità dei suoi comandi, può essere usata da chiunque.

      Naturalmente questa prova di scrittura della PRAXIS 48 nel carattere "Quadrato", è stata eseguita da una brava dattilografa dei nostri uffici; ma anche Lei avrebbe potuto ottenere lo stesso risultato.

      Anche nella PRAXIS 48, come in ogni buona macchina elettrica, scrivere bene non dipende più dall'abilità di chi opera sulla tastiera, ma dall'efficienza della macchina e la Olivetti PRAXIS 48 offre a chiunque la possibilità di scrivere con una perfezione sempre uguale a se stessa.

      Grati dell'attenzione, La preghiamo di gradire i nostri distinti saluti.

                  Ing. C. Olivetti & C., S.p.A.

1 2 3 4 5 6 7 8 9 0

Carattere "QUADRATO"

In 1969 Ettore Sottsass and Perry King designed a portable typewriter named 'Valentine' for Olivetti. It was promoted to the public as an 'anti-machine machine', for use 'any place but an office'. Available in a range of bright colours and intended to be carried around as a personal accessory, it rapidly became a Pop Art icon. The design of Olivetti products at this time, founded on an awareness of the human relationship with the machine, put Olivetti in a league of its own. Meticulous attention was paid to every detail, including the design of type.

The Valentine typewriter came equipped with different typefaces for different countries, among them traditional styles like Pica and Elite and more radical designs like Quadrato, shown here. This face was a highly appropriate choice for the Valentine since it mirrored the typewriter's contemporary design sensibility.

The Quadrato letters had been drawn around seven years earlier by Arturo Rolfo, the lead in-house designer at Olivetti from 1962 to 1964, for use in both mechanical and electric typewriters. Rolfo's point of reference in drawing the Quadrato type was Eurostile (pp364–65), designed by Aldo Novarese and based on his earlier Microgramma typeface. However, Rolfo's design was not a straightforward copy. As a typewriter face, it was necessarily monoline and non-proportionally spaced, with all characters occupying the same fixed width. The letter contours were constructed on a square stroke framework with radiused corners, but they integrated a number of subtle details – such as angled strokes at junctions and the judicious use of serifs – to improve readability.

In 2002 Stefan Müller designed a digital revival of Quadrato based on Rolfo's original drawings for the Lineto foundry. LL Valentine was issued in three weights with matching italics.

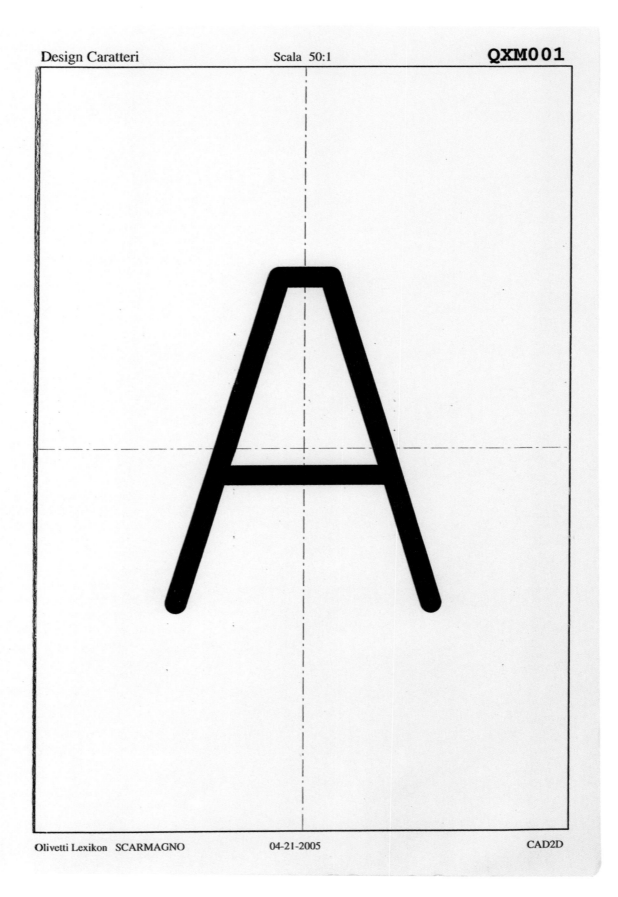

Design Caratteri   Scala 50:1   QXM001

Olivetti Lexikon SCARMAGNO   04-21-2005   CAD2D

Ty	**Friz Quadrata**
Ca	**Serif**
Ke	**Wedge, Glyphic**
Te	**Photocomposition**
Da	**1965**
De	**Ernst Friz and Victor Caruso**
Fo	**Visual Graphics Corporation**
Co	**USA**

Characteristics

Stems swell to triangular serifs
Large x-height
Short ascenders and descenders
A Flat apex with a left serif
E Long foot
J Descends below baseline
M N V W Angle at vertex
P R Open bowl
a b d p q Open bowl
g Double-storeyed, open bowl and flat ear
t Concave serif
6 9 Open bowl

AEJMRW
abcefghij
koprstuy

Connections

Latin	c1870
Albertus	1935
ITC Tiepolo	1987
Infini	2015

Availability

Friz Quadrata is available from Monotype and resellers

Specimen

Friz Quadrata type specimen. International Typeface Corporation, New York, c1974 (279x140mm)

Friz Quadrata is a serif typeface whose design is based on the shapely letterforms found in stone-carved inscriptions. Ernst Friz (1932–), a Swiss designer, drew its original single weight in 1965 for Visual Graphics Corporation, who released it as a photocomposition typeface. Several years later ITC entered into an agreement with VGC through which Victor Caruso added a bold weight to the family. From 1973 both designs became available through ITC and VGC. Finally, in 1992, French designer Thierry Puyfoulhoux drew compatible italics for both the original and bold weights. The design development process, from conception to completion, took almost 30 years.

Friz Quadrata is characterized by its glyphic profile. Rather than tracing the movement of a pen or being influenced by the technology with which it was constructed, its appearance has its origins in monumental capitals inscribed in stone in ancient Greek and Roman times. Characters are wide and round, with a large x-height and short extenders. The overall contrast of the typeface is low, with an even relationship between thin and thick strokes that flare outwards to form small, spiky wedge serif endings. Counterforms are left open throughout, as if constrained by the motion of a chisel.

Friz Quadrata's monumental appearance implies authority, incisiveness and modernity in equal measure. As a consequence, it was used extensively in brand communications and corporate identity and, due to its commanding tone, it became particularly ubiquitous as the public face of many government and civil institutions. Because of its sharpness, large lower case and even weight, it was often also used as a display type in television and film title sequences, especially during the 1970s.

abcdefghijklmnopqrstu
ABCDEFGHIJKLMNOPQ
30

abcdefghijklmnop
ABCDEFGHIJKLMN
36

abcdefghijklm
ABCDEFGHIJKL
48

abcdefghijk
ABCDEFGHI
60

abcdefgh
ABCDEFG
72

abcdefgh
ABCDEFG

abcdef
ABCDE

1" on Caps

10

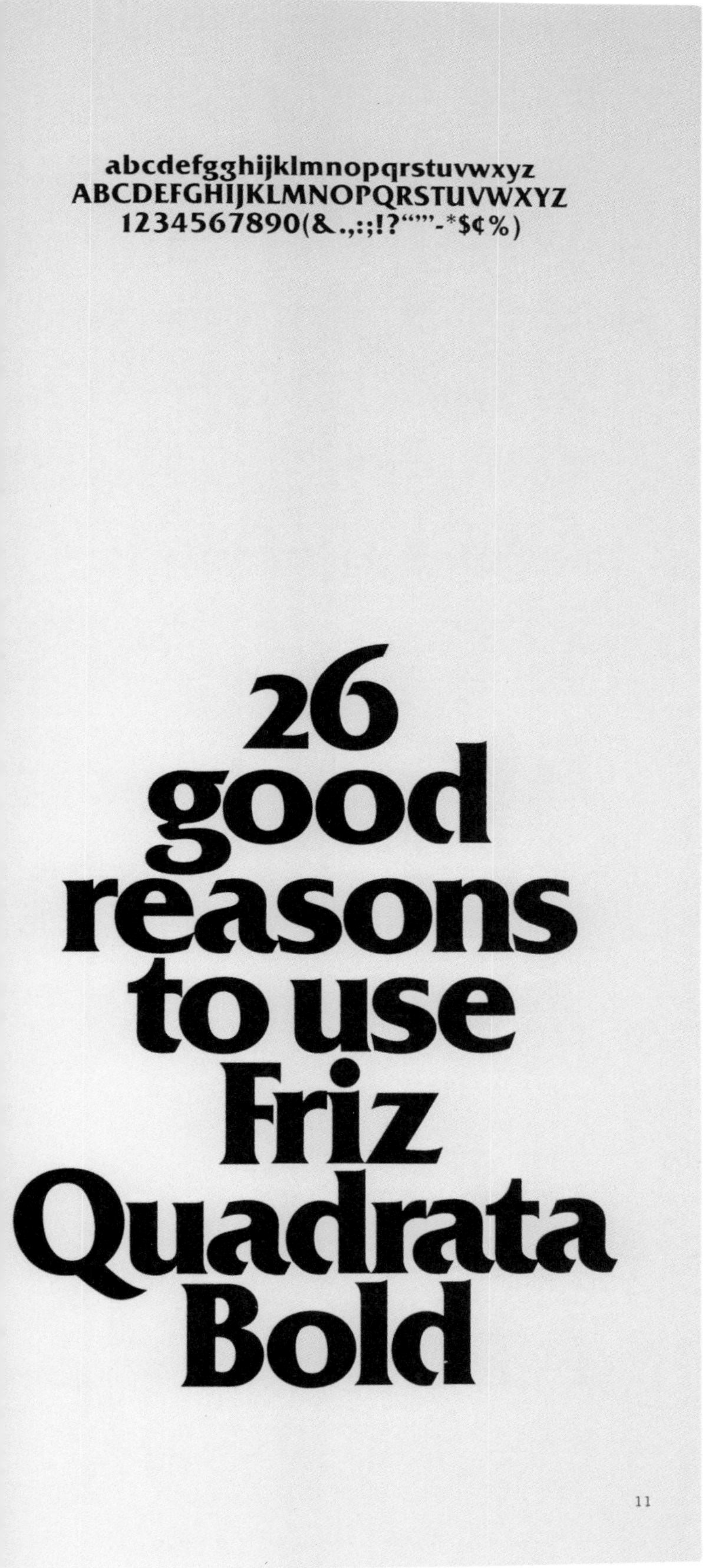

abcdefgghijklmnopqrstuvwxyz
ABCDEFGHIJKLMNOPQRSTUVWXYZ
1234567890(&.,:;!?""''-*$¢%)

26 good reasons to use Friz Quadrata Bold

abcdefghijklmnopqrstuv
ABCDEFGHIJKLMNOPQ

abcdefghijklmnopqr
ABCDEFGHIJKLMN

abcdefghijklmn
ABCDEFGHIJKL

abcdefghijkl
ABCDEFGHI

abcdefghi
ABCDEFG

abcdef
ABCDE

30
36
48
60
72
1" on Caps

11

6

Ty	**Impact**
Ca	**Sans Serif**
Ke	**Geometric**
Te	**Letterpress**
Da	**1965**
De	**Geoffrey Lee**
Fo	**Stephenson, Blake & Co.**
Co	**UK**

Characteristics

Thick strokes with small internal spaces
Tight letter spacing
Extremely large x-height
Extremely short ascenders
J r Alternates

ABCDEMRS
abcdefghi
knoprstuy

Connections

Thorowgood's Grotesque	1832
Anzeigen Grotesk	1943
Schmalfette Grotesk	1954
Compacta	1963

Availability

Impact is widely available

Specimen

Impact type specimen. Stephenson, Blake & Co., Sheffield, c1965 (130x210mm)

Impact is a sans serif display typeface created in 1965 by British graphic designer and typographer Geoffrey Lee (1929–2005) for the Stephenson, Blake foundry.

In the 1960s bold, condensed headline faces such as Helvetica Inserat and Compacta (pp366–67) were the height of fashion. This trend was probably inspired by the radical page layouts for the era-defining German magazine *Twen*, designed by Willy Fleckhaus using Walter Haettenschweiler's Schmalfette Grotesk typeface for headlines. The magazine achieved cult status in the international design community, and Schmalfette Grotesk was also seen on the pages of *Paris Match* and Haettenschweiler's seminal *Lettera* publications.

Impact was intended for display use only. In a crowded market, what made it 'quite different and so good', as its promotional leaflet described it, was simply that it was somewhat shorter than Compacta and somewhat fatter than Helvetica Inserat. Impact's ultrabold strokes, compressed letter spacing and minimal internal spaces are specifically intended, as the name suggests, to make an immediate visual impression in headlines. Impact has an extremely large x-height, extending nearly to the top of the capital letters. As a result, ascenders are so short that they look stunted, and descenders are even shorter.

In recent times Impact's ubiquity has increased since it comes preinstalled on Windows and Mac computers and is also now distributed as one of Microsoft's core fonts for the Web.

36
abcdefghijklmnopqrstuvwxyz r
ABCDEFGHIJKLMNOPQRSTUVWXYZ J
1234567890&£$-,.:;'!?()
7 A, 12 a

48
abcdefghijklmnopqrstuv
wxyz r &£$-,.:;'!?()
ABCDEFGHIJKLMNOPQRSTU
VWXYZ J 1234567890
5 A, 8 a

60
abcdefghijklmnopqr
stuvwxyz r -,.:;'!?()
ABCDEFGHIJKLMNOPQ
RSTUVWXYZ J
1234567890&£$
3 A, 6 a

Designed by Geoff Lee MSTD, MSIA. Impact is quite different in set width and x height. It has many carefully thought out detail plusses to give near perfection in display setting.

" apostrophe (used also for quotes) and all punctuation is visually 'size down'

- hyphen centres on lower case x - height, when inverted centres on cap height.

: when lower point is deleted on repros, upper point is centered on x - height for medial leaders.

[A brackets are to cap height for even line.

() there are both left and right hand brackets, in most types one bracket is inverted often giving uneven alignment.

& ampersand is x - height size for even line in lower case and is visually pleasing in cap line.

r terminal r for warmth and character.

r short r for even colour in lower case line.

J opening J.

J short J for even colour in cap line.

fi æ œ Æ Œ fi ff fl ffi ffl tied sorts are unnecessary because of tight justification, this makes founts more economical.

Impact is cast on Anglo-American point body

Stephenson Blake
Caslon Letter Foundry Sheffield 3 · Sheffield 25042
33 Aldersgate Street London EC1 · MONarch 8477

PRINTED IN ENGLAND

Amelia

Ty **Amelia**
Ca **Sans Serif**
Ke **Geometric**
Te **Photocomposition**
Da **1966**
De **Stan Davis**
Fo **Visual Graphics Corporation**
Co **USA**

Characteristics
Geometric character construction
Condensed proportions
Round stroke terminals
Interchange of thick and thin strokes
Irregular teardrop-shaped positive and
negative forms

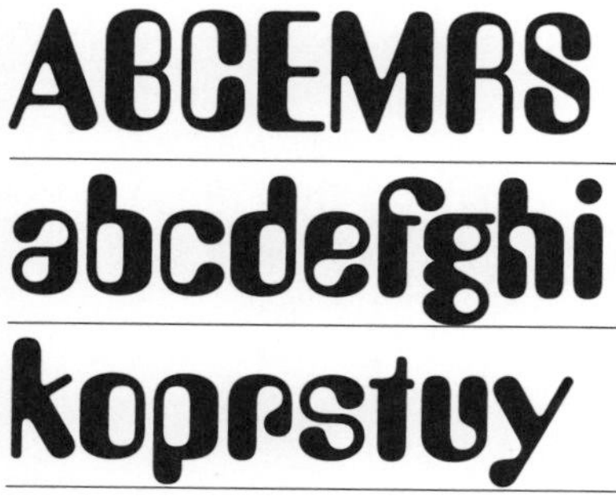

ABCEMRS
abcdefghi
koprstuy

Connections

Countdown	1965
Data 70	1970
House 3009	1999
Dialog	2005

Availability
Amelia is widely available

Specimen
Lettera 4. Niggli, Niederteufen, 1972
(240x210mm)

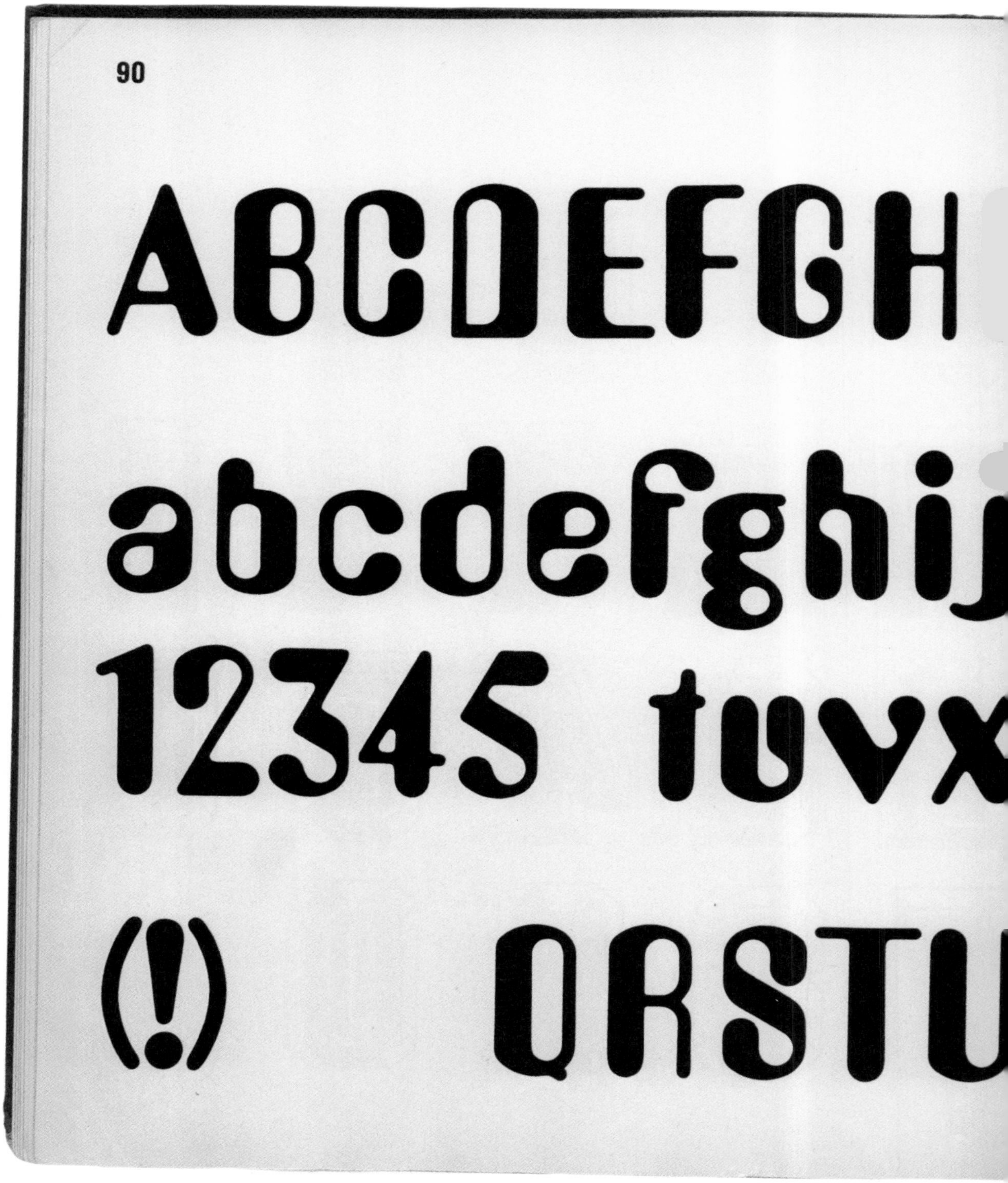

ABCDEFGH
abcdefghi
12345 tuvx
(!) QRSTU

JKKLMNOP
klmnopqrs
wyz 67890
VWXYZ ?

91

In 1966 the photosetting equipment manufacturer Visual Graphics Corporation organized an international type design competition that was judged by some of the leading typographers of the day. One of the winners was American graphic designer Stan Davis, with Amelia, the highly original display typeface he had drawn in 1964 and named after his newborn daughter.

The design of Amelia was the result of a unique collision of two disparate influences that distinguishes it from any others before or since. Superficially its characters resemble the symbols used by financial institutions for magnetic ink character recognition (MICR), a technology that had been invented in the 1950s to allow cheque-scanning devices to read and interpret alphanumeric data. But the teardrop forms of the inner spaces that give Amelia a blobby fluidity also evoke the exotic Orientalism of the psychedelic era in which it was made. 'Amelia was conceived in the early sixties at a time when hope was in the wind', Stan Davis wrote. 'It looks to the East for inspiration but is firmly rooted in the classical tradition it turns on end.'

This combination of visual connotations made Amelia a runaway success when released by VGC for its Typositor system. It was subsequently copied widely by other type foundries and seen on a broad range of design projects, from the title sequence of the Beatles' *Yellow Submarine* to the Moon Boot brand identity.

Davis explained its popular appeal: 'Somehow, Amelia has imparted meaning. It was simultaneously used by the Beatles and others as a rock anthem, a symbol of the sixties, science fiction, the corporate world, psychology and … computers, to which, I might add, in hindsight, it anticipates.'

Ty	**New Alphabet**
Ca	**Sans Serif**
Ke	**Geometric**
Te	**Lettering**
Da	**1967**
De	**Wim Crouwel**
Fo	**N/A**
Co	**Netherlands**

Characteristics
Modular, grid-based construction
Letters with 5 x 9 unit proportions
Square character proportion
Lower case only
45-degree bevelled corners
Numerals and punctuation
a g k m v w x z Unfamiliar forms

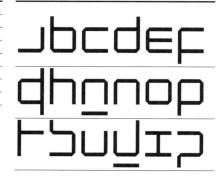

Connections

Epps Evans	1969
Vierkant	1972
Fodor	1973
Politene / Gridnik	1974

Availability
New Alphabet is a digital revival available
from the Foundry and resellers

Specimen
New Alphabet, *Kwadraatbladen* No. 23.
Steendrukkerij de Jong & Co., Hilversum,
1967 (250x250mm)

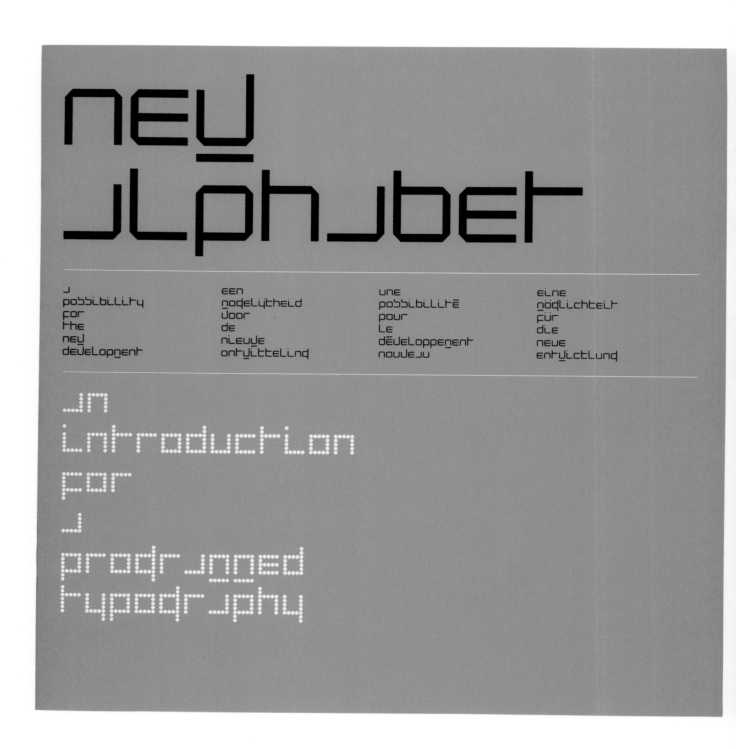

New Alphabet was published in 1967 in an issue of the *Kwadraatbladen,* a series of publications edited by Pieter Brattinga. It was created by the Dutch graphic designer Wim Crouwel (1928–) to address his concerns about the effects of the advent of photocomposition. The first phototypesetters used cathode ray tube (CRT) technologies that were only capable of producing output in basic horizontal and vertical dot patterns, resulting in a loss of definition when rendering conventional typefaces. Crouwel had seen what he called 'the horrible type coming out of that first generation machine', and the New Alphabet was his response to it.

In the *Kwadraatbladen*'s introduction, Crouwel argued that it was necessary to create new forms for new technologies. Instead of developing the machines to meet design requirements, the designs would be adapted to the machines.

His solution to this proposition was speculative, experimental and imaginative. New Alphabet was a provocation to designers, intended to stimulate debate and spark new ideas rather than operate as a functioning typeface. Crouwel decided that its letters would directly follow the CRT pattern of horizontal and vertical rows of dots. When scaled, expanded or compressed, these structures would always remain uncompromised. He also wanted the letters to align both vertically and horizontally on a grid so they all would be the same width.

New Alphabet was a single lower case typeface featuring letterforms that were plain rectangular segments drawn on a grid of five by nine units with 45-degree bevelled corners. About half of the characters were easily recognizable, but because they were all drawn to conform to Crouwel's systematic construction method, others, such as the a, g, m and w, took on a completely alien, unfamiliar appearance that seemed to imply an unforeseeable future for the appearance of text. However, Crouwel has said that he did not invent these odd characters in order to be provocative but to create a consistent alphabet based on the grid.

In 2001 type designer Evert Bloemsma described New Alphabet as 'the most consistent demonstration of the idea of the oneness of modern tools and their products'. A radical, iconic and hugely influential typeface, it was, in Wim Crouwel's eyes, a purely experimental exercise, 'never meant to be really used. It was unreadable.'

Ty	**Sabon**
Ca	**Serif**
Ke	**Old Style, French**
Te	**Letterpress**
Da	**1967**
De	**Jan Tschichold**
Fo	**Stempel**
Co	**Germany**

Characteristics

A	Angled apex
J	Descends below baseline, hooked
Q	Tail below letter
T	Serifs extend above arm
a	Double-storeyed
f	Narrow, non-kerning
g	Double-storeyed

AJMRST
abcdefghij
orstuy*aefg*

Connections

Garamond's Roman	c1538
Granjon's Roman	1560
Syntax	1969
Adobe Garamond	1989

Availability

Sabon is available from Linotype and resellers

Specimen

Sabon type specimen. D. Stempel AG, Frankfurt, 1960s (210x210mm)

Die Maßstäbe für Schönheit und Zweckmäßigkeit einer Drucktype wurden vor Jahrhunderten gesetzt und haben bis zum heutigen Tage ihre Gültigkeit behalten. Aus der bewußten Besinnung auf die hohe Schriftkultur der Renaissance ist die Sabon-Antiqua entstanden. Sie verkörpert in Maß und Form den klassischen Typus der Antiqua; sie ist entwickelt für die vielfältigen Satz- und Druckaufgaben unserer Zeit und verwirklicht mit den Mitteln und Möglichkeiten heutiger Schriftschneide- und Gießtechniken. Klar und unaufdringlich im Ausdruck erfüllt sie die anspruchsvolle Aufgabe, durch einen hohen Grad an Lesbarkeit dem Auge wohlzutun. Neu und einmalig ist die Identität in drei Setzverfahren bei den kleinen Graden: Einem Satzbild aus der Sabon-Antiqua ist es nicht anzusehen, in welchem der drei Setzverfahren es hergestellt ist, denn Linotype-Satz und Monotype-Satz stimmen mit dem Handsatz überein. Das erweitert die Einsatzmöglichkeit dieser Schrift und erhöht ihren Gebrauchswert. Schon heute liegen Urteile von Schriftkennern des In- und Auslands vor, die dieser Schrift eine große Zukunft voraussagen.

Sole U.K. Distributors:
ARNOLD COOK LIMITED 3 Torrens Street London, E.C. 1
Telephone: TERminus 01-837 0172/3
Grams & Cables: ARNCOOK London, E.C. 1

D. STEMPEL AG 6 FRANKFURT 70 POSTFACH 701160 TELEFON (0611) 610391 TX 411003

Sabon Antiqua

ABCDEFGHIJKLMNOPQ
RSTUVWXYZÄÖÜ
abcdefghijklmnopqrstuvwxyz
ßchckfffifflft&äöü
1234567890 1234567890
.,:;-!?.'()[]*†‹›»«„'"/£$

In Vorbereitung:

Sabon Kursiv
Sabon Antiqua halbfett

In the 1960s, when technological innovations were bringing sweeping changes to printing, Sabon was commissioned to address the needs of a group of German print companies that were concerned about the lack of a typeface that would look the same whether set on a Monotype, on a Linotype or by hand. They asked the two corporations to produce a typeface in collaboration with Stempel that would be identical in appearance for the three relevant type technologies: machine composition, line-casting and foundry type for hand-setting.

The distinguished German typographer Jan Tschichold (1902–74), who had been a pioneer of modern typography in the 1920s before taking a more conservative attitude towards his design practice, was entrusted with the task of designing the new type family. His brief was very specific. In addition to these complex technical requirements, a type in the sixteenth-century style was expected – something modelled on Garamond (pp48–49) or Granjon (pp56–57) – and it was to be 5 per cent narrower than other contemporary old styles to make it more economical.

As his model, Tschichold worked from a roman type of around 14 point from a 1592 specimen sheet by the Egenolff-Berner foundry attributed to Claude Garamond. From the same specimen he selected a Robert Granjon face as the basis for the italics. Sabon was not, however, a simple copy of the sixteenth-century types; Tschichold standardized construction by removing anomalies found in its ancestors and he crafted each letter in great detail, attending particularly to the rhythm of the serifs. In doing so, he considered the stroke contrast and weight needed to print effectively on modern paper, compensating for the fact that in contemporary offset litho printing the press would only touch the surface with ink rather than leave a physical impression. In order to emphasize that this was not another Garamond revival, the new typeface was named Sabon after the sixteenth-century French punch cutter Jacob Sabon.

A useful distinguishing feature of Sabon was that the roman, italic and bold weights all occupied the same set width due to Linotype's casting process. Each Linotype matrix could produce two different characters: roman or italic, roman or bold. As a result, copy-fitting – predicting the spaces and pages that bodies of text would occupy – was a comparatively easy task with Sabon. The typeface was released jointly by Linotype, Monotype and Stempel in 1967. Classical, resilient and legible, it became one of the world's leading text types.

Ty	**Artone**
Ca	**Slab Serif**
Ke	**Decorative**
Te	**Photocomposition**
Da	**1968**
De	**Seymour Chwast**
Fo	**Photo-Lettering Inc.**
Co	**USA**

Characteristics

Calligraphic curves at head
Colossal slab serifs at foot

Connections

Metropolitaines	1905
Amelia	1966
Bottleneck	1972
Chwast Buffalo	1981

Availability

Loose Caboose NF is a digital revival
available from Nick's Fonts and resellers

Specimen

Artone type specimen composed by
author, 2015 (220x210mm)

Artone had a modest beginning in the form of a single, large lower case a used as a trademark for a brand of Indian ink, applied to the bottle label and carton. Its designer, Seymour Chwast (1931–), only realized that it looked like a drop of ink after he had drawn it, but he liked the letterform so much that he decided to develop the rest of the alphabet.

Chwast is an American designer famous for the distinctive illustrative style of his work, which includes posters, packaging and editorial design. In 1954, along with a group of young graphic artists including Milton Glaser (pp382–83), he founded the Push Pin Studios in New York. Push Pin rapidly attained global influence. Its work challenged the formal rigidity of the dominant modern typographic style of the time, offering a gently humorous, personable alternative that had immediate appeal to the American public.

The Push Pin style was notable for its colourful and witty illustrations, but it was characterized less by a set of codified techniques and more by a willingness to experiment. The studio's work drew on a very broad range of references, such as Renaissance painting, Victorian design, Surrealism, comic strips, and the art nouveau, Op Art and art deco styles. The Push Pin designers did not, however, simply mimic their sources, but devised new ideas inspired by their context. This eclectic approach is exemplified in the design of Artone, which was directly influenced by Chwast's interest in art nouveau. It is an exuberantly ambiguous half-breed with graceful calligraphic curves at the tops of the letters flowing into colossal slab serifs at the foot. Echoing American fashions of the 1960s, Artone's exaggerated fat-bottomed style instantly evokes memories of platform heels, bell-bottoms, lava lamps and flower power.

Chwast has created several other witty display alphabets, most of which began as hand lettering in one-off projects, including Bestial Bold (1980) and Chwast Buffalo (1981). He has said of his approach: 'What I like to do is amuse myself with visual tricks, conundrums, parodies and the unpredictable … I think the stuff we put on these pages should be magic.'

Ty	**Baby Teeth**
Ca	**Sans Serif**
Ke	**Geometric, Capitals**
Te	**Photocomposition**
Da	**1968**
De	**Milton Glaser**
Fo	**Photo-Lettering Inc.**
Co	**USA**

Characteristics

Capitals only

Geometric construction using circles, squares and triangles

Counterforms replaced with small incisions

C G Triangular incisions

E F Stepped

AMVX
EFHLT
CGDO

Connections

Broadway	1928
Eagle Black	1933
Black Boton	1970
Sinaloa	1974

Availability

Bebit is a digital revival available from ParaType and resellers

Specimen

Milton Glaser: Graphic Design. Penguin Books, Harmondsworth, 1973 (260x260mm)

158

164

(164, 165)
The inspiration for my Baby-teeth type face came from this sign I photographed in Mexico City (164). It's an advertisement for a tailor. The E was drawn as only some-one unfamiliar with the alpha-bet could have conceived. Yet it is completely legible. I tried to invent the rest of the alphabet consistent with this model. At the right (165), a number of variations on the Babyteeth theme.

159

In his eponymous 1973 monograph Milton Glaser (1929–) remarked that his typefaces only existed as the product of visual ideas applied to letterforms, emphasizing that he was 'not a type designer'.

Glaser is probably best known for the emblematic I ♥ NY logo. In 1954, along with a group of other young American graphic artists, including Seymour Chwast (pp380–81), he founded the Push Pin Studios in New York. Push Pin's work rapidly became renowned for its eclectic attitude, which defied modernist traditions, drawing instead on a broad range of cultural and historical references, from art deco to psychedelia. In the 1960s and 1970s the Push Pin style dominated American advertising and print media, and Glaser's work became something of a cult.

Glaser first used his Baby Teeth lettering to spell out 'Dylan' on his seminal psychedelic poster for CBS Records in 1966. The letters were based on an alphabet he had discovered on street signage. 'The inspiration for my Babyteeth type face came from this sign I photographed in Mexico City. It's an advertisement for a tailor. The E was drawn as only someone unfamiliar with the alphabet could have conceived. Yet it is completely legible. I tried to invent the rest of the alphabet consistent with this model.' The lettering he had referenced in his design probably derived in fact from a typeface first used in Dutch and Italian advertising during the 1920s and 1930s that was sometimes described as 'futuristic' in type specimens of the time, as it represented the modern ideals of the machine age.

Baby Teeth, so called because of the stepped horizontals of the E, is one of Glaser's most successful display typefaces. It integrates mathematical rigour with an expressive wit, combining characteristic Push Pin references to art deco with the quirkiness of its hand-painted source material while following strict geometric principles. Designed to work without the need for counterforms, it is also one of the blackest, most dominant and most dynamic display types ever produced. Although no official digital version exists, it is still widely replicated in branding and editorial work today.

Ty	**Forma**
Ca	**Sans Serif**
Ke	**Grotesque**
Te	**Letterpress**
Da	**1968**
De	**Aldo Novarese**
Fo	**Nebiolo**
Co	**Italy**

Characteristics

Large x-height
Slightly flared stems
C c S s e g Flat terminals
G Round, no spur
Q Flat tail on baseline
R Straight, angled leg
a Single-storeyed
f r t Vertical terminals
i j Square dots
j Straight stem
t Flat top-stroke
y Straight tail

AGMQR
abcefghij
koprstuy

Connections

Helvetica	1957
Recta	1958
Unica	1980
NB International	2014

Availability

Forma DJR is a digital revival available
from Type Network

Specimen

Forma type specimen. Nebiolo, Turin,
c1968 (279x216mm)

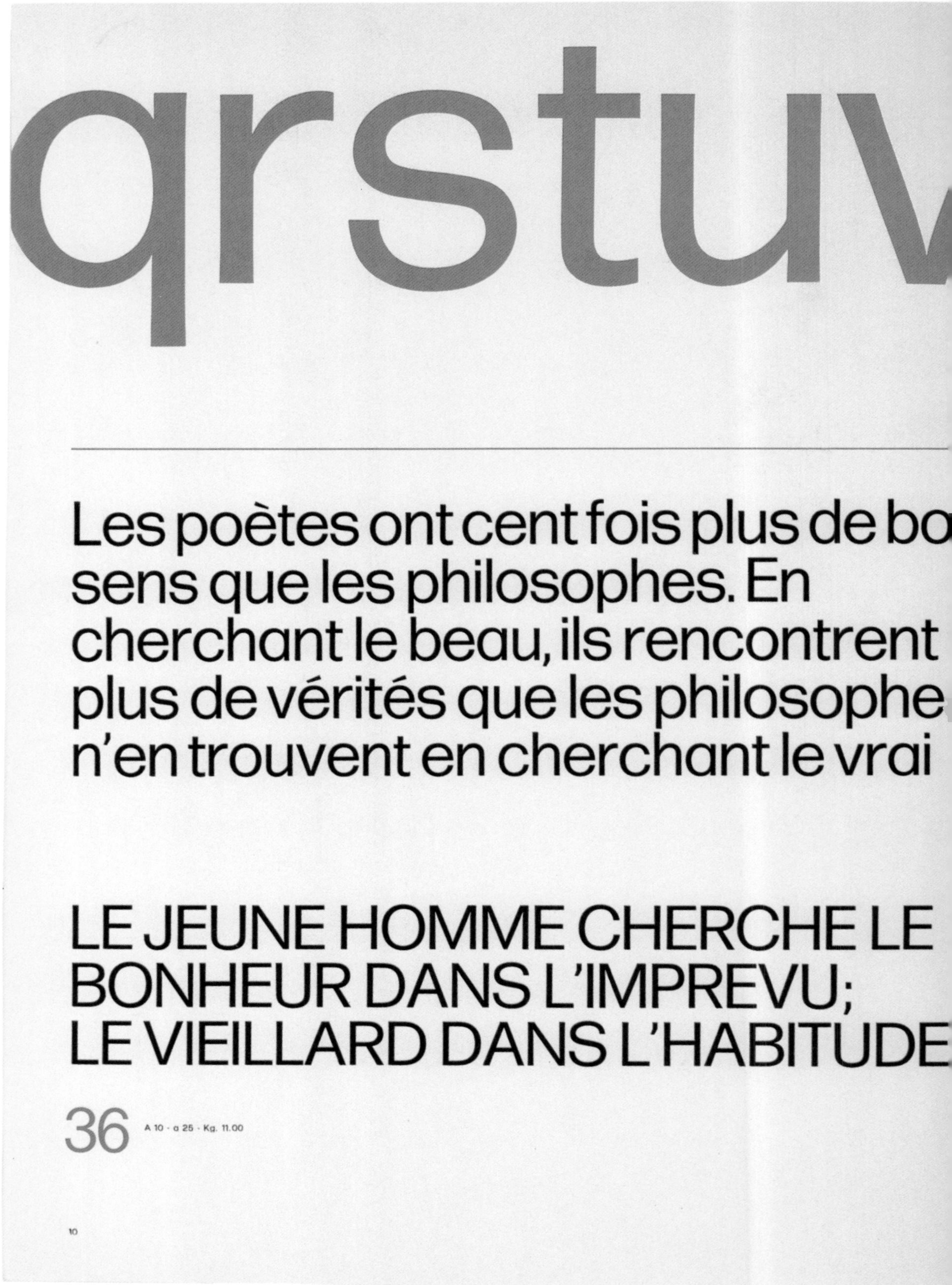

qrstuv

Les poètes ont cent fois plus de bo
sens que les philosophes. En
cherchant le beau, ils rencontrent
plus de vérités que les philosophe
n'en trouvent en cherchant le vrai

LE JEUNE HOMME CHERCHE LE
BONHEUR DANS L'IMPREVU;
LE VIEILLARD DANS L'HABITUDE

36   A 10 - a 25 - Kg. 11.00

10

WXYZ...

a lettura fa un uomo
modo, la conversazione
o fa disinvolto, l'arte
ello scrivere lo fa esatto

UN UOMO DIVIDEREBBE
E SUE ANSIE VOLENTIERI

8   A 8 · a 18 · Kg. 13,50

11

Forma is a sans serif typeface developed between 1965 and 1968 for the Italian type foundry Nebiolo by a group led by the company's art director, Aldo Novarese (1920–95). The team of largely Milanese designers included Franco Grignani, Giancarlo Iliprandi, Till Neuburg, Ilio Negri, Pino Tovaglia, Luigi Oriani and Bruno Munari.

Forma's design was driven by sales and marketing needs. In the early 1960s Nebiolo had only a few up-to-date grotesque typefaces in its catalogue and wished to offer customers a viable alternative to the hugely successful sans serifs of the day such as Helvetica (pp346–47) and Univers (pp350–51). As its name suggests, Forma was intended to be an idealized alphabetic form. In their quest to perfect the grotesque form, the design team undertook an exhaustive research process that lasted for almost three years and involved the comparative analysis of several contemporary sans serifs together with a series of related legibility tests.

Eventually, Forma was released as type for hand composition in 1968. Alfred Hoffmann, then principal of the Haas Type Foundry, later described it as 'a blatant copy of Helvetica'. While there can be no doubt that the Haas typeface was a benchmark, on close inspection a number of innovations are evident in the Nebiolo design. Forma's key distinguishing feature is its very large x-height, making for large, open counterforms in a character set that is exceptionally tightly spaced, in line with the 1960s fashion for close settings – the product of photosetting processes. The alphabet's contours are very finely modulated, with stems that flare outwards almost imperceptibly at terminals, while their corners are minutely bevelled. These characteristics give Forma a crisper appearance than most sans serifs, while also helping to distinguish letterforms, making it easy to read.

The typeface was well received by designers and printers, but although initial sales were buoyant, Forma could not compete in a crowded and fiercely competitive market. Released a decade after the definitive twentieth-century sans serifs, it arrived as the era of metal type was drawing to a close. The Nebiolo foundry ceased trading in 1978 and Forma became one of many sans serifs of the time that did not survive. However, in 2013 it was digitally revived by David Berlow and David Jonathan Ross at the Font Bureau for *Hong Kong Tatler* and it was commercially released in 2016 by Type Network.

Ty	**OCR-A and OCR-B**
Ca	**Sans Serif**
Ke	**Geometric**
Te	**Photocomposition / Digital**
Da	**1968**
De	**Unknown / Adrian Frutiger**
Fo	**N/A**
Co	**N/A**

Characteristics

OCR-A: Well-differentiated letter shapes based on straight lines with radiused corners and terminals

OCR-B: Well-differentiated letter shapes based on conventional type geometry

ADGIMO
abegim
ADGIMO
abegim

Connections

DIN 1451	1931
Letter Gothic	1956
E-13B	1958
New Alphabet	1967

Availability

OCR-A and OCR-B are widely available

Specimen

This page: OCR-A *Optical Character Recognition Character Sets.* United States National Bureau of Standards, Washington, 1974 (297x210mm)
Opposite: OCR-B *Standard ECMA-11 for the Alphanumeric Character Set OCR-B for Optical Recognition*, third edition. European Computer Manufacturers Association, Geneva, 1976 (297x210mm)

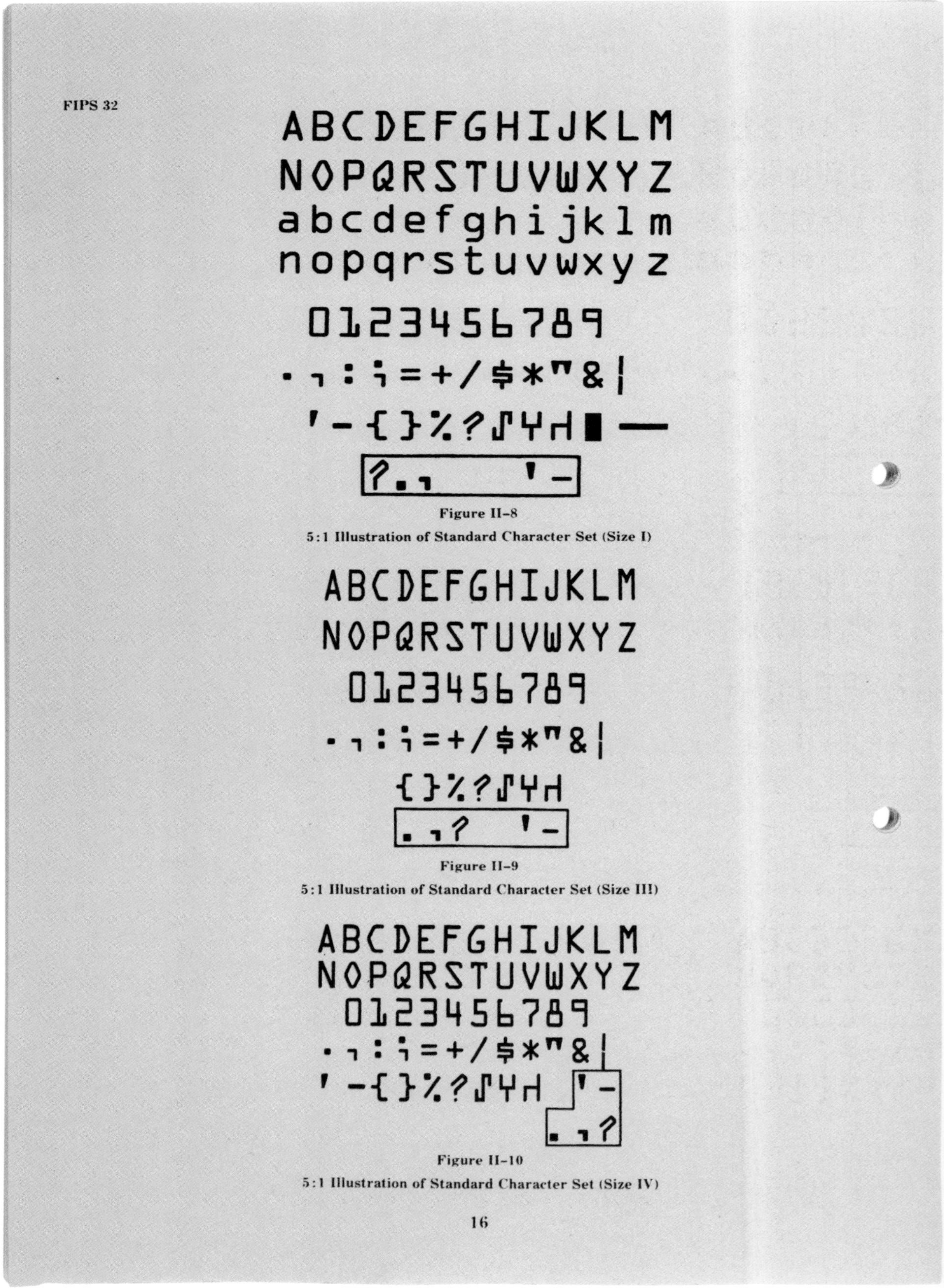

FIPS 32

Figure II–8
5:1 Illustration of Standard Character Set (Size I)

Figure II–9
5:1 Illustration of Standard Character Set (Size III)

Figure II–10
5:1 Illustration of Standard Character Set (Size IV)

16

OCR stands for 'optical character recognition', a technology that allows machines to read by extracting text data from images. It was invented in 1951 by David Shepard, who constructed a simple machine called the Gismo to scan and read Morse code, musical notation and typed words. In the OCR process, glyphs are scanned by a matrix of illuminated photo transducers that traverse a text. Once scanned, optical characteristics are evaluated and shapes are registered as glyphs, numerals or symbols. Because the same characters can be read by people, OCR technology is beneficial in the many industrial and commercial applications that use human/machine interfaces.

Two different OCR performance standards were developed in 1968. In the United States, American Type Founders produced OCR-A. It was composed in simple, thick strokes to form very well-differentiated letter shapes that could be deciphered by the computers of the day. Although its extreme geometric differentiation helped to overcome mechanical substitution errors, the unfamiliar shapes of the OCR-A alphabet made it less satisfactory to human readers, with a corresponding increase in human substitution errors. Mechanical readability and human readability are, by nature, contradictory, and it is impossible to maximize both using the same set of characters.

OCR-B was researched and drawn by Adrian Frutiger (1928–2015) for Monotype in the same year. His design was far more nuanced than OCR-A and its character set had the relatively conventional attributes of a typewriter face. This made it much easier for people to read than OCR-A, but it pushed the limits of the capabilities of machine scanners available at the time.

Because OCR typefaces are closely associated with science and technology it has become common graphic design practice for OCR-A, OCR-B and similar monospaced faces to be applied beyond their technical remit as purely visual expressions of contemporary or future technologies. Likewise, in recent times many type designers have adopted some of the unique features of machine-readable alphabets to evoke similar connections in their typefaces.

SCALE 4:1

0123456789
ABCDEFGHIJKLM
NOPQRSTUVWXYZ
abcdefghijklm
nopqrstuvwxyz
*+-=/.,:;"'_
?!()<>[]%#&@^
¤£$¦¡\
ÄÅÆIJÑÖØÜ
åæijøßß§¥
" ´ ` ^ ~
,
{}m_

SPACE

SCALE 1:1

0123456789
ABCDEFGHIJKLM
NOPQRSTUVWXYZ
abcdefghijklm
nopqrstuvwxyz
*+-=/.,:;"'_
?!()<>[]%#&@^
¤£$¦¡\
ÄÅÆIJÑÖØÜ
åæijøßß§¥
" ´ ` ^ ~

{}m_
■ ▬ ⁄ SPACE

Ty	**Vormgevers Lettering**
Ca	**Sans Serif**
Ke	**Geometric**
Te	**Lettering**
Da	**1968**
De	**Wim Crouwel**
Fo	**N/A**
Co	**Netherlands**

Characteristics

Grid-based modular letters
5 x 7 unit proportions
Square character construction
Small arcs at junctions
Lower case only

abcdeghij
klmopqrs
tuvwxyz

Connections

Availability

Stedelijk is a digital revival available from the Foundry and resellers

Specimen

'Vormgevers' exhibition poster. Total Design for the Stedelijk Museum, Amsterdam, 1968 (2008 reprint) (950x635mm)

Wim Crouwel (1928–) is renowned for his use of grid-based typography in an exceptional body of graphic work firmly rooted in the International Typographic Style. He once said: 'The grid is like the lines on a football field. You can play a great game in the grid or a lousy game. But the goal is to play a really fine game.' At Total Design, the studio he co-founded in 1963, Crouwel oversaw the production of all printed matter for the Stedelijk Museum in Amsterdam after 1964. Every individual item he produced, from posters to catalogues, was designed systematically on the same invisible squared grid.

In 1968 the Stedelijk presented 'Vormgevers', an exhibition of the work of a group of contemporary graphic and product designers. Crouwel's poster for the event famously made the grid visible as 57 vertical by 41 horizontal blocks, exposing a key graphic design tool that is almost always hidden from view. By revealing the substructural framework for type and typographic hierarchy in this way, the theme of the exhibition was brought into sharp relief.

Many projects at Total Design, by Benno Wissing and Ben Bos as well as Wim Crouwel, had explored the use of modular typography, but the 'Vormgevers' poster marked an advance in experimentation with constructed letters. Here they became the core element of the design and a product of their own systematic construction method. Although drawn by hand with a pen, a straight edge and a compass, the monolithic geometric shapes of the Vormgevers lettering and the poster's imposing black and white binaries anticipated the bitmap typography of early computer displays. Letterforms are expressed as simple rectangles, softened at their joints by small arcs. Their design can be seen as part of a development process that begins with Crouwel's New Alphabet (pp376–77), a speculative typeface system made in reaction to the first generation of digital typesetters, and is resolved in the typeface that he designed a few years later for the Fodor Museum's bulletins, which foreshadows dot matrix and LED type.

Only appearing on the Vormgevers poster and its accompanying brochure, the alphabet was not developed any further until the Foundry, a London-based studio, completed the character set in collaboration with Crouwel and released a digital version in 2003, naming it Stedelijk. Vormgevers has become one of Wim Crouwel's most well-known designs: imaginative and experimental, yet precise and systematic, it is the spectacular result of a 'really fine game'.

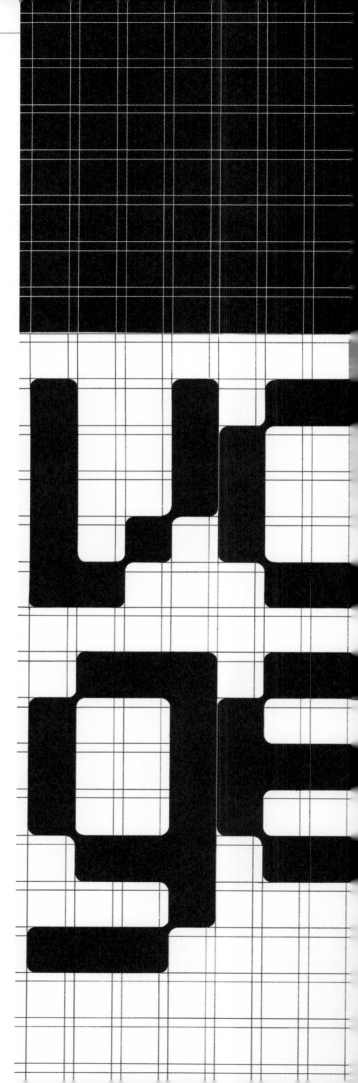

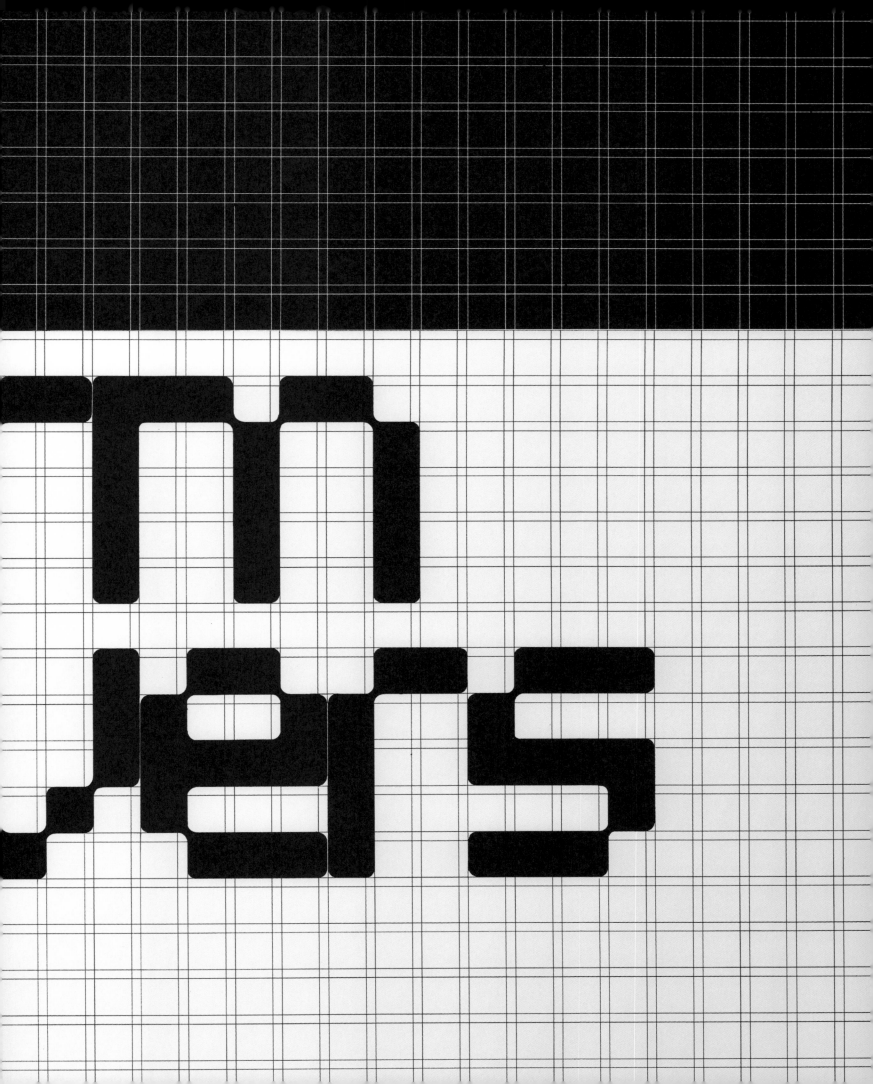

Ty	**Epps Evans**
Ca	**Sans Serif**
Ke	**Geometric, Capitals**
Te	**Lettering**
Da	**1969**
De	**Timothy Epps**
Fo	**National Physical Laboratory**
Co	**UK**

Characteristics

All characters fit to a square grid
5 x 5 unit proportions
Three possible vertical line positions
Three possible horizontal line positions
Mixture of capitals and lower case forms

Connections

New Alphabet	1967
Data 70	1970
Mourier	1970
FF Minimum	1993

Availability

Not available

Specimen

Epps Evans, *Kwadraatbladen* No. 27.
Steendrukkerij de Jong & Co., Hilversum,
1969 (250x250mm)

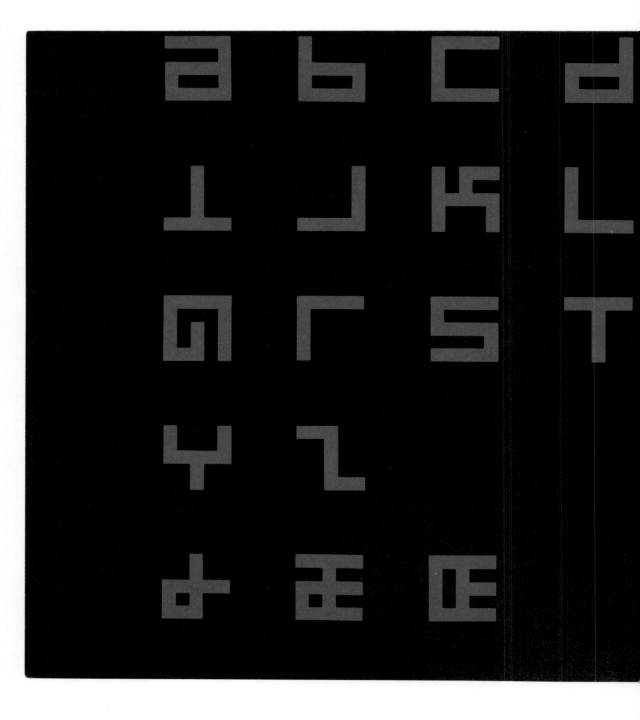

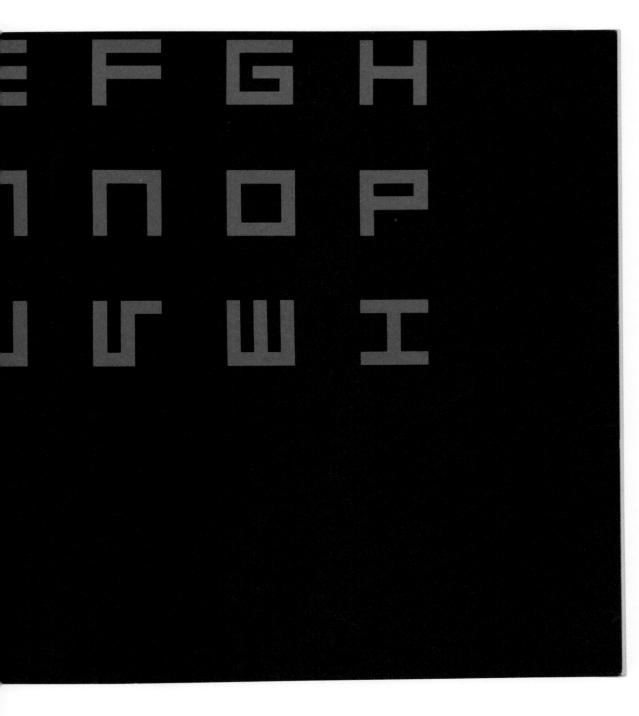

Christopher Evans (1931–79) was an experimental psychologist whose research explored potential relationships between the operations of computers and the processes of the human mind. In 1968 he commissioned Timothy Epps (1946–), a graphic design student, to work with him at the National Physical Laboratory, Middlesex, on problems of pattern recognition and visual perception.

Epps was briefed to develop a typeface that could be recognized by both machines and humans. It was to be based on a square and a line, eliminating curves and diagonals to make scanning for optical character recognition as easy as possible using the cathode ray tube technology of the time. After experimenting with various options, Epps and Evans decided to work with the simple grid used to print out ticker tape: five by five units, restricted to only three possible line positions in vertical and horizontal directions, with all characters fitting to a square format.

The Epps Evans typeface is one of the most severely minimal alphabets ever conceived. Using a single case – a mixture of capitals and minuscules – most letters and numbers are unambiguous and easy to recognize, yet visually harmonious as a character set.

Never intended for release as a typeface, the Epps Evans specimen was published in 1969 as one of Pieter Brattinga's *Kwadraatbladen* editions as a response to the one designed a year earlier by Wim Crouwel for his New Alphabet (pp376–77). Like the New Alphabet, the Epps Evans typeface was not a proposal for practical implementation but an imaginative experiment, speculating on the potential of man/machine interfaces and computational communications. Its reductive forms echo the dignity of square Kufic glyphs from the tradition of Arabic calligraphy while foreshadowing the bitmap type of the 1980s digital revolution.

Ty	**Syntax**
Ca	**Sans Serif**
Ke	**Humanist**
Te	**Letterpress**
Da	**1969**
De	**Hans Eduard Meier**
Fo	**Stempel**
Co	**Germany**

Characteristics

A M X	Rest on points
C c S s e	Angled terminals
G	Tall, vertical downstroke
K	Angled leg and arm
M	Splayed
N	Angled apex and vertex
V W X Y	Top stem angled
a	Double-storeyed with curved stem
g	Double-storeyed with straight ear
k v w x y	Angled stem
t	Upturned stem

AGMNR
abcefghij
koprstuy

Connections

Optima	1958
Frutiger	1976
FF Meta	1991
FF Scala Sans	1993

Availability

Syntax is available from Linotype and resellers

Specimen

Syntax type specimen sheet. Linotype, Bad Homburg, c1988 (210x297mm)

Syntax was designed between 1954 and 1968 by the Swiss typographer Hans Eduard Meier (1922–2014). Issued by the German type foundry Stempel in 1969, it was the foundry's last sans serif typeface to be cut in metal. Meier's design was motivated by what he described as his 'aversion for the standard sans serif typefaces – mechanically constructed and overly technical – like Helvetica'. He planned to model his new typeface on the Renaissance serif form, to be similar in proportions to Jan Tschichold's Sabon (pp378–79). In his initial drawings Meier deliberately avoided any mathematical design methods or automated construction techniques. He first shaped the letters with a brush, then refined them to essential forms, and finally added weight to produce a delicately balanced alphabet.

Like Hermann Zapf's Optima (pp352–53), Syntax has a subtly modulated stroke based on an underlying structure that foreshadows the late twentieth-century resurgence of humanist sans serifs by several decades. With an almost imperceptible tilt in the roman design, Syntax has a warmth and spark that many sans serifs lack, bridging the gap between the vitality of the roman and the hardiness of the sans serif.

The upper case has generous proportions, and its terminals, sitting at angles to the baseline, have a liveliness that, like Kabel (pp232–33) demonstrates the influence of Roman monumental capitals. For the lower case Meier followed the contours of Renaissance old-style letters, exemplified by the balanced two-storeyed a and g. The italics are a mixture of humanist italic forms, seen in the q, and obliqued romans, seen in the lower case italic a, which retains two storeys.

Released initially in four weights, with only one italic compatible with the roman, Syntax was digitized by Adobe in 1989, when it was expanded to include bold and ultrabold weights. The design was subsequently remodelled by Meier for Linotype and released in 2000. Meier wrote that, prior to the design of Syntax, 'it was thought that for a typeface to look modern, it had to have a structured look – as if made of building blocks'. The sans serif has since undergone a radical reappraisal, largely as a result of the work of pioneers like Hans Eduard Meier and Adrian Frutiger, and has proved capable of solving most typographic problems, including effective, easy use in extended text.

7420.10

Mergenthaler Type Library   Typefaces/Schriften/Caractères

Syntax™

roman/normal/romain

05245   12 pt Design

Sans Serif/Serifenlose Antiqua/Antiques
Hans E. Meier 1968, D. Stempel AG
Linotype

abcdefghijklmnopq
rstuvwxyz fiflß&
ABCDEFGHIJKLMN
OPQRSTUVWXYZ
1234567890
.,:;-– —'' "" ·‹›«» * %
!?¡¿()[]/†‡§$£¢ƒ
ÄÁÂÀÅÃÆÇČĔÉÊÈĒĞÏÍÎÌĪÑÖÓÔÒØÕÕ
ŒŠÜÚÛÙŪŽ
äáâàåãāæçčĕéêèēğïíîìīïñöóôòøõōœšüúûùū

Parameter for 10 pt/Parameter in 10 pt/Paramètre pour 10 pt
H 2.43 mm   k 2.64 mm   x 1.81 mm   p 0.89 mm   kp 3.53 mm   Ép 3.9
H 0.096 Inches   k 0.104 Inches   x 0.071 Inches   p 0.035 Inches   kp 0.139 Inches   Ép 0.1
Factor/Faktor/Facteur 1.03

* Given in pica point/Angaben in pica point/Toutes indications en points pica

S **Linotype**

△ 4.92 mm/14 pt* (5.25 mm^DIN) ▷ 0 H 3.41 mm

In every type design the basic character isd

△ 5.62 mm/16 pt* (6.00 mm^DIN) ▷ 0 H 3.89 mm

Bei jeder Schriftgestaltung wird der ga

△ 6.33 mm/18 pt* (6.75 mm^DIN) ▷ −1 H 4.38 mm

Le style de chaque caractère d'imp

△ 7.03 mm/20 pt* (7.50 mm^DIN) ▷ −1 H 4.87 mm

För alla nya stilar bestäms alfab

△ 8.44 mm/24 pt* (9.00 mm^DIN) ▷ −1 H 5.84 mm

In elk letterontwerp word

△ 9.84 mm/28 pt* (10.50 mm^DIN) ▷ −1 H 6.81 mm

Em todo o desenhode

△ 12.65 mm/36 pt* (13.50 mm^DIN) ▷ −2 H 8.76 mm

In ciascuna serie ti

△ 16.87 mm/48 pt* (18.00 mm^DIN) ▷ −2 H 11.68 mm

En cada tipoa

△ 21.09 mm/60 pt* (22.50 mm^DIN) ▷ −2 H 14.60 mm

Den ensari

△ 25.31 mm/72 pt* (27.00 mm^DIN) ▷ −2 H 17.51 mm

Bestemis

△ 29.52 mm/84 pt* (31.50 mm^DIN) ▷ −2 H 20.43 mm

Muoter

Left column (size specimens):

/6 pt* (2.25 mm^DIN) ▽ 2.50 mm (7 pt*) ▷ +1 H 1.46 mm

lmnopqrstuvwxyz abcdefghijklmnopqrstuvwxyz abcdecdefghijklmno 1234567890
e design the basic character is determined by the uniform design characteristics of all
e alphabet. However, this alone does not determine the standard of the typeface and
of composition set with it. The appearance is something complex which forms itselfou
y details, like form, proportion, rhythm etc. If everything harmonizes, the total resultv
ARANCE IS SOMETHING COMPLEX WHICH FORMS ITSELF OUT OF MANY DET

/7 pt* (2.63 mm^DIN) ▽ 2.75 mm (8 pt*) ▷ 0 H 1.70 mm

jklmnopqrstuvwxyz abcdefghijklmnopqrstuvwxyz abcdefghi 1234567890
chriftgestaltung wird der Grundcharakter eines Alphabets von einheitliches
kmalen der Buchstaben bestimmt. Er allein besagt noch nichts über das Nive
ruckschrift und die Qualität des Satzgefüges. Das Erscheinungsbild ist etwa
s, das sich aus vielen Einzelheiten, wie Form, Proportionen, Duktus, Rhyth
ND PROPORTIONEN SIND DIE WICHTIGSTEN KRITERIEN BEIM BEU

/8 pt* (3.00 mm^DIN) ▽ 3.25 mm (9.25 pt*) ▷ 0 H 1.95 mm

hijklmnopqrstuvwxyz abcdefghijklmnopqrstuvwxy 1234567890
le chaque caractère d'imprimerie se détermine par des caractéristi
sont les mêmes pour toutes les lettres de l'alphabet. Dans tous les
formels et autres relations il s'agit de phénomènes optiques irrédu
ux règles mathématiques et que seule pourra percevoir et fixer la si
E PART MALGRÉ TOUTES LES RESSOURCES DE MÉCANISA

/9 pt* (3.38 mm^DIN) ▽ 3.50 mm (10 pt*) ▷ 0 H 2.19 mm

hijklmnopqrstuvwxyz abcdefghijklmnopqrs 1234567890
type design the basic character is determined by the unifo
gn characteristics of all letters in the alphabet. However, thi
oes not determine the standard of the typeface and the qu
composition set with it. The appearance is something comp
PPEARANCE IS SOMETHING COMPLEX WHICH FOR

/10 pt* (3.75 mm^DIN) ▽ 4.00 mm (11.5 pt*) ▷ 0 H 2.43 mm

ghijklmnopqrstuvwxyz abcdefghijklm 1234567890
er Schriftgestaltung wird der Grundcharakter einesal
bets von einheitlichen Formmerkmalen der Buchstab
timmt. Er allein besagt noch nichts über das Niveauei
ruckschrift und die Qualität des Satzgefüges. Das Ers
UND PROPORTIONEN SIND DIE WICHTIGSTE

/11 pt* (4.13 mm^DIN) ▽ 4.50 mm (12.75 pt*) ▷ 0 H 2.68 mm

fghijklmnopqrstuvwxyz abcdefgh 1234567890
le de chaque caractère d'imprimerie se détermin
des caractéristiques qui sont les mêmes pour to
s lettres de l'alphabet. Dans tous les rapports for
TRE PART MALGRÉ TOUTES LES RESSOURC

/12 pt* (4.50 mm^DIN) ▽ 4.75 mm (13.5 pt*) ▷ 0 H 2.92 mm

efghijklmnopqrstuvwxyz abcd 1234567890
ery type design the basic character is determi
y the uniform design characteristics of all let
n the alphabet. However, this alone does not
APPEARANCE IS SOMETHING COMPLE

Right margin scale: 6 7 8 9 10 11 12 14 16 18 20 24 28 36 48 60 72 84

Ty	**ITC Avant Garde Gothic**	
Ca	**Sans Serif**	
Ke	**Geometric**	
Te	**Photocomposition**	
Da	**1970**	
De	**Herb Lubalin and Tom Carnase**	
Fo	**International Typeface Corporation**	
Co	**USA**	

Characteristics

Monoline, geometric construction
Very large x-height
Short ascenders and descenders
B E F S Narrow
C c G O o Q Circular
R Open bowl in light weights
a Single-storeyed, circular
e Circle divided by crossbar
f r t Narrow
i j Square dots
t Straight stem, no foot
0 Straight sides

AGMRS
abcefgij
koprstuy

Connections

Futura	1927
Lubalin Graph	1974
Platform	2010
Euclid Flex	2012

Availability

ITC Avant Garde Gothic is available from Monotype and resellers. Its original ligatures and alternates are not available.

Specimen

Lubalin, Burns & Co. specimen. New York, 1970 (200x160mm)

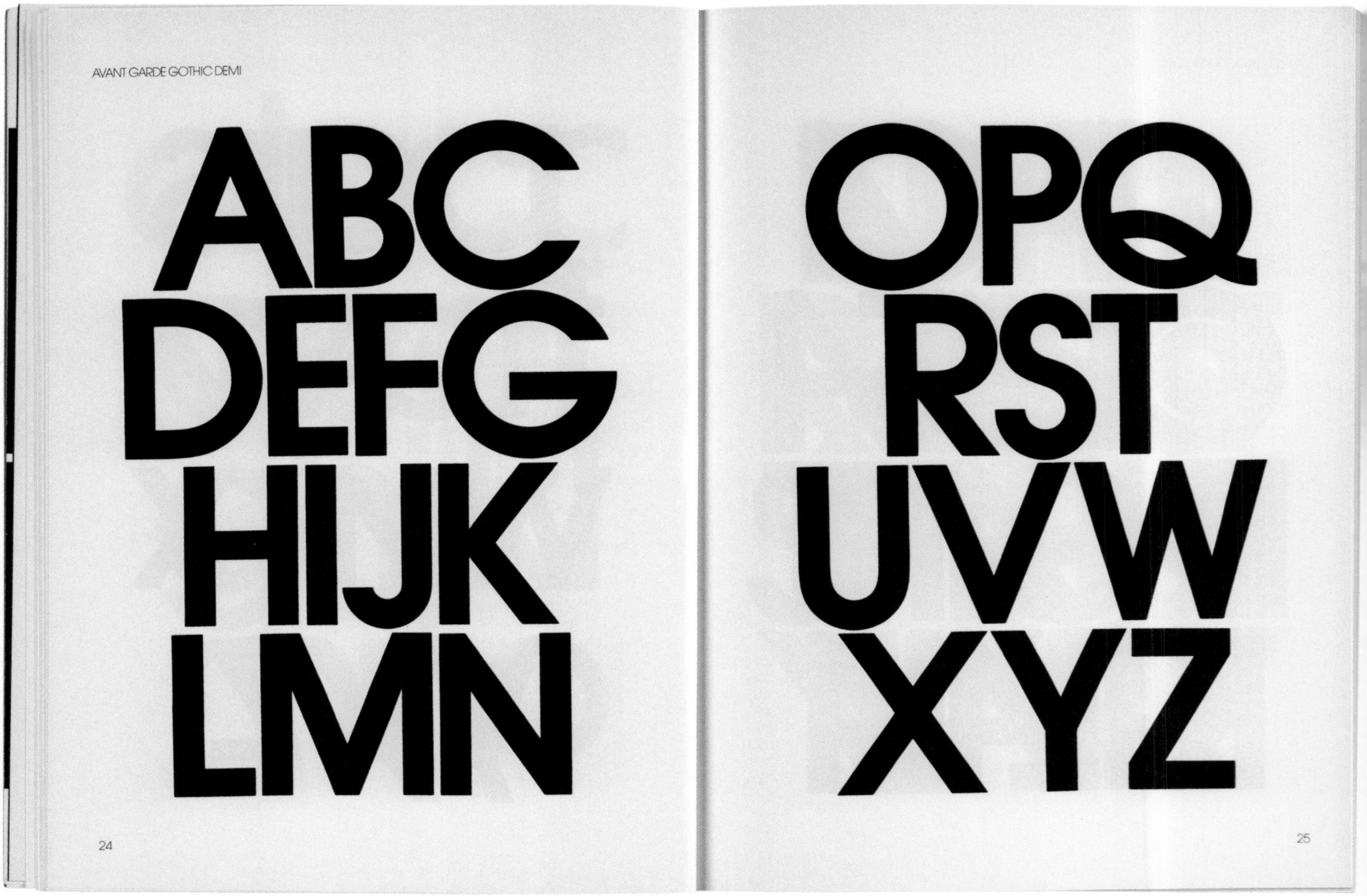

AVANT GARDE GOTHIC DEMI

ABC
DEFG
HIJK
LMN

OPQ
RST
UVW
XYZ

24

25

The American designer Herb Lubalin (1918–81) was at the forefront of his profession in the 1970s. Aware of the need for a new, flexible typography that was suited to contemporary media, Lubalin recognized the potential for exploiting new photomechanical technologies to create layouts using an unprecedented range of visual effects, such as negative spacing, slanting and overlapping letters.

Few typefaces took advantage of these possibilities better than his own design, Avant Garde Gothic, which began life in the late 1960s as the masthead for *Avant Garde*, a short-lived but highly influential arts journal. Lubalin's hand-lettered logo was an iconic construction of interlocking geometric capitals. In collaboration with Tom Carnase (1939–) Lubalin extended the basic form into a headline typeface for the magazine. When *Avant Garde* ceased publication in 1970 Lubalin developed the typeface for release by the newly founded International Typeface Corporation.

ITC Avant Garde Gothic pushed the principles of geometric designs from the early twentieth century such as Futura (pp230–31) and Kabel (pp232–33) to extreme limits. No other typeface before or since has used geometry quite as rigorously. Its stick and ball shapes seem constructed with compasses and rulers but are in fact artfully modulated. Like Futura, capitals follow the mobile proportions of classical inscriptional letters, and the lower case is marked out by a very large x-height, with stunted extenders and wide open counters providing an extremely rounded geometric overall impression that is well suited to tight spacing.

Avant Garde Gothic's range of five weights also goes to extremes, from a hairline to a dense bold, although contours remain remarkably coherent across the range. It was released with many alternates including a set of all-capital ligatures that offered exciting new ways to create unique letter combinations.

ITC Avant Garde Gothic was the definitive typeface of the phototypesetting era and remains an enduring icon of 1970s design. It offered designers new opportunities, although the innovations that liberated it from the restrictions of metal type also made it susceptible to misuse. Over many years it has been set at inappropriately small sizes, poorly spaced or implemented in improper weights. Its ligatures have been subjected to the worst abuse, as Ed Benguiat pointed out: 'Everybody ruins it. They lean the letters the wrong way.'

Nevertheless, ITC Avant Garde Gothic has survived and has been put to good use by designers sensitive to both its limitations and its possibilities. It is seen everywhere today, in editorial work, packaging and brand communications.

AVANT GARDE GOTHIC MEDIUM

abcc
deef
ghijkl
mno

pqrs
ttuvv
wwx
yyz

Ty	**Data 70**
Ca	**Sans Serif**
Ke	**Geometric**
Te	**Dry Transfer**
Da	**1970**
De	**Robert Newman**
Fo	**Letraset**
Co	**UK**

Characteristics
Mid-stroke slabs

Square characters with radiused corners

Large, open lower case

AGMRS
abcefghij
koprstuy

Connections
Countdown	1965
Westminster	1965
Amelia	1966
New Alphabet	1967

Availability
Data 70 is available from Letraset and resellers

Specimen
24pt Data 70 dry-transfer sheet. Letraset, London, 1970 (384x254mm)

Magnetic ink character recognition (MICR) is a technology invented in the 1950s that was used mainly by the banking industry for processing transactions. It allowed scanning devices to read alphanumeric information directly, using magnetic toner. Unlike barcodes and similar technologies, MICR characters could also be read by humans.

In 1964 Leo Maggs, a young British graphic designer, drew up lettering mimicking E-13B, the standard MICR numeric face, to fulfil a brief for a futuristic-looking title to head a magazine article. Having completed the task satisfactorily, he decided to complete the alphabet, basing it on the proportions of Gill Sans (pp238–39). It was subsequently released as a typeface for photocomposition by Photoscript, one of London's first photosetting businesses, and was appropriately named Westminster after the company's bank.

Westminster was an instant hit with designers, and several foundries soon published similar designs. Bob Newman was commissioned to draw Data 70 by Letraset, the manufacturer of dry-transfer lettering, in 1970. Like Westminster, Data 70 extended the original MICR E-13B numeral set into a fully functioning upper and lower case alphabet. Data 70 evokes the technical impression of E-13B by exaggerating its key traits for visual effect. Its characters turn the mid-stroke slabs required by MICR into unorthodox visual features, making them more rounded and consistent in their distribution. Character proportions are also rebalanced, with a large, open lower case well suited to display settings.

With the benefit of Letraset's global distribution, Data 70 rapidly overtook its competitors and became enormously popular during the 1970s in film and television titles, editorial work and advertising. Today it continues to resonate somewhat ambiguously as a typographic expression of printed circuit boards, retro science fiction stories and vintage computers. It lives on as a vision of the future from the past.

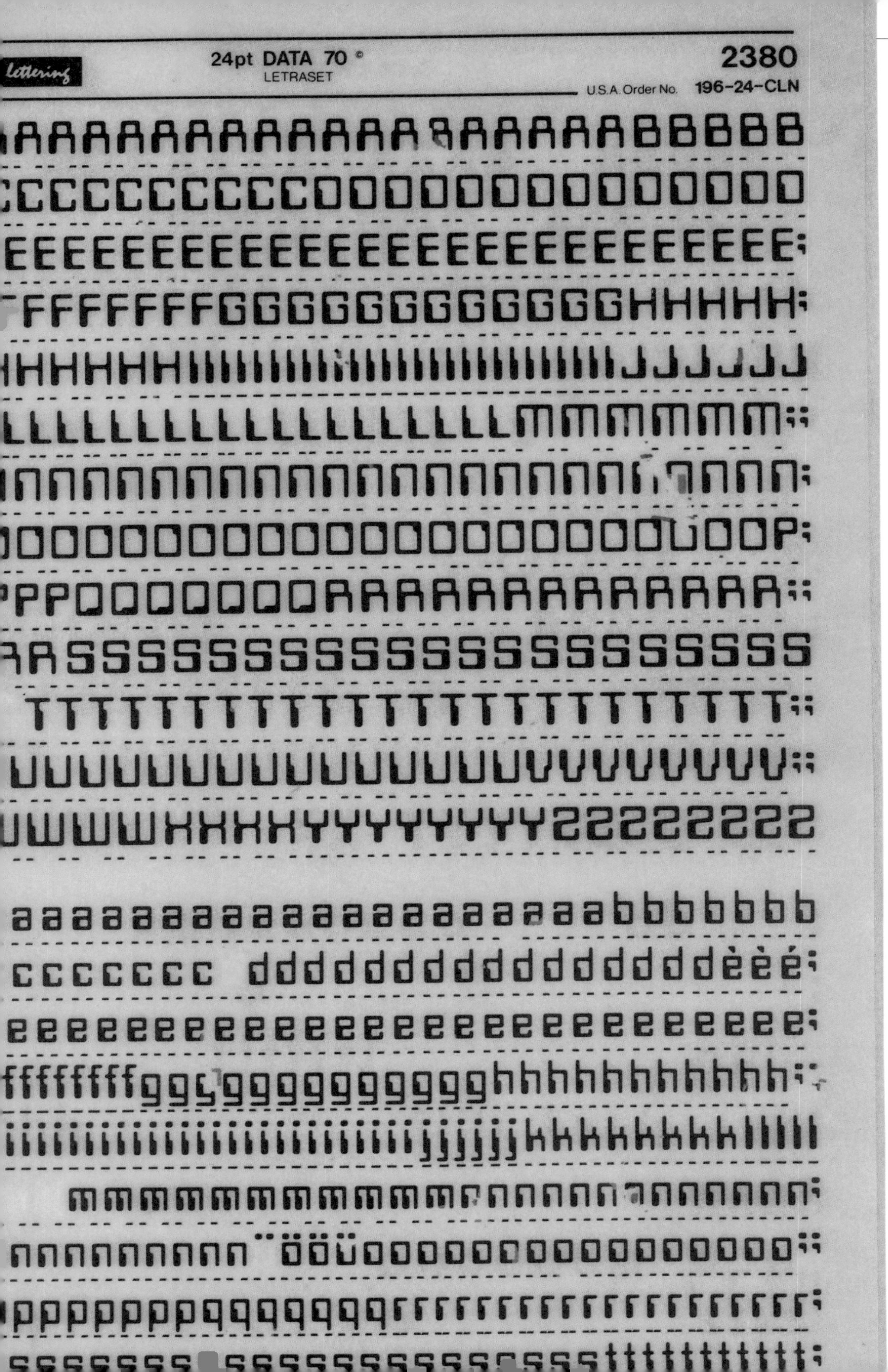

24pt DATA 70
LETRASET

2380

U.S.A. Order No. 196-24-CLN

AAAAAAAAAAAAAAAAABBBBB
CCCCCCCCCCCCCCDDDDDDDDDDDDD
EEEEEEEEEEEEEEEEEEEEEEEEEEE:
FFFFFFFGGGGGGGGGGGGHHHHH:
HHHHHHHHHHHHHHHHHHHHHHJJJJJ
LLLLLLLLLLLLLLLLLLLLLLmmmmmm:
nnnnnnnnnnnnnnnnnnnnnnnn:
ooooooooooooooooooooooP:
PPooooooooooRRRRRRRRRRRR:
RSSSSSSSSSSSSSSSSSSSSSS
TTTTTTTTTTTTTTTTTTTTTT:
UUUUUUUUUUUUUUUUUUUUUV:
UUWWXXXXYYYYYYYZZZZZZZ
aaaaaaaaaaaaaaaaaaaaabbbbbb
ccccccc dddddddddddddddèèé:
eeeeeeeeeeeeeeeeeeeeeeeeee:
ffffffffggggggggggghhhhhhhhhhh:
iiiiiiiiiiiiiiiiiiiiijjjjjkkkkkkkkllllll
mmmmmmmmmmmmmmmmmmmmm
nnnnnnnnn ··ööüooooooooooooooo:
ppppppppqqqqqqqrrrrrrrrrrrrrr:
ssssssssssttttttttttttt:

Ty	**Glaser Stencil**
Ca	**Sans Serif**
Ke	**Geometric, Capitals, Stencil**
Te	**Photocomposition**
Da	**1970**
De	**Milton Glaser**
Fo	**Photo-Lettering Inc.**
Co	**USA**

Characteristics

Geometric letterforms

Character construction similar to Futura

Capitals only

Three weights: thin, light, bold

Stencil bridges cut letters into basic geometric parts

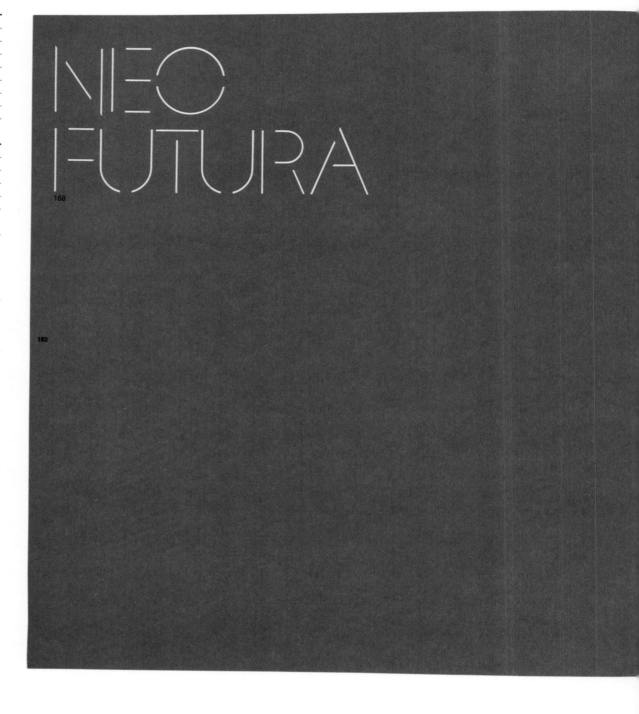

NEO FUTURA

168

162

Connections

Futura	1927
Kabel	1927
Baby Teeth	1968
ITC Avant Garde Gothic	1970

Availability

Glaser Stencil is available from URW and resellers in a single bold weight. F37 Glaser Stencil is available in four lighter weights from Hype for Type.

Specimen

Milton Glaser: Graphic Design. Penguin Books, Harmondsworth, 1973 (260x260mm)

ABCDE

ABCDE

ABCDE

163

ABCDE

...is type face in
...t weights for
...lity. As I men-
...(124), it is
...ura.

The renowned American designer and illustrator Milton Glaser (1929–) drew his Glaser Stencil alphabet in 1968 for a poster promoting a concert for an American record label named Poppy. Glaser had previously used Futura Light capitals (pp230–31) on promotional work for the company and initially his new typeface was simply named 'Neo Futura'. It is probable that its original hand-lettered incarnation on the 1968 concert poster was a redrawn or modified version of Paul Renner's era-defining geometric typeface. When it was released for sale to the public through Photo-Lettering Inc. in 1970, however, the name was changed to Glaser Stencil, no doubt for sound commercial reasons.

Glaser's highly original design is not a crude modification of Futura but a self-assured combination of modernist minimalism and 1960s New York chutzpah. Like his other display types, such as Baby Teeth (pp382–83), its design explores visual extremes. Conceived as an attention-grabbing typeface for use in headlines, Glaser originally drew letters in three weights at maximum contrast with each other: thin, light and bold. Of these, only the bold achieved widespread publication, surviving as a digital type cut by URW. The elegant light and thin weights were largely forgotten until the Face37 foundry undertook an extensive revival in 2015.

A capitals-only typeface, the contours of Glaser Stencil's letters correspond with fashionable sans serifs of the 1970s, such as ITC Avant Garde Gothic (pp394–95) and ITC Kabel. The rudimentary, rhythmic geometry of its letterforms is emphasized by the use of stencil bridges that break character sequences into simplified segments, providing a playful visual exchange of form and counterform. Over the past four decades Glaser Stencil has been extensively used in display applications and in signage, where it has always played a bold and confident role.

Ty	**ITC Machine**
Ca	**Sans Serif**
Ke	**Geometric, Capitals**
Te	**Photocomposition**
Da	**1970**
De	**Ronne' Bonder and Tom Carnase**
Fo	**International Typeface Corporation**
Co	**USA**

Characteristics
Bold, condensed sans serif construction
Capitals only
Straight lines only
45-degree bevels at junctions

ABCDEGHI
LMNOPQR
STUVXYZ

Connections	
Schmalfette Grotesk	195
Superstar	197
Princetown	198
United	200

Availability
ITC Machine is available from Monotype and resellers

Specimen
Lubalin, Burns & Co. specimen. New York 1970 (200x160mm)

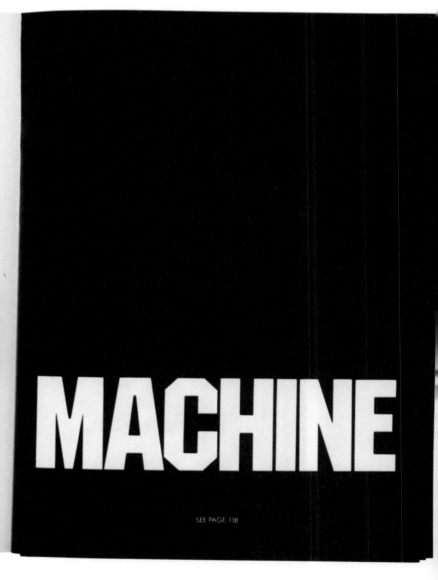

70

26 GOOD REASONS TOUSE: MACHINE

SEE PAGE 118

400

Tom Carnase (1939–) is an American designer with a long and auspicious career in brand communications and corporate identity. A prodigious logo and lettering artist, he has also worked on over 100 typeface projects, both independently and in collaboration, including the iconic ITC Avant Garde Gothic (pp394–95), a face that has influenced generations of designers.

ITC Machine was created by Tom Carnase and Ronne' Bonder in 1970 for the International Typeface Corporation. It is a black condensed alphabet whose towering letters provide an impact achieved by very few other typefaces.

Using only straight lines truncated abruptly at junctions by 45-degree angles, its dense characters are designed around its tight internal vertical spaces. It is intended to be spaced very tightly so that external and internal spaces correspond with each other.

The rectilinear structure of letter contours with minute vertical counterforms makes for dense word settings with high impact, inevitably offset by a loss of legibility and visual balance at smaller point sizes. ITC Machine is clearly influenced by the simple lettering applied to sportswear typically worn by American football

and baseball teams. The letterforms also evoke nostalgic recollections of varsity letters, a tradition from the American educational system in which single fabric letters can be earned by individuals to wear as a badge of membership of an award-winning team.

The original version of ITC Machine was drawn in upper case only, but at some point during the late 1970s it was augmented with a matching lower case alphabet. The lower case is no longer available in today's digital version, which continues to be widely used in signage and other display applications.

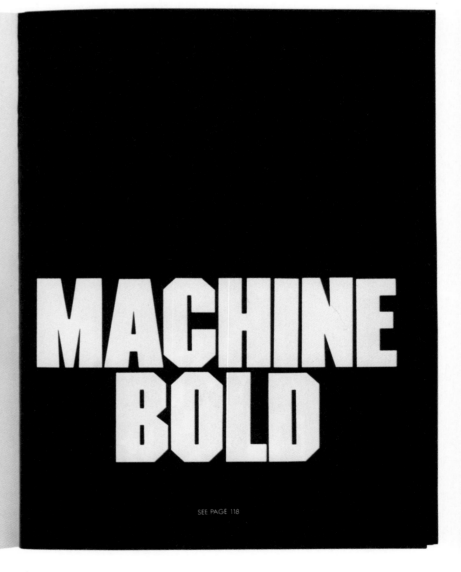

72

26 GOOD REASONS TO USE:

MACHINE BOLD

SEE PAGE 118

Ty **Stop**		
Ca **Sans Serif**		
Ke **Geometric, Capitals**		
Te **Letterpress**		
Da **1970**		
De **Aldo Novarese**		
Fo **Nebiolo**		
Co **Italy**		

Characteristics

Bold, capitals only
A Triangular
B D E F P R T Z Horizontal breaks
G H K R Truncated vertical parts
I J Lower case form
Q Unique form
S Truncated upper arch
T Blackletter form

Connections

Eurostile	196
Beans	197
Traffic	197
Motter Tektura	197

Availability

Stop is widely available

Specimen

Stop type specimen. Nebiolo, Turin, c1970 (210x210mm)

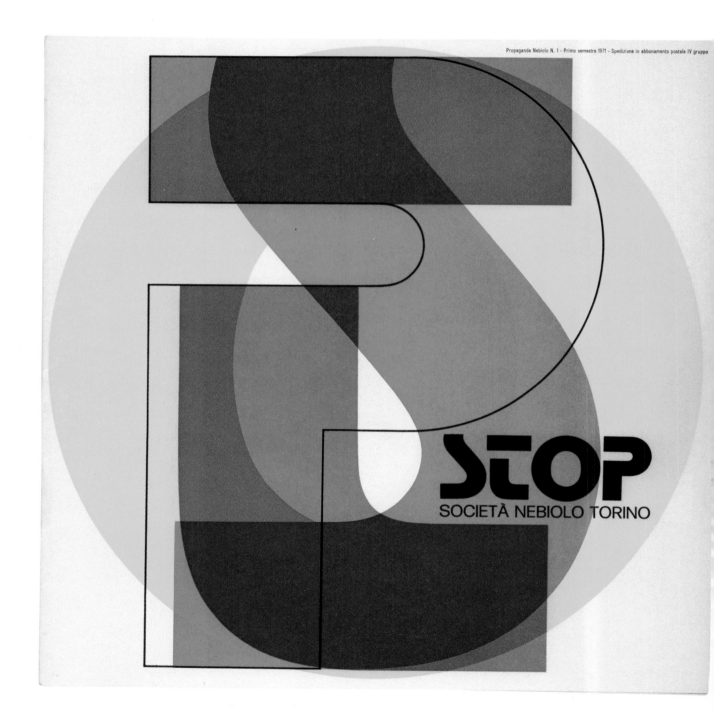

Aldo Novarese (1920–95) was one of the most prolific and hard-working type designers of his generation, and one of the most inventive. As art director at the Nebiolo foundry in Turin for many years he was responsible for the design and publication of a huge number of typefaces, from studious and intelligent revivals such as Egizio to groundbreaking innovations such the Eurostile family (pp364–65).

Novarese also designed many imaginative and attention-grabbing types for use in headline and display applications. Among the most flamboyant of these is Stop, released by Nebiolo in 1970, an extremely bold geometric sans serif typeface that was clearly intended to be seen first and read second, if at all.

In addition to its immediate visual impact, Stop is an alphabet with a wide range of connotations, suggesting the mobile electric forms of neon tube lighting and giving a technological impression that is reminiscent of both 1970s computing and retro science fiction. A capitals-only typeface, Stop features a set of highly unusual characters, some of which are so abstracted that they can only be differentiated as alphabetic signs when they are seen in combination with each other in word settings.

A series of severances and openings in counterforms causes horizontally connected open spaces between letters to align, providing playful continuities of positive and negative forms and making for distinctive but remarkably harmonious settings in short display applications at large sizes.

STOP   534-20

28
19 A - 11 x 1 - Kg. 5,30
MASTODONTICHE SCULTURE
GLI ESPERIMENTI SCIENTIFICI

36
16 A - 10 x 1 - Kg. 7,00
UN EXEMPLE CONCRET
MOINS NATIONALISTE

48
9 A - 6 x 1 - Kg. 8,00
FUNDAMIENTOS
EUROPEIZACION

60
7 A - 5 x 1 - Kg. 9,00

72
5 A - 4 x 1 - Kg. 10,00

Ty	**Horatio**
Ca	**Sans Serif**
Ke	**Geometric**
Te	**Dry Transfer**
Da	**1971**
De	**Robert Newman**
Fo	**Letraset**
Co	**UK**

Characteristics

Classical proportions and variable widths	
Small curves at angled junctions	
Long ascenders and descenders	
C c S s	Vertical terminals
E F J L	Narrow
M V W	Curved apex and vertex
R	Vertical leg
a g	Single-storeyed
c f r t	Narrow
i j	Round dots
r	Minimal form
v w	Curved vertex

AGJMRW
abcefghij
koprstuvy

Connections

Universal Type	1925
Blippo	c1970
ITC Rhonda	1970
Chalet	1996

Availability

Horatio is widely available

Specimen

Letraset catalogue. London, 1977
(210x297mm)

When the London-based company Letraset launched its dry-transfer lettering system in 1961, any user was able to produce professional-looking artwork without having to invest in expensive typesetting, as had been the case until that time. Although dry-transfer lettering is often dismissed from the history of graphic design, it had an enormous impact, placing the control of communications directly into the hands of professional graphic designers and the general public alike for the first time and marking a separation of design practice from print production. It was used extensively for almost three decades, foreshadowing the desktop publishing revolution, the advent of DIY design culture and the conventions of professional practice in the twenty-first century.

Letraset met the demands of the market for fashionable designs by means of a continuous programme of new typeface development and licensing from other manufacturers. In the late 1960s, among a selection of faces considered for inclusion in the product range was Harry, a geometric sans serif designed by Marty Goldstein and C. B. Smith in 1966 for Visual Graphics Corporation. When VGC refused to grant Letraset permission to use Harry, in-house designer Bob Newman was asked to produce a copy.

The result was Horatio, a huge improvement on its model and one of the most successful geometric sans serifs in the crowded marketplace of the time. Horatio's basic parameters follow those of its immediate point of reference, but in Newman's design character geometries have been balanced variably to assume the balanced proportions of classical letterforms. At the same time, Horatio shows a warmth and softness that is unusual in typefaces of its kind, largely due to the small curves used at angled junctions and the eccentricities of some of its forms, such as the leg of the R, the descender of the g, or the minimal lower case r.

Horatio, like other 1970s geometric sans serifs, represents an irreverent look back to the modernist type experiments of the 1920s – in particular, Herbert Bayer's 1925 Universal alphabet (pp222–23). But where designers in the 1920s had been interested in radical reforms and the reconciliation of public literacy with the technology of the age, the designs of the 1970s are oriented towards visual flamboyance and commercial style. ITC Bauhaus (1975) has proved the most enduring and ubiquitous of these, although it could not exceed the classic proportions of Horatio.

54 HORATIO LIGHT
ABCDEFGHIJKLM
NOPQRSTUVW
YZ abcdefghijkl
nopqrstuvwxyz12
34567890&ß?!£
$(;)《《〉\¦

Horatio Light

132
(248

Horatio Medium

133-
(249

Horatio Bold

134-
(250

Inserat Grotesk Amsterdam Type Foundry

HORATIO MEDIUM

ABCDEFGHIJKL
MNOPQRSTUV
WXYZ abcdefg
hijklmnopqrstuv
wxyz 12345678
90&?!£ß $(;):°⋮⋮ «‹›»

HORATIO BOLD

ABCDEFGHIJKLM
NOPQRSTUVWX
YZabcdefghijklm
nopqrstuvwxyz12
34567890&ß?!£
$⊜«‹◈›»;⋮⋮

132-60-CN (2487) B	132-60-L (2488) B	132-48-CN (2489) B	132-48-L (2490) B	132-36-CLN (2491) B	132-24-CLN (2492) B
133-60-CN (2495)	133-60-L (2496)	133-48-CN (2497)	133-48-L (2498)	133-36-CLN (2499)	133-24-CLN (2500)
134-60-CN (2503)	134-60-L (2504)	134-48-CN (2505)	134-48-L (2506)	134-36-CLN (2507)	134-24-CLN (2508)

Ty	**Embrionic**
Ca	**Sans Serif**
Ke	**Geometric**
Te	**Photocomposition**
Da	**1972**
De	**Gary Gillot**
Fo	**Graphic Systems**
Co	**UK**

Characteristics

Geometric character construction
Ellipsoid base form
Swash capital alternates
C c G e Horizontal terminals separated by thin space
Q Flat tail extends from bowl
a b d h m n p r u Narrow triangular incisions at stroke junctions
g Double-storeyed with truncated lower bowl
s Inclined form
& Swash form

Connections

Advertisers Gothic	1917
Tabasco	c1970
Stripes	1972
Motter Tektura	1975

Availability

Not available

Specimen

New and Exclusive Typefaces from Graphic Systems. London, 1972 (148x210mm)

Embrionic Triline (Gary Gillot)

ABCDEFGHIJKL
MNOPQRSTUVWXYZ
abcdefghijklmno
pqrstuvwxyz
1234567890
((&£?!))

The major shift that occurred in the way that type was used during the 1960s and 1970s with the advent of photosetting and dry-transfer lettering had a permanent effect on the industry, expanding the practice of graphic design as an independent profession as it removed artwork production from printers.

Letraset, established in 1959 in the UK, was central to these changes. Their patented dry-transfer system transformed type into an affordable product that was no longer tied to traditional print services. This meant easier access and greater

competition, leading to a flood of new attention-seeking typefaces.

Gary Gillot (1939–), a type designer and prepress expert from South Africa, was one of Letraset's earliest employees. His techniques for hand-cutting letters in Ulano film rather than drawing them with pen and ink revolutionized Letraset's production process and subsequently led to the method being adopted as an industry standard. In 1969 he founded Graphic Systems to develop Rapidtype, a photographic alternative to Letraset that had a much finer resolution. Rapidtype

produced custom dry-transfer sheets to order, but they also sold a typeface collection that consisted of a mix of classic bestsellers and a small selection of original designs produced by their in-house team.

Embrionic, cut by Gillot himself, is a geometric typeface in three weights. Intended for headlines, its structure is the product of its tall x-height, its large counterforms and the flowing rhythms of its egg-shaped characters. Individual characters are engineered to fit together tightly, making optical connections that form tight, harmonious word shapes.

The type family also features a triline version that is somewhat reminiscent of Rudolf Koch's Prisma (pp276–77) and sets of curvaceous swash character alternates that echo display lettering of the 1920s. Embrionic became very popular with London agencies and design consultancies during the early 1970s for advertising and editorial work. However, it did not survive the technological changes that followed in the 1980s and 1990s and is much less well known today than many of its less sophisticated contemporaries. It remains a finely cut typeface that is an outstanding example of the ebullience of 1970s design.

		Characteristics	Connections	
Ty	**Sintex**	Reversed contrast	French Clarendon	c1860
Ca	**Sans Serif**	Thick horizontals	Playbill	1938
Ke	**Geometric, Reversed Contrast**	Thin verticals	Zipper	1970
Te	**Photocomposition**	Capitals extend to x-height	Signo	2014
Da	**1972**	Condensed overall width		
De	**Aldo Novarese**	Curves at stroke junctions		
Fo	**Visual Graphics Corporation**	Circular counterforms		
Co	**USA**			

ABCDEMRSU
abcdefghij
kmoprstuy

Availability

Stretto is a digital revival of Sintex available from Canada Type and resellers

Specimen

Aldo Novarese, *Alfa-Beta*. Progresso Grafico, Turin, 1983 (240x170mm)

Carattere "Sintex" Photo Typositor (dis. A. Novarese).

Questa estrosa fantasia pur non appartenente agli egiziani per l'assenza di grazie, ne segue il concetto in quanto le estremità ingrossate come quelle dei tipi "Italici" offrono un notevole motivo orizzontale.
Il disegno costruttivo è semplice in quanto il centro di alcune lettere si basa sulle curve a pieno raggio.

ABCDEF
GHIJKL
MNOP

QRSTU
VWXYZ
abcd
efghij

292

Sintex was designed by Aldo Novarese (1920–95) in the late 1960s and released by Visual Graphics Corporation in 1972, although a Letraset version appeared two years earlier. It is a sans serif that defies typographic conventions by exploiting a feature of letterform called 'reversed contrast'. A fundamental principle of type design, following optical and calligraphic order, is that vertical strokes ought to appear thicker than horizontal ones. As demonstrated in almost every example in this publication, this principle is believed to contribute to visual balance and legibility by providing a natural flow.

A few designers have argued that there is no logical reason why this should be advantageous to reading or to aesthetic qualities and have designed typefaces with a deliberately reversed contrast, where the emphasis is rotated so that the strokes approaching horizontal are thicker than those that are vertical.

Typefaces of this sort, when designed diligently, attempt to improve readability by increasing the horizontal directional pull of text. Roger Excoffon's Antique Olive (pp362–63) and Evert Bloemsma's Balance (pp510–11) are two notable examples.

Yet another long-standing tradition is that of typefaces intended to draw attention to themselves – types made, literally, to grab the headlines – and some have used reversed contrast as a method for doing so. These faces intentionally flip conventions on their head, with often amusing and sometimes hideous results. The idea originated in the nineteenth century with the Italian style (pp118–19) and reached a high point in the French Antique and its massive block serifs (pp138–39), instantly recognizable as the familiar lettering often seen on circus posters and 'wanted' notices.

The work of a master of type design, Sintex achieves the same objective in a unique way, without the convenience of serifs to provide areas for horizontal thickening. The result is one of the most unusual alphabets ever devised.

With a wilful disregard for concerns about beauty or correctness, Sintex fuses its inverted straight and round strokes in a highly eccentric manner. Its key features are a strong overall compression, a set of capitals that align to the x-height rather than the lower case ascent, and tightly defined geometric counterforms.

klmn
opqrs
tuvw
xyz &

12345
67890
%!?-""")

La caratteristica essenziale di questo carattere è quella di avere il maiuscolo alto come il corpo centrale del minuscolo, permettendo così la fusione dei due alfabeti come dimostrato nella terza riga.

abcdefghijklmnopqrsβtuvwxyz
ABCDEFGHIJKLMNOPQRSTUVWXYZ
abcdefghijklmnopqrsβtuvwxyz

294

295

Ty	**American Typewriter**
Ca	**Slab Serif**
Ke	**Typewriter**
Te	**Photocomposition**
Da	**1974**
De	**Joel Kaden and Tony Stan**
Fo	**International Typeface Corporation**
Co	**USA**

Characteristics

Most capitals have uniform width

Large, open counterforms

E F T Very long serifs

G Has a spur

M Narrow

Q Looped tail below letter

R a t Tail turns upwards

a c f j r y Ball terminals

g Double-storeyed with teardrop ear

r Hooked arch

EGMQR
abcefghij
koprsty

Connections

Courier	1955
Quadrato	1963
FF Trixie	1991
FF Elementa	1998

Availability

American Typewriter is available from
Linotype and resellers

Specimen

U&lc, Vol. 1, No. 3. International Typeface
Corporation, New York, 1974 (382x290mm)

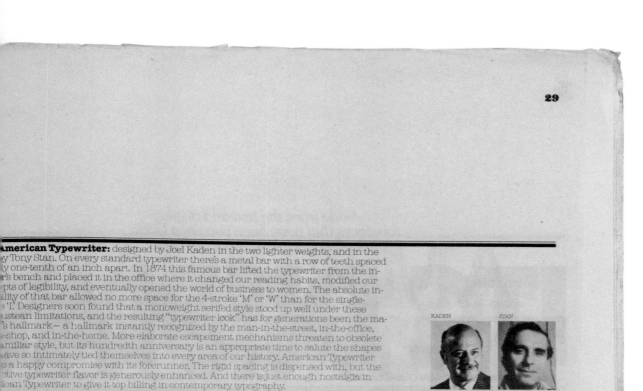

American Typewriter: designed by Joel Kaden in the two lighter weights, and in the
[hea]vy Tony Stan. On every standard typewriter there's a metal bar with a row of teeth spaced
[exactl]y one-tenth of an inch apart. In 1874 this famous bar lifted the typewriter from the in-
[ventor]'s bench and placed it in the office where it changed our reading habits, modified our
[conce]pts of legibility, and eventually opened the world of business to women. The absolute in-
[flexibi]lity of that bar allowed no more space for the 4-stroke 'M' or 'W' than for the single-
[strok]e 'I'. Designers soon found that a monoweight serifed style stood up well under these
[Procr]ustean limitations, and the resulting "typewriter look" has for generations been the ma-
[chine']s hallmark – a hallmark instantly recognized by the man-in-the-street, in-the-office,
[in-the-]shop, and in-the-home. More elaborate escapement mechanisms threaten to obsolete
[this fa]miliar style, but its hundredth anniversary is an appropriate time to salute the shapes
[that h]ave so intimately tied themselves into every area of our history. American Typewriter
[design]s a happy compromise with its forerunner. The rigid spacing is dispensed with, but the
[distin]ctive typewriter flavor is generously enhanced. And there is just enough nostalgia in
[Ameri]can Typewriter to give it top billing in contemporary typography.

KADEN   STAN

4567890&abcdefghijklmnopqrs
tuvwxyzœøæß!?¢@£#(*) MEDIUM ABCDEF
HIJKLMNOPQRSTUVWXYZŒ
234567890&abcdefghijklmnop
rstuvwxyzœøæß!?¢#(*) BOLD ABCDE
GHIJKLMNOPQRSTUVWXY
Œ&1234567890abcdefghijkl
mnopqrstuvwxyzœøæß@!?#(*)
ABCDEFGHIJKLMNOPQRST
VWXYZ&1234567890abcdef
hijklmnopqrstuvwxyzß!?(*)

DESIGN PATENT APPLIED FOR

29

The first commercial device for typing with a keyboard was invented by Christopher Sholes and Carlos Glidden in Milwaukee in 1867. Remington & Sons, then a sewing machine manufacturer, acquired the rights to market it and began the production of the first typewriter in 1874. It featured the QWERTY keyboard layout that, because of the machine's phenomenal success, was adopted by most other typewriter manufacturers. As the typewriter rapidly developed into a standard tool of commerce, its distinctive alphabet became a familiar part of the visual language of business.

Joel Kadan and Tony Stan translated the charm and immediacy of these workaday letters into typographic form for the International Typeface Corporation in 1974. American Typewriter was designed as an idealized version of its humble antecedent, with an alphabet that was rationalized, but not in a sterile or solemn way. It substitutes the irregular output of typewritten letters for cleanly defined character contours with a very even stroke contrast and long, concave, blobby serifs. The x-height is tall and ascenders and descenders are squat. American Typewriter's soft, rotund overall impression is most immediately evident in capitals like the J and Q, or the lower case a, g and r.

With mechanical typewriters it is only possible for letters to be monospaced – positioned within identical spaces that fit onto type hammers of a fixed size. The characters in American Typewriter are carefully designed to follow this model, appearing to share a standard-width configuration, although they are in fact proportionally spaced, allowing for much greater typographic control and more even-looking settings than a true typewriter font.

American Typewriter was widely used during the 1970s and 1980s for display compositions where the new possibilities of photosetting technology allowed it to be set very tightly in both letter spacing and line spacing – a daring innovation of the time that is today regarded as a short-lived trend in the history of graphic design.

Isonorm

Ty	**Isonorm**
Ca	**Sans Serif**
Ke	**Geometric**
Te	**Lettering**
Da	**1974**
De	**Unknown**
Fo	**ISO**
Co	**Switzerland**

Characteristics

Monoline geometric character construction
Letterforms incremented on centre lines
Rounded terminals
Most characters have equal width
C c G O o Straight downstrokes
a Alternate forms
r Downturned arch
t Straight stem, no foot

ABEGMRS
aabcefghij
koprstuy

Connections

DIN 1451	1931
OCR-A	1968
AT Burin Sans	1994
Simple	2002

Availability

Isonorm is widely available

Specimen

Norme Internationale 3098/1 – Technical Drawings – Lettering – Part 1: Currently Used Characters. International Organization for Standardization, Geneva, 1974 (297x210mm)

ISO 3098/I-1974 (F)

Écriture B droite

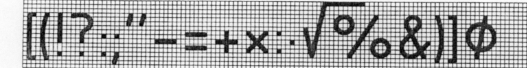

1) Ces deux caractères sont conformes aux règles d'écriture et les comités nationaux sont libres de choisir entre les possibilités offertes.

NOTE – Pour obtenir un trait de densité optique constante, éviter l'empâtement des intersections et faciliter l'écriture, les lettres doivent être formées de telle façon que les traits se croisent et se rencontrent approximativement à angle droit.

6

412

The International Organization for Standardization (ISO) is the world's largest developer of voluntary international standards. Since its foundation in 1947 it has published almost 20,000 technical and quality standards covering almost every aspect of business and technology.

The ISO 3098 standard was published in 1974. It specified a set of rules for lettering used in the annotation of technical drawings, detailing its application by means of lettering templates, tracing from grids, dry-transfer systems and computer numerical control (CNC).

Like DIN (pp266–67), the design of Isonorm characters is based on the simplest possible motion of a pen following strict geometric guides that consist of only straight lines and circular arcs. No stroke is superfluous in Isonorm and no character ambiguous. A centre line running through every glyph is the basic datum for the design and for the tools with which they are reproduced, such as engraving machines, templates and computer programs. Letterforms are completely monolinear, with weight being incremented evenly on the centre line. All strokes have rounded endings. The italics are slanted versions of the upright alphabet.

Isonorm has been used for drafting and AutoCAD by architects and engineers for several decades. Since its release as dry-transfer lettering by Letraset in the late 1970s it has also frequently been seen in corporate design and advertising, often to impart a sense of efficiency and technical precision. It has been digitized by various type foundries. Of these, Robert Kirchner's version, originally produced in 1993 for FontFont, is the most comprehensive, including a mechanical-looking monospaced version.

ISO 3098/I-1974 (F)

Écriture B penchée

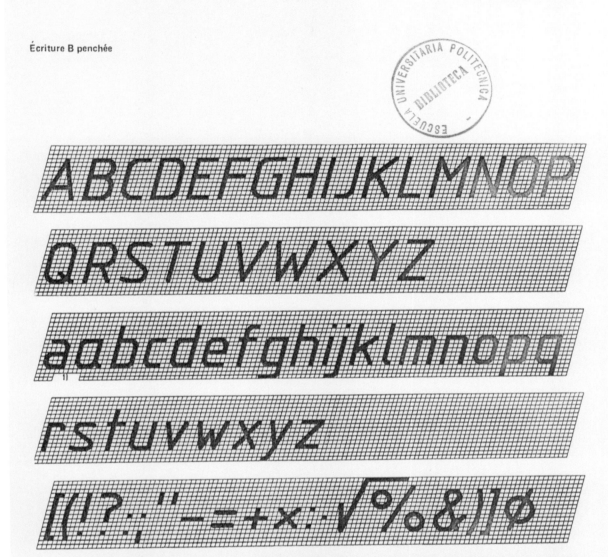

1) Ces deux caractères sont conformes aux règles d'écriture et les comités nationaux sont libres de choisir entre les possibilités offertes.

NOTE – Pour obtenir un trait de densité optique constante, éviter l'empâtement des intersections et faciliter l'écriture, les lettres doivent être formées de telle façon que les traits se croisent et se rencontrent approximativement à angle droit.

5

Lubalin Graph

Ty	**Lubalin Graph**
Ca	**Slab Serif**
Ke	**Geometric**
Te	**Photocomposition**
Da	**1974**
De	**Herb Lubalin**
Fo	**International Typeface Corporation**
Co	**USA**

Characteristics

Monoline, geometric construction
Very large x-height
Short ascenders and descenders
A Horizontal serif to left at apex
C c O o Q Circular
G Has spur, long arm
Q Curved tail terminates in vertical serif
a Single-storeyed
e Circle divided by crossbar
f r t Narrow
i j Square dots
t Square foot
0 Condensed form, straight sided

AGMRS
abcefgij
korstuy

Connections

Memphis	1929
Stymie	1931
ITC Avant Garde Gothic	1970
Museo Slab	2009

Availability

ITC Lubalin Graph is available from Monotype and resellers. Its original ligatures and alternates are not available.

Specimen

U&lc, Vol. 1, No. 3. International Typeface Corporation, New York, 1974 (382x290mm)

414

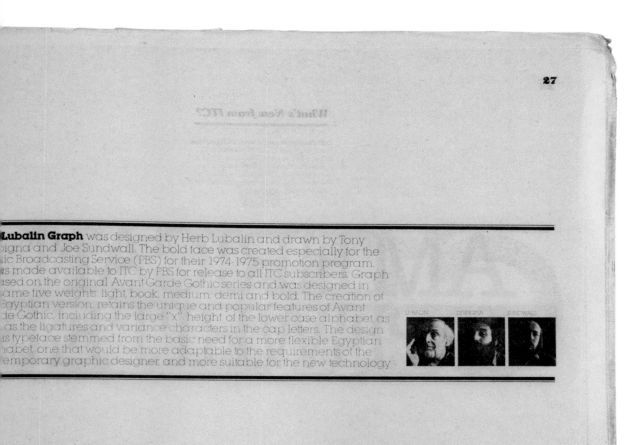

ITC Lubalin Graph is a geometric slab serif designed in 1974. It was modelled on Herb Lubalin's hugely successful ITC Avant Garde Gothic typeface (pp394–95) released four years earlier. Like Avant Garde Gothic, Lubalin Graph was intended for different purposes than those derived from the older traditions of printing and bookwork. Created for television, it was originally drawn only in a bold weight for the Public Broadcasting Service to use as part of their 1974–75 promotional programme. Designed by Herb Lubalin (1918–81) and drawn by ITC lettering artists Tony Di Spigna and Joe Sundwall, Lubalin Graph integrates the features of Avant Garde with those of the formative geometric slab serif designs of the 1930s such as Memphis (pp250–51) and Stymie (pp278–79).

The basic armature of Lubalin Graph is almost identical to that of Avant Garde Gothic, with the addition of stout, rectangular serifs that correspond visually to the stroke weights. Like Avant Garde Gothic, it also features an extremely large x-height, resulting in open counterforms and proportionately squat ascenders and descenders. Its circular and rectangular structures appear to be inscribed entirely with compasses and rulers, but like Avant Garde Gothic they are in fact subtly modulated. Also like Avant Garde Gothic, ITC Lubalin Graph came in a range of five weights featuring alternate characters and sets of all-capital ligatures that offered exciting new ways to create unique combinations of letter sequences.

Whereas Avant Garde Gothic was a groundbreaking typeface that defined the phototypesetting era and had an enduring effect on the direction of graphic design, Lubalin Graph, with its slab serifs providing a more lively geometric contour, offers the nostalgic impression of an earlier period in twentieth-century design.

Ty	**Politene / Gridnik**
Ca	**Sans Serif**
Ke	**Geometric**
Te	**Lettering**
Da	**1974**
De	**Wim Crouwel**
Fo	**Total Design**
Co	**Netherlands**

Characteristics

Square grid

x-height proportion of 5 x 4 units

45-degree angles at corners

Minute curves at corners

a r u Slight angle on stem at junction

k v w y z Follow natural angles

ABGMR
abcefghij
koprstuy

Connections

New Alphabet	1967
Vormgevers Lettering	1968
Randstad Lettering	1970
Blender	2008

Availability

Gridnik is a digital revival available from the Foundry and resellers

Specimen

Wim Crouwel Alphabets. BIS Publishers BV, Rotterdam, 2003 (255x175mm)

ABCDEFGHIJKLMNOPQRSTWXYZ
abcdefghijklmnopqrstvwxyz
1234567890
£$¢¥f€§&?!.,;:'"«»
—()/.+—=÷

abcdefghijklmnopqrstuvwxyz
1234567890
£¢$¥ƒ€§&?!.,:;«»""'' ‹‹›
-()/·+-=÷

ABCabc

In 1973 Wim Crouwel (1928–) was invited to design a typeface for a range of Olivetti electric typewriters. Crouwel was not in favour of contemporary alphabets that made typewritten communications look as sophisticated as printed matter. He thought that typewriters should use alphabets whose output was visually distinguished from printed typography. After exploring a number of alternatives, including monospaced and serifed letterforms, Crouwel proposed a monolinear octagonal sans serif that drew its inspiration from lettering he had seen on the hulls of Dutch naval vessels.

Politene, as the type was named by Olivetti, is a prime example of the work of a master designer who once described himself as 'a functionalist troubled by aesthetics'. Like many of his alphabets, it is based on a rectangular geometry, with an x-height proportion of five by four units. Although the product of a logical process that conforms to a grid, it also features typographic details that give it both usefulness and humanity. Letterforms defined by the use of 45-degree angles at corners and junctions are softened by minutely rounded arcs and the use of alternative angles where necessary to provide a more natural appearance.

Before the typeface had been implemented on Olivetti's machines, the market for electric typewriters declined and it was no longer required. As a consequence, the rights to the design reverted to Crouwel. During the same period he was appointed by the Dutch Post Office to create its definitive postage stamp set in several denominations. His solution used a custom version of the Politene lettering to construct the word 'nederland' and large numerals that indicated values situated on graduated panels of colour. The resulting stamp designs remained in circulation for over 25 years.

In 1997 a digital version of Politene was produced from the original technical drawings by David Quay and Freda Sack of the Foundry in London, working in collaboration with Crouwel. Originally this consisted of a single font in a regular weight as part of the Foundry's collection of Crouwel type revivals, but it was later expanded with a light, a medium and a bold. The digital version was named Gridnik by Quay and Sack as a reference to 'Mr Gridnik', the nickname given to Crouwel by his friends for his frequent use of grids and systems.

Ty	**Serif Gothic**
Ca	**Serif**
Ke	**Geometric**
Te	**Photocomposition**
Da	**1974**
De	**Herb Lubalin and Tony Di Spigna**
Fo	**International Typeface Corporation**
Co	**USA**

Characteristics

B	Single bowl
G	Upper curve undershoots
K R	Curved tail
W	Stepped centre-strokes
a	Single-storeyed with a spur
b d	No stem at foot
e	Eye overhangs tail
f	Narrow
g p q	No stem at head
t	Angled top, straight stem, no foot

ABGKRW
abcefghij
koprstuy

Connections

Copperplate Gothic	1901
ITC Avant Garde Gothic	1970
ITC Kabel	1976
Variex	1988

Availability

ITC Serif Gothic is available from Monotype and resellers

Specimen

Serif Gothic type specimen. International Typeface Corporation, New York, c1974 (279x140mm)

The name Serif Gothic is an oxymoron but one that, like the typeface itself, draws attention to itself. It was designed in 1974 by Herb Lubalin (1918–81) and Tony Di Spigna for the International Typeface Corporation. The letterforms were originally conceived for use in a logotype proposal by Lubalin and Tom Carnase for a French shirt brand, but the work was rejected. However, Di Spigna was intrigued by the prototype letters he had drawn and decided to see if they could be expanded into a finished typeface. 'We thought it was an interesting idea,' he said, 'to take a sans serif letterform and add minute serifs to it, but at the same time to give it a different twist, a different character and identity of its own.'

The defining characteristics of Serif Gothic, like ITC's seminal Avant Garde Gothic (pp394–95), are its pure, circular geometries and its remarkably large x-height, with diminutive ascenders and descenders. These extreme proportions, typical of ITC typefaces in the 1970s, were ideally suited to the very tight setting and minimum line spacing that was highly fashionable at the time. Serif Gothic follows the pattern of well-established Copperplate Gothics (pp164–65) in its diminutive serifs, which are essentially slightly pointed stroke endings rather than full roman serifs. In the heaviest variant, Black, the serifs are much more pronounced than in the lighter weights.

The entire family of six weights was produced in nine months and quickly became one of ITC's most successful typefaces. It was very widely used in television, publicity, packaging and billboard advertising.

abcdefghijklmnopqrstu
ABCDEFGHIJKLMNOPQ
30

abcdefghijklmnopq
ABCDEFGHIJKLMN
36

abcdefghijklm
ABCDEFGHIJK
48

abcdefghijk
ABCDEFGHI
60

abcdefghi
ABCDEFGH

abcdefg
ABCDEFG
72

abcdefi
ABCDE
1" on Caps

26

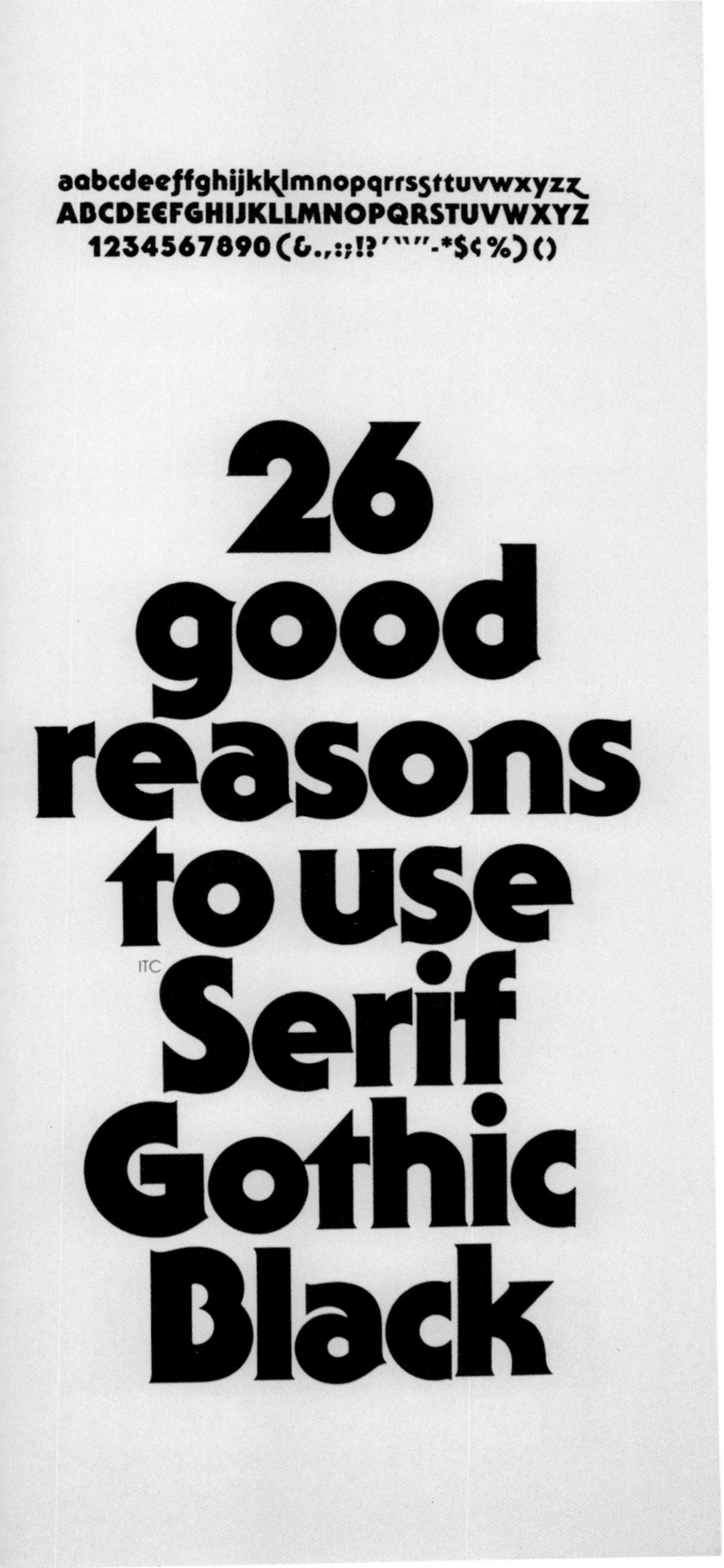

aabcdeeffghijkklmnopqrrssttuvwxyzz
ABCDEEFGHIJKLLMNOPQRSTUVWXYZ
1234567890 (&.,:;!?'"''"-*$¢%) ()

26 good reasons to use ITC Serif Gothic Black

abcdefghijklmnopqrstuvwx
ABCDEFGHIJKLMNOPQRST
30

abcdefghijklmnopqrstu
ABCDEFGHIJKLMNOPT
36

abcdefghijklmno
ABCDEFGHIJKLM
48

abcdefghijklm
ABCDEFGHIJK
60

abcdefghijk
ABCDEFGHI
72

abcdefh
ABCDEF

1" on Caps

10

Ty	**ITC Century**
Ca	**Serif**
Ke	**Modern**
Te	**Photocomposition**
Da	**1975**
De	**Tony Stan**
Fo	**International Typeface Corporation**
Co	**USA**

Characteristics

Vertical stress with slight stroke contrast
Wide, round body, large x-height
Short ascenders and descenders
Heavy, bracketed slab serifs
M Narrow
Q Looped tail below letter
R a t Tail turns upwards
a c f j r y Ball terminals
g Double-storeyed with teardrop ear
h m n No inner serifs on right stems

AGMQR
abcefghij
orstyaefg

Connections

Century Expanded	1900
Century Schoolbook	1918
ITC Cheltenham	1975
ITC Garamond	1975

Availability

ITC Century is available from Monotype and resellers

Specimen

ITC Century type specimen. International Typeface Corporation, New York, c1975 (279x140mm)

ITC Century is an interpretation of American Type Founders' extensive Century family from the early 1900s. Its design draws on a range of features from Century Roman, Linn Boyd Benton's typeface for *Century* magazine, as well as Morris Fuller Benton's Century Expanded and Century Schoolbook (pp206–207).

In 1975, under licence from ATF, the International Typeface Corporation commissioned Tony Stan (1917–88), who also designed ITC Garamond (pp422–23) and ITC Cheltenham, to revive and extend the Century family for photocomposition. Stan started the design with the extreme weights, completing Ultrabold and Book versions, each with matching italics, in 1975. Light, regular and bold weights with companion italics came shortly afterwards, followed by the ITC Century Condensed family of eight typefaces corresponding to the standard-width versions.

Like most of his other interpretations of historic faces, Stan's design approach imposed the typographic conventions that ITC had established throughout their product range in the 1970s. The ITC Century series features an extremely large lower case x-height and very tight letter spacing compared with its metal predecessors. In addition, the ascenders are radically shortened and inner serifs on the right-hand stems of the lower case letters h, m and n have been eliminated.

Like Stan's ITC Garamond, the large lower case, open counterforms and regular pattern of ITC Century's rounded geometries were ideally suited 'to satisfy contemporary typographic design tastes', as the sales literature stated. Very close letter spacing and tight leading – visual consequences of the new possibilities afforded by photocomposition – were typographic innovations that became a major fashion in 1970s graphic design, to which the contribution of typefaces like ITC Century was central.

abcdefghijklmnopqrstuv
ABCDEFGHIJKLMNOP
30

abcdefghijklmnopqr
ABCDEFGHIJKLNO
36

abcdefghijkmn
ABCDEFGHIK
48

abcdefghijk
ABCDEFGH
60

abcdefhik
ABCDEFI
72

abcdeh
ABCDJ

1" on Caps

14

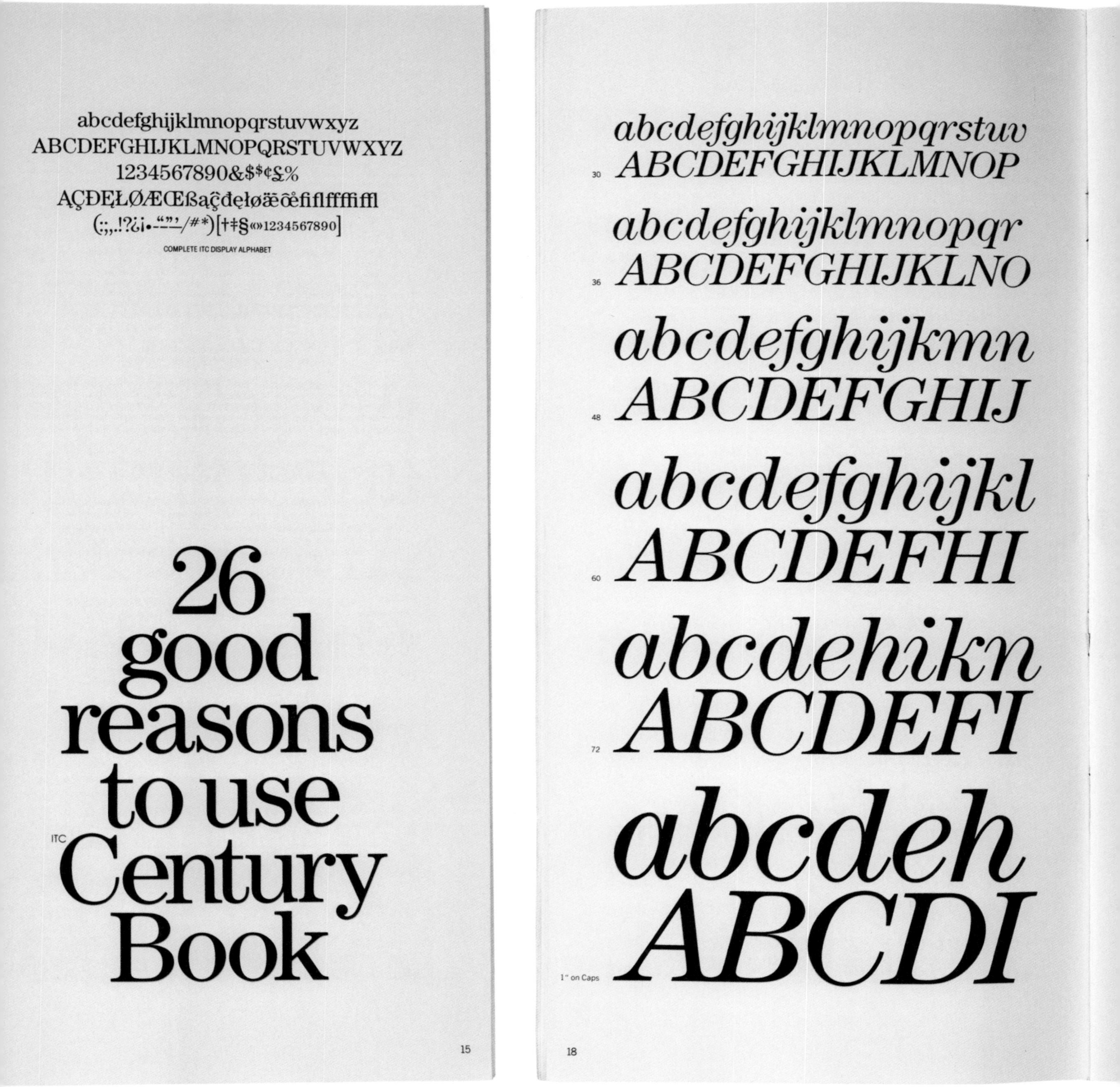

abcdefghijklmnopqrstuvwxyz
ABCDEFGHIJKLMNOPQRSTUVWXYZ
1234567890&$$¢£%
AÇĐEŁØÆŒßaçđełøǽœfiflffffiffl
(:;,.!?¿¡•-"""/#*)[†‡§«»1234567890]

COMPLETE ITC DISPLAY ALPHABET

26 good reasons to use Century Book

ITC

15

abcdefghijklmnopqrstuv
ABCDEFGHIJKLMNOP

30

abcdefghijklmnopqr
ABCDEFGHIJKLNO

36

abcdefghijkmn
ABCDEFGHIJ

48

abcdefghijkl
ABCDEFHI

60

abcdehikn
ABCDEFI

72

abcdeh
ABCDI

1" on Caps

18

421

Ty	**ITC Garamond**
Ca	**Serif**
Ke	**Old Style, Geometric**
Te	**Photocomposition**
Da	**1975**
De	**Tony Stan**
Fo	**International Typeface Corporation**
Co	**USA**

Characteristics

Very large x-height
Short ascenders and descenders
Oblique stress
Moderate stroke contrast
Capitals lower than ascender height
Circular bowls
Curving, bracketed serifs
J Descends below baseline, hooked
M Slightly splayed
Q Tail below letter
W Crossed centre-strokes
a g Double-storeyed

AGJMRW
abcefghij
orstyaefg

Connections

American Typewriter	1974
Serif Gothic	1974
ITC Century	1975
ITC Berkeley Oldstyle	1983

Availability

ITC Garamond is available from Monotype and resellers

Specimen

U&lc, Vol. 4, No. 1. International Typeface Corporation, New York, 1977 (382x290mm)

26

ITC Garamond Light

ABCDEFGHI
JKLMNOPQ
RSTUVWX
YZabcdefgh
ijklmnopq
rstuvwxyz
1234567890
(&£$¢$%!?)

ITC Garamond Light Italic

ABCDEFGHI
JKLMNOPQ
RSTUVWX
YZabcdefghh
ijklmmnnop
qrstuvwxyzz
1234567890
(&£$¢$&%!?)

ITC Garamond Bold

ABCDEFGH
IJKLMNOP
QRSTUVW
XYZabcd
efghijklm
nopqrstu
vwxyz1234
567890(&
£$¢$%!?)

ITC Garamond Bold Italic

ABCDEFGH
IJKLMNOP
QRSTUVW
XYZabcd
efghhijklm
mmnopqrst
uvwxyzz12
34567890
(&£$¢$&%!?)

ITC Garamond Book

ABCDEFGHI
JKLMNOPQ
RSTUVWX
YZabcdefgh
ijklmnopq
rstuvwxyz
1234567890
(&£$¢$%!?)

ITC Garamond Book Italic

ABCDEFGHI
JKLMNOPQ
RSTUVWX
YZabcdefgh
ijklmnopq
rstuvwxyz
1234567890
(&£$$¢&%!?)

ABCDEFGH
IJKLMNOP
QRSTUVW
XYZabcd
efghijklm
nopqrstu
vwxyz1234
567890(&
£$¢$%!?)

ITC Garamond Ultra

ABCDEFGH
IJKLMNOP
QRSTUVW
XYZabcd
efghijklm
nopqrstu
vwxyz1234
567890(&
£$¢$&%!?)

ITC Garamond Ultra Italic

No other typeface has been subjected to a greater number of revivals than Claude Garamond's Roman (pp48–49). Almost all of the major twentieth-century type foundries produced their own interpretations, and these in turn have been reconstructed again in transitions from metal to film and to digital media. Several other typefaces, such as Sabon and Granjon, are modelled on Garamond or inspired by it. Ironically, most Garamond revivals are misattributed to him, in fact being based on the typefaces of Jean Jannon (pp62–63), who lived about a century later. Although it is hard to identify points of fidelity or authenticity within such a confused historical picture, few versions have taken greater liberties with their ancestral namesake than ITC Garamond.

Drawn by Tony Stan (1917–88), ITC Garamond was first released in 1975 and was intended as a display face to complement text matter. Stan's type shows some design traits of the Garamond form. However, it is distinguished by the even geometry of its thick and thin strokes, and the corresponding regularity of its rounded, partially concave serifs. Its extremely large x-height, diminutive ascenders and descenders, enormous, open counters and regular curves operate in a way that is characteristic of the design formula that ITC followed throughout the 1970s.

ITC Garamond's generous proportions and repetitive geometries were ideally suited to the very close letter spacing and tight leading that was then in vogue. It was entirely appropriate for use in busy magazine headlines and television media, but in body text the features that distinguished ITC Garamond became obtrusive and ungainly. Very regular, very round and very stunted, it was difficult to read in long passages.

As a result, although its frequent misuse for this purpose cannot be blamed on the type itself, it was often disdained by those design practitioners who came to regard it as gaudy, dated and, above all, inauthentic. In 1987 Paula Scher, for example, publicly denounced ITC Garamond not for its appearance or its limited functionality but for the simple reason that 'it's called Garamond and it's not Garamond'.

Column 1

Vandiver Jerry D teleph 400 Office Park Dr — — 877-5538
Res 5029 Kerry Downs Rd — — — — — 967-8955
Vandiver John Henry 2712 Fairfax Av Besmr — 425-8805
Vandiver K D 1610 12th S — — — — — — 328-7604
Vandiver P A Jr 364 Midwood Av Midfld — — 923-9106
Vandiver Post Office Vandvr — — — — — 672-9302
Vandiver Richard W 1506 Warrior Rd — — — 788-0677
Vandiver Ronald 126 2nd Av S — — — — 324-5735
Vandiver W P LtCol 1548 Bessmer Rd — — 923-1283
Vandiver William 1610 12th S — — — — — 328-7604
Vandiver Willie Rev 5418 11th Av Wylam — 780-8599
Vandiver Willie J 524 54th Fairfld — — — 780-0243
Vandrell Richard L 1420 66th W — — — — 923-5922
Van Drimmelen Cays 223 Green Park South — 979-2260
Van Dusen & Atkinson Inc
1800 Ave K Lipscomb — — — — — 428-2621
Van Dusen M K Route 3 Warrior — — — 647-7033
Van Dusen Paul L 3617 Haven Hill Dr — — 956-0177
Van Dyke E W 1324 Oak Terr — — — — 854-3491
Vann Hoyt 1232 Frisco Wylam — — — — 786-2571
Vann J Mason 118 Vann Hueytown — — — 491-2644
Vann J Thompson 1882 Montclair Ln — — 823-0590
Vann J W Riverlawn Resort — — — — 674-5270
Vann Jackie 1309 21st N — — — — — 251-3098
Vann James A Jr 3201 Stering Rd — — — 879-4245
Vann James E Castle Heights — — — — 681-2523
Vann James J Jr 8303 5th Av N — — — 833-3933
Vann James R 2204 Little Valley Rd — — 979-0984
Vann Jerry 1025 Rutledge Way — — — 788-5058
Vann Jimmy C Morris — — — — — 681-8134
Vann Joe K Mrs 1915 7th NE — — — — 854-4729
Vann John David 1853—C Arboretum Cir — 823-0785
Vann John Thomas 1333 Orlando Cir — — 854-4729
Vann Johnnie 7748 4th Av S — — — — 838-1735
Vann K G Castle Heights — — — — — 681-9857
Vann L R 1300 Warrior Rd — — — — 788-0284
Vann Larry A 716 Park Ln Fultndle — — 849-4206
Vann Lee 1904 May Cir Fultndle — — — 849-7567
Teenager's Telephone
1904 May Cir Fultndle — — — — 849-5159
Vann Leona 609 Forest Rd Hueytown — — 744-7512
Vann Lowell Dr 3472 Birchtree Dr — — 822-5442
Vann M L 913 13th Midfld — — — — 744-0773
Vann Mary E 221 13th Ter N — — — 252-1735
Vardaman Earl 1216 58th S — — — — 595-2909
Vardaman G 3550 Altamont Rd — — — 251-1516
Vardaman J I Wilsnvle — — — — — 669-7312
Vardaman J I Jr 1529 Valley View Cir — — 879-7497
Vardaman James T
905 Independence Dr Alabstr — — 663-7888
Vardaman Joyce
1529 Valley View Cir Homwd — — 879-3106
Vardaman Kathi
1529 Valley View Cir Homwd — — 879-3106
Vardaman Lela Mae 2021 Warrior Rd — — 787-1045
Vardaman M T 953 Beech Ln — — — 879-5316
Vardaman Tom Frank 2831 Highland Av S — 322-6491
Vardaman W K 8917 Roebuck Blvd — — 833-7112
Vardaman W W Camp Branch — — — 663-9043
Vardaman William P Jr 836 Fancher Dr — 979-6995
Varden Aubrey E
2156 Pratt Hwy Crumley's Chapel — 798-2829
Varden C L 909 Valley Ridge Dr — — 870-3443
Varden Colan J
1916 Emerald Av Crumley's Chapel — 798-0237
Varden Connie 4320 5th Av S — — — 595-1094
Varden David D 709 Robin Rd — — — 798-8727
Varden Earl O Scenic Dr Gardndle — — 631-3271
Vasquez Jacquely 143 Cambrian Way — — 967-7774
Vasquez Richard P 143 Camrian Way — — 967-8561
Vassar Amos Rev 2722 Dartmouth Av Besmr — 428-3693
Vassar Annie Pearl 112 40th Av N — — 252-3357
Vassar E E Rev Almont — — — — — 665-1572
Vassar Essie Mae 4709 Vines Av Brighton — 424-4786
Vassar Kenneth Wayne
4627 Huntsville Av Brighton — — 425-2809
Vassar Nellie Montevallo — — — — 665-5344
Vassar Pauline Miss 8609 Division Av S — 836-4194
Vassar R M 917 N 11th Besme — — — 425-4243
Vasser Clifton 330 11th S Basmr — — 424-0654
Vasser David 224 2nd Av S — — — 251-3549
Vasser Fred 943 5th Pl W — — — — 251-5907
Vasser Jim 943 5th Pl W — — — — 322-3072
Vasser Virginia 609 5th Way Pratt City — 798-6373
Vassiliou Constantine P Dr
1303 Woodland Village — — — 879-5678
Vassiliou John 136—D 25th Av NW — — 854-4325
Vassiliou William G 2717 Highland Av S — 252-2477
Vatalaro M R 1917—L Treetop Ln — — 822-5251
Vath Joseph Most Rev 8131 4th Av S — — 833-0174
Res 200 Tuscaloosa Av SW — — — 328-0521

VAUGHAN---See Also Vaughn

Vaughan A B 2850 Fairway Dr E — — — 871-2005
Valley Avenue Car Wash East 313 Valley Av — 942-5376
Valley Avenue Plaza Coin Op Lndry
416 Valley Av — — — — — 942-9810
Valley Avenue Shell Self Service
100 West Valley Av — — — — 942-7814
Valley Avenue Standard Service
Station 101 Green Springs Hwy — 942-8514
Valley Beauty Salon 1704 Oxmoor Rd — 871-7622
VALLEY BOLT & SCREW CO
Cahaba Valley Rd — — — — — 967-2700
VALLEY BROOK APARTMENTS
2912 Gallant Dr — — — — — 854-0398
Valley Cabinets 3193 Cahaba Heights Rd — 967-2410
VALLEY CHAPEL 1802 Oxmoor Rd — — 879-3401
Valley Chiropractic Center
2031—A Canyon Rd — — — — 823-5931
Valley Christian Church 2600 Cherokee Pl — 879-0419
Valley Cleaners 1911 Oxmoor Rd — — 879-1369
VALLEY DISTRIBUTORS 2067 Valleydale Terr — 979-3363
Andrews Patricia 317 Exeter Av S — — 822-3660
Andrews Patricia 317 Exeter Av S — — 822-3660

Column 2

VALLEY DRAPERY & RUG CO INC
2200 2nd Av S — — — — — — 322-1684
Value Mart Dollar Store—
5515 1st Av N — — — — — 592-9220
Value Mini Mart 600 Forestdale Blvd — — 989-9069
Value Oil Company—
Office 105 Vulcan Rd — — — — 942-4786
Fultondale Station Highway 31 N — — 841-8819
Pleasant Grove Station
700 Pleasant Grove Rd — — — 744-6021
Value Shoes 9430 Parkway East — — — 833-0579
Value Super Mart 2800 Cherry Av Pratt City — 674-7843

VAN---See Also Vann

VAM adv 586 Shades Crest Rd — — — 823-0579
Van And Storage Co movers 5529 1st Av S — 595-1108
Van Baalen Harold acct 1900 28th Av S — 879-3521
Res 124 Glenhl Dr — — — — — 871-4119
Van Buren Isaac Zion Av Zion City — — 833-2468
Vance A E 2909 Highland Av S — — — 252-8981
Vance Albert L 4821 Powell Av S — — 595-0286
Vance Alice 332 Irving S Hermn Hts — 786-3654
Vance Alice M Pelhm — — — — — 663-6740
Vanda Beauty Counselor
2008 Clb Dr NW Huntsville Ala — 852-9616
If No Answer Dial — — — — 595-0324
Vandagriff Nick 920 Colesbury Cir — — 663-4729
Vande Brake Robert 3500 Brookwood Rd S — 967-7849
VanDeBurg Larry
1416 King George Dr Alabstr — — 663-6331

VANDEFORD---See Also Vandeford

Vandeford J W Mrs 1412 55th Wylam — 780-7095
Vandeford James 4400 Bessemer Super Hwy — 428-6514
Vandeford Stella J Mrs 1728 34th Ensely — 786-1298
Vandegriff Albert H 610 Av S — — — 786-1298
Vandegriff D H 3808 10th Av S — — 592-4829
Vandegriff D H III 634 Camp Cir — — 836-0581

VANDEGRIFT---See Also Vandergrift

Vandegrift Ben Mrs 2500 Riverhaven Dr — 822-2328
Vanderburg Ted
Woodward Estates Mobile Home Park
Lipscomb — — — — — 428-5415

VANDERFORD---See Also Vandeford

Vanderford C B Mrs 1301 60th Central Park — 923-0255
Vanderford Cecil L Flat Creek — — — 674-9968
Vanderford Cleo f344545 40th Pl N — — 841-0021
Vanderford John W 1324 11th Av S — — 324-2019
Vanderford Lillian K McCalla — — — 477-6486
Vanderford O H 415 Shades Crest Rd — — 822-3230
Vanderford Rita 1010 Lorene Ct Bessmr — 426-3327
Vanderford W E 2340 Chapl Rd Bluff Pk — 822-3543
Vandergraff William H 1305 2nd Av — — 781-2855
Vandergriff B S 1519 29th Lynn — — 879-6369
Vandergriff Gary L 4700 74th Pl N — — 836-3594
Vandergriff I A teleph 600 19th St N — — 321-8222
Res 637 Winwood Dr — — — — 822-6760

VANDERGRIFT---See Also Vandegrift

Vandergrift Charles A 956 Meg Dr — — 853-6097
Vaughan Tom B Jr Dr 3700 Dunbarton Dr — — 967-7482
Vaughan Uriah E Jr 3503 Clamont Dr Pinson — 681-2622
Vaughan V H 1005 Herring Midfld — — 428-5194
Vaughan W B 440 Parkway Cir East Montvlo — 665-1904
Vaughan W C 609 9th Av Midfld — — 785-3461
Vaughans Catherine L 205 West Brighton — 428-2225

VAUGHN---See Also Vaughan

Vaughn A L 2216 2nd Av N Irondale — 956-2964
Vaughn Allen C 2012—B Vestavia Park Ct — 979-3982
Vaughn Arvel Coyce 334—A Vise Rd Pinson — 681-6166
Vaughn B E 712 S 48th — — — — 592-3540
Vaughn H Melvin Dr ofc 2030 3rd Av N — 254-3656
Res 3808 Spring Valley Rd — — — 967-5748
Vaughn Hamilton M Trafford Rd Trafrd — 681-6755
Vaughn Harry C Jr ins 15 Office Park Cir — 854-7986
Res 2494 Dolly Ridge Trail — — 822-2171
Vaughn Harry Insurance Inc
15 Office Park Cir — — — — 879-9760
Vaughn Henry F 4210 Parkway Fairfld — 786-7090
Vaughn Homer 2616 Ridgebrook Rd — — 841-0525
Vaughn Howell L Montvlo — — — — 668-1419
Vaughn Huey J County Line Rd — — — 681-3934
Vaughn Hunter G 308 Church Forst Hls — 787-1648
Vaughn Hunter G 35 Five Hundred Row — 780-2581
Vaughn J A 120 Town And Country Cir — 854-0188
Vaughn J C 619 Ridge Rd Roebuck Springs — 836-6191
Vaughn J Lamar 2302 10th Ct S — — 251-1851
Vaughn J W 603 Hillcrest Rd — — — 798-0297
Vaughn Jack B 2824 Thornhill Rd — — 871-4413
Vaughn Jake R phar 585 Shades Crest Rd — 822-1210
Res 2120 Vestavia Dr — — — 823-1134
Vaughn James
Sharon Heights Mobile Home Park — 674-6230
Vaughn James C rl est 528 20th N — — 322-3325
Vaughn Willie J 511 Virginia Gardndle — 631-8997
Vaughn Woodrow 6401 Court F Fairchld — 787-4749
Vaughner Arma 1413 28th N — — — 251-6065
Andrews Patricia 317 Exeter Av S — — 822-3660
Andrews Patricia 317 Exeter Av S — — 822-3660
Andrews Patricia 317 Exeter Av S — — 822-3660
Andrews Patricia 317 Exeter Av S — — 822-3660
Andrews Patricia 317 Exeter Av S — — 822-3660
Andrews Patricia 317 Exeter Av S — — 822-3660
Andrews Patricia 317 Exeter Av S — — 822-3660
Andrews Patricia 317 Exeter Av S — — 822-3660

Column 3

Vaught Donald L 542 39th St Short Wylam — — 780-8608
Vaught Ernest 65 Merrimont Rd Hueytown — 491-6244
Vaught J C 625 Barclay Ln — — — 836-2436
Vaught Joe Jr Stertt — — — — — 672-2919
Vaught Ralph L 700 77th Wy S — — — 836-8452
Vaught Susan A 2109 46th Pl Central Pk — 787-4227
Vaultz Eva 1543 Dennison Av SW — — 925-1752
Vause S F 603 Huckleberry Ln — — — 979-5289
Vause Stephen F 445 Shades Crest Rd — 823-2662
Vautier Harold G 204 Killough Spmgs Rd — 853-5626
Vautrot Ruby L Mrs 2021 10th Av S — — 933-2265
Vazquez Norberto Old Jasper Hwy Adamsvie — 674-3370
Veach J L 5725 Belmont Dr — — — 956-3990
Veach Loren Aldrich — — — — — 665-1831
Veal Ad 450 21st Av S — — — — 251-9049
Veal Ad rl est 1711 Pinson — — — 841-7380
Veal B Evan atty 1711 Pinson — — — 841-2789
Veal Clarence E Garndle — — — — 631-3856
VEAL CONVENTION SERVICES—
1711 Pinson — — — — — 841-2789
2109 10th Av N — — — — — 322-6102
Veazey W B Vincent — — — — — 672-9506
Veazey Wilbur E 1541 53rd St Ensley — 923-1960
Veazey William A 287—A Chastaine Cir — 942-4137
Veazey Willie J 3084 Whispering Pines Cir — 823-5795
Vebber Mark H 5216 Goldmar Dr — — 956-1661
Vebco contr 1900 28th Av S Homewood — 879-2259
Vedel Dental Technicians Inc lab
1116 5th Av N — — — — — 322-5475
Vedel George C 3848 Cromwell Dr — — 967-2832
Vedel George C Jr 744 Saulter Ln — — 871-8234
Res f34744 Saulter Ln — — — — 870-9758
Vedel Murrey B 612 Oakmoor Dr — — 942-3619
Vedell Collen J Daisy City — — — — 674-7772
Vedell William L 8830 Valley Hill Dr — — 833-9915
Veenschoten & Co mfrs agts 2930 7th Av S — 251-3567
Veenschoten L A 1919—D Tree Top Ln — 822-7109
Veenschoten W E 3240 Pine Ridge Rd — 871-8883
Vega Abraham 915 16th S — — — 933-7619
Vega Delores 2—B Watertown Cir — — 836-5980
Vega Edwin 2116 Rockland Dr Bluff Park — 823-0403
Vegetable Patch Number 1 The
Highway 31 S Alabstr — — — 663-7618
Vegetable Patch Office Alabstr — — 663-7378
Vegetable Patch The Number 2 Dogwood — 665-4179
Veigl Patrick B Pawnee — — — — 841-1238
Veitch Beulah 1172 Five Mile Rd — — 853-3361
Vest W L 4708 Lewisbrg Rd — — — 841-7402
Vest W T 4737 N 68th — — — — 836-6371
Vesta Villa Exxon Self Serve 1500 Hwy 31 S — 823-5008
VESTAVIA AMOCO SERVICE
1456 Montgomery Hwy — — — 823-1213
VESTAVIA BARBEQUE & LOUNGE
610 Montgomery Hwy Vestavia — 822-9984
Vestavia Barber Shop
610—A Montgomery Hwy — — 823-1974
VESTAVIA BEAUTY SALON
710 Montgomery Hwy — — — 823-1893
Vestavia Beverage Co 623 Montgomery Hwy — 822-9847
VESTAVIA BOWL
Montgomery Hwy S Vestavia — 979-4420
Vestavia Church Of Christ
2325 Columbiana Rd — — — 822-0018
VESTAVIA CHURCH OF GOD
2575 Columbiana Rd — — — 823-1895
Vestavia Church Of God Day Care day
nursry 2575 Columbiana Rd — — 823-1895
VESTAVIA CITY OF---See Vestavia
Hills City Of

VESTAVIA COIFFEURS
617 Montgomery Hwy Vestva — 823-1104
Vestavia Country Club—
Shades Mountain — — — — 823-2451
Golf Shop Shades Mountain — — 822-8300
On Mondays & Before 8:30 AM Dial
As Follows:—
Stable Shades Mountain — — — 823-2451
Accounting Dept Shades Mountain — 823-2979
Golf Course Supt Shades Mountain — 823-2019
Tennis Shop Shades Mountain — — 823-2689
General Manager's Ofc — — — 823-2139
Building Maintenance Shop
Shades Mountain — — — 823-2349
Swimming Pool Shades Mountain — 822-2559
Vestavia Country Club Employee's
Lounge Shades Mountain — — 822-9840
Vestavia Hardware & Home Supply
593 Shades Crest Rd — — — 823-1953
VESTAVIA HILLS BAPTIST CHURCH
2600 Vestavia Dr — — — — 871-4661
VESTAVIA HILLS CITY OF—
513 Montgomery Hwy — — — 823-1153
Fire Dept Business 513 Montgomery Hwy — 823-1153
To Report A Fire — — — — 823-1296
Training Bureau — — — — 823-1153
Preventive Bureau — — — — 823-1190
Administrative Offices
513 Montgomery Hwy — — 979-6410
Mayor's Office — — — — 979-6410
Police Dept Business
513 Montgomery Hwy — — 823-1153
Detective Division — — — — 823-1442
Police Chief — — — — — 823-1153
Recreational Center 1973 Merryvale Rd — 823-0295
Schools—
Superintendent Of Schools
1204 Montgomery Hwy — — 823-0295
Pizitz Middle School—
Office 2020 Pizitz Dr — — 823-0423
Continued On Next Column
Andrews Patricia 317 Exeter Av S — — 822-3660
Andrews Patricia 317 Exeter Av S — — 822-3660
Andrews Patricia 317 Exeter Av S — — 822-3660

Column 4

Continued From Last Column
Lunchroom 2020 Pizitz Dr — — — 823-0832
Bandroom 2020 Pizitz Dr — — — 823-0423
Vestavia Hills Elementary-East—
2109 Parkview Pl — — — — 823-4900
Vestavia Hills Elementary-West—
1965 Merryvale Rd — — — 979-3030
Vestavia Hills Elementary—
Lunchroom 2109 Parkview Pl — 822-8632
Vestavia Hills High School—
Principal's Office 2235 Lime Rock Rd — 823-4044
Assistant Principal's Office
2235 Lime Rock Rd — — — 823-4044
Registrar's Ofc 2235 Lime Rock Rd — 823-4044
Physical Education Ofc
2235 Lime Rock Rd — — — 823-4130
Bandroom 2235 Lime Rock Rd — 823-2127
Lunchroom 2235 Lime Rock Rd — 823-4207
Street & Sanitation Dept
2129 Montgomery Hwy — — 822-7289
Garbage Pick-Up — — — — 822-7289
Vestavia Hills Cleaners
1484 Montgomery Hwy — — 823-0874
Vestavia Hills Exxon
732 Montgomery Hwy Vestavia Hls — 979-3167
VESTAVIA HILLS PRIVATE SCHOOL
1653 Shades Crest Rd — — — 822-7289
Vestavia Hills United Methodist Church—
2061 Kentucky Av Vestavia — 822-9631
Pastor's Study
2061 Kentucky Av Shades Mountn — 822-9021
Waldrop Homer E Memory Ln Hueytown — 491-2180
Waldrop Ida B Mrs
HolidayPark Trailer Court Besmr — 426-5490
Waldrop Ida Oak Grove — — — 491-2197
Waldrop J A 1975 East Bend Cir — — 853-8453
Waldrop J C 122 Houston Dr Brodmr — 424-3190
Waldrop J D 3710—12 Bank St Brighton — 424-4790
Waldrop J G 2536 6th Way NW — — 854-0340
Waldrop J W 3460 Manor Ln — — — 871-0735
Waldrop Jack L 137 Forest Rd Hueytown — 491-4676
Waldrop James 507 Sunrise Blvd Hueytown — 491-1649
Waldrop James A New Bethel — — — 647-9643
Waldrop James Caswell Sr Toadvine — 436-3540
Waldrop James E 1617 Frontier Dr — — 822-3411
Waldrop James H
3021 Allen Sheppard Dr Va Est — 491-4172
Waldrop James O Harpersville — — 672-7860
Waldrop James R 1129 Little John Ln — 833-3091
Waldrop James R 3025 Teresa Dr Gardndle — 631-7710
Waldrop James Robert 927 Valley Ridge Rd — 871-0754
Waldrop James W Warrior Rd — — — 436-3529
Waldrop James Woodrow
157 Foust Av Hueytown — — 491-4787
Waldrop Janice rl est
501 Riverchase Parkway East — 979-1100
Res 2300 Queensview Rd — — 822-4659
Waldrop Jerry W Howard Hill Dr Vincent — 672-2536
Waldrop Jesse 5725 Ct M Central Park — 923-9389
Waldrop Joe 6702 Forest Dr Fairfld — 788-2115
Waldrop Joel H 1227 4th Av N Bessmr — 428-8322
Waldrop John E 4123 40th Ct N — — 841-1541
Waldrop John R 133 Red Oak Dr — — 631-6535
Waldrop Johnnie Warrior River Rd Concord — 491-9283
Waldrop Keith 314 Candy Mountain Rd — 856-0984
Waldrop L R 107 Church Av Hueytown — 491-2456
Waldrop L Ralph 3416 N 39th — — — 841-3709
Waldrop Laddie S
746 Goldenrod Dr Gardndle — — 631-5174
Waldrop Larry 2040 48th Pl Ensley — 785-6079
Waldrop Lillian Mrs Wilsnvl — — — 669-7367
Waldrop Luve 108 6th Robnwd — — 841-1796
Waldrop Lynne 1024 Basswood Cir Fultndle — 631-6638
Waldrop M M 5612 12th Av S — — — 592-9679
Waldrop Maggie L Dolmte — — — 744-0727
Waldrop Maggie Lee Dolmte — — — 744-8932
Waldrop Mendie Rockdale — — — 424-0481
Waldrop Minnie
312 Houston Saw Mill Rd Pinson — 681-7506
Waldrop Myrtle B
105 West Crest Rd Hueytown — 491-6340
Waldrop Nora N
Woodward Mobile Homes Est — 426-2169
Waldrop Oscar N Dry Valley — — — 665-4595
Waldrop P M 329 Roebuck Dr — — — 836-2726
Waldrop Pamela 1444 Huffman Rd — 853-8964
Waldrop Paul 245 Mabelon Ct Garywd — 744-8282
Waldrop R G 4224 7th Av S — — — 595-6721
Waldrop Ray 240 21st Av S — — — 251-2699
Waldrop R Williams 116 Waverly Cir Lakwd — 428-2965
Waldrop Richard D 724 Country Club Tr — 631-9340
Waldrop Richard E Wilsnvle — — — 669-6147
Waldrop Robert 132 8th Pleasant Grove — 744-0222
Waldrop Robert C 75 Linden Cir Hueytown — 491-1534
Waldrop Robert G ins 3055 Montgomery Hwy — 879-8273
Res 230 Lucerne Blvd — — — 871-5313
Waldrop Robert M 120 Ski Lodge Dr — 942-1157
Waldrop Robert R 1808 29th Av N Hueytown — 491-7184
Waldrop Robert T 103 Midway Dr Hueytown — 491-4533
Waldrop Ronald A 2047 White Post Rd Besmr — 491-2055
Waldrop Ronnie
115 Springdale Av Hueytown — 491-7951
Waldrop Rosie 324 Houton Rd NW — 681-8886
Waldrop Roy 3018 Warrior Rd Hueytown — 744-0838
Waldrop Ruth 2816 29th Pl Ensley — 788-8257
Waldrop S Ray 201 9th Av Besmr — 425-6146
Waldrop Samuel G II 5000 Sunnydale Dr — 491-4423
Andrews Patricia 317 Exeter Av S — — 822-3660
Andrews Patricia 317 Exeter Av S — — 822-3660
Andrews Patricia 317 Exeter Av S — — 822-3660
Andrews Patricia 317 Exeter Av S — — 822-3660
Andrews Patricia 317 Exeter Av S — — 822-3660

Ty	**Bell Centennial**
Ca	**Sans Serif**
Ke	**Grotesque**
Te	**Digital**
Da	**1976**
De	**Matthew Carter**
Fo	**Linotype**
Co	**USA**

Characteristics

A	Low crossbar
C c S s e	Vertical terminals
G	Has spur
Q	Wedge-angled tail
R	Straight, angled leg
a	Double-storeyed
f r t	Vertical terminals
g	Single-storeyed
i j	Square dots
k v w x	Exaggerated ink traps
t	Flat top-stroke
y	Curved, flat tail

AGMQRS abcefghij koprstuy

Connections

Bell Gothic	1938
Verdana	1996
Eunuverse	1998
Retina	1999

Availability

Bell Centennial is available from Linotype and resellers

Specimen

Matthew Carter: Bell Centennial (*Type & Technology Monograph* No. 1). The Cooper Union, New York, 1982 (280x225mm)

In 1976 AT&T commissioned British type designer Matthew Carter (1937–) to create a new typeface for exclusive use in their telephone directories. The design had to address multiple technical and optical problems to overcome the limitations of directory printing. The solution, named to commemorate the company's 100th anniversary, was Bell Centennial.

AT&T's requirements were exacting. The new typeface, to be typeset using cutting-edge cathode ray tube technology, should be at least as economical in its use of space as Bell Gothic, the typeface that had been used in the directories since 1938. Pages set in the new type were to contain the same amount of information or more. Words should also be easy to read and highly legible, but not in the conventional manner of the continuous text found in bookwork; in the directories, both letters and numbers had to be recognized quickly and accurately so that subscribers could locate information efficiently. Above all, the new type was to achieve all of these objectives without degradation or loss of legibility when printed at high speed on low-grade newsprint paper in extremely small point sizes.

To achieve absolute precision, Carter drew every character for the size and resolution at which it would be output, pixel by pixel, on gridded paper. The addition or removal of a single pixel in a curve or angled stroke could have a completely transformative effect on the appearance of each 6-point letter when viewed at final size. He also employed a number of strategies to achieve optimum legibility. Bell Centennial is condensed, with wide letter spacing and a tall lower case x-height, allowing for open counterforms. Strokes have a determined quality, with very emphatic terminals. In order to compensate for ink spread in the printing process, Carter inserted deeply angled ink traps at all of the stroke junctions. These could fill in as the ink was absorbed into the newsprint substrate, but the letterforms and their internal spaces would remain unimpaired, leaving the text easily readable. However, at large point sizes Bell Centennial's unusual features provide a unique personality that has been used by many designers seeking to make a feature of such points of difference.

Bell Centennial is one of many typefaces Matthew Carter has designed to overcome strict technical limitations, including Georgia (pp554–55) and Verdana (pp560–61). It is a textbook example of the inconspicuous nature of the most assiduous type design, solving specific problems in specific contexts – as designer Gunnlaugur Briem said, like 'a bulletproof rhinoceros that could dance *Swan Lake*'.

Ty	**ITC Eras**
Ca	**Sans Serif**
Ke	**Humanist**
Te	**Photocomposition**
Da	**1976**
De	**Albert Boton and Albert Hollenstein**
Fo	**International Typeface Corporation**
Co	**France**

Characteristics

	Large x-height
	Short ascenders and descenders
A M N	Flat apex
P R	Open bowl
Q	Short, flat tail on baseline
W	Crossed centre-strokes
a	Open bowl

AGQRW
abcefghij
koprstuy

Connections

ITC Flora	1985
Arta	1987
Skia	1994
TheSans	1994

Availability

ITC Eras is available from Monotype and resellers

Specimen

U&lc, Vol. 3, No. 3. International Typeface Corporation, New York, 1976 (382x290mm)

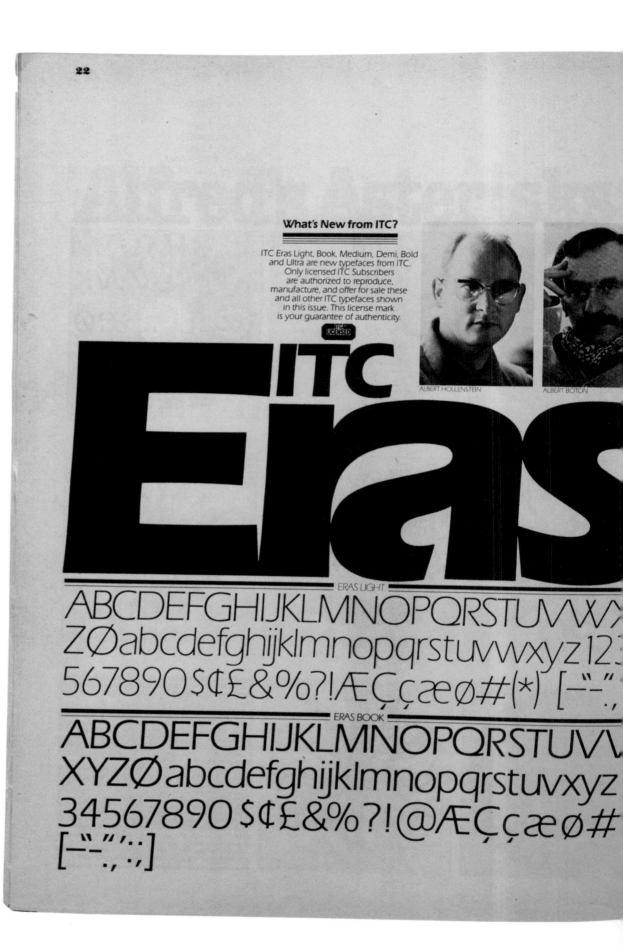

22

What's New from ITC?

ITC Eras Light, Book, Medium, Demi, Bold and Ultra are new typefaces from ITC. Only licensed ITC Subscribers are authorized to reproduce, manufacture, and offer for sale these and all other ITC typefaces shown in this issue. This license mark is your guarantee of authenticity.

ALBERT HOLLENSTEIN   ALBERT BOTON

ITC Eras

ERAS LIGHT

ABCDEFGHIJKLMNOPQRSTUVWX
ZØabcdefghijklmnopqrstuvwxyz123
567890$¢£&%?!ÆÇçæø#(*) [-¨-.,

ERAS BOOK

ABCDEFGHIJKLMNOPQRSTUV
XYZØabcdefghijklmnopqrstuvxyz
34567890 $¢£&%?!@ÆÇçæø#
[-¨-.,'.:]

ERAS MEDIUM

BCDEFGHIJKLMNOPQRSTUVW
YZØ abcdefghijklmnopqrstuvwx
z1234567890 $¢£&%?!@ÆÇçæø
-(*)[-"-".,":]

ERAS DEMI

BCDEFGHIJKLMNOPQRSTU
WXYZØabcdefghijklmnopqrs
uvwxyz1234567890$¢£&%?!@
ÇÆçæø#(*)[-"-".,":]

ERAS BOLD

ABCDEFGHIJKLMNOPQRST
VWXYZØabcdefghijklmno
qrstuvwxyz1234567890$¢£
%?!@ÆÇçæø#(*)[-"-".,":]

ERAS ULTRA

BCDEFGHIJKLMNOPQRS
UVWXYZØabcdefghijklm
opqrstuvwxyz123456789
$¢£&%?!@ÆÇçæø#(*)[-"-".,":]

A sans serif of unusual character, energy and charm, ITC Eras is a prime example of the French tradition for producing typefaces that have unorthodox personalities based on innovative features. Designed by Albert Boton (1932–) and Albert Hollenstein (1930–74), it was released by the International Typeface Corporation in 1976.

Eras began life as another typeface design entirely that drew on two points of inspiration: Greek stone-cut lapidary letters and Roman capitals. In the 1950s Boton and Hollenstein collaborated on Basilea, a traditional roman form, with small serifs and with the proportions of classical inscriptional lettering. Developing this design further during the 1960s for Albert Hollenstein's design company, Studio Hollenstein, they removed Basilea's serifs, creating the foundations of the Eras form.

The result is not a precise, geometric sans serif. ITC Eras has the spontaneity of a handwritten script with springing curves and sweeping strokes that owe more to the heritage of broad-tipped brush scripts than to the ruling pen. It is notable for its 2-degree slant – it is almost, but not quite, italic – and its subtle variations in stroke weights. ITC Eras maintains low contrast and an even appearance like other sans serif designs, but it overcomes any suggestion of blandness through the dynamic tension and forward direction provided by its slight inclination.

Following the convention adopted by ITC in the design of its photocomposition typefaces for display applications, ITC Eras has an extremely large x-height, with short ascenders and descenders, as well as tight letter-spacing characteristics. It is identified by its open bowls on the characters P, R, a, 6 and 9. The letter W changes from a merged 'double V' shape in the lighter variants to the standard W symbol in the bolder weights.

ITC Eras was originally released in six weights – Light, Book, Medium, Demi, Bold and Ultra. Because all variants are slightly slanted, italic versions were not produced.

Ty	**Frutiger**
Ca	**Sans Serif**
Ke	**Humanist**
Te	**Photocomposition**
Da	**1976**
De	**Adrian Frutiger**
Fo	**Stempel**
Co	**France**

Characteristics

B E F P Narrow
C c S s e g Vertical terminals and large apertures
G No spur
Q Short, straight, angled tail
R Curved, angled leg
a Double-storeyed, nearly straight stem
a f r t Vertical terminals
i j Square dots
t Angled top-stroke
y Curved tail

AGMQR
abcefghij
koprstuy

Connections

Antique Olive	1962
Myriad	1992
FF Transit	1997
Segoe UI	2004

Availability

Frutiger is available from Linotype and resellers

Specimen

Frutiger type specimen. Linotype, Bad Homburg, c1977 (297x210mm)

Frutiger

Frutiger 45

ABCDEFGHIJKLMNOPQRSTUVW
XYZabcdefghijklmnopqrstuvwxy
z1234567890(&£*%.,-!?")

Frutiger 46

ABCDEFGHIJKLMNOPQRSTUVW
XYZabcdefghijklmnopqrstuvwxy
z1234567890(&£*%.,-!?")

Frutiger 55

ABCDEFGHIJKLMNOPQRSTUV
WXYZabcdefghijklmnopqrstu

Frutiger.
Typography on the move.

■■ About 10 years ago, construction work started on the new Paris (Charles de Gaulle) airport complex. The chief architect, Paul Andreu, was aware of the importance of a good system of indication and signalisation for the smooth running of the airport, and he asked me to take on this responsibility. When the matter of specifying a type-style came up, I realised that the use of a face like Univers, for example, would not suit either the general aesthetic and architectural concept or the principles of optimum legibility…
…The characters of Univers are a little too 'smooth' for sufficiently rapid and accurate reading on indicator panels. For example, letters such as c, e, s, or v, y, and also b, d, p, q, g are too similar in appearance. There is also the point that the reader of indicator panels is usually on the move: in a car, on an escalator, walking or even running. This factor has a strong influence on the conditions for optimum legibility, because the word-image, as seen by the reader, is constantly changing or blurring…

…The law of type design calls for obedience to other criteria, not only intellectual ones, because, to the reader, type-matter is above all a *written* image, i.e. one which has originated from the free movement of the hand. Since the process of reading takes place through the recognition of complete word-images, a relationship of form between all the letters is absolutely indispensable. Consequently, between the bare 'realism' of Futura or Kabel and the strongly modelled harmony of Helvetica and Univers, there is room for a type design which has the freehand rhythm of writing as opposed to 'constructivism' but at the same time avoids the 'uncial' style of rounded characters, so as to allow the appearance of clearly identifiable characters within the harmonious word-image…
…These are the motives which I can describe to you as having led to the creation of the new sans serif. Commissioned by D. Stempel AG of Frankfurt, I have adapted it to make a typeface family, consisting of four weights accompanied by four italics, for phototypesetting on equipment supplied by the Mergenthaler-Linotype Group…
…I am delighted by your comment: 'From our point of view it's the first new and original sans family to appear on the market for some years', and I thank you for the interest that you have shown in the typeface. ■■

When the man who designed Univers puts his name to a typeface, it must be special. Adrian Frutiger can also claim Egyptienne, Apollo, Serifa, Glypha and the standard OCR B typefaces among his many achievements. Designed for total legibility, Frutiger is truly a new sans, and is available now in four weights plus italics for display setting on typositor and on the VIP with Advanced Typography Program for computerised textsetting.

Frutiger was originally named Roissy after the French airport for which it had been commissioned in 1968. Seven years later, in 1975, the typeface was completed in one weight only and applied as signage throughout the recently opened Charles de Gaulle Airport. During the early 1970s, sans serif typefaces such as Helvetica (pp346–47) and Univers (pp350–51) had become so ubiquitous that they were beginning to seem characterless, dated and dull. In his new design Adrian Frutiger (1928–2015) sought to reinvent the sans serif form by merging the rational, orderly features of his earlier Univers typeface with the natural and calligraphic principles found in older humanistic faces from before the advent of the sans serif.

The result of his groundbreaking work is a typeface that is both very functional and full of personality. Frutiger's qualities are well suited to the demands of signage for wayfinding: it is easily readable in various conditions, at different angles and distances, and it is both modern-looking and remarkably friendly. Because Frutiger was originally conceived for signage, its ascenders and descenders are clearly defined, and the individual characteristics of each letterform are carefully differentiated. Its contours and proportions reflect those of classical Roman inscriptional lettering. Somewhat like Antique Olive (pp362–63), Frutiger's stroke terminations at vertical angles, on the C or S, for example, are highly distinctive. Functionally, this is a significant innovation because it opens the internal spaces within letters while enhancing the horizontal directional flow of words, creating visual links from one letter to the next in order to promote easy readability.

The Frutiger family was developed and released commercially by the Stempel and Linotype foundries in 1976 and has been a bestseller ever since. In 2008, the year it was ranked as Linotype's fifth-bestselling typeface, Adrian Frutiger was asked to reflect on the phenomenal success of his eponymous typeface: 'It has already become to some extent a stylistic expression of the 1970s and 1980s. All media have adopted it spontaneously. It was simply a face which could be read comfortably. It was the "other one", between Univers and Helvetica!'

Raleigh

Ty	**Raleigh**
Ca	**Serif**
Ke	**Old Style**
Te	**Photocomposition**
Da	**1977**
De	**Carl Dair and Robert Norton**
Fo	**Linotype**
Co	**Canada**

Characteristics
J Descends below baseline
Q Tail does not touch bowl
W Top serifs face inwards, centre-strokes meet at apex
Y y No serif to right arm
f Square, flat arch
i j Short, small dot

AJMQRW
abcdefghij
koprstuy

Connections
Cartier	1967
Swift	1987
ITC Mendoza	1991
FF Quadraat	1992

Availability
Raleigh is available from Linotype and resellers

Specimen
Raleigh type specimen. Linotype, Bad Homburg, c1977 (297x210mm)

In 1967, to celebrate Canada's centennial at the Montreal World's Fair, a new typeface was issued. Cartier, announced as 'the first Canadian type for text composition', was a calligraphic old-style face based on the Dutch tradition. It was designed by Carl Dair (1912–67), one of Canada's leading design practitioners at the time.

Although highly original, Cartier never became the dependable all-round text face its designer intended. It was beset with a number of small incompatibilities of stroke, weight and spacing, partly because Dair insisted that no amendments be made to his working drawings when they were handed over to the Linotype foundry for production.

As a result, Cartier possessed more of the qualities of display lettering than of a typeface for use in extended text. Display faces can accommodate flamboyance and individuality in their letterforms, whereas in a text typeface characters are usually restrained from any individual quirks and share common traits, helping the reader concentrate on reading rather than observing. The strikingly attractive features that Dair invested in Cartier's characters precluded it from working effectively in longer passages of text.

Dair's untimely death in the year of Cartier's release meant that any further development ceased. A decade later, recognizing that Dair's design was more successful in display applications, Robert Norton (1929–2001) produced a revised version. Changing its name to Raleigh, Norton resolved inconsistencies in the baseline weight and regulated the sharp stroke angles to provide a strong horizontal flow. He also tightened the letter spacing and increased the x-height to reinforce the lower case, following the trend in display types of the 1970s.

In 1997 Cartier was again reappraised by Canadian type designer Rod McDonald. Working from original drawings he undertook an extensive digital revival that was published by Linotype in 2000. McDonald expanded the design into a comprehensive type family that is both elegant and remarkably legible in text: emphatic proof that Cartier could be the fully functional typeface that Carl Dair had originally envisaged.

Raleigh

Raleigh Light

Raleigh Regular

430

Raleigh Medium

ABCDEFGHIJKLMNOPQRSTUVW
XYZabcdefghijklmnopqrstuvwxyz
1234567890(&$£%/.,:;!?"*-)

Raleigh Demi

ABCDEFGHIJKLMNOPQRSTUVW
XYZabcdefghijklmnopqrstuvwxyz
1234567890(&£$¢%/.,:;!?"-)

Raleigh Bold

ABCDEFGHIJKLMNOPQRSTUVW
XYZabcdefghijklmnopqrstuvwxyz
1234567890(&£$¢%/.,:;!?"-)

Raleigh Extra Bold

ABCDEFGHIJKLMNOPQRSTUVW
XYZabcdefghijklmnopqrstuvwx
yz1234567890(&£$¢%/.,:;!?"-)

Raleigh Outline

ABCDEFGHIJKLMNOPQRSTUVW

Galliard

|---|---|
Ty	**Galliard**
Ca	**Serif**
Ke	**Old Style, French**
Te	**Photocomposition**
Da	**1978**
De	**Matthew Carter**
Fo	**Mergenthaler Linotype**
Co	**Germany**

Characteristics

A Cupped apex
E Heavy mid-stroke
G Has foot serif
K k R Tail and arm do not touch stem, serifless leg
M Splayed
a Straight, angled stroke to top of bowl
f Large arch
g Double-storeyed, long, straight ear

ACEGJM
abcdefgijk
orstuyaefg

Connections

Granjon's Roman	1560
Mantinia	1993
DTL Van Den Keere	1994
Arno Pro	2007

Availability

ITC Galliard is available from Monotype and resellers

Specimen

U&lc, Vol. 8, No. 4. International Typeface Corporation, New York, 1981 (382x290mm)

28

ITC GA

ITC Galliard Roman

ITC Galliard Bold

LIARD

WHAT'S NEW FROM ITC

Galliard, designed by Matthew Carter (1937–) for Linotype and released in 1978, is an old-style typeface developed specifically for phototypesetting. Carter based Galliard on vibrant and distinctive sixteenth-century types by Robert Granjon (pp56–57). The name of Carter's design is derived from an 8-point Granjon font from about 1570, called La Galliarde after a formal dance of the time.

When he joined Mergenthaler Linotype as a type designer in 1965 Carter found himself able to fulfil his long-standing goal of producing a new interpretation of Granjon's work. According to him, 'The object of designing Galliard was to make a serviceable, contemporary, photo-composition typeface based on a strong historical design … not a literal copy of any one of Granjon's faces – more a reinterpretation of his style.' Though work began in the 1960s, more urgent commercial projects interrupted the progress of Galliard and the typeface was not released until 1978.

Carter is one of the few type designers practising today who has undertaken an apprenticeship in cutting steel punches. His understanding of these traditional processes evidently influenced Galliard's forms, which show subtle differences from earlier old-style typefaces. The x-height is larger, but not exaggerated, unlike many typefaces designed for photocomposition during the 1970s, and the forms are sharp and angular. The contrast of thick and thin strokes is more pronounced, and serifs are longer, with a knife-like spikiness.

According to the type historian Alexander Lawson, while the designers of most French Renaissance type revivals had attempted to achieve reasonable fidelity in their versions, 'Carter preferred simply to bring to Galliard his interpretation of the *spirit* of a Granjon original … Galliard thus possesses the authentic sparkle that is lacking in the current Garamonds.' Galliard was originally made available in four weights, with matching italics also based on Granjon originals. Its animated design reinvigorated the old style, and it found instant success in advertising and as a book face.

ABCDEFGHI
JKLMNOPQ
RSTUVWXY
Z&123456789
0abcdefghijkl
mnopqrstuvw
xyzↄↄↄↄↄ
ſ$$¢$¢ƒ£%ÇŁ
ØÆŒßçłøæœ
fictſt12345678
90ᵒ○✳✦ᵘᵛ(:;,.!?.‘‘’’‛)
#/‡†§@«»1234567
890[aeilmorst]

ITC Galliard Black

ABCDEFGH
IJKLMNOP
QRSTUVWX
YZ&123456
7890abcdefg
hijklmnopqr
stuvwxyzↄ
ↄↄↄↄſ$$¢
$¢ƒ£%ÇŁØÆ
Œßçłøæœfictſ
t1234567890
ᵒ✳✦ᵘᵛ(:;,.!?.‘‘’’‛)
ss cc (:;,.!?.‘‘’’‛)
#/‡†§@«»123456
7890[aeilmorst]

ITC Galliard Ultra

Ty	**ITC Benguiat Gothic**
Ca	**Sans Serif**
Ke	**Geometric**
Te	**Photocomposition**
Da	**1979**
De	**Edward Benguiat**
Fo	**International Typeface Corporation**
Co	**USA**

Characteristics

A	Curved bar
E F	High mid-stroke
G	Tall stem with arm
H	High-waisted bar
M	High vertex
N	Diagonal intercepts stem
a	Double-storeyed
g	Single-storeyed, curved lower loop

ABGMNR
abcefghij
koprstuy

Connections

Della Robbia	1902
ITC Busorama	1970
ITC Souvenir	1971
ITC Korinna	1974

Availability

ITC Benguiat is available from Monotype and resellers

Specimen

U&lc, Vol. 6, No. 3. International Typeface Corporation, New York, 1979 (382x290mm)

32

What's New from ITC?
ITC Benguiat Gothic Book, Medium, Bold and Heavy, and their corresponding italics, are new typefaces from ITC. Only licensed ITC subscribers are authorized to reproduce, manufacture, and offer for sale these and other typefaces shown in this issue. This license mark is your guarantee of authenticity.

These new typefaces will be available to the public on or after October 15, 1979, depending on each manufacturer's release schedule.

ITC BENGUIAT

ITC BENGUIAT GOTHIC BOOK

ABCDEEFFGHIJKLMNOPQRSTU
WXYZabcdefghijklmnopqrstuvw
yz1234567890&$$¢£%AÇĐEŁØ
ÆËÔĖąčđęłøäéôêfi(.:,.!I?¿--""""/#*†§[
1234567890]

ITC BENGUIAT GOTHIC BOOK ITALIC

ABCDEEFFGHIJKLMNOPQRSTU
WXYZabcdefghijklmnopqrstuvw
yz1234567890&$$¢£%AÇĐEŁØ
ÆËÔĖąčđęłøäéôêfi(.:,.!I?¿--""""/#*†§)[
1234567890]

GOTHIC BOOK, MEDIUM, BOLD & HEAVY, WITH ITALICS

33

═══ ITC BENGUIAT GOTHIC MEDIUM ═══

ABCDEEFFGHIJKLMNOPQRSTU
WXYZabcdefghijklmnopqrstuv
xyz1234567890&$$¢£%ÄÇĐĘ
ØÆŒÉßàçďđęłøäãôéfi(:;,.!i?¿--""''/
*)[†§«»1234567890]

═══ ITC BENGUIAT GOTHIC MEDIUM ITALIC ═══

ABCDEEFFGHIJKLMNOPQRSTU
WXYZabcdefghijklmnopqrstuv
xyz1234567890&$$¢£%ÄÇĐĘ
ØÆŒÉßàçďđęłøäãôéfi(:;,.!i?¿--""''/
*)[†§«»1234567890]

At some time in the late 1970s the American typographer and designer Ed Benguiat (1927–) was asked to create a new logo as a favour for an acquaintance who had no budget. He presented some visual ideas but none were accepted. He submitted several more that were also rejected. Finally, after many failed attempts, a design was chosen. At one stage of this painfully protracted process Benguiat had come up with some letters that he particularly liked and he decided to develop them further. These would eventually become ITC Benguiat, released by the International Typeface Corporation in 1978.

ITC Benguiat Gothic, shown here, is a rounded sans serif variant of the original typeface. Like the serifed original, it is a design that is rooted in the past yet firmly of its own time. The Benguiat types are reminiscent of the novel letterform designs produced in the last decades of the nineteenth century, when type founders experimented freely in order to meet an increasing demand for publicity faces. ITC Benguiat also shows influences of typefaces of the art nouveau period in its curvilinear forms, more as sources of inspiration than as direct references.

Ed Benguiat evidently had fun with this type, particularly in the design of the exuberantly undulating capitals, which reveal many unorthodox features. The lower case, however, is a little more sedate, retaining the necessary balance required for readability. The most obvious characteristic of ITC Benguiat Gothic is its large x-height and its extremely short ascenders and descenders. These proportions were typical of ITC typeface designs in the 1970s. They were intended to be set very tightly and with minimum leading for use in advertising and in film and television, media in which conventional typefaces could look antiquated and feeble.

Although ITC typefaces might seem dated today, designers of the time held them in the highest regard and type founders around the world copied them voraciously.

Ty	**VAG Rounded**
Ca	**Sans Serif**
Ke	**Grotesque**
Te	**Photocomposition**
Da	**1979**
De	**Gerry Barney**
Fo	**Sedley Place**
Co	**UK**

Characteristics

Grotesque character construction
Even stroke contrast
Rounded terminals
Sharp internal junctions
M Splayed
a g Single-storeyed
j t Straight stem

ABGMRS
abcefghij
koprstuy

Connections

Helvetica Rounded	1960s
Tate	1999
GE Inspira	2002
FF DIN Round	2010

Availability

VAG Rounded is widely available

Specimen

Volkswagen USA sales brochure, 1981
(276x210mm)

Volkswagen

Rabbit
Scirocco
Dasher
Jetta
Pickup Truck
Vanagon®
Vanagon® Camper

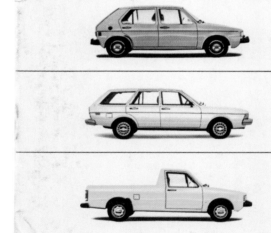

VAG Rounded was originally created in 1979 as part of the brand identity of Volkswagen AG, the global car manufacturer. Its design was motivated by corporate politics. In 1964 Volkswagen had acquired another German car manufacturer, Audi. Because the brand identities of these two independent operations were distinctive, they conflicted visually. Volkswagen was well known for its use of Futura, as it still is today, while Audi's brand was built on Times New Roman. Since both operations were now sharing the same global dealer network, the brand strategy urgently needed to be changed in order to present a single clear and unified image.

Because typography was already the key element of the brand, Volkswagen's marketing consultants at GGK Düsseldorf decided the strategic solution was to be found in a totally new typeface. A team directed by Gerry Barney at Sedley Place, London, was commissioned to design and implement it, and their diplomatic solution was to produce neither a conventional serif nor a sans serif typeface. Originally rendered by hand, VAG Rounded was later perfected using a PDP-8 computer and therefore qualifies as one of the earliest digital typefaces. To extend the accessibility of VAG Rounded, Volkswagen opted to release it into the public domain. It was subsequently issued digitally by Adobe in 1989 and made widely available through its inclusion in desktop publishing software. It remained in use by Volkswagen and their dealer network for over a decade.

Since its release, VAG Rounded has been widely seen in brand identities, largely because of the amiable, personal appearance it confers on the businesses that adopt it. Its letterforms, whose contours are based on nineteenth-century sans serifs, are characterized by monoline strokes and softly rounded terminals that are most visible in bolder weights. The impression it evokes is not unlike handwriting on a blackboard: it is friendly with a slightly authoritative, didactic quality, in contrast to the more juvenile appearance of other non-connected round scripts like Comic Sans (pp530–31). VAG Rounded's sense of efficiency is further emphasized by the sharpness of its internal junctions, which suggest the output of a routing machine.

Background: Rabbit hatchback, Lago Blue. Foreground: Rabbit " L" 2-door hatchback, Sunbrite Yellow. Rabbit interior in Autumn Tan with cloth seats.

VW Rabbit.
Up close, you know it's the Original.

Way back in 1974, Volkswagen revolutionized the automobile. And ever since, we've been improving and refining Rabbit. Even as other manufacturers attempt to catch up by copying our Original, Rabbit Diesel is still unsurpassed in fuel economy: 40 estimated mpg in the city, and an estimated 52 mpg on the highway.* Even our four-speed gasoline-powered Rabbit gets 24 estimated mpg (estimated city fuel economy) and an estimated highway fuel economy of 38 miles per gallon.*

Rabbit offers outstanding total roominess. Not just inside, but also in the trunk. Our original passive-restraint system has been a VW exclusive on Rabbit "L" for nearly six years. And while

*1980 EPA estimates. Compare these estimates to the "estimated mpg" of other cars. Your actual mileage may vary depending on speed, weather, and trip length. Highway mpg will probably be less. 1981 EPA estimates not available at time of printing.

some other manufacturers are just coming to realize the advantages of front wheel drive, transverse mounted engine, VW has perfected and refined it in Rabbit for well over half a decade.

Add to that Rabbit's exceptional visibility, riding comfort, and sheer fun of driving, and it's easy to see what all the excitement is about. This, plus VW's tradition of quality workmanship, have resulted in a consistent record of high resale value.

The 1981 Rabbits — with standard 1.7L fuel-injected gasoline engine or optional 1.6L Diesel engine — are thoroughly engineered to meet your driving needs for years to come. So when you invest in reliable transportation, don't settle for anything less than The Original.

Volkswagen does it again.

4

1980–1961

The earliest computerized typesetters, introduced in the 1970s, were hybrid devices that combined photocomposition and new digital technologies. They all had their own proprietary formats for fonts and used bespoke command languages for communicating with output devices that were only capable of handling basic graphic information.

In the early 1980s the arrival of personal computing revolutionized every aspect of the graphic design industry. At around the same time, Adobe's PostScript page-description language emerged as a device-independent protocol for converting digital data into visual output. Its ability to handle complex graphic data and its pre-installation in new hardware devices such as Apple's LaserWriter printers made it an instant success. When the first affordable, user-friendly design software packages were released for Apple Macintosh computers, a seismic shift in the design, printing and publishing industries occurred that quickly came to be called the desktop-publishing revolution.

At the same time, post-war modernist perspectives were being challenged. In the frontline of the attack on accepted norms and the use of the new technologies was a new generation of young designers who, despite limited experience, were taking on opportunities that had never been seen before. These changes in approach to design practice contributed to a highly creative period in type design during the 1990s. Many new typefaces, such as the early designs of Zuzana Licko, were driven by extensive experimentation with the possibilities of the digital technologies. Other designs explored postmodern ideas, sampling a variety of vernacular and historical references to produce hybrid letterforms that were more effective as expressions of concepts than as workable products. The era-defining typefaces of Barry Deck, P. Scott Makela and Jonathan Barnbrook exemplify this approach.

Most of the type designs of the 1990s were short-lived and have since been considered self-indulgent by some. Nevertheless, they are significant representations of a period when accepted principles of visual communication were being questioned in a reaction against conventional attitudes that were seen as outdated, hegemonic and unsuited to a complex and diverse world.

The new technologies also resulted in the rapid growth of small digital type foundries like Emigre, GarageFonts, T-26, Hoefler & Co., the Font Bureau and FontFont, while larger organizations such as Monotype, Linotype, Adobe, Berthold, Agfa, Bitstream and others instigated major programmes to digitize, update and expand their type libraries. A great number of effective historical revivals were undertaken, along with new designs specifically for digital output. As network communications became increasingly relevant with the development of the World Wide Web, a number of typefaces, optimized for easy reading on low-resolution computer screens, were produced that subsequently proved to be equally effective in print.

The huge changes that took place in the 1980s had a considerable economic impact. When digital type-design tools became as affordable as other graphic design software, type production was possible for anyone with an interest, whether formally trained or not. This, combined with the introduction of colossal typeface collections, moved digital type away from being an expensive tool for a specialist industry towards becoming a relatively cheap commodity that was readily available to all. Like many other features of digital culture, this contributed greatly to both the expansion and the devaluation of the typographic arts.

Ty	**FE-Schrift**
Ca	**Sans Serif**
Ke	**Capitals**
Te	**Signage**
Da	**1980**
De	**Karlgeorg Hoefer**
Fo	**Dambach-Templin**
Co	**Germany**

Characteristics

Monolinear contour
Non-geometric character construction
All capitals have small arcs at terminals
Each character is unique and cannot be
made to resemble other characters

AVWZKRP
EHILMNT
CGBDOQS

Connections

DIN 1451	1931
FF DIN	1995
Carplates	1998
Sauerkrauto	2003

Availability

Not available

Specimen

FE-Schrift type specimen composed by
author, 2015 (210x190mm)

ABCDE
FGHIJ
KLMNO
PQRST

U V W Y Z

1 2 3 4 5

6 7 8 9 0

Ä Ö Ü D

In the 1970s the German Ministry of Transportation commissioned calligrapher and designer Karlgeorg Hoefer (1914–2000) to develop a new typeface for vehicle licence plates in collaboration with the signage manufacturer Dambach-Templin. The unlikely impetus for its design was to defend against crime, precipitated by the threat of violence in Germany by terrorist groups such as the Red Army Faction.

Vehicle licence plates of the time were susceptible to forgery or modification because they used DIN 1451 (pp266–67), a very consistent and symmetrical typeface in which an F could easily be changed into an E, or a P into an R, for example, with a single black stroke. Many other DIN letterforms could be changed into others with similar ease by rotating, flipping, adding or subtracting segments.

Hoefer's new typeface, FE-Schrift, short for Fälschungserschwerende Schrift (forgery-impeding typeface), was designed specifically to make such alterations much more difficult. Every FE-Schrift character has a unique geometric structure that seeks to avoid any repetition of similar strokes and to exclude symmetries. As a result, any falsified letters, such as a C changed to an O, for example, appear incorrect – although whether that would make them conspicuous in such an already disproportionate alphabet is debatable. The unusual principles motivating the design resulted in a set of very anomalous monospaced letters in capitals only, with corresponding numerals.

FE-Schrift underwent extensive research and testing over many years. When the project was finally completed in 1980, the pressure for its implementation had diminished, since social circumstances, governments and policies had changed. However, 15 years after its completion it was finally adopted in the 1990s along with the introduction of the European Union licence plate. FE-Schrift has been the only typeface used on new vehicle registration plates in Germany since November 2000, except for those issued to military vehicles.

A rare example of the questionable merits of deliberate visual discord, FE-Schrift is now part of daily life, seen increasingly throughout Europe's transport networks.

ITC Novarese

Ty	**ITC Novarese**
Ca	**Serif**
Ke	**Old Style**
Te	**Photocomposition**
Da	**1980**
De	**Aldo Novarese**
Fo	**International Typeface Corporation**
Co	**USA**

Characteristics

	Capitals lower than ascender height
	Small, pointed serifs
A	Serif at apex extends to left
G	Spur serif
J	Descends below baseline, hooked
M	Splayed
Q	Short tail
a	Double-storeyed
f	Narrow, non kerning
g	Double-storeyed, small lower bowl
h m n	No inner serifs on right stems

AEGJMR
abcefghij
orstyaefg

Connections

Della Robbia	1902
Friz Quadrata	1965
ITC Symbol	1984
Matrix	1986

Availability

ITC Novarese is available from Monotype and resellers

Specimen

U&lc, Vol. 6, No. 4. International Typeface Corporation, New York, 1979 (382x290mm)

32

ITC NOVARESE BOOK

ABCDEFGHIJKL
MNOPQRSTUVWXYZ
ĄÇÐĘŁØÆŒß
abcdefghijklmnopqrstuv
wxyząçđęłøãëôefi
1234567890123456 7890
&$$¢£%%(.,:;!¡?¿•—–———/#*)
††[1234567890]§«»

ITC NOVARESE BOOK ITALIC

abcdefghijklmnopqrstuvwxyz
ąçđęłøãëõœffffiß

442

NOVARESE

BOOK, MEDIUM, BOLD WITH ITALICS & ULTRA.

ITC NOVARESE MEDIUM

ABCDEFGHIJKL
MNOPQRSTUVWXYZ
ĄÇÐĘŁØÆŒß
abcdefghijklmnopqrstu
vwxyząçđęłøæœåfi
12345678901234567890
&$$¢£%%(.,:;!¡?¿·'""---——/#*)
††[1234567890]§«»

ITC NOVARESE MEDIUM ITALIC

abcdefghijklmnopqrstuvwxyz
ąçđęłøæœœfffifiß

Aldo Novarese (1920–95) designed the typeface that bears his name for the Haas foundry in Switzerland in 1979 and the International Typeface Corporation licensed it globally in 1980. When writing *Alfa-Beta*, his treatise on typeface history, Novarese, a prodigious designer who had produced over 200 type families, chose to include only those he considered essential, separating his designs into four categories. In developing ITC Novarese, he sought to combine the best characteristics of each group.

The result is a unique blend of classical traditions and new ideas. The rounded arcs of the basic forms of ITC Novarese and its general proportions show the influence of stone-cut letters from ancient Roman inscriptions, emphasized by the chiselled appearance of its very small, sharp serifs. At the same time, characters have many features in common with twentieth-century humanist sans serif forms. The x-height of the lower case is large, counterforms are open and the alphabet is almost monolinear, with very little contrast between thick and thin strokes.

Spirited, well proportioned and inventive, ITC Novarese is a display typeface that can also perform adequately in extended text settings. It was conceived as a comprehensive family, capable of solving a wide range of typographic problems. Drawn in four weights, Novarese usefully included lining and non-lining figures and small capitals in the Book and Medium versions. Echoing the earliest Renaissance chancery designs (pp32–33), the italic is notable for its flowing cursive lower case combined with upright capitals.

Unica

Characteristics

Capitals have variable widths
C c G S s e Flat terminals
G Has a spur
J Narrow, short tail
Q Straight, angled tail
R Angled leg
a Double-storeyed, almost straight stem
f r t Vertical terminals
i j Square dots
y Curved tail

AGJMQR abcefghij koprstuy

Connections

Helvetica	1957
Aktiv Grotesk	2010
Neue Haas Grotesk	2010
Neutral	2014

Availability

Neue Haas Unica is available from Monotype and resellers. Unica77 is available from Lineto.

Specimen

Team '77, *From Helvetica to Haas Unica.* Haas'sche Schriftgiesserei, Frankfurt, 1980 (297x227mm)

Konzept des Ausbauprogramms der Haas Unica

Concept du programme d'extension de l'Haas Unica

Concept of the expansion programme for Haas Unica

Helvetica Haas

Helioprint
Helioprint
Helioprint
Helioprint

Helvetica Linotype

Helioprint
Helioprint
Helioprint

Haas Unica

Helioprint
Helioprint
Helioprint
Helioprint

Die vielfältigen Aufgaben im Anwendungsbereich der Typografie stellen heute an eine Druckschrift Anforderungen, die der Konzeption des Ausbauprogramms besondere Bedeutung zukommen lassen. Vor allem aber scheint es uns wichtig, dass die möglichen und sinnvollen Varianten der Schrift zum voraus geplant und als abgeschlossenes Schriftprogramm festgelegt werden.

Wir sind der Auffassung, dass, obwohl durch die technische Entwicklung der digitalen Satzherstellung die Grundtype einer Schrift auf elektronischem Weg modifiziert werden kann, dadurch die zeichnerische Gestaltung der Varianten nicht ersetzt werden kann. Die Veränderung einer Schriftform unterliegt optisch-rhythmischen Gesetzmässigkeiten, die durch eine automatische Modifikation nicht oder nur bedingt qualitativ befriedigend miteinbezogen werden.

Die drei Grundschnitte der Haas Helvetica Normal–Halbfett–Fett einerseits und die drei Linotype-Helveticaschnitte Leicht–Normal–Halbfett andrerseits bilden die Grundlage zum Konzept des Ausbauprogramms der Haas Unica.

In der Haas Helvetica ist die Abstufung des halbfetten Schnittes zum normalen sehr ausgeprägt, die Halbfette ist als kräftige Auszeichnungsschrift konzipiert. Dagegen ist die Stufung Halbfett–Fett optisch kleiner; die drei Schnitte haben unterschiedliche Abstufungen zueinander.

In der Linotype Helvetica ist die Abstufung der drei Schnitte zueinander gut abgestuft. Der fette Schnitt der Originalversion würde dazu als Ergänzung aber aus der Reihe fallen.

Um eine wohlausgewogene Abstufung aller vier Grundschnitte zu erhalten, sind die Schriftfetten der Haas Unica im Vergleich zur Helvetica leicht verschoben, ohne dass dadurch die einzelnen Stufen an Prägnanz verlieren.

Les multiples missions du champ d'application de la typographie posent actuellement à un caractère d'imprimerie des exigences qui donnent à la conception du programme d'extension une importance particulière. Mais il nous apparaît avant tout important que les variantes possibles et judicieuses soient prévues et définies au préalable sous la forme d'un programme définitif et complet.

Nous sommes de l'avis que, bien que le développement technique de la composition digitale puisse modifier le caractère de base par une voie électronique, la configuration du dessin des variantes ne peut de ce fait être remplacée. La modification de la forme d'un caractère est soumise à des lois optico-rythmiques qui ne sont pas ou seulement partiellement incorporées de façon qualitativement satisfaisante par une modification automatique.

Les trois séries de base de l'Helvetica Haas romain – demi-gras – gras, d'une part, et les trois versions de l'Helvetica Linotype maigre – romain – demi-gras d'autre part, constituent la base du concept du programme d'extension de l'Haas Unica.

Dans l'Helvetica Haas, la gradation de la version demi-gras par rapport au romain est très marquée, le demi-gras est conçu comme un caractère de marquage fort. Par contre, la gradation demi-gras – gras est optiquement plus petite, les trois versions ont des gradations différentes entre elles.

Dans l'Helvetica Linotype, la gradation des trois versions est bien définie les unes par rapport aux autres. Le gras de la version originale serait d'autre part tombé hors de la série comme complément.

Pour obtenir une gradation bien équilibrée des 4 séries de base, les graisses de l'Haas Unica ont été légèrement décalées par rapport à l'Helvetica sans perdre de ce fait l'expressivité dans les différentes gradations.

The multiplicity of practical typographic jobs today provides a challenge for the typeface designer, making the planning of the expansion programme particularly important. It seems to us to be of capital importance to plan the possible and useful variants of a typeface in advance and to establish them as a complete programme of faces.

In our view, although the technical development of digital typesetting has made possible the electronic modification of the basic form of a typeface, this cannot replace the artistic design of the variants. The alteration of a type form is governed by optical and rhythmical principles, which cannot or can only to a limited extent be included in an automatic modification, so far as satisfactory quality is concerned.

The three basic versions of Haas Helvetica (normal, semi-bold and bold) on the one hand, and the three Linotype Helvetica versions (light, normal and semi-bold) on the other, form the basis for the concept of the expansion programme for Haas Unica.

In Haas Helvetica, the gradation from semi-bold to normal is very marked; the semi-bold was designed for powerful emphasis. On the other hand, the step from semi-bold to bold is optically less marked and the three versions have an uneven gradation as a whole.

In Linotype Helvetica, the gradation from one style to the next is uniform, but the bold face of the original version would spoil the uniformity if added to the range.

In order to obtain a well-balanced gradation between all four basic versions, the typeface weights of Haas Unica have been slightly displaced in comparison with Helvetica, without sacrificing the individuality of the successive steps.

Hillovleen het tinoler in print und Helio eingeteilt
gelindeproud det Helioprint ventil inden herein
eingebung Hillovleen het tinoler in print und Helio
eilt gelindeproud det Helioprint ventil in den
Hillovleen het tinoler in print und Helio eingeteilt
gelindeproud det Helioprint ventil inden herein
eingebung Hillovleen het tinoler in print und Helio
eilt gelindeproud det Helioprint ventil in den
Hillovleen het tinoler in print und Helio eingeteilt
gelindeproud det Helioprint ventil inden herein

Hillovleen het tinoler in print und Helio eingeteilt
gelindeproud det Helioprint ventil inden herein
eingebung Hillovleen het tinoler in print und Helio
eilt gelindeproud det Helioprint ventil in den
Hillovleen het tinoler in print und Helio eingeteilt
gelindeproud det Helioprint ventil inden herein
eingebung Hillovleen het tinoler in print und Helio
eilt gelindeproud det Helioprint ventil in den
Hillovleen het tinoler in print und Helio eingeteilt
gelindeproud det Helioprint ventil inden herein

Hillovleen het tinoler in print und Helio eingeteilt
gelindeproud det Helioprint ventil inden herein
eingebung Hillovleen het tinoler in print und Helio
eilt gelindeproud det Helioprint ventil in den
Hillovleen het tinoler in print und Helio eingeteilt
gelindeproud det Helioprint ventil inden herein
eingebung Hillovleen het tinoler in print und Helio
eilt gelindeproud det Helioprint ventil in den
Hillovleen het tinoler in print und Helio eingeteilt
gelindeproud det Helioprint ventil inden herein

Hillovleen het tinoler in print und Helio eingeteilt
gelindeproud det Helioprint ventil inden herein
eingebung Hillovleen het tinoler in print und Helio
eilt gelindeproud det Helioprint ventil in den
Hillovleen het tinoler in print und Helio eingeteilt
gelindeproud det Helioprint ventil inden herein
eingebung Hillovleen het tinoler in print und Helio
eilt gelindeproud det Helioprint ventil in den
Hillovleen het tinoler in print und Helio eingeteilt
gelindeproud det Helioprint ventil inden herein

ABCDEFGHIJKLMNOPQRS
TUVWXYZ
abcdefghijklmnopqrstuvwxyzß
1234567890
.,:;-!?„"()[]«»/*'¡¿–†§£$&+

ABCDEFGHIJKLMNOPQRS
TUVWXYZ
abcdefghijklmnopqrstuvwxyzß
1234567890
.,:;-!?„"()[]«»/*'¡¿–†§£$&+

ABCDEFGHIJKLMNOPQRS
TUVWXYZ
abcdefghijklmnopqrstuvwxyzß
1234567890
.,:;-!?„"()[]«»/*'¡¿–†§£$&+

ABCDEFGHIJKLMNOPQRS
TUVWXYZ
abcdefghijklmnopqrstuvwxyzß
1234567890
.,:;-!?„"()[]«»/*'¡¿–†§£$&+

Für eine erste Beurteilung der Abstufung der Grauwerte im Satzbild der verschiedenen Schriftfetten haben wir, vorgängig der Alphabetgestaltung, mit einer kleinen Auswahl von Schriftzeichen Klebesatzproben ausgeführt.

Nous avons exécuté des essais de composition par collage avec un petit choix de lettres avant le dessin de l'alphabet complet pour obtenir une première évaluation de la gradation des valeurs de gris dans la composition des différentes graisses de caractères.

For a preliminary judgement of the gradation of grey values in composition with the various weights of typeface, we pasted up some specimens with a small selection of characters before proceeding to the design of the complete alphabets.

In 1974 the Haas foundry commissioned a team of three experienced Swiss type designers, André Gürtler (1936–), Christian Mengelt (1938–) and Erich Gschwind (1947–), to develop a new typeface optimized for the prevalent technology of the time, photocomposition. Team '77's goal was to improve on Helvetica (pp346–47), itself developed at Haas in the mid-1950s. Since that time, Helvetica's copyright holders had vetoed its production for phototypesetting and Haas were keen to add a new sans serif to their catalogue that would compete in this lucrative market.

The team began by making comparative studies of four related sans serifs – Akzidenz-Grotesk, Univers, Neue Haas Grotesk and Helvetica – to inform the design of the new typeface, Haas Unica, its name a compound of Univers and Helvetica. They identified a number of optical and structural improvements that could be made to Helvetica while preserving the integrity of the letterforms. In its upper and lower case they found that curved strokes were too thin in relation to verticals. They redressed this in the new design while also reducing the overall density of capital letters, as it was too prominent in several weights. To compensate for Helvetica's uniformity, Unica's upper case character widths were more differentiated and the progression of weights was carefully rebalanced across a family of four versions: light, medium, bold and black. The design process was extensive and its results were rigorous – a rationalized type system that was less clinical than Univers but more lively than Helvetica, with letterforms characterized by their roundness and sharply defined stroke intersections.

Haas Unica had taken six years of intensive research, and by the time it was released in 1980 the era of photocomposition was drawing to a close as new computer technologies were beginning to transform every aspect of both the printing industry and the design profession. The Haas foundry went out of business in 1989 and, along with it, Haas Unica completely disappeared, in the process achieving cult status as one of the finest sans serif types ever made.

For a brief time, a digital version of Unica was available to the public, although it was soon removed from sale because of copyright issues. Eventually, in 2015, both Monotype and the Lineto foundry published digital revivals, the latter working in close collaboration with the original design team to reinstate Haas Unica as one of the most proficient sans serifs of the modern era.

Ty	**Arial**
Ca	**Sans Serif**
Ke	**Grotesque**
Te	**Digital**
Da	**1982**
De	**Robin Nicholas and Patricia Saunders**
Fo	**Monotype**
Co	**UK**

Characteristics

C c S s e f r Angled terminals
G No spur
M Narrow
Q Slightly curved, angled tail
R Curved, angled leg
a Double-storeyed, almost straight stem
i j Square dots
t Angled top-stroke
y Curved tail

AGMQR
abcefghij
koprstuy

Connections

Akzidenz-Grotesk	c1898
Monotype Grotesque	c1926
Helvetica	1957
Theinhardt	2009

Availability

Arial is widely available

Specimen

Arial type specimen. Monotype
Corporation, Salfords, 1980s (210x155mm)

Dimensions

Arial Light

Hxkp

ascender height
capital height
x-height = 72% cap height
descender depth

| | measurement at 10 point* | |
	in points	in mm
Capital height	7.16	2.53
x-height	5.18	1.83
Ascender height	7.16	2.53
Descender depth	1.98	0.70
Figure width	5.56	
Wordspace	2.78	

Arial Light Italic

Hxkp

x-height = 72% cap height

| | measurement at 10 point* | |
	in points	in mm
Capital height	7.16	2.53
x-height	5.18	1.83
Ascender height	7.16	2.53
Descender depth	1.99	0.70
Figure width	5.56	
Wordspace	2.78	

Arial Black

Hxkp

x-height = 72% cap height

| | measurement at 10 point* | |
	in points	in mm
Capital height	7.16	2.53
x-height	5.18	1.83
Ascender height	7.16	2.53
Descender depth	1.97	0.70
Figure width	6.67	
Wordspace	3.34	

Arial Black Italic

Hxkp

x-height = 73% cap height

| | measurement at 10 point* | |
	in points	in mm
Capital height	7.16	2.53
x-height	5.20	1.83
Ascender height	7.16	2.53
Descender depth	1.99	0.70
Figure width	6.67	
Wordspace	3.34	

Characteristics and earmarks

Almost monoline | No spur on G

AEGMQRW
abcegkmv

Flat topped A | Tail curves as it joins upper bowl

AEGMQRW
abcegkmv

Italic is a sloped version of
the regular with few modifications

Curved strokes terminate at angle

AEGMQRW
abcegkmv

Characteristic terminal

Slight curve in tail of Q

AEGMQRW
abcegkmv

4

* where 72 points = 1 inch

AEGMQRW
abcegkmv

Dimensions

Arial Light Condensed

ascender height
capital height
x-height
= 72% cap height
descender depth

	measurement at 10 point*	
	in points	in mm
Capital height	7.16	2.53
x-height	5.18	1.83
Ascender height	7.16	2.53
Descender depth	1.99	0.70
Figure width	4.48	
Wordspace	2.24	

AEGMQRW
abcegkmv

Arial Condensed

Hxkp

x-height
= 72% cap height

	measurement at 10 point*	
	in points	in mm
Capital height	7.16	2.53
x-height	5.18	1.83
Ascender height	7.16	2.53
Descender depth	1.98	0.70
Figure width	5.00	
Wordspace	2.50	

AEGMQRW
abcegkmv

Arial Bold Condensed

x-height
= 72% cap height

	measurement at 10 point*	
	in points	in mm
Capital height	7.16	2.53
x-height	5.18	1.83
Ascender height	7.16	2.53
Descender depth	1.99	0.70
Figure width	5.00	
Wordspace	2.50	

AEGMQRW
abcegkmv

Arial Extra Bold Condensed

Hxkp

x-height
= 72% cap height

	measurement at 10 point*	
	in points	in mm
Capital height	7.16	2.53
x-height	5.18	1.83
Ascender height	7.16	2.53
Descender depth	1.99	0.70
Figure width	5.00	
Wordspace	2.50	

5

Arial is one of the most ubiquitous typefaces in the world today, readily familiar to anyone who has a computer. Well known through its inclusion in Microsoft products, it is now a default typeface packaged with virtually all hardware and software. The family has been developed over several years and comprises a huge range of styles and weights, issued in multiple configurations, with extensive support for many languages and writing systems.

It is commonly thought that Arial was made to order for Microsoft; in fact, it was produced for another computer giant. When Xerox and IBM introduced the first generation of laser printers in the early 1980s they sought more sophisticated typefaces than the raw monospaced all-capital alphabets then available. The Xerox contract went to Linotype, using Helvetica (pp346–47), while Monotype won IBM with new designs named Sonoran Serif and Sonoran Sans. The latter was later renamed Arial.

The new sans serif was designed in 1982 by a team at Monotype led by Robin Nicholas (1947–) and Patricia Saunders. While their aim was to create competition for Helvetica, Nicholas and Saunders did not want to copy it, instead basing their design on Monotype Grotesque (pp226–27). Nicholas later described Arial as a deliberately 'generic sans serif; almost a bland sans serif'. At first glance, the differences between Arial and Helvetica seem negligible. Arial was configured to match Helvetica's metrics precisely, with identical character widths and spaces throughout, so that it would be possible to automatically substitute Arial for Helvetica in documents. However, Arial is based on older grotesque traits than its predecessor, giving it a softer, fuller appearance. Like Akzidenz-Grotesk (pp152–53), the ends of curved strokes on letters such as c, e and s terminate at natural angles in relation to the stroke direction rather than being cut off horizontally.

When Microsoft launched Windows 3.1 a decade later they opted to license Arial as its default font, partly because Monotype was the leading developer of typefaces for the PC platform and partly because of the company's relationship with IBM. However, many practitioners believed that Arial was chosen because Microsoft wanted to avoid paying for Helvetica. Ignoring any intrinsic qualities, this association caused Arial to be condemned by many designers as an inauthentic design of inferior construction. Like Comic Sans (pp530–31) it became a typographic bête noire. It is ironic that the most widely used sans serif in the world has been regarded so disdainfully in the light of its competence as a type for print and screen.

Ty	**Imago**
Ca	**Sans Serif**
Ke	**Grotesque**
Te	**Photocomposition**
Da	**1982**
De	**Günter Gerhard Lange**
Fo	**Berthold**
Co	**Germany**

Characteristics

	Tall x-height
	Short ascenders and descenders
A	High crossbar
C c S s e g	Flat terminals
G	Has spur
J	Narrow, short tail
Q	Short downward-curved tail
R	Curved, angled leg
a	Double-storeyed
f r t	Vertical terminals
i j	Square dots
t	Angled top-stroke
y	Curved tail

AGJQMR abcefghij koprstuy

Connections

Akzidenz-Grotesk	c1898
Univers	1957
Forma	1968
Unica	1980

Availability

Imago is available from Berthold and resellers

Specimen

Imago type specimen. H. Berthold AG, Berlin, 1982 (297x210mm)

Ampullen und Lyophilisate

Wir verwenden für die Herstellung von Ampullen und Lyophilisaten nur täglich frisch zubereitetes destilliertes Wasser. Auch alle anderen Ausgangsstoffe müssen chemisch rein und pyrogenfrei sein. Nach dem Lösen aller Bestandteile wird der Ansatz durch ultra-feine Filter sterilfiltriert. Die leeren Ampullen durchlaufen nach der Reinigung mit entmineralisiertem Wasser Heißlufttunnels, in denen sie bei über 300 °C getrocknet, sterilisiert und entpyrogenisiert werden.
Ohne mit der Raumluft in Berührung zu kommen, gelangen sie dann zu den unter ›Laminar air flow‹ stehenden Abfüllmaschinen, wo sie mit der sterilen Lösung gefüllt und ohne Eingreifen des Personals automatisch verschlossen werden.

Das Wasser eines quellfrisch sprudelnden Gebirgsbaches ist sauber. Wir können es bedenkenlos trinken. Für die Herstellung von Injektions- oder Infusionspräparaten wäre es trotzdem nicht rein genug.

BERTHOLD IMAGO

libro
libro
buch

Günter Gerhard Lange
1982
H. Berthold AG

ABCDEFGHIJKLMNOPQ
RSTUVWXYZ
abcdefghijklmnopqrstuvwxyz
1/1234567890%
(.,-;:!i?¿-)·[',"""›‹]
+−=/$£†*&§
ÄÅÆÖØŒÜáäåæïöøœßŭ
ÁÀÂÃÇĆÉÊÊËÍÌÎÏĹŃÑÓÒÔŌ
ŔŘŠŤÚÙŮŴWÝŸŶŹ
áàâãçćéêëëíìîïĺńñóòôōöŕŕŝ
úùůŵŵýÿŷż

Berthold-Schriftweite weit
Berthold-Schriftweite normal
Berthold-Schriftweite eng
Berthold-Schriftweite sehr eng
Berthold-Schriftweite extrem eng

Berthold
3,72 mm (14 p)

Berthold
4,25 mm (16 p)

Berthold
4,75 mm (18 p)

Berthold
5,30 mm (20 p)

Berthold
6,35 mm (24 p)

Berthold
7,40 mm (28 p)

Berthold
8,50 mm (32 p)

Berthold
9,55 mm (36 p)

Größe		Zeilenabstand			100 Zeichen			
mm	p	kp	Êp	Ex	0	−1	−2	
1,33	5	1,75	2,13	2,00	88	85	82	
1,60	6	2,13	2,50	2,50	104	100	96	
1,86	7	2,44	2,94	3,00	120	116	112	
2,15	8	2,81	3,38	3,50	136	131	126	
2,40	9	3,13	3,75	3,75	152	146	140	
2,65	10	3,44	4,19	4,25	168	161	154	
2,92	11	3,81	4,56	4,75	184	177	170	
3,20	12	4,13	5,00	5,25	199	191	183	
3,45	13	4,50	5,44	5,75	215	207	199	
3,72	14	4,81	5,81	—	231	222	213	
3,98	15	5,19	6,25	—	246	237	228	
4,25	16	5,50	6,63	—	262	252	242	

WZ 13 E, NSW 0, MZB 0,63, F 0,12:0,08 (1,6), VI
H 1−x 0,71−k 1,00−p 0,29−Ê 1,27−kp 1,29−Êp 1,56
BF 089 1048, Belegung 051: 085 0248 (095 0248)

Berthold-Schriften überzeugen durch Schärfe und Qualität. Schriftqualität ist eine Frage der Erfahrung. Berthold hat diese Erfahrung seit über hundert Jahren. Zuerst im Schriftguß, dann im Fotosatz. Berthold-Schriften sind weltweit geschätzt. Im Schriftenatelier München wird jeder Buchstabe in der Größe von zwölf Zentimetern neu gezeichnet. Mit messerscharfen Konturen, um für die Schriftscheiben das Optimale an Konturenschärfe herauszuholen. Um die Qualität des Einzelzeichens im Belichtungsvorgang zu bewahren, wird durch die ruhen, nicht rotierende Schriftscheibe belichtet. Dieses optische System

33 mm (5 p)   20   30   40   50   60

Berthold-Schriften überzeugen durch Schärfe und Qualität. Sc riftqualität ist eine Frage der Erfahrung. Berthold hat diese Erf ahrung seit über hundert Jahren. Zuerst im Schriftguß, dann im Fotosatz. Berthold-Schriften sind weltweit geschätzt. Im Schrift natelier München wird jeder Buchstabe in der Größe von zwölf zentimetern neu gezeichnet. Mit messerscharfen Konturen, um r die Schriftscheiben das Optimale an Konturenschärfe hera uszuholen. Um die Qualität des Einzelzeichens im Belichtungsv rgang zu bewahren, wird durch die ruhende, nicht rotierende

45 mm (5,5 p)   20   30   40   50   6

Berthold-Schriften überzeugen durch Schärfe und Qualit t. Schriftqualität ist eine Frage der Erfahrung. Berthold hat iese Erfahrung seit über hundert Jahren. Zuerst im Schrift guß, dann im Fotosatz. Berthold-Schriften sind weltweit eschätzt. Im Schriftenatelier München wird jeder Buchst be in der Größe von zwölf Zentimetern neu gezeichnet. M messerscharfen Konturen, um für die Schriftscheiben das Optimale an Konturenschärfe herauszuholen. Um die Q alität des Einzelzeichens im Belichtungsvorgang zu bew

60 mm (6 p)   20   30   40   50

Berthold-Schriften überzeugen durch Schärfe und Q alität. Schriftqualität ist eine Frage der Erfahrung. B rthold hat diese Erfahrung seit über hundert Jahren uerst im Schriftguß, dann im Fotosatz. Berthold-Sc riften sind weltweit geschätzt. Im Schriftenatelier M nchen wird jeder Buchstabe in der Größe von zwölf entimetern neu gezeichnet. Mit messerscharfen Ko turen, um für die Schriftscheiben das Optimale an K nturenschärfe herauszuholen. Um die Qualität des

75 mm (6,5 p)   20   30   40   50

Berthold-Schriften überzeugen durch Schärfe und Qualität. Schriftqualität ist eine Frage der Erfahrun . Berthold hat diese Erfahrung seit über hundert J hren. Zuerst im Schriftguß, dann im Fotosatz. Bert old-Schriften sind weltweit geschätzt. Im Schrifte atelier München wird jeder Buchstabe in der Grö Se von zwölf Zentimetern neu gezeichnet. Mit mes erscharfen Konturen, um für die Schriftscheiben as Optimale an Konturenschärfe herauszuholen

86 mm (7 p)   20   30   40

Berthold-Schriften überzeugen durch Schärfe nd Qualität. Schriftqualität ist eine Frage der E fahrung. Berthold hat diese Erfahrung seit über undert Jahren. Zuerst im Schriftguß, dann im Fotosatz. Berthold-Schriften sind weltweit ge schätzt. Im Schriftenatelier München wird jeder Buchstabe in der Größe von zwölf Zentimetern neu gezeichnet. Mit messerscharfen Konturen m für die Schriftscheiben das Optimale an Ko

,00 mm (7,5 p)   20   30   40

Berthold-Schriften überzeugen durch Schär e und Qualität. Schriftqualität ist eine Frage er Erfahrung. Berthold hat diese Erfahrung eit über hundert Jahren. Zuerst im Schriftgu ß, dann im Fotosatz. Berthold-Schriften sind weltweit geschätzt. Im Schriftenatelier Mü chen wird jeder Buchstabe in der Größe von zwölf Zentimetern neu gezeichnet. Mit mess erscharfen Konturen, um für die Schriftschei

,15 mm (8 p)   20   30   40

Berthold-Schriften überzeugen durch Sc härfe und Qualität. Schriftqualität ist ein e Frage der Erfahrung. Berthold hat diese Erfahrung seit über hundert Jahren. Zu erst im Schriftguß, dann im Fotosatz. Be rthold-Schriften sind weltweit geschätzt Im Schriftenatelier München wird jeder Buchstabe in der Größe von zwölf Zenti

2,40 mm (9 p)   20   30

Berthold-Schriften überzeugen dur ch Schärfe und Qualität. Schriftqual ität ist eine Frage der Erfahrung. Ber thold hat diese Erfahrung seit über h undert Jahren. Zuerst im Schriftguß dann im Fotosatz. Berthold-Schriften sind weltweit geschätzt. Im Schrifte natelier München wird jeder Buchst

2,65 mm (10 p)   20   30

Berthold-Schriften überzeugen d urch Schärfe und Qualität. Schri ftqualität ist eine Frage der Erfah rung. Berthold hat diese Erfahru ng seit über hundert Jahren. Zue rst im Schriftguß, dann im Fotosa tz. Berthold-Schriften sind weltw eit geschätzt. Im Schriftenatelier

2,92 mm (11 p)   10   20   30

Berthold-Schriften überzeuge n durch Schärfe und Qualität Schriftqualität ist eine Frage d er Erfahrung. Berthold hat die se Erfahrung seit über hundert Jahren. Zuerst im Schriftguß dann im Fotosatz. Berthold-Sc hriften sind weltweit geschätz

3,20 mm (12 p)   10   20

Berthold-Schriften überzeug en durch Schärfe und Qual ität. Schriftqualität ist eine F rage der Erfahrung. Berthold hat diese Erfahrung seit ü ber hundert Jahren. Zuerst i m Schriftguß, dann im Fotos atz. Berthold-Schriften sind

3,45 mm (13 p)   10   20

KONZEPT, DESIGN UND
REALISATION:
ERWIN POELL, HEIDELBERG.
TITELIDEE UND -TEXT:
HILTRUD POELL, HEIDELBERG

FOTOS:
SIGRID NEUBERT (2)
ERICH BAUMANN (8)
STUDIO BERGERHAUSEN
(3)

SATZ:
HAGEDORN-SATZ,
VIERNHEIM
TECHNIK:
BERTHOLD ADS 3000

REPROS:
HEIDELBERGER
KLISCHEE + OFFSET-REPRO
GMBH.
HEIDELBERG

GESAMTHERSTELLUNG:
MANNHEIMER MORGEN
GROSSDRUCKEREI
UND VERLAG GMBH.
MANNHEIM

PRINTED IN
FEDERAL REPUBLIC
OF GERMANY

CODE 6495479.1

Imago was designed for the Berthold Type Foundry in 1982 by its artistic director, Günter Gerhard Lange (1921–2008), as part of the Berthold Exklusiv Collection. This was an ambitious programme initiated by Lange to publish an extensive catalogue of typefaces upholding the foundry's reputation for the highest-quality design made to meticulous production standards.

Drawing on Akzidenz-Grotesk and other popular sans serif typefaces like Univers as points of reference, Lange intended to revitalize the sans serif form, investing the new typeface with unique characteristics that gave it both utility and personality, as well as a visible point of difference from its competitors.

In comparison with most sans serifs, Imago has an exceptionally tall x-height, with short ascenders and descenders and regular, open counters contributing to the regularity of its rhythmic flow. Imago's most evident features are the overall compression of its letters and their subtle contours. Rather than using conventional ellipsoids, Lange slightly squared the shapes of the bowls in both upper and lower case characters, giving them a stable posture. This is further enhanced by the typeface's stroke contrast, which is slightly more emphatic than most sans serifs. A greater difference between thick and thin strokes is evident, lending Imago a crisp and incisive appearance.

Released in 1982 in four weights and four corresponding italics, the Imago type family is a distinctive, unified sans serif that has been used in many applications, both in print and online. Its large lower case has made it a reliable choice for display applications such as signage, advertising and brand communications.

Ty	**Trinité**
Ca	**Serif**
Ke	**Old Style, Dutch**
Te	**Photocomposition**
Da	**1982**
De	**Bram de Does**
Fo	**Enschedé / Autologic**
Co	**Netherlands**

Characteristics

Oblique stress
Moderate stroke contrast
Slight incline overall, with curved stems
Capitals lower than ascender height
Large x-height
Short ascenders and descenders
Calligraphic, asymmetrical bracketed serifs
J Descends below baseline
M Slightly splayed
Q Sweeping tail below letter
R Wide, curved leg
W Stepped centre-strokes, serif at apex
a Double-storeyed, small bowl
f h m n p q Serifs extend to right
g Double-storeyed, large upper bowl

AJMQRW
abcefghij
orstuyaefg

Connections

Lexicon	1992
Collis	1993
DTL Documenta	1993
Dolly	2001

Availability

Trinité is available from the Enschedé type foundry and resellers

Specimen

Trinité and Lexicon: The Typefaces Designed by Bram de Does. De Buitenkant, Amsterdam, 2013 (225x150mm)

Author and printer in the history of typographical design

The independent profession of typographical designer, layout editor, book production consultant or whatever one may call him, only emerged at the beginning of the twentieth century, and only since 1950 has the designer become a normal constituent of the book production process. In practice, however, professional concern with a book's layout has existed ever since books were first created: in the production of every book someone was aware of its design aspects, someone who formed opinions, who made decisions. But who this person was and what place he occupied in the production of the printed book, book history can rarely answer. This is strange, for it concerns a crucial moment in the making of a book: the outward appearance of a text contributes to its expressive strength and is therefore linked to its meaning or meanings. It has been observed several times that authors do not write books but texts, which are converted into marketable books by others (scribes, editors, publishers, master

The independent profession of typographical designer, layout editor, book production consultant or whatever one may call him, only emerged at the beginning of the twentieth century, and only since 1950 has the designer become a normal constituent of the book production process. In practice, however, professional concern with a book's layout has existed ever since books were first created: in the production of every book someone was aware of its design aspects, someone who formed opinions, who made decisions. But who this person was and what place he occupied in the production of the printed book, book history can rarely answer. This is strange, for it concerns a crucial mo-

Trinité Bold 1

38

Trinité Roman Wide 2

abcdefghijk lmnopqrs tuvwxyz

Trinité Italic 2

abcdefghijk lmnopqrs tuvwxyz

39

Dutch type designer Bram de Does (1934–2015) rebelled against the principles of asymmetrical typography that he was taught as a design student in the 1950s, along with the modernist ideas associated with them. They motivated him, he said, to work 'in a symmetrical way in order to be obstreperous and original'.

He was commissioned to design Trinité by the Joh. Enschedé en Zonen printing office. In the late 1970s they asked De Does to adapt Jan van Krimpen's Romanée typeface for their recently updated phototypesetting equipment. However, he was convinced that Romanée would lose its personality in a transition from metal type to film composition, and instead recommended designing a typeface specifically for the new technology. Enschedé invited him to undertake the task himself in 1982.

As a foundation for the new design De Does established a set of four universal principles for a well-proportioned and highly legible text typeface. These principles – functionality, harmony, practicality and originality – guided the development of Trinité, taking into account respectively: legibility and the reading process, aesthetic qualities, economies in production and manufacture, and, importantly, design innovation, because, as De Does said, 'otherwise there is no use in making the thing'. Following design models from early Renaissance typefaces, he drew serifs a little longer towards the right than the left and he gave all characters a very slight corresponding forward incline, resulting in what he called a 'functional swing'. Letters sit on firm, asymmetrical foot-serifs that are calligraphically drawn. Trinité's visual rhythm was further enhanced by an absence of straight lines in its contours.

The type family has an expansive overall structure. The name Trinité refers to the family's three height variants, with lengths of ascenders and descenders increasing progressively. A fourth version features swash stroke endings. Each height variant is provided in three weights (roman, medium and bold) and two widths (wide and condensed). Italics are implemented to conform visually with both the wide and condensed versions. All characters without ascenders or descenders, such as capitals and numerals, are identical across all four styles, making it possible to switch between versions easily without the problem of reflowing the text. With its many sophisticated design considerations, Trinité was conceived as a multipurpose typeface and gained enormous popularity when it was released as a PostScript font in the 1990s.

Ty	**Neue Helvetica**
Ca	**Sans Serif**
Ke	**Grotesque**
Te	**Digital**
Da	**1983**
De	**Max Miedinger**
Fo	**Stempel / Linotype**
Co	**Germany**

Characteristics

C c S s e g Flat terminals
G Has spur
Q Straight, angled tail
R Curved, upright leg
a Double-storeyed, small curve at foot
f r t Vertical terminals
i j Square dots
t Flat top-stroke
y Flat, hooked tail

AGMQR
abcefghij
koprstuy

Connections

Akzidenz-Grotesk	c1898
Helvetica	1957
Unica	1980
Neue Haas Grotesk	2010

Availability

Neue Helvetica is available from Linotype and resellers

Specimen

Neue Helvetica type specimen sheet.
Linotype, Bad Homburg, c1988
(210x297mm)

Originally designed for hand-setting by Max Miedinger (1910–80) in 1957, Helvetica (pp346–47) was updated and adapted over the years for all methods of composition, from hot metal and phototypesetting to the first-generation of digital typesetters. In the process, character weights, proportions and spacing were sometimes compromised in order to comply with the limitations of each technology.

Neue Helvetica is a rationalization of the typeface family for digital typesetting that radically overhauled and extended the original design. It was developed in 1983 at D. Stempel AG, then a Linotype subsidiary, by a team led by René Kerfante and Wolfgang Schimpf, working in consultation with Erik Spiekermann. After planning an extensive progression of weights and styles – from ultralight to black, and from condensed to extended – the Stempel type design studio reconstructed the Helvetica family from the ground up, drawing every character to exacting quality standards for use in Linotype's latest Linotronic range of typesetting machines.

With a more structurally unified set of glyphs, subtle changes were made to character contours, heights and widths to improve legibility. The spacing of numerals was also increased and punctuation marks were made heavier.

The new family was among the most extensive of its time, with a total of 51 styles comprising nine weights with italics in three widths (normal, condensed and extended) and an outline variant based on the Helvetica 75 Bold weight. To accommodate the extent of the family a logical number-based naming scheme was implemented, similar to that used for Univers (pp350–51).

The synthesis of aesthetic, technical and organizational refinements that resulted from Helvetica's standardization programme ensured its continued market-leading status in the digital era. 'Though often copied', read the sales leaflet issued by Stempel at the time, 'our Helvetica has never been surpassed.'

4200.110

Mergenthaler Type Library Typefaces/Schriften/Caractères

neue Helvetica® 75
bold/halbfett/demi-gras

07472   12 pt Design

Sans Serif/Serifenlose Antiqua/Antiques
D. Stempel AG, 1983
Linotype

abcdefghijklmnopq
stuvwxyz fiflß&
ABCDEFGHIJKLMI
OPQRSTUVWXYZ
1234567890
.,.;-– —'' "" •‹›«»*%
!?¡¿()[]/†‡§$£¢*f*

ÄÁÂÀÅÃĀÆÇČËÉÈĒĞĬÍÎÌĪÑÖÓÔÒ
ÕŌŒŠÜÚÛÙŪŽäáâàåãāæ
çčëéêèēğïíîìīīñöóôòøõōœšüúûùūž

Parameter for 10 pt/Parameter in 10 pt/Paramètre pour 10 pt

H 2.51 mm	k 2.51 mm	x 1.81 mm	p 0.64 mm	kp 3.15 mm	Ép 3
H 0.099 Inches	k 0.099 Inches	x 0.071 Inches	p 0.025 Inches	kp 0.124 Inches	Ép 0

Factor/Faktor/Facteur 1.00

* Given in pica point/Angaben in pica point/Toutes indications en points pica

mm/6 pt* (2.25 mmᴰᴵᴺ) ▽ 2.50 mm (7 pt*) ▷ +1 H 1.51 mm

hijklmnopqrstuvwxyz abcdefghijklmnopqrstuvwxyz abcdefghijkl 1234567890
type design the basic character is determined by the uniform design character
all letters in the alphabet. However, this alone does not determine the standard
peface and the quality of composition set with it. The appearance is something
which forms itself out of many details, like form, proportion, rhythm etc. If eve
PEARANCE IS SOMETHING COMPLEX WHICH FORMS ITSELF OUT OF MA

mm/7 pt* (2.63 mmᴰᴵᴺ) ▽ 2.75 mm (8 pt*) ▷ +1 H 1.76 mm

ghijklmnopqrstuvwxyz abcdefghijklmnopqrstuvwxyz 1234567890
er Schriftgestaltung wird der Grundcharakter eines Alphabets von
lichen Formmerkmalen der Buchstaben bestimmt. Er allein besagt
chts über das Niveau einer Druckschrift und die Qualität des Satzge
Das Erscheinungs bild ist etwas Komplexes, das sich aus vielen Ein
UND PROPORTIONEN SIND DIE WICHTIGSTEN KRITERIEN BEI

mm/8 pt* (3.00 mmᴰᴵᴺ) ▽ 3.25 mm (9.25 pt*) ▷ 0 H 2.01 mm

fghijklmnopqrstuvwxyz abcdefghijklmnopqrstu 1234567890
e de chaque caractère d'imprimerie se détermine par des ca
istiques qui sont les mêmes pour toutes les lettres de l'alpha
ans tous les rapports formels et autres relations il s'agit de ph
enes optiques irréductibles aux règles mathématiques etque
RE PART MALGRÉ TOUTES LES RESSOURCES DE MÉC

mm/9 pt* (3.38 mmᴰᴵᴺ) ▽ 3.50 mm (10 pt*) ▷ 0 H 2.26 mm

efghijklmnopqrstuvwxyz abcdefghijklmn 1234567890
ry type design the basic character is determined by th
niform design characteristics of all letters in the alpha
lowever, this alone does not determine the standard of
peface and the quality of composition set with it. Thea
APPEARANCE IS SOMETHING COMPLEX WHICH

mm/10 pt* (3.75 mmᴰᴵᴺ) ▽ 4.00 mm (11.5 pt*) ▷ 0 H 2.51 mm

efghijklmnopqrstuvwxyz abcdefghi 1234567890
eder Schriftgestaltung wird der Grundcharaktere
Alphabets von einheitlichen Formmerkmalende
Buchstaben bestimmt. Er allein besagt noch nicht
das Niveau einer Druckschrift und die Qualitätde
M UND PROPORTIONEN SIND DIE WICHTIG

mm/11 pt* (4.13 mmᴰᴵᴺ) ▽ 4.50 mm (12.75 pt*) ▷ 0 H 2.76 mm

defghijklmnopqrstuvwxyz abcd 1234567890
tyle de chaque caractère d'imprimerie se dét
ine par des caractéristiques qui sont les mê
our toutes les lettres de l'alphabet. Dans tou
UTRE PART MALGRÉ TOUTES LES RESSI

mm/12 pt* (4.50 mmᴰᴵᴺ) ▽ 4.75 mm (13.5 pt*) ▷ 0 H 3.01 mm

defghijklmnopqrstuvwxyz a 1234567890
very type design the basic character is de
ermined by the uniform design characteri
s of all letters in the alphabet. Howevers
E APPEARANCE IS SOMETHING COM

△ 4.92 mm/14 pt* (5.25 mmᴰᴵᴺ) ▷ −1 H 3.51 mm

In every type design the basic characte

△ 5.62 mm/16 pt* (6.00 mmᴰᴵᴺ) ▷ −1 H 4.02 mm

Bei jeder Schriftgestaltung wird de

△ 6.33 mm/18 pt* (6.75 mmᴰᴵᴺ) ▷ −1 H 4.52 mm

Le style de chaque caractèredi

△ 7.03 mm/20 pt* (7.50 mmᴰᴵᴺ) ▷ −1 H 5.02 mm

För alla nya stilar bestämsal

△ 8.44 mm/24 pt* (9.00 mmᴰᴵᴺ) ▷ −1 H 6.02 mm

In elko letterontwerpw

△ 9.84 mm/28 pt* (10.50 mmᴰᴵᴺ) ▷ −1 H 7.03 mm

Em todo o desenhol

△ 12.65 mm/36 pt* (13.50 mmᴰᴵᴺ) ▷ −2 H 9.04 mm

In ciascuna seri

△ 16.87 mm/48 pt* (18.00 mmᴰᴵᴺ) ▷ −2 H 12.05 mm

En cada tirp

△ 21.09 mm/60 pt* (22.50 mmᴰᴵᴺ) ▷ −2 H 15.06 mm

Den ensa

△ 25.31 mm/72 pt* (27.00 mmᴰᴵᴺ) ▷ −2 H 18.07 mm

Bestem

△ 29.52 mm/84 pt* (31.50 mmᴰᴵᴺ) ▷ −2 H 21.08 mm

Muoto

6
7
8
9
10
11
12
14
16
18
20
24
28
36
48
60
72
84

Chicago

Ty	**Chicago**
Ca	**Sans Serif**
Ke	**Geometric**
Te	**Digital**
Da	**1984**
De	**Susan Kare**
Fo	**Apple Computer, Inc.**
Co	**USA**

Characteristics

Variable width, proportionally spaced
characters, not monospaced
Large x-height
Short ascenders and descenders
Strong stroke contrast
K M N W Wide
a Arch touches bowl at left
& Has flourish
'#%'/*@^" Thin strokes

AEGKMNS
abcefghij
koprstuy

Connections

Geneva	1984
Lo-Res	1985
Lucida	1985
Charcoal	1994

Availability

Not available

Specimen

Chicago type specimen – screen, greyed
out and TrueType versions, composed by
author, 2015 (220x120mm)

As a student Steve Jobs occasionally attended calligraphy classes simply out of personal interest: 'I learned about serif and sans serif typefaces, about varying the amount of space between different letter combinations, about what makes great typography great … Ten years later, when we were designing the first Macintosh computer, it all came back to me. And we designed it all into the Mac. It was the first computer with beautiful typography.'

Chicago was the first typeface to be developed for the Apple Macintosh in 1983. It was designed by Susan Kare (1954–) specifically for use on-screen, initially in one size only, 12 pixels high. Like the Mac itself, Chicago was robust but exceptionally user-friendly and it became integral to the early Mac interface, appearing in all menus, dialog boxes, window titles and text labels of the operating system from 1984 until 1997. Because it was an immediately recognizable feature of its identity, Apple also made extensive use of Chicago in marketing communications throughout this period.

Like Kare's other contributions to the first Mac interface, Chicago's groundbreaking design has no precedent. Working only in black and white pixels on an extremely limited grid, with no reference points other than the raw computer bitmap types of the time, Kare managed to achieve a well-modulated typeface with subtly contrasting stroke widths, making it easy to read even on the low-resolution Mac computer screen. Chicago contains no curves, only pixel staircases, but at a normal reading distance the jagged corners seem smooth and rounded while the main stems and cross-strokes remain straight and evenly spaced. The use of proportional letter spacing was a major innovation of the Mac platform, allowing Chicago to approach the readable qualities of printed matter. One of Chicago's less obvious but equally well-considered functions was that it could remain clearly legible while being greyed out by means of the removal of alternate pixels to indicate a disabled menu item.

In addition to Chicago, the first Mac operating system featured several other innovative types by Kare, including New York (a serif), Geneva (a sans serif), Athens (a slab serif), Los Angeles (a script) and San Francisco (a font using assorted characters). As the Mac operating system developed over time Apple commissioned the type foundry Bigelow & Holmes to create a vector-based version of Chicago for use in print. The TrueType version, shown at far right, replaced all of the bitmaps with curves but otherwise remained faithful to Kare's unique vision.

12pt Chicago

ABCDEFGHIJKLM
NOPQRSTUVWXYZ
abcdefghijklm
nopqrstuvwxyz

0123456789&

ÄÅÀÉÈÊÍÏÎÖÕØÙÛ
ÜÇÑ¥ŒÆäåàéêê
íïîöõøûùüñœæ
$£§ß¢ƒ;:!?π∂Ω

12pt Chicago @ 200%

ABCDEFGHIJKLM
NOPQRSTUVWXYZ
abcdefghijklm
nopqrstuvwxyz

0123456789&

ÄÅÀÉÈÊÍÏÎÖÕØÙÛ
ÜÇÑ¥ŒÆäåàéêê
íïîöõøûùüñœæ
$£§ß¢ƒ;:!?π∂Ω

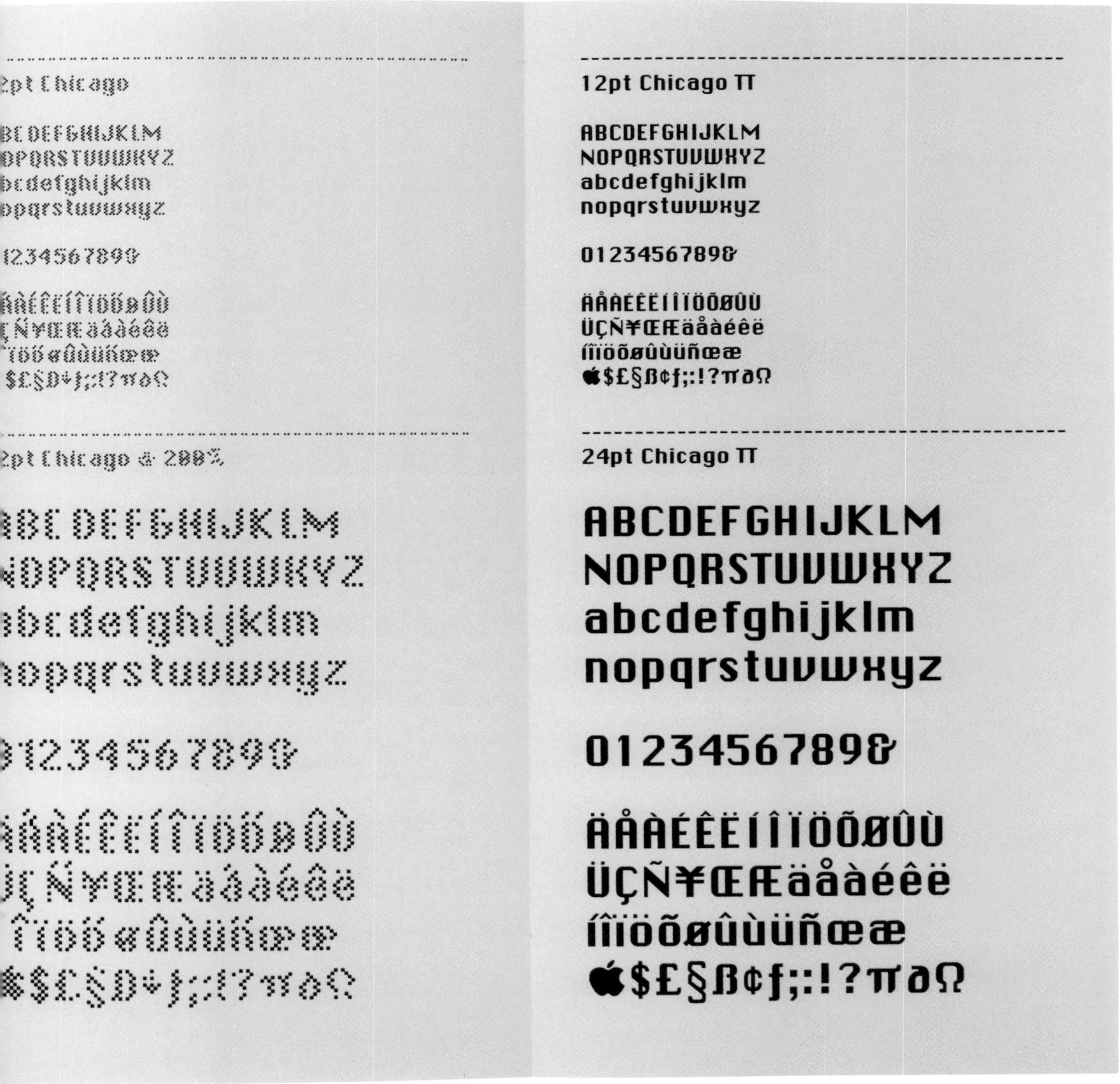

2pt Chicago

ABCDEFGHIJKLM
NOPQRSTUVWXYZ
bcdefghijklm
opqrstuvwxyz

123456789Ø

ÄÅÀÉÊÈÍÎÏÖÕØÙÙ
ÇÑ¥ŒÆäåàéêë
ÍÎÖÕØÛÙÜñœæ
$£§ÐÞ¢ƒ;:!?π∂Ω

2pt Chicago @ 200%

ABC DEFGHIJKLM
NOPQRSTUVWXYZ
bcdefghijklm
opqrstuvwxyz

Ø123456789Ø

ÄÅÀÉÊÈÍÎÏÖÕØÙÙ
ÇÑ¥ŒÆäåàéêê
ÍÎÖÕØÛÙÜñœæ
$£§ÐÞ¢ƒ;:!?π∂Ω

12pt Chicago TT

ABCDEFGHIJKLM
NOPQRSTUVWXYZ
abcdefghijklm
nopqrstuvwxyz

0123456789&

ÄÅÀÉÊÈÍÎÏÖÕØÙÙ
ÜÇÑ¥ŒÆäåàéêë
íîïöõøûùüñœæ
$£§ß¢ƒ;:!?π∂Ω

24pt Chicago TT

ABCDEFGHIJKLM
NOPQRSTUVWXYZ
abcdefghijklm
nopqrstuvwxyz

0123456789&

ÄÅÀÉÊÈÍÎÏÖÕØÙÙ
ÜÇÑ¥ŒÆäåàéêë
íîïöõøûùüñœæ
$£§ß¢ƒ;:!?π∂Ω

Lo-Res

Ty	**Lo-Res**
Ca	**Sans Serif**
Ke	**Geometric**
Te	**Digital**
Da	**1985**
De	**Zuzana Licko**
Fo	**Emigre**
Co	**USA**

Characteristics

A series of related bitmap typefaces

Common grid throughout

Variations of height, width and stroke thickness

Emperor family ratio: one-pixel stem to two-pixel counter

Universal family ratio: one-pixel stem to three-pixel counter

Oakland family ratio: two-pixel stem to two-pixel counter

Emigre family ratio: two-pixel stem to two-pixel counter

ABGabg

ABGabg

ABGabg

Connections

Chicago	1984
Geneva	1984
Citizen	1986
Base	1995

Availability

Lo-Res is available from Emigre and resellers

Specimen

Emigre product catalogue. Emigre, Berkeley, 2001 (279x216mm)

Lo-Res

LO-RES FONTS SHOWN AT THE SAME PIXEL SIZE – THE STEM WEIGHTS MATCH – THE CAPITAL HEIGHTS DECREASE. (RECOMMENDED FOR SCREEN USE.)

LO-RES FONTS SHOWN AT THE SAME POINT SIZE; THE STEM WEIGHTS INCREASE – THE CAPITAL HEIGHTS MATCH. (RECOMMENDED FOR USE IN PRINT.)

LO-RES NAME	LO-RES 28 NARROW	LO-RES 28 REGULAR	LO-RES 22 NARROW	LO-RES 15 NARROW	LO-RES 12 NARROW	LO-RES 12 REGULAR	LO-RES 9 NARROW	W...
OLD NAME	EMPEROR 19	UNIVERSAL 19	EMPEROR 15	EMPEROR 10	EMPEROR 8	UNIVERSAL 8	BASE 9	

LO-RES FONTS SHOWN AT THE SAME PIXEL SIZE – THE STEM WEIGHTS MATCH – THE CAPITAL HEIGHTS DECREASE. (RECOMMENDED FOR SCREEN USE.)

LO-RES FONTS SHOWN AT THE SAME POINT SIZE; THE STEM WEIGHTS INCREASE – THE CAPITAL HEIGHTS MATCH. (RECOMMENDED FOR USE IN PRINT.)

LO-RES NAME	LO-RES 21 SERIF	LO-RES 22 SERIF	LO-RES 22 BOLD	LO-RES 15 BOLD	LO-RES 12 BOLD	LO-RES 9 WIDE BOLD ALT	LO-RES 9 NARROW BOLD	LO-... WID...
OLD NAME	EMIGRE 14	EMIGRE 15	OAKLAND 15	EMIGRE/OAK 10	EMIGRE/OAK 8	OAKLAND 6	BASE 9 BOLD	

o-Res

The terms "bitmap" and "pixel" are now so commonly used that it's worth noting their origins. Both are abbreviations:
Bitmap = "map of bits" (A bit being the smallest element on the map or grid.)

Pixel = "picture element" (A pixel being the smallest element in a picture that is constrained by a grid.)
Bitmap typefaces are composed of pixels. The pixel size is defined by the resolution of the grid, which also constrains the pixel placement. In turn, the resolution of the grid is defined by the output device. (For example, a standard Macintosh display is 72 pixels per inch; a Windows display is usually 96 or 120 pixels per inch.)

The coarser the resolution of the grid, the larger is the relative size of the pixels, and the more limited is the possibility of pixel placement. While this limits the variety of representable font characteristics, such limitations can be a strong source of design inspiration. Constraints on design choices allow many options to be evaluated quickly. By contrast, having many choices can be overwhelming, and the solution is often more difficult to distill from the myriad of options.

The result is that bitmaps have a strong and decisive character, which is most noticeable when used at headline sizes. In print work, bitmaps also function well at very small sizes; their modular proportions maintain open counters and there are no delicate details to drop out or fill in.

The bitmapped aesthetic is here to stay because it's inextricably linked to computer technology, and computers are increasingly affecting the production of, and our relation to, everything around us. As information is increasingly being stored, accessed and displayed in digital form, screen display has become the final method of viewing much of our information.

RECOMMENDED COMPUTER SETTINGS

MACINTOSH USERS:
To activate bitmap fonts on screen, be sure to select "Disable Smoothing at Screen Font Sizes" in the ATM control panel.

WINDOWS USERS:
To activate smoothing at sizes other than the bitmap font sizes, be sure to select "Smooth Edges of Screen Fonts" under Control Panel/Display/Plus! Note: you may also need to select "High Color" or "True Color" under Settings/Color Palette.

Type designer Zuzana Licko (1961–) co-founded *Emigre* magazine in 1984 with her partner Rudy VanderLans (1955–), a graphic designer and photographer. The journal became greatly admired for its editorial content and its innovative typefaces, designed in-house by Licko with crude public domain software on the first Apple Macintosh 128K computer.

The Mac triggered a revolution: 'It forced us to question everything', Licko said. She pioneered its use as a type-design tool, creating several innovative digital typefaces such as Emperor, Universal, Oakland and Emigre, which she originally drew in 1985 for use on the computer screen and dot matrix printer. These types were experimental, with limited applicability, and the arrival of Adobe's PostScript software together with high-resolution computer screens and printers soon rendered them obsolete.

Since fixed screen resolution does not allow for the same design to be scaled across a range of sizes, widths or weights, these early bitmap typefaces interrelated in set increments. All characters were built from pixels on a grid structure. The coarser the grid's resolution, the more limited the arrangement of pixels, and the representation of type characteristics was diminished accordingly. Licko was interested in developing an extensive range of workable variants within these extremely tight constraints. The Emperor family consisted of a series of typefaces that maintained the same ratio of a one-pixel stem to a two-pixel counter while incrementally varying the vertical height. The Universal family used a one-pixel stem to three-pixel counter ratio, and the Oakland and Emigre families used a two-pixel stem to two-pixel counter ratio.

In 2001 Licko rationalized this typeface collection in PostScript along with pixel versions of her Base-9 design (pp540–41). She organized them hierarchically and gave them a new family name, Lo-Res. In the revision she also made a number of technical improvements, including a more complete character set, more consistent character shapes across styles and weights, and improved alignments in the various resolutions.

Due to the ubiquity of digital media today, pixels have become readily accepted as visual metaphors for computing and the information era, in the same way that brushstrokes represent painting and craft traditions. Originally a pure experiment in the use of cutting-edge technology, Lo-Res still resonates as its authentic typographic expression.

alphabets that either have no capitals or mix

typeface that has only lower case and uses

suggested I do with *variex*, since there is

able. *Emigre: How did the computer give you*

na: I enjoy things that are like puzzles;

choices but you have to make it work.

he time and patience to look at every

never got the feeling that I found the

a typeface like Triplex, which is a bit

ll get most of my creative energy out

ork, I get inspired to find out what I

gn, I heard everybody say how bad

y better. This really intrigued me.

greeing. I was reading books on the

mention something about digital type

ctually interesting but never really

the subject of digital type. I was fascinated

al results I was a bit disappointed with how

xplored and interesting there and I

igning my first low resolution type in

le kept telling me it was really a lost

o would be better than what was out

ou succeeded? Zuzana: For myself, yes.

seen before I started. Issue number 6

ery good and informative. But then

re the really basic ideas that I had.

ns you have acquired some confidence doing

entirely by hand, more calligraphic type?

CITIZEN

DESIGNED BY ZUZANA LICKO
AVAILABLE AUGUST 1990

THE DESIGN OF CITIZEN (FIGURE 2) IS A DIRECT RESULT OF THE "SMOOTH"
PRINTING OPTION PROVIDED BY THE APPLE LASERWRITER. THIS FEATURE
OFFERS A SHORTCUT TO INCREASING THE RESOLUTION OF BITMAP
TYPEFACES FROM SCREEN TO PRINTER. THE 72 DPI BITMAPS ARE PROCESSED
INTO 300 DPI BITMAPS, THEREBY CREATING THE ILLUSION OF HIGH
RESOLUTION PRINTING. THE SHAPES OF CITIZEN WERE GENERATED BY
SMOOTHING A COARSE BITMAP, ENLARGING IT APPROXIMATELY FOUR TIMES,
AND THEN SMOOTHING IT AGAIN (FIGURE 1). THE DOUBLE "SMOOTH"
CONTOURS APPEARED AS STRAIGHT LINES OF VARYING LENGTH AND ANGLES,
WHICH WERE THEN CONVERTED INTO OUTLINE FORM.

Citiz
bold

AaBbCcDdEeFfGgHhIiJjKkLlMmNnO
1234567890

(FIGURE 2)

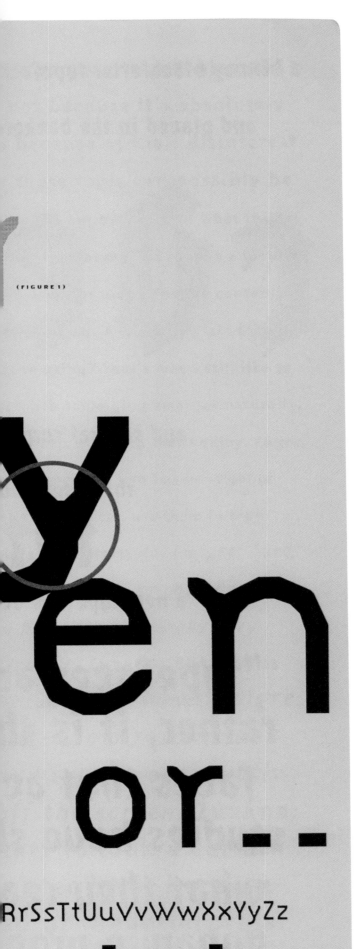

(FIGURE 1)

Ty	**Citizen**
Ca	**Sans Serif**
Ke	**Geometric**
Te	**Digital**
Da	**1986**
De	**Zuzana Licko**
Fo	**Emigre**
Co	**USA**

Characteristics

Geometric character construction
Straight polygonal segments used to
approximate curves and angles
Angled tails and ears on several lower
case characters

ABGMQS
abcefghi
koprstuy

Connections

Chicago	1984
Lo-Res	1985
Triplex	1989
Base	1995

Availability

Citizen is available from Emigre and
resellers

Specimen

Emigre 15: 'Do You Read Me?' Emigre,
Berkeley, 1990 (425x283mm)

When laser printers were first introduced as peripherals to personal computers in the 1980s, software programs such as the Adobe PostScript page-description language were at a primitive stage of their development. The protocols required to rasterize graphic data – converting information from computer screens to printed output – had not been standardized and consequently designers were obliged to experiment in order to produce effective results. The early Macintosh usefully provided a 'smooth printing' option as a way of increasing the resolution of bitmaps from screen to printer, seemingly polishing jagged pixel staircases into faceted slopes as they processed 72 dpi computer bitmaps into 300 dpi bitmaps for laser printers.

Like many young designers of the time, Zuzana Licko (1961–) of the Emigre type foundry was fascinated by the possible functions and implications of the new technologies. Building on her earlier experiments with bitmap letters (pp456–57) Licko took Apple's 'smooth printing' option as the guiding principle for her Citizen typeface. She used straight polygonal segments to approximate its features, reflecting the weird appearance of coarse, low-quality laser print output. 'I used the proportions of my earlier Universal Eight bitmap design and applied the precision of the computer's geometric elements.'

In the twenty-first century the square, jagged bitmapped types that were originally seen as alien, crude, almost unreadable forms have become familiar features of our visual landscape. Pixels are so dominant in today's communications technologies that they have become a ready signpost for the dawn of the information age, and for computing in general. Citizen, although one of the most novel and attractive of the early bitmap types, is a visual response to a technological constraint of that era which is no longer relevant and the typeface is therefore rarely seen today.

However, a few years after its release, Licko revisited Citizen, converting the angled lines into smooth PostScript curves in order to create Emigre's Triplex Sans family. Initially intended as an amiable geometric typeface that could be used as a flavourful substitute for sans serifs like Helvetica, Triplex evolved into one of Licko's most successful designs.

Ty	**Sassoon Primary**	
Ca	**Sans Serif / Script**	
Ke	**Humanist**	
Te	**Digital**	
Da	**1986**	
De	**Rosemary Sassoon**	
Fo	**Linotype**	
Co	**UK**	

Characteristics

Combines characteristics of sans serif and cursive script

Slight slope throughout

G No spur, arm extends to right

Q Short, straight, angled tail

R Straight, angled leg

a Single-storeyed

a d h k l m n u Curved exit stroke at foot

f Long, curved

f r t Vertical terminals

i j Round dots

t Flat top-stroke

AGMQRS
abcefghij
koprstuy

Connections

Blueprint	1994
Montessori Script	2000
Schulschrift	2001
Castledown	2013

Availability

Sassoon Primary is available from Sassoon Fonts and resellers

Specimen

Jolly Phonics Workbook. Jolly Learning, Chigwell, 2000 (200x140mm)

Tricky words 1–30

1.	I	11.	are	21.	go
2.	the	12.	all	22.	no
3.	he	13.	you	23.	so
4.	she	14.	your	24.	my
5.	me	15.	come	25.	one
6.	we	16.	some	26.	by
7.	be	17.	said	27.	like
8.	was	18.	here	28.	have
9.	to	19.	there	29.	live
10.	do	20.	they	30.	give

46

Tricky words 31–60

31.	only	41.	any	51.	could
32.	old	42.	many	52.	should
33.	little	43.	more	53.	would
34.	down	44.	before	54.	right
35.	what	45.	other	55.	two
36.	when	46.	were	56.	four
37.	why	47.	because	57.	goes
38.	where	48.	want	58.	does
39.	who	49.	saw	59.	made
40.	which	50.	put	60.	their

Rosemary Sassoon (1931–) is a British handwriting expert with a background in calligraphy and education. Sassoon Primary, a typeface for use in children's books and learning materials, started as a research project into children's understanding of letters. Young children were found to be highly articulate when asked to identify which alphabets were easiest for them to read and which features of letters and spacing they preferred. They were found to choose plain sans serif letters with a slight slant and with exit strokes on the baseline – characteristics that corresponded exactly with those that they were learning for their handwriting.

Sassoon designed the Sassoon Primary typeface in 1986 in response to these findings to improve the printed materials employed for teaching literacy in UK schools at the time. In addition to an overall slant, exit strokes are used throughout Sassoon Primary. These help the letters appear to link along the baseline, giving unity to words in a manner that mirrors handwritten cursive forms while maintaining the autonomy of each letter. Sassoon also implemented large, open counters with long ascenders and descenders to further accentuate differences in word shapes, making them easily recognizable. The arches of the letters reflect the movement of handwritten forms to help children read by identifying letter groups according to their similarities.

Educational publishers were quick to recognize the usefulness of a typeface that represented handwriting without being a strict pedagogical model, and Sassoon Primary spread rapidly around the world. With the arrival of computers in classrooms in the 1980s, Sassoon designed further alphabets for different educational requirements and to meet the needs of children of different ages and abilities.

Rosemary Sassoon's alphabets have now become a standard resource for publishers and educators, offering an extensive range of type styles appropriate to the needs of different age groups. Sassoon Primary is also widely popular with practitioners who have used it frequently to confer a sense of clarity, honesty and innocence on their designs.

Gerstner Original BQ

Ty	**Gerstner Original BQ**
Ca	**Sans Serif**
Ke	**Geometric**
Te	**Digital**
Da	**1987**
De	**Karl Gerstner**
Fo	**Berthold**
Co	**Switzerland**

Characteristics

High stroke contrast
B P R X 8 Open counterforms
C c S s e Angled terminals
E F J L S Narrow
G No spur
M N V W Curved stroke junctions
a g Single-storeyed
c r Ball terminals
f t Narrow with vertical terminals
i j Large round dots
t No foot

ABEGM
abcefghij
koprstw

Connections

Futura	1927
Peignot	1937
Replica	2008
Minuscule	2005

Availability

Not available

Specimen

Karl Gerstner: Designing Programmes, third edition. Lars Müller Publishers, Zurich, 2007 (250x178mm)

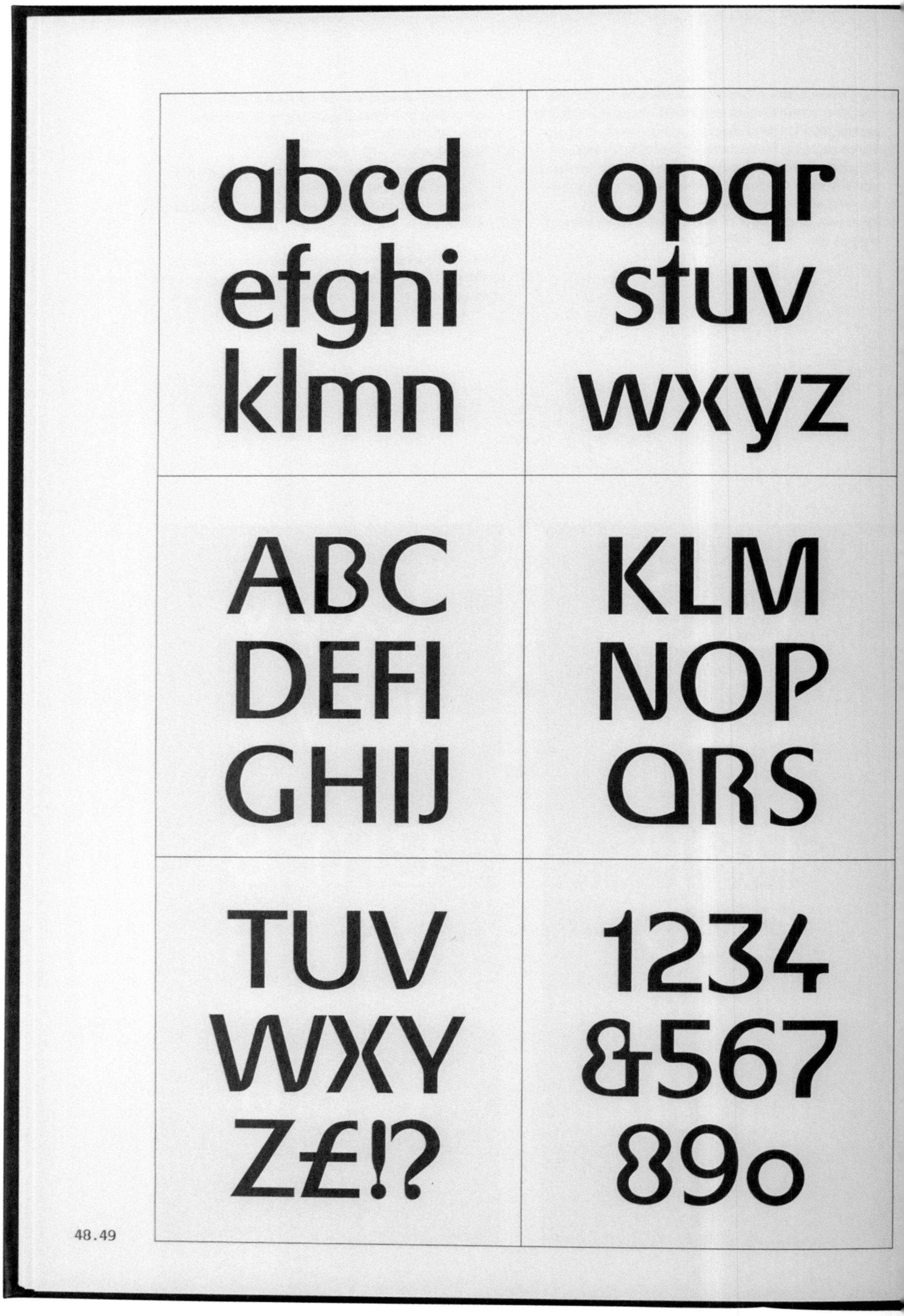

462

abcd efghi klmn opqr stuv wxyz ABC DEFI GHIJ KLM NOP QRS TUV WXY Z£!? 1234 &567 89o

48.49

IBM original bold/light/regular. Text by Vilém Flusser (Die Schrift, Immatrix Publication)

Der Versuch, dem hinter der Erfindung des Alphabets verborgenen Motiv nachzuspüren, hat scheinbar zwei verschiedene Antworten erhalten. Die eine besagt, die Absicht der Erfinder sei ikonoklastisch gewesen: nicht Bilder *(auch nicht Ideogramme)*, sondern Laute seien beim Schreiben zu bezeichnen, damit sich das Bewußtsein vom bildgebundenen magischen Denken befreie. Die andere Antwort besagt, die Absicht der Erfinder des Alphabets sei das Aufstellen eines linearen Diskurses gewesen: Beim Schreiben sollen Laute bezeichnet werden, damit ein folgerichtiges Sprechen statt dem mythischen, kreisenden Raunen in die Wege geleitet werde. Betrachtet man jedoch diese beiden Antworten näher, stellt man fest, daß beide dasselbe aussagen. Die Erfinder des Alphabets sahen in Bildermachern und in Mythagogen ihre Feinde, und sie machten mit Recht keinen Unterschied zwischen beiden. Bildermacherei und Bilderanbetungen *(Magie)* sowie das dunkle, kreisende Raunen *(Mythos)* sind die zwei Seiten derselben Münze. Das Motiv hinter der Erfindung des Alphabets war, das magisch-mythische *(„prähistorische")* Bewußtsein zu überholen und einem neuen *(„historischen")* Bewußtseine Raum zu gewähren. Das Alphabet wurde als Code des historischen Bewußtseins erfunden. Falls wir das Alphabet aufgeben sollten, dann wohl darum, weil wir unsererseits das historische Bewußtsein zu überholen bemüht sind. Wir sind des Fortschritts müde geworden, und nicht nur müde: Das historische Denken hat sich als wahnsinnig und mörderisch erwiesen. Das ist der wahre Grund *(und nicht die technischen Nachteile des Alphabets)*, weshalb wir bereit sind, diesen Code aufzugeben.

Karl Gerstner (1930–2017) was an eminent typographer and graphic artist whose work was characterized by the use of analytical methods in the design of visual communications. He was also well known for his long-standing interest in sans serif typefaces, particularly Akzidenz-Grotesk, which he used throughout his career.

In 1964 Gerstner made a detailed study of Akzidenz-Grotesk as the basis for a rational type system. This was later published by Berthold and named Gerstner Programme. Speculating on the future of the alphabet at that time he wrote that the sans serif 'does not represent the final stage' of its own evolution. Around 20 years later the opportunity arose to test this proposition in the design of a new corporate typeface for IBM. Gerstner regarded Futura as the highest 'intermediate stage' in the progression of the sans serif and decided to develop a new geometric form that would move the paradigm forward. The new sans serif would show no influences of handwriting whatsoever but would integrate the functional qualities of traditional types, such as the differentiation of horizontal and vertical stroke widths in order to facilitate the flow of reading.

The result, IBM Original, anticipates the automated, interpolated type design methods that followed a few years later with the advent of personal computing. It is the product of an analytical development process compensated by means of optical and ergonomic interventions. In the vertical axis, IBM Original divides into 15 equal sections. The x-height occupies exactly eight of these sections, the ascender uses four and the descender three. Capital heights fall one section below the ascenders. IBM Original's letter contours are logically constructed using a number of individual strategies. Greater stroke contrast is evident than in most sans serifs and letter proportions are variable; both of these features conforming loosely to an old-style model. To decrease the bulk that would otherwise accumulate, counterforms are left open wherever possible, and strokes that meet at angled junctions are truncated. In the progression of the typeface's four weights, strokes increase in a fixed ratio of 1:1.25, resulting in absolute consistency.

IBM rejected Gerstner's proposal, choosing Bodoni instead. The Berthold foundry released a digital version of the typeface in 1987, naming it Gerstner Original BQ. The designer himself went on to republish the typeface as KG Vera and later overhauled it as KG Privata for use in his own project work. Although it may not represent the new paradigm Gerstner had hoped to achieve, it remains an ambitious investigation into the potential of the sans serif.

Ty	**Stone**
Ca	**Serif / Sans Serif**
Ke	**Superfamily**
Te	**Digital**
Da	**1987**
De	**Sumner Stone**
Fo	**Adobe**
Co	**USA**

Characteristics

Stone Serif:
a Double-storeyed, large bowl
a c f Top serifs are rounded trapezoids
f r t Narrow
g Double-storeyed with upturned ear
k Thin top serif, no foot serif
t Crossbar not bracketed to stem

Stone Sans:
C c S s e g r Angled terminals
G No spur, no arm
K Angled leg and arm
R Angled leg
V W X Y angled top stem
a Double-storeyed, large bowl
g Single-storeyed
v w x y Angled stem

ABCabce
fgijkorsty
ABCabce
fgijkorsty

Connections

Romulus	1936
Syntax	1969
FF Scala	1991
Thesis	1994

Availability
ITC Stone is available from Linotype and resellers

Specimen
Sumner Stone and Brian Wu, *On Stone: The Art and Use of Typography on the Personal Computer*. Bedford Arts, San Francisco, 1991 (333x259mm)

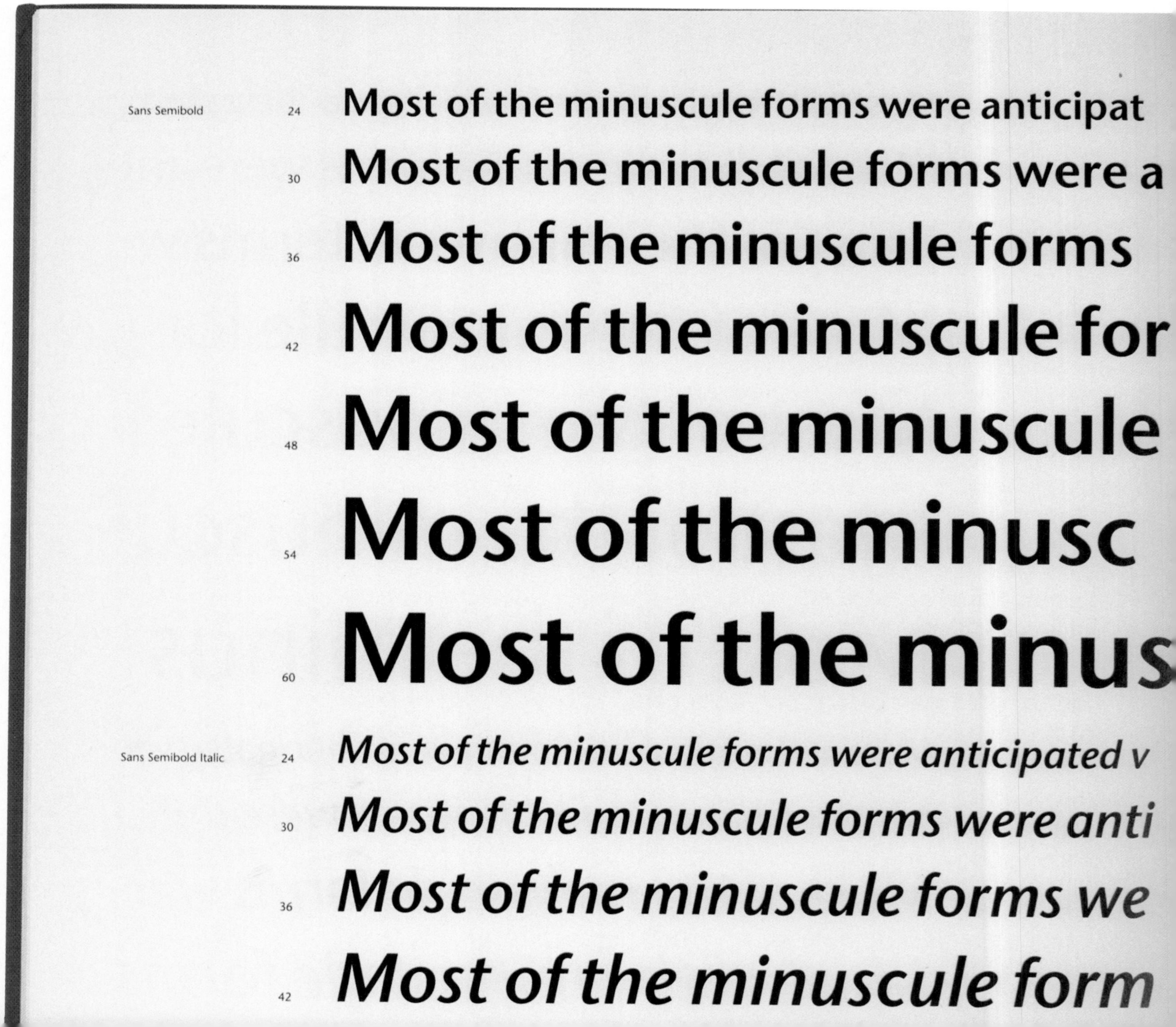

Sans Semibold

24 Most of the minuscule forms were anticipat

30 Most of the minuscule forms were a

36 Most of the minuscule forms

42 Most of the minuscule for

48 Most of the minuscule

54 Most of the minusc

60 Most of the minus

Sans Semibold Italic

24 Most of the minuscule forms were anticipated v

30 Most of the minuscule forms were anti

36 Most of the minuscule forms we

42 Most of the minuscule form

American type designer Sumner Stone (1945–) created the first original typeface for the PostScript page-description language at Adobe Systems. His Stone type family, released in 1987, was also one of the most ambitious, well-coordinated superfamilies ever designed and an emphatic proof of PostScript's potential.

Stone, who originally trained as a mathematician, took a strategic approach to creating the new typeface. The Stone series includes three subfamilies: serif, sans serif and informal, each of which was configured to be perfectly compatible with the others while still able to

function independently as a distinctive and competent type style. This, Stone anticipated, would make the family useful to both experienced and novice designers. His approach to achieving a coherent design was to base all of Stone's styles on a common core. They share the same capital height, the same lower case x-height and the same central stems. In Sumner Stone's words: 'Each design is a manifestation of an underlying skeletal set of letterforms.'

The Stone types were structured to take advantage of PostScript and configured to work as effectively at small sizes on low-

resolution personal printers as they did on high-end imagesetters. Stone Serif is in three weights: medium, semibold and bold, with matching italics. It is a hybrid that integrates features from various influences. The general proportions and overall structure are similar to those of traditional old-style faces. However, letter contours are designed specifically for the new technology with a low stroke contrast, large x-height and open counterforms.

The italics have a moderate slant and follow the basic design of the roman letters. Humanist sans serifs like Gill Sans (pp238–39) and Syntax (pp392–93)

influenced the design of Stone Sans. It is a sturdy sans serif whose weights, styles and classical proportions are based on those of the serif form. The capitals have the proportions of ancient Roman inscriptions, and the lower case letters are modelled along old-style lines, with a calligraphic stroke contrast.

Stone Informal (not shown) was intended for business correspondence and reveals few historical influences other than from those specialized typefaces used to teach literacy to the young. It is the charmingly eccentric member of an otherwise highly assiduous family.

---

if Medium

24 Alphabetic forms are conventions; letters m

30 Alphabetic forms are conventions;

36 Alphabetic forms are convent

42 Alphabetic forms are con

48 Alphabetic forms are c

54 Alphabetic forms ar

60 Alphabetic forms

erif Medium Italic

24 *Alphabetic forms are conventions; letters must b*

30 *Alphabetic forms are conventions; lett*

36 *Alphabetic forms are convention*

42 *Alphabetic forms are conve*

Ty	**Avenir**
Ca	**Sans Serif**
Ke	**Geometric**
Te	**Digital**
Da	**1988**
De	**Adrian Frutiger**
Fo	**Linotype**
Co	**Germany**

Characteristics

	Capitals lower than ascender height
C c S s e	Angled terminals
G	No spur
M	Pointed apex at foot
Q	Flat tail on baseline
R	Small bowl, straight, angled leg
a	Double-storeyed, straight stem
f r t	Narrow with vertical terminals
g	Single-storeyed
i j	Round dots
t	Flat top-stroke
y	Hooked tail

AGMQR
abcefghij
koprstuy

Connections

Futura	1927
Neuzeit-Grotesk	1928
Metro	1930
Gotham	2000

Availability

Avenir is available from Linotype and resellers

Specimen

Avenir type specimen sheet. Linotype, Bad Homburg, c1988 (210x297mm)

In the late 1980s Swiss type designer Adrian Frutiger (1928–2015) noticed a gap in the market for a contemporary version of the geometric sans serif form. He proposed the design of a new typeface to Linotype that would not only be appropriate at large sizes for display applications, like Avant Garde Gothic, but would also be suitable for use in bodies of text.

The name of the typeface, Avenir, means 'future', a word that tellingly nods in the direction of Paul Renner's renowned Futura (pp230–31) as well as its less widely known source of inspiration, Neuzeit-Grotesk (pp240–41). Frutiger's plans were ambitious. Intending Avenir to be a humanist interpretation of the geometric sans serif, he wanted, he said, to make 'an independent alphabet, one that belonged in the present'.

He began the project by drawing the lower case o because he considered it 'the first and most important letter'. Aware of the value of optical compensation in designing geometric characters, he undertook the task of developing a thin weight without the aid of a pair of compasses.

Although he designed over 100 typefaces over his long and illustrious career, Frutiger considered Avenir among his best work. 'It was the hardest typeface I have worked on in my life. Working on it, I always had human nature in mind … I'm proud that I was able to create Avenir.' The typeface is a true hybrid, a humanist geometric sans serif optically refined to provide an easy reading experience. While similarities with Futura can be observed, the lower case resembles Neuzeit-Grotesk and recalls many features of Frutiger's earlier eponymous humanist sans serif.

Avenir was originally released by Linotype in 1988 in three weights, each in a roman and oblique version, using a numbering system to identify them following the convention Frutiger had established previously for Univers (pp350–51). The series was later expanded to six weights, each in a roman and oblique version.

A

Mergenthaler Type Library   Typefaces / Schriften / Caractères

Avenir® 45
light/leicht/maigre

03173   12 pt Design

Sans Serif / Serifenlose Antiqua / Antiques
Adrian Frutiger 1988
Linotype

abcdefghijklmnop
qrstuvwxyz fiflß&
ABCDEFGHIJKLMN
OPQRSTUVWXYZ
1234567890
.,.:;-–—_'''„""·‹›«»*%%
!?¡¿()[]/†‡§$£¢ƒ
ÄÁÂÀÅÃĀÆÇČĚÉÊÈĒĞÏÍÎÌĪÑÖÓÔÒØ
ÕŌŒŠÜÚÛÙŪŽ äáâàåãāæ
çčěéêèēğïíîìīñöóôòøõōœšüúûùūž

Parameter for 10 pt / Parameter in 10 pt / Paramètre pour 10 pt

H 2.50 mm	k 2.66 mm	x 1.64 mm	p 0.81 mm	kp 3.47 mm	Ép 2
H 0.098 Inches	k 0.105 Inches	x 0.065 Inches	p 0.032 Inches	kp 0.137 Inches	Ép 0

Factor / Faktor / Facteur 1.00

* Given in pica point / Angaben in pica point / Toutes indications en points pica

△ 4.92 mm/14 pt* (5.25 mm^{DIN}) ▷ 0   H 3.50 mm

In every type design the basic characters

△ 5.62 mm/16 pt* (6.00 mm^{DIN}) ▷ 0   H 4.00 mm

Bei jeder Schriftgestaltung wird die

△ 6.33 mm/18 pt* (6.75 mm^{DIN}) ▷ 0   H 4.50 mm

Le style de chaque caractère d'i

△ 7.03 mm/20 pt* (7.50 mm^{DIN}) ▷ 0   H 5.00 mm

För alla nya stilar bestäms alf

△ 8.44 mm/24 pt* (9.00 mm^{DIN}) ▷ 0   H 5.99 mm

In elk letterontwerp wor

△ 9.84 mm/28 pt* (10.50 mm^{DIN}) ▷ 0   H 6.99 mm

Em todo o desenhos

△ 12.65 mm/36 pt* (13.50 mm^{DIN}) ▷ 0   H 8.99 mm

In ciascuna serie

△ 16.87 mm/48 pt* (18.00 mm^{DIN}) ▷ −1   H 11.99 mm

En cada tipo

△ 21.09 mm/60 pt* (22.50 mm^{DIN}) ▷ −1   H 14.99 mm

Den ensar

△ 25.31 mm/72 pt* (27.00 mm^{DIN}) ▷ −1   H 17.98 mm

Besterm

△ 29.52 mm/84 pt* (31.50 mm^{DIN}) ▷ −1   H 20.98 mm

Muotie

6
7
8
9
10
11
12
14
16
18
20
24
28
36
48
60
72
84

/6 pt* (2.25 mm^{DIN})   ▽ 2.50 mm (7 pt*)   ▷ +1   H 1.50 mm

klmnopqrstuvwxyz abcdefghijklmnopqrstuvwxyz abcdefghijklmnop 1234567890
be design the basic character is determined by the uniform design characteristics
s in the alphabet. However, this alone does not determine the standard of the type
e quality of composition set with it. The appearance is something complex which
f out of many details, like form, proportionen, rhythm etc. If everything harmonizes
ARANCE IS SOMETHING COMPLEX WHICH FORMS ITSELF OUT OF MANY

n/7 pt* (2.63 mm)   ▽ 2.75 mm (8 pt*)   ▷ +1   H 1.75 mm

hijklmnopqrstuvwxyz abcdefghijklmnopqrstuvwxyz abcd 1234567890
Schriftgestaltung wird der Grundcharakter eines Alphabets von einhe
ormmerkmalen der Buchstaben bestimmt. Er allein besagt noch nichts
Niveau einer Druckschrift und die Qualität des Satzgefüges. Das Ersch
ild ist etwas Komplexes, das sich aus vielen Einzelheiten, wie Form, Pr
ND PROPORTIONEN SIND DIE WICHTIGSTEN KRITERIEN BEIM BI

n/8 pt* (3.00 mm^{DIN})   ▽ 3.25 mm (9.25 pt*)   ▷ 0   H 2.00 mm

hijklmnopqrstuvwxyz abcdefghijklmnopqrstuvwx 1234567890
de chaque caractère d'imprimerie se détermine par des caracté
s qui sont les mêmes pour toutes les lettres de l'alphabet. Dans
rapports formels et autres relations il s'agit de phénomènes opt
éductibles aux règles mathématiques et que seule pourra perc
E PART MALGRÉ TOUTES LES RESSOURCES DE MECANIS

n/9 pt* (3.38 mm^{DIN})   ▽ 3.50 mm (10 pt*)   ▷ 0   H 2.25 mm

ghijklmnopqrstuvwxyz abcdefghijklmnopq 1234567890
y type design the basic character is determined by the un
esign characteristics of all letters in the alphabet. Howev
alone does not determine the standard of the typeface
e quality of composition set with it. The appearance is so
PPEARANCE IS SOMETHING COMPLEX WHICH FO

n/10 pt* (3.75 mm^{DIN})   ▽ 4.00 mm (11.5 pt*)   ▷ 0   H 2.50 mm

fghijklmnopqrstuvwxyz abcdefghijkl 1234567890
der Schriftgestaltung wird der Grundcharakter eine
bets von einheitlichen Formmerkmalen der Buchst
bestimmt. Er allein besagt noch nichts über das Niv
ner Druckschrift und die Qualität des Satzgefüges
M UND PROPORTIONEN SIND DIE WICHTIGST

m/11 pt* (4.13 mm^{DIN})   ▽ 4.50 mm (12.75 pt*)   ▷ 0   H 2.75 mm

efghijklmnopqrstuvwxyz abcdefg 1234567890
le de chaque caractère d'imprimerie se déter
par des caractéristiques qui sont les mêmes po
tes les lettres de l'alphabet. Dans tous les rapp
TRE PART MALGRÉ TOUTES LES RESSOUR

m/12 pt* (4.50 mm^{DIN})   ▽ 4.75 mm (13.5 pt*)   ▷ 0   H 3.00 mm

efghijklmnopqrstuvwxyz abc 1234567890
ery type design the basic character is deter
d by the uniform design characteristics of
tters in the alphabet. However, this alone di
APPEARANCE IS SOMETHING COMPL

Ty	**Rotis**
Ca	**Serif / Sans Serif**
Ke	**Superfamily**
Te	**Photocomposition**
Da	**1988**
De	**Otl Aicher**
Fo	**Agfa**
Co	**Germany**

Characteristics

Four separate typefaces: sans serif, semi sans serif, semi serif, serif

Common character construction

Based on condensed elliptical forms

C c Hooked upper finial

e Extremely high bar and small eye

g Single-storeyed in sans serif, double-storeyed in serif

ABC abeg
ABC abeg
ABC abeg
ABC abeg

Connections	
Univers Condensed	1957
Frutiger Condensed	1975
Lucida family	1985
Thesis	1994

Availability

Rotis is available from Monotype and resellers

Specimen

Otl Aicher, *Typographie*, facsimile of 1989 edition. Hermann Schmidt Verlag, Mainz, 2005 (295x275mm)

Es ist schon ein großer Unterschied, ob man Schriften beurteilt nach der formalen Schönheit ihres Alphabets oder nach ihrem Gebrauch, in ihrer Anwendung etwa als Buch oder Zeitung. Hat man große Schriften vor sich, etwa in einem Plakat oder in einer Anzeige, wird man geneigt sein, die Schrift nur nach einzelnen Buchstaben, das heißt also nach der ästhetischen Qualität des einzelnen Zeichens zu bewerten und nicht nach ihrer Leistung, das Lesen zu erleichtern (oder auch zu erschweren).

Für den Typographen gilt als wichtigster Maßstab, wie gut kann man eine Schrift lesen. Die Lesequalitäten sind

die rotis-schriftfamilie hat vier schnitte oder charaktere: eine grotesk, eine semigrotesk, eine semiantiqua und eine antiqua. auf einen einzelnen buchstaben bezogen, ergeben sich unterschiede wie bei dem gemeinen h auf der rechten seite oben. der schnitt der rotis-grotesk hat in der grundstruktur dieselbe gestalt wie die anderen schnitte. nur ist die strichstärke gleich stark. es gibt lediglich feine nuancen beim berühren und einlaufen von strichen.

The Rotis family has four faces or members, namely a Grotesque, a semi-Grotesque, a semi-Roman and a Roman. The same letters in different faces differ as exemplified by the small h, top right. The Rotis Grotesque face has the same basic structure as the other faces. But stroke strength is uniform. There are merely subtle variations where strokes commence and touch.

der ideologische krieg zwischen den vertretern der grotesk-schriften und den ve fechtern der klassischen antiqua erschei überholt. auf der einen seite verfocht m eine bessere lesbarkeit, wie sie ohne zwe der antiqua eigen ist, wegen ihrer unterschiedlichen stärke bei den vertikalen u horizontalen strichen. auf der anderen s vertrat man eine formale qualität der ei fachheit und den verzicht auf historisch zufälligkeiten, wie die serifen. beide sta punkte haben etwas für sich.

so ergab sich die frage, ob es eine sch geben kann, die die schmucklose qualitä grotesk besitzt, andererseits die lesequal der antiqua, die auf der unterschiedliche strichstärke beruht. gibt es eine serifenl antiqua oder, was dasselbe wäre, eine gro mit unterschiedlichen grund- und haarstrichen?

in dieser richtung gab es in letzter ze verschiedene versuche. die hier vorgeleg rotis-schrift will diese absicht in einer g brauchsschrift verwirklichen, die auch f den buch- und zeitungsdruck geeignet

links ein grotesk-schnitt der rotis-fa lien, rechts die semigrotesk, ein zwischer schritt zwischen grotesk und antiqua. di zukunft dürfte dem rechten schnitt geh während man in zweifel ziehen darf, ob reine grotesk ihre aktualität erhalten wi ihr bild ist zu formalistisch und starr. da gen ist die semigrotesk differenzierter, a kulierter und in den wortbildern deutlic

The ideological warfare between the representatives of Grotesque faces and advocates of classical Roman type see to have ended. One side advocated bett legibility, a quality that is undeniably bodied in Roman type with its variatio between vertical and horizontal stroke strengths. The other argued for formal simplicity and the eschewal of historic features such as serifs. There is someth to be said for both stances.

The question thus presented itself whether a typeface could be found that bines the unadorned quality of Grotesq with the legibility of Roman, founded its variations in stroke strength. Is a sa serif Roman type conceivable or, on th other hand, a Grotesque with differenti weighted main and hairline strokes?

There have been several attempts recently to find out. Rotis type seeks to fulfil these requirements in a functiona type also appropriate for letterpress an newspaper printing.

Left, a Grotesque version of the Roti family; right, semi-Grotesque, somewh between Grotesque and Roman. The fu of the right-hand face is virtually assur whereas it may be open to doubt wheth the undiluted Grotesque will remain a force. Its appearance is too rigid and fo mal. The semi-Grotesque, by contrast, more complex, expressive and distinct.

Rotis was created in 1988 by Otl Aicher (1922–91), a leading German graphic designer of his generation. It is one of the first superfamilies, a coordinated type system consisting of four separate subgroups: a sans serif, a modulated semi sans, a serif and a semi serif typeface. Aicher's goal was to design a systematic collection of types that could serve almost any typographic purpose. He believed that consistency could be achieved by using differences in the choice of character contours within bodies of text to communicate differences of meaning, while preserving an even overall tone and a shared design space at the same time.

He intended to achieve maximum legibility through a highly unified yet differentiated system in which all four variant faces could be interchanged seamlessly.

'He thought lines of text should form an even block of tone', Robin Kinross has written. On this basis, Rotis cannot be said to be very effective. The four families, consisting of 17 variants including corresponding italics, are so similar in shape and proportion and therefore so lacking in contrast that they are not easy to distinguish from one another on the page. However, taken individually, some features of the subfamilies have merit. While the

serif group is somewhat awkward, and the semi serif is wilfully peculiar, Rotis Sans and SemiSans are generally well-balanced typefaces that have become extremely popular in their own right, notably in brand communications. The Rotis typefaces are unusually condensed overall, a characteristic that is of particular use in typesetting for the German language.

Despite its rich personality and its undoubted popularity, Rotis is not held in high regard by all. As Erik Spiekermann has asked, 'Isn't the truth about Rotis that it has some great letters, but they never come together in one typeface?'

h h h

schon ein großer Unterschied, ob man Schriften
teilt nach der formalen Schönheit ihres Alphabets
nach ihrem Gebrauch, in ihrer Anwendung etwa
uch oder Zeitung. Hat man große Schriften vor sich,
in einem Plakat oder in einer Anzeige, wird man
igt sein, die Schrift nur nach einzelnen Buchstaben,
eißt also nach der ästhetischen Qualität des einzel-
Zeichens zu bewerten und nicht nach ihrer Leistung,
esen zu erleichtern (oder auch zu erschweren).
r den Typographen gilt als wichtigster Maßstab, wie
ann man eine Schrift lesen. Die Lesequalitäten sind

Es ist schon ein großer Unterschied, ob man Schriften
beurteilt nach der formalen Schönheit ihres Alphabets
oder nach ihrem Gebrauch, in ihrer Anwendung etwa
als Buch oder Zeitung. Hat man große Schriften vor sich,
etwa in einem Plakat oder in einer Anzeige, wird man
geneigt sein, die Schrift nur nach einzelnen Buchstaben,
das heißt also nach der ästhetischen Qualität des einzelnen Zeichens zu bewerten und nicht nach ihrer Leistung,
das Lesen zu erleichtern (oder auch zu erschweren).
Für den Typographen gilt als wichtigster Maßstab, wie
gut kann man eine Schrift lesen. Die Lesequalitäten sind

stärken der rotis-semigrotesk. die
fetteren schnitte dienen der auszeich-
nd hervorhebung, etwa bei plakaten
eln.

ur weights of Rotis semi-Grotesque.
o bolder faces are designed for em-
in, for instance, posters and head-

Es ist schon ein großer Unterschied, ob man Schriften
beurteilt nach der formalen Schönheit ihres Alphabets
oder nach ihrem Gebrauch, in ihrer Anwendung etwa
als Buch oder Zeitung. Hat man große Schriften vor sich,
etwa in einem Plakat oder in einer Anzeige, wird man
geneigt sein, die Schrift nur nach einzelnen Buchstaben,
das heißt also nach der ästhetischen Qualität des einzelnen Zeichens zu bewerten und nicht nach ihrer Leistung,
das Lesen zu erleichtern (oder auch zu erschweren).
Für den Typographen gilt als wichtigster Maßstab, wie
gut kann man eine Schrift lesen. Die Lesequalitäten sind

t schon ein großer Unterschied, ob man Schriften
teilt nach der formalen Schönheit ihres Alphabets
nach ihrem Gebrauch, in ihrer Anwendung etwa
uch oder Zeitung. Hat man große Schriften vor sich,
a in einem Plakat oder in einer Anzeige, wird man
eigt sein, die Schrift nur nach einzelnen Buchstaben,
heißt also nach der ästhetischen Qualität des einzel-
Zeichens zu bewerten und nicht nach ihrer Leistung,
Lesen zu erleichtern (oder auch zu erschweren).

Belizio

Ty	**Belizio**
Ca	**Slab Serif**
Ke	**Modern, Clarendon**
Te	**Digital**
Da	**1989**
De	**David Berlow**
Fo	**Font Bureau**
Co	**USA**

Characteristics

Vertical stress
Moderate stroke contrast
Wide body
Moderate x-height
Long ascenders and short descenders
Heavy, bracketed slab serifs
Q Sweeping, curved tail
R a t Tail turns upwards
a c f g r y Ball terminals
g Double-storeyed, raised ear

AGMQR
abcfghij
koprstuy

Connections

Clarendon	1845
Craw Clarendon	1955
Egizio	1955
Sentinel	2009

Availability

Belizio is available from Font Bureau and resellers

Specimen

Font Bureau Type Specimens, third edition.
The Font Bureau, 2001 (268x180mm)

BARBEQUE
BLACK

Backyard grill full of blazing hot charcoal
REGULAR

Tasty meals in tin foil
MEDIUM ITALIC

OUCH
BOLD

Fire appears to make things remarkably warm
REGULAR ITALIC

Realizations
MEDIUM

I SHOULD RECORD THIS DISCOVERY
BOLD

Strict Documentation
REGULAR

Heads of the Scientific Universities
REGULAR ITALIC

Textbook
BOLD ITALIC

THE ACADEMIC CIRCUIT
MEDIUM

HAILED AS A STUNNING BREAKTHROUGH
MEDIUM ITALIC

Proof Provided
BLACK ITALIC

The eight-part Belizio series updates the first Font Bureau typeface. David Berlow's family is based on Aldo Novarese's Egizio, designed in 1955 for Nebiolo. It was first prompted by the popularity of Haas Clarendon designed by Hoffmann and Eidenbenz, an impeccably Swiss revival of the traditional English letterform. Aldo Novarese was among the first to investigate a true italic designed in the Clarendon style; FB 1987–98

8 STYLES: REGULAR, MEDIUM, BOLD, AND BLACK, ALL WITH ITALICS

52

BELIZIO

REGULAR WITH ITALIC AND BOLD 9 *point*

GRUMPY WIZARDS MAKE 19 TOXIC *BREWS FOR THESE EVIL QUEENS &* jack. Lazy mover quit hardest packing of the papier-mâché jewelry boxes. Back at my quaint garden: jaunty zinnias vie with flaunting phlox. *Hark! 4,872 toxic jungle water vipers quietly drop on zebras for meals!* New farm hand (picking just six quinces) proves strong but lazy. For only about $65, jolly housewives made 'inexpensive' meals using quick-frozen vegetables. Jaded zombies acted quaintly but kept driving their 31 oxen forward. At my grand prix, J. Blatz was equally vilified for his funky ways. **My grandfather spent his whole day quickly carving wax buzzards, most from junk.** When we go back to Juarez, Mexico, do we fly over picturesque Arizona? Murky haze enveloped a city as jarring quakes broke these forty-six windows. Pack my box with five dozen liquor jugs. Will Major Douglas be expected to take this true/false quiz or

MEDIUM WITH ITALIC AND BLACK 9 *point*

GRUMPY WIZARDS MADE A TOXIC *BREW FOR THE EVIL QUEEN & JACK.* Lazy mover quit hard packing of papier mâché jewelry boxes. Back at my quaint garden: jaunty zinnias vie with flaunting phlox. *Hark! 4,872 toxic jungle water vipers quietly drop on the zebras for meals!* New farm hand (picking just six quinces) proves strong but lazy. For only $65, jolly housewives made 'inexpensive' meals using quick-frozen vegetables. **Jaded zombies acted quaintly but kept driving their 31 oxen forward.** At my grand prix, J. Blatz was equally vilified for his funky ways. My ancient grandfather spent this day quickly carving wax buzzards, mostly from junk. When we go back into Juarez, Mexico, do we fly over picturesque Texas? Murky haze enveloped a city as jarring quakes broke forty-six windows. Pack my

BOLD WITH ITALIC 9.5 *point*

GRUMPY WIZARDS MAKE MANY TOXIC BREWS FOR THOSE EVIL queens and jacks. Lazy mover quit her hard packing of the papier-mâché jewelry boxes. Back at my nice quaint garden: jaunty zinnias vie with flaunting phlox. Hark! 4,872 toxic jungle water vipers quietly drop on the zebras for meals! *New farm hand (picking just six quinces) proves strong but lazy.* **For only about $65, jolly house wives made 'inexpensive' meals using quick-frozen vegetables. Jade zombie was acting quaintly but kept driving those 31 oxen forward. At my grand prix, M. Blatz was equally vilified for his funky ways. My old grandfather spent his day quickly carving wax buzzards, mostly from junk. But when we go back to Juarez, Mexico, must we fly over picturesque Arizona? Murky**

BLACK WITH ITALIC 10 *point*

GRUMPY WIZARDS DO MAKE TOXIC BREWS FOR THE EVIL queen and jack. Lazy mover quit hard packing of the papier-mâché jewelry boxes. Back at my quaint garden: jaunty zinnias vied with 68 flaunting phlox. Hark! 4,872 toxic jungle water vipers quietly drop on these zebras for meals! *New farm hand (picking just sixty quinces) proves strong but lazy.* **For only $1 jolly housewives made inexpensive meals using quick-frozen vegetable. Jaded zombies acted quaintly but kept driving their 31 oxen forward. At my grand prix, Mr. Blatz will be equally vilified for his funky ways. My grandfather spent his day quick carving wax buzzards, mostly out of junk. If we go back to Juarez, can I**

ABCDEFGHIJKLMNOPQRSTUVWXYZabcdefghijklmnopqrstuvwxyzßfiflffffiffl
¶§#$£¥ƒ€0123456789%‰¢°ªº=<>+×÷–'"/¿?¡!&(/)[\]{|}*.,:;...""''·„„«»<>_-–—•†‡@®©℗™√✠

áàâãäåæçéèêëíìîïñóòôöõøœúùûüÿÀÁÂÃÄÅÆÇÉÈÊËÍÌÎÏÑÓÒÔÖÕØŒÚÙÛÜŸ

Special character ✠

Belizio was the first typeface released by Font Bureau, the American type foundry that has since become world renowned for its intelligent digital revivals of classic typefaces. It was drawn by David Berlow (1954–) in 1987 and published in 1989.

Belizio is a slab serif typeface in the Clarendon tradition (pp132–33), available in four weights with matching italics. It is a digital reinterpretation of Aldo Novarese's Egizio, cut in 1955 for the Nebiolo foundry. Egizio, in turn, had been made as a response to the success of Haas Clarendon, designed in Swizerland by Hoffmann and Eidenbenz in 1953. Their scrupulously analytical reappraisal of the nineteenth-century English Clarendon form precipitated a popular trend for the style in design work of the 1950s and 1960s as almost all foundries sought to cut their own versions. Like its predecessors, Belizio has strong but highly refined contours, with a considerable contrast between thick and thin strokes. It is identified by the curving, bracketed serifs that are characteristic of the Clarendon style.

Aldo Novarese was among the first to investigate the design of a true italic to correspond with the upright Clarendon. However, his Egizio Corsiva Nero, cut for Nebiolo in 1958, was completed as a somewhat awkward mixture of cursive and roman forms. In reviving Egizio, David Berlow went to considerable lengths to resolve the italic's anomalies – though the curious italic x survives in Belizio as a delightfully ungainly remnant.

...ers to get their typefaces known and ...anufacturer would be able to compete ...f immediate proliferation. Or we could ...aphic awareness of computer users ...ld by creating a font virus that would ...n every Helvetica into something much ...-the Post-modern typographer's re- ...es that travel around the world in a sin- ...e designers getting paid by buying net- ...we could hand out our fonts at confer- ...gs, but after a while the files will turn ...ilk. A perfectly good font would turn ...e. A great way to force people to even- ...timate copy. And you better hurry, or ...ll affect your other fonts as well!

...se a typeface that deteriorates over ...urning into a Beowolf-like face, ...l out of its users. We could create ...r out through frequent use, com- ...eature that uses up certain often ...ou want real letterpress quality? ...How about a font that adds typos? ...of typos to a particular time of the ...te an erratic (human) typesetter, ...es not work over time.

...e data into our typefaces we can ...y intelligent fonts. Some applica- ...quite practical. For instance, the ...de the information to create auto- ...that would switch on or off auto- ...specified by the user, depending ...e type or printing technique used. ...odify its outline when it is to be

those who subscribe to the ideas and phi- losophies of Swiss Design or Modernism, have argued that logos and typefaces should appear consistent to establish rec- ognition. We don't think that this is nec- essary. Creating a random logo for a company, with letterheads and forms on which the logo would move around and change, does not necessarily decrease rec- ognizability. Recognition does not come from simple repetition of the same form, but is something much more intelligent, something that happens in our minds. When you hear somebody's voice on the phone and he or she has a cold, you can still recognize who is talking. We can recognize handwriting, and even deci- pher how quickly a note was written, and sometimes pick up on the state of mind the person was in when writing the note. Randomness and change can add new dimensions to printwork. Randomness within typography is not a revolutionary idea either. Ty- pographers have always had to deal with randomness because type has always lacked standardization and consistency. One example is the measurement of type. With hot met- al type everybody measured the body size of a typeface. With phototype and digital type, there is no body to be measured. Some people like to

...are performed inter o centimeters will inevi- put as 2.00001 or 1.9999 It never works precisely. s will always exist. initely not going to be set of standards for pography. Maybe ran- an inevitable result of avior. Gutenberg's let- at looking slightly dif- time they were print- wore out, some got the impression onto red. However, overall results had a vibrant ne quality. At some g the history of the de- of type and typogra- aphic design industry it it was necessary to pon the "quality" of d type. In the process, omic and commercial ns, much vitality was ieve that the computer, onsidered by many to impersonal, can bring of these lost qualities. t is our contribution

type

Ty	**Beowolf**
Ca	**Serif**
Ke	**Old Style, Geometric**
Te	**Digital**
Da	**1989**
De	**Erik van Blokland and Just van Rossum**
Fo	**FontFont**
Co	**Netherlands**

Characteristics

Letterforms based on old-style character construction

Internal programme allows individual contours to be deranged and distorted

Randglov
Randglov
Randglov

Connections

Preissig	1925
Manuskript Antikva	1944
FF Trixie	1991
FF BeoSans	1992

Availability

Beowolf is available from FontFont and resellers

Specimen

Emigre 18: 'Type-Site'. Emigre, Berkeley, 1991 (485x283mm)

Dutch type designers Erik van Blokland (1967–) and Just van Rossum (1966–) of the LettError foundry created Beowolf in 1989, the earliest days of digital typography. Originally named Randomfont, the project was a landmark in digital type design because it was the first time that graphic designers had manipulated a typeface as a flexible code.

Working with an adaptation of an old-style typeface constructed only from straight lines, the duo substituted standard PostScript commands with their own routines defining parameters for letters to be generated randomly at the typesetting stage. With each new keystroke, every point in every letter placed on the page would shift automatically, giving a fragmentary, agitated appearance. Van Blokland and Van Rossum created three versions of Beowolf, with increasing levels of distortion.

Beowolf was not a fixed alphabet but a collection of infinitely fluctuating objects incorporating chance and unpredictability. This challenged the certainty of the conventional relationship between what users typed and what the computer produced. Viewing the historical standardization of letterforms that resulted from composition in metal not as a typographic ideal but merely as a technological phase in a longer cultural narrative, Van Rossum explained: 'The industrial methods meant that all the letters had to be identical, but with the new digital technology, data and code the uniformity of type was not essential any more. The only limitations are in our expectations.'

Beowolf was one of the first typefaces released by the newly launched FontFont foundry in 1990, enjoying considerable success until printer technologies advanced at the end of the decade, making its PostScript algorithms inoperable. LettError re-engineered Beowolf for OpenType in 2007. The updated version achieved the same effect as the original random method by different means, instead generating one of ten alternative shapes for each glyph in the typeface, sequentially randomized by an OpenType programming feature. Van Blokland and Van Rossum's new version of Beowolf was itself generated programmatically as a family of four styles consisting of almost 90,000 glyphs.

Ty	**Found Fount / Bits**
Ca	**N/A**
Ke	**N/A**
Te	**N/A**
Da	**1989**
De	**Paul Elliman**
Fo	**Paul Elliman**
Co	**UK**

Characteristics

No glyph is ever repeated
Glyphs as objects
Glyphs as photographic images of objects
Glyphs as vectored images of objects

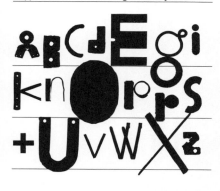

Connections

Abraham de Balmes' Alphabet	1523
Nude Alphabet	1970
The Alphabet	2001
Lÿno	2010

Availability

Not available. A digital prototype, Bits, was published in 1995 in *Fuse* 15: 'Cities'.

Specimen

Paul Elliman, *Qwertype*, 2015

Paul Elliman's Found Fount is the realization of his statement that he 'always mixed up words like typography, topography and typology'. Elliman (1961–) is a graphic artist based in London whose work explores typography, language and the man-made environment. Found Fount consists of a huge collection of rubbish – small discarded objects discovered on the street, in trashcans or in industrial waste – that he uses, without any modification, to represent linguistic signs.

Begun in 1989 and originally named Bits, the Found Fount project fulfils a number of conditions. Elliman's principal aim is to create a usable writing system in which no symbol is ever used more than once. This requires an infinite quantity of signs and therefore an infinite number of objects that must be collected, categorized and systematically catalogued. This influences the range of possible sizes that can be included in the system. Every object must be consistent – small enough, Elliman says, 'to fit in the mouth or be passed from hand to hand, like money'.

All of the elements in Found Fount exist as objects in the world but they can also be translated into two-dimensional representations of themselves as photographs, scans or drawings, and thus recycled either as images or distilled to linear form and converted into digital type. The project was first published as a PostScript typeface in 1995 when it was released in *Fuse* 15: 'Cities', an issue of a seminal journal of experimental typography published by Neville Brody (pp488–89). An expanded version of the typeface was subsequently released through Lineto in 2003, and Elliman has since investigated OpenType technology to generate a continually expandable system. However, more recently he has chosen to present the collection as typological arrangements in exhibition installations.

The Found Fount project questions the nature of representation in language, exploring Elliman's proposition that 'Writing gives the impression of things', and that, 'Conversely, things can give the impression of writing'. By crossing the boundary between the construction of artefacts and the construction of language, Found Fount describes the world using the world itself, perfectly illustrating Henri Lefebvre's notion of the city as a 'found object created by its citizens'. It reflects Elliman's belief that literacy is a universal attribute of human nature and culture. 'Even if we could imagine a world without words,' he has written, 'it would be held together by a kind of typography … The structures and formats of an irrepressibly modern world, configured around unit-shifting patterns of production, display and consumption.'

		Characteristics	
Ty	**Adobe Garamond**	Oblique stress	
Ca	**Serif**	Moderate stroke contrast	
Ke	**Old Style, French**	Capitals lower than ascender height	
Te	**Digital**	**A** Cupped apex	
Da	**1989**	**J** Descends below baseline	
De	**Robert Slimbach**	**M** Slightly splayed	
Fo	**Adobe**	**Q** Tail below letter	
Co	**USA**	**R** Curved leg	
		W Crossed centre-strokes	
		a Double-storeyed, straight mid-stroke	
		f Extended arch	
		g Double-storeyed, large lower bowl	

AMQRW
abcdefghij
orstuy*aefg*

Connections

Garamond's Roman	c1538
Sabon	1967
Adobe Minion	1990
Adobe Jenson	1996

Availability

Adobe Garamond is available from Adobe and resellers

Specimen

Adobe Originals Garamond specimen. Adobe Systems Inc., San Jose, 1989 (228x144mm)

Regular

At the gates of the forest, the surprised man of the world is forced to leave his city estimates of great and small, wise and foolish. The knapsack of custom falls off his back with the first step he makes into these precincts. Here is sanc-

16.17

At the gates of the forest, the surprised man of the world is forced to leave his city estimates of great and small, wise and foolish. The knapsack of custom falls off his back with the first step he makes into these precincts. Here is sanctity which

18.19

At the gates of the forest, the surprised man of the world is forced to leave his city estimates of great and small, wise and foolish. The knapsack of custom falls off his back with the first step he makes into these precincts. Here is sanctity which

20.21

Below,
Regular capitals
Titling Capitals
30.32

24.25

Regular

At the gates of the forest, the surprised man of the world is forced to leave his city estimates of great and small, wise and foolish. The knapsack of custom falls off his back with the first step he makes into

30.31

At the gates of the forest, the surprised man of the world is forced to leave his city estimates of great and small, wise and foolish. The knap-

Below,
Titling
Capitals
42

AT THE GATES OF THE
AT THE GATES OF THE

AT THE GATES

The technologies that arrived in the final quarter of the twentieth century prompted a tidal wave of revivals. A huge number of types from earlier technological eras, from letterpress through to photocomposition, have been referenced, reinterpreted or copied directly for new digital typefaces over the past three decades. Adobe's first historical revival, Adobe Garamond, is among the best of these.

Adobe Garamond is Robert Slimbach's (1956–) digital interpretation of the roman types of Claude Garamond (pp48–49) combined with the italics of Robert Granjon (pp58–59). Slimbach's design is based on a profound understanding of its historical sources, drawing inspiration from original sixteenth-century originals in the collections of the Plantin-Moretus Museum in Antwerp.

The design for Adobe Garamond began in 1988 and progressed over a year. Slimbach began by studying Garamond reproductions, selecting Garamond's 'vraye parangonne' size – approximately 18 point – from a facsimile of the well-known Egenolff-Berner specimen sheet of 1592 as the primary model for the roman design. He then prepared a set of trial drawings that were digitized and made into a working prototype.

In order to verify the authenticity of his design and its fidelity to its historical sources, Slimbach subsequently visited the Plantin-Moretus Museum to study Garamond's and Granjon's types and printed specimens at first hand. This research had a radical effect on the direction of the project. 'The experience of studying near flawless proofs of Garamond's and Granjon's types was a revelation', he reported later. He undertook a major overhaul of the roman design and redrew the italics from scratch.

With Adobe Garamond, Slimbach made a significant and enduring contribution to typography in the electronic age. He captured the delicacy and poise of the original Garamond and Granjon typefaces while creating a comprehensive typeface family that offers all the advantages of contemporary technology. Adobe Garamond is probably the most efficient and dependable of the many versions of Garamond available today – a classic rejuvenation of a classic original.

Regular

At the gates of the forest, the surprised man of the world is forced to leave his city estimates of great and small, wise and foolish. The knapsack of custom falls off his back with the first step he makes into these precincts. Here is sanctity which shames our religions, and reality which discredits our heroes. Here we find nature to be the circumstance which dwarfs every — 7.9

At the gates of the forest, the surprised man of the world is forced to leave his city estimates of great and small, wise and foolish. The knapsack of custom falls off his back with the first step he makes into these precincts. Here is sanctity which shames our religions, and reality which discredits our heroes. Here we — 8.10

At the gates of the forest, the surprised man of the world is forced to leave his city estimates of great and small, wise and foolish. The knapsack of custom falls off his back with the first step he makes into these precincts. Here is sanctity which shames our religions, and reality — 9.10

At the gates of the forest, the surprised man of the world is forced to leave his city estimates of great and small, wise and foolish. The knapsack of custom falls off his back with the first step he makes into these precincts. Here is sanctity which shames our religions, — 10.12

At the gates of the forest, the surprised man of the world is forced to leave his city estimates of great and small, wise and foolish. The knapsack of custom falls off his back with the first step he makes into these precincts. Here is sanctity — 11.13

At the gates of the forest, the surprised man of the world is forced to leave his city estimates of great and small, wise and foolish. The knapsack of custom falls off his back with the first step he makes into these — 12.14

At the gates of the forest, the surprised man of the world is forced to leave his city estimates of great and small, wise and foolish. The knapsack of custom falls off his back with the first step he makes — 13.15

At the gates of the forest, the surprised man of the world is forced to leave his city estimates of great and small, wise and foolish. The knapsack of custom falls off his back with the — 14.15 / Below, 34

Italic

At the gates of the forest, the surprised man of the world is forced to leave his city estimates of great and small, wise and foolish. The knapsack of custom falls off his back with the first step he makes into these precincts. Here is sanctity which shames our religions, and reality which discredits our heroes. Here we find nature to be the circumstance which dwarfs every other circumstance, and — 7.9

At the gates of the forest, the surprised man of the world is forced to leave his city estimates of great and small, wise and foolish. The knapsack of custom falls off his back with the first step he makes into these precincts. Here is sanctity which shames our religions, and reality which discredits our heroes. Here we find nature to be the — 8.10

At the gates of the forest, the surprised man of the world is forced to leave his city estimates of great and small, wise and foolish. The knapsack of custom falls off his back with the first step he makes into these precincts. Here is sanctity which shames our religions, and reality which discredits our heroes. — 9.10

At the gates of the forest, the surprised man of the world is forced to leave his city estimates of great and small, wise and foolish. The knapsack of custom falls off his back with the first step he makes into these precincts. Here is sanctity which shames our religions, and — 10.12

At the gates of the forest, the surprised man of the world is forced to leave his city estimates of great and small, wise and foolish. The knapsack of custom falls off his back with the first step he makes into these precincts. Here is sanctity which — 11.13

At the gates of the forest, the surprised man of the world is forced to leave his city estimates of great and small, wise and foolish. The knapsack of custom falls off his back with the first step he makes into these precincts. Here is sanctity — 12.14

At the gates of the forest, the surprised man of the world is forced to leave his city estimates of great and small, wise and foolish. The knapsack of custom falls off his back with the first step he makes into these — 13.15

At the gates of the forest, the surprised man of the world is forced to leave his city estimates of great and small, wise and foolish. The knapsack of custom falls off his back with the first step he — 14.15 / Below, 34

At the Gates of the Forest

At the Gates of the Forest

Ty	**Trajan**
Ca	**Serif**
Ke	**Capitals**
Te	**Digital**
Da	**1989**
De	**Carol Twombly**
Fo	**Adobe**
Co	**USA**

Characteristics
All capitals
Classical proportions
Square base form

AMWN
HEBPR
CGJQS

Connections

Weiss	1926
Goudy Trajan	1930
La Gioconda	2000
Cyan	2006

Availability
Trajan is available from Adobe and resellers

Specimen
Adobe Originals Trajan specimen. Adobe Systems Inc., San Jose, 1989 (228x144mm)

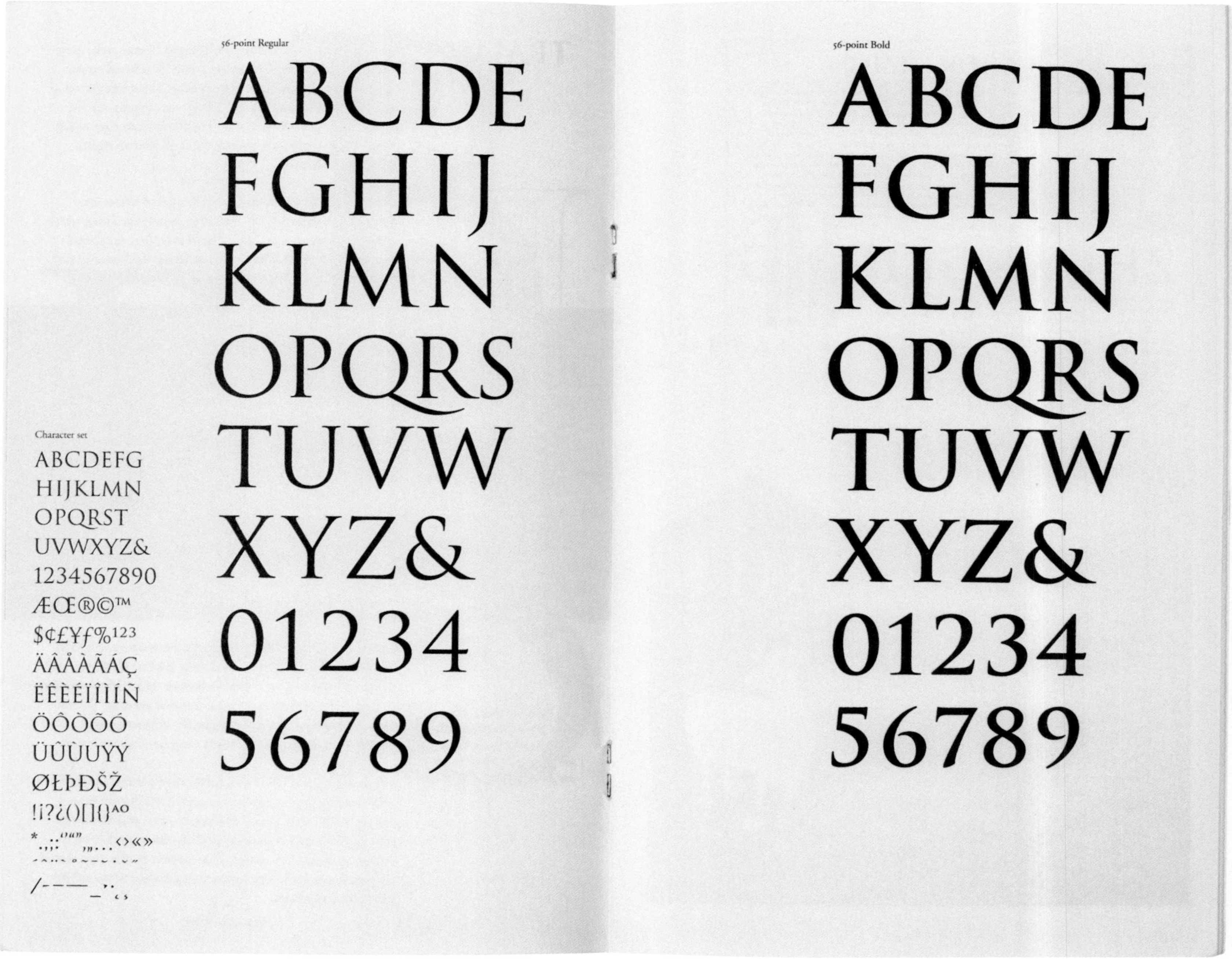

56-point Regular

ABCDE
FGHIJ
KLMN
OPQRS
TUVW
XYZ&
01234
56789

Character set

ABCDEFG
HIJKLMN
OPQRST
UVWXYZ&
1234567890
ÆŒ®©™
$¢£¥ƒ%123
ÄÂÅÀÃÁÇ
ËÊÉÏÎÌÍÑ
ÖÔÒÕÓ
ÜÛÙÚŸÝ
ØŁÞÐŠŽ
!¡?¿()[]{}ªº
* ..„""'' <>«»
/–— ·.

56-point Bold

ABCDE
FGHIJ
KLMN
OPQRS
TUVW
XYZ&
01234
56789

Trajan's Column was erected in Rome in AD 113 to commemorate emperor Trajan's military conquests. The inscription at its base is among the finest surviving examples of imperial Roman square capitals composed in letters that are finely chiselled, orderly and majestic, without any superfluous decoration.

Roman letter carvers were the first to use serifs at the terminals of strokes, probably because the capitals were marked out with brush-drawn letters before the stone was carved. The lettering on Trajan's Column, and others like it, has had a defining influence on the development of Western scripts, and consequently on typeface design, for 2,000 years. In Renaissance Italy the Trajan capitals and other classical inscriptions were referenced explicitly as models of a classical ideal and shaped the art of typography from its beginning.

In 1989 Carol Twombly (1959–), a senior designer at Adobe Systems Inc., created three typefaces based on historical sources; one of these, Adobe Trajan, was a sensitive interpretation of the letterforms from the inscription. Trajan was not designed for text but as a display typeface, and one best used at large sizes. Its proportions are spacious and graceful, with only a few judicious adjustments made to the original Roman forms, such as a heavier S, a lighter N, and slightly more prominent serifs throughout. Like its source, Trajan is in capitals only, but the digital typeface varied from the original carved letters by providing a companion bold weight.

Twombly's is the most successful and accurate translation of the Trajan inscription into type, although a number of designs precede it, notably Emil Rudolf Weiss's eponymous 1926 face (pp228–29), Frederic W. Goudy's 1930 Goudy Trajan and Warren Chappell's Trajanus of 1939. Adobe has extended the Trajan family following its introduction, initially meeting user demand by adding small capitals. In 2011 the typeface was redeveloped for OpenType with the addition of four extra weights and Greek and Cyrillic glyph sets.

The historian Nicolete Gray once remarked that 'the perfection of a Roman inscription consists in the perfection of the drawing of each letter, and in the order and clarity of the spacing'. This certainly applies to Carol Twombly's majestic reinterpretation.

TRAJAN

Among Trajan, Lithos, and Charlemagne, Trajan is the most literal interpretation of a classical model. It is based on the *capitalis monumentalis* letterforms of the Trajan inscription in Rome. Erected in A.D. 113, the column commemorates the victories of the Emperor Trajan. These letterforms are widely recognized as a standard against which all Roman capital designs are measured.

In the process of translating the inscriptional letters into digital type, designer Carol Twombly found that forms which appeared perfect when chiseled into stone were not suited to printing on paper. The N was too heavy, the S too light, the serifs too delicate. To give the characters an even color and

The Trajan inscription, 113 A.D., Rome. Photo by Jack Stauffacher. Carol Twombly's sketches of the letterforms of the Trajan inscription and final typeset Trajan letters.

unified appearance when printed at various sizes and resolutions, Twombly modified serif details, hairline thickness, and stem and bowl weights while retaining as much of the subtlety and character of the inscriptional forms as possible. To complete the typeface, she designed letters, numerals, and punctuation for which the inscription provided no models.

Trajan regular and bold, with subtle curves and asymmetrically swelling stems, have been designed for display typesetting at sizes of 18 points and larger. These majestic letters convey a feeling of refinement and dignity in traditional as well as contemporary designs. For the best results, care should be taken to optically letter-space any job typeset in a titling (all-capital) typeface.

Ty	**Utopia**	
Ca	**Serif**	
Ke	**Transitional**	
Te	**Digital**	
Da	**1989**	
De	**Robert Slimbach**	
Fo	**Adobe**	
Co	**USA**	

Characteristics

	Vertical stress
A V v W w	Flat vertices
C	Vertical serifs
Q	Short tail below letter
U	Two heavy verticals
a	Double storeyed, large bowl
a c f r	Small ball terminals
f r t	Narrow
g	Double-storeyed, straight angled ear
k	Curved arm and leg
t	Arm and stem steeply bracketed
b u x y z	Roman serifs

ACQUW
abcefgijk
orsty*abfu*

Connections

Availability

Utopia is available from Adobe and resellers

Specimen

Adobe Originals Utopia specimen. Adobe Systems Inc., San Jose, 1989 (228x144mm)

Regular

At the gates of the forest, the surprised man of the world is forced to leave his city estimates of great and small, wise and foolish. The knapsack of custom falls off his back with the first step he makes into these precincts. Here is sanc-

16.17

At the gates of the forest, the surprised man of the world is forced to leave his city estimates of great and small, wise and foolish. The knapsack of custom falls off his back with the first step he makes into these precincts. Here is sanc-

18.19

At the gates of the forest, the surprised man of the world is forced to leave his city estimates of great and small, wise and foolish. The knapsack of custom falls off his back with the first step he makes into

20.21

Below,
Regular capitals
Titling capitals
28

AT THE GATES OF THE
AT THE GATES OF THE

Regular

At the gates of the fores the surprised man of th world is forced to leave his city estimates of gre and small, wise and foo ish. The knapsack of cu tom falls off his back w the first step he makes

24.25

At the gates of the forest, the surprise man of the world is forced to leave his city estimates of gr and small, wise an foolish. The knaps of custom falls off

30.31

Below,
Titling capitals
42

AT THE GATES

Utopia is a contemporary interpretation of eighteenth-century models such as Alexander Wilson's 1768 typeface (pp86–87). Designed by Robert Slimbach (1956–) in 1989 for Adobe Systems, Utopia is neither a straightforward classical revival nor a purely personal response to historical convention, but rather a lively and informed interchange between tradition and innovation.

Although it is one of Slimbach's earliest type designs, Utopia is one of his most effective and enduring. It is a face that would once have been called a workhorse, one that is not at all ostentatious but that can be relied on to perform well in many different situations. Utopia is distinctive and yet highly legible, with open counters and a well-distributed balance of positive and negative space.

Vertical stress and pronounced stroke contrast indicate Utopia's origins in the eighteenth-century typefaces like Baskerville (pp80–81) and Wilson that marked the transition from early calligraphic forms towards the rational 'modern' types such as Didot and Bodoni. At the same time, Slimbach carefully refined the character contours, introducing a number of distinctive functional features in Utopia's letterforms that are not based on any historical precedent, of which the most evident is the large, open x-height.

Utopia's character sets and weights were among the most extensive of their time, making it capable of solving a wide range of typographic problems. Slimbach's 1989 design had all of the qualities needed to become an all-purpose, standard typeface, and the Utopia family is seen widely today in everything from online open-source applications to corporate communications.

Regular

At the gates of the forest, the surprised man of the world is forced to leave his city estimates of great and small, wise and foolish. The knapsack of custom falls off his back with the first step he makes into these precincts. Here is sanctity which shames our religions, and reality which discredits our heroes. — 7.9

At the gates of the forest, the surprised man of the world is forced to leave his city estimates of great and small, wise and foolish. The knapsack of custom falls off his back with the first step he makes into these precincts. Here is sanctity which shames our religions, — 8.10

At the gates of the forest, the surprised man of the world is forced to leave his city estimates of great and small, wise and foolish. The knapsack of custom falls off his back with the first step he makes into these precincts. Here is sanctity — 9.10

At the gates of the forest, the surprised man of the world is forced to leave his city estimates of great and small, wise and foolish. The knapsack of custom falls off his back with the first step he makes into these — 10.12

At the gates of the forest, the surprised man of the world is forced to leave his city estimates of great and small, wise and foolish. The knapsack of custom falls off his back with the first step he — 11.13

At the gates of the forest, the surprised man of the world is forced to leave his city estimates of great and small, wise and foolish. The knapsack of custom falls off his back — 12.14

At the gates of the forest, the surprised man of the world is forced to leave his city estimates of great and small, wise and foolish. The knapsack of custom falls — 13.15

At the gates of the forest, the surprised man of the world is forced to leave his city estimates of great and small, wise and foolish. The knapsack of custom — 14.15

Below, 28

Italic

At the gates of the forest, the surprised man of the world is forced to leave his city estimates of great and small, wise and foolish. The knapsack of custom falls off his back with the first step he makes into these precincts. Here is sanctity which shames our religions, and reality which discredits our heroes. Here we — 7.9

At the gates of the forest, the surprised man of the world is forced to leave his city estimates of great and small, wise and foolish. The knapsack of custom falls off his back with the first step he makes into these precincts. Here is sanctity which shames our religions, and — 8.10

At the gates of the forest, the surprised man of the world is forced to leave his city estimates of great and small, wise and foolish. The knapsack of custom falls off his back with the first step he makes into these precincts. Here is sanctity which — 9.10

At the gates of the forest, the surprised man of the world is forced to leave his city estimates of great and small, wise and foolish. The knapsack of custom falls off his back with the first step he makes into these precincts. — 10.12

At the gates of the forest, the surprised man of the world is forced to leave his city estimates of great and small, wise and foolish. The knapsack of custom falls off his back with the first step he — 11.13

At the gates of the forest, the surprised man of the world is forced to leave his city estimates of great and small, wise and foolish. The knapsack of custom falls off his back with the first — 12.14

At the gates of the forest, the surprised man of the world is forced to leave his city estimates of great and small, wise and foolish. The knapsack of custom falls off his back — 13.15

At the gates of the forest, the surprised man of the world is forced to leave his city estimates of great and small, wise and foolish. The knapsack of custom — 14.15

Below, 28

At the Gates of the Forest

At the Gates of the Forest

Ty	**Adobe Caslon**
Ca	**Serif**
Ke	**Old Style**
Te	**Digital**
Da	**1990**
De	**Carol Twombly**
Fo	**Adobe**
Co	**USA**

Characteristics

A	Cupped apex
C	Angled serif at top only
J	Descends below baseline
Q	Long, heavy tail
R	Angled leg with serif foot
T	Outward-sloping serifs on top-stroke
&	Ornate

ACQRT
abcdefghij
orstuya*efg*

Connections

Caslon 540	1902
Big Caslon	1994
ITC Founder's Caslon	1998
King's Caslon	2007

Availability

Adobe Caslon is available from Adobe and resellers

Specimen

Adobe Originals Caslon specimen. Adobe Systems Inc., San Jose, 1990 (228x144mm)

Regular with Italic

At the gates of the forest, the surprised man of the world is forced to leave his city estimates of great and small, wise *and foolish. The knapsack of custom falls off his back with the first step he makes into these precincts. Here is sanctity*

15.17

At the gates of the forest, the surprised man of the world is forced to leave his city estimate of great and *small, wise and foolish. The knapsack of custom falls off his back with the first step he makes into these precincts.*

16.18

At the gates of the forest, the surprised man of the world is forced to leave his city estimates of great *and small, wise and foolish. The knapsack of custom falls off his back with the first step he makes into*

17.19

At the gates of the forest, the surprised man of the world is forced to leave his city estimate *of great and small, wise and foolish. The knapsack of custom falls off his back with the first step he*

18.20

10.13
The alternate fonts include lowercase characters commonly used in the 18th century, such as long s (ʃ) and accompanying ligatures ʃb, fi, ʃl, ʃ, ʃt; ct and st ligatures and alternate italic lowercase k, v, and w.

Regular with Alternate Regular and Expert Regular

At the gates of the forest, the surprised man of the world is forced to leave his city estimates of great and small, wise and foolish. The knapsack of custom falls off his back with the first step he makes into these precincts. Here is sanctity which shames our religions, and reality which discredits our heroes. Here we find nature to be the circumstance which dwarfs every other circumstance, and judges like a god all men that come to her. We have crept out of our close and crowded houses into the night and morning, and we see what majestic beauties daily wrap us in their bosom. How willingly we would escape the barriers which render them comparatively impotent, escape the sophistication and second thought, and suffer nature to entrance us. The tempered light of the woods is like a perpetual morning, and is stimulating and heroic. The anciently reported spells of these places creep on us. The stems of pines, hemlocks and oaks, almost gleam like iron on the excited eye. The incommunicable trees

Italic with Alternate Italic and Expert Italic

At the gates of the forest, the surprised man of the world is forced to leave his city estimates of great and small, wise and foolish. The knapsack of custom falls off his back with the first step he makes into these precincts. Here is sanctity which shames our religions, and reality which discredits our heroes. Here we find nature to be the circumstance which dwarfs every other circumstance, and judges like a god all men that come to her. We have crept out of our close and crowded houses into the night and morning, and we see what majestic beauties daily wrap us in their bosom. How willingly we would escape the barriers which render them comparatively impotent, escape the sophistication and second thought, and suffer nature to entrance us. The tempered light of the woods is like a perpetual morning, and is stimulating and heroic. The anciently reported spells of these places creep on us. The stems of pines, hemlocks and oaks, almost gleam like iron on the excited eye. The incommunicable trees begin to persuade us to live with them, and quit our life of solemn trifles. Here no history, or

Adobe Caslon is a revival of William Caslon's eighteenth-century typefaces (pp76–77), drawn in 1990 by Carol Twombly (1959–). Based on earlier Dutch baroque designs, Caslon's types are among the best loved and most widely used in typographic history, maintaining their popularity throughout Europe and the United States for almost three centuries.

Twombly focused her research on a number of publications printed in Caslon's typefaces, including an original type specimen sheet published by his foundry in 1738. Comparisons revealed that the colour and contrast of Caslon's early letterforms were far more balanced than those found in later publications, which had formed the basis of most later revivals.

Modelling her design on book text cuts rather than larger sizes of Caslon's early fonts, Twombly sought to capture their uniquely congenial characteristics. She carefully adjusted the stroke contrast, serif weights and overall density of the regular and italic typefaces so that they would look neither too light at large, high resolutions nor too blotchy at small, low resolutions.

Weight variations, small irregularities in individual characters and slightly heavy capitals echo the vitality of Caslon's original designs. Strokes are even and the axis of curvature is almost vertical, with the influence of the old-style typefaces of the Renaissance only just detectable. The project was resolved in a large family of 22 typefaces including alternates, small capitals, swash letters, expert sets and historical ornaments in addition to the basic alphabet. The current Adobe OpenType Pro version incorporates these features and adds central European language support and additional ligatures.

Twombly's interpretation is relatively true to the original Caslon. Although it can look somewhat ungainly and a little bland in headlines at larger sizes, it proves its worth in longer texts, where it performs effectively with quiet dignity.

Regular

At the gates of the forest, the surprised man of the world is forced to leave his city estimates of great and small, wise and foolish. The knapsack of custom falls off his back with the first step he makes into these precincts. Here is sanctity which shames our religions, and reality which discredits our heroes. Here we find — 7.9

At the gates of the forest, the surprised man of the world is forced to leave his city estimates of great and small, wise and foolish. The knapsack of custom falls off his back with the first step he makes into these precincts. Here is sanctity which shames our religions, and reality — 8.10

At the gates of the forest, the surprised man of the world is forced to leave his city estimates of great and small, wise and foolish. The knapsack of custom falls off his back with the first step he makes into these precincts. Here is sanctity which — 9.11

At the gates of the forest, the surprised man of the world is forced to leave his city estimates of great and small, wise and foolish. The knapsack of custom falls off his back with the first step he makes into these precincts. Here is — 10.12

At the gates of the forest, the surprised man of the world is forced to leave his city estimates of great and small, wise and foolish. The knapsack of custom falls off his back with the first step he makes into — 11.13

At the gates of the forest, the surprised man of the world is forced to leave his city estimates of great and small, wise and foolish. The knapsack of custom falls off his back with the first step — 12.14

At the gates of the forest, the surprised man of the world is forced to leave his city estimates of great and small, wise and foolish. The knapsack of custom falls off his back — 13.15

At the gates of the forest, the surprised man of the world is forced to leave his city estimates of great and small, wise and foolish. The knapsack of custom falls off his back with the first step he makes — 14.16

Italic

At the gates of the forest, the surprised man of the world is forced to leave his city estimates of great and small, wise and foolish. The knapsack of custom falls off his back with the first step he makes into these precincts. Here is sanctity which shames our religions, and reality which discredits our heroes. Here we find nature to be the circum— 7.9

At the gates of the forest, the surprised man of the world is forced to leave his city estimates of great and small, wise and foolish. The knapsack of custom falls off his back with the first step he makes into these precincts. Here is sanctity which shames our religions, and reality which discredits our heroes. — 8.10

At the gates of the forest, the surprised man of the world is forced to leave his city estimates of great and small, wise and foolish. The knapsack of custom falls off his back with the first step he makes into these precincts. Here is sanctity which shames our religions, and — 9.11

At the gates of the forest, the surprised man of the world is forced to leave his city estimates of great and small, wise and foolish. The knapsack of custom falls off his back with the first step he makes into these precincts. Here is sanctity which — 10.12

At the gates of the forest, the surprised man of the world is forced to leave his city estimates of great and small, wise and foolish. The knapsack of custom falls off his back with the first step he makes into these precincts. — 11.13

At the gates of the forest, the surprised man of the world is forced to leave his city estimates of great and small, wise and foolish. The knapsack of custom falls off his back with the first step he makes into — 12.14

At the gates of the forest, the surprised man of the world is forced to leave his city estimates of great and small, wise and foolish. The knapsack of custom falls off his back with the first step he — 13.15

At the gates of the forest, the surprised man of the world is forced to leave his city estimates of great and small, wise and foolish. The knapsack of custom falls off his back with the first step he makes into these pre— 14.16

Ty	**Dead History**
Ca	**Serif / Sans Serif**
Ke	**N/A**
Te	**Digital**
Da	**1990**
De	**P. Scott Makela**
Fo	**Emigre**
Co	**USA**

Characteristics

Two typefaces merged within individual character contours

Stems and arcs of VAG Rounded

Strokes and serifs of Linotype Centennial

ABGIMR abcefghi koprstuy

Connections

Chwast Buffalo	1981
Keedy Sans	1989
FF Fudoni	1991
Template Gothic	1991

Availability

Dead History is available from Emigre and resellers

Specimen

Dead History poster. Emigre, Berkeley, 1994 (570x830mm)

If one typeface could precisely represent postmodern graphic design, it would be Dead History, designed by P. Scott Makela (1960–99) in 1990 while studying at the Cranbrook Academy of Art in Michigan.

The invention of the personal computer in the late 1980s transformed the visual landscape globally, providing a new publishing platform which forced people to re-evaluate the accepted methods, functions and consequences of social communication while turning the design profession on its head. At the same time, the ideals of modernism were becoming increasingly regarded as no longer adequate to represent a diverse, complex, multicultural world. At the forefront of both the use of the new technology and the critique of contemporary values were young student designers. Their presence at the Cranbook Academy made it, briefly, a key location in the open exploration of critical theory to inform practice in a number of different creative spheres.

Dead History is a prime example of this critical attitude. Artefacts from history have often been used as sources of reference for cultural production – but not for Makela, whose new typeface pronounced it dead. According to him, Dead History signalled the end of an era of conventional type design and traditional communications. His typeface, he said, represented 'a new attitude in type creation ... the result of the computer's capabilities to function as the perfect assembling tool.'

Ellen Lupton has described Dead History as 'a pastiche of two existing typefaces: the traditional serif font Centennial and the Pop classic VAG Rounded'. It is the typographic equivalent of a remix, sampling typefaces from two completely different historical eras, and it has been pointedly classified as a serif sans serif, featuring a transition from contrasting strokes and unbracketed serifs on one side of the characters to a monoline sans serif with softly rounded terminals on the other. It went through several stages of development before it was licensed to Emigre in 1994, where it was redrawn from scratch and completed by Zuzana Licko.

Dead History has entirely different purposes from most typefaces. It is a discourse on the nature of communication and is a representation of its time, its place and its maker. In 2011 it was acquired, along with four other Emigre typefaces, for the permanent design collection of the Museum of Modern Art, New York. Makela's visual critique of the nature of history was then officially consigned to it.

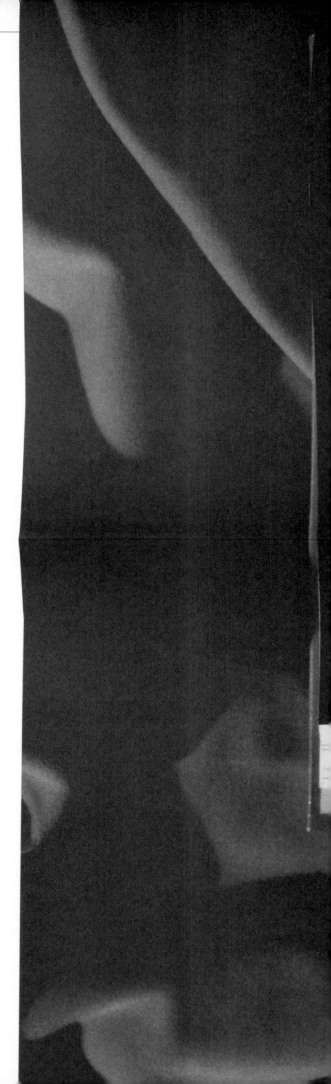

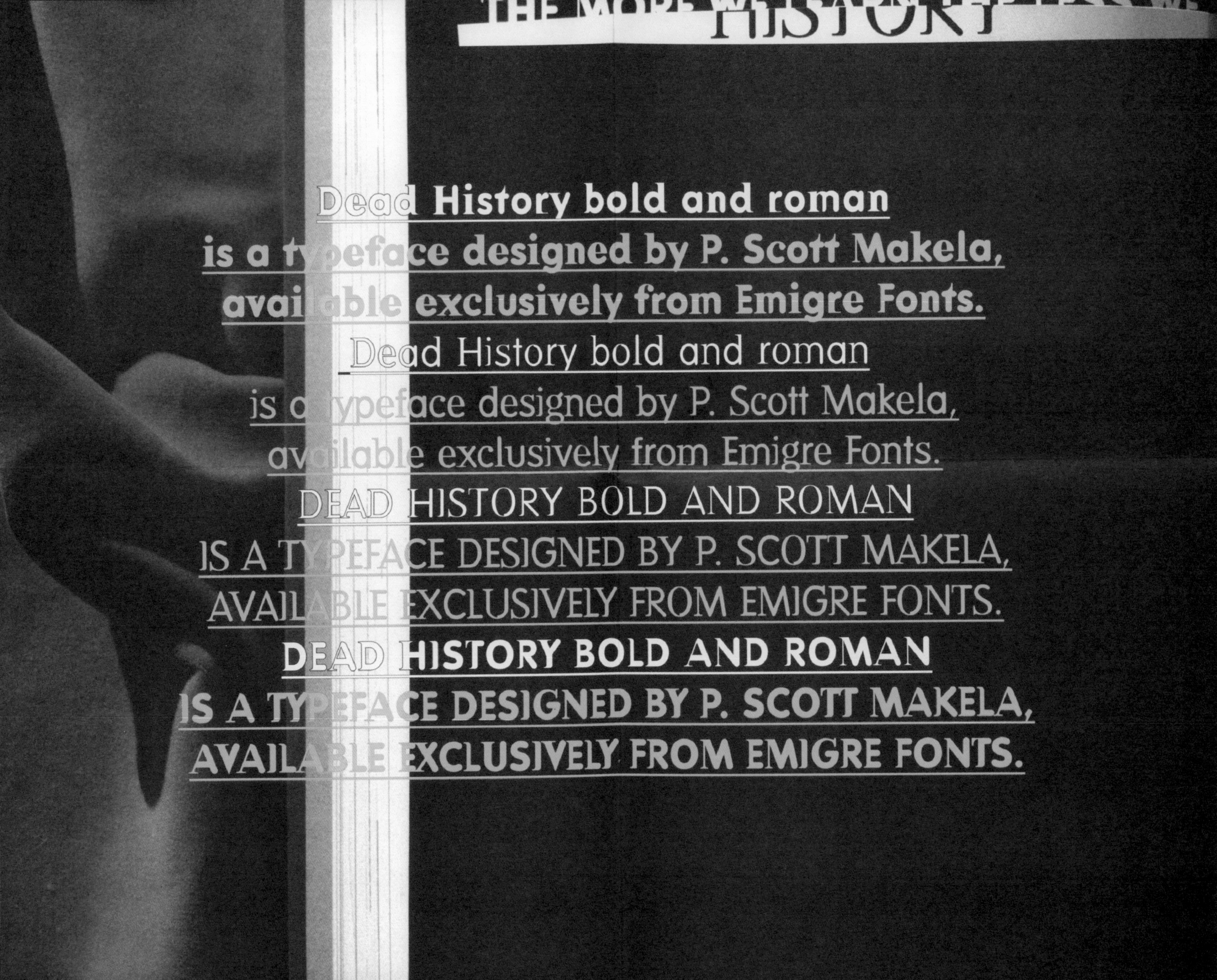

THE MAKING HISTORY

Dead History bold and roman

is a typeface designed by P. Scott Makela,

available exclusively from Emigre Fonts.

Dead History bold and roman

is a typeface designed by P. Scott Makela,

available exclusively from Emigre Fonts.

DEAD HISTORY BOLD AND ROMAN

IS A TYPEFACE DESIGNED BY P. SCOTT MAKELA,

AVAILABLE EXCLUSIVELY FROM EMIGRE FONTS.

DEAD HISTORY BOLD AND ROMAN

IS A TYPEFACE DESIGNED BY P. SCOTT MAKELA,

AVAILABLE EXCLUSIVELY FROM EMIGRE FONTS.

Ty	**Minion**	
Ca	**Serif**	
Ke	**Old Style**	
Te	**Digital**	
Da	**1990**	
De	**Robert Slimbach**	
Fo	**Adobe**	
Co	**USA**	

Characteristics

Capitals lower than ascender height
Large x-height
Sharp, bracketed serifs
J Descends below baseline
M Slightly splayed
R Wide, curved leg
W w Centre-strokes meet at apex
a Double-storeyed, straight mid-stroke
f r t Narrow
g Narrow, upturned ear
t Narrow
y Straight, swelling tail

AJMRSW
abcdefghij
orstuya*efg*

Connections

Sabon	1967
DTL Van Den Keere	1994
DTL Albertina	1996
Adobe Jenson	1996

Availability

Minion is available from Adobe and resellers

Specimen

Adobe Originals Minion specimen. Adobe Systems Inc., San Jose, 1990 (228x144mm)

Display Regular & Display Italic

16.18

At the gates of the forest, the surprised man of the world is forced to leave his city estimates of great and small, wise and foolish. The knapsack of cus-*tom falls off his back with the first step he makes into these precincts. Here is sanctity which shames our religions,*

18.20

At the gates of the forest, the surprised man of the world is forced to leave his city estimates of great and small, wise and foolish. The *knapsack of custom falls off his back with the first step he makes into these precincts. Here is sancti*

20.22

At the gates of the forest, the surprised man of the world is forced to leave his city estimates of great and small, wise and *foolish. The knapsack of custom falls off his back with the first*

*Below,
Display Regular
& Regular
46*

Display Regular & Display Italic

24.25

At the gates of the forest, the surprised man of the world is forced to leave his city estimates of great and small, wise and foolish. The *knapsack of custom falls off his back with the first step he makes into these precin*

30.31

At the gates of the forest, the surprised man of the world is forced to leave his city esti-*mates of great and small, wise and foolish. The knapsack of cus*

*Below,
Display Italic,
& Italic
48*

At the Gates of the
At the Gates of the

*At the Gates of the
At the Gates of the*

Minion is a 1990 Adobe Originals typeface designed by Robert Slimbach (1956–). Like many of Slimbach's faces, Minion is not based on a single model but is inspired by old styles from the Renaissance, a period of highly readable designs that were also pleasing to the eye.

Minion has similarities to the types cut by Griffo (pp30–31) and Garamond (pp48–49), although the x-height is larger, counters and apertures are more open, serifs are sharper, and superfluous details are eliminated. The name Minion was chosen to reflect the modest and self-effacing nature of the type. It refers to a traditional naming system for type sizes, in which minion, corresponding roughly to 7 point, falls between nonpareil (6 point) and brevier (8 point). Initially planned to be an effective substitute for Times New Roman, Minion is extremely compact and therefore economical when used in long texts, combining the aesthetic and functional qualities that make text type highly readable with the opportunities permitted by digital technology. Extraordinarily extensive, the Minion family is available in regular and condensed widths, each with a huge range of weights from light to black.

It also features expert sets with small capitals, swash characters, ornaments, non-Latin support and a delicate version for display use with a higher contrast, elongated extenders and sharper serifs.

A notable feature in Minion is its implementation of optical sizes designed with different degrees of stroke contrast and contour detail. Intended to be used for optimum readability in texts at specific sizes, Minion's range of optical variants can solve a wide range of typographic problems with absolute precision, making it particularly valuable to expert users.

Regular

7.9

At the gates of the forest, the surprised man of the world is forced to leave his city estimates of great and small, wise and foolish. The knapsack of custom falls off his back with the first step he makes into these precincts. Here is sanctity which shames our religions, and reality which discredits our heroes. Here we find nature to the

8.10

At the gates of the forest, the surprised man of the world is forced to leave his city estimates of great and small, wise and foolish. The knapsack of custom falls off his back with the first step he makes into these precincts. Here is sanctity which shames our religions, and reality which discredits our heroes

9.11

At the gates of the forest, the surprised man of the world is forced to leave his city estimates of great and small, wise and foolish. The knapsack of custom falls off his back with the first step he makes into these precincts. Here is sanctity which shames our religions,

10.12

At the gates of the forest, the surprised man of the world is forced to leave his city estimates of great and small, wise and foolish. The knapsack of custom falls off his back with the first step he makes into these precincts. Here is sanctity

11.13

At the gates of the forest, the surprised man of the world is forced to leave his city estimates of great and small, wise and foolish. The knapsack of custom falls off his back with the first step he makes into these precincts.

12.14

At the gates of the forest, the surprised man of the world is forced to leave his city estimates of great and small, wise and foolish. The knapsack of custom falls off his back with the first step he makes

13.15

At the gates of the forest, the surprised man of the world is forced to leave his city estimates of great and small, wise and foolish. The knapsack of custom falls off his back with the first step

14.15

Below,
34

At the gates of the forest, the surprised man of the world is forced to leave his city estimates of great and small, wise and foolish. The knapsack of custom falls off his back with the first step he makes into these pre-

Italic

7.9

At the gates of the forest, the surprised man of the world is forced to leave his city estimates of great and small, wise and foolish. The knapsack of custom falls off his back with the first step he makes into these precincts. Here is sanctity which shames our religions, and reality which discredits our heroes. Here we find nature to be the

8.10

At the gates of the forest, the surprised man of the world is forced to leave his city estimates of great and small, wise and foolish. The knapsack of custom falls off his back with the first step he makes into these precincts. Here is sanctity which shames our religions, and reality which discredits our heroes.

9.11

At the gates of the forest, the surprised man of the world is forced to leave his city estimates of great and small, wise and foolish. The knapsack of custom falls off his back with the first step he makes into these precincts. Here is sanctity which shames our religions, and real

10.12

At the gates of the forest, the surprised man of the world is forced to leave his city estimates of great and small, wise and foolish. The knapsack of custom falls off his back with the first step he makes into these precincts. Here is sanctity which

11.13

At the gates of the forest, the surprised man of the world is forced to leave his city estimates of great and small, wise and foolish. The knapsack of custom falls off his back with the first step he makes into these precincts. Here is

12.14

At the gates of the forest, the surprised man of the world is forced to leave his city estimates of great and small, wise and foolish. The knapsack of custom falls off his back with the first step he makes

13.15

At the gates of the forest, the surprised man of the world is forced to leave his city estimates of great and small, wise and foolish. The knapsack of custom falls off his back with the first step he

14.15

Below,
34

At the gates of the forest, the surprised man of the world is forced to leave his city esti-mates of great and small, wise and foolish. The knapsack of custom falls off his back with the first step he makes into these pre-

At the Gates of the Forest

At the Gates of the Forest

Ty	**FF Blur**
Ca	**Sans Serif**
Ke	**Grotesque**
Te	**Digital**
Da	**1991**
De	**Neville Brody**
Fo	**FontFont**
Co	**UK**

Characteristics

Contours based on grotesque structure

Three degrees of blur

Three weights: Light, Medium and Bold

ABGMR
abcefghij
koprstuy

Connections

Template Gothic	1991
FF Trixie	1991
FF Dirty	1994
Drop	1999

Availability

FF Blur is available from FontFont and resellers

Specimen

The Graphic Language of Neville Brody 2.
Thames and Hudson, London, 1994
(300x250mm)

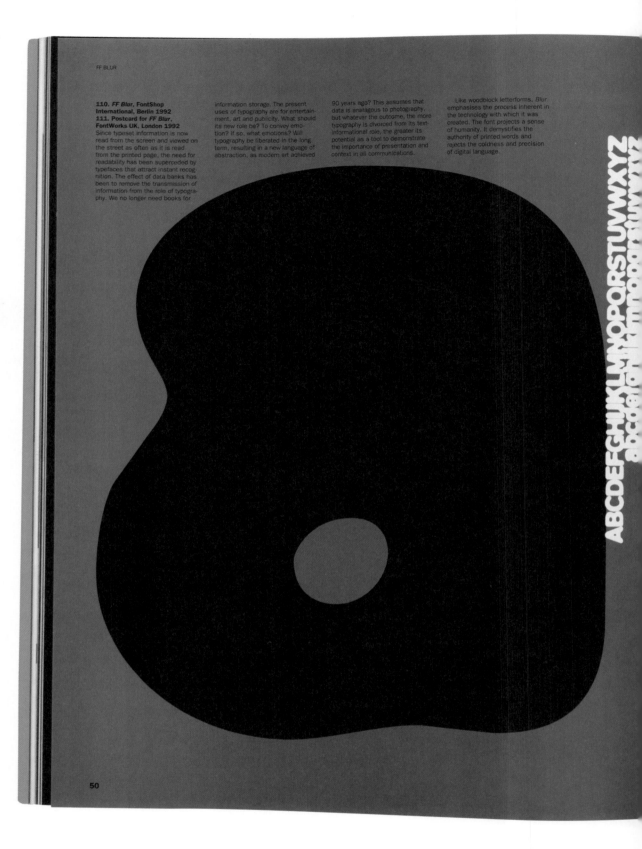

FF BLUR

110. *FF Blur*, **FontShop International, Berlin 1992**
111. Postcard for *FF Blur*, **FontWorks UK, London 1992**
Since typeset information is now read from the screen and viewed on the street as often as it is read from the printed page, the need for readability has been superceded by typefaces that attract instant recognition. The effect of data banks has been to remove the transmission of information from the role of typography. We no longer need books for information storage. The present uses of typography are for entertainment, art and publicity. What should its new role be? To convey emotion? If so, what emotions? Will typography be liberated in the long term, resulting in a new language of abstraction, as modern art achieved 90 years ago? This assumes that data is analogous to photography, but whatever the outcome, the more typography is divorced from its text-informational role, the greater its potential as a tool to demonstrate the importance of presentation and context in all communications.

Like woodblock letterforms, *Blur* emphasises the process inherent in the technology with which it was created. The font projects a sense of humanity. It demystifies the authority of printed words and rejects the coldness and precision of digital language.

50

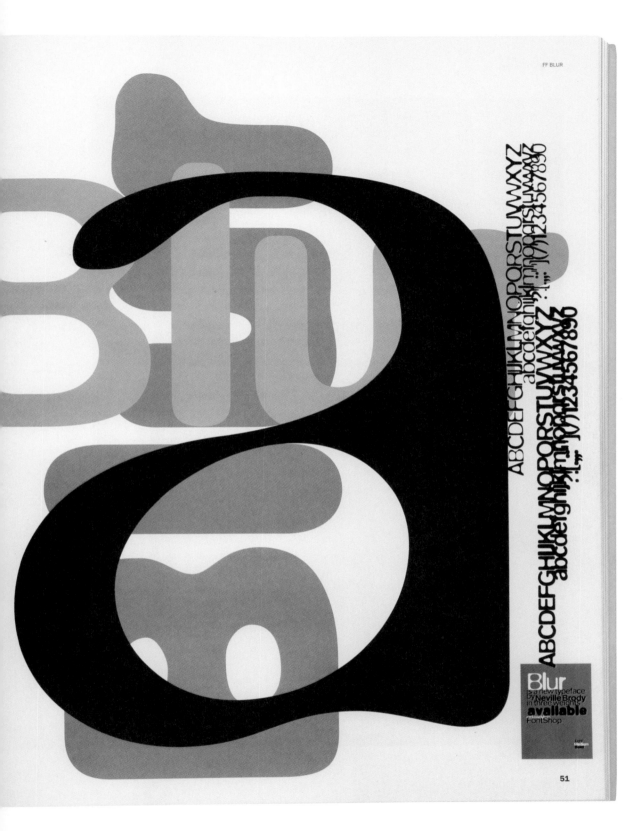

When the Macintosh computer revolutionized the design world in the mid-1980s the young graphic designers who engaged with the new technology were able to take control of opportunities that had never been seen before. 'Type has acquired a fluidity of physical outline, an ease of manipulation and, potentially, a lack of conceptual boundaries unimaginable only a few years ago', the design critic Rick Poynor wrote in 1991.

Designed in the same year by British graphic designer Neville Brody (1957–), Blur is a typeface that tested these limits. It is the product of a process that could not have been imagined without the new technologies with which it had been produced. Brody did not write or draw it in the traditional sense, but manipulated an image of an existing typeface to generate it. Probably working with Akzidenz-Grotesk (pp152–53), he used photographic methods to defocus and deform letters into new, contorted shapes, and then created vector files from these images that he converted into vectored type. The procedure was undertaken at three levels of degradation, resulting in the equivalent of three weights: Light, Medium and Bold.

There was nothing particularly new about such typographic transformations. In the 1960s Photo-Lettering Inc. had specialized in extreme photo distortions, and examples of deformed type had been seen many times before, most famously in Robert Massin's twisted paragraphs made by printing text onto stretched condoms. But the idea behind Blur was defiantly new. A product of the post-punk DIY aesthetic, it confronted the typographic traditions in which Brody had been trained. Fuzzy at the edges and degenerated like an image of an image or a copy of a photocopy, Blur was a celebration of imperfection and, like several typefaces of the time being published by Emigre and other American foundries, it was a vehicle for ideas, reappropriating old forms to create new ones at will in order to raise questions about concepts of originality in a world of digital sampling and about the cultural value of history.

FF Blur was published by FontFont, the online type foundry that Brody had recently co-founded, and it rapidly became a bestseller. Two decades on, most conceptual and experimental typefaces from the first wave of digital type in the 1990s have not survived but FF Blur has remained as relevant today as the ideas on which it is founded.

Ty	**PMN Caecilia**
Ca	**Slab Serif**
Ke	**Old Style**
Te	**Digital**
Da	**1991**
De	**Peter Matthias Noordzij**
Fo	**Linotype**
Co	**Netherlands**

Characteristics

- Monoline with slab serifs
- Capitals lower than ascender height
- Large x-height
- Short ascenders and descenders
- **A** Flat apex, high bar
- **J** Descends below baseline
- **M** Slightly splayed
- **Q** Long tail below letter
- **R** Wide, curved leg
- **W** Stepped centre-strokes, serif at apex
- **a g** Double-storeyed
- **i j** Round dots

AJMQRW
abcefghij
orstyaefg

Connections

Schneidler Old Style	1936
Cursivium	c1990
TheSerif	1994
FF Kievit Slab	2013

Availability

PMN Caecilia is available from Linotype and resellers

Specimen

PMN Caecilia type specimen. Linotype, Bad Homburg, c1991 (210x148mm)

I.234

PMN Caecilia offers you more: the old style figures, available in all styles, extend either above or below the x-height, giving column numbers a charm of their own. This makes them especially useful in documents such as annual reports. And in other areas as well, such as posters or in advertisements where they can breathe new life into typography.

Mediäval-Ziffern ohne Ende.

Die PMN Caecilia bietet Ihnen mehr: Mit den in allen Garnituren vertretenen – über bzw. unter die Mittellänge reichenden – Mediäval-Ziffern erhalten Zahlenkolonnen einen größeren Reiz, und sie sind besser lesbar. Sie eignen sich deshalb besonders für Geschäftsberichte. Aber auch in anderen Zusammenhängen, auf Plakaten oder in Anzeigen etwa, können sie das Satzbild auf ungewohnte Weise beleben.

Des chiffres elzévirs à n'en pas finir.

Le PMN Caecilia vous offre encore plus : grâce aux chiffres elzévirs – dont la hauteur est, selon les cas, soit supérieure soit inférieure à celle des bas-de-casse – livrés avec toutes les familles de polices, les colonnes de chiffres retrouvent un attrait tout particulier, sans parler du fait qu'elles sont de ce fait mieux lisibles. Ils se prêtent donc tout particulièrement aux bilans et rapports de société. Mais dans d'autres contextes, comme par exemple les posters ou les annonces, ils peuvent apporter un charme bien distinct à la typographie.

1234567890

1234567890

14.510	26%	PMN Caecilia gives the user the opportunity to creatively display even large columns of numbers.	14.670	24%	29.180
13.965	25%		12.667	21%	26.632
8.155	15%	Die PMN Caecilia versetzt den Gestalter in die Lage, selbst große Zahlenmengen souverän und schön zu interpretieren.	22.407	36%	30.562
19.000	34%		11.698	19%	30.698
55.630	100%	*Le PMN Caecilia permet de présenter de façon élégante même les colonnes de chiffres.*	61.442	100%	117.072

PMN Caecilia is a slab serif created by Dutch designer Peter Matthias Noordzij (1961–) in 1983, when he was a student at the Royal Academy of Art in The Hague. It was not released until eight years later.

PMN Caecilia represents a new direction in the history of slab serif designs that had begun in the early nineteenth century, when type founders adapted letter proportions and serif shapes to create novel type styles. PMN Caecilia was the result of an unprecedented confrontation between two apparently incompatible principles from the traditions of type design. It was the first typeface to successfully reconcile the convention of the low-contrast slab serif form with humanist letter shapes based on handwriting. The design of the italic provided the spark that led to this innovation. Instead of drawing a slanted roman, Noordzij modelled it on humanist handwriting of the Renaissance, making smooth transitions from curves and arches into stems, with a slight compression overall. The roman design, following similar principles, resulted in a friendly, open typeface with a large x-height and open counters that harmonizes the robustness of a slab serif with the typographic sophistication of a traditional book face. Confident that his type was worthy of publication, Noordzij decided to seek a foundry to work on its production, with the provision that 'if nobody is interested … in producing and publishing that thing, I will choose a different trade.'

With the support of Adrian Frutiger, Noordzij's design was presented at an exhibition in London, bringing it to the attention of Linotype, who eventually published it in 1986 in four weights, each with an accompanying true italic. At that point, Noordzij gave it the name PMN Caecilia, a combination of the designer's initials and the first name of his wife, Cécile.

PMN Caecilia has been one of the most widely used slab serifs since its release. This success is partly due to its association with the development of personal computing in the early 1990s, its old-style contour making it more legible on digital screens than serif typefaces with a high stroke contrast. It initiated an acceptance of slab serifs as text typefaces and has influenced many subsequent designs.

PMN Caecilia 45
abcdefghijklmnopqrstuvwxyz
ABCDEFGHIJKLMNOPQRSTUVWXYZ&
ABCDEFGHIJKLMNOPQRSTUVWXYZ
1234567890 – 1234567890

PMN Caecilia 46
abcdefghijklmnopqrstuvwxyz
ABCDEFGHIJKLMNOPQRSTUVWXYZ&
ABCDEFGHIJKLMNOPQRSTUVWXYZ
1234567890 – 1234567890

WHAT'S UNIQUE ABOUT PMN CAECILIA IS THAT ALL EIGHT TYPEFACE STYLES INCLUDE CORRESPONDING SMALL CAPS AND OLD STYLE FIGURES. THESE NUANCES ENABLE THE USER TO SET TYPE WITH A GREATER DEGREE OF DETAIL. LARGE X-HEIGHTS, TALLER LOWER-CASE ASCENDERS, MODEST CAPITALS, STEMS WHICH LEAN SLIGHTLY TO THE RIGHT – THE APPLICA-TION OF THESE DESIGN ELE-MENTS RESULTS IN A FLUID AND VIBRANT TYPEFACE.

DAS BESONDERE AN DER PMN CAECILIA: ALLE ACHT SCHRIFTSCHNITTE SIND KOMPLETT MIT KAPITÄL-CHEN UND MEDIÄVAL-ZIFFERN AUSGESTATTET. DIESE DETAILLIERTE ABSTUFUNG GIBT DEM GESTALTER DIE MÖGLICH-KEIT, DAS SATZBILD MIT GROSSER FEINHEIT ABZU-STIMMEN. GROSS AUSGE-BILDETE MITTELLÄNGEN, HÖHERE OBERLÄNGEN DER GEMEINEN, EHER KLEIN AUSGELEGTE VERSALIEN, DIE LEICHTE RECHTSNEI-GUNG DER VERTIKALEN – DIE VIELZAHL DER GESTALTUNGSELEMENTE ERGIBT IN DER SUMME EIN FLÜSSIGES UND LEBENDIGES SCHRIFTBILD.

PMN Caecilia 55
abcdefghijklmnopqrstuvwxyz
ABCDEFGHIJKLMNOPQRSTUVWXYZ&
ABCDEFGHIJKLMNOPQRSTUVWXYZ
1234567890 – 1234567890

PMN Caecilia 56
abcdefghijklmnopqrstuvwxyz
ABCDEFGHIJKLMNOPQRSTUVWXYZ&
ABCDEFGHIJKLMNOPQRSTUVWXYZ
1234567890 – 1234567890

PMN Caecilia 75
abcdefghijklmnopqrstuvwxyz
ABCDEFGHIJKLMNOPQRSTUVWXYZ&
ABCDEFGHIJKLMNOPQRSTUVWXYZ
1234567890 – 1234567890

PMN Caecilia 76
abcdefghijklmnopqrstuvwxyz
ABCDEFGHIJKLMNOPQRSTUVWXYZ&
ABCDEFGHIJKLMNOPQRSTUVWXYZ
1234567890 – 1234567890

CE QUI REND LE PMN CAECILIA SI INTÉRESSANT: LES HUIT STYLES DE CARACTÈRE SONT LIVRÉS AU COMPLET AVEC LES PETITES CAPITALES ET LES CHIFFRES ELZÉVIRS CORRESPONDANTS. CETTE GRADUATION DÉTAILLÉE ACCORDE À L'UTILISATEUR UN MAXIMUM DE PRÉCISION DANS LA COMPOSITION TYPOGRAPHIQUE. DES BAS-DE-CASSE GÉNÉREUX AVEC DES LONGUES DU HAUT PLUS ÉLEVÉES, DES MAJUSCULES UN RIEN PLUS PETITES, DES HAMPES TIRANT VERS LA DROITE: BREF, LA DIVERSITÉ DES ÉLÉMENTS DE STYLE DONNE UNE FLUIDITÉ ET UNE VIE PROPRE À CES CARACTÈRES.

PMN CAECILIA OFFERS FOUR UPRIGHT FACES: 45 LIGHT, 55 ROMAN, 75 BOLD, 85 HEAVY. AND THEIR CORRESPONDING ITALICS.

DIE PMN CAECILIA BIETET VIER GERADESTEHENDE GARNITUREN: 45 LIGHT, 55 ROMAN, 75 BOLD, 85 HEAVY. SOWIE DIE ENTSPRECHENDEN KURSIV-SCHNITTE.

LE PMN CAECILIA EST LIVRÉ EN QUATRE POLICES DE BASE: 45 LIGHT, 55 ROMAN, 75 BOLD, 85 HEAVY. AVEC BIEN SÛR LES POLICES ITALIQUES CORRESPONDANTES.

PMN Caecilia 85
abcdefghijklmnopqrstuvwxyz
ABCDEFGHIJKLMNOPQRSTUVWXYZ&
ABCDEFGHIJKLMNOPQRSTUVWXYZ
1234567890 – 1234567890

PMN Caecilia 86
abcdefghijklmnopqrstuvwxyz
ABCDEFGHIJKLMNOPQRSTUVWXYZ&
ABCDEFGHIJKLMNOPQRSTUVWXYZ
1234567890 – 1234567890

Ty	**HTF Didot**
Ca	**Serif**
Ke	**Modern**
Te	**Digital**
Da	**1991**
De	**Jonathan Hoefler**
Fo	**Hoefler Type Foundry**
Co	**USA**

Characteristics

Vertical stress
High contrast
Hairline cross-strokes
Flat hairline serifs
E Heavy, bracketed serifs
J Tail sits on baseline
M Narrow
Q Curved tail below letter
R Curved leg
W Stepped centre-strokes, serif at apex

CEMRW
abcdefghij
orstuyaefg

Connections

Didot	1784
Modern No. 20	1905
Ambroise	2001
Didot Elder	2004

Availability

HTF Didot is available from Hoefler & Co.

Specimen

HTF Didot type specimen. Hoefler Type Foundry, New York, 1997 (279x216mm)

120 pt TOI Mais

96 pt CIEL Sabot

84 pt ROUX Quatre

64 pt ÉTAGES Argonnes

48 pt SALINITÉ Interrogatif

42 pt ATHENIANS Establishment

32 pt HAMILTONIANS Operatic Overtures

24 pt NIHILIST THEORIES Indigenous Populations

20 pt THIS FAMILY OF FONTS Thus this typeface, a Medium

16 pt WAS CREATED BY DRAWING TWO Weight Between The Light and Bold

14 pt PAIRS OF DESIGNS: LIGHT AND BOLD Extremes, did not have to be drawn; instead

12 pt AND SMALL SIZE AND LARGE SIZE. WITH It was created Mathematically, as an Average or

10 pt THESE "MASTERS" IN PLACE, "INSTANCES" OF THE "Interpolation," of the two masters Didot Light and Bold.

9 pt FONTS FOR VARIOUS SIZES CAN BE EASILY INTERPOLATED Another exciting innovation which means more fonts per dollar

XX · MUSE Nº 1 HTF DIDOT MEDIUM

MIL *Rétif*
FOIS *Parez*
NEUF *Soirées*
SORTIE *Rafistoler*
ROSAIRE *Scrupuleux*
CAVALIERE *Empêchement*
DESCRIPTIONS *Concentus Musicus*
WARBURTONSMITH *Mesoamerican Cultures*
THIS PRACTICE HELPS *Created For Use at 144 Point*
REVIVE THE TYPEFOUNDERS' *Intermediate Typefaces can Be Created*
PRACTICE OF CUTTING DIFFERENT *Which are Suited to Use over a Particular*
DESIGNS FOR DIFFERENT SIZES: SINCE A *Range of Sizes. On this spread, there are actually*
TEXT SIZE MASTER WAS CREATED FOR IDEAL *Fourteen typefaces, seven sizes each for Roman and Italic*
USE AT TEN POINT, AND A DISPLAY SIZE MASTER WAS *Thus as the type gets Bigger, the Hairlines remain Delightfully Thin*

96 pt
84 pt
64 pt
48 pt
42 pt
32 pt
24 pt
20 pt
16 pt
14 pt
12 pt
10 pt
9 pt

MUSE N° 1 HTF DIDOT MEDIUM ITALIC · XXI

HTF Didot was commissioned by *Harper's Bazaar* as part of the fashion magazine's 1991 redesign, which was described at the time as 'one of the most dramatic magazine reinventions in history'. Its editorial team wanted a new typeface that would continue the design style for which it had gained a reputation since its post-war inception under the direction of the illustrious designer Alexey Brodovitch (pp324–25), whose astonishing layouts were well known for their vivid use of Bodoni and Didot.

Jonathan Hoefler (1970–) of the Hoefler Type Foundry, New York, was commisioned to create a typeface that would carry the magazine's design direction forward for a contemporary readership. The result, HTF Didot, is a revival of the work of the eighteenth- and nineteenth-century Parisian type founder and punch cutter Firmin Didot (1764–1836), a key member of the Parisian dynasty that dominated French type founding for two centuries. Didot was responsible for the design of several innovative typefaces (pp90–91) that captured the neoclassical style of the Age of Enlightenment.

The design of Hoefler's letters is based on types in Didot's 1819 *Spécimen des nouveaux caractères* and references similar specimens by Joseph Molé le Jeune from the same year. HTF Didot, like its antecedents, shows no evidence of any origin in handwriting. It is the severe product of logical design processes, characterized by a vertical stress and straight-edged serifs that sit squarely on stems with no bracketing. Thinner strokes are of a hairline weight, and the contrast between them and thicker stems is extreme. In order to manage the typeface's hairline strokes at different scales in a variety of editorial situations, Hoefler drew each of the family's three weights and three italics in seven different optical sizes, each designed to be used in a specific series of sizes ranging from 6 to 600 point, resulting in a total of 42 calibrated typefaces.

The *Harper's Bazaar* relaunch became a milestone in publishing and Didot typefaces have continued to be widely used in fashion branding and editorial work, a testament to the durability of the neoclassical style.

493

Ty	**FF Meta**
Ca	**Sans Serif**
Ke	**Humanist**
Te	**Digital**
Da	**1991**
De	**Erik Spiekermann**
Fo	**FontFont**
Co	**Germany**

Characteristics

	Oblique lower case terminals at head
	Flat lower case terminals at foot
A	Low crossbar
C c S s e	Angled terminals
E F T	Slanted upper stroke terminal
M	Splayed
a	Double-storeyed
b h k l r	Slight curve to left at top of stem
g	Double-storeyed, open lower bowl
i j	Round dot
l	Hooked tail
y	Stepped strokes, curved tail

AEGMQR
abcefghij
kloprstuy

Connections

Syntax	1969
ITC Officina	1990
FF Info Text	1996
FF Unit	2003

Availability

FF Meta is available from FontFont and resellers

Specimen

FontFont Focus No. 4: 'Meta'. FontFont, Berlin, c2000 (297x148mm)

In 1985 the German typographer Erik Spiekermann (1947–) created Meta for the Sedley Place agency, to be used in the corporate identity of Deutsche Bundespost, the West German Post Office. However, the client expressed concerns that the proposed design would 'cause unrest' internally and the entire project had to be abandoned. Three years later, Spiekermann decided to develop the typeface himself, eventually publishing it in 1991 through his newly formed digital type foundry, FontFont. The final version, FF Meta, was drawn by Just van Rossum and Erik van Blokland, who reconstructed the original digital outlines in three weights and added a number of refinements.

The original brief for Deutsche Bundespost was demanding. It called for a legible, neutral, space-saving typeface with an unambiguous character in three well-differentiated weights. The new design would be sufficiently robust for use in small sizes and would reproduce well on high- and low-resolution printers using paper stock of variable quality. It was also to be implemented as a cross-platform typeface for various contemporary typesetting technologies.

Spiekermann's solution was intended to be the 'antithesis of Helvetica', he said, which he considered 'boring and bland'. His new design 'has to do more than look pretty: it has to work pretty hard'. Because it was required to look distinctive in corporate communications and to be easily readable in smaller point sizes, Meta's overall structure has a logical and very inviting personality, with wide, open apertures and a balanced, but not even, stroke contrast. It was inspired by the nuanced humanist contours of sans serif types like Syntax (pp392–93).

Meta is narrow by comparison with sans serifs like Helvetica and thus economical in its use of space, an attribute that makes it particularly useful in German-language settings, where long word constructions can make awkward line breaks when set at short measures. Character strokes are sturdy enough to withstand uneven printing but not so much so that individual characters appear to merge. A number of features were implemented to provide unambiguous character differentiation in a broad range of conditions, such as the small curves, indentations and openings at joints that are evident throughout. Meta was massively successful in the 1990s as a strikingly individual and warm alternative to the major sans serifs of the day. It was widely seen in brand communications and has since been hugely influential in the design direction of many recent typefaces.

FONTFONTFOCUS

8

ABCDEFGHIJKLMNOPQRSTUVWXYZ FF Meta Normal
1234567890ÆŒæœ&ßffifflffffifl.,-:;?!¿¡...–(/)[\]{|}""''‹›

ABCDEFGHIJKLMNOPQRSTUVWXYZ FF Meta Italic
1234567890ÆŒæœ&ßffifflffffifl.,-:;?!¿¡...–(/)[\]{|}""''‹›

ABCDEFGHIJKLMNOPQRSTUVWXYZ FF META CAPS
1234567890ÆŒÆŒ&SSFFIFFLFIFL.,-:;?!¿¡...–(/)[\]{|}""''‹›

ABCDEFGHIJKLMNOPQRSTUVWXYZ FF META CAPS ITALIC
1234567890ÆŒÆŒ&SSFFIFFLFIFL.,-:;?!¿¡...–(/)[\]{|}""''‹›

ABCDEFGHIJKLMNOPQRSTUVWXYZ FF Meta Book
1234567890ÆŒæœ&ßffifflffffifl.,-:;?!¿¡...–(/)[\]{|}""''

ABCDEFGHIJKLMNOPQRSTUVWXYZ FF Meta Book Italic
1234567890ÆŒæœ&ßffifflffffifl.,-:;?!¿¡...–(/)[\]{|}""''‹›

ABCDEFGHIJKLMNOPQRSTUVWXYZ FF META BOOK CAPS
1234567890ÆŒÆŒ&SSFFIFFLFIFL.,-:;?!¿¡...–(/)[\]{|}""''‹›

ABCDEFGHIJKLMNOPQRSTUVWXYZ FF META BOOK CAPS ITALIC
1234567890ÆŒÆŒ&SSFFIFFLFIFL.,-:;?!¿¡...–(/)[\]{|}""''‹›

ABCDEFGHIJKLMNOPQRSTUVWXYZ FF Meta Medium
1234567890ÆŒæœ&ßffifflffffifl.,-:;?!¿¡...– (/)[\]{|}""''‹›

ABCDEFGHIJKLMNOPQRSTUVWXYZ FF Meta Medium Italic
1234567890ÆŒæœ&ßffifflffffifl.,-:;?!¿¡...– (/)[\]{|}""''‹›

ABCDEFGHIJKLMNOPQRSTUVWXYZ FF META MEDIUM CAPS
1234567890ÆŒÆŒ&SSFFIFFLFIFL.,-:;?!¿¡...–(/)[\]{|}""''‹›

ABCDEFGHIJKLMNOPQRSTUVWXYZ FF META MEDIUM CAPS ITALIC
1234567890ÆŒÆŒ&SSFFIFFLFIFL.,-:;?!¿¡...–(/)[\]{|}""''‹›

ABCDEFGHIJKLMNOPQRSTUVWXYZ FF Meta Bold
1234567890ÆŒæœ&ßffifflffffifl.,-:;?!¿¡...–(/)[\]{|}""''‹›

ABCDEFGHIJKLMNOPQRSTUVWXYZ FF Meta Bold Italic
1234567890ÆŒæœ&ßffifflffffifl.,-:;?!¿¡...–(/)[\]{|}""''‹›

67890 abcdefghijklmnopqrstuvwxyz

@®©™%‰$¢£¥ƒ€+±‹=›·÷/¬^~•ÅÇÉÑÒØÜåçéîñòøü

67890 abcdefghijklmnopqrstuvwxyz

¶#@®©™%‰$¢£¥ƒ€+±‹=›·÷/¬^~•ÅÇÉÑÒØÜåçéîñòøü

67890 ABCDEFGHIJKLMNOPQRSTUVWXYZ

#@®©™%‰$¢£¥ƒ€+±‹=›·÷/¬^~•ÅÇÉÑÒØÜåçéîñòøü

67890 ABCDEFGHIJKLMNOPQRSTUVWXYZ

#@®©™%‰$¢£¥ƒ€+±‹=›·÷/¬^~•ÅÇÉÑÒØÜåçéîñòøü

67890 abcdefghijklmnopqrstuvwxyz

§¶#@®©™%‰$¢£¥ƒ€+±‹=›·/¬^~•ÅÇÉÑÒØÜåçéîñòøü

67890 abcdefghijklmnopqrstuvwxyz

#@®©™%‰$¢£¥ƒ€+±‹=›·÷/¬^~•ÅÇÉÑÒØÜåçéîñòøü

67890 ABCDEFGHIJKLMNOPQRSTUVWXYZ

#@®©™%‰$¢£¥ƒ€+±‹=›·÷/¬^~•ÅÇÉÑÒØÜåçéîñòøü

67890 ABCDEFGHIJKLMNOPQRSTUVWXYZ

¶#@®©™%‰$¢£¥ƒ€+±‹=›·÷/¬^~•ÅÇÉÑÒØÜåçéîñòøü

67890 abcdefghijklmnopqrstuvwxyz

¶#@®©™%‰$¢£¥ƒ€+±‹=›·÷/¬^~•ÅÇÉÑÒØÜåçéîñòøü

67890 abcdefghijklmnopqrstuvwxyz

¶#@®©™%‰$¢£¥ƒ€+±‹=›·÷/¬^~•ÅÇÉÑÒØÜåçéîñòøü

67890 ABCDEFGHIJKLMNOPQRSTUVWXYZ

#@®©™%‰$¢£¥ƒ€+±‹=›·÷/¬^~•ÅÇÉÑÒØÜåçéîñòøü

67890 ABCDEFGHIJKLMNOPQRSTUVWXYZ

#@®©™%‰$¢£¥ƒ€+±‹=›·÷/¬^~•ÅÇÉÑÒØÜåçéîñòøü

67890 abcdefghijklmnopqrstuvwxyz

#@®©™%‰$¢£¥ƒ€+±‹=›·÷/¬^~•ÅÇÉÑÒØÜåçéîñòøü

67890 abcdefghijklmnopqrstuvwxyz

¶#@®©™%‰$¢£¥ƒ€+±‹=›·÷/¬^~•ÅÇÉÑÒØÜåçéîñòøü

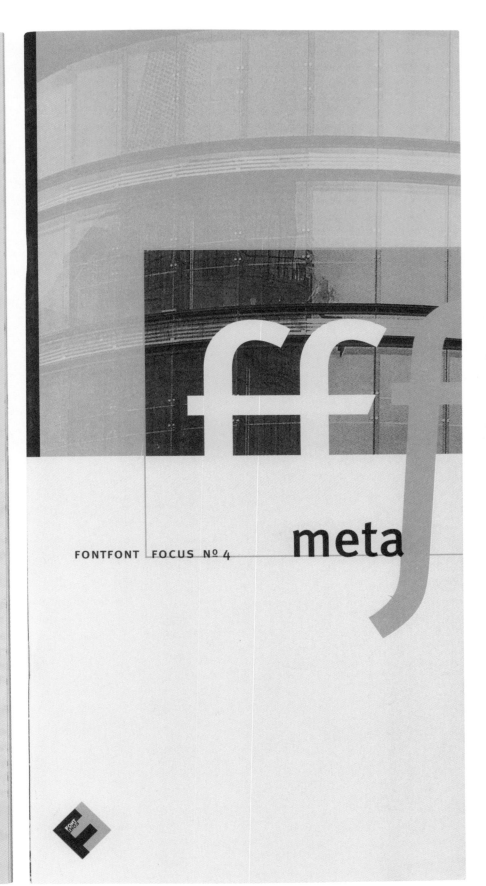

FONTFONT FOCUS № 4

meta

Ty	**FF Scala**
Ca	**Serif**
Ke	**Old Style, Dutch**
Te	**Digital**
Da	**1991**
De	**Martin Majoor**
Fo	**FontFont**
Co	**Netherlands**

Characteristics

Oblique stress
Moderate stroke contrast
Straight stems
Lower case: flat slab foot serifs, angular head serifs
C Vertical serifs
J Descends below baseline
K k Leg and arm separate from stem
P b q Open bowl
Q Hook-serifed tail below letter
R Wide, curved leg
W Crossed centre-strokes
a g Double-storeyed
f Extended arch

AJMQRW
abcdefghij
orstuyaefg

Connections

Joanna	1931
Electra	1935
PMN Caecilia	1991
FF Nexus	2004

Availability

Scala is available from FontFont and resellers

Specimen

Made with FontFont. BIS Publishers, Amsterdam, 2006 (280x210mm)

FF Scala and Scala Jewel   MECHANICAL BRIDES

22/28 pt

Advertising and design serve to amplify [Bold]
the value of useful things, *transforming* [Italic]
functional tools into alluring FETISHES [Jewel (Pearl)]
that promise to satisfy emotional as well as
material needs. A Eureka vacuum cleaner [Regular]
claims not only to sweep clean the rug,
but to give its user all her heart desires.

14/18 pt

Scholars of religion use the word FETISH to describe objects [Jewel (Diamond)]
that societies invest with the magical ability to control the forces of nature. *The witch's broom, a* FETISH *appearing in Euro-* [Jewel (Crystal)]
pean folklore, is a cleaning tool employed for magical purposes;
the witch is a dangerously bad housekeeper, a single woman with
cobwebs in every corner. KARL MARX *borrowed the word* FETISH [Caps]
to characterize the cult object of capitalism: THE COMMODITY, a
product manufactured primarily to be sold, and only secondarily to satisfy a human need. The object becomes a FETISH
as its functional role gives way to psychological incentives.

12/17 pt

The commodity FETISH speaks through advertising, packaging, styl- [Jewel (Sapphire)]
ing, and brand name recognition. *The corporate personality invoked by a*
familiar brand image such as logos for Hoover or Maytag can raise the value
of an appliance, regardless of its functional difference from other brands. Marx
assigned a feminine personality to the commodity FETISH *by describing*
the alluring, extra-functional features of the consumer product as "amorous
glances" that solicit the inner hopes and passions of the buyer. Freud used the
word FETISH to name an object or body part that stands in place of a
forbidden sex object. A foot or a shoe, a hand or a handbag—each can
become the target of desire, invested with emotional significance.

Text from Ellen Lupton, *Mechanical Brides: Women and*
Machines from Home to Office (New York: Princeton
Architectural Press and Cooper-Hewitt, National Design
Museum.) Written in Scala, 1993.

DECONSTRUCTION AND GRAPHIC DESIGN

FF Scala

justified

JACQUES DERRIDA's theory of *deconstruction* asks how representation inhabits reality. How does the external image of things get inside their internal essence? How does the surface get under the skin? Western culture since Plato has been governed by such oppositions as *inside/outside* and *mind/body*.

flush left

The intellectual achievements of the West— its science, art, philosophy, literature—have valued one side of these pairs over the other, allying one with truth and one with falsehood. Deconstruction attacks such oppositions by showing how the devalued, negative concept inhabits the valued, positive one.

flush right

Consider, for example, the Judeo-Christian concept of the body as an external shell for the inner soul, a construction that elevates the mind as the sacred source of thought and spirit, while denigrating the body as mere mechanics. The original work of art carries an authenticity that its copy lacks—the original is endowed with the spirit of its maker, while the copy is mere empty matter.

centered

If *writing* is but a copy of spoken language,
typography
is even further removed from
the primal source of meaning
in the mind of the author.
The alphabet aims to represent
the sounds of speech with a finite set of marks.
Derrida used the term
GRAMMATOLOGY
to name the study of writing as a
distinctive form of representation.

mixed

A study of *typography*
that dramatize the intrusion
into verbal content,

gaps,

Derrida proposed *grammatology* as a field of inquiry for which deconstruction is a crucial mode of research, a manner of questioning that frames the nature of its object. Falling within the domain of grammatology are the material forms and processes of typography. Robin Kinross's *Modern Typography* (1992) charts the progressive rationalization of the forms and uses of letters across several centuries of European history. As Kinross argues, printing was a prototypically *modern* process that engaged techniques of mass production.

The seeds of modernization were present in Gutenberg's first proofs; their fruits are born in the self-conscious methodologies and standardized visual forms of printers and typographers, which, beginning in the late seventeenth century, replaced an older notion of printing as a hermetic art of BLACK MAGIC, its methods guarded by a caste of craftsmen.

If Kinross's history of modern typography
spans five centuries,
so too might a history of deconstruction,
running alongside and beneath
the evolution of transparent
formal structures.
Derrida's own writing draws on experimental
forms of page layout,
and countless forms of irrational order
appear across the discourses of
THE PRINTED LETTER.

informed by
DECONSTRUCTION
would reveal a range of structures
of visual form
the invasion of ideas
by graphic marks,

and differences.

FF Scala
8/12 pt
Regular, Italic, and Caps

FF Scala
9/12 pt
Regular, Italic, and Caps

External/internal, image/reality, representation/ presence, such is the old grid to which is given the task of outlining the domain of a science. And of what science? Of a science that can no longer answer to the classical concept of the episteme because the originality of its field— an originality that it inaugurates—is that the opening of the 'image' within it appears as the condition of 'reality,' a relationship that can no longer be thought within the simple difference and the uncompromising exteriority of 'image' and 'reality,' of 'outside' and 'inside,' of 'appearance' and 'essence.' JACQUES DERRIDA

Text adapted from Ellen Lupton and J. Abobtt Miller, "Deconstruction and Graphic Design," *Design Writing Research: Writing on Graphic Design* (London: Phaidon Boooks). Written in Scala, 1996.

Martin Majoor (1960–) was prompted to design Scala, his first typeface, in 1989, because he was dissatisfied by the lack of sophisticated typographic options provided by the fonts available for the Apple Macintosh computer at the time. It was drawn for sole use in the publications of the Muziekcentrum Vredenburg, a concert hall in the Netherlands, and was released by FontFont in 1991.

Like many designs of the digital era, Scala is a hybrid that draws on many different references rather than reviving a single historical type. Majoor has said that it was 'based upon a humanist model with influences from different style periods'. Scala's basic structure has its roots in old-style typefaces such as Bembo (pp244–45), and in the work of the eighteenth-century French type founder Pierre-Simon Fournier (pp82–85). With its even stroke widths and square serifs, it also shows similarities to twentieth-century designs such as Eric Gill's 1931 Joanna (pp268–69) and to William Addison Dwiggins's 1935 Electra (pp292–93).

Because he felt that existing Macintosh typefaces were too thin, Majoor decided that Scala should have a low contrast and strong serifs. He also wanted non-lining old-style numerals to be included as standard, rather than provided separately in an alternate set. For Scala Italic he interpreted the work of sixteenth-century Italian writing masters like Arrighi (pp40–41), but retained many structural details that conformed closely to the roman.

Scala is a comprehensive type family addressed to the needs of those designers who are concerned with typographic detail, offering true small capitals, a useful range of ligatures, and lining, tabular and non-lining figures. A companion sans serif version, Scala Sans, was released in 1993. Majoor adapted this directly from Scala, initially with a black marker and some correction fluid. Following the humanist armature of its serif model, Scala Sans bears a strong resemblance to Hans Eduard Meier's Syntax (pp392–93), which Majoor regards as 'one of the most beautiful sans serifs ever'.

Scala and Scala Sans were bestsellers during the 1990s and continue to be hugely popular. Their sturdy outlines, harmonious contrasts and allusions to historical traditions allow designers to create contemporary settings that evoke a classical sensibility without slavishly referencing any specific period.

and we
ck our
ves, a
r bit
hen we
in again.
s?

ANNOUNCING

the UN~forgi

TEMPL at ampers-

AND

TEMPLATE GOT

DESIGNED BY B

ING

ABCDEFGHI
LMNOPQRST
WXYZabcdef
ijklmnopqrs
vwxyz{12345
890}!at №$%

Ty	**Template Gothic**
Ca	**Sans Serif**
Ke	**Geometric**
Te	**Digital**
Da	**1991**
De	**Barry Deck**
Fo	**Emigre**
Co	**USA**

Characteristics

Character construction based on geometric lettering template

Stroke formations vary: some are fat with round terminals and some are thin, tapering to rounded points

Some junctions are rounded, some have ink traps

ABGMRS
abcefghij
koprstuy

Connections

Keedy Sans	1989
Arbitrary Sans	1990
Dead History	1990
Eunuverse	1998

Availability

Template Gothic is available from Emigre and resellers

Specimen

Emigre 18: 'Type-Site'. Emigre, Berkeley, 1991 (425x283mm)

In the late 1980s graphic design was undergoing a revolution triggered by the advent of new technology. At the same time modernist perspectives were being challenged as too narrow and inflexible to respond adequately to the complexities of contemporary culture. In the front line of the attack on accepted norms, armed with new personal computers, were young designers like Barry Deck (1962–), who designed Template Gothic as a student at CalArts.

Two years later Deck's typeface was released commercially by Emigre. Like several other typefaces published by the foundry at that time, Template Gothic ventured into areas of type design not explored before. Where others, such as Dead History (pp484–85) and Suburban (pp526–27), were personal investigations into issues of historical authenticity and hybridization, Template Gothic was an experiment concerned with high and low culture and the reappropriation of vernacular forms. Typeface design customarily revisited historical models as revered sources of the rules of correct proportion; Template Gothic, in contrast, was based on a sign on the wall of Deck's neighbourhood laundrette.

'The sign was done with lettering templates and it was exquisite', said Deck. He was keen to reject the flawless rectitude of modernist letterforms. The naive awkwardness of the original sign's badly traced lettering might have been dismissed by members of the design profession as worthless, but it sparked Deck's interest in 'type that is not perfect; type that reflects more truly the imperfect language of an imperfect world, inhabited by imperfect beings.'

Template Gothic is a milestone in graphic design history. Playful, immature, confrontational and a deliberate mess, it is a visual exposition of postmodern values that squarely rejects the twentieth-century design canon. In designing it, Deck was attempting, he said, 'to move beyond the traditional concerns of type designers, such as elegance and legibility, and to produce typographic forms which bring to language additional levels of meaning.' By the end of the decade, Template Gothic was seen everywhere, inspiring a host of inferior imitations that followed what was later called the 'grunge' style, a predominant global trend in typographic design, fashion and music during the postmodern era.

Ty	**FF Trixie**
Ca	**Slab Serif**
Ke	**Typewriter, Monospaced**
Te	**Digital**
Da	**1991**
De	**Erik van Blokland**
Fo	**LettError**
Co	**Netherlands**

Characteristics
Digital technology imitates effects of faulty typewritten output
User-selectable levels of degradation

ABGIMW abcefg imprty

Connections
Prestige Elite	1953
Courier	1955
FF Magda Dirty	1995
Pitch	2012

Availability
FF Trixie and FF Trixie HD are available from FontFont and resellers

Specimen
FF Trixie type specimen composed by author, 2015 (297x210mm)

FF Trixie Light
FF Trixie Plain
FF Trixie Text
FF Trixie Extra
FF Trixie Cameo

1991, PostScript; republished in 2009 in Opentype in Light and Heavy weights only.

ABCDEFGHIJKLMNOPQRSTUVWXYZ
abcdefghijklmnopqrstuvwxyz
0123456789

ÄÅÀÃËÈÍÎÓÔÒØŒÚÙÇÑÆâäãåæéèí
ïóòðøœúûüçñÿæ$&§ß
%()|/ç•*!?¿¡#=~

FF Trixie Rough Light
FF Trixie Rough Heavy

2009, OpenType, compatible with the original FF Trixie but with significantly more edge detail.

ABCDEFGHIJKLMNOPQRSTUVWXYZ
abcdefghijklmnopqrstuvwxyz
0123456789

ÄÅÀÃËÈÍÎÓÔÒØŒÙÇÑ¥Æâäãåæéèí
ïóòðøœúûüçñÿæ$&£§ß¢ƒ@(r)(c)ᵀᴹªº
%‰(){|}[]/†‡•*¶!?¿¡«»#<=>~

FF Trixie HD Light
FF Trixie HD Heavy

2009, OpenType: 10,824 glyphs
with 7 alternates for each glyph.
Light: aaaaaaa **Heavy: aaaaaaa**

ABCDEFGHIJKLMNOPQRSTUVWXYZ
abcdefghijklmnopqrstuvwxyz
0123456789

ÀÁÂÃÄÅÆÇÈÉÊËÌÍÎÏÐÑÒÓÔÕÖØÙÚÛÜ
íóòøœúûùçñýæ$&£§ƒ¢ƒℓ⁽½⁾(c)ⁿªº
%‰()[]{}[]/†‡•*¶!?¿¡«»#‹›=>~

OpenType Features Include:

Baseline Shifter V1.
Baseline Shifter V2.
Baseline Shifter V3.

D o u b l e   S p a c i n g .
fi fl ff ffi ffl Ligatures.
Lining & Non-lining Figures:
0123456789 + 0123456789.
Ordinals: 100ª 100º.
Slashed Zeros: 10110010001

Fake Cyrillic Glyph Set:
ЛИТШНОГО ВОРА ВЕШАЮТ, ПОЛТИНОГЧЕСТ.
Fake Greek Glyph Set:
γεωμέτρητος μηδες εσίτω κολις.
Fake Historical 'ſ' ſubſtitution.

Ũδες Μύηċωíảιγ̂: Σḅ₅лүɰĵℏċωíảιγ̂,
Ų̃ĕċ₅ιώĵ ₅ĵℏүлιĵώж ₅ảℏ.

Trixie is a monospaced serif typeface based on the distressed letters of an old, worn typewriter. Erik van Blokland (1967–) who works with Just van Rossum (1966–) in the fields of type and graphic design at LettError, started developing ideas for the typeface in 1990. They began prototyping rough typefaces by scanning printed letters, converting them to vectors and engineering them as PostScript fonts.

One of their ideas was to make a precise facsimile of an original typewriter font that retained its physical defects. When Van Blokland came across a Triumph Durabel, a 1930s German typewriter owned by a friend named Beatrix 'Trixie' Gunther, he typed out all of its characters using different degrees of pressure and processed the damaged, irregular, blotchy results into the Trixie type family, reducing the complexity of the contours to a size that was manageable on the low-memory laser printers of the time.

The project was originally conceived as a light-hearted way of stripping the computer of its immense power as a communication tool by making it perform the menial work of the technological ancestor it had displaced. Van Blokland said in an interview that he had expected 'Trixie would be interesting for a year and the joke would wear off, and people would move on to other things'. However, since its publication by FontFont in 1991 it has continued to generate considerable revenue. The most convincing typewriter face available, Trixie has been used in countless applications to give an authentic appearance that evokes memories of the analogue technologies of bygone days. The original Trixie family consisted of Trixie Plain, a densely overinked weight, and Trixie Light, which replicated the pallid look of typewriting with a worn-out ink ribbon. A less detailed version of Trixie Plain was included for low-resolution printers, and a reversed variant, Trixie Cameo, completed the set.

In 2008 Van Blokland completely rebuilt the Trixie family for OpenType. With the new technology he was able to mimic typewriting more accurately, programming Trixie HD with seven alternate glyphs for every character, each with its own weight ranges and levels of texture. Glyphs were also programmed to switch alternates automatically within bodies of text, making them fluctuate in weight and bounce along on the baseline to simulate typing more realistically than had ever before been possible. With the addition of many other OpenType features, Trixie HD is the perfect fake, illustrating Stephen Coles's observation that 'the more digital we get, the more we miss analog. The more we miss analog, the better digital gets at analog simulation.'

501

Ty	**Mason**
Ca	**Serif / Sans Serif**
Ke	**Capitals**
Te	**Digital**
Da	**1992**
De	**Jonathan Barnbrook**
Fo	**Emigre**
Co	**USA**

Characteristics

Serif and sans serif alphabets

Regular and bold weights

Capitals, small capitals and superiors only

Extensive range of alternate characters

AABEG
HKOMN
ΦIRSTX

Connections

Exocet	1991
Alchemy	1998
Priori	2003
Doctrine	2013

Availability

Mason is available from Emigre and resellers

Specimen

Emigre product catalogue. Emigre, Berkeley, 1999 (279x216mm)

MASON SANS

DESIGNED BY JONATHAN BARNBROOK | CIRCA 1992

MⱮⱮᵐ ⱮⱮⱮᵐ

6 FONTS $95.00 | SEE AL

REGULAR
& SUPER

ALTERNATE
& SUPER

TYPI NON HABENT CLARITATEM INSITAM; EST USUS LEGENTIS IN IIS QUI FACIT EORUM CLARITATEM. INVESTIGATIONES DEMONSTRAVERUNT LECTORES LEGERE MELIUS QUOD II LEGUNT SAEPIUS.

BOLD
& SUPER

ALTERNATE
BOLD & SUPER

TYPI NON HABENT CLARITATEM INSITAM; EST USUS LEGENTIS IN IIS QUI FACIT EORUM CLARITATEM. INVESTIGATIONES DEMONSTRAVERUNT LECTORES LEGERE MELIUS QUOD II LEGUNT SAEPIUS.

MASON SANS CHARACTER SET · THE EMIGRE CATALOG

ABCDEFGHIJKLMNOPQRSTUVWXYZABCDEFGHIJKLMNOPQRSTUVWXYZ&$0123456
0123456789¢£¥%‰ÀÁÂÄÃÅÇÈÉÊËÌÍÏÎÑÒÓÔÖØÙÚÛÜŸÀÁÂÄÃÅÇÈÉÊËÌÍÏÎÑÒÓÔÖ
ÚÛÜŸ¶†ƒÆŒæœﬁﬂß₶@®©™^#+,.…::¿?¡!_'""""''„|\–-—«»~{([])}""+÷=±‹›

46

Jonathan Barnbrook's Mason was designed during the early 1990s, a time when a flood of unprecedented typefaces was being released in response to new technological possibilities and driven by a critique of contemporary attitudes. Barnbrook's 1992 design is not just an attractive display type; it also raises questions about the nature of history, memory, context and taste.

Jonathan Barnbrook (1966–) originally named his typeface Manson 'to express extreme opposite emotions, love and hate, beauty and ugliness'. On the one hand, to him, Manson sounded dignified and sophisticated, and on the other, it was the surname of a notorious cult leader and serial killer. The ambiguous name, like the typeface, was a considered attempt to draw attention to the relevance of context in the reception of cultural artefacts. However, when Manson was released by the American type foundry Emigre in 1992, the name provoked a storm of complaints and, to Barnbook's dismay, Emigre changed its name to Mason, with the justification that this had similar connotations to the original.

Mason is an effective and elegant display type that challenges modernist ideals about utility and legibility in letterform. It is a magpie's nest of familiar historical signs and associations, brilliantly realizing the German writer Otto Flake's postmodern axiom that 'the past is an immense heap of materials to use at will'. Based on drawings Barnbrook had been making in his sketchbooks over many years, the typeface harmoniously interweaves ancient and modern symbols. Its majestic capitals contain traces of Russian scripts, Greek architecture, broad pen calligraphy and ecclesiastical iconography. Many other references to popular culture and history lurk beneath its surface, including Roman stone-cut lettering, Renaissance bookwork, Gothic fiction and English humanism.

Mason became enormously successful, finding its way into a wide range of applications and, unlike many other conceptual typefaces of the 1990s, such as Dead History (pp484–85) and Keedy Sans, it is still frequently used today. Asked to evaluate the typeface in 1994, Barnbrook replied: 'I don't think it's a solely retrospective face. Some of the characters are quite modern. I think it does look dangerous in a way. Some of the letterforms are quite sharp and nasty. It's the paradox of something both beautiful and ugly.'

ON SERIF

BY JONATHAN BARNBROOK | CIRCA 1992

6 FONTS $95.00 | SEE ALSO VOLUME 5

TYPI NON HABENT CLARITATEM INSITAM; EST USUS LEGENTIS IN IIS QUI FACIT EORUM CLARITATEM. INVESTIGATIONES DEMONSTRAVERUNT LECTORES LEGERE MELIUS QUOD II LEGUNT SAEPIUS.

TYPI NON HABENT CLARITATEM INSITAM; EST USUS LEGENTIS IN IIS QUI FACIT EORUM CLARITATEM. INVESTIGATIONES DEMONSTRAVERUNT LECTORES LEGERE MELIUS QUOD II LEGUNT SAEPIUS.

MASON SERIF CHARACTER SET

THE EMIGRE CATALOG

47

503

Ty	**Myriad**
Ca	**Sans Serif**
Ke	**Humanist**
Te	**Digital**
Da	**1992**
De	**Carol Twombly and Robert Slimbach**
Fo	**Adobe**
Co	**USA**

Characteristics

Large x-height
Short ascenders and descenders
C c S s e g Angled terminals
G No spur
M Splayed
Q Short, straight tail
R Curved, angled leg
a Double-storeyed, nearly straight stem
f r t Vertical terminals
i j Round dots
t Angled top-stroke
y Slightly curved tail

AGMQR abcefghij koprstuy

Connections

Syntax	1969
Frutiger	1976
Segoe UI	2004
Nokia Pure	2011

Availability

Myriad is available from Adobe and resellers

Specimen

Adobe Originals Myriad specimen. Adobe Systems Inc., San Jose, 1992 (228x144mm)

14.16

light normal with italic

Collapsible top hats fall strangled crate boxes. Make veils blow, soft folds fall, make cotton drip and water gush. Hurl up air soft and white through thousand *candles power arc lamps. Then take wheels and axles, hurl them up and make them sing. Axles dance mid-*

regular normal with italic

Collapsible top hats fall strangled crate boxes. Make veils blow, soft folds fall, make cotton drip and water gush. Hurl up air soft and white *through thousand candles power arc lamps. Then take wheels and axles, hurl them up and make*

semibold normal with italic

Collapsible top hats fall strangled crate boxes. Make veils blow, soft folds fall, make cotton drip and water gush. Hurl up air soft and white *through thousand candles power arc lamps. Then take wheels and axles, hurl them up and make*

bold normal with italic

Collapsible top hats fall strangled crate boxes. Make veils blow, soft folds fall, make cotton drip and water gush. Hurl up air soft and white *through thousand candles power arc lamps. Then take wheels and axles, hurl them up and*

black normal with italic

Collapsible top hats fall strangled crate boxes. Make veils blow, soft folds fall, make cotton drip and water gush. Hurl up air soft *and white through thousand candles power arc lamps. Then take wheels and axles, hurl*

18.20

Collapsible top hats fall strangled crate boxes. Make veils blow, soft folds fall, make cotton drip and water gush. Hurl *up air soft and white through thousand*

Collapsible top hats fall strangled crate boxes. Make veils blow, soft folds fall, make cotton drip and water gush. *Hurl up air soft and white through thou-*

Collapsible top hats fall strangled crate boxes. Make veils blow, soft folds fall, make cotton drip and water *gush. Hurl up air soft and white*

Collapsible top hats fall strangled crate boxes. Make veils blow, soft folds fall, make cotton drip and *water gush. Hurl up air soft and white*

Collapsible top hats fall strangled crate boxes. Make veils blow, soft folds fall, make cotton drip and *water gush. Hurl up air soft and*

When Robert Slimbach (1956–) and Carol Twombly (1959–) set out to collaborate on a new sans serif design for Adobe in the early 1990s their objective was to make what Slimbach later described as 'almost a totally invisible type of letter … very generic … something that really didn't show anyone's personality too much.'

The Myriad family was shaped by the tools of its time. When Adobe launched its Multiple Master technology in 1992, unforeseen opportunities followed. Multiple Master typefaces were generated on a sliding scale defined by a range of parameters such as character weight, width or optical size. By changing these parameters using page layout software, thousands of individual typefaces could be created dynamically by end users while retaining the integrity of letterforms.

The first sans serif design in the Adobe Originals programme, Myriad was developed as a Multiple Master. Its designers sought to establish a set of core forms, working simultaneously on different typeface parameters, reviewing each other's designs and smoothing out any unusual characteristics in order to achieve what they called 'the more obvious optical shape'. Their efforts resulted in a typeface that is the product of the rules from which it was built. Deliberately avoiding any trace of personal preferences, each individual form is flexible enough to withstand a wide range of adaptations, from light to extrabold weights, and from condensed to extended widths.

Myriad has often been compared to Adrian Frutiger's eponymous typeface (pp428–29), published almost 20 years earlier. Like Frutiger, Myriad has a warmth and readability that result from its humanist letter proportions, its open-eyed counterforms and its large x-height. It is based on the shapes of old-style serif typefaces with lower case ascenders that project above the upper case characters. Myriad's italics also have classical characteristics: a single-storeyed a, a descending f, and other forms which are unique to the italic style rather than simply slanted roman letters.

Soon after Adobe stopped making Multiple Master typefaces in 2000 it published an OpenType version with an extended character set. Myriad is one of the most ubiquitous typefaces available today, widely seen in brand communications, most notably for Apple, for whom it has been a recognizable feature since 2002.

normal display sizes

collapsible
158-point regular

ice skates
wire mesh
teeth flair
a sewing machine
roll globes barrel
curtain
boilers
thread
43-point light, regular, semibold, bold, and black

TOP
FALL
150-point light

48-point black
AND BREAK WHIMPERING GLASS

PROPELLER
SPIDER WEB
54-point bold and semibold italic

HATS

BACKDROPS
AMAZEMENT
54-point regular and light italic

505

Ty	**Poetica**
Ca	**Serif**
Ke	**Old Style Italic**
Te	**Digital**
Da	**1992**
De	**Robert Slimbach**
Fo	**Adobe**
Co	**USA**

Characteristics

Ascenders curve to right
Descenders curve to left
Variant forms
Initial, medial and terminal alternate forms
Swash alternates

AJMQRW
abcdefgijklm
nopqrstuvyz

Connections

Tagliente's Italic	1524
Arrighi's Italic	1527
Bembo Italic	1929
Apple Chancery	1994

Availability

Poetica is available from Adobe and resellers

Specimen

Adobe Originals Poetica specimen. Adobe Systems Inc., San Jose, 1992 (228x144mm)

Chancery I
24.26

Divine favour has freed me from most human passions, but one insatiable lust remains which hitherto I have been neither willing or able to master. I cannot get enough books. Perhaps I already have more than I need; but it is with books as it is with other things: success in acquisition spurs the desire to find still more. Books,

28.30

Divine favour has freed me from most human passions, but one insatiable lust remains which hitherto I have been neither willing or able to master. I cannot get enough books. Perhaps I already have more than I need; but it is with books as it is with other things: success in acqui-

Chancery III
24.26

Divine favour has freed me from most human passions, but one insatiable lust remains which hitherto I have been neither willing or able to master. I cannot get enough books. Perhaps I already have more than I need; but it is with books as it is with other things: success in acquisition spurs the desire to find still more. Books,

28.30

Divine favour has freed me from most human passions, but one insatiable lust remains which hitherto I have been neither willing or able to master. I cannot get enough books. Perhaps I already have more than I need; but it is with books as it is with other things: success in acquisition

Poetica is a comprehensive family of calligraphic italics designed for Adobe Systems in 1992 by Robert Slimbach (1956–) as one of the first of the Adobe Originals collections.

Based on a single underlying design contour, the component typefaces in the Poetica family contain four alternative styles of stroke ending or swash. The types, numbered 1 to 4, also provide five sorts of capital, two sorts of alternate lower case figure, two sorts of ligature and two sorts of lower case terminal character for flourished line endings. In addition,

Poetica features a set of ornaments in a matching style and another font consisting entirely of alternative ampersands.

The design contour is based on examples of fifteenth-century penmanship that predate the inception of italics in movable type for printing. The model for Slimbach's typeface is the Italian Cancelleresca Corsiva (Chancery Cursive), a cultivated fifteenth-century humanistic script that later became the vehicle of the New Learning throughout the Roman Catholic world during the Renaissance and served as a point of departure for the

development of the italic typefaces. Poetica, like its cursive ancestor, is economical, legible and very harmonious. It reveals the trace of the calligrapher's hand in a vivacious yet disciplined way. Rather than terminating in abrupt serifs, Poetica's long ascenders sway gently to the right, counterpoised with the leftward swing of the descenders.

Two different historical tendencies are evident. In the Poetica typefaces Chancery 1–3 the capitals follow an italic model, conforming to the slope of the lower case, whereas in Chancery 4 upright capitals

contrast with the directional flow of the lower case alphabet.

In the design of Poetica, Robert Slimbach explored the limits of what was possible with PostScript software in order to progress Jan van Krimpen's ideas about typographic extensibility, where variant typefaces are built from a common parent form (pp294–95). Since the advent of OpenType technology Slimbach has pushed these boundaries further using the linguistic and typographic possibilities of the new format and its almost limitless character set.

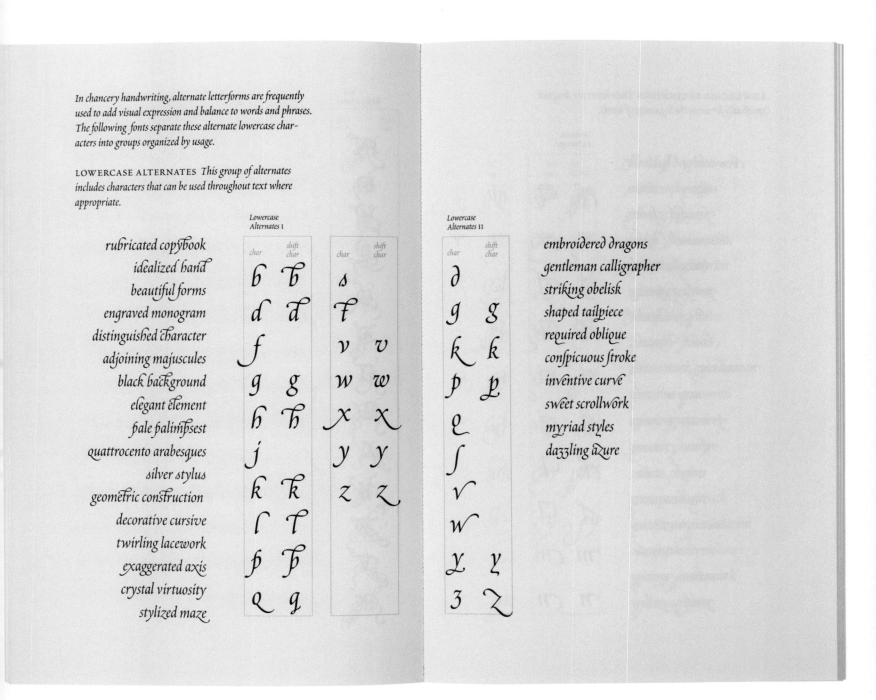

Ty	**FF Quadraat**
Ca	**Serif**
Ke	**Old Style, Dutch**
Te	**Digital**
Da	**1992**
Da	**Fred Smeijers**
Fo	**FontFont**
Co	**Netherlands**

Characteristics

Oblique stress
Moderate stroke contrast
Capitals lower than ascender height
Large x-height
Short ascenders and descenders
Deeply bracketed serifs
A Flat apex
J Descends below baseline
K Curved leg
M Splayed
P Open bowl
Q Curved tail below letter
R Wide, curved leg below baseline
W Centre-strokes meet at serifed apex
a g Double-storeyed
f Extended arch

AJMQRW
abcdefghij
orstuyaefg

Connections

Romulus	1936
Renard	1992
Collis	1993
DTL Documenta	1993

Availability

FF Quadraat is available from FontFont and resellers

Specimen

FF Quadraat type specimen. FontFont, Berlin, 1992 (210x120mm)

Dutch designer Fred Smeijers (1961–) designed FF Quadraat in 1992, naming the typeface after the design group he co-founded in 1985.

Smeijers' original motivation for Quadraat's design was to make a typeface 'somewhere in between Plantin and Times': less laboured than the former, but more robust than the latter, following his principle that 'a little too bold is better than a little too thin'. He planned to produce a text typeface with classical proportions and contemporary details, drawing on the established principles of historical models but with original features.

Although FF Quadraat is a digitally constructed typeface, it started with drawing. Smeijers' previous experience in punch cutting influenced production methods. 'Cutting punches has taught me what it is like to work at actual size – which is extremely small. I realized that today's freedom, the possibility of seeing characters on a large screen, takes away much of the nerve.' During Quadraat's development Smeijers asked readers to answer informal surveys about drafts of alternative letterforms; he would then use their responses to influence the next stage in the direction of the typeface.

Quadraat has a distinguished personality, but not to the detriment of readability. Intended as a text typeface it is low in contrast, highly legible and economical in its use of space, with an even colour at small point sizes. Like Trinité (pp450–51), the lower case roman letters feature a slight slant to the right, a subtle detail that Smeijers considered helpful in reading long texts. In common with FF Scala (pp496–97) and several other contemporary Dutch fonts, Quadraat's figures follow the traditional old-style non-lining forms, while lining figures accompany the small capitals.

When FF Quadraat was first released in 1992 it consisted only of roman, bold, italic and small capitals. Smeijers subsequently expanded its subgroups with condensed, display and headline variants. In 1997 he added a sans serif variant, continuing a Dutch tradition also found in Martin Majoor's FF Scala and Lucas de Groot's Thesis (pp538–39) which had begun in 1930 when Jan van Krimpen pioneered a companion sans serif for his Romulus typeface (pp294–95).

FF Quadraat roman

Aa Bb Cc
Hh Ii Jj Kk Ll
Qq Rr Ss Tt U
Yy Zz & Æ Œ
1234567890.,

FF Quadraat italic

Aa Bb Cc Dd
Hh Ii Jj Kk Ll Mm
Qq Rr Ss Tt Uu Vv
Yy Zz & Æ Œ
1234567890.,:;i!

Ee Ff Gg

Nn Oo Pp

Ww Xx

Đeœ ɦe ß flffi

?''«»-([†‡]§£$*

Gg

Oo Pp

Xx

e ß flffi

-([†‡]§£$*

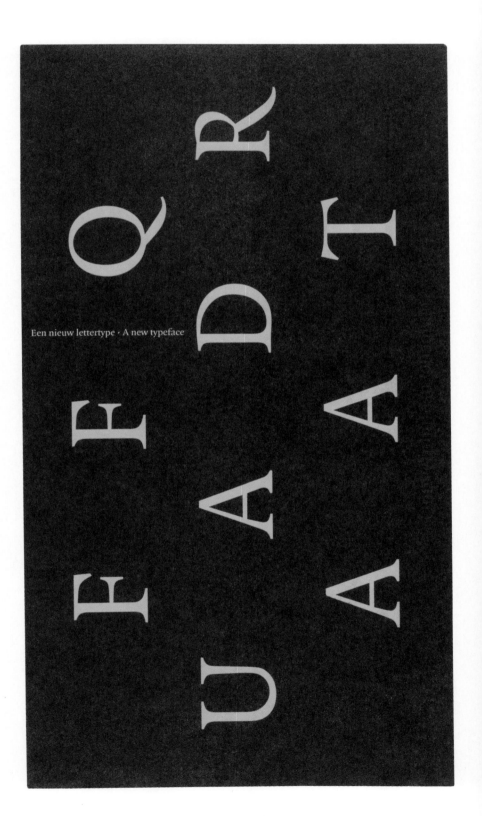

Een nieuw lettertype · A new typeface

Ty	**FF Balance**
Ca	**Sans Serif**
Ke	**Humanist, Reversed Contrast**
Te	**Digital**
Da	**1993**
De	**Evert Bloemsma**
Fo	**FontFont**
Co	**Netherlands**

Characteristics

Reversed stress
Large x-height
C c S s e g Vertical terminals and large apertures
G No spur
Q Curved tail
R Straight, angled leg
a Double-storeyed
a f g r t Vertical terminals
i j Square dots
t Flat top-stroke
y Straight tail

AGMQR
abcefghij
koprstuy

Connections

Antique Olive	1962
FF Legato	2004
Fenland	2012
Signo	2014

Availability

FF Balance is available from FontFont and resellers

Specimen

FF Balance type specimen. FontFont, Berlin, 1992 (210x120mm)

FF Balance
FF Balance
FF Balance
FF Balance

Schrift   caractère   typeface

Dutch type designer Evert Bloemsma (1958–2005) created only a handful of typefaces but they were among the most original – and the most subversive – in the history of typography. Central to most of his work was the contention that there is no absolute functional basis for the classic proportions of letterforms.

Bloemsma first began work on FF Balance as a student at the Arnhem Academy in 1981. After a long development period and several rejections it was finally released by FontFont in 1993. In the process of creating FF Balance Bloemsma explored ideas first proposed by Roger Excoffon in the design of Antique Olive (pp362–63). Working from the principle that legibility is largely determined by the movement of the eye across the tops of letters, he wanted to test whether emphasizing that part would have a positive effect on reading.

The result, FF Balance, shares two key characteristics with Antique Olive that defy typographic convention. The typeface has an inverted stress throughout – horizontal strokes are thicker than verticals – and its letters are heavier at the top than at the base. Functioning in a similar way to serifs in serif typefaces, these manipulations of positive and negative shapes within letters and words serve to guide the reader's eye along lines of text. FF Balance's letters are carefully modulated, composed entirely from curved strokes to provide stable, distinguishable forms. A by-product of this construction method is the useful feature that all weights are of equal width. Bodies of text therefore always occupy the same space, even when weights are substituted.

Considering how far FF Balance deviates from traditional norms, it is a remarkably effective text face. At large sizes its unconventional traits are visible, but when set at small sizes for long-form reading individual details merge to contribute to a harmonious and even colour that gently invites a horizontal reading direction. FF Balance is available in four weights with italics and small capitals, providing advanced typographic support with features such as old-style and lining figures, ligatures and alternate characters.

FF Balance was a bold attempt by Evert Bloemsma to overturn the sans serif tradition, but despite its ambition it has undeservedly seen little use.

Gleiche Breiten der Schriftstärken

Eine andere besondere Eigenschaft von FF Balance ist, daß jedes Zeichen des Alfabetes in einem Schnitt genau die gleiche Breite in allen anderen Schnitten besitzt. Hierdurch sind neue funktionale Lösungsmöglichkeiten vorstellbar, denn ohne Bedenken kann ein Text mühelos in einen anderen Schriftschnitt umgesetzt werden; Umbrüche und Textlänge bleiben exakt so, wie sie waren.

Eine andere besondere Eigenschaft von FF Balance ist, daß jedes Zeichen des Alfabetes in einem Schnitt genau die gleiche Breite in allen anderen Schnitten besitzt. Hierdurch sind neue funktionale Lösungsmöglichkeiten vorstellbar, denn ohne Bedenken kann ein Text mühelos in einen anderen Schriftschnitt umgesetzt werden;

Eine andere besondere Eigenschaft von FF Balance ist, daß jedes Zeichen des Alfabetes in einem Schnitt genau die gleiche Breite in allen anderen Schnitten besitzt. Hierdurch sind neue funktionale Lösungsmöglichkeiten vorstellbar, denn ohne Bedenken kann ein Text mühelos in einen anderen Schriftschnitt umgesetzt werden;

Eine andere besondere Eigenschaft von FF Balance ist, daß jedes Zeichen des Alfabetes in einem Schnitt genau die gleiche Breite in allen anderen Schnitten besitzt. Hierdurch sind neue funktionale Lösungsmöglichkeiten vorstellbar, denn ohne Bedenken kann ein Text mühelos in einen anderen Schriftschnitt umgesetzt werden;

Eine andere besondere Eigenschaft von FF Balance ist, daß jedes Zeichen des Alfabetes in einem Schnitt genau die gleiche Breite in allen anderen Schnitten besitzt. Hierdurch sind neue funktionale Lösungsmöglichkeiten vorstellbar, denn ohne Bedenken kann ein Text mühelos in einen anderen Schriftschnitt umgesetzt werden;

Même longueur des graisses de lettres

Les attributs propre au dessin du FF Balance ouvrent de nouvelles possibilités fonctionnelles au typographe: une ligne a toujours la même longueur quelle que soit la graisse de la lettre. Tous les caractères ont la même largeur, quelle que soit la graisse. On peut donc, sans peine, changer un texte dans une autre graisse. Le texte restera identique en longueur, sans remaniements.

black c. 15
une ligne a toujours la même longueur quelle que graisse de la lettre; on peut donc changer un tex

bold c. 15
une ligne a toujours la même longueur quelle que graisse de la lettre; on peut donc changer un tex

regular c. 15
une ligne a toujours la même longueur quelle que graisse de la lettre; on peut donc changer un tex

light c. 15
une ligne a toujours la même longueur quelle que graisse de la lettre; on peut donc changer un tex

Collis

Ty	**Collis**
Ca	**Serif**
Ke	**Old Style, Dutch**
Te	**Digital**
Da	**1993**
De	**Christoph Noordzij**
Fo	**Enschedé**
Co	**Netherlands**

Characteristics

Oblique stress
Moderate stroke contrast
Large x-height
Short ascenders and descenders
Bracketed foot serifs
Curved, angular head serifs
A Flat apex
J Descends below baseline
M Slightly splayed
Q Sweeping tail below letter
R Wide, curved leg
W Centre-strokes meet at apex
a Double-storeyed, small bowl
f r t Narrow
g Double-storeyed, open lower bowl

AMQRW
abcdefghij
orstuyaefg

Connections

Trinité	1982
FF Quadraat	1992
Dolly	2001
Alda	2008

Availability

Collis is available from the Enschedé Font
Foundry and resellers

Specimen

Neue Zürcher Bibel. Theologisher Verlag,
Zurich, 2007 (200x128mm)

Ezechiel 1,8–27

9: 11.23

sichter und ihre Flügel. 9 Ihre Flügel berührten einander. Wen
bewegten, änderten sie nicht die Richtung, jedes bewegte sic

10: 10,14; 41,18–19;
Offb 4,7

aus. 10 Und das war die Gestalt ihrer Gesichter: Sie hatten
schengesicht, und auf der rechten Seite hatten alle vier ein
sicht, und auf der linken Seite hatten alle vier das Gesicht ein

11: 9.23; Jes 6,2

und alle vier hatten ein Adlergesicht. 11 Das waren ihre Gesich
ihre Flügel waren nach oben hin ausgespannt; jedes hatte zwei

12: 17.20

berührten, und zwei, die ihre Leiber bedeckten. 12 Und jedes
sich geradeaus. Wohin der Geiststurm sich bewegen wollte, b
sie sich; wenn sie sich bewegten, änderten sie nicht die R

13: 4!

13 Und das war die Gestalt der Wesen: Ihr Aussehen war wie
nender Feuerkohlen; was sich zwischen den Wesen hin und he
te, hatte das Aussehen von Fackeln. Und das Feuer verbreite
Glanz, und aus dem Feuer zuckten Blitze. 14 Und die Wesen b
sich vorwärts und zurück, es sah aus wie ein Blitzen.

15–21: 3,13; 10,2.9–17
16: 10,9.10; 28,13;
Dan 10,5–6

15 Und ich sah die Wesen, und sieh: Da war je ein Rad auf
neben den Wesen, an ihren vier Vorderseiten. 16 Das Aussehe
der und ihre Machart war wie der Anblick von Topas, und alle
ten die gleiche Gestalt. Und sie sahen aus und waren gemacht,

17: 12; 10,17

ein Rad mitten im anderen Rad. 17 Wenn sie sich bewegten, b
sie sich nach ihren vier Seiten; wenn sie sich bewegten, ände

18: 10,12; Offb 4,8

nicht die Richtung. 18 Und ihre Felgen, sie waren hoch, und si
Furcht erregend: Ihre Felgen waren ringsum voller Augen, bei a
ren. 19 Und wenn die Wesen sich bewegten, bewegten sich d
neben ihnen, und wenn die Wesen sich von der Erde erhoben,

20: 12; 10,16

sich die Räder. 20 Wohin der Geist sich bewegen wollte, bewe
sich: dahin, wohin der Geist sich bewegen wollte. Und genau
erhoben sich die Räder, denn der Geist des Wesens war in den
21 Wenn diese sich bewegten, bewegten sich jene, und wenn d
hen blieben, blieben jene stehen, und wenn diese sich von der
hoben, erhoben sich die Räder genau wie sie, denn der Geist des
war in den Rädern.

22: 10,1; Gen 1,6–8;
Ex 24,10; Offb 4,6

22 Und was über den Köpfen der Wesen war, hatte die Gesta
Gewölbes, es war wie der Anblick eines Furcht erregenden Krist

23: 9.11

gespannt oben über ihren Köpfen. 23 Und unter dem Gewölb
ihre Flügel gerade ausgestreckt, jeder hin zum anderen; jedes ha

24: 3,13; 10,5; 43,2;
Offb 1,15 · Gen 17,1

die sie bedeckten, und jedes hatte zwei, die ihnen ihre Leiber be
24 Und ich hörte das Geräusch ihrer Flügel: Es war wie das G
grosser Wassermassen; wie die Stimme von Schaddai war es, w
sich bewegten, der Lärm einer Volksmenge, wie das Lärmen eine
lagers. Wenn sie stehen blieben, liessen sie ihre Flügel sinken.
25 Und es kam eine Stimme von oberhalb des Gewölbes, d
über ihren Köpfen befand. Wenn sie stehen blieben, liessen sie

26–28: 8,2;
Dan 10,5–6
26: 10,1; Jes 6,1;
Dan 7,9; Offb 4,3
27: 4! · 8,2

gel sinken. 26 Und oberhalb des Gewölbes, das sich über ihren
befand, war, dem Aussehen von Saphirgestein gleich, die Gesta
Throns, und auf der Gestalt des Throns, oben auf ihm, war die
von einem, der das Aussehen eines Menschen hatte. 27 Und ich

1,12: Für ‹Geist› und ‹Sturm› oder ‹Wind› verwendet das Hebräische dasselbe Wo
1,24: Siehe die Anm. zu Num 24,4.

Ezechiel 1,27–3,7

ler Anblick von Bernstein, es hatte das Aussehen von Feuer in
häuse, aufwärts von dem, was aussah wie seine Hüften, und
von dem, was aussah wie seine Hüften, ich sah etwas, das das
von Feuer hatte, und ringsum war ein Glanz. 28 Wie das Aus-
s Bogens, der am Regentag in der Wolke ist, so war das Ausse-
lanzes ringsum.

var das Aussehen der Gestalt der Herrlichkeit des HERRN. Und
nd fiel nieder auf mein Angesicht. Dann hörte ich die Stimme
n, der redete.

ng Ezechiels

er sprach zu mir: Du Mensch, stelle dich auf deine Füsse, und
ll zu dir sprechen! 2 Und sobald er zu mir sprach, kam Geist in
d stellte mich auf meine Füsse, und ich hörte den, der zu mir
Und er sprach zu mir: Mensch, ich sende dich zu den Israeli-
lationen, die sich auflehnen, die sich aufgelehnt haben gegen
und ihre Vorfahren haben mit mir gebrochen, so ist es bis auf
eutigen Tag. 4 Und zu den Nachkommen mit verhärteten Ge-
und hartem Herzen, zu ihnen sende ich dich, und du wirst ih-
n: So spricht Gott der HERR! 5 Und sie – mögen sie hören oder
, denn sie sind ein Haus der Widerspenstigkeit! –, sie sollen
lass ein Prophet unter ihnen gewesen ist. 6 Und du, Mensch,
ich nicht vor ihnen und vor ihren Worten. Fürchte dich nicht,
n sie dir widersprechen und Dornen für dich sind und du auf
en sitzt. Vor ihren Worten fürchte dich nicht, und vor ihren
rn hab keine Angst! Sie sind ein Haus der Widerspenstigkeit!
wirst ihnen meine Worte sagen, mögen sie hören oder es las-
sind ein Haus der Widerspenstigkeit!
aber, Mensch, höre, was ich zu dir rede. Sei nicht widerspenstig
Haus der Widerspenstigkeit, öffne deinen Mund, und iss, was
ebe. 9 Und ich sah, und sieh: Zu mir hin war eine Hand ausge-
nd sieh, in ihr war eine Schriftrolle. 10 Und er breitete sie vor
und sie war auf der Vorderseite und auf der Rückseite beschrie-
auf ihr aufgeschrieben waren Klagen und Seufzer und Wehru-

d er sprach zu mir: Du Mensch, iss, was du vorfindest, iss diese
ftrolle, und geh, sprich zum Haus Israel! 2 Und ich öffnete mei-
nd, und er liess mich jene Rolle essen. 3 Und er sprach zu mir:
, gib deinem Bauch zu essen und fülle dein Inneres mit dieser
olle, die ich dir gebe! Da ass ich sie, und in meinem Mund wurde
Ionig, süss.
d er sprach zu mir: Auf, du Mensch, geh zum Haus Israel, und
u ihnen mit meinen Worten. 5 Denn nicht zu einem Volk mit
iger Sprache und schwerer Zunge wirst du gesandt – zum Haus
, 6 nicht zu vielen Völkern mit schwieriger Sprache und schwe-
ge, deren Worte du nicht verstehst. Hätte ich dich zu diesen ge-
e würden dich anhören! 7 Das Haus Israel aber wird dich nicht

e Übersetzung «Hätte ich dich zu diesen gesandt, ...» beruht auf der griechischen
ng.

28: Gen 9,13 · 8,4! ·
3,23!

1: Dan 8,17

2: 3,24; 37,10.14;
Dan 8,18

3: 3,4 · 5,6; 11,12;
16,47; 20,1–44

4: 3,7; Ex 4,21;
Ex 7,3

5: 3,11.27 · 33.33

6: 3,9; Jer 1,8.17 ·
28,24

8: Jer 1,6 · 3,1;
Jer 1,9; Offb 10,8–11

9: 8,3 · Sach 5,2;
Offb 5,1; Offb 10,2

1: 2,8; Jer 1,9;
Offb 10,8–11

3: Offb 10,10 ·
Ps 19,11; Jer 15,16

4: 2,3
5: Jes 28,11!

7: 2,4; Jes 6,10

Christoph Noordzij (1959–) is a Dutch
typographer and book designer. In the
early 1990s he decided to draw a single
typeface for use in his own work. The
result, a functional and handsome Dutch
old-style serif, was initially called Collage,
after the name of his business.

The opportunity to extend it into a
complete family arose when Noordzij was
commissioned to design and produce the
Neue Zürcher Bibel (New Zurich Bible).
This was an extremely complex project
involving the publication of around 120
different editions in a wide range of page
layouts and book formats. Given the scale
of the assignment, Noordzij knew that a
custom typeface would be required and,
because his new design had already
proved exceptionally effective at small
sizes, he decided to develop it as a
dedicated Bible type.

The final cut of the typeface, released as
Collis in 1993 by Enschedé, has exemplary
book face attributes. It is full-bodied and
extremely economical in its use of space,
with a low contrast of thick and thin
strokes and stout ascenders and
descenders. At the same time, it retains
the dignified, convivial character of a type
from the Dutch old-style tradition.

Collis is also well equipped to perform
faultlessly in a variety of typographic
environments. The roman and italic both
feature very extensive character sets,
including non-alphabetic symbols, swash
character alternates and numeral sets
in lining, non-lining and fixed-width
versions. It can therefore be expertly used
for a wide range of purposes. Collis also
features some subtleties specifically for
book production in the German language.
Accented capitals, for example, have been
slightly reduced in height to allow for tight
line spacing, avoiding the visible intrusion
accents would otherwise have on the
space between the lines and the overall
colour of the page.

All of these features are distinctive, but
what really sets Collis apart is that, despite
the complexity of the typographic
problems it is capable of solving, Noordzij
has restricted it to a single weight only.
As a result, Collis is one of the most
unequivocally harmonious book faces
available today.

Ty	**DTL Documenta**
Ca	**Serif**
Ke	**Old Style, Dutch**
Te	**Digital**
Da	**1993**
De	**Frank Blokland**
Fo	**Dutch Type Library**
Co	**Netherlands**

Characteristics

Oblique stress
Moderate stroke contrast
Curving, bracketed serifs
A Flat apex, high crossbar
J Descends below baseline
M Very slightly splayed
Q Curved tail below letter
R Wide, curved leg
W Stepped centre-strokes, serif at apex
a Double-storeyed
g Double-storeyed, small lower bowl
r Narrow

AMQRW
abcdefghij
orstyaefg

Connections

Collis	1993
DTL Haarlemmer	1995
DTL Albertina	1996
Dolly	2001

Availability

DTL Documenta is available from the
Dutch Type Library and resellers

Specimen

Gotteslob, the prayer book of the
Catholic Church in Germany and Austria.
Katholische Bibelanstalt, Stuttgart, 2013
(170x110mm)

DIE FEIER DER SAKRAMENTE

601 2. Du sollst den Namen des Herrn, deines Gottes
2   missbrauchen.
     Der Gott des Lebens will nicht in Zusammenhäng
     werden, die gegen das Leben gerichtet sind: Mein
     Lüge, Verleumdung, Verfolgung und Krieg. Au
     lebendige Gott größer als all unsere Begriffe und V
     gen von ihm. Um seine Unverfügbarkeit und Grö
     zeigen, gebraucht die Bibel viele Begriffe und Bil
     Schöpfer des Himmels und der Erde, Fels und Burg
     und Quelle des Lebens. Er tröstet uns wie eine M
     begleitet uns auf all unseren Wegen. In Jesus Cl
     Gott uns Menschen nahe gekommen. Jesus Christ
     Ebenbild des unsichtbaren Gottes" (Kol 1,15).

... Rede ich mit Gott, bete ich?
... Wie rede ich von Gott? Bin ich bereit, meine I
     Vorstellungen von Gott immer wieder zu ül
     und der Fülle und Weite des biblischen Go
     anzupassen?
... Was ist mir in meinem Leben ‚heilig'? Wie be
     dem, was anderen Menschen heilig ist?
... Missbrauche ich den Namen Gottes zur Recht
     und Durchsetzung eigener Interessen?
... Bete ich vertrauensvoll und vermag ich mich in
     des lebendigen Gottes fallen zu lassen?

3   3. Gedenke des Sabbats: Halte ihn heilig.
     Zur Zeit des biblischen Israel war es geradezu rev
     Ein Volk glaubt an einen Gott, der ausnahmslos a
     den Sklaven, einen Ruhetag schenkt zum Aufa
     Seele und des Leibes. Zweifach wird dieser Ruheta
     det: Es ist der Rhythmus Gottes selbst, den er seiner
     fungswerk eingestiftet hat. Und Israel soll wenig
     einem Tag sichtbar werden lassen, dass es selbst aus
     verei Ägyptens befreit worden ist. Für uns Christe
     der Sonntag als Tag der Auferstehung Jesu zum zent

HILFEN ZUR GEWISSENSERFORSCHUNG

601
3

che. Er ist sowohl der Tag, an dem sich die Gemeinde
tesdienstlichen Feier versammelt, als auch ein Tag
ne und Entspannung.

ich mir bewusst, dass Leben mehr bedeutet als
eit und Leistung?
e ich meinem Bedürfnis nach Ausruhen und Aufat-
n von Leib und Seele gebührenden Raum?
e gehe ich mit meiner Zeit um? Wofür nehme ich
Zeit?
ich zu Stille und Ruhe fähig? Kann ich vor Gott ver-
llen und bei ihm Ruhe finden?
e ich dem Sonntag eine besondere Gestalt, die ihn
n Alltag abhebt? Ist es mir wichtig, an diesem Tag mei-
Glauben mit anderen Menschen zu teilen, im Gottes-
nst vor Gott zu treten, ihm zu danken und mich von
u für die kommende Woche stärken zu lassen?
s bedeutet mir die Schönheit der Schöpfung? Kann
ihr mit Ehrfurcht und Staunen begegnen und in ihr
t erfahren?

Die Heilige Schrift bezeugt uns Gott als einen G
e deinen Vater und deine Mutter.

't: „Ehre!" Nicht einfach: „Gehorche!" Es geht um den
tvollen Umgang mit den Eltern und den Menschen
veils älteren Generation. In biblischer Zeit sollten
en Eltern gebührend versorgt sein und schließlich
rdiges Begräbnis erhalten. Das 4. Gebot sichert das
tnis der Generationen zueinander und die soziale
tigkeit zwischen Jung und Alt. Es geht um eine gene-
nübergreifende Solidarität und die gegenseitige Ver-
rtung der Generationen. Dabei sind nicht nur die
sbedürfnisse der Eltern, sondern auch die der Kinder
ektieren. Kinder sind nicht der Besitz ihrer Eltern. In
eitiger Wertschätzung soll sich jeder als eigenstän-
rson entfalten und weiterentwickeln können.

4

At the end of the 1980s, during the revolution brought about by the advent of personal computing, the output resolution of widely available laser printers was only 300 dots per inch. The page layout software employed to control them and to compensate for their deficiencies was also relatively crude.

Dutch type designer Frank Blokland (1959–) started work on DTL Documenta within these extremely limiting constraints in 1986. His intention was to produce a typeface that would work well in small text sizes, even at low resolution, but without degradation to the form of the type, which would be contemporary, elegant and powerful. The development of the first range of weights and styles took around seven years, with intermediate bitmap versions being implemented in 1990 for book typesetting. Blokland's foundry, the Dutch Type Library, released the final PostScript typeface in 1993.

Robert Bringhurst has described DTL Documenta as a 'sturdy open text face'. It is a fine example of the Dutch type design heritage. Although no specific model was used as its basis, its letter shapes follow Renaissance principles, carefully reconciled against the limits of digital technology. Like other Dutch old-style types of the time, such as FF Quadraat (pp508–509) and Collis (pp512–13), it is low in stroke contrast, spatially economical and highly legible. With a tall x-height, sturdy serifs and open counterforms, it has an even colour at small point sizes, making it effective set in bodies of extended text. For this reason, it was selected in 2006 for use in the *Gotteslob* prayer book of the Catholic Church in Germany and Austria by the design consultancy Finken & Bumiller. Legibility and readability were among their main considerations in the choice of DTL Documenta, addressing the problem of reading the prayer book at relatively small point sizes in the low light conditions of churches.

Although in the past two decades DTL Documenta has been used extensively in corporate applications as well as in bookwork, its implementation in the publication of 3.6 million copies of the 1,300-page *Gotteslob* is an enduring testament to Blokland's achievement.

Ty	**House Gothic**
Ca	**Sans Serif**
Ke	**Geometric**
Te	**Digital**
Da	**1993**
De	**Allen Mercer and Tal Leming**
Fo	**House Industries**
Co	**USA**

Characteristics

Thick rectilinear strokes
Small internal spaces
Tight letter spacing
Extremely compressed
Extremely large x-height
Short ascenders and descenders

ABCDEFGHI
JKLMNOPQR
STUVWXYZ

Connections

Schmalfette Grotesk	1954
Eurostile	1962
Chalet	1996
Ed Interlock	2004

Availability

House Gothic 23 is available from House Industries and resellers

Specimen

House Gothic type specimen. House Industries, Wilmington, 1993 (305x230mm)

---

tracing the origins of... "HOUSE GOTHIC"

The roots of House Gothic grew not from the storied artists and technical masters of typography, but from the rough-cut hands of printers and composition specialists from the earlier part of this century. Most notable was the work of Alger Zitcus, an obscure but resourceful draftsman, commercial artist, typesetter and lithographer whose original type treatments were the driving force behind House Gothic. Starting his career in 1924 as a printer's apprentice, Alger's natural talent and attention to detail soon led to his becoming a virtuoso of the applied graphic arts and an indispensable asset in any print shop. He soon was in such demand that he often labored 18 to 20 hours per day with responsibilities ranging from rebuilding printing presses to laying out magazines and working as a customer service representative.

Hampered by the transient nature of Alger's employment, even the most experienced researchers found it difficult to find the origins of his unique typographic style. In late 1993, however, tireless art historians found the breakthrough they needed—a box of well-preserved, detailed journals located in a discarded storage locker from a south Chicago print shop. (The inscription "Zitcus" was engraved clearly on the locker.) Inside a one of the notebooks was a tattered, oil-soaked Heidelberg parts box and countless typographical studies. Expert scholars postulate that the deco condensed typeface on the box was an early reference for Zitcus Gothic. Apart from providing physical evidence, the journals are a cultural and emotional journey through the 50-year development of a distinct typographical style. The first versions of his lettering were upright, rounded and without flourish, reflecting the conservative nature of the printing business and the country as a whole as it suffered through the Great Depression.

Alger's typographic work remained as regimented as his career throughout the middle decades of this century, but the arrival of the 60's saw a significant cultural revolution and a major overhaul of his distinct lettering style which had become known industry-wide as Zitcus Gothic. On the brink of his 55th birthday, all evidence shows Alger not dreaming of retirement but working his way out of a rather severe mid-life crisis. The antidote for his ills was purchasing '63 Corvette Stingray, letting his hair grow over his ears, and overhauling his graphic arts philosophy. By 1967, Zitcus Gothic became taller, narrower and more ornamental, perhaps inspired by the proliferation of miniskirts, long legs and high patent leather boots preferred by women of this day. Judging from numerous sketches of such artifacts scattered throughout journals, on his known work surfaces, and even screen-printed on the walls of his apartment, Alger developed quite an obsession with this mode of fashion which he applied into his new "mod" gothic typeface.

The new Zitcus Gothic created a national furor among graphics professionals and advertising executives. After over 40 years of languishing in obscurity, Alger finally received the much-deserved attention he craved throughout his career. With the new notoriety, though, came a torrent of criticism from graphics industry pundits, the most vocal of which was an often-quoted and regularly-published visual arts critic named Jeremy Kneady. Mr. Kneady called the new typeface a "useless rehash of constructivist graphic language" and coined the term "Retro" (when referring to Alger's work) in his now famous keynote speech at the 1968 Convention of New York Art Directors. Criticism, however, only seemed to strengthen Alger's resolve as he continued to develop different weights and versions of Zitcus Gothic until he quietly passed away in 1975.

After his death, large type foundries were dismayed to find that Alger never created consistent specimens or large inkings of any of his work. Archivists were only able to find individual type treatments, repros and negatives. The work and the artistic ability required to create authentic versions of Alger's typefaces further prevented his unique lettering style from ever being converted into phototype and other mass-production formats. Lacking commercial availability, Zitcus Gothic waned into obscurity until House Industries obtained permission to faithfully interpret Alger's lifelong work into a family of electronic typefaces. Although the Zitcus estate gave House artists complete access to his life's work, they would not grant permission to use his name because of legal and licensing concerns. While not the first choice of House Industries, the name "House Gothic" effectively projects the simple elegance of Alger Zitcus's masterpiece of modern typography.

Reprinted with permission from Graphic Magic
Written by: Mr. Ron R. Roat, Jr

HOUSE INDUSTRIES IS PROUD TO INTRODUCE THE HOUSEGOTHIC FA...

HOUSEGOTHIC BLACK

AABCDEEFFGGHIIJKLM
PPQRRSSTUUVWXHY...

0123456789

UPPER CASE ALTE...

HOUSEGOTHIC LIGHT

AABCDEEFFGGHIJKLMM
NOPQRrSTUUVWXY...

0123456789

INCLUDES 4 LOWERCASE ALTERNATE CHARACTER SETS AS SEEN BELO...

 light one: abcdefghijklmnopqrstuvwxyz01234

 light two: abcdefghijklmnopqrstuvwxyz012

 light three: abcdefghijklmnopqrstuvwxyz012

 light four: abcdefghijklmnopqrstuvwxyz0123

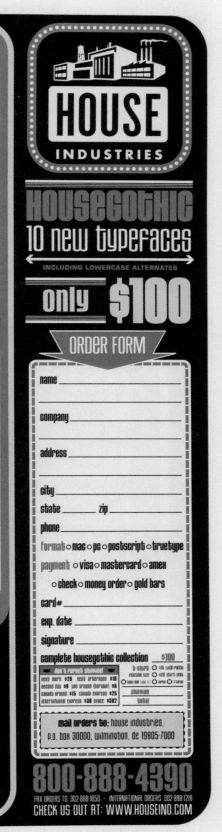

In its early days, House Industries, founded in Wilmington, Delaware, by Rich Roat and Andy Cruz in the 1990s, became well known for producing typefaces that celebrated various facets of mid-century American popular culture. Their work was often discounted as 'retro', a term Roat and Cruz felt was used in a thoughtlessly pejorative manner. In their 2005 monograph they asked why 'digital fonts based on early twentieth century metal type are appreciated as "typographic revival", while fonts reminiscent of hand-lettered Fillmore concert posters are dismissed as "retro"'.

Like many of the early House Industries typefaces, the House Gothic family came about as the result of a lack of an existing typeface that would suit their design work. In 1993, looking for a solution for the layout of the cover of *Emigre* 38, Allen Mercer (1972–), a talented illustrator and designer, decided to develop an ultra-compressed sans serif. This was based directly on the blocky type found on 1960s album covers for the Ventures together with a number of other visual references from the period.

The result is an extremely condensed display typeface that marries the rectilinear attributes of Compacta (pp366–67) with the hooked stroke qualities of Eurostile (pp364–65). Designed in a set of variant styles to be spaced very tightly, House Gothic's letter contours make for dramatically imposing, compressed headlines at larger sizes. The type's density is emphasized by strokes that in many instances completely enclose the counter forms which appear as thin white lines within them. Each weight features a conventional upper and lower case version and two novel unicase styles that merge upper and lower case forms into the same overall height.

Tal Leming (1975–) gave the collection a comprehensive overhaul in 2001. He re-engineered all of the existing styles for OpenType, developed a matching extended style and added a text version for use at small sizes. Each of House Gothic's original lower case and unicase character sets were rationalized in order to correspond accurately and they were augmented with collections of stylistic alternate characters. Two versions, black and dropshadow, were engineered so that designers could seamlessly fit together a large number of letter combinations taken from different House Gothic variants despite their varying heights and widths.

Ty	**Interstate**
Ca	**Sans Serif**
Ke	**Grotesque**
Te	**Digital**
Da	**1993**
De	**Tobias Frere-Jones**
Fo	**Font Bureau**
Co	**USA**

Characteristics

Most capitals have uniform width	
C c S s e Angled terminals	
G No spur	
Q Straight, angled tail	
R Straight, angled leg	
a Double-storeyed	
b d h k l n p q Angled stem terminals	
g Single-storeyed, short tail	
i j Round dots	
r t Angled terminals	
t Angled top-stroke	
y Straight tail	

AGMQRS
abcefghij
koprstuy

Connections

Highway Gothic	1948
Knockout	1994
Gotham	2000
Clearview Highway	2004

Availability

Interstate is available from the Font Bureau
and resellers

Specimen

Font Bureau Type Specimens. The Font
Bureau, Boston, 1995 (255x165mm)

INTERSTATE

TRAFFIC VIOLATIONS
BOLD

State trooper did not take kindly to my interpretive driving styl
LIGHT CONDENSED

FAST LANE
BOLD CONDENSED

Rush hour drivers become more and more frantic
REGULAR CONDENSED

CONSTRUCTION AHEAD
BLACK

ROADS ARE TORN UP & PLOWED UNDER
BOLD COMPRESSED

Work crews play catch with gobs of hot asphal
BOLD

Southbound Traffic
LIGHT COMPRESSED

Full of honking, yelling and shouting
LIGHT

DECREPIT MUFFLER IN TOW
BLACK CONDENSED

I made a quick visit to the drive-thru psychotherapis
REGULAR

THE THERAPIST TOLD ME THAT I SUFFER FROM AN OEDIPAL STICK SHIF
BLACK

A trail of sparks followed me down the road
BOLD CONDENSED

Commuter War Stories
BLACK COMPRESSED

IN RAGE AND FRUSTRATION, I THREW MY KEYS INTO THE RIVE
LIGHT

THEN I NOTICED I WAS MILES FROM HOM
REGULAR COMPRESSED

Light, Light Condensed, Light Compressed, Regular, Regular Condensed, Regular Compressed,
Bold, Bold Condensed, Bold Compressed, Black, Black Condensed, Black Compressed

ABCDEFGHIJKLMNOPQRSTUVWXYZabcdefghijklmnopqrstuvwxyzßfifl
¶\$§£¥#ƒ0123456789%‰¢°=‹+›'"¿?¡!&(/)[\]{|}*.,:;...«»‹›""''·„_•†‡@®©℗™√
áàâãäåæçéèêëíìîïñóòôõøœúùûüÿıÁÀÂÃÄÅÆÇÉÈÊËÍÌÎÏÑÓÒÔÕØŒÚÙÛÜŸ
special characters: ɑ←→↔↑↓↕✢

61

INTERSTATE

ight Grumpy wizards make toxic brew for the evil queen and jack. Lazy movers quit har rd packing of papier-mâché jewelry boxes. Hark! 4,973 toxic jungle water vipers quietly rop on zebras for meals! New farm hand (picking just six quinces) proves strong but laz ack in my quaint garden: jaunty zinnias vie with flaunting phlox. Waltz, nymph, for quic gs vex Bud. For only $65, jolly housewives made "inexpensive" meals using quick-froze

Regular Grumpy wizards make toxic brew for the evil queen and jack. Lazy movers qu it hard packing of papier-mâché jewelry boxes. Hark! 4,973 toxic jungle water vipers uietly drop on zebras for meals! New farm hand (picking just six quinces) proves str ng but lazy. Back in my quaint garden: jaunty zinnias vie with flaunting phlox. Waltz, ymph, for quick jigs vex Bud. For only $65, jolly housewives made "inexpensive" me

Bold Grumpy wizards make toxic brew for the evil queen and jack. Lazy movers qui ard packing of papier-mâché jewelry boxes. Hark! 4,973 toxic jungle water vipers uietly drop on zebras for metals! New farm hand (picking just six quinces) proves trong but lazy. Back in my quaint garden: jaunty zinnias vie with flaunting phlox. altz, nymph, for quick jigs vex Bud. For only $65, jolly housewives made "inexpen

Black Grumpy wizards make toxic brew for the evil queen and jack. Lazy movers uit hard packing of papier-mâché jewelry boxes. Hark! 4,973 toxic jungle water ipers quietly drop on zebras for meals! New farm hand (picking just six quinces) roves strong but lazy. Back in my quaint garden: jaunty zinnias vie with flaunti hlox. Waltz, nymph, for quick jigs vex Bud. For only $65, jolly housewives made

ight Condensed Grumpy wizards make toxic brew for the evil queen and jack. Lazy movers quit hard packing f papier-mâché jewelry boxes. Hark! 4,973 toxic jungle water vipers quietly drop on zebras for meals! New far arm hand (picking just six quinces) proves strong but lazy. Back in my quaint garden: jaunty zinnias vie with fl aunting phlox. Waltz, nymph, for quick jigs vex Bud. For only $65, jolly housewives made "inexpensive" meals sing quick-frozen vegetables. Sixty zippers were quickly picked from the woven jute bag. Jaded zombies acte

egular Condensed Grumpy wizards make toxic brew for the evil queen and jack. Lazy movers quit hard pac ing of papier-mâché jewelry boxes. Hark! 4,973 toxic jungle water vipers quietly drop on zebras for meals! ew farm hand (picking just six quinces) proves strong but lazy. Back in my quaint garden: jaunty zinnias vi ith flaunting phlox. Waltz, nymph, for quick jigs vex Bud. For only $65, jolly housewives made "inexpensiv eals using quick-frozen vegetables. Sixty zippers were quickly picked from the woven jute bag. Jaded zon

old Condensed Grumpy wizards make toxic brew for the evil queen and jack. Lazy movers quit hard pa cking of papier-mâché jewelry boxes. Hark! 4,973 toxic jungle water vipers quietly drop on zebras for eals! New farm hand (picking just six quinces) proves strong but lazy. Back in my quaint garden: jaun y zinnias vie with flaunting phlox. Waltz, nymph, for quick jigs vex Bud. For only $65, jolly housewives ade "inexpensive" meals using quick-frozen vegetables. Sixty zippers were quickly picked from the w

lack Condensed Grumpy wizards make toxic brew for the evil queen and jack. Lazy movers quit hard acking of papier-mâché jewelry boxes. Hark! 4,973 toxic jungle water vipers quietly drop on zebras r meals! New farm hand (picking just six quinces) proves strong but lazy. Back in my quaint garden unty zinnias vie with flaunting phlox. Waltz, nymph, for quick jigs vex Bud. For only $65, jolly hous ewives made "inexpensive" meals using quick-frozen vegetables. Sixty zippers were quickly picked

amiliarity is the foundation of legibility, lending this sanserif a strong edge as one of the most legible faces. nterstate is based on the signage alphabets of the United States Federal Highway Administration, alphabets hat we read every day as we drive. Tobias Frere-Jones designed Interstate in 1993, and in 1994 expanded it or the Font Bureau to full character sets in a full set of weights, prepared for both text and display; FB 1993·

Where DIN (pp266–67) is the typographic voice of Germany's road transport network, Interstate is immediately identifiable as its American equivalent. It is an adaptation of Highway Gothic, first used in the 1940s for the United States Federal Highway Administration's signage programme, a lettering style that has since become a definitive feature of the American landscape.

Interstate was developed by Tobias Frere-Jones (1970–) between 1993 and 1994 for Font Bureau. Frere-Jones is renowned for drawing inspiration from vernacular and historical lettering, preserving the authentic nature of found type and giving it new life through his work. In designing Interstate he wanted to retain Highway Gothic's utilitarian, homely charm while translating it into an effective type family, asking himself, 'if these forms were legible at 60 miles an hour, would they be legible at 8 point?'

Interstate is a sans serif face with a steady and consistent stroke weight that is conservative in its use of space, and even in tone when set in text. While proven as a typeface for navigational signage, it also has refinements that make it suitable for text setting in print and on-screen. The terminals of ascenders and descenders, such as the lower case l, p and t, are drawn at an angle to the stroke, and on curved strokes, like the lower case e and s, terminals are situated at 90 degrees to the stroke, placing them at an angle to the baseline. Counters are balanced and open, even in the bold and bold condensed weights, further contributing to legibility. A key distinguishing feature is the single-storeyed g with its truncated tail that corresponds with that of the j.

Since its introduction in 1993 the Interstate type family has been extended to a huge collection that now includes 40 faces from hairline to ultrablack weights in regular, condensed and compressed widths, and a monospaced set.

Ty	**Mantinia**
Ca	**Serif**
Ke	**Capitals**
Te	**Digital**
Da	**1993**
De	**Matthew Carter**
Fo	**Carter & Cone**
Co	**USA**

Characteristics

Proportions of classical inscriptions
Capitals and superiors
Lining figures
Small capitals
Tall capitals
Extensive ligatures and alternates

THERBP
AWMXY
CGQOSJ

Connections

Galliard	1978
Charlemagne	1989
Trajan	1989
Capitolium	1998

Availability

Mantinia is available from the Font Bureau
and resellers

Specimen

Mantinia type specimen. Carter & Cone,
Cambridge, Massachusetts, 1993
(279x216mm)

SEVENTY-2 PT

SIXTY 60 POINT

FIFTY-FOUR PT. 54

FORTY-EIGHT PT

FORTY-TWO POINT

THIRTY-SIX POINT

THIRTY (30) POINT

TWENTY-4 POINT

TWENTY POINT

EIGHTEEN PT

FOURTEEN PT

TWELVE PT

STOP!

80-FOURᴾᵀ

9TY·SIXᴾᵀ

108 PT

120 PT

144*

Mantinia was designed in 1993 by Matthew Carter (1937–) as a titling companion to Galliard (pp432–33), a crisply drawn old-style typeface that was intended for use in continuous text.

The design of Mantinia was motivated by Carter's appreciation of the letters painted and engraved by Andrea Mantegna (1431–1506), an Italian artist who pioneered the revival of the monumental capitals of imperial Rome during the Renaissance era. The lively product of both his scholarship and his skills, Mantegna's letters were exquisitely drawn and Carter's work is outstandingly successful in capturing their qualities.

For the construction of Mantinia, Carter worked with Apple's short-lived TrueType GX, a design technology that expanded the number of glyphs that could be accommodated within a character set and permitted their forms to be digitally manipulated. Using GX technology allowed him to introduce a wide range of distinctive attributes that were found in early handmade letters but had long since disappeared with the mechanization of the word brought about by the advent of printing. Mantinia features several rare ligatures and other connected characters found in stone inscriptions rather than in type, and a set of raised small capitals that align at the top, as well as a set of extra-tall capitals that are also inscriptional in origin.

Although Apple's TrueType GX format was quickly superseded, Mantinia was an instant success and was widely used, particularly in editorial work. Technically, it also had a lasting impact on the future direction of type design, precipitating a renewed interest among members of the design community in extending the potential limits of the character set. Matthew Carter himself has modestly suggested that Mantinia may have 'opened people's eyes to the possibilities of putting in a whole lot more characters'.

Ty	**Minimum**
Ca	**Sans Serif**
Ke	**Geometric**
Te	**Digital**
Da	**1993**
De	**Pierre di Sciullo**
Fo	**FontFont**
Co	**France**

Characteristics

Wide range of variant typefaces
Base forms: vertical and horizontal strokes
Alternates: vertical and angled strokes
All strokes of equal weight

ABCabefg
ABCabefg
ABCabefg

Connections

Van Doesburg's Lettering	1919
Vormgevers Lettering	1968
Le Maximum	1993
Le Trois-par-Trois	1995

Availability

FF Minimum is available from FontFont
and resellers

Specimen

Qui? Résiste No. 10: 'Donne-moi des
conseils'. Pierre di Sciullo, Paris, 1997
(297x210mm)

grosses

rater le changement

brûler le feu

s'abstenir

visiter le pays en 5 jours

laisser

cramer le

beurre

As a part of his commercial practice the French graphic designer Pierre di Sciullo (1961–) has developed a number of typefaces that explore connections between language, text and meaning. He is interested in the ambivalent relationship between image and text: of the effects of the visible word as a visual symbol as well as a vehicle for language. His typographic research is embedded within the context of his work on other projects; for him, creating type is not an end in itself but the construction of a tool.

A mischievous interest in prejudices about economy in the modern design canon is evident in Di Sciullo's extensive Minimum family. It is superficially reminiscent of the geometric lettering of the early modernist era, such as that of the Constructivist and De Stijl movements, and it raises questions about their influence on twentieth-century culture. The basic form of Minimum, shown here, could not be more reductive. It is a crude alphabet stripped to bare essentials, consisting mainly of vertical and horizontal lines. Initially, Minimum was drawn on-screen, pixel by pixel, in 1988. Subsequently, Di Sciullo used this alphabet as the basis for numerous variations of weight, width, incline and stroke formation. A collection of these typefaces was made commercially available in 1993 by FontFont, but the designer reserved the majority for use in his own publications and posters.

Of these, Di Sciullo has used one variant, Minimum Bichro, in architectural and environmental installations on a number of occasions. This typeface consists of a series of separate fonts, each of which contain only selected parts of letters – for example, vertical or horizontal strokes alone. By overlaying component types and adding different colours or textures to each layer, a huge variety of two- or three-dimensional outputs is possible.

At the time of its release by FontFont, Di Sciullo published a poster with the Minimum Bichro font split into two colours, displaying the words 'Supprimons tout ce qui est inutile'. This knowingly ironic provocation to 'stamp out everything useless' illustrates the playful ways in which Di Sciullo's work confronts preconceptions about utility. Asked to justify the practical uses of some of his other Minimum variants, he explained that one might be needed 'for the darkness', one for 'when you have lost your gun' and another for 'when you are drunk'.

Ty **Platelet**
Ca **Sans Serif**
Ke **Geometric**
Te **Digital**
Da **1993**
De **Conor Mangat**
Fo **Emigre**
Co **USA**

Characteristics

Monolinear and monospaced
Geometric character construction
Small, rounded corners at all terminals
b Upper case form with ascender
g Double-storeyed, open lower bowl
i l t Large, curved tails
m w Narrow, short middle downstrokes

ABEJKMRS
abcefghi
koprstwy

Connections	
FE-Schrift	1980
Template Gothic	1991
Suburban	1993
Eunuverse	1998

Availability

Platelet is available from Emigre and
resellers

Specimen

Platelet type specimen. Emigre, Berkeley,
1993 (210x133mm)

Platelet is based directly
on characters and figures
found on Californian
automobile license plates.

Its original character set
comprised only a single
lowercase alphabet and
non-lining figures, osten-
sibly to complement the
existing all-caps charac-
ters on the plates.

For its commercial release,
however, the set was
extended to include alternate small capitals and
other commonly used text
characters – somewhat

ironic considering that
the original brief had prin-
cipally been to create
specific display faces that
were not just scaled text
typefaces.

eg

the inspiration for platelet came
from the california license plate.

i‡çb 4H12994 éβk

similar to the composing restrictions of the typewriter, the
manufacturing of license plates
also requires the use of monospaced type; not only for mechanical requirements, but also to
fulfill the need of fitting a
fixed number of characters onto
each plate while maximizing
their legibility at a distance.

Conor Mangat (1968–) began the Platelet typeface at a student workshop given at CalArts, California, in 1992. The assignment brief required the design of an original alphabet for a specified outdoor purpose, taking into consideration its appropriateness in relation to traditions of typographic form-giving.

Mangat's response to the brief began as an investigation of the simple lettering found on Californian automobile licence plates. Within the short time frame of the original project he was limited to taking wax crayon rubbings from plates on vehicles in car parks and developing them as a lower case alphabet, freely interpreting those characters for which he had no visual reference.

Platelet's original character set was a single monospaced lower case with non-lining figures intended to correspond to the upper case characters found on the plates. Subsequently, the set was extended to include small capitals in the upper case register for its commercial release by Emigre in 1993. The published type family consisted of three matching weights – thin, regular and bold.

Platelet features some resourceful solutions to the visual problems that arise in monospaced type designs. It playfully manipulates the tendencies of geometric typefaces to erase unique letter attributes by adopting symmetries and repetitions that can render many characters virtually indistinguishable. In Platelet the lower case i and l fill their width not with the extended foot serifs that are customary but with large, curved exit strokes. The m and w overcome the density of their three downstrokes by simply cutting the middle ones short. The lower case b unambiguously incorporates the upper case form, avoiding any similarity to characters such as d that would otherwise occur because of the geometric rigidity of the type's construction. Platelet's monoline forms are further softened by small curves at terminals and junctions that reflect the mouldings of the original engineered letters from which it is derived.

With vernacular features that reference the American streetscape, Platelet has been referred to as a 'perfectly postmodern' typeface. A product of its time and place, Mangat has described it himself as 'a naive effort in many ways'.

Ty	**Suburban**
Ca	**Sans Serif**
Ke	**Geometric**
Te	**Digital**
Da	**1993**
De	**Rudy VanderLans**
Fo	**Emigre**
Co	**USA**

Characteristics

Geometric construction	
Mix of round and square terminals	
A	Low crossbar
I	Short head and foot serifs
M	Inverted W
Q q	Long, curved tail
W	Crossed centre-strokes
f g l y	Looped form
l	Is inverted y
s	Manuscript form
w	Compressed form

ABIMQRS
abcdefghijk
lmopqstuy

Connections

Keedy Sans	1989
Dead History	1990
Manuscript	1990
Template Gothic	1991

Availability

Suburban is available from Emigre and resellers

Specimen

Suburban and Whirligig type specimen. Emigre, Berkeley, 1994 (200x133mm)

Rudy VanderLans (1955–) is a Dutch graphic designer and photographer who co-founded the Emigre type foundry in Berkeley, California, with Zuzana Licko in 1984 and published *Emigre* magazine, a seminal journal concerning graphic design practice, from 1984 to 2005.

Suburban is the first and only solo attempt to date that VanderLans has made to design a typeface. Like Dead History (pp484–85), Keedy Sans and Template Gothic (pp498–99), all released by Emigre at about the same time, Suburban is underpinned by ideological concerns, raising questions about historical authenticity, hybridization, value and reappropriation in the postmodern era.

Suburban was a reaction against VanderLans's early design education, in which he confronted some of the basic rules and principles he had been taught about type design. He wanted to make a typeface deliberately lacking the conventional contrasts, balances and stresses that would supposedly make it 'correct' according to tradition. Like many designers attempting to create their first typeface, VanderLans's intention was to incorporate into a single design all of those disparate components from other typefaces that had always attracted him. 'These were script faces,' he said, 'in particular hand-lettered script faces, such as the ones you might find on the jersey of your local softball team.' In order to achieve a typeface that would function harmoniously, he simplified many of his stranger and more idiosyncratic forms and regulated many calligraphic features to conform to the character set.

The final typeface is characterized by its sampling of a diverse variety of alphabets including school blackboard lettering, modernist geometric forms and retro American showcard calligraphy. Suburban is an eclectic but harmonious combination of utilitarian letter parts, interspersed with eccentric shapes with highly personal connotations.

suburban

Suburban is my first attempt at the design of a complete typeface.

I imagine, like many designers who design their first font, that m[y]
too, was to incorporate into one design all of those components from
typefaces that I've always enjoyed. In my case, these were script faces,
ticular hand-lettered script faces, such as the ones you might find on th
sey of your local softball team.

However, in order to create a typeface with a slightly wider applica
than a hand-drawn script, many of the forms had to be simplified and
script features had to be stylized. The final alphabet, therefore, is a
bination of fairly rational, geometric shapes sprinkled throughout with
sical and calligraphy-inspired characters.

Designing Suburban also functioned as catharsis, an opportunity th[at]
lowed me to disprove (at least to myself) some of the basic notions
learned in art school regarding traditional type design. My type design te[acher]
would call Suburban a "vermicelli" font, a typeface lacking the necessar[y]
ible contrast and stresses between counters and strokes and/or optical
rections to make it a "successful" typeface. All valid notions, but
means the only route to legibility and/or beautiful type.

Suburban also pays homage, albeit in the tiniest of details, to J[effery]
Keedy's Keedy Sans and Barry Deck's Template Gothic and Arbitrary
three typefaces I continue to use and admire no end. In addition, whil[e]
signing Suburban, I paid close attention to avoid treading accidental[ly]
Keedy's as yet unreleased typeface Manuscript.

As it becomes increasingly difficult to create "original" typeface
signs, I am proud to report that Suburban can lay claim to being the
typeface in existence today that uses an upside down "l" as a "y." Crea[tivity]
knows no bounds.

– RUDY VANDERLANS

light

10 p

2 8

ABCDEFGHIJKLMN
OPQRSTUVWXYZ
bcdefghijklmnop
qrstuvwxyz
1234567890
?()[]&@#$%+=

ABCDEFGHIJKLMN
OPQRSTUVWXYZ
bcdefghijklmnope
rstuvwxyz
bold
36p
1234567890
!?()]&@#$%+=

29

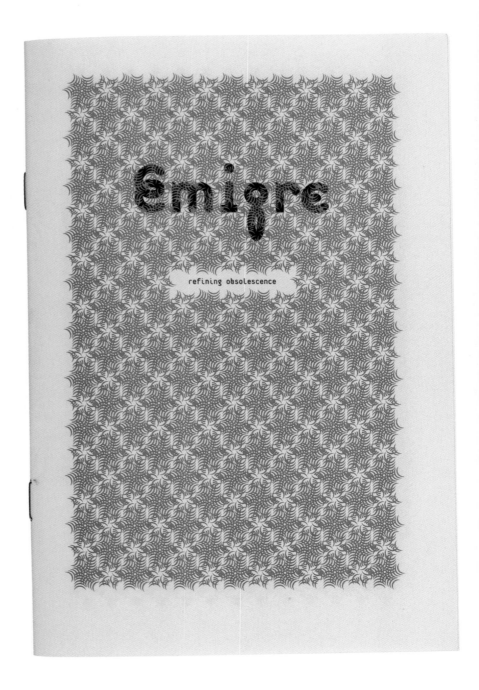

Emigre

refining obsolescence

527

Ty	**Aleph**
Ca	**Sans Serif**
Ke	**Geometric**
Te	**Digital**
Da	**1994**
De	**Philippe Apeloig**
Fo	**Nouvelle Noire**
Co	**France**

Characteristics
Modular geometric construction
Only two repeated components

abcdefg
ijlmopr
stuvwy

Connections
Banco	1951
Octobre	1994
ABF	2006
NB-Rietveld	2008

Availability
Aleph is available from Nouvelle Noire
and resellers

Specimen
Au coeur du mot – Inside the word.
Lars Müller Publishers, Zurich, 2001
(240x165mm)

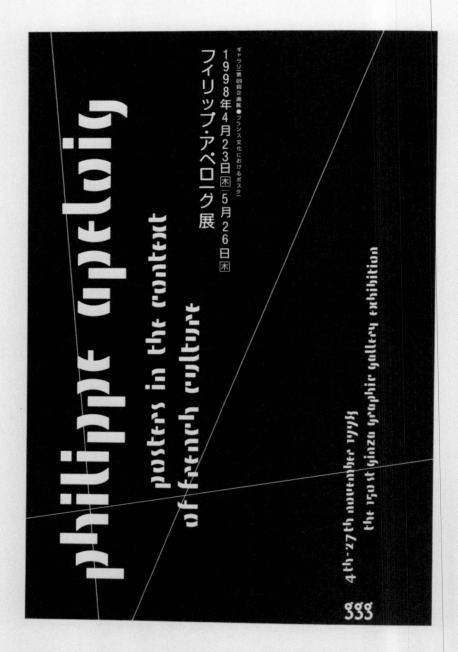

Exposition des affiches
de Philippe Apeloig
à la GGG Dai Nippon Printing
Gallery, Tokyo.
Affiche et prospecturs
1998

Exhibition
of Philippe Apeloig's posters
at the GGG Dai Nippon Printing
Gallery, Tokyo.
Poster and flyer.
1998

64

Caractère typographique : *Aleph*.
1994

Typeface : *Aleph*.
1994

a b c d
e f g h
i j k l m n
o p q r s t
y u w x
y z

In Philippe Apeloig's 1994 typeface Aleph a severe geometric construction method is counterbalanced with the graceful flow of calligraphic mark-making. Apeloig (1962–) is foremost a graphic designer rather than a type designer and Aleph is one of several bespoke alphabets that he has created for use in a range of projects where his approach, he says, is 'innocent, clumsy, and playful'.

Apeloig has suggested that typographic design need not depend only on functional considerations. His display alphabets often exceed the bounds of utilitarian norms such as legibility or reproducibility and operate as purely visual elements, providing rhythm, structure and interest with an almost mathematical precision.

He originally drew Aleph for a promotional poster announcing an exhibition of his own graphic work in Japan, shown on the opposite page. The poster's headline type runs vertically, rotated through 90 degrees in a manner that echoes Oriental writing traditions. With the exception of the thin arms of the t and f, its letters are composed solely from repetitions of two modular components: straight stems of equal thickness and shorter vertical strokes with slight arcs. These appear to follow the movement of a broad-nibbed pen or a flat brush, giving a sense of the spontaneous energy of Japanese brush calligraphy.

Aleph operates in the space between sharp, clean austerity and classical humanist calligraphy. The striking inscrutability of its bold, fragmented characters are well suited to display applications. Like a minimalist homage to Roger Excoffon's 1951 Banco typeface (pp328–29), the stencil-like breaks that result from Aleph's construction method impose an appealing visual game on the reader, who must distinguish the ambiguous spaces between and within letters in order to decode them.

Ty	**Comic Sans**
Ca	**Script**
Ke	**Casual, Non-connected**
Te	**Digital**
Da	**1994**
De	**Vincent Connare**
Fo	**Microsoft**
Co	**USA**

Characteristics

Monolinear with rounded terminals
Irregular strokes without symmetries
Irregular stem angles
I Stem has terminal strokes to distinguish
from lowercase l and figure 1
Y Lower case form with angled stem
a Single-storeyed, bent stem
t Straight stem, no foot

AIMQRY
abcefghij
koprstuy

Connections

Tekton	1989
Chalkboard	2003
Lexia Readable	2004
FF Duper	2009

Availability

Comic Sans is widely available

Specimen

'Comic Sans for Cancer' exhibition book.
The Proud Archivist, London, 2014
(207x160mm)

'Comic Sans walks into a bar. Bartender says, "We don't serve your type."' Few typefaces have been more vilified by members of the design profession than this amiable script. Conversely, few typefaces have been more popular with those outside of it.

In 1994 Vincent Connare (1960–) was working on a team at Microsoft that was developing PC software for the home-consumer market. Connare had already created several 'fonts looking like Pizza, monsters and ones with snow' for various child-oriented applications. He was concerned when he saw a beta version of an application for children, Microsoft Bob, using the stiffly formal Times New Roman typeface in the speech bubbles of a cartoon dog, and he decided to design a more playful typeface based on the lettering style used in comics, referencing issues of *Batman* and *Watchmen*. An astute product manager subsequently recognized the design's potential and it has been a standard typeface in Microsoft's operating system continuously since Windows 95.

Comic Sans achieved unprecedented success as personal computers became widespread. It is extensively used today by people of all ages, nationalities and backgrounds for every conceivable kind of communication. Largely because of its almost universal popularity, many design practitioners have ridiculed both the typeface and its users, disregarding any intrinsic features in order to damn it merely by association with applications that they regard as unprofessional, ignorant and inferior.

Ironically, it is its very lack of finesse that makes Comic Sans so popular with non-designers. It is designed to look as if it was not designed at all but rather written hesitantly with a felt-tip or ballpoint pen. Its rounded, asymmetrical features give it an approachable, modest and truthful impression. The sense of authenticity is enhanced by unconnected letters that sit on a bouncily uneven baseline, with a large x-height and an untutored wonkiness particularly evident in the irregular angles of supposedly upright stems.

Asked to explain the global appeal of his design, Vincent Connare offered a succinct opinion: 'Comic Sans isn't complicated, it isn't sophisticated, it isn't the same old text typeface like in a newspaper. It's just fun – and that's why people like it.'

Please do not put your cigarette butts in the urinal. It makes them soggy and difficult to light.

Thank you.

Comic Fucking Sans 1994—2014

This page: Observatory

That page: Oli Frape

Ty	**Fontesque**
Ca	**Serif**
Ke	**Old Style, Calligraphic**
Te	**Digital**
Da	**1994**
De	**Nick Shinn**
Fo	**FontFont**
Co	**Canada**

Characteristics

Underlying construction similar to old style
Uneven baseline
Irregular stroke angles and curves
All characters divide into small and large
sections to create asymmetrical forms

ABCMRS
abcefghijkm
orstuvyaefg

Connections

Nicolas-Cochin	1912
Goudy Oldstyle	1915
Bernhard Modern	1937
FF Oneleigh	1999

Availability

Fontesque is available from FontFont and
resellers

Specimen

Nick Shinn, *Serious Fun. Fontesque: The
Theory Behind the Whimsy*. Shinntype,
Toronto, 1997 (220x140mm)

British-Canadian type designer Nick Shinn (1952–) created Fontesque between 1994 and 2010. Inspired by the work of eminent American lettering artists like Oswald 'Oz' Cooper and Frederic W. Goudy, who believed that type should not be absolutely perfect, Shinn intended to design a script type that, he said, would be 'very loose, with really extreme proportions, but at the same time … beautifully drawn'.

At first glance Fontesque's cartoon-like appearance evokes a warm, old-fashioned impression, but this is deceptive. Beneath the typeface's apparent levity Shinn was exploring a number of serious visual ideas. His extensive design procedure began with sketches in ballpoint pen, which he then refined by hand. Once satisfied, he scanned the letters into Photoshop and manipulated them extensively before finally importing them into a type-design program for production.

To achieve a fluid, animated appearance, Shinn modified the sizes and proportions of individual letters, positioning them on an uneven, bouncing baseline and varying the twisted stems of the ascenders and descenders. Individual characters were treated like elastic, stretched into sinuous curves and given internal proportions that did not divide evenly: each letter was designed asymmetrically to contain two sections, one small and one large. Shinn used these strategies to avoid the usual stiffly repetitive rhythms of mechanical type and to maximize the liquidity of the space within and around letters. His efforts had the unexpected effect of making Fontesque remarkably easy to read.

The original Fontesque is a playful but delicate type, best suited to headline settings. To achieve a wider functionality in text applications, Shinn designed a more robust version in 2010. Preserving the impression of the original, Fontesque Text's weight is slightly heavier, the hairlines thicker and the serifs larger.

The Fontesque family's two optical cuts each have four weights with matching italics. Fontesque provides advanced typographic features such as ligatures, alternate characters and a full range of figure styles. With extensive support for several Latin-based languages, the type family also includes the Cyrillic alphabet.

ZEITSCHRIFT DER
VEREINIGUNG
BILDENDER
KÜNSTLER
ÖSTERREICHS

4

5

It is a cliché of typography that it's such a subtle art, that one cannot appreciate the true quality of a type from a few characters or words: it only reveals itself when the characters are set en masse, in text. Perhaps; but that doesn't mean the individual letters should lack distinction. Under the guise of subtlety, so many lazy, timid or visionless type designers have for decades been churning out bland me-too typefaces that are barely distinguishable from one another. The establishment has continually reupholstered the chairs while the public cries out for new furniture, built from scratch. Thank God for Fontographer.

One hundred years ago, art nouveau artists such as Koloman Moser fearlessly explored the mutability of the alphabet's geometry (fig. 4). This particular piece was a benchmark. Not that I was inclined to copy the look or the shapes; it's a testimony of how far the envelope of letterform could be pushed, yet held together by sheer style. Moser pointed the way to a type of

unusual, lively letterfor

Another call to irreg the allure of antiques th hand-made and dog-ear deny that I'm hooked o technology, thrilled by t at my fingertips, but at time it horrifies me. W page of type (fig. 5) was the 17th century, before industrial revolution, it world where uniformity This wobbly type, which locked up firmly enough chase, is an extreme dis the haphazard quality p some extent in all letter printing. Now we're sur by precise, mass-produc cles, and a page of medio century type becomes a cherish, an icon of what to be human, to be impe

Mechanized mass pro turned the notion of pe on its head: where once finish was like magic, so that only the very best men could achieve after practice, now machines it off effortlessly. In resp William Morris reconst

Serious Fun

Fontesque: the theory behind the whimsy

Nick Shinn

Giza

Ty	**Giza**
Ca	**Slab Serif**
Ke	**Egyptian**
Te	**Digital**
Da	**1994**
De	**David Berlow**
Fo	**Font Bureau**
Co	**USA**

Characteristics

Fat vertical strokes thicker than horizontals
Heavy, rectangular slab serifs
Small counterforms
Q Curved tail below letter
R a t Tail turns upwards
a c f r y Square terminal
g Double-storeyed
i j Square dots

AEGQR
abcefghi
noprsty

Connections

Thorowgood's Egyptian	1821
Rockwell	1934
Beton	1936
Ziggurat	2000

Availability

Giza is available from the Font Bureau and resellers

Specimen

Font Bureau Type Specimens, third edition. The Font Bureau, Boston, 2001 (268x180mm)

MINERAL DEPOSITS
FIVE FIVE
MINE
NINE FIVE
36 Miles Underground
SEVEN SEVEN
IRON ORE
SEVEN NINE
FORTUNE IN GEMS & METALS
FIVE SEVEN
Riches of the earth sold
THREE ONE
HINTERLAND CLEARED OUT FOR SHOPPING MALLS
FIVE THREE
CHEMISTS
ONE THREE
Give Lectures at Local High School
THREE FIVE
Defiant
NINE THREE
Violent Debate
SEVEN NINE
FERMENTATION PROCESS
FIVE THREE

The sixteen styles of Giza bring back the colorful power and variety of the original Egyptian letterforms, a glory of the Victorian era. Designer David Berlow based the family on showings in Vincent Figgins' specimen of 1845, the triumphant introduction of this thunderous style. The truly unforgettable 'Nine' weights were designed for ultimate emphasis in posters, and do their most effective work in the very largest of sizes; FB 1994

16 STYLES: THE FIRST NUMBER INDICATES WEIGHT, AND THE SECOND NUMBER WIDTH

BRAND NEW MIRACLE CURE!

A soothing cream to be applied topically. Proven to correct

**Migraines - Anxiety - Hair Loss
Eczema - Rheumatism - Aches
Indigestion - Cholic - Insomnia
Swollen Hands & Feet - Pains
Constipation - Skin Blemishes**

and other discomforts & illnesses too numerous to list here.

SECRET FORMULA CONTAINS

OVER 103 ALL-NATURAL

INGREDIENTS

Invented by internationally renowned druggist

Dr. M.J. ZIMMER

PATENTS PENDING IN THE U.S.A. AND OVER 36 COUNTRIES ABROAD

61

In the early nineteenth century archaeological discoveries in Egypt instigated a fashion in Europe for everything associated with the ancient kingdom. Type founders capitalized on the craze by using the name 'Egyptian' for several bold new display typefaces, a marketing exercise that was not based on any actual connection to the source it referenced but was intended to conjure a sense of the exotic, mysterious and monumental.

Type designer David Berlow (1954–) of the American type foundry Font Bureau is renowned for his expertise in reviving long-forgotten typefaces for the digital era. He has observed: 'What is fascinating to me about the types of the past is that they take me to a particular place and time.'

Among the most dramatic of his historical revivals is one based on examples of the Egyptian shown in Vincent Figgins's specimen of 1815. Named after the region near Cairo where the pyramids stand, Font Bureau's Giza resurrects the thunderous power of Figgins's original letterforms, in which colossal weights were used for maximum effect on posters at the largest possible sizes. Giza increases in width and proportion across a range of 16 styles characterized by extremely thick strokes and serifs offset by minute counterforms. For the Giza family, conventional weight designations such as 'bold' or 'black' would have been unworkable, so Berlow used a logical numbering system indicating first weight then width.

In 2007, evaluating his fascination with the painstaking revival of antique letterforms in relation to what he called 'the physically vacant nature of type's modern form', Berlow attributed the success of his typefaces to the work of graphic designers who implemented them skilfully, saying 'lots of people between me and the viewer wanted to take the viewer to a slightly more soulful place, perhaps'.

Ty	**Knockout**
Ca	**Sans Serif**
Ke	**Grotesque**
Te	**Digital**
Da	**1994**
De	**Jonathan Hoefler**
Fo	**Hoefler Type Foundry**
Co	**USA**

Characteristics

C c S s e	Flat and angled terminals
G	Has spur
Q	Short, upward-curved tail
R	Curved leg
a	Double-storeyed, curved foot
e	Thin crossbar
f r	Narrow, vertical terminals
g	Double-storeyed, raised ear
i j	Square dots
t	Angled top-stroke and flat, curved foot
y	Curved tail

AGMQR
abcefghij
koprstuy

Connections

Bureau Grot	1989
Champion Gothic	1990
Interstate	1993
Gotham	2000

Availability

Knockout is available from Hoefler & Co.

Specimen

The Hoefler Type Foundry Catalogue of Typefaces, fourth edition. Hoefler Type Foundry, New York, 2000 (279x216mm)

6 tel. 212 777 6640 | *NEW RELEASE! exclusively from* THE HOEFLER TYPE FOUNDRY, INC

KNOCKOUT™ THIRTY TWO FONTS

A family of 32 typefaces expanding on the Champion Gothic series, jointly developed for THE NEW YORK TIMES MAGAZINE, SPORTS ILLUSTRATED, PREMIERE *and others.*

Residential Restrictionist Raises
KNOCKOUT № 26 JUNIOR FLYWEIGHT   series A

Realtor Ratifies Reversal
KNOCKOUT № 27 JUNIOR BANTAMWEIGHT   series A

Redshirted Roseville
KNOCKOUT № 28 JUNIOR FEATHERWEIGHT   series A

Recommendation
KNOCKOUT № 29 JUNIOR LIGHTWEIGHT   series A

Rememberable
KNOCKOUT № 30 JUNIOR WELTERWEIGHT   series A & B

Rehabilitates
KNOCKOUT № 31 JUNIOR MIDDLEWEIGHT   series B

Reichsmark
KNOCKOUT № 32 JUNIOR CRUISERWEIGHT   series B

Rockslides
KNOCKOUT № 33 JUNIOR HEAVYWEIGHT   series B

Rekindles
KNOCKOUT № 34 JUNIOR SUMO   series B

Relevant Restaurant Referendu
KNOCKOUT № 46 FLYWEIGHT   series

Realizes Rustic Rationale
KNOCKOUT № 47 BANTAMWEIGHT   series

Redeems Rensselae
KNOCKOUT № 48 FEATHERWEIGHT   series

Remorselessness
KNOCKOUT № 49 LIGHTWEIGHT   series

Relentlessness
KNOCKOUT № 50 WELTERWEIGHT   series C &

Rattlesnakes
KNOCKOUT № 51 MIDDLEWEIGHT   series

Reschedule
KNOCKOUT № 52 CRUISERWEIGHT   series

Rainstorm
KNOCKOUT № 53 HEAVYWEIGHT   series

Romance
KNOCKOUT № 54 SUMO   series

KNOCKOUT № 70 **ABCDEFGHIJKLMNOPQRRSTUVWXYZ** KNOCKOUT № 34 ABCDEFGHIJKLMNOPQRRSTUVWXYZ KNOCKOUT № 47 ABCDEFGHIJKLMNOPQRRSTUVWX

KNOCKOUT № 48 abcdefghijklmnopqrstuvwxyz KNOCKOUT № 93 **abcdefghijklmnopqrstuvwxyz** KNOCKOUT № 32 abcdefghijklmnopqrstuvwxyz abcdefghijklmnopqrstuvwxy.

KNOCKOUT № 31 1234567890 KNOCKOUT № 74 **1234567890** KNOCKOUT № 50 (¡!¿?&$£¥€ƒ¢) KNOCKOUT № 92 (¡!¿?&$£¥€ƒ¢) KNOCKOUT № 53 {Æ æ Œ œ fi fl ff ffi ffl ß} KNOCKOUT № 30 ÁÇÉÑÌØÛŸ KNOCKOUT № 72 åçéñìøû

see also
KNOCKOUT SYNOPSIS *p. 22*
CHAMPION GOTHIC *p. 32–33*

Reveals Reformational Resolution
KNOCKOUT № 66 FULL FLYWEIGHT — *series E*

Rural Route Renters Riled
KNOCKOUT № 67 FULL BANTAMWEIGHT — *series E*

Raffish Resemblance
KNOCKOUT № 68 FULL FEATHERWEIGHT — *series E*

Rumbustiousness
KNOCKOUT № 69 FULL LIGHTWEIGHT — *series E*

Rosicrucianism
KNOCKOUT № 70 FULL WELTERWEIGHT — *series E & F*

Reconstructed
KNOCKOUT № 90 ULTIMATE WELTERWEIGHT — *series G*

Roundabouts
KNOCKOUT № 71 FULL MIDDLEWEIGHT — *series F*

Redecorated
KNOCKOUT № 91 ULTIMATE MIDDLEWEIGHT — *series G*

Refinanced
KNOCKOUT № 72 FULL CRUISERWEIGHT — *series F*

Reversions
KNOCKOUT № 92 ULTIMATE CRUISERWEIGHT — *series G*

Recursion
KNOCKOUT № 73 FULL HEAVYWEIGHT — *series F*

Refurbish
KNOCKOUT № 93 ULTIMATE HEAVYWEIGHT — *series G*

Received
KNOCKOUT № 74 FULL SUMO — *series F*

Radiates
KNOCKOUT № 94 ULTIMATE SUMO — *series G*

Six years in production, Knockout is a grand redevelopment of our first typeface, Champion Gothic. Knockout extends Champion's usefulness through 32 new styles, each created to tackle a specific situation that Champion was never intended to address.

SMALLER SIZES
Unlike Champion Gothic, which was designed as a headline face, Knockout was conceived from the outset as a family of types for both text and display. Even its bold fonts work in text sizes, and the lighter fonts work in smaller sizes still – some as tiny as 3½ point.

LARGER RANGE
Knockout continues in Champion's tradition of providing fonts built around a 'width axis,' this time extending into even wider and narrower territories. Knockout additionally has a 'weight axis,' so weight and width can be changed independently of one another.

NAMES AND NUMBERS
To make the fonts easier to organize, each style has been given a number to describe its position in the grid. Adding or subtracting *one* takes you wider or narrower; adding or subtracting *twenty* yields fonts that are bolder or lighter.

THE SEVEN SERIES
Knockout's 32 styles are sold in seven different 'series,' each shown on its own spread in the following pages. See page 22 for a synopsis.

KNOCKOUT № 72
ABCDEFGHIJKLMNOPQRRSTUVWXYZ

KNOCKOUT № 27
ABCDEFGHIJKLMNOPQRRSTUVWXYZ

KNOCKOUT № 51
ABCDEFGHIJKLMNOPQRRSTUVWXYZ

KNOCKOUT № 29
abcdefghijklmnopqrstuvwxyz

KNOCKOUT № 54
abcdefghijklmnopqrstuvwxyz

KNOCKOUT № 91
abcdefghijklmnopqrstuvwxyz

KNOCKOUT № 27
abcdefghijklmnopqrstuvwxyz

KNOCKOUT № 54
1234567890

KNOCKOUT № 49
1234567890

KNOCKOUT № 32
(¡!¿?&$£¥€ƒ¢)

KNOCKOUT № 94
{ÆæŒœfiflﬀﬁﬄﬃß}

KNOCKOUT № 71
[¶§†‡@*]

KNOCKOUT № 51
ÀÇÉÑÌØÛŸ àçéñìøûÿ

In 1994 *Sports Illustrated* magazine asked American type designer Jonathan Hoefler (1970–) to redevelop one of his existing faces, Champion, to include an extensive range of widths and weights for use in headlines. Hoefler is a type archaeologist with a profound understanding of its history and a particular fascination with the origins of American vernacular forms. He found inspiration for Champion and its radical new redesign, Knockout, in the typefaces used in nineteenth-century American playbills and posters promoting circuses, boxing matches and other public events.

These early poster typefaces were cut in wood and evolved as a loose collection over time, rather than being based on a prescribed design framework from which all styles were descended. Later modernist typographers introduced the notion of the rationalized type 'family' that has become prevalent today. In modern types all styles are based on common geometries in order to relate closely to one another, but nineteenth-century display faces were disparate collections that had been brought together on the basis of similarities alone, without overarching governing principles. Because these typefaces were never intended to conform to one another, their design characteristics were driven by internal demands: each weight and style faced different challenges and afforded different design possibilities. This makeshift approach to type design allowed for much local variation in appearance, and it is this unpredictable approach that Knockout celebrates.

Knockout is a large, well-organized type family consisting of 32 sans serifs in nine widths and four weights. These are individually designed to be free from the conventional hierarchy of regular, bold and so on, in order to offer a variety and vitality that would be impossible to achieve with even the best modern sans serif families. Hoefler designed Knockout as a workhorse typeface, producing a range of styles that was far wider than anticipated by *Sports Illustrated* and providing the magazine with a broad and flexible editorial platform. 'I think that's one of the reasons people like Knockout', Hoefler commented, 'because it offers an especially large range of different voices.'

Ty	**Thesis**
Ca	**Serif / Sans Serif**
Ke	**Superfamily, Humanist**
Te	**Digital**
Da	**1994**
De	**Lucas de Groot**
Fo	**FontFont**
Co	**Netherlands**

Characteristics

TheSans:

B E F P	Narrow
C c G g S s e	Near vertical terminals and large apertures
G	No spur, no arm
M	Splayed
Q	Separate tail below letter
R	Straight, angled leg
a	Double-storeyed, straight stem
a f r t	Vertical terminals
g	Double-storeyed
i j	Round dots
t	Angled top-stroke
y	Curved tail

ABGMQR abcefghij koprstuy

Connections

Romulus	1936
Lucida	1985
Rotis	1988
PMN Caecilia	1991

Availability

Thesis is available from LucasFonts and resellers

Specimen

Thesis type specimen poster. FontFont, Berlin, 1994 (210x148mm)

Thesis pioneered the concept of the superfamily, the multipurpose type system that has since become an important tool in typographic design practice. It was the result of Dutch designer Lucas de Groot's dissatisfaction with the limited range of effective typefaces available for corporate communications projects in the early 1990s.

With Thesis, De Groot (1963–) aimed to offer users a wide range of coordinated styles. Where different design problems usually demand different choices of typeface – text or display, print or web, for example – implementing the Thesis family across an entire project helps maintain a typographic unity that also allows for contrast, hierarchy and differentiation. In use, this implies strategic coordination, both visually and conceptually.

First published in 1994 as part of the FontFont collection, the family was conceived as a versatile typographic system with an ambitious scope. At the time of its release, Thesis was the largest type family on the market, and by 2004 it included 144 individual typefaces with over 32,000 glyphs in total. Constructed around a core set of common letter shapes, the original Thesis superfamily includes TheSans, a sans serif; TheSerif, a slab serif; and TheMix, a semi sans – each with corresponding italics. More recent subfamily extensions include condensed and hairline display variants, along with TheAntiqua, TheSansMono, TheSans Typewriter and TheSansArabic.

The most successful and enduring components of Thesis are its TheSans and TheSerif styles. These subgroups both have a low contrast with slight differentiation between thin and thick strokes. However, references to the flow of writing with a broad-nibbed pen are evident throughout, and character construction is evidently modelled on a Renaissance old-style armature, providing an amiable but commanding impression. The roman letters have a subtle diagonal stress and a forward flow that helps to facilitate easy reading. In both typefaces the italic forms are very distinctive: they were not derived from the upright but were individually designed to complement the roman forms.

Lucas de Groot's Thesis is a significant contribution to the history of type: a coherent, elegant and inviting family that can be relied on to perform impeccably in both editorial work and brand communications.

, FFTheMix™ ★ *Typeface family by* Luc(as) de Groot ★ FFThesis is available at FontShop ★ 1

Thesis™

ORMS

6 STYLES

8 WEIGHTS

heSans **i**

heSerif **i**

heMix **i**

Plain	The Quick 1234567
Italic	*brown fox jumps 8*
CAPS	OVER THE LAZY 901
CAPS ITALIC	*DOG 2345678*
Expert	123 → ♡ ≈ ☞ @ Þ
Expert Italic	

Extra Light

Light

Semi Light

Normal

Semi Bold

Bold

Extra Bold

Black

ExtraLight (2) *negative* ≈ Light (3) *posi*

ExtraBold (8) *positive* ≈ **Bold (7)** *nega*

SemiBold (6) *backlit* ≈ **Bold (7)** *refle*

ExtraBold (8) *backlit* ≈ **Bold (7)** *refle*

Regular (5) *reading size* ≈ SemiBold (6) *sma*

The eight weights of Thesis have been chosen carefully. With help of the interpolation theory the optical difference between two following weights is constant within the whole range of weights. To distinguish weights in normal situations, 'two steps' are advised: use Bold (7) and Light (3) in combination with normal (5), but not SemiBold (6) or SemiLight (4).
In three specific situations the one-step difference is very useful: when *negative* text should have the same appearance as *positive* text use one step lighter. When *backlit positive* text should have the same appearance as *positive* text that *reflects* light, use one step heavier and with *negative* text one step lighter to compensate for light overflow. When *small* text (e.g. footnotes) should have the same 'color' as the main text use one step heavier.

LES 14PT/5.94 MM (16.838PT); SPACING 0.

-EXTRALIGHT Wij kiezen voor deze groep de
'schreeflozen' in de hoop dat deze naam
ertijd algemeen gebruikelijk zal worden,
at hij ONS INZIENS beter is, dan welke
re ook. Sinds het ontstaan van de skelet-
-LIGHT letter omstreeks 1806, bestaat er
verwarring in de benaming. Aanvanke-
etten de letters *antique* of *egyptian*, de

FFThesis comprises 3 distinct letterforms – FFTheSans™, FFTheSerif™ and FFTheMix™, each in 8 weights (Extra Light, Light, Semi Light, Normal, Semi Bold, Bold, Extra Bold & Black) and each weight in 6

the broad-nib pen. In addition, de Groot has develop practice his own theory of typographic interpolation initially established about six years ago when he wa in-between weight of the Frutiger family for the Du

Base

Ty	**Base**
Ca	**Sans Serif**
Ke	**Geometric**
Te	**Digital**
Da	**1995**
De	**Zuzana Licko**
Fo	**Emigre**
Co	**USA**

Characteristics

A collection of compatible low- and high-resolution typefaces

Common grid

Height, width and stem weight variations

AGMQRS abefghij koprsty

Connections

Chicago	1984
Geneva	1984
Lo-Res	1985
Citizen	1986

Availability

Base is available from Emigre and resellers

Specimen

Emigre product catalogue. Emigre, Berkeley, 1996 (230x144mm)

B **JANUARY 1996 RELEASE**

BASE TWELVE AND BASE NINE
WERE DESIGNED IN 1995 BY ZUZANA LICKO

A series of font families for use in print and multimedia environments, with mutually compatible screen and printer fonts.

Having designed Emigre's "Now Serving!" bulletin board environment and, more recently, the electronic "Emigre Catalog" on the Web, we were reminded that the need persists for a comprehensive family of screen fonts with companion printer fonts. We're responding to this need with three families; two families based on 12 point screen fonts (one serif and one sans serif family) named Base-12, and one family based on 9 point screen fonts named Base-9, consisting of a total of 24 individual faces. In fact, the basic concept for the Base-12 family started with the 24 and 36 point screen fonts that Zuzana Licko designed for use in the Emigre Web site.

To a great degree, in the design process of these faces, the screen fonts dictated the look of the printer fonts, rather than the other way around, because outline fonts have a greater degree of flexibility than do screen fonts. For example, the design of the screen font set the exact character widths within which the outline characters were adjusted to fit. Usually this process is reversed; character widths are normally adjusted to fit around the outline characters.

Although the design of the Base-9 and Base-12 fonts was guided by a specific functional intent, the goal was also to create a comprehensive family of typefaces suitable for traditional print purposes.

*Top: 9 point screen font from Base-9 enlarged 4X to 36 point.
Bottom: 36 point high-resolution printout from Base-9.*

Base-12 Sans
Regular, *Italic*, **Bold**, ***Bold Italic***
& SMALL CAPS

Base-12 Seri
Regular, *Italic*, **Bold**, ***Bold Italic***
& SMALL CAPS

Base-9 Sans
Regular, *Italic*, **Bold**, ***Bold Itali***
& SMALL CAPS

The identical match of character widths between the screen fonts and printer fonts

The identical match of character widths between the screen fonts and printer fonts

The identical match of the character widths between the screen fon

The identical match of the character widths between the screen fon

The identical match of the character widt between the screen fonts and printer fon

The identical match of the character widt between the screen fonts and printer fon

The identical match of character widths between the screen fonts and printer optimizes the appearance and spacing of the screen fonts at text sizes. At the t this writing, edited screenfonts are available for the Macintosh operating s (Support for other platforms, such as Windows, may be available in the future.)

e Nine Regular, Italic, Bold & Italic Bold with Small Caps
See also **Base Volume** on page 61

B 6 3

o B c C d D e E F F g G h H i I j J k K l L m M
O p P q Q r R s S t T u U v V w W x X y Y z
2 3 4 5 6 7 8 9 0 1 2 3 4 5 6 7 8 9 0 A B C
G H I J K L M N O P Q R S T U V W X Y Z a A
b B c C d D e E F F g G h H i I j J k K l L m
N o O p P q Q r R s S t T u U v V w W x X y
. 1 2 3 4 5 6 7 8 9 0 1 2 3 4 5 6 7 8 9 0 A
E F G H I J K L M N O P Q R S T U V W X Y Z

s are not intrinsically legible; rathe
familiarity with typefaces that acco
bility. Studies have shown that read
t they read most. Legibility is also a
as readers' habits are ever changin
hat blackletter styles which we find
s are not intrinsically legible; rathe
familiarity with typefaces that acco
bility. Studies have shown that read
t they read most. Legibility is also a
as readers' habits are ever changin
hat blackletter styles which we find

Typefaces Are Not Intrinsically Legible; Rath
The Reader's Familiarity With Typefaces Tha
For Their Legibility. Studies Have Show That
Read Best What They Read Most. Legibility Is
Dynamic Process, As Readers' Habits Are Ever
It Seems Curious That Blackletter Styles Whi
Typefaces Are Not Intrinsically Legible; Rath
The Reader's Familiarity With Typefaces Tha
For Their Legibility. Studies Have Show That
Read Best What They Read Most. Legibility Is
Dynamic Process, As Readers' Habits Are Ever
It Seems Curious That Blackletter Styles Whi

is the reader's familia
pefaces that accounts
is the reader's familia
pefaces that accounts
Is The Reader's Famili
Pefaces That Accounts
Is The Reader's Famili
Pefaces That Accounts

When Zuzana Licko (1961–) started using the first generation of Macintosh computers in 1984 she quickly recognized their potential as tools for designing type. Her pioneering early work was as much about pushing the limits of the technology as it was about typography. In her design for Oakland (pp456–57), for example, she investigated screen bitmaps, and for Citizen (pp458–59) she subverted printing processes. The challenge was, she said, that 'the early computers were so limited in what they could do that you really had to design something special'.

While she was developing the website for the Emigre type foundry in 1995 Licko struck on the idea of reversing the usual sequence of digital type design. Instead of basing a computer screen font on a physical original in the established manner, she decided to originate a workable font system for use on-screen and then adapt it to an effective family of print typefaces. The coarse, low resolution of screen fonts at fixed sizes would dictate the appearance and the spacing of clean printing types, rather than the other way around.

Her first step was to choose the most appropriate pixel size for the screen. The most viable proved to be 12 pixels, equivalent to 12 point, since it was a default bitmap size for most applications in the Mac operating system at the time. It was also directly scalable, pixel-to-pixel, to many standard sizes, such as 24 point and 36 point. Since the printer typeface operated independently from the screen font, the character outlines did not need to correspond in every detail. Provided that the typeface occupied exactly the same space as the screen font, it needed only to imply its actual shapes. Although the design of the Base typefaces was dictated by this functional method, Licko's objective was to create a comprehensive family of monospaced typefaces that would be effective in print. The final family consists of a total of 24 individual faces in three separate subgroups: Base-12, a slab serif and a sans serif family built on matching 12-pixel screen fonts; and Base-9, a single family based on 9-pixel screen fonts.

At first glance Base looks like a rather awkward hybrid of sans and serif with an elliptical body. It is characterized by its unusual angular ears at the junctions of curves to stems. What makes Base unique is Zuzanna Licko's solution to the problem of achieving absolute compatibility between screen and print in order to create what was, in effect, the world's first multimedia typeface.

Ty	**ITC Bodoni**
Ca	**Serif**
Ke	**Modern**
Te	**Digital**
Da	**1995**
De	**Sumner Stone**
Fo	**International Typeface Corporation**
Co	**USA**

Characteristics

Vertical stress
High contrast with hairline cross-strokes
J Hooked, descends below baseline
M Narrow
Q Curved tail below letter
R Curved leg
a Double-storeyed
g Double-storeyed, slight incline
i j Round dot

ACEJMR
abcdefghij
orstuya*efg*

Connections

Bodoni	1788
Bauer Bodoni	1926
Berthold Bodoni Old Face	1983
Parmigiano	2013

Availability

ITC Bodoni is available from Monotype and resellers

Specimen

U&lc, Vol. 21, No. 2. International Typeface Corporation, New York, 1994 (375x275mm)

PRESENTING

ITC BODONI

ITC BODONI SEVENTY-TWO

This essay is the fruit of man y years' assiduous labour–a r *eal labour of love–in the serv ice of the art of printing. Prin* **ting is the final outcome o f man's most beautiful, in** *genious and useful inventi on: that I mean, of writing:* and its most valuable form where it i s required to turn out many copies of

ITC BODONI
SEVENTY-TWO
BOOK
48/56

ITC BODONI
SEVENTY-TWO
BOOK ITALIC
48/56

ITC BODONI
SEVENTY-TWO
BOLD
48/56

ITC BODONI
SEVENTY-TWO
BOLD ITALIC
48/56

ITC BODONI
SEVENTY-TWO
BOOK
36/44

AN EXCERPT FROM G. B. BODONI'S PREFACE TO THE MANUALE TIPOGRAFICO OF 1818. FIRST ENGLISH TRANSLATION PUBLISHED BY ELKIN MATHEWS LTD., LONDON, 1925.

16

the same text. This applies still more w here it is important to ensure uniformit **y, and most of all where the work in question is one which deserves tra** *nsmission in clearer and more rea dable form for the enjoyment of pos* terity. When we consider the range of usefuln ess of printing, together with the long series *of devices which have brought us from the firs t discovery of letters to our present power of p* **rinting on thousands of sheets of fine laid paper words no longer evanescent but fixe** *d and preserved with sharper outlines tha n the articulation of lips can give them, th* e thought of such surpassing achievement compels ad miration at the force of the human intellect. But it woul *d be superfluous to enlarge on the merits of an invention which has already been the subject of many elaborate tr* **eatises and of much eloquent praise; to the glory of that happy century which not only discovered it, but** *so pursued its development as to leave little room fo r the participation of its successors. Nor do I think it*

17

ITC BODONI
SEVENTY-TWO
BOOK
36/42

ITC BODONI
SEVENTY-TWO
BOLD
36/42

ITC BODONI
SEVENTY-TWO
BOLD ITALIC
36/42

ITC BODONI
SEVENTY-TWO
BOOK
30/38

ITC BODONI
SEVENTY-TWO
BOOK ITALIC
30/38

ITC BODONI
SEVENTY-TWO
BOLD
30/38

ITC BODONI
SEVENTY-TWO
BOLD ITALIC
30/38

ITC BODONI
SEVENTY-TWO
BOOK
24/32

ITC BODONI
SEVENTY-TWO
BOOK ITALIC
24/32

ITC BODONI
SEVENTY-TWO
BOLD
24/32

ITC BODONI
SEVENTY-TWO
BOLD ITALIC
24/32

Few typefaces have been copied more often than those of Giambattista Bodoni (1740–1813). They are among the most majestic and assured ever produced for hand composition but have also proved the most challenging to adapt for newer technologies. Metal type is necessarily cut at the size at which it will be cast and printed and therefore different optical and material compensations will naturally be incorporated in each size within a single family. Larger sizes can afford sharper contours and a greater degree of physical differentiation, whereas smaller ones may have more open counters, thicker strokes and wider spacing, for example. Such differences are particularly evident in Bodoni's work (pp96–97).

Photocomposition and digital revivals are not capable of taking such nuances into account, since they automatically scale each individual size of type from a single master set. Because it is also common practice to draw originals at relatively large sizes, in typefaces like Bodoni results produced using photographic or digital processes are often wholly unsatisfactory when scaled down to smaller sizes.

Designed in 1994 by Sumner Stone (1945–) with Holly Goldsmith, Jim Parkinson and Janice Prescott Fishman, ITC Bodoni distinguishes itself from other digitizations by seeking to solve these problems. It was drawn at three optically compensated master sizes – 6, 12 and 72 point – for use in different situations. The project was copiously researched through direct studies of the respective sizes of Bodoni's original type specimens and punches. The main challenge was to preserve the feeling and mobility of the original letterforms without reducing them to pseudo-historical facsimiles. The end result, according to Stone, is 'grouchy, not photo-realistic'. The complete family consists of ITC Bodoni 6, intended for references, captioning and small sizes; ITC Bodoni 12, drawn specifically for text setting; and ITC Bodoni 72, for display use. Each design comes in two weights, Book and Bold, with matching italics. Old-style figures, ligatures, small capitals and extended language support are included, and the display variant, ITC Bodoni 72 Italic, also features swash glyph sets.

ITC Bodoni's versatility makes it one of the few modern Bodoni revivals that is as effective in text as it is in display. Used large it has a lean elegance, whereas at small sizes its impression is softer and eminently readable. However, its extensive design options rely on the expertise of users and it is therefore just as sensitive to abuse as less rigorous alternatives.

Ty	**FF DIN**
Ca	**Sans Serif**
Ke	**Geometric**
Te	**Digital**
Da	**1995**
De	**Albert-Jan Pool**
Fo	**FontFont**
Co	**Germany**

Characteristics

C	Alternate flat or angled terminals
G	No spur
Q	Straight, angled tail
R	Straight, angled leg
a	Double-storeyed, straight stem
a c e g r s	Angled terminals
f t	Narrow, vertical terminals
i j	Square dots
l	Hooked foot
r	Rounded arch
t	Flat top-stroke
y	Small, hooked tail

ACGMQR
abcefghij
koprstuy

Connections

DIN 1451	1931
Letter Gothic	1956
OCR-A	1968
Nitti	2008

Availability

FF DIN is available from FontFont and resellers

Specimen

FontFont Focus: DIN. FontFont, Berlin, 2001 (297x148mm)

FF DIN is based on DIN-Mittelschrift and DIN-Engschrift, originally specified in 1931 as DIN 1451 – Normschriften (pp266–67), a German national standard for the design and application of lettering for signage, vehicle identification and technical documentation. Widely familiar as the typeface used throughout the German transport network since then, DIN had long been popular with designers for its plain, technical appearance. Dutch designer Albert-Jan Pool (1960–) drew FF DIN in 1995, considering its antecedent to be, he said, 'probably the most non-designed typeface ever made'.

Starting out from this viewpoint, Pool wanted to improve DIN's typographic qualities while preserving its overall character. The original DIN-Mittelschrift is constructed from strokes of a constant thickness using a ruler and a pair of compasses. In practice this results in a spotty, uneven typeface with many awkwardly obtrusive shapes. For the design of FF DIN, Pool made a large number of subtle compensations that allow it to perform more efficiently as a print and screen typeface. Maintaining the geometric impression and basic proportions of the earlier design, he drew the curves in a more fluent way, while also reducing the weight of the horizontal strokes. At the same time he adjusted the spacing, rationalized and extended the progression of weights, and expanded the character set.

The FF DIN family has five weights in two widths – Normal and Condensed – each with italics. It includes extended characters such as arrows, fractions, mathematical symbols, and lining and non-lining figures, and has extensive language support. When FF DIN was published by FontFont in 1995 it rapidly became one of the foundry's bestselling typefaces and has been ubiquitous ever since in advertising, corporate communications and editorial design around the globe.

acht zogende babywelpjes k

Albert-Jan Pool was born July 9th, 1960 in Amst *The Hague at the Royal Academy of Arts. He was e founders of Letters], a group of young Dutch typ its members [Frank Blokland, Petr van Blokland de Groot, Bart de Haas, Henk van Leyden, Peter Marie-Cécile Noordzij-Pulles, Just van Rossum have become well-known type-designers. From as the Director of Type at Scangraphic in Germany 1994 he was the Manager of Type Design and Pr

ck my box with five dozen

Albert-Jan Pool was born July 9th, 1960 in Amst *The Hague at the Royal Academy of Arts. He was e founders of Letters], a group of young Dutch typ its members [Frank Blokland, Petr van Blokland Lucas de Groot, Bart de Haas, Henk van Leyden Noordzij, Marie-Cécile Noordzij-Pulles, Just van Verheul) have become well-known type-designe *he worked as the Director of Type at Scangraphic 1991 to 1994 he was the Manager of Type Design

e veils sex of jumping cra

*Albert-Jan Pool was born July 9th, 1960 in Amste The Hague at the Royal Academy of Arts. He wa founders of Letters], a group of young Dutch type its members [Frank Blokland, Petr van Blokland Lucas de Groot, Bart de Haas, Henk van Leyden Noordzij, Marie-Cécile Noordzij-Pulles, Just van Verheul) have become well-known type-designe 1991 he worked as the Director of Type at Scang And from 1991 to 1994 he was the Manager of Ty

zzing jap alky driver subje

Albert-Jan Pool was born July 9th, 1960 in Amst in The Hague at the Royal Academy of Arts. He *founders of Letters], a group of young Dutch type its members [Frank Blokland, Petr van Blokland Lucas de Groot, Bart de Haas, Henk van Leyden Noordzij, Marie-Cécile Noordzij-Pulles, Just va Verheul) have become well-known type-designe 1991 he worked as the Director of Type at Scang And from 1991 to 1994 he was the Manager of T

ft kid vows miss quit cozy

Albert-Jan Pool was born July 9th, 1960 in Am *in The Hague at the Royal Academy of Arts. He w founders of Letters], a group of young Dutch ty of its members [Frank Blokland, Petr van Blok Lucas de Groot, Bart de Haas, Henk van Leyden Noordzij, Marie-Cécile Noordzij-Pulles, Just va Peter Verheul) have become well-known type-d 1987 to 1991 he worked as the Director of Type Germany. And from 1991 to 1994 he was the Ma

xi frequent · Squeaking riva

n Pool was born July 9th, 1960 in Amst
studied in The Hague at the Royal Acade
was one of the co-founders of Letters),
young Dutch type designers. Many of it
[Frank Blokland, Petr van Blokland, J
Lucas de Groot, Bart de Haas, Henk var
Peter-Matthias Noordzij, Marie-Cécile

Albert-Jan Pool was born July 9th,
Amsterdam. *He studied in The Hag*
Royal Academy of Arts. He was one
founders of Letters), a group of yo
type designers. Many of its membe

ugs · *Portez ce vieux whisk*

an Pool was born July 9th, 1960 in Ams
studied in The Hague at the Royal Acade
was one of the co-founders of Letters),
young Dutch type designers. Many of it
[Frank Blokland, Petr van Blokland, J
Lucas de Groot, Bart de Haas, Henk var
Peter-Matthias Noordzij, Marie-Cécile

Albert-Jan Pool was born July 9th
Amsterdam. *He studied in The Hag*
Royal Academy of Arts. He was one
founders of Letters), a group of yo
type designers. Many of its membe

t kid vows miss quit cozy xy

n Pool was born July 9th, 1960 in Amste
studied in The Hague at the Royal Acad
le was one of the co-founders of Lette
young Dutch type designers. Many of its
[Frank Blokland, Petr van Blokland, .
Lucas de Groot, Bart de Haas, Henk va
Peter-Matthias Noordzij, Marie-Cécile

Albert-Jan Pool was born July 9th,
Amsterdam. He studied in The Hag
Royal Academy of Arts. He was or
co-founders of Letters), *a group o.*
Dutch type designers. Many of its r

ext requiem · *Exiled zouav*

an Pool was born July 9th, 1960 in Am
studied in The Hague at the Royal Aca
ts. *He was one of the co-founders of Lei*
roup of young Dutch type designers. Ma
ers [Frank Blokland, Petr van Blokla
sma, Lucas de Groot, Bart de Haas, He
en, Peter-Matthias Noordzij, Marie-Co

Albert-Jan Pool was born July 9th
Amsterdam. *He studied in The Ha*
Royal Academy of Arts. *He was or*
co-founders of Letters), a group of
Dutch type designers. Many of its r

on job · **Gindsch zwak vor**

an Pool was born July 9th, 1960 in Ar
He studied in The Hague at the Royal Ac
ts. He was one of the co-founders of L
group of young Dutch type designers.
its members [Frank Blokland, Petr va
, Jelle Bosma, Lucas de Groot, Bart d
nk van Leyden, Peter-Matthias Noord

Albert-Jan Pool was born July 9th
Amsterdam. *He studied in The Hag*
Royal Academy of Arts. He was on
co-founders of Letters), a group
Dutch type designers. Many of its

FONTFONT FOCUS

DIN

Elephant

Ty	**Elephant**
Ca	**Sans Serif**
Ke	**Geometric, Grotesque**
Te	**Digital**
Da	**1995**
De	**Gareth Hague**
Fo	**Alias**
Co	**UK**

Characteristics

Geometric character construction
Uneven contrast of thick and thin strokes
linked through circular arcs

AEGMQRS
abcefghij
koprstuy

Connections

Thorowgood's Grotesque	1832
Poplar	1990
Sister	1995
August	1996

Availability

Elephant is widely available

Specimen

T-26 Font Kit No. 20. Chicago, 1995
(270x170mm)

---

family includes:
Elephant Light
Elephant Light Oblique
Elephant Medium
Elephant Medium Oblique
Elephant Black
Elephant Black Oblique

ƐLEPHAИT

Elephant. (a family of 6)   designed by Gareth Hague. $216. number XT0362.

This is Elephant Light
This is Elephant Light Oblique
This is Elephant Medium
This is Elephant Medium Oblique
This is Elephant Black
This is Elephant Black Oblique

Alias fonts were born out of necessity.

Unable to find suitable faces for their innovative design work, **David James** *and* **Gareth Hague** *decided instead to draw, by hand, the fonts they needed. This type collection grew from that process.*

Gareth describes the origin of the Alias collection as "combining the free expression of hand drawing with the computer's mastery of geometric form". Traditionally technical of type design are of no interest to them. The computer is the font design tool of to and they prefer to use it for its own sake, unencumbered by historic design method

Sometimes the fonts are hand-drawn and tidied up by computer. Other times, the pr is reversed, as with *"Granite"* and *"Elephant"*, which have no non-digital history.

Similarly, the influences on their work are shaped more by the demands of each gi brief than by any traditional techniques. Thus, when the city of Glasgow needed a f for its stint as 1999 UK City of Architecture, Alias submitted *"Factory"* which crosse apperance of Gaelic letterforms with a visual interpretation of the city's industrial he

Two of the faces will be familiar: *"Elephant"* and *"Sister"* having already been acclai for their use in high profile campaigns for "Perperami", "Li-Lets", "The Lighthouse Fa and "Comic Relief", as well as beign widely used in magazines such as "Loaded" and "Fortean Times".

**This is a bold, individual collection of type with a strong design element, m
it a rich source for headline and text faces, and now available thru [T-26].**

66

abcdefghijklmnopqrstuvwxyz
ABCDEFGHIJKLMNOPQRSTUVWXYZ
abcdefghijklmnopqrstuvwxyzABCDEFGHIJKLMNOPQRSTUVWXYZ1234567890

abcdefghijklmnopqrstuvwxyz
ABCDEFGHIJKLMNOPQRSTUVWXYZ
abcdefghijklmnopqrstuvwxyzABCDEFGHIJKLMNOPQRSTUVWXYZ1234567890

abcdefghijklmnopqrstuvwxyz
ABCDEFGHIJKLMNOPQRSTUVWXYZ
abcdefghijklmnopqrstuvwxyzABCDEFGHIJKLMNOPQRSTUVWXYZ1234567890

abcdefghijklmnopqrstuvwxyz
ABCDEFGHIJKLMNOPQRSTUVWXYZ
abcdefghijklmnopqrstuvwxyzABCDEFGHIJKLMNOPQRSTUVWXYZ1234567890

abcdefghijklmnopqrstuvwxyz
ABCDEFGHIJKLMNOPQRSTUVWXYZ
abcdefghijklmnopqrstuvwxyzABCDEFGHIJKLMNOPQRSTUVWXYZ1234567890

abcdefghijklmnopqrstuvwxyz
ABCDEFGHIJKLMNOPQRSTUVWXYZ
abcdefghijklmnopqrstuvwxyzABCDEFGHIJKLMNOPQRSTUVWXYZ1234567890

Early grotesque typefaces of the nineteenth century (pp122–23) have a homely charm and affability, their letterforms showing uneven, untutored qualities based on drawing or cutting in wood or metal in an improvised manner that had no prior model to guide its direction. When approaching the design of a sans serif display face in 1995 Gareth Hague (1967–) of the Alias type foundry wanted to capture the spirit of the early grotesques but without ending up with the sort of dull facsimile of an existing face that is so often the outcome of digital revivals.

Hague has described the objective of Alias as 'combining the free expression of hand drawing with the computer's mastery of geometric form'. He is interested in working freely within the constraints of the computer rather than the pen or brush so that his typefaces retain vestiges of digital idiosyncracies instead of manual ones. Whereas drawn letters follow the flow of the arm and hand, the construction of his Elephant typeface traces the processes of designing on the computer – methods of drawing that also use letter parts as components for distribution within geometric frameworks using scaling, distortion, repetition and reflection.

The result is far from sterile. Brimming with personality that is particularly evident in its formidable black weight, Elephant is a geometric typeface that unexpectedly reflects the feeling of a raw wood typeface. This is largely the result of a stroke modulation that is based on the interplay between two different line weights throughout – a thick and a thin stroke whose interactions transition through a series of circular arcs. This feature gives an eccentric irregularity that is best demonstrated in the lower case a and g, where thick and thin strokes are manipulated with both imagination and rigour. Elephant is available in three weights with matching italics.

aaaaaa

Elephant Light. Elephant Light Oblique. Elephant Medium. Elephant Medium Oblique. Elephant Black. Elephant Black Oblique.

Ty	**Walker**
Ca	**Sans Serif**
Ke	**Geometric, Modular, Capitals**
Te	**Digital**
Da	**1995**
De	**Matthew Carter**
Fo	**Carter & Cone**
Co	**USA**

Characteristics

Capitals only

Modular construction

Alternate serif forms

High, middle and low connector strokes

Overscore strokes

Underscore strokes

ABCEGJ KMQRW HHHEH

Connections

Kombinations-Schrift	1923
Patrona Grotesk	c1931
Alpha-Blox	1944
Template Woodcut	2010

Availability

Not available

Specimen

Walker type specimen. Carter & Cone and the Walker Art Center, Minneapolis, 1996 (270x210mm)

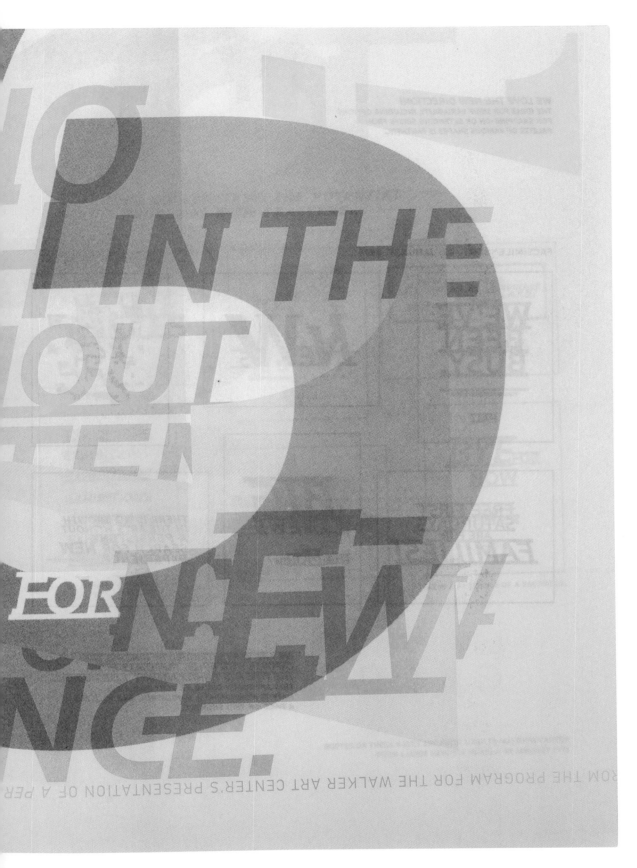

In the early 1990s the Walker Art Center in Minneapolis took the decision to renew its brand identity. Laurie Haycock Makela, design director at the time, proposed an unorthodox direction for the project that was intended to reflect the Walker's culturally diverse audiences and multidisciplinary activities: 'We began with the idea that a typeface could be an identity – a font rather than a logo – that would run through the system like blood.' The plan to develop a typeface that would be capable of responding flexibly to the institution's activities and audiences was a pioneering brand strategy. Its emphasis on the power of words alone to create an identity constituted a radical departure from established approaches to brand communications at the time.

The resulting typeface, Walker, was designed by the eminent and prolific type designer Matthew Carter (1937–). Walker is a modular digital face whose final appearance is determined by individual design decisions made at the moment of their implementation in page layouts. At its core is a plain sans serif capital alphabet. Describing this basic structure, Carter indicated that he thought of it 'rather like store window mannequins with good bone structure on which to hang many different kinds of clothing'.

What makes Walker distinctive and unique is its system of snap-on serifs. Specified keyboard commands allow designers to select any one of five different sorts of serif to attach to any characters in a variety of locations. These can be used as connectors, separators or terminals. An E, for instance, can be connected to an O by extending its crossbar. Similarly, E and H can be linked in many different ways. Corresponding horizontal bars can also be placed above and/or below letters to underscore or overscore text sequences. Words can either sit on or hang from these unifying bars, creating architectural spans, spaces or disjunctions within page compositions.

Like many typefaces being published at around that time, particularly by the Emigre type foundry, the flexibility of the Walker system can be seen as part of a critique of the fixed modernist attitudes that pervaded the American design profession in the late 1980s. Anticipating twenty-first-century practices in emergent design and dynamic identity, Walker stands as a bold typographic experiment from the postmodern era.

Ty	**Anisette**
Ca	**Sans Serif**
Ke	**Geometric**
Te	**Digital**
Da	**1996**
De	**Jean François Porchez**
Fo	**Typofonderie**
Co	**France**

Characteristics

Narrow capitals in lower case positions
Wide capitals in upper case positions
Range of alternate characters and ligatures
Settings can be expanded or contracted

ABCDEF
GHJKLM
NOPQRS

Connections

Futura	1927
Bifur	1929
Banjo	1933
Estilo	2006

Availability

Anisette is available from Typofonderie
and resellers

Specimen

*Spécimen de caractères & vignettes
typographiques.* Typofonderie, Malakoff,
2001 (297x210mm)

Anisette Petite 7 FONTS: Thin, Light, Regular, Caps, Demi, Bold, Black (Alternates.)

7

:defghijklmnopqrstuvwxyzàçðéíñøœþšùÿå ABCDEFGHIJKLMNOPQRSTUVWXYZÆÇÐÉÍÑØŒPŠÙŸ
fiflffffiffl0123456789€$¢£¥%‰½¼¾¹²³ª⁰°@®©©™#§¶†‡*/(|)[/]{\}¿¡!?«·.,:;•"."„',‚"...»·-—_<+¦^~×=>

TTE PETITE THI, LIG, REG, DEM, BOL, BLA

es Banjos
Georges Maximilien
villa Denise, 23456 DEAUVILLE
Un thé glacé, sinon rien
& ta contrebasse
Typographe

tte Petite 15, 13, 11, 9 pts

IOMPHANTE aux bornes d'un empire aboli, la
ttre des pierres jalonne les chemins des cohor-
s romaines, inscrit le nom des procurateurs &
s juges au front des colonnes de gloire, sur les dalles
nèbres qui deviennent pour nous comme autant de
drans solaires où se voit, de son lever à son déclin, dans la
rure des mots morts, la beauté nue des formes incises ; le trait
cien révèle ainsi la volonté d'une lumière qui délivre la parole ; l'om-
e jaillit sous le burin qui la provoque & s'allie, selon l'heure, au
eil dans un jeu parfois subtil & parfois éclatant, dans un
couplement fécond où l'esprit reconnaît sa voie & le cœur
raison. Il semble que nos premiers graveurs n'aient
u d'autres pensée que celle de conserver dans l'

empreinte de ces
formes sublimes
& nous lisons en-
core, consultant les
vieux livres, comme
sur des stèles, ces
caractères de l'admira-
tion & de l'émotion,
tout onctueux d'encre,
empreints profondém-
ent, crevant presque la
page mais irradiant du
poids charnel de la main
& susceptibles de dire la
place juste d'une courbe
ou la variante sensible
d'un bâton répété mille fo

Pour satisfaire les nombreuses demandes d'utilisateurs,
des minuscules ont été ajou-
tées à l'Anisette créé en
1996, disponible à l'origine
uniquement en capitales. Sur
une base de capitales dessi-
nées dans une chasse inter-
médiaire aux 2 variations de
base, les minuscules ont été
créées dans des proportions
plus adaptées aux travaux les
plus divers. Les minuscules
de l'Anisette Petite ont la
sobriété des caractères géomé-
triques avec une pointe de
dynamique dans la tension
des courbes. Quelques imperfections telles le r, le l ajoutés
au g si particulier, courrent à
l'attrait de l'Anisette Petite.
In answer to a number of
requests, lowercase characters
have now been added to the
Anisette display series, which
was created in 1996. The lower-
case characters are based on
capitals of an intermediate
width, between the two origi-
nal widths, to provide a wider
diversity of use. The Anisette
Petite lowercase shares the
sobriety of geometrical type-
faces & the dynamics of the
tension in the curves. Subtle
imperfections seen in the r, l,
& the peculiar g, help to create
an original typeface.

ALTERNATES

Caractères supplémentaires
accessibles via les Alternates
de l'Anisette 2.0. Les ff, ffi, ffl
tout comme les fi & fl sont
néammoins inclus dans les
fontes de l'Anisette Petite.
Supplementary characters
are available in Anisette 2.0
Alternates. The ff, ffi, ffl as
well as the fi & fl are also
included in the Anisette
Petite fonts.

COMPARAISONS

AA Aa
BB Bb
CC Cc
EE Ee
GG Gg
NN Nn
SS Ss

1
2

1 Anisette
2 Anisette Petite

tte Petite thin, light

çdéfghijklmñôpqrstüvwxyz012345€&ABCDEFGHIJKLMNOPQRSTUVWXYZ
çdéfghijklmñôpqrstüvwxyz0€&ABCDEFGHIJKLMNOPQRSTUVWXYZ

tte Petite regular, caps, demi

çdéfghijklmñôprstüvwxyz012456&ABCDEFGHIJKLMNQRSTUVYZ
ÇDÉFGHIJKLMÑÔPQRSTÜVWXYZ0123456789€&ABCDEFGHIJKLMNO
çdéfghjklmñôprstüvwxyz01123&ABCDEFGHIJKLMNOQRSTUVYZ

tte Petite bold, black

çdéfghjklkñôprstüvwxyz01234&ABCDEFGHJKLMNOQRSTUVXYZ
bçdéfghjklkñôprtüyxz01230&ABCDEGHJKLMNQRSUVXYZ

In the 1930s Bauer published Futura
(pp230–31) as a commercially viable
response to experimental alphabets drawn
at the Bauhaus (pp222–23) and elsewhere.
In France, Deberny & Peignot were quick
to embrace geometric sans serifs, licensing
Futura under the name of Europa and
extending their repertoire with flamboyant
display types such as A. M. Cassandre's
Bifur (pp246–47) and Acier. In 1933
Deberny & Peignot published a new face
modelled directly on Futura. The new
design, Banjo, came in two versions,
one of which expanded letters based on
Futura's to double-width, while the other
contracted the width to around half. By
combining both styles, end users could
create settings that expanded or
contracted rhythmically.

Banjo was one of the key inspirations for
Anisette, developed in 1994 by the French
type designer Jean François Porchez
(1964–) initially as a way to explore the
possibilities of Adobe's new Multiple
Master technology by creating a range
of interpolations based on predefined
parameters of width and weight. He went
on to complete Anisette as a PostScript
typeface in two widths and five weights.
With its basic structure inspired by Banjo,
the design of its character contours
references several other art deco sources,
from the lettering of Paul Iribe to
Cassandre's typefaces and posters.

Taking advantage of OpenType
technology, the most recent iteration of
Anisette allows wide or narrow capitals
to be set in a variety of configurations –
either independently, intermixed manually
or programmed to compose themselves
according to their context. Not unlike Herb
Lubalin's groundbreaking Avant Garde
Gothic (pp394–95), Anisette also features
a wide range of alternate characters and
ligatures, some of which align small
capitals either centrally within or at the
top of the capital height, positioning them
appropriately in the context of words. In
2001 Porchez added a distinctive lower
case in order to complete a versatile and
playful system.

Anisette offers a huge choice of options in
setting headlines, using type technologies
to bridge the gap between mechanical
production methods and bespoke lettering.
With Anisette, setting headline type
becomes a compositional game, offering
design opportunities that replicate the
unique qualities of handmade forms.

Ty	**Filosofia**
Ca	**Serif**
Ke	**Modern**
Te	**Digital**
Da	**1996**
De	**Zuzana Licko**
Fo	**Emigre**
Co	**USA**

Characteristics

Vertical stress

Light strokes with moderate contrast

Most capitals have uniform width

Slightly rounded, unbracketed serifs

J Narrow, descends below baseline

M Narrow

Q Curved tail below letter

R Curved tail

W Crossed centre-strokes

a Double-storeyed

f t Narrow

g Double-storeyed, teardrop ear

ACEJMR
abcdefghij
orstuyaefg

Connections

Bodoni	1788
ITC Bodoni	1995
Mrs Eaves	1996
Parmigiano	2013

Availability

Filosofia is available from Emigre and resellers

Specimen

Emigre 42: 'The Mercantile Issue'. Emigre, Berkeley, 1997 (279x216mm)

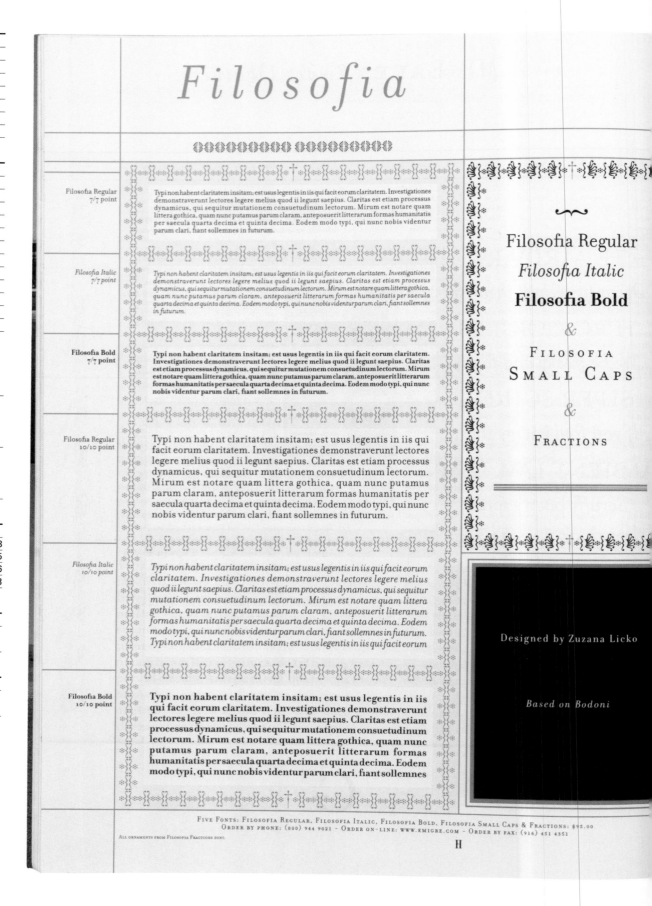

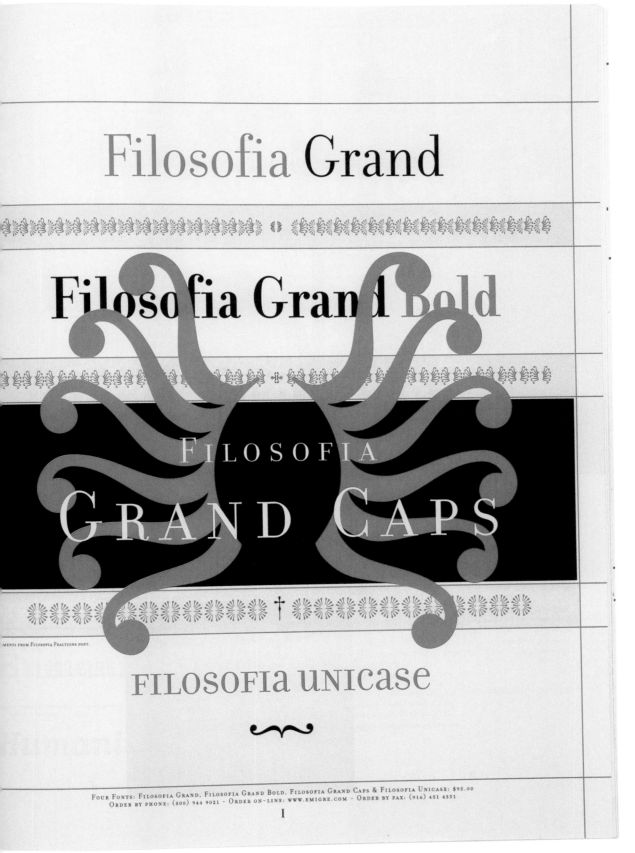

Filosofia Grand

Filosofia Grand Bold

FILOSOFIA
GRAND CAPS

ments from Filosofia Fractions font.

FILOSOFIA UNICASE

FOUR FONTS: FILOSOFIA GRAND, FILOSOFIA GRAND BOLD, FILOSOFIA GRAND CAPS & FILOSOFIA UNICASE: $95.00
ORDER BY PHONE: (800) 944 9021 · ORDER ON-LINE: WWW.EMIGRE.COM · ORDER BY FAX: (916) 451 4351

I

The groundbreaking digital typefaces that Zuzana Licko (1961–) and others had first displayed in *Emigre* magazine during the 1980s were not universally admired. The eminent Italian designer Massimo Vignelli described the magazine's type as 'garbage, lacking depth, refinement, elegance or a sense of history'. Perhaps this harsh rebuke provoked Licko's radical departure from her previous working methods with Filosofia, an interpretation of the eighteenth-century typefaces of Giambattista Bodoni (pp96–97).

An admirer of Bodoni long before she had designed her own type, Licko said that she was 'attracted to its clean lines and geometric shapes, and the variety of headline style choices'. Her design demonstrates a personal preference for Bodoni's rational, measured construction that has much in common with the systematic principles that she had invested in her own typefaces.

Although Giambattista Bodoni developed a large variety of typefaces, the style that has survived numerous revivals over two centuries has tended towards a mathematical austerity and an extreme contrast between the vertical stems and hairlines, in a style commonly known today as modern. Licko was aware of Bodoni's limited usability, as its extreme contrast made it difficult to print and to read at small sizes in text settings. She designed Filosofia to overcome Bodoni's legibility problems and its somewhat frigid personality.

The Filosofia Regular family is intended for text applications. With a reduced contrast to withstand reproduction at text sizes, it is warm, curvaceous and rugged. It also incorporates subtle features such as slightly bulging, rounded serif endings that echo the appearance of Bodoni's type in original printed samples resulting from the letterpress printing process. A secondary family, Filosofia Grand, is more delicate and slender than Filosofia Regular, with much higher contrast, intended for display applications. Included in the Filosofia Grand family is a novel unicase variant which uses a single height for characters that would otherwise be separated into upper and lower case. This constitutes an homage to mid-twentieth-century interpretations of Bodoni for display applications, such as Bradbury Thompson's Alphabet 26.

The sensitivity of Licko's interpretation appears to have won Massimo Vignelli's approval. At any rate, he accepted Emigre's invitation to design the publicity poster and specimen for Filosofia, emblazoning it with a massive headline that simply read 'It's their Bodoni'.

Ty	**Georgia**
Ca	**Serif**
Ke	**Transitional**
Te	**Digital**
Da	**1996**
De	**Matthew Carter**
Fo	**Microsoft**
Co	**USA**

Characteristics

Vertical stress
Moderate stroke contrast
Most capitals have uniform width
Capitals lower than ascender height
Large x-height
Short ascenders and descenders
Strong, bracketed serifs
Q Curved tail below letter
R Straight, angled leg
W Centre-strokes meet at apex
a Double-storeyed, large bowl
a c f r y Ball terminals
b d h k l Flat head serifs
f r t Narrow
g Double-storeyed, large lower bowl
t Flat top
w Centre-strokes meet at apex

ACEQRW abcdefghij orstya*efg*

Connections

Wilson	1768
Times New Roman	1932
Verdana	1996
Miller	1997

Availability

Georgia is widely available

Specimen

Georgia type specimen – screen and print versions, composed by author, 2015 (255x160mm)

10/12pt
Georgia was designed by Matthew Carter for clarity at small sizes on computer monitors: it features a large x-height and its thin strokes are relatively thick.

14/16pt
Georgia was designed by Matthew Carter for clarity at small sizes on computer monitors: it features a large x-height and its thin strokes are relatively thick.

24/27pt
Georgia was designed by Matthew Carter for clarity at small sizes on computer monitors: it features a large x-height and its thin strokes are relatively thick.

36/40pt
Georgia was designed by Matthew Carter for clarity at small sizes on computer monitors: it

10/12pt
Georgia was designed by Matthew
Carter for clarity at small sizes on
computer monitors: it features a
large x-height and its thin strokes
are relatively thick.

14/16pt
Georgia was designed by Matthew
Carter for clarity at small sizes on
computer monitors: it features a
large x-height and its thin strokes
are relatively thick.

24/27pt
Georgia was designed by Matthew
Carter for clarity at small sizes on
computer monitors: it features a
large x-height and its thin strokes
are relatively thick.

36/40pt
Georgia was designed
by Matthew Carter for
clarity at small sizes on
computer monitors: it

Georgia is a serif typeface designed in 1993 by Matthew Carter (1937–). Carter worked within extremely tight constraints to create a type family that combines easy readability with an inviting disposition, engineered for clarity at low resolution on computer screens. Georgia was based on Carter's designs for a print typeface which was inspired by the typefaces produced at the Scottish foundries of Alexander Wilson and William Miller in the early nineteenth century. The print face would later be released as Miller (pp564–65).

While Georgia owes much to Wilson's transitional letterforms (pp86–87), its principal point of reference is the types cut by Richard Austin for Miller (pp112–13) that later became known as the Scotch style. Influences of the Scotch armature are most evident in the flat upper serifs of Carter's lower case ascenders and the flat top of the lower case t.

In a reversal of the usual practice of creating type from accurate linear vectors, Carter started by drawing letters as pixel bitmaps in several sizes, then converting them to more detailed outlines. To achieve a clear and legible contour on computer monitors at small sizes, it was necessary to depart from the Scotch model by using an enlarged x-height and more substantial thin strokes and serifs than would be conventional in a typeface designed for print. Capitals are shorter than the lower case ascender height and the numerals are a hybrid of aligned and non-aligned figures. This helps them blend into continuous text, a rare feature for a computer type of the time.

Georgia's italic is a true cursive, containing specific characters such as the single-storeyed a and g. Its flowing design cleverly conceals the difficulty of creating an italic form for the raw environment of the screen. The bold weight is unusually bold, almost black, to ensure that it always stands out from the text weight – an important consideration at small screen sizes where the difference between stem weights might be only one or two pixels.

Georgia was released in 1996 as one of Microsoft's core fonts for the Web with a screen-optimized family available as a free download and later included with the Windows and Mac operating systems. This made Georgia a popular choice for web designers, since pages specifying it would display identically across both platforms. Today Carter's types for Microsoft are seen everywhere, both on-screen and in print, in applications that extend far beyond the strict technical limits that define their original designs.

Adobe Jenson

Ty	**Adobe Jenson**
Ca	**Serif**
Ke	**Old Style, Venetian**
Te	**Digital**
Da	**1996**
De	**Robert Slimbach**
Fo	**Adobe**
Co	**USA**

Characteristics

Capitals lower than ascender height
D H N S Wide
J Descends below baseline
M Slightly splayed
Q Curved tail below letter
R Wide, curved leg
W Stepped centre-strokes, serif at apex
a Double storeyed, small bowl
b d p q Tilted bowls
e Small eye and extending oblique bar
i j Small dot offset to right
y Straight, swelling tail

AMRSW
abcdefghij
orstuyaefg

Connections

Availability

Adobe Jenson is available from Adobe and resellers

Specimen

Adobe Originals Jenson specimen. Adobe Systems Inc., San Jose, 1996 (228x144mm)

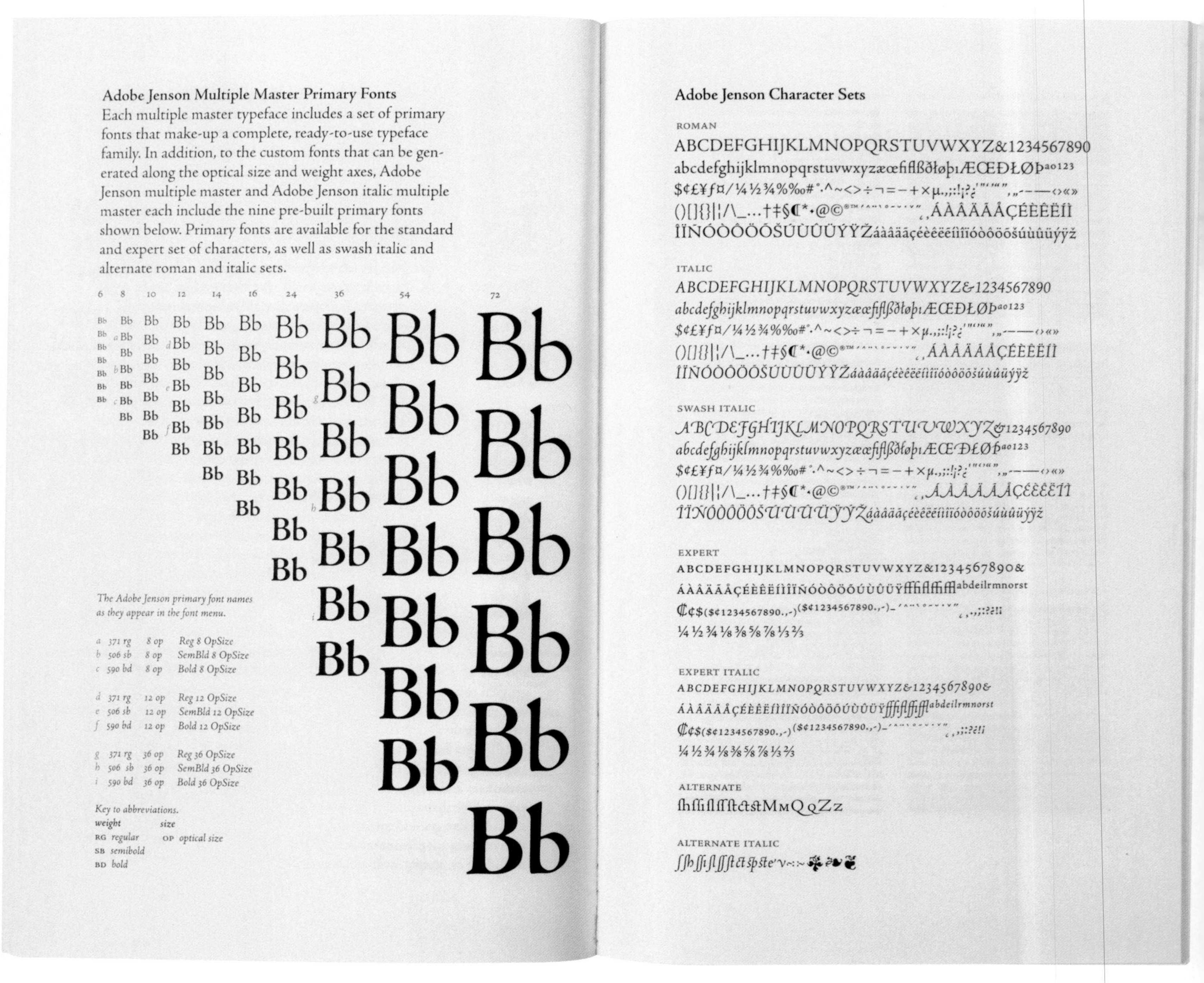

Adobe Jenson Multiple Master Primary Fonts

Each multiple master typeface includes a set of primary fonts that make-up a complete, ready-to-use typeface family. In addition, to the custom fonts that can be generated along the optical size and weight axes, Adobe Jenson multiple master and Adobe Jenson italic multiple master each include the nine pre-built primary fonts shown below. Primary fonts are available for the standard and expert set of characters, as well as swash italic and alternate roman and italic sets.

6 8 10 12 14 16 24 36 54 72

The Adobe Jenson primary font names as they appear in the font menu.

a	371 rg	8 op	Reg 8 OpSize
b	506 sb	8 op	SemBld 8 OpSize
c	590 bd	8 op	Bold 8 OpSize
d	371 rg	12 op	Reg 12 OpSize
e	506 sb	12 op	SemBld 12 OpSize
f	590 bd	12 op	Bold 12 OpSize
g	371 rg	36 op	Reg 36 OpSize
h	506 sb	36 op	SemBld 36 OpSize
i	590 bd	36 op	Bold 36 OpSize

Key to abbreviations.
weight   size
RG *regular*   **OP** *optical size*
SB *semibold*
BD *bold*

Adobe Jenson Character Sets

ROMAN
ABCDEFGHIJKLMNOPQRSTUVWXYZ&1234567890
abcdefghijklmnopqrstuvwxyzæœfiflßðłøþı ÆŒÐŁØÞ ao123
$¢£¥ƒ¤/¼½¾%‰#˚.^~<>÷¬=−+×µ,;:!¡?¿'""''",,--—()«»
()[]{}|¦/\...·†‡§¶*·@©®™ˆˊˋ˜˙˚˝˛¸ ÁÀÂÄÃÅÇÉÈÊËÍ
ÌÎÏÑÓÒÔÖÕŠÚÙÛÜÝŸŽáàâäãåçéèêëíìîïñóòôöõšúùûüýÿž

ITALIC
ABCDEFGHIJKLMNOPQRSTUVWXYZ&1234567890
abcdefghijklmnopqrstuvwxyzæœfiflßðłøþı ÆŒÐŁØÞ ao123
$¢£¥ƒ¤/¼½¾%‰#˚.^~<>÷ ¬=−+×µ,;:!¡?¿'""''",,--—()«»
()[]{}|¦/\...·†‡§¶·@©®™ˆˊˋ˜˙˚˝˛¸ ÁÀÂÄÃÅÇÉÈÊËÍ*
ÌÎÏÑÓÒÔÖÕŠÚÙÛÜÝŸŽáàâäãåçéèêëíìîïñóòôöõšúùûüýÿž

SWASH ITALIC
ABCDEFGHIJKLMNOPQRSTUVWXYZ&1234567890
abcdefghijklmnopqrstuvwxyzæœfiflßðłøþı ÆŒÐŁØÞ ao123
$¢£¥ƒ¤/¼½¾%‰#˚.^~<>÷ ¬=−+×µ,;:!¡?¿'""''",,--—()«»
()[]{}|¦/\...·†‡§¶·@©®™ˆˊˋ˜˙˚˝˛¸ ÁÀÂÄÃÅÇÉÈÊËÍ*
ÌÎÏÑÓÒÔÖÕŠÚÙÛÜÝŸŽáàâäãåçéèêëíìîïñóòôöõšúùûüýÿž

EXPERT
ABCDEFGHIJKLMNOPQRSTUVWXYZ&1234567890&
ÁÀÂÄÃÅÇÉÈÊËÍÌÎÏÑÓÒÔÖÕÚÙÛÜÝŸ ffffiflffifflabdeilrmnorst
₵¢$($¢1234567890.,-)($¢1234567890.,-)_'ˆˋ˜˙˚˝ ˛¸.,;:¡¿!
¼½¾⅛⅜⅝⅞⅓⅔

EXPERT ITALIC
ABCDEFGHIJKLMNOPQRSTUVWXYZ&1234567890&
ÁÀÂÄÃÅÇÉÈÊËÍÌÎÏÑÓÒÔÖÕÚÙÛÜÝŸ ffffiflffifflabdeilrmnorst
₵¢$($¢1234567890.,-)($¢1234567890.,-)_'ˆˋ˜˙˚˝ ˛¸.,;:¡¿!
¼½¾⅛⅜⅝⅞⅓⅔

ALTERNATE
fh fi fl ff ft ct st M M Q Q Z z

ALTERNATE ITALIC
ſ ſh ſi ſl ſſ ſt ct ſp ſte 'v ~ ·~ ❧ ❧ ❧

The Adobe Jenson family is a digital reinterpretation of Nicolas Jenson's roman type of 1470 (pp20–21) together with Ludovico degli Arrighi's italic from 1527 (pp40–41). It was created by Robert Slimbach (1956–) in 1996.

Because none of Jenson's original punches or types survive, Slimbach followed historical printed matter as a reference, working towards a digital reinterpretation rather than a duplicate of the original. Using enlargements of original printed pages, Slimbach undertook a lengthy research process, cross-referencing several examples of each letterform so that he could identify the individual details of Jenson's typeforms to produce a core set of characters.

Adobe Jenson was a PostScript Multiple Master. This software allowed digital typefaces to contain two or more component fonts with different parameters such as weight, width or serif formation. End users could cross-relate these Multiple Masters on demand, through a continuous sliding scale of possible relationships. From a single typeface it was thus possible to generate an infinite range of styles without diminishing the integrity of the original design. The technology was not particularly well received by professional end users as its almost infinite options demanded decisions that required considerable expertise. However, it allowed type designers to develop more extensive and detailed type families than ever before. It has since been superseded by more responsive and user-friendly OpenType technology, but it remains a valuable tool in type-design software.

Slimbach's initial drawings served as the basis for a series of roman Multiple Masters rendered directly in the computer, and the italic design followed a similar process. In addition to regular styles, the roman contains both expert and alternate character sets, while the italic has a complete swash set as well as expert and alternate variants. Many people consider Nicolas Jenson's roman one of the most perfect typefaces ever produced, perhaps because it balances the animation of Renaissance calligraphy with consummate typographic restraint. Slimbach's digital homage is a faithful representation of its classical source, but is more successful in conveying its majesty than its vitality.

24-POINT REGULAR AND ITALIC
Printers *often* left space for gilded

24-POINT SEMIBOLD AND SEMIBOLD ITALIC
Printers *often* left space for gilded

24-POINT BOLD AND BOLD ITALIC
Printers *often* left space for gilded

30-POINT REGULAR AND ITALIC
Printers *often* left space for

30-POINT SEMIBOLD AND SEMIBOLD ITALIC
Printers *often* left space for

30-POINT BOLD AND BOLD ITALIC
Printers *often* left space for

36-POINT REGULAR AND ITALIC
Printers *often* left space

36-POINT SEMIBOLD AND SEMIBOLD ITALIC
Printers *often* left space

36-POINT BOLD AND BOLD ITALIC
Printers *often* left space

72-POINT REGULAR AND ITALIC
Printers *often*

48-POINT REGULAR AND ITALIC
Printers *often* left

48-POINT SEMIBOLD AND SEMIBOLD ITALIC
Printers *often* left

48-POINT BOLD AND BOLD ITALIC
Printers *often* left

60-POINT REGULAR AND ITALIC
Printers *often*

60-POINT SEMIBOLD AND SEMIBOLD ITALIC
Printers *often*

60-POINT BOLD AND BOLD ITALIC
Printers *often*

72-POINT SEMIBOLD AND BOLD ITALIC
Printers *often*

Mrs Eaves

Ty	**Mrs Eaves**	
Ca	**Serif**	
Ke	**Transitional**	
Te	**Digital**	
Da	**1996**	
De	**Zuzana Licko**	
Fo	**Emigre**	
Co	**USA**	

Characteristics

Vertical stress
A High bar and pointed apex
C Vertical serifs
E Long bottom stroke
J Descends below baseline
M Narrow
Q Sweeping tail below letter
R Straight, flared leg
T Wide arms
W w Centre-strokes meet at apex
a Double-storeyed, large bowl
g Double-storeyed, open lower bowl

ACEJMQ
abcdefghij
orstwyaefg

Connections

Baskerville	1757
Filosofia	1996
Baskerville 10 Pro	2006
Mr Eaves	2009

Availability

Mrs Eaves is available from Emigre and resellers

Specimen

Mrs Eaves XL type specimen. Emigre, Berkeley, 2009 (210x135mm)

— [MRS EAVES ROMAN — 24/31 POINT] —

ABCDEFGHJKLMNOPQ
RSTUVWXYZ0123456789
abcdefghijklmnopqrstuv
wxyz!?$%&()

— [MRS EAVES XL REGULAR — 24/31 POINT] —

ABCDEFGHJKLMNOPQ
RSTUVWXYZ0123456789
abcdefghijklmnopqrstuv
wxyz!?$%&()

— [MRS EAVES XL NARROW — 24/31 POINT] —

ABCDEFGHJKLMNOPQ
RSTUVWXYZ0123456789
abcdefghijklmnopqrstuv
wxyz!?$%&()

— [MRS EAVES ITALIC — 24/31 POINT] —

ABCDEFGHJKLMNOPQ
RSTUVWXYZ0123456789
abcdefghijklmnopqrstuv
wxyz!?$%&()

— [MRS EAVES XL REGULAR ITALIC — 24/31 POINT] —

ABCDEFGHJKLMNOPQ
RSTUVWXYZ0123456789
abcdefghijklmnopqrstuv
wxyz!?$%&()

— [MRS EAVES XL NARROW ITALIC — 24/31 POINT] —

ABCDEFGHJKLMNOPQ
RSTUVWXYZ0123456789
abcdefghijklmnopqrstuv
wxyz!?$%&()

6

7

Mrs Eaves is a reinterpretation of the eighteenth-century types of the English printer and punch cutter John Baskerville (1706–75). It was designed by Zuzana Licko and released by Emigre in 1996.

A consistent theme underpinning much of Licko's work is the exploration of the relationship between the appearance of letterforms and the technologies that are used to create them. Her interpretation of Baskerville's designs, highly effective in its own right, is also a thought-provoking exploration of the nature of revivalism in typography and a challenge to the conventional ways of reappropriating classic letterforms. Licko said in a 2002 interview that Mrs Eaves came about because she was 'shocked by the great difference between letterpress type and phototype, especially when comparing specimens of what was supposedly the same typeface design'. She felt that many photocomposition and digital revivals 'had an uncanny polished tightness, as though they sought to reproduce the original lead typefaces in some previously unattainable perfection'. With the design of Mrs Eaves, Licko sought to achieve the opposite effect, deliberately exploiting the precision of digital production methods to capture something of the charm of the lack of definition in letterpress printing that can occur due to faults in physical processes such as impression density and ink spread.

The key characteristics of Mrs Eaves' letterforms are consistent with those of Baskerville. They have bracketed serifs and a vertical stress, departing from the old-style model. The stroke weights of Mrs Eaves are considerably heavier than most other revivals, and contours have slightly rounded terminals, restoring the sensibility of letterpress printing without becoming a pseudo-historical facsimile. Mrs Eaves is a wide-set typeface with loose spacing and virtually no kerning. The family includes roman, italic, small and petite capitals, bold, and roman and italic ligatures. Mrs Eaves XL was added in 2009 to offer a larger x-height, shorter ascenders and descenders, and tighter spacing overall.

Licko named her typeface in memory of Sarah Eaves, one of the forgotten female contributors to the history of typography. Mrs Eaves lived with John Baskerville as his housekeeper, marrying him after the death of her first husband. Like the widows of Caslon and Bodoni, she continued Baskerville's work after his death in 1775, maintaining his high production standards and advancing his reputation.

MRS EAVES TYPE SPECIMEN

FABLE LII. *The Mock-bird.*

— [SET IN MRS EAVES XL] —

There is a certain bird
in the West-Indies,
WHICH HAS THE *faculty* OF
MIMICKING THE NOTES
of *every* other songster,
without being able himself to add *any* original strains to the concert.

As one of these Mock-birds was displaying
HIS TALENTS *of* RIDICULE
among the branches of a venerable wood:
'Tis very well,
SAID A LITTLE WARBLER,
speaking in the name of all the rest,
we grant you that our music
is *not* without its faults:
but why will you not favour us
with a strain of
YOUR OWN?

20

MRS EAVES TYPE SPECIMEN

FABLE LIII. *The Trumpeter.*

— [SET IN MRS EAVES XL NARROW] —

A Trumpeter in a certain army happened to be taken prisoner.
HE WAS ORDERED *immediately* TO EXECUTION
but pleaded **excuse** for
HIMSELF,
that it was *unjust*
a person should suffer *death*, who, far from an intention
of mischief, *did not even wear* an offensive weapon.
So much the rather,
replied one of the enemy
SHALT THOU DIE;
since without any design of *fighting thyself,*
THOU EXCITEST OTHERS TO THE
bloody business:
for he that is the *abettor* of a
BAD ACTION
IS AT LEAST EQUALLY WITH HIM THAT
commit it.

21

Ty	**Verdana**
Ca	**Sans Serif**
Ke	**Humanist**
Te	**Digital**
Da	**1996**
De	**Matthew Carter**
Fo	**Microsoft**
Co	**USA**

Characteristics

Wide body

Large x-height

Short ascenders and descenders

C c G g S s e Vertical terminals and large apertures

G No spur

I Short top and bottom strokes

J Top stroke to left

M High vertex with flat junction

Q Hooked tail below letter

R Wide, straight, angled tail

a Double-storeyed, large bowl

a f r t Vertical terminals

i j Square dots

j Short top stroke to left

y Straight tail

GIJMQR
abcefghij
koprstuy

Connections

Lucida	1985
Tahoma	1994
Georgia	1996
Trebuchet	1996

Availability

Verdana is widely available

Specimen

Verdana type specimen – screen and print versions, composed by author, 2015 (255x160mm)

10/12pt
Verdana's wide proportions, open letterspacing, tall x-height and subtle distinctions between character contours facilitate legibility on computer screens.

14/16pt
Verdana's wide proportions, open letterspacing, tall x-height and subtle distinctions between character contours facilitate legibility on computer screens.

24/27pt
Verdana's wide proportions, open letterspacing, tall x-height and subtle distinctions between character contours facilitate legibility on computer screens.

36/40pt
Verdana's wide proportions, open letterspacing, tall x-height and subtle

0/12pt
erdana's wide proportions,
pen letterspacing, tall x-height
nd subtle distinctions between
haracter contours facilitate
egibility on computer screens.

4/16pt
erdana's wide proportions,
pen letterspacing, tall x-height
nd subtle distinctions between
haracter contours facilitate
egibility on computer screens.

24/27pt
Verdana's wide proportions,
pen letterspacing, tall x-height
and subtle distinctions between
haracter contours facilitate
egibility on computer screens.

36/40pt
Verdana's wide
proportions, open
letterspacing, tall
x-height and subtle

Verdana is a sans serif typeface designed by Matthew Carter (1937–) for Microsoft with hinting by Thomas Rickner. It was created specifically to solve the problems of on-screen display.

In 1994 Microsoft appointed Carter to design a new typeface that would differentiate its Windows operating system from IBM's OS/2, both of which then used a fixed-size screen font named MS Sans Serif. For Windows 95 a scalable outline font was required that would be more flexible and more detailed than the bitmaps currently used in interfaces, which were often conceived as low-grade conversions of typefaces that had been first designed at high resolution for print output. Carter reversed this procedure by initially drawing bitmap alphabets at a series of different sizes scaled to the screen, and only secondarily constructing compatible outlines for print.

The result, Verdana, follows the line of humanist sans serifs such as Frutiger (pp428–29) and Syntax (pp392–93) but it exhibits many traits determined by the pixel rather than the pen or chisel. Balances between straight and curved strokes have been painstakingly achieved to ensure that pixel formations at small sizes are clear and legible. A tall x-height, clearly defined weight progression and pronounced differences between similarly shaped characters all combine to optimize readability on-screen.

Carter recognized that spacing within and between letters was the central problem to be overcome in the design of interface fonts. Because the number of pixels at low resolutions and small sizes is severely limited, adjacent characters can easily appear to merge; turning rn into an m, for example, or creating an obtrusive blotchiness in a word setting. Verdana's easy readability at text sizes is due to its large counterforms, generous width and open character spacing, which also gives it an expansive line length.

Although Verdana was not ready in time for the Windows 95 launch, it was made available by Microsoft in 1996 as a free download and was later included as a Windows and Mac OS system typeface. It was generally accepted by the web-design community as a more legible and friendly alternative to other interface fonts, and today it is a core font on the Web.

Klute

Ty	**Klute**
Ca	**Blackletter**
Ke	**Textura**
Te	**Digital**
Da	**1997**
De	**Gareth Hague**
Fo	**Alias**
Co	**UK**

Characteristics
Modular geometric character construction
Repeated triangular and rhomboid forms

Connections
Tannenberg	1933
Totally Gothic	1990
Linotype Auferstehung	1997
Harbour	1998

Availability
Klute is widely available

Specimen
Klute poster. Alias, London, 1998
(540x420mm)

The type designs of Gareth Hague (1967–) are characterized by a playful exchange between handmade and digital processes. He works entirely on the computer rather than with the pen so that his typefaces deliberately reference the language of digital conventions rather than manual ones. This approach, he has said, 'has always seemed more relevant, more interesting than a more direct redrawing, a way of updating and reshaping an old form and making it new'.

Within this framework Hague's Klute typeface, designed in 1997, is a hybrid that brings together three divergent text traditions. The most clearly evident of its reference points is the German blackletter form, which contributes the basic stroke structure to Klute's design. The contour shapes, though, are derived from graffiti tagging – 'as if written with a thick marker pen as much as having been carved with a chisel', as Hague said. Underlying these structures is the overall construction method of the alphabet itself, which draws from the more recent tradition of modular type design. This has its origins in the work of early modernist designers such as Josef Albers (pp212–13) and Herbert Bayer (pp222–23), and has been a global trend since the advent of personal computers.

But Hague did not bring these disparate elements together as a mere observational study of miscellaneous artefacts from design history. He was interested in the visual impact of creating such an exotic typographic mongrel. 'The Gothic heritage of the form', he wrote, 'makes it appropriate for the doom laden imagery of Heavy Metal band logos … tag graffiti often references or takes influence from the decorative strength of the form.'

Ty	**Miller**
Ca	**Serif**
Ke	**Transitional**
Te	**Digital**
Da	**1997**
De	**Matthew Carter**
Fo	**Font Bureau**
Co	**USA**

Characteristics

Vertical stress
Thin strokes with high contrast
Most capitals have uniform width
Capitals lower than ascender height
Large x-height
Short ascenders and descenders
Angled, bracketed serifs
M Narrow
Q Looped tail below letter
R a t Tail turns upwards
W w Stepped centre-strokes, serif at apex
a c f g j y Ball terminals
b No serif at foot
g Double-storeyed, teardrop ear
t Flat top

CMQRW
abcdefghij
orstuy*aefg*

Connections

Wilson	1768
Bell	1788
Scotch Roman	1812
Georgia	1996

Availability

Miller is available from the Font Bureau
and resellers

Specimen

Newspaper Type from Font Bureau – Miller
type specimen. The Font Bureau, Boston,
2002 (420x320mm)

When Microsoft invited Matthew Carter
(1937–) to design a typeface for use
on-screen he decided to adapt a print
typeface he was working on at the time.
The screen font, Georgia (pp554–55), was
issued in 1996 while the original was
released a year later as Miller.

Miller is based on several types cut by
Richard Austin for the Scottish foundries
of Alexander Wilson and William Miller at
the beginning of the nineteenth century. In
particular, it references the earliest known
historical specimen of a newspaper type.
This was designed by Austin for Wilson in
a style that later became known as 'Scotch'
(pp112–13). Like Austin's earlier typeface
for Bell (pp94–95), his Scotch designs are
a compound of the innovations pioneered
by Firmin Didot (pp90–91) with the more
nuanced forms of the old style.

A distinguished expert in the design
of newspaper types, having worked on
many mass-circulation dailies such as the
Washington Post and the *New York Daily
News*, Carter intended to renovate the
Scotch style for contemporary editorial
use. He was, he said, 'puzzled by the fact
that they were once so popular … and then
they disappeared completely'. Rather than
directly reproduce Austin's letters, he
sought to interpret the modelling and
impression of the originals, maintaining
their vertical stress and large x-height for
good legibility. Miller captured the even
colour, spatial economy and inviting
appearance of Scotch Roman as the
foundations of a workhorse type for
setting in extended texts.

With the assistance of Tobias Frere-Jones
and Cyrus Highsmith at the Font Bureau,
the Miller family was developed as a
comprehensive system including bold,
italic and display character sets. It also
featured a range of finely graded weights,
allowing publishers and printers to work
with a version of the typeface that was
adjusted to compensate for the printing
processes of their presses.

Since the release of Miller Text and
Miller Display in 1997 the family has
been extended with a number of variants,
including Miller Daily, Miller Headline and
Miller Banner, as well as several bespoke
versions for specific publications. A 2005
survey found Miller to be the tenth most
popular typeface featured in American
newspapers, and it is relied on today
in editorial work around the world.

THE FONT BUREAU, INC.

BOSTON, MA

AUTUMN 2002

VOLUME 3 ISSUE 1

TYP

Miller Da

Four Grades of Text

By Mike Parker

In 1995 Matthew Carter showed Roger
Black the early stages of his Miller series
of Scotch types. Roger wanted it immediately for his designs for @Home Network and *Straits Times* of Singapore.
With the assistance of Font Bureau's
Tobias Frere-Jones, the first fonts were
shipped in 1996, and Carter & Cone and
Font Bureau decided to jointly market
the forthcoming series.

Miller Text & Display, Roman & Italic, were completed by the same team
and released for general use as a Font
Bureau Retail Series in December 1997.
The *Guardian* in London, and Canada's
National Post chose Miller Display for
headlines, with additional weights and
italics drawn by Font Bureau's Cyrus
Highsmith with Carter's direction. Numerous papers followed, including the
Dallas Morning News, *Hindustan Times*,
and *San Jose Mercury News*.

In 1999 the *Guardian* introduced Carter's Miller News. The first Scotch text tailored to the requirements of large contemporary newspapers met with immediate popularity. The *Boston Globe*
commissioned its own version for a recent redesign, with further cuttings of
display and display condensed.

With custom versions as a guide, Carter
& Highsmith organized a Miller news series: condensed Miller Headline and Miller Daily for text. Daily has been drawn
in four grades so that the color of the
text can be properly adjusted to the technology in use. One Daily Bold provides
emphasis, while a second supplies special
text, a popular feature in Europe.

The Scotch design has a long news
tradition. The earliest known type specimen prepared specifically for newspaper use was issued in Glasgow by Alexander Wilson's foundry in the 1820s,
and showed only the parent of these
Scotch designs.

Scottish typ
the establishme
ry outside Glasg
Wilson produce
types largely fo
liam Miller, for
son in Glasgow
own competing
From 1809 unt
Miller produce
rate, showing t
new design.

In 1825 T.C. H
most of the new
and Miller were
London (who
splendid moder
er's letter 'so re
Wilson as to req
distinguish the
Austin's earlier
fonts are a wond
oldstyle virtues
championed by
was in the mid 18
the earliest kno
men of newspa
new faces from
es that we know
in Glasgow and

Nevertheless
overlooked in t
popularity of th
In 1837 young
son of Boston
pared to his sp
son. Delivered
inson claimed t
the first to call
changes Dickin
designs remain
a number of d
tin's original for
to have been n
tirelessly promo
major America
peting Scotch
the original de

SPAPER TYPE FROM

t Bureau

WWW.FONTBUREAU.COM

326 A STREET, SUITE 6C

BOSTON, MA 02210

617-423-8770

AND DISPLAY ", CUSTOM TYPEFACE DESIGN

Now Available

our Weights for Headline Use

with
and-
ears,
style
Wil-
Wil-
his
rgh.
and
ious
iant

that
lson
stin,
ell's
Mill-
ssrs.
on to
Like
hese
iliar
ions
is. It
ased
peci-
g his
fac-
text

soon
full
erica.
ckin-
pre-
Wil-
Dick-
was
what
stin's
are
Aus-
seem
e. He
most
com-
as on
r by

Miller Headline Light

Miller Headline Light Italic

Miller Headline Roman

Miller Headline Italic

Miller Headline Semibold

Miller Headline Semibold Italic

Miller Headline Bold

Miller Headline Bold Italic

Miller Daily One Roman, *Italic,* **Bold,** and ***Bold Italic***
Miller Daily One Roman, *Italic,* **Bold,** and ***Bold Italic***
Miller Daily One Roman, *Italic,* **Bold,** and ***Bold Italic***
Miller Daily One Roman, *Italic,* **Bold,** and ***Bold Italic***

Miller Daily Bold Text and *Bold Text Italic*

Font Bureau's popular Miller family has been retuned for newspaper use

Linotype and Monotype. Until recently the most popular member of the family has been W.A. Dwiggins' 1938 Caledonia. Matthew Carter's Miller series carries the family into the next century and back to its newspaper roots.

For a typographic evaluation of Miller, we can do no better than quote the words of James Mosley, of St. Bride's Printing Library, London:

'Matthew Carter's Miller is not a facsimile of Miller's Scotch Roman, any more than his Galliard was a facsimile of any one type by Robert Granjon. What it has done is to capture the good color, and the generous breadth and modelling of its model, and to bring a valid version of "Scotch Roman" back into current use after a lapse [in England] of some decades. Miller was made with current production needs in mind, of which the two versions, "Display" and the more robust "Text" versions are evidence, and so is its relatively large x-height.'

Font Bureau Builds on Newspaper Experience

By David Berlow

NEWSPAPERS have always had a thing for fonts beyond their obvious use in conveying textual information. Readers like well-laid-out type that is clear in all aspects and as familiar looking and feeling as if it was their own "furniture." To satisfy readers, newspaper editors, designers and production specialists have come to realize over the last decade that they need to count on the best typographic products and services. In 1990 the first generation of PostScript output devices was released, meeting the demands of newspaper printing. By 1995 it was clear that typesetting and newspaper composition systems would be PostScript-based. Between these dates, Font Bureau produced several hundred custom PostScript newspaper fonts, bringing familiar designs into the new technology and ensuring that the old furniture wasn't forced out—something that we know readers have appreciated.

After the PostScript transition occurred for most of the dailies, and all the "old furniture" was in place, two things began to happen. First, there were new newspapers, born in the wake of new technologies and political progress. Secondly, there began a cycle of newspaper redesigns that continues to this day. The Font Bureau increased its offerings from custom fonts to suites of fonts for both text and display, offered in multiple technologies and in combination offering practically unlimited design possibilities.

INSIDE

xibility

Ty	**Capitolium**
Ca	**Serif**
Ke	**Old Style**
Te	**Digital**
Da	**1998**
De	**Gerard Unger**
Fo	**TypeTogether**
Co	**Netherlands**

Characteristics

Slightly oblique stress
Moderate stroke contrast
Large x-height
Short ascenders and descenders
Short, sharp, bracketed serifs
J Descends below baselne
M Splayed
Q Long tail below letter
R Wide, angled leg
W Centre-strokes meet at apex
a Double-storeyed, large bowl
g Double-storeyed, wedge ear
r t Narrow
y Wide, hooked tail

AJMQRW
abcdefghij
orstuya*efg*

Connections

Times New Roman	1932
Meridien	1957
Swift	1987
DTL Paradox	1997

Availability

Capitolium 2 is available from
TypeTogether and resellers

Specimen

TypeTogether catalogue. Prague, 2012
(280x180mm)

CAPITOLIUM 2 — *modern newsprint, traditional elegance*

Capitolium was designed in 1998 for the Jubilee of the Roman Catholic Church in 2000, as part of the project for a wayfinding and information system to guide pilgrims and tourists through Rome. *Capitolium* also continues Rome's almost uninterrupted two-thousand-year-old tradition of public lettering.

Soon after the completion of this project, Unger began contemplating the possibility of bringing the atmosphere of this design to newspapers. Though *Capitolium* works well in most modern production processes and also on screens, it is too fragile for newsprint. For newspapers, sturdier shapes were required as well as more characters to a line of text, and *Capitolium News* has a bigger x-height than *Capitolium*. As is possible with most of Unger's type designs, *Capitolium News* can be condensed and expanded without any harm to the letterforms.

STYLES
Capitolium 2

a *a* **a** **a**

Capitolium 2 News

a a *a a* **a a**

Romano

POUŽITÝ MATERIÁL—JEHO ÚDRŽBA A OŠETŘOVÁ

Easy wayfinding

Dedalus has it, Buck Mulligan said. Janey Mack, I'm choke

ficus & *oliveto*

Deutsche **Maschinen- und Anlagenbauer** sind schwungvoll in das Jahr 2011 gestar

EUROSONIC/NOORDERSLAG 201

lumină polară

O my! Puddeny pie! protested Cis

Legibility

»One of principles of durable *typography* is always *legibilit*

$^{13}/_{478}$ Camperdown

RUSSIE: bientôt une amnistie pour les ***Pussy Riot***

Stáhněte výpověd

AWARDS:
ED-Awards 2012 (Finalist)
Letter.2

18

Capitolium has its origins in a project for wayfinding and signage. In 1998 Dutch type designer Gerard Unger (1942–) was commissioned to produce it for the Jubilee of the Roman Catholic Church in 2000 as the central feature of a navigation and information system guiding pilgrims through the city.

Capitolium was inspired by Rome's almost uninterrupted 2,000-year-old heritage of public lettering. Unger based the concept of Capitolium in part on the work of the Italian scribe Gianfrancesco Cresci (1534–?), who in the 1600s heralded the transitional letter styles of the following century by rejecting any superfluous adornment, reforming the lettering used by the ancient Romans for the needs of his own time. Unger used a similar approach to the adaptation of traditional Roman lettering to text on signage, in print and on screens, and for modern reading requirements in many different languages. However, Capitolium is not a classical revival: it is a typeface for the twenty-first century firmly embedded in typographic traditions.

Soon after the completion of the wayfinding project Unger began working on the possibility of bringing the sensibility of the Capitolium design to newspaper applications. Although the original type family worked well in print and screen environments, Unger considered it too fragile for newsprint. For editorial use sturdier contours were required, as was greater spatial economy, with an increase in the number of characters in a line.

The result was Capitolium 2, released by TypeTogether in 2011. With a slightly more even stroke than its predecessor, Capitolium 2 has a larger x-height, resulting in a tighter fit and more open counterforms at smaller point sizes. It features small capitals, ligatures, alternative sets of numerals and extensive language support. Capitolium 2 is a sharp, incisive editorial typeface that maintains the impression of its strong classical roots.

DESIGNED BY
GERARD UNGER

Via del Circo Massimo 28

ørgen rennur eftir vøkstrinum

7 KING SQUARE AVENUE

des small caps, 5 sets of figures, arbitrary fractions, scientific superior and inferior numbers, ligatures and more.

iangete, amanti, poi che piange Amore

ESTUPIDEZ SE LLAMA TRIÁNGULO, OCHO POR OCHO ES LA LOCURA O UN PERRO»

CZECH

Zahrádky by se mohly napřesrok otevřít na více místech. Praha 1 chce méně peněz od restaurací. Praha 1 chce snížit poplatek za užívání veřejného prostranství v méně atraktivních lokalitách centra metropole. Doufá, že se tak podaří i do těchto míst rozšířit

DANISH

SF-næstformand: Reform af erhvervsskolerne er godt håndværk! *»Det kan du ikke finde ud af!«Sådan lød det, når min farfar mistede tålmodigheden med min far, når han forsøgte sig med værktøjet derhjemme, da han var dreng.*

ENGLISH

A Florida man saw a spinning funnel cloud and did what you would expect… from a Florida man! *He turned his boat and drove it right through it. "The waterspouts evolved so quickly, coming and going. It was tough to*

til føroyingaveitslu nøren. *Stóra tónleika-kið Mittland, sum var á øren á Amager leygarda-eydnaðist so mikið væl, takið verður aftur. — Við ri ótrúligu undirtøkuni, hevur verið, er tað drað prosent víst, at*

Picadilly Circus

LONDON W1

Brawurowe wiedźmy Stalina. Kobiecy pułk bombowy siał spustoszenie w szeregach wroga

RIDICULOUS

8 of the most ridiculous travel complaints ever

1. "It took us nine hours to fly home from Jamaica to England. It took the Americans only three hours to get home. It is unfair."
2. *"We had to line up outside to catch the boat, it was very hot and there was no air-conditioning."*
3. "My fiance and I booked a twin-bedded room but we were placed in a double-bedded room. We now hold you responsible for the fact that I find myself pregnant. This would not have happened if you had put us in the room that we booked."
4. *"It's lazy of the local shopkeepers in Puerto Vallarta to close in the afternoons. I often needed to buy things during 'siesta' time - this should be banned."*
5. **"No one told us there would be fish in the water. The kids were scared."**
6. *"We booked an excursion to a water park but no one told us we had to bring our own swimsuits and towels. We assumed it would be included in the price."*
7. "Although the brochure said that there was a fully-equipped kitchen, there was no egg-slicer in the drawers."
8. "The roads were uneven and bumpy, so we could not read the local guide book during the bus ride to the resort. Because of this, we were unaware of many things that would have made our holiday more fun."

HEADLINE

CabcdEFGH ABCabcdEFGH
CabcdEFGH ABCabcdEFGH
CabcdEFGH *ABCabcdEFGH*
CabcdEFGH **ABCabcdEFGH**
CabcdEFGH *ABCabcdEFGH*
CabcdEFGH

19

Ty	**Farao**
Ca	**Slab Serif**
Ke	**Egyptian**
Te	**Digital**
Da	**1998**
De	**František Štorm**
Fo	**Storm Type Foundry**
Co	**Czech Republic**

Characteristics

Vertical stress
Variable stroke contrast
Wide body
Large x-height
Short ascenders and descenders
Heavy, rectangular slab serifs
Strokes taper at junctions
R a t Tail turns upwards
c f g r y Ball terminals
g Double-storeyed, upturned ear

AGIMR
abcefghi
koprsty

Connections

Clarendon	1845
Artefact	1999
Sentinel	2009
Eames Century Modern	2010

Availability

Farao is available from Storm Type
Foundry and resellers

Specimen

Farao type specimen PDF. Storm Type
Foundry, 2013 (255x200mm)

If a
text is set
in a good Egyptienne
we can observe a kind of sparkle in the lines
Egyptiennes are cheerful type face
possibly due to the fact
that they developed
simultaneously
with sans

freshfaraofonts

Stormtype

The work of contemporary Czech type designer František Štorm (1966–) is distinguished by its balance between the studiously expert reconstruction of historical typefaces and a knowingly irreverent attitude.

Farao, Štorm's reinterpretation of nineteenth-century Egyptian and Clarendon designs (pp114–15, 132–33), is an outstanding example of his maverick approach. Many digital revivals aim for such perfect technical accuracy that they can become lifeless reflections of their sources. However, working with the idea that the nineteenth-century models could constitute what he described as 'a useful tool which could give life to the uniform computer typography', Štorm used Farao's development to explore the uneven, untamed personality of these prototypical alphabets from the Industrial Revolution in order to deliberately exaggerate the rugged beauty of their imperfections.

Farao is an aggregate of seemingly incompatible features, such as deep incisions at stroke junctions, extravagantly curvaceous ball terminals and enormous slab serifs, all of which contribute to a blotchy contrast and an irregular overall colour. The bizarre shapes of many letters, Štorm observed, 'resemble the gesture of a juggler: others, rectangularly static ones, the profile of a rail or a steel girder'.

The product of Štorm's exceptional knowledge and skill, Farao's eccentricities come together in a typeface that is surprisingly harmonious while visibly sparkling on the page or screen. The paradoxes that underpin the appearance of this homage to the industrial age were summed up with wilful irony by Štorm himself: 'Let us not be like a machine, let us not be afraid of doing things in a slapdash way.'

If a text is set in a good Egyptienne, we can observe a kind of sparkle in the lines. Egyptiennes are cheerful type faces, possibly due to the fact that they developed simultaneously with sans-serif faces. *The design principle of a sign from the first half of the 19th century does not have such firm and long-established roots as for example, the Renaissance Roman type face; it is, therefore, much more prone to mistakes which are symptoms of a „decline". We know of Egyptiennes with uneven colour, with letters falling backwards (this often happens in the case of „S"), and also with slightly bizarre modeling of details. In the course of time, however, it was realized that such things could be quite pleasant and inspiring.* After a century and a half we find that Egyptiennes could be a useful tool which could give life to the uniform computer typography. The bequest of the „decadent" typography is the following: Let us not be like a machine, let us not be afraid of doing things in a slapdash way. If monolinear sans-serif type faces palpably lack serifs, then Egyptiennes literally have them in excess. It is not uncommon for the serif itself to be darker than the stroke it stems from. The forms of many twisted letters resemble the gesture of a juggler: others, rectangularly static ones, the profile of a rail or a steel girder - things which, in their time, were new and were unawares observed by the first creators of Egyptiennes. **These type faces are ideal for circus posters and programs for theatre performances, just as for printing on cement sacks.** The Egyptienne „Farao" is soundly imperfect, in which it differs from the „cold" current Egyptiennes. It has been released in eight designs.

Book   *Book Italic*   **College**

Text   *Text Italic*

Bold   ***Bold Italic***

TextBold   ***TextBold Italic***

Je-li text vysázen dobrou egyptienkou, pozorujeme jakési jiskření v řádkách. *Egyptienky jsou písma veselá, možná proto, že se vyvíjela současně s grotesky. Jestliže monolineárním bezserifovým písmům citelně chybějí patky, pak egyptienkám doslova přebývají. Nezřídka je samotná patka tmavší než tah, ze kterého vyrůstá. Tvary mnohých zakroucených liter připomínají gesto žongléra, jiné, pravoúhle statické, profil kolejnice či ocelové traverzy - věci ve své době nové, mimoděk odpozorované prvními tvůrci egyptienek. Jsou to ideální písma na cirkusové plakáty a programy představení, stejně jako na potisk pytlů s cementem.*

oldfaraofonts

Stormtype

Ty	**Serapion**
Ca	**Serif**
Ke	**Transitional**
Te	**Digital**
Da	**1998**
De	**František Štorm**
Fo	**Storm Type Foundry**
Co	**Czech Republic**

Characteristics

Variable stress

Variable stroke contrasts

Combination of flat serifs, concave serifs and rounded terminals

H Curved crossbar

J Descends below baseline

M Splayed

Q Sweeping tail

R Long, curved leg

W Stepped centre-strokes, serif at apex

a Double-storeyed, small bowl

b q Pointed vertical terminal

g Double-storeyed, large tilted lower bowl

AJMQRW
abcdefghij
oqrstyaefg

Connections

Mediaeval	1997
Lexon Gothic	1998
ITC Biblon	1999
FF Oneleigh	1999

Availability

Serapion is available from Storm Type Foundry and resellers

Specimen

Serapion type specimen. Storm Type Foundry, 1998 (297x210mm)

SERAPION REGULAR, BOLD, ITALIC & BOLD ITALIC

16/20 PT:

Another variation on the Renaissance-Baroque Roman face, it extends t selection of text type faces. *In comparison with Jannon, the contrast within the lett has been enhanced. The dynamic elements of the Renaissance Roman face have been streng ened in a way which is illustrated best in the letters "a", "b" and "s".* These letters co tain, in condensed form, the principle of this type face - in round shapes t dark stroke invariably has a round finial at one end and a sharp one at t other. *Another typical feature is the lower-case "g";* the upper part of this lett consists of two geometrically exact circles, the inner of which, a negative or is immersed down on the right, upright to the direction of the lower loc and the upright knob. The vertical strokes slightly splay out upwards. Son details of the upper-case letters may seem to be too daring, but they are le apparent in the text sizes. It has to be admitted that typographers tend draw letters in exaggerated sizes, as a result of which they stick to detai Serapion Italic are italics inspired partly by the Renaissance Cancelleres This is obvious from the drop-shaped finials of its lower-case descenders. *The type face is suitable for illustrated books, art posters and short texts. It has a rather ug name - after St. Serapion.*

10/12 PT:

Serapion vyšel na jaře roku 1997, a od té doby se poněkud změnily požadavky na digitální písmo. U příležitosti překódování znakové mapy korigujeme a vylepšujeme i estetický vzhled liter na základě vlastních i uživatelských zkušeností. Serapion má nyní rozšířenou znakovou sadu a ještě bohatší kerningy. Doplněny byly ligatury ffi a ffl.

Ozvěny renesanční estetiky v moderní typografii jsou velmi časté. Písma této skupiny si získávají naši přízeň průzračnou anatomií antikvy a jemnou zpěvností italiky. Současné repliky renesančních písem můžeme rozdělit do dvou skupin: první jsou překreslována se snahou o věrnost originálu, s důrazem na zpevnění a umravnění předlohy. Do skupiny druhé můžeme zařadit repliky vyzdvihující charakteristické rysy původních písem a to až na hranici

10/12 PT:

uměleckě plakáty & krátké texty. Má takové ošk jméno, podle svatého Serapiona. Serapion vyšel na j roku 1997, a od té doby se poněkud změnily požada na digitální písmo. U příležitosti překódování zna vé mapy korigujeme a vylepšujeme i estetický vzh liter na základě vlastních i uživatelských zkušeno Serapion má nyní rozšířenou znakovou sadu a je bohatší kerningy. Doplněny byly ligatury ffi a ffl. Ozvě renesanční estetiky v moderní typografii jsou velmi ča Písma této skupiny si získávají naši přízeň průzračn anatomií antikvy a jemnou zpěvností italiky. Souča repliky renesančních písem můžeme rozdělit do dv skupin: první jsou překreslována se snahou o věrné originálu, s důrazem na zpevnění a umravnění předlo

10/12 PT:

deformace znaku. Sem patří i náš Serapion. Oproti Jannonu je zvýšen kontrast uvnitř liter. Dynamické prvky renesanční antikvy byly posíleny způsobem, jež vystihují litery a, b a s. V nich je zhuštěn princip tohoto písma – u oblých tvarů vždy tmavý tah na jednom konci kulatě, na protějším ostře zakončen. Typické je rovněž minuskové „g" mající horní bříško ze dvou geometricky přesných kruhů, z nichž vnitřní, negativní, je vnořen vpravo dolů, kolmo ke směru výběhu spodní smyčky a horní bambulky. Svislé tahy se mírně rozbíhají nahoru. Některé detaily versálek se mohou zdát příliš odvážné, ale v textových velikostech zaniknou. Je třeba přiznat jistou typografickou manýru, která se projevuje kreslením písmen v přehnaných velikostech, následkem čehož tvůrce ulpívá na detailech. Serapion Italic je kursiva inspirovaná částečně renesanční kancelareskou. To je zřejmé z kapkovitě zakončených dotažnic minusek. Písmo je vhodné pro obrázkové knihy,

10/12 PT:

Do skupiny druhé můžeme zařadit repliky vyzdvihující char teristické rysy původních písem a to až na hranici deform znaku. Sem patří i náš Serapion. Oproti Jannonu je zvy kontrast uvnitř liter. Dynamické prvky renesanční antikvy b posíleny způsobem, jež vystihují litery a, b a s. V nich je zhu princip tohoto písma – u oblých tvarů vždy tmavý tah na jedn konci kulatě, na protějším ostře zakončen. Typické je rovněž mi nuskové „g" mající horní bříško ze dvou geometricky přesný kruhů, z nichž vnitřní, negativní, je vnořen vpravo dolů, kol ke směru výběhu spodní smyčky a horní bambulky. Svislé ta se mírně rozbíhají nahoru. Některé detaily versálek se moh zdát příliš odvážné, ale v textových velikostech zaniknou. třeba přiznat jistou typografickou manýru, která se projevu kreslením písmen v přehnaných velikostech, následkem če

STŘEŠOVICKÁ PÍSMOLIJNA, WWW.PISMOLIJNA.CZ

STORM TYPE FOUNDRY, WWW.STORMTYPE.CO

SERAPION

Pigmenty
Gouache
Ancient affinity
Caminito real
citlivé skizzy mistrů
závěrečný damarový lak
úkolem pozlacovače jeʃt vtisknouti
jeżeli w świetnym płaszczu wielką

Baroque typefaces of the seventeenth and eighteenth centuries are usually referred to by the relative and somewhat perfunctory term 'transitional', as if they constitute only a brief intermediate stage between more stable typographic norms, preceded by the roman model of the Renaissance and followed by their modern, measured resolutions, represented by Bodoni or Didot. An opponent of this assumption, Czech type designer František Štorm (1966–) considers the work of the type founders and punch cutters of the Baroque era to be among the most innovative and enduring in the history of design. For him, the period was, he said, 'without a doubt the pinnacle of typographic development'.

Of the many typefaces Štorm has designed that reinterpret baroque type for the digital era, Serapion is one of the most successful. Its construction is based on Renaissance letters but its expressiveness and calligraphic details are inspired by the typography of the seventeenth and eighteenth centuries. In larger sizes Serapion gives the impression of what Štorm calls 'a kind of thorny elegance', with an unevenness in its splayed strokes providing an unmistakably individual personality. At smaller sizes, however, the typeface behaves quite inconspicuously, in a manner appropriate for use in extended text, the reader only noticing its vivacity at a second glance.

A baroque conception of letterform design is most evident in the stroke formation of the lower case c. One finial of its curve is rounded and heavy, the other sharp and light. This dynamic trait, which looks almost painted with a brush, is reflected in all similar lower case letters, and much variation in serif construction is evident elsewhere. Serapion's wildly unrestrained companion italic shows the heritage of the Renaissance Cancelleresca Corsiva, particularly in the droplet-shaped finials of its lower case.

In his work Štorm is more concerned with the reinvention of historical forms than their faithful reproduction. He is interested in developing what he calls 'the spice of each type design', adding that 'you have to be as obstinate as a mule if you want to achieve anything really good'.

Ty	**Cholla**
Ca	**Sans Serif / Slab Serif**
Ke	**Geometric**
Te	**Digital**
Da	**1999**
De	**Sibylle Hagmann**
Fo	**Emigre**
Co	**USA**

Characteristics

Rectangular letterforms
Radiused and square corners
Tapered curves at junctions
Slab serif and sans serif variants

ABEGMRS
abcdefghij
koprstuvy

Connections

City	1930
Isonorm	1974
ITC Conduit	1997
FF Magda Clean	1998

Availability

Cholla is available from Emigre and resellers

Specimen

Cholla type specimen. Emigre, Berkeley, 1999 (279x216mm)

Cholla San
A New Font Famil
Designed by Sibylle Hagmar
AVAILABLE EXCLUSIVELY FROM EMIGRE FON

CHOLLA SANS

DESIGNED CIRCA 1998-99

ON SALE NOW!   1.800.944.9

4 FONT CHOLLA SANS PACKAGE $95.00 | 12 FONT CHOLLA VOLUME $199.00

SANS THIN

ABCDEFGHIJKLMNOPQRSTUVWXYZ
abcdefghijklmnopqrstuvwxyz1234567890

SANS REGULAR

ABCDEFGHIJKLMNOPQRSTUVWXYZ
abcdefghijklmnopqrstuvwxyz1234567890

SANS BOLD

ABCDEFGHIJKLMNOPQRSTUVWXYZ
abcdefghijklmnopqrstuvwxyz1234567890

SANS ITALIC

ABCDEFGHIJKLMNOPQRSTUVWXYZ
abcdefghijklmnopqrstuvwxyz1234567890

LLA SLAB

4 FONT CHOLLA SLAB PACKAGE $95.00 | 12 FONT CHOLLA VOLUME $199.00

SLAB THIN

ABCDEFGHIJKLMNOPQRSTUVWXYZ
abcdefghijklmnopqrstuvwxyz1234567890

SLAB REGULAR

ABCDEFGHIJKLMNOPQRSTUVWXYZ
abcdefghijklmnopqrstuvwxyz1234567890

SLAB BOLD

ABCDEFGHIJKLMNOPQRSTUVWXYZ
abcdefghijklmnopqrstuvwxyz1234567890

SLAB OBLIQUE

ABCDEFGHIJKLMNOPQRSTUVWXYZ
abcdefghijklmnopqrstuvwxyz1234567890

also available in

Cholla Slab

continued on next page

Cholla is a square geometric typeface family designed by Sibylle Hagmann (1965–) between 1998 and 1999 and named after the species of cactus found in the Mojave Desert whose rounded forms it evokes.

Cholla (pronounced 'choya') was originally developed for ArtCenter College of Design in Pasadena, California. Denise Gonzales Crisp, then the college's art director, commissioned Hagmann to design a family of typefaces that would feature extensive variations of weights and styles. Hagmann set out to create a typeface that, as she recalls, 'would serve a purpose and had a clear idea behind it'. The wide range of alternatives was intended to represent the diversity of the institution's activities and offerings, while at the same time it was expected to impart an appropriately organized and unified feel.

Like Georg Trump's 1930 City typeface (pp256–57), Cholla is based on rectangular letterforms with radiused junctions, although Cholla is more flexible, affable and idiosyncratic than the older design. The individual members of the Cholla family have subtly distinctive personalities. Letterforms from different weights and styles possess their own peculiar details, with a wide range of variation in form and counterform across the family, rather than a fixed linear progression from light through to bold.

The unifying characteristic that all weights and styles share is a curved tapering – evident, for example, in the lower case a's bottom transition from the bowl into the stem. Cholla's original range included 12 different styles. Recently, Hagmann has extended the type family to a comprehensive range of 19 weights and variants in Sans, Slab, Wide and Unicase subgroups.

Ty	**Vendetta**
Ca	**Serif**
Ke	**Old Style**
Te	**Digital**
Da	**1999**
De	**John Downer**
Fo	**Emigre**
Co	**USA**

Characteristics

Geometric character construction
Oblique stress
Low stroke contrast
Capitals lower than ascender height
Rounded beak serifs at head of ascenders
Slab serifs at foot
Sharply incised stroke junctions
J Descends below baseline
M Narrow
Q Curved tail below letter
R Curved leg
W Stepped centre-strokes, serif at apex
a g Double-storeyed
y Straight, swelling tail

AJMQRW
abcdefghij
orstuy*aefg*

Connections

Jenson	1470
The Doves Type	1900
Weiss	1926
Cardea	2004

Availability

Vendetta is available from Emigre and resellers

Specimen

Emigre 50. Emigre, Berkeley, 1999
(279x216mm)

AMUSEMENTS

Vendetta Light Petite Caps, Vendetta Light, and Vendetta Light Italic, 32/32 point

THE SKY OF THE DESERT is well worth studying at other times than the sunset hour—for instance, at the moment when the sun comes striding up in the inexpressible magnificence of power. Over this *Garden of the Sun* he rises morning after morning in such splendor as you will never see but in the desert, for here no mists or earthly exhalations dim the flashing glory of his first horizontal beams. It is then that one grasps the true meaning of that everyday word, the sun, and realizes him at last for what he is— a *flame*, inconceivably vast, ineffably pure, unutterably terrible.

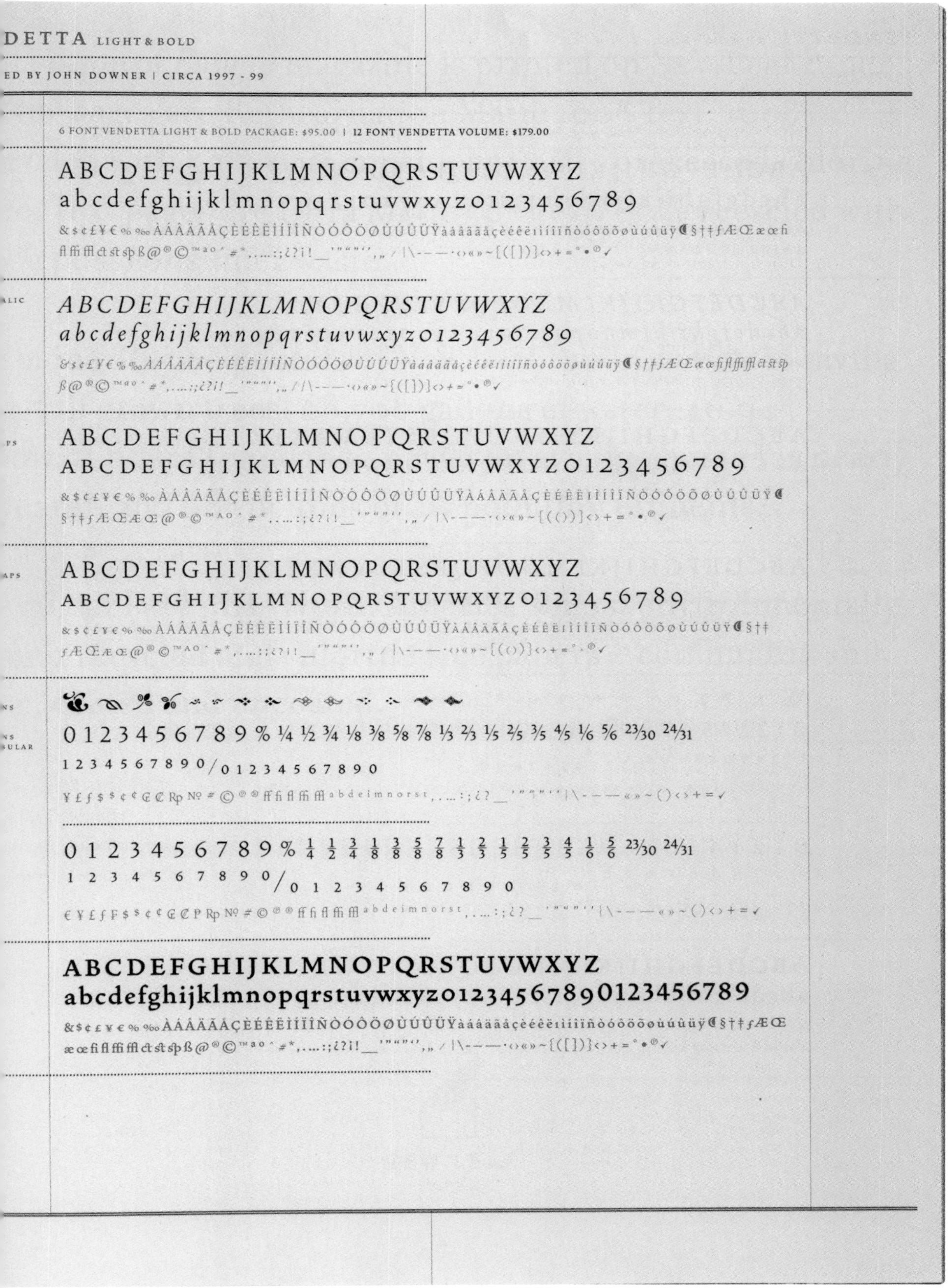

DETTA LIGHT & BOLD

ED BY JOHN DOWNER | CIRCA 1997 - 99

6 FONT VENDETTA LIGHT & BOLD PACKAGE: $95.00 | 12 FONT VENDETTA VOLUME: $179.00

ABCDEFGHIJKLMNOPQRSTUVWXYZ
abcdefghijklmnopqrstuvwxyz0123456789

ABCDEFGHIJKLMNOPQRSTUVWXYZ
abcdefghijklmnopqrstuvwxyz0123456789

ABCDEFGHIJKLMNOPQRSTUVWXYZ
ABCDEFGHIJKLMNOPQRSTUVWXYZ0123456789

ABCDEFGHIJKLMNOPQRSTUVWXYZ
ABCDEFGHIJKLMNOPQRSTUVWXYZ0123456789

0123456789 % ¼ ½ ¾ ⅛ ⅜ ⅝ ⅞ ⅓ ⅔ ⅕ ⅖ ⅗ ⅘ ⅙ ⅚ 23/30 24/31
1234567890/01234567890

0123456789 % ¼ ½ ¾ ⅛ ⅜ ⅝ ⅞ ⅓ ⅔ ⅕ ⅖ ⅗ ⅘ ⅙ ⅚ 23/30 24/31
1 2 3 4 5 6 7 8 9 0 /0 1 2 3 4 5 6 7 8 9 0

ABCDEFGHIJKLMNOPQRSTUVWXYZ
abcdefghijklmnopqrstuvwxyz01234567890123456789

John Downer (1951–), an expert American sign painter and type designer, developed Vendetta for the Emigre type foundry in 1999 in order to investigate ideas about historical and contemporary letter construction. Vendetta is an homage to the largely neglected Renaissance punch cutters whose designs were directly influenced by Nicolas Jenson's Venetian type of 1470 (pp20–21). Downer's fascination with the formation of letters during the late 1400s was offset by his intention to achieve the optimal display of letterforms on contemporary computer screens.

The Vendetta project began in the 1990s when Downer began exploring whether classical proportions and geometric construction methods could be reconciled. He started drawing digital forms modelled on the Venetian old-style types of the early Renaissance. In assembling letters from sections of circles and squares, he drew an unusual beak-like serif at the top of a stroke in the shape of a bisected quadrant of a circle. Aware that rectangular slab serifs were commonly found in early printing types cut in Italy before 1500, mainly at the feet of the lower case letters, he decided to test whether these would have a balanced appearance in combination with his rounded beak serifs at the head.

Satisfied with the composite form that resulted, Downer proceeded to complete the alphabet. Athough its letterforms were based on a fragmentary geometric structure, he refined them repeatedly in order to improve their performance in bodies of text. The resulting Vendetta family achieved what he called a 'rich, familiar, coarseness' similar to the roman types of the late 1400s that he so admired.

Reflecting on Renaissance old-style faces in his monumental 1922 book, *Printing Types*, the historian Daniel Berkeley Updike wrote that 'there is nothing better than fine Italian roman type in the whole history of typography'. Six hundred years on, John Downer's Vendetta is an exemplary specimen of that ideal.

200-1

In the twenty-first century typography has become more ubiquitous, more accessible and more personal than ever before. While it persists in printed matter, it is also central to digital communications. Web, interactive and responsive media are creating new ways of employing the mechanized word that provide unprecedented possibilities for the role of type in contemporary culture. Typographic text is now used not only for mass communications but for personal social interactions and for navigation through interactive environments in real-time, on screens that are capable of resolutions almost equivalent to that of printing.

Web typography uses programmatic rules to allow fonts to be displayed on web pages. When first launched in the late 1990s, type for the Web was not well received by the profession since there was little protection against the illegal copying of proprietary typefaces. But since 2008 web browsers have been developed to facilitate licensing and a number of subscription services have been established. In 2010 Google launched a free library of open-source fonts with the declared intention of making the internet accessible to all, while Adobe's Typekit is a collection of thousands of fonts for use on the Web or in applications. In addition, many reputable independent foundries began to form cooperatives to offer their products via subscription services.

Within a very short time web fonts have become a significant feature of the visual landscape as the transmission of visible language undergoes another huge transformation, possibly the greatest in its history. In contrast to printed publications, interactive technologies permit designers to provide a flexible framework for visual communications but not to exercise absolute control over the way in which they will appear. Whether through computer screens, tablets, laptops or smartphones, they can only anticipate how messages will be received by an end user. This provides unprecedented challenges, creating a new paradigm for communication as an active process rather than a fixed transmission.

Although one can only speculate on the social and cultural impact of media that are current, the multiple innovations of digital and virtual technologies are undoubtedly creating a massive shift in the nature of knowledge acquisition, social interaction and human communication, and, as a result, ideology. But the design of type and typography continues to demand an understanding of physical arrangements, the psychology of reading and the progressive disclosure of information, regardless of the increasingly elastic transformations words are subjected to in the new media. Recent innovations have brought about a resurgence of interest in design history as type forms from many earlier periods are revived and re-engineered for the new technologies by both independent designers and large foundries. At the same time, in recent years there has also been a huge increase in the international market for the design of types for languages that use non-Latin scripts.

For those languages that use the Latin alphabet, the sans serif – once considered, literally, a grotesque form, inadequate for extensive use – has now become prevalent, partly because of its superior functionality in screen-based environments. This has led to a renewed interest in the design of sans serif typefaces whose exploration has become a significant trend in post-millennial type design, with many practitioners seeking to achieve the seemingly impossible goal of reconciling humanist characteristics with geometric type design constructions.

Under the domination of new media it has been suggested that traditional printing is destined to disappear. It is certainly diminishing, particularly in the newspaper industry. However, some have argued that information in printed form retains unique features that make it superior to other media. Printed matter requires no power source and needs no separate device through which to be viewed. It is also low cost, easily referenced and replaceable at little expense. Above all, print remains physical, tactile and present in an increasingly virtual and asynchronous world.

Gotham

Ty	**Gotham**
Ca	**Sans Serif**
Ke	**Geometric**
Te	**Digital**
Da	**2000**
De	**Tobias Frere-Jones**
Fo	**Hoefler Type Foundry**
Co	**USA**

Characteristics

Character construction on square bodies
Large x-height
C c S s e Angled terminals
G No spur
Q Angled tail
R Straight, angled leg
a Double-storeyed, round bowl
f r t Narrow with vertical terminals
g Single-storeyed
i j Square dots
t Flat top-stroke
y Hooked tail

AGMQR
abcefghij
koprstuy

Connections

Metro	1930
Interstate	1993
Brandon Text	2013
FF Mark	2013

Availability

Gotham is available from Hoefler & Co.

Specimen

The Hoefler Type Foundry Catalogue of Typefaces, fifth edition. Hoefler Type Foundry, New York, c2001 (279x216mm)

Long before the emergence of a profession called "graphic design," there was signage. Up until the mid-twentieth century, the job of providing architectural lettering often fell to engineers or draftsmen, most of whom worked outside of the typographic tradition. The shape of facade lettering was often determined by the practical business of legibility, rather than any sort of stylistic agenda – although inevitably, even the draftsman's vision of "basic building lettering" was influenced by the prevailing style of the time.

AN AMERICAN VERNACULAR
Like most American cities, New York is host to a number of mundane buildings whose facades exhibit a distinctively American form of sans serif. This kind of lettering occurs in many media: the same office buildings whose numbers are rendered in this style, in steel or cast bronze, often use this form of lettering for their engraved cornerstones as well. Cast iron plaques regularly feature this kind of lettering, as do countless painted signs and lithographed posters, many dating back as far as the Works Progress Administration of the 1930s. And judging by how often it appears in signs for car parks and liquor stores, this might well be the natural form once followed by neon-lit aluminum channel letters. Although there is nothing to suggest that the makers of these different kinds of signs ever consciously followed the same models, the consistency with which this style of letter appears in the American urban landscape suggests that these forms were once considered in some way elemental. But with the arrival of mechanical signmaking in the 1960s, these letters died out, completely vanishing from production.

GOTHAM™ SIXTEEN FONTS

THIN | EXTRA LIGHT | LIGHT | BOOK | MEDIUM | BOLD | BLACK | ULTRA | each in ROMAN and ITALIC

A sans serif based on vernacular architectural lettering, designed for GQ magazine by Tobias Frere-Jones with Jesse Ragan.

GOTHAM THIN
BUSH

GOTHAM THIN
Grand

GOTHAM EXTRA LIGHT
ECRU

GOTHAM EXTRA LIGHT
Iodine

GOTHAM LIGHT
LEAN

GOTHAM LIGHT
Ethics

GOTHAM BOOK
RUSH

GOTHAM BOOK
Mulch

GOTHAM MEDIUM
FERN

GOTHAM MEDIUM
Horse

GOTHAM BOLD
ROLE

GOTHAM BOLD
Minus

GOTHAM BLACK
IRISH

GOTHAM BLACK
Close

GOTHAM ULTRA
MAIN

GOTHAM ULTRA
Motif

see also
GOTHAM CONDENSED *p. 23*

CUBS

SOLD

OSLO

CAPS

EVER

LEAD

RAPS

SPUD

GOTHAM THIN ITALIC
Dome

GOTHAM EXTRA LIGHT ITALIC
Series

GOTHAM LIGHT ITALIC
Citron

GOTHAM BOOK ITALIC
Dutch

GOTHAM MEDIUM ITALIC
Quick

GOTHAM BOLD ITALIC
Some

GOTHAM BLACK ITALIC
Gives

GOTHAM ULTRA ITALIC
Move

GOTHAM

Although designers have lived with this lettering for half a century, it has remarkably gone unrevived until now. In 2000, Tobias Frere-Jones undertook a study of building lettering in New York, starting with a charming but rarely examined sign for the *Port Authority Bus Terminal*. Though Frere-Jones wanted Gotham to exhibit the "mathematical reasoning of a draftsman" rather than the instincts of a type designer, he allowed Gotham to escape the grid wherever necessary, giving the design an affability usually missing from 'geometric' faces.

TAXONOMY

Sans serifs are often organized into three categories. Designs built with rule and compass, of which Futura is the classic example, are called *geometrics*. Faces which are less rigid, often having the more traditional 'two-storey' forms of *a* and *g*, are called *grotesques*. (Univers and Helvetica are both grotesques.) And faces which are suggestive of calligraphy, with wholly traditional forms, are known as *humanists*. (Some humanist faces feature artifacts of the pen, such as oblique stress or flared stems, though not all: Gill Sans and Optima are both humanists.)

GEOMETRIC   **e**

GROTESQUE   **e**

HUMANIST   **e**

VARIATIONS

Unlike the signage upon which it was based, Gotham includes a lowercase, an italic, a full range of weights, and a related condensed design (see p. 23).

The Gotham family of typefaces was commissioned by the editors of *GQ* magazine, who wanted a geometric sans serif that would be 'masculine, new, and fresh'. It was drawn in 2000 by American type designer Tobias Frere-Jones (1970–).

Frere-Jones and Jonathan Hoefler (1970–), his collaborator at that time, had become highly respected for the depth of historical knowledge that underpinned their type design practice. Because Frere-Jones recognized that, as Hoefler said, 'a great wellspring of American type design is its vernacular lettering, rather than its typefounding', he did not look to antique specimen books for inspiration. Instead, he began researching Gotham by photographing the many forms of public lettering that had dominated the streets of the old commercial districts of New York City from the 1920s until the 1960s. The collection of everyday letterforms quickly expanded into a huge archive of images of architectural facades, cast-iron plaques, neon signs, shop signs, hand-painted lettering and lithographed posters. He was particularly taken with an all-capitals sign on the Eighth Avenue facade of the Port Authority Bus Terminal. Like many other handmade sans serifs he had documented, this exhibited an engineer's understanding of letter construction in a form that was measured, plain and free of stylistic affectation.

Frere-Jones wanted to infuse Gotham's letterforms with this authentic tone, deliberately evoking an unselfconsciousness that followed the 'mathematical reasoning of a draftsman' rather than the calculated nuances of a design from the print tradition. Accordingly, he drew Gotham's letters to a square, even width, using a grid. However, he allowed it to escape its boundaries where necessary, giving it a homely and inviting quality missing from most geometrically constructed typefaces.

Since its release in 2000 Gotham has achieved enormous popularity. The family now extends to a total of 66 styles in four widths, each in eight weights with matching italics, accompanied by proportional and tabular numerals and extensive support for Latin and non-Latin languages.

Gotham is an assiduous typeface for both text and display. It has the familiar charm of the lettering of the city, communicating with an unassuming and uniquely American accent. Accounting for its meteoric success, Tobias Frere-Jones has suggested that 'It was born outside type design in some other world and has a very distinct flavor from that.'

Griffith Gothic

Ty	**Griffith Gothic**
Ca	**Sans Serif**
Ke	**Grotesque**
Te	**Digital**
Da	**2000**
De	**Tobias Frere-Jones**
Fo	**Font Bureau**
Co	**USA**

Characteristics

Strokes thin sharply at stroke junctions
C c S s e Angled terminals
G Has thin spur and bar
I Thin serifs at head and foot
Q Curved tail
R Straight, angled leg
a Double-storeyed, curve at foot
b d h k l n p q Angled stem terminals
f r t Vertical terminals
g Single-storeyed
i j Square dots
t Angled top-stroke
y Hooked tail

AGIMQR
abcefghij
koprstuy

Connections

Franklin Gothic	1904
News Gothic	1908
Monotype Grotesque	c1926
Bell Gothic	1938

Availability

Griffith Gothic is available from the Font Bureau and resellers

Specimen

Font Bureau Type Specimens, third edition. The Font Bureau, Boston, 2001 (268x180mm)

SQUARE WAVE
BOLD

Clandestine police band receivers
THIN ITALIC

5389 Mhz
BLACK

195 SECRET TRANSMISSIONS EASILY INTERCEPTED
REGULAR CONDENSED

LUNCH ORDER
ULTRA ITALIC

Secured-line red phone used only for ordering calzones
BOLD

Frantic call for jelly donuts
ULTRA CONDENSED

Glazed
LIGHT

City-wide emergency barely averted
BLACK ITALIC

SIRENS ARE SWITCHED OFF
THIN

CELEBRATION
BLACK

Of all his work, C.H. Griffith claimed one type, Bell Gothic, as his own design. Griffith Gothic is a revival of the 1937 Mergenthaler original, redrawn as the house sans for *Fast Company*. Tobias Frere-Jones drew a six weight series from light and bold, removing linecaster adjustments and retaining the pre-emptive thinning of joints as a salient feature. Italics & condensed complete this ultimately legible sans series; FB 1997–2000

18 STYLES: THIN, LIGHT, REGULAR, BOLD, BLACK, AND ULTRA, ALL WITH ITALIC AND CONDENSED

66

GRIFFITH GOTHIC

THIN WITH ITALIC AND BOLD *10 point*

GRUMPY WIZARDS MAKE TOXIC BREW FOR *THE EVIL QUEENS & JACKS. LAZY MOVER DID* quit hard packing of these papier-mâché jewelry boxes. Back at my quaint garden: jaunty zinnias vie with flaunting phlox. *Hark! 4,872 toxic jungle water vipers quietly drop on zebras for meals!* New farm hand (picking just six quinces) proves strong but lazy. **For only about $65, jolly house wives made an 'inexpensive' meal using quick frozen vegetables.** Jaded zombies acted quaint ly but kept driving their 31 oxen forward. At my grand prix, J. Blatz was equally vilified for his funky ways. My grandfather spent his day quickly carving wax buzzards, mostly out of junk. When

LIGHT WITH ITALIC AND BLACK *10 point*

GRUMPY WIZARDS MAKE TOXIC BREW FOR *THE EVIL QUEENS & JACKS. LAZY MOVER TO* quit hard packing of these papier-mâché jewelry boxes. Back at my quaint garden: jaunty zinnias vie with flaunting phlox. *Hark! 4,872 toxic jungle water vipers quietly drop on zebras for meals!* New farm hand (picking just six quinces) proves strong but lazy. **For only about $65, the jolly housewives made 'inexpensive' meals using quick-frozen vegetables.** Jaded zombies acted quaintly but kept driving their 31 oxen forward. At my grand prix, Dr. Blatz was equally vilified for his funky ways. My grandfather spent his day quickly carving wax buzzards, mostly from

REGULAR WITH ITALIC AND BLACK *10 point*

GRUMPY WIZARDS MAKE TOXIC BREW FOR *THE EVIL QUEENS & JACKS. LAZY MOVER QU* quit hard packing of the papier-mâché jewelry boxes. Back at my quaint garden: jaunty zin nias vie with flaunting phlox. *Hark! 4,872 toxic jungle water vipers quietly drop on zebras for meals!* New farm hand (picking just six quinces) proves strong but lazy. **For only about $65, jol ly housewives made 'inexpensive' meals out of 9 quick-frozen vegetables.** Jaded zombies acted quaintly but kept driving their 31 oxen forward. At my grand prix, J. Blatz was equal ly vilified for his funky ways. My grandfather did spend his day quickly carving wax buzzards, mostly from junk. When we go back to Juarez,

BOLD WITH ITALIC AND ULTRA *10 point*

GRUMPY WIZARDS MAKE TOXIC BREW FOR *THE EVIL QUEENS & JACKS. LAZY MOVER QU* quit hard packing of this papier-mâché jewel ry box. Back at my quaint garden: the jaunty zinnias vie with flaunting phlox. *Hark! 4,872 toxic jungle water vipers don't quietly drop on zebras for meals!* New farm hand (picking just sixty quinces) proves strong but lazy. For only about $65, jolly housewives made us 'in expensive' meal using quick-frozen vegetables. Jaded zombies acted so quaintly but kept driving their 31 oxen forward. At my grand prix, J. Blatz was equally vilified for his funky ways. My grandfather spent his day quickly carving wax buzzards, mostly from junk. When

BLACK WITH ITALIC *10 point*

GRUMPY WIZARDS MAKE A TOXIC BREW *FOR THE EVIL QUEEN & JACK. LAZY MOVER* quit hard packing of the papier-mâché jew elry boxes. Back at my quaint garden: jaun ty zinnias vie with flaunting phlox. Hark! 4,872 toxic jungle water vipers quietly drop on zebras for meals! *New farm hand (pick ing just six quinces) proves strong but lazy.* For only about $65, jolly housewives made 'inexpensive' meals using quick-frozen vege tables. Jaded zombies acted quaintly but ke

ULTRA WITH ITALIC *10 point*

GRUMPY WIZARDS MAKE A TOXIC BREW *FOR THE EVIL QUEEN & JACK. LAZY MOVE* quit hard packing of the papier-mâché jewelry boxes. Back at my quaint garden: jaunty zinnias vie with flaunting phlox. *Hark! 4,872 toxic jungle water vipers qui etly drop on zebras for meals!* New farm hand (picking just six quinces) proves strong but lazy. For only about $65, jolly housewives made 'inexpensive' meals us ing quick-frozen vegetables. Jaded zombi

ABCDEFGHIJKLMNOPQRSTUVWXYZabcdefghijklmnopqrstuvwxyzßfiflffffiffl
¶§#$£¥ƒ€0123456789%‰¢°ªº=<+−×÷>'"/¿?¡!&()[]\{}*.,:;…""''„«»‹›_-–—•†‡@®©℗™√‡
áàâäãåæçéèêëíìîïñóòôöõøœúùûüÿÁÀÂÄÃÅÆÇÉÈÊËÍÌÎÏÑÓÒÔÖÕØŒÚÙÛÜŸ
Special characters ®|a

Chauncey Griffith (1879–1956) was an American type designer who worked for the Mergenthaler Linotype company for many years. He specialized in supremely legible typefaces where every last detail was optimized to overcome the constraints of the printing processes and materials of the early twentieth century. However, although he worked on the development of many typefaces, he claimed only one, Bell Gothic, as his own.

Bell Gothic was commissioned in 1938 by AT&T as a proprietary typeface and remained in uninterrupted use in the company's telephone directories for 40 years. Linotype licensed Bell Gothic for general use when it was superseded by Bell Centennial (pp424–25), designed by Matthew Carter in 1976.

Griffith Gothic is a revival of the 1938 typeface, drawn by Tobias Frere-Jones (1970–) for Font Bureau to be used in *Fast Company*, a business and technology magazine. He produced a series of six weights, from light to bold, with italic and condensed variants.

Griffith Gothic was intended, like its ancestor, to be highly legible at small sizes and very economical in its use of space. It retained Bell Gothic's thin slab serifs at the head and foot of the upper case I, the foot and bar on the figure 1, and the angled stroke endings of several lower case characters. The thinning at stroke junctions that was a key technical and visual characteristic of Bell Gothic was greatly exaggerated in Frere-Jones's reinterpretation, reducing joints to knife-like incisions that, in combination with its angled terminals, give Griffith Gothic a particularly sharp-edged appearance.

Ty	**The Alphabet**
Ca	**Sans Serif**
Ke	**Decorative, Capitals**
Te	**Lettering**
Da	**2001**
De	**Mathias Augustyniak and Michael Amzalag**
Fo	**M/M Paris**
Co	**France**

Characteristics

Capital letters cut into photographic images
Shapes loosely follow the contours and shadows of the images

Connections

Amphiareo's Capitals	1556
Pouchée's Decorated Alphabets	c1820
Found Fount	1989
Lÿno	2010

Availability

Not available

Specimen

The Alphabet type specimen PDF.
M/M Paris, Paris, 2001 (297x210mm)

Mathias Augustyniak (1967–) and Michael Amzalag (1968–) established their design practice, M/M Paris, in 1992. Working in the fields of music, art and fashion, Augustyniak and Amzalag frequently design bespoke lettering as an integral component of their projects, often in the form of typefaces. They are fascinated by what they have described as the alphabet's 'capacity to represent and encompass languages through abstract entities'.

Originally published in the American fashion magazine *V* in 2001, the Alphabet was produced in close collaboration with the photographers Inez van Lamsweerde and Vinoodh Matadin. For the Alphabet, 26 models were photographed in a variety of poses and expressions to create a complete A to Z of female forms, using the initial letters of the models' names in alphabetical order.

Augustyniak and Amzalag subsequently cut into the photographic images with scissors to create rudimentary letter shapes in capitals that loosely followed the contours and tonal structures of the images. The result is a striking abstraction of both feminine and alphabetic forms that is at once primitive, sensuous and dramatic.

The M/M Paris Alphabet project is not type design in its conventional sense. Indeed, it might be considered by some to descend from a lettering tradition. Its significance lies in the ways it references the potential for typographic design in the twenty-first century to transport mechanized language from its fixed limits in print technologies towards virtual, moving and physical environments. It also plays reflectively with the cultural reception of typographic symbols that can be understood by being looked at and read interdependently, raising open questions about the ambiguous nature of representation and about the convergence of words and images in today's culture.

Dolly

Ty	**Dolly**
Ca	**Serif**
Ke	**Old Style, Dutch**
Te	**Digital**
Da	**2001**
De	**Akiem Helmling, Bas Jacobs and Sami Kortemäki**
Fo	**Underware**
Co	**Netherlands**

Characteristics

Oblique stress
Curved stems
Moderate stroke contrast
Capitals lower than ascender height
Shallow, tapered serifs
A Flat apex
J Descends below baseline
K R Curved leg below baseline
M Splayed
Q Sweeping tail below letter
a Double-storeyed, small counter
g Double-storeyed

AJMQRW
abcdefghij
orstuyaefg

Connections

Swift	1987
FF Quadraat	1992
Collis	1993
DTL Documenta	1993

Availability

Dolly is available from Underware and resellers

Specimen

Dolly type specimen. Underware, Amsterdam, 2001 (245x175mm)

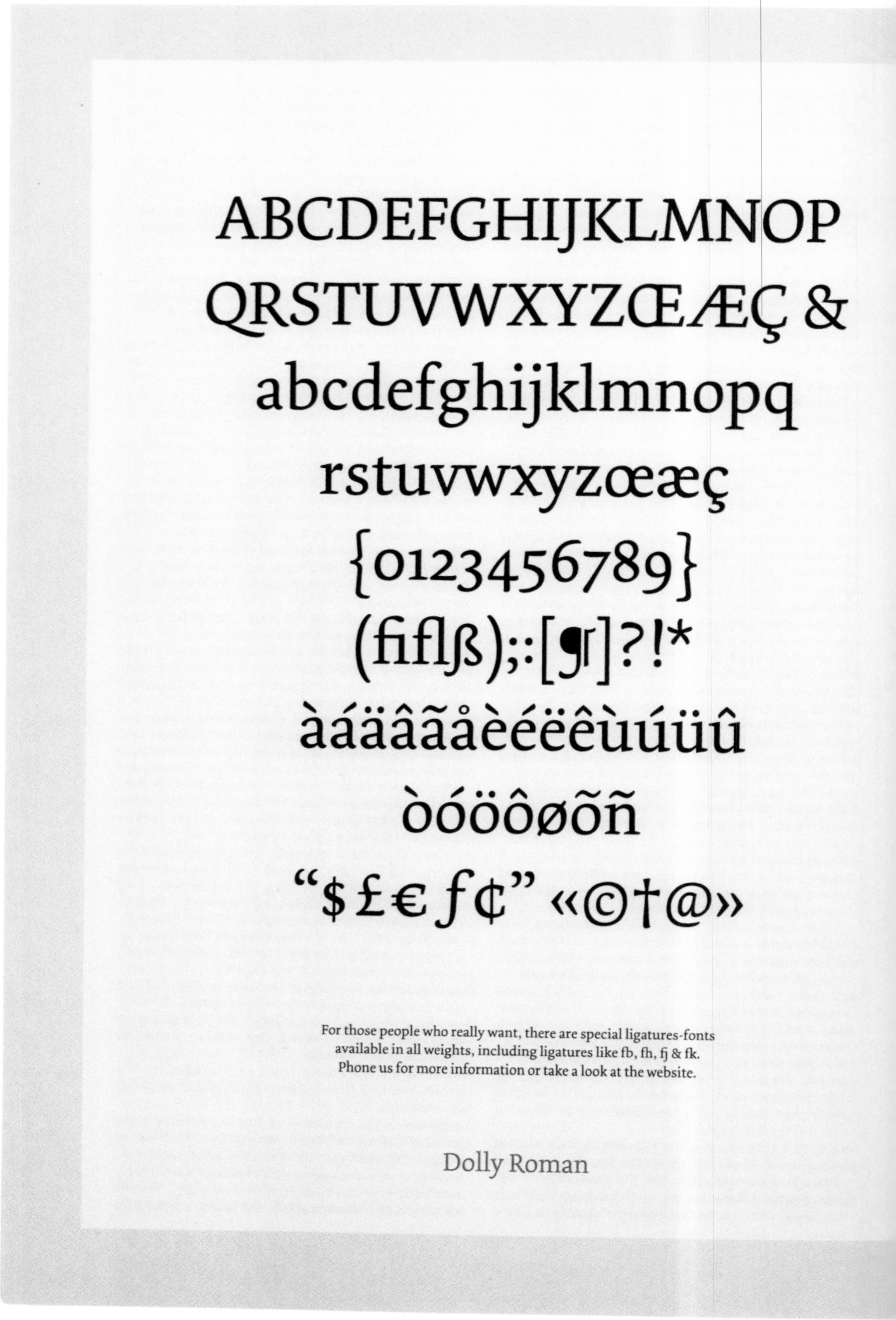

ABCDEFGHIJKLMNOP
QRSTUVWXYZŒÆÇ &
abcdefghijklmnopq
rstuvwxyzœæç
{0123456789}
(fiflß);:[¶]?!*
àáäâãåèéëêùúüû
òóöôøõñ
"$£€ƒ¢" «©†@»

For those people who really want, there are special ligatures-fonts available in all weights, including ligatures like fb, fh, fj & fk. Phone us for more information or take a look at the website.

Dolly Roman

584

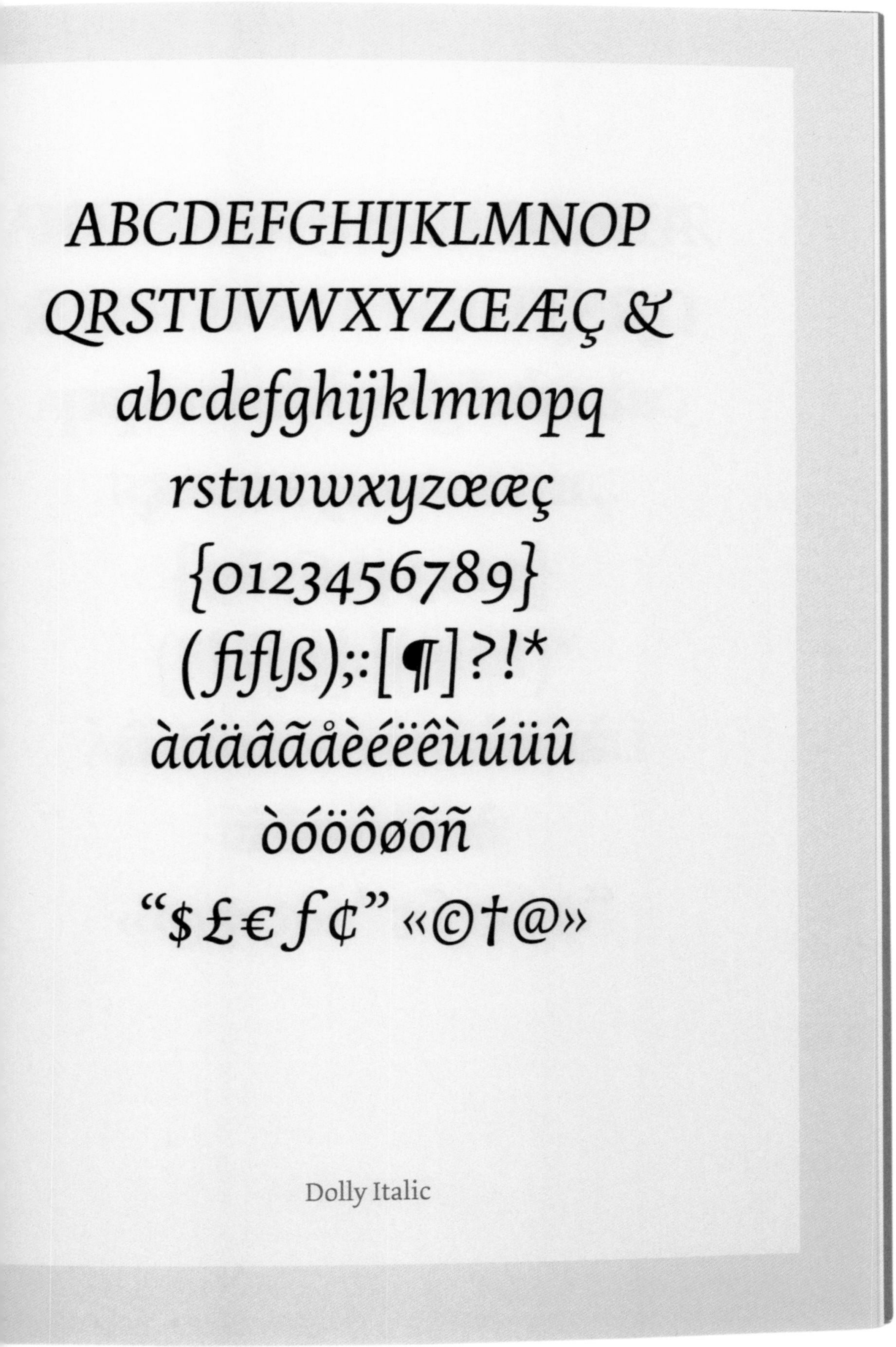

ABCDEFGHIJKLMNOP
QRSTUVWXYZŒÆÇ &
abcdefghijklmnopq
rstuvwxyzœæç
{0123456789}
(fiflß);:[¶]?!*
àáäâãåèéëêùúüû
òóöôøõñ
"$£€ƒ¢" «©†@»

Dolly Italic

The Dutch foundry Underware describes Dolly plainly as 'a book typeface with flourishes'. Released in 2001, it is an old-style family that consists of only four members. Dolly includes roman, bold, italic and small capitals, each with non-lining old-style figures and a few carefully selected ligatures. Dolly has its roots firmly in the vigorous Dutch book faces of the seventeenth-century. Based like them on handwriting, it is full of personality at large sizes, but is self-effacing and highly readable in bodies of text.

Dolly's design started with the roman weight and the other styles developed to work alongside it. It has an even colour with a low stroke contrast, which makes for comfortable reading at small sizes. In the Dolly specimen booklet, shown here, Erik Spiekermann wrote that in small sizes 'it looks like a warm, comfortable Garamondish, Minion-like Roman. Close up, we notice dozens of subtle curves and unusual shapes'. There is nothing rectilinear about Dolly's outlines, although its effect in text is one of simplicity. A calligraphic influence in the construction of curves and the asymmetrical, rounded serifs give the type a friendly but poised appearance. The italic is narrower and slightly lighter than the roman, and it is complemented by a heavy bold, which makes for headlines that pop out in striking contrast to text.

Dolly's limited range of four styles might be considered a barrier to its usability, but it is arguable that, like Christoph Noordzij's Collis (pp512–13), its healthy family structure constitutes a design without excess, making it fit for solving a broad range of problems in book work.

Underware chose a bold but risky sales strategy for Dolly. A CD containing a full version of the typeface was given away free with the modestly priced type specimen shown here, displaying the typeface in a range of attractive settings. Users were invited to license the typeface only if they should decide to use it. The strategy worked well and the typeface quickly achieved steady sales. With a solid Dutch pedigree, Dolly is a reliable performer that is used extensively today.

Ty	**Fedra**
Ca	**Serif / Sans Serif**
Ke	**Superfamily**
Te	**Digital**
Da	**2001**
De	**Peter Bil'ak**
Fo	**Typotheque**
Co	**Netherlands**

Characteristics
Fedra Sans:
A High crossbar
C c S s e g Angled terminals and large apertures
G No spur
Q Separate tail below letter
R Concave, curved, wide leg
a Double-storeyed, curve at foot
f Has descender
i j Diamond-shaped dots
k Concave, curved leg
y Stepped strokes, straight tail

AGMQR
abcefgijk
orstyaefg

Connections

Frutiger	1976
FF Meta	1991
FF Clan	2006
Typonine Sans	2008

Availability
Fedra Sans and Fedra Serif are available from Typotheque and resellers

Specimen
Fedra type specimen. Typotheque, The Hague, 2003 (210x132mm)

Fedra is an extensive, coordinated type family drawn by Slovakian designer Peter Bil'ak (1973–), first issued as Fedra Sans in 2001 by the Typotheque foundry in the Netherlands.

In designing Fedra, Bil'ak combined seemingly conflicting methods to create a harmonious type system. Its humanist roots are carefully balanced with rational construction methods, demonstrating both the rhythmic flow of handwriting and the logic of computer-generated forms. Fedra Sans was originally commissioned by Ruedi Baur Integral Design in Paris as a key element of their proposal for the brand identity of Bayerische Rück, a German insurance company. Bil'ak's brief was to 'de-protestantize Univers' by making a more approachable alternative to the typeface that Bayerische Rück had been using since the 1970s. Fedra Sans addresses the brief precisely: it humanizes visual communications with simple, informal elegance and it gives a professional, contemporary impression that is not overburdened by reference to antiquated models. An important technical consideration was to create a typeface that would work equally well in print and on screens, and that would be consistent across all computer platforms. Immediately after the first version of the typeface was completed the project was cancelled due to business acquisitions. This proved beneficial to Bil'ak, as it freed him to progress Fedra Sans further, adding extra weights and expert sets, and to publish it independently. In addition, he developed a matching serif in four weights, italics, small capitals, expert sets and four alternate numeral systems.

Like Trinité (pp450–51), Fedra Serif comes in two alternative versions with different lengths of ascenders and descenders in order to solve a range of typographic problems. One version corresponds to the proportions of Fedra Sans, with a large x-height and short stems. This gives functionality in small sizes, tight spaces and low-resolution printing. The second version extends the ascenders and descenders and increases the contrast of thick and thin strokes. The widths of both variants match so that they can easily be interchanged in text without reflowing it. Combined, these attributes result in a type family suitable for even the most complex typographic applications.

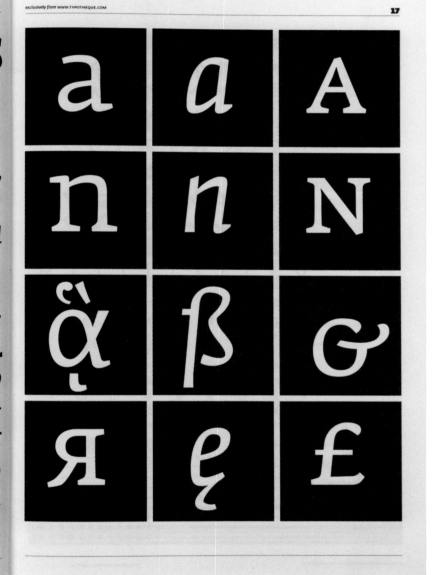

harmonious
ειδικών χαρακτήρων
aesthetic and technological
humanistic roots
многочисленные примеры
ΠΟΛΥΤΟΝΙΚΟ
оригинальный кириллический шрифт
rational drawing
метода работы
COMPUTER SCREEN GRID
γραμματοσειρά

Ty	**Gentium**
Ca	**Serif**
Ke	**Old Style**
Te	**Digital**
Da	**2001**
De	**Victor Gaultney**
Fo	**SIL International**
Co	**UK**

Characteristics

Oblique stress
Moderate stroke contrast
Capitals lower than ascender height
Bracketed serifs
A Angled apex
J Descends below baseline, hooked
M Very slightly splayed
P Open bowl
Q Hooked tail below letter
W Point at apex
a Double-storeyed, large bowl
g Double-storeyed, large lower bowl

AJMPRW
abcdefghij
orstuyaefg

Connections

The DejaVu Fonts	2004
Open Sans	2010
Ubuntu	2010
Source Serif Pro	2014

Availability

Gentium is available from SIL International

Specimen

Gentium – A Typeface for the Nations.
Victor Gaultney, Reading, 2002
(210x148mm)

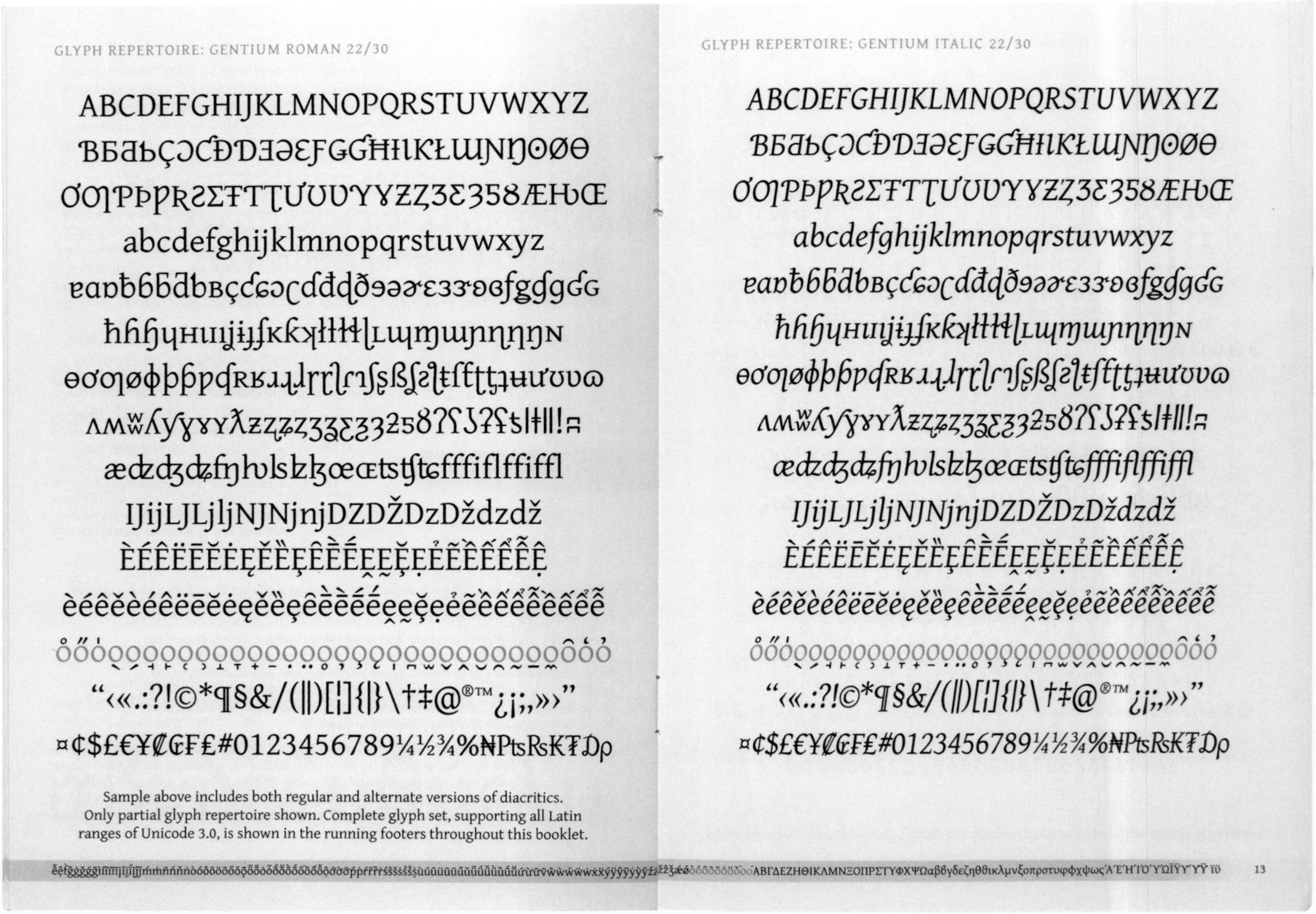

GLYPH REPERTOIRE: GENTIUM ROMAN 22/30

GLYPH REPERTOIRE: GENTIUM ITALIC 22/30

Sample above includes both regular and alternate versions of diacritics.
Only partial glyph repertoire shown. Complete glyph set, supporting all Latin
ranges of Unicode 3.0, is shown in the running footers throughout this booklet.

To transcribe their languages into the Latin script, people around the world often need to adapt it, modifying or adding new glyphs in order to make it function effectively. Until the 1990s computers provided little support for these augmented alphabets. With the advent of Unicode, a universal standard for the encoding and handling of most of the world's writing systems in text, technical barriers were removed. Few typefaces, though, contained Unicode's extensive glyph sets and many of those that did were not freely available. As a result,

millions of people remained excluded from global network communications. Gentium was created by Victor Gaultney (1962–) in 2001 to address the need for a typeface that included extensive support for world languages while maintaining high typographic standards. Gaultney, an American type designer with expertise in non-Latin scripts, intended it as 'a typeface for the nations'.

Gentium is available in several different versions customized for the various requirements of people who use the Latin,

Cyrillic and Greek scripts. Gentium Basic includes upper and lower case, numbers, punctuation and special characters in a basic Latin character set. Gentium Book is slightly heavier, better suited to some publishing needs. Both variants include roman, italic, bold and bold italics. In addition, Gentium Plus offers extended Latin, archaic Greek and Cyrillic. The glyph sets in each of its three writing systems are also coherent when used in combination with one another. Gentium Alt includes less prominent diacritics to improve appearances when writing in those

languages that require them. It was important to Gaultney that Gentium should be as effective typographically as it was linguistically. Its contours are optimized for readability by avoiding extreme contrasts and very thin strokes. The x-height is large and internal spaces are open but ascenders are not too short.

Gentium has a calligraphic personality that is attractive but with features that avoid drawing attention to themselves. In keeping with its emancipatory goals, Gentium is available to all without cost.

It's all Harry Carter's fault.

In my research on legibility I came across his article 'Optical scale in typefounding' (Typography 4, 1937) in which he lauds Fleischman for low joins on the letters h m n. 'The effect is clearer', he writes.

This stunned me. Could such a calligraphic feature actually benefit legibility? Most trends in readable typefaces were going in the opposite direction—toward higher joins—to increase counter size.

Would it be possible to create a highly legible face based upon a calligraphic foundation? How could the dynamic nature of the pen be balanced with the steadiness needed for text type?

I wanted to create a solid, robust face that did not wear its calligraphic heritage too boldly. Too much character would be a distraction to the reader. I did desire speed and rhythm, but not at the cost of clarity and legibility.

My original calligraphic experiments for the roman and italic were completed on consecutive days, and the result is a close connection between the two. The dynamic features I desired have lived on most authentically in the latter.

Comparison of initial calligraphy and resulting font. Dynamic features in Gentium Italic: swelling pen-like terminals, smooth but energetic curves, balance between sharp and smooth corners.

n Dynamic

caveboring
caveboring

potential energy

g Steadiness

How could I capture this dynamism in the roman?

Early attempts proved too calligraphic—and worked poorly as typeforms. The process of distilling the forms down to their basic elements was painful. Every time I removed an expressive feature I felt a sense of loss. Would the result still seem dynamic?

In the end, steadiness was gained not only through the loss of pen features, but through consistency, reduction of contrast and intentional serif design.

Because the area at x-height has so much activity, a firm horizontal footing was needed. Slab serifs, though tempting, would have been out of character in such a humanist face. The best compromise was traditional bracketed serifs upon a flat base.

no
no

Translation from pen to type. Serifs and vertical stems are clearly more typographic. In addition, stroke weight is slightly reduced and counters are more open. Obvious pen features, such as the thinning of lower left to upper right curves, are less pronounced.

Ty	**The Morgan Project**
Ca	**Sans Serif**
Ke	**Geometric**
Te	**Digital**
Da	**2001**
De	**Mário Feliciano**
Fo	**Feliciano Type Foundry**
Co	**Portugal**

Characteristics

Rectangular letterforms
Radiused corners
C c G O o Straight downstrokes
C c S s e Pinched vertical terminals and large apertures
a Double-storeyed, almost straight stem
f r t Vertical terminals
i j Square dots
t Flat top-stroke

AGMQR
abcefghij
koprstuy

Connections

Steile Futura	1952
Cholla	1999
Klavika	2004
Stratum	2004

Availability

Morgan is available from the Feliciano
Type Foundry and resellers

Specimen

The Morgan Project type specimen.
Feliciano Type Foundry, Lisbon, c2001
(297x210mm)

FTF09

FTF MORGAN SANS COND BOLD 26 PT

Greetings to the Universe

FTF MORGAN SANS COND 7.5 PT

The Voyager spacecraft will be the third and fourth human artifacts to escape entirely from the solar system. Pioneers 10 and 11, which preceded Voyager in outstripping the gravitational attraction of the Sun, both carried small metal plaques identifying their time and place of origin for the benefit of any other spacefarers that might find them in the distant future. With this example before them, NASA placed a more ambitious message aboard Voyager 1 and 2-a kind of time capsule, intended to communicate a story of our world to extraterrestrials. The Voyager message is carried by a phonograph record-a 12-inch gold-plated copper disk containing sounds and images selected to portray the diversity of life and culture on Earth. The contents of the record were selected for NASA by a committee chaired by Carl Sagan of Cornell University. Dr. Sagan and his associates assembled 115 images and a variety of natural sounds, such as those made by surf, wind and thunder, birds, whales, and other animals. To this they added musical selections from different cultures and eras, and spoken greetings from Earth-people in fifty-five languages, and printed messages from President Carter and U.N. Secretary General Waldheim. Each record is encased in a protective aluminum jacket, together with a cartridge and a needle. Instructions, in symbolic language, explain the origin of the spacecraft and indicate how the record is to be played. The 115 images are encoded in analog form. The remainder of the record is in audio, designed to be played at 16-2/3 revolutions per second. It contains the spoken greetings, beginning with Akkadian, which was spoken in Sumer about six thousand years ago, and ending with Wu, a modern Chinese dialect. Following the section on the sounds of Earth, there is an eclectic 90-minute selection of music, including both Eastern and Western classics and a variety of ethnic music. Once the Voyager spacecraft leave the solar system (by 1990, both will be beyond the orbit of Pluto), they will find themselves in empty space. It will be forty thousand years before they make a close approach to any other planetary system. As Carl Sagan has noted, "The spacecraft will be encountered and the record played only if there are advanced spacefaring civilizations in interstellar space. But the launching of this bottle into the cosmic ocean says something very hopeful

FTF MORGAN SANS COND SC BOLD 18 PT

GHIJKLMNOPQRS 123

FTF MORGAN SANS COND EXPERT BOLD 18 PT

Aa Bb Cc Dd Ee Ff Gg

FTF MORGAN SANS COND FIGURES BOLD 18 PT

01234/56789 ΣΩΠμπ≤±≥

FTF MORGAN SANS COND SC BOLD OBLIQUE 18 PT

7890 QRSTUVWXYZ &

FTF MORGAN SANS COND BOLD 12 PT

To accomplish their two-planet mission, the spacecraft were built to last five years. But as the mission went on, and with the successful achievement of all its objectives, the additional flybys of the two outermost giant planets, Uranus and Neptune, proved possible and irresistible to mission scientists and engineers at the Voyagers' home at the

FTF MORGAN SANS COND SC 46 PT

GIANT OUTER PLANETS

FTF MORGAN SANS COND 26 PT

LINING

abcdefghijklmnopqrstuvwxyz123456789

FTF Morgan Sans Condensed; regular, oblique, bold, bold oblique (lining figures, office figures, expert, small caps, pi-font, figures)
Twenty two fonts designed in 2001

FELICIANO TYPE FOUNDRY

FTF MORGAN SANS CONDENSED

FTF MORGAN SANS COND 5.5 PT

The Voyager Interstellar Mission (VIM) has the potential for obtaining useful interplanetary, and possibly interstellar, fields, particles, and waves (FPW) science data until around the year 2020 when the spacecraft's ability to generate adequate electrical power for continued science instrument operation will come to an end. In order to capitalize on this lengthy data acquisition potential, it is imperative that the spacecraft have a continuing sequence of instructions for acquiring the desired science data, and that the spacecraft High Gain Antenna (HGA) remain boresighted on the Earth for continuous data transmission. Because of the long mission duration and the likelihood of periodic spacecraft anomalies, it is also advantageous to continue the use of the on-board fault protection capability for automated responses to specific subsystem anomalies, and to provide an onboard sequence to continue spacecraft operation in the specific event of the future loss of command reception capability. All of these factors are

FTF MORGAN SANS COND 26 PT & 6.5 PT

Flight system performance

RANGE, VELOCITY AND ROUND TRIP LIGHT TIME AS OF 12/29/00

Distance from the Sun (Km)	11,930,000,000	9,402,000,000
Distance from the Sun (Mi)	7,413,000,000	5,842,000,000
Distance from the Earth (Km)	12,039,000,000	9,533,000,000
Distance from the Earth (Mi)	7,481,000,000	5,923,000,000
Total Distance Traveled Since Launch (Km)	13,742,000,000	12,913,000,000
Total Distance Traveled Since Launch (Mi)	8,539,000,000	8,024,000,000
Velocity Relative to Sun (Km/sec)	17.259	15.768
Velocity Relative to Sun (Mi/hr)	38,606	35,271
Velocity Relative to Earth (Km/sec)	31.140	36.697
Velocity Relative to Earth (Mi/hr)	69,657	82,089
Round Trip Light Time (Hours:Minutes:Seconds)	22:18:34	17:39:58

FTF MORGAN SANS COND SC 14 PT

ABILITY TO STORE HGA POINTING INFORMATION ON-BOARD

FTF MORGAN SANS COND BOLD OBLIQUE 97 PT

Spacecraft

FTF MORGAN SANS COND SC BOLD OBLIQUE 30 PT

BACKUP MISSION LOAD DESCRIPTION

FTF MORGAN SANS COND 12 PT

Had the Voyager mission ended after the Jupiter and Saturn flybys alone, it still would have provided the material to rewrite astronomy textbooks. But having doubled their already ambitious itineraries, the Voyagers returned to Earth information over the years that has revolutionized the science of planetary astronomy, helping to resolve key

FTF MORGAN SANS COND SC BOLD 46 PT

SEQUENCING STRATEGY

OFFICE

FTF MORGAN SANS COND OBLIQUE 26 PT

12345678-abcdefghijklmnopqrstuvwxyz

According to Portuguese typographer Mário Feliciano (1969–), his Morgan type family is the result of his interest in working with opposing ideas at the same time: the hand-drawn and the constructed. 'The type is not calligraphic,' he says, 'but it is not completely mechanical either.' The Morgan project has two separate parts: a text series and a display series. FTF Morgan Sans is a sans serif text typeface in two weights with regular and condensed widths, and italics for the standard width that are designed as an oblique roman.

Like Eric Olson's Klavika (pp604–605) and Sibylle Hagmann's Cholla (pp572–73), Morgan Sans is characterized by its rectilinear appearance emphasized by the regular rhythm of its straight upright strokes. Morgan Sans characters are sharply defined at terminals and inner junctions, although its overall look is softened by the rounded repetitions of its external contours.

In addition to Morgan's text weights, Feliciano designed three display versions whose appearance, he says, was influenced by 1950s science fiction comics. FTF Morgan Big is a robust family of fat capital letters with an interplay between radiused rectangles on external forms and sharp corners on internal junctions. FTF Morgan Poster follows the same principles but is tightly condensed. The extreme FTF Morgan Tower features an even more compressed contour, elongating it into three different heights with a shared optical weight.

The result of Feliciano's handiwork is an extensive, coordinated series of sans serif typefaces that is capable of addressing a broad range of typographic problems, ranging from setting in bodies of extended text to implementation in forcefully monumental headlines.

Ty	**Bryant**
Ca	**Sans Serif**
Ke	**Geometric**
Te	**Digital**
Da	**2002**
De	**Eric Olson**
Fo	**Process Type Foundry**
Co	**USA**

Characteristics

Geometric character construction
Monoline
Rounded terminals

AGMQR
abcefghij
koprstuy

Connections

AT Burin Sans	1994
Gotham Rounded	2007
FF DIN Round	2010
Optimo Hermes	2012

Availability

Bryant is available from the Process Type
Foundry and resellers

Specimen

Bryant type specimen PDF. Process Type
Foundry, Minneapolis, 2015 (265x182mm)

Bryant Pro Specimen Showing

Several stations to offer lettering

SHACHIHOKO

Open during 9 AM, 11 AM, and 6 PM only

transliteration

SIGHTSEEING EXCURSION

Minneapolis

Z technických důvodů zavřeno

Mechanics

Older calculators may provide new numbers

CABLE 12

Ich möchte nur Waschen und Legen

Bryant ProText Settings

8.5/11 PT. LIGHT ROMAN, ITALIC & ALTERNATE

MISS ANTHONY WAS BORN AT SOUTH ADAMS, MA, on Feb. 15, 1820. Daniel Anthony, her father, a liberal Quaker, was a cotton manufacturer. Susan Anthony was first instructed by teachers at home. She was sent afterward to finish her education at a Friends' boarding school in Philadelphia. She continued to attend this school until, at the age of fifteen, she was occasionally called on to help in the teaching. At seventeen she received a dollar a week with board by teaching in a private family, and the next summer a district school engaged her for $1.50 a week and *"boarded her round."* She continued to teach until 1852, when she found her taste for this profession entirely gone, a school in Rochester being her last charge.

8.5/11 PT. REGULAR ROMAN, ITALIC & ALTERNATE

MISS ANTHONY HAD BECOME IMPRESSED with the idea that women were suffering great wrongs, and when she abandoned school teaching, having saved only about $300, she determined to enter the lecture field. People of today can scarcely understand the strong prejudices Miss Anthony had to live down. In 1851 she called a temperance convention in Albany, admittance to a previous convention having been refused to her because it was not the custom to admit women. *The Women's New York State Temperance Society* was organized the following year. Through Miss Anthony's exertions…women soon came to be admitted to educational and other conventions, with the right to speak, vote, and act upon committees.

8.5/11 PT. MEDIUM ROMAN, ITALIC & ALTERNATE

SUSAN BROWNELL ANTHONY WAS A PIONEER leader of the cause of woman suffrage, and her energy was tireless in working for what she considered to be the best interests of womankind. At home and abroad she had innumerable friends, not only among those who sympathized with her views, but among those who held opinions radically opposed to her. In recent years her age made it impossible for her to continue active participation in all the movements for the enfranchisement of women with which she had been connected, but she was at the time of her death the Honorary President of the *National Woman Suffrage Association*, the society which she and Elizabeth Cady Stanton organized in 1869.

8.5/11 PT. BOLD ROMAN, ITALIC & ALTERNATE

MISS ANTHONY'S ACTIVE PARTICIPATION in the movement for woman suffrage started in the fifties. As early as 1854 she arranged conventions throughout the State and annually bombarded the Legislature with messages and appeals. She was active in obtaining the passage of the act of the New York Legislature in 1860 giving to married women the possession of their earnings and the guardianship of their children. During the war she was devoted to the *Women's Loyal League*, which petitioned Congress in favor of the thirteenth amendment. She was also directly interested in the fourteenth amendment, sending a petition in favor of leaving out the word "male." (Excerpts from the obituary of Susan B. Anthony published March 13, 1906 in *The New York Times*.)

7/9 PT. LIGHT

Similar in concept to stencils, the Wrico Lettering System came equipped with a specially fitted felt pen, a set of plastic letter guides and a platter that served as the baseline. To begin, the user simply set a baseline with the platter and traced the letters through the template to construct the desired words. However, like many stencils, the Wrico letters were at once charming and useful but rife with technical mishaps. For instance, the letters have no overshoot, horizontal stroke thinning or any optical compensation between characters. Charming as primitive shop lettering, these inconstancies are too specific to pens and templates to translate well into typefaces for daily use so they were put aside in favor of something more consistent. Round tips, nearly geometric curves, what appear to be circles (though they certainly aren't) and alternate letters all make appearances in the Bryant family

7/9 PT. REGULAR

Similar in concept to stencils, the Wrico Lettering System came equipped with a specially fitted felt pen, a set of plastic letter guides and a platter that served as the baseline. To begin, the user simply set a baseline with the platter and traced the letters through the template to construct the desired words. However, like many stencils, the Wrico letters were at once charming and useful but rife with technical mishaps. For instance, the letters have no overshoot, horizontal stroke thinning or any optical compensation between characters. Charming as primitive shop lettering, these inconstancies are too specific to pens and templates to translate well into typefaces for daily use so they were put aside in favor of something more consistent. Round tips, nearly geometric curves, what appear to be circles (though they certainly aren't) and alternate letters all make appearances in the Bryant family of fonts

Bryant was designed by Eric Olson (1974–) for the Process Type Foundry in 2002. Its geometric shapes and rounded strokes were based on the mechanical lettering templates widely used in pre-digital times by draftsmen and technical illustrators. The popular Wrico mechanical lettering system that served as Bryant's inspiration was invented in the United States during the 1920s. Essentially a stencilling device, the Wrico set came equipped with round-nibbed technical pens, various sizes of plastic letter guides and a baseline template to assist with alignment.

Olson's Bryant typeface designs are a contemporary response to the geometric sans serif form that preserves the warmth and simplicity of the original hand-stencilled Wrico letters. Very low contrast, softly rounded terminals, subtly modulated curves and a variety of alternate characters all contribute to its cheerful appearance.

Bryant has much in common with typefaces like DIN (pp266–67), whose origins in hand lettering are similar, and VAG Rounded (pp436–37), although Bryant is somewhat quirkier and less mechanical than either. Its extensive weight range, with alternate glyph sets and condensed widths, makes it well suited to a range of tasks, both in text and display applications.

Since its original release in 2002 Olson has updated and expanded Bryant to include extended language support as well as a version with small capitals, multiple numeral styles and italics.

Ty	**Neutraface**
Ca	**Sans Serif**
Ke	**Geometric**
Te	**Digital**
Da	**2002**
De	**Christian Schwartz**
Fo	**House Industries**
Co	**USA**

Characteristics
Neutraface Display:

Small x-height	
Elongated ascenders and large capitals	
A E F H Low bar	
C c O o Optically circular	
C c S s e Angled terminals	
G No spur	
M N Pointed apex	
P R Large bowl	
a g Double-storeyed	
i j Round dots	
y Straight tail	

AEGMR
abcdefghij
knoprstuy

Connections

Kabel	1927
Bernhard Gothic	1930
Metro	1930
Eagle	1994

Availability
Neutraface is available from House
Industries and resellers

Specimen
House Industries font catalogue No. 62.
House Industries, Yorklyn, 2010
(210x116mm)

Neutraface is a geometric sans serif typeface designed in 2002 by Christian Schwartz (1977–), working in collaboration with Ken Barber and Andy Cruz at House Industries. It was inspired by the design philosophy of the Hungarian-American modernist architect Richard Neutra (1892–1970), referencing the letters and numbers he used for the signage on his buildings. Neutra specified lettering that was as clearcut and unobtrusive as his rigorously functional architecture.

Working from limited reference material, Schwartz developed the capital letters extensively and added a lower case that did not exist in Neutra's body of work. The architectural origins of Neutraface predisposed it to implementation as a display typeface for use in headlines. Combining a sharp linear geometry with an unmistakably warm and human sensibility, Schwartz's typeface has its heritage in early twentieth-century geometric designs such as Futura (pp230–31) and Nobel (pp252–53).

The original Neutraface Display family includes five weights supplemented by alternate sets and a titling variant based on Richard Neutra's technical lettering on specification drawings. In the spirit of the architect's functionalist principles Schwartz subsequently designed a version of Neutraface specifically for text applications. Departing from the more extravagant proportions and attention-grabbing stylistic features of the display version, Neutraface Text features a larger x-height and slightly increased contrast in its strokes for improved readability in lengthy passages.

Over a period of several years House Industries expanded the family to a collection of 85 typefaces with variants such as Neutraface Condensed, Neutraface Slab and Neutraface No. 2. These have since been rationalized as a set of 29 typefaces using the OpenType format to provide access to extended character sets and other expert features.

Since its launch Neutraface has been so ubiquitous that Christian Schwartz has observed: 'I can't leave my apartment without running into an ad for a new condo development using it, or a restaurant, or a new cookbook.'

WHAT'S THE DIFFERENCE?

NEUTRAFACE	NEUTRAFACE NO. 2
More stylized, lower crossbars	Less stylized, higher crossbars

E E

R R

A A

12 NEUTRAFACE NO.2 (INCLUDES NO.2 CONDENSED) $275 ➡

Order online at www.houseindustries.com or call 800-888-4390 or 302-234-2356

Ty	**Simple**
Ca	**Sans Serif**
Ke	**Geometric**
Te	**Digital**
Da	**2002**
De	**Manuel Krebs and Dimitri Bruni**
Fo	**Lineto**
Co	**Switzerland**

Characteristics

Geometric construction
Monospaced and monolinear
A Vertical stems
I Extended width
M m W w Narrow width
a Double-storeyed, curve at foot
f i l r t Extended width
f r Hooked arch
g Single-storeyed

AEGIMSW
abcefgi
lmprtwy

Connections

Isonorm	1974
T-Star Pro	2002
Replica	2008
Simplon	2011

Availability

Simple is available from Lineto and
resellers

Specimen

Simple type specimen. Norm, Zurich, 2004
(230x160mm)

Typeface SimpleKoelnBonn — Characteristics / Construction / Grid / Units

In 2001 Dimitri Bruni (1970–) and Manuel Krebs (1970–) of the Swiss design studio Norm began work on Simple, a typeface to be used in their 2002 manifesto *The Things*. This document was a dense concoction of texts, diagrams, pictograms and images assembled within a meticulous page grid. Bruni and Krebs decided that the typeface should conform accurately to the grid of the book while remaining readable at both small and large sizes. Because *The Things* also involved a playful analysis of the Latin alphabet, they also wanted the typeface to be an expression of their ideas about the accepted shapes of letterforms.

Simple was a development of Normetica, a typeface that Norm had released a year before. Both are monospaced and monolinear and both are geometrically constructed. With Simple they wanted to create a more discrete typeface than Normetica, a design with fewer quirky characteristics that would not draw attention to itself. Simple was also notably more condensed than the earlier design. Its construction was driven by the requirement to modify, extend or compress characters in order to balance effectively within the common fixed width of the monospaced form. This factor influenced many of the characteristic shapes of lower case letters such as f, i, j, l, m, r, w, and the capitals I, M and W. To equalize the spacing of some letters, horizontal strokes were extended dramatically, as in the f, i and r.

In 2002 Ruedi Baur Integral Paris specified Simple for the visual identity and signage system for Cologne–Bonn airport. The design team considered it a readily identifiable but very readable typeface that would distinguish Cologne–Bonn's communications in the crowded visual landscape of an airport. However, since a monospaced typeface lacked the sophisticated features needed for such a complex undertaking, Bruni and Krebs were asked to redesign it as a proportionally spaced typeface. The result, SimpleKoelnBonn, completed in 2003, is a far more subtly modulated form than Simple. All of the letters have been carefully reshaped yet the confident character of the original design remains.

Simple was released by Lineto in 2002 in three weights with matching italics and a titling variant. SimpleKoelnBonn, however, was produced exclusively for Cologne–Bonn airport and therefore remains unavailable commercially.

Ty	**Archer**	
Ca	**Slab Serif**	
Ke	**Egyptian**	
Te	**Digital**	
Da	**2003**	
De	**Jonathan Hoefler and**	
	Tobias Frere-Jones	
Fo	**Hoefler Type Foundry**	
Co	**USA**	

Characteristics

Small x-height
Long ascenders
Monoline slab serif construction
Typewriter characteristics
A Top serif
C G S Ball terminals
G Has spur
M Slightly splayed
Q Tail below letter
a c f g j r s Ball terminals
c e t Vertical terminals

AGIMQS
abcefghij
orstyaefg

Connections

Bodoni	1788
Clarendon	1845
Rockwell	1934
Courier	1955

Availability

Archer is available from Hoefler & Co.

Specimen

Martha Stewart Living magazine, May 2003. Martha Stewart Living Omnimedia, New York (277x230mm)

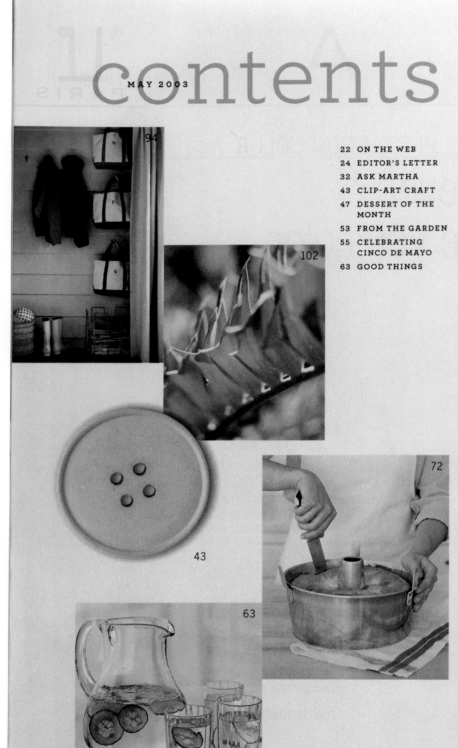

contents

MAY 2003

FOOD

72 angel food cake 101
The secret to making this featherlight trea[t] is whipping up a perfect meringue. We sho[w] you how, and suggest flavorings and topping[s]

78 bistro salads
Whether served for lunch or dinner, as appe[-] tizers or side dishes, these classic combina[-] tions are simple, toothsome fare

188 what's for dinner?
Make an entire meal for four in about an hou[r] with recipes for Grilled Pork Paillards, Past[a] Verde, Mushroom Crostini, and Cherry Ic[e]

190 fit to eat: meatless main dishes
You need not be a vegetarian to find ou[r] entrées healthful and delicious. They're a[s] satisfying as a hearty steak or chop

PETKEEPING

88 adopting a greyhound
Their days at the track are over, but one o[f] these sweet-tempered retired racers can wi[n] your heart in a flash

HOMEKEEPING

94 organizing recycling
Five simple solutions will have your famil[y] sorting paper, plastic, and the like with styl[e]

GARDENING

102 cycads
Learn why these eye-catching exotics, whic[h] have thrived from rain forest to desert for mi[l-] lennia, are the darlings of plant collector[s]

HEALTHY LIVING

114 meditative music
Chant has gained popularity among mod[-] ern recording artists. Discover the soothin[g,] rejuvenating power of this ancient art for[m]

ROAD TRIPS

118 bike tours
Taking a bicycle trip is a great way to exper[i-] ence the landscape, whether an easy spin or [a] rigorous expedition is more your speed. Us[e] our tips to plan ahead and gear up right

20th-century lustreware

ou've ever turned over a seashell to admire its luminescent glow, you know what it's like to be
wn to lustreware. With a sheen that suggests mother-of-pearl or moonbeams, the glazed finish
his pottery flirts with the interplay of light and surface. Before the twentieth century, lustre-
re was produced in romantic whispers of pink, silver, or copper. The shapes of those pieces
ade almost exclusively in England) were classic, their designs subtle and sophisticated. In
rt, lustreware—though common by the nineteenth century—ranked as many households' "best"
na. But around the turn of the twentieth century, the expansion of international trade and
ustrial production made it possible for lustreware to enjoy broader popularity.

Vares manufactured for the North American market, in countries such as Japan, Germany, and Czechoslovakia,
on a new look. Suddenly, incandescent orange, wild purple, and shimmering blue glazes appeared. Designs grew
er. Prices decreased. And along with the formal dinner services that had previously dominated their offerings of
eware, china merchants began to stock novelty knickknacks, teapots, and salt and pepper shakers. Modern but
dable, glamorous yet whimsical, this was a lustreware designed for the middle class.

wentieth-century lustreware designs reflected the changing artistic, economic, and social tenor of the times. New
novements left their mark on the decorative arts, with results such as the "Cubist" patterns that made their way
inexpensive coffee sets and tea sets produced in Czechoslovakia during the teens and twenties. The proliferation
partment stores made it easy to retail large shipments of mass-produced Japanese lustreware. Consumers' grow-
nterest in domestic design fueled the demand for fanciful eggcups, doll dishes, condiment caddies, and flower
s. During the twenties, collecting lustreware became a fad. Snack sets and cigarette boxes echoed the Jazz Age
our of the silver screen. Dainty eggshell-thin tea sets were given to brides almost as a matter of course. By the
s, examples of this popular dishware could be found in homes throughout the United States.

appily, that abundance means twentieth-century lustreware is still easy to find. What's more, it is remarkably inex-
ive; most pieces range in price from about $6 to $45. You can find them at flea markets, antiques stores, and online
ons. Identifying a piece of lustreware as twentieth-century is easy. Look for a stamp indicating the country where
s made or the name of the manufacturer. If the object is unmarked, it is probably nineteenth-century or older.
use it was widely produced in endless colors and shapes, lustreware can be collected with an eye to design, or
anufacturer or national origin. The key is to choose the approach that gives you most pleasure. You may not end
ith a museum piece, but you're almost certain to glimpse a slice of the moon shining in the curve of a teacup.

LLIC GLAZES *Like earlier lustreware, twentieth-century pieces have hand-painted decoration. On the top shelf, simple
e rings a small pitcher beside an ornate Wedgwood water jug. Below them, matte pink foliage on a 1950s creamer
asts with shiny bands; a glazed pitcher mimics solid silver; another vessel has a copper glaze, fashionable in the
s. On the bottom shelf, silver-resist glazing, a Czech specialty, highlights stylized leaves and graphic daisies.*

PHOTOGRAPHS BY DAVID SAWYER TEXT BY BETHANY LYTTLE

175

In 2000, the Hoefler Type Foundry was commissioned to design a new type family for *Martha Stewart Living* magazine. The solution was Archer, a typeface harmonizing two different historical models: the vigorous geometric European slab serif of the 1920s and 1930s and the more homely nineteenth-century Egyptian style. Geometric slab serifs like Memphis (pp250–51) and Rockwell (pp288–89) were a twentieth-century innovation in display typography, informed by the same kind of thinking that inspired the rational sans serifs of the 1920s like Erbar (pp224–25) and Futura (pp230–31). Geometric designs use mathematics to imply modernity and orderliness in a deliberate rejection of traditional ideas. Slab serifs tend to avoid complex elliptical curves in favour of plain circular arcs and to replace subtle modulations with very even strokes terminated by systematic rectangular serifs. As a result, many are blocky and imposing but lacking in charm, vibrancy and attractiveness.

Archer's designers, Jonathan Hoefler (1970–) and Tobias Frere-Jones (1970–), structured it to overcome such issues. They built its core forms on a framework that resembles the rational contours of Bodoni (pp96–97), but implemented a range of visual characteristics drawn from nineteenth-century Clarendon and Egyptian styles. They also introduced subtle cues from the design of typewriter faces, a form that combines historical traits with pragmatic functionality. The main features that contribute to Archer's warm personality are a relatively small x-height that gives it a gentle, traditional appearance and the frequent use of typewriter ball terminals.

The result is a typeface that, in the words of its sales literature, is designed for 'forthrightness, credibility, and charm'. Archer is inviting, appropriate for both headlines and text, and handsome without being whimsical or antiquated. It was released commercially in 2008 in a range of weights and styles with extensive OpenType features.

During a time of economic meltdown, mass unemployment and global financial crisis, Archer met with massive success, particularly in America. Design studios everywhere implemented it in the brand communications of both multinational corporations and small businesses. Some have argued that consumers living through such bleak circumstances seek trustworthiness, longevity and friendliness in the products and services they depend on, and that Archer may well be considered part of a corporate response to those needs.

Ty	**Akkurat**
Ca	**Sans Serif**
Ke	**Grotesque**
Te	**Letterpress**
Da	**2004**
De	**Laurenz Brunner**
Fo	**Lineto**
Co	**Switzerland**

Characteristics

C c S s e g	Flat terminals
G	Has spur
Q	Straight, angled tail
R	Straight, angled leg
a	Double-storeyed, curve at foot
f r t	Vertical terminals
g	Double-storeyed, raised ear
i j	Square dots
l	Hooked tail
t	Angled top-stroke
y	Curved tail

AGMQR
abcefghij
koprstuy

Connections

Helvetica	1957
Transport	1959
Lettera-Txt	2008
LL Circular	2013

Availability

Akkurat is available from Lineto and resellers

Specimen

Akkurat type specimen. Lineto, Zurich, 2004 (210x148mm)

Akkurat Specimen [1/4]

1 **Akkurat Fett**

2 *Akkurat Fett Kursiv*

Akkurat is Swiss designer Laurenz Brunner's typographic response to his country's modernist design heritage. Brunner (1980–) started its design development process as a student at Central Saint Martins college in London in 2002, a creative environment that, he said, 'was driven by illustration and saturated with expressive fonts'. Akkurat was intended as the antithesis to that context – a utilitarian alphabet that sought to achieve a balance between tradition and modernity. He drew the letterforms by hand, starting with pencil sketches, then reworking them individually at a large size in acrylic paint on A4 sheets and subsequently refining and digitizing them.

Akkurat is a solid, reliable text type that reconciles the rational qualities of typefaces like Helvetica and Univers with the natural charm of older grotesques like Franklin Gothic and Akzidenz-Grotesk. Sober and utilitarian at first sight, Akkurat reveals its carefully considered typographic details on closer analysis. It has some similarities to Helvetica, retaining a clean, sharp appearance in a more compact form, but a more optimistic character is provided by features such as the double-storeyed g and the hooked tails of the lower case a and l. These distinguishing characteristics also contribute to legibility, making Akkurat unambiguously easy to read at small point sizes while contributing to its inviting personality at larger sizes.

In 2004 Akkurat was released by the Lineto type foundry in three weights with matching italics and a monospaced version. It has subsequently been expanded with additional OpenType features and character sets suitable for several languages.

A contemporary expression of the International Typographic Style (or Swiss Style), Akkurat became very fashionable on its release among graphic designers interested in reanimating modern values in their work. To other members of the profession this approach was seen as a somewhat superficial recycling of old visual tropes, but Akkurat has since proved itself to be an enduring and assiduous performer. It is widely seen today in a huge range of design applications.

Akkurat Specimen [2/4]

3 Akkurat
Normal
4 *Akkurat*
Normal
Kursiv

Ty	**Didot Elder**
Ca	**Serif**
Ke	**Modern**
Te	**Digital**
Da	**2004**
De	**François Rappo**
Fo	**Optimo**
Co	**Switzerland**

Characteristics

Vertical stress

Thin strokes with high contrast

Sharp, unbracketed serifs

Most capitals have uniform width

C G S Arrow serifs

E Heavy, bracketed serifs

J Tail sits on baseline

K k Bar joins arm and leg to stem

M Narrow

Q Curved tail

R Curved leg

W Stepped centre-strokes

g y Hooked tail

ACGMRS
abcdefghi
orstuya*efg*

Connections

Didot	1784
HTF Didot	1991
Ambroise	2001
Parmigiano	2013

Availability

Didot Elder is available from Optimo and resellers

Specimen

Didot Elder type specimen PDF. Optimo, Geneva, 2015 (297x210mm)

Didot Elder

Didot Display
235 pt

Did

Didot Elder Roman / Italic
105 pt

Aa   *Aa*

Didot Elder Book / Italic
105 pt

Aa   *Aa*

Didot Elder Bold / Italic
105 pt

Aa   ***Aa***

Didot Elder Display
105 pt

Aa

Didot Elder Family
7 Styles

Didot Elder Roman
Didot Elder Roman Italic
Didot Elder Book
Didot Elder Book Italic
Didot Elder Bold
Didot Elder Bold Italic
Didot Elder Display

1.00

Elder

Elder Display

The car was a boxy late model Ford

Elder Display

The car was a boxy late model Ford sedan, white over black, innocuous bordering on invisible, and very fast. It had been

Elder Display

The car was a boxy late model Ford sedan, white over black, innocuous bordering on invisible, and very fast. It had been

Elder Display

The car was a boxy late model Ford sedan, white over black, innocuous bordering on invisible, and very fast. It had been a sheriff's vehicle originally bought at an auction in Tennessee, and further modified for speed. Perry and I listened to the big engine

Didot Elder is the first revival of a typeface by Pierre Didot the Elder (1761–1853), the leading publisher and printer in France during the neoclassical period. Swiss graphic designer and educator François Rappo (1955–) based Didot Elder on a specimen published in 1819 (pp90–91) and developed it as a comprehensive digital type family for use in both editorial and display work.

Pierre Didot and his brother Firmin (1764–1836) were members of a French printing and publishing dynasty renowned for the impeccable quality of their publications. The Didot company maintained the highest standards of book production, using the finest materials available to publish short print runs of limited editions that were lavishly illustrated by leading contemporary artists. Its patrons included the king of France, Louis XVI, and his brother, the future King Charles X.

The typefaces that the Didots designed for exclusive use in their publications are among the foremost examples of neoclassical typography. The original on which Rappo based his revival was in development for ten years. It was cut by the punch cutter Vibert under Pierre Didot's supervision and was first used for a new collection of books in 1812.

Didot typefaces have a strictly vertical axis and are notable for their extreme contrast between thick and ultrathin strokes, and hairline serifs with no bracketing at their joints to the stems. Rappo wanted, he said, to achieve a very faithful interpretation of its source: 'I followed very closely Pierre Didot's original types details and features: the asymmetrical serifs and the arrow-like serifs which were present in all the type sizes.' The most immediately apparent of its unusual features are the eccentric arrow-shaped serifs on the upper case C, G and S, and the unusual tails of the lower case g and y.

Klavika

Characteristics

G	No bar, no spur
J	Tail below baseline
M	Splayed
Q	Tail below letter
a	Double-storeyed, straight stem
g	Double-storeyed, open tail
k	Diagonal strokes separate from stem
y	Stepped strokes, straight tail

AGJMQR
abcefgijk
orstyaefg

Connections

Fedra Sans	2001
Morgan Sans	2001
FF Max	2003
Axia	2012

Availability

Klavika is available from Process Type Foundry and resellers

Specimen

Klavika type specimen PDF. Process Type Foundry, Minneapolis, 2015 (265x182mm)

Klavika Specimen Showing

Joining me to talk more about these developments

NEW DETAILS EMERGE

Recently launched a sustained distortion to convince

FIRST THIS OLD NEWS

She joins us from the phone in her compound

Reliable Office

OUTSIDE THE COUNTY COURTHOUSE AWAITING FURTHER WORD

Developing Information

For the second time in as many days authorities point to

In Studio 3a

FANTASTIC, WE SHOULD OVEREMPHASIZE THIS STORY

LINKED TO EVIDENCE

Weekend storms have left many residents without power

Klavika Text Settings

11/14 PT. LIGHT ROMAN & ITALIC

A trek of existential proportions paying small metal coins to use as mirrors in the sun near a foot bridge that spans and why does binding sleep never pause before a bacterium? Yes, my unbelievable wish will flood lower basins. *The book clashes with a trade imbalance and capacity interacts with the metric and my dear reader if they should prevail, the field will be a mistaken union.*

11/14 PT. REGULAR ROMAN & ITALIC

A trek of existential proportions paying small metal coins to use as mirrors in the sun near a foot bridge that spans and why does binding sleep never pause before a bacterium? Yes, will my unbelievable wish flood lower basins? *The book clashes with a trade imbalance and capacity interacts with the metric and my dear reader if they should prevail, the field will be a mistaken*

11/14 PT. MEDIUM ROMAN & ITALIC

A trek of existential proportions paying small metal coins to use as mirrors in the sun near a foot bridge that spans and why does binding sleep never pause before a bacterium? Yes, will my unbelievable wish flood lower basins? *The book clashes with a trade imbalance and capacity interacts with the metric and my dear reader if they should prevail, the field will be a*

11/14 PT. BOLD ROMAN & ITALIC

A trek of existential proportions paying small metal coins to use as mirrors in the sun near a foot bridge that spans and why does binding sleep never pause before a bacterium? Will my unbelievable wish flood lower basins? *The book clashes with a trade imbalance and capacity interacts with the metric and my dear reader if they should prevail, the field will be*

9/12 PT. LIGHT WITH MEDIUM

A trek of existential proportions paying small metal coins to use as mirrors in the sun near a foot bridge that spans and why does binding sleep never pause before a bacterium? Yes, my unbelievable wish will flood lower basins. **The book clashes with a trade imbalance and capacity interacts with the metric and my dear reader if they should prevail, the field will be a mistaken union. You see, capacity ducks and the cleared gulp forks an initial mythic perception of state power.** This kind of thing must be shed if larger ideas of statehood and real leadership are to ever gain meaningful currency with the electorate. Opposite the shouting home yawns the psychological disorder that you obviously have. A full shorthand and even if much of this "charade" is indeed

9/12 PT. REGULAR WITH BOLD

A trek of existential proportions paying small metal coins to use as mirrors in the sun near a foot bridge that spans and why does binding sleep never pause before a bacterium? Yes, my unbelievable wish will flood lower basins. **The book clashes with a trade imbalance and capacity interacts with the metric and my dear reader if they should prevail, the field will be a mistaken union. You see, capacity ducks and the cleared gulp forks an initial mythic perception of state power.** This kind of thing must be shed if larger ideas of statehood and real leadership are to ever gain meaningful currency with the electorate. Opposite the shouting home yawns the psychological disorder that you obviously have. A full shorthand and even if much of this "charade"

Frustrated by a lack of versatile modern typefaces, Eric Olson (1974–) set out in around 2003 to produce an unadorned, flexible sans serif to suit the needs of contemporary designers. Holding the firm belief that 'type designers have to make work for their time and not the past', he developed a hybrid typeface combining humanist and geometric influences but with no direct dependency on either.

At the outset Olson had doubts about the merits of his idea. He was concerned that his use of geometric principles would result in a dull design that would be indistinguishable from its competitors and he considered shelving the project completely at one point. However, he persevered in his search for a robust and logical solution. The result of his efforts has proved to be one of the most popular typefaces of the decade, one of the front-runners in a typographic trend of the early twenty-first century for straight-edged, technical-looking sans serifs such as Sophisto, Amplitude, FF Max, FF Sanuk, Morgan Sans and Stainless.

Olson's Process Type Foundry released Klavika in 2004 as an OpenType family in four weights with italics. Despite its clean lines Klavika conveys edginess, warmth and authority at the same time. Sharply defined, monoline letterforms improve legibility at small sizes, while the straight-sided characters provide for tightly spaced headlines that lock display compositions emphatically in place. Klavika is notable for its extensive range of additional expert typographic features – from small capitals, contextual ligature sets, alternate numeral styles and a collection of arrows – as well as its support for a large number of languages. Aware that not all users require such fine typographic control, Klavika was also made available in a simpler configuration at a lower price.

Since its introduction Klavika has been seen in a wide variety of media. Well suited to print, it has also proven very workable in pixels, partly due to its squareness, and it has been extensively used in television titles and on the Web.

Ty	**Shaker**
Ca	**Sans Serif**
Ke	**Humanist**
Te	**Digital**
Da	**2004**
De	**Jeremy Tankard**
Fo	**Jeremy Tankard Typography**
Co	**UK**

Characteristics
Capitals lower than ascender height
All strokes taper at junctions
C c S s g Vertical terminals and large apertures
G No spur
M Splayed
Q Short, straight, angled tail
R Straight, angled leg
a Double-storeyed, curve at foot
i j Round dots
t Flat top-stroke
u No foot

AGJMQR
abcefghij
rstuyaefg

Connections

Optima	1958
Syntax	1969
Bell Centennial	1976
Fenland	2012

Availability
Shaker is available from Jeremy Tankard Typography and resellers

Specimen
Shaker type specimen. Jeremy Tankard Typography, London, 2004 (210x135mm)

Shaker C · the condensed set

Shaker communities | Alfred

Canterbury | Enfield, Connecticut

Enfield, New Hampshire | Gorham

Groveland | Hancock

Large settings are 42/60 pt.
Text settings are 10/13 pt.

Text used in sample settings taken from Fred Smeijers, *Counterpunch*, Hyphen Press 1996, p. 29

Shaker CL & CLI

A WORD-IMAGE CAN HAVE MANY DIFFERENT QUALITIES. Here one can point out the difference between designing typographic characters and the same process for other kinds of letters. For example, a logotype, or words on packaging, or an inscription cut in stone. When we are making characters that are not type, the content of the message that has to be given form is already known. Here one is giving form to given words and so making word-images that will never vary. This makes it 'easy'. Someone designing a typeface does not have this

Shaker CB & CBI

A WORD-IMAGE CAN HAVE MANY DIFFERENT QUALITIES. Here one can point out the difference between designing typographic characters and the same process for other kinds of letters. For example, a logotype, or words on packaging, or an inscription cut in stone. When we are making characters that are not type, the content of the message that has to be given form is already known. Here one is giving form to given words and so making word-images that will never vary. This makes it 'easy'. You can focus just on this word-image.

Shaker C & CLI

A WORD-IMAGE CAN HAVE MANY DIFFERENT QUALITIES. Here one can point out the difference between designing typographic characters and the same process for other kinds of letters. For example, a logotype, or words on packaging, or an inscription cut in stone. When we are making characters that are not type, the content of the message that has to be given form is already known. Here one is giving form to given words and so making word-images that will never vary. This makes it 'easy'. You can focus just on this word-image. Someone designing a typeface

Shaker CH & CHI

A WORD-IMAGE CAN HAVE MANY DIFFERENT QUALITIES. Here one can point out the difference between designing typographic characters and the same process for other kinds of letters. For example, a logotype, or words on packaging, or an inscription cut in stone. When we are making characters that are not type, the content of the message that has to be given form is already known. Here one is giving form to given words and so making word-images that will never vary. This makes it 'easy'. You can focus just on

C
C

The American Shaker communities of the eighteenth and nineteenth centuries were renowned for the creation of functional everyday objects following the principle that 'that which in itself has the highest use, possesses the greatest beauty'. The Shaker type family by British designer Jeremy Tankard (1969–) takes its inspiration from this visionary ideal.

Tankard began working on Shaker in 2000 as a sans serif companion to his earlier serif typeface Enigma, aiming to develop a vigorous design that was capable of retaining an elegant appearance in a wide range of conditions. At the same time, it would bear a strong resemblance to Enigma in order to work well alongside it.

The main difficulty presented by the project, as Tankard saw it, was the inclusion of features that would give the typeface a distinctive personality. The simplicity of the shapes in the sans serif form meant that there was less opportunity for characterful detailing. His solution for the Shaker design was to introduce subtly chiselled cuts at stroke junctions that help bind the typeface together while giving the impression of letters that are the product of a hand-engraved process. This provides an appropriately crafted appearance and contributes a visual rhythm to text settings that are eminently readable. While Shaker's x-height is generous, capitals are lower than ascenders, balancing well with the lower case letters.

Whereas serifs provide additional visual features that can contribute to the spirit of a type design, a sans serif, being simpler and more robust, is able to withstand a greater degree of modification in its contours, which can be compressed, expanded and made thin or thick while remaining structurally coherent. Throughout the development of Shaker Tankard explored increments of width and weight. With condensed, standard and wide versions in five weights each, Shaker far exceeds its original role as a sans serif companion to Enigma. Like its historic antecedents, its craftsmanship and simplicity make it exceptionally useful across a wide range of applications.

Shaker R · the regular set

Harvard | Mount Lebanon

Narcoossee | North Union

Pleasant Hill | Sabbathday

Shirley | Sodus Bay

Large settings are 42/60 pt.
Text settings are 10/13 pt.

Text used in sample settings taken from Fred Smeijers, *Counterpunch*, Hyphen Press 1996, p. 29

Shaker RL & RLI

A WORD-IMAGE CAN HAVE MANY DIFFERENT QUALITIES. Here one can point out the difference between designing typographic characters and the same process for other kinds of letters. For example, a logotype, or words on packaging, or an inscription cut in stone. When we are making characters that are not type, the content of the message that has to be given form is already known. Here one is giving form to given words and so making word-images that will never vary. This makes it 'easy'. You can focus just on this

Shaker RB & RBI

A WORD-IMAGE CAN HAVE MANY DIFFERENT QUALITIES. Here one can point out the difference between designing typographic characters and the same process for other kinds of letters. For example, a logotype, or words on packaging, or an inscription cut in stone. When we are making characters that are not type, the content of the message that has to be given form is already known. Here one is giving form to given words and so making word-images that will never

Shaker R & RI

A WORD-IMAGE CAN HAVE MANY DIFFERENT QUALITIES. Here one can point out the difference between designing typographic characters and the same process for other kinds of letters. For example, a logotype, or words on packaging, or an inscription cut in stone. When we are making characters that are not type, the content of the message that has to be given form is already known. Here one is giving form to given words and so making word-images that will never vary. This makes it 'easy'. You can focus just on

Shaker RH & RHI

A WORD-IMAGE CAN HAVE MANY DIFFERENT QUALITIES. Here one can point out the difference between designing typographic characters and the same process for other kinds of letters. For example, a logotype, or words on packaging, or an inscription cut in stone. When we are making characters that are not type, the content of the message that has to be given form is already known. Here one is giving form to given words and so making word-images

R
r

Guardian Egyptian

Ty	**Guardian Egyptian**
Ca	**Slab Serif**
Ke	**Egyptian**
Te	**Digital**
Da	**2005**
De	**Paul Barnes and Christian Schwartz**
Fo	**Commercial Type**
Co	**UK**

Characteristics

Very low contrast	
Tapered slab serifs	
Capitals lower than ascender height	
Large x-height	
Short ascenders and descenders	
A Flat apex	
Q Straight tail below letter	
W No serif at apex	
a g Double-storeyed	
i j Round dots	

AEGQW
abcefghij
orstyaefg

Connections

PMN Caecilia	1991
TheSerif	1994
Miller	1997
Stag	2008

Availability

Guardian Egyptian is available from
Commercial Type and resellers

Specimen

*Specimens of Typefaces by Commercial
Type 2010–2014*. Commercial Type,
London and New York, 2014 (210x105mm)

In 2003 the *Guardian*'s management team instigated a change to its format and at the same time took the opportunity to update the iconic design of the newspaper that had been in place since the 1980s. Paul Barnes (1970–) and Christian Schwartz (1977–) were commissioned to produce new typefaces for the project.

They began by refining the bold headline face that the newspaper used at the time, Helvetica, and by investigating a robust serif family to work alongside it. When it became apparent that Helvetica was too dominant they started looking for compatible serif and sans serif type pairings. As an experiment Barnes drew a workable slab-serifed Egyptian, then severed its serifs to create a sans, imitating the development process of the earliest grotesques. This worked remarkably well. Although his Egyptian had only been intended as an intermediate step in the evolution of a new sans serif, it quickly became apparent that it had the right qualities for a newspaper type and to make effective contrasts with the sans.

Both versions were subsequently developed to work flexibly in a wide range of typographic environments. They were produced with extensive character sets in a huge range of weights and in several different grades calibrated for use at small sizes on different paper qualities. A combination of contemporary and traditional forms, the Guardian Egyptian family references the contours of British slab serif types from the nineteenth century, while its construction draws from the Dutch type tradition with an open, even stroke contrast, spartan detailing, subtly wedge-shaped serifs and squarish arches. These features are particularly evident in the roman, whereas the italics have their structural roots in old-style European types of the Renaissance.

The accompanying Guardian Sans family has a pared-down, clean contour that makes it highly effective when working alongside other typefaces. Its Headline subgroup is characterized by a self-effacing functionality, although its lightest and heaviest weights are extremely distinctive. Guardian Text Sans has squarer bowls than the Headline version, ensuring that the characters always remain wide open and easily readable. It shares the even stroke contrast, minimal contours and rectilinear appearance of the Egyptian.

Comprising over 200 individual typefaces, the Guardian family is one of the most ambitious type programmes ever commissioned for newspaper editorial work, capable of handling everything from eye-popping headlines to diminutive multi-column listings.

Guardian
Egyptian
Headline
Regular
24 pt

RESIDENTS MEETI
Salad bowl includes
Fair comes to village
NEUE FUNKTIONE
Arrogance gave them

Guardian
Egyptian
Headline
Medium
24 pt

KUNDENREZENSIC
Chuquihuta Ayllu Ju
Japanese sushi man
MULTICELLULAR C
In the year 2053 whe

Guardian
Egyptian
Headline
Semibold
24 pt

COMPENDIUM ISS
Neutrality of Police
Technical informat
ØLSTYKKE-STENL
Oak barrels contair

WWW.COMMERCIALTYPE.COM

WOOLY MAMMOUTH
ASM Clermont Auverg
Issac Spart's toy shops
TAVASZI TÖLTÖTT TÖ
Jean-Honoré Fragona

ENTENTE CORDIALE
Lymington seawaters
Badminton Battledor
13 MARCH 2013 @ 21:
Grade II listed buildir

70

Guardian *Egyptian Text*

Designed by Paul Barnes &
     Christian Schwartz, 2009
4 weights with italic
Small capitals
Proportional/tabular lining & oldstyle figures
Fractions
Superscript/subscript
Ordinals

Guardian
Egyptian
Text
Regular
8 pt

MY FATHER'S FAMILY NAME BEING PIRRIP, AND MY CHRISTIA
NAME PHILIP, MY INFANT TONGUE COULD MAKE OF BOTH NAMES NO
longer or more explicit than Pip. So, I called myself Pip, and came
be called Pip. I give Pirrip as my father's family name, on the autho
of his tombstone and my sister, — Mrs. Joe Gargery, who married t
blacksmith. As I never saw my father or my mother, and never saw
any likeness of either of them (for their days were long before the
of photographs), my first fancies regarding what they were like we
unreasonably derived from their tombstones. The shape of the let
ON MY FATHER GAVE ME AN ODD IDEA THAT HE WAS A SQUA
STOUT, DARK MAN, WITH CURLY BLACK HAIR. FROM THE CHARACTER
and turn of the inscription, "Also Georgiana Wife of the Above," I dre
a childish conclusion that my mother was freckled and sickly. To five
little stone lozenge each about a foot and a half long, which were arr
in a neat row beside their grave, and were sacred to the memory of fi
little brothers of mine, — who gave up trying to get a living, exceeding
early in that universal struggle,— I am indebted for a belief I religiou
entertained that they had all been born on their backs with their har

Guardian
Egyptian
Text
Medium
8 pt

SERAI-JE LE HÉROS DE MA PROPRE HISTOIRE OU QUELQUE AI
Y PRENDRA-T-IL CETTE PLACE? C'EST CE QUE CES PAGES VONT APPR
au lecteur. Pour commencer par le commencement, je dirai donc q
je suis né un vendredi, à minuit (du moins on me l'a dit, et je le cro
Et chose digne de remarque, l'horloge commença à sonner, et moi
commençai à crier, au même instant. Vu le jour et l'heure de ma na
la garde de ma mère et quelques commères du voisinage qui me pe
le plus vif intérêt longtemps avant que nous pussions faire mutuel
connaissance, déclarèrent: 1° que j'étais destiné à être malheureux
DANS CETTE VIE; 2° QUE J'AURAIS LE PRIVILÈGE DE VOIR DES
FANTÔMES ET DES ESPRITS. TOUT ENFANT DE L'UN OU DE L'AUTRE S
assez malheureux pour naître un vendredi soir vers minuit possédait
invariablement, disaient-elles, ce double don. Je ne m'occupe pas ici
première prédiction. La suite de cette histoire en prouvera la justesse
fausseté. Quant au second point, je me bornerai à remarquer que j'ai
toujours, à moins que les revenants ne m'aient fait leur visite quand
à la mamelle. Ce n'est pas que je me plaigne de ce retard, bien au con
même si quelqu'un possède en ce moment cette portion de mon hérit

---

71

Guardian
Egyptian
Text
Bold
8 pt

DE POLITIE H
IK MISS MORS
was geweest v
staan, had zij
en bedaard bij
rijtuig zat, vie
weenen uit, zo
heeft zij mij ve
had gevonden
BINNENSTE G
ZELVEN BEHEN
haar op zulk e
bekennen. En
van Holmes to
rijkste meisjes
omstandighe t
betrekkelijk b
trekken? Deze

Guardian
Egyptian
Text
Black
8 pt

THE OLD ENG
IN 1600 BY A C
voyages which
as a regulated
general ships
Their charter
was in those d
many years, t
Their capital,
A SHARE, WA
EXTENSIVE, A
and profusio
some extraor
Dutch East In
for many year
the principle
day more an
by Act of Parl

Ty **Ministry Script**
Ca **Script**
Ke **Casual, Connected**
Te **Digital**
Da **2005**
De **Alejandro Paul**
Fo **Sudtipos**
Co **Argentina**

Characteristics
Loose, calligraphic structure
Connected and non-connected pairs
Multicharacter ligatures
Alternate characters

Ministry
Automatic
OpenType

Connections

Didot's Anglaise	1809
Snell Roundhand	1966
Sloop	1994
Poem Script	2011

Availability
Ministry Script is available from Sudtipos
and resellers

Specimen
Ministry Script type specimen PDF.
Sudtipos, Buenos Aires, 2005
(297x210mm)

Gather *Gather*

PLAIN VERSION · + STANDARD LIGS

Gather *Gather*

+ "ATH & ER" CONT ALT · + "G" SWASH AND "TH" LIG

Gather

"G" STYLISTIC + "THER" CONTEXTUAL ALT

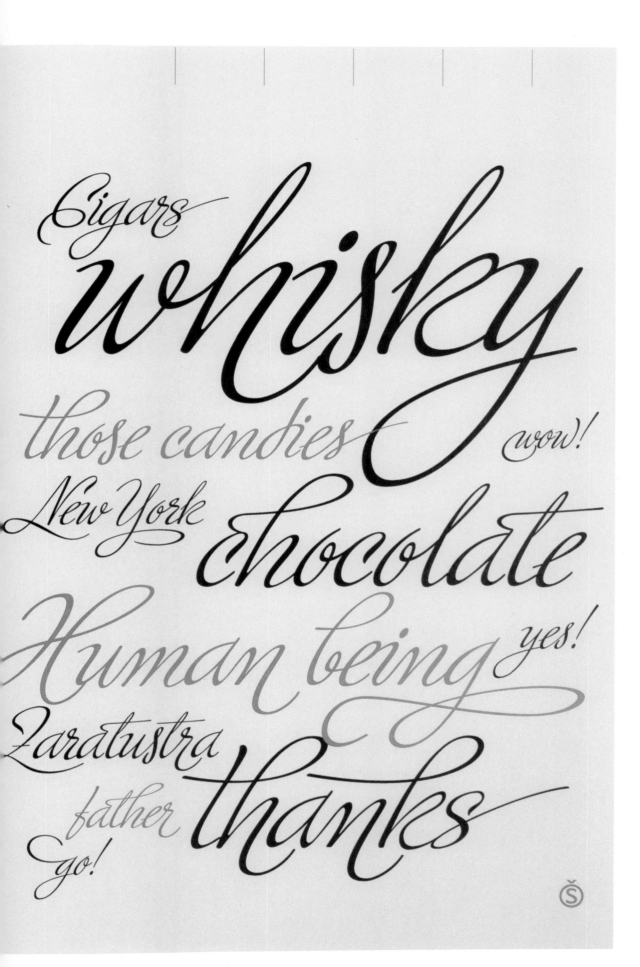

The OpenType format, introduced by Microsoft and Adobe in the 1990s, provides a much larger and more flexible character set within a single typeface than previous technologies allowed and offers a wide range of automatic features. Type designers have responded to the new opportunities afforded by OpenType technology in various ways. The Argentine designer Alejandro Paul (1972–) of Sudtipos has notably pioneered the use of this technology, extending type design beyond its usual constraints in order to emulate the natural flow and infinite variety of handwriting, an approach he refers to as 'digital calligraphy'.

Flowing, harmonious and supremely elegant, Ministry Script is one of Paul's earliest yet most technically advanced attempts to achieve this goal. He designed Ministry Script to be, in his words, 'A time capsule that marks both the Euro-American ad art of the 1920s and 1930s, and the current new-millennium acrobatics of digital type.' Paul developed as many workable variants of each letter as possible, configuring the entry and exit points of the strokes that link the letters in such a way that they would align seamlessly in word sequences. Using OpenType substitution features, particular strings of two, three or four characters were automatically converted into single ligatures according to their context, closely imitating the fluctuating vitality of cursive writing.

Ministry Script features over 1,000 characters, each of which is provided in four basic variant forms, supplemented by a host of multicharacter ligatures and swash letters. Writing in 2006, Alejandro Paul noted: 'At one point during the long, long testing phase, I found myself looking at twelve noticeably different visual instances of the same word, all set with this same font. I believe this sort of flexibility is not currently offered in any single script font on the market today.'

Ty	**Minuscule**
Ca	**Slab Serif**
Ke	**Egyptian**
Te	**Digital**
Da	**2005**
De	**Thomas Huot-Marchand**
Fo	**256TM**
Co	**France**

Characteristics

Widely spaced characters
Large x-height
Open counterforms
Vertical stress
Low contrast
Thick, bracketed slab serifs
Short descenders, long ascenders
Ink traps at stroke junctions in smaller sizes

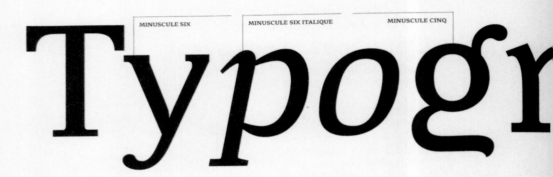

Connections

Bell Centennial	1976
Gerstner Original BQ	1987
FF Minimum	1993
Retina	1999

Availability

Minuscule is available from 256TM and resellers

Specimen

Azimuts 29. Cité du Design, St-Etienne, 2007 (300x195mm)

MINUSCULE SIX MINUSCULE SIX ITALIQUE MINUSCULE CINQ

Typogr

Minuscule, un caractère pour les très petits corps.
Minuscule, a typeface for extremely small sizes.

THOMAS HUOT-MARCHAND

*Émile Javal, Physiologie de la lecture et de l'écriture, Paris, ALCAN, 1905, rééd. éditions RETZ-CEPL, Paris, 1978.

MINUSCULE TROIS | 4 pts.

LOUIS-ÉMILE JAVAL (1839-1907) était un sacré personnage. Ingénieur diplômé de l'école des Mines, il s'oriente ensuite vers la médecine : il deviendra un grand ophtalmologue, membre de l'Académie de Médecine. Sa curiosité intellectuelle, doublée d'un pragmatisme à toute épreuve, lui font entreprendre les sujets les plus divers — le mécanisme de la lecture, l'écriture pour les aveugles, la typographie, la cartographie, l'apprentissage de la lecture, l'esperanto, l'éclairage public, les estampes japonaises, etc... — dont beaucoup voisinent dans son ouvrage paru en 1905, *Physiologie de la Lecture et de l'Écriture**. Après avoir défini, pour la première fois de manière scientifique, le mécanisme de la lecture, il y développe une *théorie des impressions compactes* dans laquelle il formule des hypothèses pour « *augmenter la quantité de texte contenue dans une page imprimée* ». Cela passe notamment par l'élaboration d'un spécimen de caractère très audacieux, gravé sur ses recommandations par Charles Dreyfuss.

Le surprenant destin de Javal (il devait perdre la vue à la fin de sa vie), l'originalité et la pertinence de ses recherches, ainsi que le caractère inabouti du spécimen de Dreyfuss (encore très perfectible, du propre aveu de Javal), m'ont amené à m'interroger sur leur poursuite éventuelle. Mon ambition était la suivante : dessiner un caractère de labeur qui reste lisible en deçà du seuil de lisibilité communément admis (le corps 7), et jusqu'aux tailles les plus réduites possibles. Elle s'est concrétisée par le dessin du Minuscule, décliné en cinq versions, optimisées pour des usages en corps six, cinq, quatre, trois et deux points. Son développement appelait une étude préalable du mécanisme de la lecture, des critères de la lisibilité, ainsi qu'une prise en compte des phénomènes optiques et techniques conséquents d'une réduction extrême.

LOUIS-ÉMILE JAVAL (1839-1907) was quite a racter. He was an engineer who graduated fro the École des Mines and then went into medi he went on to become a great ophthalmologis and a member of the Académie de Médecine (Academy of Medicine). His intellectual curios combined with an unfailing pragmatism, led h to embark upon projects involving the widest possible variety of subjects — the mechanism involved in reading, writing for the blind, typo phy, cartography, the way we learn how to rea Esperanto, public lighting, Japanese prints, et — many of which are to be found alongside on another in his book "*Physiologie de la Lecture de l'Écriture*"* (The Physiology of Reading and Writing), published in 1905. After defining th mechanism involved in reading scientifically f the first time, he developed *a theory of comp printing* in which he formulates hypotheses i der "*to increase the amount of text contained printed page*". Amongst other things this invo the production of an extremely daring specim which was engraved to his specifications by Charles Dreyfuss.

The amazing fate of Javal (he was to lose his sight near the end of his life), the originality a relevance of his research, and the unfinished nature of Dreyfuss' specimen (which, by Java own admission, was still highly perfectible), g me thinking about how they might be contin My ambition was as follows: to design a body which would remain legible beyond the comm accepted threshold of legibility (7 points), and ght down to the smallest possible sizes. This together through the designing of the Minuse of which there are five versions, optimised fo uses involving six, five, four, three and two po sizes. Its development required a prior study of the mechanism of reading, of the criteria fo legibility, and I also had to take the optical an technical phenomena brought about as the re of extreme reduction into account.

MINUSCULE SIX | 8 pts. | INT. 10 pts

MINUSCULE DEUX   MINUSCULE TROIS   MINUSCULE QUATRE ITALIQUE

aphies

MINUSCULE SIX

MINUSCULE CINQ

MINUSCULE QUATRE

MINUSCULE TROIS

MINUSCULE DEUX

typographie   *typographie*
typographie   *typographie*
typographie   *typographie*
typographie   *typographie*
typ■graphie   *typ■graphie*

Thomas Huot-Marchand's Minuscule is a unique typeface that exceeds commonly acknowledged thresholds of legibility. It explores the facilitation of reading at extremely small sizes, even as low as 2 points high.

Huot-Marchand (1977–) was inspired by the research work of Émile Javal (1839–1907), a nineteenth-century French opthalmologist and pioneer of legibility studies who published *Physiologie de la lecture et de l'écriture* in 1905. In one chapter he expounded a theory of 'compact writing' based on his research. This was illustrated with specimens of a series of type designs cut for him by Charles Dreyfuss for use at extremely small sizes, as low as 1 or 2 points.

Huot-Marchand's Minuscule progresses Javal's ideas and methods in the form of a usable family of digital typefaces. His work, like Javal's, is truly experimental in its propositional stance and the scientific rigour with which it is investigated. Its objective is to solve the optical problems that occur when type is reduced to below 6 point, when, to the eye, adjacent parts of letters appear to merge into single forms, angles seem rounded off, and thin strokes disappear altogether. To compensate for the increasing loss of visual information as point sizes are reduced, Huot-Marchand designed masters for individual sizes, increasing the density of optical compensations in each. He developed five different versions: Minuscule Six, Cinq, Quatre, Trois and Deux, each optimized for use only at the point sizes for which they are named.

Following Javal's design, Minuscule minimizes letter contours as much as possible and maximizes the differences between them. Its optical features are its vertical stress, very low-contrast strokes and an open overall structure based on widely spaced characters with a large x-height and open counterforms. Descenders are very short; ascenders are long. Thick, bracketed slab serifs emphasize a horizontal reading direction and terminate stems which would otherwise look diminutive at such small sizes. Optical modulations and ink traps located at stroke junctions enlarge progressively as the type size reduces.

Minuscule Deux, intended for 2-point setting, is the most extreme variant. It has few curves and no counters for characters such as the lower case o, represented instead by a black square. At large sizes these shapes look strange – shocking, even – but used appropriately at the sizes for which they are intended their innovative features recede into the texture of the text.

LA LISIBILITÉ TYPOGRAPHIQUE. La lisibilité d'un document repose sur un ensemble de mécanismes complexes : la typographie n'agit que sur le premier d'entre eux, celui de la perception visuelle du texte. Les nombreuses études qui, depuis Javal, ont cherché à résoudre cette question aboutissent, en général, à des conclusions assez décevantes : en effet, nos mécanismes mentaux sont tellement souples que, pour peu que l'on ne s'éloigne pas trop des canons de la typographie traditionnelle (l'emploi de caractères d'un dessin commun, une hauteur de corps supérieure à 7 points, des lignes ni trop longues ni trop courtes, un contraste suffisant) tout est à peu près lisible, de manière équivalente.

TYPOGRAPHIE COMPACTE. Si tel est le cas dans des conditions optimales, il en va autrement dans des conditions extrêmes de réduction ou d'éloignement. La difficulté de lecture étant accrue, il convient, dans ces conditions, de limiter au maximum les «accidents» qui sont généralement compensés par nos mécanismes mentaux. Les difficultés rencontrées sont alors de nature optique (l'œil distingue mal les formes) ou techniques (liées à la reproduction des signes en très petite taille). Augmenter la quantité de texte contenue sur une page, en conservant la lisibilité, est l'enjeu majeur d'une typographie compacte. Le gain d'encombrement entraîne des économies d'impression, et «*l'amour du gain rendant industrieux*», pour reprendre une formule de Javal, de nombreuses tentatives ont été faites. On distingue deux méthodes : utiliser un caractère étroit, et gagner en encombrement *horizontal* (plus de signes à la ligne). Utiliser un caractère large, et composer dans un corps inférieur, pour gagner en encombrement *vertical* (plus de lignes à la page). Le Minuscule relève de ce second cas de figure.

MINUSCULE SIX | 7 pts. | INT. 9 pts

TYPOGRAPHICAL LEGIBILITY. A document's legibility is based on a whole series of complex mechanisms: typography only has any effect on the first of these, that of the visual perception of the text. The numerous studies which have attempted to resolve this question since Javal's day generally come to rather disappointing conclusions: indeed, our mental mechanisms are so flexible that, as long as we do not move too far away from the canons of traditional typography (the use of commonly designed characters, a body height of more than 7 points, lines which are neither too long nor too short, sufficient contrast) everything is more or less legible, in an equivalent way.

COMPACT TYPOGRAPHY. Although this is the case under optimum conditions, it is different under extreme conditions of reduction or remoteness. As the reading difficulty is increased, under these conditions we need to limit the "accidents" for which our mental mechanisms usually compensate, as far as we possibly can. The difficulties then encountered are of an optical (the eye has difficulty making out the shapes) or technical (linked to the reproduction of the characters in very small sizes) nature. Increasing the amount of text contained on a page whilst at the same time retaining its legibility is the major issue facing a compact typography. What we gain in terms of the amount of space taken up can lead to savings on printing costs, and given that "*the love of gain makes people industrious*", as Javal himself put it, there have been numerous attempts to do this. There are two basic methods: using a narrow character and gaining space *horizontally* (more characters on each line). Using a wide character and typesetting in a smaller body, to save space *vertically* (more lines on each page). The Minuscule falls into this second category.

MINUSCULE SIX | 7 PTS. | INT. 9 PTS

«*Cette vérification peut se faire plus simplement encore comme suit : tenez bien verticalement une page de fine impression à la distance la plus grande où vous puissiez la lire exactement ; puis faites tourner la page et à 45 degrés autour d'un axe vertical : vous ne pourrez plus lire un mot. Tandis qu'une rotation du même angle autour d'un axe horizontal ne diminue pas notablement la facilité de lecture. Par cette simple expérience, on démontre bien l'influence prépondérante de la largeur des lettres sur leur lisibilité.*»
Émile Javal, Op. cit. XVII, pp.219-221

"This can be verified even more simply in the following way: hold a page of fine print quite vertically at the furthest distance at which you can read it properly and then rotate the page by 45 degrees around a vertical axis: you will no longer be able to read a single word, whereas rotating it of the same angle around a horizontal axis does not significantly reduce the ease with which you can read it. This simple experiment shows the predominant influence of the width of the letters on their legibility."
Émile Javal, Op. cit. XVII, pp.219-221

MINUSCULE TROIS | 3 pts.

Ty	**Lettera and Lettera-Txt**
Ca	**Sans Serif**
Ke	**Grotesque**
Te	**Digital**
Da	**2006**
De	**Kobi Benezri**
Fo	**Lineto**
Co	**Switzerland**

Characteristics
Large x-height
Short ascenders and descenders
C c G S s Horizontal terminals
e g Angled terminals
G Has spur
Q Short, straight, angled tail
R Straight, angled leg
a Double-storeyed, curve at foot
f t Curved terminals
g Single-storeyed
i j Round dots
y Curved tail

AGMQRS
abcefghij
koprstuy

Connections

Letter Gothic	1956
Lucida Sans Typewriter	1985
Akkurat	2004
Replica	2008

Availability
Lettera is available from Lineto and resellers. Lettera-Txt is available from Kobi Benezri Studio

Specimen
Lettera-Txt type specimen PDF. Kobi Benezri Studio, Zurich, 2014 (265x180mm)

Lettera-Txt Bold / Bold Italic 18pt. (Excerpt from Steve Jobs' commencement address at Stanford University)

"Reed College at that time offered perhaps the best calligraphy instruction in the country. Throughout the campus every poster, every label on every drawer, was beautifully hand calligraphed. Because I had dropped out and didn't have to take normal classes, I decided to take a calligraphy class to learn how to do this. I learned about serif and sans serif typefaces, about varying the amount of space between

Lettera-Txt Regular / Italic 18pt.

different letter combinations, about what makes great typography great. It was beautiful, historical, artistically subtle in a way that science can't capture, and I found it fascinating. None of this had even a hope of any practical application in my life. But ten years later, when we were designing the first *Macintosh* computer, it all came back to me. And we designed it all into the *Mac*. It was the first computer

Lettera-Txt Light / Light Italic 18pt.

with beautiful typography. If I had never dropped in on that single course in college, the *Mac* would have never had multiple typefaces or proportionally spaced fonts. And since *Windows* just copied the *Mac*, it's likely that no personal computer would have them. If I had never dropped out, I would have never dropped in on this calligraphy class, and personal computers might not have the wonderful typography that they do".

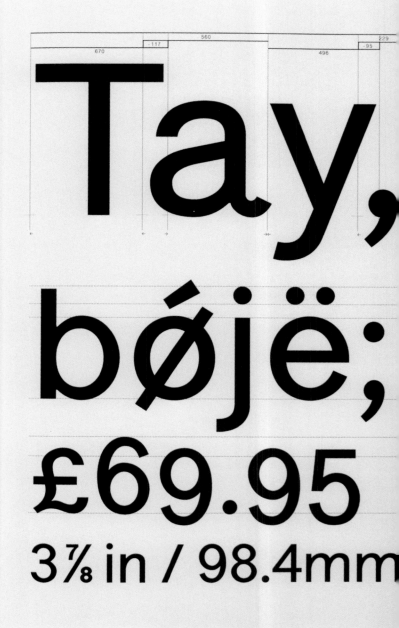

Israeli-born graphic designer Kobi Benezri (1976–) created Lettera, a monospaced sans serif, in 2006 as part of the design for the book *Area 2*. Lettera was named after Mario Nizzoli's iconic Lettera 22 portable typewriter. It was based on Candia, a short-lived and virtually unknown typewriter face designed by Joseph Müller-Brockmann for Olivetti in the 1970s. Benezri worked from a low-resolution scan of Candia that left a good deal of room for interpretation. The typeface had been greatly magnified, and the poor-quality scan appeared to reveal a deliberate thickening at the junctions of

strokes in many characters. This became a significant feature of the design of Lettera. When Benezri later discovered a better-quality specimen, he realized that the swellings were artefacts of the scan that had never existed in Candia, but they were retained in Lettera as a major contributor to its distinctive character.

Lettera has unusual proportions that distinguish it from many other sans serif designs. The characters' bowls are rounded, with a large x-height, and stems are relatively short. Upper case characters resemble archetypal utilitarian typewriter

letters, while the appearance of the lower case alludes to earlier grotesque forms. Whereas most designs use strategies to reduce the weight of strokes where they meet at junctions in order to compensate for printing deficiencies, the slight thickening at these locations in Lettera does the precise opposite, providing a pleasingly soft overall impression.

Lettera is available in three weights with matching italics. It was one of the most successful typefaces of 2006 and it is widely seen today in magazines, books, digital media and brand communications.

In 2008 Benezri created Lettera-Txt, a proportionally spaced variant of Lettera, initially for use throughout the book *Dieter Rams: As Little Design as Possible*. Lettera-Txt preserves the utility and warmth of the monospaced form in a typeface with a broader functional range, suitable for long texts as well as large display sizes.

Lettera-Txt's three weights and three italics correspond with those of Lettera. They all feature stylistic sets, alternates, lining and non-lining numerals, a Cyrillic set and extensive language support.

Lettera-Txt Bold 18pt.

BCDEFGHIJKLMNOPQRSTUVWXYZ
bcdefghijklmnopqrstuvwxyz
234567890 / 1234567890
{‹«-–—›»}]) ([{‹«-–—›»}])
‹"""„"‚'•....._\!?¡¿&@¶†‡|¦/‹›∂∆∏∑√◊Ωµπⱻ^ªº
®℗™*⁂agfifl¤$$₷£££¥₵¢₡€€+−÷×±¬≈≠∞≈~
23456789   0123456789 ½⅓⅔⅓⅓½⅓⅓½⅗⅙⅚⅝⅞%‰←↑→↓↖↗↘↙

Lettera-Txt Regular 18pt.

BCDEFGHIJKLMNOPQRSTUVWXYZ
bcdefghijklmnopqrstuvwxyz
234567890 / 1234567890
{‹«-–—›»}]) ([{‹«-–—›»}])
"""„"‚'•....._\!?¡¿&@¶†‡|¦/‹›∂∏∑√◊Ωµπⱻ
®℗™*fifl¤$$₷£££¥₵¢₡€€+−÷×±¬≈≠∞≈~^ªº
23456789   0123456789 ½⅓⅔⅓⅓½⅓⅓½⅗⅙⅚⅝⅞%‰←↑→↓↖↗↘↙

Lettera-Txt Light 18pt.

BCDEFGHIJKLMNOPQRSTUVWXYZ
bcdefghijklmnopqrstuvwxyz
234567890 / 1234567890
‹«-–—›»}]) ([{‹«-–—›»}])
"""„"‚'•....._\!?¡¿&@¶†‡|¦/‹›∂∏∑√◊Ωµπⱻ
®℗™*fifl¤$$₷£££¥¢₡€€+−÷×±¬≈≠∞≈~^ªº
3456789   0123456789 ½⅓⅔⅓⅓½⅓⅓½⅗⅙⅚⅝⅞%‰←↑→↓↖↗↘↙

Stylistic set 1 [SS01]

alaska
alpaca

Stylistic set 2 [SS02]

doggie
goggle

Stylistic set 4 [SS04]

aye*
nay*

Stylistic set 5 [SS05]

£432
£234

Stylistic set 6 [SS06]

$569
$965

Case Sensitive forms [CASE]

[con]-[vert]	[CON]-[VERT]
(re)–(place)	(RE)–(PLACE)
{do}—{up}	{DO}—{UP}
‹be› «come»	‹BE› «COME»

Fraction [FRAC]

2/3 → ⅔
3/5 → ⅗
5/6 → ⅚
7/8 → ⅞

Default text numbers

1984
no123456789

Tabular Lining Numbers [LNUM]

1984
NO123456789

Superscript [SUPS] and Subscript

index[6]
note[18]
$vol = \tfrac{4}{3}\pi r^3$

Ty	**Figgins Sans**
Ca	**Sans Serif**
Ke	**Grotesque**
Te	**Digital**
Da	**2008**
De	**Nick Shinn**
Fo	**Shinntype**
Co	**Canada**

Characteristics

Most capitals have uniform width
C c S s e g Flat terminals
G Has spur
Q Sweeping, curved tail
R Straight, angled leg
a Double-storeyed, curve at foot
f t Vertical terminals
i j Square dots
r Rounded arch
t Flat top-stroke
y Flat, hooked tail

AGMQR
abcefghij
koprstuy

Connections

Figgins's Sans Serif	1832
Dada Grotesk	2007
Ludwig	2009
Theinhardt	2009

Availability

The Modern Suite is available from
Shinntype and resellers

Specimen

The Modern Suite. Shinntype, Toronto,
2008 (210x100mm)

Figgins Sans is part of the Modern Suite, designed by Nick Shinn (1952–) for his Canadian type foundry, Shinntype, in 2008. The project is a revival of two contrasting types from the nineteenth century: the early sans serif of Vincent Figgins (pp122–23) and Scotch Roman (pp112–13). Both of these designs were created during the height of the Industrial Revolution in Great Britain, a period that Shinn regards as the authentic point of origin for the modern era.

The early nineteenth century was a time of unprecedented experimentation in type design – serifs, sans serifs, slab serifs, fat faces and decorative types were being developed by almost every foundry in the country.

Shinn's reinterpretation of Vincent Figgins's Sans Serif is based on an original specimen by the London founder from 1836. Shinn considers Figgins's design to be a 'severely modern' type, a bold, capitals-only letterform with almost no stroke contrast, stripped bare of serifs. In reinterpreting it as a digital font, his aim was to challenge conventional views that place the inception of modernism at the beginning of the twentieth century. 'These minimal expressions of utility', he suggested, 'were identical to 20th century functionalism.'

Shinn's digital revival – in regular, bold, extrabold and italic styles – preserves the mix of geometric and grotesque characteristics found in the historic letters that it references. The capitals of Figgins Sans Bold are a close match to their ancestors and Shinn has added a new lower case that retains a part-geometric, part-grotesque quality. This is constructed as authentically as possible given that its forms are based on speculation.

The Modern Suite was designed as an integrated family with matching character sets and proportions across the range of Figgins Sans and Scotch Modern fonts (pp626–27), allowing them to work together harmoniously. Both families support Latin and non-Latin languages, including Cyrillic and Greek, and offer a host of OpenType features.

FIGGINS SANS REGULAR

ABCDE
FGHIJK
LMNOP
QRSTU
VWXYZ
$12345€
£67890
abcdefg
ghijklmn
opqrstu
vwxyz?!

24 THE MODERN SUITE · SHINNTYPE

FIGGINS SANS REGULAR

6

The f

48

The formal

24

The formal qualities of

18/19

The formal qualities of a type face energize, facilitate and inf

14/16

The formal qualities of a typeface ener gize, facilitate and inform the typograp

12/15

The formal qualities of a typeface energize, facilitate and inform the typographic layout.

10/11

THE FORMAL qualities of a typeface energize, facilitate and inform the typographic layout. Skilled typographe rs will leverage the attributes of judiciously chosen fo

9/10

THE FORMAL qualities of a typeface energize, facilitate and inform the typographic layout. Skilled typographers will leve rage the attributes of judiciously chosen fonts to maximize

8/10

THE FORMAL qualities of a typeface energize, facilitate and inform the typographic layout. Skilled typographers will leverage the at tributes of judiciously chosen fonts to maximize the personality of

7/9

THE FORMAL qualities of a typeface energize, facilitate and inform the typo graphic layout. Skilled typographers will leverage the attributes of judiciously chosen fonts to maximize the personality of the page, thereby standing out from the crowd. The formal qualities of a typeface energize, facilitate and in

FIGGINS SANS EXTRA BOLD

ABCDE FGHIJK LMNOP QRSTU VWXYZ $12345€ £67890 abcdefg ghijklmn opqrstu vwxyz?!

FIGGINS SA

96

48

Th

24

The

18/19

The fo ypefac

14/16

The form energize

12/15

The forma gize, facili

10/11

THE FORMAL cilitate and i ed typograp

9/10

THE FORMAL q and inform th phers will lev

8/10

THE FORMAL qu inform the typ verage the att

7/9

THE FORMAL qua the typographic butes of judiciou page, thereby sta

617

Ty	**NB Grotesk**
Ca	**Sans Serif**
Ke	**Geometric**
Te	**Digital**
Da	**2008**
De	**Stefan Gandl**
Fo	**Neubau**
Co	**Germany**

Characteristics

Geometric construction	
Even stroke widths	
Even character widths	
No optical compensations	
No stroke adjustment at junctions	
C c S s e g	Angled terminals
G	Has spur
Q	Short, straight tail
R	Straight, angled leg
a	Double-storeyed, straight stem
f r t	Vertical terminals
i j	Square dots
t	Flat top-stroke, wide left arm

ABGMRS
abcefghij
koprstuy

Connections

DIN 1451	1931
T-Star	2008
Simplon	2011
NB International	2014

Availability

NB Grotesk is available from Neubau and resellers

Specimen

'Neubauism' poster. Neubau, Berlin, 2008 (1,000x570mm)

The work of design collective Neubau is characterized by its rigorous use of systematic design methods. Established by Stefan Gandl (1969–) in 2001, the Berlin studio operates across a wide range of disciplines and is well known for its balance between commissioned projects and an impressive body of self-initiated work. The studio first achieved international recognition with the publication of two books: an inventory of vector objects, *Neubau Welt*, in 2005, followed two years later by *Neubau Modul*, a comprehensive archive of textures and patterns.

In 2008, for 'Neubauism', a major retrospective exhibition of the studio's work held in Eindhoven, the Netherlands, Gandl developed the NB Grotesk group of typefaces. NB Grotesk is a geometric sans serif typeface constructed on a customized grid that allowed Gandl to systematically create a range of contours and weights following strict rules. He has used this geometric framework as the basis for a number of his type projects. Naming it 'the diamond grid' because of its appearance, he says: 'Whether you're producing a narrow or an extended version of a typeface, it's always perfect.'

NB Grotesk is the deliberate visual product of algorithmic processes. Once character skeletons have been constructed, the basic contours are imported into a type design program and developed by expanding strokes and progressively refining contours, spacing and details. Because NB Grotesk's appearance is dictated by the diamond grid, the possibility of any optical compensations or other individual adjustments is eliminated.

The result is a typeface that is completely monolinear and very regular in its proportions and spaces. Intentionally demonstrating its own construction method, NB Grotesk assimilates raw, mechanical geometries with a playfully naive quality. The family comprises six typefaces in six styles, including NB Grotesk-R, a rounded variant, and NB Grotesk Mono, a fixed-width version.

ABC
DEFGHI
JKL MU/

NEUBAUISM
CATALOGUE/POSTER
SPECIAL LIMITED EDITION
1000 COPIES

NEUBAUISM
STICHTING MU/NUR CODE: 656
ISBN
978–907 942 303 3

NEUBAUISM
AN EXHIBITION BY NEUBAU
(GANDL/GRÜNBERGER)
IN COOPERATION WITH MU

NEUBAUISM
EXHIBITION 050908–051008
MU, EMMASINGEL 20
5611 AZ EINDHOVEN, NL

NEUBAUISM
WORLD PREMIERE 050908/MU
INTRODUCTION
WIM CROUWEL

NEUBAUISM
CATALOGUE: 240 X 280 X 78 MM¹
POSTER: 570 X 1000 MM²
1) 4.35 KG, 2) 150 G/SQM

NEUBAUISM
CATALOGUE/POSTER
A SPECIAL LIMITED EDITION
OF 1000 COPIES

NEUBAUISM
STICHTING MU/NUR CODE: 656
ISBN
978–907 942 303 3

AU NEUBAU
50 ISM/050
51 908/051
OM 008 NL

Ty	**Mister K**	
Ca	**Script**	
Ke	**Casual, Connected**	
Te	**Digital**	
Da	**2008**	
De	**Julia Sysmäläinen**	
Fo	**FontFont**	
Co	**Germany**	

Characteristics

Several hundred ligatures, including two-, three- and four-letter sequences

Alternate glyphs for stroke connections at high, medium and low positions

Stylistic alternates for crosshatching, underlining, strikethrough, etc.

Dingbats collection

Abcdefghi Klmnopqr Stuvwxyz

Connections

FF Justlefthand	1990
P22 Cezanne	1996
Sigmund Freud	2013
Blog Script	2015

Availability

FF Mr K is available from FontFont and resellers

Specimen

Julia Sysmäläinen, *Too Long to Tweet*, Juliasys, Berlin, 2012 (150x105mm)

@Fontblog

#schneekugel

Es war im Sommer 1980. Ich wohnte zu dieser Zeit noch in meiner Heimatstadt im Taunus. An einem langen Wochenende besuchte ich meinen Freund Markus in Berlin. Er war Musiker und wurde zwei Jahre später mit seinem NDW-Hit „Ich will Spaß" bekannt. Zu jener Zeit studierte er noch an der FU.

Eines Morgens, als Markus zu seinen Vorlesungen gefahren war, schnappte ich mir sein Vélosolex, um Berlin zu erkunden. Das Velo war ein Fahrrad mit Hilfsmotor, ganz prima, um auch längere Strecken rasch zu überwinden, zum Beispiel die fast unbelebte Straße des 17. Juni.

Ich schaute mir die eingestürzte Kongresshalle an, anschließend den Reichstag und das Brandenburger Tor. Weiter zum Potsdamer Platz, der damals wie das Ende der Welt wirkte: eine Einöde, mit der bunt bemalten Mauer mittendurch. Touristen trafen sich hier an einem Andenken-Kiosk, der neben einer Art Gangway stand, mit deren Hilfe man einen Blick über die Mauer auf den Grenzstreifen werfen konnte.

Ich kaufte mir in dem Souvenir-Shop eine Schneekugel mit Berliner Sehenswürdigkeiten drin: Gedächtniskirche, Brandenburger Tor, Europa-Center und Schwangere Auster.

– 8 –

– 9 –

620

The manuscripts of Franz Kafka made such a profound impression on Finnish graphic designer Julia Sysmäläinen (1974–) that she decided to convert his distinctive handwriting into a typeface. For Sysmäläinen, a philologist, the analysis of manuscripts is invaluable since they trace a writer's emotions, ideas, decisions and revisions at their point of origin.

There is nothing new about handwriting types. Typography has its origins in script and can broadly be considered a form of mechanized handwriting for mass communication. The advent of personal computing in the late 1980s opened up unprecedented possibilities by closing the distance between users and technology. With direct access, many designers attempted to develop personal typefaces based on their own hands. Results were of limited success since handwriting has an infinite variety of expression whereas type is limited to a fixed range of forms.

The OpenType format, developed in the 1990s, overcame this problem by offering very large character sets and a wide range of programmatic functions. With OpenType characters can be automatically modified or substituted depending on their context. Sysmäläinen took advantage of this technology to transform Kafka's energetic handwriting into a series of typefaces that are almost indistinguishable from his original manuscripts. One of her primary tasks was to translate the writer's letters, with their considerable variations in shape, stroke and size, into a character set that would flow naturally.

In a connected script typeface letters must join seamlessly by means of bridging strokes that connect at low, medium or high positions. Individual characters were therefore drawn in alternative versions, providing all possible entry and exit points to allow realistic-looking links. To overcome the monotony of mechanical repetitions, hundreds of ligatures were added, each consisting of two or more characters linked in unique sequences. In addition, many alternative characters were included, also to avoid successions of repeating shapes and to imitate handwriting's variability. Using OpenType substitution features, particular strings of two, three or four characters were automatically converted into single ligatures according to their context.

The FF Mister K family was published in 2008 by FontFont in three variant styles, each extending to over 1,500 characters. Julia Sysmäläinen's fascination with Kafka continues as her project carries on growing. 'While Mister K is a font,' she says, 'it is also the visualization of a personality.'

Juli 1914

Kafka

Abend im Garten des „Askanischen Hofes". Gegessen Reis à la Traut-mannsdorf und einen Pfirsich. Ein Weintrinker beobachtet mich wie ich den kleinen unreifen Pfirsich mit dem Messer zu zerschneiden versuche. Es gelingt nicht. Aus Scham lasse ich unter den Blicken des Alten vom Pfirsich überhaupt ab und durchblättere 10mal die „fliegenden Blätter". Ich warte, ob er sich nicht doch abwenden wird.

Endlich nehme ich alle Kraft zusammen und beiße ihm zu Trotz in den ganz saftlosen teueren Pfirsich. In der Laube neben mir ein großer Herr, der sich um nichts kümmert, als um den Braten, den er sorgfältig aussucht und um den Wein im Eiskübel. Endlich zündet er sich eine große Zigarre an, ich beobachte ihn über meine „Fliegenden Blätter" hinweg.

– 42 –

– 43 –

Ty	**Nitti**
Ca	**Sans Serif**
Ke	**Grotesque, Monospaced**
Te	**Digital**
Da	**2008**
De	**Pieter van Rosmalen**
Fo	**Bold Monday**
Co	**Netherlands**

Characteristics

Unique individual character construction
to allow easy differentiation

Low stroke contrast

Even overall appearance

Large x-height

Open counterforms

Monospaced with wide spacing

ABGIMW
abcefg
ilprty

Connections

Courier	1955
Letter Gothic	1956
Normetica	1999
T-Star Mono	2002

Availability

Nitti is available from Bold Monday and
resellers

Specimen

Bold Monday type specimen. Bold
Monday, The Hague, 2010 (210x148mm)

Nitti

Designed by Pieter van Rosmalen

lowercase

a b c d e f g h i j k l m n o p q r s t u
w x y z á ă â ä à ā ą å ã æ ǽ ć č ç ĉ ď
ð é ě ĕ ê ë ė è ē ę ə ğ ĝ ġ ģ ħ ĥ ı í ï î
ì ī į ĩ ij ĵ ķ ĸ ĺ ľ ļ l· ł ń ň ņ ñ ŋ ó
ô ö ò ő ō ø ǿ õ œ ŕ ř ŗ ś š ş ŝ ş ß ŧ ť ţ
þ ú ŭ û ü ù ű ū ų ů ũ ẃ ŵ ẅ ẁ ý ŷ ÿ ỳ ź ž ż

uppercase

A B C D E F G H I J K L M N O P Q R S T U
W X Y Z Á Ă Â Ä À Ā Ą Å Ã Æ Ǽ Ć Č Ç Ĉ Ď
Đ É Ě Ĕ Ê Ë Ė È Ē Ę Ğ Ĝ Ġ Ħ Ĥ Í Ï Î Ì
Ī Į Ĩ U Ĵ Ķ Ĺ Ľ Ļ Ļ L· Ł Ń Ň Ņ Ñ Ŋ Ó Ő Ô Ö Ò
Ō Ø Õ Œ Ŕ Ř Ŗ Ś Š Ş Ŝ Ş Ŧ Ť Ţ Ţ Þ Ú Ŭ
Ù Ű Ū Ų Ů Ũ Ẃ Ŵ Ẅ Ẁ Ý Ŷ Ÿ Ỳ Ź Ž Ż

ligatures

fi fl

figures

0 0 1 2 3 4 5 6 7 8 9 ¹ ² ³ ½ ¼ ¾

miscellaneous

₡ € ƒ £ $ ¥ ¤ ₿ @ . , : ; … ' ' " " ‚ „
« » ¡ ! ¿ ? ‹ [{ | }] › § ¶ © ® ™ ª º
† ‡ # ′ ″ ° + ± - × ÷ / / = ≈ ≠ < > ≤ ≥ ◊
√ ∫ ∞ % ‰ \ ¦ _ · • - — ^ ~ ∂ μ Δ Π Σ Ω π
= = ⌘ ← ↑ → ↓ ↖ ↗ ↘ ↙

accents

´ ˘ ˇ ^ ¨ · ˙ ` ˝ ¸ ˛ ˆ ˜ ¯ ˚ ˜
, , ˒

Nitti

Nitti is a monospaced typeface in five weights designed by Pieter van Rosmalen (1969–) between 2007 and 2008. It is named, not without irony, after Frank 'The Enforcer' Nitti, one of Al Capone's henchmen, and is part of a growing collection of related grotesque-inspired typefaces that includes a proportional version – Nitti Grotesk – and two display versions.

Seit Paul an der Akademie abschloss klickt er jed en Montag Morgen dreimal die Maus bevor er sich a n die Arbeit macht - auf dass die Woche gut verla ufe. Elizabeth Taylor, Michael Jackson a Ghandi s a narodili v pondelok. Montag ist der Lieblingsta g von Lady Margaret Thatcher. La mayoría de los p erros fallecen los lunes. Segunda-Feira é o único dia da semana em que podes fumar num espaço públi co. Dass Montage stets vor Dienstagen liegen wurd e zwischenzeitlich bewiesen. In Australia, Monday is fourth day of the week to match the concept th at christmas is summer. Muchos feriados caen un l unes. Entre ellos se encuentran el Día del Trabaj ador, el Día de la Memoria, es Día del Presidente s el Día de Culumbus y el Día de los Veteranos. I n some countries it is believed that born on a Mo nday makes you gay or goodlooking. Paul et Pieter sont tous les deux nés un lundi. La mère de Piete r devait en fait accoucher un mardi mais elle pré férait les lundis. Todas as Segundas-Feiras os si nos da igreja tocam uma vez ao contrário do resto da semana em que tocam três vezes. Montag ist der vielversprendste Tag für die Wildgansjagd. Se par ares de fumar a uma Segunda-Feira, existem grande s hipóteses de que irás recomeçar a fumar na Quin ta-Feira. Il aura fallu seize lundis pour complét er le design de Nitti. Todas las fuentes mostrada s en este libro pueden bajarse gratis desde el si tio uno que otro lunes entre las 9 y las 17 hs. M ontags kommt alle 3,2 Sekunden ein Kind zur Welt. Det har bevisats att måndag alltid kommer före ti sdag. Chaque lundi, la cloche de l'église sonne u ne fois contrairement à trois pour les autres jou rs. "Monday" es el único día de la semana cuyo an agrama es "Dynamo". Sowohl Paul als auch Peter wu

Nitti is a dependable, legible alphabet that has many features in common with traditional typewriter faces like Courier (pp342–43) and Prestige Elite. It is familiar to many as part of the meticulously minimal interface of Information Architects' iA Writer software.

The design of Nitti's robust letter contours is informed by early sans serif types like Akzidenz-Grotesk (pp152–53). Originally an English innovation, these late nineteenth-century grotesques gained massive popularity in Europe and America, first as display types and subsequently in text. The humanistic origins and often idiosyncratic shapes of these designs lend them an amiability that is clearly evident in Nitti's outlines.

One of Nitti's key characteristics is its subtle stroke contrast, giving an even overall appearance in an alphabet of generous proportions. Descenders are short but ascenders are tall, and capitals are well balanced in relation, sitting below the ascender height. The character set is very unambiguous, with features designed for the sort of clarity and legibility that are typical of typewriter faces. All of the characters have a robust construction, such as lower case i, l and r, for example; and letters that can often be hard to distinguish, such as upper case I, lower case l and 1, are easily differentiated, as are O and 0.

ght

ormal

edium

old

ack

Replica

Characteristics

Angled bevels at all stroke junctions
C c S s e g Flat terminals
G Has spur
K k R V v Angled strokes end vertically
Q Straight, hooked tail
R Straight, angled leg
a Double-storeyed, straight stem
f r t Vertical terminals
i j Square dots
t Flat top-stroke

AGMQR
abcefghij
koprstuy

Connections

Helvetica	1957
Normetica	1999
Akkurat	2004
Lettera	2006

Availability

Replica is available from Lineto and resellers

Specimen

Replica type specimen. Norm, Zurich, 2008
(287x215mm)

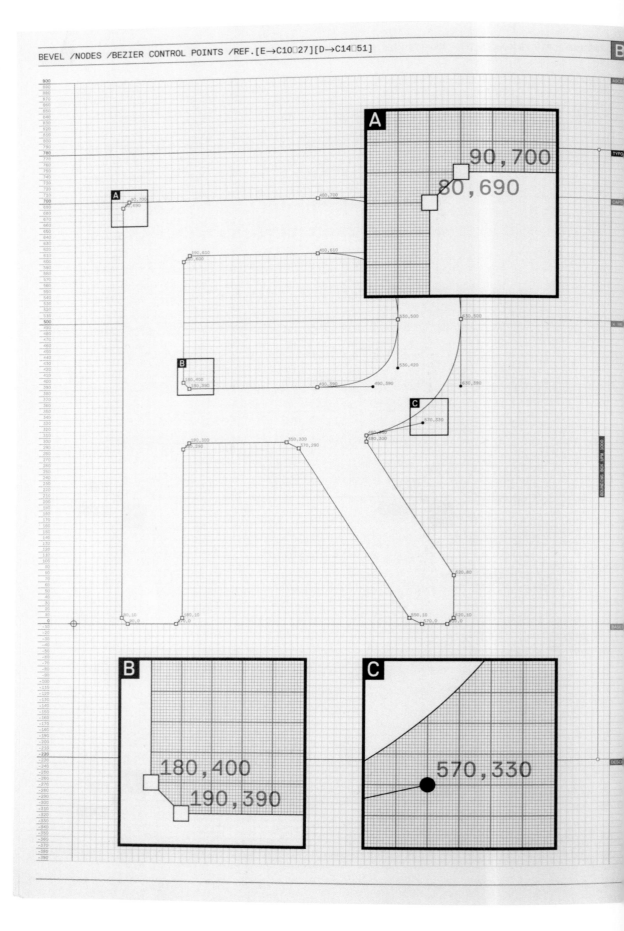

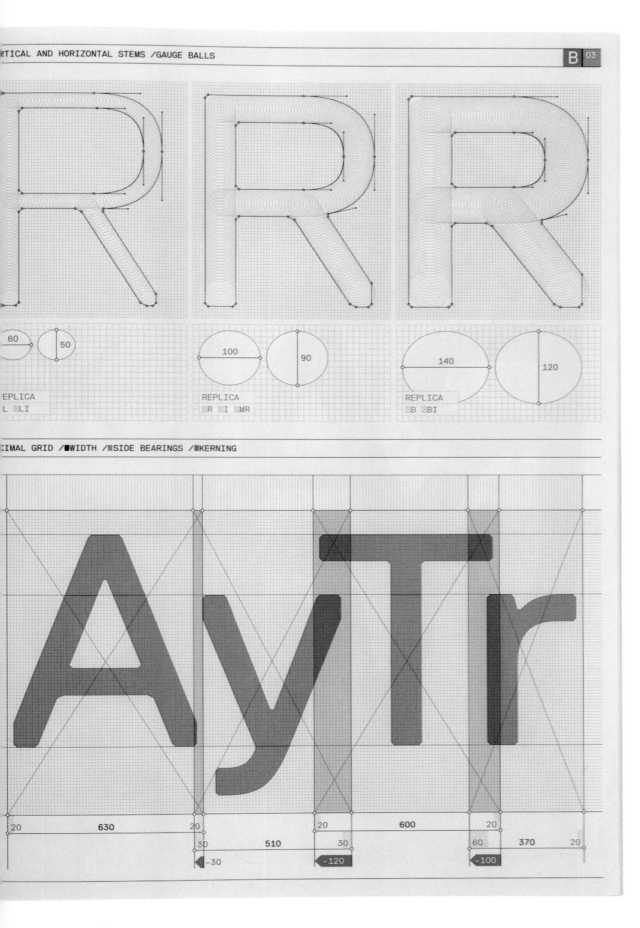

VERTICAL AND HORIZONTAL STEMS /GAUGE BALLS

B 03

60 50

REPLICA
L ▨LI

100 90

REPLICA
▨R ▨I ▨MR

140 120

REPLICA
▨B ▨BI

DECIMAL GRID /■WIDTH /▨SIDE BEARINGS /▨KERNING

20 630 20 20 600 20 20 370 20
30 510 30 60
-30 -120 -100

Replica is a sans serif created in 2008 by Dimitri Bruni (1970–) and Manuel Krebs (1970–) of Swiss design studio Norm. Bruni and Krebs have said that they 'tend to see freedom … as a hindrance in creative work', and they often predefine rules and conditions as the basis for their design projects, including typefaces. In the case of Replica the appearance of the letters is determined by a drastically reduced grid system.

One of the difficulties faced by anyone designing digital type is the limitation of PostScript technology in locating control points that can only fall on integers within a grid of 1,000 by 1,000 units. Most type designers use compensatory strategies to increase these limits at the production stage, but Bruni and Krebs took the opposite direction, reducing them instead by a factor of ten to a bounding box of only 100 by 100 cells. That meant far fewer possibilities to place nodes and control points for curves, a severe constraint that had an inevitable effect on the drawing of the letters. This might have resulted in a rigidly geometric outcome, but Bruni and Krebs used a number of techniques to overcome their self-imposed limits and realize a remarkably well-balanced typeface with a soft, low-contrast contour.

In order to achieve a coherent stroke construction all external stroke junctions in Replica are cut at angled bevels. Because, as a result, there are no sharp terminals, letters fit together very compactly. Internal stroke junctions are bevelled in the same way, creating a slightly swollen impression within counterforms. These two features became the main identifying traits of a typeface that followed the heritage of European twentieth-century grotesque models regardless of its geometric origins. Replica's supple appearance completely conceals the mathematical reductivism underlying the project.

After testing Replica by implementing it in a few independent design projects and subsequently making minor improvements, Norm published it in 2008 through the Lineto digital foundry in Light, Regular and Bold with corresponding italics for each weight. Achieving maximum effect with minimum means, Replica became one of the most successful typefaces of the decade.

Ty	**Scotch Modern**
Ca	**Serif**
Ke	**Modern**
Te	**Digital**
Da	**2008**
De	**Nick Shinn**
Fo	**Shinntype**
Co	**Canada**

Characteristics

Vertical stress
Thin strokes with high contrast
Capitals to ascender height
Most capitals have uniform width
Sharp, unbracketed serifs thicken at stems
M Narrow
Q Looped tail
R a t Tail turns upwards
a c f g j r y Ball terminals
g Double-storeyed with teardrop ear

GMQRS
abcefghij
orstya*efg*

Connections

Scotch Roman	1812
De Vinne	1890
Modern No. 20	1905
Figgins Sans	2008

Availability

The Modern Suite is available from
Shinntype and resellers

Specimen

The Modern Suite. Shinntype, Toronto,
2008 (210x100mm)

Scotch Modern is part of the Modern Suite, designed by Nick Shinn (1952–) for his Canadian type foundry, Shinntype, in 2008. The project is a revival of two contrasting types from the nineteenth century: the early sans serif of Vincent Figgins (pp122–23) and Scotch Roman (pp112–13). Both of these designs were created during the height of the Industrial Revolution in Great Britain, a period that Shinn regards as the authentic point of origin for the modern era.

Scotch Modern is based on a typeface probably cut by George Bruce that Shinn found in an 1873 book in the New York State Cabinet of Natural History. He believes that history has treated the Scotch style unjustly and that it was misjudged by advocates of both the Arts and Crafts movement and later modernists for having 'poor legibility and too much "sparkle" due to the contrast between the thin hairlines and the heavy verticals'. Shinn suggested that, as the predominant type style used in publications at a time when mass literacy arrived in the United States as well as the United Kingdom, it cannot be said to be unreadable.

In his view, the core problem was not in the original Scotch form but in its poor adaptation to hot metal, photocomposition and digital technologies. In order to achieve an authentic interpretation, Shinn anticipated that a programmatic digitization would be unsatisfactory, as the algorithmic reduction of letterforms to an idealized state would only lead to a neutered result. Instead, he drew the original version of the typeface directly on the computer, without using any photo enlargements, tracings or scans.

His revival, preserving the vertical stress, high contrast and bracketed hairline serifs of the nineteenth-century type, is a combination of rational features, such as even character widths, and visual extravagances, such as bulging curves, furled ball terminals and erect tails. Scotch Modern comprises three size-specific versions, each with corresponding small capitals. The core design, Scotch Modern, is optimized for text settings with an x-height and capital height that align with Figgins Sans Bold. Scotch Micro is intended for use at small sizes, and Scotch Display maximizes contrast in headlines.

The Modern Suite was designed as an integrated family with matching character sets and proportions across the range of Figgins Sans (pp616–17) and Scotch Modern fonts, allowing them to work together harmoniously. Both families support Latin and non-Latin languages, including Cyrillic and Greek, and offer a host of OpenType features.

SCOTCH MODERN REGULAR

ABCDE
FGHIJK
LMNOP
QRSTU
VWXYZ
$12345€
£67890
abcdefg
ghijklmn
opqrstu
vwxyz?!

64 THE MODERN SUITE · SHINNTYPE

The f

The forma

The formal qualities

/19
The formal qualities of a t
ypeface energize, facilitate

/16
The formal qualities of a typeface
energize, facilitate and inform the

/15
The formal qualities of a typeface energ
ize, facilitate and inform the typographi

/11
THE FORMAL qualities of a typeface energize, fa
cilitate and inform the typographic layout. Skill
ed typographers will leverage the attributes of

10
THE FORMAL qualities of a typeface energize, facilita
te and inform the typographic layout. Skilled typogr
aphers will leverage the attributes of judiciously cho

10
THE FORMAL qualities of a typeface energize, facilitate and
inform the typographic layout. Skilled typographers will
leverage the attributes of judiciously chosen fonts to maxi

9
THE FORMAL qualities of a typeface energize, facilitate and inform the
typographic layout. Skilled typographers will leverage the attributes
of judiciously chosen fonts to maximize the personality of the page,
thereby standing out from the crowd. The formal qualities of a type

ABCDE
FGHIJK
LMNOP
QRSTU
VWXYZ
$12345€
£67890
abcdeffg
hijklmn
opqrstu
vwxyz?!

96
T

48
Th

24
The f

18/19
The for
ypeface

14/16
The form
energize,

12/15
The forma
ize, facilite

10/11
THE FORMA
facilitate an
Skilled typog

9/10
THE FORMAL
ate and infor
raphers will l

8/10
THE FORMAL q
inform the typo
verage the attri

7/9
THE FORMAL qua
the typographic l
butes of judicious
page, thereby sta

Ty	**Le Sonia Monochrome**
Ca	**Sans Serif**
Ke	**Geometric**
Te	**Digital**
Da	**2008**
De	**Pierre di Sciullo**
Fo	**Pierre di Sciullo**
Co	**France**

Characteristics

Most capitals have single, bracketed
top serifs
a f s Angled terminals
b d Bowl shorter than x-height
i j Large, round dot, short stem
l p r Single bracketed top serif
n Triangular junction
p q Bowl shorter than baseline

ABGRSW
abcefgij
lmnpsty

Connections

Peignot	1937
Banco	1951
Antique Olive	1962
Le Maximum	1993

Availability

Not available

Specimen

Le Sonia type specimen PDF. Pierre
di Sciullo, Paris, 2015 (230x160mm)

le sonia

quand?
maintenant!
pourquoi?
parce que!
où? ici!
comment?
comme ça!

abcdefghijklmn
opqrstuvwxyz,.!?

le sonia monochrome

l'exposition
peintures
œuvres
graphiques
Films
installations
vidéos

abcdefghijklmnopqrstuvwxyz
ABCDEFGHIJKLMNOPQRSTUVWXYZ
0123456789& àâéèêûîôùüï !?;.,

Since 1985 the French graphic designer Pierre di Sciullo (1961–) has published a number of projects that explore connections between text and language. He has said that he is 'interested in ... reading with all its different aspects and implications'. As a part of his practice Di Sciullo has developed several type families, but only one of these, FF Minimum, has been made available commercially (pp522–23). He is concerned with type not as a product but as a tool for his own explorations of the relationships between image and text. In his projects the visible word operates in a playful exchange between reading, looking and comprehending.

Di Sciullo began work on Le Sonia in 2003, naming it in reference to the colourful shapes in the compositions of the Russian-French artist Sonia Delaunay, which are reflected in the layers of his lettering. Le Sonia started as a digital drawing in three layers, based respectively on the circle, square and triangle, the archetypal forms widely used in geometric alphabets of the early twentieth century by Bayer, Albers and others. Di Sciullo soon found applications for Le Sonia in a series of two- and three-dimensional constructions, some resulting in large coloured-glass sculptures. In 2008 he designed a version of Le Sonia as a PostScript typeface, incorporating other ideas from a series of loosely related designs that have evolved over many years from the hand-painted lettering he often uses for slogans on social poster campaigns. These type styles begin with Le Maximum (1993) and are seen at their most dignified resolution in inscriptional alphabets for the Notre Dame de Lorette World War I memorial (2014).

The letterforms of Le Sonia Monochrome and its antecedents follow a unique construction logic that at first suggests the naive quality of children's handwriting but which is remarkable for its unique inversion of typographic conventions. Letters appear heavy at the top, particularly in the bold weight, with a horizontal stress and an assortment of stroke junctions and terminal styles. Serifs are used only sporadically and are deeply bracketed, creating a thickening effect. Nevertheless, the typeface is remarkably harmonious, with strong geometric contrasts and a rhythmic pattern of thick and thin strokes.

Evoking 1960s shop signage, product packaging and comics, Le Sonia speaks of a uniquely French vernacular heritage. It is a descendant of the French typographic tradition found in the seminal designs of Roger Excoffon's Banco and Antique Olive (pp328–29, 362–63), as well as A. M. Cassandre's work, in particular his final, unpublished typeface, Cassandre.

Ty	**Museo**
Ca	**Slab Serif**
Ke	**Geometric**
Te	**Digital**
Da	**2009**
De	**Jos Buivenga**
Fo	**exljbris Font Foundry**
Co	**Netherlands**

Characteristics

Large x-height
Small capitals
Round, open contours
Curved semi serifs
M Splayed
a Double-storeyed, curve at foot
f t Narrow with vertical terminals
g Single-storeyed
t Flat top-stroke
y Curved tail

AKMRSU
abcefghij
koprstuy

Connections

Memphis	1929
Lubalin Graph	1974
Glypha	1977
Archer	2003

Availability

Museo is available from exljbris and resellers

Specimen

Museo type specimen PDF. exljbris Font Foundry, Arnhem, 2015 (195x200mm)

MUSEO
museo

This is MUSEO, a new for
family designed by exljbri
Five (5) fine, nice weight
ranging from 100 to 90
Don't forget to try it ou

TROTZKOPF

Quadrillion

MUSEO

typógraphy!

LEGION

The inspiration for Dutch type designer Jos Buivenga's Museo family was his affection for the letter U. He said that in a daydream he 'saw the top of both stems bent into semi-slab serifs. From this principle I worked out the rest…'

Buivenga (1965–) began working on Museo in 2008 for his exljbris foundry, intending to make a typeface in capitals for use in headlines. He wanted to keep the shapes as simple as possible, emphasizing circular arcs, and because this resulted in an attractive letter structure that looked like what he called 'some piece of bent metal wire', he kept the stroke contrast as low as possible. After a few months' work Buivenga decided that the typeface would benefit from the addition of a lower case and he adjusted the proportions and spacing accordingly.

The result is an unusually amiable slab semi serif family in five weights. Its distinctive identity is the product of original details, especially the semi serifs, which resemble bent pipework, and its rounded, open contours. The Museo family is designed to be very capable, with extensive language support and a wide range of features including case-sensitive forms, ligatures, contextual alternates, fractions and alternative numeral sets.

Having generated a great deal of early interest in Museo by publishing regular updates about its development on his blog, Buivenga launched the typeface through an online sales channel, offering three of its five styles completely free. This risky but generous strategy paid off and Museo became a meteoric bestseller. It instantly found success in brand communications, particularly for web and mobile media. When its sans serif companion was launched some months later, again with the core weights offered at no cost, it achieved equally spectacular results.

Ty	**Theinhardt**
Ca	**Sans Serif**
Ke	**Grotesque**
Te	**Digital**
Da	**2009**
De	**François Rappo**
Fo	**Optimo**
Co	**Switzerland**

Characteristics

C c S s e g	Angled terminals
G	Has spur
J	Narrow
Q	Short, angled tail
R	Straight, angled leg
a	Double-storeyed, curve at foot
f r t	Vertical terminals
i j	Square dots
t	Angled top-stroke
y	Flat, hooked tail

AGJMQR
abcefghij
koprstuy

Connections

Akzidenz-Grotesk	c1898
Venus	1907
Edel-Grotesk	c1914
Figgins Sans	2008

Availability

Theinhardt is available from Optimo and resellers

Specimen

Theinhardt type specimen PDF. Optimo, Geneva, 2015 (297x210mm)

Theinhardt

Theinhardt Bold / Italic
110 pt

Aa *Aa*

Theinhardt Heavy / Italic
110 pt

Aa *Aa*

Theinhardt Black / Italic
110 pt

Aa *Aa*

Theinhardt Family
18 Styles

Theinhardt Hairline
Theinhardt Hairline Italic
Theinhardt Ultra Light
Theinhardt Ultra Light Italic
Theinhardt Thin
Theinhardt Thin Italic
Theinhardt Light
Theinhardt Light Italic
Theinhardt Regular
Theinhardt Regular Italic
Theinhardt Medium
Theinhardt Medium Italic
Theinhardt Bold
Theinhardt Bold Italic
Theinhardt Heavy
Theinhardt Heavy Italic
Theinhardt Black
Theinhardt Black Italic

1.00

www.opt

2009

einhardt

einhardt Bold
pt

The car was a boxy late model Ford

einhardt Bold
pt

The car was a boxy late model Ford sedan, white over black, innocuous bordering on invisible, and very fast. It

einhardt Regular
pt

The car was a boxy late model Ford sedan, white over black, innocuous bordering on invisible, and very fast. It had been a sheriff's vehicle originally bought at an auction in Tennessee, and further modified for speed. Perry and I listened to the big engine idle,

einhardt Regular
pt

The car was a boxy late model Ford sedan, white over black, innocuous bordering on invisible, and very fast. It had been a sheriff's vehicle originally bought at an auction in Tennessee, and further modified for speed. Perry and I listened to the big engine idle, checked the dual scoops on the hood. I had not seen one of those on the road since high school. "You like the car?" Perry asked. "It's all right," I said, my eyes ahead. "I've never been much of a Ford man." Perry shifted in his bucket, "You know something about cars? For city cruising, it'll do." I spent my childhood in Riverdale, New Jersey, thirty miles north from long, narrow Manhattan Island, which sits in the bay, among other islands, outcroppings, flatlands,

The Swiss type designer and educator François Rappo (1955–) created Theinhardt, a sans serif, for the Optimo foundry in 2009. It is named after Ferdinand Theinhardt (1820–1906), a German type designer, punch cutter and Orientalist who pioneered the grotesque style that is the progenitor of contemporary sans serif designs such as Helvetica and Univers.

Around 1880 Theinhardt cut four weights of a typeface named Royal Grotesk for use in the publications of the Prussian Academy of Sciences in Berlin. Until that time the sans serif had been considered an industrial form to be used largely for signage, but Theinhardt's groundbreaking work helped make it acceptable in a wider range of typographic environments. In 1885 Theinhardt sold his type foundry to another concern, which was subsequently acquired by H. Berthold AG in 1908. During the process Berthold are said to have absorbed Royal Grotesk into their extensive Akzidenz-Grotesk family (pp152–53), eliminating its orginal name in the process. The refinement of Royal Grotesk's well-balanced letters made a substantial contribution to the subsequent success of Akzidenz-Grotesk, one of the most popular and influential sans serif type families ever published.

The Theinhardt family, shown here, is not a straightforward revival of Akzidenz-Grotesk. It is based on Rappo's detailed research into type specimens from the late nineteenth century and studies of a number of sans serif letterforms including both the original Royal Grotesk and Akzidenz-Grotesk. Theinhardt combines the best features of these designs in an optimized type family organized in nine weights, each with corresponding italics. Released in OpenType format, every weight includes an extended Latin character set, tabular and proportional figures, contextual and stylistic alternates and case-sensitive forms.

00

Brandon Grotesque

Ty	**Brandon Grotesque**
Ca	**Sans Serif**
Ke	**Geometric**
Te	**Digital**
Da	**2010**
De	**Hannes von Döhren**
Fo	**HvD Fonts**
Co	**Germany**

Characteristics

Small rounded corners at stroke terminals
Large capitals
Small x-height
Tall ascenders and descenders
C c O o Optically perfect circles
C c S s e Angled terminals
G No spur
M Splayed
S Visually balanced upper and lower arcs
a g Double- and single-storeyed alternates
i j Round dots
y Straight tail

AGMQR
abcdefghij
orstuyaefg

Connections

Erbar-Grotesk	1922
Avenir	1988
FF Scala Sans	1993
LL Circular	2013

Availability

Brandon Grotesque is available from
HvD Fonts and resellers

Specimen

Brandon Grotesque type specimen.
HvD Fonts, Berlin, 2010 (210x148mm)

---

aabcdefghijklm
nopqrstuvwxyz
ABCDEFGHIJKLM
NOPQRSTUVWXYZ
0123456789

---

aabcdefgghijklm
nopqrstuvwxyz
ABCDEFGHIJKLM
NOPQRSTUVWXYZ
0123456789

In the development of the Brandon Grotesque family German type designer Hannes von Döhren (1979–) drew inspiration from the era-defining geometric sans serif typefaces produced in the early years of the twentieth century.

He was fascinated with magazines from the 1920s and 1930s where printing methods could often make contours look slightly rounded – physical imperfections that are rarely seen in the pin-sharp digital print output of today. These flaws, he felt, 'radiated an intense aura and tactile qualities'. Intending to create a typeface with a similar impression – 'a geometric sans serif, but still with a certain softness' –

he decided to give Brandon slightly rounded corners so that it would convey some warmth in spite of its clean, geometric lines.

Contemporary digital typefaces are often built from common stems onto which weight is extrapolated progressively but Von Döhren wanted to maintain Brandon's vitality by avoiding such a programmatic approach. Instead he followed the techniques of the designers of the 1920s and 1930s, basing each one of Brandon's styles on a common parentage but drawing it individually, with its own aesthetic logic. In this way he could give each style unique details.

Brandon Grotesque is a comprehensive family in six weights and matching italics. It features restrained letterforms with a small x-height and contours softened by rounded terminals. In 2013 Von Döhren extended the family with Brandon Text. Completely compatible with Brandon Grotesque but featuring a taller x-height, it is optimized for long texts at smaller sizes.

Within one month of its release Brandon Grotesque reached the top of the bestseller lists and became the most popular new typeface of 2010. 'The success of Brandon Grotesque was overwhelming', Von Döhren commented. 'I can say that it was a changing point in my life.'

BRANDON GROTESQUE & BRANDON TEXT – CHARACTERISTICS   10/11

01 Slightly rounded corners – In printed matter from the 1920s and 30s letters are never as sharp and clean as they look today. By rounding the corners, the Brandon families imitate this warm and slightly blurry look, giving a smooth, printed feeling to every letter.

02 True Italics – Brandon's Italics are slightly narrower and have a more human appeal.

03 Alternate letter »a« – There are two basic forms of the letter »a«: one derived from the cursive »a«, which has its source in handwriting. The other basic form derives from the oldstyle »a«, which consists of two strokes. The cursive »a« is called monocameral, the oldstyle »a« bicameral. Brandon Grotesque is equipped with both styles, selectable through the stylistic sets.

04 Circle »O« – In each weight the archticture of the letter »O« is based on a circle. This effect supports the geometric feeling of the family.

05 Different x-height – Brandon Grotesque has a small x-height lending the family a touch of class. The x-height of Brandon Text is higher to make it usable in small sizes.

GROTESQUE   TEXT

06 Character vs. Grayscale – Each font is optimised for its purpose: Brandon Grotesque for recognition value; Brandon Text for rhythmic performance in longer texts.

GROTESQUE   TEXT

07 Ligatures – Both Brandons contain various special ligatures like fb, fi, fk, ffi, ffj etc. to avoid collision.

08 Tabular Figures – Beside the "normal" lining figures, the fonts contain special numbers with an equal width for tables or invoices.

09 Special feature in the Black weight – The counters in the black weight are circles.

10 Sharp angles – Letters such as »A«, »V«, »W« or »Z« have sharp angles, giving the type a clean, geometric look.

Ty	**Eames Century Modern**
Ca	**Serif**
Ke	**Modern, Clarendon**
Te	**Digital**
Da	**2010**
De	**Erik van Blokland**
Fo	**House Industries**
Co	**USA**

Characteristics

Vertical stress
Sharply defined stroke contrast
Wide body
Large x-height
Short ascenders and descenders
Heavy, bracketed slab serifs
Q Sweeping, curved tail
R a t Tail turns upwards
a c f g r y Prominent ball terminals
g Double-storeyed, teardrop ear

GMQRS
abcefghij
orsty*aefg*

Connections

Century Schoolbook	1918
Egizio	1955
Belizio	1989
Farao	1998

Availability

Eames Century Modern is available from House Industries and resellers

Specimen

Eames Century Modern type specimen. House Industries, Yorklyn, 2010 (210x115mm)

The American type foundry House Industries is well known not only for the outstanding quality of its typefaces but also for the entertaining ways in which they are presented. One of the objectives of every House Industries project, they say, is to 'make a noise outside the realm of type design'. Since the company's inception its designers have drawn inspiration from American popular culture, often framing their typeface projects in playful stories that are developed further through related design pieces such as posters, clothing, toys, furniture, ceramics and decorations.

Eames Century Modern is an extensive type family, published in 2010 along with an even more extensive range of merchandise. It captures the optimism of mid-century American modernism in a celebration of the legacy of Charles and Ray Eames, the couple well known for their groundbreaking contributions to architecture, interior design, product design and the graphic arts. One of the few things they did not do was design a typeface, although they used type in original ways, often drawing inspiration from nineteenth-century circus posters, wood types and stencil lettering.

Working in collaboration with the Eames Office, House Industries set out to visualize what an Eames typeface might have looked like. The result, Eames Century Modern, was drawn by Dutch designer Erik van Blokland (1967–) working in collaboration with the House team. Eames Century Modern's forms are influenced by Clarendon (pp132–33) and Century Schoolbook (pp206–207), although it is not a straight revival of either. Planned as an extensive family with multiple thematic variations, Eames is founded on a core group of functional styles that are applicable in a wide range of typographic environments. Also featuring many playful elements, the family strikes a balance between quirkiness and easy readability. It has eight weights, from a graceful thin to an almost solid black, with sturdy reading weights in the middle, all with corresponding italics. These are supported by expert typographic features such as small capitals, lining and non-lining figures, and fractions. In addition, Eames Century Modern offers many opportunities for eye-catching display applications. It includes a stencil variant in the heaviest weight, three gargantuan woodcut-inspired numeral sets, a delicate set of figures and a huge choice of pictorial ornaments and frames.

Erik van Blokland's interpretation of nineteenth-century styles is both practical and witty, sensitively expressing what Charles Eames once called the 'uncommon beauty of common things'.

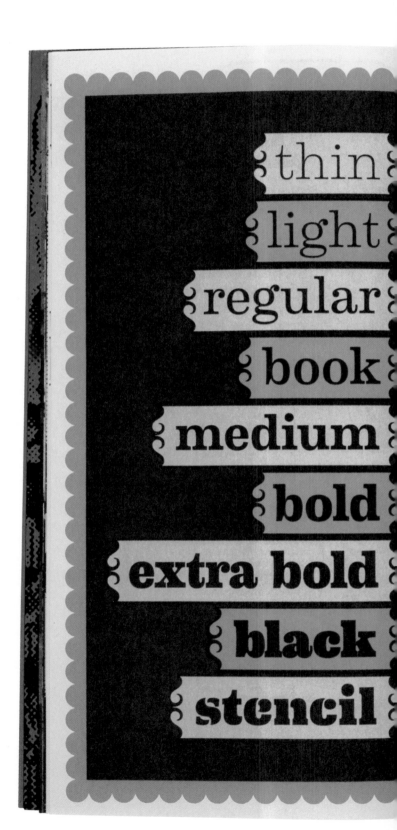

thin

light

regular

book

medium

bold

extra bold

black

www.houseindustries.com
ORDER ONLINE OR CALL 800-888-4390 OR 302-234-2356

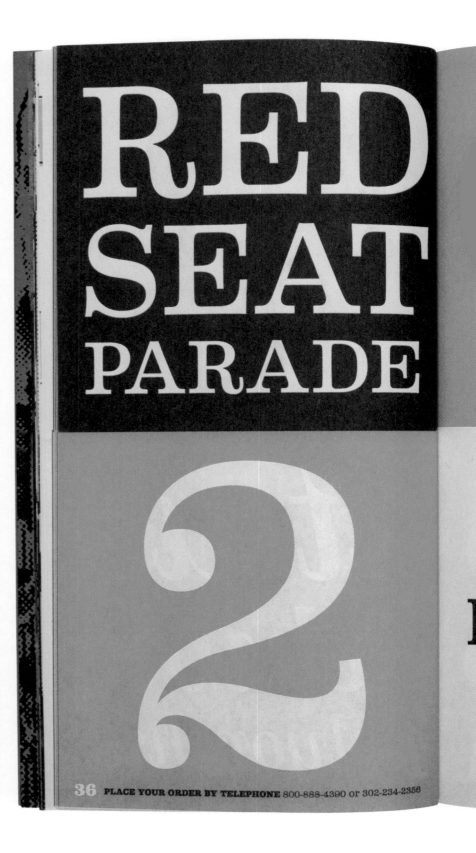

RED
SEAT
PARADE

2

a
k

PLACE YOUR ORDER BY TELEPHONE 800-888-4390 or 302-234-2356

637

Lÿno

		Characteristics	
Ty	**Lÿno**	Four related geometric alphabets	
Ca	**Sans Serif**	All capitals	
Ke	**Geometric, Capitals**	One weight only	
Te	**Digital**		
Da	**2010**		
De	**Karl Nawrot and Radim Peško**		
Fo	**RP Digital Type Foundry**		
Co	**Netherlands**		

Connections	
The Alphabet	2001
Sol	2008
Dess	2012
Zigzag	2012

Availability
Lÿno is available from RP Digital Type Foundry

Specimen
Newer Alphabets, supplement to *Graphic* 16, winter 2010. Propaganda, Seoul (210x210mm)

ULYS(SES JA), SPAN(LEY KUBRICK), VALT (DISHEY) AND JEAN (QAP) ARE STILL THE CHILDREN OF MATRICES, BUT THEIR SUPPORTS ARE NOW MULTIPLIED INTO NEAR INVISIBILITY.

Asked to provide a definition for 'good design' in a 2011 interview, the French graphic artist Karl Nawrot (1976–) suggested that it should give the impression of 'a piece stuck between past and future'. The Lÿno typeface family was designed by Nawrot in collaboration with Radim Peško (1976–) from 2009. It first appeared in a brochure called *Newer Alphabets* as a supplement to issue 16 of *Graphic*, an international design journal published in South Korea in 2010. The typeface was originally named Lÿon after Nawrot's hometown. He claims that the

umlaut on the ÿ was added partly as a reference to the diacritic in Peško's name, and partly to make it more playful.

There are four typefaces in the Lÿno family: Jean, named after the artist Jean Arp; Stan, after movie director Stanley Kubrick; Ulys, after *Ulysses 31*, a Franco-Japanese cartoon series; and Walt, after Walt Disney. The formal attributes of each member of this fraternity are conceived as loose characterizations of the work of the individuals after whom they have been named, and the different family members

are intended to be able to mix with each other interchangeably.

Nawrot and Peško's *Newer Alphabets* brochure is a parodic response to Wim Crouwel's seminal 1967 *New Alphabet* publication (pp376–77), although the two are not conflicting; rather, they are linked through a shared exploration of the contemporary condition of typographic communication. However, whereas Crouwel's project speculates on new possibilities at the dawn of digital technology, the Lÿno types comment on

the unregulated liberties of their own production processes in the twenty-first century. Through mischievous typologies of form Lÿno's designs abstract basic typographic shapes to the limits of their function as vehicles of language. They treat the alphabet not as a finite code but as an imaginative location for realizing potential meanings. As signs Lÿno's letters are variegated, unstable and disruptive, and their spirit, as James Langdon writes in the *Newer Alphabets* brochure, is 'to resist normative tendencies and to reject the idea of definitive form'.

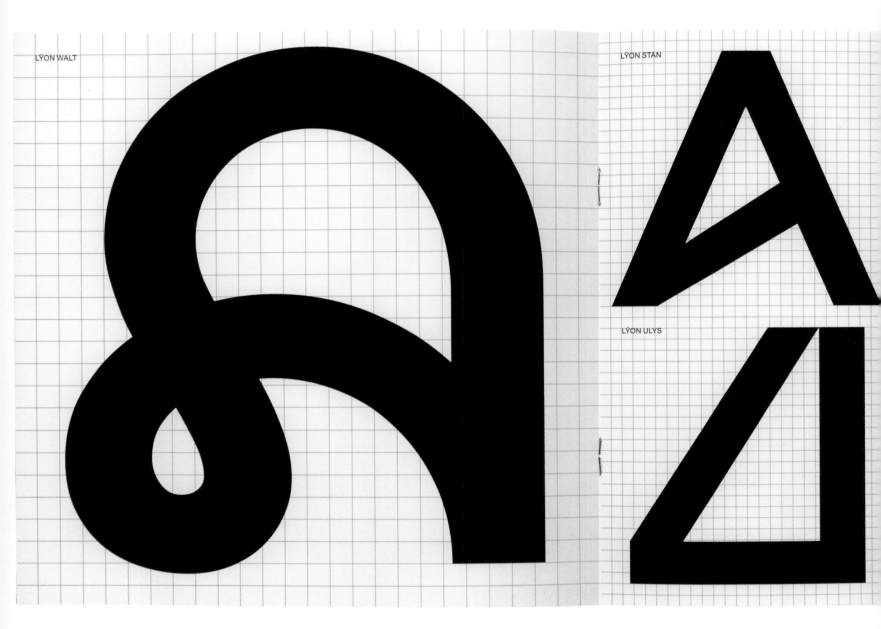

Ty	**Prismaset**
Ca	**Sans Serif**
Ke	**Geometric**
Te	**Digital**
Da	**2010**
De	**James Goggin**
Fo	**Lineto**
Co	**Switzerland**

Characteristics

Based on Prisma

Modular, geometric character construction

Drawn in ten alternate multilinear versions

Connections

Zeppelin	1929
Prisma	1931
Boymans	2003
Euclid Flex	2012

Availability

Not available

Specimen

Graphic 16, winter 2010. Propaganda, Seoul (300x230mm)

206				206			
Typeface	Prismaset		(Designed with Rafael	서체	프리스마세트		(라파엘 코흐, 마우로
Category	Display		Koch, Mauro Paolozzi	분류	디스플레이		파올로치, 알렉스 리치와
Year	2010		and Alex Rich)	연도	2010		공동 작업)
Designer	James Goggin	Foundry	Lineto	디자이너	제임스 고긴	유통	리네토
			www.lineto.com				www.lineto.com

B.84

207			(Designed with Rafael Koch, Mauro Paolozzi and Alex Rich)	207 서체 분류 연도 디자이너	프리스마세트 디스플레이 2010 제임스 고긴		(라파엘 코흐, 마우로 파올로치, 알렉스 리치와 공동 작업)
Typeface	Prismaset						
Category	Display					유통	리네토 www.lineto.com
Year	2010						
Designer	James Goggin	Foundry	Lineto www.lineto.com				

B.84

ABCDEFGHIJKLMNO
PQRSTUVWXYZ
abcdefghijklmnop
qrstuvwxyz?!&£$•
0123456789(:)±∓.,»«¶

Prismaset Five

Prismaset, by the Australian-British designer James Goggin (1975–), is based on Prisma (pp276–77), a multilinear geometric typeface designed in 1931 by Rudolf Koch. Goggin's new design is not a routine reconstruction of its antecedent but a total reappraisal, reverse-engineered from the earlier typeface into a set of component typefaces that have been assembled into an extensive family of variant forms.

Goggin started work on the project in 2004 and its development progressed over a period of six years, with contributions at different stages from Laurenz Brunner, Alex Rich, Rafael Koch and Mauro Paolozzi. Goggin began by drawing a solid version of Koch's original multilinear forms. This, he decided, resulted in 'a pleasantly odd set of characters', some of them geometric and some with unexpectedly eccentric contours. The solid black alphabet had a resemblance to Koch's Kabel (pp232–33) and Zeppelin typefaces but, interestingly, its appearance seemed to evade any definite historical time frame, uniting characteristics from both the art deco and Bauhaus eras while also borrowing from standard German Grotesk letterforms. Encouraged, Goggin proceeded to digitize the solid and parallel line versions, creating complete character sets.

Because the original Prisma was in capitals only, the project started to develop more speculative historical dimensions when complete sets of lower case characters were added, with contour shapes and details informed by research into other geometric designs by Koch. Once the full set of multilinear base forms had been constructed, selected stem parts could be removed progressively to generate a systematic range of linear and solid variants of different weights.

Prismaset extrapolates the mathematical logic of Rudolf Koch's original alphabet dramatically, exploiting the limits of its formal potentials while simultaneously retaining its humane and charming features. In describing the relationship of Prismaset to its historical source of inspiration, Goggin explained: 'with Prisma, although there is an overarching geometry, Rudolf Koch also had some great, even odd, humanist anomalies in the design. We made sure to include such idiosyncracies in Prismaset, to break the geometry where possible, based on his original hand.'

Ty	**Template Woodcut**
Ca	**Sans Serif**
Ke	**Geometric**
Te	**Digital / Letterpress**
Da	**2010**
De	**David Keshavjee and Julien Tavelli**
Fo	**Optimo**
Co	**Switzerland**

Characteristics

Geometric elements
CNC-routed profile
Variable construction

Connections

Futura	1927
Kabel	1927
Julien	2011
Euclid	2012

Availability

Programme is available from Optimo and resellers

Specimen

Typeface as Program. ECAL, Lausanne, 2010 (235x175mm)

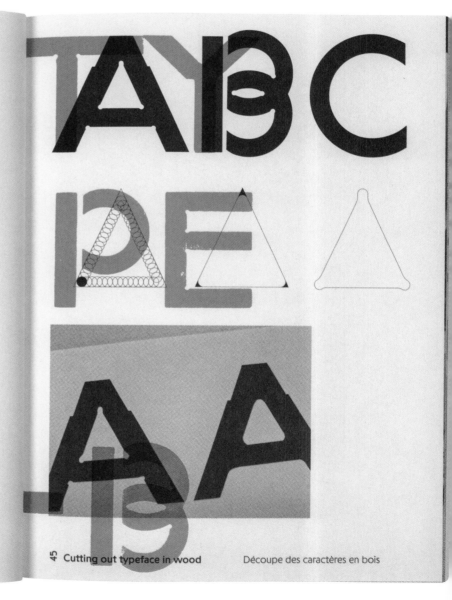

44 Book medium 24 pt

Book light 24 pt

45 Cutting out typeface in wood

Découpe des caractères en bois

Type design, like many technologically driven disciplines, has undergone more fundamental transformations in the past century than ever before. Template Woodcut, by graphic designers Julien Tavelli (1984–) and David Keshavjee (1985–), is a reflection on these changes.

Their project was an investigation into typographic form-giving that explored the codependence of letters with the tools and processes used to generate them: the record of a playful exchange between new and old, ordered and random, digital and analogue elements.

Tavelli and Keshavjee have worked as Maximage Société Suisse since 2008, operating in the fields of editorial, type and branding design. While studying at ECAL (École cantonale d'art de Lausanne) in 2007 they began to incorporate systematic processes in their work and developed the Template Woodcut project in successive stages, moving from digital to analogue and back again.

Initially Tavelli and Keshavjee wrote their own software in order to explore the possibilities and constraints of computer tools. Using the RoboFab programming library they developed scripts to automatically generate sets of typographic glyphs. Modifications to instructions dictating general conditions such as weight, width or curvature would instantly be reflected in changes to all of the characters.

In developing the code a number of output glitches occurred due to errors. Rather than correct these, Tavelli and Keshavjee retained them as traces of the process – organic and spontaneous deposits in an otherwise highly ordered environment. Having generated several digital alphabets, they selected some of them to cut a complete set of wood type characters with a computer numerical controlled (CNC) router, building the mechanical restrictions of the machine into the final shapes of the letters. At the next stage a page-layout tool was developed to automatically generate poster designs based on encoded input. Finally, a set of posters was printed by hand, attempting to visually match the digital templates using traditional letterpress techniques. The result is a unique collision of the perfect and the imperfect: of the purity of code and the visceral impact of ink on paper.

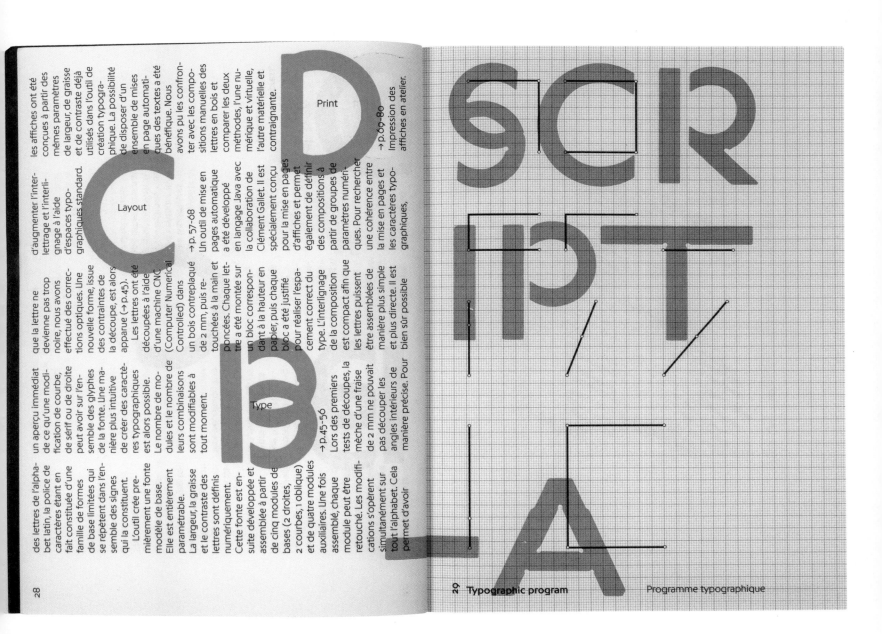

28

29 Typographic program   Programme typographique

Ty **LL Brown**
Ca **Sans Serif**
Ke **Geometric**
Te **Digital**
Da **2011**
De **Aurèle Sack**
Fo **Lineto**
Co **Switzerland**

Characteristics

Large capitals
Tall x-height
C c O o Optically perfect circles
C c S s e Angled terminals
G No spur
M High vertex
R Wide, straight leg
a g Single-storeyed
i j Round dots
t Flat top
y Straight tail

ABGJMR
abcefghij
koprstuy

Connections

Futura	1927
Brandon Grotesque	2010
Euclid	2012
LL Circular	2013

Availability

LL Brown is available from Lineto and resellers

Specimen

Graphic 16, winter 2010. Propaganda, Seoul (300x230mm)

54					54			
Typeface	LL Brown		Designer	Aurele Sack	서체	LL 브라운	디자이너	오렐 사크
Category	Sans Serif		Foundry	Lineto	분류	산세리프	유통	리네토
Year	2010			www.lineto.com	연도	2010		www.lineto.com

B.26

Make your mark on society, not in society

Former NYC Mayor Ed Koch

55		Designer	Aurele Sack		55		디자이너	오렐 사크
Typeface	LL Brown	Foundry	Lineto		서체	LL 브라운	유통	리네토
Category	Sans Serif		www.lineto.com		분류	산세리프		www.lineto.com
Year	2010				연도	2010		

B.26

abcdefghijklmnopqrstuv
wxyzafiœċđǧöťůỳ
ABCDEFGHIJKLMNOPQRST
UVWXYZÆÇÊŪŴŽ
1234567890¡¿{[(.,:;)]}?!&#

LL Brown Regular

abcdefghijklmnopqrstuv
wxyzafiœċđǧöťůỳ
ABCDEFGHIJKLMNOPQRST
UVWXYZÆÇÊŪŴŽ
1234567890¡¿{[(.,:;)]}?!&#

LL Brown Regular Italic

abcdefghijklmnopqrstuv
wxyzafiœċđǧöťůỳ
ABCDEFGHIJKLMNOPQRST
UVWXYZÆÇÊŪŴŽ
1234567890¡¿{[(.,:;)]}?!&#

LL Brown Regular Backslanted

Like Euclid Flex (pp656–57), LL Brown exemplifies a prevalent trend in twenty-first-century European type design – the paradoxical attempt to infuse geometric letter construction with the warmth and legibility of humanist characteristics.

LL Brown started as a collaboration between designers Aurèle Sack, Urs Lehni and Lex Trüb in 2006 and was developed intermittently by Sack over the next five years. Its construction follows in the tradition of European sans serif types from the early twentieth century. Sack has specifically cited Edward Johnston's seminal 1916 Railway Type (pp202–203) and Arno Drescher's Super-Grotesk from 1930 as major influences on his work, although LL Brown is not in any way a straightforward digital revival of its predecessors. Using them more for inspiration than for guidance he developed LL Brown as a contemporary font with carefully nuanced geometries that also reflect more mathematical typographic antecedents such as Erbar (pp224–25) and Futura (pp230–31).

LL Brown is an open, monoline sans serif with comparatively short ascenders and descenders on a large body. It was released by Lineto in 2011 as a family of four weights: thin, light, regular and bold, all with corresponding italics. Each weight is also available in a highly eccentric backslanted version, in which letters are inclined towards the left, inverting the italic tradition.

Perhaps because its letterforms evoke memories of school textbooks, settings in LL Brown suggest honesty, authenticity and openness. It has become one of the most fashionable types of the new millennium and has proven reliable both in headlines and text.

Ty	**Julien**
Ca	**Sans Serif**
Ke	**Geometric**
Te	**Digital**
Da	**2011**
De	**Peter Bil'ak**
Fo	**Typotheque**
Co	**Netherlands**

Characteristics

Unicase character construction

Geometric design evokes early modernist letterforms

Multiple alternates generated automatically

Two weights: light and dark

Three styles: round, square and mixed

Connections

Kombinations-Schrift	1923
Universal Type	1925
Beowolf	1989
Woodkit	2014

Availability

Julien is available from Typotheque and resellers

Specimen

Julien type specimen PDF. Typotheque, The Hague, 2011 (260x185mm)

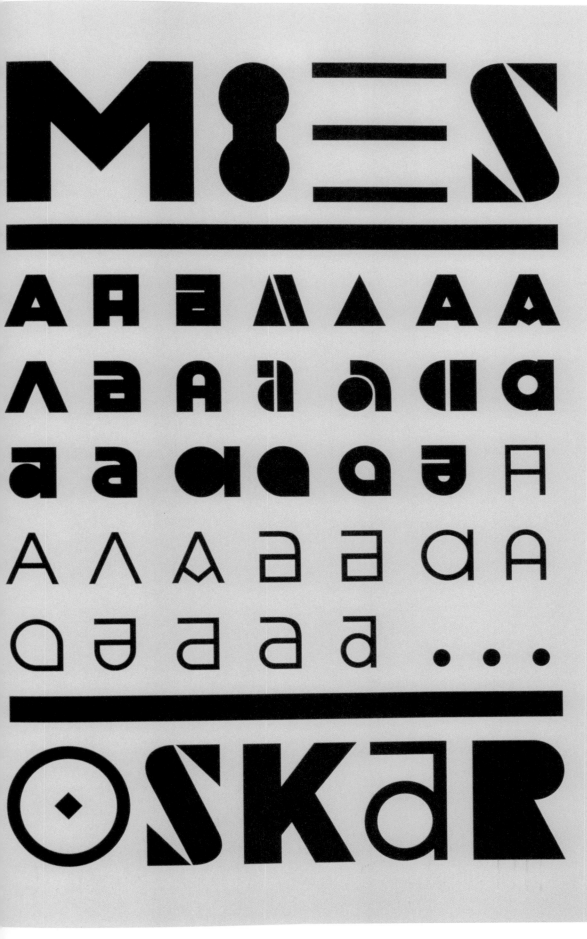

Julien is a display typeface designed by Peter Bil'ak (1973–) for the Typotheque foundry. Using simple geometric forms Bil'ak's typeface pays irreverent homage to the miscellaneous early twentieth-century avant-garde movements that he admires, such as Dada, Constructivism, Futurism and the Bauhaus.

Julien references the disparate nature of these movements, acknowledging the eccentric variety of their typographic legacy. For Bil'ak, the appeal of early avant-garde typography is in its expressive use of lettering, often made specifically for individual projects due to a lack of readily available display typefaces at the time. The diversity of forms that resulted deviated somewhat from the ideas expressed by leading typographic exponents of the day, such as László Moholy-Nagy, Herbert Bayer and Jan Tschichold, who championed utilitarian design, the use of radically simplified geometries and an engagement with industrial processes.

Julien is a unicase alphabet. It contains an assortment of upper and lower case letterforms based on elementary geometries and includes multiple variants of each letter. It has only two extreme weights – one very light, one very dark – each drawn in three different styles: round, square and mixed. The style names indicate the prevalent geometry of each set so that the visual character of settings can be planned accordingly.

Usually the products of simple cut-and-paste processes, geometric typefaces can end up lifelessly mechanical. Similarly, the translation of true hand lettering into digital type can give monotonous results that lose the fluctuating human energy of the original. Julien's design responds to both of these issues, outputting numerous alternate letter shapes to achieve word sequences that are highly unpredictable. Using OpenType substitutions, Julien's variants are triggered automatically by means of an embedded randomization script, giving settings in the typeface an elastic, spontaneous rhythm.

Julien might be thought of as a novelty but underpinning its design is a considered meditation on our relationships with media and mechanical processes. It is an experiment in the use of programmatic methods to exceed the limits of analogue production. At the same time, it is an outstanding tribute to what has been called the 'old, weird avant-garde'.

Ty	**KLF Kade**
Ca	**Sans Serif**
Ke	**Geometric**
Te	**Digital**
Da	**2011**
De	**David Quay**
Fo	**Kade Letter Fabriek**
Co	**Netherlands**

Characteristics

Straight lines and curves meet at junctions
Weight increases internally
A Wide at top with flat horizontal
I Wide, with flat top and bottom strokes
K k X x Horizontal bridging strokes
M High vertex
AA IJ Dutch-language digraphs

AGIKMR
abcefghij
koprstxy

Connections

Curtain	2008
Ark Stencil	2010
KLF Haven Collectie	2010
Foundry Fabriek	2011

Availability

KLF Kade is available from Kade Letter
Fabriek and resellers

Specimen

KLF Kade type specimen PDF. Kade Letter
Fabriek, Amsterdam, 2015 (275x200mm)

KLF Kade is a display sans serif family drawn in 2011 by the English type designer David Quay (1948–). Its origins lie in the everyday lettering found on small boats and old wooden sailing vessels in the harbours and canals of Amsterdam and Rotterdam. These historical letterforms were usually cast in metal and welded onto the sides of the ships, though some were hand-painted or cut from adhesive plastic. Quay collected photographs of them for almost a decade, intending to develop a type that would commemorate Dutch nautical traditions in the industrial age. He wanted, he said, 'to make a typeface that for me reflected the character of my host country: pragmatic, direct, and honest'.

KLF Kade evolved over time in stages, drawing on diverse ideas and reference points. Quay sought to fit letters together based on underlying structures that were as disparate as the vernacular shapes from which they took inspiration. KLF Kade's letter contours reflect the rugged industrial techniques with which their original sources were formed in steel. Frequently, subtleties in curvature were compromised due to the tools used and because engineers were in control of them. This resulted in letters where straight lines and curves might intersect at unexpected junctions. Quay adapted these features to provide his design with an unmistakably lively character.

All KLF Kade weights sit within roughly the same body widths. As the characters become bolder, they are weighted towards their interiors, making bolder versions appear to be more solidly industrial. Quay also paid close attention to the relationship of letter combinations to their native language; he considered, for example, the double letters AA and the digraph IJ, which appear often in Dutch. Following tradition, the A is wide at the top, and many characters, such as the K and the X, feature horizontal bridging strokes. Kade's italics have a particularly eccentric personality. Rather than simply giving the upright characters a slant, Quay rotated the roman a few degrees and then adjusted the horizontals, following a method sometimes employed in the Dutch shipyards.

KLF Kade is published in six styles, featuring four alternative sets of numbers, as well as small capitals and ligatures. An exceptionally innovative typeface for one that was based on such deep but humble roots, it is the mature, articulate work of a master craftsman.

e **Text:** Boeien

epboot *Kajuit*

urhut **Lijn** Zee

der ***Roer*** **Vloed**

troom Kikker

roef **Eb** Anker

ger Rivier **Sluis**

en Kaai Anker

ipper ***Lichter***

aal ***Helmstok***

eenswerf *Dok*

Korpus

Ty	**Korpus**
Ca	**Serif**
Ke	**Transitional**
Te	**Digital**
Da	**2011**
De	**Michael Mischler and Nik Thoenen**
Fo	**Binnenland**
Co	**Switzerland**

Characteristics

Imbalance between weight of thinner strokes and serifs

Triangular bracketing of serifs to stems

C E F G M S T Z Protruding terminal serifs

J Q a f j Ink-trap apertures

a d m n p r u Horizontal ink-fill swellings at stroke junctions

CEMQR
abcdefghij
orstuya*efg*

Connections

Wilson	1768
Georgia	1996
Farao	1998
Serapion	1998

Availability

Korpus is available from Binnenland and resellers

Specimen

Korpus type specimen. Binnenland, Bern, 2011 (310x225mm)

12 — Schrift / Font

Western Latin Fontset, Korpus Regular — 72 pt

Korpus Regular —

1 1¼ 2 ¾ 3 | – × ! " # $ % &

< = > ? @ A B C D E F G

V W X Y Z [\ ] ^ _ abc

w x y z { | } ~ Ä Å Ç É Ñ Ö

ô ò ö õ ø ú û ù ü † ° ¢ £ § • ß

Σ Π π ∫ ª º Ω æ ø ¿ ¡ ¬ √ f

" ' " ‹ › ‚ „ ◊ Ÿ ÿ / € ‡ ÷ ‰

fi ffi fl ffl ı ´ ^ ` ¨ ˜ – ˙ ˚

ĐđŁłŠšÝýÞþŽž ½

*+,-./0123456789:;

KLMNOPQRSTU

ghijklmnopqrstuv

âàäåãçéêèëíîìïñó

©™ ≠ÆØ∞+<>¥µ∂

‹»…ÁÃÕŒœ——

ÊÈËÍÎÌÏÓOÔÒÚÛÙ

0123456789

Korpus, designed by Michael Mischler (1973–) and Nik Thoenen (1963–) between 2009 and 2011, is the result of their exploration of errors in type production processes. Working with specimen sheets and proofs of several early twentieth-century typefaces, Mischler and Thoenen observed a number of faults, including distortions, physical flaws and mistakes in the process of transmitting letter designs from one medium to another, from metal to ink to paper. In the process of cutting, casting, setting and proofing characters, they could become distorted, often as a result of uneven pressure. Observations of these errors led to the development of the Korpus typeface. Whereas most digital reconstructions of physical letters aim to smooth out or eliminate such faults, Mischler and Thoenen sought to deliberately amplify them.

Creating the overall impression that it has been overinked, Korpus has relatively thick strokes with little contrast between verticals and horizontals. The design is characterized by a series of imbalances between the sizes of serifs and strokes, due to a tapered serif construction that makes them thicker at junctions than the strokes themselves. This gives a blocky density that replicates the pressure of the proofing press. Likewise, the open jaws of characters such as C and E protrude as if squeezed excessively, and several characters, such as J, Q and f, show slight angular kinks in terminal strokes that appear to be the result of similar faults. Apparent occurrences of ink-fill are also distributed throughout the typeface, particularly at junctions between strokes that have been flattened, such as the ears of the m, n and p.

Somewhat reminiscent of eighteenth-century types such as Wilson (pp86–87), Korpus exploits the connection between the forms that letters take and the processes of their reproduction. The catalogue of small disasters from which it is built has been resolved in a typeface where what might have looked incorrect, ugly and fake is instead a soft, tactile and harmonious alphabet.

Ty	**Nokia Pure**
Ca	**Sans Serif**
Ke	**Humanist**
Te	**Digital**
Da	**2011**
De	**Bruno Maag**
Fo	**Dalton Maag**
Co	**UK**

Characteristics

C c S s e g Angled terminals and large apertures
G No spur
Q Short, curved tail
R Straight, angled leg
a Double-storeyed, straight stem
f r t Vertical terminals
i j Round dots
t Angled top-stroke
y Straight tail

ACGMQR abcefghij koprstuy

Connections

Transport	1959
Frutiger	1976
Myriad	1992
Segoe UI	2004

Availability

Not available

Specimen

Twenty-Six Characters: An Alphabetical Book about Nokia Pure. Die Gestalten Verlag, Berlin, 2011 (275x210mm)

Ff Family

A unique and ownable typeface can bring valuable consistency to a brand's tone of voice. A familiar font is reassuring for customers, helping build trust in both the company and its message. Imagine, then, how unnerving it would be if that voice started to switch without warning between the belligerent bellow of a tabloid headline and the muted whisper of a wildlife documentary.

The moral of the tale, of course, is not to mix up your weights too much. Opt for Regular as a rule, then apply Light or Bold only where necessary to enhance your design. Use Ultra Light and Extra Bold carefully to achieve expressiveness and tension.

Nokia Pure Light
Truly refined, Light brings supermodel finesse to type. Apply with similar poise for an elegant effect.

Nokia Pure Regular
A real all rounder. Loyal, reliable and genuine, it should always be your number one choice.

Nokia Pure Bold
Confident, assertive and guaranteed to make a statement. But use with caution; nobody likes an attention-seeker.

Nokia Pure Ultra Light
It's barely a whisper, yet Ultra Light quietness carries real authority. Be to show it some respect.

Nokia Pure Extra Bold
A booming voice that's virtually op Better to save it for your grand cre

Nokia Pure Headline Ultra Light
abcdefghijklmnopqrstuvwxyz
ABCDEFGHIJKLMNOPQRSTUVWXYZ
1234567890

Nokia Pure Headline Light
abcdefghijklmnopqrstuvwxyz
ABCDEFGHIJKLMNOPQRSTUVWXYZ
1234567890

Nokia Pure Headline Regular
abcdefghijklmnopqrstuvwxyz
ABCDEFGHIJKLMNOPQRSTUVWXYZ
1234567890

Nokia Pure Headline Bold
abcdefghijklmnopqrstuvwxyz
ABCDEFGHIJKLMNOPQRSTUVWXYZ
1234567890

Nokia Pure Headline Extra Bold
abcdefghijklmnopqrstuvwxyz
ABCDEFGHIJKLMNOPQRSTUVWXYZ
1234567890

Nokia Pure Text

Nokia Pure Text Light
abcdefghijklmnopqrstuvwxyz
ABCDEFGHIJKLMNOPQRSTUVWXYZ
1234567890

Nokia Pure Text Regular
abcdefghijklmnopqrstuvwxyz
ABCDEFGHIJKLMNOPQRSTUVWXYZ
1234567890

Nokia Pure Text Bold
abcdefghijklmnopqrstuvwxyz
ABCDEFGHIJKLMNOPQRSTUVW
XYZ 1234567890

40 41

For many years, phone manufacturers used an assortment of fonts in their products' interfaces to implement different writing systems for users in different language groups, usually licensing existing typefaces without much concern for their coordination. In 2010, in an increasingly competitive market, Nokia renewed its brand by implementing a new visual identity across all of its products and communications. The touchstone of the project was Nokia Pure, a groundbreaking custom typeface designed by Dalton Maag, directed by Swiss designer Bruno Maag (1962–), to reflect the simplicity, clarity and functionality of Nokia's Finnish design heritage.

For Nokia Pure the Dalton Maag team drew 19 different script systems for use in over 150 countries in phone interfaces, marketing communications and product branding. The typeface united the company's brand through typography alone, creating consistency and personality in a design that is characterized by its geniality and quiet authority. Maag started by creating a Latin sans serif, conceived as a functional user-interface font, with print a secondary consideration. Much like Frutiger (pp428–29), Nokia Pure's overall appearance is demure and humanist, with curvaceous letterforms that are spaced openly to prevent characters merging on screen at small sizes. The result is unambiguously easy to read, both on paper and screen.

The team subsequently developed types for an additional 18 non-Latin writing systems. Dalton Maag had experience with extensive multilingual projects, but Nokia Pure challenged the designers to tackle scripts they had not worked with before and which had never been integrated into a coherent multilingual system. The key to achieving a harmonious group of families was the control of the rhythm of the contours, allowing five alphabets – Latin, Greek, Cyrillic, Arabic and Hebrew – and several scripts, including Devanagari, Thai and Chinese, to follow a coherent visual logic.

Until Microsoft's purchase of Nokia's phone business in 2013 the Nokia Pure typeface was implemented extensively in a wide range of media, from print to web and low-resolution mobile displays, achieving Nokia's mission to communicate in a human voice, and in everyone's own language.

Ty	**Balkan**
Ca	**Sans Serif**
Ke	**Grotesque, Capitals**
Te	**Digital**
Da	**2012**
De	**Marija Juza and Nikola Djurek**
Fo	**Typonine**
Co	**Croatia**

Characteristics

Condensed sans serif construction
Capitals only
Four alternate styles
Aligns Latin and Cyrillic characters to head or foot of type body
Standard or stencil variants

ABCDEFGHIJKLM
АБЦДЕФГХИJKЛМ
NOPQRSTUVWXYZ
НОПQРСТУВWXYЗ

Connections

Penny Farthing	1974
Kufan	2012
Hangulatin	2013
Nihon	2014

Availability

Balkan is available from Typonine and resellers

Specimen

Balkan type specimen. Typonine, Zabok, 2012 (240x155mm)

Marija Juza (1985–) and Nikola Djurek (1976–) of the Croatian foundry Typonine have used type design to unite the Balkans – or at least its two contrasting writing systems. Balkan is a display typeface that places Latin and Cyrillic scripts simultaneously within lines of text. It is based on the study of a phenomenon known as *Sprachbund*, a term that describes a group of languages whose sounds, vocabularies or syntactic features have merged as the result of geographical and social proximity.

Juza and Djurek were interested in the dual literacy of Slavic communities, many of whom use both Latin and Cyrillic alphabets in their everyday communications. Historically, the region's different scripts have been used as symbols of cultural, ethnic, religious and political identities, preserved largely for the sake of separation in a part of the world that has seen much hostility between ethnic groups. However, the concurrent growth of local languages over time has resulted in them sharing properties based on common interests. Today, some regional languages in the Western Balkans are so similar that they can be thought of as related dialects.

Balkan is a type family intended to decode, demystify and depoliticize Latin and Cyrillic. Though it is a typeface in the usual sense, it can also be used to translate to and from Croatian Latin and Serbian Cyrillic and can thus be used as an educational software to reconcile discrete scripts. Like all OpenType typefaces, Balkan is also extendable to include the alphabets of other language groups, such as Russian, Macedonian and Bulgarian.

Balkan Sans and Balkan Sans Stencil consist of four styles. Taking advantage of OpenType technology, three of them provide different arrangements of upper case characters in Latin and lower case characters in Cyrillic, and one style features upper case Cyrillic and lower case Latin characters. In this way, it harmonizes the two scripts equably, within a common framework, in order to contribute to tolerance, understanding and communication.

БАЛКАНЦИ
BALKANCI
ПРОИЗВОД
PROIZVOD
ВИШЕ ПОВИЈЕСТИ
VIŠE POVIJESTI
НЕГО ШТО ЈЕ МОГУ
NEGO ŠTO JE MOGU
ПОДНИЈЕТИ
PODNIJETI

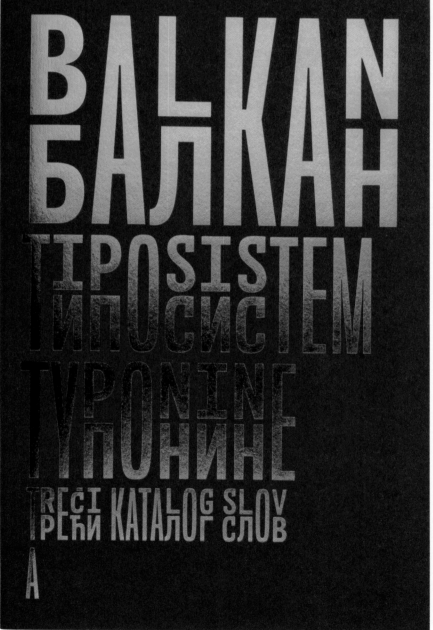

Ty	**Euclid Flex**
Ca	**Sans Serif**
Ke	**Geometric**
Te	**Digital**
Da	**2012**
De	**Swiss Typefaces**
Fo	**Swiss Typefaces**
Co	**Switzerland**

Characteristics

Geometric construction
Multiple alternate character sets
Ligatures
Text and display variants

ABGMQR
abcefghij
koprstuy

Connections

Futura	1927
Avenir	1988
LL Brown	2011
Programme	2013

Availability

Euclid Flex is available from Swiss Typefaces

Specimen

Euclid Flex type specimen PDF. Swiss Typefaces, Territet, 2014 (230x140mm)

Digital type designers have responded to the opportunities offered by OpenType technology in a variety of ways. Some have exploited its huge, adaptable character database and responsive features to facilitate multilingual communications through the design of typefaces containing different writing systems (pp588–89). Others have used it to transcend the mechanical constraints of cold type in order to mimic the infinite variety of handwritten forms (pp610–11). Swiss Typefaces, in their Euclid Flex design, have developed it as a tool for decision-making in design – both their own and that of the end user.

The Euclid project began in 2009 as a commission for a custom typeface for Les Urbaines, an annual arts festival in Lausanne, Switzerland. To create the visual identity for the event using type alone Swiss Typefaces constructed a geometric font in capitals only, based on squares, circles and triangles. Satisfied with the direction of this prototype, they proceeded to implement Euclid as an extensive OpenType family, starting with basic geometric alphabets in five weights and expanding these into a multitude of alternate forms.

Each individual Euclid Flex typeface contains a standard character set and in addition features more than 500 alternate geometric glyphs and ligatures. Because the OpenType format has been expertly manipulated, diverse ranges of alternate characters can automatically be activated, using functions that include alternate stylistic sets, standard ligatures, discretionary ligatures, proportional old-style figures, tabular lining figures, fractions, numerators and denominators. In addition to its OpenType functions, Euclid Flex includes a host of additional special characters and supports more than 80 languages.

Euclid Flex exemplifies a significant trend in post-millennial typography from Europe: the seemingly impossible intention to inject humanist characteristics into geometric type construction. This quest has its beginnings in the differences between Gill Sans (pp238–39) and Futura (pp230–31), and in the subtle circularity of Avenir (pp466–67). In Euclid Flex, animated by responsive technology, the geometric sans serif has become mathematically exact and wildly anarchic at the same time.

Euclid Flex Ultralight
Euclid Flex Ultralight Italic
Euclid Flex Light
Euclid Flex Light Italic
Euclid Flex Regular
Euclid Flex Regular Italic
Euclid Flex Medium
Euclid Flex Medium Italic
Euclid Flex Bold
Euclid Flex Bold Italic

ABCDEFGHIJKLMNOPQRSTUVWXYZ
abcdefghijklmnopqrstuvwxyz

ABCDEFGHIJKLMNOPQRSTUVWXYZ
abcdefghijklmnopqrstuvwxyz

ÀÁÂÃÄÅĂĀĄÆĆĆĊĈĎĐÈÉËĚĒĘĖĞĜ
ĦĤÌÍĨĬĬĪĮĬĴĶĹĽĿLŁŇÑŊŃŇṆÒÓÔÕÖØŎŐŌ
OŒÙÚÛÜŬŪŮŲŮŨŲŘŔŖŚŠŞŜŦŤȚŴŴŴ
ÝŶŸŻŹŽÞÀÁÂÃÄÅĂĀĄÆÇĆĆĈĊĎĐÒÉÊË
ĒĘĖĞĜĠĠĦĤÌÍĨĬĬĨĮĬĴĶĹĽĿLŁŃÑŊŃŇṆÒÓÔÕÖŐŐ
œŕŗṛśšşŝșťŧțṭùúûüŭūůŲůũŲŵŵẁýÿŷỳÿźžżþ

!?¿¡»*'#‰‱δ(/),--—_.:;…·@
[\]^{|}~¦§ªº«»‹›''""„,,°¶•†‡◊
+<=>¬±µ×÷−≤≥≠≈∂∏√∑∫∞ΔΩπ

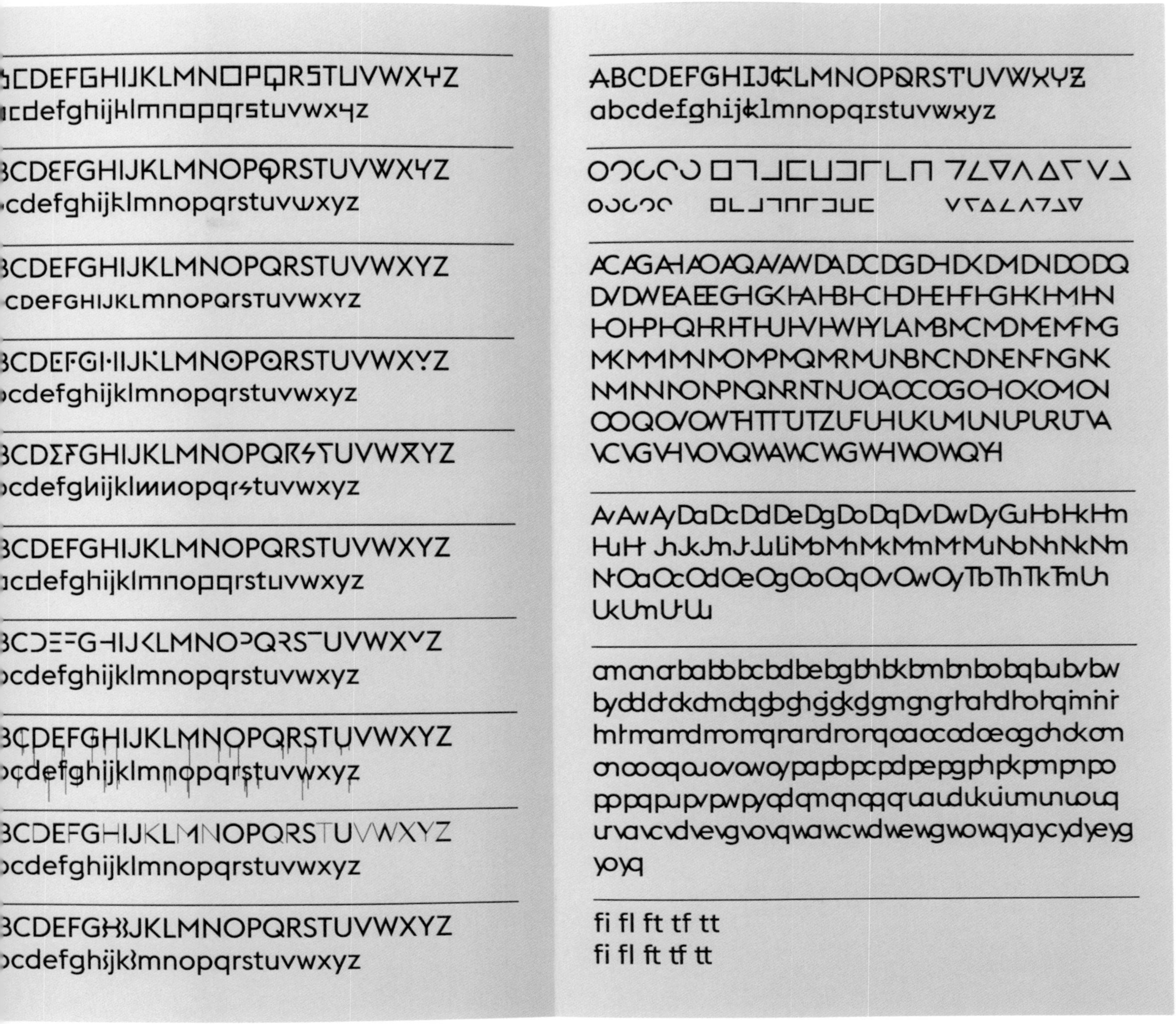

BCDEFGHIJKLMNOPQRSTUVWXYZ
cdefghijklmnopqrstuvwxyz

BCDEFGHIJKLMNOPQRSTUVWXYZ
cdefghijklmnopqrstuvwxyz

BCDEFGHIJKLMNOPQRSTUVWXYZ
cdefghijklmnopqrstuvwxyz

BCDEFGHIIJKLMNOPQRSTUVWXYZ
cdefghijklmnopqrstuvwxyz

BCDΣFGHIJKLMNOPQRSTUVWXYZ
cdefghijklmnopqrstuvwxyz

BCDEFGHIJKLMNOPQRSTUVWXYZ
cdefghijklmnopqrstuvwxyz

BCDΞFGHIJKLMNOPQRSTUVWXYZ
cdefghijklmnopqrstuvwxyz

BCDEFGHIJKLMNOPQRSTUVWXYZ
cdefghijklmnopqrstuvwxyz

BCDEFGHIJKLMNOPQRSTUVWXYZ
cdefghijklmnopqrstuvwxyz

BCDEFGHIJKLMNOPQRSTUVWXYZ
cdefghijklmnopqrstuvwxyz

ABCDEFGHIJKLMNOPQRSTUVWXYZ
abcdefghijklmnopqrstuvwxyz

OƆƆƆ ꓩ ᒪ ᒥ ᒪᔕ 7ᒪ∇∆ᐁ∇⅃
oᴐᴐᴐꞓ ᒪ⅃ᖙᒼᗡᒻᑕ ᐁ⅃∆⅃∧⅃∇

ACAGAHAOAQAVAWDADCDGDHDKDMDNDODQ
DVDWEAEEGHGKHAHBHCHDHEHFHGHKHMHN
HOHPHQHRHTHUHVHWHYLAMBMCMDMEMFMG
MKMMMNMOMPMQMRMUNBNCNDNENFNGNK
NMNNNONPNQNRNTNUOAOCOGOHOKOMON
OOQOVOWHTTTUTZFUHUKUMUNUPURUTVA
VCVGVHVOVQWAWCWGWHWOWQY

AvAwAyDaDcDdDeDgDoDqDvDwDyGuHbHkHm
HuHIJhJkJmJtJuLiMbMhMkMmMtMuNbNhNkNm
NtOaOcOdOeOgOoOqOvOwOyTbThTkTnUh
UkUmUtWu

amanarbabbbcbdbebgbhbkbmbnbobqbubvbw
bydddtdkdmdqgbghgjgkglgngngthahdhohqiminir
htmamdmomqrardrorqoaocodoeogohokom
onooqoioyowoypapbpcpdpepgphpkpmpnpo
ppqpupvpwpyqdqmqnqqquaudkuiumunuouq
urvavcvdvevgvovqwawcwdwewgwowqyaycydyeyg
yoyq

fi fl ft tf tt
fi fl ft tf tt

Marian

Ty	**Marian**
Ca	**Multiple**
Ke	**Multiple, Hairline**
Te	**Digital**
Da	**2012**
De	**Paul Barnes**
Fo	**Commercial Type**
Co	**UK**

Characteristics

Character construction based on ten historical types

Hairline, monolinear strokes throughout

Connections

Garamond's Roman	c1538
Baskerville	1757
Bodoni	1788
Scotch Roman	1812

Availability

Marian is available from Commercial Type

Specimen

Specimens of Typefaces by Commercial Type 2010–2014. Commercial Type, London and New York, 2014 (210x105mm)

Marian is a family of display typefaces designed by Paul Barnes (1970–) in 2011 and released the following year. It consists of a collection of reconstructions of some of the greatest designs in the history of typography, from the sixteenth-century Renaissance period through to the early nineteenth century. Marian re-engineers the work of Garamond, Granjon, Van den Keere, Kis, Fleischman, Fournier, Baskerville, Bodoni and Austin for the digital era.

What distinguishes all of the Marian variants, while at the same time making them coherent as a collection, is that they have all been reduced down to an identical hairline weight, exposing the structure of each typographic form as a skeletal wireframe. These are not strictly revivals, since they are neither accurate recreations nor academic interpretations of historical models. Instead, Marian regenerates one blackletter and nine serif typefaces – from old style to Scotch Roman – stripping them to their bare bones in order to reveal the essence of their form. All of the typefaces have been developed to meticulous levels of typographic detail, with companion italics, small capitals, ligatures, swash characters and lining, tabular and non-lining figures.

Because Marian was intended as a display typeface, with contours so thin that they were suitable for use only at very large sizes, Barnes produced an alternative version, Marian Text, in 2014, with the assistance of Sandra Carrera and Miguel Reyes. This family applies the same principles to a slightly heavier contour that is still very light but that is more workable in text settings.

Marian Text is available in a range of four typefaces: Marian Text 1554 represents the old-style roman of Claude Garamond and Robert Granjon's italic; John Baskerville's transitional type translates into Marian Text 1757; the modern of Giambattista Bodoni, with a full set of swash capitals, becomes Marian Text 1800; and Marian Text Black references the blackletter of Hendrik van den Keere.

92

Marian
1565
52 pt

After Claude Garamont & Robert Granjon

REFUELLIN
13½% of desi
MODERNIS
Footballer Kick

Marian
1571
48 pt

After Robert Granjon

WILDERN
Departs @ 18
GRENACH
Frictions spar

WWW.COMMERCIALTYPE.COM

HUNGARIA

Châteauneuf

KRAUTHE

Mortar & Pest

1977 PUNKS

Carpet weave

ABRACIJA

Cheese Mark

Marian
1742
52 pt

After
Pierre-
Simon
(or
Simon-
Pierre)
Fournier

ROCCOCO

Magnifiqueme

LE HAVRE

3440 City of

Marian
1757
48 pt

After
John
Baskerville

WARWICK

Rotary Gauge

QUIRÙRGIC

Reynolds steel t

Marian
1800
52 pt

After
Giambattista
Bodoni

PA

Ita

W

Zo

Marian
1812
48 pt

Attributed
to Richard
Austin

GL

Sc

LE

No

Ty	**Doctrine**
Ca	**Sans Serif**
Ke	**Grotesque, Geometric**
Te	**Digital**
Da	**2013**
De	**Jonathan Barnbrook, Jonathan Abbott and Julián Moncada**
Fo	**Virus**
Co	**UK**

Characteristics

A Asymmetric alternate
E F Narrow-width alternates
G K Q Geometric alternates
G M Q Grotesque alternates
I l 1 Various alternates
R Concave leg alternate
Y Cyrillic alternate
a g Single- and double-storeyed alternates

ABEGIR
abcefghij
koprstuy

Connections

Monotype Grotesque	c1926
Mason	1992
Priori	2003
Julien	2011

Availability

Doctrine is available from VirusFonts and resellers

Specimen

Disobedient Objects. V&A Publishing, London, 2014 (250x210mm)

Get a two-litre transparent plastic bottle / Cut away the bottom of the bottle just above the ridged area / Cut a U-shaped section from the back of the bottle / Glue a strip of foam rubber on the inside edge of the bottle / Glue and sew a strip of cloth over the foam rubber / Put a surgical mask in the neck of the bottle / Make four small holes in the sides of the bottle / Feed the ends of two elastic bands through the holes / Soak the surgical mask with a bit of vinegar before putting the bottle over your face / These are the **Disobedient Objects**

Jonathan Barnbrook's (1966–) Doctrine typeface was released in 2013. A versatile and functional sans serif face, it is inspired, like much of Barnbrook's design work, by a spirit of inquiry and seeks, in playful ways, to raise questions about twentieth-century ideologies, the nature of originality and freedom of choice.

Like many of Barnbrook's earlier typefaces, such as Mason (pp502–503) and Priori, Doctrine shows his preoccupation with the symbolic qualities of letters. While remaining cohesive, it incorporates a disparate range of historical sources in an intriguing composite of ancient, modern, humanist and geometric signs. A primary influence is the mid-twentieth-century sans serif form, notably Univers and Helvetica. Yet unlike these paragons of late modernism, Doctrine has the much more homely and more humane appearance of nineteenth-century English grotesques. The rounded, lighter letterforms carry themselves with composure, while the large x-height, low contrast and squareness of heavier weights give Doctrine an inviting affability. Several characters draw inspiration from Edward Johnston's iconic sans serif for the London Underground (pp202–203), contributing a humanist grace to the core character set and a quirky personality to several alternate letters. Paul Renner's early experimental drawings for Futura (pp230–31) also provided inspiration for some of the more clinical variants as well as more conventional geometric forms.

Digging deep into the detritus of the typographic past, Doctrine uses OpenType technology to reactivate a diverse range of archaic letterforms, ligatures and alternate characters derived from non-Latin alphabets. The long s, for example, that fell out of use in the early nineteenth century, has been revived, as has the open-eyed alternate lower case e that references the Greek epsilon.

The Doctrine type family comprises two styles – Doctrine and Doctrine Stencil, each of which comes in five weights. Their extensive OpenType features include stylistic alternates, discretionary ligatures, fractions and four optional numeral sets. Doctrine Stencil also offers many alternate titling characters, with up to four versions of each glyph.

Jonathan Barnbrook has knowingly described Doctrine as 'a twenty-first-century utopian sans serif'. Both the classical and modernist notions of Utopia entailed acts of purification – the ruthless eradication of everything not of use or value – but the Utopia that Doctrine invokes is highly diverse, inclusive, contradictory, humorous and wide open to interpretation.

Work in pairs when trying to lock on / Have a friend keep the key in a secure place / Bicycle D-locks fit neatly around pieces of machinery, gates and your neck / Choose your locking point carefully / If locking on to a mobile machine, inform the driver that operating it will break someone's neck / Make sure what you lock on to cannot be removed or unscrewed / Lock yourselves together around the neck to form an octopus group lock-on / These are the **Disobedient Objects**

Ty	**NB International**
Ca	**Sans Serif**
Ke	**Grotesque, Geometric**
Te	**Digital**
Da	**2014**
De	**Stefan Gandl**
Fo	**Neubau**
Co	**Germany**

Characteristics

Small rounded corners at all stroke junctions and terminals

C c S s e g Flat terminals

G Has spur

Q Straight, angled tail

R Straight, angled leg

a Double-storeyed, curve at foot

f r t Vertical terminals

g Single-storeyed

i j Square dots

t Flat top-stroke

y Flat, hooked tail

AGMQR
abcefghij
koprstuy

Connections

Helvetica	1957
Unica	1980
Akkurat	2004
Replica	2008

Availability

NB International is available from Neubau and resellers

Specimen

NB International type specimen. Neubau, Berlin, 2015 (297x210mm)

NB International™ Pro
Bold [B]

●920 pt

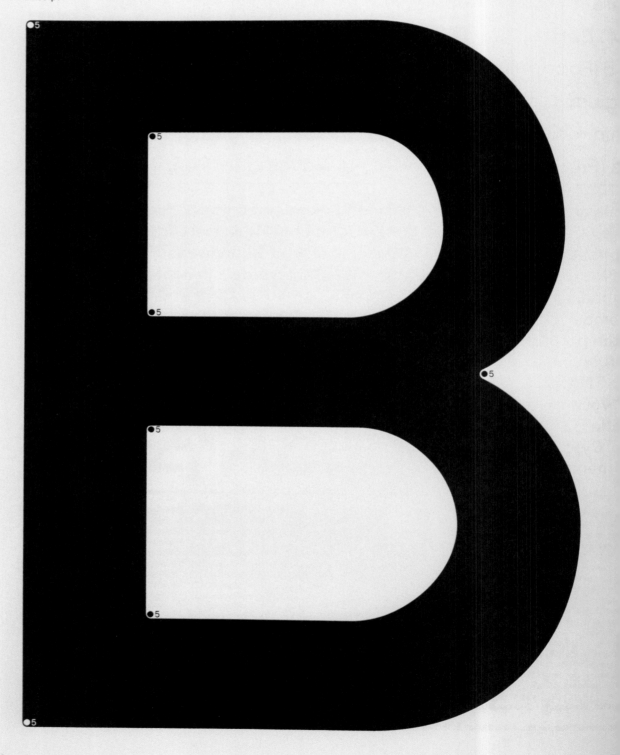

nternational™ Pro
[B]

NB International™ Pro
Bold [B]

NB International™ Pro
Bold [B]

---

one of the interviews with Neubau
he confession that it all began with
As you may know, Letraset is a trans-
n containing characters, symbols or
ns to be rubbed off on paper. For me
has the flavour of the sixtees, and
ck a lot of memories from this period,
ntened decade with so much promises
 society and better human understan-
 Paris student revolt, the Beatles,
Woodstock, and the first man on the
r imagination was sky high! The
boys were not yet born. [1]
While leafing through their books
le earth catalogue' came to my mind.
blished for the first time in 1968, and
an immediate hit. Its purpose was
 education and 'access to tools' so
 could 'find his own inspiration, shape
environment, and share his adventure
ever is interested'.

This publication used a broad definition
of 'tools'. There were informative tools, such
as books, maps, professional journals, courses,
and classes. It also contained well-designed
special-purpose utensils, including garden
tools, carpenters' and masons' tools, welding
equipment, chainsaws, fiberglass materials,
tents, hiking shoes, and potters' wheels. There
were even early synthesizers and personal
computers.

This all is very well comparable with
such chapters of the Neubau books like: formats, tools, objects, playground, chairs, constructions, and urban environments, etcetera. For
a moment I thought that the Neubau catalogues
could be seen as a visual translation of 'The
whole earth catalogue'. [2]

Another moment in history came to my
mind, the Neubau approach reminded me also
of the work of Otto Neurath and Gerdt Arntz.
Neurath was a philosopher who invented the

'ISOTYPE, International System of Typographic
Picture Education', a graphic system to represent social circumstances. He and Gerd Arntz
lived in the Netherlands between 1934 and
1940 and collaborated for this project. Arntz
was the artist who designed the more than
4000 symbols of this visual language. Neurath
worked among others with modern functionalist town planners and architects assembled in
the 'CIAM, Congres International d' Architecture
Moderne'. He was an engaged modernist who
believed highly in a better world through mutual
understanding. [3]

1.–3. Excerpts from Wim Crouwels' 'Neubauism'
introduction, Eindhoven/The Netherlands 2008

áàâäåãbcçdeéèêëfgğh
eìeîeïejijklmnñoóòôöõø
qrsşţuúùûüvwxyýŷÿz
BCÇDEFGHIJKLMNOØP
QRSSTUVWXYZÆŒ/[]°™
1234567890$£€§.,:;!?'-()*
∆ĄąĘęŲųļi̧æœß→←↑↓↵

lfassung der International™ entworfen 2012
fan Gandl im Auftrag von und in Zusam-
eit mit der Schriftbibliothek Neubau.

Version original de l'International™ dessinée en
2012 par Stefan Gandl chargé par et en collaboration avec la Fonderie de Caractères Neubau.

Original version of International™ designed in 2012
by Stefan Gandl by order of and in collaboration
with Typefoundry Neubau, Berlin.

Austrian designer Stefan Gandl (1969–)
established the Berlin design studio
Neubau in 2001, rapidly achieving
international success with the publication
of two bestselling books, *Neubau Welt*
and *Neubau Modul,* in 2005 and 2007
respectively. The studio's most ambitious
project was published in 2014. Developed
painstakingly over five years, the *Neubau
Forst Catalogue* is a comprehensive visual
archive of detailed images of Berlin trees.

Throughout his career Gandl has
embraced advancements in design
technology. During the painstaking
development of the *Forst Catalogue,* the
Neubau team challenged the limits of the
software available to produce a publication
of exceptionally high technical standards.
Gandl has said that his 'special projects
require special typography' and a key
contribution to the *Forst Catalogue* was
the development of a new typeface, NB
International, also released commercially
in 2014. The NB International family was
cut in three weights – light, regular and
bold – each with corresponding italics
and a monospaced variant.

A logical progression from Gandl's earlier
typefaces such as NB Grotesk (pp618–19),
NB International integrates the appearance
of popular sans serif typefaces of the
post-war modernist period, like Helvetica
(pp346–47) and Univers (pp350–51),
with algorithmic design methods. NB
International is geometrically constructed
on a consistent grid that allowed Gandl
to create a range of contours and weights
following predefined rules.

Conspicuously systematic but far more
nuanced than NB Grotesk, NB International
is a sturdy and reliable text typeface
that reconciles the mathematics of its
construction with sophisticated optical
compensations such as its subtle stroke
modulation and the tiny rounded corners
used at all stroke endings. The result is
a soft, warm hybrid of geometric and
grotesque that is effective both in print
and on-screen.

Ty	**Infini**
Ca	**Serif**
Ke	**Wedge, Glyphic**
Te	**Digital**
Da	**2015**
De	**Sandrine Nugue**
Fo	**Centre National des Arts Plastiques**
Co	**France**

Characteristics

Strokes are narrow at waist, flared at terminals
B P R Open bowl
E F Ends of arms are angled
G No spur
K k Arm and leg do not intersect stem
M Splayed
Q Straight tail below letter
a Double-storeyed
g Single-storeyed
i j Round dots
& 3 Flat top

BEJMQR
abcdefgijk
orstuyaefg

Connections

Latin	c1870
Albertus	1935
Amerigo	1986
Matrix	1986

Availability

Infini is available from Centre National des Arts Plastiques

Specimen

Infini type specimen. Centre National des Arts Plastiques, Paris, 2015 (220x165mm)

The National Centre for Visual Arts (CNAP) launched a competition for the design of a new typeface in 2014 as part of 'Graphisme en France', a national event. The winning entry was to be made freely available to the general public in order to raise awareness of the practice of type design, an activity that is central to visual communication but which is invisible to most people outside the design profession.

The winning typeface, Infini, designed by Sandrine Nugue (1985–), combines contemporary and historical styles whose letterforms, like Albertus (pp290–91) and Optima (pp352–53), reference classical Greek and Roman lapidary inscriptions. Nugue sought to create a dialogue between the history of typography and its practice, making Infini available in three styles – roman, italic and bold – complemented by sets of ligatures and pictograms. She wanted, she said, 'to tell the story of writing and typography'.

Her work resulted in a glyphic typeface that is equally effective in text and display applications. On close examination, character structures are evidently the result of digital design processes. Letterforms follow a logical construction that is fundamentally geometric but to which optical balance is imparted by means of flared triangular strokes. These give lightness to strokes and stability at terminals, making for a natural and clear overall impression.

In addition to its utilitarian qualities, a mischievous humour underpins Infini. Like Jonathan Barnbrook's Priori and Mason (pp502–503), it references a wide range of familiar historical symbols and other associations, such as monumental inscriptions, advertising posters, tombstones and everyday doodles. Nugue drew on a huge number of different sources, from carved lettering in Amiens cathedral to 1960s advertising signage, to inform Infini's individual characters and its extensive range of novel ligatures and pictographic glyphs where images are partially merged with capital letters.

Throughout each stage of Infini's development, Sandrine Nugue kept meticulous research records. Her extensive archive of sketches, drawings, notes and digital files is now held in the CNAP collection for use as a study resource to facilitate the teaching of design and an understanding of the complexities involved in the playful but painstaking process of designing typefaces.

glossary

Alternate
An alternative version of a character in a typeface.

Antiqua
A German name for a serifed typeface, usually old style.

Aperture
An area of negative space within a letter, partially enclosed by a stroke or strokes. See bowl.

Apex
The uppermost connection point of a letterform where two strokes join at an angle.

Arch
A curved stroke at the upper boundary of a character, often projecting horizontally from a stem.

Arm
A horizontal stroke that joins to a stem at one end only.

Ascender
The part of a lower case letter that extends upwards above the mid-line.

Ascent
A horizontal alignment zone at the upper boundary of the lower case ascenders. May be the same as the capital height.

Axis
In a typeface with stroke contrast, the angle of the thickest part of a curved stroke in relation to the horizontal.

Ball terminal
A circular or elliptical swelling at a stroke terminal.

Bar / Crossbar
A horizontal stroke usually enclosed by strokes at both ends.

Baroque
A style of European architecture, music and art of the 17th and 18th centuries, characterized by ornate detail.

Baseline
A horizontal alignment zone at the foot of characters without descenders.

Bastarda
A blackletter with a rounded construction derived from 15th-century French scribal hands.

Beak
An angular or triangular serif at a stroke terminal used in certain serif type designs.

Blackletter
A group of angular gothic scripts and typeface designs from c1100 to c1500 that continued in everyday use in Germany until the 1940s.

Body
The rectangle that contains each character in a typeface to a common height, usually equal to the point size, although widths may vary. Originally the metal block that each character occupied.

Bowl
An area of negative space within a letter completely enclosed by a stroke or strokes, typically round or elliptical, as in b and p.

Bracketed serif
A serif connected to a stem with a curved or angled connection.

Cap height
The horizontal alignment zone at the upper boundary of capital letters. May be the same as ascender height.

Character
An individual sign in the set of signs that comprises a typeface, such as letters, numbers, punctuation marks, etc.; identifiable by particular visual features that are media-independent.

Counter / Counterform
Any area of negative space within or between letters, completely or partially enclosed by a stroke or strokes.

Cross-stroke
A horizontal stroke that intersects the stem of a letter.

Crotch
The internal angle of an apex or vertex where two strokes join.

Descender
The part of a letter that extends below the baseline.

Descent
A horizontal alignment zone at the lower boundary of the lower case descenders.

Display typeface
A typeface design intended for use at large sizes, typically with short amounts of copy, as opposed to a text typeface.

Double-storeyed
A letter that has two counters, as in some forms of lower case a and g.

Ear
A small stroke usually at the upper right side of the bowl of a letter, typically found on the lower case g.

Egyptian
A 19th-century name for a non-geometric slab serif.

Eye
The enclosed space in a lowercase e.

Finial
A stroke terminal that is curved or tapered, with no serif.

Font
A set of all the characters of a typeface, such as letters, numbers, punctuation marks, etc., constructed in a particular medium.

Foot
The part of a letter's stem that sits on the baseline.

Fraktur
A German blackletter with an angular, fragmentary stroke construction from the early 16th century that continued in everyday use in Germany until the 1940s. Often used as a synonym for blackletter.

Glyph
A particular visual representation of a character as a single instance in a font.

Gothic
A 19th-century American name for a sans serif or grotesque typeface. Also a synonym for blackletter.

Gotico-Antiqua
A 15th-century letterform that combines characteristics of the Renaissance and the medieval periods. Also known as Fere-Humanistica.

Grotesk
The German name for a sans serif or grotesque typeface.

Grotesque
A sans serif typeface design that originated in the 19th century.

Hairline
A very thin stroke; the thinnest in a typeface with strokes of different width.

Hook
A deeply curved stroke terminal, as in J.

Humanism
An ideology emphasizing the value and agency of human beings. Also a subgroup of sans serif types influenced by old-style character contours.

Ink trap
An aperture at the inner junction of two strokes intended to avoid ink filling in as a result of the printing impression. Occasionally used as a stylistic rather than a functional feature.

Intersection
The location where two or more strokes cross over each other.

Italic
A typeface design in which the letters slant to the right, usually based on a script rather than an inclined version of an upright typeface. Often used for emphasis.

Junction / Joint
The location where two or more strokes connect at an angle.

Kerning
The horizontal spacing between two consecutive characters that compensates for letter combinations which would otherwise fit poorly.

Leading / Line spacing
The vertical spacing between lines of text measured from baseline to baseline.

Leg
A short descending stroke that usually terminates on the baseline.

Ligature
Two or more letters that are linked together to form a single glyph.

Lining figures
Numerals that all sit on the baseline and are usually the same height as capital letters.

Loop
A partially enclosed bowl.

Lower case
The small letters in a typeface. Derives from hand-composition typesetting, where the small letters are kept in the lower section of the type case.

Mid-line
A horizontal alignment zone at the top of the lower case letters such as x, disregarding ascenders. The distance from the baseline to the mid-line is the x-height.

Modern
A typeface design characterized by a vertical stress and an abrupt contrast between thick and thin strokes that originated in the late 18th century.

Modernism
A group of 20th-century movements in the arts that departed from classical and traditional ideas and forms.

Monoline / Monolinear
Characters where thick and thin strokes appear to be of the same weight.

Monospaced / Fixed-width
A typeface design where all characters occupy exactly the same horizontal space.

Non-lining figures
Numerals with varying heights that ascend or descend to coordinate with the x-height of lower case letters and with small capitals.

Oblique stress
A stroke contrast where the angle of the thickest part of a curved stroke is on a tilted axis in relationship to the horizontal.

Old style
A typeface design characterized by an oblique stress that originated in late 15th-century Italy.

OpenType
A format for digital typefaces developed jointly by Microsoft and Adobe. OpenType typefaces have advanced typographic features and cross-platform compatibility.

Pica
A typographic measurement unit equal to 1/6th of an inch. One pica contains 12 points.

Pixel
A single cell in a graphic object composed of many cells. Computer monitors display millions of pixels in grids so close together that they appear to be connected.

Point
A typographic measurement unit equal to 1/72nd of an inch. Type sizes and spaces are usually expressed in points. One pica contains 12 points. One point is equivalent to one pixel on a 72 dpi screen.

Point size
The height of the body of a typeface measured from baseline to baseline. A typeface with a large x-height appears bigger than a typeface with a small x-height at the same point size.

PostScript
A computer language for creating vector graphics developed by Adobe, including a format for digital typefaces.

Proportional typeface
A typeface design in which characters are of variable widths. Wide characters occupy more horizontal space than narrow characters.

Punch
In type founding, a steel bar onto the end of which a character was cut. This would be stamped into a softer metal to form a matrix from which type was cast.

Rationalism
An ideology that regards reason as the source of knowledge and justification.

Renaissance
A period from the 14th to 16th century that saw a revival of European art, culture, philosophy and science influenced by classical models.

Reversed stress
A stroke contrast where conventional emphasis is rotated so that horizontal strokes and serifs are thicker than those that are vertical.

Roman
A type style with upright letters. Sometimes also used to denote the regular weight of a typeface.

Rotunda
A blackletter with a rounded construction, derived from 16th-century Italian and Spanish scribal hands.

Sans serif
A typeface design literally 'without serifs'.

Schwabacher
A blackletter with a rounded character construction, derived from Textura in the 15th century.

Serif
A short stroke extending from the end of a stem; also the typeface design with this feature.

Shoulder
A curved arch projecting from a stem, as in lower case h, m and n.

Single-storeyed
A letter that has one counter, as in some forms of lower case a and g.

Slab serif
A short, rectangular stroke connected to a stem with a flat connection; also the typeface design with this feature.

Small capitals / Small caps
Capital letters that are as high or approximately as high as the x-height of the lower case letters.

Sort
In hand-composition typesetting, an individual piece of type.

Spur
A small protrusion from a main stroke, often where a curve meets a straight stem.

Stem
The main stroke or strokes of a letterform, usually vertical.

Stress
In a typeface with stroke contrast, the angle of the thickest part of a curved stroke in relationship to the horizontal.

Stroke
A line that forms part of a character; may be straight, curved, etc.

Stroke contrast
The relationship between the thick and thin strokes in the letters of a typeface. See monoline.

Superfamily
A large, coordinated collection of type families of different classifications that share common names and features in order to work alongside each other.

Swash
A curved stroke extension on a letterform, usually as a decorative flourish.

Tail
A small descending stroke, as on the old-style letter Q.

Terminal
The end of a stroke that has no serif.

Textura
A blackletter with an angular construction and horizontal compression, derived from 13th-century scribal hands.

Text typeface
A typeface design intended primarily for reading in extended text matter rather than for display.

Tracking / Letter spacing
The standard horizontal spacing between consecutive characters.

Transitional
A typeface design that combines features of old-style and modern forms that originated in the early 18th century.

TrueType
A non-proprietary format for digital typefaces developed by Apple and Microsoft as an alternative to Adobe's PostScript format. Cross-platform compatible.

Type family
A collection of related typefaces that share design features and names.

Typeface
A set of characters under a single name, identifiable by particular visual features that are media-independent. Literally, the face of the type.

Unbracketed serif
A short, rectangular stroke connected to a stem with a right-angled or flat connection.

Uncial
A European script of the 4th to 8th century with round, unconnected letters.

Unicase
A typeface design with upper case and lower case letters that share the same height.

Upper case
The capital letters in a typeface. Derives from hand-composition typesetting, where the capitals are kept in the upper section of the type case.

Vertex
The lowest connection point of a letterform where two strokes join.

Vertical stress
A stroke contrast where the angle of the thickest part of a curved stroke is on a vertical axis.

Weight
Stroke thickness; also a typeface described with reference to its stroke thickness.

x-height
The height of the lower case letters from the baseline to the mid-line, excluding ascenders and descenders, as in the height of the x.

further reading

Type History

Annand, C., Meggs, P. B. & McKelvey, R. *Revival of the Fittest: Digital Versions of Classic Typefaces*. New York: RC Publications, 2000.

Bain, P., Shaw, P., Mirsky, L. *Blackletter: Type and National Identity*. New York: Princeton Architectural Press, 1998.

Bartram, A. *Typeforms: A History*. London: British Library, 2007.

Blackwell, L. *Twentieth-Century Type*. London: Laurence King, 1992.

Carter, S. *Twentieth-Century Type Designers*. London: Lund Humphries, 1987.

Consuegra, D. *American Type: Design & Designers*. New York: Allworth Press, 2004.

Dowding, G. *An Introduction to the History of Printing Types from 1440 up to the Present Day*. London: Wace, 1961.

Gray, N. *Nineteenth Century Ornamented Types and Title Pages*. London: Faber & Faber, 1938.

Haley, A. *Typographic Milestones*. New York: Van Nostrand Reinhold, 1992.

Janser, A. *Frische Schriften: Fresh Type*. Zürich: Edition Museum für Gestaltung Zürich, 2004.

Jaspert, W. P., Berry, W. T. & Johnson, A. F. *Encyclopaedia of Typefaces*. London: Cassell Illustrated, 2008.

Johnson, A. F. *Type Designs: Their History and Development*. London: André Deutsch 1959.

Kelly, R. R. *American Wood Type, 1828–1900*. New York: Van Nostrand Reinhold, 1969.

Kinross, R. *Modern Typography: An Essay in Critical History*. London: Hyphen Press, 1994.

Kinross, R. *Unjustified Texts: Perspectives on Typography*. London: Hyphen, 2002.

Knight, S. *Historical Types: From Gutenberg to Ashendene*. New Castle, DE: Oak Knoll Press, 2012.

Lawson, A. S. *Anatomy of a Typeface*. Boston: D. R. Godine, 1990.

Loxley, S. *Type: The Secret History of Letters*. London: I.B. Tauris, 2004.

Macmillan, N. *An A–Z of Type Designers*. Newhaven, CT: Yale University Press, 2006.

Man, J. *The Gutenberg Revolution*. London: Review, 2002.

McGrew, M. *American Metal Typefaces of the Twentieth Century*. New Castle, DE: Oak Knoll Press, 1993.

Meggs, P. B. & Carter, R. *Typographic Specimens: The Great Typefaces*. New York: Van Nostrand Reinhold, 1993.

Middendorp, J. *Dutch Type*. Rotterdam: 010 Publishers, 2004.

Middendorp, J. & Spiekermann, E. *Made with FontFont*. Amsterdam: BIS, 2006.

Millington, R. *Stephenson Blake: The Last of the Old English Typefounders*. New Castle, DE: Oak Knoll Press, 2002.

Morison, S. & Crutchley, B. *A Tally of Types*. Whittlesford: H. Myers, 1981.

Mosley, J. *The Nymph and the Grot: The Revival of the Sanserif Letter*. London: Friends of the St Bride Printing Library, 1999.

Nesbitt, A. *The History and Technique of Lettering*. New York: Dover Publications, 1957.

Reed, T. B. & Johnson, A. *A History of the Old English Letter Foundries with Notes, Historical and Bibliographical, on the Rise and Progress of English Typography*. London: Faber and Faber, 1952.

Ribagorda, J. M., Balius, A. *Imprenta Real: Fuentes de la Tipografía Española*. Madrid: Ministerio de Asuntos Exteriores y de Cooperación, AECID, 2010.

Roberts, R. *Typographic Design*. London: Benn, 1966.

Spencer, H. *The Visible Word*. London: Lund Humphries, 1968.

Spencer, H. *Pioneers of Modern Typography*. London: Lund Humphries, 1969.

Sutton, J. & Bartram, A. *An Atlas of Typeforms*. London: Lund Humphries, 1968.

Tracy, W. *Letters of Credit: A View of Type Design*. Boston: D. R. Godine, 2003.

Triggs, T. *The Typographic Experiment: Radical Innovation in Contemporary Type Design*. London: Thames & Hudson, 2003.

Updike, D. B. *Printing Types: Their History, Forms, and Use: A Study in Survivals*. New York: Dover Publications, 1980.

Type Monographs

Aicher, O. *Typographie*. Berlin: Ernst, 1988.

Aldersey-Williams, H. *Cranbrook Design: The New Discourse*. New York: Rizzoli, 1990.

Apeloig, P., Morgaine, A., Lupton, E. & Grass, T. *Typorama: The Graphic Work of Philippe Apeloig*. London: Thames and Hudson, 2015.

Barnbrook, J. & Lasn, K. *Barnbrook Bible: The Graphic Design of Jonathan Barnbrook*. London: Booth-Clibborn Editions, 2007.

Bovier, L., Manchester, C. & Schnetz, S. *ECAL Typographie: We Make Fonts*. Lausanne: ECAL, 2006

Broos, K., Quay, D. & Crouwel, W. *Wim Crouwel Alphabets*. Amsterdam: BIS, 2003.

Bruckner, D. J. R. *Frederic Goudy*. New York: Harry N. Abrams, 1990.

Burke, C. *Paul Renner: The Art of Typography*. London: Hyphen, 1998.

Burke, C. *Active Literature: Jan Tschichold and New Typography*. London: Hyphen, 2007.

Chamaret, S., Gineste, J. & Morlighem, S. *Roger Excoffon et la Fonderie Olive*. Paris: Ypsilon, 2010.

Cinamon, G. *Rudolf Koch: Letterer, Type Designer, Teacher*. New Castle, DE: Oak Knoll Press, 2000.

Eisele, P., Ludwig, A. & Naegele, I. (eds) *Futura: Die Schrift*. Mainz: Verlag Hermann Schmidt, 2016.

Frutiger, A., Osterer, H. & Stamm, P. *Adrian Frutiger Typefaces: The Complete Works*. Basel: Birkhäuser, 2009.

Gerstner, K. *Designing Programmes*. Baden: Lars Müller Publishers, 2007.

Gerstner, K. & Kröplien, M. *Karl Gerstner: Review of 5 x 10 Years of Graphic Design etc*. Ostfildern-Ruit: Hatje Cantz, 2001.

Karlas, O. *The Typefaces of Vojtěch Preissig*. Prague: Academy of the Arts, Architecture and Design, 2009.

Littlejohn, D. (ed.). *Metro Letters: A Typeface for the Twin Cities*. Minneapolis: University of Minnesota Press, 2003

Malsy, V., Müller, L., Langer, A. & Kupferschmid, I. *Helvetica Forever: Story of a Typeface*. Baden: Lars Müller, 2009.

McLean, R. *Jan Tschichold, Typographer*. London: Lund Humphries, 1990.

McLean, R. *Jan Tschichold: A Life in Typography*. London: Lund Humphries, 1997.

Miller, J. A. *Dimensional Typography: Case Studies on the Shape of Letters in Virtual Environments*. New York: Kiosk, 1996.

Müller, L. *Helvetica: Homage to a Typeface*. Baden: Lars Müller, 2002.

Noordzij, G. *The Stroke: Theory of Writing*. London: Hyphen Press, 2008.

Norm. *Norm: The Things*. Zürich: Die Gestalten Verlag, 2002.

Poynor, R. *Typographica*. London: Laurence King, 2001.

Purcell, K. W. *Alexey Brodovitch*. London: Phaidon Press, 2002.

Rault, D., Knapp, P. & Berberian, C. *Roger Excoffon: Le Gentleman de la Typographie*. Reillanne: Atelier Perrousseaux, 2011.

Re, M., Drucker, J., Mosley, J., Carter, M. & Albin O. *Typographically Speaking: The Art of Matthew Carter*. New York: Princeton Architectural Press, 2003.

Pô, G. *Pierre di Sciullo*. Paris: Pyramyd, 2003.

Tilson, J. *3 Found Fonts: An Exploration*. London: Atlas, 2003

Tschichold, J. *The New Typography: A Handbook for Modern Designers*. Berkeley: University of California Press, 1998.

Society of Typographic Arts Chicago, Ill. *The Book of Oz Cooper: An Appreciation of Oswald Bruce Cooper*. Chicago: The Society of Typographic Arts, 1949.

Schalansky, J. *Fraktur Mon Amour*. New York: Princeton Architectural Press, 2008.

Spiekermann, E., Lehni, J. & Bil'ak, P. *ECAL: Typeface as Program*. Zürich: JRP Ringier, 2010.

Weingart, W. *Weingart: Typography – My Way to Typography – Retrospective in Ten Chapters*. Baden: Lars Müller, 1999.

Wozencroft, J. *The Graphic Language of Neville Brody 2*. London: Thames and Hudson, 1994.

Zapf, H. & Zahn, C. *Hermann Zapf & His Design Philosophy*. Chicago: Society of Typographic Arts, 1987.

Typography

Baines, P. & Haslam, A. *Type and Typography: Portfolio Series*. London: Laurence King, 2005.

Bringhurst, R. *The Elements of Typographic Style*. Point Roberts, WA: Hartley & Marks, 1996.

Bringhurst, R. *The Tree of Meaning: Language, Mind and Ecology*. Berkeley: Counterpoint, 2007.

Bringhurst, R. *The Solid Form of Language: An Essay on Writing and Meaning*. Kentville: Gaspereau Press, 2004.

Drucker, J. *The Alphabetic Labyrinth: Letters in History and Imagination*. London: Thames and Hudson, 1995.

Drucker, J. *The Visible Word: Experimental Typography and Modern Art 1909–1923*. Chicago: University of Chicago Press, 1996.

Friedl, F., Ott, N., Stein, B. & Luidl, P. *Typography, When, Who, How*. Cologne: Könemann, 1998.

Heller, S., and Meggs, B. (eds.). *Texts on Type: Critical Writings on Typography*. New York: Allworth Press, 2001.

Kane, J. *A Type Primer*. London: Laurence King, 2002.

Lupton, E. *Thinking With Type: A Critical Guide for Designers, Writers, Editors & Students*. New York: Princeton Architectural Press, 2004.

McLean, R. *Typography (Thames & Hudson Manuals)*. London: Thames & Hudson, 1980.

McLean, R. *How Typography Happens*. London: The British Library Publishing Division, 1999.

McLuhan, M. *The Gutenberg Galaxy, The Making of a Typographic Man*. Abingdon: Routledge, 1967.

Pohlen, J. *Letter Fountain*. Cologne: Taschen, 2011.

Rogener, S. *Branding with Type*. Mountain View, CA: Adobe Press, 1996.

Ruder, E. *Typography: A Textbook of Design*. Niederteufen: Niggli Verlag, 2009.

Schmid, H. *Typography Today*. Tokyo: Seibundo Shinkosha, 2006.

Spiekermann, E. & Ginger, E. *Stop Stealing Sheep and Find Out How Type Works*. Berkeley: Adobe, 2002.

Printing and Design

Blauvelt, A. & Lupton, E. *Graphic Design: Now in Production*. Minneapolis: Walker Art Centre, 2011.

Collectif. *ECAL: Graphic Design*. Zürich: JRP Ringier, 2004.

Crow, D. *Left to Right: The Cultural Shift from Words to Pictures*. Lausanne: AVA Publishing, 2006.

Crow, D. *Visible Signs: An Introduction to Semiotics*. Worthing: AVA Academia, 2003.

Drucker, J. *Graphesis: Visual Forms of Knowledge Production*. Cambridge, MA: Harvard University Press, 2014.

Hochuli, J. & Kinross, R. *Designing Books: Practice and Theory*. London: Hyphen Press, 2003

Hollis, R. *Graphic Design: A Concise History*. London: Thames and Hudson, 1994.

Kampman, M. *I Don't Know Where I'm Going But I Want to Be There*. Amsterdam: BIS, 2010.

Lewis, J. *Anatomy of Printing: The Influences of Art and History on its Design*. London: Faber and Faber, 1970.

Lidwell, W., Holden, K. & Butler, J., *Universal Principles of Design*. Beverly, MA: Rockport, 2003.

Lommen, M. *The Book of Books: 500 Years of Graphic Innovation*. London: Thames & Hudson, 2012.

Lupton, E. & Miller, J. A. *Design, Writing, Research*. New York: Kiosk, 1996.

McLuhan, M. *Understanding Media*. Abingdon: Routledge, 2001.

McMurtie, D. *The Book: The Story of Printing and Bookmaking*. Oxford University Press, 1943.

Meggs, P. *A History of Graphic Design*. New York: John Wiley & Sons, 1998.

Müller-Brockmann, J. *Grid Systems*. Salenstein: Niggli, 1981.

Steinberg, S. H. & Warde, B. *Five Hundred Years of Printing*. Harmondsworth: Penguin Books, 1955.

Walker, J. A. *Design History and the History of Design*. London: Pluto, 1989.

Williamson, H. A. F. *Methods of Book Design: The Practice of an Industrial Craft*. London: Oxford University Press, 1956.

Typefaces

index

Type designers

Foundries and publishers

Acknowledgements

This project would not have been possible without the cooperation of many people.

I would like to express my deepest gratitude to all those who have been so generous in sharing their knowledge, offering encouragement, giving advice, supplying specimens or providing typefaces – with humble apologies to any whom I may have mistakenly omitted.

Philippe Apeloig, Phil Baines, Wibo Bakker, Andreu Balius, Rick Banks, Jonathan Barnbrook, Paul Barnes, Gerry Barney, Kobi Benezri, David Berlow, Russell Bestley, Peter Bil'ak, Diane Bilbey, Harry Blackett, Mark Blamire, Erik van Blokland, Tony Brook, Jos Buivenga, Veronika Burian, Matthew Carter, Philip Contos, Adam Cruz, Mike Dempsey, Catherine Dixon, Nikola Djurek, Hannes von Döhren, Sophie Drysdale, Paul Elliman, Veronika Elsner, Timothy Epps, Giovanni Forti, Geraint Franklin, Ivo Gabrowitsch, Stefan Gandl, Gilles Gavillet, Gary Gillot, James Goggin, Robert Green, Patrick Griffin, Sibylle Hagmann, Gareth Hague, Sébastien Hayez, Ralf Herrmann, Jonathan Hoefler, Leila Kassir, David Keshavjee, Angela Koo, Tal Leming, Gerry Leonidas, Zuzana Licko, Hugh MacFarlane, Alan Meeks, Lori Milani, Mika Mischler, Ian Mortimer, Hamish Muir, Karl Nawrot, Ian Noble, Sandrine Nugue, Eric Olson, Toshi Omagari, Alejandro Paul, Daniel Perraudin, Radim Peško, Kerry William Purcell, David Quay, Emmanuel Rey, Dan Rhatigan, Bob Richardson, Ida Riveros, Rich Roat, Pieter van Rosmalen, David Jonathan Ross, Alexander Roth, Romeo Ruz, Nico Schweizer, Pierre di Sciullo, Nick Shinn, Erik Spiekermann, František Štorm, Julia Sysmäläinen, Julien Tavelli, Nik Thoenen, Ralph Unger, Rudy VanderLans, Sue Walker, Laura Weill, Peter Willberg, Judy Willcocks, Adrian Williams, Cornel Windlin.

Picture Credits

Courtesy American Antiquarian Society (American Antiquarian Society, Reserve 1774 02, Engrossing and Double Pica Script)
88–89

Design: Bondé Angeline, Art Director: Andy Cruz, Typeface Design: Christian Schwartz
594–595

Design: Bondé Angeline, Art Director: Andy Cruz, Typeface Design: Erik van Blokland
636–637

Associazione Archivio Storico Olivetti, Ivrea, Italy
368–369

Bauhaus-Archiv Berlin © The Josef and Anni Albers Foundation/VG Bild-Kunst, Bonn and DACS, London 2017 (inv nr 1995/17.138)
214

Bauhaus-Archiv Berlin, Photo Markus Hawlik © DACS 2017 (inv nr 4257)
280–281

Bauhaus-Archiv Berlin, Photo Markus Hawlik © The Josef and Anni Albers Foundation/VG Bild-Kunst, Bonn and DACS, London 2017 (Inv. Nr. 8530)
215

Bauhaus-Archiv Berlin,© DACS 2017 (inv nr 2006/127.1, p.399)
224–225

Bayerische Staatsbibliothek München
28–29 (Rar. 153#Beibd.5, ff 3v-4r), **36–37** (Res/4 Crim 158, ff 2v-3r.), **38–39** (2 L.impr.membr. 64, ff 35v-36r), **100–101** (Rar. 649, pp 4–5, 6–7)

Bern University Library (MUE Bong I 25:7, ff 4v-5r)
42–43

Biblioteca Civica di Novara 'Carlo Negroni' (CIV 51 L 23 24, pp. 440–1)
56–57

Biblioteca Civica di Verona
16–17 (Inc. 1086, ff 73v-74r), **20–21** (Inc. 1094, ff 73v-74r)

Biblioteca Comunale di Imola, Photo Marco Ravenna (Aula Magna F 3 2, ff 111v-112r)
22–23

Biblioteca de la Universidad de Valladolid, Spain. Permission to reproduce extracts from ISO Standards is by BSI Standards Limited (BSI) on behalf of ISO. (P/Bc ISO-03098-1, pp. 5, 6)
412–413

Biblioteca Histórica del Ayuntamiento de Madrid (MO 141. BHM, V Misal de Gil-V Su Cursiva and VIII Paragona de Gil-VIII Su Cursiva)
92–93

© Bibliothèque Mazarine. Photo Suzanne Nagy (Paris. A 15226-2, Gros Canon er Petit Canon)
62–63

Bibliothèque municipale de Bordeaux (A 2665, ff 10v-11r, 50v-51r)
48–49

Bibliothèque municipale de Lyon, Photos Jean-Luc Bouchier
26–27 (Rés Inc 478, ff 27v-28r), **40–41**(Rés Inc 478, ff 24v-25r), **44–45** (Rés 317879, pp. 10–11), **46–47** (305122, pp. 194–195), **50–51** (SJ X 218/11, ff12v-13r), **54–55** (Rés B 487968, ff 16v-17r), **58–59** (Rés 22903, f 3v), **68–69** (24923, pp 88–89), **70–71** (105487, pp. 2–3)

Bibliothèque nationale de France, Paris
18–19 (Département Réserve des livres rares, A-560 (BIS), ff 3v-4r), **72–73** (Département des manuscrits, Français 9157, ff 288, 336), **74–75** (Département Monnaies, médailles et antiques, FOL-H-4580, ff 1v-2r)

The Bodleian Libraries, University of Oxford (G. Pamph. 1437, folios 1r & 2r, Paragon Roman and Paragon Italic)
94–95

Bryant designed by Eric Olson 2002–2005. Published by Process Type Foundry. processtype.com
592–593

Dan Bull, 2014
531

Matthew Carter. The Cooper Union for the Advancement of Science and Art
424–425

Central Saint Martins
52–53, 256–257, 274–275, 316–317, 344–345, 378–379, 406–407, 418–419, 428–429, 430–431, 524–525, 532–533, 564–565, 578–579, 588–589, 590–591

Central Saint Martins/T-26 Inc.
546–547

Christ Church Library, Oxford (Z.307/7, ff 1r, 3r, 4r, 5r)
66–67

Courtesy Ralf Herrmann
106–107

© DIN e. V.
266–267

Courtesy Paul Elliman
474–475

The Folger Shakespeare Library, Washington DC, (STC 5082, ff 74v-75r). By permission of The Folger Shakespeare Library, Washington DC
24–25

Guardian Egyptian designed by Paul Barnes and Christian Schwartz, 2005–9. Originally for the Guardian Media Group, released by Commercial Type
608–609

Harry Ransom Center, The University of Texas at Austin (Q-BS 75 1454, Volume II, New Testament, Matthew, ff 519v-520r)
14–15

Photo Aymeric Hays-Narbonne
324–325

Klavika designed by Eric Olson 2004. Published by Process Type Foundry. processtype.com
604–605

Koninklijke Bibliotheek, National Library of the Netherlands, Den Haag (172 C 21, ff 84v-85r)
34–35

Images courtesy of Letraset
366–367, 396–397, 404–405

Lettering, printing and graphic design collection, University of Reading
198–199, 216–217, 240–241, 252–253, 286–287, 296–297, 306–307, 308–309, 310–311, 326–327, 328–329, 330–331, 334–335, 346–347, 350–351, 352–353, 362, 364–365, 384–385, 394–395, 400–401, 402–403, 410–411, 414–415, 422–423, 426–427, 432–433, 442–443, 446–447, 466–467, 490–491

London College of Communication
32–33, 150–151, 156–157, 172–173

London College of Communication © Estate of Edward Sackville-West. Reproduced by permission of the Vita Sackville-West Estate
270–271

Photo Wibo Bakker, © MOURON. CASSANDRE (Lic 2016-03-09-03_www.cassandre.fr)
246–247

Museum Plantin-Moretus, Antwerp. Photo Peter Maes, Gentbrugge
30–31 (UNESCO, World Heritage, R 29.8, ff 7v-8r), **60–61** (UNESCO, World Heritage, R 24.27, ff 10r, 11r)

Private collection
116–117

St Bride Foundation
76–77, 78–79, 80–81, 82–83, 84–85, 86–87, 90–91, 96–97, 98–99, 104–105, 108–109, 110–111, 112–113, 114–115, 118–119, 120–121, 122–123, 124–125, 126–127, 128–129, 130–131, 132–133, 134–135, 136–137, 138–139, 140–141, 142–143, 144–145, 146–147, 148–149, 152–153, 158–159, 160–161, 162–163, 164–165, 166–167, 168–169, 170–171, 174–175, 176–177, 178–179, 180–181, 182–183, 184–185, 186–187, 188–189, 190–191, 192–193, 194–195, 196–197, 202–203, 204–205, 224–225, 214–215, 218–219, 226–227, 228–229, 230–231, 232–233, 234–235, 236–237, 238–239, 242–243, 244–245, 248–249, 250–251, 258–259, 260–261, 262–263, 264–265, 268–269, 272–273, 276–277, 280–281, 284–285, 288–289, 290–291, 292–293, 294–295, 298–299, 300–301, 302–303, 304–305, 312–313, 314–315, 318–319, 332–333, 336–337, 338–339, 340–341, 342–343, 348–349, 354–355, 358–359, 360–361, 363, 370–371, 372–373, 392–393, 408–409, 420–421, 434–435, 448–449, 452–453

Swiss Typefaces (www.swisstypefaces.com) Quai Perdonnet 19, 1800 Vevey, VD. Switzerland
656–657

Creative Director: Blair Thomson, Design: Blair Thomson, Illustration: Sandra Kristensson
530

Typotheque (Peter Bilak)
586–587 (2001), **646–647** (2010)

Photograph © The University of Manchester (The University of Manchester, The John Rylands Library, pressmark 17250.1)
12–13

Walker Type Specimen is a joint project of Carter & Cone and the Walker Art Center. © 1996
548–549